WALTER KAUFMANN

Walter Kaufmann

PHILOSOPHER, HUMANIST, HERETIC

STANLEY CORNGOLD

PRINCETON UNIVERSITY PRESS

PRINCETON & OXFORD

Published by Princeton University Press
41 William Street, Princeton, New Jersey 08540
6 Oxford Street, Woodstock, Oxfordshire OX20 1TR

press.princeton.edu

Library of Congress Control Number: 2017964104

ISBN 978-0-691-16501-1

British Library Cataloging-in-Publication Data is available

Editorial: Rob Tempio and Matt Rohal
Production Editorial: Mark Bellis
Jacket/Cover Design: Pam Schnitter
Production: Erin Suydam
Publicity: Jodi Price

This book has been composed in Arno

Printed on acid-free paper. ∞

Printed in the United States of America

10 9 8 7 6 5 4 3 2 1

CONTENTS

Preface   vii

Abbreviations for Kaufmann Citations   xiii

	Introduction	1
1	Nietzsche Redivivus	11
2	Raw Life	43
3	Cleaning the Stables	75
4	Transcending the Human	100
5	The Riches of the World	128
6	A Contempt for Popularity	159
7	Stories of Religion	199
8	Living with Hegel	230
9	The Philosophy of Tragedy	278
10	Tragedy as Philosophy	311
11	Against Decrepit Ideas	351
12	The Places of Religion	378
13	This Priceless Heritage	411
14	What Is Man's Lot?	438
15	Philosophy as Psychology	476
16	Opium of the Intellectuals	503

17 Unsubdued Quarrels   532

Epilogue   563

Postscript. Contra *Nietzsche*   572

Acknowledgments 609
Notes 611
Index 703

PREFACE

PRINCETON UNIVERSITY PRESS has undertaken to reprint, with new introductions, many of Walter Kaufmann's most important books. It is a fine thing
to do, I think, for several reasons: it honors an eminent, German-born émigré
scholar who taught in Princeton's Department of Philosophy from 1947 until
his untimely death in 1980; and it honors a reading public that seems eager
to read his works, in many cases, for the second time. When I recently told
a younger scholar that I intended to write a book about the works of Walter
Kaufmann, he greeted the idea, saying how important they had been to his
father. "They came out in Anchor Books, didn't they? I wish I'd kept my
father's copies." The result was that these books were no longer immediately
available to my friend, and the implication was that he would read them if
they were.

There is furthermore a wider audience that, to take one special case, is
poised to read Kaufmann's celebrated work *The Faith of a Heretic.*[1] The Amazon
website lists twelve enthusiastic reviews by readers in the past who describe
the book as "the best critical study of religion available," "a classic application
of philosophy to religion for the layman," "the book that started my philosophical career," "a powerful, challenging and heart-felt work," "the most thought-
provoking book I have read in years," "critically engaging, life-inspiring," "[an]
outstanding book," "[a work of] distinctive genius," and, finally, with pungent
incisiveness, "Eat this book!" The commentator develops his thought: this is
"probably the most important and meaningful book I have ever read or am
likely to read."[2] It seems a good thing to give other readers the opportunity
to test this idea. My surmise about the general interest in Kaufmann's work
is supported by what the German playwright Bertolt Brecht called "plumpes
Denken" (approximately, "blunt thinking"). Consider that the cheapest hard-
back copy of *The Faith of a Heretic* found on Amazon at this time of writing
ranges between $62 and $495, the cheapest paperback between $92 and $195!
If price is indeed a measure of demand . . .

This surmise can be put even more directly. We can apply to Kaufmann the comment made by the critic Cynthia Ozick about the novelist Bernard Malamud, with one change of word: "A new generation, mostly unacquainted with the risks of uncompromising and hard-edged *criticism* ['compassion' in the original] deserves" Kaufmann "even more than the one that made up his contemporary readership."[3] What they will find in Kaufmann is a scrupulous humanistic moral philosophy. Add to Ozick's remark the words of a young professor of history, Molly Worthen, writing in 2015:

> As nonbelievers tangle with traditional Christians over same-sex marriage and navigate conflicts between conservative Muslims and liberal democracy, they will need a confident humanist moral philosophy. The secular humanist liberation movement, in its zeal to win over religious America, should not encourage nonbelievers to turn away from their own intellectual heritage at the time when they will want it most.[4]

If *not* turning away from one's religious heritage means actively turning toward it, that movement should also include the most unabashed criticism—a crucial task, following Kaufmann, whose heretical faith is the product of a lifelong critique of religion. During the Vietnam War, which appalled him, he wrote, "My plea is that in cultivating ethics, philosophy and the other fields, we examine our traditional faith and morals"—"questions of faith and practice."[5] Here is another brief for studying him: his criticism is *engaged*—meaning, it grows more personal and intense as the gravity of the matter increases.[6] Thinkers in search of a robust "humanist moral philosophy" who ignore Kaufmann's work risk courting a moral despair along the lines of Reverend Casaubon's, in George Eliot's novel *Middlemarch*, whose failure, too, was neglecting *to read the Germans.*[7]

This book is an attempt to heighten the pleasure and instruction you will find in Kaufmann's work and not a substitute for it. Emphasis falls again on Kaufmann's work: this book is an intellectual biography, in the way that Kaufmann describes *The Faith of a Heretic*: "The heretic in *The Faith of a Heretic* is myself. But the book doesn't tell the story of my life. It is an attempt to describe my views."[8] That is also the aim of the book that you now hold in your hands . . . or on your Kindle.

If you have read Kaufmann's translation of Nietzsche's *Thus Spoke Zarathustra*, you may recall that Nietzsche anticipated a time when "the nobility" would abandon their loyalty to a "Vaterland" (fatherland) for a "Kinderland" (children's land)—a time and place of the childlike courage to create new values in a playful spirit.[9] Nietzsche could not imagine that his dreamt-of "Kinderland" would turn into a "Kindleland," with its redemptive and its damnable sides, of which we are all too aware. On this topic of a promised land, Nietzsche was not as explicit as Hegel—who, as Kaufmann shows, was often Nietzsche's reference—about identifying America as the new world of courageous children. For, "far from claiming that world history would culminate in Prussia, Hegel . . . hailed the United States as the land of the future and expected it to enter world history, decisively, after its frontiers were conquered."[10] Kaufmann died just before the digital revolution; one can only imagine the intellectual frontiers he would have "conquered" with digitally enhanced tools of writing and research.

Although I have this digital advantage, I want to forecast the limitations of this book. I do not know all the things Kaufmann knew before he set pen to paper (unlike him, I read very little Aramaic . . . and no Pali at all). Many of these "things" would have been available only to a student, like Kaufmann, of a classical German *Gymnasium* and thereafter at the Institute for Jewish Studies in Berlin, where they would have been received in a way that cannot be captured today. You can attempt to read all the books Kaufmann read and excerpted in philosophy, history, comparative religion, comparative litera- ture . . . or begin to, for their number beggars belief. It may also be that all Kaufmann's philosophizing, as Nietzsche wrote, is "a return and a homecom- ing to a remote, primordial, and inclusive household of the soul" that we *share* and "out of which those [philosophical] concepts grew originally."[11] But the way they enter the individual mind owes a great deal to its selective hospital- ity—to its intellectual history and personal culture. And so, I cannot easily claim to have obeyed the famous German romantic injunction to understand the author better than he understood himself—a procedure, incidentally, vigorously defended on one occasion by Kaufmann.[12] But I want to make a beginning, and I would be happy to think that others who read this book will write their understanding in its margins and on top of it.[13]

I treat Kaufmann's major works one by one, in the order of their publication, mainly keeping to one side the foreknowledge of what he was still to write. I enjoy, and I hope you, reader, will enjoy this journey to ideas as yet unknown. Along with my admiration for most of his work, I have obviously taken liber- ties with the idea of a pure exposition: I have not followed all of Kaufmann's precepts on composition. In *Hegel: A Reinterpretation*, Kaufmann encourages the critic not to sell the philosopher's ideas short in order to expound his own views. I ignore this precept not so much to offer my own views as to offer the views of other scholars, meaning to enrich Kaufmann's presentations with the products of recent scholarship. But I have also added critical thoughts of my own and I hope useful parallels, always meaning to indicate the places where I do so. Most of my additions expand what Kaufmann set down; from time to time, I oppose him. I do so, somewhat guardedly, too, recalling Kaufmann's 1979 preface to his *Tragedy and Philosophy*: After having deplored the habit of "some philosophers . . . who read their own ideas into their predecessors," he adds, "Nor do I feel that a book about another philosopher is the place to show why one thinks that he was wrong and then to present one's own views."[14] This engaging principle is in fact one that Kaufmann honors, from time to time, in the breach. He is scathing on Aristotle's poetics of tragedy and on Hegel's view that "Christianity discovered the infinite worth of every human soul," a "cliché" he finds "ridiculous."[15] He is certain that Hegel's identification of what actually is with what is objectively right—indeed, as designed by God—is an incorrect "generalization," to say the least. I am sure that such opposition is well within the spirit of his enterprise: my own remarks are an invitation to the reader to rethink, once again, what Kaufmann has written. Reading should not be assent but a call to vigilance.[16] In 1954 Kaufmann wrote:

> What is the point of a book on a thinker? It can have mainly two valid purposes: to get people to read and understand him because he has something worthwhile to offer; or to combat him and to show that what he has to offer is unacceptable. These two aims are not mutually incompatible.[17]

At the end of his life, some twenty-five years later, Kaufmann stressed the point: "An interpreter of a philosopher, poet, or statesman must have some grasp of the mind or mentality of the subject . . . and finally the still more difficult grasp *that requires the critical rethinking of the writer's ideas*" (emphasis added).[18]

In his *Hegel*, Kaufmann also wrote that one must do better than attempt to describe everything one reads in a book; productive criticism addresses and goes deeply only into selected passages. I have not described everything in Kaufmann's books, but I have striven to give as full an accounting of their contents as I could—consistent with the desire that the account be pleasurable and interesting.[19] I am also thinking of the requirement imposed on Hegel before he could lecture at Heidelberg in 1816, exactly two hundred years ago: he had to produce *compendia*. A "compendium," as Kaufmann defines the word, is "an abridgement of a larger work or treatise, giving the sense and substance within smaller compass."[20] Such a text would be bound in turn to invite marginal commentaries from the author—demurrals, additions, and exclamation points of appreciation. That is the case here: it is a critical exposition.

At this point, readers who have glanced inside this book may wonder why it includes so many direct quotes from Kaufmann's writing. I cite him often because his voice in his work is far more resonant than that of any commentator's. A friend of Kaufmann, the philosopher Ben-Ami Scharfstein, remembers him as "an individual whose voice speaks (I hear it clearly) from each page he wrote."[21] In fact, the authority for the decision to cite Kaufmann in his own words comes directly from Kaufmann, via Freud: "Of course, Freud was right when he said that it is easier for the reader to deal with a single author and become accustomed to his voice, while constant translations [read: paraphrases] of quotations are exhausting."[22]

I also cite Kaufmann because his work is not otherwise available in so condensed and extensive a form as in this book. It would be best, of course, if readers would go directly to Kaufmann's opuses and read them through, although their volume, including the writings of others he reproduces in his anthologies (and even leaving his numerous articles and translations aside) totals some eight thousand printed pages. I especially wanted to reproduce the richness of his work in his own voice out of a feeling of dismay on reading many of the reviews his work received during his lifetime. Almost nothing of his verve, erudition, and synthetic power can be gotten from these screeds, which, on the example of Kaufmann's magnum opus *Tragedy and Philosophy*, typically read, "It is gratifying that a large publishing house saw fit to bring out so personal a book," or "Euripides receives a scant, unsatisfactory twenty pages."[23]

A final note about the arrangement: because I want to create a continuum in which Kaufmann's voice will sound and resound, it is only at the end of the book, in a postscript, that I report various critical views of Kaufmann's first major work, his 1950 *Nietzsche: Philosopher, Psychologist, Antichrist*. These pages include voices harsher than they need be and are in places fairly technical. Readers who prefer to extend their impression of Kaufmann's first *chef d'oeuvre* should go directly to this late section. But before there was *Nietzsche*, there was this remarkable man, the subject of this intellectual life story, who deserves a proper introduction.

C *Critique of Religion and Philosophy*. Princeton, NJ: Princeton University Press, 1978; originally published in 1958 by Princeton University Press.

D1 *Discovering the Mind*, vol. 1, *Goethe, Kant, and Hegel*. New Brunswick, NJ: Transaction, 1991; originally published in 1980 by McGraw-Hill.

D2 *Discovering the Mind*, vol. 2, *Nietzsche, Heidegger, and Buber*. New Brunswick, NJ: Transaction, 1992; originally published in 1980 by McGraw-Hill.

D3 *Discovering the Mind*, vol. 3, *Freud, Adler, and Jung*. New Brunswick, NJ: Transaction, 1992; originally published in 1980 by McGraw-Hill.

E *Existentialism from Dostoevsky to Sartre*. A Plume Book. New York: Penguin, 1975; originally published in 1956 as a Meridian book by World Publishing.

ER *Existentialism, Religion, and Death: Thirteen Essays*. New York: New American Library, 1976.

F *The Faith of a Heretic*. Princeton, NJ: Princeton University Press, 2015; originally published in 1961 by Doubleday.

FH *The Future of the Humanities*. New York: Reader's Digest Press, 1977.

H *Hegel: A Reinterpretation*. Anchor Books. Garden City, NY: Doubleday, 1966; originally published in 1965 by Doubleday.

Hp *Hegel: Texts and Commentary*. Notre Dame, IN: Notre Dame University Press, 1977; originally published in 1965 by Doubleday.

LL *Life at the Limits*, the first book of *Man's Lot: A Trilogy*. New York: Reader's Digest Press/McGraw-Hill, 1978.

N *Nietzsche: Philosopher, Psychologist, Antichrist.* Princeton, NJ: Princeton University Press, 1974; originally published in 1950 by Princeton University Press.

R *Religion from Tolstoy to Camus.* New York: Harper and Brothers, 1961.

RE *Religions in Four Dimensions: Existential and Aesthetic, Historical and Comparative.* New York: Reader's Digest Press/Thomas Y. Crowell, 1976.

S *From Shakespeare to Existentialism.* Princeton, NJ: Princeton University Press, 1980; originally published in 1959 by Beacon.

T *Tragedy and Philosophy.* Princeton, NJ: Princeton University Press, 1979.

TA *Time Is an Artist,* the second book of *Man's Lot: A Trilogy.* New York: Reader's Digest Press/McGraw-Hill, 1978.

W *Without Guilt and Justice: From Decidophobia to Autonomy.* New York: Peter Wyden, 1973.

WM *What Is Man?,* the third book of *Man's Lot: A Trilogy.* New York: Reader's Digest Press/McGraw-Hill, 1978.

WALTER KAUFMANN

Introduction

WALTER KAUFMANN WAS born in Freiburg in Breisgau, Germany, on July 1, 1921, and died in Princeton, New Jersey, on September 4, 1980, far too young, at fifty-nine, for someone of his vitality.[1] His colleague, the Princeton historian Carl Schorske, remained lucid until his death in 2015, after having celebrated his one-hundredth birthday.[2] Arthur Szathmary, who together with Walter Kaufmann joined Princeton's Department of Philosophy in 1947, died in 2013 at ninety-seven; and Joseph Frank, emeritus professor of comparative literature at Princeton, with whom Walter debated an understanding of Dostoevsky's *Notes from Underground*, passed away in 2013 at ninety-four, some months after publishing his last book.[3] It is hard to imagine Kaufmann's sudden death at that age arising from an ordinary illness, and in fact the circumstances fit a conception of tragedy—if not his own. According to Walter's brother, Felix Kaufmann, Walter, while on one of his Faustian journeys of exploration to West Africa, swallowed a parasite that attacked his heart. In the months following, Walter died of a burst aorta in his Princeton home.

His death does not fit his own conception of tragedy, for his book *The Faith of a Heretic* contains the extraordinary sentences:

> When I die, I do not want them to say: Think of all he still might have done. There is cowardice in wanting to have that said. Let them say—let me live so they can say: There was nothing left in him; he did not spare himself; he put everything he had into his work, his life.[4]

He would also not want it otherwise than to have his readers oppose him, for only some of this claim would prove true. Against his will, and yet at no threat to his nobility (for "nobility squanders itself"), readers will think of all he might have done.[5] This awareness, too, is heartbreaking, when one reads

1

more and more of his vast and lively work as philosopher, essayist, poet, photographer, translator, and editor. I think of all the joy of creativity denied to him—and to us, who study him with intricate pleasure and with a response that needs to be creative. Indeed, as Kaufmann's former student and colleague the philosopher Alexander Nehamas has written, we are working "in a field ['the philosophical tradition'] that sometimes considers agreement a form of discourtesy."[6]

In a disarmingly simple sentence in *The Faith of a Heretic*, published in 1961, Kaufmann writes of the commitments made by two formidable writers, Hermann Hesse and Martin Buber: "Their personalities qualify their ideas." Kaufmann means that such commitments—Hesse's apolitical reclusiveness and Martin Buber's "selfless" principles of Bible translation—may not have the same value "when accepted by men of a different character." Here we have his recurrent insistence on the exemplary importance of great personalities "if we ever are to learn the meaning of humanity."[7] He might have quoted Stephen Spender: "I think continually of those who were truly great."[8] Shakespeare, Goethe, Nietzsche, and Freud are Kaufmann's distinctive examples. This high valuation of character over culture—a character informed by what may be called *virtù*—*will, flooded with intelligence*—could make Kaufmann's thoughts seem out of season in our acquisitive, culture-besotted age. But his distaste throughout the 1950s and 1960s for the feeling that the times could no longer countenance greatness of soul would have survived him into our century. His short life gives us a good, strong taste of what such greatness of soul would be like.

Walter's father, Bruno Kaufmann, a cultivated lawyer, was born a Jew but converted to Protestantism; his mother, Edith née Seligsohn, did not convert, as we discover from a poignant interview conducted shortly before Kaufmann's death. Even as a boy of eleven, as he recalls, he was unable to understand who or what the Holy Ghost was and asked his father for an explanation. The explanation fell short, and he replied, "Well, I don't believe in Jesus and I don't believe in the Holy Ghost either, so it seems I just believe in God, and then I cannot really be a Christian."[9] He took this conclusion very seriously and, not yet twelve years old, formally abjured Christianity and received a document confirming his decision.

The abjuration of Christianity was not an abjuration of the subject he found "intensely interesting"—religion—an interest he would maintain for the rest of his life.[10] Still a boy of twelve, he converted to Judaism, ignorant of the fact that *all* his grandparents were born Jewish. He then became bar mitzvah, partly under the guidance and participation of Rabbi Leo Baeck, at that time the acknowledged leader of the Jewish community in Germany.[11] To elect, as he did, to be bar mitzvah in Berlin in the year 1933 might be called a gesture of Socratic protestantism; it might also be reckoned the expression of a self *never* inclined to bend—and might have led (or not) to the burst aorta that took Kaufmann's life at the unquiet age of fifty-nine.

In the years following his conversion, Kaufmann met the charismatic Martin Buber as well; and he was much impressed, then and long afterward, by the writings of both thinkers. He translated a volume of essays by Leo Baeck, *Judaism and Christianity*, admiring especially the essay "Romantic Religion," and Buber's *I and Thou*, often acknowledging its importance.[12]

Kaufmann would soon encounter Nazi social viciousness head-on. He was denied entrance to a university but was able to use profitably even those years of not yet lethal persecution. In March 1938, at age seventeen, having graduated from the Grunewald Gymnasium in Berlin, where his family now lived, Kaufmann entered the Hochschule für die Wissenschaft des Judentums (Institute for Judaic Studies), where he completed a semester and a half of work in Jewish history. Thereafter he went to Palestine for three weeks; he was to revisit Israel many times afterward.[13] On returning to Berlin, he began studying Talmud at the *Lehranstalt* of the institute in preparation for the rabbinate before emigrating in January 1939 to the United States. He prepared for the rabbinate, he explains, since

> in Germany at that time, there was nothing else to study. As a Jew I couldn't go to the university, so, being terribly interested in religion at that time, and in Judaism in particular, . . . [becoming a rabbi] is what I thought I would do. When I came to United States, I took all the religion courses I could take in college, majored in philosophy, and one thing led to another.[14]

Kaufmann escaped the fate of several members of his family. Their change of faith meant nothing to the Nazis; the entire family, Walter Kaufmann included, could have expected certain death had they not left Germany. One of Walter's uncles, fighting for Germany in the First World War, died in Russia; two others were murdered. The dedication to the volume *The Faith of a Heretic* reads:

To My Uncles
WALTER SELIGSOHN
who volunteered in 1914 and was
shot off his horse on the Russian front in 1915

JULIUS SELIGSOHN
AND
FRANZ KAUFMANN
both Oberleutnant, Iron Cross, First-Class, 1914–18,
one a devout Jew,
one a devout convert to Christianity,
one killed in a Nazi concentration camp in 1942,
one shot by the Secret Police in 1944,
both for gallantly helping others
in obedience to conscience, defiant

Kaufmann arrived in the United States alone in 1939 and in the fall enrolled in Williams College, in Williamstown, Massachusetts, with sophomore credit. He mastered English with exceptional speed, graduating two years later with high honors. Details of his intellectual progress at Williams are found in the alumni archives of the Williams College Library, where they have been examined by Eric v. d. Luft and inserted into a brief—and in part painfully derogatory—biography in the *Dictionary of American Biography*.[15] Kaufmann studied with John William Miller, who lectured on the philosophy of history, "grounded," according to v. d. Luft, in the "free act proposing systematic consequences."[16] Kaufmann's other mentor was James Bissett Pratt, who lectured on comparative religion, a course that Kaufmann attended zealously.[17] Pratt taught the pertinence of bodily experience to religious feeling,[18] and his comments on mysticism recur in Kaufmann's 1958 opus *Critique of Religion and Philosophy*. About these opposite ideas of freedom and bodily determinism, v. d. Luft notes that "both strains of thought were later manifested in Kaufmann's own thought."[19] Early in his undergraduate years, Kaufmann abandoned his commitment to Jewish ritual while developing a deeply critical attitude toward all established religions.

After graduation, Kaufmann's likely path led to graduate school, to write a doctoral thesis in philosophy, but his ever-present will to action, and now with a war on, urged him, after a year at Harvard, to join the US Army Air Force and thereafter serve as an interrogator for the Military Intelligence Service "in an old German penitentiary in the Rhineland."[20] His experience with the occupying troops was morally vexing, and a poem in his volume *Cain* tells of his chagrin:

"Occupation"

Parading among a conquered and starving people
among the ruins

with patches and stripes and ribbons and hash marks
one for a year in the army
for having grown callous and dumb
one for a year in the States
for learning to goldbrick and pass the buck
one for the fight and one for the occupation
for drinking and whoring and black marketeering
one for the victory that is melting away
while they parade among the ruins with ribbons and stripes.[21]

He deplored the collapse of military discipline. A piece published in 1979 in Princeton's student newspaper the *Princetonian* reports Kaufmann's remark, during a lecture on Nazism, that in 1944, as part of an American military intelligence team, he witnessed American soldiers who, in the course of their interrogations, beat and killed German prisoners.[22]

In Berlin Kaufmann bought a copy of the Musarion edition of Nietzsche's collected works and was captivated.[23] He returned to Harvard with the intention of writing his doctoral dissertation on Nietzsche, which he did in a year, earning his PhD in 1947 with a thesis titled "Nietzsche's Theory of Values." That very fall he began teaching at Princeton, where he continued to teach for the next thirty-three years.

In 1950, just three years after arriving in Princeton, Kaufmann published his remarkable first opus, with signature provocativeness, *Nietzsche: Philosopher, Psychologist, Antichrist*, which would transform the reception of Nietzsche in America and Europe. In Kaufmann's hands, Nietzsche emerged as a deeply productive philosopher, altogether more engaging than his pejorative image as wild man and proto-Nazi would suggest. Nietzsche studies in America flourish as a rigorous discipline entirely aware of Kaufmann's intellectual revision. It is hard to find a single monograph on Nietzsche in the fifty years following that does not take pains either to agree or to disagree with his work. At Princeton Kaufmann would be promoted to full professor in 1962, but as an "avowed critic of religious institutions,"[24] his rise to this position was visibly delayed, and it took another seventeen years for him to occupy the distinguished Stuart Professorship of Philosophy.[25]

There is a sort of permanent youthfulness—zest and pugnacity—in all of Kaufmann's writing, consistent with the picture of him in life that many people retain. The filmmaker Ethan Coen, who studied philosophy at

Princeton, mentions Kaufmann's special dedication to undergraduates.[26] I first saw Kaufmann in 1955, in the early summer following my graduation from Columbia College, when he came to lecture on that new and exciting philosophical movement called existentialism. To my regret, I was unable to feel myself addressed for the very callow reason that I could not expect a professor who himself looked like an undergraduate and, as I recall, wore lederhosen, to speak with much authority. (I was used to the solemnity and air of mature grandeur that attached to the great figures at that university—Quentin Anderson, Moses Hadas, Lionel Trilling, et al.).

Part of my first impression of Kaufmann was shared by others, to judge from passages in a story titled "Princeton Idyll" by Princeton's own Joyce Carol Oates. One of her two narrators writes, "I do remember the philosopher and Nietzsche translator Walter Kaufmann, who came by on his bicycle to introduce himself . . . and who became one of my grandfather's good friends. So boyish-looking, people mistook him for an undergraduate at the University." The second narrator, a semiliterate housekeeper recalls: "One of them [the geniuses] came alone on his bicycle. I thought he was a student, but this was "WK" who was so kind to me. . . . Once on Olden Lane I was walking & WK stopped his bicycle to walk with me. He wore cordroy trousers and a V-neck sweater like a boy. His hair was very dark and his eyes were dark and lively. He was not much older than I was."[27]

Kaufmann's life, even as a tenured university professor of philosophy, was full of incident and adventure, which he achieved quite possibly in earshot of the mutterings of some colleagues. In a passage from an earlier work, *Critique of Religion and Philosophy*, we read in italic, "*That those who prefer freedom to the existence of the intellectual shut-in must of necessity be unable to make up their minds or to act with a will is a myth popular in institutions.*"[28] He went his own way, with striking independence, in love with proofs of his autonomy. Something of the scope of the lands he surveyed is suggested in the 1979 preface to the book *From Shakespeare to Existentialism*, whose first edition preceded by a year the appearance of *The Faith of a Heretic*. There, he writes of discovering, in summer 1979, his penchant for returning again and again to places that had once fascinated him in the course of "traveling around the world *for the fourth time.*"[29] On returning to Rembrandt's "Large Self-Portrait" in the Vienna art museum, he had a sort of moral epiphany. Seeing "integrity incarnate" in the painter's eyes, he felt as if he were being "mustered" by that gaze. He explained: "One has to do something for a living, especially if one has a family, but I felt that I want to write only in the spirit in which Rembrandt had painted himself, without regard for what might pay or advance my career."[30]

He would write (following Stendhal) with what he called "the logic of passion" for a larger reading public. After completing his breakthrough study *Nietzsche: Philosopher, Psychologist, Antichrist* when he was not yet thirty, he finished his fourth decade by publishing four volumes in nearly consecutive years, the above-mentioned *Critique of Religion and Philosophy*, in 1958; a book of his essays, *From Shakespeare to Existentialism*, in 1959; a commented anthology of religious writings, *Religion from Tolstoy to Camus*, in 1961; and *The Faith of a Heretic*, again, in 1961. The scope of his intellectual concerns is stunning, the erudition breathtaking, and for one so young, the tempo of production uncanny: each of these four near masterpieces is around four hundred pages in hard covers. And this is to overlook his publication, in 1958, as well, of an edited translation of a volume of essays by Leo Baeck, *Judaism and Christianity*; in 1961, two volumes of a commented *Philosophic Classics* and in the same year his redoubtable translation of Goethe's *Faust*; and finally in 1962, his edition and translation of *Twenty German Poets* and a volume of his own poems, *Cain and Other Poems*. At this early stage he had already created what in German is called *ein Werk*, a substantial, coherent, interrelated body of work. And this prolific evidence of a sustained life of writing and reflection would be present to the very end of his days.

The memorial composed by Princeton's Philosophy Department on Kaufmann's death sums up the life beautifully, if too briefly:

> He lived his life with a truly dazzling expenditure of energy, giving tirelessly of himself. The life he wanted, he said, was one "of love and intensity, suffering and creation." That is exactly the kind of life he had.[31]

The pages that follow deal closely with almost all of Kaufmann's books, highlighting their relevance to arguments and issues vibrant today: the God question, the crisis of the individual subject in an age of aggrandizing technology, the fate of the humanities, and particularly the good of philosophy. Because you will read here and there in dictionaries that Kaufmann was "not a philosopher," I want to stress how his concerns are also professionally timely.[32] Consider a passage from the short biography composed by Ivan Soll, Kaufmann's student, himself a professor of philosophy. Soll writes, "In *The Faith of a Heretic* [1961] Kaufmann . . . argued that what essentially defines our philosophical tradition, and makes it valuable, is its critical or 'heretical' character." He quotes Kaufmann at length:

In medieval philosophy, apologetics triumphed over criticism. In modern philosophy, critical thinking re-emerges. Both tendencies are prominent in the great modern thinkers. But as we examine their progression, we discover that their rationalizations have proven less enduring than their criticism. And instead of seeing the history of philosophy as an accumulation of fantastic systems, one may view it as the gradual analysis of, and liberation from, one illusion after an another, a stripping away of fantasies, a slow destruction of once hallowed truths that are found to be errors.[33]

How interesting it is to compare this passage with a sentence from a book on Plato by the current and rightly much-celebrated philosopher Rebecca Goldstein:

The progress to be made in philosophy is often a matter of discovering presumptions that slip unexamined into reasoning, so why not the unexamined presumption that got the whole self-critical process started?[34]

In this matter of Kaufmann's relevance, apropos of his fundamental interest in religion, consider this citation from the *New York Times* in 1986:

I remember [Paul] de Man looking me in the eye, [J. Hillis] Miller recalls, and saying, "For me, the most important questions are religious questions." So much for [de Man's] "nihilism."[35]

It remains for us to wonder what part of Kaufmann's preoccupation with religion is an affair of devotion and what part is ethical and intellectual interest. His interviewer Trude Rosmarin-Weiss wonders as well: "He described himself as an 'agnostic' and a 'heretic,' but he wrote so much on religion and defended Judaism against Christianity with such fervor and vehemence that it seemed to me that Professor Kaufmann 'doth protest' too much against religious belief."[36] Kaufmann's credo from a later work titled *Existentialism, Religion, and Death* gives further direction to our concern: "Religion deals with faith, morals, and art. I am much less interested in metaphysics and theology than in what religions do to people—how they affect human existence." This is the position of the religious rationalist—religion matters only as it might serve human intellectual and ethical interests. But Kaufmann then adds, "In that sense, my own ultimate concern is existential."[37] The term "existential" implies a more than rational disposition. It implies commitment—*belief* in a matter to which one brings empathy and care. Equally, it does not exclude intellectual interest, for Kaufmann's existence—his *life*—is informed by an unrelenting *libido sciendi*, a craving to know. It is now wonderfully coherent that Kaufmann's first committed project would be a study of Nietzsche, the greatest modern expert on "what religions do to people."

1

Nietzsche Redivivus

NIETZSCHE: PHILOSOPHER, PSYCHOLOGIST, ANTICHRIST

I love Nietzsche although my disagreements with him are legion.

—WALTER KAUFMANN

IN SUMMER 1954, as a naval cadet in the NROTC unit at Columbia University, I lay sprawling on the steel floor of the destroyer USS *Steinaker* reading *Nietzsche: Philosopher, Psychologist, Antichrist*, the cover quite visible and flagrant.[1] An officer saw me and shouted, "Why are you wasting your time reading this book!" Ever since then, I have felt myself especially protective of this book, the author, and his subject.

It is one of those books that stand out in your past as vividly as the first glimpse of a dreamlike foreign place or a first love. I do not know whether it has such distinction for everyone who read it at twenty. Certainly, it has stood out in the older or recent past of almost every scholar who has since written on Nietzsche. Citations from Kaufmann function as a seal of authenticity, proof of a competent intellectual-historical awareness. He is so often quoted appreciatively—or attacked angrily—and presumably corrected—that all modern Nietzsche scholarship begins to read like so many footnotes to Kaufmann.[2] And where he has not been cited (as in several articles in the 2013 *Oxford Handbook of Nietzsche*), I conclude not ignorance of Kaufmann but the strongest possible disagreement.[3]

In this light, Kaufmann's *Nietzsche* has enjoyed an importance acquired by very few other books—as a work central to the humanities, as obligatory reading at the foundation of many kinds of scholarship: Nietzsche studies, of course, but also modern European history, moral philosophy, reception studies, literary history, and so on. How many books of intellectual history can claim a comparable durability? In fields I recognize, I think of Erwin Panofsky's *Studies in Iconology: Humanist Themes in the Art of the Renaissance* (1939);[4] Erich Auerbach's *Mimesis: The Representation of Reality in Western Literature;*[5] and Ernst Curtius's *European Literature and the Latin Middle Ages,*[6] the latter two works published in English translation in 1953.

Nietzsche deserves to be part of this company at the order of style as well. The book is fine-grained and scrupulous, notably well written, often with aphoristic elegance—better: aphoristic enthusiasm: "The irrational is not envisaged as something that is adverse to rationality but only as a weak form of rationality."[7] "As human beings we have ideals of perfection which we generally find ourselves unable to attain. We recognize norms and standards of which we usually fall short; we long for a triumph over old age, suffering, and death; we yearn for perfection and immortality—and seem incapable of fulfillment. We desire to be 'as gods,' but we cannot be so" (N 254). "When the overcoming of suffering is not conceived in terms of one's own exertions, it is apt to take the form of one's own triumphant elevation over the suffering of others" (N 275). "There is a sense in which every great individual is an embodiment of new norms, an incarnate value-legislation, and a promise and challenge to posterity" (N 415). "It may well be true that agony is the price of all birth, and travail the cost of creation; one may grant that all great pleasure can only be had after considerable suffering, and that those who are capable of the most extreme exultation are also most sensitive to anguish" (N 272). (One thinks of Franz Kafka, whom Kaufmann often quotes in his later work, writing: "No one sings so purely as those in deepest hell; what we consider the singing of angels is their singing."[8])

We can agree that reading Kaufmann's *Nietzsche* cannot be a merely contemplative, aesthetic affair. Having mentioned Kafka, I will note that the effect of *Nietzsche* on the alert reader is bound to be like that of Kafka's stories in the account given by Theodor Adorno:

> Each sentence of Kafka's says, "Interpret me." Through the power with which Kafka commands interpretation, he collapses aesthetic distance. He demands a desperate effort from the allegedly "disinterested" spectator of an earlier time, overwhelms you, suggesting that far more than your intellectual equilibrium depends on whether you truly understand; life and death are at stake.[9]

The allure of Kaufmann's *Nietzsche* is heightened by its surface.[10] I mean quite literally its defiant cover: the thinker, in chiaroscuro, with his small and shapely ears and bushy mustache—unheard of—descending over, sealing up his mouth. With such an obstacle to speech or food or drink, what could one do other than think and write? The title of the book is printed in carmine letters—a burning orange-red—anticipating Nietzsche's sun worship and craving to blaze like a sun. "Life—that means for us constantly transforming all that we are into light and flame . . . we simply can do no other."[11] How much of this blaze flashes out of Walter Kaufmann's early magnum opus? Thomas Mann thought . . . a lot!—calling it "a work of great superiority over everything previously achieved in Nietzsche criticism and interpretation." The Thomist philosopher Jacques Maritain judged Kaufmann's "analysis of Nietzsche's life, thought, and influence . . . extremely well-informed, thorough, and searching."[12] The book is certainly superior for its attention to very nearly the whole of Nietzsche's work. (The gap in attention implied by "very nearly" would become a bone of contention decades later.) Kaufmann meant his cultured, liberal-humanist enterprise to put an end to "readings" that sought an opportunity, in writing on Nietzsche, to foam at the mouth.[13]

Certainly, a great deal has already been written about the violent use made of Nietzsche by German warmongers in 1914 and Nazi propagandists decades later. It was precisely this sort of overt political "instrumentalization" that Kaufmann's book aimed to get past.[14] On the question of how grievously Nietzsche should be held responsible for his being so user-friendly to the wrong cause, the jury is out. It speaks in his favor that in at least one respect the Nazi attempt to use him was notably unsuccessful. The regime did not win this war of ideas. Bureaucrats responsible for selecting, publishing, and furthering the work of national-leaning writers soon abandoned a mooted critical edition of Nietzsche in favor of Hölderlin.[15] To the chagrin of his editors, too much in Nietzsche did not fit an exterminationist agenda. This is a result that should be kept in mind when scholars complain that Kaufmann criticizes too often—it was his "wont," thus the worthy Duncan Large, "to attack every previous edition and translation."[16] At least several of the objects of his criticism—such as Professor Alfred Bäumler, the publicist Heinrich Härtle, and the editor Richard Oehler—were Nazi collaborators, soldiers of ideas for the Third Reich. These conformist hacks did their best to enlist Nietzsche, who proved more trouble than he was worth. When Kaufmann's book wrests Nietzsche from readings obsessively attentive to Nietzsche's presumed fascist bearings—let alone the disfiguring, fascist-minded *use* of Nietzsche—his work amounts to more than an academic exercise: it becomes a cultural-political act. Kaufmann conceives his enterprise as a personal cultural politics as well—as Kaufmann's way to his own self-overcoming. Two thought flows accompany the writing of this chapter—one, what Nietzsche means for reestablishing a sane German intellectual tradition—and, two, what Nietzsche means *for him*.

In conjuring and measuring the depth of Kaufmann's commitment to his subject, we should begin by noting the labor of his working through his subject's German in an acquired language—in an English whose clarity no one has ever disputed. I will develop this point by understatement: Nietzsche mattered enormously to Kaufmann; he was well worth the work put in. Nietzsche describes Schopenhauer as his "educator"; in just this way, Nietzsche is Kaufmann's educator.[17] When discussing the work of the Nietzsche scholar Erich Podach, Kaufmann suggests that "likemindedness, temperament, and even the range of a writer's emotional and intellectual experience" are *not* "irrelevant when the points at issue concern appreciation or over-all interpretation" (N 439). My assumption throughout this chapter is that Kaufmann qualifies as an "over-all" interpreter. And so I shall emphasize the passages and arguments in his reading of Nietzsche that answer to the urges of Kaufmann's literary and philosophical personality. It could be that, treasuring so much of Nietzsche's thought, Kaufmann wrote this book in a mood of righteous indignation at the way the experience of reading Nietzsche had been misrepresented, perverted, etiolated by critics operating not on knowledge but on hearsay—Nietzsche *looted*. We can feel this emotion when we contrast what we read in Kaufmann with what subsequent professional critics have written, coolly disengaged in the act of identifying his "errors." Many of these alleged deficiencies, though not all, disappear on a close reading of his book; and so we have, as a result, what David Pickus has called "the Kaufmann myth"—the myth of the book's extreme bias toward a sweetly reasonable Nietzsche, its bland "liberal humanism" contrived to suit readers' interests.[18] But what we have seen so far, I think, is that there is nothing bland about the temper of the writing, a function of the depth of Kaufmann's commitment.

Kaufmann's book, in its four revisions, is as interesting for what it says Nietzsche believed as what Nietzsche *did not* believe, though much of the task of drawing conclusions as to the latter will fall to the reader, who, arriving with archaic expectations, may be in for a surprise. Kaufmann's undertaking obliges him to criticize, sometimes scathingly, and often, other respected commentators, a compliment that has been returned, after his death, by the scathed and their students.[19] Readers may wish to consult the postscript to this book, where

Kaufmann's critics' main complaints are detailed . . . and criticized in turn. My concern now is to represent his *Nietzsche* at its first birth, with this caveat: I come to study Kaufmann, not to praise him.

The most pronounced quality of this book is its probity: Kaufmann's insistent questioning, careful phrasing, dialectical *ricorsi,* many caveats—and plain disagreements with his subject. I was pleased to find in an early review that the French phenomenologist Adolphe de Waehlens had also been struck by Kaufmann's *probité.*[20] What follows, then, is Kaufmann's detestation of misrepresentation, of fraud—hence, his opening insistence that by manipulating Nietzsche's unpublished papers, Frau Elisabeth Förster-Nietzsche distorted his leading ideas.[21] Kaufmann is as harsh on studies by ideologists tributary to the Stefan George circle. They judged Nietzsche to be incoherent, whereas Kaufmann will prove the essential coherence of his work—dissolve Nietzsche's seeming "ambiguity" by painstakingly tracing the history of his writings and defining its context in every case.[22]

Kaufmann does not hesitate to declare the critical writings by Förster-Nietzsche, Stefan George, Ernst Bertram,[23] and others *dead wrong*—an "essentialist" judgment, according to the historian Steven Aschheim and hence anathema to the work that historians do: Nietzsche, in Aschheim's view, cries out for historians and not enthusiasts or hangmen in judges' robes. That is very well, but as Aschheim also notes, "the philosopher," unlike the cultural historian, "is not only free to judge and evaluate—*he is obliged to do so*" (emphasis added). Meanwhile, Kaufmann operates in the creditable spirit of the cultural historian as well, since, following Aschheim, "the historian must be alert to overt invention, expurgation, selective editing, and outright falsification of Nietzsche's texts; the notorious tampering activities of Elizabeth Förster-Nietzsche are well known."[24]

Kaufmann is devoted to context, in the sense of insisting on understanding Nietzsche's key—and, especially, controversial—ideas in light of the historical moment in Nietzsche's writing career and the detail of the argument that embeds it. Changes in context change the meaning of identical-seeming propositions. Here is an example of such reading:

> It has been overlooked that the Dionysus whom Nietzsche celebrated as his own god in his later writings is no longer the deity of formless frenzy whom we meet in [*The Birth of Tragedy*], Nietzsche's first book. Only the name remains, but later the Dionysian represents passion *controlled* as opposed to the extirpation of the passions which Nietzsche more and

more associated with Christianity. The "Dionysus" in the Dionysus versus Apollo of Nietzsche's first book and the *"Dionysus versus the Crucified"* in the last line of [*Ecce Homo*], Nietzsche's last book, do not mean the same thing. The later Dionysus is the synthesis of the two forces represented by Dionysus and Apollo in *The Birth of Tragedy* . . . (*Die Götzen-dämmerung* [The Twilight of the Idols] IX 49). (N 129)[25]

It might be supposed that, besides shifting context, Nietzsche's aphoristic style, irrepressibly allusive, would obstruct every attempt to generate a unified argument from his writings.

The elusive quality of this style, which is so characteristic of Nietzsche's way of thinking and writing, might be called *monadologic* to crystallize the tendency of each aphorism to be self-sufficient while yet throwing light on almost every other aphorism. We are confronted with a "pluralistic universe" in which each aphorism is itself a microcosm. Almost as often as not, a single passage is equally relevant to ethics, aesthetics, philosophy of history, theory of value, psychology, and perhaps half a dozen other fields. (N 75)

This description does not spare Nietzsche's style from the charge of "decadence," as Nietzsche himself conceives it:

the word becomes sovereign and leaps out of the sentence, the sentence reaches out and obscures the meaning of the page, and the page comes to life at the expense of the whole—the whole is no longer a whole. This . . . is the simile of every style of decadence: every time there is an anarchy of atoms [*Der Fall Wagner* (The Case of Wagner) 7]. (N 73)

In his lustrous book *Nietzsche: Life as Literature*, Alexander Nehamas, Kaufmann's former colleague and interlocutor, stresses Kaufmann's claim that the seeming chaos of Nietzsche's aphorisms reveals an "organic unity" behind which is "a whole philosophy" (N 74).[26] For Kaufmann, Nietzsche's central idea is the unity of created (or sublimated) *personhood*, namely, "the fact that . . . [Nietzsche's] life and work suggest an organic unity" (N 70). "The self-creation Nietzsche has in mind," adds Nehamas, "involves accepting everything that we have done and, in the ideal case, blending it into a perfectly coherent whole."[27]

Both Kaufmann (and Nehamas in his own work) are inclined to reason through so-called organic unities: Kaufmann calls direct oppositions "Manichaean" and prefers to see blended fusions, as in the claim that "Nietzsche's position can be summarized quite briefly: *happiness is the fusion of power and joy*—and joy contains not only ingredients of pleasure but also a component of pain" (N 278). The opposite direction, I'll add, is taken by Henry Staten's *Nietzsche's Voice* (1990), which speaks in detail of the restless, nonorganic, fragmentary character of Nietzsche's writing, describing it as "a problematic and fractured unity."[28] But Kaufmann means all along to resist the view of Nietzsche's fragmentation, whether in spirit (*Geist*) or method.

To strengthen his notion of an organic unity of aphorisms, Kaufmann treats the individual aperçu as an experiment. Nehamas's commentary is instructive: "In order to accomplish this [unity]," he writes,

> Kaufmann interprets the aphoristic style as an expression of Nietzsche's philosophically grounded objections to system building and of his preference for posing questions rather than for giving answers: "Nietzsche," Kaufmann writes, "is, like Plato, not a system-thinker, but a problem-thinker" (N 82). He then argues that Nietzsche transcended the limitations of the style of decadence by putting it into the service of what Kaufmann calls "his experimentalism": this is an attitude that essentially involves "the good will to accept new evidence and to abandon previous positions, if necessary" [N 86]. Each aphorism is therefore, for Kaufmann, an "experiment." And even if not all of Nietzsche's experiments confirm the same theory, they are still unified by his "intellectual integrity," which "makes each investigation a possible corrective for any inadvertent previous mistakes. No break, discontinuity, or inconsistency occurs unless either there has been a previous error or there is an error now. . . . His 'existentialism' prevents his aphorisms from being no more than a glittering mosaic of independent monads." (N 91)

Besides this unity of argument, Kaufmann strives to find in Nietzsche's aphorisms an underlying unity of *method*.[29] We have Kaufmann's elegant formulation of Nietzsche's philosophy of method:

> In *The Birth of Tragedy*, the Dionysian represents that negative and yet necessary dialectic element without which the creation of aesthetic values would be, according to Nietzsche, an impossibility. True to his method, he does not, to begin with, assume a divine providence or a purpose of nature—and lacking these, he seems to have no sanction for an absolute obligation or a moral "ought." He turns to aesthetic values which are not so firmly associated with a supernatural sanction and are conceivable without any element of obligation. (N 129–30)

This thrust to unity is Kaufmann's main task, and it will involve a change of tempo in the narration: we move from the *presto* of his exposing the ideological crimes and philological misdemeanors of Nietzsche's early (proto-Nazi) interpreters—the vigorous parry and thrust of polemic—to the andante and even largo of patient explication, not without its dramatic highlights and changes of pace. The Nietzsche scholar Richard Schacht outlines the corresponding conceptual evolution in this movement: "a record of Nietzsche's development from the author of *The Birth of Tragedy* into a psychological thinker on a par with Freud, with his further transformation into a philosopher coming somewhat later."[30] The experience of reading Kaufmann is of a relentless progress through Nietzsche's work, consistent with Kaufmann's methodological premise of a precise chronological, contextual positioning of Nietzsche's ideas.

The sought-after coherence of Nietzsche's corpus of thought involves Nietzsche's great desideratum: the organic unity of the individual personality. This idea is the keystone of Nietzsche's virtual system; as such, it supports Kaufmann's presentation at every juncture. Self-creation is the book's indispensable idea: the unity of the strong self is to be obtained by acts of self-stylization. Here is Nietzsche in *The Gay Science*:

> *One thing is needful.* "Giving style" to one's character—a great and rare art! It is exercised by those who see all the strengths and weaknesses of their own natures and then comprehend them in an artistic plan until everything appears as art and reason, and even weakness delights the eye. Here a large mass of second nature has been added; there a piece of original nature has been removed: both by long practice and daily labor. Here the ugly that could not be removed is hidden; there it has been reinterpreted and made sublime. . . . It will be the strong and domineering natures who enjoy their finest gaiety in such compulsion, in such constraint and perfection under a law of their own . . . (*Die Fröhliche Wissenschaft* (The Gay Science, 290). (N 420)

Kaufmann would paraphrase Nietzsche, with internal quotes: "'One thing is needful'—namely, 'that a human being *attain* satisfaction with himself,' recreate himself, and become 'a single one' by 'giving style' to his character" (N 420–21). This enterprise is the most valuable, the privileged form of the exercise of the will to power. Kaufmann repeatedly affirms that "the will to power is at the core of Nietzsche's thought, but inseparable from his idea of sublimation" (N xiv)—of self-overcoming (*Sichüberwinden*)—an exercise of the will to power on itself.[31]

Now, here is one serious caveat before we become too negatively exercised by the precritical idea of a perfectly unified self: the aspect of perpetual *striving* in the enterprise of self-fashioning is crucial. The implication that this process could come to rest in a single being is less prominent in Kaufmann's account than the element of contestation. Self-overcoming means an ongoing encounter with, indeed a thirst for, resistance; and what could offer greater, more stubborn resistance to the personality than forms in which the will to power had already invested itself and "attained satisfaction?"[32]

In light of this account of the will to power—its character as self-contestation—it would be quite unfair to describe Kaufmann's view of self-making in Nietzsche as a "disappointingly trite praise of personal self-control." These are the words of the Nietzsche scholar Bernard Reginster in 2007. In fact, Kaufmann's view runs chiefly in accord with Reginster's own description of the will to power as the will to the sensation of overcoming resistance, of *becoming*, a view inconsistent with the idea, as well, of achieving domination and control of other persons, social classes, parties, or institutions.[33]

In the introduction to his translation of *The Birth of Tragedy*, Kaufmann addresses the chaotic and murky writing of especially the later passages of this book and then its Apollinian harnessing in the lucid prose of the books that followed—an illustration of the very effort at self-stylization that Nietzsche saw as the soul of the individual will to power. Kaufmann *also* writes: "to be sure, the self-styled Dionysian dithyrambs of *Zarathustra* symbolize Nietzsche's departure from the Apollinian articulateness of his aphoristic style." Here, then, is evidence of the unceasing struggle between the two forces, as each resists the other's dominance. The apparent superiority of an Apollinian mode of address is attained only after long struggle and remains perpetually subject to metamorphosis.[34]

———

A sympathetic commentator, David Pickus, whose essay on the "myth" of Kaufmann's *Nietzsche* I've mentioned, observes that Kaufmann treats Nietzsche "as someone who never lets us forget that the question of *strength*— its simultaneous quality and quantity—undergirds all inquiry into value."[35] "Strength" has indeed functioned as a normative arbiter of value from Hans Vaihinger in 1902 to Reginster's *The Affirmation of Life* in 2006. This link of strength and value is vivid in a passage from Nietzsche's late writings:

The Germans think that *strength* must reveal itself in hardness and cruelty; then they submit with fervor and admiration: they are suddenly rid of their pitiful weakness and their sensitivity for every naught, and they devoutly enjoy *terror*. That there is *strength* in mildness and stillness, they do not believe easily. They miss strength in Goethe . . . !—XI [containing by-products of *Morgenröte* (Dawn) and *Die Fröhliche Wissenschaft* (The Gay Science), 112.] (N 228)

Kaufmann will represent the thought of Nietzsche as consistent with this irenic strain—a strain undoubtedly present throughout Nietzsche's work even when interrupted by a tone and argument more hectic and more violent. Kaufmann needs a set of points to organize *one* reading of this multifold, fragmented, ever-changing corpus of texts: the most important points—I will stress this fact—connect the *will to power* with the effort at *self*-overcoming, *self*-stylization, an affair if not of "mildness" then of "stillness," for nothing audible—no shouting—can be detected in such work. "At the top of the power scale," writes Kaufmann," are those who are able to sublimate their impulse, to 'organize the chaos,' and to give 'style' to their character" (N 280). Kaufmann conceives of the longed-for Übermensch, of whom most readers have heard, as the embodiment, somewhat controversially, of a maximum of the will to *self*-perfection. An account of Kaufmann's achievement by Henning Ottmann, the editor of a German Nietzsche encyclopedia, reads:

> It was basically Walter Kaufmann's book *Nietzsche: Philosopher, Psychologist, Antichrist* . . . that, for its scholarship and its comprehensive reconstruction of Nietzsche's philosophy, inaugurated the philosopher's rehabilitation. To be sure, to counteract the demonization of Nietzsche, Kaufmann harmonized and depoliticized his philosophy to the point where the Übermensch was nothing more than the moral ideal of individual self-overcoming.[36]

One wonders, however, what else Nietzsche meant the Übermensch to be, what other qualities he was meant to embody? Those of a race-hating, jack-booted killer?[37] Here Kaufmann introduces the crucial figure of Dionysus to contain many of the nonirenic moments in Nietzsche. The Übermensch is the " 'Dionysian' man . . . who has overcome his animal nature, organized the chaos of his passions, sublimated his impulses, and given style to his character—or, as Nietzsche said of Goethe: 'he disciplined himself to wholeness, he *created* himself' and became 'the man of tolerance, not from weakness but from strength,' 'a spirit who has *become free*'" (N 316). *The Will to Power* adds an engaging description of Dionysian tolerance: The "art of communication commanded in the highest degree by the Dionysian type [is] marked by the ease of metamorphosis; it is impossible for him to overlook any sign of an affect."[38] Still, Kaufmann's account of the Übermensch has been the object of persistent scholarly criticism, as we shall see in the postscript to this book.

It is at the midpoint of Kaufmann's study, which aims to establish the unity of Nietzsche's key thinking, that we touch "the crown of Nietzsche's philosophy: the dual vision of the Übermensch and the eternal recurrence; its key conception is the will to power" (N 121). The connection of these ideas lies in the optimal exertion of the will to power in the service of affirming one's individual being through the process Kaufmann—and Nietzsche, occasionally—call sublimation. What is crucial is that in so doing, "the Übermensch would also affirm all that is, has been, or will be [*Die Götzen-dämmerung* (The Twilight of the Idols) IX 49]" (N 320). Thus the terrible thought of the Eternal Recurrence of the Same can function as a boon for "the man who perfects himself and transfigures his *physis*," for such a one need "no longer feel concerned about the 'justification of the world'" (a topic, notes Kaufmann, poorly solved by aesthetic means in *The Birth of Tragedy*, which famously declares that "the world is *justified* only as an aesthetic phenomenon"[39]). Kaufmann writes: "The 'Dionysian' man who is depicted under the name of Goethe at the end of the *Götzen-Dämmerung* [The Twilight of the Idols] (IX, 49)" (N 316) "affirms the world forward, backward, and 'in all eternity.'" "The best injunction reads: 'Not merely bear what is necessary, still less conceal it . . . but love it' (*Ecce Homo* II 10)" (N 324).

It might be said (it will be said) that Kaufmann's deflection of the will to power from mastery over others to self-mastery sanitizes Nietzsche, especially when Kaufmann unblushingly declares that the "leitmotif of Nietzsche's life and thought" is "the anti-political individual who seeks self-perfection far from the modern world" (N 418). I shall return to this theme, since it is also the leitmotif of the criticism directed against his book.

Kaufmann, of course, is selective in his emphases, even within the wide range of his concerns, for an overriding purpose:[40] that in 1950 Nietzsche might be read calmly, anew, in the context of the main movement of his work, freed for a time from the rage of the "tough" Nietzscheans, who had saddled him with a Hitlerian morality of perpetual combat, struggle (with others), hardness, self-sacrifice, and thereafter of racial breeding. And as these values involve a deprecation of reason, of a lucid consciousness, Kaufmann defends Nietzsche precisely on this ground. The "crown" of Nietzsche's thought includes his "high esteem of rationality. . . . Nietzsche's position is unambiguous and unequivocal, provided that one examines his philosophy as a whole. . . . Nietzsche himself . . . attached supreme significance to what *he* took to be the conscious aspect of that state of being he called power" (N 268–69).

I have been stressing Kaufmann's view that the optimal aim of Nietzsche's will to power is self-vivification, and so I will stay with this thesis one page longer. One hears Zarathustra's plangent cry: "Behind your thoughts and feelings, my brother, there stands a mighty ruler, an unknown sage—whose name is self." "Always the self listens and seeks: it compares, overpowers, conquers, destroys. It controls, and it is in control of the ego too." Note just now how readily Nietzsche, not merely Kaufmann, erases the distinction between the exercise of "control" and a more energetic dialectic of the self that is "creative" even as it "conquers" and "destroys": "The creative self," Zarathustra declares, "created respect and contempt; it created pleasure and pain."[41] From "behind," from below, the self appropriates "thoughts and feelings" to the end of an increase in its sense of power.

Nietzsche's writing on this topic, as it is embodied in the type of the ascetic artist, is some of his most impressive.

> One should . . . not . . . think little of this . . . phenomenon ["the bad conscience"] merely because it is painful. . . . At bottom, it is . . . that very *instinct of freedom* (in my language: the will to power): only here the material upon which the form-giving and ravishing nature of this force vents itself is man himself, his . . . animalic . . . self—and *not . . . other men*. This secret self-ravishment, this artists' cruelty, this pleasure in giving form to oneself as a hard, recalcitrant, suffering material—burning into it a will, a critique, a contradiction, a contempt, a No—this . . . work of a soul that is willingly divided against itself and makes itself suffer—this whole *activistic* "bad conscience" has . . . been the real womb of all ideal and imaginative events and has thus brought to light an abundance of strange new beauty and affirmation—and perhaps *beauty itself*— . . . [*Zur Genealogie der Moral* (On the Genealogy of Morals) II 18]. (N 252–53)

The result of such insistence on a "politics of the self" is, of course, that Nietzsche's "large-scale politics" gets shorter shrift in Kaufmann's book than in subsequent studies.[42] It is not that angry politics is ignored:

Nietzsche . . . was also aware that—more often than not—the will to power manifests itself in more aggressive ways. The weak, lacking the power for creation, would fain shroud their slave souls in a royal cloak and, unable to gain mastery of themselves, seek to conquer others. [Kaufmann's rhetorical flourish here is borrowed from Goethe, who, at the beginning of the *Classical Walpurgisnacht* in *Faust II*, writes: "For everyone who does not know / How to control his inmost self would fain control / His neighbor's will according to his own conceit."][43] . . . Nietzsche speaks of the will to power; but he leaves no doubt that this drive is an Eros and can be fulfilled only through self-perfection. (N 255–56)

The claim of subsequent critics that Kaufmann's apolitical view of Nietzsche—who, in *Ecce Homo, called himself* "antipolitical"—enfeebles Nietzsche's doctrine of will to power is asserted with more noise than truth.[44] A good deal of such resistance might be owed to *our* attachment to the topical mood of warmongering, cruelty, and terror, which Kaufmann allegedly whited out of Nietzsche. The sobering reminder by the Ernst Bloch scholar Peter Thompson makes the point: "We are once again living in an eschatological and apocalyptic era . . . [in which] it is easier to imagine the end of the world than it is to imagine a different and better one."[45]

Evidently, monographs devoted entirely to Nietzsche's politics treat more thoroughly than Kaufmann's the theme of Nietzsche's "large-scale politics," forecasting terrible wars in the name of the breeding of the Übermensch. But if Kaufmann's book is short on Nietzsche's political theory—and indeed on the political theory implicit in his own way of reading Nietzsche—his book does something other than theorize. In shifting the focus of Nietzsche's "tough-minded" readers aiming at his presumptive fascist bearings, it is itself, as I've said, a cultural-political *act*. His book, no less its title, never hides its intention: it will treat Nietzsche not as a political thinker but as a philosopher, artist, and—not uncritically—saint-like ascetic.[46] Can you imagine the fate of Nietzsche scholarship after Kaufmann if he had systematically included everything in Nietzsche by the categorial name that subsequent commentators preferred? There would be nothing but a vast empty sigh of agreement.[47] Perhaps Nehamas can be allowed to settle the matter of Kaufmann's relevance for the moment, in his foreword to the new Princeton Classic edition of *Nietzsche*:

Kaufmann's *Nietzsche* is . . . a book that everyone seems to be familiar with but few have actually read, as if, having succeeded in upending the traditional picture of Nietzsche, it can now be safely ignored. But reading it (or rereading it) repays the effort. Kaufmann's . . . accounts of Nietzsche's dependence on Goethe, of his naturalism . . .—[of] the mechanisms of sublimation and his affinities with American pragmatism are genuine and lasting contributions to our understanding of this still seductive and enigmatic philosopher who is now, thanks to this book, part and parcel of our intellectual heritage. Kaufmann's Nietzsche is still very much alive, and for that reason his *Nietzsche* deserves to come alive once again.[48]

————

The legacy of Kaufmann's *Nietzsche* will occupy us more fully in due course, but the right question for *this* book involves a Copernican turn: not what is Kaufmann's *Nietzsche* for its posterity, not even who is Kaufmann's Nietzsche (though this is a matter we must address), but what, chiefly, is Kaufmannesque in Kaufmann's view of Nietzsche? To answer this demand means: reading Kaufmann, in Nietzsche's own punning words, *rück- und vorsichtig* (backward, forward—and *carefully*).[49] He is owed this attention: this project went deep into him. Through it Kaufmann begins to *become* his own (Nietzschean) intellectual self on the Nietzschean logic that you are truly what you love (others would add: *fated* to love).[50] In creating his Nietzsche, Kaufmann creates—or *sublimates*—himself. This claim is different from saying that he fell into the arms of Nietzsche's corpus—or did not try not to. His caveat reads: "I have always tried to resist the exegetical temptation of reading my own ideas into the text" (N iv). The work is replete with caveats. Some signal illustrations will define the hard edge of his profile in contradiction to Nietzsche's; they will also have the benefit of giving us a window onto Kaufmann's main concerns:

> The content of Nietzsche's message . . . no less than the form it entails, offers the most striking contrast to the Biblical prophets. He lacks their humility which, while defying the judgment of mankind, yet knows itself no more than a mouthpiece of God. Nietzsche seems less appealing than the ancient prophets because his outrageous conceit steps between him and us. Yet if there is any sense in which he seems more appealing, it is that he thus appears more wretched, more forsaken, and more tragic. (N 99)

In *Ecce Homo*, Nietzsche writes—in some distinction from Kaufmann's passing view of him—"My lot is that I must be the first *decent* human being, that I know myself to be in opposition against the mendaciousness of millennia."

But Kaufmann is quick to point out "the touch of madness in the uninhibited hyperbole of Nietzsche's phrasing" (IV 1) (N 111).

Kaufmann objects to a confusion between Nietzsche's reading of history as a naturalistic—read: "biological"—sequence of events and Nietzsche's view of these events as symbols and in their fullness a work of art. "Nietzsche speaks of sensing in history 'a whole world of deep meaning, power, and beauty' without making clear of what exactly historical events are supposed to be symbols and whether the value of history is still naturalistic" (N 149).

He raises an objection to Nietzsche's positing a single principle—will to power—informing the totality of being: "The assumption that the cosmos can, and must, be reduced to one principle" might be "due only to the Western heritage of monotheism," though this caveat prompts an inspired illustration and defense of this "decisive point of Nietzsche's cosmology":

> Nietzsche was a *dialectical monist*. His basic force, the will to power, is not only the Dionysian passionate striving, akin to Schopenhauer's irrational will, but is also Apollinian and possesses an inherent capacity to give itself form . . . Thus the spirit is a unity that is not an "inert simplicity," nor an "unstained self-identity," but essentially a process . . . , a dialectical monism in which the basic force is conceived as essentially creative. . . . The will to power is, as it were, always at war with itself. The battle between reason and impulse is only one of countless skirmishes. All natural events, all history, and the development of every human being, consist in a series of such contests: all that exists strives to transcend itself and is thus engaged in a fight against itself. (N 235, N 239, N 241–42)

Something of the richness and survival power of this conception is illustrated in a passage from Staten's *Nietzsche's Voice*. Staten makes little obeisance to Kaufmann—indeed he finds fault with some of Kaufmann's translations of Nietzsche in key places (see the postscript)—but I think his refined, analogous discussion of the eristic component of Nietzsche's view of the self is illuminating here. According to Staten, Nietzsche's philosophy cannot be a philosophy of immediate self-actualization because the individual self is a scene of conflict: the "restricted" economy, which aims at appropriating and holding fast, constructing and enduring as a particular being, fights against the "grand economy," which urges that it spend itself and die. (Kaufmann quotes Nietzsche pertinently: "True goodness, nobility, greatness of soul . . . which does not give to take, which does not want to *promote* itself by being good, *squandering* as the type of true goodness, the wealth of personality as prerequisite" [N 114n15]). In Nietzsche's thought, Staten continues, the contest is not only or even principally a contest of themes and concepts, one of which might be proved more truthful and valuable than its opposite, with the result that the other is annihilated. Instead, it is a play of rhetorics and styles—of cross-conceptual attractions and repulsions, advances and withdrawals, driven by the Dionysian "pathos" of the will to power. Words like "contest" and "play" are more nearly apt here than "structure." Nietzsche proposes not so much arguments as contests within arguments fought at a micrological level: at every moment key terms strive toward and away from one another. It can never be a matter of eliminating an apparently weaker term when Christ the Jew inheres in Dionysus.[51]

We have been citing several of Kaufmann's caveats as evidence of his readiness—indeed, his eagerness—to put critical distance between Nietzsche and himself. And so here is another of his key objections:

> It is one of Nietzsche's most serious shortcomings—and has contributed seriously to his "influence"—that he failed to give any emphasis to this common human potentiality and did not consider the possibility that this potentiality might be quite sufficient to re-establish that "cardinal distinction between man and animal" which Darwin seemed to Nietzsche to have denied. Nor did Nietzsche stress the element of secrecy which surrounds the mystery of election and precludes man's ability to judge his fellows. (N 286)

This is to say: The omnipresent human potentiality for the good that Kaufmann sees as establishing the firm distinction between man and animal flies in the face of Nietzsche's chief insistence: that precisely no such firm distinction exists between animal and man, *with the exception of the artist, philosopher, and saint.* Or let us temper Kaufmann's caveat a bit, for he is not entirely easy at being dismissive of Nietzsche: "There is," he writes, "a certain plausibility to Nietzsche's doctrine, though it is dynamite. He maintains in effect that the gulf separating Plato from the average man is greater than the cleft between the average man and a chimpanzee" (N 151). Still, serious doubt about Nietzsche's dangerous elitism has been put in place.

Kaufmann's criticism of Nietzsche's "hypothesis" of the Eternal Recurrence of the Same is especially vigorous:

> Nietzsche is plainly guilty ... [of turning] a profound and valid insight into an exclusive "doctrine"—and he might be criticized in the very words he

used to pass judgment on Christianity: he "transformed the symbolic into crudities." . . . One can grasp Nietzsche's conception of "Dionysian" joy while feeling that the more explicit "doctrine" transforms a fruitful notion into a rigid crudity. (N 332)

It is interesting that there then follows a familiar dialectical ricorso, aiming to ease criticism of Kaufmann's educator. He adds: "One should remember, however, that the doctrine of the eternal recurrence—as distinguished from the profound experience of joy that comes to the overman—was presented by Nietzsche not as a dogma but as a hypothesis, true to his method" (N 332). This is part of a recurrent No-but-Yes pattern informing Kaufmann's presentation of arguments: he produces correctives at the end from a sought-after fair-mindedness tilting toward the thing or person criticized when that thing or person still deserves consideration. A vivid example from another context reads: "To be sure, Luther did not mean to repudiate love and works of love, however many extreme passages one could quote from his works almost at random" (N 348).[52]

Kaufmann will return unhappily to Nietzsche's tone, especially at the end of Nietzsche's writing life: "There is something shrill about much of Nietzsche's writings: he delights in antitheses to what is current; it is as if he were swimming against the stream for its own sake; and he makes a sport of being provocative" (N 413).[53]

Finally, toward the close of his book, he sees Nietzsche failing "to distinguish sharply enough between that internal criticism of 'contemporary virtue' which is properly the revaluation, and that creation of new norms which is characteristic of all creativity." This point might be made clear by an analogy one hears in seminar rooms: If I can prove that the (intellectual) currency in your pocket is counterfeit, I still have not put good (intellectual) currency into your pocket. Kaufmann continues by noting that

the confusion may have been due in part to the fact that one man—whom Nietzsche supremely admired—represented both the critical and the creative function in the highest degree: Socrates. He was not only the "gadfly" of Athens and the "vivisectionist" of contemporary conceit and hypocrisy; he also created his own character and embodied new values which generations of philosophers after him sought to explicate in their ethics. (N 414)

Here we have yet another example of the ricorso that aims to put the criticized tone or argument in a better light, as well as an early statement of a principle that will become ever more prominent in Kaufmann's work: the value of personality and of the thought arising from great personality. This view borrows Nietzsche's paean to "true goodness, nobility, greatness of soul . . . which does not give to take, which does not want to *promote* itself by being good; *squandering* as the type of true goodness, *the wealth of personality as prerequisite* (final emphasis added)" (N 114).

Despite this recurrent show of critical distance, it would be impossible for Kaufmann not to come away (to speak with Milton) with a "new acquist of true [conceptual] experience."[54] In our discussion of Kaufmann's thought, this means that it will not be mainly a question of the ideas (from Nietzsche) he brought into his work but the ideas that emerged (for him) from a way of reading exemplified by Nietzsche, of thinking *boldly*, of forever increasing the pressure of thought, indifferent to the risks it might run.[55] (After all, this is a man—Kaufmann—who converted to Judaism in the year the Nazis seized power!) One concrete desideratum surfaces often—Kaufmann's signature thought: the indispensable power of reason, or what Lessing called "the diligent drive for Truth, albeit with the proviso that I would always and forever err in the process."[56]

> Nietzsche . . . insists that, though the intellect is an instrument, its figments should be frankly labeled as fictions. . . . The question arises, of course, from what point of view the fictions of the intellect could possibly be criticized and found out to be only fictions. With Kant, Nietzsche believes in reason's capacity for self-criticism—and the fictions in question may be found either to be self-contradictory or to contradict each other. To be bold in offering such criticisms is part of the service of truth. (N 356–57)

This claim interests Kaufmann, a fugitive from the deranged irrationalism of the Nazis, mightily and lastingly: he finds this claim justified in Nietzsche, and it produces some of Kaufmann's most invested writing. An aphorism cited earlier supports this view: "The irrational is not envisaged [in Nietzsche] as something that is adverse to rationality but only as a weak form of rationality." Kaufmann continues: "The will to power is neither identical with reason nor opposed to it, but *potentially* rational" (N 234–35).

Such evident gestures of Kaufmann's taking Nietzsche to heart and mind can be read through the book's many conceptual emphases but also through Kaufmann's method and style—his exegetical signature. (It is, of course, one of his explicit concerns to show that "Nietzsche's literary style reflects a way of thinking—indeed, a method that has philosophic significance" [N xiv].) I will point out, throughout this book, how this experience of reading Nietzsche— in content and form—colors Kaufmann's future work, and here is a direct foreshadowing of this procedure. A good portion of the Kaufmann-to-be can be found in the following:

> A philosopher, says Nietzsche, . . . must not allow "concepts, opinions, things past, and books" to step "between himself and things." He must not rationalize the valuations of his own society. As Nietzsche sees it, the temptation to do this is particularly great for the German professor who is an employee of the state. Of course, that is a chief reason for his choice of Schopenhauer as his protagonist in the essay in which he attacks the State so fearlessly; Schopenhauer was, unlike Kant and Hegel, no university professor. (N 104–5)

Kaufmann will rate his "existential" identification higher than his rank as a university professor, to wit,

> [Nietzsche's] . . . own philosophy even shows many decided affinities to Kant's; but Kant's failure to question the existence of the universal moral law provoked Nietzsche's attacks, which further illustrate his reasons for opposing systems and his "existential" identification of any failure to question with a desire not to experience fully. (N 103)

He would attempt "to experience fully" even and especially outside the walls of the university, to which his more than four scrupulously attentive trips around the world would testify.

———

These early pages have aimed to describe what Nietzsche meant *for* Kaufmann as a scholar of the history of philosophy. His Nietzsche appears as a retrospective educator of the great figures in the intellectual tradition, ranging from Heraclitus, Socrates, Luther, Lessing, Kant, Hegel, Dostoevsky . . . to John Dewey, André Malraux, and onward. Kaufmann inserts Nietzsche's writings into a traditional history of philosophical reflection, as announced in the preface to the first of the four editions: "Nietzsche is here assigned a place in the grand tradition of Western thought and envisioned against the background of Socrates and Plato, Luther and Rousseau, Kant and Hegel—not as has often been done, as Schopenhauer's wayward disciple or a lone epigone of the pre-Socratics" (N xiii). And as Schopenhauer was Nietzsche's educator, so is Kaufmann's Nietzsche ours. The book *educates*, faithful to its etymological sense of "leading out" of stupor into knowledge, in line with Kaufmann's professional interest in teaching via competent analysis, erudition, and style.

Since Nietzsche means so much for Kaufmann's personal history, it will be interesting to ask about the genealogy of his interest, the conditions of the possibility of Nietzsche's importance for him. An accidental encounter is crucial to this story: while still a soldier and interrogator in Germany, Kaufmann came across the rare and celebrated Musarion edition of Nietzsche in Berlin and was fascinated. From this point on, his own implicit convictions dovetailed with what he saw as Nietzsche's life goal of a strenuously virtuous self-stylization. Nietzsche—and the entire enterprise of getting him right in a book—is Kaufmann's primary educator. In the spirit of good moral ecology, I will once again take my bearings from David Pickus. "At this point," Pickus writes,

> it is possible to stop and take a step backward in German intellectual history in order to clarify why Kaufmann's work is nether apologetic in the polemical sense of the word or "humanist" in the vague but pejorative sense used as an accusation. Indeed, the notion of humanism, even if used in Kaufmann's favor, hinders an understanding of what he was about. Kaufmann's "constructive refutation" of the Nietzsche legend is not so much aimed at anyone like the Nazis as at writers . . . [insensitive] to *an intellectual tradition centered around self-confrontation in the service of Bildung* and other German ideals of self-cultivation (emphasis added).[57]

The historian David Sorkin elaborates this ideal:

> The ideal of *Bildung* . . . denoted a process of integral self-development on the basis of a form that was an inherent part of the individual. Form no longer resulted from imitation of an external, religious model, but from the development of what was innate. Man achieved a unity of essence and existence through a self-initiated process for which he was his own model.[58]

These descriptions illuminate Kaufmann's interest in Nietzsche as a theoretician of Bildung: he "rescues" Nietzsche for a tradition of German thinking and writing that became the mainstay of the *Bildungsbürgertum*.[59] The *Bildungsbürger*, as described by Ian Buruma, is

> a member of the pre–[World] War II bourgeois German elite whose status was marked less by birth than by a solid classical education. Some of the proudest *Bildungsbürger* were Jews. . . . The minimum requirement for a *Bildungsbürger* was a sound knowledge of Latin and Greek, the classics of European literature, and of course German classical music. The German bourgeois [was shaped] by the Gymnasium.[60]

Kaufmann's family belonged to this Bildungsbürgertum, the "natural" social and cultural class from which the Nazis drove him out. (In short order, almost the entire class was eliminated from German social life.) Kaufmann remembers his grandmother saying, "A teacher is a hallowed person" (*eine geheiligte Person*).[61] At seventeen, Kaufmann already belonged to the Bildungsbürgertum on his own merits, having completed his classical education with distinction at a first-rate (Berlin/Grunewald) Gymnasium.[62] His formal academic development, however, came to an abrupt end under the Nazis; as a Jew, he was denied entrance to a university. He did, however, complete a year of study at the Hochschule für die Wissenschaft des Judentums (Institute for Judaic Studies), whose disciplinary "science" (Wissenschaft), as Sorkin informs us, was originally conceived as addressing "all extant sources, irrespective of language or an author's religion" and including

> relevant works by non-Jews. This was but another form in which Judaism was subsumed to the larger category of *Bildung*. The academic study of Judaism was the scholarly outgrowth of the ideology of emancipation.[63]

Individual "Bildung," it was supposed, would fuel the drive to Jewish emancipation. Kaufmann's Nietzsche project presents an opportunity to evoke, revive, and enlarge the cultural ideal of the Bildungsbürgertum.

Obviously, only a certain view of Nietzsche and his intellectual context could function this way. It is remarkable that Buruma finds "in many respects the perfect example of a *Bildungsbürger*" in Johannes Fest—father of the well-known German "liberal-conservative" writer Joachim Fest—who "took pride in his complete works of Goethe, Shakespeare, Heine, and Lessing."[64] These are among the most important writers in the intellectual tradition in which Kaufmann locates his Nietzsche and, indeed, his own subsequent thinking. We can begin to intuit the *salvational*—the *personally* salvational—potential of this feat. In taking Nietzsche away from the Nazis and returning him to an "authentic" Germany, Kaufmann recovers the idea of Germany—the line of Lessing-Kant-Schiller-Goethe—that Jews dreamt of in their assimilationist craving, the dream of the *haskalah* (Jewish Enlightenment). Moreover, in bringing Nietzsche to America, Kaufmann brings with him the entire galaxy of German classical-idealism, no longer shrouded and under suspicion. Finally, and not trivially, as Kaufmann, at Harvard and Princeton, embeds Nietzsche, his educator, in a sane German cultural tradition—one that amounts to the course of study in the *Geisteswissenschaften* at a German university—he recoups the missing years of his own education.

It remains to note that this benevolent account of the *Bildungsideal* does overlook its inherent liability. The very title of Fritz Ringer's celebrated *The Decline of the German Mandarins* gives the game away: "The word *Bildung,*" he writes, "contained the single most important tenet of the mandarin tradition." This is its "highly distinctive model of the learning process," which involves much more—or something other—than absorbing and transmitting information and even increasing one's analytical powers. It is an affair of "'inner growth' and integral *self*-development." This development feeds off

> the moral and ascetic examples contained in the classical sources. . . . The whole personality is involved in the act of cognition. If the materials to be learned are properly selected, their contemplation could lead to wisdom and virtue. They can attract, elevate and transform the learner. He can thus acquire an indelible quality, also called *Bildung,* which is a potential rival to the characteristics of the aristocrat.[65]

The last word is a deal breaker. There is little in this personal bootstrapping program to encourage empirical political work on behalf of a just and equitable society. The defects of so individual an ideal, with its fantasy of spiritual nobility ("Seelenadel"), would prove disastrous for Germany, blatant in the horrific breakdown of the Weimar Republic. Ringer writes of "a decisive reversal of priorities. Geist (spirit) and its representatives had lost control of society. The new politics and economics had become emancipated from the influence of the cultured sage and of his values."[66] But the unpolitical component of the Bildungsideal was hardly foremost in Kaufmann's mind in 1950, fighting for a coherent self and a coherent life far from home.

The claim that Kaufmann was bringing the best possible notion of the German Bildungsideal to America might still be refuted by a point made by Pickus, writing on Kaufmann's view of the future of the humanities in America (see chapter 13). Unlike other German Jewish refugees—for example, Hannah Arendt, Leo Strauss, and Theodor Adorno—Kaufmann, writes Pickus, "never felt the nostalgia for Europe or the German patriotism common in the older generation. Indeed, unlike them, his education was as much American as it was European."[67] This latter point, however, is moot. According to Ivan Soll, who writes with the authority of a former graduate student, personal friend, and biographer of Kaufmann, he "was not so much educated by the two American institutions [Williams College and Harvard University] he attended as a student, as that he . . . used them as the required institutional backdrop for an intellectual and personal development whose mainsprings and general configuration already lay within him."[68] Kaufmann's view of the humanities in America was shaped by his personal involvement in the German cultural tradition—which, nota bene, always included a sustained internal critical distance. (Kaufmann: "There is no such thing as 'the' tradition.") On this point, we might think of the ongoing logomachy within this "universe of discourse"[69] aiming to give it its proper definition (Hegel versus Kant; Schopenhauer versus Hegel; Nietzsche versus Wagner; Nietzsche *in favor* of Hegel; Thomas Mann—the "ironic German"—for *and* against Nietzsche, etc.—or think of Nietzsche, for that matter, critical of [almost] every gesture of the culture of Wilhelmine Germany).

This mention of Thomas Mann invites further reflection on Kaufmann's sense of a sane German cultural tradition, which involves a determined critical triage: the ill (the irrational) must be excluded first. Kaufmann's empirical relation to Thomas Mann is a muted affair. Kaufmann arrived in Princeton in 1947, some five years after Thomas Mann had left, so there is no evidence of personal contact. Mann, the liberal humanist, might seem an exemplary figure for Kaufmann, a potential educator, but he is not—chiefly, I suspect, on the grounds of the diminished respect Kaufmann had for Mann's alleged misreadings of Nietzsche. Mann and Kaufmann, like many other notable minds, met on the threshing floor of Nietzsche criticism, with Kaufmann typically the more aggressive and Mann, quite possibly, skeptical behind his praise of Kaufmann's book. In *Nietzsche*, Mann is remembered as one who got the dates wrong of any provable influence of Dostoevsky on Nietzsche and as one who also thought wrongly of Nietzsche's Dionysianism as an efflux of German romanticism. On the other hand, Kaufmann casually terms Mann "illustrious" and, in this later edition, includes him, inevitably, in the reading list of all those writers who were subsequently "influenced" by Nietzsche. Kaufmann is thinking especially of Mann's *Doctor Faustus* for its modern elaboration of the legend of Nietzsche's encounter with a prostitute in a Dresden brothel.

The figure of Mann is relevant to Kaufmann's relation to the German cultural tradition in establishing it as complex and divided. Mann never tired of affirming his place in German intellectual and literary history—"the great tradition of Germanism from Luther to Bismarck and Nietzsche."[70] "What I owed to the German tradition of thought and how deeply rooted I am in the tradition is perfectly clear."[71] When Mann conceives of his relation to Nietzsche's thought, it is as Nietzsche's gift. He writes: "I have often felt that Nietzsche's philosophy might be able to become the good fortune and the lucky find of a great writer . . . , the source of the loftiest, most erotic and slightest irony

playing between life and mind."[72] Mann tirelessly claims Goethe, Schopenhauer, and Nietzsche as "vessels" of the intricate literary-philosophical tradition into which he "pours his soul." Later, however, in *Doctor Faustus*, he
dismissed the constitutive irony of Germany, its perpetual self-criticism and
self-division, as a mad adventure. In a letter of August 13, 1941, Mann writes:
"One would have to drive pretty far upstream along the course of German
history before one found no sign of that spirit which today has reached the last
degree of baseness and threatens to barbarize and enslave the world. At least
as far as the Middle Ages; for Luther . . . already had decidedly Nazistic traits.
And what horrors are to be found in Fichte! What menaces in the music, and
even more in the writings of Wagner! What a muddle of clarity and obscurity
in Schopenhauer and Nietzsche!"[73] There is very little in this picture of Mann's
No and Yes that would not apply as well to Kaufmann.

This list of opposing contenders for authority within this "universe of discourse" is infinitely expansible.[74] Consider Karl Jaspers and Kaufmann, as we
come closer to home, who for many years were highly critical of one another's
view of Nietzsche. Jaspers summed up their differences, as well as offering a
glimpse into the tone of the German philosophical conversation, in his correspondence with Hannah Arendt. Arendt had written to Jaspers, "[In Prince-
ton] I got to know Walter Kaufmann, who attacked me furiously—which
was his perfect right. . . . He is not (please keep this completely entre nous)
very well liked there because he is given to the German and German-Jewish
mode of discussion, which is so very intent on having the last word." To which
Jaspers replied, even after acknowledging Kaufmann's prodigious memory
and erudition, "In [Kaufmann's] . . . eyes, Kant's pre-Critical writings make
him a great philosopher, for in that period Kant was a European and enlightened. After *Critique of Pure Reason*, he started wandering on German byways.
That shows how little Kaufmann understands of philosophy. For him, I am a
German, of course, a non-European, with only one foot in the Enlightenment,
and therefore a highly suspect figure."[75]

In the next chapter I will confront Jaspers with Kaufmann once again, but
at this point we have a view on this German tradition for Kaufmann: it is a
mansion in which, to abuse the metaphor, its many rooms contend; it is an
invitation to enter and contend in turn; it is, when the times are dark, export-
able, a portable house, into which others may be invited.

Before leaving *Nietzsche* entirely, I want to develop a bit further the ethical
tradition of personal Bildung, which gives background and aura to Kaufmann's
reading of the will to power as bent on self-creation. Consider the proposition:

the stronger the passions, the wilder the chaos, the more strenuous the organization, the more effective the result. One scholar, Fritz Breithaupt, building on Marc Redfield's powerful reflections, prefers to translate "*Bildung* by the English word 'extension' instead of the more common 'formation' to emphasize [its] . . . dynamic nature. . . . For the early Romantics and Goethe," he continues, "*Bildung* was less a finished product and not even a shaping but rather a process of a *Horizonterweiterung* (a widening of horizons). This extension does not result in any describable entity, gestalt, or form; in fact, this very indescribability belongs to the notion of *Bildung*."[76]

"Expansion" would be a better word choice than "extension," though the latter gets the concept moving.[77] For, describing "the will to life," Nietzsche writes, "The great and small struggle always revolves around . . . growth and expansion."[78] Once again, there is nothing bland or ordinary about this process, since, citing Kaufmann, "the will to power is, as it were, always at war with itself. . . . All that exists strives to transcend itself and is thus engaged in a fight against itself" (N 242). "I assess the *power* of a *will*," Nietzsche writes, "by how much resistance, pain, torture it endures and knows how to turn to its advantage."[79] Such "self-perfection"—thus Kaufmann—"is possible only through suffering, and the ultimate happiness of the man who has overcome himself does not exclude suffering" (N 368). These remarks are especially telling in light, once again, of Bernard Reginster's skepticism—and not only his. Reginster pleads for a Nietzschean ethics based on the high value of suffering, suffering properly exacerbated by the striving to achieve one's highest ideals, a will to suffer perpetual resistance.[80] But where, once more, is this proposition *not* in Kaufmann? In fact, Kaufmann's stress on the *agony* of self-making hardly invites the charge that he is captive of what Michael Tanner calls "the *ideology* of liberal humanism," while accusing Kaufmann of having invented a Nietzsche in his own image.[81] The *agony* of self-making is not a common property of liberal humanism. This point should temper the objection that Kaufmann has improperly *embourgeosified* Nietzsche's aristocratic ideal of self-perfection. This construction of a *Nietzsche for everyone* willing to submit to the discipline, the torment, of ascetic self-making improves the case, especially in Austria, that the Bildungsbürgertum often included an aristocratic model, as we have learned, in its image of upward cultural mobility.[82]

Kaufmann is surely correct to lay stress on another of Nietzsche's key words for the cultivation of the self: *organization*. I will add a word or two about this term, for it is central to Nietzsche's thought from the beginning as the great antipode to the nihilism of personal and social formlessness, passivity, and fatigue. In notebook entries from 1882 on, which Kaufmann publishes in his edition and translation of Nietzsche's *The Will to Power*, Nietzsche writes of the danger of European nihilism, warnings directed to "us," whose "morality of freedom" impels us to affirm life.[83] For "we" are opposed by an enemy called "hatred of life," a sort of "Buddhism." The scene is all of Europe—a Europe informed by a will to power (*Thatkraft*) bent perversely on self-extinction. In the midst of this crisis, the idea of "recurrence" adds "a terrible burden." Nietzsche is anticipating the thought of the Eternal Recurrence of the Same, the meaningless life cycle implying endless, inescapable nullity. Five years later, in 1887, he will write down this idea "in its most frightful form: existence, as it is, without meaning and purpose, but irresistibly returning, without a finale into nothingness: 'The Eternal Recurrence.'"[84] Here, as in Kaufmann's central thought, the will to power and the Eternal Recurrence of the Same are linked in an essential way—at its highest pitch, the will to power, when exercised by the superior man, joyously affirms the eternal recurrence of his life cycle.

But how is this new capability to be achieved? Through the *organization* that the elect are able to confer on themselves. Where Kaufmann's inquiry into Nietzsche turns on this issue, as Kaufmann makes clear, Nietzsche usually has Goethe in his sights: after Schopenhauer, he is Nietzsche's highest educator. This superior being *suggests* the internal balance of the Übermensch, the incarnation of the strongest yea-saying will to life. The Übermensch, as we recall, is

> the "Dionysian" man who is depicted under the name of Goethe at the end of the *Götzen-Dämmerung* (The Twilight of the Idols) (IX 49). He has overcome his animal nature, *organized* the chaos of his passions, sublimated his impulses, and given style to his character—or, as Nietzsche said of Goethe: "he disciplined himself to wholeness, he *create*d himself" and became "the man of tolerance, not from weakness but from strength," "a spirit who has *become free*" (first emphasis added). (N 316)

This organization would indeed have to be superhuman, I'll add, to resist its fracturing by never-ending self-contestation, not to mention the aporia of inserting its mooted perfection into the mud and chaos of "factical" existence—the empirical, social world. Yet there needs to be a beginning. "If we do not maintain ourselves," Nietzsche's notes from 1882 continue—"we, ourselves, through organization—everything will come to an end." And only if we do are we "life's friends."[85]

This model of friendship implicitly involves organization—now, between "ourselves" and life. An intersubjective relation functions as an ontological category. This is a point of some importance in all of Nietzsche's writings, beginning with his plangent address, in *The Birth of Tragedy*, to "my friends": "Yes, my friends, believe with me in Dionysian life and the rebirth of tragedy."[86] "Friendship," like "organization," entails the concerted activity of various "centers." Without such centers—which in the period between fall 1887 and March 1888 Nietzsche subsequently calls "ruling centers" (*Herrschaftsgebilde*)—we have only a great, diffuse *noia*, a disaggregation of the will, which augurs worse: "Nihilism as a brief prelude."[87] All this is to confirm, with Kaufmann, that the crucial, life-saving expenditure of the will aims at an organization of the self in relation to life—a life that must be thought of as impressing itself on the entire sensorium, hence, chiefly, an organization of reason and sensibility.

Earlier in this chapter, I mentioned the figure of Hölderlin, a rival to Goethe, whose poetry today, I believe, is found more demanding and more beautiful than Goethe's. Kaufmann is interested in Hölderlin, as we shall see, and often has recourse to him, although it is Goethe who plays the greater tutelary role—Goethe, who, for Kaufmann, occupies so central a position as educator in Nietzsche's thought and who will also occupy so central a position in Kaufmann's own.[88] Early on in *Nietzsche*, Kaufmann produces this elegant contrast between the figures of Goethe and Jakob Burckhardt:

> Perhaps Burckhardt, like Goethe, looked back upon the storm and stress of his own youth, sensed in himself *a still dangerous medley of passions that could be controlled only by maintaining a subtle equilibrium*, and deliberately refused to become involved in the younger man's comet-like career which for Burckhardt could mean only destruction. While Goethe, however, deeply wounded men like Hölderlin and Kleist—the poets whose meteoric lives, ending respectively in insanity and suicide, invite comparison with Nietzsche's—Burckhardt managed to let Nietzsche feel his sympathy (emphasis added). (N 27)

Such aperçus and allusions, which are owed to Kaufmann's formidable knowledge of German literary and philosophical culture, are a special source of the pleasure and instruction in Kaufmann's *Nietzsche*. A smart insight into the continuity of Nietzsche's thought with his late eighteenth-century forebears sees Nietzsche's contrast of the Apollinian and Dionysian as indebted to Kant's contrast of the beautiful and sublime (N 133)—and, in another century, that Nietzsche's "monumentalistic" or "supra-historical" approach to history . . . was further developed by Stefan George's disciples. While some of them perversely denied this insight to Nietzsche in their contributions to the Nietzsche literature, claiming that he had envisaged such individuals only as unattainable goals, other members of the Circle composed studies of the very men whom Nietzsche himself had held up as examples: Caesar, Frederick II, Shakespeare, Napoleon, Goethe. (N 415n2)

These are fine observations, and there are many more at hand, though we are concerned with them chiefly as they bear on the logic of Bildung—the act by which "a still dangerous medley of passions . . . could be controlled only by maintaining a subtle equilibrium" (N 27). Here we are again alluding to Goethe, who, as a young man, just before his writing *The Sufferings of Young Werther*, was driven half-mad by the chaos of his passions, swinging through moods, desires, and impulses at an unmanageable "high velocity." He was a threat both to himself and to anyone with whom he came in contact—the prime example, before Lord Byron, of someone mad, bad, and dangerous to know.[89] His Bildung was an affair of sublimation, a will to power that turns on more nearly contingent forms of itself—"your thoughts and feelings"—in the name of a perfection of reason, the self being "your great reason . . . an unknown sage."[90]

———

Kaufmann, by his own admission, visible in his work to come, was deeply interested in religion—indeed, it very likely remained his chief preoccupation. Hence, it is not altogether surprising to find him frequently referring his subject, Nietzsche, to Christianity; this is also a date stamp. You will scarcely find this mention in the ever-increasing corpus of technical Nietzsche commentary, which focuses on Nietzsche's epistemology and the unspoken presumptions underlying his teachings on morality. In such treatments, few philosophers seem inclined to discuss Nietzsche's thought, with a sort of obligatory courtesy, in its likeness or unlikeness to Christianity. Kaufmann, on the other hand, will write that "what Nietzsche has in mind" in respect of "power" "is an empirical fact of nature and as such, he adds, not contrary to Christian morals" (N 260). Furthermore, "in his keen appreciation of suffering and self-sacrifice as indispensable conditions of self-perfection, Nietzsche seems more 'Christian' than most philosophers" (N 271). Kaufmann cites "R. B. Perry, *The Present Conflict of Ideals* (1918), 158, [who] suggests that one would do better not to insist on Nietzsche's affinity with Christianity, because he himself was so eager to repudiate it. It seems important, however, to distinguish between those elements which Nietzsche attacked and those with which he agreed" (N 271). It is the latter elements that lead to Walter Sokel's notorious criticism:

> [Kaufmann's] tendency . . . was to spiritualize Nietzsche and to narrow at all costs the gulf between him and Christianity. Not being able to declare Nietzsche a Christian, Kaufmann at least makes him an existentialist not too far removed from Kierkegaard. Kaufmann sees Nietzsche, in close analogy to Kierkegaard, as addressing only "den Einzelnen," the single individual soul outside and beyond all political concerns. . . . The spiritualization and Christianization of the Will to Power miss . . . something essential in Nietzsche. While it is true that self-overcoming is a constant theme in his work . . . , it is, I believe, impossible to dissociate it from exercise of power over others.[91]

Sokel's commentary requires a good deal of adjustment. First of all, as Pickus points out, Kaufmann in fact "sharply distinguishes between Kierkegaard's existentialism and Nietzsche's. The former he associates with both Schelling and Christianity, and he compares him unfavorably to Nietzsche for precisely that reason. . . . To be sure, Kaufmann did draw a link between the ways both Kierkegaard and Nietzsche addressed the individual [N 161]. But not only did he not say the individual was outside of political concerns, he suggested that Kierkegaard's romanticism made his stance fundamentally different from Nietzsche's" (N 125). Secondly, consider the entire chapter in *Nietzsche* called "Nietzsche's Repudiation of Christ."[92] Finally, to Sokel's point that self-overcoming in Nietzsche implies the exercise of power over others—a topic we have discussed above—Kaufmann shows that in Nietzsche's account of the exercise of the will to power in particular peoples, the will to power over *others* is ranked lowest. On the other hand, contrary to Pickus, and however counterintuitive it may seem, it is wrong to say that Nietzsche banished every friendly reference to Christianity. Consider, above all, the foundational claim in his second meditation on Schopenhauer:

> This is the basic idea of *culture* insofar as it assigns only one task to every single one of us: *to promote inside and outside of ourselves the generation of the philosopher, the artist, and the saint, and thus to work at the perfection of nature* (emphasis added). (N 172)

I stress: "saint." This figure embodies (or disembodies) Nietzsche's highest valuation of the ascetic ideal.

None of these concessions, however, should be construed as supporting Sokel's charge that Kaufmann "narrowed *at all costs* the gulf between Nietzsche and Christianity" (emphasis added)." This claim, stated at the outset, deprives the new, as yet untested reader of the opportunity to refine and qualify this association on his or her own. It is curious that even without alluding to this allegedly all-too-friendly Christian involvement, subsequent critics of Kaufmann's work should so often target it as "tender." This is a charge discussed in detail in the postscript to this book.

———

The German sociologist Niklas Luhmann, writing on the creation of "individuality" in modern society, describes three modes: one, the copying of role models; two, a sort of cleavage of the self—self-doubling—when the pressure of experience becomes too great; and, finally, three, the experience of a career, in which the self, while constantly changing, remains compatible with "yesterday's."[93] Do we not have in outline here the main motives of self-creation in the life of the author of Walter Kaufmann—motives sharply revealed through his interpretation of Nietzsche?

On role models, first: chief among Kaufmann's exemplary personalities is the German poet, novelist, dramatist, scientist, privy councilor, and crafter of shrewd aphorisms Johann Wolfgang von Goethe. Nietzsche—Kaufmann's Nietzsche, who idolized Goethe—is not far behind. Kaufmann reads Nietzsche through Goethe, as in this telling passage from Nietzsche's *The Twilight of the Idols*, which includes elements that resonate with aspects of Kaufmann's own self-styling:

> Goethe— ... sought help from history, natural science, antiquity, and also Spinoza, but, above all, from practical activity; he surrounded himself with limited horizons; he did not retire from life but put himself into the midst of it; he was not fainthearted but took as much as possible upon himself, over himself, into himself. What he wanted was *totality*; he fought the mutual extraneousness of reason, senses, feeling, and will ... he disciplined himself to wholeness, he *created* himself. In the middle of an age with an unreal outlook, Goethe was a convinced realist: he said Yes to everything that was related to him in this respect. Goethe conceived a human being who would

be strong, highly educated, skillful in all bodily matters, self-controlled, reverent toward himself, and who might dare to afford the whole range and wealth of being natural, being strong enough for such freedom; the man of tolerance, not from weakness but from strength because he knows how to use to his advantage even that from which the average nature would perish; the man for whom there is no longer anything that is forbidden, unless it be *weakness*, whether called vice or virtue. Such a spirit who has become free stands amid the cosmos with a joyous and trusting fatalism, in the *faith* that only the particular is loathsome, and that all is redeemed and affirmed in the whole—*he does not negate anymore* [*Die Götzen-Dämmerung* (The Twilight of the Idols) IX 49]. (N 281)

"Self-cleavage" is the act of registering a second self in oneself, which then becomes the object of self-consciousness. Kaufmann's life story, emphasizing persecution, alienation, exile, and putative assimilation, would have included more than one scene of consternation, a collision of opposite affects, as well as the temptation to cultivate *ressentiment*, to seek revenge for the harm done by the Nazis to him and his family. At this point we can register the special importance for Kaufmann of Nietzsche's resistance to this feeling—its longed-for extinction. Kaufmann quotes Zarathustra: "For *that man be delivered from revenge, that is for me the bridge to the highest hope* . . . (Z II 7)" (N 373). And comments: "To have claws and not to use them, and above all to be above any *ressentiment* or desire for vengeance, that is, according to Nietzsche, the sign of true power" (N 372). At such moments of self-doubling, a judgment as to a disparity asserts itself: the will to power of the higher part aims to sublimate the lower. Kaufmann cites Nietzsche, and I will cite him again:

> the material upon which the form-giving and ravishing nature of this force ["bad conscience"] vents itself is man himself, his . . . animalic . . . self— *and not . . . other men.* This secret self-ravishment, this artists' cruelty, this pleasure in giving form to oneself as a hard, recalcitrant, suffering material—burning into it a will, a critique, a contradiction, a contempt, a No— this . . . work of a soul that is willingly divided against itself and makes itself suffer—this whole *activistic* "bad conscience" has . . . been the real womb of all ideal and imaginative events and has this brought to light an abundance of strange new beauty and affirmation . . . (*Zur Genealogie der Moral* [On the Genealogy of Morals] II 18). (N 253)

Kaufmann adds: "The one self . . . tries to give form to the other; man tries to remake himself, to give 'style' to himself, and to organize the chaos of his passions" (N 253).

With regard to the creation of individuality through a career: it goes without saying that Kaufmann found definition as a prominent teacher of philosophy at Princeton and subsequently as a moral legislator to a wide reading audience.

Toward the close of his book, Kaufmann writes what will serve as a finale to this chapter.

> In many ways Nietzsche is close to what one might call the temper of existentialism. He fused philosophy and psychology, he took a special interest in what Jaspers later called *Psychologie der Weltanschauungen*, he wrote of the death of God, he discussed nihilism and alternative attitudes toward an absurd world, he was a penetrating literary critic, and he mobilized the resources of literature to communicate his philosophy. (N 422)[94]

These pages include a summary statement of Kaufmann's own credo (explicitly paving the way to his later book *The Faith of a Heretic*): it is the philosopher's credo to enforce the urge to ask radical questions, which Kaufmann finds in Nietzsche and *his* sources: "The philosopher must always stand opposed to his time and may never conform; it is his calling to be a fearless critic and diagnostician—as Socrates was" (N 405). This urge comes under the head of "Nietzsche's Socratic protestantism and chronic heresy" (N 417). As a motive to criticism and dissent, it once more looks "backward and forward" to Kaufmann's personal life and work.

I would like to remind readers that they will find in a postscript a medley of voices, sometimes technical and sometimes abrasive, criticizing Kaufmann's *Nietzsche*.

2

Raw Life

EXISTENTIALISM FROM DOSTOEVSKY TO SARTRE

Existence precedes and commands essence.

—JEAN-PAUL SARTRE

FOLLOWING THE RECEPTION of *Nietzsche: Philosopher, Psychologist, Antichrist* (1950), Kaufmann continued to produce, as one encomium reads, "work of high quality at an awesome rate."[1] In the years following, he wrote a number of essays taking up key themes of *Nietzsche*, which proved that his vision of Nietzsche was ever more usable—themes of autonomy, self-making, struggle, affirmation of life on earth, especially as they are developed in Kaufmann's "educators," Goethe, Hegel, Kierkegaard, and . . . Nietzsche once more. These essays would be elaborated and republished in *From Shakespeare to Existentialism* in 1959.[2] Essays written in the following decade, which treat issues of bare existence, would appear in 1976 as *Existentialism, Religion, and Death*, with Kaufmann a student but by no means an uncritical adherent of existentialism.

Along with the writing of these pieces, the years following the publication of *Nietzsche* are years of accomplishment: Kaufmann translated Nietzsche's *Thus Spoke Zarathustra*, *Twilight of the Idols*, *The Antichrist*, and *Nietzsche contra Wagner*, which he collected in *The Portable Nietzsche* (1954), still a gold standard, very much in use; and he compiled a widely read, widely assigned anthology, *Existentialism from Dostoevsky to Sartre* (1956), consisting, as the book jacket reads, of the "basic writings of Existentialism by Sartre, Kierkegaard,

Nietzsche, Kafka, Heidegger, and others" (the others are Dostoevsky, Rilke, Jaspers, Ortega y Gasset, and Camus).[3] These projects, fulfilling enough, were accomplished alongside the demanding tasks of lecturing, advising, and grading at Princeton ("Grader love hath no professor") and by night-time preparations for two major volumes published at the end of the decade: *Critique of Religion and Philosophy* (1958) and *The Faith of a Heretic* (1961).

Existentialism from Dostoevsky to Sartre is a collection of short texts by ten major modernist writers and thinkers, accompanied by Kaufmann's brief prefaces and a forty-page introduction suggesting how "existentialism" might be defined as an object of study and reflection, if not, indeed, as a "way of life."[4] Its key terms are quickly announced: "perfervid individualism," the rejection of systematic thinking, and a disdain for academic philosophy in its remoteness from what Dostoevsky's Underground Man calls "really lived life" (E 11). Somewhat hastily, Kaufmann terms these negative features "the heart of existentialism," but categories a good deal more gripping emerge in the course of the book: the primacy of thought rooted in feeling, the demand for decision, the struggle for authenticity, especially in the face of a mooted godlessness, nothingness, thrown existence.[5] And so we have grounds for the apt concerns of the scholar of phenomenology and existentialism Calvin Schrag, who wondered why Kaufmann had not offered, at the outset, the far more substantive account of existentialism of which he was capable. Such an account would profile "common 'structures' of existence," which, following Schrag, all existentialist thinkers address, even if with varying significance: "concern or care, possibility, anxiety, despair, death, time, history, conscience, guilt, and decision."[6] But readers of Heidegger's *Being and Time* will recognize this inventory as Heidegger's. And Kaufmann's irritation at this work, central to his general irritation with most of Heidegger's work, which will soon concern us, can have worked against this list of features. The signature of Kaufmann's thought is rather to insist on the stark individualism—that is, the differences between—the writers whose works he has collected. He is not offering a system, an unfolding protocol of thought.

These writers, like himself, consider themselves loners, belonging to no school,[7] even if they are not immune to a description that discovers family resemblances—as we can, in Kaufmann's case—between himself and other humanist cultural historians and critics of his time, like Erich Heller (1911–1990), Peter Gay (1923–2015), George Steiner (1929–), and the somewhat older Isaiah Berlin (1909–1997).[8] All were transplanted Europeans, unapologetic, elitist defenders of European high culture, hostile to Marxism, and critical of egalitarian movements and the debased pseudoculture they saw around them. The mantle of cultural criticism was passing to the émigrés.[9] To these outsiders, we could add the names of some homegrown marginal or latecoming avatars of an elitist alienation, namely, the provincial Englishman Colin Wilson (1931–2013), the youthful author of *The Outsider* (1964); the Americans Philip Rieff (1922–2001), author of *Fellow Teachers* (1973); and even Allan Bloom (1930–1992), author of *The Closing of the American Mind* (1987). All were at odds with the mainstream philosophical and literary critical professoriate and wrote in a tone of defiance and resentment. There was an audience in America, especially among younger readers, for books identifying and encouraging "alienation." Certainly, the vapid optimism, trivial pursuits, lip-service religion, mass-medial entertainment, and the "can-do," business-as-usual middle-class ethos pervading American social life in the years following World War II amounted to a provocative, even infuriating contrast to the extreme, convulsive experiences of European society before, during, and after the war. Younger Americans wanted words conveying intensity, and they devoured Kaufmann's anthology. "Hardly a college student in the 1960's could be found without a dog-eared copy of Walter Kaufmann's collection *Existentialism from Dostoevsky to Sartre* (1956)."[10] The book—though not necessarily dog-eared—was in the backpacks of younger Americans on campus and on the road, unlike and not unlike the copies of Hölderlin's poetry in the rucksacks of younger Germans on the war front.

One aspect of Kaufmann's introduction is immediately striking—and bemusing: two pages are devoted to Dostoevsky (a fine piece of impressionist literary criticism) and not much more than that to Nietzsche. Karl Jaspers, however, gets eleven pages, consisting almost entirely of relentless criticism (E 22–23). This cold diatribe sticks out oddly in an introduction meant to show us the exemplary work of the founders of existentialism. It is unfortunately relevant that Jaspers had declared both publicly and privately (in his correspondence with Hannah Arendt) that he was unable to take Kaufmann seriously. It will not be the only place in Kaufmann's corpus where his criticism of others' work in fields close to his own would run away with his argument. But how bizarre that his editors at Meridian gave this roughhouse a pass: Kaufmann must have been very insistent, and being insistent came easily to him. It is true that in a lengthy and detailed essay, David Pickus produces good and honorable grounds for Kaufmann's criticism of Jaspers;[11] but these objections belong elsewhere, as Kaufmann must have concluded, since he reproduces the gist of his criticism of Jaspers in the essay "Jaspers in Relation to Nietzsche" in 1959 in a collection of his essays titled *From Shakespeare to Existentialism*.

Kaufmann's six-and-one-half page introduction to Heidegger continues in the same critical, even sarcastic mode, which suggests that Kaufmann's year abroad in Germany prior to publishing this volume, where he could "listen to lectures by Jaspers and Heidegger and talk with them," drastically diminished the awe the more parochial reader might feel in the face of the massive dimensions of their books and reputations.[12] In a review published in 1954, Kaufmann's opinion of Heidegger was decidedly more respectful: after dismissing the scholasticism of the authors under review, Kaufmann wrote:

> Does anyone suppose that Heidegger exerted a spell over generations of students, and that he continues to fascinate millions of Germans, Frenchmen, and Spanish-speaking people, by virtue of the sort of thing that [Kurt F.] Reinhardt and [James] Collins report so carefully?
>
> When I read Heidegger's essay on Nietzsche, for example, I can disagree a hundred times and perhaps also demonstrate outright errors; but I am moved, excited, in suspense: he takes words, phrases, sentences which had seemed clear, and makes you feel the insufficiency of any previous understanding. He creates that wonder in which, according to Plato and Aristotle, philosophy begins.[13]

Kaufmann's current view on Heidegger grants Heidegger no such distinction. Kaufmann's criticism displays a combative wit that becomes even sharper in subsequent writings, when he could be more assured of his audience. After declaring that classical scholars found Heidegger's reading of a fragment of Anaximander to be untenable; that Heidegger's interpretation of Kant "was widely repudiated by Kant scholars"; and that professors of literature considered Heidegger's readings of Hölderlin, Rilke, and Trakl, among others, way stations to the destruction of German literature, Kaufmann concludes: "Even so, some who know their Kant are awed by the erudition of Heidegger's classical interpretations; Nietzsche scholars find his Rilke essay stimulating and profound; and Rilke scholars bow before his Nietzsche exegesis" (E 36). Kaufmann's remarks on Jaspers and Heidegger bring to the relatively innocent American reader a whiff of the atmosphere of academic dogfighting in and around the German university, as scholarly reputations are aggressively created and then torn apart. In 1956, the eminent Basel Germanist Walter Muschg, in a volume literally titled *The Destruction of German Literature*, would speak of Heidegger's philology as "chattering poetry to pieces."[14]

Since Kaufmann's own contribution to this volume is relatively small, I have designed this chapter as a companion to a renewed reading of the anthology. I will continue to comment on Kaufmann's introduction but also on the authors he has selected, intending to define but also to enlarge the argument of his book.

The introduction begins with a "hortation" (to use a word Kaufmann favors, especially in his critical description of Jaspers) that will recur in the prefaces to the subsequent volumes—*Critique of Religion and Philosophy* and *From Shakespeare to Existentialism*: you, reader, must read this volume from beginning to end with no sidetracking, no impulsive rummaging around in its contents; it is not a grab bag but a teleologically designed artifact. The skeptical hypothesis would be: all three volumes are made up of bits and pieces; here the editor or author is merely insisting that they constitute a coherent story (and Kaufmann, as we know from *Nietzsche*, is a devotee of coherent wholes). His hortation is designed to shame you if you are unable to grasp the connection of its parts "when read straight through," for only then will you appreciate "the growing variation of some major themes, the echoes, and the contrasts" (E 10). Yet . . . the professor doth protest too much, methinks—or may I think so? How warranted is my skeptical surmise?

Answer: Reader, test the matter pragmatically! Learn from Nietzsche's experimentalism. Read these texts with "caution, patience, subtlety,"[15] and read them "straight through" (E 10).

And yet there is a problem in this procedure—the general problem of apparent contradiction. On the one hand, you can read this volume for unity, *because it is a unity*. On the other hand, you can read this book skeptically, unmoved by the author's hortation, *because it* (evidently) *is not a unity*: you can pick out the fractures in that alleged wholeness. These contradictory instructions are based on contradictory propositions. Can they in turn be unified?

Generally speaking, one can expend energy on attempting to prove that two apparently contradictory propositions are in fact compatible. This is Kaufmann's inclination: the fractures are only apparent; with the right attention to context and history, they will be *aufgehoben*—"sublated" (for Kaufmann, "subsumed"). Or one can expend the same energy in attempting to prove that two apparently compatible propositions are in fact inconsistent (the postmodernist urge). What knowledge, what principle can produce in every case the appropriate fidelity to the text—what Nietzsche, in *The Antichrist*, calls "philology?"

Philology is to be understood . . . as the art of reading well—being able to read off a fact without falsifying it by interpretation, without losing caution, patience, subtlety in the desire for understanding. Philology as *ephexis* in interpretation.[16]

What does *ephexis* mean?

In *Nietzsche and the Ancient Skeptical Tradition*, Jessica Berry examines "Nietzsche's claim in this passage that philology means 'ephexis in interpretation.' . . . As Nietzsche is well aware, the Greek term ephexis means 'a stopping or checking,' and it comes from the verb *epechein*, which itself means 'to hold back' or 'to check.' . . . To think of philology 'as ephexis in interpretation' indicates that what makes good interpretation or good philology is a type of suspension of judgment."[17]

But the problem is one that goes beyond the philological expertise of the reader; it also involves his or her presuming to know—or having the courage to claim to know—or having the naïveté of not needing to know—when and how long to "hold back" in his or her penetration. And because such knowledge is likely to be motivated by contingencies of personality, which Kaufmann calls the thinker's (or reader's) "subjective make-up"—variant notions and degrees of "caution, patience, subtlety"—it remains, of course, a highly unreliable knowledge, and will no doubt perpetuate a different reaction in the next vigorous reader (N 79). I add on to this aporia Nietzsche's own declaration, in his last papers, that "it is precisely facts that do not exist, only interpretations."[18] This claim eliminates any possibility of a dispositive closure to this conflict of interpretations.

Since Franz Kafka will figure in *Existentialism from Dostoevsky to Sartre* and, then again, all throughout Kaufmann's writings, I shall solicit an incisive contribution by an unlikely character in *The Castle*. (In Kaufmann's *Existentialism*, Kafka is represented by three short parables.) Olga, the taproom prostitute, comments on the difficulty of interpreting a letter from the castle correctly, as follows:

And staying in the middle between the exaggerations, that is, weighing the letters correctly is impossible, their value keeps changing, the thoughts that they prompt are endless and the point at which one happens to stop is determined only by accident and so the opinion one arrives at is just as accidental.[19]

This state of affairs puts us in a whirl of competing "accidents" that can be settled only by the application of a principle extrinsic to the more or less pure intuition of a meaning—in a word, an application of power. This inevitable conclusion is a thought allegedly formulated by Nietzsche as "All things are subject to interpretation. Whichever interpretation prevails at a given time is a function of power and not truth." The quote, however, is apocryphal,[20] although a number of Nietzsche's aphorisms from *The Will to Power* demonstrably link the activity of interpreting with the will to power, a point that Kaufmann has foregrounded and which dictates the gist of my conclusion. Ergo, as Nietzsche declares, "The very same milieus [read: texts] can be interpreted and exploited in opposite ways: there are no facts."[21] "It is the selfishness of the judges which interprets an action, or its performer, in relation to its utility or harmfulness to themselves."[22] "One may not ask: 'who then interprets?' for the interpretation itself is a form of the will to power, exists (but not as a 'being' but as a process, a becoming) as an affect."[23] "That the value of the world lies in our interpretation . . . ; that previous interpretations have been perspective valuations by virtue of which we can survive in life, i.e., in the will to power, for the growth of power; that every elevation of man brings with it the overcoming of narrower interpretations; that every strengthening and increase of power opens up new perspectives and means believing in new horizons—this idea permeates my writings."[24] "This 'will to power' expresses itself in the interpretation, in the manner in which force is used up; transformation of energy into life, and 'life at its highest potency,' thus appears to be the goal."[25] "The will to power *interprets*. . . : it defines limits, determines degrees, variations of power. Mere variations of power could not feel themselves to be such: there must be present something that wants to grow and interprets the value of whatever else wants to grow. . . . In fact, interpretation is itself a means of becoming master of something."[26] A note in *Will to Power* is headed: "To What Extent Interpretations of the World Are Symptoms of a Ruling Drive."[27]

At this juncture, a sobering injunction by Luther seems called for: "I am not in favor of a theologian's setting about allegorizing before he is perfectly familiar with the rightful and plain meaning of the text."[28] Indeed, this was the very point taken up by Nietzsche in the passage we have been considering: Nietzsche also began with an attack on impetuous theologians, ending with the motto: "philology is *ephexis* in interpretation."[29] But, as we saw, this argument swiftly became an aporia about the *right amount* of hesitation. So, a second injunction of Luther applies with special pertinence to the act of interpreting: "Sin boldly!"[30]

Kaufmann hardly ever needed encouragement to sin in this way. He is an assured interpreter, displaying, often, a frank awareness of the contrary evidence that every interpretation needs to get past.[31] This movement of thought is vivid in *Nietzsche* in the "Yes—but No—but Yes *but* . . ." pattern informing, with variations, Kaufmann's arguments: he produces correctives, relativizations, and at the end, a fair-mindedness tilting toward the thing or person criticized when that thing or person is of deserving quality. This procedure runs throughout Kaufmann's introduction to *Existentialism from Dostoevsky to Sartre*. Jaspers gets bad marks for his reluctance to draw conclusions, to make a solid landing on conceptual soil, at the same time that Kaufmann points up Sartre's unacknowledged debt to Jaspers for the value of asystematic, noncognitive-truth-only "philosophizing." Heidegger, too, is travestied but held in some awe for the adventurousness of his thought.

Of course, both Jaspers and Heidegger have pride of place in the anthology as primordial existentialists (despite their refusing the title). In this matter of introducing a No into every Yes before that Yes is affirmed, Kaufmann, in years to come will hold this method of argument to be irrefutable. And it is a fact that whether done intentionally or willy-nilly, Kaufmann's paragraphs are marked by their *many* countercurrents, by the presence on its surface of *many* embryonic arguments running counter to his main conclusion, allowing for as many openings out for criticism—or renewed agreement—or . . . In this way, Kaufmann's reader is especially beset by the practical demands of ephexis, the famous need to decide where and when and how long to suspend judgment. We will do what we must.

Kaufmann's introduction of Heidegger discusses the philosopher's late work under the head of "*das andenkende Denken*, a thinking that *recalls*"—a thinking that "Heidegger proposes to put in the place of representational thinking" (E 39). He notes that this translation has Heidegger's "enthusiastic approval," which conjures the remarkable picture of this sworn enemy of "Anglo-Saxon pragmatic-technical thinking" turning anglophone and enthusiastic at an example of such thinking, since no *translation* from German, the one language in which authentic thought is conceivable—thus Heidegger—could be anything but a pragmatic-technical makeshift.[32] This preferred mode of thought is inspired by Heidegger's immersion in the late poetry of Friedrich Hölderlin, the author of the great hymn "Andenken," which is, indeed, a memorializing, a "recalling" thinking. Kaufmann's main worry about Heidegger's chosen immersion is whether a poetry written forever on the brink of schizophrenia would be the best enabler of Heidegger's avowed goal—a renewed thinking of Being. A first reaction might be to consider Kaufmann's resistance as merely banausic, but the case hardens when we consider that another of Heidegger's exemplary pathways to an "andenkendes Denken" is the poetry of another madman, Georg Trakl. So the "new acquist of true experience" (Milton) that comes off Kaufmann's disaffection is actually quite eye-opening: it says something, at the least, about Heidegger's aesthetic inclinations, confirmed in Heidegger's own poetry.[33] He is a romantic, in love with the "poetry of genius," with words darkly inspired (Kaufmann describes Heidegger's Hölderlin as "the dark poet whose splendid rhythms carry ordinary readers over vast abysses of obscurity" [E 38]). Kaufmann loves poetry, but loves reason in equal measure. This cannot be said of Heidegger, and the opposite claim has been made explicitly by Heidegger: "Thinking begins only at the moment we realize that reason . . . is the fiercest enemy of thinking."[34]

Kaufmann means to doubt Heidegger's later findings through Heidegger's recourse "not merely to what is extraordinary but . . . what is pathological" (E 38–39). This being so, it is a pity that Kaufmann wrote too soon to discover, in the work of Walter Muschg (see above, p. 46) and the Hölderlin scholar Peter Szondi, that Heidegger's treatment of Hölderlin's poetry is itself extraordinary . . . and from a certain philological point of view pathological.[35] Heidegger's astonishing approach to Hölderlin's hymn "Wie Wenn am Feiertage" (As when on a holiday) is to reprint a mutilated version of the text, all the time declaring that "the text which shall serve here as the basis for the present lecture, and which has been repeatedly checked against the original manuscripts, rests upon the following attempt at an interpretation."[36] This interpretation concludes, quite falsely, that in this poem Hölderlin conveys positively the experience of *parousia*, a realized access to sacred Being with the poet as unscathed mediator of the divine lightning bolt. Unfortunately, the sublimity of Heidegger's reading is checked and dispersed by the manuscript lines that Heidegger chose *not* to print, as *not* conducive to his interpretation:

1. But, oh, my shame! when of
2. ————————————————————
3. ————————————————————
4. ————————————————————
5. My shame!

   ————————————————————————

   ————————————————————————

6. And let me say at once————————
7. ————————————————————————
8. That I approached to see the Heavenly,

9. And they themselves cast me down, deep down

10. Below the living, into the dark cast down

11. The false priest that I am, to sing,

12. For those who have ears to hear, the warning song.

13. There————————————————————————[37]

By virtue of the very lines that Heidegger chooses to omit, the poem says the very opposite of what Heidegger makes it say. At the same time, Paul de Man would add, even if Heidegger's actual interpretation were dead wrong, it redounds to the interlocutor that his interpretation takes place at the right, rather exalted ontological level.[38] It is not hard to imagine Kaufmann's reaction to this line of argument. It would be akin to arguing that a "high enough-level," Nazi racialist citation of the Übermensch deserves credit, for it does after all take us to the level of thought where the question of the nature and necessity of this arcane, yet so crucial a being, can be debated.

This is not the place to continue to expand the range of Kaufmann's suspicions of Heidegger, since—with impressive authority, especially in a subsequent work, *Discovering the Mind*, vol. 2, *Nietzsche, Heidegger, and Buber*—Kaufmann will excoriate the shortcomings of Heidegger's magister opus.

The chief attraction-grabbing feature of Kaufmann's introduction to *Existentialism from Dostoevsky to Sartre* is, as I've suggested, the extended, persistent criticism of the work of Jaspers and Heidegger. It will be no less interesting to consider the work that Kaufmann finds absolutely seminal: Dostoevsky's *Notes from Underground*. Kaufmann was fascinated by this novella from early days, his enthusiasm perhaps especially mediated by Nietzsche's discovery of it, which Kaufmann reports early in his *Nietzsche*: "When [Nietzsche] wrote of pity and resentment, solitude and conscience, he knew whereof he spoke. And when [in 1887] . . . he discovered Dostoevsky's *Notes from Underground*, he instantly recognized a matchless psychologist" (N 59–60). In *Existentialism*, Kaufmann spells out Nietzsche's dramatic discovery:

> I did not even know the name of Dostoevsky just a few weeks ago. . . . An accidental reach of the arm in a bookstore brought to my attention *L'esprit souterrain*, a work just translated into French. . . . The instinct of kinship (or how should I name it?) spoke up immediately; my joy was extraordinary. (E 52)

Nietzsche continues to describe the part of the story that Kaufmann reprints (the omission of the conclusion is regrettable) as "really a piece of music, very strange, very un-Germanic music" accompanying "a kind of self-derision of the γνῶθι σεαυτόν [know thyself]" (E 52). In this strange music Kaufmann hears an "altogether new voice," and he is surely right.[39] *Notes* begins: "I am a sick man. . . . I am a spiteful man." Kaufmann writes,

> The pitch is new, the strained protest, the self-preoccupation. To note a lack of serenity would be ridiculous: poise does not even remain as a norm, not even as an element of contrast; it gives way to poses, masks—the drama of the mind that is sufficient to itself, yet conscious of its every weakness and determined to exploit it. What we perceive is an unheard-of song of songs on individuality: not classical, not Biblical, and not at all romantic. No, individuality is not retouched, idealized, or holy; it is wretched and revolting, and yet, for all its misery, the highest good. (E 12)

How well do these remarks hold up against the best contemporary scholarship on *Notes from Underground*? Marcus Bullock's way of expanding this paraphrase of the Underground Man's insistent individuality runs parallel with Kaufmann's own: "It is much closer to a person's real desires," writes Bullock, "that one's acts and choices be one's *own* than they be to one's advantage, and this freedom of choice can only be confirmed where it deviates from advantage. Thus the cruelty of a private self-laceration is ultimately more desirable than to be obliterated in a calculable public order."[40] In his magisterial five-volume study of Dostoevsky, Joseph Frank, Kaufmann's Princeton colleague, pinpoints the ideological identity of the terms "advantage" and "calculable public order": they belong to the utilitarianism of Chernyshevsky, the target of Dostoevsky's satire. Frank makes clear that the work aims to depict the misery of the being who has once made an honest attempt to live according to the "rational" ideology of Chernyshevsky and the radicals among the Russian intelligentsia. These are writers and intellectuals bent on creating a more perfect society based, they propose, on man's innate goodness—better: man's lucid awareness of what lies in his greater interest. But, as Frank writes, beginning with the view of a Dostoevsky scholar V. V. Rozanov,

> No world order based on reason and rationality could possibly contain this seething chaos of the human psyche. . . . Chernyshevsky had believed that man was innately good and amenable to reason, and that, once enlightened as to his true interests, he would be able, with the help of reason and science, to construct a perfect society. Dostoevsky may have also believed man to be capable of good, but he considered him equally full of evil, irrational, capricious, and destructive inclinations.[41]

Well and good as a beginning, but Frank is quick to reject the possible implication of these lines—namely, that the Underground Man, in declaring mankind "loathsomely bloodthirsty" (E 70), is a transparent mask of Dostoevsky and that all his invective can be ascribed to Dostoevsky. Surely, *Notes* does *not* mount a straightforward attack on utilitarianism, which would give an incontrovertible prestige to the figure of the Underground Man—a plain absurdity. In this respect, Frank and Kaufmann are of one mind. Kaufmann writes, "It is the besetting fault of Dostoevsky criticism that the views and arguments of some of his characters are ascribed, without justification, to the author" (E 15). But Frank is on his own ground in advancing the original thesis that "the underground man *dramatizes within himself* the ultimate consequences of the position that Dostoevsky was opposing (emphasis added). . . . His diatribes . . . do not arise because of his rejection of reason; on the contrary they result from his acceptance of *all* the implications of reason in its then-current Russian incarnation."[42] This incarnation includes a strong element of Chernyshevsky's denial of free will. Kaufmann, we might note, is, like Chernyshevsky, a lover of reason—with a penchant, at the same time, for mystical experience—but none of these biases could possibly amount, for him, to a denial of free will. In this matter, the fictive existentialist, the Underground Man, and Kaufmann, the anthologist—in his lucidity and confidence the Aboveground Man par excellence—join hands.

Kafka, who—following Kierkegaard, Nietzsche, and Rilke—appears in Kaufmann's book as Dostoevsky's kin, makes Dostoevsky's point anew, dramatizing the urge to self-destruction when man has been subjected to a purpose: "Human nature, essentially changeable, unstable as dust [flying into the air], can endure no restraint; if it binds itself, it soon begins to tear madly at its bonds, until it rends everything asunder, the wall, the bonds, and its very self."[43]

The outcome of these remarks is to ward off a wrong conclusion often drawn from Kaufmann's presentation of *Notes*: it is to treat the Underground Man as Dostoevsky's existentialist *hero*. Kaufmann took pains to say, "I can see no reason for calling Dostoevsky an existentialist"; on the other hand, Kaufmann's next comment might very well have encouraged this misreading of *Notes*: "I do think that Part One of *Notes from Underground* is the best overture for existentialism ever written. . . . The major themes are stated here that we can recognize when reading all the other so-called existentialists from Kierkegaard to Camus" (E 14). In the authoritative reading by Frank, the Underground Man is in no way exemplary except as the monster who has become what he is by being loyal to defective ideologies. And yet, at the same time, some credence must be given to Kaufmann's claim. In this very *composite* text, a good many aperçus flow as irrefutable wisdom sentences from the lips of the Underground Man—remarks that can be assimilated to an existentialist worldview:

> Perhaps the only goal on earth to which mankind is striving lies in this incessant process of attaining, in other words, in life itself, and not in the thing to be attained. . . . And why are you so firmly, so triumphantly, convinced that only the normal and the positive—in other words, only what is conducive to welfare—is for the advantage of man? . . . Does not man, perhaps, love something besides well-being? . . . Man is sometimes extraordinarily, passionately, in love with suffering, and that is a fact. . . . Suffering is the sole origin of consciousness. (E 77–78, 80)

To preserve the integrity of Frank's reading, which insists on distinguishing the mind of Dostoevsky from the heightened "consciousness" (a key word) of the Underground Man, one could say that from time to time the plan to project the Underground Man as an exemplary derelict got away from the author. And indeed Frank appears to be of this view, which he puts subtly, first by acknowledging "the force of . . . [the Underground Man's] imprecations and anathemas against some of the most cherished dogmas of modern civilization." Frank continues: "As a result the parodistic function of his character has always been obscured by the immense vitality of its artistic embodiment."[44] This argument is a vivid example of how a thesis can be maintained in the face of acknowledged objections. To my mind, it brings together the writings of the liberal humanist colleagues Frank and Kaufmann to show that conclusions can be reached on the strength of preponderant though not exclusive evidence, where the value of the conclusion is shored up by the frank demonstration of obstacles in its way.

In a brief essay in the *Dictionary of Modern American Philosophers*, Edward P. Antonio notes Kaufmann's distinctive way of "expounding [his extraordinary knowledge of the history of philosophy] through his equally expansive knowledge of literature." Kaufmann's "interdisciplinary approach to philosophy," thus Antonio, would then connect to his "interest in existentialism, a philosophical movement that was often mediated through works of literature."[45] The latter point is, of course, very evident; we have it from the source. In *Existentialism*, Kaufmann writes: "In the end, Rilke, Kafka, and Camus pose a question, seconded by Dostoevsky and by Sartre's plays and fiction: could it be that at least some part of what the existentialists attempt to do is best done in art and not philosophy?" Kaufmann imagines an answer:

> It is conceivable that Rilke and Kafka, Sartre and Camus have in their imaginative works reached heights of which the so-called existentialist philosophers, including Sartre, not to speak of Camus's essays, have for all their efforts fallen short. . . . Whether this is so or not, that is a crucial question which no student of this movement can avoid. (E 49)

Hence, Antonio's asserted *priority* of "the philosophical movement" to "works of literature" might well be rewritten as an affair of reciprocal mediation. In fact, at other moments, in this book and in later work, especially on considering ancient Greek tragedy, Kaufmann is inclined to award primacy to literature. Consistent with this surmise, one sees the philosophers in *Existentialism*—Kierkegaard, Jaspers, and Heidegger—treated by and large scathingly while the literary avatars of existentialism—Dostoevsky, Rilke, and Kafka—are shown pure. (If Heidegger is acknowledged, it is in part because, with his scholastic apparatus, "he made discussion of death and despair and dread and care and other previously unacademic subjects quite respectable. He made it possible for professors to discuss with a good conscience matters previously considered literary, if that" [E 34–35]). The two philosophers who, along with Ortega, are acclaimed by Kaufmann—Sartre and Camus—are themselves represented by "works of literature"; and Camus's *The Myth of Sisyphus* concludes the anthology as its "excellent finale" (E 375). I cite Camus as a philosopher, because that is how he is generally regarded; Kaufmann, in several of his works, takes pains to prove that, while a powerful writer, he does not deserve that title.

Other commentators on this volume have covertly acknowledged this reciprocity between philosophical writing and literary fiction in noting the resistance to existentialism among American professional philosophers—a resistance focused chiefly on Sartre. The philosopher Walter Cerf applauds Kaufmann for "defending Sartre . . . against those academic philistines who suspect him simply because he has published novels and plays," adding too, that the merit of Kaufmann's presentation of Sartre also lies in opposing "those who, justly annoyed by Sartre's dialectical apparatus and semantic confusions, refuse to see his Cartesian commitments and what may be called the picturesque insights of his psychology."[46] "Picturesque insights" might refer to such fugues as, for example, Sartre's phenomenological analysis of the caress in *Being and Nothingness*,[47] viz., "I make myself flesh in order to impel the Other to realize for herself and for me her own flesh. My caress causes my flesh to be born for me insofar as it is for the Other flesh causing her to be born as flesh."[48]

The inclusion of Kierkegaard in Kaufmann's anthology as the next avatar of the existentialist worldview has been the most frequently contested. The Harvard Germanist Henry Hatfield observed that existentialism appears in Kaufmann's volume as "the agglomeration of the personal philosophies of a series of thinkers and artists who often disagreed with one another, rather than a consistent body of doctrine." Hatfield is inspired to draw this conclusion by taking Kaufmann himself as one in this series, who makes "particularly sharp comments about the limitations of Kierkegaard."[49] As if the point needs to be emphasized, Kaufmann comes to his wider topic in a critical spirit, selective about whom to show intellectual support. His standard is consistent with his view on Nietzsche in *Nietzsche*, which can be summed up, after many caveats, in Kaufmann's most sympathetic description of Nietzsche's philosophy as "Dionysian Enlightenment." This doublet will function apotropaically vis-à-vis whatever in existentialism kills passionate joy and lucid science by means of what the aforementioned Cerf calls its "vague Nothings and ambiguous Absolutes."[50] On the other hand, Hatfield is wrong in seeing Kaufmann's anthology as a mere congeries of separate voices. Kaufmann supplies markers along the way about how these writers can be read together—how they exhibit family resemblances—and his selection aims to make the point. The point is a complex coherence that Kaufmann earlier described as a play of recurrent motifs, echoes, and intelligible variations. We read, for example, that "some of Kierkegaard's motifs are clearly continuous with *Notes from Underground*. Some are taken up and developed by Jaspers and Heidegger. But Kierkegaard on faith should be compared with Sartre's 'Portrait of the Anti-Semite'" (E 85). These pages give Kaufmann the opportunity to mark a distinction that means a great deal to him and that he will amplify in future writings. For Kierkegaard, "ethics is not a matter of seeing the good but of making a decision. The crucial difference between an informed and uninformed, a reasoned and un-reasoned, a responsible and irresponsible decision, escapes him" (E 17).

Cerf also balks at the way Kierkegaard has been included. Kaufmann's Kierkegaard is no way a *religious* thinker, testifying to what, for Cerf, is "Kaufmann's lack of interest in the religious aspects of existentialism." Cerf gets a bit testy: "Kaufmann, one is inclined to suspect, went through Kierkegaard's works with a list of certain existentialist themes before him, snapping to attention any time Kierkegaard writes something that fits the list and slumbering the more frequent times that Kierkegaard is Kierkegaard." This leads him to wonder why Kaufmann has not included "contemporary" religious existentialists.[51] Kaufmann explains why. First, he paraphrases Kierkegaard: "The self is essentially intangible and must be understood in terms of possibilities, dread, and decisions. When I behold my possibilities, I experience that dread which is 'the dizziness of freedom,' and my choice is made in fear and trembling." And then to the point: "These are motifs that remain central in all so-called existentialism: we recognize them in the non-denominational religiousness of Jaspers and in Sartre's atheism as well as in the mutually opposed theologies of [Karl] Barth and [Rudolf] Bultmann" (E 17). He has not specifically included their writings, or those of Buber or Paul Tillich or Gabriel Marcel, since "religion has always been existentialist . . . always preoccupied with suffering, death, and dread, with care, guilt and despair." Many prominent modern theologians have been influenced by Heidegger and Jaspers, who, of course, are represented in the anthology. It might be enough to show these concerns in their migration and settlement in philosophy and fiction, "severed from their earlier religious context." These theologians, too, "have availed themselves of a specifically modern language to remind us of what their diverse religions have always said" (E 49–50).

I bother to stress Cerf's last complaint, because in works to come—especially Kaufmann's *Critique of Religion and Philosophy*—Barth and Bultmann, amid a plethora of contemporary liberal theologians, come in for severe criticism. It is as if Kaufmann took Cerf's brief objection very seriously and then answered it in a massive way. This pattern might be said to persist, since, as we saw earlier, Kaufmann's subsequent book, *The Faith of a Heretic*, was written at least in part owing to the querulous suggestion by an English theologian that Kaufmann, after displaying his powers of criticism in *Critique of Religion and Philosophy*, might pay his dues with a frank statement of his own beliefs: "One wanted to know where I stood."[52] In *The Faith of a Heretic*, Kaufmann says so, amply.

I mentioned earlier the objection of the philosopher Calvin Schrag to Kaufmann's attempt to get at "the heart of existentialism" by negations alone: existentialism is not academic, it eschews system, and so on. Schrag, like the others, saves his most mordant criticism for Kaufmann's presentation of Kierkegaard ("one of the least adequate sections of the Introduction"). Since Schrag's remarks are productive, I will quote them at length. (In the course of this book, I will have occasion to offer Kaufmann's counterstatement.)

Kierkegaard is described as a "frequently befuddled thinker"; "in revolt against the wisdom of the Greeks"; "anti-philosophical" in general, and specifically "anti-Plato," "anti-Hegel," "anti-Thomas," and "anti-Copernicus" [E 16]. In short, according to Kaufmann, Kierkegaard abandons reason and thought altogether and anathematizes philosophy. To be sure, in Kierkegaard's writings one can find isolated passages that seem to suggest a thoroughgoing anti-intellectualism and disparagement of philosophy. (Kaufmann quotes one such passage from the *Concluding Unscientific Postscript*: "The conclusions of passion are the only reliable ones" [E 18]). But this is to neglect the tension between passion and reason, imagination and thought, voluntarism and intellectualism, which permeates the whole of Kierkegaard's works. Kierkegaard, in reaction to the "pure thought" of Hegelian rationalism, places a high premium on pretheoretical awareness and the revealing function of mood and feeling, but he also affirms the validity and relevance of thought. In the *Postscript* he writes: "If thought speaks deprecatingly of the imagination, imagination in its turn speaks deprecatingly of thought; and likewise with feeling. The task is not to exalt the one at the expense of the other, but to give them an equal status, to unify them in simultaneity; the medium in which they are unified is *existence*." One must not overlook the fact that for Kierkegaard "the subjective thinker is an existing individual and a thinker at one and the same time." The subjective thinker strives to penetrate his concrete particularity with thought. Kierkegaard did not proclaim an end to philosophic thought but insisted that the passional and the rational, the ethical and the intellectual, are inseparably bound up at their very source—existence.[53]

This account of Kierkegaard would make him a Nietzschean after Kaufmann's heart—this is to say, a Nietzschean in light of Kaufmann's *Nietzsche*—but there Kaufmann takes pains to distinguish them precisely on the grounds of Nietzsche's, unlike Kierkegaard's, devotion to rational thought, his "Cartesian commitments." What entitles both to count as avatars of existentialism, despite the different thrusts of their writing and thinking, is the intensity of their focus on the individual subject craving dignity. "The question that Nietzsche puts," Kaufmann writes, "is essentially *Die Frage an den Einzelnen* [Kaufmann is citing the title of a book by Martin Buber], a question for 'the single one alone for himself'—Kierkegaard's *hiin Enkelte*, who is the antithesis of the crowd."[54] Kierkegaard's fancied an epitaph that would read "That Individual" (E 16). On the other hand, we were reminded earlier by Pickus that

Kaufmann decisively connects Kierkegaard with Schelling—and hence, by association, with Christianity—which puts Nietzsche and Kierkegaard, once again, at an unbridgeable distance.

In another essay, Pickus develops at considerable length a counterargument to the criticisms of Kaufmann's presentation of Kierkegaard mentioned above.[55] Kaufmann's eye-catching selection of texts follows from a conscious decision to "tell the story" of existentialism: after all, Kierkegaard had been dead for nine years when Dostoevsky published *Notes from Underground* in 1864, so how does it come about that the mutterings of the Underground Man—let alone a fictional being—*precede* in this account the once-live philosopher Kierke-gaard? It is clearly part of Kaufmann's strategy—above all the valorization of fictive presentations of the existentialist mood—to model Kierkegaard, given the bounty of his very heterogeneous writings, on the Underground Man, and so Kaufmann begins with "Kierkegaard's account of how he first became a writer. . . . It is as if he stepped right out of Dostoevsky's pen" (E 14).

This connection amounts to a positive conceptual element in Kaufmann's definition of existentialism (radical subjectivity; compulsory horror of the crowd, the "They-self"). Earlier on, we discussed Kaufmann's definition of a generalized existentialism chiefly by negation, a strategy that invited criticism. And so it is interesting that now—some half century later—Stephen Crowell, a contempo-rary authority on existentialism, gives Kaufmann's argument more credit.

> To approach existentialism in this categorial way may seem to conceal what is often taken to be its "heart" . . . , namely, its character as a gesture of protest against academic philosophy, its anti-system sensibility, its flight from the "iron cage" of reason. But while it is true that the major existential philosophers wrote with a passion and urgency rather uncommon in our own time, and while the idea that philosophy cannot be practiced in the disinterested manner of an objective science is indeed central to existential-ism, it is equally true that all the themes popularly associated with dread, boredom, alienation, the absurd, freedom, commitment, nothingness, and so on—find their philosophical significance in the context of the search for a new categorial framework, together with its governing norm.

Crowell's new categorial framework is built on the category *authenticity*.[56] We might note that Crowell's "categories" are in fact anticipated by the "motifs" that Kaufmann finds in Kierkegaard: "possibilities, dread, decisions, . . . 'the dizziness of freedom,' fear and trembling" (E 17). It often seems the case that Kaufmann draws criticism that never quite hits the mark; or to put this complaint more liberally, critics rely on what they take to be the "preponderant" evidence of a fault, leaving it to Kaufmann's well-disposed readers, who come afterward, to point up the suppressed contradictions that work to his advantage.

I want to return to Schrag's point in support of a "feeling" sort of thinking. Kaufmann writes eloquently on this trope all throughout his work. For a number of reasons, he would not be surprised by the idea that Schrag sees represented most vividly in Kierkegaard. It is present in *Nietzsche*; it is reiterated again and again in the modernist literature Kaufmann knew well, in many vivid rhetorical conjunctions. The Germanist Gerhard Neumann observes that "from Pascal and Novalis on, at the latest [both writers are discussed in Kaufmann's *Nietzsche*], the limits of what can still be termed thought are extended further and further into the domain of something indeterminately 'like feeling.'"[57] To cite a source that Kaufmann knew very well—Thomas Mann's *Doctor Faustus* (1947)—Mann writes that the imaginary musical masterpiece *The Lamentations of Doctor Faustus* makes "the highest and profoundest claim of feeling to a stage of intellectuality and formal strictness."[58] This passage may have prompted Philip Rieff—who shares a family resemblance with Kaufmann as a fellow promulgator of mandarin alienation—to title a volume of his writings *The Feeling Intellect*.[59]

To return, finally, to Kaufmann's Kierkegaard: What is the reader to do if Kierkegaard, as Schrag argues, both exults in and disdains rational thought? I will adapt some lively remarks by the philosopher Tom Stern, who, thinking of Nietzsche's contradictions, imagines how critics might deal with such an aporia. They can write:

> While he [Nietzsche . . . or Kierkegaard . . . or, for that matter, Kaufmann] seemed inconsistent in places, his "considered position" (what he would think if he had thought about it more, or better, and therefore hadn't published some inconvenient sentences) was not inconsistent on fundamental points. . . . Either he [Nietzsche . . . or Kierkegaard . . . or, for that matter, Kaufmann] held such-and-such a very complicated, exegetically speculative "theory," or he was simply inconsistent. Fear of the second option is meant to compel the reader into the awkward embrace of the first: your money or your life.[60]

This is a conversational way of describing what I have called conclusions based on a preponderance of evidence set down alongside its contradictions, a method implicit in Frank's reading of *Notes from Underground* and one that John Wilcox pursued in his book on Nietzsche's theory of knowledge—a method that Kaufmann applauded (see below, p. 628n31).

After Kierkegaard, Kaufmann returns to Nietzsche in a brief introduction charged with polemical flair, spectacularly opposite to that "desiccated writing" for which even Kierkegaard, and Kaufmann, harbor "a violent distaste" (E 18). This section strengthens further the idea of this anthology as a story ("The present volume is intended to tell a story" [E 10]), showing its connections and echoes and repetitions.

> In the story of existentialism, Nietzsche occupies a central place: Jaspers, Heidegger, and Sartre are unthinkable without him, and the conclusion of Camus' *The Myth of Sisyphus* sounds like a distant echo of Nietzsche. Camus has also written at length about Nietzsche; Nietzsche is the first name mentioned in Sartre's philosophic main work, *L'être et le néant*; Jaspers has written two whole books about him and discussed him in detail in several others; and Heidegger, in his later works, considers Nietzsche even more important than Jaspers ever did. (E 21–22)

There is a sort of jubilating mood that runs through this entire section. It is as if Kaufmann, in returning to his much-loved philosopher, psychologist, and antichrist, catches his joy, "a 'Dionysian' joy and exultation that says Yes to life not in a mood of dogged resolution, which is prominent in later German existentialism, but with love and laughter" (E 21).[61] In Kaufmann's elation there may be a reminiscence, too, of his own *Nietzsche* and the joy of creation that accompanied it, which gives him a sense of renewed prowess, like Antaeus, who was unconquerable as long as his feet touched the ground.

Kaufmann celebrates Nietzsche's joyous Yea-saying, and it is true that Nietzsche gives an account of joy that is nonpareil in writing I know; it might be as interesting, however, to stress that that joy flows less from Nietzsche's *saying* Yes to life than from his *writing* its necessity. He will say Yes, again and again, to music—to *Bizet's* music:

> Has it been noticed that music liberates the spirit? gives wings to thought? that one becomes more of a philosopher the more one becomes a musician?—The gray sky of abstraction rent as if by lightning; the light strong enough for the filigree of things; the great problems near enough to grasp; the world surveyed as from a mountain.—I have just defined the pathos of philosophy.—And unexpectedly answers drop into my lap, a little hail of ice and wisdom, of *solved* problems.—Where am I?—Bizet makes me fertile. Whatever is good makes me fertile. I have no other gratitude, nor do I have any other *proof* for what is good.[62]

Note how his joy develops as he attests to it: Nietzsche's joy is, will be productive, and it is sustained by production, by the very writing of joy. Such writing brings gratitude in its wake.

> On this perfect day, when everything is ripening and not only the grape turns brown, the eye of the sun just fell upon my life: I looked back, I looked forward, and never saw so many and such good things at once. It was not for nothing that I buried my forty-fourth year today; I had the *right* to bury it; whatever was life in it has been saved, is immortal. The first book of the *Revaluation of All Values*, the *Songs of Zarathustra*, the *Twilight of the Idols*, my attempt to philosophize with a hammer—all presents of this year, indeed of its last quarter! *How could I fail to be grateful to my whole life?*— and so I tell my life to myself.[63]

At the acme, there is *inspired* writing—a writing inspired by its own joy:

> Has anyone at the end of the nineteenth century a clear idea of what poets of strong ages have called *inspiration*? If not, I will describe it.—If one had the slightest residue of superstition left in one's system, one could hardly reject altogether the idea that one is merely incarnation, merely mouthpiece, merely a medium of overpowering forces. The concept of revelation—in the sense that suddenly, with indescribable certainty and subtlety, something becomes *visible*, audible, something that shakes one to the last depths and throws one down—that merely describes the facts. One hears, one does not seek; one accepts, one does not ask who gives; like lightning, a thought flashes up, with necessity, without hesitation regarding its form—I never had any choice.
>
> A rapture whose tremendous tension occasionally discharges itself in a flood of tears—now the pace quickens involuntarily, now it becomes slow; one is altogether beside oneself, with the distinct consciousness of subtle shudders and of one's skin creeping down to one's toes; *a depth of happiness in which even what is most painful and gloomy does not seem something opposite but rather conditioned, provoked,* a necessary *color in such a superabundance of light* [emphasis added]; an instinct for rhythmic relationships that arches over wide spaces of forms—length, the need for a rhythm with wide arches, is almost the measure of the force of inspiration, a kind of compensation for its pressure and tension.
>
> Everything happens involuntarily in the highest degree but as in a gale of a feeling of freedom, of absoluteness, of power, of divinity.—The involuntariness of image and metaphor is strangest of all: one no longer has any notion

of what is an image or a metaphor: everything offers itself as the nearest, most obvious, simplest expression. It actually seems, to allude to something Zarathustra says, as if the things themselves approached and offered themselves as metaphors: ("Here all things come caressingly to your discourse and flatter you; for they want to ride on your back. On every metaphor you ride to every truth. . . . Here the words and word-shrines of all being open up before you; here all being wishes to become word, all becoming wishes to learn from you how to speak").[64]

This is *my* experience of inspiration; I do not doubt that one has to go back thousands of years in order to find anyone who could say to me, "it is mine as well."[65]

Kaufmann's closing signature brings joy to wit, writing, "Existentialism without Nietzsche would be almost like Thomism without Aristotle; but to call Nietzsche an existentialist is a little like calling Aristotle a Thomist" (E 22). The tone droops considerably as we turn to Kaufmann's rather captious treatment of Jaspers.

Kaufmann dislikes him, and the core of that dislike, in addition to the rumor of Jaspers's dislike of him, is Jaspers's reading of Nietzsche. In this instance, and others, Jaspers deplores the view of philosophy as a fount of "knowledge" to which one journeys to receive "a total conception of man's being" (E 27–28)—the offering in scare quotes is the brunt of Jaspers's rejection of Heidegger's *Being and Time*. Aside from their shared dislike of *Being and Time*, Jaspers and Kaufmann are unlike in their expectations of, let us say, Plato, Spinoza, Schelling and, above all, Nietzsche. For in Jaspers's reading— thus Kaufmann—"all of Nietzsche's definite ideas, theories, and arguments are dissolved" by a show of contradictions—specious contradictions that do not affect Kaufmann's own view of Nietzsche's work as a teaching, a vehicle of knowledge, as soon as contradictory propositions are seen in the right philological and historical perspective. True, Jaspers gives Nietzsche's work the salutary function of "endlessness," akin to the permanent "philosophizing" that Jaspers represents—"endless reflection, sounding out and questioning everything, digging without reaching a new foundation," although, in Nietzsche's reprehensible case, it reaches irritably for "new absurdities" (Jaspers) (E 31). But even Nietzsche's absurdities, following Jaspers, have a practical function: they set you whirling, they keep your certainties in suspense. Kaufmann quotes Jaspers: "Out of every position one may have adopted, i.e., out of every finitude, we are expelled; we are set *whirling*." Kaufmann continues:

Jaspers' characterization of "all true philosophizing" is eminently applicable to the effect at which he aimed in his big book on Nietzsche: It loosens us from the fetters of determinate thinking, not by abandoning such thinking but by pushing it to its limits. . . . The plunge from the rigidities which were deceptive after all turns into the ability to stay in suspense; what seemed abyss becomes the space of freedom: the seeming Nothing turns into that from which true Being speaks to us. (E 31)

But Kaufmann also charges Jaspers with terrible philology in Jaspers's effort to produce contradictions—his cavalier disregard of dates, context, and local argument, his lack of feeling for development, for the "story" in which competing halves of these factitious antinomies are embedded. But precisely here we have the amiable recrudescence of Kaufmann's dialectic of polite concession. *Yes*, the charge of the invalidity of Jaspers's reading of Nietzsche is true; but also, *No*, it is untrue that Jaspers's performance is without merit, for it is "stimulating and deeply disturbing" (E 31); but, finally, *Yes*, it is a disaster, far less than the philosophical "shipwreck" ripe with existential implications that Jaspers's readings strove for, since Jaspers's Nietzsche book on the whole "makes its subtitle a mockery: 'Introduction to the Understanding of His Philosophizing.'" Kaufmann adds: "A far fairer estimate is found toward the end of Jaspers' essay on his own philosophy . . . where he says: 'My *Nietzsche* was to be an introduction to that shaking up of thought from which *Existenzphilosophie* must spring'" (E 31–32). This is the stimulating and disturbing element.

On the question of the cogency today of Jaspers's thinking, we note immediately that the effect at which Jaspers's *Nietzsche* aims—the "plunge from rigidities . . . into the ability to stay in suspense"—has a hermeneutic counterpart in Nietzsche's "*ephexis* in interpretation." Such suspense, such *ephexis*, has a long life in both past and present literary theory and was vigorously revived, for one, in Paul de Man's elaboration of Friedrich Schlegel's definition of irony as "permanent *parekbasis*"—a perpetual shifting away of subject matter or form from the subject matter or form at hand. A palpable shift occurs every time a proposition is succeeded by its opposite, as, for example, when our understanding of Nietzsche's definition of the *self* in *Zarathustra* as "a mighty ruler," possessed of "a granitic *fatum*," appears in the *Will to Power* as a boil of striving impulses without substance ("no subject 'atoms.' . . . no 'substance'").[66] The romantic irony of permanent parekbasis, following the philosopher of history Frank Ankersmit, is a sort of "'dialectics without the happy closure' (that is, there is no moment of synthesis, as in Hegel and Marx). Instead, the moment of synthesis is exchanged for a permanent impasse in which the mind comes to stand in a relationship to itself."[67]

So, on the face of it, there is a family resemblance between Jaspers's "suspense" and the deconstructionist's "irony": in the former, the mind comes to stand in a relationship to authentic *Existenz*. Still, the categorial slippage is significant. The passage of the subject's ruling concern from existential suspense to irony could seem a linguistic edulcoration of the swirling possibilities of commitment, of decision. The drift of the change is dramatic in Paul de Man's sinister *jeu d'esprit*: "Death is a displaced name for a linguistic predicament."[68] It is bemusing to conjure the mighty figure of Karl Jaspers, relentless thinker of death and "deathlessness," responding to that remark—or for that matter his energetic disputant, the subject of this book.

Thanks to Kaufmann's year abroad in 1955 as a Fulbright professor at the University of Heidelberg—just before the publication, the following year, of *Existentialism*—we hear rumors of the secret life of the great professors, which Kaufmann describes with novelistic intimacy. For example, before Kaufmann's introduction, we did not know that there was a time when Heidegger would seek out Jaspers for conversation and they would philosophize together for days on end. It comes as another surprise that Heidegger's failure to deliver the manuscript of the second half of *Being and Time*, meant to be devoted to the temporality of Being, which Heidegger had promised in the published first half, can have been owed to his reading or recoiling from Jaspers's three-volume *Philosophie*.[69] The project of authenticating this surmise would make an excellent separate chapter on the history of the German existential philosophical movement between the wars; but it would have to stress Heidegger's counterclaim that this omission was owed, not to anything Jaspers might have written, but to "our abandonment by Being," a modern emptiness, an inauthenticity of machination and waging gain against which no mortal thought could prevail (E 35). It would follow, as Kaufmann informs us, that Jaspers would then have had little patience with Heidegger's later writing, which the critic Gerald Bruns describes, altogether positively, as a dark "comedy of thinking in its uncontainability, its refusal of control, its lapse from reason . . . its nearness to poetry," but Kaufmann, in a trenchant phrase, as an evidently reprehensible "search for an esoteric gnosis" (E 28).[70]

For his part, Heidegger soon proved impatient with Jaspers's insistence on a philosophical thinking that never concludes, that never delivers positive knowledge, whose task is only to "suspend," to "whirl," to "shatter" assumed certainties. This project fits badly with the decisiveness (*Entschlossenheit*) that

Heidegger requires; ergo, according to Kaufmann, Heidegger returned Jaspers the compliment of no longer reading his books. (Jaspers's project might have fit better with the *Gelassenheit*, the existential mode of "letting-be" that Heidegger adopts after the alleged *turning* of his thought, but even that decision represents a determinate end point to a whirl of thought.) In either perspective, Heidegger's separation from Jaspers degrades the triumphant conclusion of Jaspers's thought that the beginning of truth lies "*zu zweien*, in a situation where there are two human beings" engaged in a "loving fight," which guarantees that each will come to doubt the certainty of his or her position. But that breach certainly never healed and, moreover, widened fatefully when Jaspers, after World War II—following a request from the French occupiers of southeast Germany—urged that Heidegger be deprived of the *venia legendi*, permission to teach at a German university. Jaspers explained his verdict:

> In our present situation, the education of the younger generation needs to be handled with the utmost responsibility and care. Total academic freedom should be our ultimate goal, but this cannot be achieved overnight. Heidegger's mode of thinking, which seems to me to be fundamentally unfree, dictatorial and uncommunicative, would have a very damaging effect on students at the present time. . . . He should be suspended from teaching duties for several years, after which there should be a review of the situation based on his subsequent published work and in the light of changing academic circumstances. The question that must then be asked is whether the restoration of full academic freedom is a justifiable risk, bearing in mind that views hostile to the idea of the university, and potentially damaging to it when propounded with intellectual distinction, may well be promoted in the lecture room. Whether or not such a situation arises will depend on the course of political events and the evolution of our civic spirit.[71]

There is little in this statement that is not affirmed in Kaufmann's abundant criticism of Heidegger in this and a number of his books to follow.

Kaufmann's renewed discussion of Heidegger again takes up Jaspers's immanent logomachy with Heidegger, which Kaufmann projects onto their readings of Nietzsche. Inspired, Kaufmann produces a cogent figure of thought to get at their differences:

> In his Nietzsche image each of them has drawn his own portrait as his rival sees him: in Heidegger's eyes, Jaspers is as inconclusive as his Nietzsche,

philosophizing endlessly without ever evolving a philosophy; to Jaspers, in turn, it seems that Heidegger who began by using terms that look existential and who once spoke with an existential pathos is really a metaphysician like his Nietzsche. (E 34)

Matters then take a substantive turn, and Kaufmann considers this criticism a sort of side chapel to the great cathedral of thought that each seeks to erect. Where Nietzsche foundered in perpetual statement and counterstatement, there Jaspers will build his *Existenz-philosophie* that allows for an unmediated event of "Transzendenz." Where Nietzsche's will to metaphysics is apparent, as a continuation of the great post-Socratic deviation of thought, there Heidegger will "overcome" it in his various prolegomena to a history of Being.

The confrontation of Heidegger with Jaspers is otherwise fruitful (in ironies) when Kaufmann remarks again on Jaspers's "hortatory" tone, which Heidegger allegedly resists. But, declares Kaufmann, with Rilke much in mind (Rilke figures in the anthology), Heidegger also asks us in a way not always heard by readers of *Being and Time* "to change our lives" (Rilke: "Du mußt dein Leben ändern"). Kaufmann illustrates Heidegger's point negatively when he writes, "Heidegger's enthusiastic exhortations, immediately after Hitler came to power, that the students and professors at the German universities must now think in the service of the Nazi state . . . are a very noteworthy exception" (E 34). But it is unclear why Kaufmann would think that the Rektoratsrede of 1933 was *not* an appeal to his audience to change their lives: it can't be taken for granted that all those in attendance were already convinced Nazis. But that this speech—and other evidence of Heidegger's allegiance to the Nazi program—represents a betrayal of the excoriation of the "They-self" (*das Man*) of public convention in *Being and Time* has been vigorously asserted by J. P. Stern, whom we will encounter later in his charge that Kaufmann failed to deal fairly with Nietzsche's political thought. Stern emphasizes the disturbing cleavage between Heidegger's philosophy and his actual life decisions by introducing this description, in *Being and Time*, of *das Man*,

> by which . . . [Heidegger] means that aspect of our being in the world and with other people which is constitutive of inauthentic conduct, conduct legitimated by an appeal to "the average" or "the everyday", and summed up in such phrases as "one does", or "they say" or "it is thought that":
>> We enjoy ourselves and take pleasure in things the way *one* enjoys them, we read, see and judge literature and art the way *one* sees and judges; but

we also distance ourselves "from the crowd" the way *one* distances *oneself*;
we find "*shocking*" what *they* find shocking. The *One* [or: the *They*] which is
indeterminate and which is what all are, though not as their sum, prescribes
the mode of everyday being.... Togetherness as such constitutes [*besorgt*]
the average. *The average* is the pattern [*Vorzeichnung*] of all that can and may
be ventured, it watches over every exception that asserts itself. Every kind
of priority is silently suppressed. Overnight, everything original is instantly
glossed over as long since familiar. Everything that has been fought for
becomes readily available. Every mystery loses its power. This care of the
average discloses once more the essential tendency of being in the world
[*Dasein*], which we call the leveling-out of all possibilities of Being [*Sein*].⁷²

Here, in 1989, Stern confirms Kaufmann's point, made more than three
decades earlier, that, in Stern's words, "the philosopher who has analyzed inauthenticity more profoundly than any other, and given it its place not as an
adventitious psychological phenomenon but as part of an ontological analysis
of man's being, his *Dasein*, is among its most astute practitioners."⁷³

In preparation for his introduction of Sartre, Kaufmann clarifies the notorious commonplace of Heidegger's rejection of the title of existentialist and
his firm statement of his difference from Sartre. Heidegger's protest is found
in his "Letter 'On Humanism,'" evidently provoked by Sartre's famous lecture "Existentialism Is a Humanism," which Kaufmann reprints in its entirety.
Kaufmann quotes the crux of Heidegger's distinction:

Sartre formulates the basic principle of existentialism in these words:
existence precedes essence. Here he uses the terms *existentia* and *essentia* in the old sense of metaphysics which says since Plato: the *essentia*
precedes the *existentia*. Sartre reverses the sentence. But the reversal of
a metaphysical sentence remains a metaphysical sentence. Being such a
sentence, it remains, like all metaphysics, in the oblivion of the truth of
Being. (qtd. in E 37)

Heidegger then grants Sartre the aptness of the term "existentialism" for *his*
philosophy but makes clear its inappropriateness to his own project, which
is concerned from the start with the meaning and truth of Being, a steadily
deanthropologizing itinerary of thought.

Kaufmann's smart move is to include Heidegger's late works in a modernism defined chiefly by its "revolt against representation." He had previously
noted that Heidegger's late works involve "multiple plays on words," a point

that might be radicalized as Heidegger's approach to poetic language as "the house of Being." Nor would it be wrong to see Heidegger's own "memorializing language" of commentary (on the pre-Socratics; on the provincial poet J. P. Hebel, "deeply rooted in the Alemannic homeland"; on Rilke; on Trakl) as participating in radical forms of nonrepresentational expression.[74] Earlier I cited Bruns, who discussed Heidegger's late writings in their "nearness to poetry." Bruns's extraordinary construction of a canon of modern writers to which Heidegger might be assigned—one need hardly add that they are chiefly nonrepresentative stylists—now seems, after Kaufmann's suggestion, slightly less absurd. What Bruns sees as the intrinsically punning and parodic character of Heidegger's "estrangement" of language allows him to appear "closer in spirit to Flaubert, Joyce and Beckett, to Mallarmé, Kafka, and Blanchot, to Gerard Manley Hopkins and Edmond Jabès . . . (and also to . . . postmodern [writers] like John Ashbery and Thomas Pynchon) than to Hölderlin—or anyhow to Hölderlin as Heidegger read him in the thirties."[75] Kaufmann's surmise predates an advanced contemporary critic's by thirty years. He finds in Heidegger something like a modernist "ceding of the [poetic] initiative to words" (Mallarmé), noting, "We are aware of the relations between words which have the same roots, but much less clear about the connections between the phenomena which he [Heidegger] describes; *the thought process seems determined by the words*"(emphasis added) (E 40). Kaufmann's conclusion is plain: "Even as modern prose and painting are no longer satisfied with the representation of events or things, Heidegger feels that the time has come for philosophy to break with what he calls representational thinking" (E 39).

In this final mention of what is original in Kaufmann's understanding of Heidegger, Kaufmann discusses the "almost legendary" difficulty of translating him, noting "that like Aristotle and Hegel before him . . . he often deliberately defies the idiomatic vernacular, although at other times he appeals to it. Moreover, the 'weight' of a word [today, we might say 'the signifier' or 'the materiality of the sign: its sound-look'] is scarcely less important to him than its meaning" (E 234). Kaufmann then reprints Heidegger's "My Way to Phenomenology" in Joan Stambaugh's translation. It is precisely here, in the translator's preface, that Stambaugh repeats Kaufmann's point that Heidegger's neologisms "typically . . . have strong connections to everyday phrases or words, and so exhibit a curious mix of strangeness and familiarity."[76]

Kaufmann is happy to move on to Sartre, not least for the fact that "Sartre is much closer to Nietzsche than to German existentialism." It goes without saying that *this* Nietzsche is the Nietzsche of Kaufmann's massive study of

1950, preoccupied with themes of "passion and its mastery, independence of convention, and that creative freedom that finds ultimate expression in being a law unto oneself" (E 41–42). This view of Nietzsche, as we well know today, seems privative to many, especially when Kaufmann's common labeling of Nietzsche and Sartre as existentialists means that they "have developed no political philosophy." Developing their political philosophy (especially Nietzsche's) is a cottage industry today.[77] On the other hand, Kaufmann's conclusion that "so-called existentialists have made widely different political decisions" is unlikely to provoke any backtalk (E 48).

Unsurprisingly, Kaufmann admires a kind of thinking impregnated with the impulses of lived experience: "Sartre's comments on commitment and decision, dread, and death are charged with life. . . . He does not consider it subphilosophical to base discussions of despair, decision, dread, and self-deception on experience" (E 40–41). Much of Nietzsche's writings too—one can conclude, extending Kaufmann's perspective—are the efflux of powerful states of mind; witness the grafting of joy onto inspiration and inspired writing, so that Nietzsche's prose can be said to communicate the *experience* of thought. This sense of Nietzsche is consistent with Kaufmann's view of Sartre, and more: "Not the least thing Sartre shares with Nietzsche is the multiplication of styles that gives expression to a new experience of life and a new vision of man, dazzling variety that is still one at heart" (E 41). One thing that Sartre will not share with Kaufmann's Nietzsche is his embrace of political Marxism; in his later books, Kaufmann has harsh words for Sartre's, in his view, leap of bad faith and excoriates his flight from existential solitude into submission to Marx's *Das Kapital.*[78]

At this point, however, needing to supply additional philosophical company for Sartre, Kaufmann conjures "the French tradition"—again, no surprise—a lineage "that, more often than not, has produced men who stand at the borderline of philosophy and literature: Montaigne, Pascal, Voltaire, Rousseau" but far more originally, the Buddha. Many an intellectual historian might prefer to see Sartre's revelatory encounter with Husserl's phenomenology in place of the Buddha, but "let be." How, then, does the Buddha fit in? Kaufmann speculates that much of the resistance to Sartre among American academic philosophers at the time of writing (1956) stems from Sartre's atheism. Sartre makes a point of his disbelief, a position bound up with his "insistence on the relevance of ideas to life." And the Buddha? He too "made a point of his lack of belief, and for essentially the same reason as Sartre" (E 46). This provocation requires a good deal of justification, and so I will quote Kaufmann at length, at his contrarian best:

The differences between the two men could scarcely be more striking, even though the Buddha stressed despair and suffering no less than the existentialists. It would be folly to paint Sartre in the image of the Buddha: he is not saintly but aggressively human; he does not preach disenchantment but commitment in the world; like Nietzsche, Sartre remains "faithful to the earth" and says, "Life begins on the other side of despair." Few men could be more unlike each other.

Nevertheless, the Buddha, too, opposed any reliance on the divine because he wanted men to realize their complete responsibility. His final, and perhaps most characteristic, words, according to tradition, were: "Work out your own salvation with diligence." And if the diligence is rather uncharacteristic of the existentialists, the Buddha's still more radical dictum with which the Dhammapada opens is nothing less than the quintessence of Sartre's thought: "All that we are is the result of what we have thought." (E 46)

This extraordinary yoking of contrarieties evidently tells us as much about Kaufmann's style of thought as it does about Sartre and the Buddha. First, it is one of the earliest declarations in Kaufmann's oeuvre of his intense and probably capital interest in world religion. This passion will come to the fore in his next book, *Critique of Religion and Philosophy* (1958) and in many works thereafter, especially *Religions in Four Dimensions* and *Existentialism, Religion, and Death* (1976). Secondly, it might be added that at the present time of writing we possess a large enough list of works applying Buddhist notions of nothingness to existentialism and especially to Sartre's concept of the empty self. Among them is a remarkable work by Steven W. Laycock, *A Buddhist Engagement with the Ontology of Jean-Paul Sartre*, which, while not entirely critical, would "resolve the incoherence implicit in the Sartrean conception of nothingness by opening to a Buddhist vision of emptiness."[79]

Finally, we might note the No but Yes ductus in Kaufmann's claim to this comparison that has more than once emerged as his signature dialectic. It is also interesting to see this Buddhist "quintessence of Sartre's thought," following Kaufmann, in the proposition "All that we are is the result of what we have thought" recur as the quintessence of Nietzsche's philosophy, according to Kaufmann's former colleague Alexander Nehamas, who writes: "Each 'thing' [the subject-'thing' included] is nothing more, and nothing less, than the sum of all its effects and features."[80] Supposing this to be true, Nehamas lends Kaufmann's association of Sartre with Nietzsche (and by implication with the Buddha) the luster of further confirmation.

Along with the Buddhist association, Kaufmann invokes "the world of Shakespeare," to which Sartre's world is certainly closer. What they share is the drama of impossible situations: no matter what escape route you choose, you will not escape guilt. Kaufmann's dictum invites further reflection. Given this tragic sense of life, the object, presumably, is still to do, in some qualitative sense, the right thing rather than attempt to diminish quantitatively the collateral burden of guilt. This consideration will arise whenever the performance of an inflexible duty would nevertheless inflict concrete and immediate harm on a love-object. Kaufmann is not now concerned with such a predicament although it will figure in his later critical account of Kant's moral theory (chapter 15). Here we note that references to Shakespeare's tragedies will often recur, as in the book that Kaufmann is about to write, *From Shakespeare to Existentialism* (1959). In this light, "secular existentialism is a tragic world view" (E 47). This proposition also prepares the way for another later, important book titled *Tragedy and Philosophy* (1968).

What is meanwhile surprising and noteworthy about Kaufmann's final remarks is that he shows himself quite able, in the end, to supply a categorically rich, phenomenologically saturated definition of existentialism. Like religion, as we noted, it is "preoccupied with suffering, death, and dread, with care, guilt, and despair" (E 49–50). Here we can recall the criticism of Calvin Schrag, who was dismayed that Kaufmann had failed to supply existentialism with positive categories—with phenomenological "substance"—and drew up this list for him: "concern or care; possibility, anxiety, despair, death, time, history, conscience, guilt, and decision."[81] I judged this list unacceptable to Kaufmann for being too much a copy of the table of contents of Heidegger's *Being and Time*. But now Kaufmann does note the existential preoccupation with "suffering, death, and dread, with care, guilt, and despair." This could make a hash both of Schrag's criticism and my own account of Kaufmann's resistance to it. But on inspection, observe the categories from Schrag's list that Kaufmann's list excludes: concern, possibility, anxiety, time, history, conscience, and decision. These categories do cry out *Being and Time*, and once again we observe Kaufmann defining a religious tradition and thereafter an existential tradition that do not inhabit Heidegger's landmark book.

Existentialism nonetheless closes with Kaufmann's own assertion of an intellectual *historical* crisis that circa 1950 pits analytic philosophy versus existential philosophy. Here we have the drastic separation of age-old philosophical tendencies that, following Kaufmann, were joined productively in Socrates and were active in Nietzsche, too, and to some extent in all philosophers before him—but now no longer.

> It is one of the saddest features of our age that we are faced with an entirely unnecessary dichotomy: on the one hand there are those whose devotion to intellectual cleanliness and rigor is exemplary but who refuse to deal with anything but small, and often downright trivial, questions. . . .
>
> The existentialists have tried to bring philosophy down to earth again, . . . taking up the passionate concern with questions that arise from life, the moral pathos, and the firm belief that, to be serious, a philosophy has to be lived. The analytical philosophers, on the other hand, insist—as Socrates did, too—that that no moral pathos, no tradition, and no views, however elevated, justified unanalyzed ideas, murky arguments, or a touch of confusion. In Nietzsche—and more or less in every great philosopher before him, too—philosophy occurred in the tension between these two timeless tendencies, now inclining one way, now the other. Today this dual heritage has been developed in different camps, and between them they have made us aware of the pitfalls of traditional philosophy no less than of each other's faults. That the existentialists and analysts will get together is not likely. But if the feat of Socrates is really to be repeated and philosophy is to have a future outside the academies, there will have to be philosophers who think in the tension between analysis and existentialism. (E 51)

This description is altogether true to our current situation. But implicit in it there is a program: in Kaufmann's books to come, he will think and write in the tension between analysis and existentialism.

3

Cleaning the Stables

CRITIQUE OF RELIGION AND PHILOSOPHY/1

A temperate cleaning of the stables and a restoration of the Socratic flame.

CRITIQUE OF RELIGION AND PHILOSOPHY (1958), an intensely personal book, is written with "liveliness and truth" (Wordsworth), with fervor and conviction.[1] The persona in *Critique* is the philosophical self, full of noetic verve, lightened by the absence of empirical characteristics: we could not learn from it whether Kaufmann was married (he was) or what he liked to drink (cold water) or especially savored (a crisp apple).[2] It is the voice of critical reason, meaning to "compel the assent of every reasonable person," as Kaufmann will define "knowledge," and informed by an aversion to the faith of the *true believer*, the irrational support of defective knowledge (C 113). In *Critique*, we come closer to the man who acknowledges in its many guises (not to coin a phrase) the ineluctable modality of the irrational.

The preface to *Critique*, probably written as the finale to the manuscript, defines genuine philosophical writing in a way that organizes both it and, importantly, most of Kaufmann's oeuvre. Such writing must be playful, if the "must" does not cancel the play element: it must not seem too strenuously achieved. This notion of a play of thinking and writing is modeled on the Socratic manner, a play with real-world implications.[3] Such a flow of thought—or "flight" of thought, the phrase Kaufmann prefers—is full of verbal wit, a flair for dialectic, and surprising, cross-grained argumentative moves.[4] Nonetheless, the stake is genuine instruction. Here, Kaufmann implicitly sets up a standard by which he will be judged.

The second requirement appears to stem from Kaufmann's commitment to a Nietzschean idea of self-making via thought that is deep enough, daring enough. This urge brings seriousness into the play of thought: the philosopher "may be serious in . . . his willingness to be changed himself in the course of his inquiries." This philosophic readiness implies the tentativeness, the being-in-time of the flight (of thought). The change might occur "forward," as a positive element, resulting in "information that may still be worth sharing," or it might occur as an undoing of older elements, biases, and certainties even in the course of this very flight—this very critique. If we look ahead to the third preface of 1978, we find this surmise confirmed: "Looking back on *Critique* now, I find that today I would do countless things differently. There are some ports at which I would no longer stop at all—because of what I discovered when I called there" (C xii).

This process of self-undoing leads to a third quality of genuine philosophical thought (Kaufmann likes numbered points): it can proceed by criticism, as long as that criticism is not trivial.

> Directed at enduring dangers that confront men in all ages, it may be of lasting importance. The critic who attacks idolatry does the most serious thing of which a man is capable. . . . One can try to sustain a consistent positive outlook and define it in terms of a critique of idol upon idol. (C xviii)

We could learn from the postscript that Kaufmann's critic Arthur Danto found one feature of Kaufmann's *Nietzsche* to be beyond reproach: Kaufmann's reading of "idols" in Nietzsche's *The Twilight of the Idols*, "in the sense in which Bacon used it, where idols are merely pernicious habits of beliefs which hold men in thrall to error."[5]

Kaufmann holds iconoclasm (the "attack on idolatry") to be the most serious requirement of genuine philosophy; this judgment contains the bud of a thought that will unfold all throughout *Critique*. It is its main thrust and will invigorate some readers and irritate others. This oppositional stance, for Kaufmann, is exemplarily personified in the Greek Socrates and the prophets of the Old Testament, not to overlook the Buddha: all agree on the importance only of the work of thought that disturbs the pieties of the age. But what is most striking in this argument is less the claim than its declared sources in Greek thought and Hebrew thought—"Jewgreek is greekjew. Extremes meet"—[6] conspicuously omitting the Christian tradition, which Kaufmann will excoriate throughout *Critique*, although with the expectable three-beat dialectic of No—but Yes—but No *but.* . . .

It is not simply that, for Kaufmann, much Jewish biblical thought is compatible with Greek philosophy, the prophets with Socrates; to put this directly, the Jewish Bible *overpowers* the Christian Bible in its argument and majesty. This is Kaufmann's bold refrain throughout many of his books. As a topic of passionate concern, Jewish Bible criticism responds well to the historical moment, since, in the decades to follow, we find a good deal of sympathetic work aiming to include Jewish biblical thought and commentary in a philosophical tradition hitherto dominated by Heidegger's exclusionary Graecophilia. This restoration is richly elaborated, for one, in the work of Emmanuel Levinas, which Kaufmann does not acknowledge. It is work that runs parallel to Kaufmann's writings at the end of the 1950s, though certainly not always in agreement.[7] The impact of Walter Benjamin's biblical metaphorics and Jacob Taubes's revisions of St. Paul should also be mentioned. For his part, Kaufmann's sense of the tradition can be readily traced to his intellectual formation: in the 1930s at the Institute for Jewish Studies in Berlin, he studied the Hebrew Bible, Talmud, and Jewish history and a decade later developed a marked antipathy to Heidegger on grounds internal to Heidegger's work, just at the time that Levinas was turning away from Heidegger, with dismay, on learning of his Nazi past.

In a requirement familiar from the introduction to *Existentialism*, Kaufmann wants this book to be read straightforwardly, in the given order of its one hundred sections, without flipping pages or skimming along the way. Serious readers, he warns, had best heed his instruction or they will be misled. What is interesting here is the allowance made for the curious, the impatient, or the reader easily tempted to disobey. In their case, declares Kaufmann, let them go immediately, if they must, to a long biblical quotation in section 79. Without thinking at the moment of readers of this page as curious or impatient, I will ask them to suffer my own disobedience in order to make a point. Section 79 wonders whether a commentary on the book of Job could not have done the essential job of work that the entirety of *Critique* does. A long quotation from Job 13:1, in which Job answers his comforters, is the crux. Kaufmann translates Job's passion anew, in this way too producing a discreet monument to his Jewish studies at the time that he felt the Nazi assault most brutally.

Behold, my eye has seen all this,
My ear has heard and understood,
What you know, that I also know . . .
But you, you beautify with lies,

Idol-physicians that you are. . . .
Would you speak wickedly for God
and deceive for his sake?
You think, you favor him?
You think, you take his side? . . .
Be still and leave me that I speak,
And let come on me what will.
Wherefore? I will take my flesh between my teeth,
and my life I will put in my hand.
He will slay me? For that I hope.
But my ways I will maintain to his face.
And let this be my salvation
that no hypocrite comes to face him. (C 348–49)

"My critique of theology," Kaufmann declares, "and my polemic against fin-ished philosophic edifices and the finding of dubious reasons for what we believe anyway, could have been forced into the mold of a commentary on Job" (C 349). He hints at an exegesis with an observation very much in his preferred style: quirky, original, disturbing. In a full exegesis, "the verse 'I only am escaped alone to tell thee' might have evoked the reflection that beasts earn survival by being fit while men must justify their survival after the event" (C 349). The artistic consciousness that presides over his book—which Kaufmann directly terms "a work of art"—remembers the origin of this section 79 in the preface, instructing the restless reader to come to this passage from Job if he or she must. This section repeats, with a slight revi-sion, a citation in biblical cadence from André Gide's *The Counterfeiters*. There Gide wrote: "What is the use of doing over again what other people have done already, what I myself have done already, or what other people might do?" (C xviii). Now, in section 79, Kaufmann rewrites Gide to mean: "What *right* has a survivor to do over again what other people have done already or might do as well?" Kaufmann adds: "A commentary on *Job* need not be dry or impersonal," which is a modest way of inviting an existential turbulence into it (C 349).

This book is a critique, which Kaufmann defines, in opposition to a polemic, as "showing the limits of what is criticized, what it can and cannot do, its value and abuses" (C xx). It means to extend the line of Bacon and Descartes, whose "analysis of human knowledge made cosmic and theolog-ical speculations problematic . . . for, in the 'spirit of Socrates,' they brought philosophy down to earth again" (C 1). (One could deplore the absence of Kant and Marx in this lineage, both of whom specifically wrote "critiques," but Kaufmann's later writings reveal a constitutional resistance to both writers.) This "earth" is man and his preoccupations—Socratic man, following Kaufmann's Plato, thirsts for knowledge by the rule of reason, the ideal of the type present at the beginning of Plato's philosophy and its end: "In the *Apology* of Socrates, we behold the ideal man of Plato, as yet unencumbered by metaphysics and epistemology" (C 38). The restoration of man into the center of philosophy prepares for the rethinking of mankind as a community. In a following aperçu, Kaufmann writes:

> The bifurcation of the world is always rooted in a prior bifurcation of mankind and man. Wherever two worlds have been postulated [as in the later writings of Plato], man was first divided into two parts—senses and reason, body and soul, phenomenon and noumenon—and often there were also thought to be two kinds of men: the mass and the elite. The doctrine of two worlds goes hand in hand with a superior evaluation of the other world, the unseen one; and prior to Kant the central theme of all such teachings was the path by which a man could hope to reach this other world. (C 39)

For all their disagreement in subject matter and approach, both analytic philosophy and existentialism share the creditable purpose of "bringing philosophy down to earth again." In a signature formulation, Kaufmann writes:

> bothered by the abstractness and artificiality of so much traditional philosophy, [both movements] try to bring philosophy down to earth again: that is what the appeals to ordinary language and extraordinary language, to common sense and uncommon experiences, have in common. They have, all of them, kindled their flame from the fire lit by Socrates. (C 31)

The moral thrust of *Critique* is apparent from beginning to end: Kaufmann is writing as one of many "who stand appalled at the present situation in philosophy" (C 61).[8] This thrust will lead to the strong commitment of Kaufmann's next book, *The Faith of a Heretic*, which means to acquaint readers with the possibility of changing their lives.

At the moment, his goal—a temperate cleaning of the stables and a restoration of the Socratic flame—is obstructed by the prestige enjoyed in America by Protestant theologians. In criticizing the work of Bultmann and Tillich and Reinhold Niebuhr, Kaufmann answers the questions put to *Existentialism* about his exclusion of religious existentialists. That book and this one stand in the conceptual continuity that will inform *all* of Kaufmann's work, the sort of coherence, a household, he detected and loved in Nietzsche:

> Individual philosophical concepts . . . grow up in connection and rela-
> tionship with each other . . . they belong . . . to a system . . . something
> within them leads them, something impels them in a definite order, one
> after the other—to wit, the innate systematic structure and relationship of
> their concepts. Their thinking is, in fact, far less a discovery than a recog-
> nition, a remembering, a return and a homecoming to a remote, primor-
> dial, an inclusive household of the soul, out of which those concepts grew
> originally.[9]

Kaufmann's *Critique* aims to attack beliefs, but in our time we may not be quick to identify our beliefs or even to admit that we have any.[10] We tend to think of beliefs as what takes the place of information in minds less well informed than our own. Belief might be "distinguished by the lack of evi-dence sufficient to compel the assent of every reasonable person," a definition even "calmly conceded" by St. Thomas Aquinas (C 113–14). For St. Thomas, for Kaufmann, for "us," beliefs supplement while also indicating defects in knowledge.

Unlike St. Thomas, however, we, who address the beliefs of others—the gaps and muddle in their knowledge—expect to be without them. The profit of Kaufmann's reflections might be to acquaint us, after all, with our beliefs. And if we insist that we are unaware of having any, it becomes our duty to say how this certainty has come about. Is all our presumed infor-mation verifiable? "The motto [of great philosophy and poetry] is always: What is well known is not known at all well" (C 5). This work of clearing remains ours to do. Reading this book, we will follow Kaufmann's work of critical thought, and, as convinced hermeneutists, enlarge it, drawing con-clusions from his imitable exposure of commonly maintained—especially religious—beliefs.

A nagging concern might be to ask who Kaufmann imagines his audience to be in all this. I think the reader who takes him up is likely to be (1) of the same liberal humanist community as the author's—which raises the question of what, after all, Kaufmann has to teach such a reader beyond cultural infor-mation otherwise obtainable and lacking the power to change him or her; (2) among his adversaries—theologians par excellence—who have heard of his critique and are interested in resisting it—Christians who would like to test the muscle of their faith against it; (3) the undecided, the trimmers, the vague, the curious, who wish their minds conceptually articulated—an interest that does not exclude members of communities (1) and (2).

If we are persuaded by his work, will we all become humanists like the author? What is it to be a humanist? For Kaufmann, it is he who *is* this very enterprise of "understanding man"—an obligatory enterprise, since, following Kaufmann, modernity (its philosophers included) has failed to produce a *whole* picture of man, without which we will gasp and stumble. But what is it to be the man or woman who is this very enterprise? It would be to run in parallel with the kind of being claimed by Kafka, who wrote his fiancée: "I have no literary interests; I am made of literature," meaning: "I am nothing else and cannot be anything else."[11] Everything inhuman—by which *he* will have meant the all-too-human—is alien to me. I live for one thing only: the literary—read: for Kaufmann, the philosophical "flight," an intensity of the experience of the thought of man.

It might be possible to distinguish the humanist from a nonhumanist or anithumanist care for man. Kaufmann's humanism implies an anthropological study centered on man's *subjectivity*—his thoughts, feelings, velleities, moods—accompanied by a sense of self.[12] Consider Hölderlin's novel *Hyperion* "Man wants to have a sense of self. . . . Not to have a sense of self is death."[13] In contrast, a number of important philosophical thought flights originating from Paris—shadowed by Heidegger's *Being and Time*—study man through impersonal "existentials," wider categories of human being, like Being, Language, Interpretation. Stefanos Geroulanos's *An Atheism That Is Not Humanist Emerges in French Thought*, for one, discusses antihumanist flights spearheaded by "the human sciences" of structuralism and so-called negative anthropology.[14] The "self" is in retreat.[15]

On this point of impersonality, however, Kaufmann's humanist inquiry does not begin with *your* own experiment: there is a vast history to it, which it behooves you to know and to criticize.

> To build—not a small chapel for myself,
> using what stones my native land provides,
> but, drawing on the best the world can give,
> the wisdom of the Greeks, the subtle learning
> of Jews and Arabs, and the Holy Scriptures,
> construct the universal church of man.[16]

Some past "stones," however, are so empty of "substance" that, contrary to the conventional view, they deserve to be excommunicated from the church of man or forced to play a much-diminished part—: for example, most of Christianity, Kantian (systematic) epistemology, and "ordinary language" philosophy. Kaufmann's *Critique* will devote a good part of its energies to defending this exclusion.

Two foundational features of genuine philosophical thought involve information that philosophy has tended to overlook. First is the data of an empirically based psychology: "we need a new empiricism which neither flees experience nor ravishes it but tries to do justice to it" (C 37).[17] Second are the synoptic insights of "great psychologists, [though they] are exceedingly rare" (C 3). Nietzsche is one of them: recall the title of Kaufmann's Nietzsche study, where Nietzsche is presented as philosopher, *psychologist*, and Antichrist. (And while we're here, let's quickly note that Kaufmann's translation of Nietzsche's [German] word "Antichrist" as the English "Antichrist" has been much contested and that Kaufmann subsequently considered but finally did not accept a revision: the word can mean the Antichrist of the Apostle John's First and Second Epistles but it also [merely] means "Anti-Christian"; in German "ein Christ" is "a Christian").[18] But now we are interested in Kaufmann's valorization of the disciplinary name and practice of psychology, for "in some of the most interesting philosophic works, psychological analysis and analysis of concepts illuminate each other. Indeed, any philosophical work that pursued one to the exclusion of the other does so at its peril" (C 2). In this pantheon, the Buddha and Freud flank the writings of Nietzsche: they are shining examples.

In advocating a turn to psychology, Kaufmann is in fact advocating a *return* to psychology. His plea occurs at the downward curve of the antipsychologism of modernist literature, criticism, and epistemology. One thinks, in the latter case, of Husserl and Heidegger (of their war cry: *zu den Sachen selbst*: let the mind address things before they have been psychologically disfigured). Think, too, of Ortega y Gasset, cited as an exemplar of existentialism in Kaufmann's anthology but the author of *The Dehumanization of Art*, for which we might substitute the nonce word *Depsychologization*: Ortega pleads for an art of felt *objects*, not feelings. Think of Mallarmé's *Un coup de dés*; of Rilke's "thing"-poems—Rilke is also cited as existentialist in Kaufmann's anthology—and Joyce's nonpsychological, nonreferential epiphanies. This list of avatars of depersonalization in the arts can be vastly enlarged.[19] But perhaps Kaufmann's vaunted recovery of psychology is best understood through its polemical intent, once again, as a countering thrust to Heidegger's *Being and Time*, with its contempt of psychology. The plausibility of this hypothesis will grow stronger throughout this study. If a book could be a "self," *Being and Time* would be Kaufmann's antiself.[20]

Kaufmann very much wants the tool of psychological analysis: its main role in his thought world is its power to detect special pleading, the production of bad reasons for convictions held on instinct and interest. This is a Nietzschean legacy. If Kaufmann has a quarrel with ordinary language philosophy, it is because it fails both standards: ordinary language philosophers show "a flagrant disregard for observation and develop strangely unempirical psychologies." This lack in fact facilitates, in Kaufmann's claim, the school's apologetic bias for Christianity and bourgeois morals, since its work simply does not go deep enough, to the brute fact of existence before amelioration (C 3).[21] As for modern psychology itself, it has taken for its subject matter "not Homo sapiens [in its higher registers] but, for the most part, man's irrationality and abundant sub-humanity" (C 4). This is a subset of irrational practice. I will add that if Freud's method was indeed to bring the searchlight of reason to the lower depths of the irrational, it was also to bring the agency of the irrational into the field of sensible reason, man's higher register. In *The Interpretation of Dreams*, for one, Freud assigns an unwonted "theoretical value" to the dream, conceiving of it as "a window, to cast a glance into the interior of the mind."[22] This sort of conceptual richness throughout all of Freud's writings is the product of an exemplary work ethic, "the devotion, the scientific hunger of a Freud" (C 5). Freud now stands foremost among Kaufmann's "educators." He contributes to Kaufmann's method and postulated character: a philosopher inaugurates basic inquiries, consonant with his major premise that what is well known is not at all known well. He brings endless intellectual curiosity to the task, a libido sciendi supported by seriously won erudition and the disciplined courage of a point of view.

On the question of literary style, which philosophical works must contend with, Kaufmann makes the point—one much developed in the following years in other people's studies of modernism—that the works of eminent writers in the first half of the twentieth century do not have endings ... and struggle to profile clear beginnings as well. They survive as hulks, as fragments. A look around us confirms Kaufmann's aperçu: Robert Musil's massive *The Man without Qualities* disintegrates into a mass of fragments. The same is true of Marcel Proust's *In Search of Lost Time*: as he lay dying, Proust was still at work on the contradictions, sketches, and unincorporated passages of the last three volumes. Kafka's novels exist only as fragments and do not have genuine endings (if *The Trial* ends with the protagonist's death, it is because Kafka wrote down the ending in the same flight as the beginning pages; but if he fills in the gap of the last place, he leaves scandalous gaps in places leading to the end: beginning and end do not rhyme). Kafka hated the ending of "The Metamorphosis," and

The Castle ends with the words, "It was Gerstäcker's mother. She gave K. her trembling hand and had him sit down next to her, she spoke with difficulty, it was difficult to understand her, but what she said . . ."

Kaufmann begins his point with Joyce's *Finnegans Wake*, which has neither beginning nor end in the sense that the last words begin a sort of sentence that the first words sort of complete. For Kaufmann, this snake-biting-its-tail narration means "to bring out the essential integrity of the work that, in a sense, has neither beginning nor end" (C 6). The idea of the essential integrity of the work that does not situate its beginning action at a point of fictional time and does not conclude at a later point of fictional time invites Joseph Frank's idea of "spatial form" and suggests Roland Barthes's notion that the modernist novel cannot be read, but only reread: what is meant is that the sense of the putative beginning can emerge only when one has got to the putative end. But, as we have noted, Kaufmann's dismay is not appeased by either of these formulations.

He advances by putting our "contemporary predicament" into historical-philosophical perspective, leading to the view that our predicament is not optional.

> Hegel already did not know where to begin because every sentence was bound to presuppose all the rest. Nietzsche's major works lack the kind of structure one expects of pupils. Wittgenstein's logistic arrangement in his *Tractatus* often differs only superficially from a very loose aphoristic style, and in the end he found himself literally unable to complete a book containing his philosophy. Heidegger has given us a fragment of one book, and then lectures and essays. . . . The problem transcends the age. A philosophic book is almost a contradiction in terms. Socrates knew this and did not even try to write; Plato knew it and wrote dialogues—in which arguments alternate with myths, and epigrams with digressions—as well as a letter in which he insisted that his dialogues did not really contain his philosophy. In a sense, Plato's dialogues, however artfully organized, are fragments of the mind's soliloquy: invitations to a philosophic life.

Kaufmann is on a philosophic flight:

> Spinoza put down his philosophy in a single volume, apparently *ordine geometrico*, but had recourse to a stunning diversity of styles. Much of Leibniz's philosophy has to be gleaned from his letters. Kant could write brilliant essays, but his *magnum opus*, the *Critique of Pure Reason*, is one of the worst-written great books of all time. And yet it would be impertinent to ridicule the style, for the problem is universal. (C 6–7)

What, then, is the conclusion for the present enterprise—Kaufmann's meaning to record his philosophic life, sprung in the "tension between analysis and existentialism"?

It will require another form, taking shape from the exigencies of a household of thoughts that would incorporate the *substance* of philosophy and religion—an impossible form, the form of an aspiration in exactly one hundred chapters but no less an aspiration only. Kaufmann's view of man is centered on man the *aspiring* creature, which numerical constraints, however witty, will not realize. This Faustian stress on philosophic longing was already set down in Kaufmann's *Nietzsche*:

> As human beings, we have ideals of perfection that we generally find ourselves unable to attain. We recognize norms and standards of which we usually fall short; we long for a triumph over old age, suffering, and death; we yearn for perfection and immortality—and seem incapable of fulfillment. We desire to be "as gods," but we cannot be so. (N 254)

Early on in *Critique*, Kaufmann's summarizes his prospectus:

> One can study man's distinctive endeavors—[art, religion, philosophy, morality, and science]—as aspirations which usually fall short of what is wanted. If one asks in this spirit about the relation of philosophy and religion to truth, the implicit foci of the discussion are two questions that have been at the center of philosophy since Socrates—questions that are found in the Bible, too, albeit with a different accent: "What is man?" and "What is truth?" (C 6)

One is inclined to subtend another question: What would guarantee the form of an authentic answer to either of these questions?[23]

Something like *greatness* is the answer. In the matter of the philosopher's chief aspiration, writing great books could take him or her some way closer to an ideal of perfection, but, following Kaufmann, the way now seems unreachable (C 7). This is a point, I'll add, that Thomas Mann develops with magisterial richness in *Doctor Faustus*. Kaufmann perceives a way out; the idea of this book begins to form.

> To present everything is impossible, but one can present several images, each boldly etched, to bring out what truth there is in it, unretouched, as sharp as possible. One can also offer criticisms of retouched pictures. At its best, philosophy offers a great deal of truth and an invitation to a different way of life. (C 7)

In light of the fact that several of Kaufmann's late great books are photo-graphic *picture* books, with commentaries, one can see this imagery as a budding passion. It reappears in the "avowed aim" of this book, as Kaufmann puts it in a later chapter: "to show the utter inadequacy of the popular pic-tures, to see the familiar in new perspectives, to make suggestions for a new map" (C 220).

These pictures amount to Yes-pictures—crystal clear, "boldly etched," full of truth—and No-pictures, exposing the distortions in what ought to be clear lines. Positions are then frequently triptychs: the one flanking element is clear; the middle is dark; the concluding element is again clear—and triumphant. Or the reverse, where the position enjoys an only intermittent clarity. For example, in considering Kaufmann's pictures of analytic philosophy, we have the first dark frame: its only superficial, politely social field of verbal objects. Take the distinction between belief and perception: Though I am right to say I *believe* in the existence of a teapot even where there is no teapot, I am wrong to claim I *perceive* a teapot when there is no teapot in view, Q.E.D. The middle picture gives analysis a certain brilliance as a gregarious enterprise:

> Analytic philosophy does not only develop the intellectual conscience, train the mind, and combine subtlety with scrupulous precision; above all, it teaches people to think critically and makes them instinctively anti-authoritarian. There is something democratic in this way of thinking: a proposition is a proposition, whether written by a student, a professor, or a Plato; the laws of logic are no respecter of persons. (C 25)

Many candidates vie for the position of the third triptych, which is dark, full of inanity. "At this point, however, all modesty is suddenly abandoned, and every student can tell you what is wrong with Kant without troubling to read more than a few pages" (C 25). But darker shortcomings have already been announced in philosophy's constitutive tension between analysis and existentialism, where the intensity of existentialism's concerns points up the risklessness of analysis: its resistance to the felt mood of existence (*Dasein*), to the hermeneutics of complex texts, to the historical context of meanings, as might be required by Nietzsche's aperçu: "All concepts in which an entire process is semiotically concentrated elude definition; only that which has no history is definable."[24]

> The charge against the tradition of British philosophy [from Berkeley and Hume to Broad and Ryle] should not be that it has been too critical—on

the contrary, its critical power has been its chief excellence—but that it has avoided an awareness of its relevance to experience, or indeed of the nature of the experiences to which various beliefs and arguments owe their significance. (C 43)

Kaufmann warms to his topic and characterizes the "British philosopher" of his day with a nice irony that Kaufmann's casual readers are not inclined to attribute to him: "[The British philosopher] has a feeling for nature as far as it is visually apprehended, but much less for music; a strong sense of propriety and little sympathy with mysticism; and not much appreciation of the difference between moral perplexity and indecency, passion and bad manners" (C 43). Analytical arguments turning on the perception of teapots and—as we shall see—carpets and gooseberries do not come from just any field of experience: they carry the dust of ancient college interiors. There is not a trace in them of hospitals, battlefields, mines, prisons, factories or, let us say, sofas (think: Crébillon *fils* or Sartre). "The whole philosophical tradition of which G. E. Moore forms an important link," Kaufmann concludes, relies on a very narrow range of experience, supposing it were pertinent even to attempt to remedy that lack. "The movement that is generally called empiricist really spurns experience," foremost aesthetic and religious experience (C 46).

As I glance at what I have written above, I have the feeling—I deplore it—that I have by and large made Kaufmann plainer than he is, his claims somewhat ordinary. I may be only partly to blame; Kaufmann is wittier, more surprising in the *detail*. Can anything of what one has read so far prepare for Kaufmann's plea for laughter in philosophy, a claim that actually might be as tedious as it sounds without illustration, but here is one: it is not a joke, but about Hegel's jokiness: "Hegel, who was far from humorless, concealed his jokes behind so many pronouns that they have to be construed" (C 13). Or given Kaufmann's solemn side deploring some of the bizarre triviality of Oxford philosophizing, one is surprised—and delighted—that his other side exults in its gaiety, calling Austin's piece "Pretending" "perhaps . . . the most hilarious piece of philosophy ever written" (F 57). (It's about whether a man gives definite proof of his anger when he bites the carpet on the model of whether it is the case that by a "'gooseberry,' we [definitely] mean simply a hirsute grape—and by a 'grape' likewise simply a glabrous gooseberry."[25])

It might be profitable—and certainly amusing (and we therewith satisfy a Horatian standard) to consider the author who sparked Kaufmann's perception of a witty Hegel. Since that author is Nietzsche, we have the benefit of learning of Hegel's hold on Nietzsche and being reminded of Nietzsche's on Kaufmann:

> *Esprit and morality.* The Germans, who know the secret of being boring with spirit, knowledge, and feeling, and who have accustomed themselves to feel boredom as moral, fear the French *esprit* lest it prick out the eyes of morality—fear and yet are charmed, like the little bird before the rattle-snake. Of the famous Germans perhaps none had more *esprit* than Hegel; but for all that, he too feared it with a great German fear, which created his peculiar bad style. The essence of this style is that a core is wrapped around, and wrapped around again and again, until it scarcely peeks out, bashful and curious—as "young women look through their veils," to quote the old woman-hater, Aeschylus; that core, however, is a witty, often pert perception about the most spiritual things, a delicate and daring connection of words, such as belongs in the company of thinkers, as a side dish of science—but in those wrappings it presents itself as abstruse science itself, and by all means as the most highly moral boredom. Thus, the Germans had their permissible form of a *esprit*, and they enjoyed it with such extravagant delight that Schopenhauer's good, very good, intelligence froze at the mere sight: all his life he stormed against the spectacle offered him by the Germans, but never could explain it to himself.[26]

Hegel, along with Nietzsche, is the modern philosopher who supplies Kaufmann the best precedent for the project of his books: "to attain knowledge of what is known by acquaintance, what is familiar," and to show, as Hegel did in his *Phenomenology of Spirit*, "how different philosophic positions are stages in the life of the spirit. . . . [Here] Hegel recorded his own voyage of discovery" (C 11). Kaufmann will devote a good deal of the second half of his writing life to interpreting Hegel, most importantly in the full-length volume *Hegel: Reinterpretation, Texts, and Commentary* in 499 pages (1965).[27] Even Kaufmann's hostile biographer Eric v. d. Luft considers Kaufmann's works on Hegel "benchmarks of the Anglo-American Hegel renaissance that began in the 1950's," adding, "Kaufmann's forte was in dispelling prevalent myths about the thinker—for example, the allegations that Hegel regarded Napoleon as 'the world soul on a horse' and history as the inexorable 'march of God' through time."[28] There are many other fortes in Kaufmann's Hegel interpretation, which we will take up in chapter 8, but we do not want to get too far ahead of ourselves. It remains to ponder a certain inconsistency in Kaufmann's procedure about his source. If he is writing a critique, then Hegel must not be central, for Hegel attacked Kant, the author of critiques, on this very point. Hegel is a speculative philosopher and not a critical one. *Néanmoins . . .*

Early on in his *Critique*, Kaufmann sets up the logical plan that prepares the thrust from his criticism of analysis, positivism, or "ordinary language" philosophy to his criticism of contemporary religion. Beginning with the philosophical concerns of Wittgenstein and his academic predecessors, mostly British, he writes:

> whatever one says about the foundations of mathematics or about sense data, and whatever reasons one considers best for saying that sometimes *I know* that you are angry or bored, at that level our most persistent quandaries are ignored, *the challenge to change one's life is not heeded, and a void remains—to be filled unfortunately without the benefit of philosophy*. Whether it is Kierkegaard that rushes in, extolling the "absurd," or rather common sense, whether it is Calvinism or Catholicism or the fashions of the day, philosophy has abdicated its responsibility (emphasis added). (C 56–57)

As *Critique* gathers momentum, Kaufmann identifies the main culprit that has come to fill the void and represents the present danger. It is not, let us say, "Calvinism" but the lukewarm Protestantism of uncritical Americans, who must be brought to their senses. This is the Socratic project of attacking "the fateful confusions of theologians, statesmen, and whatever other oracles we have . . . [for] confusion is not merely an occupational disease of philosophers . . . : a philosopher can be of some service by exposing the rank confusions of non-philosophers" (C 58). It need hardly be pointed out that when Kaufmann later speaks of the severely dampening effect on his career in academic philosophy produced by his project of speaking truth to power, or to ordinariness, the offense would have been his rather ostentatiously assuming this *mi*-Socratic mantle. In the agenda of philosophy departments in England and America, the work of elucidating confusion was very clearly restricted to the writings of other philosophers.

Kaufmann is thinking about the interesting contrast of Wittgenstein and Socrates:

> If Wittgenstein had a tendency to be too respectful before the wisdom of simple people and perhaps actually felt some slight nostalgia for the strong faith of Augustine or at least Kierkegaard's faith in faith, Socrates, albeit in

the marketplace, went to the opposite extreme and tended to view with scorn his intellectual inferiors. He came close to despising the common people. (C 60)

Despising is not Kaufmann's final stance. He puts the attitude of disrespect in its extreme form to shock respectable readers into recognition of its at least discussable character. For all his boldness, Kaufmann is not inviting trial, condemnation, and death by hemlock for impiety and corrupting youth. He will bring a German (and French) Enlightenment temperateness—*pace* Adorno and Horkheimer—to Socratic arrogance, thinking, perhaps, of the young Kant, who wrote:

> I myself am a researcher by inclination. I feel the entire thirst for knowledge and the eager restlessness to proceed further in it, as well as the satisfaction at every acquisition. There was a time when I believed this alone could constitute the honor of humankind, and I despised the rabble who know nothing. Rousseau has set me right. . . . Rousseau discovered for the very first time beneath the manifold of forms adopted by the human being the deeply hidden nature of the same and hidden law, according to which providence is justified.[29]

This "law" is "the consciousness of a feeling" that in its depth releases "the true voice of conscience," enlarging the scope of the self to include other minds and hearts. Among Kaufmann's "educators," Kant, despite his execrable style, would assume, along with Socrates, Goethe, and Nietzsche, an honorable, if marginal place, even as a negative example. *Critique of Practical Reason*, I will add, following Kant's indebtedness to Rousseau in his "Remarks," above, famously organizes Rousseau's celebration of conscience in the *Profession de foi du vicaire savoyard* as an autonomous source of ethical certainty.[30] On the other hand, "Kant's postulate of God" in this work might simply be "funny" (C 13). *Critique of Pure Reason*, we recall, despite being ill-written, remains for Kaufmann a "great book," and its stylistic aberrations cannot conceal its "profound originality" (C 6, 16).

Kaufmann, as I have noted, is a great suspecter of *beliefs*, though I earlier worried that he may have little to say to those who, like the fictional writer Elizabeth Costello, in a novel of that name by John Coetzee, "do not believe in beliefs," even their own.[31] And so it is important to note that Kaufmann gives the term a wide governance. His unshakable supposition is our love of truth—of evidence and logical consistency. For all the energy we might invest in the pursuit of personal excellence, we want "above all . . . to triumph over falsehood and deception."

Now, these abstractions are socially embodied in "custom and convention . . . inseparable from ignorance, misinformation, and hypocrisy," and these embodiments together constitute—and here is the relay—"a whole world of *beliefs*" (C 64). This world, for the greater part, is our environment *tout simple*, which means, however, that in the idea of a world of beliefs, there is leeway for us, "the chance to choose or build our *own world* of beliefs." So it not that beliefs as such are the placeholders of ignorance, misinformation, and hypocrisy: there are others, full of truth and the potentiality for right action, but we must choose and build them. At this point, however, "we" will feel the constraint of "they," who do not choose and do not build: our action will meet with resistance or torpor at every turn, and only "a bold effort" will be any good. It would be easier if this resistance were hard and identifiable: today we might identify it in the constraints of government, which, in its colossal credo—"the ongoing war on terrorism"—has produced instruments of surveillance inspiring timidity and fear. But while this constraint is one that Kaufmann cannot have had in mind— the war around him was a different war, the Cold War—he does have in mind a constraint that, in our day, is as much with us, as, in his day, it was with him: "The power that constrains our freedom is seen to be arbitrary and indifferent, a slothful despotism of surpassing cynicism." This power runs through our world as the mute power of self-repression. I would like to conjure Kafka at this point.

> Since the Fall we have been essentially equal in our capacity to recognize good and evil; nonetheless it is just here that we seek to show our individual superiority. But the real differences begin beyond that knowledge. The opposite illusion may be explained thus: nobody can remain content with the mere knowledge of good and evil in itself, but must endeavor as well *to act* in accordance with it. The strength to do so, however, is not likewise given him, consequently *he must destroy himself trying to do so*, at the risk of not achieving the necessary strength even then; yet there remains nothing for him but this final attempt. . . . Now, faced with this attempt, man is filled with fear; he prefers to annul his knowledge of good and evil . . . ; yet the accomplished cannot be annulled, but only confused. It was for this purpose that our rationalizations (*Motivationen*) were created (emphasis added).[32]

The crux of this aperçu, I believe, is the phrase "consequently he must destroy himself trying to do so." It will not be in everyone's moral lexicon to suppose that destroying oneself might produce all the strength necessary for one to do the right thing. This aperçu is important for our study of Kaufmann, of course, only insofar as it touches Kaufmann's project of doing right philosophy. So how can the idea of a self-destruction that gives strength be apposite to a thinker who lends such prestige to self-*making*, to the acquisition of "personal excellence"? The answer is that Kaufmann has not been chary either of pointing up the empirical risk of the project of authenticity.[33] *To change one's life*—the sovereign task of philosophy—quite evidently means destroying the old for the new. Less than Kafka, however, is Kaufmann willing to assert the separate superiority of the life of action, of doing "the right thing"; he wants to keep the value of philosophy, after all, the higher life of the mind, but he will always conceive of philosophy as valid only insofar as it does moral work, shattering the idols of the age. This moral work, too, will need the authority of both evidence and logical prowess. Bernard Williams makes this point, in the form of a warning:

> The search for an authentic life is always questionable, and it is not a secret that it can lead to ethical and social disaster.... Given an actual situation of choice or reflection in which the pursuit of authenticity needs the virtues of truth, one reason why they may fail is that there, in the nature of the case, the need for them may be concealed.[34]

The criticism of beliefs is not immune, either, to criticism of the personality of the believer, which includes attention to his or her place in time.

> We must ask what the author meant by the terms he used, and whether he used these terms in the same sense in his early and his late works, or even throughout the work at hand. All this will seem a matter of course only to those who have never read much theology or philosophic criticism. To give a single example: almost the entire Nietzsche literature flouts those rules. (C 72)

Here is one reasonably up-to-date example, which I shall pursue in some detail.

Some time ago, I criticized a translation made by the deconstructionist critic Paul de Man. In an essay on Nietzsche's *The Birth of Tragedy*," de Man cited an aphorism of Nietzsche: "Von Intelligenz kann nur in einem Reiche die Rede sein, wo etwas verfehlt werden kann, wo der Irrthum stattfindet— im Reiche des Bewußtseins."[35] A literal translation reads: "Intelligence can exist only in a realm in which something can go amiss, in which error takes place—a realm of consciousness." De Man, however, translated the sentence as "Intelligence can only exist in a world in which mistakes occur, in which *error reigns*—a world of consciousness" (emphasis added). Recall that Kaufmann considers a key question for interpreters "whether [the author—and in this case, precisely, Nietzsche] . . . used these terms in the same sense in his early and his late works, or even throughout the work at hand" (C 72). The crucial term we're discussing is "Irrtum" (error).

To stress all the consequences of de Man's "translation"—good for his theory of the omnipresence of erroneous consciousness, disastrous for human-kind—would take us far afield. We are interested in his defense of his trans-lation. Consciousness, he argues, would be the perennial scene of *necessary* error, *the* fateful error inhering in all consciousness; and, according to de Man, there was a good deal of evidence in Nietzsche's writings to support his thesis.

> Nietzsche says "wo der Irrtum stattfindet" which, especially after the use of "Reiche" for "world" and with the temptation of alliteration, is better rendered by "error reigns." . . . "Der Irrtum" has for him a very specific and precise meaning. It is, as in *The Will to Power*, "the old error of the ground [*der alte Irrtum vom Grunde*], the error which consists of mistaking the figure of a ground for an actual cognitive grounding." . . . Error is not, here, just any error, let alone "such a thing as error" [as Corngold proposed] but the error that cannot be separated from cognition to the precise extent that cognition cannot be separated from discourse. But if error is thus "funda-mentally" linked to cognition, etc.[36]

De Man is appealing to a famous aphorism in *The Will to Power* for proof of "the very specific and precise meaning" that the term "Irrtum" (error) *always* has for Nietzsche—"the old error of the ground [*der alte Irrtum vom Grunde*]." He cites this aphorism from Kaufmann's and R. J. Hollingdale's translation and edition of *The Will to Power*:

> The whole of "inner experience" rests upon the fact that a cause for an excitement of the nerve centers is sought and imagined—and that only a cause thus discovered enters consciousness: this cause in no way corre-sponds to the real cause—it is a groping on the basis of previous "inner experiences," i.e., of memory. But memory also maintains the habit of the old interpretations, i.e., of *erroneous* causality—so that the "inner experi-ence" has to contain within it the consequences of all previous false causal fictions. Our "outer world" as we project it every moment is indissolubly tied to *the old error of the ground*: we interpret it by means of the schematism of "things," etc.[37]

My point now is merely to stress that Nietzsche composed this aphorism, which links *all* cognition of the outer world to error, in the spring of 1888, *seventeen* years after the aphorism under discussion. This latter aphorism is supposed to supply evidence for de Man's interpretation. It is a big assumption to make in favor of an interpretation in which one has a vested interest. In preceding aphorisms, written in the same period (spring 1888), Nietzsche repeatedly speaks of error in the plural: there are various sorts of errors, having different causes, those of "good will," even those of a *physiological* origin, which will prepare for Kaufmann's next point about a psychophysiological criticism of erroneous beliefs.[38] Here I want to cite the conclusion of this very aphorism, since it has a special relevance to our discussion: "I call that *a lack of philology*; to be able to read off a text as a text without interposing an interpretation." At another place, close by, Nietzsche writes: "The lack of philology: one constantly confuses the explanation with the text—and what an 'explanation'!"[39]

I return to Kaufmann's account of the proper method of "criticizing beliefs," which is to say: doing philosophy, the first having been, as in our discussion above, to link the value of key terms in the philosopher's development to the moment in his career when he employs them. But

> besides the systematic and the developmental meaning there are the many symptomatic meanings. The proposition may be symptomatic psychologically: the author's choice, and especially his abuse, of words, his imagery and his examples, his style and attitude, may invite psychological study. (C 72)

Kaufmann is skillful in reading philosophical texts this way, especially when it comes to his reading of Hegel, as we shall see—a method he has developed on Nietzsche's example and from his dedication to Freud. A passage from the brief, unsympathetic biography of Kaufmann composed by v. d. Luft and cited earlier in connection with Kaufmann's abundant work on Hegel addresses this skill but with a good deal of exaggeration: "Kaufmann's fundamental method," writes v. d. Luft, "was to discover the private consciousness of the thinker. . . . Scholarly detractors claim that Kaufmann's conclusions about Hegel's and Nietzsche's psyches are too speculative—for example, his idea that Hegel's fathering of an illegitimate child materially affected the content of *Phenomenology of Spirit*. These detractors have dubbed his posthumous psychoanalysis of philosophers 'Kaufmannization.'"[40]

I, for one, have nowhere found "detractors" dubbing Kaufmann's posthumous psychoanalysis of philosophers "Kaufmannization." I strongly suspect that these detractors are none other than the author of the idea of such detractors. V. d. Luft, to judge from his curriculum vitae, knows a good deal about the history of medicine, and so he knows, as few readers will realize, that "Kaufmannization" refers to an especially vicious sort of psychiatric therapy involving electric shocks and verbal abuse, practiced in veteran's hospitals in Germany at the end of World War I. V. d. Luft's essay, with its insider's "joke," has been published as a seemingly authoritative short biography of Kaufmann in a reputable reference work. One certain use of the book that you are now reading is to set v. d. Luft's squib in another perspective.

Since Kaufmann exhorts us to read ideas for symptoms of psychological needs, the question will arise, sooner or later, of the reasons underlying Kaufmann's own investments. At the risk of destroying the suspense involved in this question, I'll note that in the introduction we have encountered—and will continue to encounter—evidence of Kaufmann's drives and motives. They precipitate—or do they arise from?—such acts as his youthful conversion to Judaism even in the year the Nazis seized power; his Napoleonism stemming, perhaps, from his small stature and boyish appearance; his physical energy and good looks; his loss of rightful membership in the social class of the German Bildungsbürgertum; the deprivation of university study in Germany; other unrecorded insults he will have suffered as a persecuted Jew in Germany; the radical change of identity entailed in his immigration to America; the tension of being an American Army conquistador in his occupied homeland; the romantic ideology of what David Pickus, in the supplement to chapter 6, calls his death work ethic; and, finally, his Nietzscheanism, his sense that what he achieved was owed to a relentless exercise of a will to power—all converging on an intense sense of self.

Nietzsche's jottings on what is "perhaps," as he writes, the indissoluble attachment of error to observation, if "true," would disqualify any perception, cognition, or intuition as false.[41] This does not speak to Kaufmann's subchapter "Theories of Truth." There are many theories of truth, and Kaufmann's own bias is to recast them in the mold of interpersonal relation by figuring truth as what is "trustworthy." We are after all inclined in the first instance to say that *persons* are trustworthy: they have earned our trust. This way of figuring truth may not be self-evident, and may be many steps in clarity behind theories of truth based uniquely on correspondence (between objects and their representations) or coherence (between elements of propositional sequences) or pragmatic success (between hypotheses and their applications). If we consider the description of contents on the back of a medicine bottle or on a Kerman rug to be true for being trustworthy, it is because we have implicitly decided to trust the manufacturer of these labels.[42] There is nothing on the face of a similar label floating on water to confirm its trustworthiness any more than cloud shapes or wave writing on the sands point to the intent of a creator to communicate his or her vision. How then can a state of affairs that we assume to be true indicate the trustworthiness confirming our assumption? Kaufmann answers as follows: "Truth is what is trustworthy and truth always involves a correspondence of appearance and reality or of expectation and fulfillment.... Truth is what keeps its promise" (C 74). One must have heard the promise. Evidently Kaufmann's use of the term "correspondence" signals the impossibility of doing without it—and he will employ the term of "coherence" as well—if kept within the constraints of his discourse of interpersonal figuration (again, "truth is what keeps its promise"). Such correspondence as between appearance and reality, between expectation and fulfillment, relies on an inevitable coherence:

> we have no second sight to see whatever appearance and reality correspond, and if we would know whether a proposition is true we must see whether it is consistent with what else we know, with our other experiences.
>
> Even as correspondence is not known intuitively, coherence here is not a matter of consistency with a fixed number of other propositions. ... As rival theories which would exclude each other, both theories go beyond what they have seen: one notes that truth involves correspondence, while the other one notes the importance of coherence—and both state their insights in a manner that necessitates objection. ... Truth—even that of the Biblical God—is experienced by man only in time as a series of events, of promises fulfilled. This temporal and open character of truth has been stressed by the pragmatic theory, which ... is very close to the Biblical conception of truth. ... The Hebrew *emeth*, which means firmness, reliability, and trustworthiness, and is sometimes rendered as *aletheia* in the Septuagint, has been explained ... as essentially not a static quality but something that manifests itself in time in the fulfillment of expectations and the justification of claims. ... Truth is the correspondence of promise and performance, a consistency that is not established once and for all but continuing and open toward the future. Truth is what proves itself continually. (C 74–75)

It would seem that Kaufmann's lexicon derives the interpersonal figure of truth from the relation between man and God.

Trustworthiness is a feeling, and Kaufmann is a great proponent of truth in emotion:

> What we ordinarily call moods, feelings, and emotions are, are least in many of us, nine-tenths thoughts. It maybe physiological processes that predispose us toward certain kinds of thoughts, but moods and emotions are, to a large extent, complexes of thoughts. (C 84)

In this, Kaufmann joins a significant modern tradition of thought that empowers *moods* as prime revelators of being. This type of feeling, I'll note, which, as *Befindlichkeit* (how one is faring, what sort of mood one's in), is, in Heidegger, an existential category. At least as early as in Kant's *Critique of Judgment*, mood acquires "a function of disclosure which, before Kant, had been attributed only to logical cognition. Kant implicitly gives mood a significance that, only recently, in the work of Heidegger and Scheler, has received the explanation that is its due."[43] Kaufmann's educator Nietzsche belongs centrally to this positioning of mood (the category) in the arc of German reflection on art, aesthetics, and play that leads from Kant through Heidegger and Scheler (and to which terminus both Walter Benjamin and now Walter Kaufmann need to be reckoned).[44] In Kaufmann's *Critique*, as in his previous anthology *Existentialism*, a mood-saturated art is the great revelator of human being in depth. Musil's novels *The Perplexities of Young Törless* and *The Man without Qualities*, that great hulking fragment, suit his thesis very well. Under the glut and pressure of profit-driven media, "one sometimes wonders whether differentiated emotions will soon become extinct. But good writers have not died out, and richly differentiated emotions have always been the forte of the few." And so "those who do feel deeply and intensely will instinctively turn to art" (C 82, 83).

The words of art, like the expressive words of emotion, do not name objects in the world: they are not "the names of objects of experience" (C 78). The relation of naming to properly nonobjective experiences—"the uncanny, the mysterious"—is a fraught one: it can objectify what is elusive or tremendous. "A noun is not the name of a thing but an attack on a thing: a noun tears a thing out of its environment, strips it of its defenses, and hales it into court for an indictment" (C 78). The ancient Hebrews were well aware of the loss of aura through displacement onto common things: they "resolved that God must not be named, or that the name must be pronounced only once a year on a most awesome occasion. Eventually, the very pronunciation of the name was forgotten. Nor does the Christian God have a name" (C 87). Words are not constitutive of all experience, least of all the language of the tribe (common *beliefs*) and the language of the scribe, for what has he *seen*? He may "hide a paucity of insight behind a façade of verbiage." The temptation of common sense to adulterate experience with words aforethought is persistent: it resists "all penetrating perception," hampers intensity: "[words] gain admittance, clipped by stereotyped expectations, and are 'understood' before they have been fully felt. We overpower them lest we feel their power, and remember them almost before we have had them" (C 95–96). The latter temporality, however, may not be so easy, or desirable, to circumvent in every case. We have the testimony of its benefit, for one, in the stunning passage on crossing the Alps in chapter 6 of Wordsworth's *The Prelude* titled "Cambridge and the Alps." Here is evidence for the inevitability—and even the glory—of such a reversal of mental states, in which memory overpowers the putative moment of lived experience, with this variation: the traveler remembers but does not *literally* remember; just after he has *not* had the experience of crossing the Alps, he remembers the hope of having it. Having set his sights on the moment of passage through the Simplon Pass, some peasants inform him that he has already passed the moment by, whereupon a sort of memory, not empirical, but intensified as imagination, "an unfathered vapor," sublimates the loss. Common sense does not block the intensity: the intensity transcends common sense, drastically. Scholars continue to ponder this "irruption of the imagination at the moment when Wordsworth realizes he has already crossed the Alps . . . , concluding that the passage, for all its grandeur, is a 'poetic failure' on logical grounds."[45] Indeed this objection runs parallel to Kaufmann's logical objection to the obstructive practice of common sense, but in another, extraordinary sense, which is not logical, Wordsworth prepares the mind for a glimpse, precisely, of its "uncanny, its mysterious" depth. His journey has come to an end before, as it were, it had reached its end—its goal—in the anticipated moment of passage. The completion is chronologically later, but, in the mind's temporality, it comes before the desired end. What I have called a sort of potentiated memory—Imagination—rises

> Like an unfathered vapour; here that power,
> In all the might of its endowments, came
> Athwart me.[46]

This discovery is followed by an epigrammatic commentary on the experience of anticipation:

Our destiny, our nature, and our home,
Is with infinitude—and only there;
With hope it is, hope that can never die,
Effort, and expectation, and desire,
And something evermore about to be.[47]

In the long run, Wordsworth and Kaufmann are one in their "uncompromising denial that the normal faculties of consciousness are adequate to discover 'our destiny, our nature, and our home'"—even when the normal faculties are behaving logically.[48] Poetry knows this; it teaches the point to philosophy, and in philosophy's increase of such knowledge is a way of life. This result is consistent with Kaufmann's discussion in the sections titled "Words as Categories" (section 30), "Works of Art as Categories" (section 31), and "Common Sense" (section 32), which concludes that part of *Critique* addressing philosophy. The remainder of the book, with the exception of its coda, called "Reason and Eros," goes to Kaufmann's critique of religion. In this critique, Freud will make several crucial appearances.

4

Transcending the Human

CRITIQUE OF RELIGION AND PHILOSOPHY/2

These writers represent our incessant effort to transcend the human without
forsaking humanism.

—HAROLD BLOOM

ON THE THRESHOLD of *Critique of Religion and Philosophy* stands the theme
of "man's aspirations," an idea charged with passionate conviction.[1] It is indispensable to Kaufmann's humanism and the basis of the religious impulse
everywhere alive and to which he is no stranger. The phrase looks backward to
Kaufmann's *Nietzsche* and forward to the first half of *Critique*, where it figures
as the philosopher's "aspiration for truth," and then, as an afterthought, "not
only the philosopher's" (C 63). Indeed, in a coming discussion of the idea of
perfection as it appears in St. Anselm's ontological proof of the existence of
God—a proof that Kaufmann finds vacuous—Kaufmann defines perfection
as "the absence of flaws that generally characterize human beings. . . . What is
ascribed [to a perfect being] is a triumph over some inadequacy that weighs us
down. This is best understood in connection with man's aspirations" (C 164).[2]

Wouldn't this latter feature be the sine qua non of humanism, for how
could we respect a creature equipped to aspire yet who will not aspire to the
knowledge of its condition? The socialization of this failure is *convention*, the
substance of an agreement not to care about the truth. At the time of this
writing—to drop a few levels in this narrative—we discover the existence of a
new convention, one transparent to the nature of conventions as such, among

American politicians running for office (in October 2014 and after). Asked for their views on climate change, party members, again and again, shrug and say, "I'm not a scientist."[3] This convention betrays its essence as a convention: it is the agreement *not* to aspire to the truth of one's condition.

Kaufmann's view of convention as a principled opposition to the aspiration to truth anchors his analysis of religious belief. This analysis, sustained for some fifty chapters, is the great content of the second half of his *Critique*. My concern in this chapter is to relay a sense of the range of Kaufmann's commentary by dwelling on what I take to be moments particularly illustrative of his bent of mind. This must be a personal reading: it cannot do full justice to the hundreds of Kaufmann's pages of battling thought, engaged erudition, and—yes—aspiration to truth in a momentous matter. The possibility, validity, honor of religious experience—something not to be taken for granted— is at stake. Most of Kaufmann's contemporary reviewers declared that they could not see the thread running through the one hundred chapters. It is very unlikely that there is such a thread, except as the testimony ("l'essai brillant") of what the French philosopher Gérard Deledalle called "un esprit vif doublé d'un érudit."[4] I want to try to convey a sense of Kaufmann's enterprise that will encourage you, reader, to go to the source.

Religious belief, to put it directly, is belief in the existence of God, in which context it is called faith. St. Thomas Aquinas's "calm concession" that belief is "*not* based on evidence sufficient to compel the assent of every reasonable person" merely prepared the way for acceptance of "the crucial articles of faith." Kaufmann writes vigorously of the several (appalling) tonalities in which this concession appears in Christian authors—"bold defiance if not truculence. Paul boasted that what he believed was 'to the Greeks foolishness'; Tertullian, that it was 'impossible'; Luther, that it contradicted reason; Kierkegaard that it was utterly absurd." But there can be no virtue in believing without evidence (C 114).

In the matter of the presumed evidence used to bolster the main articles of Christian belief wherever faith is hard to come by, Kaufmann discriminates three types: the first is historical evidence. Such evidence must be adequate to the claims based on it. Consider the proposition "*Jesus himself said*, 'no man comes to the Father, but by me'" (emphasis added).[5] What is the evidence for the truth of this statement? "There are no eyewitness accounts but only documents written decades after the events which they discuss, by men who were demonstrably influenced by the needs and violent polemics of a later age and often disagree on vital points." To put the matter gently, older times did not always have the same sense of historical accuracy scholars today require. Kaufmann cites Matthew 27:52–53:

> And the graves were opened; and many bodies of the saints which slept arose, And came out of the graves after his resurrection, and went into the holy city, and appeared unto many.

Kaufmann then remarks, wryly, that "the resurrection did not seem to Matthew as extraordinary as it does to our contemporaries: it was to his mind, and his audience's, unusual—a little more so than the earthquake he reports in the preceding verse—but by no means unique" (C 121).

Some evidence works *against* conclusions, as for example, against the virgin birth of Jesus Christ, since Paul, whose Epistles, as Kaufmann reminds us, antedate the Gospels, never mentions it, a point that would certainly have interested his community. This absence is evidence against a conclusion, although it does not disprove the conclusion.

Again, on the matter of good—and missing—evidence, the birth in Bethlehem is reported by Luke and Matthew but not by Mark or John. Other pieces count against the claim that Jesus was born there, but here the point is the degree of implausibility of different claims and, hence, the weight of the sort of evidence they require for proof. The claim "that Jesus literally rose from the dead on the third day" calls for weightier evidence than does the claim that he was born in Bethlehem or, for that matter, passed his childhood in Nazareth—in the latter case, there is a lot less at stake.

The second type of religious proposition—the first being historical evidence—is the robust generalization. One proposition that Kaufmann would have heard during his army days argues for the self-evidence of religious belief: "There are no atheists in foxholes," meaning, everyone's weak refusal turns to ardent faith when death lowers. This is patently untrue, I'll note, if only on the example of David Hume (Boswell, ever curious, saw no trace of a conversion); of Thomas Paine, who allegedly cried, to the Presbyterian ministers come to console him, "Let me have none of your Popish stuff"; and of the eloquent atheist Christopher Hitchens, who was mortified at the imputation that, dying of a fever, he would relent.[6]

The third type of religious proposition Kaufmann calls "speculative": it cannot be supported (or refuted) by either historical evidence or by the criteria appropriate (or inadequate) to generalizations like those above. What is to be made of such propositions as "In the earth's molten core, souls burn everlastingly" or "After death, consciousness survives"? These are evidently not propositions of the same kinds, but the point is that they elude proof and contribute to Kaufmann's major thought, which stresses the disparity in the types of proposition to which "a religion attaches decisive significance and in terms of which it defines itself." Hence, the critique of religion must begin by identifying the kind of proposition it is addressing and the "kind of evidence that is relevant for deciding whether the proposition is true, probably true, probably false, or certainly false" (C 124).

Revelation—the notion that God reveals himself and his requirements in a book he has composed through a privileged secretary—gives proof of all three types of propositions. But the evidence it brings is circular: it is good enough only as it is held on faith to be better than good.

> Are we to believe that God exists because a book asserting his existence was revealed by him and therefore must be right? Or that Jesus was God because Jesus said he was, and if he was God he could not be wrong? After all, when Father Divine makes the same claim, most of us do not believe him. Even if we assume that Jesus made this claim—which is highly doubtful in view of the evidence—why should we believe him, unless it were because we think he really was God, which begs the question. (C 124–25)[7]

Kaufmann lists the criteria generally employed to validate mystic experience; this is also an opportunity to cite his influential teacher at Williams College, James Bissett Pratt. "The Absolute may explain *everything*; it cannot explain anything in particular."[8] (Hear Hegel turning in his grave.) Kaufmann's impulse is to take seriously the topic of mystic revelation, while concluding that such alleged revelation cannot *establish* any belief that makes recourse to it (C 128). There are too many obstacles, which he lays out, in the way of taking its substance as true. "A miracle requires faith: to those who lack faith it is not a miracle" (C 129).[9]

What drives religious belief? Regrettably, Kaufmann passes over Freud's invocation in *Civilization and Its Discontents* of "the oceanic feeling." Instead he has Freud identify—and incriminate—a single psychological motive: wishful thinking. But this picture of an original founder contriving an illusion responsive to the wishes of a deluded mass is false. It misses, above all, the element of tradition, of cultural transmission, shaping a religion at every moment of its existence. "The founders of religions have either codified or modified traditions that preceded them," traditions animated by a variety of illusory and also real world interests (C 134). Nietzsche's apothegm from *Genealogy of*

Morals is perfect: "For every kind of historiography there is no more important proposition than this . . . : the cause of the origin of a thing and its eventual
usefulness, actual employment, and incorporation into a system of aims lies
worlds apart."[10]

Freud's large-scale simplification might itself be driven by a structural
requirement of his thought. There are his parallel simplifications in the field
of dreams—"censorship and self-deception"—and of art—substitutive gratification, the compensations of the daydream. And so, according to Kaufmann,
when Freud writes of religious doctrines in *The Future of an Illusion*, "They are
all illusions," he is stressing the one motive to piety: the craving to be deceived,
to be gratified by illusion. For all his admiration of Freud, Kaufmann thinks
this explanation paltry in the name of the greater respect owed to "man's creative impulses," although the sway of mass belief today is less creative than
imposed. On the other hand, we now encounter the familiar third term of
Kaufmann's habit of argument, the temperate Yes; for "faith, secular or religious, is by nature close to wishful thinking" (C 135).

Beyond wishful thinking, faith, and the craving to be deceived, there exist
ostensibly logical "proofs" to shore up religion. Kaufmann's discussion of
St. Thomas Aquinas is impressive and deserves slow reading: alas, it is too
detailed to be included here, except as an opportunity to like a number of
Kaufmann's intellectual-historical jeux d'esprit. The Latin translations of Aristotle had made inroads into dogmatic Christian belief and in the early thir-
teenth century were banned from the curriculum of the University of Paris.
Aquinas studied Aristotle, though his knowledge of the texts was imperfect,
since he did not read Greek. As Kaufmann writes, "St. Thomas went forth, but
did not slay the dragon [of reason]. He pulled its fangs and made it subservient
to the Church" (C 143).

There are odd moments in Thomas's magisterial *Summa Theologica*, often
expectably overlooked though even emphasized by his faithful editor Étienne
Gilson, who insists, along with Thomas, on the absolute certainty of angels.
Kaufmann deals calmly with this claim, no excrescence but, according to
Gilson, one necessary to maintain the equilibrium of Thomas's system.[11] There
would be a number of ways to deal with such dogmas, the most arduous being
"to construct a rival system without God or angels, or perhaps, as C. D. Broad
comes close to doing in *Religion, Philosophy, and Psychical Research*, without
God but with angels" (C 153).[12] This glancing mention of Broad, as in so many
instances of glancing mentions of scholars whom Kaufmann has read, awakens
the reader's possibly dormant antiquarian impulse.

One looks forward to Kaufmann's citation of the ontological proof of the existence of God, which, contra expectation, is *not* among the five proofs of the existence of God found in the *Summa* to buttress a faith-based system. In systematic argument, Kaufmann judges Thomas's five proofs to be logically weak, then turns to address the original version of the ontological proof attributed to St. Anselm, which builds on the claim that God's perfection entails God's existence. The concept of perfection, as Kaufmann points out, is not a clear concept, perfection being a matter of fitness to a purpose, or else vaguely aesthetic, as one might say of the marble torso of the Aphrodite from Cyrene in Rome, "How perfect she is!" This much granted—or rather withheld from the proof—it is then altogether moot whether existence is to be regarded as an accompanying perfection. Kaufmann sums up the matter:

> it might be a possible definition of God that he is the incarnate triumph over man's inadequacies, thought of as existing, that he is the embodiment of that state of being after which all men—or most men—aspire, thought of not as a logical possibility but as existing. From this definition, however we could not infer that God actually exists. (C 165–66)

Here Kaufmann follows Kant's earlier destruction of a "proof" based on the premise that "existence" is a predicate. The fact of "existing" adds nothing to the essence of a thing, let alone caps its perfection. Following Kant, you could conceive of a perfect being as not existing. Pascal's wager fares no better: the core of Kaufmann's objection is that God might be reluctant to bless a creaturely faith based on a prudent risk assessment analysis.

What about visionary evidence? Isaiah had a vision of "God on a throne surrounded by seraphim—probably fiery serpents, not angels—with six wings." There is a way of absorbing this vision without necessarily believing either its detail or its main claim of proof of the existence of God. It is not necessary to believe, for example, "that one of the seraphim literally touched Isaiah's lips with a live coal, or that the Lord [literally] sat upon a throne surrounded by six-winged seraphim" (C 174). Nonetheless, like Blake's drawings, I'll add, it can shape a *conception* of divinity through awe and fascination without entailing belief in its existence. Kaufmann puts the matter in a cross-grained, surprising way that is close to humor, remarking: "Asked whether Odysseus was phenomenally stupid, we could say No without committing ourselves regarding his historical existence" (C 175). That is, one can judge even a fiction on its verisimilitude, alter its details, approve it in the main, and yet by no means grant real existence to a character conjured by the fiction.

Kaufmann is engaged by the concept of ambiguity, which acquires different values in the course of his writings. At this point in his discussion of religious faith, he notes that "most statements about God are essentially ambiguous." This predicate does not amount to a refutation; it does not amount to the death of the claim it veils (C 181). Neither, I'll add, does it create ipso facto a uniquely literary value, as in the New Critics' celebration of ambiguity as the hallmark of great poetry, although, considering Kaufmann's citation of Kafka—"the clarity and precision" of whose style "hides unfathomable ambiguity"—"such ambiguity [in an artist] is not objectionable" (C 196). Kaufmann implicitly links Kafka's prose with the language of the Hebrew Bible, whose "essential ambiguity" has always been a spur to exegesis—to even "truly daring interpretations." The crux is that the ambiguity of such writing must be taken *ad ovo* as "poetic and only symbolically true" (C 270). But such judgments are disputatious. Ambiguity is, indeed . . . ambiguous.[13]

In religious discourse, ambiguous propositions are neither true nor false. For example, what is the truth value of the bare proposition "God exists"? Clearly, the concept of "existence" here is ambiguous: few would be prepared to say that God's mode of existence is the familiar mode of existence of windows, clocks, and, for that matter, hirsute grapes (see above on Austin). Are there other modalities of existence? "Those asserting the existence of God have sometimes . . . contended that God's mode of existence is unique, that he . . . exists in a sense peculiar to himself. Logically, however, this is not different from saying that God does *not* 'exist.'" (C 178). Readers of Heidegger are acquainted with the effort to assign another mode of being to the god-term Being (*Sein*; later, *Seyn*) unlike that of merely existing entities (*Seiendes*). Kaufmann's distinctions help to resituate Heidegger's seductive distinctions anew—and more clearly.

I mention Heidegger's ontology because it is a recurrent topic in Kaufmann's work, a persistent object of concern and refutation. Reenergized via its deconstruction by Derrida and his legatees, its influence touches many more fields than the Protestant theologies with which Kaufmann is immediately concerned. Moreover, with the 2014 publication of Heidegger's *Black Notebooks*, Heidegger's "phenomenological ontology" is once again drastically contentious. In the present chapter, titled "God and Ambiguity," Kaufmann addresses the nearer target, the Harvard professor and German American theologian Paul Tillich, who had published his major works—*Systematic Theology, Part I* (1951) and *The Courage to Be* (1952)—in the years when Kaufmann was conceiving his *Critique*. Characteristically, when Tillich writes that "God is being-itself, not *a* being," Kaufmann stresses the affinity between Tillich's theological thought and the ostensibly atheological thought of Heidegger.

> Tillich's affirmation suggests that theists affirm something after all, and that this affirmation is denied by atheists. But no atheist would deny the affirmation that "God is being-itself"; he would only say that in that case we might as well dispense with all reference to God and—like Heidegger, for example, to whom Tillich is exceedingly close—speak of "being." (C 178–79)

If we are to speak of God, thus Kaufmann, He cannot be "being-in-itself," since to speak of Him this way is to dispense with the testimony of Scripture. The term "God" is overdetermined, charged with the history of the thoughts and feelings aroused by His words and deeds recorded in the Bible. At first Kaufmann specifies *Hebrew* Scriptures, addressing the God of Abraham, Isaac, and Jacob, but there is much more to add in the Judeo-Christian tradition alone:

> And now there have been added to this overrich conception of the Scriptures the sayings of Jesus and the stories of the Gospels, the theologies of the fourth evangelist and Paul, the ideas of the other authors of New Testament Epistles, the visions of the Revelation of St. John the Divine, and the vast lore, if not of the Talmud, Midrash, and the Jewish mystics, of the church fathers and the Christian mystics, the scholastics, and innumerable theologians and philosophers. (C 180–81)

God is far from being a univocal term: He is the subject of ambiguities.

Kaufmann's view of Christianity, however, is scarcely unambiguous: it is scathingly critical, and, as we will see, it spurs fierce opposition from Christian scholars. Kaufmann cannot accept the harsh exclusionary thrust in Christ's teaching—in a word, its emphasis on hell and damnation. He asks, on a theological flight:

> Why should God have so ordered the world that all men were headed for everlasting damnation and that he was unable to help them except by begetting a son with a woman betrothed to Joseph, and by then having this son betrayed and crucified and resurrected, by having him fetch Abraham and a few of the damned out of hell while leaving the rest to their lot, and by saving only that small minority among men who first heard this story and then believed it? Surely, such a God is not an unequivocal symbol of love. (C 200)

The word "unequivocal" appears as a concession to his Christian readers. The fact remains that "the God of traditional Christianity . . . relegates the mass of mankind to eternal torment" (C 203).

How is this strain—"the deification of superhuman cruelty"—to be accommodated to a religion that is known to preach love? Kaufmann, no Christian theologian, cannot or will not answer this question; instead, he addresses flagrant shortcomings in the traditional picture. There is first of all Hegel's notorious claim, which asserts—falsely—that the idea of the infinite value of every human soul comes into the world through Christianity, "according to which the individual as such has *infinite* value, being the object and end of God's love."[14] "In Hegel's time," writes Kaufmann, "one could plead extenuating circumstances or one's ignorance of other religions. . . . Christianity comes into the world over five centuries after Buddha, and the [Hebrew] prophets had introduced . . . the high estimation of love," based on the recognition of the intrinsic value of *every* human being. "In Judaism, Hinduism, and Buddhism no soul is damned eternally" (C 204). Moreover, the traditional Christian conception of love is a jealous love, "the love of a God so jealous that he condemns to eternal torment all those who have failed to love him as he wants to be loved, including those who, for one reason or another . . . never had a chance of loving him" (C 205). Kaufmann is tireless in rejecting Christianity:

> Given the belief that man was created in the image of God, or that God will save all who go on crusades to kill infidels and to conquer the supposed sepulcher of Jesus; or that God will torment everlastingly all who reject one of the Christian dogmas and . . . permit the saved to watch this spectacle eternally . . . we must ask not only about the evidence for such beliefs, but also about their moral implications. (C 206)

The critique goes on. Luther wrote: "Whoever wants to be a Christian should tear the eyes out of his reason."[15] Granted, but not to their credit, few Christian apologists are prepared to read this injunction literally. The *Interpreter's Bible* speaks of Luther's "Oriental hyperbole," his point being merely that reason is a danger, for it can proffer inducements to sin, and *such* a thing must be torn out. Here Kaufmann surprises the reader with a Nietzschean reminiscence, remarking that such cuts would thoroughly undermine "an ethic of self-realization or sublimation"; they would rob the "sinner" of the opportunity to make a good thing of his sin. For what, after all, is reason, if not "a thrust beyond the present and an education in self-contempt. . . . Reason enables man to strive consciously to transcend himself" (C 354). Is this point not being made too drastically?[16] A reminiscence of Kafka would formulate this ethic as "not shaking off the self but consuming the self."[17] It was Moses, after all, "[who] said to his people: 'Ye shall be unto me a kingdom of priests' and 'Ye shall be holy'—not merely some but all; everyone is called to make something of himself. Perhaps *this* was the most revolutionary idea of world history" (emphasis added) (C 218).

The Christian limitation of "self-realization" extends to the body politic. It would stand to reason that where there is "sin" in government—the corruption of power—it is the right of the abused to take arms against this evil. But Kaufmann cites Romans 13:1, which reads: "Let every person be subject to the governing authorities. For there is no authority except from God, and those that exist have been instituted by God. Therefore, he who resists the authorities resists what God has appointed, and those that resist will incur judgment" (C 211). Kaufmann takes pains to highlight the courage of certain leading Christian thinkers under Hitler, who disregarded Romans in order to speak truth to power. He finds abundant fault with the "demythologizing" theology of Rudolf Bultmann but honors the words he spoke on behalf of the persecuted Jews of Germany.

Bultmann's treatment of Jesus's apocalyptic expectations causes Kaufmann (and believers in the divinity of Christ) further trouble. Bultmann writes in *Das Urchristentum* (proto-Christianity): "It is not necessary to mention that *Jesus was deluded in his expectation of the proximity of the end of the world.*"[18] A good deal of Bultmann's work claims the extraordinary superiority of Jesus's thought to the thought of others of his era. How can Jesus's delusion be squared with this claim? Albert Schweitzer is exceptional among Christian theologians in his disturbed attentiveness to this contretemps (French, originally, "motion out of time"). Kaufmann cites him:

> "All attempts to escape the admission that Jesus had a conception of the kingdom of God and its impending arrival which remained unfulfilled and cannot be taken over by us mean trespasses against truthfulness." Among Jesus' ideas are some "which we can no longer experience as truth or accept. . . . Doesn't he cease then to be an authority for us? . . . I have suffered deeply from having to maintain out of truthfulness something which must give offense to the Christian faith." (qtd. in C 213–14)[19]

Bultmann wrote abundantly on Jewish topics, a subject that invigorates Kaufmann's critique. On the topic of *everlasting perdition*, Kaufmann invokes the volatile Isaiah 66, which has been taken as a Jewish source of this cruel idea. But Rabbi Akiba, in an interpretation that became canonical in the Mishnah and the Talmud, reads Isaiah nonliterally, introducing a note of humility in regard to knowledge of the world to come. "This blend of a reverent agnosticism with charity," Kaufmann writes, "contrasts sharply with the Evangelists and the Revelation of St. John the Divine" (C 215–16).

> Again and again, the Jews accorded the highest honor to men like Hillel, Akiba, and Maimonides, while the Christians have consistently condemned the relatively humane teachings of Origen regarding hell, of Arius concerning Christ, and of Pelagius against original sin. The church persecuted those who championed these views, and it canonized St. Athanasius and St. Augustine. Calvin still burned Servetus, the Unitarian. (C 216)

The declared aim of *Critique* is this ongoing critical destruction of the views that inform common religious belief. A key thrust rejects the standard account of the main achievement of early Christianity, Jesus's "protest against Jewish legalism, i.e. against a piety which finds the will of God in a written law and in the tradition which interprets it" (Bultmann).[20] Kaufmann stresses that "the protest against the law which Bultmann . . . ascribes to Jesus is at best highly equivocal in the Synoptic Gospels, while it is found emphatically and unequivocally in the [Hebrew] prophets" (C 221). Still, current Protestant theology will go its own legalistic way, selectively quoting and revising Scripture in the mode of interpretation comminated by Nietzsche that Kaufmann calls "gerrymandering." It is the way of Tillich and Bultmann, with a good deal of help from Heidegger's *Sein und Zeit*; both theologians attempt to rejuvenate doctrine with the jargon of existentialism. "Bultmann and Tillich try to show that one can be an existentialist and a Protestant, too, and that nothing could be more existentialist than true Protestantism. Meanwhile, Maritain argues that nothing could be more existentialist than Thomism" (C 223). These exegetes merely confirm that "theology is the systematic attempt to pour the newest wine into the old skins of denomination" (C 221).

On the tactic of "gerrymandering," Kaufmann is sufficiently self-aware that, especially as a result of his critique of Christianity, he can expect to be excoriated in turn. Of course, he will resent it if it is unfair, as he is inclined to suppose it is.[21] "Quotations can be slander / if you gerrymander," he declares. In the hands of the superior poet, it is Antonio, in *The Merchant of Venice*, who puts the idea definitively: "Mark you this, Bassano / The devil can cite Scripture for his purpose."[22] The gerrymandering critic as devil: it is an idea, I'll add, enacted by Goethe in the "Bible-translation scene" of *Faust*, part 1, if you will follow the critic Friedrich Kittler in *Discourse Networks, 1800/1900*. Faust translates the Bible freely; he imposes his meaning on the Λόγος (logos) embedded in the opening sentence of the Gospel According to St. John: "In the beginning was the Word," translating Λόγος as "deed" (*Tat*), one meaning that Λόγος does *not* have. In Faust's study, however, there is a poodle, "whose barking triggers the translation attempt and later puts a stop to it." This hellhound is Mephistopheles in dog's disguise. Throughout this scene of text torturing, "the translator Faust is watched over by the devil in poodle's garb," who will forever after, when German scholars practice hermeneutics, haunt them as the very image of textual abuse.[23] Kaufmann's anticipatory blackening of his virtual assailants—devils all—"critics cursed with short breath, structure blindness, and myopia"—is an apotropaic gesture (C 220).

Foremost among these devils are theologians, that genre of thinker all of whom owe their original impulse to Paul. It is one of Kaufmann's strongest, most interesting, and most contentious claims to argue that

> Christianity defined itself in terms of its theology. To speak of a pretheological original Christianity which was unfortunately Hellenized at an early date is downright wrong. Before Paul there was only another Jewish sect and no Christian religion. Nor was Christianity rejected by the Jews. Christianity was born as a separate religion when Paul developed a theology and rejected Judaism. (C 226)

These critical passages are followed by a thirty-page "Satanic Interlude or How to Go to Hell," a cheerful, higher-order parody of the dialogue between God and Mephisto in Goethe's *Faust* and Adrian Leverkühn and the devil in Thomas Mann's *Doctor Faustus*. Here, in lieu of the heroic Faustus, we have the Theologian as fall guy. The piece calls for reading aloud—or, better, staging—on its own. Satan is Kaufmann's mouthpiece, recognizable for his insistence that "play and seriousness do not preclude each other."[24] A good deal of seriousness is in play. "What is satanic," asserts Satan, "is not egoism but the love of truth at the expense of happiness—to find one's happiness in truth, to oppose illusion, to value integrity above God, and character above salvation" (C 239). Readers may wish to note that this wisdom-sentence dovetails with an apothegm of Walter Benjamin defining the "primordial satanic promise as what is alluring: the semblance of freedom in the fathoming of what is forbidden."[25] There is also a good deal of play at work in this piece. Satan rather proves the point, acknowledging the Theologian who insists on a difference between theology and philosophy: "In theology the stakes are higher—and people used to get burned on them" (C 231). This is Kaufmann's nice application of the trope called zeugma.[26]

Kaufmann's Satan, like Socrates, is an ecumenical dialogist: he engages more than one opponent in this playlet—the Theologian but also the Christian and the Atheist. They are earnest and intelligent after a fashion and are given good lines, but none escapes whipping. Of course, Satan is equipped with Kaufmann's superior erudition and dialectical prowess. He is "a theoretician and a critic," not unlike the devil in Thomas Mann's dialogue, who suddenly appears in the mask of the sagacious Theodor W. Adorno.[27] Contrary to casual expectations—and this point is dispositive of Kaufmann's worldview—his Satan does not love the Atheist any more than he loves the Theologian or the Christian, for the Atheist can be presumed to know very little of such scriptures and sages as "the Bible and the Buddha, the Upanishads and the Bhagavad-Gita, Lao-Tze and the Tales of the Hassidim, . . . for what matters is that they speak to you and in some way change you" (C 258–59). With Rilke, another of Kaufmann's educators, I'll add, forever "Wolle die Wandlung,"

> *Will* transformation. Oh be inspired for the flame
> in which a Thing disappears and bursts into something else;
> the spirit of re-creation which masters this earthly form
> loves most the pivoting point where you are no longer yourself.[28]

Satan enlightens the Atheist: "Religion is one of the most fascinating subjects in the world. . . . I don't agree with the people who accept these scriptures, but I can talk with them and, to be frank, I rather enjoy talking with them. But you! I wish you'd go to heaven" (C 258–59). The atheist's omissions are a litany of missed opportunities for conversation . . . and change.

This Satan has élan: he is relentless—a scholar and ethicist, fiercely interested in the (misbegotten) origins of Christianity. With a virtually raised index finger, he points out: "The early Christians conceived of God in terms of the Greek or Hellenistic *Logos*" (C 234).[29] (He would have very little use for Faust's translation of *logos* as "deed" [*Tat*], even while implicitly admiring Faust's [one] ennobling characteristic: striving. For, asked by the Christian to think of God as justice, he replies: "Is it not an idea, or if you prefer, an ideal? Something toward which men aspire?" [C 247].)[30] Satan enlarges his philippic: the fatal Hellenistic addition is present right at the outset of the New Testament. Moreover, that is the beginning of Christian theology. It was a fantastic misunderstanding, the worst mismarriage on record. At first the theologians tried to wed the God of Abraham and Jesus to *Hellenistic* philosophy; then, in Augustine's time, to Plato's; still later to Aristotle's; and finally Luther went back to the Hellenism of the Fourth Gospel and Paul. To think that the God of Job could be identified with Aristotle's magnetlike attractive God!

The Theologian is not tongue-tied; he is quick to counter:

> In the first place the New Testament is not Hellenistic but profoundly Jewish as W. D. Davies and David Daube have shown, and as the Dead Sea Scrolls prove beyond a doubt [etc.]. (C 234–35)[31]

Such ripostes are only stimulants to Satan's brief. Dissatisfied with these authorities, he is instead happy to enlist Bultmann to his wider argument, bent on revising the "received images" of early Christianity, for, as Bultmann himself admits:

> In no case may one suppose that Jesus' ethical teaching so infuriated the Pharisees and scribes that he finally fell victim to their hostility. The constant opposition of the Pharisees and scribes rests upon the schematic imagination of the late Christian. (C 236)

Satan is richly provisioned to prove Christian *theology* untenable.

A final citation of Satan's engaging words: in his conversation with the Christian, he takes umbrage at the vagueness of the Christian's diction of "salvation" and "damnation": "*You are repeating words that once designated very understandable superstitions. Now you denounce the superstitions but cling to the same words and believe that you are still saying something*" (C 254). I am interested in Kaufmann's evocation of "once understandable superstitions." In today's jargon these would be elements of an older symbolic order that, following Kaufmann, are no longer viable yet live on, a state that the philosopher Eric Santner calls "undead." They continue to produce baffling, irrational effects in the individual and the social body, having become a sort of "nature morte" but not for that reason ineffectual. They can be manipulated to increase state power; they have an exchange value in biopolitics.[32]

As Kaufmann widens his scope to survey other-than-Christian religions, Kaufmann writes appreciatively of Buddhism for the noncognoscenti:

The Buddha considers . . . [metaphysical] speculation frivolous because the
world is burning and "the one thing needful" is salvation. . . . He disparaged
metaphysics because it dominated the religious thought of his time, still
preserved in the Upanishads. . . . [His] supreme concern was not truth but
salvation: a state of being. Peace of soul comes closer to it than accumulation of knowledge. (C 262)

Like Kaufmann, Kaufmann's Nietzsche had a lifelong interest in Buddhism,
disparaging it as world denying and will negating (N 131) (see chapter 1), yet
admiring it for its absence of resentment.[33] It will come as no surprise, I'll
add, that a good deal of European literary modernity has been Buddhistic
in one important respect—its denegation of the impulse to make one's life's
goal the accumulation of knowledge. I say "*de*negation" because there is at
once denial and affirmation in the knowing stance of a repudiation of propositional truth. Here, too, Kafka speaks for many, writing that the knowledge
of good and evil, in which we are essentially equal, demands that we act in
accordance with it; but as we do not have the strength, we flee from this
awareness. "It is for this purpose motivations arise. The whole world is full
of them: indeed, the whole visible world is perhaps nothing more than a
motivation of man's wish to rest for a moment—an attempt to falsify the fact
of knowledge, to try to turn knowledge into the goal."[34] The "fact of knowledge" demands from life, actions for the good on the strength of knowledge
and not the accumulation of knowledge. Kaufmann is very well aware of this
temptation, the scholar's vice, and especially in his 1961 volume *The Faith of a
Heretic* makes clear that he means his work to bring about change in all those
who would read him.

Kaufmann's respect for Judaism, which authorizes his faith but imposes
no dogma, is based on its primary concern, which is not with Halachah—the
interpretation of the laws, its prohibitions and commandments—but "with a
way of life":

This way of life involves a strong sense of tradition and a determination
to realize certain ideals. Both may well be stronger than in any other
religion. This unique directedness from a historical past into a messianic
future, from Mount Sinai to justice for orphan, widow, and stranger and
the abolition of war, has saved Judaism from death by ice and death by
fire, from freezing in all of a rigid tradition from evaporating into utopian
reverie.

It was Scripture that defined this direction and, for more than two thousand years, nourished the thought and imagination of the Jews. It was Torah which in the wider sense is the whole of Scripture and in the narrow sense the Five books of Moses, and in neither case merely *nomos*, "the Law," as Paul would have it. Surely, Genesis is not a compilation of laws, but it received at least as much loving attention as any other book. The Hebrew word *Torah* means not law but teaching. (C 268)[35]

The received image that repeatedly invites Kaufmann's iconoclasm is that of Judaism as a religion of positive law—the dead letter.[36] Its love of the book should not be confused with the sporadic tyranny of the lawyer, the pedant, the judge—the hangmen of Reason. It is a permanent stay against the temptation advanced in other religions to perform a sacrifice of the intellect. The charge of Jewish legalism evaporates on a rereading of the prophetic books— try Isaiah, Jeremiah, Lamentations, Ezekiel, Daniel—Kaufmann's educators all. Judaism is "a religion without theology"; it sponsors an "undogmatic piety"; "no effort was made to define God, and the way was left open for a multitude of different ideas" (C 276, 286–87).

It is bemusing to consider today Kaufmann's quietly prophetic conclusion: "This anti-theological piety may well have a future. Today the many want theology and Socrates, too. Infidel piety is for the few whose beliefs are not dictated by their emotions and whose emotions are not shriveled by their unbelief" (C 287). We are speaking about religion without the God of idolatrous monotheism. Mark Johnston, a Princeton philosopher, has written a rich work of natural theology titled *Saving God: Religion after Idolatry*, which modifies this prophecy in ways faithful to its Socratic gist, sans Socrates'— thus Johnston—defective affirmation of death. It is a work that Kaufmann would have been glad to consider and debate at close quarters. Johnston addresses "the large-scale structural defects in human life," including "arbitrary suffering, ageing . . . our profound ignorance of our condition, the isolation of ordinary self-involvement, [and] the vulnerability of everything we cherish to time and chance, and, finally, to untimely death"—shortcomings that do not go unaddressed by Kaufmann, who writes, "What the great religious scriptures and tragedies know is the sheer misery of being human and the experience that only self-immolation can redeem this misery." But this point allows Kaufmann to enlarge his criticism of Christianity, whose "conception of heaven and lack of sympathy for the damned militate against tragedy: hell is not experienced as tragic but as part of a divine comedy" (C 343).

This criticism, let it be noted, takes little account of what Johnston considers Christianity's core instruction: "Thou shalt love the Lord thy God with all thy heart, and with all thy soul, and with all thy strength, and with all thy mind; and thy neighbor as thyself."[37]

"One kind of ideal reader" of Johnston's book, as Johnston conceives of him or her, "would be an intelligent young person who is religious, but who feels that his or her genuine religious impulses are being strangled by what he or she is being asked to believe, on less than convincing authority, about the nature of reality."[38] This advertisement could equally be attached to Kaufmann's proposal. At the same time, one should keep in mind Kaufmann's caveat apropos of authoritarianism in religion: "If the authoritarianism of [let us say] Rabbi Akiba and the Zen masters detracts from their humanism, . . . one must face the fact that there never has been any completely humanistic religion" (C 338). Or, one might add, "any completely naturalistic religion." Johnston's religion sustains the authority of Christ as exemplary. This is a claim that might be founded on the Gospels: At the close of the Sermon on the Mount, we read that "when Jesus had ended these sayings, the people were astonished at his doctrine: For he taught them as one having authority, and not as the scribes" (C 333).[39] This point is at least cogent to Kaufmann's insistence that there has *never* been any such thing as a "humanistic religion; . . . there have only been humanistic tendencies in most religions, and occasionally, but rarely, these humanistic tendencies have found clear and striking expression in some tale, a page of Scripture or a marginal figure" (C 345).

In his unappeased critique of Christianity, however, in the matter of its source figure, Kaufmann wonders how Jesus can be regarded as a supreme teacher of morals. There has never been any general agreement about the viability of his demands even when they are explicit, while many of his parables are dark (C 294). Christ's example of literally *dying* for men's sins can hardly qualify as a categorical imperative; by contrast, the notion of self-sacrifice, in the Hebrew prophets, is a "profoundly original reinterpretation of the ancient notion of self-sacrifice: . . . one could sacrifice oneself, living; self-sacrifice could be a matter of suffering for others without necessarily dying for others" (C 344). A sort of morality of self-immolation survives in Christianity in the form of obedient belief. Following Paul's and then Luther's revisions, salvation is assured by an intensity of belief and devotion to the sacraments, but these directives do not shape the whole of a life, and they are without any bearing on the sufferings of others. Morality is driven by a notion of a perfection available to man.

In the Hebrew Bible, this higher state of being—boundless creative power and love everlasting—is represented by God. But this conception of God is not experienced as the incarnate futility of man's aspiration, as perfection from which man is cut off by original sin, as power before which men must grovel in the dust. God is the great promise: "Ye shall be holy: for I the Lord your God am holy." . . . Soon, [however,], it became the distinction of Christ that he alone among men had achieved perfection; and he was God to begin with: perfection was now envisaged as being beyond the power of man. (C 356)

Kaufmann links Luther, among other Christian theologians, with Plato for this fatal error of thought: they erected absolutist dualisms, with Luther's dualism figuring as the inversion of Plato's. (Recall Kaufmann's evident enthusiasm for a Hegelian-Nietzschean dialectical *monism*.) A number of more recent writers would situate the impulse to think in absolute dualisms in the flux of Gnostic thought—later than Plato and earlier than Luther—occurring circa the late first century AD in nonrabbinical Jewish and early Christian sectarian milieus.[40] But this additional source does not disqualify Kaufmann's account of Plato, who distinguished between founded knowledge and untenable belief: these two types of cognition correlate with the distinct worlds in which such cognitions are possible—knowledge with "eternal objects, such as his 'Forms' and mathematical objects, and belief with the world of sense experience" (C 303). It is obvious that this perspective stands in the way of science, predicated on a "disciplined study" of the (treacherous, forever) changing objects of worldly experience.

Luther's dualism reads: "I have often said and wish powerfully that we might sever these two realms: the word and reason. For reason, however beautiful and glorious she may be, belongs nevertheless only in the realm of this world; there she has her dominion and regions. But in the realm of Christ, there God's word is alone supreme."[41] Kaufmann's flair for patterned relationships—here, for inversions—is evident:

For Luther there are two worlds as there were for Plato; and Luther, like Plato, disparages this world in favor of a supersensible world to which the soul belongs. But for Plato this higher world was the world of reason, and for Aristotle, too, man's dignity depended on his capacity for rational inquiry and philosophic discourse. Luther banishes reason from the supersensible world and links it contemptuously with "the wisdom of this world." (C 307)[42]

We might recall that Nietzsche stood the test of Kaufmann's intellectual loyalty only on Kaufmann's discovering and proclaiming Nietzsche's praise of reason. It is this love of a reason that resists dogma, which inclines Kaufmann to celebrate Judaism in its deep differences from Lutheran Christianity. His argument contra Luther centers on the Jews'

> intimate awareness of the multifarious riches of their Scripture, [where-upon] no dogma could ever gain authority.
>
> Under the influence of Greek philosophy and Muslim theology, Mai-monides attempted some definitive formulations, but Judaism never accepted them as sacrosanct nor allowed them or any other such attempts to come between itself and the inexhaustible texts. Hence one kind of ten-sion between religion and the quest for truth is almost unknown in Juda-ism: no sacrifice of the intellect is demanded. (C 269)

But here is Luther: "Faith must trample under foot all reason, sense, and understanding, and whatever it sees it must put out of sight, and wish to know nothing but the word of God."[43]

All religions gain support from the testimony of mystics. Kaufmann is inter-ested in mysticism, not least of all because his Williams College teacher J. B. Pratt wrote extensively on mysticism, and "Pratt is surely right" (C 317). This phrase needs qualification: Pratt is perceptive in countering the common claim that mystic experience is ineffable. Pratt—and Kaufmann—stress what Heideg-ger calls the "fore-structure" of the truths mystically conveyed. Following Pratt,

> the mystics are by no means always unable to communicate the truths which they have intuitively perceived during their ecstasy, although it must be noted that the "revealed" truths which they can communicate are always old truths which they knew.[44]

So-called mystical revelations are revelations of what the mystic already knows; his or her vision is a fitting conclusion to preparatory lucubrations. The dreamlike imagination works up religiose material and delivers that material again in livelier form. Kaufmann imagines this procedure in practice:

> Let us imagine a case in which a person desires to have a particular expe-rience of which he has some preconception. He may, for example, crave a vision of the Virgin Mary. He may go into seclusion, forgo sleep, fast, practice austerities, pray and meditate and hope for his vision all the time. When the moment of his vision comes, we should hardly expect him to see Shiva in his glory, dancing. Lutherans do not usually see the Virgin Mary, and Catholics do not see Martin Luther, unless it were in hell. (C 319–20)

This very brief discussion, which hardly touches on the utterability of mystic experience, calls for further study. Michel de Certeau, for one, has analyzed "the elements in mystic texts related to utterance."[45] Returning to Kaufmann's prolegomenon to any future vision, I'll add a touching literary example. Kafka's dog narrator in his "Researches of a Dog" fasts, dreams, sings quietly to himself, in pursuit of his end: a fullness of sought-after experience: "food would spontaneously fall from above and, without paying any attention to the ground, come knocking on my teeth for admittance" (153).[46] Do not expect, in Kafka, the most straightforward results, but an elliptical form of this imagined compensation occurs. Tormented by starvation, the dog "could no longer conjure up even the slightest magic incantation out of the huge jumble of them in his memory, not even the little verse with which newborn pups duck down under their mother."[47] Still, his reward will be great, as long as he remains beside himself and the reward occurs in the register of what he has lacked but wanted in its absence, which he fills with the name of the thing he is lamenting the loss of: music.

He sees another dog, "handsome but not very extraordinary," a doppelgänger, perhaps—with "a beautiful strong searching gaze," whereupon he believes he

> perceived something that no dog had ever experienced before me; at any rate, cultural memory does not contain even the slightest hint of it; and in infinite anxiety and shame I hurriedly lowered my face into the puddle of blood in front of me. What I seemed to perceive was that the dog was already singing without his being aware of it—no, more than that: that the melody, detached from him, was floating through the air and then past him according to its own laws, as if he no longer had any part in it, floating at me, aimed only at me.

I believe that the narrator-dog's conclusion is of a piece with Kaufmann's (he recounts the fact of having had an important mystical experience without saying what the content was):[48]

> Today, of course, I [the dog!] deny any such perceptions and attribute them to my overstimulation at the time, but even if it was an error, it nevertheless had a certain grandeur and is the sole reality, even if only an apparent reality, that I salvaged and brought back into this world from the time of my fast, and shows, at least, how far we can go when we are completely out of our senses.[49]

Kaufmann's clearest, driest statement about his own relation to religion and the religious impulse needs citation:

> Those who would renounce authoritarianism entirely must renounce religion, though they may wish to keep religiousness. Whether such religiousness without religion can be passed on from generation to generation is very doubtful. Probably, it can exist only on the fringes of the historic religions and is unable to survive without them. . . .
>
> The idea of a spiritual but not authoritarian mass movement is utopian.
>
> The hope that spirituality may be nourished by a few scattered individuals with no commitment to each other but a common respect for the great spirits of the past, in whose works they seek comfort and strength and to whose achievements some of them add in turn, is compatible with a pervasive resignation. It requires no faith in religion. Those who believe that religion has a future, not merely as a vulgar mass movement or a mess of chronic superstitions, should reflect on the idea of the remnant. (C 346)

The idea of the remnant is found in many places in the scriptures but earliest in Isaiah 10:

> And it shall come to pass in that day, *that* the remnant of Israel, and such as are escaped of the house of Jacob, shall no more again stay upon him that smote them; but shall stay upon the LORD, the Holy One of Israel, in truth.
>
> The remnant shall return, *even* the remnant of Jacob, unto the mighty God.
>
> For though thy people Israel be as the sand of the sea, *yet* a remnant of them shall return: the consumption decreed shall overflow with righteousness.[50]

If religion is to have a creditable future, it must be loyal to its root in "man's aspiration to transcend himself." Kaufmann continues:

> It does not merely satisfy needs . . . religion has, if not created, cultivated needs which no longer allow man to feel at home among the other animals. [Consider Rilke:
>   "the sly animals see at once/
>   how little at home we are/
>   in the interpreted world."][51]

William James turned to religion because he wanted to feel at home in the universe. But *the greatest accomplishment of religion has been that it did not allow man to feel at home in the universe,* that it raised a hope in man's heart

which the world could not quench, and that instead of telling man to abandon such a foolish hope, religion staked its life on it. (C 355)

Kaufmann's own vision grows more vivid and more passionate as his *Critique*
draws to a close. You will detect the Nietzschean worldview filtering through
the language of a philosophic flight charged with Nietzsche's rhetoric:

> Religion can channel man's aspiration to transcend himself into many dif-
> ferent ways of life: on the one hand there is asceticism, ranging from stern
> demands on oneself to systematic and elaborate austerities, and there is
> moral effort, ranging from a sustained attempt to perfect oneself to a devo-
> tion to social reform; on the other hand, there is inactive adoration of that
> which transcends the self, ranging from meditation to prayer and hope for
> grace, and there are beliefs and rites and sacraments.
>
> The basic choice is this: either man hypostatizes the object of his pro-
> foundest aspirations, projects his boldest hopes, and in the most extreme
> case strips himself of all that distinguishes him from the apes, and then the
> ape that remains grovels on his belly; or man seeks to leave the ape behind
> on the ground and tries to raise himself to a higher level of being. Whether
> he worships idols or strives to perfect himself, man is the God-intoxicated
> ape. (C 359)[52]

The conclusion to *Critique* alludes to many of the themes and genres of
writing that Kaufmann will explore at length in later works. A chapter critical of Erich Fromm's attempt to conjure a thoroughly humanistic religion is
titled "Contra Fromm: Religion and Tragedy." The essay contains germs of
the revisionary theory of tragedy that Kaufmann expounds in *Tragedy and
Philosophy*, a major work published some ten years later, in 1968. Religion and
tragedy are at loggerheads: both Judaism and Christianity in different ways
show man the straight way, which he ignores at his peril. There is no redemption for the sinner who defies right action, the religious assumption being
that there is a right action. Tragedy, on the other hand, concerns "situations
in which one cannot act, nor abstain from action, without incurring guilt;
that is the common theme of Oedipus and Antigone, and of Hamlet, too. . . .
Tragedy occurs where society dissolves and man stands alone," where "society"—proof against tragic solitude—may mean inclusion in a great idea that
will ultimately win out. In the Hebrew Bible, this idea is the task of a people
chosen by God and determined on righteousness. Wrapped in the mantle of a
great idea, no one dies tragically: this is the mythic consolation of martyrdom

(C 342–43). These reflections would make one see modern political terror as aiming to destroy the very consciousness, the ground of minimal lucidity, of the individual who might otherwise find in himself or herself the power of a saving idea.

Martin Buber appears in Kaufmann's discussion of Moses's encounter with the Tetragrammaton "I am that I am"; Kaufmann writes:

> Moses protested against any objectification of the divine whatsoever and offered an altogether new conception of the divine is essentially an embodied—or rather, *unembodied*—moral challenge. . . . Moses' God is nonmythical: he has no private life, no objective existence; in the language popularized by Buber, Moses' God is no It but only a Thou. (C 364)

Buber will turn out be a vitally important reference for Kaufmann; Kaufmann admitted to having been "haunted" by his ideas.[53] He met Buber for the first time at age thirteen; their relationship deepened from meetings in Princeton, New York, and Jerusalem during the years 1951–63. Buber's chef d'oeuvre *I and Thou* was translated by Ronald Gregor Smith in 1952; Kaufmann retranslated it with notes and a prologue in 1970.[54] Buber figures alongside Nietzsche and Heidegger in the second volume of Kaufmann's epic *Discovering the Mind*, suggesting his importance; but in this work, published ten years after the translation, Kaufmann had changed his mind about the validity of the I-Thou dichotomy ("Manichean"!) and other aspects of Buber's thought, including its oracular style.[55]

There might be a reason to wonder at Buber even through Kaufmann's celebration of his thought in *Critique*. Kaufmann takes up Moses's meeting with God once again, stressing that there is no agreement as to "the derivation and meaning, if any" of the name "Yahweh." He continues interestingly:

> But there is agreement that Exodus 3:14 is intended as an interpretation: "And Moses said to God: When I come to the children of Israel, and say to them, The God of your fathers has sent me to you; and they ask me, What is his name? what shall I say to them? and God said to Moses, EHYEH ASHER EHYEH: and he said, say this to the children of Israel, EHYEH has sent me to you." The King James Bible renders the first phrase "I AM THAT I AM" and the second "I AM."

Kaufmann goes to Buber's interpretation of this "interpretation," which relies on the counterfoil of Egyptian thought, the assumption that if only you know the name of the god, you can conjure him. Kaufmann puts the matter wittily. "God's reply means: I shall be there, but you cannot *predict* the mode of my presence" (emphasis added). Buber: "In sum, you do not have to conjure me, neither can you conjure me."[56] Kaufmann: "The Tetragrammaton, with the initial J or Y which indicates the third person, would then mean: HE IS PRESENT" (C 381).

Now the question naturally presents itself: If the being represented by the Tetragrammaton is a third person, how can he be a "Thou?" A visit to Buber's *Königtum Gottes* might resolve the matter; I indicate only the slight perplexity Kaufmann's précis provokes, remarkable since almost everything else he writes is clear.

We noted Kaufmann's burgeoning preoccupation with tragedy, which compels him now to speak of Hamlet. Ever vigilant, he disputes, if not by name, T. S. Eliot's reading of *Hamlet* as faulty for its lack of an "objective correlative" for Hamlet's delays; there are "correlatives" enough for his extreme ambivalence toward the demand to murder his mother's lover. In subsequent unsurprising pages on literary interpretation, Kaufmann speaks of Lear and Coriolanus as courageous; this is the virtue that redeems their faults. They will win the reader's sympathy through the "appeal of courage, older than poetry itself. . . . Courage is the tragic virtue par excellence" (C 372). In *The Faith of a Heretic*, the successor to *Critique*, Kaufmann spells out a tetrad of chief virtues: honesty, love, "humbition" (a neologistic fusion of "humility" and "ambition," an ambition that knows its bounds), and finally, this very courage. It is crucial, indispensable to the fully lived life. In Kant's formulation from *What Is Enlightenment?* that Kaufmann admiringly quotes, we read: "Sapere aude! Have the courage to avail yourself of your own understanding—that is the motto of the Enlightenment." "The great enlighteners, including Kant and Freud—[educators both!]—possessed this courage to a high degree" (C 413).

Reviewers of *Critique* have frequently noted, with pleasure or with resistance, the many genres in which it is executed: prose analysis, prose flights, drama, poetry, aphorisms. I hope to have given examples throughout of Kaufmann's activity in these several genres, but the lure of citation grows very strong in the closing chapters as Kaufmann's writing takes on the exhilaration of his coming to the end of his century, his hundred chapters. His personal statements about his hopes for religion are eloquent; there are fine sentences cast about in a Malrauxian vein, as for example: "Only the passage of five thousand years brought out that haunting look on the face of Zoster who built the step pyramid at Saqqara, the world's first large stone structure" (C 373).[57] He reaches back to German, to his mother tongue, to conclude:

Alles starb in meinem Herzen
was nicht reines Feuer war:
in den Gluten meiner Qualen
bracht ich's Gott im Himmel dar.
Nur das flammenhafte Sehnen,
das sich grad am Brande nährt,
hat die Gluten überstanden
noch nachdem sie Gott verzehrt. (C 431)[58]

A plain prose translation reads: "Everything that was not pure fire died in my heart. In the glowing embers of my torments, I offered it, my heart, to God in heaven. Only the flamelike longing that just now feeds on the conflagration still outlived the glowing embers *after they consumed God*" (emphasis added). The logical conclusion: God is neither pure fire nor the "objective correlative" of flamelike longing. For all the crabbed concision of the poem (and the awkwardness of this rendering), it helps to know the author's final word: what remains is not God but the flames of the purest aspiration for a higher order of human being.

Nonetheless, a teasing complication is present throughout these final pages. They strike a tone markedly different from the major tone of *Critique*, which is set by the pointed criticism of Christianity that runs through the preceding ninety-odd chapters. Much religion—worshipful of the Highest, inviting fantastic theological elaborations—especially as its character emanates from the book's attacked Christian center, would appear to be an unredeemable error, a great misleader of men. Judaism as a set of moral teachings and Buddhism for its calm of mind escape the harshest brunt of Kaufmann's criticism.[59] But the attack on theology of whatever sort represents the major thrust. These last chapters, however, speak of religion as a great prompter of man's aspiration for ontological richness, for life at a higher order than is by and large accessible to him. The tone, the lighting, the moral weather, changes.

Kaufmann employs the good phrase "*ontological* privation" to mark the basic character of (flawed) human existence. "Whether man is aware of it or not, he needs to rise above that whole level of being which is defined by his psychological and physiological needs and their satisfaction: he needs to love and create" (C 423). This formula is immediately remarkable for its introduction of love; "love," unlike "courage" and "charity" and, for that matter, "sex," is found nowhere in the index.[60] The omission could come as a surprise, if not for the fact that Kaufmann very rarely speaks of God as love, let alone to affirm this equation. You do not find Kaufmann quoting 1 John 4:8: "He that loveth not knoweth not God; for God is love." Kaufmann allows John to supply his commentary: "This is my commandment, That ye love one another, as I have loved you. Greater love hath no man than this, that a man lay down his life for his friends. Ye are my friends, *if ye do whatsoever I command you* (1 John 15:12–14) (emphasis added). What condition has the primacy here: love or obedience? Kaufmann adds: "Might not a man lay down his life . . . for men who do not do whatever he commands them?" (C 200).[61]

Christian love is not the answer to man's higher need. "As long as we cling to the conception of hell, God is not love in any human sense—and least of all, love in the human sense raised to the highest potency of perfection" (C 201). What then might sponsor and sustain the need to love and create? Kaufmann's rather uncritical answer is surprising: "We have a surpassing interest in works of art, and this interest is closely related to our determination to emerge from our 'self-incurred minority' *and our religious quest*" (C 415) (emphasis added).[62] He continues:

Historically, it has been religion above all that has awakened and cultivated men's ontological interest and raised the sights of the mass of men to some idea at least of a higher level of being. In the form of gods it has hypostatized this higher being and represented it, more or less visibly, as a possibility; and in the name of these gods it made demands on the mass of men to change their mode of existence, to be dissatisfied with a life on the physio-psychological plane and to aspire to something higher. (C 425)

"Historically," in one sense, yes; historically, in the sense of what is deeply afoot in the middle of the twentieth century, art can no longer be simply, neutrally linked to religion as the saving power, being "closely related." At the same time, Kaufmann's sentence says, no doubt unintentionally, that art is there to abet "our determination to emerge from . . . our religious quest." What this sentence glides over without blinking is the salient cultural fact of the supersession of religion by art. I shall quote from an essay "Art and Religion" by the philosopher Richard Shusterman:

Artists of the nineteenth century . . . saw art as superseding religion and even philosophy as the culmination of contemporary man's spiritual quest. Artistic minds as different as Matthew Arnold, Oscar Wilde, and Stephan Mallarmé predicted that art would supplant traditional religion as the locus of the holy, of uplifting mystery and consoling meaning in our increasingly secular society dominated by what Wilde condemned as a dreary "worship of facts."[63] By expressing "the mysterious sense . . . of existence, [art] endows our sojourn with authenticity and constitutes the sole spiritual task," claims Mallarmé.[64] "More and more," writes Arnold, "mankind will discover that we have to turn to poetry to interpret life for us, to console us, to sustain us. Without poetry, our science will appear incomplete; and most of what now passes with us for religion and philosophy will be replaced by poetry."[65]

Especially in the perspective of Kaufmann's antiself and bête noire Arthur Danto, art has superseded religion (a claim asserted some decades after *Critique*) by conveying "'the kind of meaning that religion was capable of providing': the highest spiritual truths and meanings, including the 'supernatural meanings' of 'metaphysics or theology.'"[66]

Kaufmann develops his brief for divine aid in what he previously celebrated as *man's* effort "to raise himself to a higher level of being."

> The conception of gods provides a setting for an aspiration that reaches out beyond all physical objects. It makes possible a language in which superhuman love and gratitude, despair and grief, can be expressed. . . .
>
> What could equal the pathos of the cry: "My God, my God, why hast thou forsaken me?" To be able to utter these words with a whole heart and not as a mere trope is almost reason enough to accept the religion of the Bible. (C 425–27)

How can the reader take this defense and celebration of religion in stride following the stunning quote from Hegel that Kaufmann supplied earlier in his book:

> Hegel speaks [in 1807] of those who want "not so much knowledge as edification," but Hegel's comments are applicable to some men in every age: "The beautiful, the holy, the eternal, religion, and love are the bait that is demanded to arouse the desire to bite; not conceptual analysis but ecstasy, not the coldly progressing necessity of the matter at hand but fermenting enthusiasm." (C 34)[67]

Is or is not Kaufmann, on the strength of these effusions, one of these men? Is this acclamation part of Kaufmann's great habit of mind: to modify his measured but principal "No!" to religion with a generous "Yes!" at the end, concluding his critique of religion with its incisive description as "authoritarian . . .

poetry"? Here is the core of a thesis for ongoing reflection—a prompt to Kaufmann's reader and an accomplishment of Kaufmann's own, for "even humanists should reflect on the meaning of God though they may believe that apart from man there is no god."[68] Kaufmann's future work is shot through, even sustained by this reflection.

5

The Riches of the World

FROM SHAKESPEARE TO EXISTENTIALISM

Shakespeare "celebrates the riches of the world without God."

—WALTER KAUFMANN

FROM SHAKESPEARE TO EXISTENTIALISM is Kaufmann's first collection of his essays, consisting of work done between 1949 and 1959, the year of its publication.[1] It covers a period even wider than its title indicates, since Socrates and Sophocles and Aristotle figure as moral and intellectual touchstones from the start. The range of authors and topics treated in this volume is also very wide, many of which we have not encountered in Kaufmann's work until now, or else only in passing, for example, "Goethe versus Romanticism," "The Hegel Myth," "German Thought after World War II." But the title repeats Kaufmann's regular emphases: Shakespeare, who figured importantly in *Critique of Religion and Philosophy*, especially at its close, as the author of *Hamlet* and *King Lear*; and existentialism, which, with varying degrees of conviction, resonates from Kaufmann's second book—the very influential *Existentialism from Dostoevsky to Sartre* discussed in chapter 2.[2] Existentialism reappears as a topic in Kaufmann's second book of essays titled *Existentialism, Religion, and Death*, published in 1976, to which I shall return at the end of this chapter, since the final, 1979 edition of the present volume, *From Shakespeare to Existentialism*, contains a retrospective preface composed that year—a year before Kaufmann's sudden death. In that way, and in its prefigurative power, *From Shakespeare to Existentialism* subtends the essays in the 1976 volume *Existentialism, Religion, and Death*.

The late third preface to *From Shakespeare to Existentialism* has the special value of identifying Kaufmann's basic intellectual concerns: "the intimate connection between [authorial] character and work" and "the philosophical dimension of much of the greatest poetry" (S ix). Goethe is his main example of the presence of the producer in his work; Kaufmann qualifies this relation in a way that will satisfy every literary-critical orthodoxy. "The question [is] of the man behind the work," he writes, "or rather *in* the work" (S xi). The key example of Kaufmann's second concern—poetry's philosophical implications—is Shakespeare's mainly non-Christian, mostly Sophoclean (and also existentialist!) *tragic* worldview.

> He is far closer to Socrates and Nietzsche, to Aristotle and Goethe than he is to the evangelists or St. Augustine, to Aquinas, Calvin, Kierkegaard, or T. S. Eliot. His work ... celebrates the riches of a world without God. (S 22)

This constructed tradition is meant to refute T. S. Eliot's notorious claim that Shakespeare had no philosophy.

Kaufmann saw the shape of both of his concerns in his writing on Goethe thirty years earlier, themes that then "recur in many of the other essays in this volume and have remained characteristic of my work ever since," which is to say through until 1979 (S ix). With the exception of Jaspers and Toynbee, whom Kaufmann thinks he has disposed of, he has returned again and again in his other books to all the writers discussed in this volume. Heidegger often reappears in Kaufmann's work, regrettably, for Kaufmann would have dearly loved to have "finished the job" on him earlier: he abhors Heidegger's "repudiation of logic," authoritarianism, covert theology, sham originality—and worse. But the job on Heidegger has not been done, so Kaufmann's concern with him is not a matter of admiration, enthusiasm, let alone love as with his other "educators" but the desire that he be critically dispatched, once and for all. (Heidegger's star, even today, and despite the *Black Notebooks*, is still in the ascendency.) Kaufmann will deal with his shortcomings at great length in a work titled *Nietzsche, Heidegger, and Buber*, underway in 1979; it is the second volume of the trilogy *Discovering the Mind* (1980). Neither Heidegger nor Buber comes off well.

From Shakespeare to Existentialism contains twenty essays, another round number; *Critique of Religion and Philosophy* contained one hundred. The essay form is Kaufmann's natural métier. It suits his main stylistic interests: trenchancy, clarity, and verve, qualities regularly noted even by critics of his abrupt polemical thrusts. Each essay contains numbered sub-essays;

each makes its point swiftly, favoring movement. In case one were inclined to take Kaufmann's clear, rapid, emphatic writing lightly, the first preface contains his impassioned declaration of his *faith in writing*: many of these essays, he says, were written *twenty* times over. In their new constellation in this volume, they called for still more "worry and work . . . for writing is a form of seeing and of suffering, of life and love" (S xii). Meanwhile, the task for readers is to capture the red thread running through Kaufmann's basic concerns—better: perceive, within the thread, its telltale knots. Or, to vary the figure: if these essays are thought of as constituting an extended family, then the critic's task is to detect its mutual celebrations, as well as its quarrels and its alibis.

The volume displays Kaufmann's leading critical ideas as ways of reading the work of canonical cultural figures. Their "greatness" is crucial: these writers—Socrates, Aristotle, Shakespeare, Goethe, Hegel, Kierkegaard, Nietzsche, Rilke, Freud—are great *because* they celebrate the "great-souled man," *because* they celebrate courage and the virtues one attaches to "nobility." (One relegates Jaspers, Heidegger, and Toynbee to second rank, not because they are not, in their own way, concerned with great men but because even their concern will not justify their intellectual aberrations.) Thinking of Shakespeare—thinking, surely, especially of *King Lear*, of Lear's "Nothing will come of nothing. Speak again" (act 1, scene 1), Kaufmann writes:

> Even with the word "nothing" Shakespeare had his sport; the confrontation with death is there no less than resolution, man's abandoned state, and above all the sheer absurdity of life. And what remains to man? The liberating feeling of pervasive disillusionment, the joy of honesty, integrity, and courage; and the grace of humor, love, and comprehensive tolerance: in one word, nobility. (S 18–19)

Note the intrusion of a refugee from another order of discourse—"the absurdity of life"—that is to say, existentialism, into this discussion. In thinking about tragedy, which is Kaufmann's underlying concern, one might readily speak of the "confrontation with death" and with "resolution"—the first as a virtue, in the sense of the hero's resolve, and the second as an (absent) compensatory ending to the tragic action. One might also speak of the tragic figure's dereliction: these terms may even have a home in existentialism as well. But "the absurdity of life" has no customary place that I know of at the table of tragic theory.[3] Still, Kaufmann's book not only proceeds "to" existentialism; more, the existentialist life view, short of its despair, penetrates all its chapters.

These noble virtues are obligatory in the "great-souled man" because, following Aristotle's definition of the type, he is bound to come into lethal conflict with others. Following Aristotle, he is

> "justified in despising other people;" ... "haughty towards men of position and fortune;" [one] who cares "more for the truth than for what people will think" ... and who speaks evil of his enemies only "when he deliberately intends to give offence." (S 18)

We are anticipating the lineaments of Shakespeare's tragic hero and Shakespeare as the knowing exemplar of the tragic view of life. Aristotle's description contains the character traits found in Brutus and Hamlet and Lear and Antony and Coriolanus. "Surely," writes Kaufmann, "Shakespeare's acid contempt for men and women is one of the central motifs of his tragedies"—and others' (S 11). The predicament of such figures and their authors, and the way they bravely cope, becomes a steady refrain. By celebrating the dignity of the tragic view of life, Kaufmann can continue his anti-Christian polemic, because Christianity, he asserts, does not know tragedy: "The tragic world view involves an ethic of character, not, like the Gospels, an ethic of otherworldly prudence." Kaufmann quotes Günther Bornkamm, a German Protestant theologian: "The New Testament does not know the idea of the good deed that has its value in itself."[4] On the other hand, for Kaufmann, "The tragic hero has no reward. The tragic view knows, as Christianity does not, genuine self-sacrifice." Such a claim is bound to inspire the Aristotelian response of whatever great-souled scholars abound in the camp of Christian belief, but Kaufmann has produced some hard, inarguable facts to support his claim, thus, "In the Sermon on the Mount alone, the word 'reward' recurs nine times, the idea of reward at least another nineteen times, and the threat of dire punishments at least a dozen times" (S 15).[5] The thrust of this polemic aims to protect Shakespeare's worldview from its proposed Christian remedy, a critical idea that at the time of Kaufmann's writing had adherents thinking in the train of T. S. Eliot, who regretted the absence of Christian humility in the closing speeches of Hamlet, Antony, Coriolanus, and Othello and saw the modern world divided up by the contrary figures of Dante and Shakespeare. To the commonplace presumption that where there has been love, Christianity has been present, Kaufmann replies, "Goethe's *Iphigenie*, Sophocles' *Antigone*, Hosea, and the Song of Songs remind us of the baselessness of this Christian imperialism that would monopolize love" (S 4). Shakespeare celebrates love, but with even greater intensity portrays the courage that lovers need.

The logical figure running throughout *From Shakespeare to Existentialism* is the unstabie binary of power and control, expansion and binding up. Kaufmann wants them joined on the model, I surmise, of the figure of thought found in Nietzsche's *Birth of Tragedy*: "An 'idea'—the antithesis of the Dionysian and the Apollinian . . . is *aufgehoben* [in tragedy] into a unity; and in this perspective things that had never before faced each other are suddenly juxtaposed, used to illuminate each other, and comprehended" (N 395). This procedure knows the cardinal exception detailed above: the irresolvable conflict of tragedy and Christianity. Christianity knows the Last Judgment and the possibility of eternal compensation; the judgment of tragedy is death without reprieve. Here, ironically, Kaufmann and T. S. Eliot converge in the formulation of the modern conceptual world order, but—it hardly needs to be said—they come down on opposite sides.

This binary can figure in Shakespeare's rage, as in his *Timon of Athens*, and its outcome: Shakespeare, "having poured out his fury, . . . did not become converted, nor did he renounce this world. He achieved a poetry of disillusionment without resentment" (S 13).[6] This binary shapes Goethe's Faust's unbounded aspiration and his subsequent learning, however fleetingly, the concept of measure. It is compressed in Nietzsche's vision of "the Roman Caesar with Christ's soul" (or, I'll add, in the figure of the "*musiktreibender Sokrates*" [Socrates who makes music] of *The Birth of Tragedy*) (S 6). It shapes the reader's response of empathy and criticism, where both energies are required. The binary is resolved in the "logic of passion," the energetic concept that Stendhal made famous in *The Charterhouse of Parma* (1839) and that Kaufmann will use to describe Hegel's dialectic.[7] Kaufmann very likely knew that Goethe read Stendhal attentively and recorded his appreciation.[8] Kaufmann certainly knew that Nietzsche linked and praised Goethe and Stendhal together, both "preparing in the mysterious labor of their soul, the way for that new [European] synthesis."[9] It is from Stendhal's "logic of passion," presumably, that Nietzsche learned to employ this very expression in German, "die Logik des Gefühls."

It will be productive, I think, to glance at the "logic of passion" in Stendhal's *The Charterhouse of Parma*, since this concept means a great deal to Kaufmann. The novel turns on Fabrizio del Dongo's hopeless love for Clelia Conti, the daughter of his jailer. Fabrizio succeeds in obtaining a clandestine interview with her, in which Clelia means to ward off his attentions, as she is engaged to be married to another man.

Clelia, who was trembling all over, had prepared a fine speech: her object was to make no compromising admission, but *the logic of passion* is insistent; the profound interest which it feels in knowing the truth does not allow it to keep up vain pretenses, while at the same time the extreme devotion that it feels to the object of its love takes from it the fear of giving offence.[10]

This is Stendhal's swift, elliptical prose in action: we might have expected that passion's devotion to the object of its love would rein in the heady drive to know the truth. No—passion-love presumably feels a kind of protection in the purity of its intentions, and that is why it is not afraid of giving offense. The logic of passion is insistent because passion "knows" its rights. As in Pascal, "The heart has its reasons, which reason does not know."[11]

The phrase "the logic of passion" is, of course, richly ambivalent: it can mean the character and the structure of passion, here, of the passion of devotion to another. Weight falls on this passion; its logic is to be forceful even in its pretense of devotion, it craves an *extreme* form of itself, it is fearless in its craving, and, knowing no limits, it will err, necessarily. But the logic of passion can also mean the logical hunger, the hunger for logic, the hunger for truth that passion transports in its forward movement. Stendhal gladly admitted that his "great, unrequited passion for Métilde Dembowski . . . [was] his 'first course in logic.'"[12] And how instructive is grief!

What have we learned? Passion seeks (more of) its own intensity, it would forever increase as passion, but with the same extremity it seeks *to know*, it is a *libido sciendi,* and hence necessarily a passage to knowledge through error. Even in the meeting between Fabrizio del Dongo and Clelia Conti, Clelia's passion will have disastrous repercussions.

A good deal of this precise train of thought is present to Kaufmann. The entire final section of his essay "The Young Hegel and Religion" is titled "The Logic of Passion." It begins with a quotation from Goethe's *Wilhelm Meister* (7: 9), published in 1796:

Not: to keep from error, is the duty of the educator of men, but to guide the erring one, even to let him swill his error out of full cups—that is the wisdom of teachers. Whoever merely tastes of his error, will keep house with it for a long time . . . but whoever drains it completely will have to get to know it unless he be insane. (S 160)

The "draining" is evidently an affair of *passionate* consumption, since the knowledge of what is consumed appears to follow it in time. Kaufmann notes the happy consequence of passionate error for Hegel, who writes at a time before the collapse of the hope of Stendhal's "the happy few"—a pervasive melancholy linked with the defeat of Napoleon. Kaufmann comments:

> Those who merely nibble at a philosophic position may never get beyond it, while those who take it even more seriously than its creator did and push it to its final consequences will get to know it and pass through it to a more mature position, propelled higher and higher by their very serious-ness. This is the sense in which the dialectic of Hegel's *Phenomenology* is a *logic of passion.* . . .
>
> Hegel's own development illustrates the logic of passion. He embraced his puzzling faith in the essential rationality of tradition and its assumption that the great philosophies of the past are all partially true only after he had gone through the very opposite attitude and, in Goethe's phrase, swilled it out of full cups.
>
> Hegel always remained faithful to some elements of the Enlighten-ment, such as the belief in inalienable human rights and the faith in reason, but he reacted violently against other aspects.[13] Where he had previously condemned Christianity for its irrationality, he later celebrated Christian dogmas as ultimate philosophic truths in religious form.

It is again interesting that Stendhal's novel ends with Fabrizio's burning com-mitment to an ascetic Christianity: the "charterhouse" is, after all, a monastery. Hegel does not "submit" to Christianity:

> Instead of achieving a crowning synthesis, he unwittingly illustrated his own dialectic by overreacting against the views of his youth and by going to the opposite *extreme.* Yet he did not atone for his early opposition to Christianity by submitting to it, as some of the romantics did. Though the tone of his later remarks about Christianity is approving, he approves of Christianity only as an admirable but inadequate anticipation of his own philosophy, at a subphilosophic level [emphasis added].
>
> Hegel always remained the heir of the Enlightenment, opposed to romanticisms and theology alike, insofar as he maintained until the end that there is one pursuit that is far superior even to art and religion: phi-losophy. (S 161)

Error and extremity en route to cognition: the internal logic of passion appears to recapitulate the external logic of the historical passage of feeling into a cognitive tool. The logic of passion in Goethe and Hegel is a dialectical logic, built on error and recovery. "In the eighteenth-century," writes the historian Balduin Schwarz, "concern for the phenomenon of error reached a quantitative maximum. At no time either previously or since were so many attempts made to investigate the conditions of human error. . . . Kant [for example] studies the way in which the error of the entire metaphysical tradition must arise as a necessity of the human spirit."[14] Of course, whether the perception of error *necessarily* results in the perception of a higher truth remains moot. We are back at the point that surfaced in our chapter 1: if I discover that the intellectual currency in my pocket is counterfeit, I do not thereby put good money in my pocket. More darkly, as T. S. Eliot—Kaufmann's nemesis—remarked of the historical succession of errors of interpretation of Shakespeare, "Whether truth ultimately prevails is doubtful and has never been proved; but it is certain that nothing is more effective in driving out error than a new error."[15]

So much for the logic of passion, which, for Kaufmann, collapses and puts into dialectical unity the binary of feeling and reason. This connection achieves, a half century after Hegel and Stendhal, I will add, a rhetorical maximum in Oscar Wilde's *The Picture of Dorian Gray*, namely:

> To note the curious hard logic of passion, and the emotional colored life of the intellect—to observe where they met, and where they separated, at what point they were in unison, and at what point they were at discord—there was a delight in that![16]

And an intellectual maximum, perhaps, in a diary notation by Franz Kafka: "A special method of thinking. Shot through and through with feeling. Everything feels itself as thought, even what is least definite" (1913).[17]

I have stressed the polarity "empathy" versus "criticism" that informs Kaufmann's readings of great texts. We saw it above in Kaufmann's appeal to a reader's empathy that would allow him to understand the author better than the author understood himself, praising "those who take ['a philosophic position'] even more seriously than its creator did and push it to its final consequences" (S 160). The question of the possibility, or merit, of understanding an author better than himself was a burning issue in the romantic philosophy of the German "Sattelzeit" (roughly, 1750–1850), pursued notably by Fichte and Friedrich Schlegel. What is unfortunate is that Kaufmann should embed his remarks in an attack on "romanticism" when it is the romantic theorists Fichte and Schlegel—not "misty" thinkers at all—who explored most fully the notion of understanding a text at once better and worse than its author.[18] On

the general relation of romanticism to the values of Enlightenment—values
that Kaufmann would defend to the death—one needs to make distinctions
between its early (*Frühromantik*), middle (*Hochromantik*), and later phases
(*Spätromantik*). In general, as the movement (if it be such) unfolds, it becomes
more conservative, in the words of Frederick Beiser, "more hostile to some
of the central values [namely, reason, individualism, the separation of church
and state] of the *Aufklärung* [Enlightenment]." But romanticism in its beginnings must be seen "as both [its] affirmation and negation. . . . Like a phoe-
nix, the *Aufklärung* was consumed by its own flames. From its ashes arose
romanticism."[19]

Goethe and Nietzsche stand behind Kaufmann's aversion to German
romanticism *tout court*: they deplore its turn to medieval Christianity and
its ethic of extravagant (merely assumed?) emotion. These claims prompt
Kaufmann's distinction between the Romantic mind and that of the great-
souled man (he has Nietzsche's support: "*There is nothing romantic about greatness of soul*" [italic is in Nietzsche's original]).[20] One side of the great-souled
man is passion, feeling, sensibility *under restraint*—on occasion he despises
others, intends to give offence, but all with good reason. At his other side,
rather, is restraint unmoved by passion, feeling, and sensibility—an iron
refusal to be moved, high impassiveness. Where do we find such a schema?
There are elements of it in Aristotle's account in the *Nicomachean Ethics*, as
above; the strongest is Shakespeare's description of the type in his very contentious sonnet 94:

> They that have power to hurt and will do none,
> That do not do the thing they most do show,
> Who, moving others, are themselves as stone,
> Unmoved, cold, and to temptation slow:
> They rightly do inherit heaven's graces
> And husband nature's riches from expense,
> They are the lords and owners of their faces,
> Others but stewards of their excellence.
> The summer's flower is to the summer sweet
> Though to itself it only live and die,
> But if that flower with base infection meet,
> The basest weed outbraves his dignity:
> For sweetest things turn sourest by their deeds;
> Lilies that fester smell far worse than weeds.

Here Kaufmann links formulations from Aristotle and Shakespeare, as glimpsed through Nietzsche, to affirm an ideal of self-sufficiency—a perilous ideal too: impassiveness that falls into passion is viler than the merely impassioned state it once despised. This seems to be knowledge especially congenial to Hamlet. It is knowledge, I would add, very useful to share today, when a heightened sense of contingent determinations held to be responsible for personal debility (world capitalism, kleptocratic government, the medial theft of individual mind, the lost ideal of transcendence) has made the stance of self-sufficiency, as defined above, seem a quaint remnant of the past. But with this vacuous refrain comes, perhaps, a recognition that the greatness of Aristotle's prodigal man was forever reserved to an unhappy few; the time and men around them were no better than what we might despise today. Kaufmann is surely unique in the examples he chooses to make this otherwise evident point: "We think of the age of the great prophets as a kind of golden age, struck by the succession of the titans from Elijah and Amos and Jeremiah and the second Isaiah; but to them the their own age could scarcely have been worse" (S 30). Modernity's godlessness in every respect offers unlimited opportunity for character development.

The fact of "godlessness," it is worth stressing, does not extinguish Kaufmann's feeling for religious experience: that opening remains alive. His way of linking the experience of tragic drama to the "numinous" makes the connection plausible. He begins a flight on the uncannily nonpsychological character of the motivations of Shakespeare's tragic figures, whose condition "retains something of the sacramental quality of the Greek drama and the Bible" (S 39). Shakespeare's tragedies abound in dei ex machina propelling the action: they are not extraneous to the action but

> point to a suprapsychological significance that raises the drama beyond mere accident. They create that "numinous" atmosphere—to use Rudolf Otto's word for what is simultaneously majestic, awe-inspiring, overpowering, and fascinating—that is the essence of Shakespeare's great tragedies and gives them the depth and intensity of the religious experiences that Otto describes. (S 39–40)[21]

A contrast between Shakespeare's heroes Hamlet and Macbeth, on the one hand, and Faust, on the other, refines the last point. We are in the midst of the chapter "Shakespeare versus Goethe," a conversation between two (along with Nietzsche) of Kaufmann's greatest educators. Goethe's Faust is not the equal of Shakespeare's great-souled men: like them, he is confronted by a supernatural figure—the Earth Spirit—but he cannot stand the encounter and flinches; in Faust's reaction, Kaufmann concludes, unsurprisingly, he is more like "us." "There is an implicit contrast here with more heroic times—an anticipation of Joycean irony" (S 46). (Kaufmann's choice of Joyce over T. S. Eliot, the rival candidate, could be foretold.) Kaufmann is not modest in his summing up the differences: "Faust, unlike Hamlet and Macbeth, is not a titan but as human as we are, and a would-be superman as some of us are" (S 46–47). If he is generous to "some of us," he is as generous to Hamlet in lending him "titanic stature." (Here is the ghost of T. S. Eliot shaking his head sadly.)

If Faust fares badly vis-à-vis Hamlet and Macbeth, he shines even when paired with the great Dostoevsky, in whose novels, we find, in a striking phrase, "terror in congenially crushing proportions" (S 49). It is not unusual for Kaufmann, even in the midst of his clarity and speed, the latter the product of perfect conviction, to write a phrase that could haunt the reader for a minute or an hour or longer. The interpreter might reach for help for whatever is in his head, but . . . "congenially" and "crushing"? I find help in Rilke, as I believe Kaufmann did—the modern poet whom Kaufmann loved the best— and Kafka, the modern seer whom Kaufmann admired equally. Rilke's first *Duino Elegy* begins:

> Who, if I cried out, would hear me among the angels' hierarchies?
> and even if one of them pressed me suddenly against his heart:
> I would be consumed in that overwhelming existence.
> For beauty is nothing but the beginning of terror, which we are still
> just able to endure.[22]

Here we have it all: terror; beauty in its attractiveness (who would find beauty uncongenial?); a subject, "I," being crushed ("pressed . . . against his heart, . . . consumed"); and even "proportions" ("the angels' hierarchies").
And Kafka? Kafka writes:

> How much more oppressive (*bedrückend*, literally, "crushing") than the
> most inexorable conviction of our present sinful state is even the weakest
> conviction of the coming eternal justification of our temporality.[23]

The elements of the terror that Dostoevsky assails us with are all here, if more diffuse than in the Rilke citation, whose priorities it inverts. Contrary to expectation, it is now our coming (congenial?) justification that terrifies us even more than the consciousness of our sinfulness: this inverted proportion is "crushing."

But we need to stay with the point of Kaufmann's invocation of Dosto-evsky: his novels serve as a foil to Goethe's art, different but "not less intense for being far from terror, and [with a] scope and unity outside the pale of dogma, not purchased for a sacrifice of vision" (S 49). The latter is a reflec-tion on Dostoevsky's promiscuous lack of tolerance. Here we should look to Goethe, and most particularly to Goethe's *Faust*—to lines spoken by Faust on the essence of passion:

> Do you not hear, I have no thought of joy!
> The reeling whirl I seek, the most painful excess,
> Enamored hate and quickening distress.
> Cured from the craving to know all, my mind
> Shall not henceforth be closed to any pain,
> And what is portioned out to all mankind,
> I shall enjoy deep in my self, contain
> Within my spirit summit and abyss,
> Pile on my breast their agony and bliss,
> And thus let my own self grow into theirs, unfettered,
> Till as they are, at last I, too, am shattered.[24]

This is aspiration gone mad: it is megalomania. Kaufmann's explication res-cues it for reasonableness: the plot of *Faust*, he explains, unlike that of Hamlet or Macbeth,

> is no longer centered in a man raised above his fellows by inscrutable fate, one made to perform a hideous deed to which his own will stands in a questionable and mysterious relation (the crux of *Oedipus*, *Hamlet*, and *Macbeth*); instead the hero *wishes* to raise himself above other men, is eager to experience agony as well as joy, but suffers like the rest of us when con-fronted with grief. (S 47)

This attempt at humanizing a madman, muting the vision of a passion for *everything*, will not make it jibe with sentiments more nearly fundamental to Goethe, who wrote, at the close of *Wilhelm Meisters Lehrjahre* (The Appren-ticeship of Wilhelm Meister): "Man cannot be happy until his unconditional striving limits itself" (S 65). Admittedly, Faust has said "I have no thought of joy," but he has also asked for bliss. There is, presumably, bliss in the mad ven-ture to break down even the limits imposed by the consecutive nature of time.

This speech of Faust haunts Kaufmann, and he will continue to be of two minds about its value and its representativeness. In a following chapter titled

"Goethe's *Faust* and Faust's Redemption," Kaufmann cites the aphorism from *Wilhelm Meister* just quoted, and adds: "Goethe must have felt how ineffective the dry antitheses of *Meister* were, compared with such intoxicating lines [citing Faust's great speech above]; and by now he was loath to be identified not only with the hero but with the drama itself" (S 66). This "and" is odd; the logic would seem to require "but." In this formulation, there is evidence of Kaufmann's uncertainty about what in Goethe to love.

A second cavil concerns Kaufmann's celebration of the "unity" of Goethe's art; the acid test would be the posited unity of *Faust*. But how is this claim to be maintained? Kaufmann does not argue the point: however, if we want to pursue the matter, we do find a good suggestion in the essay "Reading Faust" by the late Cyrus Hamlin, an eminent devoté of Goethe.[25] Hamlin describes the "striving and searching" of scholars to show "the ultimate structural coherence" of the drama (which, following Hamlin, cannot be defined "in strictly dramatic terms, nor even by reference to the concerns of Faust the character," since in the later parts of the work Faust isn't even present!). Still, Hamlin continues,

> some principle of thematic interaction must be applied to the work as a whole, whereby the various figures, motifs, forms, and styles may be seen to interact within a myriad of interlinking patterns to constitute a vast fabric, which ultimately comprehends much of what Goethe had to say about human life, about the world, about time, and history, about the ultimate values and the ultimate powers which govern everything in our *experience* (emphasis added).[26]

There may be some higher mimicry at work here; Hamlin, like Kaufmann, may be responding to the language of Faust's encounter with the symbol of the macrocosm: "Wie alles sich zum Ganzen webt" (How everything weaves itself into a whole). But the all-comprehensive pattern that Hamlin strives to "see" by dint of an application of "principle" is likely to disappoint him just as much as it did Faust—it is only a glamorous icon, "ein Schauspiel nur!"—the commentator's spectacle. Still, the conclusion to Hamlin's idea is interesting; here is that plangent word, anchoring the search for the whole: whatever vision of the whole might be offered, it must be tested for its basic adequacy to our *experience*.

A thematic adequacy of Faust's experience to our own, conferring unity on the whole? It would be reasonable to look into the text of *Faust I* and *Faust II* for Goethe's own use of the concept—be it *Erfahrung* or *Erlebnis* or one of its cognates, the verb *erfahren* or *erleben*. But when we do, it is only to be met with a great surprise, for none of these terms makes more than a scant appearance in *Faust*. The verb "erleben" appears twice in *Faust I*, altogether casually, and once in *Faust II*; and aside from a single appearance of the nominal form "Erfahrung" in *Faust I*, there is no further instance of even a single form of the verb "erfahren" in *Faust I*. Forms of this verb do appear a couple of times, though again rather casually, in *Faust II*, but the word does not designate the adventurous thrust of Faust's new being.[27]

In the absence of any explicit thesis on the adequacy of Faust's experience to our own, we must look elsewhere for its principle, but, trusting Goethe's own declaration that the work is "incommensurable," it will be, I believe, impossible to find. What we find is every extreme of passion, only *very* intermittently constrained by reflection. Faust errs persistently, doing murderous harm to himself and others, and appears to make very little of it—for long. We do not have a sense of closure, limit, boundary even to the work: the end it comes to, a celestial medieval passion play, is in all respects factitious. The scholar Irving Singer, relying on Kaufmann, stresses Goethe's explicit anti-Catholicism: in 1831, the year in which he finished *Faust*, Goethe wrote of the cross as "the most disgusting thing under the sun, [which] no reasonable human being should strive to exhume." Singer, too, concludes, "In view of this self-conscious paganism, the echoes of Dante in Goethe [in the final scene] must be taken as a literary device, a mythological contrivance."[28]

Kaufmann does not justify or cast much light on the closing pageant in heaven. He thinks of the main legacy of *Faust* as "reflective wit—chiefly won through the contest of Faust and Mephistopheles—which does not halt before the numinous" (S 50), but I doubt he is thinking here of Goethe's Dantesque paradise. Kaufmann's stress on "wit" and "the numinous" does not tally with a view on this tragedy as a work of development, an organic unity—a view that, for Kaufmann, represents Goethe's finest teaching about art and life. The title of Goethe's autobiography, *Dichtung und Wahrheit* (Poetry and truth), announces, in an original way, the imaginative factor in its composition. For Kaufmann, it "created a new perspective for the study of an artist or, indeed, of man in general: life and work must be studied together as an organic unity and in terms of development" (S 52). Again: "It was Goethe's example—his life and his self-understanding—rather than any explicit teaching that led others more and more to study works of art and points of view and human beings in terms of development." It is this Goethean perspective that undoubtedly inspired Kaufmann to attribute to Nietzsche this coherence of the work in time, but the work of art *Faust* will not answer to this expectation.

In a rather wonderful passage Kaufmann finds a way to differentiate Nietzsche's admiration for Goethe: it goes not to the Faustian young Goethe but rather to the endlessly creative, finely controlled, self-styling older savant.

> One of Nietzsche's least plausible notions, his doctrine of the eternal recurrence of the same events at gigantic intervals, is intended partly as the most extreme antithesis to Faust's repudiation of the present. While Faust is willing to be damned if ever he should say to the moment, "abide," Nietzsche says in the penultimate chapter of *Zarathustra*: "If ever you wanted one thing twice, if ever you said, '... Abide, moment!' then you wanted *all* back. All anew, all eternally. ... *For all joy wants—eternity.*" (S 58)

This is the sort of aperçu about the German intellectual tradition that will delight readers interested in such things. Kaufmann is very good at seeing connections between ideas, even and especially relations of opposition, and will at first foreground the resulting binaries for the sake of their rhetorical punch. This makes him a modernist writer; he has not yet acquired the postmodernist, neostructuralist scorn of binaries and its dogma: "Always triangulate—incessantly!" At the same time, as we have seen, he will complicate this second-stage figure—(not p)—to a three-stage figure of thought to produce an enriched first term ($p+$) as the most truthful. We very often find examples of this intellectual procedure throughout his work; it is Kaufmann's signature logic. For example, Hölderlin appears early as an artist who, in the company of Rembrandt, Mozart, Villon, Cézanne, and van Gogh, was great, unconventional, and badly treated in his lifetime (S 2). Thereafter, narrating Goethe's view of Hölderlin, speaking not in propria persona but with the gusto of extreme sympathy, Kaufmann gives us a poet whose

> poetry quite lacks that exultation in the present that inspires Goethe's hymns. What struck Goethe was that this new poetry was an incarnate repudiation of the present, a pining for the past without all possibility of fulfillment or compromise. ... Hölderlin ... subordinated his life and sanity to his art: he sang himself insane. (S 80–81)

This view may be chiefly the pardonable view of Goethe who was not happy to respond to Hölderlin's importunities. Still, it is not clear where Kaufmann parts company from Goethe, since the above is at best half-true. In fact, before the chapter is over, Kaufmann will enrich and reaffirm Hölderlin's centrality, namely,

The differences between Goethe and Shakespeare, Kleist, and Hölderlin should not distract attention from the crucial fact that all four belong to tradition that many a modern critic has tried to read out of history, often using the device of calling the three Germans "romantic" and thus covering up the differences between them and the medievalists.

What is crucial for Kaufmann is that, as he puts the matter hyperbolically, but with graphic conviction, they are *un-Christian*, "untutored by any creed, philosophy, or revelation" (S 82).

Here, we note, we have an instance of an only truncated three-stage dialectic. It begins with a striking binary opposition, whence the first proposition is starkly "bettered" by a second (recall the drastic example: the opposition of Christianity to tragedy, and the decisive superiority of the second term—period).[29] The upshot is that Kaufmann is not consistently dialectical but is inclined to dialectic when he is not polemical, though even his three-stage dialectic points to Hegelian *closure* rather than to a neostructuralist incessant openness to one *Aufhebung* after another—an abolishing, preserving, and raising up of thesis upon antithesis without end. To strengthen this point about Kaufmann's being behind the time of the rolling caisson of deconstruction, consider that neostructuralism had after all moved into the universities by the 1960s and Kaufmann might even have read in Kafka's *Diaries* of his "repugnance for antitheses."[30] He will persistently deplore, in books and classroom, the anithumanistic threat of this movement of ideas.

A contentious point in these Goethe chapters is Goethe's and, hence, Kaufmann's aversion to the *romantic* mind. His dislike of romanticism, encouraged by Nietzsche's recurrent diatribes, centers on the generation of German poets who, circa 1800, idealized or converted to Catholicism. The flamboyant title of a study by Siegmar Hellerich says it all: *Religionizing, Romanizing Romantics: The Catholico-Christian Camouflage of the Early German Romantics; Wackenroder, Tieck, Novalis, Friedrich and August Wilhelm Schlegel.*[31] On behalf of Goethe, Kaufmann deplores so-called romantic subjectivity: "Goethe rather liked Schelling, . . . [for] he seemed . . . to have corrected one of the most serious faults of romanticism: its limitless subjectivity" (S 79). On the other hand, here are Georges Poulet and Peter Szondi, eminent scholars of romanticism, celebrating the romantic moment writing as an inescapable "*act of reflection on the fundamentally subjective character of the spirit,*" on "the isolated self thrown back upon itself."[32] Paul de Man, who thought long and deeply about romanticism, had no hesitation in seeing romantic writers as furthering "the most audacious and advanced form of contemporary thought."[33] To romantic writers is owed "the experience of an *act*, in which, to a certain extent, we ourselves have participated," an act "contributing in an immediate way . . . to the constitution of our consciousness of temporality."[34]

Kaufmann's sole perspective on romanticism as resurgent Gothic medievalism produces a puzzling effect today, when "we ourselves" are inclined to think of romanticism as a boundlessly creative European and Latin American phenomenon. But here we are dealing with a confusion of terms: de Man's romantic writers—Wordsworth, Keats, Solger, among them—are not the Romanizing writers of the first generation of German romantics. And Kaufmann has the good literary sense to detach Hölderlin and Kleist from the cluster of writers he is thinking of: Wackenroder, Tieck, Novalis, Friedrich and August Wilhelm Schlegel.

Kaufmann's several chapters on Goethe conclude by advancing a productive insight: Goethe's celebrated paganism—his admiration for the Greeks and the Romans—"deflects attention from another model that was almost equally important for his work: the Hebrew Bible" (S 89). Kaufmann's investment in the originality and ongoing importance and penetration of the thought world of the Hebrew Bible informs his work from beginning to end.

> The full story of the impact of the Hebrew Bible on Western thought and art and literature has never yet been told, partly because so much that was Hebrew originally has long been absorbed with such complete success that one no longer thinks of it as having any source at all. Even as hundreds of phrases from the Hebrew Scriptures have become part of the language, whether it be German or English, crucial ideas, too, are commonplaces now and are often falsely considered part of man's natural endowment. Reading the Greeks, some critics simply read these ideas into them: for example, that all men are brothers who, unlike the other animals, are fashioned in the image of the one and only God; that the stranger is essentially like oneself; that war is evil and should be abolished; that one ought to rest one day in seven; and that *every* man ought to make something of himself. (S 89)

The project Kaufmann calls for, a fair estimation of the influence of the Hebrew Bible on German and English literature, had begun many decades earlier. A growing sense of the originality and independence of the Hebrew Bible had been felt during the years of Goethe's youth (he was born in 1749)—one that no longer turns "the rich and varied texts of the Hebrew Torah into a vast typological waiting room for the Christian Messiah."[35] Kaufmann would have been aware of the eminent critic and pastor Northrop Frye's documenting the depth with which the Bible informs the whole of Western literature while indeed treating both the Old and New Testament as a single "continuous narrative beginning with the creation and ending with the Last Judgment, and surveying the whole history of mankind, under the symbolic names of Adam and Israel, in between."[36] This is the assumption undergirding Frye's project that biblical scholars—Kaufmann included—could not abide, being acutely aware of the multiplicity of authors and languages constructing the Bible; but no one was more adamant than Frye in proclaiming Scripture as the chief source of Western literary ideas. The Bible—Frye calls it "the Christian Bible" but has both testaments in mind—"forms the lowest stratum in the teaching of literature. It should be taught so early and so thoroughly that it sinks straight to the bottom of the mind, where everything that comes along later can settle on it."[37] From Kaufmann's standpoint: right temple, wrong pew.

Since then, many scholars have continued to describe the penetration of the Hebrew Bible into modern literature. Among the most productive is Robert Alter, whose *Canon and Creativity: Modern Writing and the Authority of Scripture*, for one, shows the extent to which the novels of modern writers— in this case even iconoclasts like Kafka (in *The Missing Person*, aka *Amerika*) and Joyce (in *Ulysses*)—are saturated with the stories, language, and imagery of the Hebrew Bible.[38] Kaufmann's demand at the end of the 1950s has borne fruit, and it is interesting that Frye would very nearly repeat Kaufmann's words in describing "the fact that the cadences and phrases of the King James translation are built into our minds and way of thought" while omitting the point that, once again, "so much that was Hebrew originally has long been absorbed with such complete success that one no longer thinks of it as having any source at all."[39]

Kaufmann is especially concerned with the informing presence of the Hebrew Bible in *Faust*. Foremost, of course, is the prologue, a noble parody of the book of Job; behind the scene of Faust's destruction of the modest house of Philemon and Baucus is the story of Naboth's vineyard in First Kings. "Faust's encounter with the specter of Care seems to have been influenced by Genesis 32. . . . [His] treatment of Faust's death was influenced decisively by . . . the death of Moses. The main point is, of course that Faust, too, dies after envisaging [but not entering] the Promised Land" (S 91).

Goethe's response to Jewish culture was varied and frequent—both antipathetic and yet with an imagination deeply influenced by the Hebrew Bible and his view of "the" mobile and energetic Jewish character. "In contrast to . . .

Christian otherworldliness," observes Karin Schutjer, "Goethe viewed Judaism as active and existential in its orientation. His maxim on 'Jewish nature'
reads: 'Energy the basis of everything. Immediate ends. No Jew, not even
the most lowly, unimportant one, who would not betray a decisive striving
and certainly of an earthly, temporal and present-oriented sort.'" One sees
immediately the consonance—though surely not the identification—of Faust
and the Jew, a relation that cannot have been lost on Kaufmann. "Goethe's
encounter from his youth with the Hebrew Bible," adds Schutjer, "was crucial
to his entire literary development. His modern wanderers lead paradoxically
back to this very ancient set of texts, which became for Goethe a surprising source and model for modern literature."[40] This is a fine elaboration of
Kaufmann's insistence.

The literary critical consensus of his time, from which Kaufmann dis-
sented, seemed to him spanned between two impossible alternatives: one is
a twentieth-century neo-Christianity (he has T. S. Eliot in his sights, as well
as the neo-Thomism of Étienne Gilson and Jacques Maritain and quite possibly the Robertsonian-Christian typologizing engine in Princeton's English
Department). The second alternative Kaufmann terms "nineteenth-century
romanticism," by which he appears to mean a poetized mindset rather than
an uncontroversial cluster of poets, although the medievalizing German poets
of the first decades figure here as its chief purveyors: "the romantic accents
of vague sentiment, the pose of pining, yearning, fainting, ecstasy, and lofty
pantheism" (S 93), equally "monkish barbarism" (Goethe) (S 67). An off-the-
cuff comment that Keats and Wordsworth also "mastered" these "accents" and
this "pose" but with a "perception" far inferior to Goethe's is simply unfortunate, a product of Kaufmann's zeal to strengthen Goethe's reputation at a time
of Goethe's diminishing prestige. Karl Jaspers had claimed that Goethe had
become obsolete after 1945, given his defective understanding of the problem
of radical evil—what the formidable Habsburg-born Germanist Erich Heller
called his "avoidance of tragedy"—and T. S. Eliot had published a scathing
repudiation of Goethe both as poet and philosopher, calling him a mere "dab-
bler" (Eliot was subsequently to withdraw his curse).[41] Kaufmann's refusal
to make this choice, which comes as no surprise, allows him to summon up
the load-bearing writers of world literature who constitute his main supports:

> "There is a world elsewhere," as Coriolanus says. Indeed, almost all
> of world literature lies outside this frightening alternative: not only
> 'Greek and Roman' . . . but also Indian literature . . . the world of the

Old Testament, which, one sometimes feels, has not been discovered yet, though Michelangelo had more feeling for it than most professors of theology and Bible; Shakespeare; Goethe himself; and, more recently, Nietzsche and Rilke. (S 67)

"Nietzsche and Rilke" is the title of one of Kaufmann's best essays in this volume. It appears further on in an itinerary that includes three chapters on Hegel, one on Kierkegaard, and one on Nietzsche's revolution in ethics. I am eager to get to "Nietzsche and Rilke" but want to acknowledge the vigor and generosity of the Kierkegaard chapter (we will attend to the content of the Hegel chapters in our own chapter 8, which deals with Kaufmann's entire conspectus of Hegel). The Kierkegaard essay is especially interesting because in its acknowledgment of Kierkegaard's strength as a writer, Kaufmann comes closer to the view of Poulet and Szondi quoted earlier on the power of romantic subjectivity (as Kierkegaard so little touches Kaufmann's religious center, to that extent he touches Kaufmann's sense of him as an artist). Kaufmann calls Kierkegaard a romantic, once again, in the Christianizing, otherworldly, sentimental, ultrasubjectivist sense but also celebrates the power of Kierkegaard's subject-saturated artistry:

> His style, however aggravating, is a splendid medium for his purpose [of foregrounding his preoccupation with himself]. With its epic digressions and its urgency, and even with its philosophic acrobatics, dancing on the tightrope between seriousness and satire, Kierkegaard's prose never permits us to lose ourselves in a story or an argument: we are constantly confronted with the author's individuality—and are made to think about our own. His psychology is a vortex psychology that draws us into self-reflection against our will and never permits us to rest content with impersonal results. (S 202)

At the close Kaufmann has caught fully the pseudonymous, dialogical, parodistic, self-dissembling play impulse from Kierkegaard. After assuming the mask of "Brother Brash" and producing a highly critical "Preliminary Expectoration," Kaufmann concludes, "Brother Brash's critique may stand; but it does not do justice to Kierkegaard, 'that individual.' Thus spoke Brother Brief" (S 206).

Let us return to Nietzsche (1844–1900) and Rilke (1875–1926). By putting them together, Kaufmann can address one of his main concerns—"the philosophical dimension of . . . the greatest poetry."[42] Nietzsche and Rilke produce a plausible field for comparison: very great, they wrote in the same language during very nearly the same decades. Moreover, they allow Kaufmann to comment on another of his declared intellectual interests, "the intimate connection between [authorial] character and work." He has exceptional treasure here: if the point of the comparison is to show a consonance of intellectual spirit in the work, and if one allows for the imprint of character on the work, then the proof has an advantage from the start, since they are brother-lovers. "Both men loved the same woman—probably more than any other."

> Nietzsche loved Lou Salomé in 1880 when she was barely over twenty, and she listened to his innermost ideas without quite reciprocating his feelings. Their relation was short-lived but intense, and their break and Nietzsche's subsequent solitude precipitated his first attempt to develop his whole philosophy in a single major work, his *Zarathustra*. When Rilke met her fifteen years later, in 1897, Nietzsche was slowly dying; he was known the world over; Lou herself had recently published a book about him; and she was mature while Rilke, at twenty-two, was not. (S 219–20)

Rilke's early poem "The Song of the Idiot" reveals his talent for speaking out of extraordinary states of mind and giving an account of the world just at it appears to the afflicted person. By *choosing* the mask of the idiot, the poet signals his doubt of the rationality of the world: this ventriloquizing, I'll add, is the contrary principle of the "dyer's hand," as articulated by Goethe's sometimes darling, Byron: "And feeling, in a poet, is the source / Of others' feeling; but they are such liars, / And take all colours—like the hands of dyers."[43] Byron's poem resists Kaufmann's imputation that the idiot's "dimness" is—"perhaps"—familiar to Rilke as his own. With a twist of taste that no one would oppose, Kaufmann turns to the greatest poem among the so-called *Dinggedichte* ("thing poems") in Rilke's *Neue Gedichte*. This is "The Panther," who challenges the limits of the poet's imagination: he must present the world in the perspective of a big caged cat. Rilke's performance is heart-stopping. Kaufmann's translation is fine: "The soft gait . . . / is like a dance of power that embraces / a core containing, dazed, a mighty will"; here is quick evidence of his skill as a translator of German poetry.[44] Kaufmann suggests a link between the extinguished sensibility of Rilke's man-panther and *Kafka's* worldview, because the mood of Rilke's poem is the confinement, the burden, the weariness of "the human condition"—but then withdraws the surmise. Despite their "historical and geographical proximity," it is "exceedingly doubtful" that Rilke might be literally drawing on Kafka as a philosophical source

(S 222). Indeed, it is. In his great story "A Starvation Artist," Kafka *replaces* a caged ascetic by a panther with fiery jaws.

> He did not even seem to miss his freedom; this noble body, equipped just short of bursting with everything it needed, seemed to carry its freedom around with it; it seemed to lodge somewhere in the jaws; and the joy of life sprang from its maw in such a blaze of fire that it was not easy for the spectators to withstand it.[45]

If there is to be a claim of influence, it must go the other way around: "The Panther" was published in 1902, Kafka's "A Starvation Artist," twenty years later. Kaufmann's suggestion is a stimulating one, a productive error. We can well imagine that Kafka chose to put a panther and no other wild beast—no other Nietzschean figure of overbearing vitality—in place of the emaciated artist as a reminiscence of—better, a tribute to—the poet who explicitly encouraged and admired his work. Indeed, Kafka does so in the very terms of a "decisiveness," an effect of vitality that Rilke found in Kafka's 1913 story "The Stoker" (Rilke's word is "Konsquenz"—also, "Verbissenheit," doggedness) but which Rilke thought missing from "Metamorphosis" and in "In the Penal Colony." Kafka, we could further imagine, put the fierce consistency that Rilke had missed in him—this "Verbissenheit"—back into the jaws of (Rilke's) panther. Kaufmann's point, however, is not so much to drive the Kafkan sense of being encaged out of Rilke's panther but to enlarge Rilke's sensibility to include its projection into so much more: "an orphan, the Buddha, a prisoner, a woman's fate, Orpheus, Eurydice, and Hermes (all three in turn), the birth of Venus, Leda, and countless others" (S 222).

In his core an ethical philosopher, Kaufmann finds Rilke's truest voice (and his own) in the well-known "Archaic Torso of Apollo." Confronted by a mutilated stone body, the speaker "discerns" the glow of the god's missing eyes, even "the smile that wanders in the loins' faint turn," and attributes to the marble by the device called prosopopoeia an exhortation rivaled for its fierce eloquence in the German tradition perhaps only by Kant's (originally Horace's) *Sapere aude*, "Dare to know!" The torso proclaims the charge: "You must change your life." The choice of poem is apt for the comparison of the two poet-philosophers, since the main ethical injunction of both Nietzsche and Rilke is: suffer change! Recall Nietzsche's dithyrambic "Only he who changes remains akin to me" ("Nur wer sich wandelt, bleibt mit mir verwandt").[46] The crux of the statue's injunction is "a call for a decision" (S 223). This is the rhetoric of Sartrean existentialism that continues to inform Kaufmann's ethical vocabulary: his late work is titled *Without Guilt and Justice: From Decidophobia to Autonomy*. This latter key word and topic can be thought of as the end frame of Kaufmann's entire corpus and, incidentally, of this book you are reading; it was there at the beginning too, in our first chapter, in Nietzsche's words: "Life—that means for us constantly transforming all that we are into light and flame . . . we simply can do no other."⁴⁷ But, for Kaufmann, that "we" does not obviously include us, Kaufmann's readership, or else we would still not need to be encouraged. Kaufmann reads the passage from Rilke's "The Panther" to his "Archaic Torso of Apollo" as a conceptual progress, in small, of Nietzsche's own development, now reading the last line of "The Panther" as an aesthetic justification of existence:

> Rarely the pupil's curtain, soundlessly
> is raised—and then an image enters him,
> goes through the silent tension of the limbs—
> and in his heart ceases to be.

For Rilke, however, the "Archaic Torso of Apollo," unlike "The Panther," is "a challenge and a promise." His attitude is that of Nietzsche in his third book, *On the Advantage and Disadvantage of History for Life*—the monumentalistic attitude, which, not without its traps and delusions, looks to monuments of greatness of the past as a motive to produce equivalents—not to imitate but to reproduce "along the lines" of the model. In its very resistance to imitation, this act is an ethical one.

This urgency to renewal, in both Nietzsche and Rilke, is sponsored by a shared historical situation in which all anthropological moorings have given way. Kaufmann quotes the splendid lines of Rilke, which also inspired Erich Heller's earlier linkage of the two writers:

> Every brute inversion of the world knows the disinherited
> To whom the past no longer belongs, and not yet the future.

What stay on are remainders, hardened stereotypes—conventions—that offer themselves as holding places but are dead set against reality. Recall Kaufmann's discussion of conventions in our chapter 4: they are contracts not to inquire into the truth of the situation that puts them on offer. These writers are open to another sort of calling: it must seem to address them as individuals. "They feel that if only they will be entirely receptive, they will be addressed personally and experience a necessity, a duty, a destiny that will be just theirs and nobody else's, but no less their duty than any categorical imperative" (S 226). Rilke wrote, "What no man has yet dared to will / shall one day be instinctive with me." It is a frightening openness, in which, as in a figure in a lyric found among his papers, one is "exposed on the mountains of the heart." Nietzsche and Rilke—they bless "the terribleness and bliss of life," in Rilke's words, "this *single* face that merely looks this way or that, depending on the distance from which, or the mood in which, we perceive it" (S 227).[48] Their stance is part and parcel of a "complete repudiation of otherworldliness" (S 228).[49] There is no talk of God: theirs is a religious emotion without God. "Rilke recalls how he once used to speak of God and adds: 'Now you would hardly ever hear me refer to him. . . . His attributes are taken away from God, the no longer utterable, and return to the creation'" (S 229). In his urge to celebrate Nietzsche's and Rilke's Dionysian affirmation of life in *this* creation, Kaufmann declares, "Nietzsche's attitude is not found in German literature before him; but it is the central mood of Rilke's elegies and sonnets" (S 231).

The second half of this proposition is surely true, though the first half is not. It is perhaps Kaufmann's one-sided view of the German romantic writers, whom he dislikes as a body, that allows him to ignore the famous Dionysian-ism, for one thing, of the novel *Ardinghello* of Heinse, to whom Hölderlin explicitly addressed his great hymn, "Bread and Wine." The expert on the German romantic appropriation of Dionysus and the Dionysian spirit—Max Baeumer—singles out Winckelmann and Hamann and Herder (and other less familiar figures—authors of works on "natural philosophy" and mythology) as "bearing eloquent witness to the natural-mystical and ecstatic stance [read: Dionysianism] of the German Romanticists, which reached its final culmina-tion in the works of Friedrich Nietzsche."[50]

This point does not mean to undercut Kaufmann's claim of a yea-saying that connects Nietzsche to Rilke but rather to enlarge the trajectory of their experience. The remarkable intensity of this connection appears to gather up the force of an entire history, and as philosopher-*poets* they are apt inheritors. Recall Nietzsche's aperçu in *The Will to Power*: "The art of communication commanded in the highest degree by the Dionysian type [is] marked by the ease of metamorphosis; it is impossible for him to overlook any sign of an affect."[51] Such Dionysian poetry peaks, for Kaufmann, in Rilke's *Duino Elegies* and the *Sonnets to Orpheus*—a significant pairing, since, as he reminds us, Greek legend blends the features of Dionysus and Orpheus: "The myth of Dio-nysus's martyrdom and rebirth, which is crucial for Nietzsche's conception, is related of Orpheus as well" (S 229).

Earlier we cited Kaufmann's insight into the distinction between Goethe and Nietzsche as to the value of a privileged moment. Faust knows that were he ever to bless such a moment of experience to the point of asking it to "tarry" awhile ("Verweile doch, Du bist so schön!"), he will be damned. Nietzsche damned the idea. Now reflection must go to the beginning of Rilke's Ninth Elegy, where the task of being human is fulfilled in the knowledge that "being here is much." In Kaufmann's translation:

> *Once*
> everything, only *once. Once* and no more. And we, too,
> *once.* Never again. But having
> been this *once*, even though only *once*:
> having been on *earth* does not seem revokable.

Do these lines put Rilke at odds with Nietzsche's doctrine of the Eternal Recurrence of the Same? That is not, finally, the appropriate "theoretical explication of the [relevant] mood," as Kaufmann puts it. Consider the roundelay from Zarathustra's Drunken Song:

> O man, take care!
> What does the deep midnight declare?
> I was asleep—
> From a deep dream I woke and swear:
> The world is deep,
> Deeper than day had been aware.
> Deep is its woe;
> Joy—deeper yet than agony:
> Woe implores: Go!
> But all joy wants eternity—
> Wants deep, wants deep eternity.[52]

"What Rilke's insistent 'once' is meant to rule out is not an eternal recurrence but a beyond; and what he, like Nietzsche, affirms rapturously is this world" (S 232).

Of all these conjunctions, one of the most suggestive concerns the angels of Rilke's *Elegies*. On November 13, 1925, in the year before his death, Rilke wrote a letter to his Polish translator discussing his intentions, saying, "The 'angel' of the elegies has nothing to do with the angel of the Christian heaven (sooner with the angelic figures of Islam). The angel of the *elegies* is the creature in whom that transformation of the visible into the invisible at which we work appears completed." Kaufmann's insight reads: "In other words, he is the image or incarnation of the accomplishment of our striving, and his features thus merge with those of Nietzsche's *Übermensch*" (S 233).

I can barely hint at the beauty of the closing sections of Kaufmann's essay, and so I will turn to the more capable narrator and cite Kaufmann and his poets at length. He quotes Rilke's glorious third Sonnet to Orpheus:

> A god can do it. But how can one follow,
> mere man, oh, tell me, through the narrow art?
> Man's sense is discord. Where ways of the heart
> are crossing stands no temple for Apollo.
>
> Song, as you teach it, does not reach nor yearn,
> nor does it woo what is at last attained;
> song is existence. For the god, unstrained.
> But when do we exist? When will he turn,
>
> to help us to exist, the earth and sky?
> It is not this, youth, that you love, although
> your voice then opens up your lips—oh, try
>
> forgetting that you ever sang. That flees.
> Singing in truth is breath that does not flow.
> An aimless breath. Flight in the god. A breeze.

Kaufmann comments:

> In some translations the last word is rendered as "gale." But what Rilke exalts here is precisely the absence of any storm; and even if it is granted that god, angel, overman, Orpheus, and Dionysus become indistinguishable at this point, this lack of strain may seem to establish a marked difference with Nietzsche, who is generally held to have conceived a more ferocious ideal. In fact, however, Zarathustra follows up his discourse "On Self-Overcoming" with one "On Those Who Are Sublime"; and this is strikingly similar in content to Rilke's sonnet:
>
>> I do not like these tense souls. . . . If he grew tired of his sublimity, the sublime one, only then would his beauty commence. . . . His deed itself still lies on him as a shadow: the hand still darkens the doer. As yet he has not overcome his deed. Though I love the bull's neck on him, I also want to see the eyes of the angel. He must still discard his heroic will;

he shall be elevated, not merely sublime: the ether itself should elevate him, the will-less one.

Surely, this is the theme of the third sonnet to Orpheus. . . . The wind is that which never locks itself up in any form, which never seeks or finds shelter, the symbol of the utterly abandoned and exposed life that is yet unstrained. . . . Rilke and Nietzsche proclaim that a certain kind of life is its own reward, that a certain mode of experience makes life infinitely worth while, and that "the secret of the greatest fruitfulness and the greatest enjoyment of existence is: to live dangerously!" (S 234–39)[53]

We have had Kaufmann saluting Nietzsche in his sublime mode; it is a mode congenial to Kaufmann, as is his other competent drive: reflection and analysis. Predictably, this paean to Dionysianism is followed by a consideration of the untested presupposition of the Nietzsche-Rilke link: the affinity of poetic language and philosophic thought, and to this end he comments on Erich Heller's own work on Nietzsche and Rilke.

Heller sees Nietzsche and Rilke as *inverting* "the tradition" of "great art," whose basis consists in "a fundamentally fixed correspondence between the impact of external experience on man and man's articulate answers." In the works of Nietzsche and Rilke, however, "doubt has dislodged all certainties. . . . It is a world in which the order of correspondences is violently disturbed" (S 243). Kaufmann's point is that the basis of great art, the heart of the "the tradition"—if it is to include Shakespeare, Milton, Goethe, Dostoevsky—has forever been an upsetting of certainties: "all great poetry and philosophy is deeply subversive" (S 244). This is a truism, no doubt, but Kaufmann is determined to employ it. There are difficulties, however, in his treatment of Heller, which is also partially supportive. Heller also writes, interestingly, "In the great poetry of the European tradition . . . the emotions do not interpret; they respond to the interpreted world. In Rilke's mature poetry the emotions do the interpreting and then respond to their own interpretation."[54] The second half of this proposition is surely right, and Kaufmann appears to agree; this is the logic of passion. But having dated the logic of passion, we know that this mode of reading the world is not original with Rilke.

Throughout this discussion we have Kaufmann's claim, too lightly assumed, that the basis of poetry consists of experienced emotions. It is a thesis whose contestation is at the soul of modern literary theory. Certainly Kaufmann has raced too quickly past his original surmise: "the question [is] of the man behind the work, or rather *in* the work," which is to say: experience may be *in* but not behind poetry. Indeed, in a sort of concessive afterthought, after asserting his main conviction of "the wealth of experiences that are not dreamt of in the poetry we have," he adds, "no less, in fact, than are dreamt of *only* in poetry" (emphasis added) (S 245).[55] In his incisive book *Poetry as Experience*, the French philosopher Philippe Lacoue-Labarthe, for one, speaks strongly to the latter.[56] Poetry is not the efflux of personal experience; it *constitutes* a fullness of experience—or indeed its perfect nullity—in its real absence. But it is not necessary now to pit Kaufmann against deconstructive theory written a half century later. There is the opposing position of T. S. Eliot, whom Kaufmann is loath to listen to, although it is his decision to make! Eliot writes:

> It is not in his personal emotions, the emotions provoked by particular events in his life, that the poet is in any way remarkable or interesting. . . . The emotion in his poetry will be a very complex thing, but not with the complexity of the emotions of people who have very complex or unusual emotions in life. One error, in fact, of eccentricity in poetry is to seek for new human emotions to express; and in this search for novelty in the wrong place it discovers the perverse. The business of the poet is not to find new emotions, but to use the ordinary ones and, in working them up into poetry, to express feelings which are not in actual emotions at all. And emotions which he has never experienced will serve his turn as well as those familiar to him.[57]

This claim, for Kaufmann, is beyond the pale. He comes to poetry as a reader who has had a great deal of experience; he feels at one with his experience, to which he brings an allowable portion of self-love. He is acquainted with the way that religious belief, for one, can "prevent the believer from savoring the full range of his own inimitable experience" (S 256). And in his love of poetry, he is not about to attribute to the experience of great writers anything less than the love he has for his own.[58]

It is greatly to his credit that his love is not blind. Just as, in later work, he will ask readers of Heidegger to think the unheard-of thought: "Can Heidegger be mistaken?," he asks readers to think the unheard-of thought that Rilke's "inspiration" is no warrant of perfection.[59] "Rilke's facile belief that his [Duino] elegies and sonnets [to Orpheus] were gifts of inscrutable inspiration undoubtedly reflects a lack of strength and a sense of his own inability to effect any improvements. There are lines in the elegies that appear to be the mere padding of pathos, and many passages in the sonnets make little sense" (S 249). This is not a sentence that you will see *anywhere* in the near-universally idolatrous Rilke criticism. But a love that is not blind can love what it sees:

> *Earth, is not this what you want: to arise in us*
> *invisible?—Is it not your dream*
> *to be invisible once?—Earth! Invisible!*
> *What if not transformation is your urgent command?*

RILKE—THE NINTH DUINO ELEGY (S 260)

We have repeatedly heard from Kaufmann how literary works are made: they are the records—"authentic and incomparable"—of experiences (S 264). But what aesthetics could justify this claim? The answer is a predictable reprise of the vitalist strain, consistent with the views of Wilhelm Dilthey, whose stress on *Erlebnis* ("the experience of the hour") as the groundwork of poetic expression is famous and inevitable. Kaufmann writes:

> Poets . . . have not only the gift of lending expression to single feelings and attitudes but also the power to create characters, enabling the reader to gain experiences for which any possibility would otherwise be lacking in a single human life. Poetry makes possible a vast expansion of our world, an extension of sympathy, and a profounder understanding not only of human possibilities but also of human realities. (S 278)

This is as straightforward a statement of the uncomplicated symmetry of verbal expression and reception as can be imagined. In an earlier passage, however, Kaufmann's rhetoric raised the *question* of the very possibility of truly understanding the works of great artists. The result is interestingly at odds with the confident Diltheyan formulation above. In this earlier passage, Kaufmann addresses the sacrifice of "comfort, life, and sanity" that some great artists have made for the sake of their art, but this tragedy is nothing next to the bitter fate that might await their art. At the end, opponents of the artist's work—opponents besotted with the indignation of their (false) interpretations—"speak with fiery tongues to a posterity that—ultimate irony—believes itself to be listening to the poet himself" (S 264). No names are named, but Goethe and Nietzsche as philosopher-poets are obvious candidates (Goethe had recently been insulted by T. S. Eliot and others in the English-speaking world, and the ubiquitous scorning of Nietzsche could explain Kaufmann's excited rhetoric). At this point we would expect a straightforward statement of the need for rectification. "But is this tragedy," Kaufmann wonders, "not purely personal, and immaterial to mankind, unless we make a point of projecting ourselves fictitiously, and somewhat sentimentally, into the artist's consciousness, which is mercifully blotted out by death or madness?" (S 264).

The hesitation of this answer is haunting: one easily detects a skeptical undercurrent questioning the possibility of a genuine fusion of consciousness in artist and interpreter. There is, first of all, the fact that the answer is put as a rhetorical question, as if a direct declaration of the success of such interpretation were too much said. Second, there is the pejorative flavor of a projection whose "fictitious" and even "sentimental" character is stressed. And thirdly, whether intended or not, there is the ambiguous power of the "merciful" blotting out of the artist's consciousness by death or madness. This mercy appears to apply to his or her not having to endure the misprision of his or her work. At the same time, this mercy is the very condition of possibility of a reader's interpretation that can proceed freely, not fearing the reprisals of the poet: there is no Nietzsche, as there is, say, a Toni Morrison to say, "That is not what I meant at all." But an act (of interpretation) obtained only on the condition of the writer's "death or madness" could raise a question as to its value.

What are we to make of these doubts built into Kaufmann's description of a tragic misunderstanding? I think that if they were put to him, he would reject them, declaring them an overinterpretation—a warning, if only a weak intimation, of "the very voice with which . . . opponents speak with fiery tongues to a posterity that . . . believes itself to be listening to the poet [read: scholar] himself." But if Kaufmann—large-hearted, as he has shown himself to be in his readiness to submit contestable claims to dialogue—submitted his rebuttal to dialogical resolution, his "opponent" might very well argue that here scholarly reason (to paraphrase Mallarmé) has *ceded the theoretical initiative to words*.[60] Or, to paraphrase Goethe's Mephistopheles:

> Yes, stick to words at any rate;
> There never was a surer gate
> Into the temple, Certainty. . . .
> For just where no ideas are
> The proper word is never far,
> With words a dispute can be won,
> With words a system can be spun,
> In words one can believe unshaken.[61]

Here the discourse of philosophy, the rhetoric of thinking, it is claimed, has "made merry" with the prime intentions of the thinker, who holds, he tells us again and again, that legitimate interpretation is an affair of an unproblematic "recapturing the experience behind ['all great poetry and philosophy']" (S 244). But we cannot ask Kaufmann to reply: in his own words, death has made it impossible to resolve this doubt. It is an undercurrent that erodes the certainty of Kaufmann's experiential-expressive-communicative theory of poetic production and reception.

These issues are discussed further in the chapter "Philosophy versus Poetry," distinguished by several of Kaufmann's epigrammatic judgments of philosophers and poets. His competence to speak on this topic is demonstrable, since he himself can be reckoned a poet-philosopher: he published a volume of poetry, as we know, and many poems elsewhere, but even without them, there is plain evidence of his deep understanding of poetry in his superb translations and, for the most part, in his scrupulous, loving criticism of poetry. (A senior member of the Philosophy Department at Princeton, it is said, was glad to grant Kaufmann this title of distinction—"Ah, Kaufmann: he is a poet"—though intending no praise by it.) All this to say that Kaufmann knows his way around this "versus," and with such knowledge comes (the will to) judgment. He is not hesitant to criticize to the left and to the right of it. No great maker escapes scrutiny: not Plato, not Aristotle, not Shakespeare. Of distinguished moderns, Heidegger and Camus are the hardest hit.

A final point: at the outset of this chapter, I referred to Kaufmann's 1976 collection titled *Thirteen Essays*. We will discuss the very striking essays "Existentialism and Death," "On Death and Lying," and "Death without Dread," which conclude the collection, in a short essay following the next chapter, devoted to Kaufmann's seminal *The Faith of a Heretic*. In fact, a good deal of the material in *Existentialism, Religion, and Death* originally appeared in *The Faith of a Heretic*, suggesting their importance for Kaufmann: they constitute a thanatology.

6

A Contempt for Popularity

THE FAITH OF A HERETIC

A character outstanding in its uncompromising courage, its defiant obstinacy, and its proud contempt for popularity.

—KAUFMANN'S DESCRIPTION OF CAPTAIN AHAB

THE FIRST OF THE EPIGRAPHS of *The Faith of a Heretic* goes directly to Jeremiah: "They have healed the wound of my people, lightly, saying, 'Peace, peace,' when there is no peace." Kaufmann will show the true face of this "light peace."[1] It is a feeble, unreflected conformity of opinion, mainly in matters of religious belief. At the outset, *The Faith of a Heretic* states its chief concern: to undo a common faith in organized religion. He is notably harder on Christianity than on Judaism.

Kaufmann, as we have heard, was born into a Protestant family with Jewish forebears. When at the age of eleven he rejected the Christianity acquired by his parents and decided to become a Jew, he was unaware of his Jewish heritage. He soon learned the true state of affairs—which came as a surprise, as if from a higher source, and spurred his intellectual interest in Judaism. This commitment was bound to strike him, some years later, as right and full of fate when he read in Goethe's *Faust*, the best book of his great "educator": "What you have inherited from your fathers: earn to possess it." He began Hebrew in earnest and became a bar mitzvah ("the son of a Commandment"). In the years following, he studied the Hebrew Bible and Talmud at the Institute for Jewish Studies in Berlin under Leo Baeck and missed no occasion to assert the superiority of Judaism to Christianity. This attitude was no doubt strengthened by the appalling perception of a Christian country embracing Nazi barbarism. Throughout *The Faith of a Heretic*, Kaufmann contrasts the Hebrew prophets' love of social justice with what he calls Christianity's "Manichean" division of the world into children of light and children of darkness. This very radically asserted opposition between the two testaments prompts critics' complaints of Kaufmann's *furor judaicus* as *his* slide into permanent Manichean error.

He traces his early rejection of Christianity to the moment his father was unable to explain the Trinity of God the Father, the Son, and the Holy Ghost. Does Kaufmann's abjuration of Christianity, then, on the grounds of its incoherence, testify, already at an early age, to a *heretical* disposition?

The title of Kaufmann's 1961 book *The Faith of a Heretic* and the words of his prologue make this claim, although the application of the concept of "heresy" can seem puzzling, since a heretic, according to one authority, "is one who deviates from an established orthodoxy under the conviction that he more truly represents the faith than do its orthodox adherents."[2] In Kaufmann's case the orthodoxy certainly cannot be either Christianity or Judaism. It will be a subtle matter to explain how his intellectual stance qualifies as heretical—a subtle matter and also a necessary one, if his use of this charged word is to escape the fault that he defines very precisely in a later book:

> One can always redefine old words in such ways that the new concepts are no longer open to the old objections. . . . The result if not the purpose of this practice is that the new concept carries the emotional charge and something of the moral authority of the old term, and does this illicitly. . . . Some individuals can manage to use the old words while realizing very clearly how precisely they are using them, and their autonomy may not suffer.

Others will not be as successful.[3] Defining the special sense in which Kaufmann thinks of himself as a heretic will be the brunt of this chapter. To stay with the standard definition as above would require more than identifying the orthodoxy that Kaufmann rejects; it would require identifying the new orthodoxy that his criticism establishes. But this is to suggest a vision of religious proportions, which is far from the mark. Kaufmann's humanist premises are not meant to establish a new religion: "Great men who deride organized religion in the name of some religious vision of their own, like Lao-Tze and many of the [Old Testament] prophets, have disappeared with Kierkegaard and Tolstoy" (F 254). (This sentence epitomizes Kaufmann's art when he is good: the pungent claim, direct and clear, borne on the strength of substantial erudition.) Kaufmann is a critic—with principles; he is no visionary; he is a dissenter, stronger in critique than in doctrine.[4] But he is a bearer of a *faith* in critique as the lifeblood of the autonomous personality.[5] This qualification of faith, this stipulation of its object—criticism—acquits Kaufmann of what would be Nietzsche's charge and warning: "The need for faith, for some kind of unconditional Yes and No . . . is a need born of *weakness*. The man of faith, the 'believer' of every kind, is necessarily a dependent man—one who cannot posit *himself* as an end."[6] *That* is one cap that does not fit Kaufmann.

At the same time, it is important to remember that his rejection of Christianity—and thereafter his conversion to orthodox Judaism and thence its rejection in turn—was not an abjuration of religion and religious feeling—a subject matter that would occupy him for the rest of his life: an angel to wrestle with, a vast enclosure, a sphere of life that embraced him—and which he would have embrace others, creating, on his example, indispensable encounters "with Luther and the prophets, Tolstoy and St. Francis, Confucius and the Buddha," "exposure to [not indoctrination by!] the Bible and the Dhammapada, to the Analects and Lao-Tze, the Upanishad and the Law of Manu, to Servetus and Calvin, to the persecutors and the persecuted" (F 278–79). From beginning to end, religion is the essential subject of *The Faith of a Heretic*, studied in the lens of philosophical criticism.

In the years following his conversion to Judaism at age eleven, Kaufmann thought of studying for the rabbinate—a not surprising impulse, since in the late 1930s there was no other higher purpose for which a Jew could study. He could not go to the university, so, as he explained, "being terribly interested in religion at that time, and in Judaism in particular, that is what I thought I would do."[7] By the time he left Williams College in 1941, however, partly as a result of his study of comparative religion, he had ceased to belong to any established church. In his case this ethical separation does not end with disenchantment but with detachment—a critical cast of mind directed at the matter that continued to interest him the most. He claims to have had a number of (unspecified!) mystical experiences in this period, which would have additionally charged his interest with a fatality that began with his conversion, as a boy in a Jewish family, to Judaism. It would be interesting to know whether Kaufmann took to heart the fact that as a Jew—however disestablished—he was, on historical precedent, cast in the role of a heretic. Already at the beginning of the Christian formation, as Steven Aschheim writes, "the Jew not only embodied dissent, he also became a metaphor for heresy itself, symbol of subversion whether or not its agents were themselves Jewish."[8]

Kaufmann once said in an interview that he conceived *The Faith of a Heretic* partly in response to a review of his *Critique of Religion and Philosophy* that appeared in the (London) *Times Literary Supplement*, in which a dissatisfied reviewer, Professor Denis J. B. Hawkins, a scholar of Catholic philosophy, asked him, after all, for his doctrine—his own beliefs.[9] In the back of his mind, however, there might also have been a desire to repair an old harm. In the previous chapter, we encountered Kaufmann's many animadversions against the literary-critical pronouncements of T. S. Eliot. Among Eliot's questionable dogmas, the famously deplorable sentence in his volume *After Strange Gods* stands out: "Reasons of race and religion combine to make any large number of free-thinking Jews undesirable."[10] On Kaufmann's reading, in plain words, which I supply: "For reasons of race, 'we' do not wish to have a large number of 'you' extant." Eliot can have stuck in Kaufmann's craw when he set about to write *The Faith of a Heretic*. It is in its own way a solid antithesis to Eliot's book of lectures, which is subtitled *A Primer of Modern Heresy*.

In *Critique*, Kaufmann had written the words "among the things that remain is the aspiration which is the soul of religion." "But," returning to Hawkins's *TLS* review, "it is an aspiration to what? That is the kind of question which an intellectual conscience condemns you to try to answer." (In Kaufmann's *Nietzsche: Philosopher, Psychologist, Antichrist*, Hawkins could have found the plain statement that man aspires to be a god whose attributes, however heretically, might be imagined [N 254].)[11] "At least," Hawkins continues, "[an intellectual conscience] . . . should lead to some attempt at a statement of ethical principle, for moral aspiration without moral principle is apt to lead to odd results."[12] Kaufmann would reply, immediately.

A preliminary sketch of his response was commissioned by *Harper's* magazine, to which *The Faith of a Heretic* alludes. Kaufmann, clearly in favor of "evidence and reason" and plainly heretic to the "church" of ordinary irrationality, writes:

> If we discard our reason, mortify our understanding, and take leave of our senses, how can we be sure that what we accept is the word of God? The mere fact that something is presented to us as the word of God is clearly insufficient. One has only to write an article on matters of religion in a popular magazine to be swamped with letters, little pamphlets, and big books that claim to offer nothing less than God's own truth; but, alas, they are far from agreeing with each other. . . . How are we to choose if evidence and reason are thrown out of court? (F 76–77)

The outcome is a substantial book of four hundred pages, in which Kaufmann takes stock of his well-stocked mind for greater stakes than a need to flesh out a magazine article. The key terms of its plangent title draw the outlines of the bigger project. We need again and again to look more closely at Kaufmann's concepts of "faith" and "heresy." One route to understanding this title is the history of Kaufmann's decision to choose it.

> Soon after my *Critique* appeared, I was asked to write an article for a projected series on religion. There were to be a Protestant, a Catholic, a Jew—and I was to represent a critical, rationalist point of view. It was a ticklish assignment, and the magazine was not a scholarly journal, but one could hardly say: congratulations, gentlemen, on your decision to present this point of view along with more popular attitudes, but if you don't mind, ask someone else. I stipulated that I must be under no pressure to pull my punches, and that the editors must not rewrite my essay. They did not change a word, but thanked me for "The Faith of an Agnostic." I preferred "The Faith of an Infidel." That would not do: it would look as if, along with two Christians and a Jew, a Muslim had been included. The editors proposed "The Faith of a Pagan." I did not think I was a pagan and, after some further thought, hit on "The Faith of a Heretic." (F 8–9)

His book is more than an identifiable expansion of this essay, even if the title gives it shape. These key words—"faith" and "heresy"—are complex and open to competing definitions. To take the latter term anew—: how does Kaufmann escape the enclosure set up at the beginning of this chapter by his critic R.B.Y. Scott, who defined the heretic, contra Kaufmann, as "one who deviates from an established orthodoxy under the conviction that he more truly represents the faith than do its orthodox adherents?" Keep in mind that the driving force of Kaufmann's book is an attack on *all* established religion. How does he get past this aporia? Answer: He does after all offer another definition! This definition functions entirely outside the theological enclosure: "Heresy is a set of opinions 'at variance with established or generally received principles'" (F 1). There is no talk here of a *correction* of "generally received principles" so that the frame of the orthodoxy in which they are contained might be preserved, let alone strengthened.

A number of other theological definitions of heresy cited by Kaufmann echo Scott's objection. One such definition holds heresy to be an "opinion that is contrary to the fundamental doctrine or creed of any particular church." This definition is not at odds with Kaufmann's critical enterprise, if "church" is taken to mean any High or Low Church or any clique possessed by dogmas. The maverick theoretical physicist Freeman Dyson, for one, writes as such a heretic, having a "science church" in mind—the consensus on climate change:

> I will be telling stories that challenge the prevailing dogmas of today. The prevailing dogmas may be right, but they still need to be challenged. I am proud to be a heretic. The world always needs heretics to challenge the prevailing orthodoxies. Since I am heretic, I am accustomed to being in the minority. If I could persuade everyone to agree with me, I would not be a heretic.[13]

Inviting the charge of invidious comparison, I'll note too that I once wrote heretically, in deconstruction's palmy days, about "The Little Church of Deconstruction around the corner in which the oblates sang, 'I believe, yea, I believe: All is Textual.'"[14]

There is, however, the particular and stringent sense of heresy that Kaufmann himself cites from *Webster's Universal Unabridged Dictionary*: "an offense against Christianity consisting in a denial of some of its essential doctrines, publicly avowed, and obstinately maintained" (F 1). This definition is not a far cry from Kaufmann's procedure, since he does continually dispute the truth of "the essential doctrines" of Christianity. A religion celebrated for its message of loving-kindness to others—whose essence, one hears, is "altruism and self-sacrifice"—is in the last resort self-centered: "In the New Testament, each man's overruling concern with his eternal happiness—his salvation—is central" (F 207, 211). It is opposite to the perspective of the Hebrew prophets, in whom

> the accent had been on the neighbor and the stranger, the orphan, the widow, and the poor. Social injustice cried out to be rectified and was no less real because it meant a lack of love and a corruption of the heart. Man was told to love others and to treat them justly for their sake, not for his own, to escape damnation. To the Jesus of the Gospels, social injustice as such is of no concern. Heaven and hell-fire have been moved into the center. . . . "Render to God what is God's"; the social sphere is not God's and merits no concern. (F 208, 210)[15]

In its main design, the Gospels "reject all concern with social justice and reduce morality to a prudent concern for one's own salvation" (F 213). And insofar as that concern means paying compulsory heed to ritual above the needs of others—a disaster not unique to Christianity and prevalent, too, in Judaism at a later stage—

the [Hebrew] prophets took as radical a stand as any great religious figures ever did: they found the essence of their ancestral religion in morality,
denounced the fusion of careful attention to the rites with indifference to
social justice as a rank abomination, and suggested that rites, unlike social
justice, were dispensable. (F 262)

Kaufmann is furiously discontented with those apologists—he emphasizes
Christian theologians—who "gerrymandered" both Bibles to dissolve such
tensions and make amazing doctrine seem less incredible:

> Let those who like inspiring interpretations be no less forthright in telling
> us precisely where they stand on immortality, the sacraments, and hell; on
> the virgin birth and resurrection; on the incarnation and the miracles; on
> John's theology, and Paul's, and James'; on Augustine and Aquinas, Luther,
> Calvin, and the various creeds. And on: "Resist not evil." And: "Let him
> who would sue you in court for your coat have your cloak, too." And: "No
> one comes to the Father but through Me." (F 127)

And yet the heresy Kaufmann practices cannot be defined by any one
system it attacks. "Heresy" means, in two words, *critical thinking* poised against
the conformist views making up the "common sense of . . . [one's] time and
[the opinions of] some of the most revered names of the past" (F 15). That
common sense needs to be specified in each case. Kaufmann's project is
defined by this task, which is, however, mainly and repeatedly focused on a
"common sense" of *religion*, turning on questions of God, the soul, morality,
and lesser beliefs, forms of worship, and public agitation as well. This para-
phernalia, more or less consciously understood, is the object of his criticism
as part of the faith commonly held in America in 1960: modern Christianity.
"What the [Old Testament] prophets criticized, mocked, and denounced was
precisely the kind of religion that has been revived since the Second World
War," with its "inconsistencies, hypocrisies," and increase of priestly privilege,
ritual practices, and demand for public inscriptions of trust in God. And where
"conformity grows, so does intolerance" (F 252-53).

Another word for Kaufmann's faith in critical reason is, simply, philosophy.[16] "In philosophy," he writes,

> it is respectable to give elaborate accounts of bygone theories on matters on
> which it would not be respectable to theorize oneself. Similarly, an exposi-
> tion of Kant, Hegel's, or Nietzsche's criticisms of Christianity is considered

a worthwhile and useful contribution which deserves an honored place in philosophic journals. . . . But the very same people who are grateful for a documented exposition of past criticisms are far from grateful for contemporary criticisms of Christianity, even if some of the strictures should be more judicious. To report other men's unsound criticisms is considered worthy of a philosopher; to offer sound criticisms of Christianity on one's own is not considered part of a philosopher's job. (F 51)

This is an example of heretical thinking aimed only indirectly at Christianity: it is foremost a criticism of conformity, an unreflected silence within the guild of academic philosophy—and not only there. Thinking of Sartre, Kaufmann quotes enthusiastically from a passage in "The Responsibility of the Writer":

If a writer has chosen to be silent on one aspect of the world, we have the right to ask him: Why have you spoken of this rather than that? And since you speak in order to make a change, since there is no other way you can speak, why do you want to change this rather than that? Why do you want to alter the way in which postage stamps are made rather than the way in which Jews are treated in an anti-Semitic country? And the other way around. He must therefore always answer the following questions: What do you want to change? Why this rather than that? (F 65)[17]

A secular example of what Kaufmann wants to change is the conformity in academic philosophy that considers such fundamental questions as the search for justification and "the quest for excellence" as outside its competence (F 59). Here, for one, is Wittgenstein: "My whole tendency and I believe the tendency of all men who ever tried to write or talk Ethics or Religion was to run against the boundaries of language. The running against the walls of our cage is perfectly, absolutely hopeless." Thinking of this revolution in philosophy elaborated by the British analytic school, which radically shrank the province of philosophical concerns considered habitable, Kaufmann concludes, "What matters is not to revolutionize philosophy, but to make philosophy once again revolutionary" (F 59–60).

In declaring his faith in critical thinking, Kaufmann involves us in the irony of a profession of faith aimed against the dominant faith of his time, where the point of his attack is indeed the ordinary Christian's faith, a *quality* of conviction or belief rather than, strictly speaking, conviction or belief in the obscure objects of this religion. Kaufmann's own faith in the activity of heretical thought calls for a continual description of a *secular* faith. But how, after all, can one distinguish the faith of the heretic from the faith of "the true believer"? (F 3). For one thing, unlike the faith invoked and assumed in established religion, the faith of the heretic is not decorous or pleasant: it exposes itself continually to "the bite of thought" (F 27). On this parlous path lies the justification of the humanist, based on a passion for articulate criticism and a taste for difficulty, for "difficulty becomes a challenge and even a delight; critical thinking, a way of life" (F 21). Kaufmann echoes William Butler Yeats, who wrote of "the fascination of what's difficult," but which, quite unlike for Kaufmann,

> Has dried the sap out of my veins, and rent
> Spontaneous joy and natural content
> Out of my heart.[18]

The distinction arises because Kaufmann, the younger scholar, is only half in love with difficulty: he is also in love with the luminous product of clear thinking.[19]

Kaufmann's principles, which mean to be strong and lively, are not merely hermeneutic in the strict sense, as, for example, the rules governing Talmudic disputation. Kaufmann's are axioms of value: they aim to supply reason its energy, its fearlessness, its probity, its aspiration to the truth. The principles are advanced throughout the book: they survive every specific critical encounter, for here, as Kaufmann writes in his preface, more than in his previous books, "criticism is subordinated to a constructive attempt" (F xxvii). Four leading principles of value—he insists on this number—support his faith in reason: they are the operative virtues of love, courage, honesty and, with a certain central European drollness, "humbition"—"humility winged by ambition" (F 306).[20] In a summing up to his anthology *Religion from Tolstoy to Camus*, Kaufmann adds "humor" to this neologism as well (R 42). His faith in these principles is long-standing: they are present in his first reflections on Nietzsche or already inform such reflections. "Late in life," he writes,

> Freud wrote Arnold Zweig, the novelist, speaking of Nietzsche: "In my youth he signified a nobility which I could not attain. A friend of mine, Dr. Paneth, had got to know him . . . and he used to write me about him."[21] We know what Paneth wrote his fiancée about Nietzsche: . . . he emphasized Nietzsche's humility, his ambition, his courage, and his honesty. (F 336)

The support of such virtues does not arise from rational certainty: they are rooted in beliefs that, together with the things that reason knows, constitute a faith. Kaufmann concedes:

Faith means intense, usually confident, belief that is not based on evidence sufficient to command assent from every reasonable person. Many people assume that an intense belief must be held with a closed mind—that it necessarily involves no longer "wanting to know what is true"—and that any willingness to look with an open mind at further evidence or at objections shows that one's faith is lacking in intensity and therefore not worthy of the name. (F 3)[22]

That exemplary openness is put on offer as the book advances: it is a matter of one's wanting "to retain in one's emotional, no less than in one's intellectual, life a high degree of openness—a readiness for the unprecedented call, experience, or demand" (F 266). Kaufmann's originary definition continues:

The use of "faith" in the title of this book depends on the assumption that a man who cares intensely may have sufficient interest to concern himself with issues, facts, and arguments that have a vital bearing on what he believes. In sum, there are at least two types of faith, though possibly many more: the faith of the believer and the faith of a heretic. (F 3)[23]

Even as *The Faith of a Heretic* constructs its table of values—love, courage, honesty, "humbition"—it remains closer to the spirit of aspiration than to a laying down of doctrine, for "a heretic wants no articles of faith." One is struck by Kaufmann's decent qualification of his beliefs: his trust in his values is not, once more, founded on certainty: "The premises are not really certain, not based on evidence sufficient to compel assent from every reasonable person" (F 10). "My own ethic is not absolute but a morality of openness. It is not a morality of rules but an ethic of virtues. It offers no security but goals. . . . [It is] the ethic of a heretic" (F 306). And so the faith of this heretic is not "merely a matter of faith" (F 10). "What saves my ethic from being anarchic and irresponsible is not portentousness or the sweep of its claims but the attention given to objections and alternatives" (F 329–30). In a word: this faith owes itself reasons for the premises it believes. And in so doing, it exemplifies the independence of morals from religion—or what commonly counts as religion, "the faith of the believer."

This independence does not have to be absolute; the matter calls for a differentiated view. In the Hebrew prophets, for example, "and in parts of the New Testament—though certainly only in parts—love, justice, and humility appear to be all that is asked of man, and questions of belief entirely peripheral, while precise formulations about God, 'his attributes, and his relations with man and the universe'—[the business of theology]—are altogether out of the picture" (F 129).[24] This does not make a morality of love, justice, and humility dependent on the Hebrew Bible and the New Testament, but it draws support from these books. At the same time, the "old morality" of the Hebrew Bible and the "new morality" of the New Testament are not the same.

> On reflection, the old morality is not protected but undermined, not extended but dissolved; and no new morality is put in its place. Where murder is not considered importantly different from calling a man a fool, nor adultery from a lustful look, the very basis of morality is denied: the crucial distinction between impulse and action. If one is unfortunate enough to have the impulse, no reason is left for not acting on it. (F 214)

One might insist on the essential independence of religious faith and morality, but is this claim consistent with the position—if it is one—of the *agnostic*? A contestable feature of Kaufmann's attack on the "common sense" of religious belief is his attack on the view that agnosticism, as opposed to frank atheism, is a position on which the critical mind can rest. The trimmer's agnosticism is conceptually vacuous. What sort of evidence is he waiting for, en route to his final decision that God exists (or does not exist)? To count as meaningful, his decision would have to be preceded by a prior understanding of the proposition "God exists (or does not exist)," with equal stress on the noun and verb. Just what is it, precisely, that the agnostic is uncertain about?

> The agnostic is supposed to be the man who finds that there is not suffi-cient evidence to be sure either that God does or that God does not exist; so he suspends judgment. But for what is there not sufficient evidence? About what precisely does he suspend judgment? Like most people, he, too, overlooks the staggering ambiguity of that strange formulation, "God exists." Without determining first what is meant by that, one cannot say in candor whether one believes that it is true, that it is false, or that there is lack of evidence both ways. To say that whatever could be meant by it is false is militant, but shows vast ignorance of the attenuated and innocuous beliefs theologians and philosophers, preachers and laymen have been reading into this hallowed phrase for centuries. (F 29)

Furthermore, it makes little sense to declare oneself "agnostic" with respect to the requirement that a moral community be founded on religious belief since we do not know of religions that are bare of moral consequences: they hang together. To be agnostic is to be without a view on their interdepen-dence: as a result it leaves morality in a precarious, unspecified relation to

Scripture. The result, for Kaufmann, is that the agnostic cannot give a fundamental account of what moral principles are, in general and in particular. This claim can seem apodictic, but Kaufmann states its basis. The positions of the agnostic and the true believer are damaged in the same way: both suspend judgment. "In his splendid book *The Greeks and the Irrational*," adds Kaufmann,

> E. R. Dodds . . . remarked that "when the archaic Greek poured liquids down a feeding-tube into the livid jaws of a moldering corpse," he wisely refrained, like a little girl feeding her doll, from thinking about what he was doing.[25] Surely the same consideration applies to most religious practices: ritual, prayer, and religious affirmations generally involve a suspension of one's critical faculties a refusal to be completely honest with oneself. (F 32)

That is the general, the theoretical point: for Kaufmann there is no principled argument for the absolute dependence of moral behavior on religious belief. He can also cite balky empirical data to reinforce his argument: "The proportion of religious affiliates is at least fifty per cent higher among convicts than among the general population" (F 270).[26] "Indeed, organized religion after the Second World War is still doing what it did in Jeremiah's days: It gives men a good conscience, crying 'peace, peace,' when there is no peace" (F 274).

Clearly, *The Faith of a Heretic* is more than the work of a reclusive theorist or a philosophical dilettante: it answers to a personal compulsion, and it is only in this respect a personal memoir. Kaufmann explains that when he was young, he read that van Gogh went down to be among the miners but also how little it helped them. Zola did not go down among them, but he wrote *Germinal*, as a result of which there was immense publicity and a good deal of legislation to better their condition. Kaufmann wills that effect. In 1959 he had already made his mark as an academic writer and thinker; he now wants to write with effect. "For centuries," he writes,

> Heretics have been persecuted by men of strong faiths who hated nonconformity and heresy and criticism while making obeisances to honesty— within limits. In our time millions have been murdered in cold blood by the foes of non-conformity and heresy and criticism, who paid lip service to honesty—within limits.
>
> I have less excuse than many others for ignoring all this. If even I do not speak up, who will? And if not now when? (F 13)

Kaufmann would forever want to be more than a professor: his way of being more is to be a heretic. We might recall from our first chapter Nietzsche's animadversions on "university scholars": "A university scholar [*ein Gelehrter*]," he wrote, "can never become a philosopher; for even Kant could not do it and remained to the end, in spite of the innate striving of his genius, in a quasi cocoon stage." Kaufmann developed this point: "A philosopher . . . must not allow 'concepts, opinions, things past, and books' to step 'between himself and things.' He must not rationalize the valuations of his own society. As Nietzsche sees it, the temptation to do this is particularly great for the German professor who is an employee of the State" (N 105). Despite being a university professor—subject, it is true, not to a state but nonetheless to a private corporation, to Princeton University, bristling with actual and potential critics of heresy—Kaufmann is determined "not to allow 'concepts, opinions, things past, and books' to step 'between himself and things.'" Nietzsche's example is an invitation to heresy.

This category "heresy" is a work in progress throughout the whole of the book: the heretic Walter Kaufmann is the sum of the most plangent and incisive of his pages. Here, at once, is a crucial example, which turns on his scorn of theologians, a subgenre of professors, who do not live the religion of the book they interpret and do not break with convention.

> The religious thinkers of our age whose books have some prestige and influence on intellectuals are not bold innovators who, like Jeremiah, have the courage "to pluck up and to break down, to destroy and to overthrow, to build and to plant." They are professors who disdain to overthrow and do not seem to have anything to plant: they are theologians and interpret. Some interpret St. Thomas, and some interpret the New Testament, and their notion of reviving is exceedingly literal: like Elijah and Jesus, they prostrate themselves over what seems dead and breathe their own spirit into it to bring it back to life. But unlike Elijah and Jesus, they avoid conflict with the organized religion of their day. (F 254)

Kaufmann's way of practicing heresy is to ask untoward questions—these arise from a critical reflection on a vast range of cultural materials. It extends from the civilization of ancient Egypt, circa 4000 BC, to his contemporary America, circa 1960, with easily recoverable references to General Eisenhower's faith in organized religion, Joseph McCarthy's slanders, race tensions, the shadow of the atom bomb. Were it not for a few unmovable place and time markers, one could easily attach these references to present-day persons and events, especially in Kaufmann's examination of the "religious revival" and organized religion as such. But it is not so much that he—and by invitation, we—are to put questions to these particular persons and issues as that a sustained reflection on these questions widens out to a deeper concern for individual justification.

His chief concerns are present at the beginning: the quest for honesty, the important but also questionable value of "commitment," the masquerade of theology, the problem of suffering, the moral core of the Hebrew Bible and the New Testament, Freud and the tragic virtues, the meaning of death, and a jeu d'esprit, a "Trilogue on Heaven, Love, and Peace," confirming that Kaufmann is a stylish writer, a superior translator of German thought and writing, and a poet of considerable (if uneven) quality himself, witness his volume *Cain and Other Poems*. We still need to see how his historical and philosophical chapters support the primary values that shape his answers to the questions he poses to his reader. Here, to make a beginning, "style" also has a role to play. The authority of Kaufmann's arguments owes a great deal to the force of their articulation, of which we've had proofs from his Nietzsche book. To make the point directly, consider some examples from *The Faith of a Heretic*.

The only *honest* theism, Kaufmann claims, is built on suffering, built on a great In-spite-of. Consider Job and Jeremiah:

> Their piety is a cry in the night, born of suffering so intense that they cannot contain it and must shriek, speak, accuse, and argue with God—not about him—for there is no other human being who would understand, and the prose of dialogue could not be faithful to the poetry of anguish. In time, theologians come to wrench some useful phrases out of Latin versions of a Hebrew outcry, blind with tears, and try to win some argument about a point of dogma. Scribes, who preceded them, carved phrases out of context, too, and used them in their arguments about the law.

"But for all that," as we have seen, "Jewish piety has been a ceaseless cry in the night, rarely unaware of 'all the oppressions that are practiced under the sun,' a faith in spite of, not a heathenish, complacent faith because" (F 169).[27]

Kaufmann's picture of Moses in his distinction from Jesus of Nazareth can have enabled his celebration of the virtue he calls "humbition"—ambition tempered by humility:

> He [Moses] went away to die alone, lest any man should know his grave to worship there or attach any value to his mortal body. Having seen Egypt, he knew better than the Buddha how prone men are to such superstitions. Going off to die alone, he might have left his people with the image of

a mystery, with the idea of some supernatural transfiguration, with the thought that he did not die but went up to heaven—with the notion that he was immortal and divine. He might have created the suspicion that, when his mission was accomplished, he returned to heaven. Instead he created an enduring image of humanity: he left his people with the thought that, being human and imperfect, he was not allowed to enter the promised land, but that he went up on the mountain to see it before he died. (F 189)

This is sublime—one of the several tonalities in which Kaufmann writes. He is adept at polemic, a skill that even his angriest critics acknowledge. A professor of philosophy who minds Kaufmann's "honesty" as "intrusive," a virtue in Kaufmann's hands lacking philosophical "discipline," finds "insights which stimulate the reader, as the following quotation indicates":

Some of those who say that man must have a god, also say that every scientist is a hidden theologian because he is a human being. The stratagem is a . . . *tu quoque*—you are doing it, too. To do justice to its kindly intent, one can call it instead conversion by definition . . . or christen it the bear's hug. (F 91)[28]

A friendlier critic, an eminent professor of theology, puts the matter wittily:

Kaufmann is one of the most "readable" of writers. Indeed, though, as a *genre*, his book belong to that class of writings which specialize in "debunking" and in slaying the sacred cows, the hand wielding the slaughtering knife moves so gracefully and so deftly that even the intended victim will be quite unable to stifle a last ecstatic cry of pleasure and admiration.[29]

Kaufmann can assume a nicer tone as well, merely emulating the lightly mocking cadences of the Enlightenment *conte philosophique*: this tone comes to the fore in a late chapter, when he has organized religion in his sights. How generally useful *as a sexual ethic*, he asks, with a droll savior faire, is the Golden Rule of Christianity: "Therefore all things whatsoever ye would that men should do to you, do ye even so to them"? He is Swiftian on the level of religious literacy at American universities in 1960, certainly no higher a half century later:

It is all right to suppose that the Buddha was . . . even some sort of Zen beatnik; it is natural never to have heard of Habakkuk; half the students at top colleges don't know in what language the New Testament was written, and some students "know" that Voltaire invented electricity, that Goethe is a style of architecture, and that Isaac was one of the prophets. They spell medieval "mid-evil" and, without irony, write "crucifiction"; but they do not criticize theologians. In fact, they aren't too sure what a theologian is. But if a man wears a round collar or has the title of Reverend, he is above criticism. What he says may be dull, but one does not question it. (F 255–56)

He can imitate the cadences of Oscar Wilde—almost: "Not all religions have the same aim: some are designed to save souls, some are not. . . . [But] not all religions that aim to save souls wish to save them from the same fate. Hinduism and Buddhism try to save souls from transmigration, Christianity from hell. In both cases it is impossible to estimate success or failure" (F 257). You can detect the signature aphoristic balance of his prose. He writes of the refined rituals of the French aristocracy before the revolution: "One can view this period through the eyes of Rousseau and deplore its artificiality. But one should not forget how a generation of aristocrats went to the guillotine with exquisite manners, noble poise, and a proud lack of fear. Their regard for ritual was emphatically not based on superstition, though they may have lacked any keen social conscience. Their lack of superstition distinguished them from most of the great Christians; their lack of a keen social conscience did not" (F 260). Kaufmann writes of Mormonism in a vein of vaudeville: "Mormons believe that couples joined in holy matrimony in a Mormon temple will enjoy each other's company in all eternity, while those married elsewhere are married for this life only. What strikes them as enviable would be more likely, in most cases, to be hell itself" (F 257). These stylistic variations suggest something of the grace of this book, along with its argumentative muscularity.

In a very serious later chapter "Morality," Kaufmann celebrates Plato, who, he declares, is unsurpassed in his philosophical power to educate: "At every turn he challenges the reader to consider new ideas, to examine striking arguments, to be surprised at unforeseen conclusions, and to reconsider" (F 290). Herewith, a model of intellectual honesty. There is more to add to Kaufmann's invocation of critical courage in dealing with historical-philosophical questions. Scholars whose task has been the obedient exegesis of past authorities will be struck by a writer contrarian enough to ask: "Does Heidegger ever entertain the possibility that Hölderlin or Sophocles, Heraclitus or Parmenides might be mistaken about anything?" (S 360). Kaufmann does not

hesitate—indeed it is the leading edge of his thought—to dare to criticize . . .
Plato, Hegel, Kierkegaard, Heidegger. . . .

What of the virtue love? Kaufmann gives "a splendid definition" with which
he is content: it comes from a tale retold by Martin Buber, in which a Hasidic
rabbi concludes: "I understood: that is love of men, to sense their wants and
bear their grief." This definition implicitly contains a thesis on justice as well.
Kaufmann develops the definition almost ad absurdum: In the matter of this
"love of men . . . , for this much we can aim in relation to all men with whom we
deal, all men toward whom we must adopt some attitude: members of our family,
colleagues, employees, employers, writers—even men like Hitler" (F 309).

I would like to point up a different source for this virtue love: Kaufmann's
love of beauty, including the beautiful comparison. His love of elegant relation extends, beyond figures of speech, to entire cultures: the arts of ancient
Egypt and ancient Israel—sublime, magnificent, connected at the root. There
are evidently differences—they might even outweigh the continuities (he is
honest!)—but the continuities are captivating:

> First, we find in Egypt, albeit restricted to a special class, a love of learning
> and respect for wisdom. Here the difference in similarity was expressed in
> a single imperative by Moses: "You shall be unto me a kingdom of priests."
> And again: "You shall be holy." Not one class but all. Every man is called
> upon to make something of himself. Perhaps this was the most revolution-
> ary idea of world history. . . .
>
> Secondly, we find in Egyptian architecture and sculpture an embodi-
> ment of the sublime that has never been surpassed. In parts of the Old
> Testament this sublimity has been transmuted into prose and poetry. . . .
> Perhaps nowhere else in the ancient world, and nowhere at all except under
> the influence of the Hebrew Bible, do we encounter such a fusion of austere
> simplicity and overwhelming power.
>
> There remains one similarity which . . . has attracted far more attention
> than any other: in the fourteenth century B.C., perhaps a hundred years
> before the Exodus, there was a monotheistic Pharaoh in the eighteenth
> dynasty in Egypt, Ikhnaton. (F 173–74)

Here Kaufmann examines the engaging idea—for him, it is no more than an
airy speculation—that Hebrew monotheism is a borrowing of the Egyptian.
There is evidence both to affirm and to oppose this view. The current authority
on this matter is Jan Assmann, who writes, in one of his many books on this
subject,

Was Akhenaten the Egyptian Moses? Was the Biblical image of Moses a mnemonic transformation of the forgotten pharaoh? Only "science fiction" can answer these questions by a simple "yes." But mnemohistory is able to show that the connection between Egyptian and Biblical monotheism . . . has a certain foundation in history; the identification of Moses with a dislocated memory of Akhenaten had already been made in antiquity.[30]

These remarks neither clearly oppose Kaufmann's insistence on the originality of the (pseudohistorical) Moses nor do they affirm it. But in Kaufmann the "mnemohistorical" sense of the connection between original aspects of the two cultures—the Egyptian and the Israelite—survives, even as it is heightened and elaborated in Freud's "novelistic" *Moses and Monotheism*.[31] Kaufmann's conclusion is important for our understanding of his attachment to a disestablished, stand-alone Judaism:

> Hebrew monotheism cannot be understood as a quantitative reduction of any traditional polytheism or as an exclusive declaration of loyalty to one of the established gods: all the established gods of the nations are set aside, and the whole lot of them is considered beneath comparison with God, who not only does not happen to be identified with the sun [as did Ikhnaton], but who is not at all an object in this world. No object in this world deserves worship: . . . not the Pharaoh nor any other human being; nor any animal. Only God who is utterly unlike anything in the world. Man alone, according to the First Book of Moses, is made in God's image and breathes his spirit. And that means every man and every woman, not just some king, emperor, or hero, or one family or people only . . . (F 175)

The same distinction emerges when one compares the older Code of Hammurabi (ca. 1754 BC) with the Law of Moses (ca. 1440 BC): "in the latter *the unique worth of man* as such is proclaimed and implicit—for the first time in human history" (emphasis added) (F 178). *The Faith of a Heretic* continually stresses the originality of this idea.

Our archaeological discoveries in Egypt leave the originality of the religion of Moses as stunning as it ever seemed. The experience of Egypt may have awakened the Hebrews to a haunting sense of the sublime, to dissatisfaction with the ephemeral, to respect for learning and to a lasting revulsion against any concern with the afterlife, against polytheism, and against idolatry and any form at all of sculpture. We must leave open the possibility that faith in the God of Abraham antedated the sojourn in Egypt. What the Bible claims, and what we have no good reason to doubt, is that the Hebrew religion was hammered out in response to the experience of Egypt not by way of accepting the religion of Egypt but rather as an enduring reply to it. (F 176)

Jewish universalism comes into special focus, for Kaufmann, when compared with a central tenet of Christianity at its beginning: its particularism, its exceptionalism, especially in death.[32] According to early doctrine, there will be Christians in everlasting glory and there will be the rest, whose eternal suffering will furnish Christian spectators a distinctive form of enjoyment. It is remarkable, Kaufmann more than once observes, how this promise of ultimate Christian bliss, based on the hell of others—found in St. Augustine and St. Thomas Aquinas, to name just two—has been repressed in every modern restatement of an original Christian teaching. There is no doubt of the centrality of hellfire as early as the Sermon on the Mount. "German theologians," writes Kaufmann, "prefer to discuss whether the fire (the 'flame,' repeated in Luke 16:24) is physical fire, when the serious question which one would expect . . . [them] to discuss is how they propose to reconcile eternal torment, no matter how 'spiritual,' with divine perfection" (F 97).[33] In a similar vein, "Those who believe in God because their experience of life and the facts of nature prove his existence must have led sheltered lives and closed their hearts to the voice of their brothers' blood" (F 168).

If Christian doctrine knows suffering as the hellish suffering of the infidel, Judaism well knows the earthly suffering of the faithful. Kaufmann dwells on the inevitable fact of human suffering throughout this book and, as a philosopher of Judaism, frames his meditation with the Jewish view. There is no more poignant account of sorrow in literature than that of Isaiah 53:

> He is despised and rejected by men; a man of sorrows, and acquainted with grief. . . . Surely he has borne our griefs and carried our sorrows. . . . He was wounded for our transgressions, he was bruised for our iniquities. . . . The Lord has laid on him the iniquity of us all. (F 165–66)

The passage has been interpreted differently by Christians and Jews. Christians consider these words an anticipation of the sufferings of Jesus; Jews see in this man of sorrows a personification of their own people. That this suffering comes from "the Lord" represents an attempt to give this suffering meaning and purpose: it is the normal way of making it bearable, a stay against the metaphysical anxiety that compounds the suffering. But "Jewish piety has been a ceaseless cry in the night, rarely unaware of 'all the oppressions that are practiced under the sun,' a faith in spite of, not a heathenish, complacent faith because" (F 169).

Thinking hard, as a universalist *and* as an existentialist—no easy act—Kaufmann addresses this threat of metaphysical anxiety:

> It does not follow that the meaning must be given from above; . . . that nothing is worthwhile if the world is not governed by a purpose. On the contrary, the lack of any cosmic purpose may be experienced as liberating, as if a great weight had been lifted from us. Life ceases to be so oppressive: we are free to give our own lives meaning and purpose, free to redeem our suffering by making something of it. (F 166)

What is called for, given "the weirdness of the world," is the *will* to make something of it.

It bears repeating: Kaufmann's attachment to a Judaism without theology—and without God—is centered on its soi-disant universality, its empowering of every single human being, free to earn his own justification on earth: "You shall have one law for the stranger and for the native" (F 316). This principle, he will insist, is overturned by Pauline Christianity. "When Paul turned his back on the old notion of forgiveness for the repentant sinner and embraced the doctrine of predestination, he gave up the idea of the equality and fraternity of all men" (F 227). This leads Kaufmann to make what I take to be the single most interesting intellectual-historical, *heretical* statement in his book:

> I am rejecting two clichés: that of the Judaeo-Christian tradition as well as the claim that Western civilization is a synthesis of Greek and Christian elements. Against the former, I stress the discontinuity between Jesus and the pre-exilic prophets: one might as well speak of the Judaeo-Islamic tradition or of the Greco-Christian tradition. Against the latter, I point to the fact that Christianity itself was a child of Greek and Hebrew parents; that the Gospels are a product of Jewish Hellenism; and that Paul, though he claimed to have sat at the feet of Gamaliel, was in important respects closer to Plato and to Gnosticism than to Micah or Jonah. (F 227)

For all Kaufmann's intensity, what effect can his work have on "us" in "the West," in an age like ours with so few beliefs, so few commitments, so little faith? In his *Nietzsche*, Kaufmann points up a key passage from the end of the first part of *Zarathustra*, which Nietzsche quoted again in the preface to

Ecce Homo: "[All] faith amounts to so little." Thomas Mann, too, wrote, in 1952, "I have not much faith—or even faith in faith."[34] But, as Kaufmann also wrote in his *Nietzsche*, "I love Nietzsche's books but am no Nietzschean" (N vii); ergo, faith has a role to play in his philosophy. It is his faith in "the Socratic heritage":

> The philosopher . . . must always stand opposed to his time and may never conform; it is his calling to be a fearless critic and diagnostician—as Socrates was. And Nietzsche feels that he is only keeping the faith with this Socratic heritage when he calls attention to the dangers of the modern idealization of equality, and he challenges us to have the courage to be different and independent. (N 405)

He concludes by asking a specific form of the question we have asked above: "In the modern world, however, is *that* [faith] still possible?" (N 405).

A closer look at Kaufmann's version of this heritage reveals its relation—a necessary relation—to the idea of heresy. He sees this heritage as the history of authentic philosophical thought, and that is as a series of heresies, a series of overturnings of conventional beliefs. Authenticity in thought is a matter of keeping faith with this heritage. "In all ages," he writes,

> philosophy contains two different tendencies: one is heretical, iconoclastic, critical; the other is apologetic and conservative. [Another instance of his Manichean slide?] The first has been illustrated from Xenophanes and Heraclitus; the second has been summed up beautifully by a nineteenth-century British philosopher, F. H. Bradley, when he said that "metaphysics is the finding of bad reasons for what we believe on instinct." (F 16–17)

These pages contain a gripping summary of such tendencies in action, as in the pre-Socratic philosopher Anaxagoras, who was tried for heresy for maintaining "that the sun and the moon were made of earth and stone instead of being gods." Recall Socrates, perishing for heresy, and Aristotle as well, who at the end of his life had to flee Athens, saying "that he left 'lest the Athenians should sin twice against philosophy.'"

> Even St. Thomas Aquinas ventured a few propositions which the Bishop of Paris and the Archbishop of Canterbury, who was a Dominican like Aquinas himself, censured in 1277; but when Thomas was sainted, the censures were withdrawn as far as they affected him. . . . Spinoza was quite literally a heretic and expelled by the synagogue of Amsterdam. He expressly

denied the authority of Scripture in matters of truth; he rejected the God of Judaism and Christianity, though he used the term "God" for what he believed in; and he repudiated the belief that the world is governed by a purpose. Berkeley is remembered as a great philosopher not because he was a bishop and believed in God but because he argued most ingeniously that the belief in matter in untenable and that there is no material substance. Hume, another generation later, criticized the notion of spiritual substance, too, and questioned many other commonplaces, including the axiom that every event has a cause. Kant, yet a little later, smashed the foundations not only of so-called rational cosmology and rational psychology but also of natural theology. He showed that all proofs of God's existence are fallacious, etc. (F 16–18)

More than once while writing on Kaufmann, I've been energized—as I hope you too, reader—to discover, along with a sense of the bold untimeliness of his questioning, his bright anticipations of what is thought and written today. We have heard of Paul de Man's alleged confession that what interested him most deeply was "religious questions," an interest that is generally rampant and survives even among advanced academic literary scholars of different schools. In the introduction, I noted Rebecca Goldstein's account of progress in philosophy as "often a matter of discovering presumptions that slip unexamined into reasoning" and hence overturning accustomed certainties. With little difficulty, her words can be applied to Kaufmann's view of the history of philosophy as a sequence of defiant objections—read: heresies. There will be more of what Avital Ronell calls such "Dasein-rhymes," that is, existential—here, philosophical—coincidences between Kaufmann's thoughts and those of contemporary thinkers. Kaufmann attacks the complacency of American Christians who today enlarge their belief in the authority of Christian teachings by the belief that America was founded on the authority of the Christian Church. Kaufmann attacked this historical falsehood in 1960. Fifty years later, this argument continues to attract belief and spark scholarly rebuttals,[35] including a fierce journalistic refusal of this claim.[36] But for all his contemporary relevance, it is, in the long run, Kaufmann's defense of *faith* that is his most decisive contribution, one that will strike even sympathetic readers, I believe—certainly at first—as hard to accept. "In the modern world, however, is faith [in *any* heritage] still possible?" (N 405). In a recent interview, the psycholinguist Steven Pinker defended his resistance to a proposed compulsory course at Harvard titled "Faith and Reason," saying, "I didn't like the euphemism 'faith.' Nor did I like the juxtaposition of 'faith' and 'reason,' as if they were just two alternative ways of knowing."[37]

Many other readers, I think, will be skeptical of Kaufmann and inclined to reply: Well, I will scratch at my consciousness to see in what I have faith (and I intend to conclude that I have faith only in the mechanisms that have brought me to see and know what I see and know). I have faith in the results, what I know to be true, the facts of the case—a conclusion that then makes the qualifier "faith" unremarkable. So . . . what are the propositions *without* anchoring facts that rely on the intellectual mechanisms in which I have faith? Like the psychiatrist D. W. Winnicott's "good enough" mother, one might assume they are "good enough" mechanisms—they function harmlessly, if not indeed usefully, in one's psychic economy: they have not threatened one's sanity so far, perhaps they are crucial to one's sanity. But inspecting these cognitive and intuitive mechanisms is not a task I am eager to undertake in my scarce leisure—it seems meddlesome, de trop. Can't they be left unsaid?

No, they cannot—under the radical ban of *The Faith of a Heretic*, a radicalism, to quote Kaufmann from a later essay, that

> facilitates progress by pushing old errors to the extremes of absurdity, making plain what is wrong with ideas that had seemed quite tolerable as long as they were taken none too seriously. Traditional morality had become reasonably comfortable by means of endless compromises, and it had come to be taken less and less seriously.[38]

This thought cuts to the quick.

Of course, if I accept this task of moral self-scrutiny, and aim for results, the task may seem less difficult if I am given some leading lines of inquiry by another thinker—a stranger. It is the way that teachers are happy at the new ideas they think they are producing to meet the (imagined) expectations of an audience of students—to whom they are strangers. Or the way that the casually hostile remark of an even well-meaning colleague or counselor or, indeed, any authority—in short, *anyone* who will utter such a remark—will set off a flight of searching, self-justificatory thought.[39] On this matter, Kaufmann quotes Franz Rosenzweig, the author of the arcane religious text *The Star of Redemption*, who wrote a farewell letter to bookish speculation: "The search for knowledge no longer seems to me an end in itself. . . . It is here that my heresy against the unwritten law of the university originates. Not every question seems to me worth asking. . . . Now I only inquire when I find myself *inquired of*" (F 78).[40]

Kaufmann objects:

> To arrive at that conclusion, one requires an additional presupposition: that no problems at all are left that bother us ourselves or, to approximate Rosenzweig's formulation, that no question whatsoever seems to me worth asking as long as I am left to myself. Having finished his book, Rosenzweig appears to have reached a state of intellectual satiety—a state most other people reach without writing a book first. (F 78)

So, readers taking Kaufmann's admonition to heart will have to be struck by the questions coming from *his* book; they require commitment, belief in their possible efficacy. "This book invites the reader to commit himself to the quest for honesty" (F 89). Still, how does one suppress the feeling that the questions Kaufmann asks are awkward or unattractive, such as: What is your "God"? What, specifically, is holy to you? (F 83).[41] Are you governed by a single, over-riding concern or many different concerns? How good is your theology—or do you prefer to contemplate a religion without one? (Do you mean to say you are living a life in which you never contemplate any religion thoughtfully?)[42]

Or one might consider his questions as oversubtle, and unaccustomed, as, for example, one implicitly asked: How theological is your literary criticism?[43] Though a recent study of Kafka's "atheology" by the scholar Paul North makes Kaufmann's question more immediate: by overturning every supposition on which traditional theologies have been built, Kafka, according to North, at the same time demolishes the leading concepts of secular modernity and hence the principles of literary criticism, founded as they are on (the original con-fusions of!) theology.[44]

And so, granted—many of Kaufmann's questions are unsuited to the mood of our time. But on second thought one might very well be inclined to ask *why* such questions are untimely. On what grounds?

Kaufmann raises question after question that one has not asked oneself, questions that change you by making you realize how few questions you (may) have asked yourself. "*Can* morality be based on religion?" "Is an absolute morality possible"? (F 280). (A lead-in: to the first question, Kant answered: "It cannot be"; to the second, consider Justice Holmes's alleged remark: "I prefer champagne to ditch water, but I see no reason for believing that the cosmos does" [F 305]). Here is the main force of Kaufmann's book: it will not allow you to dismiss the questions it asks on the grounds that they are questions no longer relevant to the times or . . . the *Times*—"what Nietzsche . . . called 'the wretched ephemeral babble of politics' and the papers" (F 80). The sort of relevance they have does not turn on the journalistic moment. As individual questions and as insistent questioning, they will put you out of joint with your time. Kaufmann reflects on fashion through the careers of his educators:

> At all times men are subject to insidious pressures to accept the prejudices of their age and to rationalize them, whether theologically or scientifically. Nietzsche and Freud found that the best, if not the only, way to resist this danger is not to humor the hypersensitive ears of one's contemporaries by choosing comfortable words but to emphasize precisely that which is not fashionable, not heard gladly, that which gives offense. . . . [This will entail] obstinacy, hardness, and the willingness to pit one's own integrity against the judgment of the world. (F 343–45)

The prospect is bottomless—and anxious-making—since it is not only this or that prejudice that demands question and answer: what comes into view is the manner in which you have lived your whole life. Have you lived attentively? What have you done with the gift of your life? With imputed permission from Kaufmann, here is a comparable adjuration from Heidegger, who, in his *Fundamental Concepts of Metaphysics*, asks: "What is world, finitude, individuation?," concepts not finally remote from Kaufmann's questions: "Each of these questions inquires into the whole. It is not sufficient for us to know such questions. What is decisive is whether we really ask such questions, whether we have the strength to sustain them right through our whole existence."[45]

To respond well to Kaufmann, we may need to read the history of philosophy (and Sophocles and Shakespeare and Goethe and Nietzsche and . . .) to get very far with these questions. Their force arises again and again from the philosopher's faith that Kaufmann finds, again . . . in Nietzsche—and *his* sources: "The philosopher," as we have heard, "must always stand opposed to his time and may never conform; it is his calling to be a fearless critic and diagnostician—as Socrates was" (N 405). This charge comes under the heading of "Nietzsche's Socratic protestantism and chronic *heresy*" (emphasis added) (N 417).

In chapter 1, I discussed an essay by the German sociologist Niklas Luhmann on the creation of "individuality" in modern society, referring its three modes to Kaufmann's life: one, the copying of role models; two, a sort of cleavage of the self—self-doubling—when the pressure of experience becomes too great; and, finally, three, the experience of a career, in which the self, while constantly changing, remains compatible with "yesterday's." I proposed to put the main motives of Kaufmann's self-stylization under these headings. In a relevant case, writing about Arthur Koestler, the scholar Neal Ascherson identified "a generation of Central European intellectuals, especially those of Jewish origins," in whom one "will recognize some of the traits in Koestler's character":

> The roots of his recurrent miseries and explosions are less interesting than the roots of his furious creative energy. He shared with that generation a profound, Hegelian sense of dialectic process. "Being" was also "becoming," or it was nothing. Every context, every person was a seed with a destiny that must be realized.[46]

Whatever the merits of its metaphor, this account of a life, with which Kaufmann, I believe, would have vigorously agreed, fleshes out Luhmann's analysis.

The encomium composed by members of the Princeton Philosophy Department on Kaufmann's death supports this surmise: "He lived his life with a truly dazzling expenditure of energy, giving tirelessly of himself. The life he wanted, he said, was one 'of love and intensity, suffering and creation.' That is exactly the kind of life he had." The inner quote comes from a late, powerful chapter in *The Faith of a Heretic* headed "Death." The quotation deserves to be given in full:

> If one lives intensely, the time comes when sleep seems bliss. If one loves intensely, the time comes when death seems bliss.
>
> Those who loved with all their heart and mind and might have always thought of death, and those who knew the endless nights of harrowing concern for others have longed for it.
>
> The life I want is a life I could not endure in eternity. It is a life of love and intensity, suffering and creation that makes life worthwhile and death welcome. There is no other life I should prefer. Neither should I like not to die. (F 374–75)

I should like to quote in full his entire death fugue: it is a magnificent coda, undoubtedly sublime (but it is also a very controversial piece, which I—and others—will discuss in a short essay at the close of this chapter titled "The Death Work Ethic"). Kaufmann's thanatology challenges Heidegger and Camus, the contemporary authorities for whom death is the crown of anxiety. He denies the alleged omnipresence of anxiety in human experience. Life need not end in fear and defeat: that is the gist of his argument. His credo reads: "To try to fashion something from suffering, to relish our triumphs, and to endure defeats without resentment: all that is compatible with the faith of a heretic" (F 169).

This faith is also compatible with that of the Hebrew prophets, who figure throughout this book, controversially, as exemplary heretics—and educators. What fills them with the fire to teach and rectify is the failure of "the chosen people" to be equal to their patrimony:

> In the Old Testament itself, the idea of the chosen people is not offered by way of justifying lower moral standards, as if it were claimed that, being chosen, one need not live up to standards intended only for the mass of men. On the contrary, the conception of the chosen people is inseparably linked with the twin ideas of a task and of an especially demanding law. (F 193)

Amos, as "the first prophet to compose poetic speeches that were committed to writing," thunders: "Behold, the eyes of the Lord God are upon the sinful kingdom, and I will destroy it from the surface of the ground; except that I will not utterly destroy the house of Jacob, says the Lord" (9:7–8). What Kaufmann takes from this commination is, I believe, a sense of himself as a survivor—on the condition that he devote himself to a "task and an especially demanding law" that Kaufmann will modify. "Not [destroy the kingdom] utterly," he repeats,

> for, as Isaiah puts it a little later when he names his son Shear-jashub: a remnant shall return that is the meaning of the name. What matters is not the glory of the people: most of them, almost generation after generation, shall be destroyed. What matters is the task: maintaining and spreading what has been revealed to them, namely, the belief in God and the morality that goes with it. And that is why a remnant shall return, lest the flame be extinguished entirely. (F 193–94)

Kaufmann does not believe in this god or any god, but he does avow "the morality that goes with it." As he repeats these lines from Amos, I believe he addresses himself as this remnant, both in the wider sense as a Jew and in the special sense of one who survived the Shoah.

> The dedications of at least some of my books, including this one, point to deep concerns, but hardly to "gods" or to any one "ultimate" concern. Some sense of responsibility to the six million Jews killed in my lifetime, especially to some whom I loved and who loved me, and to millions of others, Jew and Gentile, killed in our time and in past centuries, is certainly among my deepest feelings. (F 83)

What he then writes does not make it easy for us to understand him completely.

> Still, that [feeling of responsibility] is hardly my ultimate concern. Neither is this book, though I am deeply involved in that. Nor is it at all plausible to say that these are symbols for something more ultimate. (F 83–84)

He has left it to his readers to intuit his ultimate concern. *The Faith of a Heretic* is not, as he has told us, a personal confession. Perhaps this journey through *all* his work will bring us closer to the heart of his mystery. It is *not* the pursuit of personal happiness.

> Those of us who feel that happiness, however important, is not the ultimate consideration and that it would be an impermissible betrayal to sell our birth-right for a mess of bliss are probably haunted by the challenge of the Hebrew Bible. Here a voice was raised that has aroused a large portion of mankind, albeit a distinct minority, from their pre-Israelitic slumber. (F 206)

This conviction inspires Kaufmann to plant his tabernacle far from the New Testament, in which "each man's overruling concern with his eternal happiness—his salvation—is central and defines the whole milieu" (F 207).

And so, what is his ultimate concern? It is after all a concept he asks us to reflect on. Consider Jacques Derrida's remark, even in an autobiography: "No one will ever know from what secret I am writing, and the fact that I say so changes nothing."[47] We have every reason to want to find it, and we will come closer to it—to its context—I think, as we approach Kaufmann's conclusion:

> The prophets who depreciated and denounced ritual pinned their hopes on the remnant, not on large masses of men. The heretic who is a non-conformist on his own may similarly pin what hopes he has on a new conception of the remnant as consisting of individuals scattered over the continents and centuries, different from each other in national and religious background but related to each other in their quest, heretics all of them, each in his own way. They kindle flames across oceans, give comfort and issue a challenge, and raise the hope that in time to come there will be others like them, though never more than a remnant. (F 266–67)

In the books that Kaufmann was still to write, there will be more contexts to the personal mystery of an ultimate concern. And what is altogether intriguing is that *this* book dwells in apparent innocence, at its close, on the two most important subjects with which Kaufmann will occupy himself in coming years. His commentary on the anguish of colliding loyalties envisages—implicitly—the years of his most concentrated writing on Hegel. *Hegel: Reinterpretation, Texts, and Commentary* will appear four years later in 1965 and his edited anthology *Hegel's Political Philosophy* in 1970.[48] At the close of *The Faith of a Heretic* Kaufmann writes that this "theme of 'collisions'—'great collisions,' following Hegel, 'between the old, recognized duties, laws, and rights and, on the other hand, possibilities that stand opposed to this system, violate it, even destroy its basis' and yet 'also appear good' [is a theme] long familiar to tragic poets" (F 328). This aperçu will bear fruit in his *Tragedy and Philosophy* of 1968, though, before this book ends, its outline takes shape before our eyes:

> I should say that tragedy requires that at the very least two, if not three, conditions are satisfied. First, the hero must be a great human being. . . . Second, he (or she) must fail, and still be great and admirable in failure usually, more so than ever before. Third, and this may be more doubtful, the failure must be inevitable because the hero is in a situation in which he cannot possibly satisfy all legitimate claims and is therefore bound to incur some great guilt, whatever he does. (F 346–47)

I want to persist in this quest for Kaufmann's ultimate concern—and I hope you will too, reader. Then we will follow him as he makes his critical way through the thickets of historical philosophy and religion, bent on constituting by example the human being of humility, ambition, love, honesty, and courage.

The Death Work Ethic

> Their ethos might be summed up briefly: you must die anyway, and the only choice we have is whether we try to stretch out our lives a little longer and forgo glory, or whether we show great courage and are honest in death and remembered in song.[49]

Kaufmann's meditations on death run throughout his entire work and constitute a credo we might call heroic humanism. They are developed in *The Faith of a Heretic* and again in the essay collection, *Existentialism, Religion, and Death* of 1976, where they employ a time-honored "Orcus motif."[50] The term derives from a poem of Schiller's titled "Nänie"—a German word for the Latin *nenia*, "a funeral song." The closing lines of Schiller's elegy read:

Behold! The gods weep, all the goddesses weep,
That the beautiful perishes, that the most perfect passes away.
But a lament on the lips of loved ones is glorious,
For the ignoble goes down to Orcus in silence.[51]

The poem speaks of the death that awaits us all—beautiful or not, perfect or not—and a consolation: to have loved, to have been loved by others, who know you, who are able to celebrate you, because you have given them reasons to celebrate. It is important that the acknowledgment be articulate—ideally—a song of lament, a work of art. Brahms celebrated his deceased friend the painter Anselm Feuerbach by setting this very poem "Nänie" to choral music.

Schiller also wrote a distich on the Orcus theme titled "Immortality":

You are frightened of death? You wish you could live forever?
Make your life whole! When death takes you that will remain. (ER 232)[52]

Now "Make your life whole" is Kaufmann's translation of Schiller's phrase "Leb' im Ganzen." Kaufmann's phrase exhorts the individual to a perfection of the life as a stay against a meaningless death. This translation redounds to his Nietzschean ideal of a life fashioned as a work of art. But then the question arises: in what sense does the whole life survive when a life felt to be fragmented or incomplete—and what life can be said to be complete?—dies away? A new argument would have to be introduced, in which the life said to be whole is celebrated precisely on the grounds of its admirable wholeness. But by whom? And in what way, guaranteeing immortality?

I find this argument, which rests on a questionable translation of "Leb' im Ganzen!" to be incoherent, and I therefore prefer the translation "Live in the Whole" by Will and Ariel Durant, meaning: live a life oriented toward—let us call it—the general will; make your concerns in every case wider than your individual interests; live in accord with the best thoughts and actions of your time, the greater human universe, for *that* continues.[53] This reading is strengthened by reference to a distich of Goethe, who, together with Schiller, published a series of short poems titled *Xenien*, which includes "Immortality," in the journal *Musenalmanach*, which Schiller edited. Goethe's poem reads, in the Durants' translation:

Always strive for the whole, and if you yourself cannot become a whole, tie yourself to some whole as a serving part.[54]

The whole means a good deal more than the individual who has achieved completeness.

Kaufmann views death as justified by this sort of cultural immortality, for which he finds support in Hölderlin's beautiful lament:

To the Parcae
A single summer grant me, great powers, and
   a single autumn for fully ripened song
      that, sated with the sweetness of my
         playing, my heart may more willingly die.
The soul that, living, did not attain its divine
   right cannot repose in the nether world.
      But once what I am bent on, what is
         holy, my poetry, is accomplished:
Be welcome then, stillness of the shadows' world!
   I shall be satisfied though my lyre will not
      accompany me down there. Once I
         lived like the gods, and more is not needed.[55]

With this refrain, we approach what the scholar David Pickus calls Kaufmann's "death work ethic," which conjures a life of achievement so fulfilling that death would be a source of satisfaction.[56] Pickus's commentary is provocative and prompts a discussion—in this instance—in several voices. In addition to Goethe, Schiller, Hölderlin, and Kaufmann, it includes the humanist Corliss Lamont, Kaufmann's dedicated reader Pickus, and the Nietzsche scholar Henry Staten. In this matter of a good death, the idea of *work*—or of a work—is central: it is a key and also a contentious term. Pickus sums up the dilemma in Kaufmann's thanatology as follows: "On the one hand, it is primarily an argument—or exhortation—to live fully. On the other, I feel an undercurrent of the more famous work ethic, i.e., let me show that I'm *deserving* (and that others are not)."[57]

Commenting on these two currents, Staten emphasizes their disparity. "Granted," he writes,

the idea that it is good to "live intensely and fully" is an idea to which practically everyone subscribes. No one would argue that it is better to live in a desultory and incomplete fashion. But what is its connection with a work ethic, unless you supplement it with some kind of argument that the only way to live fully is by way of work? Then, what does living fully have to do with deserving, with being rewarded? It seems odd to think that in order to live fully you have to *deserve* to live fully; and, then again, what does a work ethic have to do with desert (although I know how these two can be connected, as they were in the Protestant ethic, but would one really want to argue that Kaufmann follows the Protestant ethic in this)?

Pickus agrees, to an extent, noting "Not everyone would treat 'To the Parcae' as a practice manual."[58] As for Kaufmann's posited *Protestant work ethic*, Pickus continues, it is beside the point. To treat the matter literally, Kaufmann, though originally brought up as a Lutheran, was only nominally Protestant, and only during his childhood. At twelve, as we know, he converted, only to discover that he had converted into what he had been in the first place: the son of a baptized Jew. The hard work he did thereafter was not for a heavenly reward—that is, the Protestant factor falls away—but for the reward of recognition, an affair both of good conscience and fame, producing confidence in one's skill, the expectation of an audience, and then—ideally—a whirl of creative activity.

There is no overlap, Pickus concludes, between the death work ethic and the Protestant work ethic: "They are not the same thing. The original adherents longed for salvation; their secularized descendants did not think of death while alive and active. However, I can admit an overlap in the matter of compulsion. No opting out for the family firm for the would-be poet."[59]

Pickus and Staten are certainly not the first to object to Kaufmann's thanatology. In an acerb piece titled "Mistaken Attitudes toward Death," the humanist Lamont stares in disbelief at Kaufmann's views now stated more fully:

If one lives intensely, the time comes when sleep means bliss. If one loves intensely, the time comes when death seems bliss. . . . The life I want is a life I could not endure in eternity. It is a life of love and intensity, suffering and creation, that makes life worthwhile and death welcome. There is no other life I should prefer. Neither should I like not to die. . . . For most of us death does not come soon enough. Lives are spoiled and made rotten by the sense that death is distant and irrelevant. One lives better when one expects to die, say, at forty, when one says to oneself long before one is twenty: whatever I may be able to accomplish, I should be able to do by then; and what I have not done by then, I am not likely to do ever. One cannot count on living until one is forty—or thirty—but it makes for a better life if one has a rendezvous with death. Not only love can be deepened and made more intense and impassioned by the expectation of impending death; all of life is enriched by it. (F 374–75)

"In some forty years of reading in the religious and philosophic literature concerning death," observes Lamont,

> I have rarely found a statement that seems so perverse as the one just cited. . . . Just why should the rapture of love make us "welcome" the nothingness of death? Why not the continued rapture of love? . . . Death is about the last thing to occupy the thoughts of a man and woman passionately in love; and the more intense their feelings, the more unlikely it is that they regard the complete extinction of themselves and their love as some sort of "bliss."

> As for Kaufmann's assertions, "For most of us death does not come soon enough" and "One lives better when one expects to die, say, at forty," I am frankly dumbfounded. For these remarks imply that it is preferable to die in the very prime of life. . . . Evidently, Kaufmann expects the generality of mankind to be youthful geniuses and accomplish all their best work by the time they are forty. Yet the briefest glance at the history of highest literary, artistic, and cultural achievement shows what an enormous proportion of it has resulted from the energies of persons well beyond that age.

> "Whatever I may be able to accomplish," avers Kaufmann, "I should be able to do by then" [by forty]. Not a word about enjoyment or pleasure. . . . Kaufmann adds: "What I have not done then [by forty], I am not likely to do ever."

> The plain facts do not bear out this judgment. . . . The truly creative individual, no matter what his age, rarely feels that his work is done; new tasks, new vistas keep opening up for him. . . .

> Finally, I take issue with Kaufmann's assertion that "all life is enriched" by "the expectation of impending death." The joys and values of human living are valid and worthwhile in and of themselves; they stand on their own feet and need no ratification, either by some supernatural god or through comparison with the realm of death. The great consummatory experiences, the moments and moods of exaltation that come from knowing beauty or love, do not depend in the slightest on any sense of imminent death. Psychologically, an individual who is constantly aware of impending death is usually saddened by the thought in a way that hardly enriches his day-to-day existence. When Kaufmann declares that "it makes for a better life if one has a rendezvous with death," he is suggesting an exaggerated consciousness of death that is only too reminiscent of the Christian viewpoint

All in all, then, Kaufmann's attitude toward death, in the passages I have cited, appears to me fantastically out of joint. Even if in these comments he intended merely to strike a poetic pose, it does not come off and remains essentially a strained and lugubrious meditation on man's fate.[60]

Lamont's essay speaks of, but does not doubt, the connection between a life full of intense emotion and, on the other hand, a life full of "accomplishment," "achievement," and "work"; but these things are hardly the same. They pose the very problem that continues to concern us. Lamont's remarks hold the two currents together, in loose suspension. He does not point up their disparity but does deepen the question of Kaufmann's motive, especially at the close, when Lamont considers "poetry" the source of Kaufmann's celebration of an early death. This is a valuable clue.

It is not every poetry to which Kaufmann appeals: it is a certain romanticism, including, centrally, the figures of Schiller and Hölderlin (but *not* Goethe). Schiller died at forty-six. In the florid words of a bygone literary historian,

> Nothing is commoner among Germans . . . than to ascribe to Goethe a genius far transcending Schiller's. The comparison is made between the whole body of Goethe's literary work, extending over upward of eighty years of exceptionally healthy activity, and the product of poor Schiller's mutilated existence stretching to scarcely more than one-half that term. . . . But had Goethe died at the same age as Schiller, he would have had a poorer result to show than Schiller has. . . . There is no doubt that Schiller, when he died at forty-six, had reached a loftier height of dramatic art than Goethe had at the same age. . . . Schiller had left behind him a long roll of immortal dramas, some of them lit up with the radiance of a fine poetry, and many of which will keep the stage as long as the stage exists.[61]

Kaufmann is thinking of Hölderlin's wretched decline, along with that of the poet Novalis, who died of tuberculosis at twenty-eight, and the dramatist Kleist, who died of a self-inflicted pistol shot at thirty-four. One might include, too, the fictional character Werther in Goethe's *The Sufferings of Young Werther*. He loves and despairs with extravagant intensity and commits suicide young. Would Kaufmann consider his death justified? Goethe does not. In consonance with Kaufmann's idea, he presents Werther's suicide as abetted—or at any rate never obstructed—by his *failure* to produce a work. In a subsequent poem, Goethe has the ghost of Werther declare: "Be a man, and do not follow me!" Kaufmann, who has been "educated" by Goethe, wants to keep intensity of experience together with intellectual or artistic achievement: "The life I want is a life . . . of love and intensity, suffering and *creation*, that makes life worthwhile and death welcome" (emphasis added) (F 375). But what is the philosophical relation of these things?

Lamont, as we've noted, suggests that it is *poetry* that inspires Kaufmann's death work ethic, one that puts the peak years at forty, whence death may follow. It is likely to be true that one of Kaufmann's sources is the death of poets. (Recall, too, that at this point Kaufmann is himself a forty-year-old poet!) In Kaufmann's *Tragedy and Philosophy* we learn that Aeschylus's "birth in 525 may have been inferred from his victory in [the annual tragedy contests] in 484," for "the Greeks dated their writers by the year in which they 'flourished,' which convention had fixed *at the age of forty*" (emphasis added).[62] In addition to the roughly four decades in which most German romantic poets accomplished their best work, there is the chronology of Nietzsche's achievements. In *Ecce Homo*, he famously celebrates the "good things," altogether "immortal," of the preceding year on "burying" his *forty-fourth* year (his mental death exceeds this climacteric by several months: he was found unconscious on the cobblestones of the Piazza Carlo Alberto in Turin, on January 3 of the following year). But the deep current of Kaufmann's thanatology has other tributaries.

From Kaufmann's general reticence about the Holocaust—aside from the dedications of two of his books—a reader could be startled to realize that Kaufmann was death-besotted. For him or her, that awareness should not come as a surprise. "It would have been quite unusual," Kaufmann is quoted as saying, "for somebody who lived, as I did, through the Second World War not to have been preoccupied with death."[63] He may never have been free for long from thoughts of the fate of his family. Of three of his uncles, all of whom served in the First World War, one was killed in battle and the other two murdered by the Nazis: they are commemorated at the outset of *The Faith of a Heretic*. The dedication to the earlier volume *From Shakespeare to Existentialism* reads: "To the Millions Murdered in the Name of False Beliefs by Men Who Proscribed Critical Reason," though there is a dryness and philosophical reserve in this formulation. And yet, as Pickus notes, "I don't think that Kaufmann spent a day of his life without thinking: 'They are dead, and I am not. What right have I?'"

Among his educators, Nietzsche stands out, along with Socrates and Freud, for his exhortation to "live dangerously" (*kühn leben*), a slogan coded in Thomas Mann's novel *Doktor Faustus* in the name of the audacious creator Adrian Leverkühn, a Nietzsche simulacrum. Here this dangerous life is clearly a life of "geniative" creation as well.[64] We also have Nietzsche's invitation to die boldly: consider these apothegms from *The Twilight of the Idols*, to which Kaufmann alludes:

> To die proudly when it is no longer possible to live proudly. Death freely chosen, death at the right time, brightly and cheerfully accomplished amid children and witnesses: then a real farewell is still possible, as the one who is taking leave is still there; also a real estimate of what one has achieved and what one has wished, drawing the sum of one's life—all in opposition to the wretched and revolting comedy that Christianity has made of the hour of death. One should never forget that Christianity has exploited the weakness of the dying for a rape of the conscience; and the manner of death itself, for value judgments about man and the past.
>
> Here it is important to defy all the cowardices of prejudice and to establish, above all, the real, that is, the physiological, appreciation of so-called natural death—which is in the end also "unnatural," a kind of suicide. One never perishes through anybody but oneself. But usually it is death under the most contemptible conditions, an unfree death, death not at the right time, a coward's death. From love of life, one should desire a different death: free, conscious, without accident, without ambush. (ER 206)

Kaufmann's early preoccupation with existentialist writers—Heidegger, Sartre, Camus—requires him to think about death, especially contumaciously vis-à-vis Heidegger, a familiar antiself. "A common fault of Heidegger, Sartre, and Camus is that they overgeneralize instead of taking into account different attitudes toward death" (F 371). Kaufmann's active repudiation of Christianity leads him to say, "Christianity became the great teacher of fear of death, and dread of purgatory and damnation became fused with a hope for a few more years in *this* world" (F 373–74). This is a freewheeling commentary on the passage from Nietzsche quoted above, which excoriates a Christian death as inspiring the dying man with violent fears of Hell and mythic hopes of salvation. I find this elaboration of Nietzsche one of the more implausible features of Kaufmann's thanatology.

To what extent, after all, is Kaufmann's a death *work* ethic? He writes, "If I ask myself who in history I might like to have been, I find that all the men I most admire [presumably his 'educators'—Goethe, Nietzsche, Freud] were by most standards deeply unhappy. They knew despair. But their lives were worthwhile—I only wish mine equaled theirs in this respect—and I have no doubt they were glad to die" (F 375). The men he admires are inexhaustible makers, workers, creators. I would stress, however, that Goethe, for one, was certainly not glad to die.

One must suspend further disbelief to enjoy Kaufmann's conclusion: "Is it possible that the fear of death and the prohibition of suicide have been as deliberately imposed on men as laws against incest—*not owing to any innate horror, but because dying, like incest, is so easy?* (emphasis added) (F 377). Pickus comments: "There is no reason to agree that the strength of the prohibition against suicide is owed to the fact that it is so easy to do. Kaufmann may have been influenced by the 'peaceful' view of death presented in Rilke's poem 'Orpheus. Eurydice. Hermes.'"[65]

Kaufmann concludes his essay "Existentialism and Death" with the declaration that there is nothing useful in existentialism for this issue: "we . . . must go it alone" (ER 218). I doubt he is thinking of "we" at this moment. I believe he means, "I, Walter Kaufmann, must go it alone; and, reader, observe that this is what is being done before your eyes." An unfriendly reviewer, whom we will encounter in chapter 11, described Kaufmann as looking "vaguely like a maverick"—a plausible complaint at such a moment.[66]

Pickus continues to question the claim to justification by work. He quotes Kaufmann:

> When I die, I do not want them to say: Think of all he still might have done. There is cowardice [viz., Nietzsche, above] in wanting to have that said. Let them say—let me live so they can say: There was nothing left in him; he did not spare himself; he put everything he had into his *work*, his life (emphasis added). (F 404)

I suspect Kaufmann can speak so comfortably of death because precisely at the age of forty, *in the exhilaration of writing the epilogue to this book,* he feels he has now done enough, worked hard enough, to justify a life. This point returns to Pickus's concern. Both elements in the aporia are necessary: live intensely *and* achieve a work—and yet they cannot be so easily fused. Here are some chastening lines from Yeats's "The Choice":

> The intellect of man is forced to choose
> Perfection of the life, or of the work,
> And if it take the second must refuse
> A heavenly mansion, raging in the dark.
> When all that story's finished, what's the news?
> In luck or out the toil has left its mark:
> That old perplexity an empty purse,
> Or the day's vanity, the night's remorse.[67]

Kaufmann is claiming to have lived fully both inside and outside his writing—a writing sensitive to his lived experience and not merely constituted by his writing or invoked as an aura in his writing. Kaufmann hints at great intensity, many metamorphoses, although we do not know their details. But they appear to be fulfilled—this is his claim—in his writing; his writing testifies to their real existence.

And he also argues—intermittently—that experiences come into their own *only* as writing: that there are important experiences found *only* in the writing of great poets. He needs this claim to justify the Orcus theme: the celebratory work must be very great in being very original. But does Kaufmann finally think that his extreme experiences—his intensities, his metamorphoses—are indeed only accomplished in his writing, or do they stand alone? In the first case, the work ethic prevails; in the second, far less so, except in the general sense that one needs to make good *use* of one's time. In the first case, he would be lining up his work with that of his great educators and the poets he translates. What should one imagine are his views on their comparative "greatness of soul," false modesty aside? In his late book *Man's Lot* (the subject of chapter 14), he has no compunction about introducing his own poems among the great anthology pieces of canonical poets that document "life at the limit."

In another locution we again address this dilemma: how central is work to Kaufmann's idea of living intensely? "But for those who reach old age," he writes, "the best insurance against hopelessness is surely to have lived rich lives, to have *used* our time so well that it would make little sense to feel cheated" (ER 247). This clash is accompanied by the lines that Lamont thought deranged: "In our youth we ought to make a rendezvous with death, pledging to be ready for it at the age of thirty; and then, if we live that long, make another date at forty. Granted that much life, one might feel that anything beyond that is a present."

The relevant point, however, is whether the verb "use" in the phrase "time used well" implies "work." It might do so, since one cannot "use" the time to undergo metamorphoses or experience intensity. Since Kaufmann had by now, at forty, written so much, so well—he could claim, with felt truth, though perhaps "poetically" deluded, that he was altogether ready to die. He can then say: Live fully, as I have lived, putting my time to *use*, profitably. This is the interpretive difficulty that continues to disturb this issue.

In another respect, one need not argue that Kaufmann's case is based entirely on the Orcus principle, on what we have called, even in the absence of benevolent gods, "cultural immortality." For there is his argument about accomplishing a work in which one would have put everything one can and then saying: "I need no more [life, time]. Dissolve me!" But not every worker is thinking subliminally or otherwise of so high a thing when he publishes his words.

I once asked Paul de Man, "So why does Hölderlin *publish*?" De Man replied: "To be encouraged." And after one's published work has been denounced, abused, and yet one continues to write, is it because one hopes that this time one will be encouraged? Or is it still another higher thing, an affair of personal justification? There is a good deal of the latter in Franz Kafka, who sought the justification that might make death easier through his writing, namely, "If there is a higher power that wishes to use me, or does use me, then I am at its mercy, if no more than as a well-prepared instrument. If not, I am nothing, and will suddenly be abandoned in a dreadful void."[68] He tasted this void so often that he had to conclude—the void *was* the conclusion—that he had not achieved it.

Is there *anyone* who is not favorably acquainted with the notion of carpe diem? On scrutiny, however, Kaufmann's "death work ethic"—I am relying now on Pickus's good summation—involves a good deal more than an exhortation to live well. Kaufmann's demand is strenuous. It requires you to give up all hope for an afterlife and the frank admission, moreover, that you do not want it anyway. You do not want it because you have accomplished a task that justifies your life, *this* life, and "more is not needed." This thought, as one reads Kaufmann, should be at the forefront of your consciousness: having accomplished what you are bent on, death is now welcome; after all, the great, the noble creators in history were "doubtless" glad to die.

Pickus also detects an unattractive interpersonal corollary in Kaufmann's thanatology: "You should not be held back from insinuating that those who do not feel this way do so because they have squandered their chances and now need consolation." Pickus continues at a more generous place: "Prepare to die with dignity: suicide may demonstrate such dignity: it is superior to an ignoble death. But if you should have the misfortune, to vegetate without dignity for some decades, then what is really important is whether, earlier, you *earned* your place. That is your justification." Finally, accept this injunction and be as one who "likes to keep talking about this subject in the manner mentioned above, [who] writes and translates poems about death that repeat these sentiments, all the while taking many photographs in which age and death are treated as (beautiful) transformations made by the 'artist' Time." Pickus is referring to Kaufmann's late photographic work in *Man's Lot*.[69]

Henry Staten's final comment jibes with my own. "I understand the question of the 'death work ethic' better. There is work in the everyday sense, and then there is work in the literary-artistic sense; and there is a big gap between them. And then there is a big gap between work of the kind we do and the kind that Hölderlin, author of 'To the Parcae,' and Franz Kafka, author of 'The Metamorphosis,' do. Encouragement is one thing, cultural immortality quite another. All this strikes me as very far from the idea of 'living fully' or a 'fulfilled life' or something like that. Everyone wants to live fully, but not everyone thinks pouring oneself out into cultural work constitutes living fully."[70]

We are set thinking further, hearing, too, in the background the great choral ode from *Oedipus at Colonus*, which Kaufmann quotes with approving awe in his book *Tragedy and Philosophy*:

> At 90, shortly before his death, Sophocles had written one of the most magnificent choral odes on the theme that any man who wished to live beyond the common span was a fool, and that long days bring on a growing burden of intolerable pains, while pleasure is no longer to be found in anything. In words reminiscent of Job and Jeremiah, the chorus exclaims:
>> nothing surpasses not being born;
>> but if born, to return where we came from
>> is next best, the sooner the better. (T 199)

Here there is no warrant for any justification, any sanctification of death through any form of activity throughout any number of years. Kaufmann's introduction to these lines softens their absolute character by salvaging the normal idea of "the common span" of life—of forty years?

7

Stories of Religion

RELIGION FROM TOLSTOY TO CAMUS

Religion is most moving in the form of stories.

—WALTER KAUFMANN

KAUFMANN'S NEW ANTHOLOGY of writings on religion, tendentiously titled *Religion from Tolstoy to Camus* (1961), was conceived under the sway of *The Faith of a Heretic*.[1] The two works are intimately connected. In his introduction to the new anthology—a short book on its own—Kaufmann stresses that one of the mottoes originally framing *The Faith of a Heretic* comes from Tolstoy's "Reply to the Synod's Edict of Excommunication," which the new anthology reprints in full. Moreover, in *The Faith of a Heretic* Kaufmann discusses Heidegger's treatment of death as little more than an "unacknowledged commentary" on Tolstoy's *The Death of Ivan Ilyitch*, a work this anthology also includes—and extols. Tolstoy is much more than a formal marker, a *terminus post quem*: he is a guiding light in this work as well as in the *Faith of a Heretic*—although at times even his light flickers. Nonetheless, Kaufmann has fashioned an arc from Tolstoy to Camus as a circle that returns to its source: "What is so remarkable about Camus is that he had the courage to accept the heritage of Tolstoy, when no one else had dared to stand before the world as Tolstoy's heir.... *The Plague* is the posthumous child of *The Death of Ivan Ilyitch*" (R 40). This sequence of stories and essays is exceptionally interesting for the many dialogical threads between them, as well as for Kaufmann's bold and incisive commentary, which alternates between respect and criticism.[2] One can sink into this book with fascination for hours, for days.

Traces of the earlier anthology *Existentialism from Dostoevsky to Sartre* (1956) are also present in Kaufmann's introduction—notably the terms "inauthenticity" and "self-deception," forms of the existentialist dereliction that, *for Tolstoy*, Christian faith can correct. Like the earlier anthology, the new book immediately appealed to both a general and an academic audience hungry for wider perspectives in a meager time and soon became the basis of college courses on religion.[3] In *The Faith of a Heretic*, Kaufmann had declared that "few things are as important for an education" as "encounters with Luther and the prophets, Tolstoy and St. Francis, Confucius and the Buddha," "exposure to [not indoctrination by] the Bible and the Dhammapada, to the Analects and Lao-Tze, the Upanishads and the Law of Manu, to Servetus and Calvin, to the persecutors and the persecuted." The *Religion* anthology goes some way to offering these "immensely desirable" encounters in a single paperback (F 276–77).

I mentioned from the start the problematic tendency in the title: Kaufmann's bias is to consider *literature* a privileged medium for the communication of ideas on religion: note the arc from the (great) writer Tolstoy to the (appealing) writer Camus. Partly on the strength of this decision, the volume soon acquired a bit of superfluous notoriety through the bitter criticism by Susan Sontag in her widely read collection of essays titled *Against Interpretation*. (It consists, expectedly, of interpretations, as critics can do no other.) Her notoriety brings Kaufmann's book to life again as the object of her indignation in her *Essays of the 1960s and 1970s*, recently republished by the Library of America.[4] The two points made above come together, since one of the chief maledictions Sontag fires against the anthology—popular among readers only in an atmosphere of "piety without content, religiosity without either faith or observance"—is Kaufmann's treating Camus as "religious," a word she finds, one, impossible when applied to Camus and, two, empty in general.[5] She understands "religious" to mean one thing only: you are a member of this or that church, usually Christian, Jewish, Muslim, Hindu, Buddhist, Zoroastrian, Shintoist, or Taoist. (Sontag adds "Tallensi," the religion of a polygamous people of northern Ghana who worship certain—but not all—crocodiles). Being religious—*in general*—would be, for her, like being able to speak language—*in general*—a putative skill that makes little sense.[6]

There is a good deal of information in Kaufmann's anthology, however, to suggest that the word "religious" means something different from being "an adherent ... to a specific symbolism and a specific historic community" or, I'll add, declaring allegiance to theological doctrine or the rituals of an established church.[7] The concept-word "religious" measures the force of your interest in religion, drawing on so-called numinous experiences in bodily life; the contemplation of fine arts inspired by religious belief, such as Bach's *St. Matthew Passion*, Grünewald's Isenheim altarpiece, and Georges Rouault's *Crucifixion*; and ideas and convictions drawn from the study of religions, including, especially in Kaufmann's case, immersion in the sites of the origin of religions.[8] If writers assert these implications, it will not do to say they are "without content." Kaufmann himself has no doubt in setting the thematic unity of the book under the headings of the justification of faith and the relevance of religion to morals and society—each topic having its subheadings.[9] This variety of implication expands throughout a work of nearly five hundred pages, with final weight falling on religious *stories*, for "religion is most moving in the form of stories, [which] ... can be read as a species of literature, along with the plays of Shakespeare and Sophocles ... as a source of profound experiences" (R 42). This conviction explains Kaufmann's including even several fairy tales of Oscar Wilde—"The Doer of Good," "The Master," and "The Nightingale and the Rose"—prose poetry that provides an answer to Kaufmann's question "whether anyone between Tolstoy and Buber has written more memorable religious parables" (R 19). Sontag considers it a conceptual scandal to term "religious" what might finally be only *serious* thinking; but epidemiologists, say, also think seriously, and Kaufmann does not include their writings or claim they are religious.

Kaufmann dedicated his celebrated *Nietzsche* volume (1950) "To My Wife and Children, Hazel, Dinah, and David"; *Critique of Religion and Philosophy* (1958) to his father, "Bruno Kaufmann, 1881–1956"; *From Shakespeare to Existentialism* (1959), as we recall, to "The Millions Murdered in the Name of False Beliefs by Men Who Proscribed Critical Reason"; and *The Faith of a Heretic* (1961) to three uncles, all of whom served in World War I, two as highly decorated officers, both of whom were subsequently murdered by the Nazis. The sense of these dedications is clear: they honor Kaufmann's family in its trapped immersion in the wider catastrophe of the Holocaust. I repeat these words to prepare for the contrast with Kaufmann's dedication of *Religion from Tolstoy to Camus* (1961) "To Herman and Sarah Wouk," and then, even more surprisingly, the relative clause, "Who Led Me to Love St. Thomas, V.I." This formulation calls for comment, not mainly for the surprising breach of tone in the relative clause.

Herman Wouk, 102 years old at this writing (April 2018), has not been in the limelight for several decades but in the years from about 1950 to 1980 enjoyed exceptional fame as the author of the novel and play *The Caine Mutiny* (1951) and thereafter the voluminous novels *The Winds of War* (1971) and *War and Remembrance* (1978). The latter book, a sequel, includes a devastating depiction of scenes from the Holocaust. Kaufmann's dedication to Wouk in 1961 obviously precedes the publication of these novels—which were, incidentally, praised for their higher truthfulness by several formidable scholars and critics, among them Martin Gilbert and (with reservations) Paul Fussell. The subject matter would have engaged Kaufmann—and provably did. Wouk's archives include a letter to Kaufmann, thanking him, in 1970, for his editorial scrutiny of an early manuscript of a fictive German general's war memoirs that would appear in *War and Remembrance*. From a study of Wouk's oeuvre by Arnold Beichman, based on a sifting of the Wouk archives at Columbia University, we learn that

> it was from Kaufmann that Wouk received a trenchant critique about the memoirs of the fictive German general Armin von Roon, titled *World Empire Lost*. . . . The Princeton adviser analyzed the German general's memoir in highly critical language including von Roon's original name, Wolfgang von Goethe, which, said Kaufmann, is "like having a British general called William Shakespeare or an American general, Abraham Lincoln." The letter, dated 17 June 1970, led to a Princeton meeting between Wouk and Kaufmann on 14 July, which lasted five and a half hours, during which both men reviewed Kaufmann's analysis page by page. Kaufmann singled out for special criticism Wouk's discussion, via the German general, of the philosophical and cultural sources of Nazism.

Thereafter, in a letter composed but never sent, Wouk thanked Kaufmann for his help. "And on your specialty—German culture and its relationship to Nazism—you made the clarifying attack which more than anything I looked for from you."[10]

"Clarifying attack" might be a first-rate watchword for almost all of Kaufmann's writings. His correspondence with Wouk proves their friendship to be solid and long lasting, but what would have crystallized it as early as the years just before the appearance in 1961 of *Religion from Tolstoy to Camus*? The answer turns on Wouk's work of 1959, *This Is My God*, the subject of which would have once again interested Kaufmann very much. It is an expression of Wouk's Jewish orthodox faith, based on an explication of "what is timeless" in Jewish belief, including Sabbath, the high holy days, prayer, Kashrut, circumcision, bar mitzvah, Kaddish, Torah, Talmud, Zionism, and more. We do not need to be reminded that Kaufmann was committed to a sort of conceptual love of this religion (unlike Wouk he was not an observant Jew) and would have been glad to see the elements of his love accurately portrayed. Equally binding would be two scholarly footnotes in which Kaufmann is mentioned respectfully by name. Wouk's concern is Kaufmann's assault on the grievous shortcomings of Julius Wellhausen's "higher criticism" of the Bible—the so-called Graf-Wellhausen hypothesis or Documentary Theory. Wouk writes: "There is some murderous demolition of Wellhausen's 'idiot forgers' in Walter Kaufmann's *Critique of Religion and Philosophy*, but the work will be of small comfort to pietists. It is a serious, often very witty, statement of a non-religious man, the best of its kind I have read since Bertrand Russell's books in that field."[11]

The phrase "idiot forgers" obviously calls for some explanation. Here I will turn to rabbinical authority for a brief exposition of the Wellhausen theory to see what is involved in this exchange of reproofs. According to Rabbi Nathan Lopes Cardozo, who acknowledges the commentaries of both Wouk and Kaufmann—in the latter case to the extent of reprinting entire sentences from Kaufmann's *Critique of Religion and Philosophy* without attribution, sentences marked in italic, below—:

> Wellhausen wanted to prove that the Torah and the Book of Joshua [in which the death of Moses is related] were, in large measure, "doctored" by priestly canonizers under Ezra in the time of the Second Temple. Their purpose was to perpetuate a single falsehood: Moshe's authorship of the Torah and the central worship, first in the Tabernacle and later in the Temple. According to Wellhausen, there never was a Tabernacle and no revelation at Sinai ever took place. Moshe, if he ever existed, considered the Deity a local thunder god or mountain god. The Torah had, therefore, to be seen as a complete forgery and not as a verbal account of God's words to Moshe and the People of Israel. . . .
>
> Wellhausen's method is clear and straightforward. *Every passage that fits his theory is authentic; all others are forgeries.* Whenever possible, he points out poor grammar, corrupt vocabulary, and alleged internal inconsistencies. In cases where he felt some "need" to change the plain meaning of a Hebrew word to fit into this theory, he offered what he called "conjectural emendation." The fact that thousands of verses contradicted his theory never disturbed Wellhausen. He contended that there was a master forger

or interpolator at work who anticipated Wellhausen's theory and consequently inserted passages and changed verses so as to refute it. Wellhausen *assumed that the forger had worked, as it were, with scissors and paste, taking all kinds of liberties: carving up the original* [Kaufmann: "received"] *texts; moving half a sentence here, a few sentences down, and three and a half sentences there, and a few sentences up, while altogether suppressing and omitting large portions of each source that could not be fitted into this patchwork* [Kaufmann: "mosaic"].[12]

So much for forgers. But Wouk cites Kaufmann as referring to "idiot forgers," so where does the question of idiocy come in? Kaufmann's adjective is meant to demean absolutely the work of the putative "master forger" of the Bible. In *Critique of Religion and Philosophy*, he says, very directly, "The detection of the most highhanded transposition of sentences and half-sentences is the forte of the Higher Critics. On these assumptions, the editor would have had to be *an idiot* if he ended up by offering a text as full of inconsistencies as the Higher Critics find it" (emphasis added) (C 383). Problem solved.

It is also interesting that both Kaufmann, writing in the years shortly before he published *Critique* in 1958, and Wouk, in the years before he published *This Is My God* in 1959, take special pains to describe W. F. Albright's *From the Stone Age to Christianity* as an indispensable reference.[13] Kaufmann notes that "Albright lists many salient Hegelianisms in the Higher Criticism, concluding with 'the Hegelian view that the fully developed religion of Israel unfolded gradually from primitive naturalism to lofty ethical monotheism'" (C 379). Wouk, for his part, "knows no book to equal" Albright for what was once "an up-to-date and gracefully written picture of critical Bible scholarship."[14] This coincidence of taste would have contributed to the mood in which friendship forms: an opposing judgment or no judgment at all would have gone some way to kill the impulse from the start.

Wouk's second reference to Kaufmann in *This Is My God* touches a point more nearly central to Kaufmann's concerns. Wouk writes about the presumed influence of Nietzsche's writings on the Nazis. He is eloquent:

If Nietzsche's first crop of dancing, laughing, sunlit supermen, the clear-eyed glad-hearted yea-sayers, the hard immoralist worshippers of Dionysos, turned out to be the scum of the German psychotic wards, that fact does not prove or disprove Nietzsche's critique of Europe. It is a historic comment that men of intelligence are still digesting.

And he is reasonable: this last proposition is perfectly true. One finds in an excellent, relatively recent book on this topic titled *Nietzsche—Godfather of Fascism?* a convincing remark by the editors entirely consistent with Wouk's. It reads: "Nietzsche was more a herald and prophet of the crisis of values out of which Nazism emerged, rather than a godfather of the century's fascist movements per se."[15] Wouk concludes:

> The Nazis vulgarized Nietzsche, misconstrued him, used him falsely. But that he was wide open to this misuse, that his influence on mediocre minds was gravely and massively pernicious, and that he unwittingly gave murdering nihilists a respectable and coruscating vocabulary of ideas and party cries—these things remain to my mind, with all deference to Nietzsche's formidable defenders, plain facts of the recent past. These facts do not render Nietzsche's masterpieces any the less worth serious study.[16]

I think it would be difficult for Kaufmann to quarrel with Wouk on this point; he might want to shift the accent of value even more in Nietzsche's favor, to what is liberating in his immoralism. But Wouk would make that an easy task as well. Just before the previous citation, he wrote:

> Thinkers like Albert Camus and Walter Kaufmann, dedicated to the proposition that man must find his integrity in a world without God, are rightly at the greatest pains to dissociate Nietzsche from the Nazis. The case for godlessness has never been stated more vigorously than Nietzsche put it, nor is it likely to be soon; and the godless men of good will in our time (such men have existed ever since Epicurus) cannot abide the calculated perversion of this master statement into a mere anticipation of the ravings of Goebbels. In Kaufmann's excellent book on Nietzsche, there is a final refutation, fully documented, of this error.[17]

We can now imagine an exchange of letters between Wouk and Kaufmann (if they exist, they are not accessible) that would have led to evenings of palm-shaded conversation in the British Virgin Islands, gratefully acknowledged in Kaufmann's dedication in *Religion from Tolstoy to Camus*. It is finally bemusing to know that as of anno 1984, Wouk's work was read in China in a volume (millions!) that vastly eclipsed the writings of Susan Sontag (her works circulated in the "low thousands)." This would mean, supposing that *This Is My God* was among them, that fair-minded Chinese readers would have been well prepared to take Sontag's attack on Kaufmann's *Religion* with a grain of MSG.[18]

On the model of his earlier anthology *Existentialism from Dostoevsky to Sartre*, the anthology *Religion from Tolstoy to Camus* contains a substantial introduction, consisting of Kaufmann's comments on each of the twenty-five (plus one) pieces included—note Kaufmann's liking, once again, for charismatic round numbers—and a brief biographical introduction to each author. I shall give an account of what I think is most salient and interesting in Kaufmann's remarks.

His commentary on Tolstoy turns on a surprising criticism of a judgment made by the usually irreproachable essayist Lionel Trilling. Kaufmann begs to disagree—and does not wait for permission to do so. Trilling finds the main effect of a reading of *Anna Karenina* to be the reader's "happiness." How could this be? It is because of the immense and consistent amount of affection that Tolstoy feels for each of his characters. Trilling writes: "This love is so pervasive, it is so constant, and it is so equitable, that it created the illusion of objectivity.... For Tolstoi everyone and everything has a saving grace.... It is this moral quality, this quality of affection, that accounts for the unique illusion of reality that Tolstoi creates."[19] Trilling's conclusion is surprising: "It is chiefly Tolstoy's moral vision that accounts for the happiness with which we respond to *Anna Karenina*" (R 2)—as if all Tolstoy's affection were rolled into a ball and then on to the reader. Kaufmann can barely contain his astonishment at this judgment, which runs counter to everything that warranted Tolstoy's inclusion in this book of religious writings. Following Kaufmann, Tolstoy does not regard his characters with affection: he finds them hopeless (though surely Levin escapes this charge). "Exoterically, the topic is unfaithfulness, but the really fundamental theme is bad faith" (R 4). Every one of these characters is a victim of self-deception, something that Tolstoy says explicitly. They would need to be saved by something larger and wider than the grace of their charm—the likeableness imputed to them (*dit* Trilling) by their author.

In fact, they are not charming: they are "on trial," in the sense that Kaufmann gives to the phrase: "Even if we confine ourselves to *Anna Karenina*, I know of no other great writer ... perhaps even in the whole of world literature, to whom I respond with less happiness and with a more profound sense that I am on trial and found wanting" (R 2–3). Kaufmann's readings of particular books tend to be intense and appreciative to the degree that they put *him* on trial—a trial that provokes the language of inner prosecutor and inner defendant. The conversations they induce may be a model of what it is to do serious moral philosophy. Kaufmann's conviction is that such books can and should put all readers on trial, and that is the measure of their value.

The "aspiration" to "authenticity" is just such a regular affair of encountering books that find you wanting—and indeed, with a good deal of "relentlessness" and asperity. It can seem as if the one goal of the serious experience of culture were to have *every* book, painting, and piece of music say to you: "You must change your life!" As this claim means so much to Kaufmann, it will be interesting to consider an opposing view (besides the obvious argument for aesthetics—or, to cite Sontag once again, erotics),[20] which, if it cannot unsettle his claim, will throw it into relief. Putting oneself on trial can brush uncomfortably with an only arranged self-contempt, an emotion that the psychoanalyst Adam Phillips, for one, is at pains to deplore. He would have us recognize that, *pace* Kaufmann, scrutinizing one's guilt can also be an obscure form of self-love. "Freud's insistence about our ambivalence," Phillips writes,

> is also a way of saying that . . . where there is self-hatred or guilt there is also self-love. . . . Self-love is always in play. Self-criticism can be our most unpleasant—our most sadomasochistic—way of loving ourselves.[21]

> But the self-critical part of ourselves, the part that Freud calls the super-ego, has some striking deficiencies: it is remarkably narrow-minded; it has an unusually impoverished vocabulary; and it is, like all propagandists, relentlessly repetitive. It is cruelly intimidating—Lacan writes of "the obscene super-ego"— . . . it insists on diminishing us. It is, in short, unimaginative; both about morality, and about ourselves.[22]

Here, then, are two views on the *morality* of judiciary introspection. A fair judgment on the assumed connection between self-examination and authenticity could be reached only in each individual case, and it will not be reached unless one takes up the adventure. (To "experience," etymologically speaking, means literally "submitting to a trial.") To this extent, Kaufmann's insistence that this adventure has to be undertaken again and again is irrefutable—indeed, in the face of *Anna Karenina* and *The Death of Ivan Ilyitch* the project of self-undeceiving isn't optional, it is inescapable—but whether book-launched introspection is the high road to authenticity remains moot.

On the point of whether there may even be pleasure in self-incrimination, Kaufmann's account of the close of Anna's life supplies material that may actually confirm this idea. At the end of the novel, we read, "Now for the first time Anna turned that glaring light in which she was seeing everything on to her relations with him [Vronsky, her lover], which she had hitherto avoided thinking about."[23] Kaufmann comments: "Thus begins her final, desperate struggle for honesty. On her way to her death she thinks 'that we are all created to be miserable, and that we all know it, and all invent means of deceiving each other."[24] Yet Tolstoy's irony is relentless." He will not let her keep her insight. "What she sees 'distinctly in the piercing light [that revealed to her now the meaning of life and human relations]' is wrong; she deceives herself until the very end and, instead of recognizing the conscience that hounds her, projects attitudes into Vronsky that in fact he does not have" (R 6).[25]

In the light of Phillips's take on inextirpable Freudian ambivalence, the reader is free to reverse Kaufmann's interpretation: Anna's thought that "we are all created to be miserable" may have arisen in response to an authenticating conscience but at the same time suggests a certain painful pleasure in enlisting "all [of us]" into her predicament. Equally, what Kaufmann sees as her flight from the truthfulness of this perception, her desperate effort to escape her fate—"to get up, to drop backwards" away from the train—is the authentic cri de coeur of the hapless creature in pain who *wants to live*.[26]

The terms "Faustian" and "Faustian . . . struggle" appear frequently in Kaufmann's discussion of *Anna Karenina*. Why this allusion to Faust? Kaufmann's main reference reads:

> Exoterically, the novel present a story of two marriages, one good and one bad, but what makes it such a great novel is that the author is far above any simplistic black and white, good and bad, and really deals with the ubiquity of dishonesty and inauthenticity, and with the Promethean, the *Faustian*, or, to be precise the Tolstoyan struggle against them (emphasis added). (R 4)

Is Kaufmann saying that only "the religious position intimated here . . . [and] articulated with full force in the works reprinted in the present volume"—"My Religion," "The Death of Ivan Ilyitch," and the "Reply to the Synod's Edict of Excommunication"—will fulfill Faust's striving for "transcendence"? (R 6–7). Now "Faustian" can mean at least two things, but not everything. In the main reference cited above, it means "relentless," "untiring"; Faust is the creature who, from his "bed of rest," may never say to any momentary constellation of things, however pleasing, "Tarry a while! You are so fair." "Faustian" can also mean the aspiration to approach "the mirror of eternal truth" (*Faust I*) or—to borrow a phrase from Goethe's eminent interpreter, Franz Kafka—to raise oneself—if not, indeed, the world—into "the Pure, the True, the Unchanging."[27] "The world" is the important reference for Kaufmann's use of the Faust figure, because it leads him to make an important distinction. "What matters ultimately is neither Gretchen nor Anna," he writes, both of whom are "squashed by the way of some Faust or Levin, a Goethe or a Tolstoy. . . . What matters ultimately is that in a world in which such cruelty abounds Faust and Levin should persist in their 'darkling aspiration.'" Here is the Faustian urge in the sense of tirelessness. "Their aspirations, however," Kaufmann continues, "are different. Faust's has little to do with society . . . ; his concern is pre-eminently with self-realization. . . . Tolstoy, on the other hand, was quite determined to attack society and bad faith" (R 6). Kaufmann's point answers well to Tolstoy's declaration of principle in "My Religion": "I was troubled *most* by the fact that all human evil, the habit of judging private persons, of judging whole nations, of judging other religions, and the wars and massacres that were the consequence of such judgments, all went on with the approbation of the Church" (emphasis added) (R 48–49). Kaufmann has linked Faust, who has little to do with such opinions, to Tolstoy's religious impulse and then dropped him, though not without leaving us the remainders of a stimulating idea. This point needs to be made quite clear.

Earlier, in our discussion of *The Faith of a Heretic*, I stressed Kaufmann's own grounding principle as Faustian in the sense of "man's aspiration to transcend himself" (C 355). And religion, he wrote, is "rooted" in this very aspiration. It's important to understand what he is *not* saying with these citations: it is not that man's aspiration achieves its *highest* fulfillment in religion, even as he puts religion *among* its highest desiderata, namely, "Religion can channel man's aspiration to transcend himself into many different ways of life: . . . there is moral effort, ranging from a sustained attempt to perfect oneself to a devotion to social reform," along with altogether less attractive outcomes, such as hypostasizing an anthropomorphic deity (C 359). That religion can channel man's aspiration in the direction of social reform answers to Kaufmann's view of *Tolstoy's* conceptual use of the Faustian in *Anna Karenina*. In this way, and to put the matter privatively, Kaufmann escapes the scorn of Morris Raphael Cohen, whose scathing, antireligious essay "The Dark Side of Religion" Kaufmann fair-mindedly includes in the anthology along with Tolstoy. Cohen writes:

One of the effective ways of avoiding any real discussion of religion or discriminating its darker from its brighter side is to define or identify it as "our highest aspiration." This is very much like defining a spouse as the essence of perfection or our country as the home of the brave and the free. Some particular religion, like some particular wife or country, may perhaps deserve the praise. But we must first be able to identify our object before we can tell whether the praise is entirely deserved. To define religion as our highest aspiration, and then to speak of Christianity, Islam, or Judaism as a religion, is obviously to beg the whole question by a verbal trick of definition. . . .

Consider the vast varieties of religions ancient and modern. Are they all expressions of our highest aspirations? Is each one an effort at universal benevolence? If so, why do they differ? And since they do differ, and each regards the others as inferior, can they all be true? Nor is the case improved if we say that each religious group seeks what is highest or noblest, for there can be no question that error, ignorance, stupidity, and fanatical prejudice enter into what men think. (R 280–81)[28]

I cite Cohen for the clarity with which he states an argument not inconsistent with Kaufmann's. In the words of the encomium composed by his colleagues at Princeton, Kaufmann "wanted us to see philosophy and religion as passionate, ceaseless efforts of the human spirit towards the ideals of truth and perfection."[29] But this path of religion is *not* his own: it is set down by others and is "immensely desirable" to know. Philosophy—read: "critical thinking"—takes precedence. And it is via critical—and indeed *self*-critical—thinking, and its articulation, that Kaufmann's ultimate value of self-realization, which is Nietzschean rather than Faustian, might come about.

Kaufmann's distinction between a pathos of social reform, as in Tolstoy's view of the gospel of Christ, and the torment of the sin-besotted soul in anguish, as in Dostoevsky's novels, allows Kaufmann to define the religious impulses of the two greatest novelists "of all time" (R 8). He reprints the Grand Inquisitor scene from *The Brothers Karamazov* and rightly prefaces it, as Sontag notes, with Ivan's uncomprehending outcry at the suffering of little children. Ivan's despair would appear to obviate absolutely the possibility of the happiness that the Grand Inquisitor promises his squashed subjects at the price of their liberty.

Kaufmann, however, reserves at the very least the possibility of happiness—and indeed one compatible with liberty—in reproof of the view of the Grand Inquisitor. The matter, Kaufmann says, is arguable. The key words are "compatible with"; he believes in the possibility of their coexistence, although this possibility is in no way the necessary or sufficient condition of individual freedom. *The Faith of a Heretic* highlights a famous sentence by the German Enlightenment thinker Gotthold Ephraim Lessing, one of Kaufmann's "educators" (H 297), which I will cite and then vary to make the point.

If God were to hold all Truth concealed in his right hand, and in his left only the steady and diligent drive for Truth, albeit with the proviso that I would always and forever err in the process, and offer me the choice, I would with all humility take the left hand.[30]

A version true to Kaufmann and useful now for our discussion would read:

If God were to hold all Happiness concealed in his right hand, and in his left only the steady and diligent drive for Freedom, albeit with the proviso that I would always and forever err in the process [*and suffer as a consequence*], and offer me the choice, I would with all humility take the left hand.

The Faith of a Heretic insisted repeatedly on the inferiority of happiness (for the one and the many) to each of his high-ranked virtues: "humbition" (humility-cum-humor-cum ambition), love, courage, and honesty. This credo would have made Kaufmann preternaturally allergic to Trilling's characterization of the author of *Anna Karenina* as the epic poet of happiness and intensify his sense of how much agreement he would find in Ivan's rebellious, anti-utilitarian rage. Ivan's "Rebellion" concludes with his refusal of a final reconciliation—a world of harmony and mutual forgiveness between torturer and tortured—when the creature who has been tortured is a little child. How deeply this refusal will have penetrated Kaufmann's heretical faith can be read from this passage from *The Faith of a Heretic*:

But suppose that it were possible to ensure the greatest possible happiness of the greatest possible number either by having recourse to a few injustices or by reducing man's creative powers, whether by drugs that reduced men to blissful imbecility or by operations that reduced their intelligence. What then? Those of us who feel that happiness, however important, is not the ultimate consideration [would feel] . . . that it would be an impermissible betrayal to sell our birthright for a mess of bliss. (F 206)

Rebellion, heresy, is justified, Q.E.D., and Dostoevsky is its most articulate advocate. But the condition of rebellion is a seizing hold of liberty!

"The Grand Inquisitor" allows Kaufmann to meditate on totalitarianism in the wider and unaccustomedly anodyne sense that individuals might be happy to have their lives "regulated" by a benevolent authority. The idea, in this wider sense, certainly does not begin with Giovanni Gentile (Mussolini's ghostwriter) or end with the destruction of his demented cohorts. Kaufmann is original on the latter point. We are done with Hitler and also with Stalin but not with "the dogmatic and naïve self-righteousness of Western statesmen who simply take for granted their own good faith, benevolence, and virtue and the lack of all these qualities in statesmen from totalitarian countries" (R 9). The crux of an understanding of Ivan Karamazov's "argument"—which I put in quotes, since it figures as a fiction inside a fiction—is that, following Kaufmann's usage, the totalitarian idea is not as such vicious: he terms a version of this concept "benevolent totalitarianism" (R 9). It is the view of the Grand Inquisitor: the crux is the assumption by an authority that it has the right to regulate every aspect of the life of its subjects and thereby relieve them of the freedom they dread. The first detailed document in defense of benevolent totalitarianism is Plato's *Republic*. "Some writers," Kaufmann notes, "balk at calling it totalitarianism, mainly because they associate the word with malignancy. Others, seeing clearly that the doctrine of *The Republic* is totalitarian, have charged Plato with malignancy" (R 10). The perspective of the Grand Inquisitor rebukes both arguments.

A couple of Kaufmann's propositions might be misleading and deserve to be put in the light of recent scholarship on Dostoevsky, foremost the work of Joseph Frank. Kaufmann writes: "Reading the story merely as a diatribe against the Roman Catholic church and supposing that it stands or falls with its applicability to one religion is almost as foolish as supposing that the Inquisitor speaks the author's mind" (R 9). The vigor of this remark, while essentially correct, might lead the unwary reader to suppose that its character as an attack on the Roman Catholic Church is merely marginal. It is not, in the light of Dostoevsky's intentions. Frank quotes from a letter Dostoevsky wrote to his editor, pointing out that "the Legend was directed [in Dostoevsky's words] 'against Catholicism and the papacy, and particularly . . . the period of the Inquisition, which had such awful effects on Christianity and on all of humanity.'" Frank continues: "Even though Dostoevsky said nothing about Socialism in these remarks, both Socialism and Catholicism had become identical for him as embodiments of the first and third temptations of Christ, the betrayal of Christ's message of spiritual freedom in exchange for bread, and the aspiration toward earthly power."[31]

At the same time, other passages from *The Brothers Karamazov* also relativize Kaufmann's a priori distinction between Tolstoy's and Dostoevsky's Christianity, in which the former is social in its orientation and the latter an affair of individual salvation. Consider this well-known statement of Ivan Karamazov—not Dostoevsky's very own voice, true, but one of his voices in this polyphonous novel: "The Church ought to include the whole State, and not only occupy a corner of it, and, if this is, for some reason, impossible at present, then it ought, in reality, to be set up as the direct and chief aim of the future development of Christian society!" In Frank's presentation of the conversation between Ivan and Father Zosima, we hear Zosima, another of Dostoevsky's constituent voices, develop this idea: "Christian society, he says, though not now ready, 'will continue still unshaken in expectation of its complete transformation from a society almost heathen in character into a single, universal, all-powerful Church. So be it! So be it!'"[32] Again, this position is uttered within a fiction, but it is clearly alive in Dostoevsky's consciousness.

Let Anatoly Lunarchasky, the first Bolshevik "Commissar of Enlightenment," join this conversation with a cogent reprise:

> "Let it be!" exclaim the inspired monks of Dostoyevsky's works. What is it they thus invoke? What is "to be" is that the Church, with its love and brotherhood, will, at some stage, overcome the state and all society founded on private property, that—at some future time—the Church will build a special, almost unearthly socialism. This ecclesiastical Utopia will be based on that coinherence of souls by which Dostoyevsky tries to replace the once-glimpsed and later rejected ideal of socialism to which he was introduced by his friends in the Petrashevsky circle.
>
> However, Dostoyevsky's "ecclesiastical revolution" takes place in an atmosphere of even greater humility than Tolstoi's sectarian revolution. It is a task which will take many hundred years, a matter for the distant future, perhaps even for the next world. It is possible that Dostoyevsky, like Tolstoi, is led by the very logic of his thought to perceive this harmonious coinherence as a purely nominative ideal, as something that will be realized only in eternity, in infinity, in the sphere of metaphysics.
>
> In this way, God, Orthodoxy, Christ as a democratic, individual, purely ethical principle of the Church—all this was quite essential to Dostoyevsky, for it gave him the opportunity to avoid a final spiritual break with socialist truth while, at the same time, anathematizing materialist socialism.[33]

In this one formidable if partial statement, Kaufmann's distinction between Tolstoy's and Dostoevsky's Christianity is not erased but properly nuanced.

Kaufmann's inclusion of the encyclical of Pope Leo XIII *Aeterni Patris* ([Of the] Eternal Father) of 1879 is original and cogent—it puts Catholic thought in a different and more expansive light, to say the least, than the dusky gloom of Ivan's Legend of the Grand Inquisitor. Furthermore, as a document essentially about the relation of philosophy and faith, it bears immediately on

Kaufmann's basic concern—namely, his *Critique of Religion and Philosophy*. Kaufmann precedes this text with excerpts from several encyclicals of Pius IX, whom Leo XIII succeeded as pope: the most striking is "A Syllabus of Errors" (1864), which supplies a negative foil to the approved positions on philosophy and religion in Leo XIII's *Aeterni Patris*. Pius IX is historically important in his own right as the author of the dogmas of the Immaculate Conception (1854) and Papal Infallibility (1870). In light of the encyclicals of both Pius IX and Leo XIII, Kaufmann doubts "whether any later pope has equaled their influence" (R 16).

Leo XIII's *Aeterni Patris* is decisive in bringing about the instauration of Thomistic philosophy. Many older readers, I believe, will have read the work of Étienne Gilson, the foremost scholar of Thomistic thought at least at the time of Kaufmann's writing. In a chapter of his book on the teachings of Leo XIII, Gilson conjures the difficult predicament of the critical reader of the encyclicals. If he or she objects to some formulation, he or she must realize that

> he [or she] is pitting his [or her] own personal judgment, not against the personal judgment of another man, but against the whole ordinary teaching of the Catholic Church, as well as against her entire tradition. . . . The church alone [which is to say, the pope] represents the point of view of a moral and spiritual authority free from all prejudices.[34]

Kaufmann smartly disrupts this claim on the strength of a close reading of the encyclical, which turns out to nuance in many ways its celebration of the teachings of St. Thomas:

> The reader should not overlook that the Pope qualifies his call "to restore the golden wisdom of St. Thomas" by explaining: "We say the wisdom of St. Thomas; for it is not by any means in our mind to set before this age, as a standard, those things which may have been inquired into by Scholastic Doctors with too great subtlety; or anything taught by them with too little consideration, not agreeing with the investigations of a later age; or, lastly, anything that is not probable." (R 14–15)

This is a refreshing caveat by Leo XIII, good to consider in the wake of the very cruel Legend of the Grand Inquisitor.

The fulminations of Nietzsche's *Antichrist* are inevitably present; and since my chapter is about Kaufmann, and his introductory essay is extremely brief, I shall now refer the reader, just as Kaufmann does, to chapter 12 of his *Nietzsche: Philosopher, Psychologist, Antichrist* (N 337–90) for an analysis of "Nietzsche's

Repudiation of Christ." Equally, Kaufmann's views on the character of Paul and the historical Jesus, which are *opposed* to Nietzsche's, can be found in chapter 8 of *The Faith of a Heretic*, "Jesus vis-à-vis Paul, Luther, and Schweitzer" (F 207–48). This punctual opposition should not mask Kaufmann's general indebtedness to the spirit and rhetoric of Nietzsche's polemic.

Absent convenient access to Kaufmann's books, "it could be fruitful" (to use a favorite locution of his when considering opposing or experimental opinions) to give a brief account of these views. The chapter in Kaufmann's *Nietzsche* titled "Nietzsche's Repudiation of Christ" foregrounds Nietzsche's objection to a spirit of resentment, of welled-up revenge: "To have claws and not to use them," writes Kaufmann, "and above all to be above any *ressentiment* or desire for vengeance, that is, according to Nietzsche, the sign of true power" (N 372). Kaufmann quotes Zarathustra: "For *that man be delivered from revenge*, that is for me the bridge to the highest hope . . . (Z II 7)" (N 373). These points connect immediately with Nietzsche's ironical animadversions against the spirit of vengeance in section 45 of *The Antichrist*, which Kaufmann drolly recommends as giving "some idea of Nietzsche's importance as a critic of Christianity" (R 17). Nietzsche writes:

> I give some examples of what these little people put into their heads, what *they put into the mouth* of their master. . . .
>
> "And whosoever shall not receive you, nor hear you, when ye depart thence, shake off the dust under your feet for a testimony against them. Verily I say unto you, It shall be more tolerable for Sodom and Gomorrah in the day of judgment, than for that city" (Mark 6: 11). How *evangelical*!
>
> "And whosoever shall offend one of these little ones that believe in me, it is better for him that a millstone were hanged about his neck, and he were cast into the sea" (Mark 9:42). *How evangelical*! . . .
>
> "Judge not, that ye be not judged. . . . With what measure ye mete, it shall be measured to you again" (Matt. 7:1 f.). What a conception of justice and of a "just" judge! . . .
>
> "But if ye forgive not men their trespasses, neither will your Father forgive your trespasses" (Matt. 6: 15). Very compromising for said "Father." (R 199–200)

These parallel passages from Kaufmann and Nietzsche should suggest a sympathetic analysis, a coincidence of views.

To gauge his disagreement with Nietzsche's "concept of Jesus," Kaufmann refers to the chapter in *The Faith of a Heretic* titled "Jesus vis-à-vis Paul, Luther, and Schweitzer." For Nietzsche, Jesus is a *décadent*—an unholy mix of "the sublime, the sickly, and the childlike"[35]—a portrait that Kaufmann considers "implausible." Kaufmann stresses, rather,

> Jesus's exalted conception of his own person that caused astonishment; and if he said half the things about himself that the Gospels relate, it must have seemed the most shocking blasphemy to the Pharisees. The three Synoptics agree that the scribes condemned Jesus not for being too liberal but for blasphemy for what he said about himself. They relate that he not only called himself the Messiah, or to use the familiar Greek translation of that term the Christ, but that he went on to say, alluding to Daniel: "You will see the Son of Man sitting at the right hand of Power, and coming with the clouds of heaven." Then, they say, the high priest tore his mantle, said, "You have heard his blasphemy," and they condemned him. (F 215)

Meanwhile, Kaufmann's main dispute with Nietzsche as it might be glimpsed in *The Faith of a Heretic* turns on the Christian concept of reward. Here we are dealing not with the character of Jesus but with the character of the Gospel. If Kaufmann's chapter is certain of one thing, it is that the concept of reward is central: indeed the concepts of reward and faith are intimately connected. Kaufmann writes:

> Each of the nine [*sic*] Beatitudes in the beginning announces a reward, and they conclude with the promise: "Rejoice and be glad, for your reward is great in heaven." In the Sermon [on the Mount] itself, promises and threats alternate continually: "shall be called great in the kingdom of heaven"; "will never enter the kingdom of heaven"; "judgment"; "hell fire"; "your whole body should be cast into hell"; "if you love those who love you, what reward have you?"; "will reward you"; "have their reward"; "will reward you"; "your heavenly Father also will forgive you"; "neither will your Father forgive your trespasses"; "they have their reward"; "will reward you"; and more in the same vein. (F 210)

Nietzsche himself quotes Luke: "Rejoice ye in that day, and leap for joy: for, behold, your reward is great in heaven" (Luke 6:23), and yet section 33 of *The Antichrist* curiously excludes the Christian concept of reward. (This is a section of *The Antichrist* that Kaufmann does not anthologize, presumably not wanting to foreground their dispute and disconcert the reader of *The Faith of a Heretic*.) Nietzsche writes:

> In the whole psychology of the "evangel" the concept of guilt and punishment is lacking; *also the concept of a reward* [emphasis added]. "Sin"—any distance separating God and man—is abolished: precisely this is the "glad tidings." Blessedness is not promised, it is not tied to conditions: it is the only reality—the rest is a sign with which to speak of it.
>
> The consequence of such a state projects itself into a new practice, the genuine evangelical practice. It is not a "faith" that distinguishes the Christian: the Christian acts, he is distinguished by acting differently: by not resisting, either in words or in his heart, those who treat him ill; by making no distinction between foreigner and native, between Jew and not-Jew ("the neighbor"—really the coreligionist, the Jew); by not growing angry with anybody, by not despising anybody; by not permitting himself to be seen or involved at courts of law ("not swearing"); by not divorcing his wife under any circumstances, not even if his wife has been proved unfaithful. All of this, at bottom one principle; all of this, consequences of one instinct. . . .
>
> What was disposed of with the evangel was the Judaism of the concepts of "sin," "forgiveness of sin," "faith," "redemption through faith"—the whole Jewish ecclesiastical doctrine was negated in the "glad tidings."
>
> The deep instinct for how one must live, in order to feel oneself "in heaven," to feel "eternal," while in all other behavior one decidedly does not feel oneself "in heaven"—this alone is the psychological reality of "redemption." A new way of life, not a new faith.[36]

Kaufmann, on the contrary, would reserve the importance of a "way of life" for Judaism ("The primary concern of Judaism is with a way of life") and see Christianity as utterly faith-centered ("In Christianity, as in no other major religion, faith is central)" [C 268, C 311]).

I will note in passing that Kaufmann's insistent habit of referring the reader to one or more of his other books for fuller clarification appears to have been inspired by Nietzsche. At the close of the very potent section 45 of *The Antichrist*, Nietzsche quotes Paul:

> Not many wise men after the flesh, not many mighty, not many noble, are called. But God hath chosen the foolish things of the world to ruin the wise; and God hath chosen the weak things of the world to ruin what is strong;

And base things of the world, and things which are despised, hath God
chosen, yea, and what is nothing, to bring to naught what is something:
That no flesh should glory in his presence (Paul, I Cor. 1:20 ff.).

Nietzsche then comments: "To understand this passage, a first-rate document for the psychology of every chandala morality, one should read the first
inquiry in my *Genealogy of Morals*: there the contrast between a *noble* morality
and a chandala morality, born of *ressentiment* and impotent vengefulness, was
brought to light for the first time. Paul was the greatest of all apostles of vengeance" (R 200). This is one of the many instances in which Nietzsche sends
the reader to one of his earlier works.

I said at the outset that I found Kaufmann's anthology extremely interesting, not least for voices that Kaufmann has revived, witness that of the Cambridge mathematician William Kingdon Clifford (b. 1845), who died young
of consumption at the age of thirty-three. His scintillating but contestable
essay "The Ethics of Belief" decries the immorality of belief without evidence;
today, it is known mainly for having provoked a response by William James
in "The Will to Believe," which, following Kaufmann, is the less persuasive of
the two.[37]

Clifford's essay clearly left a strong impression on Kaufmann's thoughts on
belief, evidence, and faith, since a number of Clifford's references surface in
The Faith of a Heretic. In the matter of Kaufmann's intellectual development
as it might be read off his books, a discussion of Clifford's essay *precedes* that
of *The Faith of a Heretic*. *Faith* begins with the saying of Jeremiah: "They have
healed the wound of my people, lightly, saying, 'Peace, peace,' when there is
no peace" (F vii). But here is Clifford:

Men speak the truth to one another when each reveres the truth in his own
mind and in the other's mind; but how shall my friend revere the truth in
my mind when I myself am careless about it, when I believe things because
I want to believe them, and because they are comforting and pleasant? Will
he not learn to cry, "Peace," to me, when there is no peace? (R 206)

Clifford then quotes Milton's *Areopagitica* to "fortify the judgment" that
assigns sin even "to those simple souls . . . who have been brought up from the
cradle with a horror of doubt." Milton wrote: "A man may be a heretic in the
truth; and if he believe things only because his pastor says so, or the assembly
so determine, without knowing other reason, though his belief be true, yet the
very truth he holds becomes his heresy" (R 206–7). In *The Faith of a Heretic*,

Kaufmann employs this very quote from Milton—though he does so in order to revise it for his purposes:

> Neither would I [Kaufmann] redefine heresy, as Milton did in his *Areopagitica*: "A man may be a heretic in the truth; and if he believe things only because his pastor says so, or the assembly so determine, without knowing other reason, though his belief be true, yet the very truth he holds becomes his heresy." Of the man accused by Milton I approve as little as he did, but I should not call him a heretic. Rather, his faith is that of most of the orthodox. (F 2)

Finally, to further fortify his argument that naïveté cannot justify belief, Clifford quotes Coleridge: "He who begins by loving Christianity better than Truth, will proceed by loving his own sect or Church better than Christianity, and end in loving himself (his own peace) better than all" (R 207). Kaufmann cites this aphorism at the head of *The Faith of a Heretic*, although he finds it already embedded in Tolstoy's "A Reply to the Synod's Edict of Excommunication." Both texts—Tolstoy's "Reply" and Clifford's "Ethic of Belief"—sit cheek by jowl in the anthology of religious writings. Tolstoy—but now Clifford as well—appear to have served as intellectual lodestars throughout *The Faith of a Heretic*. Clifford's claim that only proper evidence can justify belief—and it is a grave sin to believe on lesser grounds—surely informed Kaufmann's reflections on the adequacy of historical evidence in *Critique of Religion and Philosophy* as well.

For an extended and stinging criticism of William James's "The Will to Believe" ("his slipshod but celebrated essay" [C 115]), Kaufmann again refers us to his *Critique*. A few excerpts from both commentaries will sum up his objections. Earlier, we cited the argument from *Critique* that James had "turned to religion because he wanted to feel at home in the universe. But *the greatest accomplishment of religion has been that it did not allow man to feel at home in the universe*" (C 355). Now, in the anthology, Kaufmann dismisses James's "attempt to define 'the permissible cases' in which it is intellectually reputable to believe in the absence of 'sufficient' evidence.'" The first is that religion "must represent a 'live' option; but one man's live option," writes Kaufmann, as he strides into spirited combat, "is another man's dead option." The second condition is that the option must be "forced," the demand "either to accept this truth or go without it" (James). Kaufmann thinks this "forcing" is owed to nothing more than "a little skill in phrasing." Even when this option is phrased as it is, it is hard to see why a prudent answer, asking for further evidence of this "truth," could not circumvent the bind. To the third requirement—"the option must be 'momentous'"—Kaufmann, replies: "What else is this but an invitation to wishful thinking, provide we are tempted very much?" (C 116).

James's essay gets no better: just before the end, writes Kaufmann, it arrives at "its nadir, when . . . he [James] formulates '*the religious hypothesis*' which confronts him . . . with a live, forced, momentous option." This hypothesis, on close reading, is unintelligible. (What does it mean to claim: "Religion says that the best things are the more eternal things?") Whatever this hypothesis is—a form of Pascal's wager, I'll add—it is clear, according to James, that "it cannot yet be verified scientifically at all" (C 118). Kaufmann wonders with considerable energy about the qualifying word "yet," writing, with an incisiveness that can stand as his signature:

> He writes as if "the religious hypothesis" (James: we lose the good, *if it be true*) were a more or less scientific hypothesis for which no crucial experiment has been devised as yet; one almost gets the feeling that a colleague is working on it even now in the next room, that verification is around the corner, and that we should be stupid if we did not take a chance on it without delay. (C 118)

James's theistic puff piece is enlarged by a meditation by Josiah Royce, a neo-Hegelian Idealist and James's colleague in the Harvard Department of Philosophy. Royce turns somewhat quixotically to the book of Job in an attempt to justify the existence of suffering—his topic echoing Ivan Karamazov's despairing cry: "Why must children suffer?" Kaufmann is displeased that Royce has missed the fundamental point in claiming that "Job's problem is, upon Job's presuppositions, simply and absolutely insoluble"; these presuppositions include God's absolute justice and moral perfection. In fact, Kaufmann writes, "Job emphatically denies both, and the Lord in the end says twice that Job has 'spoken of me what is right'" (R 19). For a better understanding of Job, Kaufmann refers us to the chapter "Suffering and the Bible" in *The Faith of a Heretic*. The outcome of the book of Job cannot be a sort of moral homeostasis in this, God's world, consisting, as Royce has it, of man's ongoing, effortful "subordination" of evil by his will to goodness. The book of Job contributes nothing to this conclusion. Job's "piety is a cry in the night, born of suffering so intense that he cannot contain it and must shriek, speak, accuse, and argue with God" (F 180). The cry goes on and on . . .

It is muted in the sobriety and science of Freud's prose, which, in *The Future of an Illusion*, does not address the cry but rather the attempt to pacify it. "Critics [even of orthodox believers] persist in calling 'deeply religious' a person who confesses to a sense of man's insignificance and impotence in face of the universe, although it is not this feeling that constitutes the essence of religious emotion, but rather the next step, the reaction to it, which seeks a remedy against this feeling" (qtd. in R 278). This is the language that appears to have informed Kaufmann's first argument with William James, when he wrote that James had "turned to religion because he wanted to feel at home in the universe" (C 355).

We will hear more of Kaufmann's admiration for Freud in the following chapters (it was already spelled out in his *Critique*); this admiration is spontaneous and full-throated, since Freud gives him the example of a thinker who is at once courageous, clear-sighted, and profound. And yet no authority, however admirable the person who represents it, is immune to Kaufmann's puncturing. Readers may recall his critique of the bulk claims of Freud's "The Future of an Illusion" (above), chapters of which are reprinted in this anthology. Kaufmann's discussion of the Bible criticism of Morton Scott Enslin, a reliable, dispassionate close reader of the New Testament, becomes an opportunity for him to reveal once more that he is no respecter of great personalities when their ideas turn bad. Enslin is not the target; Enslin's claim to the impossibility of writing a life history of Jesus, there being no adequate materials for such a project, is not contentious. Kaufmann's discussion becomes (additionally) interesting for prompting an unexpected criticism of Tolstoy. To characterize the style of Kaufmann's criticism, I will conjure a word that Kafka wrote, perhaps in error. That word, if it is one, is "Vergeistichung": Kafka spoke of a national literature as amounting to a "detailed 'Vergeistichung' of the broad scope of public life."[38] "Vergeistichung" is an odd variant of the word "Vergeistlichung," meaning sublimation, purification. The orthographical slip—the loss of the "l" from "Vergeistlichung"—is bemusing; it releases a *Stich*, the stab of a knife, the sting of an insect, the pang of a pain—the stroke of a pen. . . . Kaufmann's purifying rectification of a writer's error never lacks a sting. Just where has Tolstoy erred?

Tolstoy was negatively exercised by Bible criticism. The so-called Higher Criticism, which we have described as a way of reading Scripture strongly resisted by both Kaufmann and his friend Herman Wouk, treated the Old Testament

more mistrustfully and destructively than any other classic. . . . New Testament criticism has remained largely free of this taint, except for the assumption of many critics that material common to Matthew and Luke but not found in Mark, whose Gospel is generally considered earlier and the primary source for the two others, must be assigned to a hypothetical source called "Q" (for *Quelle*, the German word for "source"). (R 24)

Enslin is controversial in rejecting this engaging hypothesis (he holds it more plausible that there is no "Q" behind these Gospels, and Luke copied from Matthew); but in this respect he shares the opinion of Tolstoy, who reacted indignantly to the entire enterprise of Bible criticism. "Take away the Church," he said, "the traditions, the Bible, and even Christ himself: the ultimate fact of man's knowledge of goodness, i.e. of God, directly through reason and conscience, will be as clear and certain as ever, and it will be seen that we are dealing with truths that can never perish—truths that humanity can never afford to part with" (R 24). Kaufmann sees this extreme formulation as sowing confusion among the certitudes of Tolstoy's "My Religion," which cannot survive, really, this departure from "reliance on exegesis and from appeal to Christ. If the appeal to 'reason and conscience' is pressed," writes Kaufmann, "we are led from religion to philosophy, unless 'reason and conscience' is nothing but a euphemism for what seems obvious to the speaker, though very different ideas may seem no less obvious to others" (R 25). Tolstoy was ready, perhaps hyperbolically, for the Bible critics even to "demonstrate that Christ was never born. No matter. It will be all the more evident that the fortress of religion is impregnable" (R 24). Kaufmann considers this surmise a fruitless heresy. What Tolstoy is in principle saying is that Christ's teachings, even in their literal absence—Christ allegedly never having been born—would necessarily have "conformed perfectly to our own personal conscience." And Kaufmann continues: "Bible criticism opens up the disturbing possibility that there may be excellent evidence that Jesus lived—and taught what our reason and our conscience do not happen to approve" (R 24–25). (The fact that Bible criticism might prove that Jesus lived is *not* the ground for Kaufmann's—and Wouk's—objection; they are dismayed by its untenable philology.) In another essay, "How to Read the Gospels and What Is Essential in Them," Tolstoy offers a propaedeutic for Bible reading. You blue-pencil everything that is "quite plain clear and comprehensive." Kaufmann continues to correct his master: "But what is plain is perhaps what we can easily assent to, while what seems outrageous to us is not 'comprehensible.' If so, Tolstoy would actually be exhorting us to construe everything in such a manner that it will conform to what we especially like" (R 25).

Kaufmann admires Enslin for his sober scholarship. He also admires the German pastors Martin Niemöller and Paul Schneider for their courage in preaching despite Nazi prohibitions. Kaufmann's passion in telling the stories of their resistance cuts to the bone; but here, too, piety cannot withstand the uprush of determined logic. In this delicate matter, it would be best to stay with Kaufmann's phrasing:

> What Niemoller's heroic sermons during the weeks before his arrest by the Gestapo prove is not that neo-orthodoxy is true or that liberalism is false, but only that neo-orthodoxy, like Nazism and Communism, was capable of inspiring martyrdom.... Every time one reads [Niemöller's sermon] "The Salt of the Earth," one's skin creeps....
>
> In an important sense, religion flourished under Hitler, in spite of Hitler. Measured against the revival of religion during that period, the mid-century revival in the United States seems shallow indeed. One may well ask whether religion does not often gain intensity and depth in times of persecution, while it loses both in ages of prosperity. Certainly, many Old Testament writers thought so.
>
> An intensity that permeates a man's whole being is always impressive; but the question of content remains. And if one pauses to reflect on Niemöller's message, one notes a striking lack of content. Transposed into a different setting where there is no persecution, his challenge evaporates and becomes trivial. Words that chilled the spine lose significance. The call to come to church and to profess allegiance to Christ and the Bible, and to obey the orders of one's church council, regardless of the consequences, is charged with meaning and daring in Berlin in 1937, but scarcely exciting in New York or London or West Berlin a quarter of a century later. (R 26)

These comments are, to my mind, good enough evidence of a heretical disposition, a commitment to independent thought—to philosophy—above everything, indifferent to popularity and to every pathos that could blur right reason.

In the context of the generally deplorable stance of the Christian Churches to Nazism, Kaufmann reprints a chapter of Malcolm Hay's *Europe and the Jews*, with its deceptively anodyne subtitle, *The Pressure of Christendom over 1900 Years*.[39] Hay's erudite, well-documented thesis is that the Nazi annihilation of the Jews—the peculiarly atrocious character of which he had firsthand evidence—was in many respects enabled by millennia of published Christian hatred of the Jews, from the Gospel according to St. John through the polemics of the dominant Catholic Church to the notably vile rhetoric of French anti-Semitic polemicists in the years just before the Holocaust. Kaufmann is a great admirer of Hay, an admiration that began in the years before 1960 when he wrote an enthusiastic preface to this remarkable book. Hay was himself a Roman Catholic, and so his teaching burning truth to members of his own congregation prompts Kaufmann to see him as an Old Testament prophet. Kaufmann is very direct and unusually exercised—and therefore revealing—when he writes, in "History and Honesty," his preface to Hay's book:

> It is well to know that these unflattering vignettes of great saints, popes, and some of the most celebrated Christians, these terrible quotations from their writings, and the unforgettable sketches of the Crusades were not drawn by an exultant rationalist but by a true heir of the Hebrew prophets who, without the comfort of the least delight, accuses, spurred by honesty, his own fold and whatever it holds sacred—and does it in the name of standards that are publicly professed but shamefully belied in worship and in action. . . . Malcolm Hay confronts us as a heartening exception, a true heir of Amos and Hosea. . . . If most priests and ministers resembled Malcolm Hay, I should still feel that Christianity is intellectually, and today emotionally, too, a failure; but I should not feel, as I do now, that it is such a dismal moral failure.[40]

Kaufmann's admiration for Hay's position is supported by his admiration for his character, his book being "a monument of honesty, humanity and . . . hope" (Hay greeted enthusiastically the founding of a Jewish homeland in Palestine) and surely, too, for his style—laconic, erudite, and touched by a prudent gallows humor.[41] Here, typically, is Hay: "There are therefore still some people who believe that the Jews were cursed out of Palestine because they had behaved in a manner displeasing to God. If nations were liable to be dispossessed for such a reason, very few of them would enjoy security of tenure. 'The Curse,' as J-P Sartre has recently pointed out, 'was geographical'" (R 348).

Kaufmann's passion for clear thought and incisive writing leads him to include, in this anthology of religious texts, a number of technical pieces on the epistemology of religious belief. In a paper titled "Gods," the Cambridge philosopher John Wisdom shifts the leading question from reasoning from signs of divinity to a reasoning from "meaning." Wisdom's argument leads him to consider how so-called facts are a product of what one "notices"—and noticing can lead to giving emphasis to details that other observers have seen but not emphasized. This emphasis produces the name of something import-ant to relationships, for example, the names "love" ("She loved him"), "hate" ("Really, she hated him"), "God" ("There is a God"). Wisdom elaborates:

> The line between using a name because of how we feel and because of what we have noticed isn't sharp. "A difference as to the facts," "a discovery," "a revelation," these phrases cover many things. Discoveries have been made not only by Christopher Columbus and Pasteur, but also by *Tolstoy and Dostoevsky and Freud*. Things are revealed to us not only by the scientists with microscopes, but also by the poets, the prophets, and the painters (emphasis added). (R 395)

One can readily imagine the pleasure these lines would have given Kaufmann. In fact, he explicitly notes the aesthetic factor in formal philosoph-ical analysis, a lesson in taste that will swiftly migrate to the reader. "While James' 'The Will to Believe' is a popular piece that does not stand up under analysis," Kaufmann writes, "Wisdom's 'Gods' is a delicacy for thinkers, and concentrates on a crucial matter which is ignored altogether in James' essay: the question of meaning" (R 36). Wisdom's arguments inspired commentar-ies by three of Kaufmann's British contemporaries, the philosophers Antony Flew, Richard Hare, and Basil Mitchell, who engage in subtle and imaginative dialogues on the great question of justification and faith. Flew sees no justifi-cation. I'll add that Jerry Coyne's recent admirable *Faith vs. Fact: Why Science and Religion Are Incompatible* develops Flew's conviction in detail and with the authority of his scientific achievement, incidentally building explicitly on Kaufmann's definition of "faith" along the way.[42]

As a sort of afterthought, in the second edition of the anthology, Kaufmann decided to include an essay "God, Evil, and Immortality" by John McTaggart, a Cambridge philosopher contemporary with Josiah Royce, which in its details is anything but a delicacy for thinkers. Here is one of McTaggart's arguments for the absoluteness, in a certain sense, of evil.

> We do not wait to call a man wicked till he does more evil than good. If a man should, at the risk of his life, save all the crew of a sinking ship but one, and should then, from mere caprice, leave that man to sink, whom he could easily have saved, we should say that he had acted wickedly. Nor is it necessary that a man should do evil for the sake of evil. To desire to attend a concert is not a desire for evil as such, but if I killed a man in order to acquire his ticket, I should have acted wickedly.

Here is another:

> The production of sin may under certain circumstances be justified. Supposing that it were true—*fortunately there is no reason to believe that it is true*—that employment as an executioner tended to degrade morally *a large proportion* of those who were employed, it would by no means follow that men ought not to be induced to act as executioners. The evil results which might follow from having no hangman might far outweigh the evil done to morality by having one (emphasis added). (R 457)

These examples range from the fatuous to the reprehensible. The latter meditation is particularly odious when it is appears almost immediately next to the closing pages of Camus's "Reflections on the Guillotine," which declares capital punishment vile and indefensible. Earlier we asked whether our literary criticism is not a form of theology, building on mostly unobserved theological premises. In that case, what we appear to be doing on seeming aesthetic grounds is in fact theology. I think the vulgarity of McTaggart's examples helps to display the clumsiness of his argument for a theodicy next to the elegance of Wisdom and his three commentators. I am very willing to say that Kaufmann nodded.

Major contributors I have not mentioned include the neo-orthodox Protestant theologians Karl Barth and Emil Brunner and the liberal Christians Rudolf Bultmann and Paul Tillich. It comes as no surprise that Kaufmann finds them all wrongheaded and uninspiring, in the sense that, for him, the Hebrew prophets, in their passion for social justice, are inspiring. Here, for one, is Kaufmann's characterization of Barth: "Barth counted culture among the things that are Caesar's and associated faith in man, reason, and progress with idolatry" (R 32).

Albert Schweitzer provides, in one respect, a salutary contrast: "His work on *The Quest of the Historical Jesus* helped to undermine liberal Protestantism by showing that the popular assumption that Jesus was, in effect, a liberal Protestant, if not a Reform Jew, was highly implausible on historical grounds. . . . Schweitzer's conception of the kingdom [of God] is much closer to the Hebrew prophets than to Jesus" (R 37). But Kaufmann's fuller discussion of Schweitzer in *The Faith of a Heretic* is again critical. Schweitzer degrades the ethic of the Sermon on the Mount as an "interim ethic," in light of the absolute connection of Jesus's otherworldliness with his view of the coming of the end of this world. On the other hand, in a leap of reason, Schweitzer dogmatically salvages "a living faith in the kingdom of God," even if, as he declares, an exact conception of this kingdom is of secondary importance. This is a regrettable qualification, since, according to Kaufmann, few men, in the last resort, "have done more than he [Schweitzer] to demonstrate the complete incompatibility of Jesus' conception of the kingdom with any social or this-worldly aspirations" (F 239).

Martin Buber, whom Kaufmann knew personally and whose influential *Ich und Du* (I and Thou) Kaufmann was to translate anew, is evidently the more engaging thinker and enables a number of new perspectives. Kaufmann notes that although there have been abundant Jewish thinkers writing in accessible Western languages, very few have influenced Christian thought. *I and Thou* is an exception. And yet, although "it has profoundly influenced Protestant theology," it may not be Buber's best book. His translation, together with Franz Rosenzweig, of the Hebrew Bible into German is, for Kaufmann, a great and congenial feat, understandably in light of the fresh insights into the Bible it makes possible as well as its rhetorical force (R 38–39). It does need to be noted, however, that during the Weimar Republic, Siegfried Kracauer and Walter Benjamin—two writers who go almost unnoticed in Kaufmann's canon of German intellectuals, as he is mainly put off by the suspicious difficulty of their writings—strongly objected to the translation. Had Kaufmann read them, he would have encountered, in the words of Martin Jay, the charge of the misplaced confidence behind "the messianic act aimed at moving us closer to primal speech. . . . There is a potential danger in the very search for an *Ursprache* (a primordial language), which is shared by all forms of gnostic hubris."[43]

Kaufmann's contentious rank ordering continues: "No other work of Buber's seems as firmly assured of a lasting place in world literature as his collection of *The Tales of the Hasidim*." Here we might be inclined to recall Kaufmann's summary conviction: "Religion is most moving in the form of stories, [which] . . . can be read as a species of literature, along with the plays of Shakespeare and Sophocles, . . . as a source of profound experiences" (R 42). In the years to come Kaufmann will often be occupied with the mind of Buber—and, in a later work, will come to challenge and dislike it (chapter 16).

Camus, who gets a poor report from Kaufmann as an existentialist philosopher, nonetheless serves as a final pivot to this anthology. Although "he is not primarily concerned with religion . . . he attempted great things: . . . his inspiration was moral." It is worth stressing once more that what matters most to Kaufmann in religion is the support it lends to morals, which are maintained by another sort of faith infused with reason, the expression of a "profound humanity" (R 39–40). In this sense Camus is a writer *on the model of Tolstoy*, a point empirically supported by the fact, for example, that a long monologue by the figure Tarrou in *The Plague* in many places echoes Tolstoy's *Resurrection*.

Sontag, whose harsh review we mentioned earlier, offers what seems a decisive objection to Camus's appearing in Kaufmann's anthology of *religious* writings:

> Camus was not, nor ever claimed to be, religious. In fact, one of the points he makes in his essay ["Reflections on the Guillotine"] is that capital punishment derives its only plausible rationale as a religious punishment and is therefore entirely inappropriate and ethically obscene in our present post-religious, secularized society. . . . If Camus is a serious writer and worthy of respect, it is because he seeks to reason according to the post-religious premises. He does not belong in the "story" of modern religion.[44]

What Sontag fails to see, in light of the later essays in Kaufmann's book, is that the "'story' of modern religion" as told by Kaufmann and especially Malcolm Hay is a story of the inhumanity—the moral ineptitude—of the Christian churches, for whom the desolation of the Jews was, for many centuries, a divine imperative and in modern, "post-religious, secularized" times a matter of cold neglect. In the vile decades of the twentieth century, the churches were in diplomatic league with ideology-besotted states for which murder was a bagatelle.[45] Like Kaufmann, repeatedly—like Malcolm Hay—Camus makes this very point. "The Catholic Church . . . has always admitted the necessity of the death penalty. It has imposed the penalty itself, without avarice, at other periods. Today, its doctrines still justify capital punishment, and concede the State the right to apply it." Camus then quotes a certain M. Grand, a Swiss councilor from Fribourg, present in 1937 at a discussion of capital punishment by the national council: "Without becoming precisely a matter of doctrine, the death penalty, *like war itself*, can be justified by its quasi-divine efficacity" (emphasis added) (R 444). One can surely agree with Sontag that Camus "was not or never claimed to be religious." But Kaufmann's book is an anthology of the writings of various intellectuals and not a gallery of authentic believers and canny theologians. It is therefore very much to the point that Camus thinks through the category of the "religious," as when he writes, in the text included by Kaufmann,

> Our society has become as diseased and criminal as it is only because it has set itself up as it own final justification, and has had no concern but its own

preservation and success in history. Certainly it is a secularized society, yet during the nineteenth century it began to fashion a kind of ersatz religion by proposing itself as an object of adoration. . . . It has regarded as a crime and a sacrilege everything that contradicts its own intentions and temporal dogmas. (qtd. in R 446)

Camus belongs in this anthology, indeed at this critical place. The lines I want to quote now, because they are so interesting, bear more on the state liable to murder than to the church liable to indifference:

Confronted with crime, how does our civilization in fact define itself? The answer is easy: for 30 years crimes of state have vastly exceeded crimes of individuals. I shall not even mention wars—general or local—although blood is a kind of alcohol that eventually intoxicates like the strongest wine. I am referring here to the number of individuals killed directly by the State, a number that has grown to astronomic proportions and infinitely exceeds that of "private" murders. There are fewer and fewer men condemned by common law, and more and more men executed for political reasons. The proof of this fact is that each of us, no matter how honorable he is, can now envisage the *possibility* of someday being put to death, whereas such an eventuality at the beginning of the century would have appeared farcical at best. Alphonse Karr's famous remark "Let my lords the assassins [be the first to] begin," no longer has any meaning: those who spill the most blood are also those who believe they have right, logic, and history on their side. (R 446)[46]

These lines build a bridge to Kaufmann's next project, and our next chapter: Hegel's mooted divinization of the state.

8

Living with Hegel

HEGEL: A REINTERPRETATION

In a sense I have lived with Hegel since I was four.

—WALTER KAUFMANN

One should try, if one bothers at all with the views of others, really to master each in turn—as an existential whole, keeping in mind that each belief is part of a larger view, and that each view requires a point of view which involves a human reality.

—WALTER KAUFMANN

IN JANUARY 1961, a frosty reviewer of Kaufmann's *From Shakespeare to Existentialism* declared that Kaufmann should stop collecting articles which, when assembled in books, reveal no distinctive argument and get to work on a serious academic monograph.[1] When "Professor Kaufmann is at his best," wrote Professor William Kennick, it is "as an expositor and critic of German philosophy. In this role he has no peer in America. It is regrettable, therefore, that he has wasted his talents and energies in this book . . . instead of devoting them to, say, a full-dress book on Hegel."[2] Kennick might very well have been recalling the impression made by Kaufmann's "landmark" essay on Hegel, "The Hegel Myth and Its Method," originally published in 1951 and discussed in our chapter 5.[3] In April 1961, shortly after Kennick's review appeared, Kaufmann published his lengthy review of an indeed full-dress book on Hegel—J. N. Findlay's *Hegel: A Re-examination*—concluding with these captious words:

230

Instead of coming close to feigning completeness by compressing the contents of big books into big chapters, one should single out what is especially important: important insights and important errors; views that, whether right or wrong, have had historical significance by giving subsequent thought new directions; and ideas which, although not influential so far, ought to be considered. Findlay's book does some of this, but not enough. It is one of the best books yet written on Hegel, and it may help to stir up enough interest in Hegel to lead someone else to write an even better one.[4]

How deeply Kaufmann felt committed, in writing that sentence, to be that someone is unfathomable, but he must surely have realized that knowledgeable readers would consider him implicated; and a little like Babe Ruth allegedly calling his shot in the 1932 World Series by pointing to the bleachers at Wrigley Field, he, Kaufmann, had better now damned well hit a home run. If it's unlikely that this hardball image went through Kaufmann's head at the time of his writing his review, he certainly had read Thomas Mann's *Reflections of an Unpolitical Man*, in which Mann writes, "I've often felt that Nietzsche's philosophy might be able to become the good fortune and the lucky find of a great writer. . . . Unlike Schopenhauer, Nietzsche has not found or not yet found his artist."[5] But it is hard to believe that Mann at this moment was not supposing that the project of completing Nietzsche would be his and no one else's. In Mann's light, the final sentence of Kaufmann's review does indeed look like his final sentence: he would now feel bound to produce the book that would accomplish everything Findlay had failed to do. Four years later Kaufmann vindicated his dare and published *Hegel: A Reinterpretation* in about four hundred pages. In *his* review of Kaufmann's reinterpretation, Findlay was hardly convinced that Kaufmann's book had met every one of Kaufmann's criteria, though he generously considered Kaufmann's book a handsome effort.[6]

There are other factors to consider in judging Kaufmann's motives for writing an entire book on Hegel. Earlier, in *The Faith of a Heretic*, Kaufmann had himself raised the possibility of a monograph on Hegel—he had been encouraged to write it a decade before Kennick's review—but had then rejected the idea in favor of books that would mean more—existentially—to more readers.[7] How can we now imagine the impulse to realize this project?

Several motives appear to have flowed together. As a recently promoted full professor of philosophy at Princeton, Kaufmann would have felt the urge coming from his home department to write books along conventional disciplinary lines. But overcoming that demand, in light of his character and a sense of his fate—Kaufmann had considerable powers of resistance to voices that might lure him off course—there was his growing love and interest in Hegel, even if, as he now writes, "the honeymoon has long passed" (H ix). That love and interest would have been much developed during the twelve years of his marriage to Hegel, so to speak, teaching graduate seminars on Hegel at Princeton.

Kaufmann's fascination with Hegel began long before his tenure at Princeton. He remembers, while growing up, the works of German Enlightenment thinkers in his parents' bookshelves—books by Lessing, Kant, Goethe, and Schiller; but above a green tile corner stove, there hung "a large picture of Kant . . . flanked by smaller portraits of Fichte and Hegel. In a sense I have lived with Hegel since I was four" (H viii). Such intimacy notwithstanding, Kaufmann did not *read* Hegel until he reached the United States, which, he reflects, added a certain distance, crucial for criticism, to his relation to Hegel, where the first requirement, intimacy, had been easily come by. Following Kaufmann, Hegel criticism (before 1965) had suffered from a hypertrophy of one or the other of these two types of relation. Closeness led the German scholar Theodor Haering in 1929 to devote thirteen hundred pages to Hegel's youthful writings without managing to address his mature work; while the English-born W. T. Stace, who taught at Princeton with Kaufmann, polished off Hegel decades earlier, in 1924, in a monograph, *The Philosophy of Hegel*, devoted entirely to Hegel's *Encyclopedia*.

After intermittent sojourns underground in the history of ideas, Hegel became very much alive in 1965, and it would have suited Kaufmann's temperament to correct a variety of tendentious readings: his book is called, after all, a "*Reinterpretation.*" In an informative essay, Anthony Quinton has charted the irregular arc of Hegel's reputation:

> Hegel's reputation in the English-speaking world was at its lowest ebb in 1945. That was the year of Russell's *History of Western Philosophy*, with its genially dismissive treatment of Hegel, and of the stormy invective of the Hegel chapter in Karl Popper's *The Open Society and Its Enemies*. In Britain the last embers of resistance to analytic philosophy, itself inaugurated at the turn of the century by Russell and Moore in total rejection of British neo-Hegelianism, had been stamped out. . . . In all branches of philosophy Hegel's ideas were not thought worth consideration even as an exemplary form of error. . . .
>
> In Europe the revival of Hegel came about at much the same time as the philosophical revision of Marx and in much the same way: by attention to

the earliest writings, which had for the most part been newly discovered. The *Realphilosophie* of Hegel's Jena period provided a new approach to *The Phenomenology of Spirit*, as did Marx's *Economic and Philosophical Manuscripts of 1844* to *The German Ideology*. Kojève's *Introduction to the Reading of Hegel*, now available in English, is a version of his famous and influential lectures of the 1930s. These awakened an interest that was further fed by Hyppolite's translation of the *Phenomenology* (1934), his long commentary on it (1946), and the essays of 1955.[8]

At this point Quinton addresses the matter most immediately at hand, Kaufmann's reinvigoration of Hegel scholarship in the United States. "In the United States the revival of interest in Hegel was initially the work of Walter Kaufmann, first in the Fifties in a series of articles, of which the most notable is 'The Hegel Myth and Its Method,' . . . an analysis of Popper's attack that is all the more effective for the general sympathy it shows to Popper, and later, in 1965, in the slightly inchoate mixture of translation, commentary, and general discussion that makes up his *Hegel*." Quinton's survey fails to include the earlier impact of Herbert Marcuse's *Reason and Revolution*, first published in 1941, which, incidentally, Kaufmann considers "remarkable" for its study of Hegel's political writings (H 247).[9] We will let Quinton's casual characterization of Kaufmann's *Hegel* pass for the moment.

Quinton's essay continues with a general orientation to Kaufmann's achievement, which will not surprise readers who have stayed until now: "Kaufmann's interest in Hegel is part of his general project of rescuing post-Kantian philosophy in Germany from the largely unsubstantiated charge by Anglo-Saxon philosophers that it is intellectually grotesque and morally outrageous. Hegel took second place to Nietzsche in this project, Kaufmann's aim being to dissociate the intellectual tradition in which they stand at either end from the Heideggerian philosophy."[10]

I will stress that Parisian Hegelmania was energized in the late 1940s by Hyppolite's massive commentary on the *Phenomenology* following his translation. The commentary was translated some decades later as *Genesis and Structure of Hegel's "Phenomenology of Spirit"* by Samuel Cherniak and John Heckman, with a valuable introduction discussing the importance of this book for Sartre, Foucault, Derrida, Lacan, and others.[11] Hyppolite's translators—Cherniak and Heckman—were my classmates at Paul de Man's seminars at Cornell in 1964, which coincided with the upsurge of poststructuralist literary theory in the United States. It was important then to know at least the chapter of the *Phenomenology* devoted to the master-slave relation and its products—stoicism, skepticism, and the unhappy consciousness—so as to come to grips with Jacques Lacan's post-Freudian permutations on this dyad.

In this chapter, I will paraphrase and cite the passages from Kaufmann, as I have done in previous chapters, that best convey the thrust of his argument—here, his *reinterpretation* of Hegel. His interpretation is more a matter of a selection of aspects of Hegel's life and work for exposition than it is an explicit and sustained argument. But his choice of key moments is presumably informed by the intellectual pleasure and instruction he takes from them. My selection answers to the same principle, although I am especially drawn to passages that give me the opportunity to comment. This procedure will not surprise the reader who has been patient enough to accompany us along this way—I say "us" deliberately. Since, when I am not commenting, I will often be paraphrasing Kaufmann on Hegel, it will be impossible to avoid, in many places, a fusion of voices.

Kaufmann has a notable view on the right way to write and think about Hegel. No longer do the categories of intimacy versus distance have any place in his method, which he locates, surprisingly, at the pole of comprehension *in opposition* to exegesis. Comprehension includes the reading modes of identification and also criticism: one must understand an argument before one can judge it to be right or wrong. To practice exegesis, on the other hand, appears to imply the decisive superiority of the source text, which comes enwrapped with the authority of its (presumably unassailable) author and toward whom the explicator adopts a subservient—a slavish?—posture. Anathema! Secondly, the exegete—as I imagine Kaufmann's resistance to the type—is likely to overcome his subservience by producing what Adorno calls "ein orientiertes Verständnis" (a "motivated" reading):[12] the exegesis makes the thought of the writer fit wonderfully the reader's own unexamined preconceptions. Kaufmann takes slight pains to mention Heidegger as its exemplary practitioner, who then gives exegesis a bad name. In *From Shakespeare to Existentialism*, Kaufmann asked: "But does Heidegger ever entertain the possibility that Hölderlin or Sophocles, Heraclitus or Parmenides might be mistaken about anything?" (S 360).[13]

In Kaufmann's study of Hegel, phylogeny recapitulates ontogeny, so to speak: just as the books of Lessing, Kant, Goethe, and Schiller preceded Hegel as visual objects of importance in Kaufmann's living room, when he was young and German, so too his book on Hegel, which he wrote as an

American, sees Lessing, Kant, Goethe, and Schiller in their historical profusion as presences in Hegel's early writings. They were, of course, more than books: they were Hegel's older contemporaries. Here are their birth dates: Georg Wilhelm Friedrich Hegel was born in 1770; Lessing, in 1729; Kant, in 1746; Goethe, in 1749; Schiller, in 1759. The masterworks of these older writers were published in Hegel's first years of study, had an impact, and leave vivid traces in his writing. Prominent among them are Lessing's *The Education of Mankind* in 1780; Kant's *Critique of Practical Reason* in 1788; Goethe's *Faust—a Fragment* in 1790; and Schiller's *On the Aesthetic Education of Man* in 1795. In his early writings on religion, Hegel cited Lessing's treatise more often than any other source.

Many other works of this efflorescence of German genius entered his conceptual world; Kaufmann strikes an original note in Hegel scholarship by stressing the abundance of literary and literary-aesthetic figures in Hegel's early writings—and this inclusion persists into Hegel's masterworks. Hegel's critical preoccupation with German romanticism is especially understandable when we realize that (Karl Wilhelm) Friedrich Schlegel, August Wilhelm Schlegel, Friedrich Schleiermacher, and Novalis (Georg Philipp Friedrich Freiherr von Hardenberg) were all virtually Hegel's age; he experienced them as intimately present contemporaries—and hence as irresistibly inviting criticism. He would deplore their romantic "inwardness," a certain subjectivity that, as he was to write in his reflections on comedy, had lost all interest in *representing* itself. He was sooner inclined to incorporate Goethe, the coryphant of German "classicism," being especially indebted to the classic vision of Goethe's play *Iphigenia in Tauris*.

> Hegel fully accepts and shares Goethe's . . . association of the Greeks with an ethic of harmony and humanity. . . . Goethe's *Iphigenia* is cited by Hegel in 1795 . . . and again in "Faith and Knowledge" in 1802; and above all we have comments on Iphigenia in his lectures on aesthetics: "With Goethe . . . [as opposed to Euripides], Iphigenia becomes a goddess and trusts the truth in herself, in the human heart." "Goethe . . . interprets the ambiguous divine pronouncement . . . in a humane and conciliatory manner: the pure and holy Iphigenia is the sister, the divine image, and the protector of the house." (H 17–18)

I'll add that in Kaufmann's presentation of Hegel, the opposition between this "classic" vision and the "romantic"—which Goethe described as a "passionate schism" ("leidenschaftlicher Zwiespalt")—is no longer held to be conceptually adequate, especially in the more drastic of Goethe's formulations, which holds the "classic" to be "healthy" and the "romantic," sick.[14] Hegel's stricture against the romantics could never be applied to Hölderlin, Hegel's closest friend—although he is often called romantic—who wrote mythically and historically saturated poetry from a fully expanded subjectivity.

Their friendship was formed and strengthened by ethics and ideas they shared in the boarding school they attended from 1788 to 1793, the renowned Tübinger Stift—both Rousseauists, both enthusiasts of the French Revolution: together they planted a "freedom tree." Some years later, however, the starting-off point of Hölderlin's philosophical itinerary, after an anguished love affair, would become something very different from Hegel's. I'll note that it begins with a moment of felt plenitude that Hölderlin calls "beauty." The hero of his eponymous novel *Hyperion* celebrates the immediate presence (*Vorhandenheit*) of "that infinite unification—Being, in the unique sense of the word. It is present—as beauty," even though fated to tragic disintegration when a subject-object consciousness resurges to shatter it.[15] By contrast, in Hegel's *Phenomenology*—his great philosophical flight—the starting-off point is the radical incompleteness, the deficient, merely part truth of sense perception.

Their mutual attentiveness continued until Hölderlin gradually succumbed to a schizophrenic near-silence, a sickness of the body and not of a poetic style. I stress "near" silence. Even in this parlous state, Hölderlin wrote short lyrics that astute critics have seen as presaging a certain second-order modernist naïveté if, let us say, the lyrics of Georg Trakl (1887–1914) for one, another schizophrenic poet, can be so described.[16] Kaufmann is brutally out of step in terming Hölderlin's late stage as "little more than [that of] of a vegetable" (H 3).

In the matter of the early influences of Hegel's contemporaries, Hegel's general opposition to Kant is significant. In chapter 5, dealing with Kaufmann's essays on Hegel in *From Shakespeare to Existentialism*, we noted Kaufmann's leading idea of Hegel's "logic of passion": the final section of the essay "The Young Hegel and Religion" is titled "The Logic of Passion," and Kaufmann would thereafter describe the thought movement of *Phenomenology* as a "logic of passion." In *Philosophy of History*, we now read, Hegel wrote: "*Nothing great in the world has been accomplished without passion*." This claim is, to say the least, quite contrary to Kant. Kaufmann quotes at length Kant's vivid diatribe against ruling passions from the latter's *Anthropology*:

Passions are cancers for pure practical reason and often incurable. . . . It is folly (making a *part* of one's aim the *whole*) that strictly contradicts reason even in its formal principle. Therefore the passions are not only, like the affects, *unfortunate* moods that are pregnant with many evils, but also, without exception, wicked, and the most benign desire, even if it aims at what belongs (considering the matter) to virtue, e.g., to charity . . . yet is (considering the form), as soon as it degenerates into a passion, not only *pragmatically* pernicious but also *morally* reprehensible. An affect brings about a momentary collapse of freedom and of the dominion over oneself. Passion renounces them and finds its pleasure and satisfaction in a slavish mind. (H 5)

Hegel also disputed Kant on the priority owed to the different moral principles of *Moralität* (a region, following Kant, of putative autonomous determination) and *Sittlichkeit* (the ethical order shaped by family life, civil society, and the state). The precedence of the latter is one that Hegel maintains throughout his entire work: "His image of Kant was always determined decisively by Kant's *Moralität* and its striking contrast with the *Sittlichkeit* of the Greeks, as interpreted in Goethe's *Iphigenia* and in Schiller's 'Letters' *On the Aesthetic Education of Man*" (H 8). We will return to this opposition in discussing Hegel's writings on the state, which attenuate this principle in envisaging the eventuality of tragic conflict. There, Hegel will write:

In the course of history, the preservation of a people, a state, and the preservation of the ordered spheres of its life, is one essential moment. . . . The other moment, however, is that this stable persistence of the spirit of a people . . . is broken because it is exhausted and overworked; that world history, the world spirit proceeds. . . . But this is tied to a demotion, demolition, destruction of the preceding mode of actuality. . . . It is precisely here that the great collisions occur between the prevalent, recognized duties, laws, and rights and, on the other hand, possibilities which are opposed to this system.

Kaufmann puts the matter directly, "In times of transition, the old mores no longer offer certainty, and the ethical world is rent by tragic collisions" (H 269). He would have us think Socrates, think Antigone, think . . . existentialism.

In Hegel's citing "the course of history," we are reminded of Kaufmann's insistence that it was not only works of literature and philosophy that affected the young Hegel. Material *events* helped to determine just which works of literature and philosophy would matter most to him. In 1792, when Hegel was twenty-two, the French began repeatedly invading Germany. Kaufmann writes vividly of

> what happened in France during the quarter of a century from the Revolution to Waterloo: . . . [it] was not just French history but also German history, and not just history but again and again a matter of life and limb. Napoleon's meteoric rise and brilliant campaigns were never far from one's mind—or body—and Hegel finished his first book, the *Phenomenology*, in Jena, the night before Napoleon finished the Holy Roman Empire, which had lasted over a thousand years, in the Battle of Jena. (H 3–4)

In this light, the importance for Hegel of Schiller's "Letters" *On the Aesthetic Education of Man* (1795) must be seen as inevitable. Schiller's work, on the surface a theoretical argument for the primacy of aesthetic activity—art, decorum, and play—is rooted in his immediate history and composed as an answer to a crisis: the brutal excesses of the French Revolution. In Schiller's view, these were owed, and would always be owed, to the tyranny of a dispirited Reason, a "formalism" that today we would call ideology. The domination in man of his natural element (Nature) produces a no less destructive "barbarism." Only a mediating force of the mind could save us—and this Schiller locates in the play drive (*Spieltrieb*), for "only there, where man plays, is man fully human" (H 29). His journey to this conclusion takes a rich path of negation that, for Kaufmann, exercised a decisive influence on Hegel's (subtle) sense of dialectic.

Schiller's Sixth Letter abounds in such examples: It is no good thing that "among us . . . the faculties of the mind [*Gemütskräfte*] express themselves as separately in experience as the psychologist differentiates them in theory" (H 20). Schiller's comment might imply a rebuke to Kant, "whose dissection of man," writes Kaufmann, "reflects the modern condition" (H 20). As Wordsworth's poem "The Tables Turned" has it—Wordsworth is Schiller's younger and Hegel's exact contemporary—"Our meddling intellect / Mis-shapes the beauteous forms of things:— / We murder to dissect."[17]

The Sixth Letter formulates a rather brilliant dialectic involving the salvaging of fragmentation by a conflict of opposites:

> The appearance of Greek humanity was unquestionably a maximum that neither could tarry nor climb higher on this stage. It could not tarry there because the understanding one possessed even then could not possibly

help separating itself from feeling and intuition to strive for distinctness of knowledge; and it could not climb higher because only a certain degree of distinctness can coexist with a certain fullness and warmth. The Greeks had reached this degree, and if they wished to progress to a higher form [*Ausbildung*], they, like we [*sic*], had to give up the totality of their nature to pursue truth on separate ways. To develop man's manifold dispositions, there was no other means than to oppose them to each other. *This antagonism of forces is the great instrument of culture* (emphasis added). (H 21)

Schiller's work ends "with a call for the restoration of the harmonious totality of our nature." This appeal, Kaufmann stresses, cannot conjure "a return to a past golden age but rather a harmony that is higher and more advanced than was the Greeks', because it will retain the advances made possible by the sacrifice of such harmony in the intervening centuries" (H 22). This conception of "stages of development"—through which the individual, like "the general spirit," passes—informs Hegel's burgeoning conception of the *Phenomenology*. Disintegration, tension, and thereafter production at a higher level forecast his dialectical thinking throughout.

Kaufmann points up a second figure of thought usually associated with Hegel but already present in Schiller's *Letters*: the contrast of two types of infinity—"the lack of all [spiritual] determination, an *empty infinity* . . . and the aesthetic freedom of determination [that] must be considered a *replete infinity*" (Schiller) (H 26). The many other energetic oppositions that Hegel and Schiller share suggest a thoroughgoing conceptual kinship. Schiller's text is an excellent propaedeutic to reading Hegel: consider Schiller's use of the key word *Geist*. "*Geist*," Kaufmann explains, "is the heir of the sensuous drive *and* of the form drive; it is not—and this is important for understanding Hegel—primarily an epistemological faculty or organ of knowledge, like 'mind,' but above all . . . *a creative force*" (H 27). There is ample textual support for this coding: at the very end of the "Letters," Schiller writes, "An animal *works* when a lack is the driving spring of its activity, and it *plays* when an abundance of force is this driving spring, when the excess of life spurs itself into activity" (H 28). What a happy association this contrast of abundance and lack inspires in Kaufmann, who is put immediately in mind of Nietzsche's contrast of romantic and Dionysian art: "Regarding all aesthetic values I now avail myself of this main distinction: I ask in every single case, 'Is it hunger or overflow which has here become creative?' (*The Gay Science* [1887, par. 370])" (H 28). I'll note that this association is not casual: the presence of Schiller's aesthetic writings in Nietzsche's *The Birth of Tragedy*, especially a fine discussion of *moods*, is well established. It is only much later that Nietzsche begins to jeer at the moral idealism of the thinker who brought a certain intellectual music to his first book, calling him, in 1888, the "Moraltrumpeter von Säckingen" (the trumpeter of morals from the village of Bad Säckingen, an allusion to the title of the romantic story of the *Trompeter von Säckingen*).[18]

On the continuing presence of Schiller even in Hegel's mature work, Kaufmann notes that Hegel's *Phenomenology* concludes with an "adapted quotation from a Schiller poem" (H 30). (We were admittedly "adapting" chronology when we connected Schiller's *Letters* of 1795 with the *Phenomenology* of 1807; but, for Kaufmann, it is here that Hegel's intellectual signature is clearest.) The quotation from Schiller concludes Schiller's early poem "Friendship" (1782), the final stanza of which reads (in my literal translation)

> Friendless was the great World Master,
> Felt *a lack*—thus he created spirits,
> Blessed mirror of *his* bliss!—
> [While] the highest being still found no likeness
> From the chalice of the great realm of souls
> There foams for *him*—Infinity.

Here is Hegel's version of the last two lines:

> From the chalice of this realm of spirits
> There foams for him his infinity. (H 30)

The Hegel scholar Donald Phillip Verene offers this explanation for the "adaptation":

> The infinity that Schiller leaves us with suggests what Hegel in the *Science of Logic* [and Schiller in the *Aesthetic Letters*] calls the "bad infinite" (*Schlecht-Unendliche*), the infinite that just goes on and on. By transposing the line to "his" (*seine*) infinity, Hegel suggests the "true infinite" (*wahrhaft Unendliche*), the infinite of an existing whole that systematically and determinately recapitulates itself. What is recapitulated is the *Geisterreich*, the realm of spirit in all of its various moments and stages that is presented in the *Phenomenology of Spirit*. At the end of Schiller's poem the World Master or God is left in pathos. The divine fails to create a companion equal to himself. In Schiller's version pathos prevails because God's existence is left in the condition of the bad infinite. [But see Kaufmann's dissenting view,

below.] In Hegel's version God's existence has a tragic face. God's relation to the forms of his creation is that of fellow sufferer. Although his being is that of the true infinite, he suffers the quest to make actually and determinate all the movements within his infinite.[19]

Hegel's habit of misquoting, I'll add, belongs to a German idealist trait that Friedrich Kittler ridicules wittily in his *Discourse Networks, 1800/1900*.[20] I'll take the liberty of once again invoking this brilliant scene. When, in Kaufmann's translation of Goethe's *Faust*, Faust undertakes to translate the Greek New Testament, Faust begins with "the Word" (Λόγος), which he comments thus:

It says: "In the beginning was the *Word*."
Already I am stopped. It seems absurd.
The *Word* does not deserve the highest prize,
I must translate it otherwise
If I am well inspired and not blind.
It says: In the beginning was the *Mind*.
Ponder that first line, wait and see,
Lest you should write too hastily.
Is mind the all-creating source?
It ought to say: In the beginning there was *Force*.
Yet something warns me as I grasp the pen,
That my translation must be changed again.
The spirit helps me. Now it is exact.
I write: In the beginning was the *Act*.

"The spirit speaks." And now the question arises: who or what is this spirit that speaks to Faust as no dictionary or concordance or commentary does— and, in Hegel's case, requires the substitution of "realm of spirits" for "realm of souls"? The spirit of scholarship—*that* spirit does not speak. But there's only one other spirit in the room at the time: "If I am to share my room with you, / Poodle, stop moaning so!"[21] The poodle is Mephisto! This little scene might be called, following Kittler, the origin of a hermeneutics of poetry from the spirit . . . of the poodle—Mephisto, the great negator, the great perverter of right reason. Thus Kittler: "Out of the poodle, aroused by vexatious biblical words, a Spirit emerges. The mask drops—Mephisto was seconding the entire scene of writing. Indeed, there cannot be more than one Spirit in the same room. The scene of the Logos has never been read literally enough: it describes the birth of German poetry from the spirit of hell."[22]

In dwelling on Schiller and Goethe, we must not forget one of Kaufmann's chief interests in Hegel's early work—his writings on religion. Kaufmann's belief in their foundational importance is held to be a decisive novelty of his critique (although one could find such an insistence in an early work by Paul Asveld).[23] Young Hegel boldly thinks of Jesus as a teacher of virtue but not in any way superior to Socrates. Socrates, unlike Jesus, "did not offend anyone by swaggering self-importance or by using high-flown and mysterious phrases of the sort that impress only the ignorant and credulous" (Hegel) (H 33). In general these texts are fearless, vivid, and surprising; they even include a criticism of the Sermon on the Mount's attack on an ethic of established law. Hegel sides with the judges and the administrators of law: his insistence comes from his respect for *Sittlichkeit*, the ethical order shaped by family life, civil society, and the state.

Hegel's writings from his twenties are the work of a humanist in Kaufmann's fullest, blooming sense of the word; the young Hegel is Kaufmann *avant la lettre*. Hegel's "prime concern . . . was from the start 'to restore the human being again in his totality.' He felt that this all-important task, left undone by Kant, could not possibly be accomplished by Christianity. . . . He demands only 'the service of reason and virtue' and rejects faith" (H 34–35). And so it follows that he, like Kaufmann, became convinced that "a humanistic religion is an impossibility" (H 36). In discussing a long early essay titled "The Spirit of Christianity and Its Fate," Kaufmann sums up his first major perspective on Hegel:

> Here Jesus is made to teach the *Sittlichkeit* of the Greeks, of Goethe's Iphigenia, and of Schiller's *Letters* rather than Kant's *Moralität*. "A man who wished to restore the human being again in his totality," after Jewish *Moralität* and insistence on the law had led to "the human being's division against himself," had to offer an ethic that did not involve "acting from respect for duty and in contradiction to one's inclinations" (inner quotes from Nohl) (H 38).[24]

To the reader's surprise, Hegel's next important essay on religion *contradicts* this position. Here we have Hegel's irrepressible invocation of the negative. One cannot overlook, thus Hegel, the historical factor in a correct conception of Christianity—namely, the torrents of criticism by contemporaries exposing its shortcomings. Hegel finds this sort of criticism inane, because one-sided, meaning: the critic cannot be "really serious about it" (H 131). Surely it can be shown that Christianity, in light of its history, also has its share of truth and moral distinction? This logic of a higher recapitulation of one-sidedness—the logic of *Aufhebung*, of a cancellation that preserves and raises up the negated item—persistently informs Hegel's own procedure. But this logic is shifting, organic, alive. Its motto, evidently, is: Always triangulate—at least! In his earlier criticism, Hegel had contrasted Christianity "unfavorably with the popular religion of Greece," but, as Kaufmann clearly—and fatefully—shows, "Hegel came to believe that the harmony of ancient Greece had to be disrupted to make way for a higher development which could now be consummated—not in religion, which is incapable of restoring man in his totality, but in philosophy" (H 41).

Christianity is a way station to the Absolute, a journey of the mind that only philosophy could complete. Such way stations are also crucial and constitutive. In his late lectures on the philosophy of history, Hegel would write: "To this point the world spirit has got now. The last philosophy is the result of all earlier ones; nothing is lost, all principles are conserved. This concrete idea is the result of the *exertions of the spirit* through almost 2500 years (Thales was born 640 B.C.)" (H 44). A historical process of *Aufhebung* coincides with Hegel's own logic of thought and writing and lecturing in the sense that these lectures assume "the standpoint of the present time, and the series of spiritual formations is for the present concluded with this.—Herewith, this history of philosophy is *concluded*" (H 45). This conclusion provides an audacious—though still only temporary—end to the historical process that is philosophy itself. A wonderful summation from an 1801 essay very informatively titled "Difference of the Fichtean and Schellingian System of Philosophy in Relation to Reinhold's Contributions toward a Readier Examination of the Condition of Philosophy at the Beginning of the Nineteenth Century, First Installment" defines the energetic motor of philosophical development as this historical development of *oppositions*:

> To sublimate such oppositions that have become fixed is the sole interest of reason. This interest does not mean that reason is against opposition and limitation in general; for necessary bifurcation is a factor of life which forms itself through eternal opposing, and totality is possible in the highest liveliness only through restoration out of the highest separation. Reason is only against the absolute fixation of bifurcation by the understanding. . . . When the power of unification disappears from the life of men and opposites have lost their living relation and reciprocity and gain independence, then the need for philosophy originates. (H 49–50)

This might be the clarion call, sounding through the ages, to which Parisian and satellite deconstruction, a century and a half later, powerfully responded. *This* essay, "The Difference," contains a second argument of considerable cogency: it settles the war between philosophy and common sense with the invocation of a higher inclusiveness: "As soon as such truths of common sense are taken by themselves and isolated . . . they appear slanted and as half-truths. . . . Speculation therefore understands common sense, but common sense does not understand what speculation does" (H 50). Here too we have the operation of the *Aufhebung*, since common sense is not vacuous: it does, however, contradict itself, its truths being half-truths. As such it has the use value of prompting speculation, which perceives the analogy of common sense with . . . the dream. Just as common sense is "unable to integrate the insights of philosophy," so too dreams are unable "to furnish us with a coherent view of the world in which both our dreams and waking experiences [like philosophy, like reason] can find their place" (H 51). Perhaps with unacknowledged resentment, common sense—"the geographical and temporary limitations of a group of men" (Hegel)—looks on philosophy as a topsy-turvy world. *Tant pis pour le sens commun.* This essay "Difference" criticizing common sense appeared in the first issue of the journal *Kritisches Journal der Philosophie*, edited, with Schelling, by Hegel. In the second issue, Hegel attacked skepticism.

This important essay, harbinger of a key chapter in the *Phenomenology*, begins with a historical scrutiny of skepticism's early forms. Sextus Empiricus is exemplary: "such skepticism recognizes the untruth of the finite." In plain words, it directs its attack against the dogmatism of common sense: "It may therefore be considered the first stage on the way to philosophy" (Hegel) (H 69). Hegel's treatment of modern, Humean skepticism, which, as he points out, is unlike Greek skepticism, becomes especially interesting when redefined as empiricism. "Ancient skepticism was so far from making feeling and intuition the principle of truth that, on the contrary, it turned first of all against the senses." Hegel's critique of empiricism is cogent today:

> The basic illusion in scientific empiricism is always this: that it uses the metaphysical categories of matter, force, and of course, one, many, generality, also infinite, etc., and furthermore makes *inferences* following the thread of such categories, while presupposing the forms of inference and using them—and all the while it does not know that it thus contains and does metaphysics and uses these categories and their connections in an entirely uncritical and unconscious manner. (H 72)

Kaufmann stresses that the arguments described above, though they form part of texts that could be called Hegel's juvenilia, nonetheless echo down the course of his mature writings. A third essay from this stock titled "Faith and Knowledge" (1802) points to one of Hegel's deepest philosophical convictions. It is "an important stage on Hegel's way from a critique of the 'positive' and irrational face of Christianity to the attempt to find knowledge by means of philosophy" (H 74). Hegel finds a vivid example in "the negative procedure of the Enlightenment" for the distinction that Schiller made between "knowledge" (which, on Kaufmann's suggestion, we earlier termed "dispirited reason") and *philosophical* reason. The Enlightenment

> whose positive side was . . . without any kernel, obtained a kernel by grasping its own negativity and by liberating itself from shallowness by means of the purity and infinity of the negative. On the other hand, the objects of its positive knowledge could therefore be merely finite and empirical things, while the eternal had to remain beyond. For knowledge, the eternal thus remains empty, and this infinite empty space of knowledge can be filled only with the subjectivity of longing and intimation. (qtd. in H 75)

What implication does this aperçu have for the task of philosophical reason? Just as, for Hegel, there can be religion without the religious spirit, so there can be

> a reason devoid of the spirit of reason. . . . Hegel opposes the philosophers who deny themselves the contemplation of the infinite and eternal, supposing that it dwells forever beyond reason; on the contrary, it is the task of reason and philosophy to contemplate the spirit in *this* world. (H 77)

The italicized article is crucial.

This point about the immanence of spirit touches on a key ethical distinction, which we have noted before, but which appears with renewed emphasis in Hegel's manuscripts from this period of 1802–3. Hegel's criticism of Kantian moral theory leads to his valorizing actions termed *"sittlich"* in opposition to those based—as Kaufmann puts it—"on the solitary individual's ratiocination about his maxims. . . . Kant had introduced the word *Moralität*, which, unlike *Moral*, is a rather artificial term; and Hegel, wanting to distinguish the Kantian ethic from his own, employs this label for Kant's while appropriating *Sittlichkeit* for his own" (H 82). But what is this—to be *sittlich*? In the words of Diogenes Laertius, which Hegel's text cites approvingly, "being ethical [*sittlich*] means living in accordance with the customs [*Sitten*] of one's country" (H 82–83).

The question then arises, from comments made by the Hegel scholar Rudolf Haym, whom Kaufmann often cites, whether Hegel did indeed believe at this time that "the real realization of the absolute spirit in ethical *communal* life was . . . the altogether true and highest realization of the spirit; [that] the ethical spirit *was* . . . the absolutely absolute" (first emphasis added) (qtd. in H 83). Kaufmann quite decisively disagrees. "When Hegel in effect declared himself for the primacy of the ethical realm, this *included* art, religion, and philosophy; he *never* set the state above these. . . . In the *Phenomenology* . . . art and religion, which are treated together, and philosophy, which is treated next and last, occupy the top rungs, above both *Sittlichkeit* and *Moralität*" (H 84–85). In Hegel's late system, the height of what he would call "objective spirit" is achieved in the ethical life and the state, but "absolute spirit," comprising art, religion, and philosophy, stands higher. By the end of his philosophical career, the primacy of the latter domain had been firmly established. This, I think, is the single most important element in Kaufmann's reinterpretation.

With a novelist's narrative empathy, Kaufmann stops to describe the claustric horror of Hegel's personal life on the eve of composing the *Phenomenology*. The basic idea of the work, Kaufmann says, is to penetrate to *the human reality* reflected in propositions, views, particular forms of consciousness: "Every outlook, in other words, is to be studied not merely as an academic possibility but as an existential reality" (H 115). Kaufmann takes this ruling principle to his lower-case phenomenology of the philosopher's agonizing existence during the time of composition: Hegel's fundamental doubt whether now, in his late thirties, he would ever be able to complete the system he had been conceiving for years; the imminent birth of an illegitimate son; and the loss of a teaching position at Jena—hence, impending financial ruin. Hegel needed to finish the manuscript by October 18, 1806—Kaufmann explains—for it was only on that condition that he had received an advance from his publisher.

> Hegel got off half of the manuscript ten days before the deadline, but then Napoleon moved in, finished off the Holy Roman Empire founded by Charlemagne in 800, in the battle of Jena, and on October 13 occupied the city. The night from the twelfth to the thirteenth Hegel finished the book—appalled by the thought that the first half might well have got lost on the way, and wondering whether he dare to mail the second half. On the eighteenth, he writes Niethammer [Hegel's most loyal friend] that he has been advised "that such circumstances set aside all obligations," but when the first mail leaves again he will send the balance. Meanwhile there

has been a big fire in Jena as well as some looting. That is how the book was finished—except for the preface, which was done in January. (H 91)

No one would think that Kaufmann or any other scholar could produce a one-to-one correspondence between Hegel's state of mind and the states of mind he analyzes in the *Phenomenology*. Still, one might profitably take from this report a feeling for the extreme—even aberrant—originality of the work: Hegel apparently had no precise conception of the whole when he put pen to paper—a work achieved, I'll add, only "by patience under torment" (Bentham).[25]

The *Phenomenology* needs to be approached, Kaufmann suggests, as a literary work of art. This is in fact the decisive element in his general reinterpretation of Hegel's masterwork. In 1857 the Hegel scholar Haym wrote in passing of "the character of the Hegelian system. I call it *a work of art of knowledge*" (H 112). This association of ideas does cry out for a consideration, missing at this point, of Hegel's own thoughts on the relation of artistic to philosophical truth, but Kaufmann will address this topic later in his book. There is, meanwhile, art and knowledge in Kaufmann's thesis, in the wit and sympathy he brings to its description. His opening is engaging:

> The preface to the *Phenomenology* is full of excellent aphorisms—a few of them quite naked and unconcealed, so no reader can miss them. To be sure, they are buried in mammoth paragraphs to forestall any popular appeal. The book is called *System of Science*, First Part, and the appearance of the pages is forbidding enough to frighten away browsers. But the reader who perseveres is brought up short every now and then by a striking epigram. The pity is that Hegel, too, is brought up short, shocked at his own unscientific manner, and intent on making amends immediately. But after a while it happens again. It is as if wore a garment that did not fit: the buttons keep popping, revealing his chest and, as it were, baring his heart; but every time he stops to sew them on again before he feels free to make another move, though it keeps happening again. It never seems to occur to him to give up the garment as a bad fit that might conceivably suit somebody else but obviously not him. (H 100)

The *Phenomenology* purports to be a science; and Hegel—Kaufmann will show—gives good reasons for thinking so, when he closely studies the preface to the *Phenomenology*.[26] But meanwhile, a certain "existential reality" manifests itself in the work in the stylistic tension between a collection of aphorisms and a bible of systematic science marked by "tapeworm" sentences performing the elucubration of arcane truths. This reality is a function, Kaufmann shows, of a logomachy among Hegel's philosophical rivals, where Kant and Fichte stand for the tapeworm model and Friedrich Schlegel and Schelling, at the time, the aphoristic bee sting.

Kaufmann's readiness (on the model of Hegel!) to detect great literature in philosophical works, and its importance for an understanding of these works, prompts him to see the *Phenomenology* as a *Divine Comedy* and as a kind of *Faust*. (These two associations were already present in the main nineteenth-century commentaries on Hegel by Karl Rosenkranz and Rudolf Haym. They can also have been inspired by Meyer Abrams's vision of Wordsworth's *Prelude* as a kind of Hegelian *Phenomenology*—the latter being "a work which manages the feat of epitomizing the cultural history of the maturing spirit entirely in terms of the diverse separations, conflicts, and incremental reconciliations of subject and object.")[27] The parallel with Dante is based on the *comedic* aspect of the *Phenomenology* as a journey from darkness and delusion into the light of absolute spirit. Each stage of the way, I'll add, requires the pilgrim's full immersion in the exemplars of error he meets. Just as Dante suffers sympathetic anguish with many a sinner along the way—fainting, for example, when he hears the tale of Paolo and Francesca—so Hegel identifies himself conceptually with each of the one-sided errors in the spirit's effort to coincide with absolute truth. Kant concludes the second edition of his *Critique of Pure Reason* with the hope that before the end of the century, philosophical workers might "give human reason complete satisfaction about that which has always engaged its curiosity" (H 103). Inspired by Fichte, a forerunner in speculative daring, Hegel means to outdo Kant in passing beyond critique. The goal of the Hegelian system—thus Kaufmann, citing Haym—is

> not to dissolve the world of being and knowledge critically but to achieve the comprehensive unity of a beautiful whole. It wants not to uncover the perplexities of knowledge or gain clarity about the limits, the contradictions, and antinomies in the world of the sprit, but on the contrary to beat down these embarrassments and to reconcile these contradictions. It is . . . the *presentation of the universe as a beautiful, living cosmos.* (qtd. in H 112)

Faust, following Kaufmann, also articulates the goal of total immersion in the way stations of the spirit to the Absolute, but the path is surely a broken one and often murderous. In our chapter 5, we quoted relevant lines from *Faust*:

And what is portioned out to all mankind,
I shall enjoy deep in my self, contain
Within my spirit summit and abyss,
Pile on my breast their agony and bliss,
And thus let my own self grow into theirs, unfettered.[28]

Here the parallel with the *Phenomenology* is engaging. But, as Kaufmann does point out, the following line of Goethe's verse does not apply. Faust concludes:

Till as they are, at last I, too, am shattered.

Still, the analogy is rewarding: Hegel "considers it necessary to re-experience what the human spirit has gone through in history, and he challenges the reader to join him in this Faustian undertaking. . . . The reader, like the author, is meant to suffer through each position and to be changed as he proceeds from one to the other. *Mea res agitur*: my own self is at stake" (H 116–17). The idea of Goethe's presence in the work continues to be engaging. *Faust*, like the *Phenomenology*, proclaims, through the figure of Mephisto—"the spirit that negates"—the constructive working of negativity. Here, Kaufmann evokes the "uninterrupted rest" that Faust must shun at the cost of losing his divine wager and links it to Hegel's "inert simplicity," the "immediacy" that must be surpassed if there is to be an increase of human consciousness. The best that can be said for "the negative" is that "every finite position is destroyed, but tragic as this perpetual destruction unquestionably is, in the long run it serves a positive end by leading to a greater good. History is the realm of sin, destruction, and evil, but out of these terrors and human agonies freedom emerges and grows" (H 118). This pattern may be plainly true for Hegel but—it needs repeating—*Faust*'s conclusion is far less anodyne. It is interesting that, looking ahead, the critic Terry Eagleton will praise Kaufmann's *Tragedy and Philosophy*, only once dimming his approval by objecting to Kaufmann's "excessively sanguine view of tragic suffering, which allows us to 'see how countless agonies belong to one great pattern.'"[29]

Kaufmann's scrutiny of the many allusions to the works of other poets and philosophers in the *Phenomenology*—we have the considerable presence of Sophocles and Aristotle, Schiller and Shakespeare . . . and a dozen more (H 125)—allows him to make one of the most revealing statements in his entire corpus. This reflection makes for a chastening contrast with the rather sanguine language of the "greater good" and the "one great pattern":

Indeed, never before [Hegel] had any major philosopher so patently enjoyed allusions, and so lavishly indulged in this pleasure. Let the cultured reader be rewarded for his pains; let the less educated be shamed into reading what they ought to have read long ago. Cliquishness is contemptible, but the mutual affinity and enjoyment of those members of the invisible church whose highly developed humanity gives them a great deal in common is one of the legitimate consolations for the misery of life. (H 120)

This "invisible church" also gives a habitation and a name to Kaufmann's religious impulse—it is at home in the congregation of specimens of "a highly developed humanity." Those who can make some headway into the *Phenomenology* are en route to joining it: let this reading adventure, thus Kaufmann, be a synecdoche for the permanent, the glorious adventure of Bildung. Others, not drawn to the "invisible church," might continue to consider this adventure in self-perfection an unfortunate distraction from social engagement aimed at alleviating "the misery of life" (chapter 1).

This supersaturation of the *Phenomenology* with allusions to the heroes of works of literature—like Antigone and Rameau's nephew—might also be considered a drawback: it produces an overspecific personification of (what Haym calls) "abstract forces" (H 129). The allusion devours the idea. We will see this fault identified in our discussion of Arthur Danto's criticism of Nietzsche (and, implicitly, Kaufmann) when Danto sees the figure of the Übermensch as overpowering an ideal of human fulfillment: here, Nietzsche's "illustrations have obscured his principles."[30]

To the great issue of the putative logical development of each form of consciousness into the next, Kaufmann offers this account, seeing Hegel as influenced by Goethe, whose sense of relation is developmental:

Probably, he was influenced by Goethe's development from style to style, which suggested that there was a "logical" sequence—not "logical" in the ordinary sense, but rather in the way in which, to use a Hegelian image from the beginning of the preface, bud, blossom, and fruit succeed each other. Hegel assumes an organic necessity. (H 132)

But however generously envisioned, there is no consistently logical passage in the *Phenomenology* from stage to stage in any sense of the word. Kaufmann soon abandons Hegel's "assumption," writing: "Any attempt to relate all points of view in a single chain is going to be at best a virtuoso performance." The transitions of the *Phenomenology* fluctuate from the one extreme—brilliantly managed—to the other—indefensible (H 133). This question has proved vexatious: for more detail on transitions in the *Phenomenology*, see, among others, Robert Pippin's "You Can't Get There from Here: Transition Problems in Hegel's *Phenomenology of Spirit*."[31]

Earlier we discussed the quote from Schiller that concludes the *Phenomenology*, citing the view of the critic Verene that Hegel's conclusion is as sanguine as Schiller's is not. Kaufmann has an important stipulation to add:

> the tone of the ending seems affirmative; but we should not overlook a crucial word that Hegel has placed before the concluding quotation—a word that, being foreign to Schiller's text, carries an immense weight: *nur* (only). In Schiller's last stanza the presumption is that the infinity of the supreme being is mirrored by the whole realm of souls: though no single one equals the master's infinity, all the souls together do mirror it. For Hegel, the infinite God is dead: "only/
>> from the cup of this realm of spirits/
>> foams his infinity for him."
> To put it into our own words: there is no supreme being beyond; the spirit is not to be found in another world; the infinite spirit has to be found in the comprehension of this world, in the study of the spirits summoned in the *Phenomenology*. "History comprehended" must replace theology. (H 147–48)

For Kaufmann, the chapter on self-consciousness in the *Phenomenology* is, after the preface, the most interesting, and so he now cites it at some length. It would add very little to the sum of human knowledge merely to reproduce Kaufmann's extensive quotes from this chapter in *Hegel*, but the material is too interesting to overlook. Here, partly for reasons earlier suggested, I would like to revive Hyppolite's valuable summary of the argument that Kaufmann admires:

> The independence of the master and the harsh education of the slave become the self-mastery of the stoic who is always free, regardless of circumstance or the hazards of fortune, or the skeptic's experience of absolute liberty, which dissolves every position except that of the I itself. Finally, the truth of this stoic or skeptic liberty comes to be expressed in unhappy consciousness, which is always divided within itself, a consciousness both of absolute self-certainty and of the nothingness of that certainty. Unhappy consciousness is the truth of this entire dialectic. It is the pain felt by pure subjectivity, which no longer contains its substance within itself.[32]

Now we are positioned to appreciate Kaufmann's interpretive comments, as when he remarks, "Skepticism is serious [not merely 'half-serious'] about what stoicism merely says." Or when he is inspired to construct an illustrative scene à la Hegel:

> The two poles of the skeptical self-consciousness of which Hegel speaks may perhaps be illustrated more vividly by considering the psychoanalyst's self-consciousness: On the one hand, he views his consciousness as empirical, accidental, and individual; he considers it unreliable and confused. On the other hand, he relies on it, considers it trans-empirical and objective, not merely personal but an instance of a general scientific consciousness. (H 139–40)

It is hard to see, however, why the figure of the academic philosopher, in lieu of the psychoanalyst, would be any less vivid an illustration.

A distinctive feature of Hegel's sentences in the *Phenomenology* is the immixing of Latinate syntax and Latinate abstractions with concrete images. It is no accident that Kaufmann is promptly reminded of Shakespeare ("Almost like Shakespeare, Hegel often thinks in pictures" [H 143]); but, following Kaufmann's own train of thought, there is a more telling comparison. This is Shakespeare's power to produce exhilarating aesthetic effects by counterpoising Latinate words with concrete "Anglo-Saxon" words, as, famously, in Macbeth's imprecation at the blood spilled at his murder of Duncan:

> No, This my hand will rather
> The multitudinous seas incarnadine,
> Making the green one red.[33]

Furthermore, in the matter of Hegel's "peculiar" diction, Kaufmann stresses that many of Hegel's key words, which are regularly translated with Latinate English words, in fact belong to ordinary speech or have familiar material connotations missing from the English. One such word is the German word *Begriff* ("concept"), which in Hegel's usage has a tactile feel to it. The phrase "*etwas begreifen*" means "to understand something," "to conceptualize something," but it has another implication, from its German root, of "grabbing hold," of grasping and gripping. *Begriff* retains something of this sense in the diction shared by Hegel's closest friend Hölderlin, who describes what is necessary for genuine comprehension as *schneller Begriff*—a swift grabbing hold of the right proportion of the many elements in a complex.[34]

"The word *Phänomenologie*," Kaufmann writes, "is true of most of Hegel's terms; they had been used before Hegel, but he gave them a new *nuance*." One revision, certainly, is the way that *Schein* (appearance or semblance) "is not, for Hegel, 'mere appearance' in the sense of error and illusion." Earlier, in chapter 5, we discussed the place of productive error in Hegel's thinking. In respect to Hegel's revision of older technical terms, Kaufmann continues, he "usually carries over into their technical use something of their sensuous core. . . . He knows that the Greek, like the German root [of 'phenomenology'] also means to shine, become visible" (H 150). Certainly, not all of Hegel's style in the *Phenomenology* is remarkable for its "sensuousness." It is safe to say that the particular sort of pleasure that Hegel's prose affords is only intermittently aesthetic: "Frequently his terminology . . . degenerates into a jargon that obscures his meaning instead of making it more precise." It is interesting that shortly before making this point of the rebarbative "scientificity" of Hegel's prose, Kaufmann identifies Sartre as "the only major figure who admittedly owes a great deal both to Husserl's 'phenomenology' and to Hegel's *Phenomenology*" (H 151). Sartre is doubly apposite when we consider his deliberate—in his case—antibourgeois refusal to write well, or in a style, in his later work, which, by no stretch of the imagination, might be called natural, beautiful, or pleasurable. These concerns allow Kaufmann to speak very much *in propria persona* when he addresses the willful obscurantism of "professors"—present textual company, surely, excluded:

> Symbolism, technical terms, and footnotes can all be extremely useful, but it is common for professors to employ such devices beyond all reason, with an eye more to their preconceptions about what looks scholarly than to the clarity of their work. Just as some modern philosophers and literary critics . . . give themselves scientific airs and say at length obscurely what might easily have been said briefly and clearly, Hegel, too, succumbed to this vice. (H 151)

It is reasonable to think of Kaufmann as tireless in his effort to be faithful to this virtue.

As he has offered a brief history of the term "phenomenology" in the German philosophical tradition—from Lambert to Husserl—Kaufmann does the same with the term "dialectic." It belongs to his reinterpretation to erase the casual identification of the three-stage dialectic with Hegel—the notorious "thesis, antithesis, synthesis." Hegel never uses the term dialectic to mean this three-step; in fact, he takes pains to criticize Kant's use of this particular form of the triad, which is Fichte's, not Hegel's contribution. Kaufmann has an earlier model for this insight: Marcuse's *Reason and Revolution* (1941), which he acknowledged earlier in this chapter. It is quite clear that no such thing as a self-sufficient "thesis" could find a place in Hegel's *Logic*, for, as Marcuse points out:

> By virtue of the inherent negativity in them, all things become self-contradictory, opposed to themselves, and their being consists in that "force which can both comprehend and endure contradiction." "*All things are contradictory in themselves*"—this proposition, which so sharply differs from the traditional laws of identity and contradiction, expresses for Hegel "the truth and essence of all things."[35]

This topic of the alleged three-step dialectic has a history of large proportions, even as the history of a legend. "There is a legend abroad," writes Kaufmann, "that the student of Hegel must choose in the end between the system and the dialectic, and it is widely supposed that the right wing Hegelians chose the system while the left wing, or the 'young' Hegelians, including Marx, chose the dialectic" (H 160). Neither of these alternatives is cogent: Kaufmann does not so much reject the one or the other alternative as he denies the validity of the choice. That is because there is no dialectic in Hegel, *if the word is to be understood as one relentless ruling logic.*[36] It will function, now and again, as a style of exposition, but it is not an instrument of discovery (H 162). Consider the *Phenomenology*—a concrete instance running counter to the false ideal of a "scientific" (*wissenschaftlich*) method of truth-baring. The *Phenomenology* is "undisciplined, arbitrary, full of digressions, not a monument to the austerity of the intellectual conscience and to carefulness and precision but a wild, bold, unprecedented book that invites comparison with some great literary masterpieces" (H 158). So, absent a usable dialectical method, what does the Hegelian corpus, at this point in our account, have to offer in the way of a "form of [logical] consciousness"? Kaufmann sums up:

> We find a vision of the world, of man, and of history which emphasizes development through conflict, the moving power of human passions, which produce wholly unintended results, and the irony of sudden reversals. If that be called a dialectical world view, then Hegel's philosophy *was* dialectical. . . . This is certainly an immensely fruitful and interesting perspective, and from the point of view of pedagogy, vivid exposition, and sheer drama it may be unsurpassed. But the fateful myth that this perspective is

reducible to a rigorous method that even permits predictions deserves no
quarter, though by now half the world believes it. (H 161)

It is obligatory to quote the last lines of this paean, since the book we are
dealing with is *Hegel—a Reinterpretation* (H 161). Today, however, we might
say—in the words of Iris Murdoch, writing in 1952, and echoed without attribution by innumerable commentators since—that belief in Hegel is not the
privilege of *half the world* but rather *all the world*, for "we are all Hegelians."
This is so whether or not "we" identify Hegel as the author of our belief.[37] The
reason for making this totalizing claim, however, varies from commentator to
commentator, preferably in the way in which they refer, now in the words of
Andrew Cole, "to a specialized dialectical tradition that is *not* reducible to the
hokum of thesis, antithesis, and synthesis."[38] But this is a topic that deserves a
book in its own right.[39]

It is no secret that the biography of philosophers matters to Kaufmann.
He is loyal to Nietzsche in seeing philosophies—"forms of consciousness"—
as very much the efflux of an *embodied* mind, which is to say, of the entire
personality, shaped by cultural inheritance and lived experience. This leads
Kaufmann to announce, with a great deal of satisfaction, a solution to a puzzle
not sufficiently noted in previous studies: the transformation of the young
Hegel, a bold, sarcastic "firebrand whose vitriolic criticisms of Christianity
invite comparison with Nietzsche and do not even stop before the person of
Jesus," into the mature professor, contriver of a dense, dogmatic, oracular prose
well suited, say, to the project of the *Logic*—"the account of God as he is in his
eternal essence before the creation of nature and any finite spirit" (H 173–74).
For Kaufmann, there is a reason for this change: it lies in the habits of mind
and exposition Hegel acquired during the eight years he spent—between stints
as the editor of a newspaper in Bamberg and his call to a professorship in philosophy at Heidelberg—as the headmaster of a small college in Nürnberg. As
principal and tutor in philosophy, he was obliged to batter philosophical the-
orems into the heads of adolescents as economically as possible, in trenchant,
weighty, implacable form. That is the solution (which might also very well
be called reductive) to the mysterious metamorphosis of the Hegelian style!

As Kaufmann approaches the *Logic*, he refers to his own earlier thoughts
on dialectic, whose definition, for him, is something of a work in progress. He
quotes an important passage from Hegel's introduction to the *Logic*, which
demands that Kant's discussion of "the forms of understanding" be submitted
to a radical critique as "a review and analysis of our categories":

This is what Hegel attempts in his *Logic*. The point is to comprehend the concepts of being and nothing, of finite and infinite; then we shall see that they are all one-sided abstractions from a concreteness of which they are merely partial aspects. [Furthermore, "any two opposite categories are always both one-sided abstractions."] That is the heart of Hegel's *Logic*; that is the meaning of its much-misunderstood dialectic. The dialectic of the *Logic* is ... different from the dialectic of the *Phenomenology*: one could not possibly call it a logic of passion. (H 183)

Let us begin with Kaufmann's first point. It is with Hegel, he writes, in italic, that the "*analysis of categories*"—the categories that structure what Hegel calls "the forms of thinking"—"*replaces speculative metaphysics.*" In a word, Hegel defines metaphysics as higher-order epistemology—ergo, "a revolution ... which is as timely one hundred fifty years later as it ever was" (H 185). Hegel is altogether penetrating about this enterprise. He writes,

the forms of thinking are first of all articulated and laid down in the *language* of man. ... In everything that becomes for him something inward, any kind of notion, anything he makes his own, language has intruded; and what man makes into language and expresses in language, contains, shrouded, mixed in, or elaborated, a category. (qtd. in H 185)

He rather wittily undoes past and future opponents by supplying them

the simple reflection that their ideas and objections contain categories which are presuppositions and themselves require criticism before they are used. Unconsciousness of this point goes amazingly far; it makes for the basic misunderstanding, the uncouth and uneducated behavior of thinking *something else* when a category is considered, and not this category itself. (qtd. in H 186)

Readers may be interested to find in Hegel the point that has since become ubiquitous in hermeneutic theory, as, for example, in Heidegger's "*Vorgriff*"—namely, the "obvious, undiscussed assumptions" that the reader brings to his interpretation. Kaufmann, with Hegel, enlarges the point beyond hermeneutics:

If these categories have application only to the objects of experience [thus Kant] ... then we have no grounds whatsoever for assuming anything beyond experience. But in that case we also have no grounds for considering the categories merely subjective. So far from merely telling us something about the structure of the human mind, they are part of the structure of all knowledge and of discourse on any subject whatsoever—whether that subject be knowledge and discourse, nature, ethics, art, religion, or philosophy. Therefore, the system of science—to recall the title Hegel originally gave the work to which the *Phenomenology* was meant as an introduction— should begin with the *Logic*. (qtd. in H 187)

Hegel's *Logic* performs the required analysis.

Hegel's youthful essay on skepticism (above) is a harbinger of the "Unhappy Consciousness" chapter in the *Phenomenology*. More than this, its critique of the suppositions undergirding empiricism anticipates the key passages from the *Logic* cited above. Here, then, is additional evidence for Kaufmann's claim of the ongoing importance of Hegel's late juvenilia for understanding the mature writings for which he is chiefly known.

Hegel's early stress on the omnipresence of language in all forms of thought leads him to discover a richness in this element. His concern is not restricted to German words or German grammar, for, thinking, too, of other languages, he notes that "the spirit and culture of a people reveal themselves . . . in the grammar of its language; the same rules and forms now have a full, living value. Through the grammar he [who has mastered a language] can recognize the expression of the spirit, the Logic" (H 189). Hegel is especially interested in the philosophical potential of some common German words having antithetical meanings. Here philosophy and style join hands. These words rehearse the tensions informing more complex entities even as they are contained in a unity. Hegel admires, as he says, this

> speculative spirit of the [German] language; it can afford thinking a delight to hit upon such words and to find the reconciliation of opposites, which is a result of speculation but an absurdity for the understanding, present lexicographically in this naïve manner in a single word of opposite meanings. (qtd. in H 179)

It is interesting that where the common understanding of Hegel would expect the word "dialectical," we have "speculative" ex cathedra.

Philosophy makes the potential of the German language explicit; it "therefore requires no particular terminology at all" (H 179). "The prime example of an ordinary word that shows the 'speculative spirit of the language' by having seemingly opposed meanings," as Kaufmann (and Hegel!) point out, "is, of course, *aufheben* (sublimate)" (H 180–81). Hegel defines this key word in a manner that we might have suspected all along:

> *Aufheben* has . . . a double meaning in that it signifies conserving, *preserving*, and at the same time also making cease, *making an end*. Even conserving includes the negative aspect that something is taken out of its immediacy, and thus out of an existence that is open to external influences, to be preserved.—Thus what is *aufgehoben* is at the same time conserved and has merely lost its immediacy but is not for that reason annihilated.—Lexicographically, the two definitions of *aufheben* can be listed as two *meanings* of the word. But it should strike us that a language should have come to use one and the same word for two opposed definitions. For speculative thinking it is a joy to find in the language words which are characterized by a speculative significance. German has several such words. . . . Something is *aufgehoben* only insofar as it has entered into union with its opposite; in the more exact definition, as something reflected, it can suitably be called a *moment*. (qtd. in H 181)

What strikes Kaufmann is the "clarity and vigor" of Hegel's aperçu, his readiness "to overcome the rigid prejudices of the understanding by showing how both reason and intuition can make perfectly good sense of something that the understanding might be inclined to rule out . . . because opposite meanings *must* be mutually incompatible and therefore, if nevertheless combined, yield nonsense" (H 182). The word "intuition" might be moot, for consider Hegel's exclusion of this element from the *Logic* below. But we can see in Kaufmann's praise, his passion for *wholeness*—the whole man, the whole mind of man—a word that is integral to Nietzsche's writings and abounds in Kaufmann's *Nietzsche*—ergo, a good deal more for him than an easy cliché.

In the passage above, Hegel signals his late modernity. His "joy" anticipates Freud's essay on the antithetical sense of primary words and Heidegger's reflections on the intrinsically philosophical character of the German language—the only modern language allegedly suited to philosophy—as when Hegel claims, however incorrectly, the parallel etymologies of the words "*Ding*" and "*denken*" (H 179).[40]

Kaufmann is creative in inventing literary figures—both persons and tropes—to characterize Hegel's major works, the *Phenomenology* and the *Logic*. He is encouraged by the depth and richness of Hegel's own rhetorical powers. In the introduction to the *Logic*, Hegel conjures the field of its concern: "*truth as it is without any shroud in and for itself*," "the realm of shadows, the world of the simple essences (*Wesenheiten*), freed from all sensuous concretion. The study of this science, the sojourn and the work in this realm of shadows ... pursues tasks remote from sensuous intuitions and aims, from feelings, from the merely intended world of notions" (qtd. in H 182–83). Hegel's magic inspires Kaufmann to a literary parallel:

> Hegel still confronts us as another Odysseus: in the *Phenomenology* we followed his Odyssey, the spirit's great voyage in search of a home where it might settle down; in the *Logic* we are asked to follow him into the realm of shadows. There we moved in a world where the passions had their place; here the passions [but not all hope] are left behind. (H 184)

This realm of shadows, and the crossings it holds—Kaufmann is eager to show—is not without influence on the daylight world—or on that brittle daylight in which disputes are conducted "that fill thousands of articles and books." These disputes are benighted in an excess of specious light, in the sense that they turn on categories—such as the *immediate* and the *mediated*—that they take to be absolutes, when they are not, for Hegel has shown that there is nothing that is entirely the one or the other. Let this stand as one of the antinomies that Hegel deconstructs at the outset of the *Logic* and which will be immediately familiar, I'll note, as the sort of opposition that modern literary theorists have undone—or seen undone in literary works of a sufficient complexity. Hegel's point is that the category embedding an assumed opposition is null and void. I will venture a crying example from Kafka, a past master of this nondistinction: the pain felt by the culprit laid on the rack in "In the Penal Colony." The pain is bodily, organic, excruciating—and it is at the same time a script parsed by the sufferer in and through the wounds it inflicts. Hegel performs the same demystifying operation on the categories "being" and "non-being": they are always encountered as an "undifferentiated unity." For whatever *is, is not* yet itself: it always has its being to be accomplished, the condition of which is its nonbeing. This perspective on this assumed antinomy makes an auspicious beginning to a description of consciousness (H 191).

It is impossible to avoid an element of Kaufmann's "reinterpretation" that has been criticized for the centrality he gives to it: the difference between the first edition of the *Logic* (1812)—a great rarity, as Kaufmann puts it, but which he holds in his hands—and the revised edition of 1831, which is the normal text of choice. A knowledgeable commentator, Professor W. H. Walsh, notes that this point of editorial scholarship, and the difference between the triads in the two tables of contents, is a less important matter than what may be missing—a more substantial account of the aims and arguments of the *Logic*. "A jaundiced student," Walsh writes, "might even think that Kaufmann is so taken up with the variations between one Hegelian edition and another that he forgets to tell the reader what the whole discussion is about."[41] But it is not so much that Kaufmann forgets as that he remembers to invite the reader to study the *Logic* on his or her own: "This discussion cannot serve as a substitute for reading Hegel's *Logic*." I will borrow his words for my own pages: they cannot serve as a substitute for reading Kaufmann. Like his, "this discussion is meant to clear away misconceptions and impediments and to show how the book is to be read" (H 200).

How, indeed, is Kaufmann's book, at this point, to be read? It is an engaging essay on Hegel's life and work, a cut above *haute vulgarisation*, stimulating the desire for a deeper knowledge of the *Phenomenology* and the *Logic*, along with a sharper sense of what views on Hegel are being reexamined and the adequacy of Hegel's works to Hegel's own systematic intentions. Of course, one must *read* the *Phenomenology* and the *Logic*—together with commentaries such as Charles Taylor's *Hegel* (in 596 pages), even if this book was reviewed scathingly, although informatively, by Kaufmann;[42] Terry Pinkard's *Hegel: A Biography* (in 812) pages; and all of Robert Pippin's books: *Hegel's Idealism: The Satisfactions of Self-Consciousness*; *Hegel's Practical Philosophy: Rational Agency as Ethical Life*; and *Hegel on Self-Consciousness: Desire and Death in "The Phenomenology of Spirit"*—each work shorter than the first two mentioned but not less rich.[43] In the meantime, let us read a compact account of Hegel's systematic intentions written by Professor Stephen Crites in the course of his identifying precisely what is missing, for all its merits, from Kaufmann's study. It reads:

> Kaufmann's more relaxed view of the system and its method may at least spare the student many unfruitful preconceptions. But it will also fail to prepare him for Hegel's philosophical seriousness, his tremendous intellectual eros and his rigor.
>
> The construction of the system was for Hegel the attempt to think self-reflexively. For Hegel saw that it is not merely the ideas about which one thinks, but the categories through which one thinks, the basic categories of interpretation, which are problematic. It is not enough for consciousness to grasp an object, a proposition, a "truth"; the philosophical task is the comprehension and criticism of consciousness itself, not in abstraction from its object, but in its grasp of the object (*Begriff*). Since consciousness

is an historical emergent, this task involves in the first place the herculean labor of comprehending the historical development of thought and symbolic representation through its evolving forms. Hegel believed that history had reached the point in this development at which it might be possible for reason to be self-conscious about this very process which gave it birth, and finally to grasp all forms of consciousness, and therefore reality itself as it is mediated by the successive forms of consciousness, as a succession of internally related and hence necessary forms within reason's own process of thought. So reason's knowledge of itself is in one sense its final task, since this knowledge completes its investigation of all truth. In another sense it is its first task, since nothing can be known essentially, in its transparency to reason, which is not known as a mode of reason itself. Hence, the need of reason to grasp every truth in its necessity, as a dialectical moment in reason's own inner life. Reason's disciplined effort to know all things in itself is the philosophical system. This conception of the system and its method belongs to the heart of Hegel's philosophy.[44]

If Kaufmann is less than explicit on the views of Hegel he is reinterpreting, he does turn directly to views of Heidegger's, repudiating them in the light of the *Logic*. He objects to Heidegger's invocation of Being as the desideratum of philosophical thinking, since, as Hegel has maintained, the concept of Being, when immediately addressed, is indistinguishable from the concept (if it is a concept) of Nothing. Kaufmann has no patience for what he calls Heidegger's "neglect of Hegel's discussion of these terms . . . [as well as] his suggestion . . . that knowing something of human existence is relatively paltry; . . . a philosopher should not bother with it . . . if it were not for the hope that we might acquire at least a little knowledge of Being" (H 204).

A scrutiny of the third part of the *Logic* makes an important interpretive point, namely, "how misguided all attempts are to construe the *Logic* as a relentless ascent from 'Being' to 'the Absolute.' . . . Hegelian metaphysics comes at the bottom, traditional logic above it" (H 213). This claim arises from a close reading of its table of contents. I think it only fair at this juncture to let J. N. Findlay have his say on Kaufmann's reading of the *Logic*:

Kaufmann rightly points out that Hegel did not believe in a single inexorable order in which the various thought-stances of the logic have to be arranged. . . . But it is quite a different thing to maintain, as Kaufmann maintains, that Hegel "kept accumulating material and ideas and then faced the terrible problem of writing an orderly book" and that his sequence of categories involves "no relentless ascent from being to the absolute" but "rather an attempt to organize an excess of material." What is here maintained seems to me simply false: the material has throughout an order of deep logical relevance, each new category arguably bringing out something which its predecessor implied but did not explicitly bring out, even though the same material could sometimes have been differently ordered with an equal degree of profound relevance. Even rigorously deductive chains can take a variety of alternative courses, and the same ought obviously to be true of Hegel's looser logic. In neither case need the logical mean the "relentless." I have in fact found that, as I studied Hegel over the years, the impression of sheer arbitrariness in many Hegelian transitions has been increasingly dissipated, and I hope ultimately to see the full point of them all. If this were not so, I should not think Hegel worthy of continued study.[45]

On Kaufmann's behalf one could conclude that Hegel is worthy of continued study apart from the degree of contingency in his transitions! His fascination continues, not least for its human interest: Kaufmann reminds us of the existential constraints under which Hegel produced this "work of overabundance"—his job, as we have heard, as the headmaster of a provincial high school. Kaufmann relays an anecdote from a letter written at the time by Clemens Brentano (an important romantic), which, apocryphal or not, deserves to be kept in circulation. "In Nürnberg," wrote Brentano, "I found the honest, wooden Hegel as the principal of the Gymnasium; he read the Edda and Nibelungen, and to be able to enjoy them he translated them, as he was reading, into Greek" (H 215).

In Hegel's oeuvre, the *Logic* is followed by the compendium that became the *Encyclopedia*, containing—as Kaufmann writes, to bring some clarity into a confusing philological matter—"an abridgement of the *Logic*, and then an abridgment of his as-yet-unwritten, or at least unpublished, philosophy of nature and philosophy of spirit" (H 218). From these humble beginnings the *Encyclopedia* grew, in the editions appearing soon after Hegel's death, to be a work—a system—of some sixteen hundred pages, incorporating every sort of reminiscence by students who had heard his lectures and every sort of editorial intrusion for the sake of a coherent narrative. Kaufmann hails the revised critical edition being produced under the imprint of the Felix Meiner publishing house: fifty years later, at the time of this writing, it is still underway, with twenty volumes in print and more in preparation. The editorial complexity is Proustian in its dimensions. Consider Rosenkranz, whom Kaufmann often quotes, writing on the spirit behind Hegel's lectures and style of composition:

> This struggle with the presentation to find the definitive, penetrating expression that would leave nothing behind; this incessant search; this wealth of possibilities made more difficult for him as the years passed— the richer his education became, the more many-sided his thought, and the greater his position—not only speaking in general but also writing; and one cannot find anything more hacked to pieces, more crossed out, more constantly rewritten than one of Hegel's drafts for a letter from the Berlin period. (qtd. in H 227)

We need to hear about the place of the *Encyclopedia* in the perspective of the system. Here Hegel writes compellingly of a key transition; Kaufmann quotes him at length.

> In my *Phenomenology of the Spirit*, which was therefore designated on publication as the first part of the System of Science, I took the way of beginning with the first and simplest appearance of the spirit, *the immediate consciousness*, developing its dialectic up to the standpoint of philosophical science, whose necessity is demonstrated by this progression. But to this end one could not stop with the formal aspect of mere consciousness; for the standpoint of philosophical knowledge is at the same time the most contentful and concrete. . . . [Hence,] it also presupposed the concrete forms of consciousness, such as, e.g., morals, *Sittlichkeit*, art, religion. The development of the *contents*, of the objects of characteristic parts of philosophical science, therefore falls at the same time within this development of consciousness, which at first seems to be limited merely to the form. (H 240)

Kaufmann's concern at this point is to talk less about these contents than about their arrangement in the three editions of the *Encyclopedia* in a "philological excursus," as he puts it, which leads to several provocative theses, bound to raise the hackles of other Hegel scholars. Kaufmann's aim is to show, on the strength of a close examination of the *Encyclopedia*, "how Hegel himself handled his system; not as so much necessary truth, deduced once and for all in its inexorable sequence, but rather as a very neat and sensible way of arranging the parts of philosophy—not even the neatest and most sensible possible, but only the best he could do in time to meet the printer's deadline" (H 243). J. N. Findlay was astonished[46]:

But the philological work that Kaufmann does in reconstructing the order of the chief sections of the *Encyclopedia* is not casual or contingent: it is the basis of his reinterpretation, which aims to undo the appearance of an intrinsic conceptual necessity driving Hegel's transitions from stage to stage. With the idea of its supposed necessity retired, we nonetheless arrive at a crucial transition in the *Encyclopedia*. It marks the introduction of a philosophy of history, which, in its original conception in the *Philosophy of Right*, is a history of *states* and always to be understood as belonging to the realm of *objective* spirit, "below art, religion, and philosophy, which comprise absolute spirit." Kaufmann reflects:

> History is not the culmination of Hegel's system; neither is the state. Hegel's relatively high estimate of the state depends on his belief that the development of art, religion, and philosophy, and their cultivation, depend on the state. Given the state, which provides the framework for the development of a culture, the continuity of cultural traditions, of language, education, and techniques, as well as the necessary security, an individual can occasionally form himself in solitude; but Hegel himself remarks that even if this should be the rule, it would not show that the state was altogether dispensable. The pinnacle of Hegel's system is absolute spirit; and within that, philosophy. (H 245–46)

Kaufmann trusts to the best pieces of the existing Hegel literature to deal with Hegel's philosophy of nature, which is "not that important"; of subjective spirit, also "not that important"; and of "Right" and other political writings. It is interesting to read Kaufmann's praise of Marcuse's treatment of Hegel's political thought in his *Reason and Revolution*, but it is not unexpected. In Kaufmann's landmark essay "The Hegel Myth and Its Method," which we cited at the outset of this chapter, Kaufmann wrote, "One may agree with Herbert Marcuse when he says in *Reason and Revolution*, 'There is no concept less compatible with Fascist ideology than that which founds the state on a universal and rational law that safeguards the interests of every individual, whatever the contingencies of his natural and social status'" (S 112). (Kaufmann's views on Marcuse's political and psychoanalytical writings would change drastically.[47]) To return to the *Encyclopedia*, Kaufmann makes clear that the pages that do need vigorous reinterpretation are the concluding lectures on the history of philosophy and the philosophy of history, whose central idea is "the story of the development of human freedom" (H 250).

In Hegel's view the grand triadic structure of philosophical history centers on a growing consciousness of the idea of freedom: "the spirit, or man as such, is free in himself" (Hegel) (H 249). In its first stage of the triad, oriental despotism, only one man is free: his freedom is arbitrary, and the *knowledge* of freedom is unknown. The second stage is the consciousness of freedom in Greek and Roman civilization, which knows that only *some* men are free; this imperfect awareness makes of their freedom something "accidental, undeveloped, ephemeral, and limited" (Hegel). Only in the *Germanic* nations, in stage three, is the concept of a universal entitlement to freedom fully understood—"the consciousness, in Christianity, that man as man is free, that the freedom of the spirit constitutes his most distinctive nature" (qtd. in H 250). But this awareness hardly amounts to its objective realization.

In thinking about these claims, Kaufmann wants to stress, first of all, that by "the Germanic nations" Hegel means the Protestant nations of northern Europe and not Germany alone. Furthermore, Hegel is hardly blind to the fact that the road to realized freedom is full of unspeakable horror and destruction: history is a single "slaughter bench, on which the happiness of peoples, the wisdom of states, and the virtue of individuals have been sacrificed." But Hegel is driven by philosophical eros to seek what redemption can be had from this apparent chaos of suffering and misfortune, and so Kaufmann has him stress "the goal rather than the sacrifices, the growing recognition of freedom rather than the slowness of its implementation, and reason rather than unreason" (H 251–52).

Kaufmann's reading of Hegel's "world-historical individual" is radically Kaufmannesque: in his existentializing perspective, in stressing the objectivation of individual identity, Hegel appears as a forerunner of Nietzsche and Sartre. This means, in Hegel's words, that "the organic individual produces himself: it makes of itself what it is implicitly; thus the spirit, too, is only that which it makes of itself, and it makes of itself what it is implicitly." Sartre hardly departs from Hegel in writing, "Man is nothing else but that which he makes of himself. That is the first principle of existentialism. . . . Man is therefore nothing else but the sum of his actions. . . . In life, a man commits himself, draws his own portrait, and there is nothing but that portrait" (H 254–55).[48] Kaufmann continues to quote, with evident enthusiasm, a series of such like-minded aperçus from Hegel: "What man is, is his deed . . . is the series of his deeds, is that into which he has made himself." Again, "often a difference is made between what a man is internally and his deeds. In history this is untrue; the series of his deeds is the man himself. . . . The truth is that the external is not different from the internal" (qtd. in H 255).

Early on, Kaufmann asserted a propaedeutic to the reading of philosophy: it requires a comprehension that includes moments of both identification and criticism. He demonstrates this practice in a tour de force—a reading of Hegel's extraordinary statement, in his philosophy of history, that the actuality of history is a fulfillment of God's plan, namely, that "the actual world is as it ought to be. . . . God rules the world; the content of his government, the execution of his plan, is world history . . . the ideal accomplishes itself . . . only what accords with the idea has actuality" (H 256). What can this mean? That God is the designer of an ineluctable slaughter bench?

This proposition is a vast, impermissible generalization. There will be moments of bliss in history—although, in Hegel's words, "History is not the soil of happiness. The times of happiness are empty leaves in it" (H 253). But "whether the positive or the negative is easier to see," writes Kaufmann, "and which it is more important to point out, depends greatly on the historical context." Kaufmann's second concern addresses what he calls Hegel's "verbal trick." Hegel has defined the "actual" as *only* those moments of harmony and success that suggest the realization of the idea. Whatever falls short of such embodiment is simply not *really* actual. This is a can't-lose theodicy. And yet "if Hegel's comfort and reconciliation to misfortune and madness depended solely on this redefinition of terms, his philosophy of history would be far worse than it is" (H 258). An astute salvaging argument follows.

Hegel's claim, in *1820*, that the idea and the realization of personal freedom had reached a maximum in Prussia is not absurd. Should he have recommended the United States, with half its population consisting of slaveholders? But Prussia was never conceived as an endpoint in this development: there would be a good deal more history—a good deal more slaughter, sacrifice, and . . . the cunning operations of reason. This means: there will always be interesting results quite apart from what men imagine to be their purposes. They will act, and they will suffer; the bodies of active men are the collateral damage of an impersonal consciousness of freedom on the march. Some are fully world-historical individuals. A poem from Walt Whitman's *Leaves of Grass*, titled "Roaming in Thought (*After Reading Hegel*)," reads: "Roaming in thought over the Universe, I saw the little that is / Good steadily hastening towards immortality" (qtd. H 370). The hastening path of Reason runs cunningly through those, writes Hegel, "who lose and suffer harm" (H 262).

Inseparable from the developing concept of freedom is the growth of the state, the genuine "actualization" of individual freedom—its bulwark, its guardian. Hegel's lectures repeat the point that freedom is realized *only* within the state:

> It is the actuality in which the individual has and enjoys his freedom.... All that man is he owes to the state.... All value man has, all spiritual actuality, he has through the state alone.... It is the absolute interest of reason that this ethical whole should exist; and this interest of reason constitutes the right and merit of the heroes who established states.... Only on this soil, i.e., in the state, can art and religion exist.... In world history one can discuss only peoples who have formed a state. (qtd. in H 265)

In an especially penetrating codicil, Hegel adds: "Indeed, all great men have formed themselves in solitude, but only by working for themselves upon what the state had already created." Only then does it follow that "the state is the more precisely defined object of world history in which freedom gains objective existence" (H 265). Kafka, who is Kaufmann's (explicit) educator—although here an unlikely witness—echoes Hegel's insistence. In a letter written at the age of twenty, Kafka declared, "God does not want me to write—But I, I must.... There are so many powers in me tied to a post, which might perhaps become a green tree while they are liberated and become useful to me and to *the state*" (emphasis added).[49]

Kaufmann joins Hegel in his celebration of the state and advances his own brief for its essential character. "A collapse and the sudden removal of the restraints associated with a state does not mean freedom" (H 266). After citing the preamble to the American Constitution, Kaufmann writes:

> That men who revere their constitution and learn this preamble by heart as children should find Hegel's association of the state with freedom perverse and talk as if it were self-evident that the state merely abridges our natural freedom is a triumph of thoughtlessness....

Hegel—a Reinterpretation was published in 1965. These comments inevitably address the student revolts of the 1960s.[50] Kaufmann's conservative stance connects with that of a collegial humanist, Lionel Trilling, who has also been called "Hegelian" at this juncture.[51] (In this book, I—and others—have linked Kaufmann's sensibility with Trilling's, although their congruence is far from perfect.[52]) There is, however, an interesting complication here: How does Kaufmann's sympathy for Hegel's celebration of the state jibe with the intended influence of Kaufmann's anthology of existentialist writings, which became the *Lonely Planet* of the sixties in its refusal of ethical conformism, what Hegel has been calling *Sittlichkeit*?[53]

There are two evident conflicts here. The first: If Kaufmann agrees with Hegel on the primacy of the state and its ethic of cultural obedience, what happens to Kaufmann's prime value, adapted from Nietzsche, of individual authenticity and self-perfection? Earlier, in chapter 5, we addressed a similar issue, citing the work of Steven B. Smith, who questioned Kaufmann's claim to the survival in Hegel of inalienable Enlightenment rights. I concluded that what might be inalienable, for Hegel, is the *possibility* of a free personality but solely in the setting of "the institutions of ethical life—family, civil society, and the state . . . as the necessary categorial framework within which our individual powers and capacities can flourish."[54] This means: the achievement of authenticity is conceivable only within a "well-enough" ordered state. (Think, once more, of D. W. Winnicott, who asks for a "good-enough" mother as the condition of the sane development of her child.) But this is not a matter easy for readers of Kaufmann on Hegel to decide, especially as the category of authenticity is irremediably obscure, intuitable only as a "sense of self" and quite possibly nurtured as an imperative precisely when states fall into chaos. The existence of a state is the categorial condition of authenticity, which can be the goal of a *free* subject; but what must be the condition of the state and the degree of freedom it allows? In *Hegel's Retreat from Eleusis*, a study of Hegel's political thought, George Armstrong Kelly quotes a youthful poem by Hegel containing these lines: "to live for free truth only; but for a peace with statutory law that regulates opinion and men's feelings—never, never to consent to that!" As Hegel continues to think of statutory law, "the free truth was not forsaken; but Hegel also sought to achieve peace—the peace of the intellect [read: 'authenticity'] and the peace of the city." His solution, which enriches our notion of the "well-enough" ordered state, is the "neutral state," which Hegel "theorized . . . amid the contrary thrusts of Revolution and Reaction, featuring an armature that protects the collectivity equally from irrational demands of religious domination and from the empty willfulness of subjective conviction."[55] After quoting from Kaufmann's anthology of essays titled *Hegel's Political Philosophy*, the political philosopher Shlomo Avineri stresses, equally, that "it is the *idea* of the state with which Hegel is dealing."[56] In this figure, a sort of Überstaat in relation to all "particular states or institutions" as they are encountered in actual modernity, "the laws are not something alien to the subject" (thus, the *Philosophy of Right*):

the subject is . . . directly linked to the ethical order by a relation which is more like an identity than even the relation of faith or trust. . . . The essence of the modern state is that the universal be bound up with the complete freedom of its particular members. The universal must be furthered, but subjectivity on the other hand must attain its full and living development. It is only when both these moments subsist in their strength that the state can be regarded as articulated and genuinely organized.[57]

This type of argument, if it is one, invokes Gandhi's probably apocryphal reply to the question, "What do you think of Western civilization?" He answered: "I think it would be a good idea." In short, in Hegel's conception of the (ideal) state, the values of authenticity and ethical "identity" are, to cite a Heideggerian trope, "equiprimordial."

In actual states, these values may (or may not) compete. In the former case, we need to find, in Kaufmann's account, Hegel's provision for civil disobedience, for a pointing up of a conflict between what freedom tells the citizen and what the state requires. Is there no provision here for tragedy—for a splitting apart of the claims of *Sittlichkeit* and the claims of tyranny?

The provision follows. Earlier in this chapter, I cited Hegel's thought as it prepares for "the great collisions" of tragedy. Kaufmann, too, is open to these catastrophes. This openness proves attractive to existentialism, which, as we've seen, profiles the extreme situation of a conflicted object choice, where life and death of one sort or another are at stake. And yet the greater weight for both Hegel and Kaufmann *in this book on Hegel* falls on the primacy of the "ethical." It is important to realize that when Hegel, with Kaufmann's enthusiasm, celebrates Antigone as "the most glorious figure ever to have appeared on earth," she is disobedient to her city not in the name of the assumed rationality of a subject-self—her morality—but in the name of *das Sittliche*, the ethics of inherited custom, for Hegel, the truly rational: "The laws of *Sittlichkeit* are not accidental but the rational itself." Antigone's integrity, courage, and intensity serve a conservative ideal, which now makes Kaufmann's conclusion hard to follow: "Had he [Hegel] been the statist and totalitarian he has been called, how could he possibly have so loved this play, which is a song of songs on civil disobedience?" (H 270) One answer to this aporia might lie in Kaufmann's earlier claim, that "when Hegel in effect declared himself for the primacy of the ethical realm, this *included* art, religion, and philosophy" (H 84–85). Depending on details of this inclusion, rebellion, nurtured by "art, religion, and philosophy"—whether in the name of custom or against the tyranny of custom—would still be valid *within* the "ethical realm."

Kaufmann is less Hegel's defender when it comes to Christianity, whose superiority to Judaism Hegel—now at loggerheads with Kaufmann—is glad to affirm. Nonetheless, Christianity occupies third rank in Hegel's three-part division of the realm of absolute spirit. It stands lower than art. "It is," Kaufmann writes, "a less developed form of what finds mature expression in philosophy," which occupies top position. Hegel spells out the logic of his ranking, in a longer citation, of considerable interest:

> The second form of the union of the objective and subjective in the spirit is *art*: it steps more into actuality and sensuousness than religion; at its most dignified it has to present, not the spirit of God but the form of the god [think: classical Greece statuary] and what is divine and spiritual in general. The divine is to be presented to intuition by it.
>
> But the true does not only reach notions and feelings, as in religion, or intuition, as in art, but also the thinking spirit. Thus we come to the third form of union—*philosophy*. This is in the manner indicated the highest, freest, and wisest form. (qtd. in H 271)

Kaufmann summarizes: "In philosophy, mythical notions (*Vorstellungen*) and subjective feeling (*Gefühl*), as well as intuition (*Anschauung*), are transcended at last by genuine comprehension. . . . Hegel merely finds the Christian myths more suggestive and appropriate anticipations of his philosophy than the myths of other religions" (H 271–72). Kaufmann is concerned to desubstantialize Hegel's Christian "God" at every turn, and there is no lack of evidence. Here is Hegel, the excellent humanist: "To grasp in thought, correctly and definitely, what God is as spirit, that requires thorough speculation [i.e., philosophy]. . . . God is only God insofar as he knows himself; his knowing himself is, furthermore, a self-consciousness in man and man's knowledge *of* God that goes on to man's knowing himself *in* God" (qtd. in H 272–73). A reminiscence of "The Rhine," a hymn composed by Hegel's friend Hölderlin, surely plays into this formulation:

> But the gods have enough
> In their own immortality and need
> If anything
> Heroes and men
> And other mortal creatures. For since
> The supremely blessed feel nothing themselves
> Doubtless another must

If it is permissible to say such a thing
Feel in their name, in sympathy and that
Someone they need.[58]

Kaufmann's commentary goes to the heart of his own worldview—at various times a heroic, a heretical, and now a conservative humanism:

> What does this mean if not that God does not know himself until man knows him; and since "God is only God in so far as he knows himself," God comes into being only when man "knows" him. Findlay has therefore called Hegel "the philosopher . . . of liberal Humanism." One may cavil at "liberal": the temperament of the mature Hegel was conservative rather than liberal. But his religious position may safely be characterized as a form of humanism. (H 273)

God, world spirit, the Idea: all are realized as "an organic system," unfolding its stages in human consciousness; they are the world as it is known to philosophical man, "essentially *concrete, the unity of differentiated determinations*" (Hegel) (H 281–82). These determinations are at once historical and logical; indeed, in their development, they are, as Hegel declares, *the same*: "The sequence of the systems of philosophy *in history is the same* as the *sequence in the logical derivation* of the conceptual determinations of the idea" (H 283). But in his later lectures on the history of philosophy, Hegel attenuated the absolute form of the parallel, thinking now that it was "mainly" true.

Kaufmann comments on this claim, holding it to be valid in parts. He has already shown that "the sequence of the categories in the *Logic* was not determined by any strict necessity, logical or dialectical; that there was no relentless deduction from Concept to Concept" (H 284). One guide for Hegel's sequence, however, might well have been a steady glance at the history of philosophy. The second part of Hegel's claim engages Kaufmann more deeply: it raises the question once more of the history of philosophy as an "organic system" or a series of reprehensible but corrigible errors. He endorses Hegel's position, if somewhat modestly: "The possibility arises that . . . different philosophies might be partially true, might supplement each other, and might therefore be worth studying one after the other" (H 283). This meditation on truth and error could once again evoke Kafka *en bonne hégélienne* when he writes of the near-impossibility of a truthful articulation of the spirit: "One cannot express what one is, for that is precisely what one *is*; one can only communicate what one is not, ergo the lie. It is only in a chorus that a certain truth may be present."[59] Hegel's "chorus" would march across the stage of world history, one chorister-philosopher at a time. In their march a certain truth is present: nothing less than the truth of absolute spirit.

Considering Kaufmann himself a historian of philosophy in the spirit of Hegel, there are evidently prominent philosophies of almost nugatory value, namely, Heidegger's ontology and Marx's "scientific materialism." What might be valuable in *Being and Time*—the radical perspective of human being in time, "time as the horizon of the understanding of being in terms of temporality"[60]—is scarcely original with Heidegger, for "Hegel equates *Dasein* (existence) with *In-der-Zeit-Sein* (being-in-time)." And here Kaufmann advances Hegel's polemic against the notion that authentic philosophizing has been lost with, say, the pre-Socratics, for "the *first philosophy* is *the wholly general, indeterminate thought* and the *simplest*. . . . One must know this lest one seek for more *behind the old* philosophies than they contain" (H 284–85).

Kaufmann deals somewhat cursorily with "Hegel after Hegel"—but he does undertake to refute Marxism philosophically. Hegel's dialectic was never

> the rigorous method that Marx and his followers sought to make of it. . . . By depriving it of its primary reference to ideas and applying it instead to modes of production, one cannot make the dialectic more precise; or materialism, "scientific." On the contrary, beliefs are at least *capable* of being literally contradicted and then subsumed in a higher synthesis, while any dialectic of modes of production or material circumstances is bound to be utterly lacking in rigor.

At the same time Marxism cannot be ignored, to say the least—but when studied must be grasped, if Lenin is to be trusted, in light of a mastery of the whole of Hegel's *Logic* (H 286–87).

It is interesting to note that Adorno appears to have done just this in disputing Kaufmann's claim of the "nugatory value" of Marxian dialectic. Adorno has another indisputably productive "path of dialectic" in mind, which is that of *immanent* critique.

> When Marx submits a form of society to critique, he does so by measuring it against what the society in question claims of itself to be. Thus Marx will say: "This society claims to be one of free and just exchange, so let us see if it lives up to these its own demands." Or again: "This claims to be a society of free subjects engaged in exchange as contracting parties; let us see how it stands with this demand."[61]

We conclude as we began—recalling Anthony Quinton—with the revolt against Hegel in the first half of the twentieth century—especially after G. E. Moore's influential "Refutation of Idealism" in 1903. The turn was marked by a reactive one-sidedness, a point that allows Kaufmann an irrepressible aside on the New Criticism (of literary theory), which again connects him to the humanism of Trilling. In its one-sidedness, this new critical approach is like the earlier British reaction to Hegel's historicism: "The Hegelian as well as the Marxist approach is rejected in favor of close analysis, often with a deliberate disregard for historical context. What has been neglected tends to be made the alpha and omega." In the course of visiting Kierkegaard's attack on Hegel's allegedly bloodless, shallow, mechanical "scientificity," Kaufmann is able to sum up the impulse to his book. He means to oppose the stigmatizing view of Hegel "as an 'essentialist' and academician, a professor who constructed a system that bore no relation to his concrete existence, a philosopher who paid no heed to living experience" (H 288).

None of the reviews of Kaufmann's book are uniformly positive, but none deny Kaufmann's success in achieving his goal stated this way. He is also entitled to conclude that his book helps put Hegel's work on a solid scholarly, bibliographical foundation by identifying the worst lacunae. It doesn't harm one's confidence in his skill when he casually footnotes "Carl Roos's *Danish* study of *Kierkegaard og Goethe*" (emphasis added) to point up Kierkegaard's lack of objectivity and dependence on secondary sources, as in the case of his only rickety knowledge of Hegel's writings. Further, in this matter of influence, Kaufmann gladly repeats mention of Sartre's "immense debt to Hegel" acquired through his prewar study of Hegel in the celebrated classes of Alexandre Kojève. A sentence from Kojève's "Phenomenological Method in Hegel" would have been of special interest to Sartre: Kojève notes "that 'Logic' is dialectical (in the broad sense) only because it implies a 'negative' or negating aspect."[62] Kaufmann's comparison of Hegel with Nietzsche concludes to Hegel's disadvantage: Nietzsche excelled by far in the continual originality of his work, sustained until the end of his mental life. This contrast prepares for Kaufmann's definitive declaration of taste in philosophy: "As a human being, Hegel seems more interesting than Aristotle and Kant; as a writer, he does not brook comparison with Plato and Nietzsche. Few will find their favorite philosopher in him. I, for one, do not. But there are not many who offer us so much" (H 297).

This could be said of Kaufmann's work as well, both for the richness of his aperçus and the verve and boldness of his rhetoric. I leave his *Hegel* holding

in my mind such a sentence from his discussion of *Antigone*: "Actuality therefore contains, concealed, the other side, foreign to knowledge, and does not
show itself to consciousness—does not show the son the father in the man
who insults him and whom he slays, nor the mother in the queen whom he
wifes" (H 128).

Hegel: Texts and Commentary

The second part of Kaufmann's reinterpretation of Hegel consists of his translation and commentary on the preface to the *Phenomenology*—a generally appreciated contribution that also appeared as a separate book.[63] The project answers to
Kaufmann's passion for translation and close reading. I shall borrow Kaufmann's
trope of thought when he writes of Hegel's system, "There is no need here to go
through the system, bit by bit" (H 247) and resist offering, in turn, a complete
commentary on his commentary, although, out of respect, I shall make a start.
Kaufmann's pages are very accessible—lucid and engaging, especially when he
shows Hegel criticizing a number of the abstruse theses misattributed to him, as
for example, the lifeless pseudotriplicity of the Concept (Hp 77).

The commentary has been praised by many reviewers, for example, by the
scholar of Marxism George Lichtheim, otherwise noted for his withering
impatience with the half-educated, who writes: "[Kaufmann's] . . . translation
of the lengthy and important Preface, with a textual commentary on facing
pages, . . . not only clarifies Hegel's famous obscurities, but offers the reader a
guide to the often very puzzling connotations of Hegel's elaborate punning in
German. . . . His lengthy commentary is a minor masterpiece of concise and
erudite interpretation."[64]

Earlier in this chapter I mentioned Kaufmann's resistance to the concept
of explication as a way of coming to grips with philosophical texts. But, as we
learn from his introduction to his translation and commentary, the idea of
explication was put forward too forcefully by Hegel himself to be ignored. "In
an aphorism of the Berlin period, Hegel said, 'a great man condemns men to
explicate him.'"[65] Kaufmann continues: "For a commentator this is an appropriate motto, but Hegel was almost certainly not thinking of himself, and the
motto is as apt for his preface as it is for my commentary" (Hp 3).

This is an intriguing sentence. Questions (and answers) spring up, especially in light of Kaufmann's earlier remarks on method. Now he appears to
be redefining the originally rejected word "explication" as "commentary."
Commentary, which spells out comprehension *and* criticism, is Kaufmann's

preferred practice. But how can he let go the oppressive valence of the word "condemned," which, in Hegel's aphorism above, is then followed by neither comprehension, criticism, nor commentary? Kaufmann recovers the somewhat casual-sounding figure of condemnation as a substantial concept "apt for Hegel's preface" in a quite wonderful formulation. He writes:

> We are all condemned, as Hegel sees it, to try to *comprehend* what man has thought up to our time and to relive, in condensed form, the experiences of the world spirit [emphasis added to Kaufmann's preferred term!]. The preface ... is of a piece with the conclusion of Hegel's introductory lectures on the philosophy of history: "The moments which the spirit seems to have left behind, it also possesses in its present depth. As it has run through its moments in history, it has to run through them in the present—in the Concept of itself." (Hp 4)

Conceptual analysis recapitulates historical accumulation. Here one begins to see a suggestive parallel between Hegel and Freud (another of Kaufmann's prime educators). Referring to Hegel's conclusion, Kaufmann reflects, "The first of these two sentences might well have been written by Freud, except that he would probably have said 'soul' [better, 'Seele,' psyche], not 'spirit'" (Hp 4). This felt linkage heightens Hegel's ongoing attractiveness for Kaufmann.

The history of Kaufmann's reading, as a young man, in the thinkers of the German Enlightenment, is recapitulated in his remarks on Hegel's preface. Kaufmann notes, for example, that Hegel's "*Weltgeist* (World Spirit) had been used by Kant, Herder, and Mendelssohn before him, and is also encountered in Schelling's and Schopenhauer's works." Kaufmann's *present* understanding of the preface contains trace layers of the uses to which each of Hegel's predecessors had put it. For example, Schiller's *On the Aesthetic Education of Man* makes a ghostly appearance. "*An und für sich* (in and for itself), *an sich* (in itself), and (*für uns*) occur together on page 37 of Fichte's *Sun-clear Report* (1801)" (Hp 3).

That Kaufmann would wish to comment in some detail on Hegel's preface comes as no surprise. It is also understandable that he should want to translate it. Hegel's diction is famously intricate: you cannot decide with any certainty what nouns Hegel's pronouns refer to, since *all* the nouns in a given sentence are likely to be abstractions in the feminine gender. Such decisions can be made clearly and economically in translation. But translating Hegel presents another sort of challenge, an intriguing one, discussed in detail many years before Kaufmann in a famous essay by Alexander Koyré on Hegel's terminology.[66]

Relying on Koyré, Heckman, in his preface to his (and Cherniak's) translation of Hyppolite's *Genesis and Structure of Hegel's "Phenomenology of Spirit,"*
stresses Hegel's "revolt" against "the overly technical and abstract terminology
that prevailed in contemporary German philosophical writing."[67] I will add,
however, as we noted just above, that this revolt was not thoroughgoing. Still,
the point is fair. Heckman is right to point up Hegel's use of ordinary words. It
follows, of course, that their meaning will differ from the meaning they have in
ordinary usage. This play of ordinary words with highly technical words could
intrigue a translator, who would enjoy the challenge of bringing this play home
to his target language. Kaufmann describes the variation in levels of diction,
which we have heard about, in a related way: "The alternation between cumber-
some sentences that go on much too long and powerful epigrams that spell temporary relief is one of the most striking characteristics of this preface" (Hp 2).
Kaufmann, philosopher and poet, is suited to this task of translation, and the
result is refreshingly clear, as consider his translation of Hegel's own description,
in a journal announcement in 1807, of the project of the *Phenomenology*:

> This volume deals with the *becoming of knowledge....* It includes the various
> *forms of the spirit* as stations on the way on which it becomes pure knowl-
> edge or absolute spirit. In the main parts of this science, . . . consideration
> is given to consciousness, self-consciousness, observing and acting reason,
> the spirit itself as ethical, educated, and moral spirit, and finally as religious
> in its different forms. The wealth of the appearances of the spirit, which at
> first glance seems chaotic, is brought into a scientific order which presents
> them according to the necessity in which the imperfect ones dissolve and
> pass over into higher ones which constitute their next truth. Their final
> truth they find at first in religion, then in science as a result of the whole.
> (qtd. in Hp 4–5)

As the preface unfolds, Kaufmann makes two important points—one
substantive, taking up Hegel, in an act of comprehension; the other, critical,
a moment required by comprehension, for "a philosopher must combine
grasp and critical evaluation" (Hp 11). The positive moment stresses "one of
the most interesting and fateful paragraphs" in Hegel's preface. Hegel writes
with respect to other philosophical systems, "Opinion considers the opposition of what is true and false quite rigid, and, confronted with a philosophical
system, it expects agreement or contradiction." That is an error, and it is Hegel's
great achievement to recast this relation as one of sublation (*Aufhebung*) in a
"progressive development of the truth." Previous systems are "elements of an

organic unity in which they not only do not conflict, but in which one is as necessary as the other; and it is only this equal necessity that constitutes the life of the whole" (Hp 8).

The first part of this proposition is underscored by Kaufmann. We cannot underestimate Hegel's achievement of seeing earlier systems, as Kaufmann writes, not "laid out next to each other in a spatial arrangement; they cannot be fully understood as long as their temporal relationship is ignored" (Hp 9). What we see forming here is the germ of a new discipline: the *history* of philosophy. The second part of Hegel's proposition calls for criticism. "When a philosopher disagrees with his predecessors, we should not reject the lot because they cannot agree with each other; rather we should ask how the later thinkers correct the partiality of the former, and how each contributes to the gradual refinement of knowledge. Hegel notwithstanding, this does not imply any genuine necessity. Hegel often uses 'necessary' quite illicitly as the negation of 'utterly arbitrary'" (Hp 11). The Hegel scholar Robert Pippin, in a major essay on the transitions between stages of consciousness in the *Phenomenology*, doubts, like Kaufmann, that Hegel has shown the *necessity* of such passages as, for example, the early movement from an essentially passive or dependent consciousness—the relation to an object—to a self-transforming, self-experiencing consciousness, a "mutually recognizing, social self-consciousness," the domain of "the Absolute as Spirit" (Hegel).[68] On the other hand, commentators have argued that Kaufmann's sense of Hegel may be too caught up in ideas of Shakespearean "overabundance" and the "incommensurability" that Goethe attributed to *Faust* to want to tease out the logical connections informing the *Phenomenology* or the structure of the System.

At this point, with the reintroduction of what is probably the most pressing aporia in all of Hegel studies—in the hope that having whetted the reader's desire to pursue these matters on his or her own—I am obliged, by reasons, too, of "spatial arrangement," to break off this compendium. Thanks to Kaufmann's skill and energy, the preface, among the most fruitful of Hegel's writings, is now widely accessible. It is ready be read and studied, handsomely republished in a single volume by the University of Notre Dame Press. In the following chapters, we will have an opportunity to survey more of Kaufmann's views on Hegel, especially Hegel's views on the tragic collision of ethical values.

9

The Philosophy of Tragedy

TRAGEDY AND PHILOSOPHY/1

The philosophy of tragedy is in its childhood.

—WALTER KAUFMANN

KAUFMANN WAS ENORMOUSLY productive in the years following the appearance of *Hegel* in 1965 and even while occupied with the writing of *Tragedy and Philosophy* (1968).¹ In addition to this new major work and a range of scholarly articles, many of them focusing on literary theory and existentialism, he published several new Nietzsche translations. Every one of these volumes, still in print, is commented and cross-referenced (although critics have objected to Kaufmann's overbearing presence as commentator). In 1966, he brought out his translation of *Beyond Good and Evil*; a year later, *On the Genealogy of Morals*, *Ecce Homo*, and *Will to Power*. In 1968, along with *Tragedy and Philosophy*, he published the indispensable Modern Library *Basic Writings of Nietzsche*, which included all these translations (except *Will to Power*) plus *The Case of Wagner* and—to return to Nietzsche's beginnings—*The Birth of Tragedy*.

Tragedy—the sorrow, the terror, and its theory—were on his mind. In *From Shakespeare to Existentialism*, Shakespeare's tragedies, backed by Aristotle, set the standard for the noble type, those who can harm but will not. *Critique of Religion and Philosophy* stressed the distinction between Judaism and Christianity as the distinction between a tragic and a nontragic worldview: if in Christianity the good death is rewarded, Christianity obliviates tragedy. Kaufmann's Hegel study begins with Goethe's tragedy *Iphigenia*, exemplary for

Hegel of the richer morality—a social ethic—*Sittlichkeit*. A stay in Jerusalem, the heart of Jewish antiquity, provided the conditions, in 1962, under which Kaufmann could think and lecture intensively on tragedy. The following years produced a manuscript, the book, and a retrospect.

The book and retrospect have survived. Terry Eagleton, a critic not readily given to praise, calls Kaufmann's *Tragedy and Philosophy* "one of the most perceptive modern studies of tragedy," focusing on Kaufmann's refusal "to distinguish between the tragic and the merely pitiful, and doubt that the ancient Greeks or Shakespeare did either."[2] This distinction is clearly one of the more difficult issues in the theory of tragedy and one that Kaufmann will discuss in detail. He will also deal closely with the suffering that Eagleton alludes to in praising the "humane, shrewd Walter Kaufmann":

> Even if suffering appears shapely on stage, this may come as scant comfort to its real-life victims. A forlorn clutch of critics, such as Walter Kaufmann in his splendidly acute, acerbic *Tragedy and Philosophy*, written at the height of the Vietnam war, see the value of tragic art as lying in its "refusal to let any comfort, faith or joy deafen our ears to the tortured cries of our brethren."[3]

Kaufmann's book is so dense with thought as to make *Hegel* seem like a feuilleton.

A retrospect appears at the outset of the 1979 Princeton reprint of *Tragedy and Philosophy*. It belongs to Kaufmann's decades-long criticism of what is wrong with philosophy—very well, with certain philosophies: above all, the distance they take from the great fact about humanity, its immitigable suffering. One wonders whether in writing these thoughts in 1979 Kaufmann already had a mordant intimation of his own shocking death a year later. There is the great tragedy of humankind; there are redoubtable literary works on stage performing tragedy; and there is the "lesser" tragedy of someone's dying by natural means. In Kaufmann's view, philosophy has taken little notice of any of it.[4]

A British philosopher, A. C. Grayling, is an exponent of a humanism consistent with Kaufmann's own. Grayling, who was recently voted president of the British Humanist Association Society, defines the key contemporary philosophical debates as follows:

(a) A metaphysical debate about what the universe contains; denying that it contains supernatural agencies of any kind makes ... [one] an atheist.

(b) A debate about the basis of ethics; taking the world to be a natural realm of natural law requires that humanity thinks for itself about the right and the good, based on our best understanding of human nature and the human condition; this makes ... [one] a humanist.[5]

There is no explicit mention of human suffering, where it might be expected, in either of these "debates." This omission adds urgency to Kaufmann's claim, a decade after the publication of his study of tragedy: "A great many ... people must feel as I do that the enormous sufferings of so much of humanity pose a profound problem for us." His book deals persistently with this crisis, in line with the ethical absolutes that Kaufmann (and Grayling, as well) profess: "Love and be courageous!" Kaufmann is quite explicit about the values that inform his book: "In *Tragedy and Philosophy* I write about what I love" (T xii). This enterprise, which challenges canonical authority, will require a good deal of scholarly courage: "What is sought is not bliss but risk" (T xxi). It might be observed that "love and be courageous" alone does not constitute an ethical program, but Kaufmann has more than once fleshed out these values with "honesty" and (the unfortunate neologism) "humbition."

In his study of tragedy, he will try to leave no stone unturned, quite literally. The conviction that widely held views on tragedy are wrong can lead to one's "finding buried treasures under the accumulated rubbish of centuries" (T xxi). Here Kaufmann may be unwittingly invoking Walter Benjamin's memorable aperçu, a "thesis on the philosophy of history" apropos of Paul Klee's drawing *Angelus Novus*. The mood of Benjamin's piece is in line with the mood of the brief prose poems that constitute a prologue to Kaufmann's book. Benjamin's thesis describes an angel,

> his face turned toward the past. Where we perceive a chain of events, he sees one single catastrophe that keeps piling wreckage and hurls it in front of his feet. The angel would like to stay, awaken the dead, and make whole what has been smashed. But a storm is blowing in from Paradise; it has got caught in his wings with such violence that the angel can no longer close them. The storm irresistibly propels him into the future to which his back is turned, while the pile of debris before him grows skyward. This storm is what we call progress.[6]

One of Kaufmann's pieces reads like a prologue to Benjamin's thesis: "The Christian dream of heaven with its sexless angels and insipid harps betrays the most appalling lack of imagination, moral and aesthetic. ... Wretched brutes ... [who] would enjoy their heaven while the mass of mankind suffers ceaseless torments" (T xix–xx). This pile of debris and wretchedness consists of many an inadequate view on tragedy—even, and especially, as held by Plato, Aristotle, and Nietzsche. Kaufmann forcefully rejects the latter's account of the birth and death of tragedy as well as his judgments on the Greek tragedians (and hereby testifies to his critical—and not apologetic—reading of Nietzsche). From this point on, I will continue my plan of reproducing—with commentary, where called for—the observations of Kaufmann that I consider most interesting.

I am struck from the start by his conceiving of Plato's views on tragedy as comparable with early Christian views on the Hebrew Bible: Plato turned against the morality of the tragedies in a radically oppositional spirit, as texts requiring correction at the root. Like Plato, and to some extent Aristotle, the church, too, "seeing itself as the new Israel, found little good in contemporary Judaism. Plato writes about the tragic poets as their rival." Aristotle's extreme formalism—his "perverse concentration on [the] plot and diction" of tragedy—might in turn be owed to his revolt against Plato, who, in the name of philosophy, had appropriated tragedy's central concerns (T 2). The outcome of Kaufmann's reflections is to deflate what he takes to be "the presumption of Socrates, Plato, and Aristotle that they were superior in wisdom to the tragic poets" (T 7). This is Kaufmann's persistent refrain: tragedy is a form of knowledge whereof philosophy knows little.

When we deal with Plato, we deal with a genius of paradox: his unrelenting attack on poetry as well as his creativity in tutelary mythmaking is couched in language of surpassing elegance. "Everything is expressed so beautifully" (T 20). This is a judgment Kaufmann had already made in *Critique of Religion and Philosophy* (C 37–41), but this distinction is no point of honor:

> Plato loved poetry and felt thoroughly at home in Homer and Hesiod; [on the other hand] dramatic passages and situations came to his mind much less often; he never once quotes or mentions one of Sophocles' plays; and he argued at length, both in the *Republic* in the *Laws*, that the influence of tragedy was evil and that tragic poets should not be allowed in an exemplary city. (T 10)

What have the poets done to deserve his scorn?

First—and here Aeschylus is mainly to blame—they have impeached the morals of the gods; poets should not accuse divinities of bringing evil into the world.[7] The divine is imperturbable; the gods do not lie—but you will not hear such statements from the poets.[8] Nor will the republic allow poets to say that "wrongdoers are often happy and the good miserable." This argument,

Kaufmann writes, would effectively ban Sophocles's *Antigone* and *Electra* and Euripides's *Medea* and *Hippolytus*, for starters: Plato's strictures suggest the production code of the Hays office in the early days of the movies (T 15).[9] Nor, on this note, is Plato tolerant of the idea of *acting* as such—of falsifying the being that one is.

We know that the *Republic* ends with the glorious myth of Er, which seems inevitable in this composition, Plato's republic being a sort of "salvation institute." The myth of Er fills in the protocols for a happy passage through the afterlife. This is not the lifeworld of the tragedies, which, for Plato, create the wrong myth, teaching, with downcast eyes, devotion to the values of *this* world. If we are ready to consider him, in this sense, a *de*mythologizer, we will value Kaufmann's second surmise about Plato, who demands that one turn away from a world of treacherous semblances, for such devotion is idolatry. "It seems safe to conclude," writes Kaufmann,

> that at least one of the ways in which Plato reached his theory of Forms came from the traditional polytheism of the Greeks and led through a radical repudiation of anthropomorphism. The Forms of beauty and wisdom are the ancient goddesses, Aphrodite and Pallas Athene, *demythologized*. . . . Those of us who turn to Homer and Sophocles should realize that in Plato's eyes we are idolators who put our trust in images (emphasis added). (T 17–19)

At this point a likely surmise would be that Plato had been influenced by the Jewish prohibition on making or contemplating images. The second of the Ten Commandments reads: "Thou shalt not make unto thee any graven image, or any likeness of any thing that is in heaven above, or that is in the earth beneath, or that is in the water under the earth: thou shalt not bow down thyself to them, nor serve them: for I [*am*] the Lord thy God." The notion that classical Greek philosophy was influenced by Jewish thought belongs to what has been called mnemohistory—meaning: the trope has circulated, but no scholar today has been able to establish solid traces of the language of the Hebrew Bible in the works of Plato—or, for that matter, Aristotle (see chapter 14).

To return to Kaufmann's Plato: The *Laws*, a description of "the second best city," is no more welcoming of tragic poets than the *Republic*, unless their work, scrutinized by magistrates, is declared fit to be recited and published. We know the sticking point: they must not present the gods as immoral or show evil men flourishing. Kaufmann reminds us that Plato destroyed *his* early poems upon turning to philosophy: the thought of this gesture throws down the gauntlet to Plato, if ever reconciliation were possible. Kaufmann himself turned to philosophy not and never at the cost of destroying *his* poems. He wrote poems until the day he died; the critical prose of each of his books is accompanied by an imaginative flight. Plato's negative example can only have encouraged him to take his own words to heart, when he wrote, on behalf of Homer—author of the "first great tragic poem of world literature"—: "The best a man can hope for is to be remembered evermore in poetry" (T 162).

What is striking in Kaufmann's discussion of Plato's poetics is his sense of Plato and the tragedians as locked in mortal combat to be remembered *in their writing*: "Plato not only writes as the rival of the fourth-century tragedians, claiming in effect that he is the rightful heir of the promise; he feels that he has come to deliver men from that kind of tragedy" (T 29). Plato does not lack a view on suffering: Kaufmann is eloquent on the Platonic alternative, much colored, I'm sure, by the Nietzschean ideal, in Kaufmann's view, of becoming the artwork that you are:

> Plato's portrait of the unjustly punished martyr who does not lose tran-
> quil self-control, who succumbs before tyrannical power without losing
> his integrity, and who faces death with complete equanimity need not fear
> comparison with the very best creations of the tragic poets. Time has not
> dimmed it; its promise stands unbroken. Here is a response to suffering
> different from the poets': not a call to discover beauty, power, and nobility
> where, without art, we might have seen only misery, but a summons to
> make ourselves into artistic masterpieces that withstand human injustice
> and natural suffering. (T 24)

This ideal is on display in the dialogue *Phaedo*, in which Phaedo recounts the exemplary death of Socrates, Kaufmann's first, altogether formidable "educator."

Kaufmann's heightened sense of philosophical rivalry, of the history of ideas as a series of corrections of the mooted errors of a powerful precursor, encourages him to see Plato on tragedy as a provocation to Aristotle on tragedy. Plato, like any philosopher, must be answerable; Aristotle will take him up, Kaufmann suggests, first, on the matter of emotion in tragedy. Aristotle has read in the *Republic* how

> we are corrupted by listening to the heroes of Homer or of the tragic
> poets when they lament and moan. "Can it be right that the spectacle of a
> man behaving as one would scorn and blush to behave oneself should be

admired and enjoyed, instead of filling us with disgust? . . . The emotions of pity our sympathy has strengthened will not be easy to restrain when we are suffering ourselves." . . . This is familiar by now but worth quoting in this formulation because Aristotle's famous doctrine of *catharsis* may have been developed to meet this point. (T 21–22)

Again note that

> Plato makes . . . remarks [in the *Laws*] that ought to be considered because Aristotle took exception to them. He says that small children prefer puppet shows; older children, comedy; "educated women, young men, and people in general favor tragedy"; and "we old men would have the greatest pleasure in hearing a rhapsodist recite well the *Iliad* and *Odyssey*, or one of the Hesiodic poems." This may have prompted Aristotle's awkward attempt, near the end of his *Poetics*, to establish the superiority of tragedy over the epic. (T 27)

In turning to Aristotle, Kaufmann turns to the second of the three philosophers who have had the greatest impact on theories of tragedy—the third, after Plato and Aristotle, being Nietzsche in *The Birth of Tragedy*. All three, it appears, are unequal to the task. The *Poetics* arrives with the unpromising legend of "terseness carried to the point of obscurity" (T 32). (An aside tars Wittgenstein with the same brush.) From the start, the reader wonders how the time-honored concepts of *catharsis* and *hamartia*, reversal and recognition, pity and fear will fare: they have excited reverent exegesis—in other theorists. Exegesis has a history and will continue to excite exegetes: "Ducks like what quacks," writes Kaufmann, flexing his rhetorical muscle (T 30). He will strive, on principle, for comprehension and criticism; he will find the *Poetics*, with its straitened perspective, inadequate to the substance of tragedy—but a good deal more adequate than the effort of many a contemporary critic, such as I. A. Richards or Lionel Abel.

Kaufmann's task at the outset is to enrich the first of the *Poetics'* key words—*tragōidia* and *mimēsis*. Conventional etymologies and translations are less than perspicuous. According to the famous thesis of Nietzsche and Gilbert Murray, and many a classical philologist, *tragōidia* means "goat song": after all, the original chorus of satyrs, with their goatish lusts, looked like goats. Kaufmann borrows his revision from the Aristotle scholar Gerald Else, on whom he often relies. Else writes, alternatively, "*tragōidoi* was the official title of the contestants in tragedy, those who actually competed for the prize." The prize was a goat. "The original competitor in the tragic contest," continues Else, "and therefore the sole possessor of the title *tragōidoi* before the year 509 or 502, was the tragic poet. And the poet was also his own actor" (qtd. in T 34).

Kaufmann offers a thoughtful account of *mimēsis*, for which a good enough translation is "mimesis," which is the title of Erich Auerbach's celebrated study of "the representation of reality in Western literature."[10] Mimesis understood, however, either as imitation or representation, makes little sense, as Kaufmann suggests, in several key places in the *Poetics*. For example, the famous second sentence reads: "Epic, tragedy, comedy, dithyrambic poetry, most music on the flute and on the lyre—all these are, in principle, *mimēsis*." Kaufmann advances boldly: "Even if we were prepared to swallow the suggestion that epic, tragedy, and comedy 'imitate' something—what does dithyrambic poetry imitate? And what does most music on lute and lyre imitate?" (T 37). The matter is soon vexed to difficulty when, citing the *Politics*, Kaufmann notes Aristotle's claim that music surpasses all other arts, including visual art, in its mimetic powers. What can mimesis mean here? In music, rhythms and melody can convey, writes Aristotle, moral qualities like "anger and mildness, and also . . . courage and temperance, and all their opposites." But Aristotle cannot have meant that music *imitates* these qualities. Kaufmann's leading thesis, in this section, is productive: the Greeks, unlike us, do not distinguish sharply between imitating, "creating striking images" (thus Kaufmann), and expressing (T 37).

Kaufmann's reenvisioning of mimesis as "creation"—as an autonomous activity using the imagination—is part of a long cultural-historical interpretation of Aristotle's theory. In their survey of the fortunes of mimesis, Gunter Gebauer and Christoph Otto Wulf observe that "the power of mimesis grows with the historical development of the individual psyche, in particular since the eighteenth century." Kaufmann's educator Lessing figures importantly in this revision. For Lessing, mimesis has an "autonomous status" although conditional on an imagination "whose general laws work together with the laws of the artistic medium."[11]

Kaufmann's cooperative dethroning of mimesis as *imitation* anticipates, in the received history of poetics, the dramatic passage from a poetics of imitation to a romantic poetics of expression, from art as mirror to art as lamp.[12] Kaufmann knows this history: "Those who would go back to theories of 'imitation' in order to enlist Aristotle's authority on the side of attempts to combat romantic theories that speak of expression, creation, and imagination mistake Aristotle's meaning and do him violence" (T 37). This comment conjures the debate in literary theory occurring in the 1950s and 1960s, with Meyer

Abrams amiably charting the romantic emergence of an expressive theory of poetry and Ronald Crane and Elder Olson and other theorists of the Chicago School—foes of romantic figuration and romantic irony—calling for a return to an older, rigorous, neo-Aristotelian "objectivism."

Kaufmann's suggestion, then, about the right paraphrase of mimesis is "make-believe, pretend, ways of pretending. . . . When Aristotle speaks of tragedy as the mimesis of an action . . . a make-believe or pretend action comes closer to his meaning than the imitation or copy of an action" (T 38). Really, the last thing Aristotle can have had in mind with mimetic art—notably tragedy—is Hamlet's image of "hold[ing] the mirror up to nature." Kaufmann supplies this haunting quote from Aristotle's *Physics*: "Art partly completes what nature cannot bring to a finish" (T 39).[13]

Of course, there is more, of great interest, to Aristotle's theory of tragedy, which he calls "the mimesis of a good [better: noble] action." Kaufmann's emendation of "good" to "noble" is based on a generalized Greek worldview, where the adjective in question—*spoudaios*—distinguishes between types of persons. Kaufmann quotes Else: "Greek thinking begins with and for a long time holds to the proposition that mankind is divided into 'good' and 'bad,' and these terms are quite as much social, political, and economic as they are moral." This line of argument resonates, as Kaufmann well knows, with the first essay in Nietzsche's *On the Genealogy of Morals* titled "Good and Evil, Good and Bad." And so Kaufmann is led to paraphrase a celebrated sentence differently, writing "poetry is more philosophical and *nobler* than history" (T 41–42). The implication of this paraphrase is fruitful: it makes clear that when Aristotle writes, "Poetry is more akin to philosophy and is a better thing [*spoudaioteron*] than history, [since] poetry deals with general truths, history with specific events," poetry's distinction cannot lie in its powers of imitation. It is the historian, following Aristotle, who copies specific events. The poet, on the other hand, as Kaufmann concludes,

> does not copy or imitate; he reflects on what *might* happen and thus rises to the contemplation of universals. . . . He does not copy what he finds in the old books or what has been related before; he merely uses material of this sort to construct a make-believe action, something that *might* happen and is of universal import. (T 42)

This point, I'll add, seems methodologically valid. What remains interesting, however, is to consult the relevant "old books" or "what has been related before" so as to take the measure of the poet's genius. If we will understand literature, we cannot do without the lesser stuff, what Adorno, speaking for Freud, calls "the refuse of the world of appearances," which the poet consumes—not tracelessly.[14] Of course, this is not a point generally lost on Kaufmann.

This section of his essay on the key elements of Aristotle's poetics of tragedy concludes on a note revealing more of Kaufmann than Aristotle. Kaufmann's eagerness to have readers—specialist and general—drop all scruples when criticizing authority where called for, begins to seem intemperate, hyperbolic, truculent. The occasion becomes less an invitation to criticize than an invitation to kick out. Kaufmann writes: "Those who consider Aristotle's *Poetics* definitive ought to pause over . . . [Aristotle's] remark about history." Aristotle wrote: "History has to expound not one action but one period of time and all that happened within this period to one or more persons, however tenuous the connection between one event and the others." This formulation, continues Kaufmann, "falls laughably short of doing justice to Thucydides." He goes on: "It stands to reason that a philosopher who characterized history in such an incredibly inadequate manner, without the least understanding of its nature and problems, was not infallible in his *Poetics*" (T 42). We can think of this tone as owed to pedagogical zeal, in some slight degree to the stance of the "true saint," following Baudelaire, "who uses his whip . . . and kills the people for their own good."[15] Here is Kaufmann playing the saint of humanism, who whips and kills authority for the readers' own good, to set us free from our own self-imposed diffidence.

No discussion of Aristotle on tragedy can do without scrutiny of the famous conclusion: by means of pity (*eleos*) and fear (*phobos*), tragedy accomplishes the catharsis of such emotions. "Actions that evoke this emotional response are felt to be tragic; or rather, . . . a play to which we respond in this way is a tragedy" (T 48). Are these emotions aroused by a final catastrophe? Contrary to every conventional view of the *Poetics*, Aristotle does not stipulate a "tragic ending" as a defining feature of tragedy. More than once, he discusses plays that do not end badly for the protagonist—and neither do other exemplary Greek tragedies. Nonetheless, as Kaufmann writes, "it is perfectly clear that Aristotle considered . . . [these emotions] a distinctive and defining characteristic of tragedy or, as we might say, the tragic emotions par excellence" (T 44).

With respect to the words for these emotions, and despite the magnitude of extant commentary, Kaufmann finds much of it superfluous, for the concept is simply *wrong*. Eleos is commonly defined as "pity," but pity is the last thing one feels on gaping at the torments inflicted, for example, in *Agamemnon*:

I did not feel pity . . . for the hare with its unborn brood that is torn by the eagles, for the individuals involved in the terror of Troy's fall, for Menelaus who was overcome by grief when he found that Helen was gone, for the warriors who experienced the terrors of war, for those who stayed behind and suffered misery at home, and those overtaken by the terrible fate that struck much of the Greek fleet on its way home. All this is but part of the sufferings to which I am exposed in the first half of the play—and *I* suffer, I am overwhelmed by the terrors of life. By the time Cassandra cries out— who am I to feel sorry for her? It is not as if I were secure and comfortable and looked down on her misery; it would come closer to the facts if we said that when my suffering had become unbearable, she suddenly lent it her voice. (T 45)

Pity requires a higher stance, an observation booth that is simply not available at tragedy: one is overwhelmed by those sufferings, one suffers with the hero—ergo, the truer emotion is closer to "sympathy," though that is not quite right either. (It hardly needs saying that Kaufmann's discernable contempt of pity would have been heightened by the opinion of a prime educator, Nietzsche.) To make good sense in English, eleos must be paraphrased. Lines from Goethe, another distinguished educator, lead Kaufmann to write that what is being said here—if it is to be right—is "sympathy and suffering, being deeply moved and shaken" (T 46).

To strengthen Kaufmann's point, I will once again cite Adorno's trope for another man's modern literature: "Through the power with which Kafka commands interpretation, he collapses aesthetic distance. He demands a desperate effort from the allegedly 'disinterested' spectator of an earlier time, overwhelms you, suggesting that far more than your intellectual equilibrium depends on whether you truly understand; life and death are at stake."[16] It may not be irrelevant that Kafka's shorter pieces are populated with figures from archaic Greek literature, many of whom suffer tragic fates: Odysseus, Prometheus, Poseidon, Sisyphus (who "was a bachelor"!).[17] But pity plays no role: "We do not 'pity,'" Kaufmann continues, in dealing with the Greek canon, "those we greatly admire, much less those to whom we look up [to] in awe. 'Pity' is not what we feel for Prometheus or Oedipus [in *Oedipus Tyrannus*, 430 BC] or Sophocles' Heracles [in *Women of Trachis*, 450 (?) BC]" (T 45).

Phobos—"fear," perhaps—also raises the question of meaningful translation. "Fear" is defective, as Kaufmann argues: it is too weak; and, I will add, unlike anxiety, it requires an object. But what, then, does one fear in witnessing

a Greek tragedy? It would be far-fetched to argue that while suffering vicari-
ously Oedipus's fate, you are also afraid that this very thing will befall you. But
if you deobjectify "fear," and it becomes merely a sort of vague foreboding—in
the words of the Aristotle scholar W. D. Ross, "fear of the unknown fate that
lies before each of us"—then you have departed utterly from Aristotle, who
maintains that "fear is for the hero" (T 46). "Terror" is better—or something
between fear and terror.

The matter of a right understanding of eleos and phobos is enriched but
not adjudicated when one turns to Aristotle's *Rhetoric*, where the terms are
treated in detail. Kaufmann's conclusion is conciliatory: Aristotle's "meaning
seems to lie somewhere between what *we* consider right, on the one hand, and
the traditional 'pity and fear,' on the other" (T 48). This pattern of reasoning
will remind us of the conciliatory dialectic also alive in Kaufmann's *Critique
of Religion and Philosophy*. A proposition—the standard reading of Aristotle's
tragic emotions—is stated, then denied utterly, then modified in relation to
the negative, so that both thesis and antithesis survive.

What of catharsis—should it mean "purification" or "purgation"? This is
no contest. Scrutiny of Aristotle's more extensive treatment of the term in his
Politics makes the choice of the second term obligatory. It is a very straightforward matter that persons who are liable to the emotions of eleos and phobos
when aroused "under the influence of religious music and songs that drive
the soul to frenzy . . . calm down as if they had been medically treated and
purged [*katharseōs*]." The result is "pleasurable relief" (Aristotle). Kaufmann
surmises that "Aristotle may have been struck by the paradoxical phenomenon
that tragedy gives pleasure" and answers the riddle as if he, Aristotle, were a
physician. Kaufmann's comment puts Plato and Aristotle, as well as his own
views, in perspective:

> Plato had argued for the exclusion of tragedy from his ideal city, partly
> because it would undermine courage and sobriety. Aristotle's concept of
> catharsis suggests that a performance of *Philoctetes* or The *Women of Tra-
> chis* will have more nearly the opposite effect on the audience: it will purge
> them of pent-up emotions and sober them. If that was Aristotle's meaning,
> he was right. (T 50)

Kaufmann's exact attention to Aristotle and his entrenched skepticism of
scholarly authority encourage him to revise several key terms and emphases.
Consider this crucial sentence from the *Poetics*: "the most important means by
which a tragedy stirs the emotions reside in the plot [*mythos*], namely reversals

[*peripeteiai*] and recognitions [*anagnōriseis*]." Kaufmann underscores the point: "The plot is the soul of tragedy . . . because it is the plot more than the other five elements [character (*ēthē*), diction (*lexis*), thought (*dianoia*), spectacle (*opsis*), and music (*melopoíia*)] that produces the distinctively tragic effect of engendering phobos and eleos" (T 55–56). The effective mythos involves peripety, drastic vicissitudes of fortune—from misfortune to good fortune and good fortune to misfortune, though the latter passage, which we would call "tragic," is not decisive. All Greek tragedies convey the surprise of a *drastic change of state*. This obligatory passage from one pole to another can beset any character, who need not be the hero or heroine. You need only consider the fate of Creon, for example, in *Antigone*.

On the great topic of the dramatic unities, Kaufmann repeats the view, now commonly held by scholars, but not by everyone, that Aristotle nowhere demands unity of either place or time in tragedy: this is the much-publicized assumption of classical French dramatists and theoreticians. Kaufmann conjures "Aeschylus and Sophocles, [who] cast a kind of spell over their audience and readers and transport them into a realm in which neither hours nor days are counted" (T 58).

The key term *anagnōrisis* means "recognition," involving as Aristotle writes, "a change from ignorance to knowledge." It is the adjunct to a reversal of fortune: as the main axes of the plot, reversal and its recognition are the chief conveyors of the tragic emotions. Here, to one's surprise, Kaufmann discovers "a passage in the Marquis de Sade that is relevant." Even the Marquis de Sade has fallen prey to this omnivorous reader, though, were he present, he would surely wonder at what had brought him to this galley; he writes:

> In the final analysis, what are the two principal mainsprings of dramatic art? Have all the authors worthy of the name not declared that they are *terror* and *pity*? Now, what can provoke *terror* if not the portrayal of crime triumphant, and what can cause *pity* better than the depiction of virtue a prey to misfortune? (qtd. in T 60).

What is the point? It is a point made per contrarium. Kaufmann's Aristotle would reject the Sadean view: "The plot should arouse *eleos* [for which Kaufmann now suggests the archaic word 'ruth'] and *phobos*, and such a plot would engender neither; it would simply be shocking."[18] As we study what Aristotle appears to consider the optimal plot, involving the optimal hero—thus Oedipus and Thyestes and their change of state—we encounter the celebrated term *hamartia*, instigator of a fall. Aristotle writes, "We are left with a character in between the other two [neither the virtuous person nor the criminal] who is neither outstanding in virtue and righteousness, nor is it through wickedness and vice that he falls into misfortune, but through some *hamartia*" (T 60).

Now, it is generally assumed that hamartia means a moral failure, a defect of character; but one important scholar, S. H. Butcher, on examining "passages in the *Nicomachean Ethics* where *hamartia* is mentioned, came to the conclusion that 'as applied to a single act, it denotes an error due to inadequate knowledge of particular circumstances'" (T 61–62). Hence, the term, for Kaufmann, "*could* designate a tragic flaw (the traditional interpretation) or an intellectual error," a cognitive failure. Following Kaufmann, this dilemma gives us a lesson. The point of our being unable to decide whether the term's weight should go to lack of character or lack of knowledge is that for the Greeks these two mental items are inseparable. What is especially interesting is that the commonly supposed link between the terms hamartia and hybris is, in fact, spurious.

> Many who speak easily of the tragic flaw, without being aware of the problems posed by Aristotle's term, *hamartia*, assume that *hybris* (which is not mentioned once in the *Poetics*) means pride or arrogance, and that this was the typical tragic flaw of the heroes of Greek tragedy. But the meaning of *hybris* has almost nothing to do with pride. . . . The Greek verb *hybrizein*, found in Homer, means to wax wanton or run riot. . . . The noun, *hybris*, means wanton violence and insolence. (T 64)

It is a Christian conception of the sin of pride that has illicitly inserted itself into this conversation. The scholar Cedric Whitman puts the matter with finality: "If a Greek boasted that he was better than a god, it was folly, impiety, and presumption. It was also very dangerous, but it was not *hybris*" (qtd. in T 65).

Kaufmann is not only skeptical—he values answerable authority. The word has nothing to do with "proud self-reliance" of whatever degree: it is its opposite, the self run amok (T 65). As such, it illuminates the behavior of Creon in *Antigone*, who runs riot, as it were, in accusing Antigone of having run riot, as it were, in covering the body of Polyneices with sand, contrary to the law of the land, and then boasting of her action. A consideration of the word in the context of *all* of Sophocles's plays confirms Kaufmann's reading. And so it is a good thing that "the best recent translators usually render hybris . . . as outrage, crime, and insolence, rarely as pride" (T 68).

In case the point has not been clearly made, Aristotle favors the *plot* that brings misfortune out of good fortune—meaning, the play should end with a catastrophe. How caused? The protagonist must have a role to play in it. He is a man (or woman) of some virtue, "better rather than worse"; hence, his (or her) fall is not caused by his (or her) evil nature but rather by "a great *hamartia*." In Kaufmann's paraphrase, "The suffering that evokes our phobos and eleos should neither be patently deserved nor totally unconnected with anything that those stricken have done." A better formulation of Aristotle's idea than we find in Aristotle's prose would specify more clearly the cause and result. "Had he said, 'a character whose virtue does not remain pristine, unstained by all guilt,' he would have come closer to Sophocles, Hegel, and the truth"—Kaufmann's own (T 68–69)!

Kaufmann has little patience for Aristotle's formalism, whose celebrated precision tolerates some serious contradictions: Does the better tragedy end catastrophically—or not? Aristotle is of at least two minds about this. For example, in chapter 13, he shuns the plot in which a good man passes from happiness to misery. "Where recognition and reversal have a place in the plot," explains Kaufmann, "even a story with a happy ending can elicit a soul-stirring *phobos* and *eleos*, and the misfortune may occur neither at the beginning nor at the end but in the middle" (T 71). What finally vexes Kaufmann is that tragedy, for Aristotle, is in the last resort not a distinguished product "of the human spirit," nor does it occur to Aristotle that tragedy is a form of knowledge from which philosophers could profit. If you are interested in the articulations of a tragic worldview or what might be called the "philosophical substance" of the plays, you will learn little from the *Poetics*. This defect prompts Kaufmann to strike a rather abrasive tone once more in *denouncing* criticism that "deals more with diction, less with plot, and traces imagery and symbols" (T 73). It is reasonable to suppose that he had not gone very deeply into the *rhetorical* criticism—structuralism and neostructuralism (aka deconstruction)— streaming out of Paris and Johns Hopkins at the time of writing, which is scarcely shallow or void of a tragic worldview. Moreover, a theory of tragedy, like Aristotle's, that defines its efficacy by the sorrow and terror it inspires has obviously crossed the line from strict formalism to theory of a spectator- or reader-orientated type. Never mind: formalist criticism, Kaufmann observes, having once been bold in the hands of Aristotle, "has become a source of livelihood for a mushrooming industry. A grasshopper is one of the marvels of nature; myriad locust are a plague." How regrettable, how forgettable is such an unfocused jeremiad. But that scruple immediately occurs to Kaufmann too, who, in a familiar ricorso, comes around again with a temporizing gesture: "Of course studies of form can be very illuminating, particularly if form is

considered as a clue rather than an end in itself." Furthermore, formalist practitioners are not worse than the "Platonizers, who look for the poets' philosophies, mistaking the characters' speeches for lectures and treatises." Indeed,
it is "high time for us," as Kaufmann has made us feel, "to move beyond both
Plato and Aristotle"—and have as a reward a new poetics (T 74).

Kaufmann undertakes this theoretical journey; his venture "Toward a New
Poetics" will be perpetually underway. Here is a first principle: the work of art
has transcendental authority. (I will refer such claims to today's critical consensus, with its strains of modernist, postmodernist, and post-postmodernist
sensibility.) Kaufmann's principle sits very badly in a critical atmosphere
informed by the absolute certainty of art's contamination by what Walter Benjamin calls "the refuse of history" and what Adorno, speaking for Freud, once
again calls the "refuse of the world of appearances."[19] Kaufmann persists: "Art
is the triumph of form over finitude.... [Art] defies the limits forced on us by
physical existence.... A work of art is a small world whose limitations spell
repose and control" (T 78). Nothing could be further from the ethos of modernism: think of Kafka, of Beckett, or to stay with the Germans ... Rilke's *The
Notebooks of Malte Laurids Brigge* or Musil's *The Perplexities of Young Törless.*
"Triumph," transcendence, "repose and control" ... Analyzing Derrida's concept of contamination in philosophy—a concept readily applicable to modern
art—the literary theorist Henry Staten writes,

> The point of departure of deconstruction from philosophy [or, by exten-
> sion, "art"] is ... quite subtle. The value and necessity of pure concepts
> and categories are not denied, but they are no longer the last word. We no
> longer simply note and then set aside the factual or empirical contamina-
> tion of our unities, but see that they are impure always and in principle, and
> pursue the implications of this essential impurity.[20]

The literary scholar Martin Hägglund takes up Staten's point, adding, "Derrida's thinking should be understood in relation to the philosophical notion of
form. If pure form traditionally has been conceived as an indivisible unity ...
for Derrida the pure form of self-identity is inhabited by a 'constitutive outside' that makes it essentially open to contamination."[21] This is only one of
the myriad opportunities to cite a modern poetics, which incorporates the
rhetoric of continental philosophy, stressing the gaps, breaks, and tensions
inhabiting such writing. A scholar of modernism, Richard Sheppard, describes
a generally modernist style as one responsive to a "metaworld of ... decen-
tered, multi-dimensionally, fluctuating energies ... involving leaps, jerks, gaps,

irregularities, and discontinuities," the whole "threatening to run out of control."[22] Where Kaufmann sees great art producing some sort of "recognition," one tends today to see this disclosure as offering not the pleasure of "repose" but a complex, troubled pleasure, a vertiginous irritation.[23] This aspect might be present in Kaufmann as the mood of the *trial* that great art imposes, the trouble it gets you into; but here we have him writing in his idealizing vein: "The artist's voice—whether music, words, color, or shapes—soars beyond him, leaving his body and ours, his life and ours, behind" (T 78). I would think rather that this poetic self "comes to life with the fire and mud of the empirical personality still clinging to it."[24] But this debate, which gives (or does not give) some measure of aesthetic or philosophical transcendence to complex writing, does not end here.

Italo Calvino, for one, lends oblique support to Kaufmann's claim in 1971, "at the height of the structuralist moment. . . . The existence of the work," writes Calvino, "is a sign that the author is dead, *happily dead* if the work is worthwhile, the work being the negation of the writer as empirical living being" (emphasis added).[25] A separation occurs, but the kind of being of the parties involved—the hand that writes and the work it inscribes—remains at issue: How "dead" is the author, how "pure" the work? Kaufmann would have the author still *happily alive*, even if abandoned, and the work *very* pure. Current theory would have the author no more dead or alive than when he began to write, his vitality an entirely contingent matter, but the work at odds with itself and altogether roiled by traces of the author's empirical obsessions, the material history of the day, and the many different discourses they have produced.

En route to his own definition of tragedy, Kaufmann evokes a performance of *The Trojan Women* and *Iphigenia in Aulis* at a small theater in New York. He speaks on behalf of every spectator: "Repressed sorrows flood my mind—my own grief and the sufferings of those close to me, past and present. I recall specific incidents and persons and the wretched lot of man." The tragic poet—Euripides—"chose a story he could use to represent the suffering that he knew"; "he wished to communicate or elicit certain thoughts and feelings" in those who read or see his play (T 82). It is moot, of course, as Kaufmann knows, to imagine the artist in possession of thoughts and feelings he means to communicate before he has ever grappled with his mythic matter. A better view, I think, holds that it is only with his immersion in the image that the impulse could arise to produce precisely these and no other thoughts and feelings. For Benjamin, of course—most radically,

In the appreciation of a work of art or an art form, consideration of the receiver never proves fruitful. Not only is any reference to a certain public or its representatives misleading, but even the concept of an "ideal" receiver is detrimental in the theoretical consideration of art, since all it posits is the existence and nature of man as such. Art, in the same way, posits man's physical and spiritual existence, but in none of its works is it concerned with his response. No poem is intended for the reader, no picture for the beholder, no symphony for the listener.[26]

It would be more than interesting to hear the voices of these two Walters in discussion. Would Walter Kaufmann be overmatched by the incomparable refinement—and obscurantism—of Walter Benjamin? Some umpires—though not many—are out. We should still not forget Jaspers's description of the younger man's—the *benjamin*'s—astonishing memory and erudition.

Kaufmann will not be dislodged from his own insistence on the felt sorrow of the "receiver" flowing from the artist's intention. It reappears in Kaufmann's own definition of tragedy, which should be cited in full:

Tragedy is (1) a form of a literature that (2) presents a symbolic action as performed by actors and (3) moves into the center immense human suffering, (4) in such a way that it brings to our minds our own forgotten and repressed sorrows as well as those of our kin and humanity, (5) releasing us with some sense (a) that suffering is universal—not a mere accident in our experience, (b) that courage and endurance in suffering or nobility in despair are admirable—not ridiculous—and usually also (c) that fates worse than our own can be experienced as exhilarating. (T 85)

Kaufmann's definition is impressive but lacks, I would think, a basic element: the suffering hero's pursuit of a design, his "quarrel with God"—a key part, surely, of what Kaufmann will call the *philosophy* of the work, its uptake.[27]

Yet his theorizing is not over by a long shot. Advancing in his "New Poetics," he begins to nuance considerably the triumphalist, intentionalist, and ahistorical tenor of his first principles. He is aware that authors' statements about their intentions are unreliable (they too are literary texts inviting interpretations that could readily undo their apparent unity of statement). On the other hand, he believes that "there may be sufficient evidence without . . . [explicit testimony] for reconstructing the authors' intentions with a very high degree of probability" (T 87). Here he appears to be saying that the meaning of the work of art depends on the meaning the author intends.[28]

But, somewhat later, it will emerge that this suggestion is circular: the reconstructed intention is convincing only insofar as it matches the reader's or spectator's precritical sense of the meaning of the work. For "suppose [the maker's] primary intention was . . . to keep himself from thinking about something. That would hardly be the meaning of the play in the sense sought after" (T 96).

Still in pursuit of a relevant intention, a worthy project, one must know something about what the author knows, which may be more and different from what the reader knows.

> To understand Milton's sonnet on his blindness, I must know the New Testament parable of the talents and also what the poet means by "God." Whether "that one Talent which is death to hide, / Lodg'd with me useless" is an autonomous image, a polemical reference to some contemporary tract, an echo of one of the poet's earlier works, or an interpretation of a Gospel parable makes a difference in meaning. And to understand the problem Milton confronts—the strong presumption that God requires man to be active and exert himself—one has to know whether this is a poetic conceit, a strange idiosyncrasy, or, as happens to be the case, a crucial feature of the Calvinist image of God. (T 88–89)

This is where knowledge of history directs the pursuit of the author's intention. You cannot fail to hear a trace of the author's own empirical interest, the "refuse" of his drives, in Kaufmann's expansion of this point: "Where historical context is ignored, pastiche and caricature may be mistaken for something else, *rebellion and extreme irreverence may go unrecognized*, and whatever mattered most to the artist and to those who were the first to witness his creation is quite likely to remain unnoticed" (emphasis added) (T 89). The emphasized phrase resonates with Kaufmann's credo, implicit in his paraphrase of Nietzsche on Socrates: "The philosopher must always stand opposed to his time and may never conform; it is his calling to be a fearless critic and diagnostician—as Socrates was" (N 405). This distinction needs to be acknowledged!

We are still in pursuit of the meaning of a work of art. Kaufmann strongly underplays the effort to unearth an author's "psychology" as a set of clues to that meaning: "We are concerned with . . . the use of psychology . . . the effort to illuminate a poem or a novel by attending to the psychology of the author. Such analyses are as irrelevant as similar attempts to analyze philosophers are to the philosophic study of their works" (T 91). Here, surprisingly enough,

Kaufmann can be seen making common cause—of course, quite uninten-tionally—with the deconstructionist thinker Paul de Man, who, in his bleak diction, also cedes epistemological primacy to the objective structure of the literary work:

> the concept of intentionality is neither physical nor psychological in its nature, but structural, involving the activity of a subject *regardless of its empirical concerns*. . . . The structural intentionality determines the rela-tionship between the components of the resulting object in all its parts, but the relationship of *the peculiar state of mind of the person engaged in the act of structurizaton* is altogether contingent (emphasis added).[29]

In later places in his oeuvre, however, following Nietzsche, Kaufmann will state the opposite claim: philosophical writing bears the imprint of an author's dominant drives, and *that* is where the nuclear meaning lies. "Gradually it has become clear to me," wrote Nietzsche, "what every great philosophy so far has been: namely, the personal confession of its author and a kind of invol-untary and unconscious memoir."[30] The thought system is the expression of the psychological character, "the peculiar state of mind" of the thinker. The literary scholar Anthony Julius, writing on T. S. Eliot, offers a crisp illustration of this idea: "If the work, or some notable part of it, is anti-Semitic, it is the work of an anti-Semite."[31] For Kaufmann, this general equation will play out attractively for Goethe but especially badly for Kant on the grounds of *his* "peculiar state of mind." This "antinomy" (Nietzsche on Kant and Goethe) is spelled out in *Nietzsche, Heidegger, and Buber*, volume 2, of Kaufmann's late work *Discovering the Mind*.

The question of the meaning of the work of art—the artist's intention as it is structured in the work—still begs for an answer. Earlier we read that the tragic poet—Euripides "chose a story he could use to represent the suffer-ing that he knew; . . . he wished to communicate or elicit certain thoughts and feelings" in those who read or see his play (T 82). Now, however, we encounter Walter Kaufmann's (not Walter Benjamin's) disqualification of this model of literary activity. "While there are cases," writes Kaufmann, "in which poets employ plots and characters and diction as vehicles for their thought, this model is misleading more often than not: most poets do not first have thoughts and then embody them in poems" (T 93). Admittedly, this "more often than not" and "most poets" suggest indecision about this thesis. Rather unexpectedly, Kaufmann now attempts to escape this trouble by introduc-ing another—alas, vaguer—category: "What the poet communicates is his *experience of life*—the way he feels about man's condition, the way he sees the world." But it is a hypothesis only, soon discarded; the difficulty remains. Imagining the author of the book of Genesis, *Oedipus Tyrannus*, Plato's *Republic*, or *Hamlet*, or much of Nietzsche, "one is working," Kaufmann writes, "as an artist whose primary concern is not with those who will eventually see his work" (T 100). A later discussion cites Shakespeare, who, "plainly, was not moved by a consuming desire to communicate his experiences and views to his readers."[32] This is to say, *communicating* anything is not foremost in the artist's mind.

Kaufmann finally ends with the idea that the meaning of a work of art is its thought content or "philosophical dimension." The thesis implied in the very title of this book—*Tragedy* and *Philosophy*—is spontaneously confirmed. True, other dimensions continue to require attention—namely, "form" and "historical context"—the place of the work within the history of its precursors, such as previous treatments of its mythos. Still, it is the philosophical dimension of its content that matters most. Note, however, "when we speak of content, it is clearly suggested that this dimension is to be found *in* the work of literature, while talk of thought or the poet's experience of life points beyond the work to the artist" (T 94). Interestingly, in his chapter on *Oedipus Tyrannus*, Kaufmann bases a correct understanding of the poet's "experience of life" on "the poet's other works," which will (or will not) "support or contradict one's findings." In this way this category—"the experience of life"—is more and more deeply established as legitimate only when "found *in* the work of literature" (T 114, T 94). The struggle to find the right terms of this "New Poetics" goes on and on, as it should. Kaufmann reasons, finally: "One discovers the most fruitful way [of understanding a tragic poem] not by deducing it from general principles but by reading and seeing and rereading again and again a particular tragedy" (T 95). Since part of my intent in this discussion is to situate Kaufmann's poetics in a more or less contemporary theory milieu, I'm bemused by the overlap once again with a passage from his antipode de Man's *Blindness and Insight*, namely, "A literary text . . . merely solicits an understanding that has to remain immanent because it poses the problem of its intelligibility in its own terms."[33] But *this* overlap means only to suggest that if one thinks long and hard enough about a problem of general interest about which a great deal has already been thought and said, one will sooner or later touch on features of other peoples' systems without any awareness or intention of espousing the whole. And so, it is on a note of radical specificity that Kaufmann finds his conclusion (which is not a conclusion): "It is time to redeem these generalizations by becoming specific and dealing with some of the greatest tragic poems" (T 100). Amen. Kaufmann's work on the topic of meaning and authorial intention would have been sharper and more self-conscious had he referred to the rich position statements even by older literary theorists available to him, such as Cleanth Brooks, W. K. Wimsatt and Monroe Beardsley, René Wellek and Austin Warren, and others.[34]

We have looked at three chapters; the work has seven more—of even greater detail and density. Lest what is coming should drift out of sight, here are their names at the outset: "The Riddle of *Oedipus*," "Homer and the Birth of Tragedy," "Aeschylus and the Death of Tragedy," "Sophocles: Poet of Heroic Despair," "Euripides, Nietzsche, and Sartre," "Shakespeare and the Philosophers," and "Tragedy Today," plus an epilogue. It will scarcely be possible, given the confines of this chapter, to do much more than suggest the richness to be found there, but here is an attempt.

Kaufmann looks at earlier versions of the Oedipus story in order to shatter the commonplace that Sophocles's story of Oedipus is *the* myth. There are many variants, in works both rumored and extant. It is important to suggest this way the originality and greatness of Sophocles's "treatment": *Oedipus Tyrannus* was not enclosed in a mythic shell, which Sophocles merely needed to crack open. "All the motifs he adopts from the myths are sublimated and spiritualized. And Sophocles' version of the recognition scene is evidently original with him." Meanwhile, the mythic element of "the piercing of the feet," he adds, "plays no part ... and Francis Fergusson's assumption that Sophocles' Oedipus has a 'tell-tale limp' is surely false" (T 113). I think Kaufmann would regret this reproof.[35]

The particular mythos of Sophocles's tragedy—for Aristotle, "exceptionally taut and well-constructed, [with] reversal and recognition" (Kaufmann)—is designed to convey crucial features of the hero and his predicament (T 103). On scrutiny, the story rules out a false assumption: that Oedipus's misfortune is in principle owed to hamartia, a tragic flaw; nor should this misfortune be seen as the iron workings of *fate*. The distinctive strength of the work lies in the fact that "Oedipus is somehow representative of all men" (T 105). This insight is owed to Freud, who, in *The Interpretation of Dreams*, was the first to perceive its universal relevance as the source of the unwearying impact of the play, for "perhaps all of us were destined to direct our first sexual stirrings toward our mothers and the first hatred and violent wishes against our fathers" (T 106). Kaufmann does not fail to note that this claim from *The Interpretation of Dreams* would carry very little weight in explaining why the play might strike women every bit as forcefully as men (T 108).

It is time to get to the core meaning of *Oedipus* through Kaufmann's "philosophical" interpretation. "First of all, *Oedipus* is a play about *man's radical insecurity*" (T 115). Personal nobility is no warrant against suffering an unfortunate fall. Greek tragedies are, as such, "plays about great suffering." Deianeira, the wife of Heracles in Sophocles's *The Women of Trachis*, calls her own life one full of sorrow despite the fact that, as Kaufmann writes, with some emotion, "she is not only outstanding in virtue but, along with Antigone and some of Euripides' heroines, one of the noblest women in world literature. . . . [Sophocles] showed that while less outstanding men and women tend to shun the extremes of suffering, like Ismene in *Antigone* and Chrysothemis in Sophocles' *Electra*, the noblest have a special affinity for the greatest suffering." On this evidence one can conclude "man's radical insecurity formed part of Sophocles' experience of life" (T 116–17).

I shall set down, with Kaufmann, other features of this core experience, with the same apodictic certainty. "*Oedipus* is a tragedy of *human blindness*"; as such, it is "representative of the human condition." Blindness is an irremediable portion of every insight, for, Kaufmann writes, echoing a line from Rilke's first *Duino Elegy*, "we ourselves are not too reliably at home with those closest to us" [Rilke: "already the knowing animals are aware that we are not really at home in our interpreted world"].[36] This means: we fail to recognize those who are closest to us for what they are (T 117). At the end of the play, Oedipus is physically blind . . . and only now can he "see."

Oedipus is the tragedy of the *curse of honesty*. The hero, the sufferer, is a truth seeker, bent on knowing at whatever cost the reasons behind the curse that has struck his city. He is wise, "possessed of more knowledge of the human condition than other men, and hence the only one to solve the riddle of the Sphinx; he is no less imposing in his relentless desire for knowledge and his . . . insistence upon taking pains to find out what is true" (T 120–21). In this sense *Oedipus Tyrannus*, once again, is *not* a tragedy of inhuman fate: the action springs from the intensity of Oedipus's libido sciendi, his craving to know the truth.[37] (Interestingly, the old mythic material concerning Oedipus had nothing of this topic of honesty.)

In making the drive behind the quest for truth equivalent to "honesty," a virtue featured so prominently in *The Faith of a Heretic*, Kaufmann gives us a fuller picture of this quality. It contains very little of a promise of happiness. He is incisive in this matter of dissociating honesty from the rewards of "the best policy":

There is a type of virtue, very different from that of Homer's and Sophocles' heroes, which involves a serenity, immune to misfortune. Socrates, who was the first to propound this paradox, embodied this kind of virtue and happiness, even as he went to his death in prison; and he became an inspiration for Plato, the Cynics, and the Cyrenaics, and later also for the Epicureans and, above all, the Stoics. These philosophers offered new ideals to mankind—variations on a theme by Socrates; and a century before Socrates, the Buddha had preached a way of life in which virtue and tranquillity were also fused. Sophocles' experience of life was no less profound than theirs, but he celebrated another human type.

We need not choose between the warlike heroism of the *Iliad* and the ascetic heroism of the Stoics, nor even between the mocking composure of Socrates and the peacefully detached compassion of the Buddha. Sophocles' heroes are closer to Homer's than to the others, for they fathom all the terrors of almost unendurable suffering. . . . In *Antigone* and *Oedipus Tyrannus*, the hero and heroine choose their own virtue to be undone by it. (T 124–25)

Next, *Oedipus* is a play about a tragic situation—"a drama that shows how some situations are characterized by the *inevitability of tragedy*" (T 126). Kaufmann is evidently aware of the distinction between "fate" and "inevitability" although without making the difference explicit. We are apparently meant to refer the inevitability of disaster, once again, to Oedipus's *determination* to know the truth; it is not "fate" that causes his predicament but his character as truth seeker, bent on healing Thebes as its king. But his passion for honesty comes at a cost: he will be destroyed, and so will his wife, Jocasta, and the happiness of his children. This tragic situation contributes to the universality of the play: "Millions have found themselves in situations in which they either had to incur the guilt of breaking the law and suffer a cruel death (like Antigone) or had to continue to live with the knowledge that they had abetted a moral outrage." One hears the voice of the untold number of survivors of the hell visited by totalitarian regimes in the decades before Kaufmann's writing these pages. This echo is well prepared for when, in the preceding paragraph, Kaufmann conjures an Athenian audience watching *Oedipus* being performed: "There were probably few in the audience who had not lost members of their families and close friends to plague" (T 128). But there is nothing that Oedipus can do to escape his "tragic situation." Readers of *The Faith of a Heretic* will anticipate the very conclusion of Kaufmann's meditation, now, in *Tragedy and Philosophy*: "There is no way out. Luther realized this and insisted that in a life devoted to works failure was inevitable, but he believed in salvation through faith in Christ's vicarious atonement and in eternal bliss after death. Sophocles' experience of life was different" (F 354, T 128–29).[38] This insight makes the point that Kaufmann frequently foregrounds: the tension between the Christian and the tragic humanist worldview, which is the object of his faith.

"Finally," writes Kaufmann, "*Oedipus* is a play about *justice*," quite particularly in the way that it puts the very notion of justice in question—first, in the evident sense that Oedipus does not deserve to be destroyed. He is the victim of the "plight [into which] the gods thrust" him; the play worries "the question of the injustice of men's fates and their sufferings" (T 129–30). At another level it is the idea of *human* justice that is challenged. "Jocasta kills herself; Oedipus blinds himself and insists on being exiled. These self-punishments . . . are acts of human justice and profoundly problematic." The lesson of "the dark side of justice" that Kaufmann takes from *Oedipus Tyrannus* made a lasting impression. Our next chapter treats Kaufmann's 1973 essay on autonomy titled, no longer surprisingly, *Without Guilt and Justice*.[39]

Kaufmann's "philosophical" interpretation of *Oedipus* invites detailed study, especially since its salient features amount to a definition of tragedy that fits *many* exemplars of the genre—though not all. These themes deserve emphasis; they recur in many tragedies: "man's radical insecurity, epitomized by a sudden fall into catastrophe; his blindness . . . the curse of virtue . . . inevitability . . . questions about justice." Perhaps insecurity and blindness can come under the single head of human finitude. Equally, "the curse of virtue and doubt about justice" are interconnected: Kaufmann's key, contentious argument, trailing a Nietzschean genealogy, reads, "tragedy calls morality into question" (T 131).

Of the salient features above, the least generally applicable to tragedies and contrary to the received view is the *inevitability* of catastrophe. (We saw from Aristotle that catastrophe was not an essential feature of the tragedies he knew.) Especially in Shakespeare this element is not essential. To strengthen Kaufmann's view and his view of Sophocles that the consciousness of finitude does not lead straight to piety, Kaufmann again invokes his master educator Freud. What Freud writes in *The Future of an Illusion* (1927) is the recurring signature of Kaufmann's religious philosophy (he has cited it in *Critique of Religion and Philosophy* and will cite it again in *Discovering the Mind*, volume 3):

It is not this feeling [of finitude, of dependence] that constitutes the essence of religiousness, but only the next step, the reaction to it, which seeks a remedy against this feeling. He who goes no further, he who humbly resigns himself to the insignificant part man plays in the universe, is, on the contrary, irreligious in the truest sense of the word.

This is a high point of the confluence of wisdom sentences, in which Kaufmann sees two of his foremost educators—Sophocles and Freud—holding out their hands to one another, *to him*, in corroboration, across the millennia (T 132). A second reflection arising from Sophocles's tragedies leads *back* to Kaufmann's ethical philosophy as we encountered it in *The Faith of a Heretic*. There Kaufmann lists the attributes of the whole man that the humanist assembles—the first, a neologism called "humbition," the marriage of ambition and humility. Kaufmann reflects that

Sophocles surely meant to teach humility. . . . [But] it does not follow that Sophocles opposed pride [read: ambition]. Not only do all of his heroes appeal to us in large measure by virtue of their great pride, but the heroes of the three late tragedies, who are not ruined but vindicated in the end, are even more unbending in their pride than the poet's earlier heroes, For my taste, Electra, Philoctetes, and Oedipus Coloneus are too lacking in humility, and Sophocles may never have made *a discovery that few men down to our own time have made*: the most admirable kind of pride is totally compatible with a profound humility. (emphasis added) (T 134)

It is striking that Kaufmann thinks of his ethical reflection as constituting a *discovery*: he has no compunction in regarding philosophy as a force greater than a protocol for correcting nonsense sentences. Philosophy is a fervently undertaken adventure, a risky exploration of the psychic world that can make robust, immutable discoveries. His last published works are a trilogy called, as we now know well, *Discovering the Mind*.

With a touch of chastening mischief, Kaufmann concludes by asking about the role that catharsis plays in the reception of a work whose hero "goes to the opposite extremes" of "moderation, accommodation, resignation." Catharsis scarcely needs to be in play, namely:

What neither Plato nor Aristotle realized was that most men's daring is so slight that it can be spent in an hour's identification with Oedipus or Antigone; then their spirit, having taken its brief fight, settles down again on the level of Antigone's sister Ismene, or Electra's sister, Chrysothemis, or Oedipus' foil Creon. In that sense, Sophocles becomes a teacher of traditional piety.

Swinging now to the opposite extreme himself and taking Plato, surprisingly, as a radical, an avatar of the "Oedipean spirit," Kaufmann concludes that it "may take a reader trained by Plato—a philosopher—to read *Oedipus Tyrannus* as I have done" (T 135). Here a personal comment by David Pickus is apt: "I think Kaufmann is at his best, and I like him most, when he plays the role of Mephisto, puncturing the pious illusions of others. I'm less enthusiastic about his affirmations, at least the rhapsodizing ones. The thought, of course, did cross my mind that the reason he was so devastatingly effective in puncturing the pious illusions of others was that he, himself, was susceptible to them."[40]

Kaufmann's next major chapter is called "Homer and the Birth of Tragedy." It had just as well been called "The Birth of Tragedy from the Spirit of Homer," in plain acknowledgment of Nietzsche's early troubled masterpiece *The Birth of Tragedy from the Spirit of Music*. At this point we may see Kaufmann preparing to contend with his "educator," brushed with the wing of the anxiety of influence and spurning it. "As we turn to 'Aeschylus and The Death of Tragedy,' we will discover how untenable some of the central ideas of Nietzsche's *Birth of Tragedy* are" (T 161). We have been put on notice to expect strong writing, but we are not yet there—we are with Homer and preoccupied with a different question, namely, What is the *Iliad*, an *epic*, doing so prominently in a book on *tragedy*?

Kaufmann has a convincing reply. This epic is in many ways *dramatic*: somewhere between half and three-fifths of the *Iliad* consists of direct speech. It is organized around a single theme—the wrath of Achilles—confined to a relatively short span of time and developed as a series of contests. The *Iliad* is pervaded by a spirit of what Kaufmann is content to call "humanity"—"a profound *humanity* that experiences suffering as suffering and death as death, even if they strike the enemy" (T 138). As if as a temporizing afterthought, Kaufmann adds on "the emphasis of the terrors of existence" (T 141), remembering a speech of Zeus: "Of all creatures that breathe and creep about on Mother Earth there is none so miserable as man. . . . And later Apollo calls men 'those wretched creatures, who, like the leaves, flourish for a little while on the bounty of the earth and flaunt their brilliance, but in a moment droop and fade away'" (T 157–58). Readers of Greek tragedy will perceive the aptness of these qualities to the form and theme of a number of plays. Homer supplies the tragedians with prototypes.

Consistent with Kaufmann's "naïve" Goethean poetics, which claims to recover from the work the artist's "experience of life—the way he feels about man's condition, the way he sees the world"—Kaufmann develops a general vision of life portrayed in the *Iliad*. Despite the profusion of gods, Homer's lifeworld is naturalistic. Kaufmann makes this point by example, meditating on an extended Homeric image of great beauty and power. At the beginning of canto 7, we read:

> They all sat down, and Agamemnon made the Achaean soldiers do the same. Athene and Apollo of the Silver Bow also sat down, in the form of vultures, on the tall oak sacred to aegis-bearing Zeus. They enjoyed the sight of all these Trojan and Achaean warriors sitting there on the plain, rank upon rank, bristling with shields, helmets, and spears, like the darkened surface of the sea when the West Wind begins to blow and ripples spread across it.

Here Kaufmann is truest to the great vein of his convictions:

> In large parts of the Western World today one sees no vultures; and death, disease, and old age are concealed. In Calcutta, vultures still sit in trees in the city, waiting for death in the streets; and sickness, suffering, and the disintegration of age assault the senses everywhere. But it is only in Homer that, while death is ever present to consciousness, the vultures in the tree are experienced as Athene and Apollo, delighting in the beautiful sight of a sea of shields, helmets, and spears. In this vision death has not lost its sting; neither has life lost its beauty. The very vultures are no reproach to the world. (T 145)

Kaufmann is quick to connect passages in literature with his ethical concerns. Consider a fateful moment in book 4 of the *Iliad*. Athene, disguised as a man, slips into the Trojan camp and beguiles Pándarus, telling him "that if only he would 'shoot Menelaus with an arrow, you would cover yourself with glory'; and 'Athene's eloquence prevailed upon the fool'—and thus the truce was broken and war resumed." Kaufmann reflects:

> The event is clearly of momentous importance. . . . Homer is closer to Camus and Sartre [than unnamed poets who attempt to *motivate* Pándarus' behavior] and lets a man do something basically irrational and foolish without any claim that, if we only knew enough facts, we should discover that the deed was necessary and in some sense rational. Least of all did

Homer feel, as so many people do in our time, that caprice is possible only in minor matters but out of the question when it comes to fateful actions like the shooting of a president or the ultimate decision to drop an atomic bomb or to resume the bombing of North Vietnam. On the contrary, he sees the unpredictable, irrational, capricious element precisely in deeds and decisions that mean cruel suffering and hideous death for large masses of people. (T 147–48)

This is the sort of wide-gauge meditation "written at the height of the Vietnam War" that led Terry Eagleton to admire this book.[41]

Consistent with his humanism, Kaufmann is keen to stress the continuum of personality in Homer's heroes: they are never divided into body and soul. That distinction is owed to later ages, the precondition of the supernatural. The supernatural is discovered on the basis of a split introduced between body and soul, whence the invisible soul is said to be the true self, truly at home only in a supernatural domain. "Only where this visible body is not my real self is this visible world subordinated to another, more real world" (T 150). This argument would clinch Kaufmann's claim that the gods in the *Iliad* are poetic fictions (T 147); there is no realism in them; the gods are a manner of speaking, a vivid way of describing human motivations and outcomes. Certainly, they do not command belief. Within the frame of their fiction, they operate as parts of nature—again, not supernaturally—"more similar to us than they are to the Lord of the [Hebrew] prophets" (T 151).

"It is time," as Kaufmann says, closing his reflections on the *Iliad*, "to return to man." "Yet for all their greatness they [men] live on the edge of night" (T 154). "Death is always near and never forgotten for any length of time; so is the striving to excel and the desire for glory. Indeed, heroic glory is inseparable from courage in the face of death and danger" (T 158). It is impossible to miss the gusto with which Kaufmann writes these characteristic sentences. "In the *Iliad* the brevity of life is no objection to the world but an incentive to relish its pleasures, to live with zest, and to die gloriously. The shadow death casts does not stain the earth with a slanderous gloom; it is an invitation to joy and nobility" (T 160). A good deal of that zest is *in* his sentences; a good deal of remembrance, too, of the good German classic-romantic tradition that he sketched out earlier in the elegies of Schiller, Goethe, and Hölderlin. This surmise is soon confirmed: "There is no immortality and no reward for heroism, except the glory of being remembered in some great poem" (T 161). The argument recalls Schiller's "Immortality" and Hölderlin's "To the Parcae," but the conclusion is not simple. If we are returned to the poets, we are returned to the aporia discussed at the end of chapter 6: Does the full life that relishes its pleasures and lives with zest foretell a glorious death? Is such a life enough, even in the absence of "being remembered in some great poem"—one's own or another's? Eliding this debate, Kaufmann concludes on a note of exaltation. "While the atmosphere of the *Iliad* is drenched with death, the first great tragic poem of world literature is also a song of triumph because it grants the dead their wish for immortal glory in song" (T 162). This is very grand oratory, but how much of the individual identity of "the dead" is preserved in the details of their slaughter?

We pass, happily, from the death of men to "the death of tragedy"—this very interesting, much contested theme, argued famously and for the first time in Nietzsche's *The Birth of Tragedy*. Nietzsche's argument runs: tragedy, perfect in the works of Aeschylus and Sophocles, died with Euripides and Socrates from a burgeoning spirit of optimism and rationalism. Kaufmann deserves his intellectual triumph in submitting Nietzsche to incontestable criticism, a victory for scholarship achieved by what Kaufmann suggests is a rare thing for philosophers: the close reading of individual tragedies *as evidence*. The presumption of Nietzsche's theory is that the works of Aeschylus and Sophocles are model tragedies, informed by the spirit of pessimism and despair of the power of reason. On close scrutiny, however, very few works of Aeschylus and Sophocles are tragedies of the kind that end in catastrophe and the ruin of reason. On the contrary, to consider Sophocles first—since his *Oedipus Tyrannus* is generally considered exemplary—it is rarely noted that after *Oedipus*, Sophocles "wrote no more tragedies like it: neither *Philoctetes* nor *Oedipus at Colonus* ends in catastrophe, and *Electra* ends on a note of triumph. . . . In other words, of Sophocles' extant tragedies, only three [*The Women of Trachis*, *Antigone*, and *Oedipus Tyrannus*] end tragically" (T 164). Kaufmann is effective in this argument, and so I shall quote him at length:

> My argument might be countered as follows. Although Sophocles was older than Euripides, both died in 406—Euripides a few months before Sophocles. If Euripides was responsible for the death of tragedy . . . it stands to reason that Sophocles, particularly in his old age, during the last twenty years of his career, was infected, too.
>
> Nevertheless, the admission that Euripides' tragedies were not really tragedies and that Sophocles, too, wrote only three bona fide tragedies would reduce the whole notion of the death of tragedy . . . to the absurd—unless

we could introduce Aeschylus at this point, saying that *he* was the creator of tragedy and that we must turn to his plays if we want to know what real tragedies look like. This is what Nietzsche clearly implies, and if this point could be sustained his argument would not be absurd. For in that case we could say that Aeschylus' seven extent tragedies are the paradigm cases of the genre to which Sophocles contributed three great masterpieces before he, like Euripides, succumbed to the essentially untragic outlook of the dawning fourth century. (T 164)

The facts, however, are otherwise, and indeed a close reading of the plays of Aeschylus shows that the very attitudes philosophers "associate with the death of tragedy are found preeminently in Aeschylus." This is an engaging premise. Kaufmann proceeds by rephrasing the features of Nietzsche's argument: Nietzsche "professes to find [a lethal optimism] not only in Socrates but also in Euripides, along with a delight in dialectic and an excessive faith in knowledge." A third motif, which links these two, is "the faith that catastrophes can and ought to be avoided. If men would only use their reason properly—this is the optimistic notion of which tragedy is thought to have perished—there would be no need for tragedies."

Here is the crux of Kaufmann's argument:

> I will argue that this was the faith of Aeschylus. Euripides, far from being an optimist, was indeed, as Aristotle puts it, albeit for different reasons, "the most tragic of the poets." Aeschylus was, compared with Sophocles and Euripides, the most optimistic; he alone had the sublime confidence that by rightly employing their reason men could avoid catastrophes. His worldview was, by modern standards anti-tragic; and yet he created tragedy. (T 165)

Kaufmann concludes with the idea that is the very heart of this entire volume, linking a discussion of ancient tragedy with the new, with works of Bertolt Brecht, Rolf Hochhuth, and others: "We should cease supposing that great tragedies must issue from a tragic vision that entails some deep despair or notions of inevitable failure and, instead, read Aeschylus with care. . . . Tragedy depends on sympathy, ruth, and involvement." It has never "perished of optimism: its sickness unto death was and is despair" (T 165–66).

Kaufmann's praise of Aeschylus turns on the splendid use he made in the *Oresteia* of the mythic material available to him in Homer's scant mention of Agamemnon, little of it laudatory. In the *Iliad*, Achilles, in anger, calls

Agamemnon an "unconscionable cur ... a drunken sot with the eyes of a dog and the courage of a doe" (T 170). This is not a helpful picture for the tragedy that Aeschylus imagines. More helpful is the fact that in the *Odyssey*, Orestes is represented as famous for the "noble" action of killing his father's murderer. Kaufmann cites Gilbert Murray, writing of Aeschylus: "He raised everything he touched to grandeur. The characters in his hands became heroic; the conflicts became tense and fraught with eternal issues."[42] This charge inspires Kaufmann's smart remark, "The Greeks did have many myths, but if Aeschylus and Sophocles had not brought off this feat, nobody could have said that these myths furnished good material for great tragedies or for serious literature of any kind" (T 174–75). Their creative powers give the declaration of Blake's Los an additional sense: "I MUST Create a System, or be enslav'd by another Man's."[43] And so, in *Eumenides*, opposite to the drift of the mythic material in Homer, "we encounter in absolutely climactic form that rationalism and optimism of which tragedy are said to have died—and find them at the culmination of the greatest work of the so-called creator of tragedy" (T 176).[44] Kaufmann embraces his discovery with pleasure; it confirms his belief in the perpetual strength of reason, a little acknowledged power that, in Nietzsche, for one, Kaufmann emphasized in his first book. It is commonly held that you will only find what you look for (although Kafka, en passant, is of the opposite view, writing "He who seeks will not find," while adding the ontological reward, "he who does not seek, will be found").[45] But Kaufmann's own strong refutation of Nietzsche's argument is a tribute to the reason he loves.

His criticism of the commonplace view of Aeschylus as the patriarch of the tragedy of negative endings leads to some of his most important conclusions. In the case of Aeschylus's *The Suppliants*, Kaufmann quotes Philip Vellacott: "as in *The Eumenides*, reason and persuasion are put forward as the proper principles of civilized life" (T 178). The *Oresteia* represents a decisive departure from the Homeric age of agonistic life to the "founding of the supreme court of Athens":

> Pride wins Aeschylus' admiration, and he finds words for it more majestic than almost anyone else; but what must be learned, not only by men but also by titans and Furies and gods ... is the willingness to reason with one's opponents and to come to terms. It is violence that makes for catastrophes that prudence could prevent; and in democratic institutions such prudence is embodied. Plainly, Aeschylus himself embodied the very spirit of which tragedy is said to have died first in the ancient world. (T 179)

This finding allows Kaufmann to make the decisive distinction between a tragic sense of life rooted in ultimate despair and the genre of play called "tragedy."

> Tragedies, alas, are not what they're supposed to be. Aristotle . . . came far closer than recent writers to doing justice to the wide range of Greek tragedy when he said that tragedies are plays that evoke *eleos* and *phobos* but provide a sobering emotional relief. Such relief is obviously quite compatible with non-tragic conclusions. What is decisive is not the end but whether we participate in tremendous, terrifying suffering. (T 181)

Kaufmann attempts to resolve this burgeoning paradox: "Aeschylus is more tragic than Homer and everyone else before him in his determination and ability to show *how* tragic life is without reason, compromise, and sanity." And here we find the passage that Eagleton admired as the soul of this book and is certainly worth repeating: "What lies at the heart of it [tragedy] is the refusal to let any comfort, faith, or joy deafen our ears to the tortured cries of our brothers. . . . The founding of the Areopagus does *not* erase Cassandra's anguish"—and herewith a manifestation of personality with a jolting alienation effect, to remind us that we are no longer in fifth-century Athens but in Jerusalem at the behest of a German Jewish refugee—"any more than the establishment of the state of Israel wipes out the terrors of Auschwitz" (T 181–82).

10

Tragedy as Philosophy

TRAGEDY AND PHILOSOPHY/2

Antigone is the absolute example of tragedy.

—G.W.F. HEGEL

The more substantial an individual's aesthetic experience, the sounder his taste, the sharper his moral focus, the freer—though not necessarily the happier—he is.

—JOSEPH BRODSKY

AT THE END of the previous chapter Kaufmann posed several questions central to his argument: What is "the tragic view of life," what kind of drama is properly called "tragedy," and what is the connection between the two?[1] It will take the whole of *Tragedy and Philosophy* to produce complete answers, but a few definite features have emerged. Tragedies depict persons suffering in such a way as to arouse our *eleos* ("ruth") and *phobos* ("something between fear and terror") and yet effect a purgation of these emotions. Shattering sympathy and healing calm can come from works whose actions end catastrophically as well as those that end peacably, all passion spent. Kaufmann stresses the puzzling fact that tragedies may have irenic endings—he has Aristotle's authority for this claim—or else we are forced into the obtuse view that very few plays of Aeschylus and Sophocles are "Greek *tragedies*." The play that concludes the *Oresteia*—the *Eumenides*—ends with a celebration of rational justice. Should we exclude the *Oresteia* from the canon of Greek tragedy? *Oedipus Tyrannus*, an indisputable tragedy, ends on a note of suffering and despair; but after writing *Oedipus Tyrannus* Sophocles never composed another work with a catastrophic ending. Should we think of Sophocles as the one who initiated the death of tragedy? This idea is absurd; even more absurd, if this is thinkable, is that the "death of tragedy" begins with the *Eumenides*, a work in love with justice.

We must be able to say, if this conversation on *tragedy* is to make sense, that tragedy is the form of verbal art invested with a tragic view of life, yet one *not* marked by utter desolation—"some deep despair or notions of inevitable failure" (T 165). Tragedy, for Kaufmann, is thus simpler than supposed; so too is the tragic view, which, at its core, holds that human suffering is immitigable and refuses to tolerate any faith or comfort that allows us to ignore the sufferings of others. La Rochefoucauld wrote, "We all have strength enough to endure the misfortunes of others."[2] This is the tragic view slanted through mordant irony.

We have nonetheless arrived at a dilemma. Is not Aeschylus's faith in the good of reason a kind of deafness to suffering? What has happened to "immitigable suffering"—is it not tempered by a faith in the curative powers of reason? Kaufmann reasons dialectically. Aeschylus has an unlimited interest in showing how suffering dominates the soul when it is *bereft of reason*: "Nothing is more moving than a noble mind gone mad; and Aeschylus was the first poet to realize this" (T 182). Since Aeschylus persists in depicting suffering, we cannot fail to conclude that where the mind has been abandoned by reason, suffering is immitigable. Will there be a time when it has not been abandoned? That has forever not yet been the case. One could evoke Giorgio Agamben's general reflection on the predicament of the heroes of many Greek tragedies, who seem to be arrested in the unbridgeable interval between "what has happened" (Aristotle) and what is to be.

> At the time of Greek tragedy, when the traditional mythic system had begun to decline under the impulse of the new moral world that was being born, art had already assumed the task of settling the conflict between old and new, and had responded to this task with the figure of the guilty innocent, of the tragic hero who expresses in all his greatness and misery the precarious significance of human action in the interval between what is no longer and what is not yet.[3]

That "precariousness" of action is owed to the default of reason. Will there *never* be a time when right action can be confidently assumed? The tragic view of life averts its face from the question. This view has degrees of despair that vary in historical periods, and no obviously stable, single normative character can be assigned to the drama that would contain it. The tragic criterion is a matter of due affect—and comprehension—where the formula of the Swiss Germanist Emil Staiger is apt: "Begreifen was uns ergreift" (Comprehend what has gripped us)![4]

One feature of Aeschylean tragedy can seem alien to a general expectation about tragic heroes. It is the absence of the consciousness of their predicament so acute as to change them. They are arrested, impervious to development, a prime example being Agamemnon, "*hamartia* in the flesh. Though the Chorus tells us twice . . . that through suffering one learns wisdom, Agamemnon's sufferings have failed utterly to teach him wisdom" (T 186–87). Kaufmann, I will add, can have been alerted to this relation—a suffering that does not instruct—by the model of Faust in Goethe's tragedy (Goethe is Kaufmann's earliest educator). Faust does not learn from experience. In the words of a specialist,

> The candidate [for salvation] Faust is damned poorly prepared for that "thrusting upwards" into the Beyond. "Es irrt der Mensch, solang er strebt" (Man errs as long as he strives): this *grandseigneur*-ish sentence of "The Lord" does its work throughout the whole length of the poem. Faust—and the formula can be reconstructed thus—has an immense number of experiences but learns nothing as a result of them.[5]

In the whole of the *Oresteia*, Kaufmann writes, no single person "acquires wisdom; rather we are shown how humanity—or, more precisely, Athens—can learn from the sufferings of the past by heeding the wise counsel of Athene" (T 187). But this is not a general plaidoyer for the superior wisdom of the gods, for, as we pass from the figure of Apollo in *Agamemnon* to the Apollo in the *Eumenides*—though now no longer "the savage god"—

> we do not see him change, nor are we told of experiences that changed him. Within a single play, he does not change. . . . Even in the *Eumenides*, Apollo is so unreasonable that he would fail utterly to realize his purpose and to keep his promise to Orestes, if Athene, the goddess of wisdom and patron of Athens, did not manage the matter for him. (T 186)

This feature of Aeschylean tragedy associates it with the epic form, for Homer's heroes, similarly, do not grow older or change their character. Or, if they seem to change, it is as a function of caprice or possession (T 184–85). "Aeschylus' concern was not with character but with long-range developments that encompass generations. Even calling his interest historical would suggest too narrow a perspective; his concerns were, in Aristotle's apt word, 'more philosophical'" (T 189).

Kaufmann's philosophical critique of retributive justice, central to his next book, *Without Guilt and Justice: From Decidophobia to Autonomy*, is partly inspired by the *Oresteia*, a work

> preeminently about justice. Not only are Agamemnon and Orestes incidental to this larger theme, even the house of Atreus is. . . . The whole final quarter of the drama is concerned with the very matter that modern critics consider most incompatible with tragedy: the founding of an institution that will resolve conflicts by eliminating the causes of disaster, namely a court of justice. (T 190)

The conversations provoked by this founding act allow Kaufmann to speak of its Platonic (dialogical) element: "The step Aeschylus took from Homer's world"—although not a giant step, as we have seen, in respect of character development—"toward the realm of the Platonic dialogue was far bigger than the further step in that direction taken by Euripides" (T 190). If Kaufmann's sensitivity to questions of justice arcs toward his next book—a work skeptical of justice as an ideal—his remarks on the moments in which characters are "out of character" run backward to his writings on existentialism: "What Homer [and one may add, Aeschylus], like Sartre, recognizes is the element of caprice—what some call the irrational and others the absurd" (T 184). Every single sentence in Kaufmann, it might be assumed, arrives from past portions of his work and moves toward as yet unaccomplished—but dimly intuited—future narratives.

He concludes with a surprising thought but one whose logic, on reflection, is by now familiar to us: he "takes back" his repudiation of Nietzsche's thesis on the death of tragedy, for there is, after all, nothing to rival the achievement of Aeschylus, Sophocles, and Euripides for many centuries afterward; the death of tragedy is fact. And so, "Was Nietzsche not right after all that there was a somewhat sinister development from Aeschylus to Euripides? He was" (T 193). This is the familiar pattern of the repudiation of a claim that gives way to a modest acceptance, that moves from a not-this to an and-both. Something happened or kept happening in Athens that is not easy to account for; although these reasons, whatever they might be, are not, as Nietzsche claims, the late efflorescence of optimism and dialectic. Kaufmann suggests as a reason the mood of exhaustion following the disastrous war between Athens and Sparta beginning in 431 BC and continuing on for more than twenty-five years, until 404 BC, when Athens surrendered. In 430 BC Athens had been struck with a plague that killed nearly a third of its population. By the time of the surrender to Sparta, Euripides, Sophocles, Thucydides, and Socrates were all dead. "War was no longer the glory of Marathon and Salamis," writes Kaufmann; "heroism seemed futile, and Euripides' skepticism" prevailed. His "mistrust of convention and pretension, his social criticism, and his pioneering tragicomedies (*Ion*, for example, and *Alcestis*) became paradigms for the new age" (T 194). Doubt and heightened self-consciousness flourish; tragedy gives way to the New Comedy. Kaufmann implicitly raises the question that will come to dominate his book: what are the social and cultural conditions enabling tragedies?

> Tragedy is generally more optimistic than comedy. It is profound despair that leads most of the generation born during and after World War II to feel that tragedy is dated; they prefer comedy, whether black or not. Tragedy is inspired by a faith that can weather the plague, whether in Sophoclean Athens or in Elizabethan London, but not Auschwitz. It is compatible with the great victories of Marathon and Salamis that marked the threshold of the Aeschylean age, and with the triumph over the Armada that inaugurated Shakespeare's era. It is not concordant with Dresden, Hiroshima, and Nagasaki. Tragedy depends on sympathy, ruth and involvement. It has little appeal for a generation that, like Ivan Karamazov would gladly return the ticket to God, if there were a god. Neither in Athens nor in our time has tragedy perished of optimism; its sickness unto death was and is despair. (T 165–66)

Kaufmann's following account of Sophocles's achievement profits from a discussion of Hegel's thoughts on tragedy (here we have again the throbbing arc that leads back to previous portions of his work). Hegel is cited at the outset for having overturned the opinion of Aristotle that *Oedipus Tyrannus* was the model tragedy, as it was for theorists of tragedy for millennia thereafter. For Hegel, as we might recall, it is *Antigone* that is "the absolute example of tragedy" (Hegel) (T 195). Hegel's ruminations on tragedy will fare a lot better than Nietzsche's, whose reading of *Oedipus Tyrannus*, even in a Hegelian vocabulary, Kaufmann considers altogether wrong. Nietzsche writes: "The genuinely Hellenic delight at this dialectical solution is so great that it introduces a trait of superior cheerfulness (*Heiterkeit*) into the whole work, everywhere softening the sharp points of the gruesome presuppositions of this process." He could not be more misguided. "As a poet," writes Kaufmann, "Sophocles was no more 'cheerful' than the author of Job; and like that book, his *Tyrannus* is infinitely more terrifying than the folk tale on which it is based" (T 197).

Sophocles's worldview is altogether terrifying: there is a futile history of critical talk that holds Sophocles to be, all in all, a capable craftsman and mollifier of conflict—indeed, as Nietzsche has it, "the most charming and beloved of all Athenians" (T 195). Kaufmann reports an antithetical anecdote recounted by Cicero: "Several ancient authors also relate that Sophocles' sons hailed him before a court to establish that, owing to his extreme age, he was incapable of managing his own property, and that he was acquitted after reciting something from 'his latest play, on which he was still working, *Oedipus at Colonus*, and then asking if that poem suggested imbecility.'" We do not know what lines Sophocles read aloud: it might have been the great choral ode, to which we earlier alluded.

> Nothing surpasses not being born,
> but if born, to return where we came from
> is next best, the sooner the better. (T 199–200)

Hegel's basic idea is mainly right for Sophocles. It reads (in italic): "*At the center of the greatest tragedies of Aeschylus and Sophocles we find not a tragic hero but a tragic collision . . . the conflict is not between good and evil but between one-sided positions, each of which embodies some good*" (Hegel). Kaufmann agrees: "Our admiration for a human being who suffers or dies clinging stubbornly to his ideas [does not] entail the judgment that there is no good at all in the position of those who oppose him" (T 201–2). A Hegelian criticism of the *Bacchae*—to jump to Euripides—would reason thus:

> Must the poet either denounce reason, criticism, and sobriety or be blind to the claims of passion, ecstasy, and enthusiastic vision? . . . A life without reason turns men into beasts, and a life without passion and vision is a living death. . . . What makes for tragedy is the relentless one-sidedness of both antagonists.

In its incredible conclusion, the lecherous Pentheus pleads with his mother Agaue to recognize him, but, maddened by Dionysus, she proceeds to tear her son to pieces. "Prudent fear of passion becomes prurient, and the man blind to the sweeping beauty of irrational experience is destroyed by those who, abdicating reason, revel in the blindness of their frenzy" (T 204). The Shakespeare scholar A. C. Bradley paraphrased Hegel memorably: "The essentially tragic fact is the self-division and *intestinal warfare of the ethical substance*, not so much the war of good with evil as the war of good with good" (emphasis added) (T 205). "Let us . . . recall," adds Kaufmann, "that Greek tragedy had roots in Homer's *Iliad*, where the noble clash with the noble and no hero is evil, and that Aeschylus sublimated the contests of Homer into moral collisions." Shakespeare, on the other hand, is not Aeschylean. The Christian influence on him is strong—Christianity, which "taught for centuries that not only evil but also evil human beings did exist" (T 207).

Not all tragedies are essentially the same; not all respond equally to general principles—for example, the idea of the tragic collision—however effectively this idea can be applied to certain plays, as, for example, *Antigone*, *The Bacchae*, and *Hippolytus*. Indeed, where Hegel could have registered the moral collision in *Oedipus Tyrannus*, he did not. At this point Kaufmann does not hesitate to reassert his own "philosophical" reading of *Oedipus* with features that Hegel overlooked: "the curse of honesty" and "the emphasis on the dark side of justice." We know these principles as an already well-established part of Kaufmann's ethical worldview (T 207).

Hegel's second contribution, again applicable only to those tragedies marked by tragic collisions, is the concept of tragic suffering. Men suffer external misfortunes—sickness, loss, even death—but these events are not tragic unless they arise from the sufferer's own action. Such action, in Hegel's *Aesthetik*, "[is] no less justified than it is fraught with guilt, owing to the collision it involves; and they [the actors] are also answerable for it with their whole self" (T 208). Kaufmann approves this concept: it is another element in his arsenal of moral principles, suitable for use throughout all his work. To the extent that—though no existentialist—he borrows from Sartre's existentialism, as we shall see, the principle of responsibility for one's own self-destructiveness is crucial from the very beginning:

> We must make a crucial distinction between *tragic guilt* and *moral fault*. Those raised on the tragic flaw too often balk at recognizing innocent suffering; following Aristotle, they consider it shocking; and though in life it stares them in the face, they do not wish to admit it in literature. Like Job's friends, they impute moral faults. But a man's destruction may be brought about by his choice, his act, his heroism, though he is morally admirable. (T 208)

Furthermore, following Hegel, now in his *Philosophy of Right*, the sufferer may not extenuate his guilt by distinguishing between his premeditated deed and its unintended consequences. "The *heroic* self-consciousness . . . accepts its guilt for the whole range of the deed." And from Hegel's lectures, we have this distinction between the heroic age and "our" own:

> In the heroic age . . . the individual was essentially one [i.e., in him there is no "opposition between subjective intention and objective deeds and consequences"]; whatever was objective was and remained his, if it had issued from him; hence the subject also wants to have done entirely and alone whatever it has done. (qtd. in T 209–10).

Hegel inspires Kaufmann's thoughts of Sartre, whose "existentialism revives the heroic ethos of Sophocles. A man is his deeds and his life; and to plead that one's intentions were better than one's works is, according to Sartre, a mark of bad faith." This linkage of ideas is satisfactory up to a point but also cries out for revision. "The *mot juste* is not tragic guilt," thus Kaufmann, "but tragic *responsibility*; for responsibility, like pride, is something one can *take*. . . . Responsibility can be free of guilt feelings" (T 209–10).

In the course of studying Sophocles, Kaufmann mentions the best performance of *Oedipus* he has ever seen, the Hölderlin translation, with Carl Orff's music, in Vienna, October 12, 1962, which he finds "incomparably the best and altogether magnificent" (T 212n24). It is interesting that Kaufmann earlier spoke demeaningly of Hölderlin's later development, which ends in madness, and contemporaries judged Hölderlin's translations to be its harbinger. The Hölderlin translation is strange, difficult, unheard of, altogether captivating in its way, but an object, too, of Goethe's and Schiller's savage derision. Here Kaufmann stands in proud independence of his educators![6]

In thirty tightly printed pages Kaufmann now produces close readings of all of Sophocles's plays. To summarize each of these in turn would burst the bounds of this chapter, so I shall stay with a discussion of his main discoveries.

His remarks on *Oedipus* close with panache: "In the end, righteous indignation and retributive justice are called into question, and the impact is shattering" (T 212). We have already heard Kaufmann identify the failure of such justice in the *Oresteia*. This insight, as I've indicated, will richly inform Kaufmann's subsequent writings on the inevitability of undeserved suffering and his doubt of a belief in the efficacy of retributive justice. This insight is linked to a rejection, in the case of *Oedipus*, of Hegel's otherwise fruitful view on tragedy as a collision of equally valuable convictions. "Hegel assumed not only that in such conflicts some good was to be found on both sides but also that both sides were *equally* justified." In the plays by Aeschylus and Euripides—whom Kaufmann calls the "more philosophical tragic poets"—this is often the case, but it is never true of Sophocles (T 212). Sophocles's tragedies abound in characters suffering heroic despair, an ordeal that, given the inevitability of human suffering, prompts Kaufmann to adopt the epithet coined for Sophocles by Cedric Whitman: "heroic humanism." This phrase comes into Kaufmann's arsenal of ethical concepts (as the Germans say) "as if summoned." He is the first "to place a hero's despair in the center of a play and to insist on the finality of tragedy"—this is the central event of his early drama *Ajax*—and as such anticipates "the modern or Shakespearean sense" of tragedy (T 213).

Sophocles's originality is especially vivid in his creation of Antigone, who is without precedent in Greek drama—a *heroine* who, like Oedipus, is possessed by despair—a despair "at the center of the action" that leads to "the absolute finality of tragedy" (T 217). Despite her overwhelming appeal, her death is not the death of an all-righteous principle but the result of a collision of moralities in the Hegelian sense; her tragedy asks you to understand that her position is not "simply and unquestionably right" (T 216). Creon holds the stage after Antigone has left, and in the end Creon speaks more lines than she does, to considerable emotional effect (T 222).

Pondering *Antigone* allows Kaufmann to clarify his general understanding of tragedy. Essential and definitive for Greek tragedies were "scenes that evoked ruth ['the feeling of sorrow for another; compassion, pity']; they did not require either a tragic collision or what Hegel called 'truly tragic' suffering, *though both are to be found in Antigone*" (emphasis added) (T 218). Here we recall Kaufmann's earlier claim that the tragic view of life invested in tragic drama is not necessarily marked by utter desolation—"some deep despair or notions of inevitable failure" (T 165). The core of *Antigone* is Antigone's suffering—her deep despair—but does even this suffering count as proof of "inevitable failure?" No. She has chosen to die *nobly*; and we have the saving refrain that we had before in respect of Homer's heroes: "There is *some* consolation, as in the *Iliad*. She may hope to be remembered for what she did" (T 221). Kaufmann is evidently ready to lend his own prestige as a thinker to the ever-recurring hope of cultural immortality: earlier we saw him celebrate this "Orcus-motif" in German classic-romantic literature—in poems of Goethe, Schiller, and Hölderlin, poets subject to the "tyranny" of ancient Greek and Latin literature.

At the end of his commentary Kaufmann emphasizes the salvific point: "Even when tragedy is ultimate, as it is in several Sophoclean tragedies, it is not wholly crushing. Like the heroes of the *Iliad*, Sophocles' heroes do not go to their doom unsung, unremembered, suggesting utter futility. Their supreme despair is recorded in poetry of transcendent power" (T 224–25).

This claim, however—I am convinced—is a category mistake. It is *not* Antigone, alive and then dead within this play as a flesh-and-blood figure, who is celebrated in lines of "transcendent power" within her world by Theban bards. In fact, the contrary is true; a great part of the ruth and terror of the play springs from Antigone's fate as one who will *not* be sung, *not* be celebrated in poetry. The chorus addresses her as a woman "Not crowned with glory, or with a dirge, / you leave for the deep pit of the dead."[7] True, the chorus reports earlier that "the man in the street . . . murmurs in the dark,"

> "No woman," they say, "ever deserved death less,
> and such a brutal death for such a glorious action.
>
> ———
>
> Death? She deserves a glowing crown of gold!"
> So they say, and the rumor spreads in secret, darkly. (Ant 95)

But this is *rumor* speaking, in demotic accents. Creon resists it as of no account, holding Antigone to be flattered for nothing more than "the sickness that's attacked her" (Ant 97). His son, her fiancé Haemon persists:

> The whole city of Thebes denies it, to a man.
> And yet, of course, it's a great thing
> for a dying girl to hear, even to hear
> she shares a destiny equal to the gods,
> *not* crowned with glory. (Ant 102–4)[8]

Because there is a controversy about the last line, the Greek scholars Robert Fagles and Bernard Knox take the view that "the chorus is expressing pity for Antigone's ignominious and abnormal death; *she has no funeral at which her fame and praise are recited* [emphasis added]. . . . The chorus reproves Antigone for comparing her own death to that of Niobe, who was not strictly a god, but moved on terms of equality with the gods. The chorus's condescending tone accounts for Antigone's indignant outburst in the next few lines" (Ant 400–401).

> And you, you springs of the Dirce,
> holy grove of Thebes where the chariots gather,
> you at least, you'll bear me witness, look,
>
> ———
>
> No tears for the destiny that's mine,
> no loved one mourns my death. (Ant 102–4)

The reader or spectator, who is not in Antigone's Thebes, must mourn for her; we do not read of her being celebrated there after death. She may be *implicitly* celebrated by Sophocles but only from a place outside the one universe she inhabits.

Consider this analogy: In this book I aim chiefly to celebrate Walter Kaufmann (though not uncritically); and so, in the mind of generous readers, he is better remembered and, by his ethics, he can die more nearly justified. *The Faith of a Heretic* gives us the opposite case, analogous to that of *Antigone*. In a "Trilogue on Heaven, Love, and Peace," Kaufmann gives superb lines to a fictional character named Irene, who, at the end of the trilogue disappears. By his eloquence on her behalf, *we* remember this fictional character, but she leaves no trace in the minds of her counterparts in the story world (F 380–98). On this analogy, there is no flesh-and-blood person corresponding to Irene whose way of dying in *our* world is thereby justified. Irene is only a model of nobility awaiting—perhaps forever—its real-world celebration. In the end, it is the agonizingly keen portraits of suffering in Sophocles's plays—a suffering that, in the case *Antigone*, is nowhere celebrated—that dominate every idea of its ennobling. In the one moment above, of wanting to add an adulated triumph to suffering, I believe Kaufmann is carried away.

I spoke earlier of Cedric Whitman's phrase for Sophocles's mode as "heroic humanism"—and hence as a gift for Kaufmann. It is a gift to which Kaufmann later gives a closer look. "Humanism" may not be the right word—for Sophocles and, in the long run, for Kaufmann—who, as heretic, would prefer to escape that label and indeed any such pinpointing by genre. "That label," Kaufmann writes nicely "is too imprecise to be wrong, unless one goes on to associate humanism with the view, so often attributed to Sophocles, that 'wonders are many, and none is more wonderful than man'" (T 236). This is the beginning of Kaufmann's wonderful close reading, which asserts that the words "wonders" and "wonderful" for *deina* and *deinos* are mistranslations.

> Reading Sophocles' tragedies, one certainly does not gain the impression that he found man as such very wonderful. Rather, the poet's world is governed by merciless powers, and men are strange, even frightening. . . . To be sure, some men and women really command the greatest admiration, and Sophocles confronts us with a few human beings of immense nobility, only to show how their very virtues lead them to brutal destruction. As the Chorus in Antigone says elsewhere, "Never does greatness come to mortals free from a curse." (T 237–38)

What bearing do these reflections have on Kaufmann's belief system as a whole? In a footnote he adds: "Humanists as well as believers tend toward more hopeful views than life, Sophocles, Euripides, or Shakespeare warrant" (T 240n55). Where does Kaufmann fit in? Is "Kaufmannism" not a humanism? He would have it be a *tragic* humanism—a heretical humanism that invites collision and readies itself ("heroically") for tragic quandaries. This is a matter exceeding definition and might finally be intuited as the total of his pragmatic and literary effects.

For now, amateurs of classical tragedy may not be aware that although Euripides was sixteen years younger than Sophocles, they were contemporaries, both of whom died in 406 BC. Their parallel lives, which allowed the poets to take notice of each other's work and to compete, was made possible by Sophocles's unusual vitality: he died at ninety, months after mourning the death of Euripides in the last play he directed.[9] Sophocles is said to have called Euripides the "whetstone" of his art. The mutual influences are traceable but, as Kaufmann would have it, their "experience of life" was different, leading to the even more drastically tragic character of Euripides's plays. Indeed, if "Aeschylus is more tragic than Homer, and Sophocles more tragic than Aeschylus, then Euripides [following Aristotle] is indeed 'the most tragic of the poets,'" the least optimistic of them all (T 243).

The latter point of course flies in the face of Nietzsche's view of Euripides in *The Birth of Tragedy*, where he figures as the instigator of the death of tragedy on three counts. These counts return to three Socratic maxims; citing Nietzsche, they are: "Virtue is knowledge; man sins only from ignorance; he who is virtuous is happy. In these three basic forms of optimism lies the death of tragedy" (qtd. in T 243). Kaufmann holds each of these claims to be false. Nietzsche has inverted the real relation of Euripides to Socrates and Plato, and there is no evidence of Euripides's intellectual and moral devotion to Socrates. If there is abundant dialectic in Euripides's plays, he can have certainly drawn this habitus from the Sophists. The more important point is that in no play of Euripides does dialectic bring about a happy ending. This outcome may be the result—the realization—of the aperçu ascribed by Aristotle to Sophocles, who saw himself as portraying "people as they ought to be, Euripides as they really are" (T 245).

The existence of an *Electra* by both Sophocles and Euripides allows for a productive comparison: Euripides's prior treatment appears to have been very much Sophocles's whetstone. Kaufmann close-reads comparable passages from both plays to show how readers' expectations of a prosy, argumentative and counterargumentative Euripides and a Sophocles rich in "poetic power and tragic feeling" will be disappointed; the far more accomplished passage is Euripides's. But it is also possible Sophocles has borrowed an impulse to parody from Euripides's playbook, for the recognition scene in Euripides's *Electra* plays out as a parody of Aeschylus.

Meanwhile, thinking of Euripides as a poet *engagé*, Kaufmann turns once again to the forever-interesting Sartre, whose play *The Flies* (*Les Mouches*) also treats the Electra story, as did the *Odyssey* and the works of the three Greek tragedians. The mention of Sartre smuggles in ideas on tragedy flowing in from Kaufmann's educator Nietzsche and not confined to *The Birth of Tragedy*. Sartre, along with Heidegger and Jaspers, is Kaufmann's prize existentialist exponent of Nietzsche's thought: here "theory is gray,"[10] for the creative root of all tragic dramas, classic and modern—Kaufmann repeatedly insists—is the author's "experience of life."

This alleged life source is once again not transparent and calls for analysis. Consider: If a man were asked to give counsel, one would expect and have the right to refer his counsel to his experience of life. But is the author of a tragic drama a counselor and is his work a practice manual for right living? What of Kaufmann's crucial distinction between the philosopher of ethics and the artist-craftsman? It is no small matter that in the case of the artist who writes, his life was chiefly spent writing.[11]

Then—at least to a great extent—such writing has no other template than itself, a zone of literary invocation and imagination. Both Euripides and Sophocles, writes Kaufmann, "mention . . . that Clytemnestra slew Agamemnon with an ax; but this detail does not function the same way in the two plays. Euripides' intent is evidently to add to the horror; in Sophocles it appears as an archaic *touch*—his Agamemnon was slain at a banquet, as in the *Odyssey*" (emphasis added) (T 248). Can these decisions be traced back to the poets' "experience of life"? Let "the experience of life" stand for the possibly otiose "x" that confers the distinction enjoyed by every literary work vis-à-vis others, but that "x" cannot be conceived as a singular thing and had best be laid out *objectively* in a differentiated way. Bemusingly, Kaufmann's choice of the word "touch" does connect a proposed subjective agency—"the experience of life"—with the exercise of *techne*, the practical know-how by which the work was made. Let us refer that "touch" chiefly to the celebrated *Fingerspitzengefühl*—the tact and "sure instinct"—of the designer.

Existentialism continues to resound, for Kaufmann, in his discussion of Euripides's *Electra*. When, finally, Orestes "protests to Electra: 'was it not some fiend commanded it, assuming the god's likeness?'" Kaufmann comments: "It sounds like a question a modern reader might ask about Kierkegaard's *Fear and Trembling*. But is it not a question that a poet of the Greek enlightenment, a contemporary of Socrates, the Sophists, and Thucydides, *had* to ask when once more treating Aeschylus' old story of Orestes?" (T 251). Note here the double provision for both an experience of life shared with contemporaries and the practical, writerly task of "treating Aeschylus' old story" anew, which is once again an affair of poetic techne.

The mention of Sartre focuses Kaufmann's gaze on a famous, arch-Euripidean line: the warning of "the Old Man, in Euripides' play, [who] tells Orestes that success 'depends altogether on yourself—and chance.'" Here, for Kaufmann, with Euripides "we actually seem closer to Sartre than Aeschylus" (T 250), for the term of "the gods"—Apollo's commandment of matricide—has been removed from this warning, and the responsibility of the subject for his action remains his own. Euripides "was not only concerned with the emotions of his audience; he was *engagé* in Sartre's sense, and at this point even comparisons with Sartre or Shaw may be less helpful than recalling Brecht, whose debt to Euripides was immense" (T 251). In the latter case, one can think of both writers' penchant for trial scenes. Euripides invites the participation of *critical* thought. After Orestes slaughters Clytemnestra,

> the Chorus applauds the dead [*sic*] as righteous, but soon condemns it as horrible. Orestes, too, stresses its utter horror, and Electra strikes a note of ambivalence: "We cast these mantles over her we hated—her we love." . . . Like Sartre's Electra, she regrets her deed in the end. Feeling broken by the ancestral curse, she bids a heartbreaking farewell to her brother and her native city. Aeschylus, Sophocles, and Euripides all treated this story, but Euripides was the only one who gave it a tragic ending. (T 252–53)

This does little for the Nietzschean claim of seeing Euripides as the poet of optimism.

Kaufmann is distinctive—even heretical—for reserving his highest praise for Euripides, who fuses an Aeschylean concern for moral issues with Sophocles's power to draw characters. In fact, Sophocles's prowess in sketching character can have been learned from Euripides, though they are different in the way in which they portray *heroic* characters: "Euripides' noble martyrs," who are almost entirely women, "are living—and dying—reproaches to the men surrounding them. . . . His intent is critical; he is indicting cruelty and callousness. Sophocles' heroic figures are inspiring; his perfection," concludes Kaufmann, "comforts," but isn't this last claim at odds with Kaufmann's chief revisionary claim about Sophocles, that he is a poet who gives no comfort, no quarter to suffering? (T 253). I think this dilemma points to the inspiration that Kaufmann takes from his vision of *heroic* men and *heroic* actions, where such action is another word for "heresy."

In his combative mode, Kaufmann cites a number of propositions about Euripides from the scholar E. R. Dodds, intending to refute them.[12] For Dodds, who is at first entirely in accord with Kaufmann—"grist to . . . [his] mill"— Euripides steadily opposed the claim "that reason (what the Greeks called rational discourse, *logos*) is the sole and sufficient instrument of truth" (qtd. in T 255).[13] Kaufmann could not agree more, just as he could not agree less that the "decisive contribution of the Greeks to human thought" was the exaltation of reason as adequate to the structure of reality and the perfect specific against moral failure. This view, Dodds continues, is affirmed by Socrates. But quite apart from the question of whether Socrates did indeed affirm a rational universe, Dodds's claim that, to put the matter bluntly, Euripides got his ideas from Socrates is dead wrong. "The truth of the matter might be that Socrates, of whom ancient tradition relates that he attended only the plays of Euripides, was stimulated by this poet—to develop countertheses." Kaufmann develops the point that interests him from the very beginning of his study: poetry's superiority over philosophy:

> Philosophers have rarely had any great influence on poets, and that a young philosopher [Socrates] should have decisively influenced a mature poet [Euripides] in whose *oeuvre* we can find no break at all is so improbable that we can safely discount it. The philosophers who did influence important poets did it posthumously; for example, Aquinas, Kant, and Nietzsche.

I shall supply the references: Aquinas—Dante; Kant—Kleist; Nietzsche— Rilke. Kaufmann continues: "That a mature poet whose work obviously has strong philosophical relevance should influence younger philosophers, even some of his contemporaries, is much more likely; Goethe's strong influence on Schelling, Hegel, and Schopenhauer provides a striking example" (T 256). Kaufmann is well informed on this point. I'll note that the philosophical vocabularies of Hegel's *Phenomenology of Spirit* and *Aesthetics*—and let us add Kant's *Third Critique*—enriched themselves with key words from German preromantic and romantic poetry. The "beautiful soul" (*die schöne Seele*), for one thing, figures in Hegel's *Phenomenology* as an exemplary if aberrant form of narcissistic consciousness, but this figure was inspired by Hölderlin, by the eponymous fictional character Hyperion, and by the aunt of book 6 of Goethe's *Wilhelm Meisters Lehrjahre*. This connection has its own history. Wilhelm Dilthey noted, "In their systems Schelling, Hegel, and Schleiermacher carry through on logical and metaphysical grounds the view of life and of the world developed by Lessing, Schiller, and Goethe"; and the philosophy professor Wilhelm Windelband declared that Kant's *Third Critique* justifies Goethe's (symbolic) poetry, a justification that might extend to unconscious imitation.[14]

When Kaufmann returns to Sartre's *The Flies*, he finds palpable strains of Nietzsche and makes the (surprising) point that its ethos is neither existentialist nor Marxist but one I'll call "individualistic."[15] The distinction of the play, aside from its densely Nietzschean texture, lies in features decidedly non-Greek: Orestes's murders appear as all but unmotivated, as *actes gratuits*: "tired of detachment, Orestes seeks a commitment," but is this not the language of existentialism? The play speaks against remorse: "Aegisthus, struck, asks Orestes: 'Is it true you feel no remorse?' And Orestes replies: 'Remorse? Why? I am doing what is right'" (T 259–60). The responsibility for his action is his; one may not leave one's act in the lurch. Is this, too, not existentialism? In this perspective, which tilts into the ready acceptance of guilt and the resistance to the punishment that would absolve the doer—strongly Nietzschean ideas— Sartre's Orestes acquires heroic stature. Kaufmann is concerned to stress how non-Christian this stance is.

This meditation also allows him to return to his persistent concern: Is this or that work a tragedy? And especially: Can this or that work written in *our* time be a tragedy? The first answer, in the case of *The Flies*, is that it is not; the second is: we must wait and see. But why is *The Flies* not a tragedy? Not because its ending does not seem to be tragic. After all,

> we call the Oresteia and Sophocles' *Electra* tragedies although their endings are not tragic—and the end of *The Flies* is far more tragic than the end of Aeschylus' and Sophocles' versions of the story. But the necessary condition of a play's being tragedy is not that it ends badly but that it represents on the stage *suffering so intense and immense that no conclusion can eradicate this impression from our minds.* (emphasis added)

The Flies does not answer to this requirement. "What we are shown on the stage is not the staggering suffering that leads to despair but the young man who triumphs over despair" (T 268).

These sentences concern issues at the heart of Kaufmann's view of tragedy. In reading Aeschylus, we were already encouraged to "cease supposing that great tragedies must issue from a tragic vision that entails some deep despair or notions of inevitable failure" (T 165). But such vindication may not be shown at the cost of minimizing the suffering that precedes it. It is not Orestes's "triumph" over despair that disqualifies *The Flies* as a tragedy: we saw that "Sophocles' heroic figures are inspiring; his perfection comforts" (T 253).

For all their right thinking, Sartre's plays are in the last resort too "cerebral," too replete with "self-consciousness" and "irony"—especially in the case of *Dirty Hands* (*Les mains sales*)—to count finally as tragedies (T 264). Consider:

HUGO: I have no gift for anything.
HOEDERER: You have a gift for writing.
HUGO: For writing! Words! Always words!

"Des mots! Toujours des mots! The title of Sartre's autobiography *Les mots*," Kaufmann notes, "sounds like a wounded cry," but it is not of the "intense and immense" sort (T 266). The crux of tragic drama is its power "to evoke ruth and terror," for which there is no prescription beyond the talent of the author to shape the terror lowering in his "experience of life."

Kaufmann could cross centuries in passing from Aeschylus to Sartre on the strength of their shared plot material. Brecht, too, enters the conversation once Sartre and Euripides have been identified as dramatists *engagés*, bent on heightening the awareness of their audience to the way in which politics derives from "imagination and mind" (Lionel Trilling).[16] But as playwrights, I'll add, Sartre and Brecht do not take their bearings consistently from fifth-century Greece, as if there were no exemplary intermediaries: no Senecan tragedies, no baroque tragedies of the seventeenth century, including works by Shakespeare, Calderón, Corneille, and Racine. Owing especially to Walter Benjamin's rejected postdoctoral thesis *Origin of the German Mourning Play* (*Ursprung des deutschen Trauerspiels*) (1928), this German form of tragic drama, with its portrayals of non-Christian courtly intrigue and violence, has grown in importance. These are plays written in the years circa 1630–80 by Martin Opitz (who translated *Antigone*), Andreas Gryphius, Johann Christian Hallmann, August Adolf von Haugwitz, and Daniel Caspar von Lohenstein. Kaufmann's account omits these writers, as well as, except in very brief phrases, French classical theater and the plays of the Spanish baroque: for example, "It is clear that Racine's plays are tragedies, though possibly of a somewhat different kind than those of the Greeks" (T 270). He will treat a few dramatists thoroughly rather than deal sketchily with many, so there is only Shakespeare to prepare for a closing discussion of Rolf Hochhuth's barely remembered *The Deputy* and the undead *Death of a Salesman*, with asides to novels of Faulkner and William Styron and random contemporary hits. But Kaufmann has devised an original way to present Shakespeare to satisfy his chief predilection, which is to think tragedy and philosophy together. Kaufmann will study the theoretical perspectives on Shakespeare by Aristotle, Hegel, Hume, Schopenhauer, and Nietzsche. It comes as no surprise that none of them proves wiser than the poet, but Kaufmann will "check" their theories against Shakespearean tragedy. This procedure runs in line with his decision to consider "the most fruitful typologies . . . associated with the names of poets: Aeschylean trilogies, Shakespearean tragedy, and so forth" (T 271).

He invokes again the eminent chapter 14 of Aristotle's *Poetics*, in which Aristotle declares his preference for tragedies that end well. No such tragedy will be found in Shakespeare's canon: "all Shakespeare's tragedies end in catastrophe" (T 273). This may be the "fore-conception" that has led most readers to misremember the *Poetics* and believe that Aristotle requires disastrous endings. In fact, there is scarcely a line in his chapter 14 that says anything to Shakespeare, since Aristotle assumes "that the deed evoking *phobos* [terror] and *eleos* [ruth] is the killing of a parent, child, or brother." But, following Kaufmann, you will not find a single tragedy of Shakespeare in which the hero actually performs such a murder, unlike, let us say, Oedipus or Medea. (Richard III, one sort of villainous historical-tragical hero, arranges to have his nephews murdered— but that is something different, yet not enough to prevent us from grudgingly admiring him![17])

In *Hamlet*, it is Claudius, the hero's opponent, who has committed fratricide. In explaining Hamlet's celebrated delay in avenging his father's murder, one could consider, following Kaufmann, that Hamlet's mother's new husband Claudius is also a kind of father, who, in light of this Shakespearean axiom, Hamlet may not kill.[18] It could be the exceptional outrageousness of Claudius's crime that produces in Hamlet the nausea Nietzsche speaks of and which inhibits his will to action, for to act in any way whatsoever is only to contribute to the vile nullity into which *all* existence has sunk. Hamlet's antic disposition works to sever the connection between the agent and such a world of (ab)uses.

Kaufmann's treatment of *Hamlet* via Aristotle invokes a factor in tragedy a good deal less sublime than fate or the workings of "the spirit that . . . may be the devil": it is an error in judgment "that, upon reflection, strikes us as entirely avoidable" (T 274). This failure of judgment or "intellectual error" appeared earlier in *Tragedy and Philosophy* as one way of understanding hamartia; but Kaufmann wants to reserve this latter Greek term for the way it has been traditionally understood, namely, as a constitutive "character flaw." "So unilluminating is Aristotle's doctrine of *hamartia* as far as Greek tragedy is concerned that it would not be the most celebrated term in literary criticism if it did not seem to work so well with Shakespeare. Not only is *Macbeth* the tragedy of a noble man who was excessively ambitious, Othello was noble but too jealous, Hamlet was noble but unable to make up his mind" (T 275). The tone of this argument, however, suggests little conviction.

Still, one feels the hermeneutic temptation to attribute Hamlet's irresolution differently: to the hamartia of a failure of judgment based on an inadequate grasp of circumstances. At first Kaufmann resists the connection, which would link hamartia to a delay of recognition (anagnōrisis), claiming that *Hamlet*'s case is different from that of, say, *King Lear, Timon of Athens*, and *Othello*, where, "recognitions are central and come too late; had they come sooner, there would have been no need for catastrophe" (T 274). In support of Kaufmann's thesis, one could hardly say that it is a *failure* of good judgment for Hamlet to demand more certainty as to the ghost's identity: it is no light matter to kill a king—and on whose authority? The matter calls for delay. But without arguing in too much detail, Kaufmann holds the play's final disasters, like those of the world, to "flow from avoidable mistakes." He wants the play—and its hero—to be like "the world"—"confused, chaotic, and complex" (T 274). Noting the heap of bodies lying on the stage, he observes, "This immense catastrophe that claims so many lives was not inevitable but brought about by a series of confusions and intrigues." Like a plague, poor judgment infects many principals at many places.

In the long run, Kaufmann insists on the only limited usefulness of Aristotle's *Poetics* to Shakespeare's tragedies, although the term of anagnōrisis (recognition) might still be interesting when applied to Hamlet's craving for the truth of his father's ghost. It is otherwise with hamartia, however, the appanage of "hamartia addicts" who mistakenly consider Hamlet's irresoluteness owed to "gentle hypersensitivity" (T 276). But here Kaufmann is chiefly scoring points. His discussion proceeds to leave Hamlet's character, like his plot, "an unclassical experience of life," flawed, yes, but not by "only one great flaw," and riddled with bad judgment (T 274). At the same time, and key to his final sense of tragedy, his imagination of what Aristotle "failed to see" allows him to define its crux: "*no flaw* or error is required for a noble human being to do something that eventually leads to his or her destruction or some other great catastrophe" (emphasis added). Kaufmann sees this uncanny pull at the heart of Sophoclean tragedy (T 276). He also finds it in the Hebrew Bible *ad contrarium* in Job's comforters: "Least of all [is] it essential to find some *hamartia* [as 'one great flaw'] because all suffering has to be deserved." This latter pair of concepts splits apart in Shakespearean tragedy into a division that "philistine" readings cannot bear to acknowledge (T 277).

Hegel's theory of tragedy involves colliding forces, each with (some) right on its side: it suits Shakespeare badly. What can be said, after all, on behalf of Claudius's case vis-à-vis Hamlet and, except for their fiendish energy, the likes of Richard III, Iago, and Edmund (in *King Lear*)? "Even if all three have grievances, there is no right on their sides. . . . [And] thus *Hamlet, Othello, Lear*, and *Macbeth* are not constructed around the moral conflict between two parties who have some legitimate claims but are too one-sided" (T 279–80). The modern tragic character, whom Hegel calls "romantic," stands, he writes, "in a wealth of more accidental circumstances and conditions, within which one could act this way or that, so that the conflict that, to be sure, is occasioned by external preconditions, is essentially grounded in the *character*." Unlike the Greek, this modern character acts out of the being that he simply is; the individuality of the Greek hero, on the other hand, is a "self-contained ethical pathos." The modern character is driven by only "subjective desires and needs"; as a result, his fate, "whether he chooses what is justified or is led into injustice and crime, remains a matter of accident" (Hegel) (T 280). This aperçu, though opposite to Hegel's basic idea of tragedy, reads like a brilliant description of Hamlet.

"The tragic figures of the French and Italians" might be an exception: they appear to embody a "self-contained ethical pathos" armed to collide with an opposite pathos. The phrases are Hegel's, but he continues in a different sense: these are figures "who, having been inspired by imitation of the ancients, may be considered more or less as mere personifications of certain passions for love, honor, fame, domination, tyranny, etc." They are barely characterized; they are abstract, formal figures, lacking the concrete vitality of the "full individuals" of the English playwrights.

> For even when some merely formal passion as, for example, the lust to rule in *Macbeth*, or jealousy in *Othello*, claims the whole pathos of one of . . . [Shakespeare's] tragic heroes, nevertheless such abstractions do not consume the full reach of the individuality; even given such a determination, his individuals still remain whole human beings . . . ; he gives them spirit and imagination, and by virtue of the image in which they contemplate themselves objectively, in theoretical reflection, like a work of art, he makes them free artistic creators of themselves. (T 281)

This is a superb insight. Hegel's critical judgment is fearless: this "fusion of direct vitality and inner greatness of soul" in Shakespeare's heroes has no equal in the work of modern writers. "Goethe, in his youth, strove after a similar faithfulness to nature and particularity, but without such inner force and height of passion, and Schiller came to cultivate a violence whose tempestuousness expansion lacks any real core" (qtd. in T 281–82).

However stimulating Hegel's ideas on tragedy, there is nothing systematic about them. The best are aperçus about Shakespeare's plays, in formulations whose elegance is owed in part to Kaufmann's translations. For example, tragic conclusions cannot be merely "the effect of unfortunate circumstances and external accidents that might just as easily have turned out differently, bringing about a happy ending." These accidents must rhyme with the genuine nature of the character.

> Viewed externally, Hamlet's death seems to be brought about accidentally through the duel with Laertes and the exchange of rapiers. But in the background of Hamlet's soul, death lurks from the beginning. The sandbank of finitude does not suffice him; given such sorrow and tenderness, such grief and such nausea over all the conditions of life, we feel from the outset that in this abominable environment he is a lost man whom inner disgust has almost consumed even before death comes to him from outside. (qtd. in T 285)

In their book *Stay, Illusion! The Hamlet Doctrine*, Simon Critchley and Jamieson Webster cite a "brutal" passage from Lacan's essay "The Mirror Stage as Formative of the I-Function" that they find brilliantly apt to *Hamlet*. They quote Lacan:

> Existentialism can be judged on the basis of the justifications it provides for the subjective impasses that do, indeed, result therefrom: a freedom that is never so authentically affirmed as when it is within the walls of a prison; a demand for commitment that expresses the inability of pure consciousness to overcome any situation; a voyeuristic-sadistic idealization of the sexual relationships; a personality that achieves self-realization only in suicide.[19]

The tonality of this "characterization" matches the tonality of Hegel's view on *Hamlet*. A citation from Hegel brings Kaufmann to the situation of tragedy at the time of his writing, still under the shadow of World War II. Hegel states his preference for happy endings. "And why not? For prizing mere misfortune, only because it is misfortune, above a happy solution, there is no other reason but a certain elegant sensitivity that feeds on pain and suffering, finding itself more interesting in the process than in painless situations, which it considers everyday affairs" (qtd. in T 286). Kaufmann turns impatiently from that "elegant sensitivity," noting only that "it seems dated." He reflects:

> We no longer think of everyday life as painless, and misfortune and catastrophe no longer seem exotic and "interesting." . . . So dark seems reality to us that yet more darkness on the stage may not be what we want; but serious plays with happy endings do not help. . . . The solution that meets with the widest favor is black comedy of some sort, whether theater of the absurd or not—an image that depicts the horrors we know from reality but makes us laugh at them. (T 287)

Think *Dr. Strangelove, or How I Learned to Stop Worrying and Love the Bomb* by Stanley Kubrick (1964); think *Brazil* by Terry Gilliam (1985); think the ghastly "tragi-comedy of Auschwitz," *La vita è bella* by Roberto Benigni (1997).

The richness of David Hume's treatise "On Tragedy" (1757) comes as a surprise because it is so little known. The essay is especially incisive since—unlike Schopenhauer, as we shall see—Hume aims directly at the enigmatic heart of tragedy: Why is it that tragedies can be enjoyable when suffering is not? "It seems an unaccountable pleasure," he writes, "which the spectators of a wellwrote tragedy receive from sorrow, terror, anxiety, and other passions, which are in themselves disagreeable and uneasy" (qtd. in T 287). Hume includes a history of attempts to answer the question, which Kaufmann retells: "L'Abbé Dubos suggested that anything that roused the mind from 'the languid, listless state of indolence, into which it falls upon the removal of every passion and occupation' [Hume], was felt to be pleasurable." Kaufmann takes up Hume's objection to compose a self-portrait: "Tragedy may be keenly appreciated by those who are in no case prone to boredom, men and women who have more projects than they have time for and passions strong enough to need no titillation of this kind."

Other aspects of Dubos satisfy Hume, especially his stress on the enjoyable character of *all* imitation: "tragedy is an imitation, and imitation is always of itself agreeable" [Hume] (T 288). Several of what Hume modestly calls his "additions" to Dubos are smart and jibe with Kaufmann's own concerns. For one thing, Hume holds that representations of extreme, unmerited suffering are unacceptable, such as "the mere suffering of plaintive virtue under the triumphant tyranny and oppression of vice." The "master of the theater" knows this, and he will show "virtue converting itself into a noble, courageous despair." In a word, he will portray the heroic attitude.

Kaufmann welcomes Hume's notes on painting as an occasion to discuss his own preferences. Hume is writing about the representation of suffering in painting: "Most painters appear . . . to have been very unhappy in their subjects. As they wrought for churches and convents, they have chiefly represented such horrible subjects as crucifixions and martyrdoms, where nothing appears but tortures, wounds, executions and passive suffering" (qtd. in T 289). These pictures delight and instruct no one. From his own experience, Kaufmann produces a counterexample in "Grünewald's panel of the crucifixion, for the Isenheim altar in Colmar, [which] would surely have struck Hume as especially horrible." Here a decalage in the history of taste makes itself felt: it was not until Kaufmann's century that Grünewald has "come into his own."

> The reason why this particular crucifixion . . . no longer offends us as barbarous is that we no longer think of it as a "history" that brings before us some remote and ugly incident . . . for us it has become "natural or probable enough," an image of our own experience, akin to a tragedy. What Hume failed to see . . . was that in great tragedies *mea res agitur*: I am involved, and part of the pleasure is the joy of recognition as I see *my* sorrows on the stage or on the printed page. . . . I am no longer alone; the terror that the poet fashioned liberates me from the prison in which *my* terror had held me captive [this reflection throws a searchlight on the workings of the play within the play of *Hamlet*]; and if the pain, grief, and anxiety suffered by the figures in the play exceed my own, I feel the comfort that, so far from being singled out by fate to suffer a worse fate than anyone, I have been relatively lucky. (T 290)

Kaufmann's questionable comment anticipates an ironic aperçu by André Gorz, Sartre's amanuensis and a philosopher in his own right. Gorz asks: Do you know that *chaud bonheur* on realizing that someone other than you has suffered even more than you for the same great cause?

Kaufmann turns to Schopenhauer, whose insistence on the distinction between tragedy and poetic justice can only have offended him: it is wrongheaded with particular Schopenhauerian malevolence. "The demand for so-called poetic justice," writes Schopenhauer, "rests on a total failure to understand the nature of tragedy, indeed of the nature of the world. . . . Only the shallow, optimistic, Protestant-rationalistic, or really Jewish world view will raise the demand for poetic justice and feel satisfied when this demand is satisfied. The true meaning of tragedy is the more profound insight that what the hero pays for is not his particular sins but original sin, i.e., the guilt of existence itself" (qtd. in T 291). Kaufmann's response is acerb and pointed: he is a capable counterpuncher, armed with superior scholarship:

> Schopenhauer fails to mention how much poetic justice we do find in Shakespeare. . . . But his notion that the insistence on poetic justice is peculiarly Protestant or Jewish is odd; after all, Luther's Reformation hinged in part on his extreme emphasis on original sin, and one might almost say that he insisted on vindicating God's injustice, for he taught that we are justified by faith alone. . . . And finding the essence of Judaism in the wisdom of Job's friends . . . is like finding the essence of Platonism in the wisdom of Thrasymachus in the *Republic*. The Hebrew prophets also knew . . . that the just man often has the worst of it, while the wicked flourish. (T 291)

What then is Schopenhauer's contribution to the core enigma of why we "find pleasure in what is downright repugnant to the will"? His answer: "What lends to everything tragic . . . its peculiar impetus to elevation, is the dawning realization that the world, that life cannot grant any true satisfaction, and hence they do not deserve our attachment: in this consists the tragic spirit: hence it leads to resignation." "The main objection to this theory," replies Kaufmann, "is that it does not accord with the facts." Some of the facts are supplied by Schopenhauer himself, who scrutinizes a few eminent Greek tragedies to show that none end in resignation. Here, he alleges, is proof of their inferiority: they do little beyond "showing the human race under the most horrible dominion of accident and error." Shakespeare is better than Sophocles, Goethe's *Iphigenia* is much superior to Euripides's *Iphigenia in Taurus*, and "the *Bacchae* of Euripides is a revolting fabrication for the benefit of pagan priests." This is the tone of a kind of writing—a perennial—that we find two centuries later in the work of our iconoclasts, as, for example, the ferocious atheist Richard Dawkins: "When you are actually challenged to think of *pre-Darwinian* answers to the questions 'What is man?' 'What are we here for?' can you as a matter of fact think of any that are not worthless?" (emphasis added).[20] Kaufmann concludes that Schopenhauer simply "lacked a sense for understanding tragedies" (T 293). His suggestion that "*our* pleasure in tragedy and our exhilaration are due to our 'dawning realization that the world, that life cannot grant any true satisfaction, and hence they do not deserve our attachment,'" whence "*we* [unlike the Greek spectator] are led 'to resignation' . . . comes as close to absurdity as any major theory of tragedy" (T 295). In his judgment on Schopenhauer, who has even figured previously as his "educator," Kaufmann gives us a model of critical intrepidity, but one would do well to be supplied with what Jaspers—in 1953!—correctly called Kaufmann's prodigious memory and erudition.[21]

Nietzsche rued the lingering Schopenhauerian odor of his own *Birth of Tragedy* because nothing could be plainer than its basic thrust, which cleanly rejects Schopenhauer's pessimism. For Nietzsche, the effect of tragedy is not resignation: it teaches "that life is at the bottom of things, despite all the changes of appearances, indestructibly powerful and pleasurable." The Greek stares into the abyss, stares into the terribleness of history and the cruelty of nature and, while "in danger of longing for a Buddhistic negation of the will," . . . he is rescued: "art saves him, and through art—life" (T 296). Kaufmann is glad of this vision: it is another reason, he writes, "why tragedies are felt to be enjoyable—they suggest to us that life and the world are beautiful in spite of all the suffering, cruelty, and terrors of existence" (T 297). This conclusion, I think, runs the danger of limiting the perception of tragedy to the few plays in which Dionysus speaks to Nietzsche and excludes, for one, the representations of life defiled by the crimes of murderous state religions.

Nietzsche—no surprise!—becomes the shining foil in which many of Kaufmann's better perceptions are reflected. Nietzsche's reading *Hamlet* is deeply satisfying and has remained normative until today:

> The Dionysian man resembles Hamlet: both have once looked truly into the essence of things, they have *gained knowledge*, and nausea inhibits action; for their action could not change anything in the eternal nature of things; they feel it to be ridiculous or humiliating that they should be asked to set right a world that is out of joint. Knowledge kills action; action requires the veils of illusion: that is the doctrine of Hamlet, not that cheap wisdom of Jack the Dreamer who reflects too much and, as it were, from an excess of possibilities does not get around to action. Not reflection, no— true knowledge, an insight into the horrible truth, outweighs any motive for action, both in Hamlet and in the Dionysian man.
>
> Conscious of the truth he has once seen, man now sees everywhere only the horror or absurdity of existence . . . he is nauseated. Here, when the danger to his will is greatest, *art* approaches as a saving sorceress, expert at healing. She alone knows how to turn these nauseous thoughts about the horror or absurdity of existence into notions with which one can live. (qtd. in T 298)

Since Nietzsche is so perceptive about *Hamlet*, it would often occur to Kaufmann that he is perceptive about other things. He remains a continual resource—for him and—as Kaufmann repeatedly points out—for Sartre as well. Roquentin, the hero of *Nausea* [*La Nausée*], will master his nausea by writing a novel that we are to imagine is titled *Nausea*. And when Nietzsche defines "the *comic* as the artistic discharge of the nausea of absurdity," we can imagine him anticipating the French theater of the absurd.

Reading Nietzsche on tragedy once again takes Kaufmann to the center of his own reflections on tragedy and comedy. In one of the most revealing passages of his study, forever en route to sharper formulations, he writes:

> I should rather say that comedy can express a despair compared with which even great tragedies are relatively hopeful. Tragedy suggests that nobility is possible, that courage is admirable, and that even defeat can be glorious. But comedy suggests that nobility is a sham, that courage is preposterous, and that triumphs no less than defeats are ridiculous. And while Nietzsche suggests in a famous passage that "What constitutes the voluptuousness of tragedy is cruelty," I submit, on the contrary, that tragedy depends for its effect on sympathy with those who suffer and is therefore a profoundly humanizing force, while *comedy* depends on cruelty. (T 299)

One might still be inclined to compare Kaufmann's claim that "tragedy depends for its effect on sympathy with those who suffer" with one he made earlier. There he held that spectators react to the suffering of a tragic figure *that exceeds their own* with relief, not sympathy. "If the pain, grief, and anxiety suffered by the figures in the play exceed my own," he wrote, "I feel the comfort that, so far from being singled out by fate to suffer a worse fate than anyone, I have been relatively lucky" (T 290). But even that relief would require an initial sympathy, an emotional comprehension of all that suffering before it could be compared with one's own good luck.

Max Scheler is the last of the philosophers of tragedy to attract Kaufmann's combative intelligence. Scheler's essay "On the Phenomenon of the Tragic" offers Kaufmann two targets: phenomenology and a view on the tragic as such. The gist of the phenomenological method derives from Husserl, Scheler's teacher; it is a logical operation that brackets out the real existence of the contemplated object, along with its effects on the will and emotions of the subject, for the sake of a "pure intuition" of its perceptual qualities. Scheler considers the phenomenon of the tragic in works of art as "an essential element in the universe itself. The material appropriated by artistic presentation and the tragic poet must contain the dark ore of this element. If we are to judge what is genuine tragedy, we must first have gained as pure an intuition as possible of this phenomenon itself." Which is: "to begin with, a characteristic of events, fates, characters, etc. that we perceive and intuit in them. . . . It is a heavy, chilly breath that emanates from these things themselves, a darkly glimmering light that surrounds them and in which a certain quality of the world—and not of our ego and its feelings or experiences of pity and fear—seems to dawn on us" (qtd. in T 302).

When Kaufmann discusses the approach *dit* phenomenological, he stresses tendentiously its "rigorous" disdain of the disciplines of psychology and anthropology. This stress does not bode well for phenomenology if it were supposed to bring Kaufmann over to its side, for it is this "phenomeno-logical method of inquiry" that, for Kaufmann, informs the opening sections of Heidegger's *Being and Time*. The meaning of this method, according to Heidegger—Kaufmann's antiself—is "to allow to be seen from itself what shows itself, as it shows itself from itself." This formula, Heidegger adds, "is not saying anything at all different from [Husserl's] maxim . . . 'To the things themselves.'"[22] Husserl says it better. In Scheler's phrasebook "what is at stake here is not proving but making see [*sic*], *showing* [the things them-selves]" (T 303).

It comes as no surprise when the allegedly presuppositionless findings of phenomenology soon slide into dogma. The phenomenologist, writes Kaufmann, "is telling us what he sees plainly and what we, taught by him, *should* see, too" (emphasis added). Now, this would be one way of mobilizing the hermeneutic circle of interpretation—but legitimate only if it were sup-plied with concrete examples. Scheler fails this test. What he sees in tragic dramas happens to be mainly what Hegel saw, namely, what Hegel *wanted* to see and what Scheler now *wants* to see: "The appearance of the tragic is . . . conditional upon the fact that the forces that destroy the higher positive value emanate themselves from bearers of positive values, and the appearance of the tragic is purest and sharpest where bearers of *equally* high values seem . . . 'damned' to destroy and annul (*aufheben*) each other" (qtd. in T 304). But beyond this unacknowledged echoing of Hegel, Scheler reveals the congen-ital flaw of theorists of tragedy, whose claims are "stripped almost entirely of literary examples and insights; and if we furnish our own examples, examining Greek and Shakespearean tragedies, we find that they are for the most part not tragic at all." Either this is so, or, as in Scheler's case, the theoretical "stipula-tions are implausible" (T 303).

Scheler serves as the dark side of a foil for Kaufmann's argument: what Scheler says, Kaufmann systematically rejects. Scheler writes, "In the tragic we are confronted by the paradox that the destruction of values, *once accomplished*, seems completely 'necessary' to us, but nevertheless takes place completely 'incalculably'—*unberechenbar*, unpredictably" (qtd. in T 305). This claim is wrong as soon as one examines the main tragedies of Sophocles and Shakespeare, though even to begin to do so would mean abandoning the "phenomenological" method, which deals in seen *essences*. The sheer opposite of Scheler's last claim is closer to the truth: "The tragic outcome is predictable," writes Kaufmann; "it is what we expect, but it does not seem completely necessary to us." Kaufmann's objection goes back to the claim he advanced earlier: the final catastrophes of *Hamlet* do "flow from avoidable mistakes." Scheler's revised formulation of his point could begin to carry greater weight: "Tragic necessity means above all '*inevitability and inescapability*. . . . Therefore, *two* kinds of destructions of values are, according to their essence, untragic: all those that can be blamed on an action or omission that can be definitely specified, and all those that could have been avoided by the use of apter means and techniques'" (T 305–6). In the spirit of Paul de Man's well-known insistence on the impossibility of distinguishing between error (necessary) and mistake (contingent and hence corrigible), Kaufmann includes *mere* error (akin to mistake) within the circuit of the tragic. But he remains resistant to Scheler's apodictic claim to have set down the truth of the tragic in the light of what he has *seen*—namely, the "essence" of the tragic—for "what he 'sees,'" says Kaufmann, writing in *his* essential manner, "is predictably a few things he has *read*," again, "especially in Hegel" (emphasis added).

Kaufmann concludes by rephrasing the questions posed at the beginning of this chapter, though their goal is the same: "What is 'the tragic view of life,' what kind of drama is properly called 'tragedy,' and what is the connection between the two?" These questions have not yet found dispositive answers: Kaufmann's book is an inquiry following several tracks, continually elaborating and subtracting from its "tragic" object—and beset by constitutive difficulties. On the one hand, tragedies are ancient Greek plays, by no means consistent with one another in their action and in their presentation by diction and spectacle. And then, surely, there are the properly named tragedies of Shakespeare. But beyond this inventory, and beyond the eleos and the phobos these plays inspire, what, if any, are their invariant conditions? And so the core questions need to be asked again with small, perhaps productive variations: "Are events tragic in the same sense in which plays are? Are there any criteria for what is tragic?" as well as the question supplying the thrust of the book's final narrative: "Is it possible to write tragedies today" (ca. 1965)?

Kaufmann recalls the genocidal horrors known at the time of his writing to prove that "except for a few professors of philosophy or literature," the commonalty of men holds such events to be tragic (T 309). At the same time men's judgments are founded more nearly on a moral mood—a Rousseauvian *sentiment*, a Kantian *Gefühl*—than on incisive thought. The case is not made easy by the fact that "there is no word" for the thing that tragedy might in every case denote—

> except insofar as the Greek word . . . has been taken over and adapted. The concept is based not on a common human experience but on a form of literature that was created by Aeschylus and his immediate predecessors. The plays in question are not called tragedies because they were so tragic—they merely had some connection with goats, and the Greek word for goat is *tragos*—but the word tragic was derived from tragedy. (T 310)

It is hard to know where Kaufmann can go from here if he is after a universally binding definition of the tragic "thing" transparent to its sense and use, but he is nothing if not relentless. Once he has stressed the evident fact that the word "tragic" has *many* senses and *many* uses, he is actually free to write freshly and powerfully. The best theories of tragedy and the tragic, from Aristotle through Nietzsche to Sidney Hook (and even including a few accents from Scheler), produce the many attributes that continue to adhere to them. But even if the most interesting recur, that fact is no argument for protecting them from criticism. A consensus of widely held views would read as follows:

> Many writers distinguish sharply between what is merely pathetic and what is truly tragic. . . . The major point is that not all suffering is held to be truly tragic. The suffering hero must be great or noble; he must fail but be more admirable in catastrophe than ever before; the unhappy end must be inevitable and issue from the hero's own decision in a moral conflict in which disaster was inescapable whatever choice he made. (T 311)

The repeated "must" gives the game away. These attractive views, along with the equally attractive commonplaces to follow, are displayed only to be rejected. The "must" is what ruins them because we will recognize some of these items as elements of Kaufmann's own explications of only *individual* plays. For example, Antigone is noble in her humiliation. Kaufmann says directly, "In *Oedipus Tyrannus* we do have a genuinely tragic situation in which catastrophe is inevitable whatever the hero decides to do," although it would be absurd to claim "that only dramas and events that closely resemble *this* tragedy are truly tragic" (T 313). A footnote refers to his reading of *Othello* in *From Shakespeare to Existentialism*, in which one can find "a measure of inevitability." (Kaufmann's celebrated memory extends, very likely, to every word he has published before, which suggests that he writes every new word in full awareness of what he is continuing and capping and concluding.)[23] The rest of his implied consensus is incisive:

> Some writers stress that there must be a moral conflict; others, the importance of the belief that failure is compatible with greatness, that greatness and the universe remain mysterious, and that failure must be final and inevitable. It would be foolish to deny that some such views have been supported with great eloquence.... Nevertheless, our exploration of Greek and Shakespearean tragedy suggests that these very attractive views ought be given up.
>
> The claim that some suffering is merely pitiful and not truly tragic can be neither proved nor disproved. But it can be shown to rest on an assumption that is false. This assumption is that both Greek and Shakespearean tragedy concentrated on the tragic and disdained the merely pathetic, and that the loss of this crucial distinction is a modern phenomenon. In fact, we have found that neither the Greeks nor Shakespeare did make this distinction. (T 311–12)

This dialectic advances, stipulating a good deal of the best that has been thought and said about tragedy and showing that, if it were to apply to Greek and Shakespearean drama, it cannot be generalized—and if it cannot, what good is it? You can specify ineluctable impending doom as a general feature of tragedy only if you are willing to exclude a great deal—indeed all—of Aeschylus. With the glaring exception of Sophocles in *Oedipus Tyrannus*, Greek tragedians labored "to convince us that catastrophe was *not* inevitable"—and this is the case of Shakespeare as well. Kaufmann's conclusion here is significant: both the Greek poets and Shakespeare considered "*disasters that could easily have been avoided . . .* to be preeminently tragic" (emphasis added) (T 313).

For all these exceptions, a lasting characteristic of Greek *and* Shakespearean tragedy is the protagonist's high-flown diction—which Kaufmann, relying on Aristotle's word *spoudaios*, defines as "noble, heroic" while stripping these words of moral connotation. This means: not all characters in tragedies who speak grandly behave as moral beings. This point becomes cogent when it exempts *tragically* suffering men and women in life from the requirement that they assume an archaically tailored verbal habitus. You cannot reserve the tragic fate in life for *heroes*, and their *tragic* fate may be other than a collision of their just ethos with the imposing ethos of their tormentors when, let us say, they are the victims of a state-sponsored famine or religious terror. "Aeschylus' Clytemnestra and Eumenides, Sophocles' Heracles and second Oedipus, no less than Macbeth and Lear have this [noble] quality, while many of Euripides' heroes do not. . . . Morality has nothing to do with it" (T 314). What is tragic inspires ruth and terror: it will be hard—or otiose—for Kaufmann to generalize further than this.

It is painfully clear: tragedy in life rarely results from grand moral collisions. Vivid and discrete moral conflicts, as par excellence in Corneille, are minor next to the vast suffering inflicted on entire populations, which surely has a tragic character. A judgment like this does not depend on conformity with Greek and Elizabethan theater, although these models might be pertinent. Tragedy need *not* be philosophically interesting, however much the spectator or survivor wants it to be. The murderous spree of Daesh in Paris in November 2015 cries out for understanding, but you cannot ask victims, witnesses, or spectators to repress their tragic feeling until its moral logic has been established. Is it retaliation for the crimes of nineteenth- and twentieth-century French colonialists in the Maghreb? For the bombings in Syria by the French Air Force? For a social system that effectively confines a great many French Muslims to foul banlieus? Or is it for what the French *are*: laicists, ostensible lovers of spontaneity and secular pleasure? It would be a parody of Hegelian seriousness to found the tragic character of this event on a substantial collision between (more or less) equally one-sided belief systems.

The French intellectual Marc Weitzmann addressed the poverty of reason in these killings by citing Joseph Conrad's *The Secret Agent*, "a novel that now seems prophetic: 'What is one to say to an act of destructive ferocity so absurd as to be incomprehensible, inexplicable, almost unthinkable; in fact, mad? Madness alone is truly terrifying.'"[24] A down-to-earth commentator, Liel Leibovitz, finds the attacks "comprehensible" *as* madness:

> Would you rather, it [Daesh] asks the largely poor and often ignored in Brussels and London and Lyon, be a dentist with a small car and a mortgage—or a lieutenant riding shotgun in a Toyota Land Cruiser with the power to take life whenever you please? . . . Wouldn't you love to live life without any earthly consequences for your actions, which are sacred in the eyes of all true believers, and run amok?[25]

One might reply that these are merely psychological incentives—they do not respond *philosophically* to the conditions of possibility of such a mad wanton object and the ruth and terror it inspires. And yet, given the absence of a competent philosophy that goes to the root of the tragic event and its alteration of consciousness in the spectator—given the absence of a serious moral *collision* and the irrelevance of grandeur in the life and death of the victim—must we deny the adjective "tragic" to the pain and anguish and term it merely pitiful or pathetic? We do not *need* to go back to Euripides to refuse to consider it less than a tragedy, but we can do so, with profit: "Euripides found vast human suffering, the ever increasing brutality of war, and the inhumanity of those who came to see his plays so serious that he did not want any clash of good with good or right to distract his audience" (T 314–15). This bold comment becomes pertinent when responders to the Paris killings try to *justify* random and atrocious murders on the grounds of distributive justice, namely, "They had it coming to them."

Kaufmann reserves his main Euripidean indignation for the conduct of the Vietnam War. It was the power of his denunciation of this *tragedy* in several closely printed pages—and his refusal to distinguish, like the Greeks and the Elizabethans, between pitiful and tragic suffering—that was picked out as admirable, to the surprise of some readers, by the Marxist Terry Eagleton. Kaufmann's jeremiad is well suited to the horror in Paris, with Daesh, this time, as perpetrator:

> The American involvement in Vietnam is tragic in the most exacting sense. The suffering it entails is immense and by no means merely incidental; the horror of it is magnified by the avowed intention of the American effort to spread death, destruction, and pain. In the two world wars the aim was for the most part to conquer or regain territory. . . . In the Vietnam war, the American daily communiqués report, not incidentally but mainly, how many human beings—called enemies, Communists, or Vietcong—have been killed. . . . Although the daily reports of the numbers of people killed put one in mind of the Nazis' genocide, the rhetoric used to justify the American intervention is as noble, or rather self-righteous, as can be.
>
> We are bombing Vietnam at a rate at which Germany in World War II was never bombed. . . . The terror has been increased vastly, always in the false conviction that just one more increase would produce the victory that would justify all of the suffering, death, and terror. If we stop, our guilt is palpable: all this hell for nothing. Hence we must incur more guilt, and more, and always more to cleanse ourselves of guilt.

Here is a parallel to *Macbeth*; only the *American* tragedy has *more* of the elements of the greatest tragedies; not only the themes of power and guilt, and the ever-deeper involvement in guilt, but also the terrifying irony implicit in the contrast between lofty moral purposes and staggering brutality, and *hamartia* in its purest, starkest form. Is it a mere error of judgment or moral fault? . . .

When we speak of events as tragedies, we use the word figuratively; but sometimes this is not merely legitimate but illuminating: it sharpens our perception and permits us to see what, without the benefit of literary insight, we might overlook. Not only philosophers could learn much from the tragic poets. (T 316–17)

We are brought back to the alleged impossibility of tragic drama in our time—a time charged with tragic events. The resemblance of the implied Henry Kissinger to Macbeth adds to the tragic character of this terror. It comes as no surprise that Kaufmann was ready to welcome enthusiastically Rolf Hochhuth's drama—*The Deputy, A Christian Tragedy* (*Der Stellvertreter—ein christliches Trauerspiel*); we should note, however, that a *Trauerspiel* (mourning play) is not of the same genre as Attic tragedy.[26] In its first performances in Europe in 1963, *The Deputy* caused a storm of protest with its accusation of the moral failure of Pope Pius XII, allegedly God's deputy, to intervene on behalf of the victims of the Nazi genocide. Since then, a half century later, the play has itself become, so to speak, the tragic victim of two opposing historical and ideological standpoints—that of the intrinsically one-sided papacy and that of one-sided historians, like Daniel Goldhagen, who are little disposed to extenuate.[27] The play has faded from public consciousness, although its author continues even today to generate scandals regularly publicized in the German press.

The play is rarely performed, partly because its criticism of Pius XII is not assured and cannot be assured until the opening of the Vatican archives. It is also dramaturgically lame, as Kaufmann points out, especially in its fourth act, where the pope is a puppet, icy and banal, an utterly inadequate foil to the hero of the play, a Jesuit priest named Riccardo Fontana demanding that this Vicar of Christ repudiate the persecution and murder of the Jews. Kaufmann corresponded with Hochhuth shortly after the play was first performed; but one wonders, had Kaufmann lived, what he would have made of the interview with Hochhuth published in 2005 in *Junge Freiheit*, a far-right German magazine. Here Hochhuth enthusiastically praises the "magnificent" works of history composed by the Holocaust denier David Irving, who, in the Lipstadt trial, was judged to be an implacable anti-Semite and liar.[28] It took some doing, but Hochhuth was finally induced to explain away his words.

To Kaufmann's satisfaction, *The Deputy*—a tragedy of sorts—did run for a year on Broadway, in 1964, thus giving the lie, at least for much of that time, to the "commonplace that in our age tragedies cannot be written" (T 317). Kaufmann sets down several reasons for this rumor: "1. we lack a shared, all-informing *myth*; 2. few in 1964 are ready to see *greatness* in men; finally, and most telling, 3. there is the modern—and especially—American—infatuation with success. This does militate against tragedy, as our audiences are reluctant to admire noble failures" (T 318). None of these reasons, Kaufmann, concludes, has merit. The historian Barbara Tuchman recently made the same point in writing on Woodrow Wilson, a personality arguably "great" and deeply flawed: "Since Americans are not, by and large, a people associated with tragedy, it is strange and unexpected that the most tragic figure in modern history—judged by the greatness of expectations and the measure of the falling off—should have been an American."[29] In fact, no American would have any difficulty, especially after reading Freud and Bullitt's study of Wilson, in seeing him as a tragic figure.[30]

Yet, for Kaufmann, there remains a genuine obstacle to conceiving and embracing tragic drama at the time of his writing. "The most distinctive and universal feature of Greek tragedy was that immense and overwhelming suffering was presented to the audience" (T 319). And now? Here, I think, Kaufmann's explanation of its absence falls short. He presents this difficulty of presentation not as an obstacle to be overcome but as a fait accompli: modern playwrights resist the idea of putting an intensely suffering individual on the stage because to do so would seem "pompous." In staging horror, they would appear to imitate the Greeks, courting the aura of past greatness, only, very likely, to fall short and seem ridiculous. Why would one even expect plays to be written on the model of an antique form? And so writers temper serious suffering with prose or wit, producing the contrasts of black comedy.

Kaufmann's argument supposes that modern playwrights see Greek tragedy in *his* main perspective as staging extreme suffering on the example of Cassandra, Heracles, and Philoctetes screaming in pain. I would think that following the horrors of World War II, audiences would be quick to situate extreme suffering in specific, historically localizable scenes of terror—the concentration camp, the gulag, the Gestapo prison—so that no poetry of tragedy could fail to include recognizable documentary elements.[31] And that insistence explains the achievement of Hochhuth but also the chief reason why *he* does not call his play a "Tragödie." His other reasons might include an awareness of the rhetorical question that Kaufmann sets down some pages later: "Is it relevant that Greek tragedy almost always turned to myth" and not to history? (T 354). The answer is Yes; but, nonetheless, for Kaufmann *The Deputy* is "the most ambitious tragedy of our generation." With very few caveats, he finally celebrates Hochhuth's documentary boldness as proof "that tragedies *can* be written in our time" (T 356).

The normal development against which to gauge Hochhuth's achievement is the gradual replacement of "the suffering hero . . . by the suffering victim, the noble agent by the passive anti-hero." Yet "such contrasts can be overdone. Philoctetes and Lear come close to being suffering victims who endure more than they [the passive victims of modern drama] do; Willy Loman's tragedy resembles Oedipus' in that he gradually discovers what he is" (T 322). Not every reader will be struck by this resemblance. But Kaufmann is concerned that the chief elements of tragedy—ruth, terror, and the suggestion of heroic failure, the whole charged with a demand for critical thought—survive into the day.[32] One might also have foretold his sympathy for Hochhuth's work from a typical provocation. In the published text Hochhuth writes: "[It is] in keeping with our experience that in the age of universal military service it is not necessarily a matter of merit or guilt . . . whether a man wears this or that uniform and whether he stands on the side of the hangman or that of the victims" (T 323). Hochhuth insisted that the same actor play each of these roles. Curiously, this proposition undercuts the main thrust of the play, which advances heroic action as a choice for every individual to make or refuse; the priest acts, the pope does not.[33]

It is not such dramaturgical niceties, however, that excite Kaufmann's enthusiasm:

> *The Deputy* . . . attempts to deal with the immense suffering of the Jews at the hands of the Nazis. Hochhuth decided to move into the center of his play the ultimate outrage: Auschwitz. The point was to put an end to the moral vacuum that persisted in Germany. . . . Not since *The Trojan Women* had a play indicted the author's fellow citizens with such uncompromising passion. (T 324–25)

Hochhuth also succeeded in imagining a genuinely tragic hero—Father Riccardo Fontana, who *chooses* to die in Auschwitz. Such a figure answers to Kaufmann's scorn of the weak reasons for denying the possibility of greatness. The Jesuit priest is an active hero; here Kaufmann's diction tips into almost Hannah Arendtian, *yekkish* scorn as he lauds Hochhuth for making it possible, with the figure of the Jesuit, to have his German countrymen "reflect on Auschwitz without *simply* bringing on the stage a chorus of doomed Jews and letting them *chant about their misery*" (emphasis added) (T 325). Aside from the question of moral tact, the question arises whether such indirection wouldn't encourage Hochhuth's *German* countrymen to assign the main responsibility for the Holocaust to the refusal of the *pope* to act.

In pitting an agonized priest against a derelict Pope Pius XII (or so he is depicted), *The Deputy* raises—for Kaufmann—the very interesting question of whether there can be a *Christian* tragedy, since a worthy hero, in proportion to his lived suffering, can expect to be rewarded after death. When he raised this question in *Critique of Religion and Philosophy*, Kaufmann denied this possibility. But now he reverses himself, for "so far from being anti-Christian *The Deputy* is a modern Christian tragedy"—whence the bold claim—"perhaps even the only Christian tragedy" (T 329). Again, a study of the German baroque *Trauerspiel* would certainly find reasons to dispute the latter claim, not to mention Goethe's *Faust—a Tragedy*, on the strength of its finale, a baroque pageant of angels and penitents. But that is not the point in our book about *Kaufmann*, who fights to maintain both his No and his Yes. He rescues Hochhuth's play for the idea of a Christian tragedy by arguing that it nowhere alludes to divine justification.

> The priest does not die as triumphant martyr. Confronted with the terrors of Auschwitz, he loses his faith and dies in an attempt to kill the Doctor.... Instead of worrying about his own soul, he takes in the misery that surrounds him and despairs.... At the end we are not asked to feel that the fate of the hero's soul is more important than the agony of millions. The play ends tragically, and the hero . . . is one who tries desperately to become a Christian in the most demanding sense of that word. I doubt that a tragedy more Christian than that is possible. (T 331)

For Kaufmann, the Jesuit priest Fontana exemplifies a rare "greatness" not easy to find in our times. "Our times" is the time of his writing, circa 1965, but I doubt that Kaufmann would find its rarity any less acute half a century later—indeed they would be field days for the absence of great figures. The question of what Kaufmann understands by "greatness" arises with special clarity in *The Deputy*, where the figure of Fontana is directly inspired by the Polish Franciscan monk Maximilian Kolbe, who in 1944 volunteered to die of starvation in a filthy cellar at Auschwitz, taking the place of a fellow Polish citizen who was anguished at the thought of abandoning his wife and children.

Kolbe's greatness is concentrated in the profoundly ethical character of his deed. And yet this deed, although it did not affect a *Jewish* inmate, still sits poorly with Kolbe's history as an anti-Semitic ideologue. How are we to understand and judge a deed that points to greatness at one moment but is in no way the coherent expression of a life lived in its preparation?

Precisely this case is taken up in Slavoj Žižek's critique of Jacques Lacan's definition of an ethical life: it is one, according to Lacan, that gives no ground relative to "the desire that is in you."[34] But is this desire ever just one thing—and especially *not* its opposite? The Masonic "Rhetor" in Tolstoy's *War and Peace*, essentially Lacan's antipode, demands that Pierre Bezukhov reveal his "*chief* predilection" with a view to renouncing it. Pierre responds tellingly, "My predilection? But I *used* to have so many of them!"[35] Žižek's criticism of Lacan's ethical maxim proceeds from the *many* contradictory activities in Kolbe's past. During the 1920s and 1930s, he "was involved in writing and organizing mass propaganda for the Catholic Church, with a clear anti-Semitic and anti-Masonic edge. With the outbreak of World War II, he helped people threatened by the Nazis, among them many Jews, and for this he was arrested and sent to Auschwitz."[36] We have read that he volunteered to take the place of another man who had been selected to die. He died himself three weeks later of starvation and for this deed was thereafter beatified by Pope John Paul II.

> How to fit these two aspects of Kolbe's life together? Most commentators take one of the many easy ways out. Some simply try to deny or minimize Kolbe's anti-Semitism (even dismissing the rumors about it as a KGB plot).[37] Some insist on the scholastic distinction between anti-Semitism proper and anti-Judaism—a "mere" prejudice against Jews, not a murderous hatred of them—claiming that Kolbe's error was of the second, minor sort. Others interpret his helping the Jews and final sacrifice as acts of repentance: having witnessed the suffering of the Jews under the Nazi occupation, Kolbe changed his view and tied to assuage his guilt. Still others take the risky step of minimizing not his anti-Semitism, but his final self-sacrificing gesture, pointing out that the man he saved was not a Jew but a Catholic Pole. All these versions are desperate attempts to avoid the embarrassing fact that the two attitudes (and activities) can easily coexist: a person who is anti-Semitic can also be capable of a dignified act of ethical self-sacrifice and—even more embarrassingly, the (explicit) motivation for Kolbe's noble self-sacrifice may very well have been the conservative Catholic ideology which had sustained his anti-Semitism.[38]

The case of Kolbe—which Žižek calls a "weird but crucial ethical dilemma"—bears on Hochhuth's portrayal of the martyrdom of the Jesuit Fontana, which Kaufmann sees—not as triumphant—but as artistic proof of individual greatness. The point of Žižek's reflection, which I find impressive, is that a "great" act, of the sort that lends itself to a dramatic spectacle, need not imply a "great" history, of which it is the presumed expression. But under these circumstances, what does it mean to impute "greatness" to a man?

In Hochhuth's second important play, *Soldiers: Necrologue for Geneva; A Tragedy* (here Hochhuth boldly employs the word "*Tragödie*"), it is Churchill who is shown to be "great" despite "the truly tragic nature of his guilt." He is guilty of having supported the vile, destructive saturation bombing of German cities during World War II. What is of special interest today is how this play, and Kaufmann's support of it, anticipate by many decades a distinction attributed to W. G. Sebald. His book *On the Natural History of Destruction* is said to have awakened the Germans from their amnesiac repression of the thousands upon thousands of deaths inflicted on German civilians by the Allied bombs, but *Soldiers* had already awakened them, at least during the time of its notoriety in late 1967.[39] On the other hand, Hochhuth's historical speculations, especially concerning Churchill's participation in plotting the fatal airplane crash of the Polish prime minister in exile Władysław Sikorski, who was arguing stubbornly against a military alliance of Britain and the Soviet Union, are less convincing than those that shape *The Deputy*.

Brecht, whom Kaufmann can barely abide, needs to be drawn into this conversation, for here, especially, in his play *Life of Galileo*, we have another smashing together of history and spectacle with even worse results:

> The notion that Galileo missed a rare opportunity to provoke great social upheavals and was a traitor for that reason is as fantastic as Brecht's moral judgments in the play are unthoughtful, [viz., "the only aim of science is to alleviate the burdensomeness of human existence" (T 343)]. That the real Galileo was incomparably greater and more fascinating than the figure in the play did not matter from Brecht's point of view. He was no more concerned with the historical record than he was with writing a tragedy or acknowledging tragic choices. . . . When Brecht was a nihilist, he expected to be applauded for being so naughty, and when he was a moralist, he expected applause for being right. (T 344, 347)

At the same time, to this No!—quite in conformity with Kaufmann's horror of one-sidedness—we also have a (tepid) Yes. "Bertolt Brecht stages a superb spectacle with fine actors, good songs, and many very interesting effects," but the No! is very much stronger for a good reason: Brecht's famous antitragic, anti-Aristotelian resistance to sympathy and identification with heroic figures is designed to leave us room to think, yet his interesting *effects* only distract us from the drama's ideas, which when detected are, in any case, according to Kaufmann, "puerile." Brecht contributes to the wrong view that tragedy is out of place in our age at the same time that his ban on sympathetic suffering fails to produce a Euripidean richness of ideas. In asking "the audience to suspend their human sympathies and . . . their critical intelligence, he asked them to become as children, listen to a tale, and accept a moral" (T 346). What remains is a man who "set himself deliberately against *this whole tradition of humanism*" (emphasis added), a statement that reminds us that Kaufmann's humanism is constitutively imbued with a tragic view of life. It could strike us that the ability, indeed the predilection to modify a No with a Yes is itself, precisely, the outcome of an education in tragedy, for, as Kaufmann stresses, "Aeschylus, Sophocles, and Euripides usually took sides, without suggesting that every right was on the side they took, none on the other. Life's most interesting choices are not like that; neither are they between gray and gray. The world of tragedy is not drab" (T 351)—and given the abundance of opportunities for tragic suffering, the agon of intellectual choice is not drab. Kaufmann uses Brecht to revise, incisively and memorably, an intellectual-historical commonplace:

> The notion that the "Aristotelian" theater was bent on illusion and that it was Brecht's great innovation to introduce what he called a *Verfremdungseffekt* or *V-Effekt*—to estrange the audience from the action on the stage, to break the illusion, to create a psychic distance—is untenable. Myths, masks, and music were so many V-effects; so were the chorus, dances, stylized acting, and the fact that all the women, too, were played by male actors. (T 354)

This argument belongs to Kaufmann's fundamental brief that classical tragedy, *pace* Brecht, is by no means aimed at illusionist imitation, even including the device of the play within a play. Euripides, for one, "keeps interposing V-effects to make us think" (T 355). Ancient Greek tragedy is modern, and its example—in its endless dramaturgical variation, its "restless spirit of experiment—gives hope, though not certainty, for the writing of tragedy in the future" (T 356). But is tragedy a chief desideratum?—Yes! and No! "In theory there is no reason why comedies should not be as great as tragedies, and laughing at the follies of mankind is no less philosophical. . . . It would be exceedingly surprising if the next hundred years should produce tragedies as great as the best we have. But they might well produce comedies as brilliant as any" (T 358). Indeed, we have Samuel Beckett to stake this prophecy firmly to the ground.

Throughout this book, Kaufmann has attempted to close the distance that he saw philosophy keeping from the great fact about humanity, its randomly distributed suffering. It is in this sense an ethical philosophy. In our next chapter, we shall deal more directly with Kaufmann's critique of distributive justice.

11

Against Decrepit Ideas

WITHOUT GUILT AND JUSTICE:
FROM DECIDOPHOBIA TO AUTONOMY

Against "decrepit ideas like justice and equality."

—WALTER KAUFMANN

Would that you might invent for me the love that bears not only all
punishment but also all guilt! Would that you might invent for me the justice
that acquits everyone except him that judges!

—FRIEDRICH NIETZSCHE

DURING TWO STAYS at the Villa Serbelloni in Bellagio, on the halcyon shores
of Lake Como, in 1970 and again in 1975, Kaufmann wrote near-final versions
of two books: *Without Guilt and Justice: From Decidophobia to Autonomy* (1973)
and *The Future of the Humanities* (1977).[1] Both books mean to appeal to lay
readers. They are written in a plain, vigorous, didactic style, without flourishes
or quantities of detailed information. The first, *Without Guilt and Justice*, is
confident, even triumphal; it announces a new moral philosophy, its verve
attuned to the beauty of its workplace. This "heavenly place" makes an appearance in the book as "the case of the beautiful garden"; "I have paid tribute to
it," writes Kaufmann, "in the chapter on guilt" (W 262). One looks forward to
the solution to this antinomy.

The optimism of *Without Guilt and Justice* is evoked by Nietzsche's conclusion to *Ecce Homo*, completed on his forty-fourth birthday (Kaufmann,

writing from Lake Como, a mere two hundred kilometers from Turin, was forty nine at the time). Nietzsche wrote:

> Not in vain have I buried my forty-fourth year today; I had the right to bury it—the life within it has been saved and is immortal. . . . How could I not be grateful to the whole of my life? That is why I am now going to tell myself the story of my life.[2]

Kaufmann's ruminations on justice and guilt belong to the whole of his life. At the close of the later book, *The Future of the Humanities*, which he again wrote "in the midst of so much beauty, written in a study with stunning views of the Lago di Como," he wonders, "how could these pages fail to be suffused with gratitude?" (FH 216–17). And surely the fate of the humanities occupied him from what he calls the very birth of his "intellectual conscience" (W 11). Nonetheless, this book, faithful to its disappointment, is written in anger.

Although he wrote a full draft of *Without Guilt and Justice* in 1970, it had taken more than thirty years of reflection to shape its argument. A crucial impulse came from Kaufmann's "experience of life" during the months in 1945, which he spent as an émigré from Nazi Germany and then as a US military interrogator in a prison in the Rhineland.[3] Many of the pieces in *Cain and Other Poems* (1962) reflect his moral turbulence, which came to be focused in this new book as an attack on "decrepit ideas like justice and equality," as well as a refusal of guilt and "the demonstration of the need for alienation," with a view toward developing "a new conception of autonomy—a new integrity—a new morality" (W vii). The argument advances with robust, aggressive, even hectoring intellectual confidence.

The tone of the later book, *The Future of the Humanities*, is bleaker: it is not "mellow"—it is both elegiac and caustic (FH 216–17). It struggles to shore up the ruin of the humanities as taught in American universities, much of whose future lies in its past. Kaufmann points up the discrepancy of tone between the two; the second book is mordant the way the paradisiacal environment of the writing was not, in kinship with an older literary tradition that situates painful reflection in ravishing landscapes.[4] From his Italian eyrie, Kaufmann surveys his essentially American experience: both books are decisively rooted in Kaufmann's experience of life in the New World, an identity that his years in the army would have done much to consolidate.[5] This legacy is conveyed in miniature in Kaufmann's account of the writing of *Without Guilt and Justice*: he reports with pride that when he presented his ideas at a conference at the University of Pennsylvania on May 1, 1965, he was seated next to Martin Luther

King, to whom he was to dedicate a fuller version of his paper.[6] Lincoln and the slaveholding Jefferson—the latter only intermittently—figure as moral preceptors in this book; they were scarcely present in his first books. We will focus now on *Without Guilt and Justice: From Decidophobia to Autonomy*, the earlier and more substantial of the two Bellagio projects.

The word "decidophobia" in its title could seem rebarbative; but once justified, it becomes a good enough formulation of Kaufmann's leading idea. On the model of "claustrophobia," which links Latin and Greek roots, "decidophobia" brings to "phobia" the Latin root *decido*, which means at once "to decide" but also "to fall (down)." In the word "decidophobia" there is fear of falling, both literally and figuratively, because the need for decision exposes the fear that habit conceals. Weight falls, again and again, on fear. It is the fear of passing from the habit of obedience to the dreadful freedom of autonomy.

Is this rallying cry to decide, a throwback to Carl Schmittian "decisionism"? In one attenuated, nonvicious sense only: if for Schmitt the validity of a decision is not a function of its "meaning" but a function of the authority behind it, then Kaufmann's concern is to authorize decision by the honesty, courage, and sense of responsibility at its source.

In a 1942 essay titled "The Yogi and the Commissar," Arthur Koestler constructed a spectrum of social behaviors, distinguishing radically the "spectral line" of the social revolutionary from the "spectral line" of the mystic personality. "On one end of the spectrum . . . we would see the Commissar. The Commissar believes in Change from Without. He believes that all the pests of humanity, including constipation and the Oedipus complex, can and will be cured by Revolution, that is, by a radical reorganization of the system of production and distribution of goods." On the other pole of the social spectrum sits the Yogi, whose subject is the individual mind in nourishing connection with the greater universe. This ascetic priest "believes that nothing can be improved by exterior organization and everything by the individual effort from within; and that whosoever believes in anything else is an escapist."[7] This essay—though surely not it alone—forecasts the thrust of Kaufmann's book, which declares the personal self the absolute primary locus of change. The fate of the individual mind precedes the fate of the social body. One enjoys no freedom when devoted to any system of social thought—Marxist, socialist, or otherwise utopian—unless the believer is fearless and autonomous in his first decision to join.

From the start, Kaufmann's reflections are couched in general language but contain—to speak with Keats speaking to Shelley—rifts laden with the ore of lived experience. When Kaufmann speaks of *fateful* decisions, he surely refers to the decision that took him, a solitary nineteen-year-old, from Nazi Germany to the United States. When he speaks of the obstacles to independent decision, such as, in the very first place, *religion*—how, born into the fold, one stays in the fold—he surely refers to the decision he made as a child of twelve to leave the Lutheran Church, into which he was born, and devote himself to the study of Judaism. Under the pressure of rational scrutiny, this enthusiasm settled and grew detached from the organization of Orthodox Judaism, although its pieces stuck to elements of Jewish learning, including, especially, biblical stories and biblical emotion. In citing Nietzsche's aperçu "Of necessity, the party man becomes a liar"—which mocks the wish "*not* to see what one does see" with the aid of the blinkers of a party agenda—Kaufmann remarks: "Those who realize [like Kaufmann himself!] how closely words like 'party' and *Parteigenosse* were associated with the German anti-Semitic movement even then [ca. 1880] may pardon his hyperbole" (W 10).[8]

We spoke of change along the spectral line of the individual personality as if it were a readily available option. But the social line does what it can to resist that readiness. "Anyone who would unhesitatingly plunge into choices that are likely to mold his own character and future would be so unpredictable that he, too, would endanger the social fabric. The easiest way to insure stability is to engender fear." How does the individual bent on change through decision deflect his attention from the clearest awareness of his options, whose risks would make him afraid? In an essay that contains many numbered lists, Kaufmann lists three basic subterfuges: "(1) avoid fateful decisions; (2) stack the cards so that one alternative is clearly the right one, and there seems to be no risk involved at all; and (3) decline responsibility" (W 4). He then breaks down these devices into the ten strategies that decidophobes employ to escape the vertigo of decision. I think it will be interesting to reproduce this series.

I mentioned the first—*religion*. In preceding chapters, we saw Kaufmann examine the kinds of authority exercised by organized religions: the dictation of ethical rules contrived by theologians who claim to have drawn them from holy scripture; the solicitation of brotherhood and communal worship; the inducement, in some cases, to monasticism in its various forms; and others. To vary one of Kaufmann's sentences: "One does not so much *decide* to obey [original: 'stay'] as one does *not* decide to disobey [original: 'leave']." If this is Kaufmann's No—his caveat—one can expect it to be followed by his Yes in a minor key: "Nor is allegiance to a religion always prompted by decidophobia"—a concession curiously prompting Kaufmann to "choose suicide as an illustration." As an illustration of what? It cannot be that allegiance to a religion is driven in every case by voluntary menticide. Rather, the parallel of religious membership with suicide lies in the fact that a *sacrificium intellectus* and worse can also come about as the result of a lucid decision, made in light of other options. "Suicide can be wholly admirable. Nor need it be primarily an act of either fear or courage; it can also be an attempt at revenge or a form of protest. Similarly, not every member of every religion is a decidophobe" (W 8). The parallel remains somewhat inscrutable.

A second strategy Kaufmann terms *drifting*, which exists in two "models"— one suited to older people, that is, those over thirty; the other, mainly to students. In the first case one simply remains within the status quo and "drifts along." The second, the younger model, leads to dropping out, without tradition, without "a code, a plan, a major purpose." Things happen if they happen; otherwise, nothing happens. Both models are likely to need lubrication with drink or tranquilizers or strong drugs (W 9).

A shiftless life can grow tedious, as in the form of tediousness that dawns from a reading of the novels of Hermann Hesse, and sponsor a turnabout: a lust for commitment, any commitment. "*Allegiance to a movement* is the third strategy," but such allegiance may represent no real choice at all. Enrolling can be done heedlessly, with little or no grasp of the moral implications involved (W 10). Again, the opposite case is also possible; this is Kaufmann's minor Yes. As with suicide, one can also declare an authentic allegiance to a party. To deny this possibility would mean to denigrate unreasonably the "common cause" made with the Communist Party, for example, by Sartre, who, for Kaufmann, is a by-and-large admirable reference (W 11). His case dictates Kaufmann's concession. It might be worth considering, as an alternative, the psychoanalyst Lacan's doubt of *any* such cost-free political commitment. Jacques-Alain Miller, Lacan's acolyte, argues that, unlike enthusiasm, anxiety (I am citing Žižek's account) "remains the only affect that does not cheat (as Freud already put it), which means that there is in *every* (political) enthusiasm for a Cause an element of imaginary misrecognition, . . . politics being a domain of imaginary or symbolic identification and as such the domain of illusions." Rejecting this claim, Žižek invokes Alain Badiou's authority to assert that political commitment, based on the enthusiasm of a principled engagement, can be no less authentic than detached cynicism, the putative preserve of a rewarding anxiety.[9] In *The Faith of a Heretic*, of course, Kaufmann also spoke directly of the value of commitment as a function of the integrity—read: lucid decisiveness—of the personality. As he says now, joiners will need to live "in a tension, occasionally acute, between their loyalty and their intellectual conscience. As usual, there are innumerable possibilities and degrees" (W 11).

Kaufmann's indicts a fourth strategy for avoiding resolute decision—*allegiance to a school of thought*. This ploy would be of immediate interest to him as a university professor, his world replete with schools and devotés who wear the colors of a particular way of thinking without having ever decided to. Kaufmann mentions various schools of philosophy: Aristotelian (in three ways: Heideggerian, Oxford analytic, Thomist), Marxist, phenomenological, psychoanalytic, and others. In literary studies today, we have deconstructionists and cultural studies devotés, formalists and computational analysts, who study novels with "new techniques in sentiment analysis drawn from the field of computer science," and others.[10] "One becomes a member of a school of thought not by making a decision but by being trained by someone who was there"—at the college where one landed (W 14).[11]

Kaufmann attacks the next device, which he calls *exegetical thinking*, with evident relish. We have already heard of his dislike of this sort of facsimile interpretation, which proceeds by projecting one's own (ideally) deep and obscure thought into texts renowned for their depth and obscurity and then "getting them back endowed with authority" (W 16). This is the case, for Kaufmann, of Heidegger's readings of Hölderlin and Rilke and Trakl. In such thinking, intellectual and moral energy is invested in works having canonical authority: they must display "a fascinating incoherence and an oracular quality." The idea, it is claimed, is to escape errant subjectivism, for the source text can do no wrong; the critical faculty is buried under awestruck mimicry, and the outcome is untestable, vatic assertion. To read Kaufmann's repudiation of exegetical thinking is to read him at his most vigorous. It figures often in his writings, at one point argued under the head of *the existentialist pattern*, shockingly visible in Kierkegaard, Heidegger, and Sartre as the flight from solitude into submission, respectively, to the Bible, the pre-Socratics, and Marx's *Das Kapital* (W 15–18). At the same time, it is hardly conceivable that Kaufmann's reading of canonical authors would escape the slide into exegetical thinking. Proving this contention could inspire a pamphlet that a willing author might be moved to write: "Contra Walter Kaufmann."

The sixth strategy for avoiding decision is Manichaeism, the applied logic of black-and-white, of one one-sidedness versus another—its opposite—an error of thinking that is deplored again and again, as we have seen, throughout Kaufmann's corpus. It is the (false) principle most opposed to the (truthful) tragic view of life, where alternatives—witness the *Iliad* and Greek tragedy—are never clear-cut and where the color of one washes into the other. (This corrective view is also the founding perspective of deconstructionism.)[12] How does radical Manichean opposition figure as an aid to the decidophobic? It makes decisions easy, if not just, by setting up choices as radically opposed, with only the one considered valuable, so that it costs nothing to have that one choice carry the day although it has never been rightly evaluated. But it is contrary to the experience of life.

> As a rule, wrong clashes with greater wrong, not only in Greek tragedy but also in life and history. . . . [Meanwhile], Manichaeism is far from dead if the name is used inclusively [following Zarathustra and Mani] to label views in which history is a contest between the forces of light and darkness, with all right on one side (emphasis added). (W 19–20)

In this discussion, writes Kaufmann, consider Heidegger, for whom behavior is either inauthentic or authentic.[13] Authenticity is an affair of resoluteness, inauthenticity, not; yet how good is this distinction when in 1933 Heidegger resolutely joined the Nazi Party? Kaufmann: "A resolute leap into faith or into a movement is quite compatible with dishonesty, decidophobia, and heteronomy" (W 20–21).

Kaufmann calls the seventh of the decidophobe's ploys moral rationalism, to which he is opposed, as he is to its titular opposite, moral irrationalism, which is evidently no better. The latter position is readily explained. It is the view that reason cannot supply adequate grounds for life-shaping decisions, which require a fateful leap, à la Kierkegaard and, in certain respects, Heidegger. But how is this view different from the allegedly bad strategy of moral rationalism? In moral rationalism, it is claimed, "purely rational procedures" can, precisely, supply all the evidence needed to make the right decision as to "what one ought to do or what would constitute a just society" (W 22). So how does such a view stand in the way of making an authentic choice? For Kaufmann, the basis of decisions cannot be reason alone: rationalism falsifies the conditions of choice, which inevitably, really, are "tragic quandaries." Certainly, I'll add, Kaufmann's objection will need more evidence, implying, as it does, that the moral positions of both Kant and Heidegger, respectively, are untenable. We find better reasons in his later critique of the idea of justice—both retributive and distributive. This entire canon of strategies of avoidance—especially Manichaeism and moral rationalism—are then put to use when it comes to criticizing, very severely, the work of an opposing thinker, Herbert Marcuse, author of Repressive Tolerance, a book that argues for "intolerance against movements from the Right, and toleration of movements from the Left" (Manichaeism); furthermore, that "the distinction between liberating and repressive, human and inhuman teachings and practices . . . is not a matter of value-preferences but of rational criteria" (moral rationalism) (W 24).[14]

The names of the three remaining ploys for postponing decision are transparent to their meaning: pedantry (i.e., microanalysis); "riding the wave of the future," a strategy ignorant of caprice as a factor in history; and, finally—perhaps surprisingly—marriage. All three are No's accompanied, ultimately, by minor Yes's: not every pedant, future rider, or spouse has acted in bad faith. Since Kaufmann will soon cite the names of famous men and women who did decide authentically and autonomously, I will add Kafka to the mix, to complicate matters. Kaufmann cites Aeschylus's Prometheus and Clytemnestra, Heraclitus, Socrates, Goethe, Nietzsche, above all, and then: Eleanor Roosevelt. Enough said: many of these claims invite objections. If the hallmark of genuine decision is a tragic quandary, a brave contemplation of alternatives, what of the decision to maintain such a quandary short of the decision that would end it? Can it rightly be said of Kafka—and by his example countless others—that he *decided* to endure the anguish of deliberation for much of his life? He did not finally flee loneliness into marriage, though—true—not for want of trying. He did, however, debate the matter very clearly, drawing up reasons For and Against in neat columns in his diary, as if moral rationalism would come to his aid, concluding, perhaps with infinite irony, "And whatever you decide, you will regret," for this sentence is also a *citation* from Kierkegaard's *Either/Or*. A citation would make a mockery of moral rationalism.

Now, Kafka's state of affairs answers to Kaufmann's requirement that decision arise from severe concern: "The best one can do . . . is to bring these preferences out into the open, to state them honestly, and to consider objections and alternatives, [but] this is the last thing a decidophobe would want to do" (W 87). In Kafka's case, however, no superior decision could result from such an accounting. Kafka did not marry but in the end needed an eleventh ploy to save him decisively from marriage with Felice Bauer—that ploy is illness, alleged or real: in Kafka's case, lethal tuberculosis. He might be judged a partial decidophobe, but he does not fit under the head of any of Kaufmann's articles.

Kaufmann's attack on the idea of retributive justice is a keystone of his critique, especially since it entails the rejection of distributive justice as well. We can intuit his argument by looking to its conclusion: "Desert is incalculable"; our interest in designing proportionate punishment is inhuman (W 64).

Although "we cannot dispense with punishments . . . we should realize that punishments cannot be just . . . [and] that a less disproportionate punishment is not always morally preferable" (W 62). The last point needs an example: we can consider the fate of Adolf Eichmann. Kaufmann writes:

> Visiting on Hitler's leading henchmen at least some of the tortures to which they had subjected millions of people and all but putting to death these mass murderers again and again [waterboarding was still in its infancy in the 1960s and 1970s] would have been more proportionate to their crimes than hanging them. (W 58)

I will add that many deemed that locking Eichmann away in semi-isolation in a maximum-security prison would have been a more nearly proportionate punishment. That judgment, however, might also be considered a gesture of leniency, a provocation to ongoing neo-Nazi agitation, or a form of torture. If the latter, then it might be concluded that considerations on a "higher moral ground" did in fact prevail: Israeli law calls for the execution—and not life imprisonment—of those guilty of crimes against the Jewish people. Since Eichmann's verdict was the sole judgment of capital punishment ever produced by an Israeli civilian court, it is clear that the extraordinary difficulty of determining a proportionate, a *just* punishment for Eichmann threw the court into the sort of quandary that, following Kaufmann, the decidophobe prefers to avoid.

Kaufmann's plaidoyer for the repudiation of retributive justice proceeds by historical and logical analysis and citation from the Gospels, Dante, Kant, and Jefferson, among others, none of whom fares well. Behind his reflections, certainly, stands Nietzsche's discussion, in *On the Genealogy of Morals*, of the *historicity* of criminal retribution. Kaufmann is also au courant with his contemporary analysts (Foucault's *Surveiller et punir* [Discipline and punish] appeared in 1975, too late to be included). His next chapter, however, "An Attack on *Distributive* Justice," contains an extensive criticism of John Rawls's celebrated *A Theory of Justice*, which appeared in 1971 and helped to spur Kaufmann to bring his dissenting opinion into print.

History, Kaufmann observes, offers no support whatsoever for the alleged progress in the refinement of distributive justice. Historical notions of justice have rarely been made autonomously; tradition gives the rule to judgment, and tradition is often monstrous. He quotes a scene from the *Iliad* in which Agamemnon rebukes Menelaus for intending to take a Trojan prisoner of war and sell him for ransom: "No, let us not leave even one of them alive, down to the babies in their mothers' wombs—not even they should live. The whole people must be wiped out of existence and none survive to think of them or weep." Homer comments: "He turned his brother's heart, for he urged justice" (W 38).

There have been occasional advances. For Plato and the Hebrew prophets, justice is dictated by a higher, a "natural law"; the just man lives in conformity with the law. For Aristotle, justice is a *virtue*, although, thereafter, "justice is no longer primarily a virtue but rather a quality of punishments and distributions." This is the modern sense: "*justice consists of meting out to men what they deserve*" (W 38–39). But just desert—"the dream of proportionality"—as we have heard, remains forever incalculable, and the grotesque wars and genocides of the past century suggest that nothing has changed from the encouragements to slaughter (in the name of justice) that fill our ancient books and scriptures.

But where in this genealogy do we observe the emergence of the ethic of love and mercy in the New Testament, and why has it been omitted? As we expect from his earlier work, Kaufmann will not grant Christianity this distinction. "Many," he writes, "associate 'an eye for an eye' with the Old Testament and . . . believe that this conception of justice was transcended in the New Testament. Often one goes on to associate the former with justice and the latter with love. . . . Yet this sermon [on the Mount] is studded with promises of rewards and punishments, and the Gospels are punctuated by threats of judgment, damnation, and hell" (W 42–43).

In either case, following Paul Reiwald:

> Men were not even able to confine themselves to the law of talio, the law of eye for eye, tooth for tooth, which seems so primitive and barbarous to us. In truth, the principle of an eye for an eye, a tooth for a tooth, with which the Jews are occasionally reproached to this day because it is held to be typical of their God of vengeance, belongs with the great and decisive advances of humanity, as is now generally recognized in the world of scholarship. (W 44)[15]

Now, if we abandon the idea of retributive justice, since it cannot be applied fairly, do we then abandon the concept of punishment? No. We cannot do without punishment for a variety of reasons—but the concepts of *punishment* and *justice* need to be separated: punishment does not deserve the name of justice. Here, in brutal summary, is Kaufmann's list of nonnegligible reasons for punishment:

A penal code deters people from committing crimes not only (1) by engendering fear but also (2) by inculcating a moral sense ... (3) by informing ... [people] of what is forbidden ... (4) by preventing private vengeance, lynchings, and a general breakdown of order ... (5) by seeing to it that the breaking of the law does not become an invitation to other men to emulate the law breaker ... (6) by providing a safety valve for the unlawful desires that smolder below the surface and are fanned to the danger point by the commission of the crime.

He develops this point.

Many people have wanted to do what the criminal did but were kept from doing it by the law or by their conscience. ... The penal code provides an outlet for this criminal desire. He has killed someone, and now you—many of you—also want to kill? All right; kill him! ... Thus the desire for talion— for doing to the criminal what he has done to someone else—does not evidence any profound sense of justice or a primordial conviction that this is clearly what the criminal deserves. (W 54)

We can read an interesting recent confirmation of this idea: Robert Gewarth, the author of a biography of the Nazi mass murderer Reinhold Heydrich, was asked whether the Germans, after the war, had made things simpler for themselves by turning the perpetrators of the Holocaust into sadistic monsters.[16] Gewarth replied: "That is perfectly clear. If the perpetrators were from good bourgeois families, university graduates bent on bettering their social position, without perceptible psychological disorders, then suddenly *the perpetrators are a lot closer to one than one would like*" (emphasis added).[17]

Lest this list seem incomplete, Kaufmann describes further grounds for punishment.

(7) Punishment is often justified as a means of reforming the offender. ... (8) When the offender is humiliated, inconvenienced, made to suffer in turn because this is held to be some recompense for the offended party, we enter the realm of punishment. ... (9) Expiation is also form of recompense. ... (10) Finally there is the claim that *justice* requires retribution, and that justice is done when, and only when, the offender is punished. (W 54–55)

We know from the foregoing that this claim is dubious; it is this notion of a *just desert* that is untenable.

Kaufmann's conclusion does a good deal of the work in advance to prove the emptiness—and hasten the "death"—of *distributive* justice as well. The tenor of this argument is again the impossibility of producing rock-solid judgments, especially those that build on an infallible principle. One might think of Hamlet's retort to Polonius: "Use every man after his desert, and who should 'scape whipping?"[18] Following Kaufmann's train of thought, we will conclude that the implied answer to this rhetorical question—namely, "No man!"—is false: Hamlet leaves undiscussed the possibility of the exception, namely, the man or woman whose life (just?) falls short of meriting extreme pain and humiliation; and, even here, where the question calls for the answer "No man," it leaves undiscussed the appropriate quantity of suffering. Hamlet, of course, is not investigating retributive justice but is about to change the subject to distributive justice, adding: "The less they deserve, the more merit is in your bounty."[19] This conclusion, however, also leaves undiscussed the quantity, let alone the nature, of a proportionate bounty. Apart from the increase in the reputation or self-esteem of the giver, what would be the appropriate *reward* for a sadistic killer? Here, Hamlet would get no help from Dante—nor from Kaufmann, who claims: "The good and the evil [that] men receive cannot be said to be deserved" (W 70).

Kaufmann is bent *not* on destroying the idea of punishment ("whipping") or reward ("bounty"); both belong to the functioning of a well-ordered society. He is bent on destroying the decidophobe's confidence that in assigning these gifts, he has served justice. The decidophobe's exultant "Justice is done" spares him the genuine anguish—Kaufmann calls it the *humanity*—of having chosen among alternatives that he has invoked, studied, and deeply realized. "As we face up to choice to which many variables may be relevant, we have to decide which are relevant and how much weight to give to each. . . . That many mutually incompatible solutions are tenable is felt to be profoundly disturbing because *this* plurality calls for excruciating choices and engenders decidophobia" (W 68, 71). Confident that one has done "justice" is, in Kaufmann's strong sense of the word, not to have *decided* at all.

Perhaps the problem of just retribution—a just distribution of goods— could be solved on the assumption that all are equally deserving. But this would presuppose that all recipients *are* in some way equal. Now, how could that determination be made? On the basis of what they are by birth (or, perhaps, at the time of distribution, since the benefits of citizenship are in play); or what they have, or what they do, or what they need, or what they desire, or what they have contracted for, or what they *have* done? (W 73–75). Of course, such discriminations can be endlessly multiplied, but all stand in the way of the requirement of absolutely equal treatment (W 81).

Since the nonalikeness of the projected recipients of a bounty, especially in the matter of merit and need, is an obstacle to doing justice, the weaker principle of *equality of opportunity* might serve instead. But a moment's abstruse thought—done just ahead of us by Kaufmann—suggests the reductio ad absurdum of this "minimal prerequisite" for equality of opportunity—namely, "the abolition of the family." (We are quickly returned to earth on learning that "no more than about 4 percent of Israelis [in ca. 1970] choose to live in kibbutzim" [W 84].) Ergo, Kaufmann concludes, "giving the same to all is not particularly reasonable, seeing that they are not alike, do not have the same desires, and cannot use the same things or opportunities" (W 85).

Kaufmann's criticism of guilt begins with a poignant citation from Kafka's journals, in which Kafka describes the near-origin of his "profound sense of guilt." Addressing his father in a letter he never sent, Kafka writes: "From these many times when, according to your clearly manifest opinion, I deserved a thrashing but, owing to your grace, barely escaped it, I accumulated a profound sense of guilt" (W 98). The crux can be restated very plainly. The breeding ground of guilt is an unfulfilled expectation of punishment: something indefinably nasty will come your way, since, after all, "You've got it coming to you" (W 100). Is there any higher sort of justice at work or play in this scenario? Not at all. In the beginning of time, these scenes arose unsystematically: a parent or soldier or governor or priest says, "If you do this thing, you will be punished." And in the expectation that that promise will be fulfilled—though it may never be fulfilled—you will suffer guilt.

But let it be clear that there are no reasons here to claim that justice is being done beyond the acceptation of certain empirical practices, customary "commands and prohibitions." We are speaking now of a mythical time before law. Kaufmann takes pains to disagree with Nietzsche, who sees the origin of justice and guilt in the imposition of a law on a conquered people. Kaufmann writes, "Arguing against the theory that had sought the origin of justice in resentment [as advanced by John Stuart Mill], Nietzsche claimed that justice comes into being only after a 'stronger power' imposes a law to put an 'end to the senseless raging of *ressentiment* among the weaker powers that stand under it.'" Kaufmann objects. "The conclusion that 'just' and 'unjust' make sense only after 'the institution of *law*' is wrong. In childhood one acquires the notions of 'just' and 'unjust' without the benefit of laws; unsystematic prohibitions and commands, delivered *ad hoc* and coupled with spontaneous promises of rewards or punishments, suffice." The origin of guilt, and thereafter the general considerations establishing justice, lies in a speech act—a command and an attendant promise, namely, "what one is *told* is deserved or to be expected" (W 102). It is important that these scenes of origin do not involve notions of equality, since, let us say, "Priests, noblemen, and servants are not expected to perform the same acts, and are not treated alike if they do the same things.... Zeus marries his sister and rapes the daughters of kings as well as some kings' wives; but what is permitted to Jove is not permitted to an ox." Kaufmann gives us the pleasure of learning this adage in Latin for our personal use: *quod licet Jovi, non licet bovi*—still, however, to be employed with caution, since less and less, in recent years, "is it taken for granted that those in positions of privilege are like Jove" (W 103–4). Surely, equality is rather the justified rage.

The assumption of the death of God entails the death of any higher law assuring justice. Hammurabi's code, for one,

> provided that if a man should strike another man's daughter, and she died, "they shall put his daughter to death." Moses' sense of proportion was different, and that in the Law of Manu different again. Few of those brought up under these laws ever doubted that the penalties provided in them were proportionate, deserved, and just. And those raised to believe in hell rarely had any qualms about that. Indeed, St. Thomas proved at length how eternal punishments for temporal offenses were *not* disproportionate. (W 106)

Ideas of proportion, justice, and desert depend not on a Platonic idea of law but on secular authority. One might be inclined to dignify one's own intuition as law, but that is the delusion of tyrants. We have positive law, which we obey, but obedience is not entitled to take its high place in a court of justice. It is all over with guilt and justice. For, as Kaufmann's next chapter tells us,

> Without justice, there is no guilt. To say that anyone is, or feels, guilty is to say that he deserves, or feels that he deserves, punishment. Once it is seen that nobody *deserves* punishment [crucial emphasis in original], it follows that nobody is guilty or should feel guilty. (W 112)

Does this mean that no one is responsible for having done something wrong—something grievously wrong? Of course not. Or that punishment should always be withheld? The sticking point is whether anyone can confidently say that the criminal *deserves* his or her punishment. Again and again we realize how closely linked are the terms *justice* and *desert*—and the guilt or resentment that arises in the accused when these imaginary things fail to cohere or arrive when expected. It is time, claims Kaufmann, to let all these things die together.

There will be opposition to this idea—presumably along these three lines: (1) Guilt feelings are crucial to the moral health of the accused: they breed remorse. (2) Guilt feelings and remorse are *owed* to the injured party. (3) Most tellingly, "Guilt feelings are held to be necessary for the protection of society. Nobody can watch people all the time in order to keep them in line. Hence, it is held to be imperative for them to internalize punishment and to torment themselves when they do something immoral" (W 113). Here Kaufmann is willy-nilly reproducing the argument that runs through Stendhal's novel *The Charterhouse of Parma* (Stendhal is one of Nietzsche's acknowledged "educators"). It is the logic of the Catholic teaching that rules the (imagined) city of Parma. The city holds a vast citadel, in which culprits can be incarcerated, but there is not room for *everyone*. So, let inculcated guilt be their jailers.

There is *not* much to be said for guilt as contributing to the humanist project of studying man's lot in a clear-sighted, critical way. One would need to do away with the Buberian-Jewish, Christian, and existentialist-phenomenologist saving of sin—or its satellite, guilt—for its alleged inspiriting, normalizing, or authenticating function. For Buber, in one case, guilt and the possibility of atonement are the indispensable basis of becoming what one is. Christian thought equates finitude—everyman's—with sin and guilt. Jaspers and Heidegger see guilt as "constituting a summons to authentic existence." And so it is, writes Kaufmann, "high time for a full-fledged attack" (W 113–14).

The crux of the attack is that guilt mutilates the personality: "It makes men vindictive and inhibits the development of generosity." It is the enemy of honesty and truth, since "guilt feelings have no particular tendency to be proportionate to the wrongs they feed on" (W 115). Guilt retards enterprise, is besotted with the past: it would be much better if it were replaced by the active virtue Kaufmann terms "humbition."

You will not find "humbition" in the *Oxford English Dictionary*; it means "humility winged by ambition" (F 306). Kaufmann coined it, but it is quite wonderful to learn that it is now used, without attribution, by organizations that aim to teach *leadership in business*, including, quite Web-prominently, a major *Jesuit* academy. In his address to his students at Marquette University, Father William Byron S.J. observes:

> The leadership lesson to be derived from a consideration of the Third Degree of Humility can be explained by reference to a secular setting

completely unrelated to the context of Ignatian spirituality, namely, a back-office service company SEI Investments in Oak, Pennsylvania, where the word "humbition" is held up for praise and imitation. "At SEI, the most effective leaders exude a blend of humility and ambition—humbition—that relies on the power of persuasion rather than formal authority."[20]

Would that Walter Kaufmann had been alive in 2015 to comment on this contretemps (it is not unthinkable: he would be ninety-five)! He might temper his sarcasm with the generous thought that after all, as his very chapter suggests, a scholar might leave his cloister to write a book to raise individuals to a "higher level of existence" and thus benefit "humanity" without specification as to clan or cult. In effect, though, it would take a new Aristophanes to do full justice to this turnabout.

Humbition is only one of the cardinal virtues that Kaufmann reprises from his discussion of a humanist ethics in *The Faith of a Heretic*: the others are love, courage, and honesty. These virtues enter his discussion of the futility of guilt (though "keen regret" is acceptable) as alternative sources of energy (W 120). Perhaps a sense of guilt may inspire some reformers to campaign for improvements in society, but it comes with side effects, distorting vision and twisting the personality. Moreover, these effects do not stay dormant in the soul of the guilt-ridden man or woman but are easily spread to others, especially those with whom they act in concert or live in intimacy. Guilt is contagious.

It might be argued that a sense of guilt is a motive to take up arms to change an intolerable situation, but it is far more often merely an impediment. The soul of guilt is repetition, not the instinct for change. Taking stock of one's peccadillo or worse—noting its features, taking responsibility for it, and planning ahead to do the thing better is infinitely more efficient. Indeed, "a profound self-examination opens up for an advance to a higher level of existence" (W 124).

What is implied here is the absence of any firm line between what might be called moral failure and technical failure—or mistake. One's customary, and in the best case, reasonable response to a technical mistake is to correct it—not agonize over it and thereupon call one's worth into long-lasting question. It is easy to provide a rational justification for an attributed mistake (a "sin of technique"); in the case of inculcated guilt feelings, however, no rational justification is necessary—and in most cases would be impossible to provide. One has internalized the voice of an authority that derives his or her authority from an older authority whose source has long since vanished into a distant past. On the other hand, much can be said for the person with humbition:

> he has a conscience, but neither a good conscience nor a bad conscience. He cultivates self-criticism, finds fault with some of his past deeds and omissions, realizes that but for those deeds and omissions he would be a different person now, in a different situation, and accepts his present self and situation (and by extension also his past) provisionally—as the raw material of his future. (W 125)

At this point, Kaufmann introduces the compelling question of collective guilt. "The proposal to replace guilt feelings with humbition spells relief from some very painful confusion. When John F. Kennedy was killed, Americans were told from many sides—first by a Christian minister—that *all* of them were guilty. But they were not" (W 122). I take this strongly worded proposition to suggest how fiercely Kaufmann would have resisted the Goldhagen thesis that holds all Germans under Nazi rule to be murderous anti-Semites. In this context, Kaufmann attempts to address and strive to exorcise the guilt felt by the millions who survived World War II and realize how many others did not. It is obviously not a question of "earning the right to our survival"—note the personal pronoun—

> after the event. Desert is out of the picture. The world is capricious and cruel, and some of the most admirable human beings suffer hideously while many of the most unconscionable flourish. . . . A liberated human being redirects his thoughts and energy toward the future, toward a worthy project. . . . Humbition aims higher and asks to what extent our own particular experience might be turned to advantage. (W 129)

This *economic* concept of self-aggrandizement is integral to the Bildungsideal.

Early on we were promised a report of "*the case of the beautiful garden.*" Kaufmann is thinking of the glorious villa in which he is writing these lines, which prompts some immediate ethical concerns:

> Suppose you were offered a chance to live in a lovely place, in the middle of a large garden, with a view of lakes and mountains. You had no chores to do; the company was splendid, the food excellent. . . . If you had some project and wanted to write, that, too, could be easily arranged. Considering the condition of most of your fellow men, should you poison this paradise

with guilt feelings? It is the thrust of my whole argument that you should not, but that you would be lacking in humanity and love if you considered the situation quite unproblematic. I am against the good conscience and the bad, but not against having a social conscience. . . .

   This case is very similar to that of the survivor. It is a common mistake to think of either case as somehow quite exceptional. Every one of us is a survivor, and most writers and readers have always dwelt in gardens. Desert is a confused notion, and the world is cruel and capricious. The question facing us is what we are to do with the opportunities that come our way. . . .

   The best solution is to find a project that will benefit humanity, in line with your limited talents, and to make the most of your situation. If you can acquire or teach skills and knowledge in the garden or write books that may help others more than what you could accomplish outside, stay without remorse; and when you no longer can, leave without remorse. . . . Surely, self-criticism and a social conscience can survive the death of guilt. (W 130, 136)

Kaufmann advances to a plaidoyer for the autonomous state of mind, without ideas of guilt and justice, which entails *alienation*—it is an anti-Marxist brief, the superficiality of which has been criticized. But that felt shortcoming might be due to the fact that Kaufmann is not so much energized by his dispute with Marx as with other celebrated German Jewish émigré intellectuals, notably Hannah Arendt, Erich Fromm, and Herbert Marcuse, whose existentially-tilted Marxism he takes to task. He is curiously reticent about the Marxist critical theory of the Frankfurt School—of Adorno, Benjamin, Bloch, Horkheimer, Kracauer, and others: I cannot say why with any certainty except for Kaufmann's judging them as figures too recondite for his anticipated readership, although it would certainly have been interesting to see him address Adorno, who was little attracted to the humanist alternatives that figured in twentieth-century Marxist debates. Another reason for Kaufmann's reticence might also be the narcissism of small differences: they are German Jewish intellectuals of a different rhetorical stripe, who think and write in, so to speak, a different language.

   Kaufmann's prose, back-translated into German, with its pithy clarity, is nothing like the clotted mandarin beauty of the prose of the Frankfurt School. Clive James, no mean critic, it may be worth noting, took very little pleasure from the prose of Walter Benjamin, claiming that "the lowly journalism of others [namely, Alfred Polgar and Joseph Roth], then and since, leaves his [Benjamin's] paroxysms of verbiage sounding inarticulate."[21]

Of what use to Kaufmann's choice of targets is this remark in praise of journalists? I am thinking now of Karl Jaspers who, believing "how little Kaufmann understands of philosophy," allegedly called Walter Kaufmann a "journalist in philosophy."[22] To this offence my source, the Nietzsche scholar Geoffrey Waite, adds on: "Possible *attacco?*"[23] A good question. Following Clive James, it is no attack at all; it is a compliment. Stendhal, who is cited admiringly in Nietzsche's *Beyond Good and Evil*, demands that a proper philosopher possess the qualities of a banker's mind: "sec, clair, et sans illusion."[24] Kaufmann, who repeatedly recommends these qualities, might be held to share them with the very best journalist, but only in the sense that the latter is dedicated to "the things themselves" and must not be obscure in describing them (he must "avoid abstractness") (FH xv, 87). I think, with these caveats in mind, this argument can highlight the documentary clarity of Kaufmann's prose—which, furthermore, both in *Without Guilt and Justice* and *The Future of the Humanities*, is scathingly attentive to the here and now of American culture at the time of writing and is not reluctant to draw on newspaper articles for support. It is important to add, however, that Kaufmann would be only partially open to this flight of ideas: several pages of the chapter "The Politics of Reviewing" in *The Future of the Humanities* are devoted to a scornful indictment of the "journalists" Hannah Arendt and Edmund Wilson, whose names we are omitting from this more positive account of the good of newspapers. Finally, after all, in the mild dialectical ricorso with which we are familiar, Kaufmann writes: "Many men and women who are by profession journalists" might "contribute a great deal" to "the Socratic probing of the faith and morals of the age" (FH 24). We are not far from Kaufmann's professed ideal.

Kaufmann's discussion of alienation is dictated by the abundant use of the term in the days—the late 1960s—when this book was being drafted. In common parlance, the word sported a Hegelian-Marxist flair; Kaufmann cites Marx's *Economic and Philosophical Manuscripts of 1844*, which "stress alienation from one's work, from the product of one's labor, and from man's true nature or essence" (W 143). It is crucial, of course, to cure such alienation, but Marx's conceptual locus is not at all Kaufmann's. The early Marxist term had better be called "dehumanization": "Alienation," for Kaufmann, means the condition of felt strangeness to oneself and to others; it is the precondition of philosophical wonder. Such alienation does not ask to be cured but to be generally distributed.

If the two senses of alienation are confounded, then errors arise—the notions "that alienation is bad; that alienation is a distinctively modern phenomenon; and that alienation is a function of capitalism, or at least of advanced industrial society" (W 141). None of these propositions is true. For Kaufmann, alienation is the ineluctable condition of "self-consciousness, autonomy, and integrity." These features entail pain for the subject in a world that is, and has always been, an inexhaustible mine of dishonesty, capitulation, and deceit, which it behooves us to identify in a condition of alienation, the loss of which no amount of economic reform could ever make good. "The notion that those who are liberated from self-alienation in the Marxian sense will no longer suffer from *any* alienation is false" (W 147). Alienation is the beginning of freedom, and "no revolution or reform could make men free" (W 144).

We need more, not less alienation—as the precondition of philosophical wonder. I'll add, though, that more work needs to be done, and has been done, on the concept of alienation to distinguish it from the agitation, dementia, or sense of hopelessness that frequently accompanies it: it is not always an agent of productive change.[25] The workings out of distress may not be life-enhancing, for the patient or for others. Furthermore, if alienation is a productive detachment from the given, what work does the concept do that, say, "criticism" does not? The concept of alienation is desperately in need of further nuancing.

What would humanity look like if its exemplary members were not alienated? Kaufmann's reflections are anticipated in Ortega y Gasset's *The Revolt of the Masses*:

> The most radical division it is possible to make of humanity is that which splits it into two classes of creatures; those who make great demands on themselves, piling up difficulties and duties; and those who demand nothing special of themselves, but for whom to live is to be every moment what they already are, without imposing on themselves any effort toward perfection; mere buoys that float on the waves.[26]

Here is Kaufmann:

> It is those who are easily satisfied that we should worry about. . . . Where those who shut their eyes and lull their minds to sleep, as well as those reduced to brutishness in one way or another, find it possible to feel at home, the autonomous spirit who insists on keeping his eyes open to examine critically his own position and alternatives finds it impossible to feel at home. (W 146–47)

In defining alienation as "not being at home," Kaufmann is taking up and reabsorbing the neoromantic sensibility of several fin de siècle German poets—such as Stefan George (1868–1933), Rainer Maria Rilke (1875–1926), and Hugo von Hofmannsthal (1874–1929)—poets whom he knew well and whose poems he translated. Of myriad examples, there is the first Duino Elegy of Rilke, who, along with "the canny animals," is aware "that we are not really at home in our interpreted world." Behind these poets is Nietzsche, who makes it plain that not being at home can be more painful than an inducement to self-criticism:

The crows caw
And move in whirring flight to the city:
Soon it will snow,—
Happy is he who still—has a home!

Now you stand rigid,
Gazing backwards, oh! for so long!
Why, you fool,
Did you steal away into the world before winter?

The world—a gate/a fool
To a thousand wastelands mute and cold!
Whoever has lost
What you have lost, will never stop anywhere.

Now you stand pallid,
Cursed to winter wandering,
Like the smoke,
That always seeks colder skies.

Fly, bird, rasp out
Your song to the tune of a wasteland bird!—
Hide, you fool,
Your bleeding heart in ice and scorn!

The crows caw
And move in whirring flight to the city:
Soon it will snow,—
Woe to him who has no home![27]

And behind Nietzsche there is Goethe's Faust, whose cry continues to resound: "Bin ich der Flüchtling nicht? Der Unbehauste? / Der Unmensch ohne Zweck und Ruh" (Am I not fugitive without a home? / Inhuman; without aim or rest).²⁸ A more cogent translation of the key word "Flüchtling" is "refugee."²⁹

This citation of the poets suggests a relation between Bildung and the felt necessity of standing apart. Kaufmann is well aware of this link, noting that

> the sense of alienation has spread with the unprecedented expanse of education. . . . If the world and the societies we live in are, and always have been, abhorrent, brutal, and cruel, then it follows that the more one comes to know about them, the less can one feel at home in them. With an increase in self-consciousness and sensitivity, the sense of alienation deepens. (W 153)

At the same time, it is not surprising that Kaufmann would revise this half-truth by introducing the distinction between the depth and breadth of the sense of alienation. He revisits the specter of the half-educated: what of the "alienation" on the lips of the half-educated?

> While even the best education must increase alienation, some aspects of the modern sense of alienation are due to the *faults* of modern education. . . . Not only have vast numbers of pupils been exposed after a fashion to great art, great novels, and to the achievements of great scientists, but pupils have also been encouraged to believe that they can paint and write as well as anyone, or make brilliant experiments and great discoveries. But men are not equal in talents, and this well-intentioned but misguided egalitarianism has resulted in the vast growth of the sense of disappointment. (W 154)

Whether consciously or not, Kaufmann has taken up a meditation by the great Czech statesman and philosopher Thomas Masaryk, writing in 1881 on the "semi-educated,"³⁰ the gist of Masaryk's important book *Suicide and the Meaning of Civilization*:³¹

> At first, writing itself counts for him [Masaryk] as the indicator of the suicidal inclination of a given society. A simple factor like the national use of paper . . . points to a stage of development of the respective writing network of "schools, libraries, art collections, presses, book trades, means of commerce and communication for the exchange of ideas in general."³² This network is once more the modern milieu of that "dangerous" "middle education or, more properly, semi-education," which is "identical with an inharmonious, disunified, and unmethodical organization of the mind."³³ Semi-education stands in an unmediated relation with suicidal impulses,

for "knowledge which cannot be used makes its possessor a victim of fantasy, of hypercritical nonsense, destroying the desire for useful labor, creating needs that cannot be satisfied, and leading in the end to boredom with life."[34]

To return to the suffering—and the "profit"—of alienation, Kaufmann alludes to its reward via a passage from Freud's autobiography. Freud speaks of the anti-Semitism he suffered, which, however, taught him to "stand alone among the opposition." Kaufmann is very satisfied to see alienation as redounding to the Bildungsideal of aesthetic self-fashioning. As a "steppingstone to autonomy," Freud's confident renunciation of a home among the Volk is "a perfect example of fruitful alienation" (W 169–70).

I judge this perspective, however, to be an impermissible edulcoration of reality, a point that comes to the fore when Kaufmann criticizes *German Jewish* thinkers for failing to consider their "alienation" as personally "fruitful":

> For those who seized on Hegel's term "alienation" and made of it a *cri de coeur* and a word for all that was wrong with society were—virtually all of them—Jews. First, Marx; then, a century later, Georg Lukács and Herbert Marcuse, Erich Fromm and Hannah Arendt, to mention only the most influential. All of them were cast in the role of aliens, and the alienation thrust on them became a source of suffering for them. But they did not react like Freud. . . . *Instead*, they began to dream of some community in which there would be no alienation. (emphasis added) (W 166)

I also judge this proposition of Kaufmann to be extraordinarily insensitive to the individual fate and the different degrees of pain suffered by these exiles and the conceivable merit of their wanting to rectify the social insanity that lay at the source of their troubles rather than have their alienation contribute to the "autonomous" personality—in effect, on reflection, a naked impossibility.

Something of this impossibility is noted in a cogent, conscientious review of Kaufmann's book by the late Douglas Sturm, an activist professor of religion and political science, who writes,

> Decisions must be made. But the principle as principle is unaffected. It must be acknowledged that illiteracy, ignorance, malnourishment, poverty, and racism are obstacles to the full effectuation of due process and therefore to the full effectuation of personal autonomy. This means that if, as Kaufmann seems to be asserting, autonomy is a specifically human

goal given the human condition, then distributive justice, in the sense of assuring, so far as possible, that each person has access to those goods, services, and opportunities needed to make fateful decisions within the natural and social world, should be considered part and parcel of autonomous morality.[35]

As there are degrees of pain, there will be degrees of autonomy, nor is even a high degree of autonomy enough, since, as Kaufmann says—and not just to startle us—autonomy may be compatible with lying. The *new* integrity, which Kaufmann calls for, requires the cooperation of the four cardinal virtues—humbition, love, courage, honesty. This definition of "integrity" is "new," because it is no longer signifies a classical wholeness of personality. Indeed, the application of all four virtues can evidently lead to collisions fracturing wholeness; these virtues are not all compatible. Consider, for example, the honesty that threatens love. But honesty is crucial.

It is not easy to say what honesty is, but Kaufmann offers what he calls "the canon" of honest inquiry, "which commands us to ask seven questions; (1) What does this mean? (2) What speaks for it and (3) against it? (4) What alternatives are available? (5) What speaks for and (6) against each? And (7) What alternatives are most plausible in the light of these considerations?" (W 178). I think the most impressive element in Kaufmann's formulation of his ethic is the need to envision *alternatives*. This thrust informs the recurring pattern of his thought: a negation tempered by a weak affirmation or an affirmation tempered by a weak negation; but this pattern, while leaving a residue of uncertainty, nonetheless empowers one dominant judgment—a Yes or a No. "What matters is that one gives oneself an honest account of the grounds for one's beliefs, and that one makes a deliberate effort to overcome decidophobia. . . . Those who have the new integrity have intellectual integrity and also live in accordance with it" (W 179–80). Honesty is not the inevitable companion of autonomy; autonomy is not enough. All weight falls on honesty as the decisive contribution to the new integrity. Honesty is in every sense of the word canonical.

We watch Kaufmann worrying a corollary proposition: is autonomy consistent with happiness? He puts the question in an original setting: "Are liberty and the pursuit of happiness . . . compatible?" Surely not if you think that autonomy, which is free, and which enjoys its freedom, serenely exercises its powers of judgment from a position of uncontested strength. An *honest* autonomy wrestles with alternatives—and we are promptly reminded that all happiness is an affair of alternation with something entirely different: searing unhappiness, pain, or, finally, listlessness. The human sensorium—the moment of happiness needs untroubled senses—cannot sustain the same response to the same stimuli: "A state of mind marked by pleasure and the absence of all pain and discomfort *cannot* last" (W 208). When good excitement dwindles, it takes happiness with it.

The reader who stays all the way to the postscript of *this* book will encounter a relevant proposition—Kaufmann's reading of the will to power, which, bent on autonomy, "is, as it were, always at war with itself. . . . All that exists strives to transcend itself and is thus engaged in the fight against itself" (N 242). Autonomy is consistent with happiness only when both are defined by the tension of opposites—of alternative decisions or feeling-states. Considering "men as different as Socrates and Caesar, Beethoven and Goethe, and most of the famous generals, statesmen, philosophers, artists, poets, novelists, explorers, and discoverers whose lives continue to fascinate more ordinary men" and opposing them to "ordinary men," Kaufmann concludes: "Despair is to be found in both camps; among ordinary people it is chronic but covered by a thin crust of contentment; among the others it flares up occasionally with immense power, alternating with eruptions of no less intense joy." But the very fascination that links ordinary men to men of genius suggests "there is a continuum, and millions live far from both extremes." The continuum is the rhythm of the pain and then the lesser pain that we all suffer (W 212).

There is another element in this continuum: it is creativity. All men play, all men dream, but very few produce creative works that last. But that difference is not the point. Though the claim is admittedly unprovable, *all* men desire to prolong the creative impulses they had as children and continue to have as dreamers. This sort of creativity does not stand apart from personality and experience: works of high scholarly value—Kaufmann cites Thucydides and Gibbon—"reflect the authors' personalities and experience of life, and do not carefully avoid all normative judgments. They are models of *creative scholarship*" (W 227). It scarcely needs pointing out that this is Kaufmann's implicit path. Think of yourself as a *survivor*, and think of the responsibility that this privilege entails. It is an opportunity for intensity that you may not neglect. The right life boils down to what comes out alive from this most acute consciousness.

On reflection, Kaufmann's emphasis on consciousness (with the exception of a nobly conceived "quest for Nirvana") prompts at least one concern: he is attached to the goal of the most acute *self*-awareness and its inescapable corollary, self-*criticism*. He is also attached to the creative life—indeed, as the highest goal. Are these two flows compatible? Kaufmann sees no interference. "It is a romantic prejudice that a highly developed reason and a critical intelligence are not compatible with the creation of great art" (W 219). Yet "reason" and "critical intelligence" are the hallmarks of "the autonomous individual," who, in pursuit of the new integrity, practices relentless and "uninhibited self-criticism" (W 33). And so it is not a mere romantic prejudice to see these combinations as problematical. Would not the exercise of a *self-centered* critical intelligence obstruct a creative openness to new forms of life? Kaufmann elides the tension between a self that actively, critically, seeks itself; and a self, confident of itself, or unconcerned with itself, that leaves everything behind for the sake of the creative rapture. (Nietzsche noted apropos of Goethe the creator: If you need to seek your self, you will not find it; the game is already lost.[36]) Again, Yeats put this ordeal in "The Choice":

> The intellect of man is forced to choose
> perfection of the life, or of the work.[37]

Other critics have disputed other theses in this book: for one, that Kaufmann's account of Marx's concept of alienation ignores its full development. Kaufmann's Marx protests the loss of the human essence, the inevitable conclusion from a reading of the *Economic and Philosophical Manuscripts of 1844*. But given Kaufmann's failure to address *Das Kapital*, we hear nothing of Marx's rage against the social crime of distributive *injustice*.[38] Kaufmann's emphasis invites the commonplace "humanist" homily: "Erst kommt die Moral, dann kommt das Fressen" (Morality comes first, then comes feeding your face), an inversion of the Marxist Brecht's notorious "Erst kommt das Fressen, dann kommt die Moral."[39] A strongly worded paper by Sidney Hook, "In Defense of Justice (A Response)," attacks Kaufmann's destruction of the concept of distributive justice. Hook argues insistently that the impossibility of *absolute* justice, based on the claim of the *absolute* difference of persons, has no bearing whatsoever on the legitimate effort to apply reasonable criteria in practice. He writes (in italic): "*An equal distribution can be reasonably called just when, after intelligent inquiry, no apparently relevant differences exist among those who are the recipients of distribution.*"[40]

In a lengthy critique that deserves study, Douglas Sturm, whom I cited above, also argued that approximate justice can be done in the absence of absolute rules:

Few, if any, sophisticated theorists of justice in law or morality have been proponents of mechanical jurisprudence. It is unclear why one cannot appreciate the relativity of moral and legal systems, the open texture of rules, the difficulties of rule interpretation and application, the sense of what legal realists call "rule-skepticism" and "fact-skepticism," and yet make an effort to do justice understood as meting out to persons what they deserve.

Furthermore, the pursuit of autonomy (in lieu of respect for the "decrepit" concept of justice) cannot be done on an empty belly: "The more immediate question is whether, within the actual world, autonomous morality is possible in the total absence of procedural and distributive justice."[41] The sociologists Judith Buber Agassi and Joseph Agassi put the matter directly, addressing Kaufmann's "chief regrettable omission: the need of the autonomous individual for [a sense of] civic responsibility, including social and political concern and obligation."[42] (This is a point we discussed in chapter 1 while attending to the shortcomings of the Bildungsideal.) One might now ask: Which of Kaufmann's cardinal virtues, after all—humbition, love, courage, honesty—would prevent the man who stands above the consensus (think: the Übermensch) from expressing his most violent impulses?

Finally, in a scathing review, John Moran, a professor emeritus of philosophy, derides Kaufmann's casually assumed elitist pretentions. Few would disagree with his judgment on a passage from Kaufmann like this: "What makes people inauthentic (and what makes their talk of food and clothes and petty failures and successes so utterly pathetic) is not that they have forgotten that they must die before long. It is that they have forgotten that they are survivors" (W 231). "In the main," writes Moran, "what Kaufmann proposes are nostrums of auto-suggestion for mandarins yearning to be cavalier; while for 'those who see themselves as radicals and revolutionaries,' and join in comradely struggle to eliminate oppression and exploitation, he proffers a bad conscience: guilt feelings."[43] How fair are these diatribes *tout court*? Reader, the jury is out; you must decide. But taking Kaufmann's own words seriously, you cannot offend him: "I have never craved uncritical acceptance.... Affirmations without negations are empty, and I aim to present my views as alternatives" (FH xxl).

12

The Places of Religion

RELIGIONS IN FOUR DIMENSIONS:
EXISTENTIAL AND AESTHETIC,
HISTORICAL AND COMPARATIVE

There is no subject more important than religion.

—WALTER KAUFMANN

RELIGIONS IN FOUR DIMENSIONS: Existential and Aesthetic, Historical and Comparative, published in 1976, stands apart from the thrust and tone of Kaufmann's previous book, *Without Guilt and Justice*.[1] In many ways, as serious as the latter's subject matter is, it is a work of superior journalism—a personal, even egotistical book, (excessively) topical, all too attentive to the ideological and mass psychological minutiae of the day. Despite its long gestation, it can seem opinionated and hastily written, and Kaufmann must have felt, soon after, the need to compose a work of greater gravitas, not least in response to some of the critical reviews the earlier book received. Kaufmann's "philosophy," drawn from Nietzsche's *Gay Science*, reads: do not requite evil with evil, but not with charity and love either: it would merely confuse one's enemy. Try to conceive of the wrong done to you as a spur to betterment. Fail better.

In *Religions in Four Dimensions* Kaufmann turns to a vastly wider scene and subject matter with, above all, a strikingly different method—erudite commentary, yes, but also art photography and poetry—including 250 of his own photographs as well as dozens of his own poems, composed in the course of

378

journeying around the world in pursuit of his chiefest predilection—his "love child" (RE 13):

> There is no subject more important than religion. It involves the most fateful questions, to which different religions give different answers. . . . What I write about is not inconsequential notions that one might review and judge but the most fateful ideas that have deeply affected the lives of people. (RE 14, 19)

Behind this book are decades of study and reflection; the book itself is capacious and wide ranging. As it deals with "the lives" of no fewer than ten religions, including Zoroastrianism, Jainism, and Sikhism, among others better known in the West, and includes immense amounts of esoteric information, it would seem impossible to suit it to the narrative of *this* book, which until now has been entirely rooted in Western Judeo-Christian culture from its earliest beginnings to the best sellers of the 1970s. But it soon emerges, wonderfully, that Kaufmann's story of the growth of religions belongs essentially to the history of lands far west of the Far East. Kaufmann overturns Hegel's famous vision of the indefatigable march of the religious spirit from the East—from China to India—to Germany. The gorgeous hymn of Hegel's friend Friedrich Hölderlin, "The Ister" (an archaic name of the Danube), begins "We, however, sing from the Indus, / Arrived from afar." Hölderlin's tragic ode *Dichterberuf* ("The Poet's Vocation") begins: "The banks of Ganges heard how the god of joy / Was hailed when conquering all from far Indus came / The youthful Bacchus.[2] The Westering of the spirit is a powerful idea, but, in fact, the religious culture of ancient Israel predates Confucius and the Buddha by a millennium.

The direction of the march is not *always* constantly west to east. Buddhism may have affected some Jewish sects and the Gospels, and Indian thought may have influenced Plato. On the other hand, "What is obvious is surely that Islam has to be understood against the background of Judaism, Zoroastrianism, and Christianity; that religion in India owes little to China; and that Buddhism spread east from India, first to China and then to Japan. In Asia the movement of religions was mainly from west to east" (RE 18). That this movement is by and large Hesperidean *at its source* is a well-founded thesis that, incidentally, once again puts Kaufmann squarely in the way of Heidegger's path of thought.

We should begin at the very beginning. To the question of what is meant by "religion," Kaufmann refers insistently to *experience*—religion at its core is a type of religious experience (tautological); it is a type of existential experience (what experience would not be "existential"?) (RE 13). We are returned to the dispute profiled in our chapter 7 concerning Kaufmann's anthology of religious writings. Susan Sontag argued that several of the texts selected by Kaufmann made sense only in a contemporary atmosphere of "piety without content, religiosity without either faith or observance." The qualifier "religious," she continued, is empty in general, as was Kaufmann's use of the word.[3] "Religious" can mean only one thing: You are a member of this or that church, faithful to its tenets and its observances. Only experience within this frame counts as religious. But Kaufmann's stance opposes hers . . . and is consistent. As early as 1958, in his *Critique of Religion and Philosophy*—as he reminds us—he wrote that "the importance of beliefs was widely overestimated, that theology was one of the worst aspects of religion, and that"—as we have often heard—"it was wrong to dissociate religion from experience" (RE 14).

What, then, is the specific character of the religious experience unique to Kaufmann at this time of writing and from which, with the help of his exceptional memory, he will address the religious experience of others? It can be approached by subtractions. It is religion (by and large) without theology, without metaphysics, without dogma, and, above all, without the assistance of the clergy. It is, I conclude—following his first, quietly intimated mystical experiences in college and thereafter his break with organized religion— chiefly the intellectual, visual, and emotional experience of an immersed *study* of religion (see chapter 7). Even as mediated, vicarious experience, it does not lack for intensity. It is fueled by Kaufmann's passion for history, for ideas, for forms involved in the great religions conveyed by books and material traces and works of visual art and architecture. It is, furthermore, the experience of religions as the virtual intersection of four dimensions—crucial points in the subject matter and protocols of the four disciplines given in the title of this work: aesthetic, historical, comparative, and existential (the latter answering especially to a sense of crisis, intimacy, and commitment). Kaufmann's encounters in the field—relayed in this book in commentary, poetry, and photographs from the very cradles in the Near and Far East where the major religions grew—animate, indeed set ablaze, for him and us, these four dimensions of religion. His sense of religious experience is embedded in these many explorations and reports.

Kaufmann knows, as does the reader, that, in the words of Wayne Proudfoot, "If the distinguishing mark of the religious is that it is assumed to elude natural explanation, then the labeling of the experience as religious by the subject includes the belief that it cannot be exhaustively explained in naturalistic terms."[4] The closest Kaufmann comes to such an explanation is the experience of being intimately addressed through art and literature by an ego-transcendent being as a Thou/You: both entities address and feel addressed by each other. The encounter has the aura of "the numinous." But this book of religious discovery marches, in both senses of the word, with its feet on the ground. Its motto is to endorse the expression "religious experience" without exceptional meticulousness of description in order to make a beginning,[5] viz., "It involves the most fateful questions, to which different religions give different answers" (RE 14). In what follows—a compendium, inevitably subjective in its choice of materials—I can only suggest the wealth of historical detail and engaging images and verses packed into it.

A sympathetic critic, the Harvard-educated, ecumenical-minded Jewish conservative scholar Jacob Agus, finding Kaufmann's book, in good Horatian, "challenging to the mind and pleasing to the eye," also stressed its "wealth of interesting data" that, for him, "illustrate the slow and agonizing ascent of mankind along the many and diverse paths winding tortuously toward the summit of 'the mountain of the Lord.'"[6] This is the sort of dizzying enthusiasm that the volume can elicit in the receptive reader. Christian critics of this book, as we will see, will have very little of this: in their view of Kaufmann's presentation, there is but *one* path winding—not all too tortuously—to the summit, and that is Judaism, with the Christian path, to speak with Kafka, less of a highroad than a tightrope slung along the ground. The articulate pastor Elijah White, objecting to Kaufmann's celebration of Judaism at the expense of Christianity, concludes that without the core teaching of "the grace of Jesus Christ" (never mind Kaufmann's generous attribution to Christianity of "ethical ardor"),[7] Kaufmann's Jewish-inflected humanism will expire in the poverty of its supports. For all of Kaufmann's "brilliance," White writes, "it is trapped in Goethe's three mindsets simultaneously: the Weltschmerz of *Young Werther*, the Shelleyesque defiance of *Prometheus*, and the pessimist-despite-himself of *Faust II*. As with most romantics and many humanists, neither people nor their religions finally live up to Kaufmann's aspirations for them."[8] It is not clear how the implied superiority of the Christian complement to Judaism follows from this conclusion.

Kaufmann ennobles the Old Testament: its conception of the one transcendental God is an achievement whose originality, Kaufmann declares, is beyond dispute. There is nothing like it earlier in ancient Egypt. Today these propositions need a great deal of qualification: there is the pharaoh Akhenaten's monotheism to reckon with (see chapter 6). The Old Testament contains echoes of the earlier Babylonian Code of Hammurabi (ca. 1700 BC), but the echoes are mainly there as laws to be modified or contradicted. "The words of the ancient, pre-Mosaic law of talion," for example, "are employed to announce the new principle of equality before the law" as in Leviticus 24, which insists on "one law for the stranger and for the native" (RE 31). Here, and throughout much of his work on comparative religion, Kaufmann holds "the essence of the religion of the Old Testament" to be a wholly revolutionary relation of God to man.

> This religion is not metaphysical, not speculative, not mythical: it does not concern itself with the nature of God . . . [or] speculate about his activities before the creation of the world or, quite generally, insofar as they do not affect man. . . . The religion of the Old Testament is concerned with God only as a Thou or You, only as related to man, only as addressing men and as addressable by man. His deeds are a subject of concern and related only insofar as they constitute an address to man. . . .
>
> This conception of this God and his relation to man leads to a revolutionary new conception of man. Neither man in general nor any kind or race of men is a brother or cousin . . . of any other animal or object in nature. (RE 41–42)

This passage evokes the definition of liberal humanism earlier proposed by Catherine Belsey: "Man, the center and hero of liberal humanism, was produced in contradistinction to the objects of his knowledge."[9] She is referring to the constitution of the type in Renaissance drama. In Kaufmann's vision, Judaism already includes such a liberal humanism.

This vision is admirable, but, as Kaufmann puts it, "logic is the weak side of history." At the moment that the Declaration of Independence, inspired by biblical sources, was proclaiming the "self-evident" truth of the equality of all men and their entitlement to life, liberty, and the pursuit of happiness, its author—Thomas Jefferson—could take stock of his hundreds of slaves (RE 42). Admittedly, at the same time, Jefferson was conscious of this appalling conflict of values and again and again sought a remedy.

The Old Testament discusses the treatment of slaves, although "there is no Hebrew word for 'slave' other than *ewed*, which means 'servant.'" (RE 42). Kaufmann sees indications of the decision to abolish even such servitude. However, it is perfectly evident that the Old Testament also includes expressions of inhumanity—much worse, passages of insensate cruelty, as in the book of Joshua, "which relates the conquest of Palestine and ascribes to God the command to slaughter 'both men and women, young and old, oxen, sheep,

and asses, with the edge of the sword'" (RE 46). Add on the Hebrew God's
genocidal imprecation against the Amalekites, as told by Samuel to Saul:

> Thus saith the LORD of hosts, I remember that which Amalek did to Israel,
> how he laid wait for him in the way, when he came up from Egypt. Now go
> and smite Amalek, and utterly destroy all that they have, and spare them
> not; but slay both man and woman, infant and suckling, ox and sheep, camel
> and ass. (1 Samuel 15:1–3)

With such madness in mind, it becomes difficult to calmly absorb Kaufmann's
claim, which is not false, that "no other sacred scripture contains books that
speak out against social injustice as eloquently, unequivocally, and sensitively
as the books of Moses and some of the prophets" (RE 42). There is another
stumbling block, internal to Kaufmann's thought: How does his extolling the
idea of social justice in the Hebrew Bible square with his repudiating, in his
previous book, the "decrepit" idea (of justice)?

What continues to be cogent is the way the Hebrew Bible does not exult in
the humiliation of a class of man, *among the Hebrews*, just as it does not exult
in the divinization of a single man. This teaching is "one of the most extraordinary facts about the religion of the Old Testament and by far the most important reason for the Jews' refusal to accept Christianity and the New Testament"
(RE 43). Kaufmann did elaborate this point earlier in *The Faith of a Heretic*.[10]

He does not omit the vexatious ascription to the Israelites of "the chosen
people," an epithet that became a cudgel in the hands of their enemies inflicting tremendous harm. It has never been, even remotely, a source of complacent pride, since

> the conception of the chosen people is inseparably linked with the twin
> ideas of a task and of an especially demanding law: . . . maintaining and
> spreading what has been revealed to them, namely, the belief in God and
> the morality that goes with it. And that is why [despite the godly ordained
> destruction of generation after generation] a remnant shall return, lest the
> flame be extinguished entirely. This theme runs through the books of the
> ancient Hebrew prophets—and beyond that, through most of the Hebrew
> Bible (RE 46–47)—

and, I will add, beyond that, through most of the tragic literature of the West.
This conception persists. It is a ruling idea that has never lost its efficacy. It is
the idea of tragedy. Horatio, at the close of *Hamlet*, will tell "the yet unknowing
world" for the lesson they will draw:

How these things came about: so shall you hear
Of carnal, bloody, and unnatural acts,
Of accidental judgments, casual slaughters,
Of deaths put on by cunning and forced cause,
And, in this upshot, purposes mistook
Fall'n on the inventors' heads: all this can I
Truly deliver.[11]

His aim is that a remnant endure, armed against sin, "lest more mischance /
On plots and errors, happen." At the conclusion of his *Doctor Faustus*, Thomas
Mann, having recorded the destruction by the Nazis of an entire generation, and
anticipating a Jewish destiny of persecution for the surviving Germans, pursues
a biblical inspiration—from the Old and the New Testaments—for affirming a
remnant of hope. There is hope of a remnant, if only a remnant of hope.

Hope "for us" is a matter different from proselytization: throughout their
history, the Jews have been indifferent convertors of other people of other
religions—a fact that has been turned into a criticism. In reality, however,

> when it was feasible, the Jews made proselytes—in the Roman Empire,
> among the Khazars in the Crimea, and elsewhere. But it is harder to per-
> suade men to submit to circumcision than it is to baptize them; it is harder
> to convert to the law than to trust in grace; and those who demand works
> will always make fewer converts than those who stress faith and the remis-
> sion of sins. (RE 48)

That Jews do not divinize their great men is consistent with a lesser principle running throughout the Hebrew Bible—an antimonarchical strain. This
tendency "was not lost on such close students of the Old Testament as Cromwell and Milton." In the beginning, there is no state—Paradise has no officers.
The state "originates within history; it is not the natural condition of man."
The book of Judges adverts to early days, when "there was no king in Israel;
every man did what was right in his own eyes" (RE 49). Throughout the Old
Testament, you find resistance to the idea of the state and any mode of sovereign rule. According to the first book of Samuel, in Kaufmann's extreme but
accurate paraphrase, "The institution of human kings . . . and the establishment of a state after the model of 'all the nations' is considered as a betrayal of
God." Today we know this resistance as the refusal of Jews of the Haredi sect
to acknowledge the legitimacy of the state of Israel: there may be one ruler
alone, and that one is God.

The Hebrew Bible does not deny all value whatsoever to the state or to king-ship. But the Hebrew Bible consistently denies any claim of the supremacy of the state in human affairs or of the superiority of kings as such. Above the state and king and any government there is a higher moral law by which states, kings, governments, and any laws that they enact are to be judged. The influence of this idea can hardly be overestimated. (RE 50)

Under what higher power or law might good men then be governed? That law is crystallized in the famous sentence of the prophet Micah (ca. 800 BC): "He has told you, man, what is good and what the Lord requires of you: only to do justice, to love mercy, and to walk humbly with your God" (RE 50–51). Kings and commoners alike are subject to this higher demand. Here, we approach the core Hebrew conception of an ideal soci-ety, one "in which the poor, the orphan, the widow, and the stranger are treated with special consideration; a society in which justice rolls down like water, and righteousness like an ever-flowing stream; a society based on justice, mercy, and humility." In the visionary verses of Isaiah, in "the word of the Lord from Jerusalem . . . they shall beat their swords into plowshares, and their spears into pruning hooks; nation shall not lift up sword against nation, neither shall they learn war any more" (RE 52). It must still be noted, however, in counterpoint to the antistatism of the Jewish tradition, that the Hebrew Bible does contain models of Jewish statehood, which were often invoked at the time of the founding of the state of Israel. Yael Tamir describes several

> religious understandings of the state . . . [that appeal to] earlier non-
> messianic authorities, well known from Jewish history. These authorities
> are basically of three sorts: the non-Davidic kings of Israel; "the good men
> of the town" (berurim) [lay leaders whose authority came from the com-
> munity]; and the Gentile rulers of the lands of the exiles. Each of these was
> religiously sanctioned.[12]

It is vital to Kaufmann's story of the Jews to consider ancient Persia, the birth land of Zarathustra (ca. 600 BC), the prophet of Zoroastrianism: his teachings are contemporary with the second Isaiah and were well known to the Jews. Zarathustra himself is a contemporary of "the Jina [the 'Conquerors,' the first enlightened exemplars of Jainism] and the Buddha—and perhaps also of Confucius, who was born in 551" (RE 55). Zoroaster was the teacher of the Per-sian king Darius I, builder of Persepolis; moreover, his teachings—essentially a dualism—influenced Christianity and Islam as well, the latter two to a far greater degree than Judaism (RE 56).

Zarathustra speaks in his own right, in what appear to be not overly complex formulations, in the seventeen hymns of the Gathas, which in their linguistic detail have nonetheless baffled translators. But their key tenets, "revelations of his god Ahura [Lord] Mazda [Wise]," signal an evident advance over the "polytheism and animal sacrifices" of his ancestors. The most important of the Gathas is the often-cited Yasna 30, "which has been called 'The Twin Gatha,' because it pictures the two spirits [the Holy One and the Evil One] as twins" (RE 57). Kaufmann quotes these 66 lines in full, in his translation; here are two key passages:

> 4. These two spirits met in the beginning
> and ordained life and death
> and that in the end the worst
> existence should await
> the followers of the Lie,
> and the best mind the fighters for Truth.

> 11. When you remember, O man,
> the commandments of Mazda—well-being
> and suffering—enduring torment
> for the followers of the Lie
> and salvation for the fighters for Truth,
> all will be well henceforth.

The dualism that speaks of two great principles—one good and one evil—and asks us to side with the good and fight against evil—is, for Kaufmann, the opium of simple minds. It is a reprehensible beginning for ethical thought: "It hallows hatred, glorifies an inhuman self-righteousness that denies the enemy all moral qualities, and assures those who oppose the wicked of a glorious final triumph" (RE 57).

It may not be idle to see this standpoint as having crystallized in Kaufmann's war experience as a German Bildungsbürger *and* an American Army interrogator: a poem cited earlier in the introduction told of Kaufmann's moral turmoil at the behavior of the army of occupation.[13] He was not about to take one or the other side absolutely, the "other" being the view of the Germans, identified with the British diplomat Robert Vansittart, "as a 'race' that had blinded the world about its true militaristic character by a 'side-show of German literature, medicine, music, philosophy.'"[14] The poem makes the point that Kaufmann was not attached to the mores of one nation, culture, or religion. Charged with excessive pity for a corrupted people or ingratitude to his host country, he would reply that the right position would depend on a measured understanding of the claims of both parties—neither one all Truth or Lie.

There is also, of course, a Nietzschean dimension to Kaufmann's aversion to a moral dualism. It is not always asked why Nietzsche should have titled his prophetic book *Thus Spoke Zarathustra*. This naming would appear to make no sense, Nietzsche and Nietzsche's prophet being arch antidualists. Nietzsche's masterstroke is to conjure a new, transfigured Zarathustra, preaching an inverted Zoroastrianism, for Zarathustra must be made to "take back" "this most calamitous error," his belief in categories of good and evil that are objectively founded and wholly divided. "The self-overcoming of [such] morality, out of truthfulness . . . that is what the name of Zarathustra means in my mouth."[15]

Zarathustra's eschatology divides evildoers from doers of good in the starkest way imaginable: "Immortal shall be the soul of the follower of Truth, but enduring torment awaits those who cleave to the Lie" [Gatha 45:7]. This endless distribution of pain and bliss after death is, for Kaufmann, Zoroastrianism's enduring legacy to Christianity. What follows is his familiar excoriation of Christian representations of hell and especially the enjoyment that awaits the saved who, from their heavenly loge, will savor the spectacle of the damned on fire, but here he overstates his case: "Christian attempts . . . to picture the rewards of goodness have rarely got beyond such phrases as listening to angels who play on harps or—at a higher level of sophistication—being close to God" (RE 60). This claim ignores Dante's *Paradiso*, for one, or the musical "attempts" of Bach and Mozart, among countless others, to conjure a sense of higher enjoyment. Kaufmann's anti-Christian philippic in the midst of his discussion of Zoroastrianism feeds the indignation that riled his Christian reviewers.

There is no tempering, however, his indignation at what Nietzsche termed "morality," the dualistic worldview that sees all of human history as a clash between good and evil, which then becomes a scourge inflicting a corresponding fate forever:

Moses and the prophets had developed a religion that was centrally concerned with ethics and left no room whatsoever for torture either in this life or in the hereafter; indeed they did not recognize any hereafter. Christianity and Islam followed Zarathustra in dividing humanity into two camps—the followers of the Truth and the Lie—and in looking forward to the eternal bliss of the former and the eternal torment of the latter. This moral and eschatological dualism became central in the New Testament and in the Koran. (RE 62)

Unlike Nietzsche, Kaufmann will not praise Zoroaster for his truthfulness. There is little truth in the "third pillar" of Zoroastrianism—the ritual ingestion of "the fermented juice of a plant called Haoma." Kaufmann comments: "This sacrament provided a royal road to salvation, and the juice itself—like *Soma* in the Vedas—was considered divine. As a god, it is Ahura Mazda's son." Kaufmann quotes the (fascinating) scholar-adventurer Robert Charles Zaehner: "In the ritual, the plant-god is ceremonially pounded in a mortar; the god, that is to say, is sacrificed and offered up to his heavenly Father. . . . After the offering, priest and faithful partake of the heavenly drink, and by partaking of it they are made to share in the immortality of the god. . . . The conception is strikingly similar to that of the Catholic Mass" (RE 62).[16] Kaufmann elaborates Nietzsche's claim of Zarathustra's truthfulness, inverting it, even with recourse to Nietzsche:

> Section 46 of Nietzsche's *Antichrist* . . . ends: "The noble scorn of a Roman, confronted with an impudent abuse of the word 'truth,' has enriched the New Testament with the only saying *that has value*—one which is its criticism, even its *annihilation*: 'What is truth?'" What did Jesus say in John 18? "I have come into the world, to bear witness to the truth. Everyone who is of the truth hears my voice." Whereupon "Pilate said to him, 'What is truth?'" Jesus' use—or abuse—of the word "truth" in this passage is surely entirely Zoroastrian, and it wholly misleading to say [as Nietzsche writes] that Zarathustra "posits truthfulness as the highest virtue." Zarathustra assumed that those who were persuaded by him and followed him were followers of the Truth and would be rewarded, while those who did not were followers of the Lie and would be tormented in all eternity. (RE 63)

The redeeming feature of Zoroastrianism after the death of the prophet Zoroaster is its vision of a final triumph over the Lie. "The vision of the final triumph became more humane than the vision of Zarathustra had been and than that of Jesus was to be." Zoroastrianism elaborates a principle of salvation *for all men*, quite in contrast with steadfast Christian doctrine (RE 64).

We have had "logic as the weak side of history." Now, in a nice fusion of esoterica and aphoristic elegance, we have the irony of the prophet Mani, for "the history of religion is full of ironies." Kaufmann observes that "Zarathustra's dualism is now chiefly remembered as the central doctrine of Manichaeism. Indeed, this dualism is not only considered the quintessence of Manichaeism but virtually synonymous with Manichaeism—although Mani, the founder of Manichaeism, was martyred by Zoroastrian priests" (RE 64). One remembers Manichaeism in its heyday chiefly as the religion that ensnared Augustine and which he violently repudiated. Its persuasiveness for him was not accidental: this religion was widely accepted in Egypt and Syria; and "in the East, Manichaeism spread to Samarkand, Tashkent, and beyond central Asia to China. The planets have Iranian names in China, and it has been surmised that Manicheans may have introduced China to the Western planetary calendar" (RE 69). Manichaeism, for Kaufmann, "is really a form of Gnosticism" . . . the latter generally understood, following the scholar John Gordon Davies, as claiming

> to mediate a gnosis of knowledge that would bring salvation. . . . It affirms a complete antithesis of spirit and matter; it postulated a primordial catastrophe in heaven when the original man fell and his being was shattered into a myriad fragments. These elements were seized upon by demons as nuclei to create a world out of the chaos of darkness, and they still survive as the souls of men. Although stupefied and held in bondage by the evil powers, they yearn to ascend to their former home in eternity. The supreme deity, who is at an infinite distance from evil matter, takes pity on these imprisoned sparks of light and sends a savior, who descends to overcome the demons and ascends in triumph.[17]

Hence, Manichaeism has also come "to mean a radical dualism that see history as a perennial contest between the children of light and the children of darkness" (RE 68).

I'll note that there is nothing solid to say against this association of Gnosticism and Manichaeism, since "Gnosticism" has never been a single set of doctrines; and it is represented in Kaufmann mainly in its second-century form—antithetically. The category *gnostikos* first appeared circa 180 in the polemics of Irenaeus of Lyon and the pseudo-Tertullian in the course of a general harrying of writers like Valentinus and Marcion as heretics. Until the Gnostic scrolls found at Nag Hammadi in 1945 (which Kaufmann does not mention), the Gnostic visionaries, and their teachings, existed only as these scapegoats of second-century heresiologists. We know it differently now; and what we know so complicates the figure of

the "demons," and hence the story of "evil," that, as Michael Williams proposes, in his *Argument for Dismantling a Dubious Category*, "Gnosticism"
had better be termed "Biblical demiurgical" thought.[18] The demiurge is
no longer systematically malevolent. This understanding actually loosens
the connections between Gnosticism and Manichaeism.[19] But this point
is not finally crucial to Kaufmann's concern, which is to allude to "the
many 'Manichean' elements in the New Testament, including the antithesis of flesh and spirit, while [the Manicheans] repudiated as a falsification of Jesus' teaching whatever did not agree with their own doctrine"
(RE 69–70). With this flourish, neither religion satisfies the moral complexities of real, living human life.

It is interesting, by default, that Kaufmann does not mention the political
philosopher Eric Voegelin's view of Nietzsche as an avatar of Gnostic thinking.
In *The New Science of Politics* (1952) and *Science, Politics, and Gnosticism* (1962),
Voegelin argued that Nietzsche was a secular—and catastrophic—vessel of
Gnostic thought, having sought to "immanentize the eschaton."[20] (In Christian theological diction "eschaton" means the "divinely ordained climax of
history."[21]) According to Voegelin, Nietzsche's project of transhumanizing the
earth in summoning up a race of *Übermenschen*—"die Herren der Erde (the
masters of the earth)"—counts as an "immanentization" of the Gnostic ideal.
This immanentizing of a perfect world order is enabled by the illumination
that guides an elite at war with the unlawful ordering of the world. This gnosis
provides a springing-off point for world reform. Here are, for Voegelin, "the
six characteristics ... of the gnostic attitude ... : (1) The gnostic is dissatisfied
with his situation ... ; (2) [believing] that the drawbacks of the situation can
be attributed to the fact that the world is intrinsically poorly organized. ...
(3) Salvation from the evil of the world is possible ... (4) [if] the order of
being ... [is] changed in a historical process ... (5) a change ... possible
through man's own effort ... (6) [to] a perfect one ..., the task of the gnostic
[being] to seek out the prescription for such a change ... [and] come forward
as a prophet who would proclaim his knowledge about the salvation of ... self
and world."[22] Nietzsche, for Voegelin, is this prophet. This picture would have
little in common with *Kaufmann's* Nietzsche, master psychologist and skep-
tic of any gnosis higher than *artistic* inspiration. (Cf. once more, *Ecce Homo*:
"Has anyone at the end of the nineteenth century a clear idea of what poets of
strong ages have called inspiration?"[23]) But Kaufmann's view of Nietzsche as
superartist marginalizes, for Kaufmann's critics, Nietzsche's bigger, upending
world-historical visions of reform.

In a book titled *God Interrupted: Heresy and the European Imagination between the World Wars*, which I mentioned earlier, Benjamin Lazier unfolds the Nietzschean implication of the "return" of the Gnostic worldview: it became a compelling subject for a number of important modern German thinkers (among them, Hans Jonas, Leo Strauss, and Gershom Scholem). They tend to reduce the Gnostic worldview to an absolute dualism of earth versus divinity. In this respect, Lazier shows Jonas to be one with Voegelin in seeing Nietzsche as the thinker of man without God, bereft of the Gnostic "absconded God": he is the *homo absconditus*. Jonas takes this "concept of man" to be "characterized solely by will and power—the will for power, the will to will. For such a will even indifferent nature is more an occasion for its exercise than a true object." Jonas's thrust is explicitly anti-Nietzschean.[24] But the subject of Nietzsche and Gnosticism is a wide, engaging field that would divert us from the matter at hand, which is "the Jews since Jeremiah."

This book of Jeremiah, conceived during the Babylonian exile, is a great poetry of suffering. "A later age ascribed to Jeremiah not only his own book but also the Book of Lamentations over the destruction of Jerusalem" (RE 72). A people conquered by a people of another religion might be tempted to bring their devotion to the conquering deity—Marduk and the several deities of the Babylonians or the Zoroastrian "bible" of their liberators, the Persians under Cyrus. "Consider," wrote Kaufmann, "Plato's contempt for democracy after Sparta had defeated democratic Athens"; or—somewhat surprisingly—"the attitude of the Japanese toward the West after their defeat in 1945" (RE 72). The surprise of a naked contemporary political reference in the middle of a novel—here, a personal, pictorial encyclopedia of world religions—which Stendhal likened to a "pistol shot a concert," is not the first such instance in this book.[25] Earlier Kaufmann contrasted the ethic of Hammurabi's law—"the man who accuses another of murder and then cannot prove his charge is put to death"—with that of Senator Robert A. Taft, who encouraged Senator Joe McCarthy "to go on making his accusations, in the hope that 'if one case doesn't work out, another may'" (RE 32).[26] But the major narrative drives on: the Jews kept their faith in the one god, "who makes peace and creates evil" (Isaiah 45:7), "resisting Zarathustra's dualism much more successfully than the other people of the Near East" (RE 72). The subtext is by now a familiar refrain. Meanwhile, Kaufmann's impulse to include *every* association on his mind at a given moment of his writing informs all his later work—it was already prominent, as I've suggested, in *Without Guilt and Justice*.

If the eloquence of Jeremiah is very great, the so-called second Isaiah none-theless surpasses it: "It is arguable that since his death the world has not seen a religious poet or prophet who could brook comparison with him" (RE 73). His marvelous verses are familiar as the main text of part 1 and the opening text of part 2 of Handel's *Messiah*. In chapter 53 Isaiah speaks of a man of suffer-ing, "despised and shunned by men," on the strength of which Jesus's passion was imagined. "Christians have long read passages like these as prophesies of Christ," but "we cannot know whom the prophet meant" (RE 75).

The prophet Ezekiel introduces a new strain into the Hebrew Bible—"apoc-alyptic books that describe visions of things to come." Here is vivid evidence of Zoroastrianism's penetration—yet one that Kaufmann declares finally marginal to an older, well-established, "imposing" literature. We will not be surprised by Kaufmann's commentary, which celebrates Judaism's resistance to the "galloping eclecticism of the Near East." "We find three or four verses that suggest some sort of afterlife or resurrection, and no development at all of the 'Manichean' theme of heaven and hell." The nearly complete refusal by the Jews of these tropes is "almost incredible," a source of wonder. What persists is a "normative" Judaism established by a definite "taste" for what deserves to be included in the Hebrew Bible and what not: that taste had been "formed by Moses and the prophets—the great prophets from Amos and Hosea, Isaiah and Micah, down to Jeremiah and the Second Isaiah. The apocalyptic literature in which the influence of Zarathustra's eschatology is undeniable" remains a "fringe phenomenon" and owes its survival to a Christian embrace (RE 75–76).

This argument persists. Kaufmann is eager to show again and again how the Hebrew Bible resisted Zoroastrianism—especially in refusing to concede an independent principle of evil endangering its monotheism. To speak with Job, "The Lord has given, and the Lord has taken away." But what of the appearance of Satan, "the adversary" in the book of Job? He is essentially "a literary device to set the stage for profound discussion of the problem of innocent human suffering." The strength of the literary qualities of this tract—

> the economy of style, the compression of a maximum of meaning into a couple of pages, the vivid simplicity that invites endless reflections—all this is worthy of the author of Genesis and may help us to understand why some rabbis attributed the book to Moses. (RE 78)

It is crucial that the physical torments that Satan inflicts on Job to test his devotion are authorized from above. After receiving instruction from the Lord, he disappears from the stage: "Satan is mentioned no more, and in the forty chapters after this the idea that God might *not* be responsible for Job's suffering is never considered even for a moment." Kaufmann reads the outcome of the book of Job, consistent with his views, as less interesting in its theological and metaphysical implications than it is in its ethics. It is a primer in respect of human suffering.

> Job's steadfast insistence that there cannot be any presumption that suffering is just implies that we must not harden our hearts to the misery of our fellow men as if they merely got what they deserved. . . . This humane attitude towards suffering remains part of normative Judaism and has become so deeply ingrained among Jews that millions of them have retained it even after giving up their belief in God [*verum sit!*].

This way of reading, I'll add, is consistent with Kaufmann's reading of Nietzsche's doctrine of the eternal return, as well: it has an essentially ethical consequence. Act so as to affirm, eternally, the repetition of that act, which you must endure: here that act would entail compassion for the sufferings of others. It is pertinent that "according to the Talmud, Job was always recited by the high priest shortly before Yom Kippur" (the Day of Atonement) (RE 78–79).

Throughout his account of early Judaism, Kaufmann stresses the rabbis' determination to resist the influence of competing Near Eastern religions, their "spelling out in painstaking detail a way of life that precluded assimilation" (RE 81). This will to orthodoxy explains the rigorous codification of ritual—the setting of a liturgy, the law of the Sabbath, and exacting dietary laws. The latter exceed in their detail all plausible reasons of hygiene—or how does one explain, for example, the prohibition on eating the meat of the hoopoe? Once, however, "this enterprise of laying down rules for all occasions was begun, it became—like scholastic philosophy in the Middle Ages . . . a kind of madness." Yet undeniable even in this madness was the ongoing construction of a world with hard contours, a dike against "the flood of syncretism" (RE 82). Furthermore, this obsession with legal details, in the case of the most honored rabbis—namely, the Pharisees Hillel and Akiba—never overpowered their moral concerns.

A wonderful anecdote concerns the Gentile who came first to the Rabbi Shammai, saying:

> I will become a convert if you teach me the whole Torah . . . while I stand on one foot. But Shammai chased him away with the rod he had his hand.

Then the man went to Hillel, who accepted him, saying: What is hateful to you, do not do to others; that is the whole Law, the rest is commentary, go and learn! (RE 83)

Readers of Kafka's *The Trial*, recalling the penultimate scene in the cathedral, will be struck anew by the priest's words to Joseph K.: "The scripture is inalterable; interpretations are often only an expression of the commentators' despair"![27] Hillel is a relevant reference for Kafka and, as a creator of hermeneutical rules for biblical exegesis, for Kafka exegetes.

Kaufmann's narrative ductus from Hillel to the fall of Masada is compelling: Hillel, who died in AD 10 was a contemporary of Jesus; Kaufmann's point is that

> for the Jews of the first century A.D., the teaching and crucifixion of Jesus did not seem earthshaking at all, nor did the Romans take the slightest notice of it in their annals. For the Jews the cataclysmic event of the first century was the destruction of Jerusalem and the second temple by the Romans in A.D. 70, after three years of war. (RE 85)

The Jews held out at Masada with extraordinary courage, as Flavius Josephus recounts in book 7 of his *History of the Jews*. His narrative is seminal in a deeply personal way for Kaufmann, since it tells of the Jews' decision to kill themselves before they might be enslaved by the Romans and, together with their wives and children, humiliated, tortured, and killed. The Jews slit the throats of every one of their community until the last slaughterer killed himself. Again and again, the advocates of mass suicide had praised the dignity of a life of freedom and the puniness of death next to the horror of its loss. In the conclusion to our earlier chapter 6, we read of Kaufmann's extraordinary ease in contemplating an early death ending a life of creative work, of ethical valor. It is irresistible to consider the view of life and death of the Jews on beleaguered Masada as a source and standard for Kaufmann's own view, vigilant in its resistance to any "unseemly dread of death" (RE 90).

Kaufmann makes some basic but indispensable distinctions. The Pharisees (the word "Pharisee" meaning "separatist") were chiefly bent on maintaining the original identity of Judaism, including the oral tradition of commentary (Mishnah and Gemara). The Sadducees rejected both the Pharisees' attachment to "oral law" as well as their belief in an afterlife. The most reliable Hebrew text of the Old Testament is the Masoretic recension; in the third century BC the Hebrew Bible text was translated, not always reliably, into

Greek, and this version—the Septuagint—is the Old Testament known to the earliest Christians. Reputable scholarship, especially on the basis of findings among the Dead Sea scrolls, has established the greater authenticity of the Masoretic text. It is interesting to learn that

> both the Septuagint and Philo's philosophy [inspired by Plato and the Stoics] made a great impression on many Gentiles. So did the Jewish conception of God, the Jews' religious services in their synagogues, and the Jewish religion as a whole. Many Gentiles were converted; others became . . . God-fearing. Around A.D. 120, Juvenal, . . . deploring the erosion of ancient Roman customs, cited as a typical example the way in which so many become more and more Jewish, accepting first the Sabbath and then the God who is worshiped without images, then the dietary laws, and finally even circumcision (Satire 14). This process of proselytizing continued until Christianity became the state religion of the empire,

the Christians being significantly less tolerant of the Jews than the Romans (RE 89). The Romans, however, were not so relaxed as not on occasion to forbid the Jews to study the Torah, an edict that led to a show of defiance by the venerable Rabbi Akiba, who, as the Talmud relates, paid the price of an atrocious martyrdom, his flayed flesh, having been ripped from him with iron combs, being afterward "weighed in a butcher's shop." Akiba is remembered for his courage and devotion but also for his exaggerated exegetical skill—in Kaufmann's familiar phrase—the art of reading one's own views into distinguished texts and thus taking one's own views back, crowned with the authority of their source. Akiba's greatest hermeneutic feat was addressed to a passage in Isaiah that appears to speak of a hellish afterlife for sinners, allowing Akiba to conclude, against the grain of the text, that a single virtuous act would save a Jew from any such fate.

Kaufmann's pages are as full of meat as an egg has yolk: dense with fact and anecdote from Jewish history and thought, scholarship and incident, extending to the state of Israel at the time of Kaufmann's writing, circa 1975. I will offer a brief anthology of the moments that especially interest me—and I hope will interest you, patient reader—in the spirit of Kaufmann's own procedure, as the scholar Agus describes it: "The author may dwell lovingly on some aspects of the subject and ignore vast areas in which he is not particularly interested."[28] Each of these brief markers invites further study.

The first concerns Jewish canonical writing and Jewish learning: "The Palestinian or Jerusalem Talmud was finished around 400, and the Babylonian

Talmud a hundred years later." In the centuries following, and up until Islam's incursion in the seventh century, "Palestine and Babylonia remained the chief centers of Jewish intellectual life" (RE 94). What follows is a roll call of eminent Jewish scholars: Rashi, a name derived from the initials of the Rabbi Shlomoh Yitzhaki, "wrote commentaries [in the eleventh century] on the whole Hebrew Bible as well as the Babylonian Talmud." Jewish culture flourished in Spain: the poet and philosopher Shlomoh ben Judah ibn Gabirol was "often cited by the Christian scholastic philosophers as Avicebron" (RE 94–95). Of course, unmissable from such a register are Yudah ben Halevi, who composed a dialogue "between a Jewish scholar and a Khazar king whom he converts to Judaism" (it is said that while reciting his elegy "To Zion" at one of the city gates of Jerusalem, ben Halevi was murdered by an Arab); and Rabbi Moses ben Maimon (1135–1204)—also known as Rambam and as Maimonides—Saladin's personal physician, who wrote a commentary in Arabic on the Mishnah and, in Hebrew, the well-known *Moreh Nevukhim* (A Guide to the Perplexed) (RE 95). The *Zohar*, "a major work of Jewish mysticism and the fountainhead of the so-called Kabbalah," is the work of Moses de Leon. Studies in Jewish mysticism were thereafter centered in Tsfat, where "Isaac Luria . . . became the leading kabbalist of his time and founded a school that survived him" (RE 95). These citations, and the citations that follow, suggest something of Kaufmann's encyclopedic scholarship, intellectual curiosity, and pithy writing (Isaiah Berlin: "He has an enviable capacity for writing clear, lively, and readable prose").[29] Here, as elsewhere, Kaufmann's work strikes me as fair-minded even when displaying a relentless polemical edge. It is sharpest when he turns it on other religions.

Modern Europe "boasts" (would that it would boast) of a profusion of Jewish scholars and artists: Montaigne can be numbered among them, as his mother was of Jewish lineage. The names of the many German luminaries from Moses Mendelssohn to Einstein are well known. Among "humane agnostics," perhaps like Kaufmann himself, such distinction leads to pride in being Jewish, an emotion that could mask the tenuousness of Jewish citizenship in the European countries that witnessed their achievement. Jewish scholars and intellectuals thought of themselves as German and French and British and so forth, as if thinking a thing hard and often enough would make the thing real. Zionists saw through this delusion of security; and though Herzl, a secular Austro-Hungarian Jew, organized the movement in Europe, even contemplating Uganda as a possible homeland, the passion for a return to Jerusalem had long swollen in the pious East, which then flowed into the Holy

Land from there. This passion was age-old: Israel was ever the Holy Land, the land of the Hebrew Bible. Even before the founding of the State of Israel, the population of Jerusalem in the decades before and after 1900 was two-thirds Jewish. Kaufmann's conclusion about this embattled country is, I think, altogether honorable, as time has told: "If Israel became a state with an established religion that discriminated against those who did not share that, while treating as second-class citizens those of different descent who have no desire to convert to Judaism, then the ancient dream has come to nothing" (RE 107). Here, too, Kaufmann's acknowledged passion for social justice clashes with his quixotic attempt, in *Beyond Guilt and Justice*, to rid the world of the shibboleth of "justice" as an idea that has allegedly seen its day. In one unfortunate sense of the phrase, it appears to have.

At this point we make a fundamental turn to the founding of Christianity, in which the sheer weight of the presence of Judaism is unmistakable (RE 109). The first Christians were Jews who, being neither Sadducees nor Pharisees, were "hospitable to all kinds of foreign influences." Jesus preached in Aramaic, the dialect of ordinary Jews, and only to them, but what he taught was foreign to the general ethos of the Hebrew Bible—his claim to be the Messiah—and it was for this blasphemy, and not for any violation of Jewish law, that he was crucified by Pilate. In a striking instance of the Jewish presence in Christianity, Mark's attribution of the words "My God, my God, why have you forsaken me" to Christ on the cross is a citation from the twenty-second psalm of the Hebrew Bible. Kaufmann anticipates his unsympathetic argument in full:

> The early Christians were people who believed not only in life after death but also that the world might soon come to an end and that the final judgment might well be at hand. They felt at home not in the prophetic demands for social justice, nor in the biblical scholarship of the Pharisees, but in the apocalyptic books that dealt with the end of things and offered frightening images of damnation. The central concern of those who had come to listen to Jesus and those who, after his crucifixion, cherished his memory was with salvation—their own salvation. According to the Gospels, it had not been necessary for Jesus to convert people to his rather Zoroastrian . . . world picture with its heaven and hell and its day of judgment. He preached that the end was at hand, and many who were frightened and wondered what when needed to do to be saved came to hear him. (RE 109)

Some sectarian Jews were converted; the great majority of Jews were not. Israel clung to its autonomy deep into Roman times and afterward. Of course,

Judaism underwent decisive changes under changed circumstances: for one thing, rabbinical exegesis, never celebrated in the Bible, grew in importance following the Babylonian exile. Still, it maintained the ethical core of the Bible, with its dream of this-worldly justice—of care for the poor and oppressed, for their and God's sake, without a thought of personal salvation. This is Kaufmann's refrain.

With the growth of Christianity, unconverted Jews were subjected to relentless hostility. Their "obstinacy" in refusing to acknowledge Christ as the resurrected Messiah fueled the antagonism of the evangelists—a sin they attributed, first, to students of the Torah (*nomikos*), whom they incorrectly called "lawyers," and then to "all representatives of normative Judaism" (RE 111). In their indignation, they advanced the lethal fiction that the Jews and not the Romans had killed their savior. In fact, countless Jews had already been crucified by the Roman governors, a form of terror and torment that came easily to them. But the urge in the Gospels to make the Jews responsible for the crucifixion had a crucial political purpose—that of quelling Roman antipathy toward the Christians. The aim was to prove that, like the Romans, the Christians hated the Jews but hated them even more.

The other side of this "Manichean" Christian hatred was love for the believer and his or her eternal reward. The so-called Sermon on the Mount, which, following Kaufmann, most scholars believe is an invention of the evangelists, begins with the "beatitudes." "Each announces a personal reward, and the poem ends: 'Rejoice and be glad, for your reward is great in heaven'" (RE 113).

The love of Christ entails contempt for possessions and more. To a questioner, Jesus said, "Sell all you have and distribute it to the poor, and you will have treasure in heaven; and come, follow me" (RE 112). To the disciples, he added, "Truly, I say to you, there is no man who has left house or wife or brothers or parents or children for the sake of the kingdom of God, who will not receive many times as much in this world, and in the world to come eternal life." Kaufmann is skeptical. "The questioner has been told that he should distribute all he has among the poor, but the disciples seem to be told that it is quite enough to leave one's wife or one's children, or one's parents, or one's brothers, as long as one does it in order to be saved" (RE 113). These biblical passages are not the most transparent or the most reasonable, for obvious reasons. Moreover, if anyone abandons his household—his possessions and let us add his wife and children—and this act should benefit another—let us say the poor—then this gesture has been made not for their sake but for the sake of the believer, who will receive "many times as much in this world."

"Indeed," adds Kaufmann, "our passages clearly suggest that whoever exerts himself to help the poor *for their sake* does *not* fulfill the conditions of salvation" (RE 113). Kaufmann finds very little intellectual satisfaction in the New Testament.

These conditions of salvation are very severe. The question arises whether all those who would believe, but are unable to comply with these demands, must be cast into hell. It is hard to imagine that if these scruples were imposed to the letter, the evangelium would have made many converts on its way to becoming the official religion of the Roman Empire. The demands were lightened: baptism, belief in the resurrected Messiah, and the eating of the sacramental bread and the drinking of the sacramental wine became sufficient to assure the convert an eternal reward (RE 126).

Kaufmann's brief against Christianity includes his expectable disdain for monasticism, which has no place in normative Judaism. He is witty and elliptically sympathetic in ruing the Christian practice of celibacy. Since some of Christianity's finest intellects were monks and priests, this custom induced a genetic disaster, always supposing that a bit of Lamarckism is operative in scholarly families.[30] The denigration of sex and the body, Kaufmann notes, is a remnant of the teaching of Mani; it is found in some forms of early Gnosticism; but it can be derived from sayings of Jesus. St. Jerome wrote an essay "in praise of virginity, and his sentiments are summed up in two striking aphorisms: 'Marriage peoples the earth, but virginity peoples heaven'; and, again, contrasting virginity and matrimony, 'a cup is for drinking and a chamber pot for the secretions of nature'" (RE 115–16).[31]

Kaufmann repeatedly denies Jesus the quality of moral genius. "Jesus believed . . . that the mass of men was headed for eternal torment; and there is no evidence that this conviction troubled him" (RE 116). He is not the revolutionary creator of a new, generous morality. Mark's gospel makes it clear that Jesus's renown was an affair of the miracles he performed and not "his moral message" (RE 118). But what of John 13:34–35: "A new commandment I give to you, that you love one another; even as I have loved you, that you also love one another. By this all men will know that you are my disciples, if you have love for one another"? Kaufmann is again skeptical:

A reader with critical faculties must surely ask: What is new about this commandment? After all, the commandment to love one's neighbor, and the stranger as well, goes back to Leviticus 19 and was central to the teachings of the most respected Pharisees, such as Hillel. Moreover, Jesus' disciples will be distinguished by the fact that they love *one another*, while their attitude toward unbelievers is closer to Zarathustra's than it is to Hillel's. (RE 126–27)

Still, in accord with Kaufmann's habit of reining in his "No" on the way to a moderate "Yes," and thereafter to a mediated, a dialectical "No," he finds reasons to admire the New Testament:

He [Jesus] prophesies his end but not necessarily his own return—also in Mark 9:1: "Truly, I say to you, there are some standing here who will not taste death before they see the kingdom of God come with power." The obvious reaction to these prophecies is surely that Jesus was a false prophet.

Still, some of his sayings, no less than many of his parables, have a haunting quality and stay in the mind; many bits have a strange beauty even if they are morally disturbing, and the imagery is often inspired. But much of what is impressive is not new but collected from a variety of Jewish and Hellenistic sources—whether by Jesus himself or by those who soon attributed these words to him. (RE 120)

At his arrest Jesus is a man forsaken. His disciples, men of small virtue, abandon him. They could not wake with him; Peter denied him three times. Confronted by "a great multitude with swords and staves," they flee. By any standard they are mediocrities, and yet it was on Peter that Jesus chose to found his church. Still, adds Kaufmann, "precisely this [the behavior of the disciples] made the Gospels more appealing. With God all things were possible, and he could elect mediocre people while making sure that many who might have seemed far superior would go to hell. That held out hope for millions" (RE 121).

The cross on which Jesus was crucified bore the words IESUS NAZARENUS REX IUDAEORUM, Jesus of Nazareth, King of the Jews. These words were fateful.

On the literal level, one may speculate that this formula provided the meeting ground for the Jewish charge of blasphemy and the Roman governor's interest in the matter. The representatives of normative Judaism felt that Jesus' manner and conception of himself were intolerable. Pilate may have thought that if the man had called or proclaimed himself king of the Jews he was a threat to the imperial authority.

The Romans, as we've noted, did not need many reasons to crucify people who displeased them. In fact, it is unlikely that Pilate considered the matter all too finely. "At times the Romans crucified so many people that the stench filled the air" (RE 123). Much contemporary scholarship, I'll add, stresses the Romans' conviction that Christ and his noisy, sword-bearing followers were a political danger. Fernando Bermejo-Rubio, a historian of early Christianity, sums up his recent work as follows:

> One of the objections raised against the hypothesis that Jesus was involved in anti-Roman seditious activity runs as follows: if Jesus was put to death as an insurrectionist, why was he arrested and crucified alone, whilst his followers were left unharmed? Although this is regarded as a real conundrum by the guild, the present article proposes that the question has been incorrectly formulated, because it uncritically assumes that Jesus was indeed crucified alone. The article argues that . . . some followers of Jesus—or at least people related to him through a shared ideology and/or activities—were sought after and crucified along with him.[32]

Kaufmann perceives in the Gospels' account of the crucifixion of Jesus a perfect tribute to the syncretistic character of Christian writing.

> The crucified king strikes ancient chords. . . . In the Gospels this old theme is fused with the imagery of the servant of God in Isaiah 53, the man not recognized for what he was while he suffered. He is crucified between two robbers, and the scene is embellished with motifs from the 22nd Psalm as well as Isaiah 53 until it becomes a masterpiece . . . in which Greek and Jewish elements are fused with Zoroastrian dualism and ancient Near Eastern lore. (RE 123)

This twenty-second psalm, in the Christian mind the so-called "Crucifixion Psalm," is, I'll add, the scene of a contentious textual conundrum. According to the King James Bible, the text of psalm 22, verse 16 reads: "Dogs have compassed me; the assembly of the wicked have enclosed me; they pierced my hands and my feet." Rabbi Tovia Singer observes:

> Understandably, Christians are confident that this passage contains a clear reference to Jesus' crucifixion. "Of whom other than Jesus could the Psalmist be speaking?" missionaries ask. . . . Paradoxically, well-educated Jews are utterly repelled by the manner in which the church rendered the words of Psalm 22:17.1. . . .

To understand how Christian translators rewrote the words of King David, let's examine the original Hebrew words of this verse with a proper translation.... Psalm 22:17 (16) Hebrew King James Version (16): "For dogs have compassed me, the כְּלָבִיםכִּי ,סְבָבוּנִי: assembly of the wicked have enclosed עֲדַת מְרֵעִים (For dogs have encompassed me; a company of evil-doers have enclosed me; like a lion, they are at my hands and my feet)." Notice that the English translation from the original Hebrew does not contain the word "pierced." The King James Version deliberately mistranslated the Hebrew word kaari (אֲרִיכ) as "pierced," rather than "like a lion," thereby drawing the reader to a false conclusion that this Psalm is describing the Crucifixion.... Had King David wished to write the word "pierced," he would never have used the Hebrew word *kaari*....

Bear in mind, this stunning mistranslation in the 22nd Psalm was not born out of ignorance. Christian translators were well aware of the correct meaning of this simple Hebrew word. They fully understood the meaning of the word אֲרִיכ and deliberately twisted their translations of this text. The word *kaari* can be found in many other places in the Jewish scriptures and they correctly translated אֲרִיכ "like a lion" in all places in Christian Bibles where this word appears with the exception of Psalm 22—the Church's cherished "Crucifixion Psalm."

This charge provoked a fierce rebuttal.[33] This angry denominational dispute is perennial. Of a piece with it is the angry response of Christian reviewers to Kaufmann's general unloving characterization of Christianity as an unloving, indeed immoral creed.

We have mentioned the few requisites to Christian fulfillment. Kaufmann cannot easily bear the thought that "all who had lived exemplary lives without such faith and sacraments were condemned already." You hear his very own voice in conjuring a protest by a disconsolate follower:

Master, if that is God's way and you see nothing wrong in it, I will not believe in you, nor will I eat your body and drink your blood to gain eternal life. I would rather go into oblivion with there is no remembrance of you and your God, sleeping forever in the dust. And if that cannot be, if those whom you do not raise up must suffer the wrath of God, then let me dwell among them and, if I have the strength, I shall try to comfort them. (RE 126)

Kaufmann appears to accept Nietzsche's view of Paul, who argued, in *The Dawn*, that without Paul, "there would be no Christianity; we should scarcely have heard of a small Jewish sect whose master died on the cross" (RE 128). This is the gist of Paul's teaching:

> "Christ died for our sins in accordance with the Scriptures," the allusion being to Isaiah 53. The crucified Messiah took upon himself the punishment for sins and thus became our Savior. What is required of us is the faith that he died for us. The antinomy of law and faith is central in Paul. Since the Messiah or Christ died for our sins, we need no longer satisfy the law; what is required for salvation is faith in Christ. (RE 130)

Kaufmann quarrels with Paul and with his superior knowledge of the Hebrew Bible appears to be on solid ground. Paul's argument is that the Jews have been cursed by the affliction of a law that is impossible to satisfy and therefore cannot be saved. Thus, argues Kaufmann,

> it seems that prior to the Crucifixion no one could be saved, because no one, neither Jew nor Gentile, could satisfy all the laws. We were all sinners, but now Christ has died for our sins, and if we believe this we are saved.
>
> Paul's assumptions, however, are flagrantly at odds with the spirit of the Hebrew Bible and the Pharisees. The whole notion of a judgment in which some are saved while the rest of mankind is damned is alien to Moses, and the notion that everyone who transgresses any commandment whatsoever, no matter how small, is damned, is, in one word, Pauline. In the Hebrew Bible and among the rabbis there never seems to have been the slightest doubt that God could at any time freely forgive those who repented.... But Paul simply could not acknowledge this without conceding that—in the pregnant words he used to rule out alternatives—"then Christ died in vain."

Considering the entire Christian soteriological story, with salvation coming available only a millennium after Moses and requiring a human sacrifice, Kaufmann concludes that "a more unlikely story would be hard to invent" (RE 131).

In Paul, love ostensibly trumps even faith, a love that Nietzsche took to be wholly inspired by the Hebrew Bible, "neither Greek nor Indian, nor Germanic. The song in praise of love that Paul composed is nothing Christian but a Jewish outburst." This thrust in fact runs counter to Paul's basic message and must be taken as including *faith*, since it is a love that "believes all things"! Kaufmann's downright angry repudiation of such a paean, traceable from his table of values in *Without Guilt and Justice*, where love occupies a second place to honesty, leads him to describe the faith that Pauline love includes as "most promiscuous, uncritical, and indiscriminate" (RE 132). He takes up the great thought experiment of what would have become of the teachings of Jesus without Paul's advocacy.

> It seems clear the little Christian sect in Jerusalem had no future among the Jews; it is obvious that it could never become the state religion of the Roman Empire without first making it much easier to be a Christian than it had always been to be a Jew; and that Paul and John found a way of making it easy by stressing belief and sacraments. . . . The New Testament . . . offered something for almost every taste, including a large number of very striking sayings, haunting parables, and unforgettable stories. In this respect, no other religion in the Roman empire had so much to offer. At the same time the new religion seemed to *require* very little. (RE 134–35)

Paul affirms the generosity of Christian doctrine, and this again fires Kaufmann's Jewish indignation. "In the First Epistle to the Corinthians, Paul said of himself: 'I have become all things to all men.'" Thinking especially of Moses and the prophets, this stance, of course, will seem altogether alien to the Jewish standpoint. They taught their people to be uncompromising; here we return to what Kaufmann stresses—and celebrates—as the Jewish resistance to "syncretistic' borrowings. Indeed, "post-Biblical Judaism became very rigid and separatist" (RE 140).

These remarks should not suggest that further interest in Paul might be found today only in the works of defensive seminarians. In fact, recent decades have witnessed an explosive adoption of readings of Paul into a new universalist political theology, as composed by Jacob Taubes, Giorgio Agamben, Alain Badiou, and Slavoj Žižek. At its polemical extreme, this "universalist" use of Paul associates the Jews' love of Halacha, of law and jurisprudence, with support of the modern biopolitical state, and Jewish elective nationhood with the crimes of twentieth-century fascist nation-states. Further discussion of these arcane disputes, however engaging, would lead us too far away from our subject, the work of Walter Kaufmann.[34]

The pages that follow explore the history of post-Pauline Christianity in its various departures from the ethos of the New Testament, which is itself a triumph of syncretism: the resurrected god, for one, is a "concept so ancient that we do not know where it came from" but is one embodied in Egypt's god Osiris and Mesopotamia's god Tammuz. To this borrowed motif there came the cult of the goddess: recall her precursors Athene and Artemis. And yet, although "the Mary of the Gospels has hardly anything in common with them . . . [she] was venerated before long as 'the Virgin,' 'the Mother of God,' and 'the Queen of Heaven.' . . . The New Testament was a product of syncretism; as Christianity spread, it absorbed more and more of the ideas of the people who adopted it" (RE 138–40).

Other practices that have come to be regarded as essential to the church have no foundation in the Bible. Consider merely the worship of saints, the society of monks, and the penchant for martyrdom. By the time of the Nicene Creed, adopted in 325, which settled the relations between the Father, the Son of God, and the Holy Spirit, "we are closer to the world of medieval scholasticism than to the 'man of suffering' in Isaiah 53." The creed asserts positive doctrine, and it anathematizes many subtle errors, for which heretics will pay dearly, however fine the metaphysical distinction, viz.,

> But those who say: Once he [Jesus Christ] was not; or: Before he was begotten he was not; or: He came into being out of nothing; or who claim that the Son of God is: of another substance or essence [than the Father], or created, or changeable, or mutable—these the Catholic and Apostolic Church anathematizes. (RE 142)

The persecutory fervor of the church was stilled briefly when the Roman Julian—subsequently Julian the Apostate—became emperor in 361. He advocated the tolerance of all religions even while supporting a Neoplatonic paganism, but his imperial generosity came to a swift end with his death after only two years of rule.

> When Julian was killed in a skirmish against the Persians, tolerance died with him; Christianity was restored as the official religion, and no similar plea prevailed for well over thousand years. Indeed, as long as there seemed to be a chance that persecution might succeed it flourished, and it was abandoned only when Europe had been utterly exhausted by the slaughters of the Thirty Years' War (1618–1648) and become persuaded that the killing was futile. (RE 143)

I am one of the "many people" Kaufmann addresses who are insufficiently aware of the differences among the Christian churches. Aside from such well-known distinctions between Lutheranism, say, and Anglicanism and between the Catholicisms of France, Italy, and Ireland, "at least one third of Christendom is neither Protestant nor Catholic but divided among various Eastern churches. The Orthodox Eastern church is merely one of these and is subdivided into many semiautonomous or 'autocephalous' churches," which employ different languages in their rituals. And there are many Eastern churches that are not Orthodox, namely,

> the Coptic churches of Egypt and Ethiopia, the Jacobite churches of Syria, Iraq, and India, and the Armenian Church. All of them are Monophysite, meaning that they believe that Jesus had only one nature, and that this was divine. . . . The Monophysites . . . were solemnly excommunicated at the Council of Chalcedon in 451. This was the first of the three major schisms of Christianity, and these very ancient churches are neither Orthodox nor Catholic nor Protestant. . . . Moreover, the Christians who influenced Muhammad were neither Catholic nor Orthodox. (RE 144)

The second of the three major schisms split apart Roman Catholic Christianity and Orthodox Christianity, a division that persisted for another six hundred years after circa 451. The third is Luther's halving of Western Christianity. Kaufmann stresses that doctrinal differences were endlessly disputed but the lines finally drawn

> coincided geographically with boundaries that were far older than these issues. The Roman Empire had been divided among Constantine's sons into an eastern and western empire, and eventually the Eastern church did not wish to recognize the primacy of Rome. And in northern Europe the countries that had not been under Roman rule eventually seceded from the church of Rome and became Protestant, and after long and bloody wars the Germans in the south and in the Rhineland, who had lived under Roman rule fourteen centuries earlier remained Roman Catholic, while the rest of Germany became Lutheran, and the religious boundary coincided with the ancient Rome *limes* or border fortifications. (RE 145–46)

Kaufmann has obtained such information—the history of the schisms, including the heretical stance of Monophysitism against Nestorianism, which focused on Jesus's birth as a human being, and later, Luther's "grand refusal"—from sources available to us as well. And so I will continue to single out those facts that convey something of Kaufmann's own sensibility—facts that surprise me and which I think must have surprised Kaufmann as well. But no selection of facts can distract from the dominant tone of his history of Christianity, which stresses its unutterable cruelty, especially at the time of the Crusades, of which there were *eight*, each rivaling one another for bloodthirstiness and hypocrisy in its claims, upon its success, to a "magnificent" fulfillment of divine will.

Kaufmann is notably intolerant of encyclopedic accounts of the Crusades that palliate its horrors. A German reference work declares, "In the Crusades, the unity of the Christian occident, which sacrifices blood and treasure for a religious idea, gains its most magnificent expression." In his book-length article for the *Encyclopaedia Britannica*, the eminent Ernest Barker observes: "When the first Crusade finally came, what was it but a penitentiary pilgrimage under arms—with the one additional objective of conquering the goal of pilgrimage?" Kaufmann comments: "That the Jews of Jerusalem were burned alive in their largest synagogue Barker did not consider worthy of note." With minimal comment, Kaufmann establishes instead—drily—its factual character as a relentless pogrom, as an energetic slaughter of thousands, as reported by an eyewitness: "Indeed, it was a just and splendid judgment of God that this place should be filled with the blood of the unbelievers, since it had suffered so long from their blasphemies. The city was filled with corpses and blood" (RE 147).

You can hear Kaufmann's voice in his account of the disputes debated at the Council of Florence in 1439, where the so-called *Filoque* clause was the first item for deliberation—"the question whether the Holy Spirit issued from the Father or from the Father 'and the Son'" (RE 144).

> One might suppose that when Islam appeared on the scene in the seventh century and within a hundred years wrested from the Christians Palestine, Egypt, North Africa, and Spain ... Christians might have come to see their differences in a larger perspective, feeling that the many things they had in common were far more important. But what happened ... at the Council of Florence, a mere fourteen years before the Muslims conquered Constantinople, was altogether typical. The squabbling among the Christians facilitated the expansion of Islam, and the bizarre complexities of Christian controversies over the relation between God the Father and the Son, and over the relation of the Holy Spirit to both, must have made the sublime simplicity of Muslim monotheism doubly appealing to many minds. (RE 146)

He will not always characterize Islam as "sublime." The rise of Islam, specifically the Muslim conquest of Acre in 1291, marks the end of the idea of the crusade. "A little less than two hundred years after the First Crusade, the madness stopped. But meanwhile the pogrom in the Rhineland," with which the First Crusade began, leading to the murder of ten thousand Jews—"the

first fruits of crusading zeal" (Barker)—"and above all the Albigensian crusade," sometime between the Fourth and the Fifth Crusades—"had proved,"
Kaufmann observes, "that there were easier ways of expressing one's religious
zeal" (RE 149).

We have the Inquisition, which Kaufmann conceives of as the chief model
for totalitarianism (in his next two books he will fault Hannah Arendt for
omitting this point). He finds a way—wittily, cruelly—to "justify" in theory
the tortures inflicted on heretics and those who were assumed to be heretic
and weren't heretics at all—although, perhaps, they were *inclined* to heresy.

> For a long time it has been fashionable to absolve, if not Christianity, at least
> the New Testament. But if God tortures unbelievers in all eternity, then it
> is arguable that Pope Gregory was much more charitable than Jesus who,
> according to the Gospels, contemplated this prospect with equanimity. To
> let heretics lead other men stray is cruel, and to torture them for a few days to
> save them from eternal torment is anything but cruel. . . . St. Thomas Aquinas
> (1225–1274) . . . argued at length in his *Summa Theologica* that heretics deserve
> "to be severed from the world by death." . . . Heretics should be admonished
> first, but if stubborn should be delivered "to the secular authority to be exter-
> minated." In support, he cited St. Jerome: "Cut off the decayed flesh, expel the
> mangy sheep from the fold, lest the whole house, the whole paste, the whole
> body, the whole flock, burn, perish, rot, die." (RE 152)

Compare, I'll add, the following speech delivered by Adolf Hitler in Salzburg
on August 7, 1920:

> This is not a problem you can turn a blind eye to—one to be solved by
> many concessions. For us, it is a problem of whether our nation can ever
> recover its health, whether the Jewish spirit can ever really be eradicated.
> Don't be misled into thinking you can fight a disease without killing the
> carrier, without destroying the bacillus. Don't think you can fight racial
> tuberculosis without taking care to rid the nation of the carrier of that racial
> tuberculosis. This Jewish contamination will not subside. This poisoning of
> the nation will not end until the carrier himself, the Jew, has been banished
> from our midst.[35]

Hitler referred his aperçu to Koch's discovery of the tuberculosis bacillus, calling himself the "Robert Koch of politics," giving a familiar Christian trope a
stain of scientific respectability.[36]

St. Thomas Aquinas was a Dominican friar and a Catholic priest. "In 1232, when Thomas was five, Pope Gregory IX entrusted the Dominicans with the sacred task of being the bloodhounds of the Lord and rooting out heresy" (RE 153). One would think that there would be a permanent division of activity and attitude between the Dominicans and the Franciscans: after all, a striking motif in the Rule of St. Francis is love.

> A common reaction to Francis is that he was a true Christian—unlike Tertullian and Augustine, Constantine and Innocent, the Crusaders and inquisitors, Luther and Calvin. On the face of it, it would make more sense to suggest that his rule that "anger and indignation hinder love in ourselves and others" is Buddhist. . . . [But this institution of love] was doomed to be no more than a momentary flash in a dark sky. Within a few decades after the death of Francis, his order vied with the Dominicans to implement the Inquisition.

Indeed, one reads in the *Cambridge Medieval History* that "Clement IV had to forbid the inquisitors to prosecute each other" (RE 154).[37]

It is often held that Luther returned Christianity to its authentic beginnings in Scripture. But his outpourings of brutality against the Jews, against heretics, against the revolting peasants, against *reason*, certainly vitiate this claim—except that there is another sense in which this claim is true. "The power of his language has rarely been equaled in any tongue, and his German Bible . . . caught something of the spirit of the originals." With this feat (of translation), Luther did really bring about a return to the Bible (RE 155).

At this point readers will not be shocked to hear of the Christian oppression of Jews and heretics and unruly subalterns, but the intensity and vividness of Luther's commination against *reason*—this "whore," "the devil's bride"—is startling:

> There is on earth among all dangers no more dangerous thing than a richly endowed and adroit reason, especially if she enters into spiritual matters which concern the soul and God. For it is more possible to teach an ass to read than to blind such a reason and lead it right; for reason must be deluded, blinded, and destroyed. (qtd. in RE 156)

For Luther, faith trumps the most violent of sins; forgiveness is all. Indeed, "Christ has brought about such a violent salvation that he deprives the Ten Commandments, too, of all their claims. . . . Be a sinner and sin vigorously" (RE 155-56). I have often noted that Christian reviewers seriously disliked what they considered Kaufmann's one-sided account of Christianity, in which the uplifting, the affectionate side of Christ's teaching was omitted. Kaufmann might reply that he "reads" Christianity as the good philologist Nietzsche called for, though, in light of Kaufmann's leading principles, his reading is *selective*. This mode of reading and writing informs *Religions in Four Dimensions* until its very end. It informs Kaufmann's account of the birth and destiny of Islam;[38] of the ancient religions of India: Hinduism, Jainism, Sikhism, Buddhism; the religious writings of China, including Zen; Shintoism; and the relation of several of these religions to the arts. The latter chapters display Kaufmann's growing passion for photography and the visual arts, which will be elaborated at length in his next book of texts and photographs, the 1978 volume *Man's Lot*.

I regret that I must break off this present compendium. It would require another hundred pages and would no doubt exhaust the resources of author, reader, and publisher. As one advances in this massive book, through text and stunning photographs, one becomes more and more aware of Kaufmann's aesthetic sensibility, his range and erudition, as well as his drive to criticize what he detects as the moral shortcomings of each of these religions, having exempted only Judaism. In each of his accounts one will also detect grace notes of admiration. The reader must go to the original to see how this is done.

13

This Priceless Heritage

THE FUTURE OF THE HUMANITIES

"This priceless heritage" must not be squandered.

—WALTER KAUFMANN

Over the years these fierce unconditional loyalties—to a country, a God, an idea, or a man—have come to terrify me. The thin veneer of civilization rests upon what may well be an illusory faith in our common humanity. But illusory or not, we would do well to cling to it. Certainly, it is that faith—and the constraints it places upon human misbehavior—that is the first to go in times of war or civil unrest.

—TONY JUDT

WE COME TO *The Future of the Humanities* (1977), a book conceived in "wrath," with the sadness and anger of a betrayed lover (FH 217).¹ Kaufmann dedicates this work "to those from whom I acquired my first love of the humanities." But what has happened to the love of wisdom in disenchanted times? We have had inklings all along, especially in Kaufmann's *Critique of Religion and Philosophy*, of his disappointment, his indignation, at the betrayal of the promise of philosophy. It has become another profession— an academic department—an opportunity for specialists bent on cleverness or sport or peer approval.

Along with philosophy, the humanities have lost their way and need to be orientated to their proper goal, for they are indispensable to the survival of

411

what we think of as humanity. Here, to begin, are four reasons for teaching them ("There is a virtue in conciseness" [FH xiv]):

> Much of history is utterly depressing, a ceaseless tale of human folly, blindness, and brutality. Yet not all this misery has been pointless; occasional triumphs redeem at least some of the suffering. . . . We should be traitors to humanity if we did not try to transmit . . . ["this priceless heritage"] to generations to come. (FH xvii)

A second reason is the aptness of the humanities to address "the ends of life . . . [the] possible goals of human existence, our ultimate purposes" (xviii); a third, its value as a medium for teaching *vision*—Kaufmann will clarify this idea; a fourth, as a platform for the study of comparative religion, for "few works of literature can brook comparison with the Bible, the Dhammapada, or the Tao Teh Ching." Moreover, you cannot understand paintings, sculptures, architecture, and music if you are ignorant of their religious context (FH xx).[2] Here we have a glimpse of what Kaufmann understands in the first place by "the humanities": they are works created by men and women that admirably convey their experience of life, present worldviews, and critically examine "our values, faith, and moral notions" (FH 37). If books, they are books that need to be read more than once (FH 47).[3] Finally, they are persuasive in being (like) subjects, not objects: by channeling the intellectual personality of their authors, they bring the reader into an I-You (*Du*) relation.

A humanist culture is produced chiefly by two kinds of mind—"visionaries" and "scholastics." The latter are open to scorn for they "travel in schools" and as professionals are merely parasitic on the discoveries of the grand innovators—the likes (somewhat pell-mell) "of Einstein and Goethe, Beethoven and Michelangelo, Plato and Moses" (F 7). But to value these types in so opposing, so Manichean a way is to overlook the fact that "not every distinctive vision is plausible, beautiful or fruitful. And it may require the concerted efforts of a great many scholastics to work out the details of a vision before we can judge its value" (FH 8).

Readers who have come this far will note the presence of diction like this, straining for effect. Or else the tone could be described more charitably as one of "existential urgency."[4] The book has pamphlet-like qualities, which may also be the result of its hasty composition: Kaufmann describes having finished a complete draft in five weeks (FH 217). In what he calls the "Prologue," Kaufmann addresses "we" who are conscious of past works of art and science as "blessed with the priceless heritage of these rare triumphs" (FH xvii). In the case above, it is not easy to form a clear picture of plural visions that are "plausible, beautiful, or fruitful" as opposed to visions that are not. A second concern might well be the identity of this blessed "we," confident in its out of hand rejection of the visions of pseudo-Einsteins and pseudo-Goethes, pseudo-Beethovens and pseudo-Michelangelos, pseudo-Platos and pseudo-Moseses. At least in the latter case, we can make a beginning from Kaufmann's frank admission, at the close of the book, that "I certainly do not see myself as another Moses" (FH 217).

Visionaries are not likely to feel at home in academic departments, and Kaufmann is informative about specific cases: "Spinoza knew [this] when he declined an invitation to become a professor at Heidelberg, as Nietzsche found out before he resigned his chair of classical philology at Basel, and as Wittgenstein found out at Cambridge University" (FH 11). It will be difficult *not* to think that with this mention of his "educators" Kaufmann is thinking of himself at Princeton. How can the reader avoid feeling this undertow? So, what kind of mind is his? A visionary's? A "creeper's"? (Scholastics are creepers because they are anaclitic on these giant oaks.)

Consider, first, that "teachers who question the consensus of the dominant schools of thought in college departments are not likely to be hired or promoted. . . . Visionaries, being loners, do not stand much of a chance in academia" (FH 12). The tension of curiosity increases: Kaufmann, assuredly a loner, nevertheless stood his ground in academia; but it was not until 1962, after an eight-year wait, that he was promoted to full professor of philosophy at Princeton. At this time he had already published thousands of pages, not a few of them, as I hope to have shown, visionary in their character (he has laid claim to "mystic experiences"; he would abolish guilt and justice).[5] When he wrote *The Future of the Humanities* in 1975, after a decade of extraordinary achievement, he was still four years away from his appointment to the prestigious Stuart Professorship at Princeton. Clearly, though, he is also an explainer—so which type is he?

Inevitably, "we have to introduce a third type"—the Socratic: "the most striking feature of this type is its concentration on criticism." Like Socrates, the critic "examines the faith and morals of his time, ridicules claims to knowledge that are based on an uncritical reliance on consensus, and exerts himself to show how ignorant, confused, and credulous most people are—including the most famous teachers, politicians, and popular oracles" (FH 14). This, surely, is Kaufmann's own preferred—and deserved—profile, and it is this (Socratic) ethos that he would want to be taught in all humanities departments as "an indispensable ingredient" (FH 24, 28).

At this point, however, he appears to distract both himself and readers from this mooted identification with Socrates, pretentious but never discarded. And so he proceeds to attack an external enemy—an inferior kind of critical mind, that of the journalist. The latter's bad character is established a priori and then augmented with a buffoonish quote from G. B. Shaw attacking the "congenital erroneousness" of the type (FH 16). This argument, however, is circular. Let us concede that there exists a disgraceful ethos of carelessness in thinking and writing, where what counts is speed and being interesting. Now, by fiat, let us collect these faults under the head of the journalistic ethos. Henceforth, anyone who writes in a journal can be suspected of peddling lies and scandal until proved otherwise.

Hannah Arendt published portions of her *Eichmann in Jerusalem* in the *New Yorker* in 1963. Earlier, in 1959, in *The Faith of a Heretic*, Kaufmann excoriated "people who do not know what to do with themselves in this life, but fritter away their time reading magazines" (FH 386). As she is a journalist, it can be supposed that Arendt's pieces will contain errors of fact—after all, she did write for a magazine. But what are the facts that she has ignored or misrepresented? Kaufmann does not say what they are; he also does not want to be confused with those critics of the book who, in pointing out its factual mistakes, seem bent on destroying its main thesis. That is not his concern, since, as he points out, he had already published a poem in 1962 likening Eichmann to a mouse—and he will not say anything further on the idea of the banality of evil except to find that "many critics have found [the notion] quite offensive" (FH 18).

On the topic of the slipshod journalist type of mind and Hannah Arendt, Kaufmann also finds the main theses of *The Origins of Totalitarianism* untenable (these origins do *not* lie in imperialism and anti-Semitism, and why has she not mentioned the Nocturnal Council in Plato's *Laws* or Dostoevsky's Grand Inquisitor?).[6] The title of her book seems just grabbed from the vulgar press. Of course, Kaufmann and Arendt had clashed bitterly at Arendt's Princeton Gauss lectures "Marx and the Western Political Tradition" a dozen years before, but let that anecdote pass—it is journalistic fodder.

Kaufmann also cannot rest before dismissing Edmund Wilson, another writer for the *New Yorker*: Wilson misreads *Philoctetes* (he does); and *To the Finland Station* contains a chapter on Hegel that Kaufmann considers deeply unsatisfactory. But just how did Wilson get Hegel wrong, and are his alleged blunders important? Kaufmann does not explain what they are—or why. At this point, we might find that his attacks on various elite journalist-critics have taught us very little. And did not Kaufmann publish his first version of *The Faith of a Heretic* in *Harper's Magazine*? When did Kaufmann know that *The Future of the Humanities* would be published by the Reader's Digest Press? The attacks discussed above would seem to be an aberration. But . . . there will be a caveat. "Not *all* people who are journalists by profession belong to the type under consideration here; much less do *all* people who sometimes write for journals. What matters is the ethos" (emphasis added) (FH 20).

This emphasis comes a bit late. Again, why, in writing that "scholastics, no less than visionaries, often feel contempt for journalists," does Kaufmann disingenuously omit the type of the critic that he is? (FH 15). The damage has been done. These pages are unfortunate, despite his last-ditch stand to integrate this resentful jeremiad into "the future of the humanities." The journalistic orientation—essentially, *topicality*—"poses an immense threat," he concludes, to the humanities, which rest on the imputed forever-lastingness and depth of its concerns (FH 21).

I will add that until it can be proved that the Internet has decisively contributed to the decline of the humanities, Kaufmann's praise of only those works that shun the "journalist's day" is unreasonable. I am saddened by the thought that if it should be true, Kaufmann would find very little merit in *this* book describing his achievement. It remains only to be said that his entire denunciation of the journalist type—his vigorous No—does not fail to receive at the end, as we might expect by now, its temperate Yes, for "men and women who are by profession journalists" might "contribute a great deal," after all, to "the Socratic probing of the faith and morals of the age" (FH 24).

It is perhaps in this perspective that Kaufmann characterizes Kierkegaard as one who combines the mind of the creeper-scholastic with that of the journalist, but without a trace of the visionary or the Socratic element; and he describes the (quite forgotten) German novelist Heinrich Böll as a mix of the qualities of creeper-scholastic and visionary! If anything, surely Böll, the author of *The Lost Honor of Katharina Blum*—a notorious story about a woman destroyed by a sensation-mongering journalist—should qualify as the pure type of the critic, but it is compilers of dictionaries whom Kaufmann judges to be of this pure Socratic type. How surprising! He does revert to good form, though, conceding, at the end, "One could have a great deal of fun arguing about individual cases" (FH 23).

The more serious matter, however, is the urgency, as I mentioned, that professors—the pure type of the scholastic, with a residual element of the Socratic waiting to be aroused—commit themselves to the Socratic task. Let them reverse the precedence of types in their intellectual character and assume their bounden duty of "rigorously examining the faith and morals of the time, giving pride of place to those convictions which are widely shared and rarely questioned" (FH 22).

Interestingly, in his introduction to *The World, the Text, and the Critic* (1983), the late literary scholar and activist Edward Said also supplies a four-part typology of literary critical minds, at several points paralleling Kaufmann's typology while presumably being unaware of it.[7] For Said these habits of mind also consist in (1) the journalistic (although not for him a reprehensible category) and (2) the visionary, such as the mind of many a French literary theorist at least at the beginning of the heyday of literary theory in the early 1960s;[8] and two types of the scholastic: (3) the "academic literary historian," whose practice returns to "such nineteenth-century specialties as classical scholarship, philology, and cultural history"; and (4) the appreciative, whose "beneficiaries . . . are all those . . . who have learned in a classroom how to read a poem, how to enjoy the complexity of a metaphysical conceit, how to think of literature and figurative language as having characteristics that are unique and not reducible to a simple moral or political message."[9]

Although Said's own work necessarily partakes of each of these approaches, he means to align the essays in his book with none of them individually in order to approach more nearly Kaufmann's Socratic type: "If what in this volume I call criticism or critical consciousness has any contribution to make, it is in the attempt to go beyond the four forms as defined above" and to attend, as the blurb has it, "to political, social, and human values."[10]

This ethic, which is Kaufmann's, butts heads, I'll note, with the professorial ethic that will be familiar to the many readers of Stanley Fish, the Socratic critic *and* journalist who made his views plain in the *New York Times* two decades after Said and four after Kaufmann. The crux of his *opposing* argument is that academics—meaning scholastics—should do their social criticism far from the university classroom. "Academic freedom" means just what the words say—in an unexpected sense. That such freedom is *academic only* is a point of truth for Fish, but a point for ironical reversal for Kaufmann, who wants that freedom to be more than "academic." Writing in the *Times* of January 8, 2009, on the question of what use are the humanities? Fish replies:

The only honest answer is none whatsoever. And it is an answer that brings honor to its subject. Justification, after all, confers value on an activity from a perspective outside its performance. An activity that cannot be justified is an activity that refuses to regard itself as instrumental to some larger good. The humanities are their own good.[11]

As an exchange between professor and student on the meaning of books and art objects, the study of the humanities is *least of all* an arena for "the rigorous examination of the faith and morals of the time."

Fish's "formalism" invited many thunderous rebukes from readers of his piece. Kaufmann's response—had he lived to see the day—like the name of Abou ben Adhem would have "led all the rest." But the bitter question does remain open, whether the fact that more and more professors, ostensibly consorting with Kaufmann's ideal, today use their classroom as a pulpit for attacking social injustice, has weakened the idea of a Socratic education. Kaufmann was concerned in 1970 "that the prestige of the scholastics has grown enormously . . . while that of the Socratic ethos has declined." In fact, I'll add, the rise of something like a new Socratic ethos, in Kaufmann's words, bent on "the critical examination of our values, faith, and moral notions" but including their materialization in the actual life of society, may have prolonged the future of the humanities, reinvigorating their relation to immediate experience (W 37).

Meanwhile, it is not that Kaufmann was unaware of the demand for "relevance": he lived through the 1960s in America. And so he was qualified to make important discriminations in this matter and was appalled at what he considered the general breakdown of all standards of (Socratic) competence, with unqualified professors delivering emotionally charged dicta and obiter dicta outside the classroom but conjuring with the authority of their status. It had not yet come to the theater of today, when broadsides, in lieu of precise and deeply thought-out positions, are delivered *in* the classroom. For him this new academic turn would signal one thing only: the end of the republic of letters!

It is relevant to invoke the figure of Philip Rieff, in the same years author of *Fellow Teachers* (1973), who shares an intellectual family resemblance with Kaufmann. From a high-cultural, mandarin standpoint, both critics attack the demise of higher values in American society and its institutions. Rieff's chief value is a sense of the sacred *pure*, "holy terror," without which no society can keep order—and his time, and not alone his, is derelict. Kaufmann is content with less terrifying intimations of the higher voice in great art, philosophy, and religious literature. Both are especially akin in their dismay at the journalistic politicization of the university; both write with wrath of classrooms being turned into revolutionary theater. I will quote a passage from Rieff at some length, since it immediately anticipates Kaufmann's tendentious *Without Guilt and Justice*. Kaufmann's concern was to explain the "decrepitude" of the idea of justice:

> To those whose minds are not liberated, wars, revolutions, and radical movements will never bring freedom but only an exchange of one kind of slavery for another. That is one of the most tragic lessons of the twentieth century.
>
> Liberation of the mind is no panacea, but without it angry rhetoric and cruel bloodbaths are of no avail, and tyranny endures. Most of those who see themselves as radicals and revolutionaries still cling to decrepit ideas like justice and equality and depend on guilt and fear, as our fathers and mothers did. What we need is a new autonomous morality (W vii).

Now here is Philip Rieff:

> I, for one, am not keen on being where the direct action is; there brutality and the horror of total politics, uninhibited by any presiding presence, will be. One necessary thing that we inactivists, we academic men, suspicious of all politics, have to teach our students is how not to invest in the nostrums of direct action now being hawked. It is our duty to protect and nurture, in our academies, a few enclaves within which to practice an inhibiting subtlety, to think in something like late Jamesian sentences. If we are not allowed indirections, slowly ordered, if we must serve some program, one side or another, then the academy has no unique service; it is least fit of all institutions to take stands or rationalize them. The more directly political it becomes, the more certainly the university must commit itself to shifting positions, in the endless war for advantage, and so destroy its intellectual integrity.[12]

To return to Kaufmann—to what can and should be done to stem the angry tide—it remains teasing, although impossible, to know whether Kaufmann's vision of an enlightened professorial mind in theory and practice diverges in any way from his own classroom persona. Was his ideal of teaching the humanities freshly developed for this treatise—I would like to think it was—or was it already at hand in the empirical facts of Kaufmann's professorial style and merely dictated as "Be like me"?

We pass readily to the mooted injunction *"Read* like me," the subject of Kaufmann's next chapter and one of the most illuminating he has written. The issue of reading is clearly crucial to the entire enterprise of the humanities. The relation between teacher (visionary, scholastic, Socratic, or [reprehensibly] journalistic) and student, I'll add, is mediated by the books they read and study in the classroom. Their relation is, in principle, in no way immediately intersubjective, with the professor playing the role of father or mother or analyst and the student appropriately subaltern; their relation is ideally shaped by the texts they share. This is a hard lesson to learn and not one easily accepted, as consider the normal way of naming the dissertation director in several academic departments *Doktorvater* or *Doktormutter*.

Even in this theater of false consciousness, reading goes on. The correction, as Kaufmann writes, lies in encouraging a certain manner of reading, a way of being in relation to the text. There are many false starts, such as the "exegetical," which Kaufmann often codes with the name "Heidegger," that holds the text to be authoritative: it knows what I, the reader, do not know, and the more arcane it seems, the more deeply I am ready to submit to it. In the kind of exegesis that Kaufmann pillories, exegetes "endow the text with authority, then read their own ideas into it, and then get them back endowed with authority" (FH 48).

I'll add that this is precisely the mode of reading practiced by Paul de Man, the visionary promulgator of a form of literary deconstruction in universities in the 1970s that has kept its momentum until today. De Man and Kaufmann were well known to one another. In 1967, in Princeton, de Man, like Hannah Arendt, gave the venerable Gauss lectures, which have subsequently been published;[13] in 1967 Kaufmann was acting director of the Gauss Seminars in Criticism. As Nietzsche scholars, each found the other's work, arising from such radically different critical presuppositions, beneath discussion.

De Man aimed to align his own readings with the process of deconstruction that every text of a certain rhetorical complexity allegedly performs on itself. The text dictates how it is to be understood; the reader is the secretary of the void of indetermination. In a certain sense, therefore, deconstruction (or rhetorical criticism) is, as de Man himself rather casually suggests, "totalitarian": "'Technically correct' rhetorical readings," he writes, "may be boring, monotonous, predictable and unpleasant, but they are irrefutable. They are also totalizing (and potentially totalitarian), . . . consistently defective models of language's impossibility to be a model language."[14] The authoritative teaching of all texts of a certain rhetorical complexity is the unreliability of "language."

There has been no lack of criticism of this faceup incoherent position. A superior scholar of rhetoric, Brian Vickers, has shown, in a biting critique, how de Man falsifies the texts he reads—in many cases quite literally—in order to read his own ideas into them more conveniently and get them back faster, as Kaufmann writes, "endowed with [their] authority" (F 49).[15] Of course, this does not ipso facto prove that de Man's ideas are not stimulating or powerful.

Another variation of the exegetical mode is the claim to understand an author better than himself. Kaufmann cites Rabbi Akiba, who "in the late first and second centuries of the Christian era . . . read his often strikingly humane ideas into the Torah, using exegetical devices that would have surprised Moses." Akiba and his fellow rabbis "believed that God had revealed to Moses or through Moses more than Moses himself had understood" (FH 49). Their approach, I'll note, anticipates a brilliant exchange among German romantic theorists, including J. G. Fichte (1762–1814) and Friedrich Schlegel (1772–1829), on this very topic. Unnerved by the limitations Kant set on understanding, they advanced the proposition that a reader must understand better than the author what the author had intended or might have intended if he were as perceptive as his reader. Schlegel's famous aphorism reads: "To understand someone, one must first of all be cleverer than he, then precisely as clever, and then also precisely as stupid." Schlegel continues: "It is not enough that one understand the true meaning (*den eigentlichen Sinn*) of a confused work better than the author has understood it. One must also be able to know, characterize, and reconstruct (*construieren*) the confusion itself."[16] Kaufmann would appear to be of two minds about this practice. On the one hand, we read in his *Hegel*: "Insofar as possible we must take the author's positions more seriously than he himself took them" (H x). On the other hand, exegesis leads in the wrong direction of ascribing superior powers of divination to the exegete. And when the exegete's feeling that such powers have abandoned him, he is inclined to use—and recommend—a salvific "violence," as do Heidegger and thereafter de Man. What is missing in this approach is the sense of the "object" of the scrutiny as a You (*Du*).

Kaufmann sums up the first-mentioned way of reading with the words, "We don't know and he does"; but we have seen how readily the pattern slips into its obverse, a second way: "We know and he doesn't." This is the *dogmatic side* of exegesis (F 55). Kaufmann breaks down this mode into three types of condescension: in plain language there is stance (a): "Had he known X, he would not have said what he did"; (b) "Had he possessed our superior techniques, he would not have said what he did." (N.b. that this is the stance of Arthur

Danto and thereafter Brian Leiter on Nietzsche, discussed in our postscript.) Type (c) reads: "He wasn't altogether hopeless and at points came close to some of us" (FH 56–57). Here Kaufmann instances American scholars who, for example, "have read Heidegger, trying to show that in places he says what John Dewey . . . has said better." It is quite certain that he is thinking somewhat impertinently of the work of his colleague Richard Rorty.

A third type of reader essentially declares, "We don't know and suspend judgment about truth." The truth of the text is not at stake. This is the "agnostic" way of reading, which is also practiced in three modes: the "antiquarian"; the "aesthetic," which is concerned solely with the "beauty and style" of the text; and the "microscopic," which now (at the time of Kaufmann's writing) runs rampant. By focusing on a single small portion of a work, let alone avoiding the author's oeuvre as a whole, "the author is spirited away, the encounter with a challenging You is avoided, and one deals with small pieces that can be taken apart" (FH 58). This is Kaufmann's prescient formulation of what has lately come under the head of "the death of the author," as witness essays by Roland Barthes, Michel Foucault, Jacques Derrida, and others. But Kaufmann was not responding to the thrust of French theory of the 1960s and 1970s; he drew a borderline around his reading, leaving Paris isolated, *outre-mer*. What he is resisting is the American New Criticism, with which he had become well acquainted during his years of study at Harvard, and its centerpiece, the so-called intentional fallacy, which politely demands that the reader *not* make the acquaintance of the author and his presumed and in some cases explicit intentions. Kaufmann is shrewd in noting that here "once again the reader reigns supreme and does not risk himself, his views, and his preconceptions" (FH 58). This very objection to the New Criticism of the 1950s appears again in the criticism leveled against the deconstructive theory of the last fifty years. In a very revealing text, de Man, whom we have identified as the progenitor of a form of deconstruction in America, traced his "own awareness of the critical, even subversive, power of literary instruction" to a course taught by Professor Reuben Brower at Harvard in the 1950s, in which students were told

> not to make any statements that they could not support by a specific use of language that actually occurred in the text. They were asked, in other words, to begin by reading texts closely as texts and not to move at once into the general context of *human experience or history*. Much more humbly or modestly, they were to start out from the bafflement that such singular turns of tone, phrase, and figure were bound to produce in readers attentive enough

to notice them and honest enough not to hide their non-understanding behind the screen of received ideas that often passes, in literary instruction, for *humanistic* knowledge (emphasis added).[17]

Of course, Kaufmann would have no objection to Brower's—and de Man's—first requirement—close reading. He quotes a professor who, when shown by a student that a passage in Hegel's *Phenomenology* said exactly the opposite of what the professor had claimed Hegel had meant, replied, "What is dialectical is precisely that the text contradicts the author's intention" (FH 60). This jest is instructive in highlighting the distinction between Kaufmann and de Man (who, in this discussion, can stand in for deconstruction *pur sang*). Whereas the reply of Kaufmann's professor is an exemplary mistake, fully corrigible, de Man, takes the mistake further, into the domain of ineluctable error, writing, "Not only does the critic say something that the work does not say, but he even says something that he himself does not mean to say."[18] Kaufmann would have none of that. Their divergence is most vivid when de Man's own parti pris declares its hand in the last words of his memoir: he speaks derisively of a "humanistic knowledge" counterfeited by clichés.

Kaufmann's distress is echoed by William Empson, the brilliant, eccentric English literary critic, who (in a recent comment by Michael Wood) considered "French theory, with deconstruction specifically . . . as just one more instance of what he saw as happening to the study of language and literature everywhere: the human stakes were being removed, words were playing among themselves, no agents or intentions were to be seen."[19] At no point does Kaufmann encourage reading for the payoff of what deconstruction boosters call—rarely specified—"humanistic cant."[20] The phrase "human stakes" is more accurate. Kaufmann wants not to recover certainties from books but to experience the shock of a disturbing newness that comes from encountering another *subject* who tests you. The condition of this adventure is the existence of an author in the work. Thinking, in the past, of Kaufmann's poetics, I called this intuited authorial presence a "poetic self" and sought to develop Kaufmann's idea:

> The poetic self cannot be known in advance of its articulation. It can come to life only for a reader. But it is not produced *ab ovo* by that reader. It is present to him as the being that intended by an act of writing to be present to the future of that act. Yet the poetic self is more than the work's ghostly, hypothetical double, its pure aesthetic correlative. It comes to life with the

fire and mud of the empirical personality still clinging to it, conveying the thrust of the writer's being to enact, identify, constitute, or bear witness to itself. Literature, for these writers, is the discourse of a subject whose saying, by virtue of how it is said, stands for the self in the future.[21]

We can now expect to hear, finally, of a fourth, more appropriate way of reading that assumes "we don't know everything, and he (the author) doesn't; but we have some intelligence and he does; and we shall try to transcend some errors by engaging in a common quest, confronting the voice of the text as a You" (FH 59). This view is once again opposite to the deconstructive view that considers error an irremediable feature of linguistic exchange.[22] What Kaufmann has in mind is a procedure he calls, with little originality, *dialectical*. He is no naive purist, imagining a future of the humanities in which all reading would be dialectical in his elaborated sense. Experience in and around universities makes it plain that professors, and their students, will read, on occasion, in the different ways marked exegetical (say, reading Isaiah), antiquarian (say, reading *Gilgamesh*), aesthetic (say, reading Santayana), dogmatic (say, reading the Upanishads), microscopic (say, reading Nietzsche—wrongly) and, let us add, deconstructive (say, reading Yeats to show how "cognitive" and "performative" aspects of the poetry tear it apart).[23] But dialectical reading is a pedagogical consummation devoutly to be wished.

Certainly, the term "dialectical reading" needs to be defined anew, and Kaufmann does so by having it subtend a familiar triad: its labels are Socratic, dialogical, and philosophical-historical, each of which answers to an ethical or experiential good essential for full personal development—the ultimate desideratum. The *Socratic* mode invites an experience of multiplicity, a full consciousness of the abundance of standpoints that one has failed to consider—what Kaufmann calls, again and again, *alternatives* (unlike today's term of choice, "otherness," for which Kaufmann deserves our gratitude). A Socratically inflected dialogical reading "seeks vantage points outside the various consensuses by which . . . [the reader] has been conditioned. The text is to help him to liberate himself" (FH 61).

For Kaufmann, dialogical reading requires you to engage with a forever-audible voice, a forever-apprehensible meaning in the text flowing from a living mind, the maker of this meaning. In "*many* texts [this meaning] reflects a distinctive experience of life" (emphasis added) (FH 66). The qualifier is striking; there were no such qualifications in Kaufmann's previous iterations of the idea. We can assume that the new criticism and neostructuralism have made serious inroads into this mimetic ideal, and they are ineluctable. Kaufmann offers another, even finer qualification of his thesis: "The new critics never tired of insisting how important it is to attend carefully to an author's language. In this way students were *at least* brought face to face with a distinctive sensibility" (emphasis added) (FH 66). The author comes into the text as an afterthought, by a concession, through a somewhat restricted entrance. In the last resort, dialogical reading does not go to words to find connections with other words but goes behind words to what Kaufmann considers a humanly accessible substance, a conveyance of spirit from one subject to another. This is the "'You'—the subject's distinctive voice and meaning" (FH 69). This drama presupposes that a rare questioning can take place—not only the expectable questioning of the text by the detached reader but the reader caught in the force field of a questioning triggered by the text. "Force field" is apt: there is a point to Kaufmann's emphasis on culture shock, challenge, and offence. Every reading experience asks Kaufmann—and *you!*— "What have you done with the gift of your life?" and prompts the injunction: "You must change your life!" (see the epilogue for some concerns about the reasonableness of this demand).

Earlier we stressed that Kaufmann had rejected an intersubjective model of correct reading, in which the professor imparts the meaning of books to the student-reader without mediation, as if pouring clear water from a translucent pitcher into a glass. It is noteworthy, however, that Kaufmann's rejection of this model by no means "spirits away" the intersubjective factor but instead displaces it into the relation of the student-reader to the authority—though one not absolute—of the person in the text. It is far from certain that in all this Kaufmann has discarded the robes of what Martin Jay calls "intellectual historians who seek the holy grail of subjective intentionality that ostensibly lies behind texts."[24] Something of a solution to the awkwardness of this smuggled intersubjectivity emerges a bit further on, when Kaufmann protests the thoughtless expense of scholastic labor in producing complete critical editions of eminent writers—voluminous series drowning in minutiae, usually indefinitely incomplete, which few readers can live long enough to master. Before entering this labyrinth, the reader needs to pose the question: "Why [am I studying] this writer rather than that one? And why this work rather than that? What is the point of it?" What makes it worth studying? Now, surely there is more at stake than making the difficult acquaintance of what Kaufmann calls the "geistige Persönlichkeit" (intellectual-spiritual personality) of the author. "The obvious reason" for such a study, he declares, is to make available to others something one considers especially beautiful or important—a work that says something vital that should not be ignored. It may be new information or a new way of seeing things, a striking criticism of accepted views, or perhaps a book, fragment, or sequence of letters that places a person, movement, or a period in a new light. (FH 123)

The encounter with the person in the book does not end with the giving and taking of offence; it must end with the reader's conveying to others the import of this intellectual shock.

The final component of dialectical reading, the philosophical-historical approach, will be familiar to us from Kaufmann's chapter in *Tragedy and Philosophy* titled "Toward a New Poetics." It is the self-evident demand that the reader know as much as he can about the history of the work and the entire oeuvre in which the work belongs before venturing to claim an understanding.

The eminent Germanist Gerhard Neumann describes the requirement for serious reading at the University of Freiburg in the 1950s; it would conform to Kaufmann's ideal. Neumann praises the seminars of Professor Gerhart Baumann, which were

> schools for the precise reading of texts, sometimes only of a few lines during an entire seminar. . . . Baumann's requirement: you will read the entire works of an author before daring to read in such [and such] a way. It is only then, after such seclusion [alone with the author], that understanding dawns; and it is only then, entirely from the reading of the text, that conceptual categories take shape; and it is only then, at the very end, that you can write something about these texts. . . . This school, if it was such a thing and if they were not merely ascetic spiritual exercises, appealed to me. And so I read the ca. one hundred and forty volumes of the Sophie-edition in order to participate in a Goethe seminar; I read the Steiner edition of the works of Hugo von Hofmannsthal; I read the oeuvre of Robert Musil in the giant three-volume edition of Adolf Frisé, etc.[25]

Such discipline is not much seen in American universities in the decades following.

Dialectical completeness requires that the reader supplement his or her reading with a sense of the historical moment of the work. Walter Benjamin's dogmatically asserted thesis that "no poem is intended for the reader, no picture for the beholder, no symphony for the listener" would now strike Kaufmann as by and large implausible.[26] He also asks that the text by which the commentator defines the author's meaning be central to his or her oeuvre and not—let us say, as in the case of Hegel—his students' notes or, in the case of Nietzsche, a scrap from his unpublished writings. A confirmation for the reader that the meaning he has taken from the work is better than his or her own projection might lie in the fact that that meaning can be found *in other works* of the author—although a moment's reflection will show that this is a poor argument. One can project meaning illicitly into one work of the author but find it elsewhere in the oeuvre. I shall remind the interested reader of the example taken from the work of de Man (discussed in some detail in chapter 3) where de Man mistranslates a sentence from Nietzsche's paralipomena to make Nietzsche say that where there is consciousness there is (necessary) error.[27] The sentence says no such thing. It says that where there is consciousness, and only there, the *possibility* of error arises. But de Man can cite a sentence from *The Will to Power*, again from Nietzsche's unpublished work, to argue the necessary domination of error in all acts of consciousness, where error is *the* error constitutive of all acts of thought or willing—the error of positing a continuum between consciousness and material nature.[28] Even here, however, other of Nietzsche's aperçus published on pages next to the one that de Man has chosen discuss error in ways that lend no support to the view that Nietzsche has this *one* allegedly essential, inextirpable error in mind.

Kaufmann repeatedly calls readers' attention to the human being behind the texts. In this way they will read like "Nietzsche and Freud, [who] are of special importance for the dialectical reader because, more than anyone before them, they called attention to the human being who finds expression in a text" (FH 71). In repeating his insistence, I am writing like Kaufmann, who in this way makes all literary criticism a psychology, thereby anticipating the major work he was to complete just before his death—his three-volume *Discovering the Mind*, a study of important philosophers, several of whom are distinguished readers.[29] The works of all of them are, in Kaufmann's view, only as good as they display the insights of great psychologists: it will come as no surprise that Nietzsche and Freud are exemplary figures. Here, at a place in *The Future of the Humanities*, which could just as well be marked the future of the humanist Walter Kaufmann, we encounter Nietzsche's and Freud's "enormous interest in *nuances*" (emphasis added). Kaufmann's intent is to heed the patient *in* the text, again and again that invisible but felt author, whose sensibility exceeds any range of "nuances" one might find in a work read merely as a weave of words. We have arrived at the clearest understanding of the principle behind Kaufmann's "humanism": it is the claim that the human being is a richer object of study than any of his works, the value of which is measured in turn by the degree of felt presence of the man. Kaufmann's postulate stands boldly formulated: "The antipsychological bias of so many scholastics in the humanities is ultimately anithumanistic" (FH 71).[30] It is a war of extreme banners swung by readers who, on the one hand, listen to the author's wildly beating, (mostly) broken heart; and on the other, detect various textual sites of "disjunctive ensemble operations."[31] Kaufmann strikes a well-placed blow: "If we do not care what the author meant, why take his name in vain? In that case we might just as well stay home and play real chess" (FH 81).

He makes no distinction between "a philosophical dimension" of the text and what he rather surprisingly reintroduces as "the experience of life [that these texts] express or their challenge to us" (FH 81). Some of the rich pondering of alternatives—including the view that certain experiences are *constituted* for the author, as his own reader, in the text and are in no sense the expression of an already mastered "experience of life" —is here reduced to doctrine for Kaufmann's less experienced reader. This chapter concludes with the demand—it is a tall order—that Kaufmann means to place on the professor of the humanities now assigned to teach "the art of reading." In all likelihood he or she will be unable to execute "the dialectical approach" because he or she does not know enough. This (missing) competence would attempt to address frontally "the great philosophers [who] were not ordinary people":

> Plato and Aristotle made all the knowledge then available in Athens their province. Descartes and Leibniz where as great as mathematicians as they were as philosophers. Spinoza was an encyclopedic philosopher, wrote a Hebrew grammar, and pioneered Biblical criticism. Hobbes translated Homer and Thucydides. Hume wrote a multivolume *History of England*. Kant advanced a major astronomical theory and, almost as much as Hegel after him, dealt with almost all the major fields of knowledge. Nietzsche, a classical philologist, was also the first great psychologist as well as a major poet.
>
> In different ways, the Greek tragic poets and Dante, Goethe, and Tolstoy are no less awesome. [And yet] no reform of education, especially in the humanities, can hope to get far if it does not pay attention to the ways in which students are taught to read. . . . Neither television nor computers can save the humanities if the art of reading texts is lost. (FH 81–83)

This catalogue contains a suggestion of Kaufmann's own competence; he would not list these strengths if he did not possess a great many of them, absent the sciences.

The passage to Kaufmann's witty reflections on book reviewing and, thereafter, on translation and editing, follows easily from his persiflage on journalists and journalism ("reviewers and translators often have a journalistic ethos" [FH 104]). Kaufmann is entitled to strong opinions, having reviewed, translated, and edited books for decades. In fact, "a writer who has contributed dozens of reviews to scholarly journals as well as weekdays, monthlies, and quarterlies really has no excuse for keeping silent" (FH 85). What is refreshing is the way in which he breaks the general silence about the meaning and importance of most reviews, a judgment that does not exclude his own: "Plainly, most reviews should not be taken very seriously" (FH 87). He, for one, would rather be writing books of his own than reviewing other people's books, a feeling he generously attributes to his colleagues as a rule. As a result, the reviews we read may often be the product of irritableness or low motives. "Not enough readers realize how many reviewers are returning or hoping for favors, or settling personal scores, or pulling their punches because it would be impolitic to be forthright. They do not wish to make enemies of certain people but can be sure of making friends by attacking others" (FH 92–93). Because, to put this mildly, not every book reviewer is ready to stand behind his or her judgments with heart and soul—or intellectual capability—we can expect a good deal of casual misrepresentation. This dismal business is egregious when a book that claims to be taken seriously is lauded in one journal and destroyed in another.

Kaufmann's own work was by no means immune to such treatment. A review of *Without Guilt and Justice* by John Moran, a professor of political science, whom I mentioned in chapter 11, found the book as a whole awkward, superficial, and morally distasteful: "Announced as a new autonomous morality, and dedicated to Alexander Solzhenitsyn, the present book is a hodgepodge of pseudo-scholarship, neologisms, self-help lists and sophistic attacks on such mildly liberal concessions as equal opportunity and affirmative action."[32] Meanwhile, Donald Kuspit, a formidable art critic, writing in *Philosophy and Phenomenological Research*, judged *Without Guilt and Justice* "an extraordinary, lucidly written book," concluding that Kaufmann's "ethos of autonomy makes superb sense. Praise for this book cannot be too great."[33] Assuming that Kaufmann read his reviews—and, even if he was disinclined to take them seriously, he was nonetheless bound to be vexed—he would want to create opportunities for redress, and so he proposes that the journal that published an attack on an author's book allot the author 150 words for his or her defense. Yet, I'll add, if contemporary practice is followed, the author who takes the bait may find himself or herself even more abusively misrepresented in the additional three hundred words that, to his or her dismay, have been allotted to the reviewer, who, to protect the reputation of the editor, must not be proven wrong, whence the conversation is closed and the new, even more abusive attack left unanswered.

At universities I know, where, let us say, dissertations or exams receive grades at polar extremes—one reader giving the work an A and the other a C—a third reader is asked to adjudicate, and his or her grade is the final one. This situation would be a model for inviting a mediator when a book is reviewed so differently in two places; and this mediator might once again be the wretched object of this exercise, the author himself, allowed in a third journal to offer a reasonable explanation for the disparity.

As there is a mostly neglected ethics of reviewing, we encounter similar shortcomings among translators. Most cannot be helped, owing to the disparity in quality between the classic work to be translated and even the stylistic competence of the translator. This is a wide, already well-ploughed field: nonetheless, Kaufmann makes a number of instructive points. From Buber and Rosenzweig's translation of the Hebrew Bible, Kaufmann introduces the concept of *Leitworte* ("leading words"), understandable in its parallel with *leitmotifs*. Philosophical texts, especially, will elaborate such key words, and it is crucial to keep them constant throughout the translation. "The German *Geist* has no perfect equivalent in English, but if in a philosophical work we should render it now as spirit and now as mind, and sometimes as ghost, wit, and intellect, we would make it impossible for students as well as others who rely on our version to discuss the author's conception of *Geist* or his attitude toward reason without misconstruing many passages" (FH 100). This example obviously refers to Kaufmann's claim, in his study of Nietzsche, of Nietzsche's fundamental advocacy of Geist as reason. It would be amusing to learn of Kaufmann's reaction to Kenneth Burke's contribution to this problem. In his *Language as Symbolic Action*, he writes, "Once, when I was translating a German biography, I found the word [*Geist*] particularly bothersome. We were told that the character's *Geist* did this, the character's *Geist* did that, . . . and so on. Did his spirit do it? Did his mind do it? Did his wit do it, or his essence, or disposition, or demon? I tried all sorts of synonyms, and none seemed quite natural in English. Then, of a sudden, a breakthrough; whereupon, lo! I translated simply: '*He* did it.'"[34] But *Geist*, in a philosophical work, cannot just be translated by the subject's pronoun.

In an instance of the sort of inconsistency that Kaufmann deplores, at a crucial juncture John E. Woods, translator of Thomas Mann's *The Magic Mountain*, translates the word *Donnerschlag* as "thunderbolt"; when it reappears, at an equally crucial juncture, it is as "thunderclap."[35] As a result, the reader is deprived of the opportunity to perceive the explicit parallel made by Mann between the commotion leading to Hans Castorp's abrupt flight from his sanatorium on the "magic mountain" and the breakout of war on the flatlands of Europe in 1914.

Kaufmann is strongly in favor of a practice he believes does not exist but ought to: equipping the translations of modern works with footnotes to explain subtleties, puns, or obscure terms—in a word, "untranslatables." He was evidently unaware that Norton Critical Editions follow this practice; he would be happy to see that one of his many suggested lifelines to the humanities had been grasped. The goal of translation, as with all interpretation, is, once again, to bring to life the unique You of the text, "different from all other writers" (FH 95). A sophisticated literary critic, one of our finest, writing now, fifty years after Kaufmann, has recently written succinctly of a rule in interpretation, which can function as a rule in translation, wholly in line with Kaufmann's emphasis: the question of all such operations on a primary text is whether it "adds emotional depth or only an odd and undigested complication."[36]

"Complication" is the *Leitwort* for Kaufmann's objection to critical editions. "The besetting fault of most critical editions," the product of the toil of scholastics, "is that they show extraordinarily little feeling for the author," who was very likely a visionary.

> The ancients spoke of the mountain that was in labor and brought forth a mouse. What we are witnessing is rather how colonies of ants bury giants under unsightly hills that are of use mainly to the ants who live there. . . . I am certainly not against all critical editions. The crux is whether the editors help the author speak to us, or whether they get in his way. (F 104)

On the question of editing, the most interesting of Kaufmann's comments concern the critical edition of Nietzsche by Giorgio Colli and Mazzino Montinari.[37] Of course one is curious to know whether Kaufmann will exempt their work from his general animadversions against the massive investment in trivial pieces of the writer's corpus. The answer is Yes: he considers their solution to the question of Nietzsche's *letters* ingenious, although it is hard to gauge his tone when he continues:

> They have decided to publish *all* of Nietzsche's cards and letters in chrono-logical order in six and a half volumes, and *all* extant cards and letters to him also in six and a half volumes, in chronological sequence. The first volume, which begins with Nietzsche at the age of five and ends before his twentieth birthday, contains the material he wrote, including many such items as "Nietzsche requests permission to purchase ink," on pages 1–297, and the material written to him on pages 299–436. After that, the letters from Nietzsche and to him are presented in separate volumes. A selection of letters about Nietzsche will comprise four volumes, and the editorial apparatus three more, making for a total of twenty volumes. . . . It would be premature to judge this particular endeavor. (FH 110–11)

This rather discreet approval soon becomes a more explicit concern:

> Let us assume that Nietzsche's case is exceptionally favorable for a "criti-cal total edition," also because few writers since 1800 were so interesting and influential. Even then some serious problems remain. First and most important, all the books he wrote have been issued in two volumes on thin paper. If it were not for these books, his letters would not be of any inter-est to anybody, and the very thought of publishing the letters sent to him would be absurd. It would seem that those interested in Nietzsche should above all read and study the books he wrote. But now they are invited to divide their time and energy between his books, the *Nachlass*, and the let-ters, not to speak of secondary literature. Hardly anyone has time enough for Nietzsche to digest all that, and what naturally happens for the most part is that the time spent on the nonbooks comes out of the time that might well have been spent on Nietzsche's books. In this way, what is most significant always tends to be drowned in a sea of what is relatively insignif-icant. To vary the metaphor slightly: Nietzsche's voice is drowned out by the voices that addressed him and that talked about him. (FH 112)

This is all essentially good Kaufmann—we have his precision, the consider-ation of alternative views, and the driving force of sincere conviction. One comes away, to speak again with Milton's Samson Agonistes, bearing a "new acquist of true experience" present in a single, trenchant distinction: an archive is one thing, a critical edition another. "An archive may aim to make 'everything' available'; books require editorial judgment" (FH 110). Hegel's youthful theological writings deserved to come out of the archive as a separate book, as did Marx's early *Economic and Philosophic Manuscripts of 1844*—Kaufmann made important use of both texts in his book on Hegel and then again in *Without Guilt and Justice*—but other citable examples of such importance are rare (FH 108).

The crux of this discussion of critical editions is that they must not bury their subject in minutiae, no amount of which will generate objective readings—at last! This extreme efflux of the scholastic spirit misses the mark; more than that, it never aimed at the heart of the matter.

> None of the dead who are worth listening to can be wooed with sweat, and they are loath to reveal their inmost thoughts and their personalities to scholars who shrink from the dangers of subjectivity. The writers, composers, and artists of the past . . . were people of passion, people who loved and perhaps also hated; and anyone would like to make them speak must be congenial to them at least in some measure. (FH 124–25)

The question arises how this call for congeniality jibes with the equally important demand that this encounter, once again, be an affair of culture shock, challenge, and offence. Perhaps it is in one's finding in oneself a ghost of the hater in the great writer under study and learning to hate that ghost in turn. It is not so easy to conjure an example, but I will venture one: let us imagine T. S. Eliot reading Louis-Ferdinand Céline.

I think Kaufmann would find congenial Kafka's extreme meditation on this matter of subjectivity and truth: we have this daring trial of thought. Kafka saw the "commentators' despair" as follows. "That which one is"—"one" being the reader now *changed* by the act of reading—"one cannot express, for it is precisely *this* that one is. One can only communicate what one is *not*, ergo, the lie. It is only in the chorus [of lies] that a certain truth may be present."[38] Kaufmann would, I think, agree: There is more truth in the work of a community of bold interpreters than a team of scholastic editors aiming at literal totality.

Reading what I will call Kaufmann's "humanist poetics of reading," one is faced with the challenge of organizing into a coherent theory at least these four strains: (1) the task of encountering a large You, a flesh-and-blood author whose iconic shadow is cast by the lines of the text; (2) equally, of being, beforehand, as a reader, congenial to the *author*—that is, one having the character to be able to profit from the rich negativity of the encounter; for (3) it must give culture shock, challenge, and offence but only because (4) the author's words strike the reader as beautiful, incomparably interesting, or new. I conclude that this organization is something to which no verbal description is equal but which occurs as an *event*. This outcome, if it were to arise from the marriage of shock and beauty, would be a type of the feeling of the sublime, nascent in every humanist encounter. Roland Barthes, more humanist than supposed, advanced the aphorism that "all criticism is affectionate," in which I will stress less *liking* than the fact of *affect*. Barthes went on to say, "This [point] should be carried even further, almost to the postulation of a theory of affect as the motive force of criticism."[39] I often feel such elation in reading Kaufmann, and that is why I write these pages, with the hope that you, too, reader, will find them, in Kaufmann's sense, a congenial object of study.

It would be unthinkable, thus Kaufmann, to construct a reading program for the humanities without attending to the authors of texts held to be sacred: hence Kaufmann's chapter-long insistence on "the place of religion in higher education" (FH 126–53). For him, there is no more privileged source of reflection on "faith and morals and the ideologies and values of . . . society"—in short, on the great question of how one is to live a justified life—than the study of comparative religion (FH 129–30). Readers of earlier chapters will not be surprised by his insistence.

This chapter is composed with a great deal of verve, wisdom, and fascinating information. As part of Kaufmann's demonstration of the *superficial* honor in which religion has been held for a century, at least, in colleges and universities, Kaufmann recalls that before Firestone library was built at Princeton, its base had to be lowered several feet into the ground so that it would not be as tall as the revered Princeton chapel, a chiefly unattended Gothic hulk (FH 126–27). But books that might be spoken of, piecemeal, in the chapel call for solid study in the library and classroom. "Indeed, we should seriously consider whether some knowledge of comparative religion *should not be required* of all college students" (emphasis added). At the very least, "knowledge of the Old and New Testaments adds a dimension to the study of European and American history and literature" (FH 130–31). These assertions have worn well: among many examples, one can instance Robert Alter's *Pen of Iron: American Prose and the King James Bible* of 2010, which, as the capable critic Adam Kirsch wrote, "makes a convincing case that it is impossible to fully appreciate American literature without knowing the King James Bible—indeed, without knowing it almost instinctively, the way generations of Americans used to know it."[40] Kaufmann then constructs a one-semester syllabus, emphasizing texts from the Old and New Testaments, the Koran, and thereafter the Dhammapada, the Bhagavad-Gita, the Confucian Analects, and the Tao Teh Ching. "That students are able to graduate from elite institutions, having read a vast amount of drivel but never any of the books mentioned here, is certainly grotesque" (FH 132). But Kaufmann's challenge does not profit from such overkill.

Since the rest of Kaufmann's chapter is devoted to a plan for the study of comparative religion at universities, I am tempted to break off this narrative, as surely you are too, reader, to rush off and begin immediately reading (at best, rereading) the sacred books mentioned above—above all, Genesis, which Kaufmann loves the best: there is no book "greater or more beautiful, profound and influential" (FH 136). The right translation must capture its extraordinary spareness, although that is not the King James Bible, which "makes it sound remote, rhetorical, and churchly, and blinds us to its unsurpassed directness and simplicity" (FH 138).

> The great virtues of the King James Bible are a commonplace, but having been "appointed to be read in churches" it deliberately flattens out the differences between the authors and their styles . . . The tone is uniformly elevated everywhere. The effect is numbing. One feels impressed but ceases to hear what is being said. (FH 133)

Kaufmann's judgment is echoed by the formidable critic James Wood, who, reviewing Robert Alter's translations of the psalms, observes how "the result greatly refreshes, sometimes productively estranges, words that may now be too familiar to those who grew up with the King James Bible."[41] In Kaufmann's syllabus, of course, there would be no risk of false notes, since "I shall abide," he declares, "by my practice of quoting the Bible in my own translations" (F 134). These would strive

> to give the student some idea of the distinctive style of Genesis. . . . It is not lush and gorgeous but has the austere beauty of the Sinai desert and of the scenery around Jerusalem that is littered with rocks and ancient olive trees. . . . Nowhere is the light more lucid and the air so clear. Nor is there any other prose that equals Genesis in its terse and simple grandeur. (FH 136–37)

The Hebrew Biblical myth is the foundation of humanism. It has special importance for Kaufmann's humanism. He argues forcefully:

> The notion that all men were descended from a single couple led to the conception that all men are brothers; and the story that man was made

in the image of God and that God breathed his spirit into him led to the notion that man, and by no means just some king or priest, was more similar to God than to the other animals. Flatly contradicting what strikes us as the abundant evidence of senses, men was held to be by no means a mere speck in nature but essentially discontinuous with it and vastly more important. (FH 142)

There are many different accounts of the root of humanism; some fix the root some seven centuries later, in the Italian Renaissance, singling out Pico della Mirandola's *De hominis dignitate* (On the dignity of man). Or its program might be attached to the development of the notion of *Bildung*, of self-cultivation, associated with early seventeenth-century German pietism. Many commentators have perceived the connection of the ideas of humanism and such self-cultivation, which involves a substantial knowledge of classical texts. Mark Greif notes,

> Humanism has always been animated by texts. The fifteenth-century *umanistsi* projected their philosophical focus onto man to escape supernaturalism and Christianity, and develop Renaissance learning. They were capable of doing so because they had inherited and plumbed . . . the manuscripts of classical antiquity.[42]

The link to the classics was there from the start.

In thinking about humanism, Greif quotes a number of thinkers who have contributed to the humanist debate, one of the most trenchant being Peter Sloterdijk, who points out that humanism has always also had an aggressive, an antithetical face: it is poised to attack barbarism.[43] Thomas Mann's novel *Doctor Faustus* constitutes a grand meditation on this struggle.

This is a wide field in which Kaufmann has planted his imperturbable banner: "What was distinctive in Genesis was the implication that all men are brothers and have a divine *dignity*" (emphasis added) (FH 142–43). This word has become a much discussed key word in current political philosophy: witness George Kateb's *Human Dignity* and Michael Rosen's *Dignity: Its History and Meaning*.[44] Rosen's discussion of dignity leads him inexorably to a reflection on humanism, a concept that he finds, for reasons troublesome to readers of Kaufmann, ineffectual. He quotes a provisional definition of humanism from Joseph Raz's *The Morality of Freedom*: "The humanistic principle" claims "that the explanation and justification of the goodness or badness of anything derives ultimately from its contribution, actual or possible, to human lives and its quality." This thesis runs in perfect accord with Kaufmann's under-standing of the term. For Rosen, however, "humanism is not an ideal label, both because it is currently used in so many other senses and because many utilitarians give weight to the well-being of animals and humans equally."[45] One might immediately wonder at the cogency of this objection. Kant's sense of the dignity of humanity, for one, would depend on the fact that men are capable of acting morally, which is not an affair of "usefulness" to anyone. True, Kaufmann does not reflect on the rights of animals, finding human rights more urgent, and he abhors Kant's conception of moral duty. Nonetheless, Rosen's objections would do nothing to shift him off course.

We can return to Genesis by contrasting it with the intellectual foundations of Chinese thought. Here we discover (1) the distinctive absence of a creation myth and (2) the earliest landscape painting in which the presence of human figures is virtually eclipsed. To find landscape painting in the West, one would have to wait until the sixteenth century, according to Kaufmann, for Pieter Brueghel the Elder's *Landscape with the Flight into Egypt* (FH 142–43).

Kaufmann would have all students study and learn to value the magnificent first nineteen verses of Genesis 22—the *Akedah*, the binding of Isaac. "The Christian idea that 'God so loved the world that he gave his only begotten son,' in the Gospel according to John (3:16) clearly harks back to Genesis 22." The notion that no sacrifice could be greater than giving up one's son—this intense love of the father for his son—is found in many places in the Hebrew Bible: one hears it in David's cry of grief at his rebellious son Absalom: "There is nothing comparable to this in ancient Indian, Greek, or Chinese literature" (FH 147). Here Kaufmann's scholarship shows to his advantage.

> It would also be instructive to compare the ancient Jewish mosaic of the *Akedah* in the synagogue of Bet Alpha in Israel with later Christian mosaics. The story is also illustrated in medieval Hebrew Bibles and prayer books, and the early Christians dealt with it in paint, glass, and ivory. Major Italian artists who took up this theme include Ghiberti, Donatello, Andrea del Sarto, Sodoma, Titian, Caravaggio, Guardi, and Tiepolo. Ghiberti's two bronze doors at the Baptistery in Florence are world-famous. The one com-pleted first is adorned with scenes from the New Testament, the second door presents Old Testament themes and is known as the Gates of Para-dise—a tribute first paid to Ghiberti's artistry by Michelangelo. It is less well known that each of the seven artists who competed for the original assignment had to do a bronze *Akedah*. Ghiberti won, and his version and

that of the runner-up, Brunelleschi, who later built the dome of the cathedral of Florence, are now in the Bargello in Florence. Rembrandt treated the story in an etching and a famous painting. And in our time, Igor Stravinsky composed *Akedah Yizhak*, a ballad for baritone and chamber orchestra set to a Hebrew text. (FH 150–51)

I will quote Kaufmann at some length once more, meaning to honor the extraordinary work that he had just accomplished—the encyclopedia in five hundred closely printed pages titled *Religions in Four Dimensions*: *Existential and Aesthetic, Historical and Comparative.* The passage concluding the chapter "The Place of Religion in Higher Education" in *The Future of the Humanities* alludes to *Religions*. In asking how one would set about teaching Buddhism to undergraduates as an indispensable element of their education Kaufmann writes:

> Buddhism is not only literature but also Angkor Thom in Cambodia and Borobodur in Java, Thai bronzes and Japanese statues carved from wood, people pouring water over gilded images on the great terrace of the Shwe Dagon pagoda in Rangoon and palmistry in Mandalay; the emperor Ashoka and the caves at Ajanta as well as Zen and the art of swordsmanship. Any notion that religion is mainly theology is a betrayal of man. Religion is far too important to be left to theologians. (FH 152)

14

What Is Man's Lot?

MAN'S LOT: LIFE AT THE LIMITS, TIME IS AN ARTIST, WHAT IS MAN?

The creative life involves suffering versus Nirvana.

—WALTER KAUFMANN

Try to be one of the people on whom nothing is lost!

—HENRY JAMES

Temples, friezes and music may be opiates, and some who have suffered much may scarcely know how to live without them.

—WALTER KAUFMANN

Finally, I think it is Man's Lot to get egg on your face; in K.'s case later rather than sooner. Time is, among other things, a comic artist.

—DAVID PICKUS

IT IS INDICATIVE OF A FREER, ever more audacious Kaufmann that he begins *Man's Lot*, a work celebrating human tenacity and human genius, with a diatribe against "most philosophers," in a tone taken from his book on the deplorable future of the humanities. It is a tone that that will dominate his future work.[1] According to Kaufmann, most philosophers have failed to attend to man *in extremis*, "at the limit," although they have been warned: according to Montaigne, Cicero wrote famously "that to study philosophy is nothing but to prepare one's self to die."[2] It is hardly the case that twentieth-century German philosophers ignored that warning or were unconscious of limit situations: the literal concept of the *Grenzsituation* is the work of Karl Jaspers, and Heidegger's analysis of Being-toward-death does not suggest ignorance of the concept. Kaufmann knows that "existentialism poses as the one great exception. . . . Indeed, the most important feature that the so-called existentialists have in common is the belief that our most extreme experiences furnish the proper starting point for philosophy" (LL 65). But having Jaspers and Heidegger in his sights, Kaufmann continues to denigrate the work of the German "existentialists," quick to point out that there are a great many kinds of limits—many approaching ecstasy—that they fail to address. Above all, not all extreme experiences are lethal or inspire dread and despair. Recall the "report" of Kafka's articulate scientist-dog in "Researches of a Dog," which refers to his vision of a melody floating in the air—Kaufmann's first example of a limit experience is inspirational music. The dog declares:

> Today, of course, I deny any such perceptions and attribute them to my overstimulation at the time, but even if it was an error, it nevertheless had a certain grandeur and is the sole reality, even if only an apparent reality, that I salvaged and brought back into this world from the time of my fast, and shows, at least, how far we can go when we are completely out of our senses.[3]

Kaufmann invokes Clifford Geertz's description of the Balinese Barong dance to illustrate another sort of limit situation he calls "Dionysian abandon":

> By the time a full-scale Rangda-Barong encounter has been concluded, a majority, often nearly all, of the members of the group sponsoring it will have become caught up in it not just imaginatively but bodily. . . . Usually sheer pandemonium breaks out at this point with members of the crowd, of both sexes, falling into trance all around the courtyard and rushing out to stab themselves, wrestle with one another, devour live chicks or excrement. (LL 67)

Kaufmann's signature insistence throughout is that death, for many, is Nothing to be afraid of (Julian Barnes's magnificent pun is unintentional).[4] Man is essentially the being who "can rise above his circumstances, leave father and mother, live dangerously, and when all else fails . . . choose to die—and how to die."[5] Kaufmann's opening trope on the limited imagination of even existentialist philosophers reads like a highly personal act of philosophical defiance.

Man's Lot consists of three short books—*Life at the Limits, Time Is an Artist,* and *What Is Man?* Each book contains didactic texts from great books and philosophical comments, poems (many are Kaufmann's own), and a great many photographs taken by Kaufmann on his journeys around the world. The titles of the three books are essentially dictated by the photographs: the first group is taken entirely in India—some in Benares, some in Calcutta, and most in Khajuraho, known for a cluster of Hindu and Jain temples, some with astonishing erotic sculptures. The second cluster of photographs illustrates the gorgeous displays and ravages of time; the third, poignant portraits— famously exotic—of people in Australia, New Guinea, and Java among others in 1974, Burma in 1975, and then in many different cities—in Madrid, Amalfi, Jerusalem, and even in Princeton, New Jersey, where Kaufmann photographed children and philosophers of science. Along with photographs, *Man's Lot* contains short disquisitions on famous thinkers and their books—in many cases spelled out more persuasively in early and later works.

The desire to preserve and display the photographs, which the author admits he loves, appears to be the main motive of *Man's Lot*, and "it is hardly decent to ask a man why he loves what he loves" (WM 137). This main motive is tempered a bit at the end by a brief access, almost an afterthought, of sociability—of Kaufmann's wanting to "share" his love (WM 139). It does not erase the impression that this is not a book written for the express pleasure and instruction of readers. Walter Benjamin's dictum, which we contrasted earlier with Kaufmann's deeply held faith in the communicative function of great art, again seems more apt: "No poem is intended for the reader, no picture for the beholder, no symphony for the audience."[6] *Man's Lot* is Kaufmann's personal lot.[7]

Might there be more to the inspiration of this book than self-pleasuring? Kaufmann acknowledges Edward Steichen's famous exhibit of photographs titled *The Family of Man,* which was afterward published as a best-selling book. *The Family of Man* and *What Is Man?* display a family resemblance—yet the narcissism of small differences appears to predominate. Kaufmann is complimentary: "Some of the images . . . are unforgettable, and the whole was greater than the parts." On the other hand, "many of the photographs were not especially remarkable considered by themselves"; and, what is crucial for Kaufmann in specifying his distinction, "by no means [did] all of the pictures show life at the limits" (LL 114).

On independent inspection, the differences grow larger and more significant. Steichen's assemblage of photographs dates from 1955, a quarter century before Kaufmann's, and they were taken by many hands; Kaufmann's photographs are all his own, steeped in the experience of taking them. Steichen aims to show a sort of human everydayness: in Mark Greif's description of his rationale, "All men (or, rather, men, women, and children) were born, ate, played, worked, made love, lived in families, and died, to be succeeded by others. These most minimal but touching arrangements formed the basis for collages of photographs."[8] Again, Kaufmann's photographs strive to depict only extreme situations.

Steichen's concern is explicitly moral: he means to picture "the essential oneness of mankind throughout the world," and this thought should nourish a universal resistance to war.[9] In *Man's Lot* Kaufmann subordinates moral to aesthetic concerns. He alludes to Nietzsche's notorious justification of the world by aesthetic means—"Only as an aesthetic phenomenon is existence and the world eternally justified"—and concludes: "Morally, the world is unjustifiable, hideous, and cruel; but looked at aesthetically, it requires no justification. Nowhere is this more striking than in the streets of India. What outrages our moral sense is nevertheless beautiful" (LL 119).

This reduction of a way of being in the world to a gaze that elides the shock of another's suffering can seem obtuse; it is as if Kaufmann, hearing this objection, seeks a way, at the very end, to enlarge his perspective. He dismisses the claim that "photography reduces everything to what Martin Buber called 'the It,' meaning, 'an object of experience and use.' Most of the images in *What Is Man?*," Kaufmann maintains, "are meant to reveal the 'You' [*Du*] that addresses me and *you*" (WM 137). Man is the being who can feel addressed by a transcendental *Du*. But this flight mainly conjures with the authority of Martin Buber, supposing that Kaufmann's thought is meaningful; and in a work written soon after, he will repudiate the key argument of Buber's *I and You* (see chapter 16).

Of the three books constituting *Man's Lot*, the first part of the trilogy, *Life at the Limits*, is the least dominated by an aesthetic ideology. It is conceptually informed: its basic concepts are presented early on in conspicuous detail in two tables, which, while eye-catching, are certainly more than a little odd. There is Table "A" and Table "B." "A" describes predicaments "at the limit"; "B" describes the emotional response to these predicaments. Each table has twelve items, and each item begins with the letter "d."

Table A

   1. delivery (birth and giving birth)
   2. deformity

3. disaster

4. defeat

5. disgrace

6. destitution (including extreme hunger and thirst)

7. distress

8. desolation and darkness (including deafness and blindness)

9. dehumanization

10. danger

11. decay

12. death

Table B

1. dread

2. depth (intensity, profundity)

3. disillusionment

4. despair, depression, despondence, dejection

5. derangement, delusions, dreams, drunkenness, drugs

6. debauchery, dissipation, disinheritance

7. degradation of others

8. destruction (including suicide and murder)

9. defiance

10. devotion, love

11. Dionysian joy (often associated with music)

12. Dionysian abandon (often associated with dance)

Kaufmann attempts to justify his construction by claiming that the recurring Latin prefix "dis-" implies separation from normality; hence, its appropriateness in this scheme, "a separation from a sheltered state that brings a confrontation with the limits" (LL 67). Alas, it rings hollow and does not invite confidence in the conceptual rigor of what follows. Kaufmann is not deaf to this objection: some ten pages later he worries, with respect to his tables, "whether *any* predominantly conceptual approach does not have serious limitations" (emphasis added) (LL 78). Surely any conceptual approach consisting of twenty-four concepts all beginning with the letter "d" might run into some danger..

Man's Lot gestures toward "the limit" in words *and* images. Philosophy has implicitly ceded that task to art, and not graciously, as witness the abundance of inferior aesthetics in the philosophical canon. But here Kaufmann holds himself to be the rare philosopher who has a highly developed feeling for visual art—especially in those works where a sort of limit is shown, not said. In the spirit of Wittgenstein, who distinguished between *saying* and *showing*, Kaufmann notes, "What makes not only much work on aesthetics but most philosophy so academic is not the common failure to understand what art *is* but the refusal to see what art *shows*" (LL 65). Wittgenstein wrote, "What can be shown cannot be said," which means, to quote an authority, "what cannot be formulated in sayable (sensical) propositions can only be shown." The pictorial form of the world is shown in symbolic art. The unsayables, writes Wittgenstein, are "things that cannot be put into words. They make themselves manifest. They are what is mystical."[10] This is Kaufmann's point, precisely.

Man's Lot includes a great many of Kaufmann's own poems, but they are not as good as the works he celebrates. The jacket praises this book of text, photographs, and poems as inaugurating "a new art form"; it is unclear what this form in others' hands would include and exclude. A less exalted view would consider *Man's Lot* a high-minded miscellany of museal citations, personal comments, fusées, recollections of things read, unacknowledged sentences from earlier works, and photographs taken on tour—many of them, certainly, beautiful. For all that, it is an impressive work for the labor involved on both sides of the production process—not least for weighing in at more than four pounds.

Are there earlier indications that Kaufmann would have turned with passion, at the end of his short life, to photography? His love of thinking, reading, and writing is well attested; he confessed earlier to his inadequate mastery of music. Are there hints of visual intensity in his earlier work? There are mentions of great painters: it is Rembrandt, we recall, who returned Kaufmann's gaze when, on contemplating "Large Self-Portrait" in the Vienna art museum, he had a sort of moral epiphany. Seeing "integrity incarnate" in the painter's eyes, he felt as if he were being "mustered" by that gaze: "I felt that I want to write only in the spirit in which Rembrandt had painted himself, without regard for what might pay or advance my career" (C xi). His love for Rilke's "Archaic Torso of Apollo" includes an image of the statue's returning the gaze of the observer and demanding that "you must change your life." Kaufmann displays a more than passing familiarity with the history of painting in a fugue in *Tragedy and Philosophy* when, charting increasing mimesis in the arts, he begins with the immediacy of "Flemish and German Renaissance painting (including Jan van Eyck, the younger Holbein, and Dürer) . . . then Rembrandt," and so on . . . as we advance from mimesis toward the freedom of "pure music" (T 80). He compares Sophocles's dramas to monumental Asian architecture. But there is more than a hint of passion for religious art in the closing chapters of *Religions in Four Dimensions*—descriptions that I briefly mentioned at the close of chapter 12 and are quite splendid. Kaufmann explicitly calls *Religions* an "Overture" to *Man's Lot*, which he holds to be the more ambitious and the even more personal work (LL 68). *Religions* is founded on historical data culled from extant, scholarly sources; to the extent that this is possible, everything in *Man's Lot* originates with Kaufmann.

This book is part of a Bildung in never-ending progress. Consider that Kaufmann, as he previously admitted, is weak in music, yet the very first chapter of *Man's Lot* celebrates music as the art form best qualified to convey the experience of "the limit." This disquisition will not satisfy experts. We learn that music is sheer *defiance* of God and gods, yet Kaufmann cites Bach's "St. Matthew Passion" as exemplary. What comes through is Kaufmann's love of canonical works: he finds Mozart's "Eine kleine Nachtmusik," which he already evoked at the close of *The Faith of a Heretic*, to be unsurpassable. There are Handel's "Hallelujah Chorus," *Don Giovanni*, Verdi's Shakespearean operas, Beethoven's Ninth, and—thankfully—his late quartets. This music is not analyzed. They are "little more than reminders of familiar compositions . . . that should be seen [not heard?] in a new perspective if we want to understand human existence." One wonders whom Kaufmann is addressing? Music "gives expression to what had seemed inexpressible," but some things remain unexpressed in great books because they are beneath mention, being merely trite (LL 70). It grieves me to think how few of Kaufmann's many admirers will welcome this fugue:

> Few if any landscapes are more moving than those suggesting life at the limits: the sea in a storm, surf pounding rocks, mountains, desert, the outback, the renewal of life in the spring, and the colors of fall. But to supplement the black-and-white photographs and the poem in the opening pages of this volume, it may suffice to quote three short poems from my *Cain and Other Poems*. (LL 71)

The poem he printed as a frontispiece read:

> Drab is the sun's endless motion
> compared to the burst
> of life when it slakes
> its fiery thirst
> in the sea and drowns. And the ocean
> is most beautiful where it breaks.

The diction of the first line is dull and its syntax archaic; the "poem" is interrupted prose, its power of invocation slight, its music almost inaudible. The three short poems mentioned are of comparable quality. In a late preface to his earlier *Tragedy and Philosophy*, Kaufmann described his project: "If we want to gain a deeper understanding of the human condition and consider life at the limits, *vita in extremis*, or the question 'What is Man?' we are quite apt to learn more from the great tragic poets and from a few other writers and artists than from philosophers" (T xii). One is entitled to wonder what Kaufmann's own poetry contributes to this project.

At this point I confess that I—and you, patient reader—may experience some loss of conviction as we continue our reading of *Man's Lot*. Kaufmann's writing and thinking in this project is personal to the point of being couldn't-care-less idiosyncratic. His value judgments are unsupported. The substance of *Man's Lot* is not the product of fresh research but an inventory of what Kaufmann already has in mind—and in his earlier books. The prose execution is not up to his standard.

Unlike previous books, the manuscript of *Man's Lot* does not appear to have been read in advance by scholars. We have not seen such sentences before as these: "*The* poet does not reduce those who suffer to objects that we might view as tools of our pleasure. He leads us to look up to them as superior" (emphasis added). Is it true that "the plays [i.e., tragedies] that are judged the most beautiful [judged by whom?] surpass all the rest in terror"; that *Hamlet*, while "beautiful," is "packed with horror"; and that, while granting the power of *Hamlet* and *Lear*, it is an acceptable judgment that "almost nothing in Western literature is in the same league" (LL 72)? Not *The Divine Comedy*, not *Don Quixote*, not *Paradise Lost*? There will be two views on why *Man's Lot* has never caught on. One is plain from the above: the level of argument is at once too high for casual readers and too low for scholars.

Kaufmann maintains his very high opinion "of the masterpieces of Dostoevsky and Tolstoy," with which, without further ado, he adds, "no novels written in Western Europe can brook comparison." Is it reasonable to claim that none of the novels of Stendhal, Balzac, or Flaubert, none of the novels of Goethe, Dickens, or George Eliot, of Thomas Mann or James Joyce, can be mentioned in the same breath? But, Kaufmann concludes, "if anyone after Tolstoy or Dostoevsky has written novels that can be compared to theirs"—and here Kaufmann is at his most idiosyncratic—"it is . . . Solzhenitsyn" (LL 73).

It is true that in the years of his writing Solzhenitsyn was compared—not "to"—but "with" Tolstoy, although he was found to be altogether unlike his master. The critic Clive James makes the point that Tolstoy wrote about a society available to him; Solzhenitsyn, about a world that lacked one. Tolstoy wrote from observation; Solzhenitsyn, from memory. "Solzhenitsyn's contemporary novels—the novels set in the Soviet Union—are not really concerned with society. They are concerned with what happens after society has been destroyed."[11] Still, James, whose opinion matters, does not dispute the evidence of Solzhenitsyn's vast creative imagination.

Throughout the 1970s Kaufmann was an ardent supporter of Solzhenitsyn. He dedicated *Without Guilt and Justice* to him. In an essay titled "Solzhenitsyn and Autonomy," published in 1976, he wrote, typically: "In the early fifties Sartre and many others in France were arguing about two seemingly unrelated questions; whether it was permissible to admit that there were two camps in the Soviet Union, and whether the novel is dead. At one blow, Solzhenitsyn made these debates ridiculous."[12] But after figuring at the center of American political discourse during the 1970s and 1980s, and creating ideological enemies among critics less anticommunist, less Christian, and less likely to deplore Western democracy than himself, Solzhenitsyn became less honored. With the waning of his personal celebrity, his books suffered neglect, so much so that a massive novel written at the end of his life—*Krasnoe Koleso* (The Red Wheel)—has not been fully translated into English. Today he is little read and less taught. Kaufmann's judgment has not survived.

"As we survey Western literature from *The Iliad* to Solzhenitsyn's war novel *August 1914*," Kaufmann continues, "we find an impressive unity in the most celebrated tragedies, epics, and novels." The unity is presumably supplied by their topic "life at the limits," but it is unclear now what limit is intended. I am also unsure what agreement about taste and clarity the following citation can elicit:

> The greatest comedies [deal relentlessly with life at the limits but] . . . seek relief not in tears but in laughter. And works whose subject matter is really light are judged to be mere *divertimenti*.
>
> The point is not to impose my value judgments. Far from it. I would gladly trade most non-Greek and non-Shakespearean tragedies for the *divertimenti* of Mozart. But Mozart's *divertimenti* are not the works of a man who stops short of the limits, averting his eyes. They are the gifts of one who has crossed the limits. (LL 74)

Questions arise. Are those judges misguided who deem "works whose subject matter is really light" to be *mere divertimenti*? Normally, the invocation of judges produces Kaufmann's agreement. Evidently there must be a distinction between "mere" *divertimenti* and *divertimenti* (Mozart's) that are worth saving even if it should mean the extinction of the totality of non-Greek and non-Shakespearean tragedies, including those of Lope de Vega, Marlowe, Calderón, Corneille, Racine, Goethe, Schiller, Ibsen, Strindberg, Beckett, and others. Mozart "crossed the limits," but what does it mean, finally, "to cross the limits"? Which limit? Where does one arrive? How does one return?

In this vein of making extreme value judgments—granted: he says he does not mean to impose them—Kaufmann writes: "Unlike *The Iliad, Oedipus,* or *The Trojan Women,* odes to flowers and birds *no longer matter*" (emphasis added). He continues: "In 'A Journal in Verse,' written in 1961 and included in my *Cain,* the poem preceding 'The Eichmann Trial' is . . . 'I heard an old harlot sighing . . .'" (LL 74). What matters is . . . "an old harlot sighing"! This short poem has three voices and two "I"s: it is difficult to empower either of the speakers—but the refrain is intelligible, if unappealing. It says that romantic poets strain for effect but do not feel what they say. They are inauthentic, and Kaufmann's poem about an old harlot asserts this claim boldly. It is not convincing. Keats's "Ode to a Nightingale" puts Kaufmann's poem in the shade; readers might (briefly) close his book and open Keats. Kaufmann should not shun romantic poets, for that would mean shunning even Byron, who made Kaufmann's point sharper, as we earlier saw, when he wrote of the song of a "Greek Bard":

> His strain display'd some feeling—right or wrong;
> And feeling, in a poet, is the source
> Of others' feeling; but they are such liars,
> And take all colours—like the hands of dyers.[13]

Of course, this argument itself falls victim to the liar paradox, invalidating the statement of the speaker, who is a self-confessed liar.

Several of the propositions that follow this revision of the canon could prompt further concern: "Shakespeare has left his mark on world literature"; "short poems . . . probe the depths of the human soul" (LL 75). One wonders why Kaufmann has ceased to imagine readers who read his *Critique of Religion and Philosophy* or *The Faith of a Heretic* with fervor and admiration. In such a mood, we might recall the complaint of Professor William Kennick, who said, while reviewing Kaufmann's *From Shakespeare to Existentialism*—a work full of innovative truth—that Kaufmann should restrict himself to his competence "as an expositor and critic of German philosophy."[14] How Kennick would have been exercised by this parade of weary bromides—words that might seem fresh to a junior high school class in English literature—and words that are incorrect: "Since Keats, Shelley, and Byron died, still young, in their twenties, there have been no poets in English of equal stature" (LL 77). Byron died at thirty-six. And have there been no English poets equal to Byron? Not William Wordsworth or Walt Whitman or Emily Dickinson or William Butler Yeats? Not T. S. Eliot or Wallace Stevens? It would be one thing to read such a claim in a book titled *Stories and Poems for Extremely Intelligent Children of All Ages* (an honorable book of this name was published by Harold Bloom). But . . . *Man's Lot*? To be fair, Kaufmann appears to intuit this objection to Byron's unequalled distinction by mentioning several of these excluded poets and giving each a poem, but he does not adjust his table of values. Later he cites Paul Celan—while writing, incorrectly, that Celan "survived Auschwitz." Kaufmann may be thinking of Adorno's famous apothegm "to write poetry after Auschwitz is barbaric."[15]

On the other hand, *en bonne humaniste*, Kaufmann is certainly right to refute the error of judging poetic intensity by the (negative) intensity of the poet's life, where intensity might mean proximity to "limits" like madness and suicide. Personal derangement is not a prerequisite for poetry of the limits: "Sophocles, who was utterly sane and lived to the age of ninety, wrote poetry of madness, despair, and suicide second to none" (LL 78). T. S. Eliot wrote famously on poetry and emotion in a way cogent to Kaufmann's claim: "For it is not the 'greatness,' the intensity, of the emotions, the components, but the intensity of the artistic process, the pressure, so to speak, under which the fusion takes place, that counts."[16]

It is not clear why Kaufmann reprints a medley of anthologized poems displaying the social conscience of several unimpressive American and German poets, including Franz Werfel, Edwin Markham ("The Man with the Hoe"), Louis Untermeyer, and Erich Kästner, the author of sarcastic light verse. It is clear why he turns to Rilke, who is "*perhaps* the greatest [poet] of the last hundred years" (emphasis added)—"perhaps" is a locution that recurs throughout these pages when preceding statements of absolute superiority. Rilke, Kaufmann avers, "seems remote from the horrors of two world wars" (LL 82), but Kaufmann does not appear to know that Rilke wrote a cycle of flagrantly warmongering poems in 1914. "These poems," as Adam Zagajewski notes, "sang the praise of a god of war as a great renewer of humanity. Later on, Rilke never joined those poets who wept over the disaster of the same war, which failed to renew anything except the death industry."[17] A good deal of Kaufmann's discussion of Rilke is taken from his previously published collection of essays, *From Shakespeare to Existentialism*.[18]

What is new, in *Man's Lot*, is Kaufmann's singling out the one great theme of Rilke's short poems, which is "as significant as any theme can be. It is the choice between two modes of existence that might be called intensity and peace; the creative life that involves suffering versus Nirvana; Eros and Thanatos; or, in the words of Moses: 'Choose life or death this day'" (LL 82). And thereby hangs a tale. If this should not be Rilke, it is surely Kaufmann, with Kaufmann's choice unstated but everywhere implied throughout his work. What now and again leap out brilliantly from this chewed-over "philosophy"—it is clear that what Kaufmann understands as the "philosophical dimension" of art is the "experience of life" allegedly recoverable from it—are Kaufmann's translations of Rilke. Here is the twelfth of part 2 of the *Sonnets to Orpheus*:

> Choose to be changed. Oh experience the rapture of fire
> in which a life is concealed, exalting in change as it burns;
> and the projecting spirit who is master of the entire
> earth loves the figure's flight less than the point where it turns. (LL 87)

Concerning a later section of *Life at the Limits*, "Western Philosophy," it will by now come as no surprise to find an iteration of what Kaufmann has already written in his previous works about Christianity ("a confirmation and increase of human callousness"); Kierkegaard ("infinitely more concerned about his own dread and despair than about human misery"); Nietzsche (he recommended "living dangerously"); Jaspers ("much preoccupied with his mortality, he took such exceedingly good care of himself that he lived to be eighty-six") and Heidegger ("essentially a comic figure" [who] "by being careful also lived to be eighty-six") (LL 91–93). One section nowhere to be found in Kaufmann's earlier work is a long, approving quote from *Hell's Angels* by Hunter S. Thompson, the founder of "gonzo journalism," which describes breathlessly the feel of a "windscream," of "wind-burned eyeballs," of hurtling toward "the Edge." Kaufmann's commentary is one of the very few passages in the entire eight-thousand-plus pages of his published writings that I find hard to understand:

> At first glance the great poets who wrote of their own despair or celebrated the beauty of the most intense suffering seem poles apart from the few who expressed a social conscience, writing about a brutalized toiler, the leaden-eyed, or the coal mines. But as soon as we compare them with youths who

take drugs or lose control on an oil-slick and kill themselves and perhaps others as well, Shakespeare and Mozart appear in a different light. (LL 95)

The new philosophical material is also often oddly angled, for example, "Sartre's being wall-eyed did not keep him from taking great risks when the Nazis occupied France," although this formative experience "does not exempt his work from criticism. When he tried to philosophize he came to grief" (LL 95). On the topic of what great philosophers knew in addition to their philosophy, Kaufmann writes:

> Aristotle was a scientist as well; Descartes and Leibniz were mathematicians of genius; Hume and Hegel were in their different ways also historians; Hobbes translated Homer as well as Thucydides. Spinoza wrote a Hebrew grammar and pioneered Biblical criticism; Kant advanced a major astronomical theory.

These remarks are very interesting but would be more so if we did not already remember them from *The Future of the Humanities* (as well as from *The Faith of a Heretic*, with small variations [F 45]):

> Descartes and Leibniz were as great as mathematicians as they were as philosophers. Spinoza was an encyclopedic philosopher, wrote a Hebrew grammar, and pioneered Biblical criticism. Hobbes translated Homer and Thucydides. Hume wrote a multivolume *History of England*. Kant advanced a major astronomical theory. (FH 82)

There a great deal of evidence that Kaufmann is now ready to publish sentences he has already published elsewhere, without attribution. There is an intermittent slackening of attention, tact, and a concern for transmitting reliable (falsifiable) knowledge. Perhaps this tissue of improvised texts can be accepted as a means to bind together the photographs, many of which are once again splendid.

Certainly, one might welcome the opportunity to turn to Kaufmann's discussion of Western art after his brief forays into Western literature and philosophy. Kaufmann lovers might hope to learn from him, value his taste, and share his enthusiasms. But again the range is too ambitious for accuracy: Kaufmann will pass from Hammurabi "in greenish blue steatite" (LL 97) to the film *Bad Day at Black Rock* (LL 114) in seventeen pages. From the outset there is no lack of eye-opening but slightly consternating declarations. Consider the case of the so-called Carnarvon head of the pharaoh Sesostris III, who, writes

Kaufmann, "looks like a man without illusions who had an exceptionally keen sense of human frailty, suffering, and death" (LL 97–98). Kaufmann quotes a description found in literature at New York's Metropolitan Museum, which considers "the expression of the mouth ... melancholy rather than disdainful," but he will have little of that. He observes that the head is carved in very hard stone—quartzite, in one version, granite in another—in order to conclude that "the choice of stone seems more felicitous than adjectives like 'melancholy' or 'disdainful.'" On the other hand, "What we see is total disillusionment and strength enough to live with it. Sesostris clearly knew what Sartre said in *The Flies*: 'Life begins on the other side of despair.'" One could wonder whether Kaufmann really knows what Sesostris, who lived in the nineteenth century BC, "clearly knew"; and what precisely, once again, is this knowledge of a life "that begins on the other side of despair"? The latter question might be pointless, since Kaufmann has made it clear that art expresses the inexpressible. On the other hand, perhaps one should then not preempt this voice of silence so confidently.

The same concern arises when Kaufmann proceeds to divulge "the secret" of Nefertiti's beauty, who, the more modern figure, nevertheless lived sixteen centuries ago: "there is nothing bland about it ... hers is an unsheltered spirit that masters grief with pride and fortitude." Kaufmann generalizes about the Egyptian sculptures that have come down to us: these "sculptors and the men and women they portrayed knew life at the limits" (LL 98). I doubt that any Egyptologist or "common reader" could find much use in this assertion. But it signals the freewheeling manner of Kaufmann's interpretations of stone and canvas throughout the ages. And so we have, in his discussion of classical Greek sculpture, the proposition: "The tragic poets explored life at the limits, while the sculptors and painters did not." And yet one might ask, What about the bronze Zeus—or Poseidon—from the sea off Cape Artemision, who is about to launch a spear, or Discobolus, the disc thrower? They do not seem to stand far off from "the limits."

A casual phrase in this discussion might advance Kaufmann's general thesis: "Great architecture and sculpture are Apollinian in the sense that they are content to stay within drastic limits and try to achieve harmonious perfection, the triumph of proportion, *not of defiant will*" (emphasis added) (LL 98). But here another question arises. Kaufmann wonders rhetorically whether "a subtle taste" might not "find more life and intensity in the tiny ebony head of Queen Tiye [the mother of Akhenaten] and more energy in a battered portrait of Sesostris than in this huge marble group"—the Hellenistic *Laokoon*. Very well, but might not this very subtle taste recoil from a definition of "the limits" as chiefly a display of "defiant will"? Here, Kaufmann's heroic humanism has been plainly projected onto speechless stone.

Kaufmann's discussion of Christian art centers on a striking theory about the sudden emergence of representations of anguish in "the high Middle Ages" (LL 100). Since his thesis is based on his personal experience of works of art—the sculptures adorning Romanesque churches—it "cannot be proved—nor disproved"—as he has maintained: one's personal experience of an art object "is not subject to refutation" (T 89). On the other hand, one may find one's experience diminished by a consensus of views by established scholars, including the renowned Meyer Schapiro. Kaufmann's argument proceeds:

> The Christ of early Christian and Romanesque art [ca. 1000–1200] was not the Suffering Servant of Isaiah 53; he was the Lord. The cross was not seen as an instrument of torture before the high Middle Ages, and it was only then that the torments of the damned began to capture the imagination of sculptors. Why this sudden concern with anguish? It was clearly not derived straight from the Gospels, seeing that it emerged only after the Crusades had begun and then became much more pronounced in the fourteenth century. (LL 100)

The agent of this new artistic consciousness was "the Crusades." In what way? The Crusades were abundant in the production of death, torture, and anguish. But whose? To our surprise, Kaufmann says it was the murdered Jews, the victims of the terrible pogrom in the towns on the Rhine with which the First Crusade began. He quotes sources that he has already quoted in his fierce discussion of the Crusades in *Religions in Four Dimensions*. This new mood of anguish would presumably have come from the contemplation of the sufferings of the Jews and Muslims slaughtered in Jerusalem. (Kaufmann omits mentions of the massacred Saracens.) A certain Raymond, an eyewitness, reports:

> Some of our men . . . cut off the heads of their enemies; . . . others tortured them longer by casting them into the flames. Piles of heads, hands, and feet were to be seen in the streets of the city. . . . Men rode in blood up to their knees and bridle reins. Indeed, it was a just and splendid judgment of God that this place should be filled with the blood of the unbelievers since it had suffered so long from their blasphemies.[19]

After the Crusades we have the Inquisition and "a papal bull that [in 1252] officially authorized torture in cases of heresy. This," continues Kaufmann, "is the context in which the concern with suffering and death, anguish and torture emerged in Christian art" (LL 101).

According to Kaufmann it is the suffering of the Jews, (implicitly) Muslims, and heretics that for the first time conveys the experience of anguish to Christian artists. These sculptors, under the sway of the church, would have been covertly inspired by the suffering of the "blasphemers" to portray the suffering of the damned. Again, it is true that Kaufmann claimed that thoughts inspired by such art experiences are irrefutable. In this instance, however, doubts increase.

Was there not enough suffering around *until* the time of the Crusades to inspire an art bearing witness to it, supposing, as Kaufmann does, that it is the lived experience of suffering that inspires its representation? The certain fact of an available abundance of experiences of human agony even in the eleventh century suggests that something in addition—an affair of the emergence of generic types and formal constraints immanent to the history of sculpture— was also at work in producing newer representations of anguish and death. An inscription on the tympanum of the Abbey Church of Sainte Foy at Conques, circa 1000, warns:

> "O sinners, if you do not change your lives, know that a harsh judgment awaits you." ... The tympanum [is divided] into two zones: the chosen on the right, the damned on the left. ... On the side of the chosen, calm, happiness, order and rhythm are opposed to the disorder, agitation, ugliness and horror prevailing on the side of the damned. ... Among the damned, languishing in despair, torments and the horror of deformity and monstrosity, the sins of Christian society, lust, lying, adultery, avarice and pride, are punished with tortures.[20]

A historian writing on "religious certainty" in the period of the construction of the Romanesque churches observes:

> Romanesque architects peopled the earth with churches and chapels symbolizing eternity. Yet their sense of anguish and consciousness of sin invested these buildings with strange, unhappy monsters representing a melancholy, heartfelt appeal to redemption. This bestiary of monsters, which took such a hold on Romanesque imagination, represented far more than a reservoir of forms and decorative themes. It was a type of classification of a haunted,

frightening world and its resources, of evil. Everything there was linked in an infernal dance: nightmare animals, gryphons, monsters from the East, sciapods, dog-headed beasts and dwarfs with huge ears. They formed a strange picture of intellectual abandonment and sheer terror.[21]

The great art historian Meyer Schapiro should have the last word, from the seventh of his Charles Eliot Norton Lectures of 1977:

> The word *remorsus*, from which we get our word *remorse*, is not classical Latin but Christian Latin. It appears first in early Christian writings; it means, "to bite oneself." Or the word *angustiare*—to be in anguish—means to be in a tight, narrow place. It is based on a Latin word, but in this intense verbal form it first appeared in Christian writing. Hence, we recognize that the concept of the Romanesque beast who mutilates, or bites, or destroys himself is already built into language and into folklore. . . . But we recognize too that within a community in which concepts of penitence and guilt are immensely important, the model of the individual assumes more and more features of such a conflicting character. The art that results, the art that is built upon such concepts, when it is open to free fantasy . . . is not surprisingly, then, filled with imagery of the animal as the carrier of such motifs of self-torment, or involves conflict, and self-constraint.[22]

It would appear then that anguish, and the means to its representation, were well known to Romanesque sculptors centuries before the Crusades.

Kaufmann's interpretive style throughout this book is aggressive, though it is an understandable if not entirely justifiable manner. He is devoted to the etchings and paintings of Francisco Goya, which he has seen and loves and knows about—a range of work far exceeding *The Disasters of War*, which is generally appreciated. Kaufmann's passion for Goya's work is inseparable from his passion for his own interpretations, for which he feels he must fight, since the media are full of the opinions of irksome know-nothings. For example, "some" art historians who have published their views of Goya's extraordinary "black paintings" have clearly failed to understand them. Keizō Kanki, for one, writes about the painting "Duel with Cudgels":

> My own explanation of this gloomy scene, in which two men fight ferociously knee-deep in mire, is that Goya was trying to give expression to the two conflicting personalities within himself: mindless Aragonese tradition warring with the enlightenment the artist acquired in middle life. If this is

not a scene depicting the artist's inner turmoil, the painting may be thought of as expressing the two contradictory ways of life prevalent in Spain at the time. (qtd. in LL 105)

Kanki creditably highlights the difficulty of one assured reading, offering alternatives that respect Kaufmann's own principles in his "Toward a New Poetics" (see chapter 9). An interpretation may not overlook the artist's historical and conceptual milieu at the time of composition; here is Kaufmann:

> We cannot be sure about the artist's intentions, nor can we gain more than a very partial understanding of a work, unless we study its *historical* context. . . . One's personal experience of the object confronting one . . . may actually be more sensitive than the experience of a better informed scholar; or it may be less sensitive as well as more ignorant. (T 88–89)

Kaufmann continues, certainly not eager to contemplate the latter option. He is very displeased with the interpretations of the Goya scholars Pierre Gassier and Juliet Wilson. "The authors of the *Life and Complete Work of Francisco Goya* do not seem to have understood the picture either." They write:

> *The Duel* (1616) would be a barbarous but straightforward fight with cudgels between two peasants if it were not for the nightmare suggestion that the combatants are sinking into quicksand as they bludgeon each other to death; and *The Dog* (1612)—[another of the "black paintings"], perhaps the strangest of all the scenes, produces its powerfully disturbing effect by leaving everything to the spectator's imagination, with no possible answer to the question of the artist's own intention. . . . A dog is sinking into the quicksand, only his head still visible, alive—how much longer?—in a totally base and abstract setting. Such a subject defies analysis and belongs to the irrational world of dream and hallucination. (qtd. in LL 105)

Kaufmann's indignant comment could raise eyebrows:

> Nightmare? Irrational? Hallucination? No possible answer to the question of Goya's intention? Are some people who write about art as illiterate as people writing philosophy often are ignorant of the visual arts? Have they never read or seen Samuel Beckett's *Endgame*? Do they not know the conclusion of Kafka's *Trial*? "'Like a dog!' he said; it was as if the disgrace should survive him." (LL 105)

It is not obvious that the ideas of "nightmare" and the "irrational" imply an ignorance of Kafka, who, after all, invoked his "talent for portraying . . . [his] dreamlike inner life," which had "thrust all other matters into the background. My life has dwindled dreadfully, nor will it cease to dwindle."[23] Even so, Kaufmann's expectation that Gassier and Wilson should share Kaufmann's view that the death of Josef K. is the rational representation of a real-world event is not his most questionable point. More questionable still is his view that Kafka's view of Josef K. is equal to Goya's view of Everyman!

Kaufmann now presents his own confident interpretation of the "The Duel with Cudgels" and "The Dog":

Assuming that the identification of quicksand is right in both cases, no "analysis" is required, and the name of the "Duel" in the inventory of 1828, "Two Provincials," seems as apt as a scholar's attempt, in 1867, to identify them as "cattle herdsmen from Galicia" seems irrelevant. The first chapter of the *Dhammapada*, one of the oldest and most venerable Buddhist scriptures, is more to the point: ". . . The world does not know that we must all come to an end here; but those who know it—their quarrels cease at once." We are all dying slowly, and the end is not far off, but many people bludgeon each other to death, unaware that they are sinking. In the eleventh chapter of the *Dhammapada* it is said that "A man who has learnt little, grows old like an ox; his flesh grows, but his knowledge does not grow." Goya suggests that a man who has learned little dies like a dog—and one who has learned much is at least aware of the fact that he is dying as helplessly as a dog.

His interpreters have preferred not to understand him. (LL 105–6)

Again, it would hardly seem incumbent on Gassier and Wilson to be well acquainted with the *Dhammapada,* let alone incumbent on Goya to share the Buddhist view. And Kaufmann has certainly made it easy for himself by attributing to these scholars a deliberate "preference" for "not understanding," which means, once more, a deliberate preference for avoiding the Buddhist instruction that would have made perfect sense of Goya's two black paintings. It is interesting that the superior Goya scholar Robert Hughes agrees with the two art historians: apropos of Goya's *The Dog,* he writes, "We do not know what it means, but its pathos moves us on a level below narrative."[24] There are times when the subject of Kaufmann's book—*man in extremis*—appears more truthfully as *Kaufmann in extremis*—Kaufmann as Nietzsche's ascetic priest, laying down morals.

His essay on Goya concludes with a glimpse of "the terrifying drawings of a certain album "C," which, for their subject matter, could have been done in the mid-twentieth century:

> Above one drawing he wrote: "Poor man in Asia who sets his head aflame until they give him something." . . . A whole series shows victims of the Inquisition with such captions as: "For being of Jewish ancestry" . . . "For wagging his tongue in a different way" . . . and "For discovering the motion of the earth." . . . Yet we have been told again and again that only the Nazis persecuted Jews for being of Jewish descent, and a celebrated existentialist wrote a big book, *The Origins of Totalitarianism* (1951), without as much as mentioning the Inquisition. (LL 107)

It is dismaying that Goya's album "C" should become the vehicle of a slur directed against Hannah Arendt. In fact in an earlier work—*The Future of the Humanities*—Kaufmann had already indicted her for failing to find the origins of totalitarianism in Plato and in Dostoevsky's Grand Inquisitor. What is even more curious is that Kaufmann calls her a celebrated existentialist, presumably on the knowledge of her having been intimate with Martin Heidegger. This squib is an example of the rather offhand manner in which Kaufmann takes the readers of *Man's Lot* into his confidence. Arendt's early writing on existentialism gives no support to Kaufmann's descriptor: her view of the movement is negative. In 1946, she wrote in the *Nation*:

> Yet if the revolutionary élan of these writers [Sartre, de Beauvoir, Camus] is not broken by success . . . the time may come when it will be necessary to point out those aspects of their philosophy which indicate that they are still dangerously involved in old concepts. The nihilistic elements, which are obvious in spite of all protests to the contrary, are not the consequences of new insights but of some very old ideas.[25]

To put this matter in a somewhat wider light, it is true that recent scholars such as Odin Lysaker and Richard Wolin have attributed to Arendt, especially on the strength of *The Human Condition* (1958), a philosophy of "political existentialism." Lysaker notes that "even in times of crisis, Hannah Arendt writes, all human beings have the right to a humane politics. Such politics should be based on what she refers to as existential conditions, such as natality, plurality, and freedom. This is the core of Arendt's political existentialism."[26] Richard Wolin also speaks of Arendt's political existentialism but reserves the same title for the work of Carl Schmitt, but herewith tarring

Arendt with the same brush.[27] On Arendt's credentials as an existentialist thinker, the jury is out.

In his preceding book, *Religions in Four Dimensions*, Kaufmann wrote in detail about the four great Indian religions—Hinduism, Buddhism, Jainism, and Sikhism—and commented on art in ancient and medieval India. The ancient civilization of Mohenjo Daro yielded a few small sculptures—a slim girl who might be "a prototype of the dancing Shiva, of which no examples are known until about two thousand years later" (RE 209). Shiva, the dancing god, acquires considerable interest for Kaufmann as a figure for Nietzsche's prose, which we will discuss; this intuition may explain his willingness to see the prototype of a god in a girl. Scholars of ancient India see a prototype of Shiva not in the girl but in the seated heavyset figure, almost certainly male, in a surviving seal. Little else remains of the civilization of Mohenjo Daro, which was destroyed by Aryan horsemen in the sixteenth century BC.

Its annihilation leads to a claim that bears on Kaufmann's treatment of Indian art in *Man's Lot*. In *Religions in Four Dimensions*, Kaufmann wrote, "From about 1550 B.C. until after the invasion of Alexander the Great we have no evidence of any art in India, except literature. No temples, no other stone buildings, no sculpture, nor even an inscription survives. There is nothing until the third century . . . and *most of the glories* of Indian architecture and sculpture are medieval" (emphasis added) (RE 209). Devoted readers of both books who recall these lines will be struck by the contrasting style of the chapter on Indian art in *Man's Lot* titled "India *versus* the West." There is nothing here about the medieval glories of Indian architecture and sculpture. But we do have a repetition of Kaufmann's language from the preceding book. "From 1550 B.C. until the time of the Buddhist emperor Ashoka, thirteen centuries later, we have no evidence of literacy or of sculpture, temples, or other buildings in India. . . . The sculptures and painters of India remain cloaked by medieval anonymity, and their subjects are either nameless or gods." There is no suggestion in *Man's Lot* that their work deserves mention (LL 116). That is one worry. Another is how to square the claim that "from 1550 B.C. . . . until thirteen centuries later, we have no evidence of literacy" with Kaufmann's statement in *Religions in Four Dimensions* that "from about 1550 B.C. until after the invasion of Alexander the Great we have no evidence of any art in India, *except literature*" (emphasis added). Or are we being too particular? It can be safely assumed that *texts* of the Upanishads date from long before the reign of the emperor Ashoka.

Kaufmann's procedure is again freewheeling. Here is a glorious example of the *associative* ductus that characterizes the writing in *Man's Lot*.

> Hindu sculptors carved marvelous horses—by the hundreds; for example, in the so-called Hall of a Thousand Pillars in Srirangam. But there is no statue in Indian art remotely resembling the defiant individualism of Andrea Del Verrocchio's bronze statue of Bartolommeo Colleoni on horseback. Contemplating that work in Venice, or even looking at pictures of it, one understands how the ethos that emerged in the Renaissance differs from that of the Middle Ages and how people with such an image of man would feel drawn to the Old Testament. (LL 116)

The point seems to be that there is no reminiscence of the Hebrew Bible in the horse statuary of Hindu sculptors. Surely the Hindu horse statuary is not alone in this regard. It would not be easy to imitate the associative logic that informs this paragraph.

In the spirit of *Religions in Four Dimensions*, Kaufmann's narrative in *Man's Lot* includes moralizing judgments on the superiority of Judaism to Hinduism and Islam, with criticisms of Christianity at the ready: we have Kaufmann's dismay once more at the absence of a general social ethic of compassion in Christianity—a fault grievous and insupportable in the caste system of Hinduism—and his assertion of the intellectual debility of Islam. In light of the Bhagavad-Gita,

> compassion for the oppressed and downtrodden would be as ill-conceived as compassion for the damned . . . according to St. Augustine and traditional Christian teaching. . . . To many Western people the misery they see in India comes as a profound shock, but no more so than the attitude toward it of most upper-class Indians. . . . A religion could, after all, refuse to accept such misery as inevitable. (LL 117)

Such a religion is Judaism. "Ancient India never heard a voice like that"—the voice of the prophets Amos, Isaiah, and Micah, who taught the love of justice and an end to oppression, who commanded the Jews to "defend the orphan, plead for the widow."

> Ancient India . . . did hear the Buddha's teaching of compassion, and the Buddha rejected not only the authority of the Vedas . . . he also repudiated the caste system. But the Bhagavadgita soon after pointed a different path. The caste system survived. . . . The destitute are held to merit their lot as the more fortunate deserve theirs, for the Lord is just. (LL 117)

I shall simply mention one rather misleading judgment made by Kaufmann in this context. "Jews and Buddhists cultivated medicine as Christians and Muslims did not" (LL 117). The statement lacks chronology. No historian of Islam could allow so broad a judgment: for one thing, Muslim medicine was far superior to that of the Christian West during the Dark and Middle Ages.

Dear reader, I am aware that you may find this captious way of going on to be tiresome and possibly one-sided. Nevertheless, *Man's Lot,* for all its pungent claims, its passion for its material, and the beauty of the photographs, is a slap-dash product. It is not a rival to Hölderlin's "To the Parcae" in the sense that this is the work whose splendor could justify Kaufmann's own descent into Orcus. Let us leave it at that and try to celebrate some of its beauties as well, in line with Kaufmann's insistent view that art, including street photography in Calcutta, makes terrible things beautiful.

It is precisely apropos of Calcutta that Kaufmann produces some memorable—and characteristic—reflections. The Old Testament remains the gold standard for a religious ethic of which Hinduism knows nothing. I will quote Kaufmann at some length.

> It is widely considered proof of India's spirituality that Hindu teachers have made much of meditation and the quest for one's own ultimate transphenomenal self. The Hebrew prophets would have seen this teaching in a very different light, and we really fail to understand its import if we close our eyes to its social context and results. . . .
>
> It is high time to contrast the Hindu ethos with that of Moses and the prophets and to realize that the individual human being of flesh and blood is not seen in India as being made in God's image and not respected as a person, regardless of social status. . . .
>
> Until modern times most Christians felt much the same way about the torments of the damned. The main difference is that in India you can find the damned in the streets. You do not have to go to a cathedral to discover them in stone friezes. (LL 117–18)

In following passages Kaufmann alludes to his initial thesis, which links horror and beautiful art: "The point is not that the horrors of destitution are not to be found in Indian art. It is rather that the extraordinary realities of Indian life, including its enormous and distinctive beauty, have no place in Indian art" (LL 118). It is notable that Kaufmann defends the *sublimity* of horror in art without once using this word, overriding the Kantian distinction between Kaufmann's preferred word—the "beautiful"—which is direct and has one immediate flow of feeling, and the sublime, a "negative Lust," which involves the radical overturning of terror, "pleasure which is possible only by means of displeasure."[28] But Kaufmann is by and large hard-pressed to produce convincing examples of Calcutta's "distinctive beauty"—a city drenched in human misery—aside from colorful saris and the firm posture of women who have been carrying loads on their heads since they were little (LL 123). It may be the haunting plays of light and shadow encompassing street misery in his photographs that are meant to supply the proof, though they appear without titles, descriptions, or commentary of any sort.

As promised, Kaufmann is certainly interesting on the topic of Shiva.

The peculiar spirituality of India has been largely misunderstood in the West. But that is not to say that Hinduism lacks profundity. Its most profound and distinctive symbol is the dancing Shiva. At one time, Christians made too much of the Hindu "trinity" of Brahma, the creator; Vishnu, the preserver; and Shiva the destroyer; for this trinity plays no very prominent part in Indian thought or religion. Shiva, on the other hand, and his worship are ubiquitous, and he is seen importantly though not solely as a destroyer. (LL 118–19)

This leads him to an original aperçu into Nietzsche, of the type that embellishes his first Nietzsche book, owed to Kaufmann's formidable knowledge of German literary and philosophical culture. He writes in *Man's Lot*:

Without ever mentioning Shiva, Nietzsche, who called himself a disciple of Dionysus, had his "Zarathustra" say in the chapter "On Reading and Writing": "I would believe only in a god who could dance." In that context Nietzsche was attacking the spirit of gravity and solemnity while extolling "light feet." But in Nietzsche's first book, *The Birth of Tragedy*, there is a haunting remark . . . "existence and the world seem justified only as an aesthetic phenomenon." . . . In the preface [to this book] the immediately following sentence brings to mind Shiva—though I am not sure that it ever *has* brought to anyone's mind Shiva: "Indeed, the whole book knows only an artistic meaning and crypto-meaning behind all events—a 'god,' if you please, but certainly only an entirely reckless and amoral artist-god who wants to experience, whether he is building or destroying, in the good and in the bad, his own joy and glory—one who, creating worlds, frees himself from the *distress* of fullness and *overfullness*." (LL 117–19)[29]

Kaufmann's remark about Nietzsche's sentence bringing Shiva to his mind—and almost certainly no one else's—reads like a sudden gesture of modest self-irony—or of plain superiority. Once again the jury is out, though Kaufmann's scorn of half-blind, intellectual readers, especially "professors," is irrepressible.

> Some professors, of course, are deeply interested in the visual arts. But they are apt to insist that buildings make powerful statements. They intellectualize art, feeling that this is needed to make art respectable. They look for world views in architecture and for truth in paintings. Yet the value of art to a human being might well be that it offers us alternative approaches, different experiences—that it opens our eyes.

What might be the best way to justify the importance of visual objects? Surely one need not respond, "'because it makes such and such a true statement.' One might instead proceed more or less as we did in the chapter on art" (LL 122)

Unfortunately, the pronouns are once again unreliable. "A human being" mutates into an indistinct "us," which then appears to acquire the meaning of the editorial "we," which is to say, Kaufmann. It is Kaufmann speaking on behalf of "human beings." This is not quite the meaning of humanism. Attentive readers will also recall, in the manner of "over-intellectualizing professors," that Kaufmann found the point of Goya's "The Dog" to be a true statement about the passage to death, wholly in line with the preachment of "the first chapter of the *Dhammapada*, one of the oldest and most venerable Buddhist scriptures" (LL 105–6).

Kaufmann wants you to look at his pictures. They make an ineffable statement about "life at the limits" that is not entirely an affair of "death, dread, and despair." This is the cant of "existentialists." Kaufmann is not—or no longer—of their ilk. He wants you to cultivate a subtler, *moral* taste that will allow you to see and feel in his photographs what people might feel beyond or to one side of their apparent destitution—sublime acceptance or even exhilaration. Here, more than in the next two books in the trilogy, the dominantly aesthetic demand shades off into a moral demand. It is the idea, the requirement that runs through all his work: see differently, consider alternatives, try new perspectives. It is consistent with his view of himself as an absolute loner.[30]

We now leave the first part of the trilogy of *Man's Lot*—*Life at the Limits*—for the second brief volume titled *Time Is an Artist*, which means to prove just what it says with stunning photographs and once again with an idiosyncratic text.[31] Many but not all the photographs showing the workings of time are captivating, having been taken in a great variety of settings around the world: they depict old people, sunsets, ancient rock formations, uncanny textures of aged wood, weathered stone buildings, stone sculptures. The great Hungarian photographer André Kertész praised them: "Professor Kaufmann's work is good, sensitive, intelligent, honest, and absolutely human. This is, to me, most important in photography."[32] I would have expected to hear Kertész add that they are very beautiful. If he withholds this adjective, it may be because his aesthetic is different: he prefers miniatures of subjects that have been composed; Kaufmann's format is uniformly grand. In Kertész's work, one immediately detects his mastering eye; in Kaufmann, the subject speaks for itself with a visual force that overwhelms the receptive gaze.

The art of time is once again sublime—the kind of beauty that Kaufmann prefers. (In suggesting that the sublime might be a type of *beauty*, I revert to a pre-Kantian aesthetic, which does not make a sharp distinction between the two kinds of pleasure.) It has terribleness in it—Michelangelo's *terribilità*. Such art is consistent with an aesthetic that includes the ugly: Kaufmann would have us think of Rembrandt, Turner, Goya. In the end Kaufmann's master artist, however, is Nature, the mother of the sense of beauty, as he has earlier argued in this book—Nature taking its own good time in producing such "works" as the Grand Canyon, the Dolomites, and the volcanoes of Bali.

> One can think of art as a bold attempt to conquer time, as setting its face against change and decay. Yet ancient glass, buried, becomes iridescent; and bronze statues, too, are transfigured by time and made much more beautiful than they were in their prime. Time paints the foliage of fall, evening skies, old trees, and many things made by man. . . . Old faces can be much more expressive than young ones, old walls and sculptures much richer than new ones. (TA 25)

This is very fine: it is based on precise seeing. These are propositions that can be verified. But in this work, as in *Life at the Limits*, one is soon, alas, jolted away from such admirable grace. One reads a plaidoyer for this "essay": Kaufmann writes: "To go to one's death without having thought about man's lot is to die like a dog" (TA 25). There are no internal quotation marks. We realize that the only foundation for this remark is a previous citation from *Life at the Limits* buried in Kaufmann's confident reading of a "black painting" by Goya. Without this (disputable) reference, the brutality of the comment above—not "the unexamined life is not worth living" but "the unreflected life turns man into a dog"—is shocking and even with the reference is scarcely endurable.

At times we are overhearing a man who cherishes his verbal impulses while talking to himself.

And then, in a moment of considering breaking off one's friendship with Kaufmann, one is drawn, happily, into a lively, erudite, opinionated excursion into ancient history, centering on the discovery of time, and featuring Genesis, the Hebrew prophets, the Upanishads, Plato, Sophocles, and the other usual educators. Some of its liveliness is owed, once more, to its contentiousness.

There is an odd resistance to thinking about time in the King James (mis) translation of the Hebrew Bible. Where the King James Bible has Genesis 29:14 say, "And he abode with him the *space* of a month" (emphasis added), the Pentateuch has "a month of days." "In Leviticus 25.8, the King James says: 'and the space of the seven sabbaths of years shall be unto thee forty and nine years.' Here the Hebrew has 'days' instead of 'space.' . . . The ancient Hebrews' attitude toward time revolutionized civilization"; as we learn later, it is in the way "they overcame the widespread, if not universal, terror of change" (TA 26, 35). Still, one might feel that this is not a thesis simple enough to be defended by a brief photographic essay.

Earlier, in *Religions in Four Dimensions*, Kaufmann wished to make it clear that religious culture did not *always* move from East to West, from the desert to Rome. And so he wrote, "I would be even willing to argue elsewhere that Indian thought influenced Plato." But elsewhere is soon at hand, immediately following this proposition. Kaufmann continues:

> After all, the Persians had conquered part of India before they tried to conquer Greece and were stopped at Marathon and, ten years later, at Salamis; and Greek philosophy began in the Persian empire, on the coast of Asia Minor. The points of similarity between Pythagoras and Plato on the one hand, and Indian thought on the other, are too numerous to be due to accident. (RE 18)

These are the rudiments of an argument, but what in the earlier book is a hypothesis, is in *Man's Lot* a certainty: "[Plato's] views of change and time drew heavily on another culture: India" (TA 27). No sooner has this statement been made, which today is regarded as unprovable,[33] than Kaufmann *imagines* an adversary voice, which he must take pains to stifle.

> One of the unwritten rules for scholars concerned with Greek philosophy is to ignore non-Greek sources, including even Persia, not to speak of

India.... Most historians of Greek philosophy and Plato scholars treat the non-Greek world as if it had not existed. (TA 28)

Black Athena, by Martin Bernal, another polymathic loner—a much-contested book, unfortunately published a decade after Kaufmann's thesis that argues for the African and Asian elements in classical Greek culture—would have interested Kaufmann very much. But here, in *Man's Lot*, Kaufmann makes his thesis plain in a declarative manner:

> The notion that time, change, and multiplicity are unreal, and that ultimate reality is one, unchanging, and timeless, was born in India, like the belief in transmigration, which Plato adopted from Pythagoras. These ideas are found in the Upanishads before they appear among the Greeks.... The idea that perfection is timeless and change is a blemish was an import from India; and in most important respects Plato represents a break in Greek culture.... His world view ... was distinctive and emphatically not *the* Greek view.

One would reasonably conclude that the content of Plato's worldview was precisely the Indian claim that "ultimate reality is one, unchanging and timeless." But then, to one's puzzlement, we read that "Plato certainly did not succeed in proving that the world of change is mere appearance and that ultimate reality is timeless. He *differed* from the school of Elea and the Upanishads by *not* accepting their doctrine that ultimate reality is one and that multiplicity is also merely apparent" (emphasis added). To make sense of Plato's failure, one would need to know a great deal about his ontology, especially his contradictory dialogue *Parmenides*; but what accomplished Greek scholar would tackle propositions meant to serve as conceptual ballast for a selection of photographs destined for the coffee table of the common reader? Perhaps we must make do with the intellectual profit of Kaufmann's summing up: "One must allow change and time some reality, and one has to be content to claim that in the last analysis something timeless is in some sense 'more real'" (TA 28).

This section contains a number of overemphatic generalizations: "People in India have not taken time seriously and have taken no interest in historical questions" (TA 28). On the other hand, Kaufmann surely does, and he sets a vivid example.

> In some ways Hinduism changed very drastically—although few Hindus know it, for a sense of history is still very rare in India. During the centuries

when it competed with Buddhism, Hinduism absorbed the old native cults that antedated the invasion of the Aryans whose religion we find in the Vedas and the Upanishads. Hinduism adopted the worship of Shiva, who is not mentioned in the Vedas and the Upanishads; the phallic worship of the lingam that is associated with Shiva; the use of idols and temples, of which there is no trace in the Vedas and Upanishads; and a profusion of gods and goddesses not found in the old traditions either. But the very idea that the use of temples and idols might have an origin in time and history is foreign to Hinduism. It is assumed that everything in one's religion has always been as it is now. (TA 30)

One assimilates the concrete instruction with gratitude; the generalization about *the* Indian mind is rebarbative.

The Greeks fare only a little better than the Hindus, but they too "had very little historical sense. . . . We have a few quotations from the works of the earliest Greek philosophers . . . [but] it is clear that not one of them took an interest in history, despite the proximity of civilizations that did" (TA 31). The "only" civilizations that "kept studying their own traditions" were the Jews and the Chinese (TA 30). One might wonder about the several "civilizations" whose proximity should have awakened an historical sense in the Greeks, who, after all, "had surprisingly little interest in history" (TA 32). Egypt, Mesopotamia, and Iran are ruled out, for there "it also remained for foreigners"—though not the Greeks!—"to unearth and begin the study of the ancient art and literature" (TA 30). With their extraordinarily well-developed sense of time, history, and tradition, the Jews were the only plausible candidates as educators, for they "changed human attitudes more than any other ancient people. They experienced time differently. They overcame the widespread, if not universal, terror of change" (TA 35). This is a claim that can be difficult to understand when we read, first, that "the Hebrews accepted death as final" and, thereafter, that "for the Jewish people, the children of Israel, there is no death" (TA 40). The crux is presumably the distinction between the life of the individual and that of his or her people, but, in a treatise on time and death, one would expect, following this crux, the refining fire of additional thought. Why should the meaning of death in this context vary so? *Man's Lot* gives abundant insight, pleasure . . . and consternation.

It is encouraging that the great historian of ancient civilizations Arnaldo Momigliano does confirm one of Kaufmann's assumptions. He considers a recent (ca. 1944) papyrological discovery, which shows that "in the fourth century BC a story like the judgment of Solomon was known in Greece *(Pap. Oxy.* 1944), but there is no sign that it came from the Bible." This is one of the very few references to encounters between these peoples before the time of Alexander.

> We ask the obvious question: what did Greeks and Jews make of these serious opportunities for meeting and knowing each other? As for the Greeks, the answer is simple. They did not register the existence of the Jews. The little nation which was later to present the most radical challenge to the wisdom of the Greeks is mentioned nowhere in the extent pre-Hellenic texts.[34]

It is entertaining to consider, in the context that Kaufmann has established, the likely response of the Jews to the Greeks whom they encountered when Judah became the vassal of the Macedonian state under Seleucus. We read in the *Jewish Virtual Library:*

> Like all others in the region, the Jews bitterly resented the Greeks. They were more foreign than any group they had ever seen. In a state founded on maintaining the purity of the Hebrew religion, the gods of the Greeks seemed wildly offensive. In a society rigidly opposed to the exposure of the body, the Greek practice of wrestling in the nude and deliberately dressing light must have been appalling! In a religion that specifically singles out homosexuality as a crime against Yahweh, the Greek attitude and even preference for homosexuality must have been incomprehensible.[35]

Thinking about the attitude toward time in the Hebrew Bible, Kaufmann stressed its irrevocableness. You would imagine, he wrote, that the first words of the Bible

> would have struck people like the opening chords of Beethoven's Fifth Symphony, but they did not. "In the beginning God created the heaven and the earth." *There was a beginning!* And from there the story proceeds relentlessly, relating what happened *just once* [emphasis added]. Here, surely, is the origin of this passage in Rilke's Ninth Duino Elegy:

> > ... *Once*
> > everything, only *once. Once* and no more. And we, too,
> > *once.* Never again. But having
> > been this *once,* even though only *once:*
> > having been on earth does not seem revokable.

(TA 36)

In his sustained reflection on time, supported by the many beautiful, even life-changing photographs, one would expect some mention of the unique moment of time in the photograph, on the once-ness of the image, its "that-has-been" (Roland Barthes).[36] But Kaufmann published his book a year before the appearance of Barthes's epoch-making *Camera Lucida*, which prompted searching reflection on the phenomenon of the photograph in its specific difference from the thing it studies. On the other hand, Kaufmann was in a position to read Susan Sontag's *On Photography*, consisting of essays published in the years 1973–77 in the *New York Review of Books*, a journal that Kaufmann read and contributed to. And except for a 1962 work by the photographer van Deren Coke, *The Painter and the Photograph*, which treats the effect of photography on the history of painting—in studying Kaufmann's book, one would have preferred to learn about the reverse effect—there is no mention in Kaufmann's extensive bibliography of a single work on photography. He evidently does not require counsel on a matter so close to him: it is enough that the photograph is simply something that he saw. This is his declaration concluding *Man's Lot*: "I have seen some things that you have not seen, and I would like to share them with you because they have added to my understanding of man's lot" (WM 139).[37]

When one thinks about this claim, however, it becomes clear that the photograph is not *the thing* he saw. It is a *photograph* of the thing he saw, and that is the thing that in *Man's Lot* escapes sustained reflection.[38] In the previous section of this trilogy—*Life at the Limits*—Kaufmann briefly refers to a series of photographs by Margaret Bourke-White published in 1937 as *You Have Seen Their Faces*. His commentary is of a piece with his insistence on the immediacy and authenticity of what Hegel would call "the object of sense-certainty." These are photographs of "poor people, black-and-white, in the American South, and Erskine Caldwell, who was her second husband, supplied a text" (LL 114). Caldwell's text reads: "The legends under the pictures are intended to express the authors' own conceptions of the sentiments of the individuals portrayed; they do not pretend to reproduce the actual sentiments of these persons." This thoughtful admission points to the inevitable subjective bias in the photographer's representation of "actual sentiments." Kaufmann comment is: "Shades of Goya and Daumier" (LL 114). We are to understand that Goya and Daumier would be appalled at realizing that they had accomplished something so little and so mean with their drawings and their inscriptions. At the very end of *Man's Lot*, Kaufmann appears to perform a volte-face, writing, "Nor do the photographs in *Man's Lot* compete with the realities they portray."

This means, as the phrase goes, that the reality—here, "the sentiments of the individuals portrayed"—has "ontological priority" vis-à-vis the portrayal. It exists in radical independence of the image, forever eluding the genius of the artist-photographer who would capture it (WM 139).

Time is another sort of artist; cultures should be aware of its artistry—and cherish it. Most cultures, however, are cruel to women who grow old. Why are so many cultures like this? In one of Kaufmann's more astonishing explanations, we read that "most probably one reason why widows were burned in India, and witches in Europe and in America . . . is because such women have stopped menstruating and become a living reminder that the passage of time is irrevocable, and that there is no restoration." What was that? Kaufmann catches himself. "To be sure, not all widows and witches were old, but most widows are; and why wait?" (TA 78). There is nothing in this explanation to account for the fact that impotent males are not burnt.

At the same time Kaufmann appears to know—and want to forget—what he calls "time's cruelty" to the body. He instances the ageing of Rembrandt's face in his self-portraits. He also considers Michelangelo, who "caricatured his own features in his 'Last Judgment' on a flayed skin dangling from the left hand of St. Bartholomew. He was over sixty by then, and when he looked into the mirror, he evidently did *not* feel that time was an artist" (TA 59). Old bodies are not beautiful—or, better, in Kaufmann's final view, in this part of his book, they are not *only* beautiful. He explains his idea: "Time is an artist. But an artist is not only an artist. Old is beautiful. But old is not only beautiful. As long as we fail to see the artistry of time and the beauty of age, we are far from understanding man's lot"—and of course that is the intention of this volume (TA 79).

I am not sure how to understand these lines except for Kaufmann's wanting to have the old body beautiful, as it were, *and* let time ruin it, though honorably. He returns to the plight of old women. Why are their old bodies not honored—not even by themselves, because in this they fail "to face up to time"? In Kaufmann's not overly felicitous simile, "They have tried to hide time the way undertakers hide death, with cosmetics" (TA 79). If time strikes them as their archenemy, the attitude of the cultures in which they live seconds the insult. What Kaufmann is chiefly concerned *never* to say, never to hint at, in light of his photographs, is that time's "cruelty" makes bodies *ugly*.

In the final pages of this second part of *Man's Lot*, Kaufmann is chiefly concerned to insist that time's work cannot be undone—and in most cases it is a good thing. Restoratives efforts bungle the beauty of objects rejected for being old. Patinas enhance bronze statues; "the play of light and shadow can be time's way of restoring nature's claims" (TA 61). The new is not always beautiful.

Kafka, one of Kaufmann's perpetual if second-order educators, addressed this topic elegantly and in sympathy with Kaufmann. We can imagine Kaufmann's pleasure in reading him, but Kafka's remarks on this topic were not available in his lifetime. In the very first diary entry of Kafka's that has survived, he wrote a series of comments on Max Brod's thesis that the beautiful is the new; like Kaufmann, Kafka was skeptical:

> One may not say that only the new impression awakens aesthetic pleasure, but rather: every impression that does not fall into the sphere of the will awakens aesthetic pleasure. What is new? . . . Everything is new, for since all objects are caught in a forever changing time and illumination, and it is no different with us observers, we therefore must always encounter them at a different place.[39]

It could hardly be the case, then, that *everything* is beautiful. But even this non sequitur helps us to acknowledge what Kaufmann wants us to see. He wants to enlarge our capacity for taking aesthetic pleasure—and, ultimately, moral encouragement—in a range of objects at *the limit* of conventional affirmations of beauty—images shot through with traces of "disaster, destitution, distress . . . dread, and despair" and a sublime elation as well (LL 121).

The third section of this trilogy *Man's Lot* is titled *What Is Man?* It reads like a mélange of the associations of a richly furnished mind without a thesis, ranging from Rabbi Bunam to Mark Twain, Emperor Ashoka to Vincent van Gogh, Immanuel Kant to Eleanor Roosevelt. Kaufmann's work comes late to the literature that Greif treats in *The Age of the Crisis of Man*—a burning topic in American literary culture at the mid-twentieth century. Kaufmann ignores the array of books written by his near-contemporaries who were also reacting to the worry that a general human nature was on the verge of dissolution. Their answers to the question "What is man?" tended toward brutal abstraction, oblivious of the endless differentiations the concept requires—as, for example, pragmatically insistent distinctions of race and gender. And yet these distinctions are not strongly marked in *Man's Lot*.

At the outset of his *What Is Man?* Kaufmann declares that the question is unanswerable. A definition would have to aim at the essence of man; but man, as Kaufmann will teach us, on the strength of Goethe, Hegel, Nietzsche, and Sartre, among others, is not a creature of essences but the sum of his effects.

A proper answer would require an unattainable knowledge of the history of everyone. "What can we do?' (WM 53) He turns to his library and proceeds to amass citations, often contradictory and many culled from previous works, which he terms "touchstone passages about man's lot" (WM 75). The writing is clear and lively, if unpredictable in its twists and turns, and often rewarding.

Kaufmann stresses that the consciousness of others precedes self-consciousness: "Hegel," for one "did not know himself well at all" (WM 56). "Our intelligentsia is for the most part blind to what is not verbal" (WM 59): this comment, in 1978, is a date marker of the pause before all our intelligentsia became film critics, though Stanley Cavell's *The World Viewed: Reflections on the Ontology of Film* did appear in 1971. "A book reflecting on what man is should make people more thoughtful by calling dubious assumptions into question and by pioneering a new approach" (WM 60); Kaufmann would hold his book *What Is Man?* to be very adequate to this normative demand. There are fine aperçus.

> Typically, it is the death of a person to whom one has been very close that leads one to think about the meaning of life and the human condition. But it is part of the poignancy of such experiences that most of one's fellowmen are not at all prepared to share one's thoughts and feelings. It is therefore not surprising that the most celebrated statements of our first theme were written under the impression of momentous wars, when large numbers of people had been killed and empires were crumbling. At such times there was an audience for this theme. (WM 61)

Kaufmann discusses this grim theme as one of three topics bearing centrally on the nature (or history) of man: man is ephemeral—a plaything of the gods, a view supported by Homer, Plato, and Seneca. A second theme asserts the inequality of men (a view supported by the Rig-Veda and the Laws of Manu, the New Testament, and subsequently, with nuances, by Kaufmann himself; his position, however, shaped by Nietzsche, rejects the brutal Christian inegalitarianism of the saved and the damned, an insistent refrain from previous works). A reason for Plato's banning theater from the ideal city, Kaufmann suggests, is Plato's belief that each man was equipped in life to play only a single role: hence, he could not abide the thought of actors playing several roles. Finally, we have the third thesis, which declares: "Man is a wolf to man," first formulated by Plautus in *The Comedy of Asses*. This discussion is the freshest of the thematics, spangled with memorable citations from Cicero and Seneca—here, Cicero: "While we derive great utility from the cooperation and agreement of men, there is also no detestable disaster that does not come to man from man" (WM 70). The fact that the profit of this section is supplied even more than a little by the *Encyclopedia Britannica* is not finally discouraging; Kaufmann has always been a great reader-through of encyclopedias: the *Britannica* is his favorite, but he is also partial to the *Encyclopedia of Religion and Ethics*.

What Is Man? centers on its "touchstone passages"—familiar extended aphorisms from Shakespeare and slightly less familiar passages from Pascal and Nietzsche. Kaufmann is new and informative on Nietzsche, who wrote:

> "What is the ape to man? A laughingstock or a painful embarrassment. And man shall be just that for the overman: a laughingstock or a painful embarrassment." Naturally, the generation that read this or heard about it around the turn of the century thought of Darwin. Who, to this day, excepting Nietzsche himself, thought of Heraclitus, Nietzsche's favorite among the early Greek philosophers before Socrates? Yet Heraclitus' fragments 82 and 83 (known to us because Plato quotes the sentences in the *Greater Hippias* 289) read: "The most beautiful ape is ugly compared with the human race." "The wisest of men, when compared to a god, will appear but an ape in wisdom and beauty and all else." (WM 79)

In the course of stressing Nietzsche's devotion to Pascal, Kaufmann cites a revealing passage from *Human, All Too Human*: beyond Schopenhauer, Nietzsche invokes the names of eight "educators." It is a sterling, a seminal example of the relationships that Kaufmann would emulate *with his educators*:

> 408. The Journey to Hades. . . . I too have been in the underworld . . . that I might be able to converse with a few dead souls. . . . There were four pairs who responded to me in my sacrifice: Epicurus and Montaigne, Goethe and Spinoza, Plato and Rousseau, Pascal and Schopenhauer. With them I have to come to terms. When I have long wandered alone, I will let them prove me right or wrong; to them will I listen, if they prove each other right or wrong. In all that I say, conclude, or think out for myself and others, I fasten my eyes on those eight and see their eyes fastened on mine. . . . [They] seem to me so living that I feel as if even now, after their death, they could never become weary of life.[40]

These writers and their touchstones are run-ups to the great change in humanity produced by "paradigmatic individuals"—that is, great men and women. They "change our perception of what it means, or could mean, to be human." There is one literary work that displays "the greatest collection of such individuals, more so than any single book to be found in any one culture: that is the Old Testament"; Kaufmann's passion for the Hebrew Bible (always heightened by Nietzsche's celebration of it) was bound to produce this choice.

> In the Jewish Old Testament . . . there are human beings, things, and speeches in so grand a style that the Greek and Indian literature have nothing to compare with it. One stands with awe and reverence before these tremendous remnants of what man once was. . . . The taste for the Old Testament is a touchstone for "great" and "small." (*Beyond Good and Evil*, section 52)

Through Abraham (via Kaufmann's exegesis) and Jacob, who is "the first example in world literature of character development"; through Moses, who would not be deified, and Samson, the first recorded Jewish suicide; through Saul, whose kingship was disputed, and David, who consoled him, Kaufmann foregrounds the great theme of "man's growth through suffering" (WM 113, 117).

Greek literature is also a source of paradigmatic individuals: Homer gives us Achilles, but from Aeschylus we have Clytemnestra and Prometheus; from Sophocles, Antigone and Oedipus; from Euripides, Medea and Phaedra. Hegel called "the heavenly Antigone the most glorious figure ever to have appeared on earth," though there are numerous figures in the Old Testament who could compete for this distinction, having also "defied kings in the name of a higher law." Socrates's greatness—his autonomy, his epistemological minimalism—emerges from Plato's dialogues with a rough fidelity to the historical Socrates (WM 118–19). To these heroic individuals Kaufmann adds the names of Rembrandt, Goethe, and van Gogh, who fill the last rooms in the museum. They are the first artists to gain entry; each adds a facet to Kaufmann's construction of a full human personality, but there are few novelties in his short summaries of their character and achievement. Kaufmann speaks with contagious enthusiasm about Rembrandt's series of self-portraits, a rare record of personal development, consistent, as he says, with the "conventional wisdom" about Rembrandt; but he repeats the canard that Goethe's *Sufferings of Young Werther* was "in the hands" of countless young men and women who committed suicide, victims of what is still today called the "Werther effect" (WM 123). A "Werther effect," a spike in copycat suicides following a widely publicized suicide, is a fact, but the alleged wave of suicides that spread in the 1770s in imitation of Young Werther is a fiction.[41] Kaufmann is an unconditional admirer of Goethe, "autonomy incarnate," whom he thinks of as the prime theorist and exponent of human *development*; and Kaufmann promises to celebrate

Goethe's achievement at length in a new book, for, after all, "to be human takes time and involves development" (WM 124). In speaking with appreciation about the subsequent development in German writing on "the history of art and literature, philosophy, religion, science, and innumerable works that dealt with individuals," all allegedly on Goethe's example (although the growth of a historical consciousness long precedes Goethe), Kaufmann revealingly cites his philosophical antiselves, namely, twentieth-century "revolts against this tradition: the new criticism in literature, analytical philosophy, and structuralism" (WM 125). His shockingly early death did spare him the full blooming of deconstructionism and "the death of the subject" at Yale, Cornell, and Johns Hopkins Universities. He goes on to celebrate van Gogh with expressive selections from his letters, his enthusiasm stoked by the felt likeness of the mental worlds of van Gogh and Nietzsche; they are "two pastors' sons from the north who created some of their finest works within a few miles of each other in the late eighteen-eighties" (WM 127). This relation, as Kaufmann rightly remarks, is little studied—and is worth the effort, on Kaufmann's example: in a word, both treasured their work above everything, lived dangerously, and were bent on creation and not long life. They were prepared, like Zarathustra, "to go under" for more intensity.

Man's Lot ends poignantly, with thirty-four poems written by the author on the death of his mother, meaning to exemplify the feeling core of Man: in the midst of his suffering, he strives for justification. It would be disrespectful to submit them to analysis.

A word needs to be said about the photographs that accompany this text and occupy as many pages. They are less soul-enlarging than those attached to *Life at the Limits* and *Time Is an Artist*. Many are ordinary tourist's shots of village life in remote places (New Guinea, Java); and one, consisting of the still bleeding, chopped-off heads of goats strewn on rough grass—despite all the masking suada of its title—is more than ugly; it is hideous. The title reads: "After the sacrifice: Central Java, the Muslim festival commemorating how Abraham almost sacrificed Isaac." As an exhibit of man's lot, this image appalls.

Leaving *Man's Lot*, one is "irritated' in the German sense of the word, meaning, both "vexed" and "stimulated." How is one to grasp a book that moves so quickly from exotic color photographs to potted encyclopedic surveys, from intimate revelations to the most problematic theses? One can also feel a certain light-headed affection for a mind so rich, a personality so energetic . . . and so often outrageous, indeed preposterous, in its judgments, yet so self-secure in its right to pronounce—an ascetic priest in Dionysian sheep's clothing. In the end one is simply challenged, as Kaufmann would have it, by a book that stares back at you, asking: Are you, reader, equal to this work?[42]

Skeptical and enlightened, elated and troubled, we pass from a serious coffee table trilogy to a serious café table trilogy titled *Discovering the Mind*, shaking our head in anticipatory astonishment at what manner of achievement awaits us at the end of Kaufmann's life.

15

Philosophy as Psychology

DISCOVERING THE MIND, VOLUME 1, KANT, GOETHE, AND HEGEL

Who among philosophers was a *psychologist* at all before me?

—FRIEDRICH NIETZSCHE

Although he was a very small man physically, in other ways, he was more than life size.

—WALTER KAUFMANN ON IMMANUEL KANT

KAUFMANN'S FINAL BOOK, *Discovering the Mind*, is another remarkable—indeed, startling—undertaking in eleven hundred pages, consisting of three volumes, each devoted to the work of three philosophers.[1] The freewheeling, opinionated style of late Kaufmann is on display throughout. All three volumes are shaped by a leading idea cued by Nietzsche, who called himself the first depth psychologist—"Who among philosophers was a *psychologist* at all before me?" (D2 6). Kaufmann will explore the psychological underpinnings, in volume 1, of Goethe, Kant, and Hegel;[2] in volume 2, of Nietzsche, Heidegger, and Buber; and in volume 3, of Freud, Adler, and Jung. In each volume it is the first-named—Goethe, Nietzsche, and then Freud—who carries the day as the best-constituted individual, as a "paradigmatic individual," truly creative, supremely accomplished, undeceived, courageous in his enterprises. We have known them all along as Kaufmann's educators.

476

The trilogy, for want of a clear-cut genre, has been called, with much originality, "romance."[3] This could sound odd. By a happy coincidence we are free to lend it qualities from a conventional account of romance fiction—namely, it must be "smart, fresh, and diverse."[4] Kaufmann's discussions are smart—this description comes as no surprise. They are fresh in the sense of flying off the pen of a man who takes dictation from the heart and could not care less, it seems, how he will be judged by other professors of philosophy. And they are diverse—to a fault, consisting of all manners of writing, pell-mell: solid analysis, declared preferences, "philosophical"-sounding truisms, pictures from ordinary life, chunks of personal experience—it is a sort of American writing in the genre of "On the Road."[5]

A glance at the first pages of the first volume—*Goethe, Kant, and Hegel*—gives us a fresh and confident author, with a thesis in mind, like Antaeus at home on the earth of the German intellectual tradition. We were told at the close of *Man's Lot* to expect a new book featuring Goethe's incomparable contribution to a discovery of "the mind"—under which heading Kaufmann will include "feeling and intelligence, reason and emotion, perception and will, thought and the unconscious" (D1 4).[6] Each of these vectors is writ large in Goethe's protean sensibility and its working-out in some 143 volumes (WM 120). It is an awe-inspiring production, Kaufmann wants us to know, especially when we realize that Goethe, for the greater part of his adult life, was fully occupied as cabinet minister of a grand duchy.

The mind of Goethe (1749–1832) is radically different from the mind of Kant, the older man (1724–1804); it is productive to consider their difference. It was Goethe, not Kant, who contributed more to the discovery of the mind than anyone before him (D1 6). This claim of a perfect opposition of mentalities is not original with Kaufmann. It was conceived by Nietzsche, as Kaufmann suggests: "What Goethe wanted was totality; he fought the mutual extraneousness of reason, senses, feeling, and will (preached with the most abhorrent scholasticism by Kant, the antipode of Goethe); he disciplined himself to wholeness, he created himself."[7] Their contrasting legacies were much debated: the neo-Kantian Karl Vorländer's still very readable *Schiller-Goethe-Kant* attempts their reconciliation: "The differences between Kant and Goethe are not unbridgeable, they are differences of personality and method rather than of basic convictions; it is rather that the personalities of both *complement* one another."[8] In a word, Vorländer concludes: we must have Goethe *and* Kant!

Kaufmann is in no such conciliatory mood. In his account, Kant, with his false idea of scientific rigor, which he advanced as a model for the humanities, impeded the discovery of the mind more than anyone else, with the possible exception of Hegel, whose preface to his first book, the *Phänomenologie des Geistes* (Phenomenology of Spirit), makes a similarly unfortunate obeisance to science (D1 5). Their mistake is to believe that science progresses without error. Consider the phrase "the secure stride of science," which Kant repeats more than a dozen times in the preface to the second edition of his *Critique of Pure Reason*, whereas, as Kaufmann writes, "to make discoveries one must not be too anxious about errors" (D1 4, 8). This is the wisdom inscribed in Goethe's head and body, a "rebellious individualist" to the end.

A conversation about Goethe *and* his art must soon enough raise the question of the role of personality *in* art, and here Kaufmann bestrides both normative positions, in the manner we have seen earlier in chapters 5 and 9. Yes, greatness of soul is a prerequisite for great art in the sense, putting the matter modestly, that "a poem expressing the highly individual sensibility and experience of a poet is not for that reason worthless" (D1 8). On the other hand, the splendid poem may be merely a mask of a flaccid personality. Throughout Kaufmann's work we have seen him shift priority from the person to the work and back again. It would have been helpful for him to say forthrightly that the relation between the poet's sensibility and the product of his art is a purely contingent one, in the sense that it cannot be generally stipulated, but he is at heart the devoté of an art that appears to convey great personal experience—ideally, great suffering! We learn, for one, that "Hegel's insistence on demonstrating some *necessity* in his work was . . . born of deep suffering. . . . What Hegel sought in . . . in his *Phenomenology* was a view, a demonstration that would reconcile him to the misery of humanity by showing that all the suffering had not been pointless" (D1 236–37).

Kaufmann's poetics is a propaedeutic for the psychological method he will employ in his study of nine thinkers, one that aims to form a picture of the mentality of the thinker on the evidence of the work *and* the life with a view to a judgment on the value of the work. And so he quotes at length from a famous character sketch of the fiercely unorthodox young Goethe, made in 1772 by a friend, J. C. Kestner, the gist of which was repeated by the philosopher F. H. Jacobi two years later: "This man is autonomous (*selbstständig*) from tip to toe." Ergo: "Goethe's first major contribution to the discovery of the mind is that he provided a new model of autonomy" (D1 15).

What are we understand by this model? "Autonomy" suggests that "one gives or has given laws to oneself; that one is self-governing; that in essentials one obeys one's own imperatives. Kant made 'autonomy' the centerpiece of his philosophy and discussed the term at length in his first major work on ethics, in 1785." Kant's notion of autonomy, however, implies the rejection of all personal "inclinations," of "all spontaneity and enthusiasm," and dutiful obedience to the imputed rationality of oneself *and others* (D1 164).[9] Goethe refuted this bleak notion by example. In this very year 1785, we have the first "clear indication that Goethe is planning a complete interruption to his official work in Weimar," leading to his departure, the next year, incognito, to Rome.[10] "Kant offered an anatomy of the mind, based not on experience but on what *must* be the case to make possible human experience and knowledge." By *his* knowledge and experience, Goethe rejected that procedure and that picture. It is Goethe's rather than Kant's version of autonomous mind that we find at the heart of Nietzsche's philosophy and Freud's psychology, as we shall see in volumes 2 and 3 (D1 15, 24).

Kant's idea of autonomy holds that a choice is free only when imputed to everyone else as the right choice to make. He "associates morality with universality, and autonomy with universal laws that are binding for all rational beings, not with *individuality*" (emphasis added) (D1 17). "Am I free," Kaufmann asks, "when my acts bear no relation to my phenomenal self, my individuality?" (D1 141). Recall his celebration in *Man's Lot* of the paradigmatic *individuals* Moses and Goethe, Rembrandt and van Gogh. Kaufmann himself, I hasten to add, belongs somewhere in this table, by the qualities of passionate seriousness, diligence, and intellectual desire that I hope these many pages have conveyed—a judgment that would not lack his own consent. *He* is the subtext of this prolonged brief for autonomy (it is also the explicit topic of his earlier work *Without Guilt and Justice*). Kaufmann will discuss Kant's view of autonomy in detail three chapters later in this book; we have to do now with Goethe's wider contributions to the discovery of the mind, which are all in all four.

Kaufmann's introduction to Goethe's personality prompts a number of provocative sentences that again bear intimately on the author. "That a human being could have a significant impact on human thought by virtue of his character or personality may seem strange to many professors who assume that contributions must be made in terms of articles or books." Clearly, Kaufmann is not *this* professor, as he is arguing for the formative power of Goethe's personality, not to mention Goethe's grand precedent, Socrates, whose independence and courage have informed philosophical and literary thought until today. But, as a professor, what is Kaufmann's view on the force of "contributions . . . made in terms of articles and books"? Surely he is not dismissing the expectable force of his own publications—or if their impact is bound to be small, why go on writing the next one thousand pages of this trilogy? Is he then so eager to polemicize against conventional professors, so eager to be considered a professor only nominally and as a person distinct from that mask—like Goethe, "a rebellious individualist," a heretic—that he is willing to forget himself? I think this is the case. What does the next sentence add to this conundrum? "Even those who do *not* sacrifice character to scholarship are apt to feel that personality is something private that has no place in their writings [emphasis added]. It is assumed that science is impersonal and that scholarly work ought to be scientific" (D1 20–21). But this invoked scholar is once again *not* Kaufmann, since he is one of those who have indeed *not* "sacrificed character to scholarship," in the sense that for several decades, on his own admission, he has felt, even as a professor of philosophy, that he must write unconventional books closer to his own deeply felt concerns. In doing this, however, he has by no means suggested that "personality is something private that has no place in . . . [his] writings." So the scholar he has invoked must be a lesser breed of academic who does *not* sacrifice character to scholarship only in the sense that his work is dominated by egoistic polemic and a pursuit of his own undistinguished interests and idées fixes. At the same time he is blind to what he has done: he does not know himself. And Kaufmann? A review of this very book by his friend, Ben-Ami Scharfstein, a professor of comparative philosophy, contains the haunting remark: "He died before his own self-discovery—furthered by this series of books—reached the limit of which, granted a longer life, he was capable." He died, in the midsentence of his life, as these books were being published.[11]

The one straightforward, fully committed idea emerging from this discussion is that progress in the humanities, such as it is, depends on abandoning a scientific—better, scientistic—model. This advance follows from a willingness of scholars to write with the full force of their personal concerns and prepare to undergo change and accept error. Here I believe it is unfortunate that Kaufmann's intense refusal to profit from Heidegger blocks out Heidegger's more precise contribution to their shared goal of defining a nonscientific humanities. Humanistic *reading* arrives at the meaning of the whole of a work or a lived phenomenon on the strength of its details, yet that selection of details inevitably proceeds in light of a foreconception of the meaning of the whole. This state of affairs appears to doom humanistic reading to an empty circularity, but it must not fear this result. If the humanistic reader appears to be trapped in a defective circularity, unlike the alleged presuppositionless scientist in his or her research, still, Heidegger concludes, this circularity—properly, the hermeneutic circle—is not a limitation, not to be fled from or shunned, but "to be gotten into in the right way"—maintained, enjoyed, and explored to the limit.[12]

Goethe's second principle has come down to us as the first existentialist principle: man has no essence; he is his deeds. But Goethe already put the point vividly in 1810 in his *Doctrine of Colors*:

> We really try in vain to express the essence of a thing. We become aware of effects [*Wirkungen*], and a complete history of these effects would seem to comprehend the essence of the thing. We exert ourselves in vain to describe the character of a human being; but assemble his actions, his deeds, and a picture of his character will confront us. (D1 23)

Under these circumstances, what is the meaning of the concept-word "mind"? It is a shorthand term for a bundle of intuited energies, called, with equal inaptness, "feeling and intelligence, reason and emotion, perception and will, thought and unconscious." Indeed, following Goethe, "we can dispense with the concept of mind as an entity."

Of course, when Kaufmann adopts this claim, he implicitly grants himself a great deal of narrative freedom. If mind is not an entity but a conglomerate of sensibility, understanding, velleity, and so on, then the discussion of "mind," the goal of this trilogy, may easily become an impulsive commentary on whatever "mental" topic Kaufmann finds interesting—including, especially, what Kaufmann finds wrongheaded in his nine authors. (Goethe, Nietzsche, and Freud escape whipping—the others do not.) This freedom need not be a fault as such; the reasonableness of Kaufmann's practice will be a function of its deeds, its effects.

Goethe meanwhile deserves credit for insistently showing that "the mind can be understood only in terms of development." This insight, in Kaufmann's story, is the third principle establishing Goethe's genius at discovering the mind. The succession of his literary works is marked by continual experimentation, a continual variation in theme, genre, and style. Apart from his novel *Wilhelm Meister*, which inaugurated the phantom Bildungsroman (novel of education), Goethe publicized his ideas of development and of skepticism toward a unified concept of mind on the example of his life; his tragedy *Faust*, which appeared in many stages; and finally his autobiography, especially significant in the way its title *From My Life: Poetry and Truth* (*Dichtung und Wahrheit*) forecasts a hybrid, problematic form of writing about the self (D1 19).[13] Kaufmann had already stressed Goethe's powers of renewal in earlier books, most explicitly in *From Shakespeare to Existentialism* and *Man's Lot*: see chapters 5 and 14. His summary of Goethe's life and works, concentrating especially on the figure of Faust, is also not new, either in Kaufmann's bibliography or in "the literature." What is surely new is his conceit that the old Faust, alone in his study at the outset of the tragedy, moaning about the elusiveness of the life he craves, is . . . Immanuel Kant!—though this conceit has no historical basis. Kaufmann discussed *Faust* accurately and at length in our chapter 5 as well as in his introduction to his (admirable) translation and edition of *Faust, a Tragedy*. Kaufmann is not quite Goethe in the latter's drive never to repeat himself. (It must be noted too that the present discussion of Goethe is prolix and repetitive in ways that Kaufmann's earlier criticism is not.) It continues to be interesting, however, to encounter Kaufmann's "existentialist" view of the figure of Mephistopheles, Faust's antiself, who provokes in Faust the web of self-deception—certainly an irreducible component of mind. Goethe's demonstration of a mind in continual development contrasts most decidedly with Kant's

> conception of the mind . . . [in which] development has no place. He claimed to describe the human mind is it always is, has been, and will be. . . . Goethe did not prove the opposite view by argument. . . . But the question whether showing something is inherently inferior to proving it or deducing it from pure concepts is part of Goethe's legacy. (D1 25)

The last point is excellent and suggests Kaufmann's thought is most productive when he has narrowed his focus and has a text or texts to work with. Here he writes fruitfully in this vein:

> As a poet, too, [Goethe] . . . kept developing, and at the age of seventy he revolutionized German poetry once more with the publication of his *West-Eastern Divan*, a collection of his most recent poems in which he imitated Persian and other Near Eastern models, thus contributing to a lively concern with what he himself called, coining this term, "world literature." (D1 31)[14]

But the narrative is not always this steady or this good. The freewheeling mode of writing we called "romance" is not proof against couldn't-care-less writing—or some failure to envision an audience. Remarking that Goethe had become of perennial interest to schoolboys *like himself*, Kaufmann writes:

Nor was Goethe himself innocent of this development. In 1811 he began to publish his autobiography, *Out of My Life: Poetry and Truth*. The German subtitle, *Dichtung und Wahrheit*, which is usually cited as if it were the main title, is ambiguous. *Dichtung* could mean fiction as well as poetry. The second volume appeared in 1812, the third in 1814—and eventually the sixth and last in 1822. The impact of this work was immense. It pointed the way for subsequent studies not only of Goethe but also of other poets and artists, and eventually of every human being. (D1 32)

The question might arise as it did very often with respect to *Man's Lot*: For whom is such writing intended? Persons who have never heard of Goethe before, or little beyond his name, do not need to know the exact dates of publication of the second, third, and sixth volumes of Goethe's autobiography. Scholars of German literature, supposing they were otherwise ignorant of the publishing order of Goethe's autobiography and who happened to turn to this volume of *Discovering the Mind*, would presumably want to know the dates of publication of volumes four and five as well. Furthermore, what is the evidence for and against the statement that Goethe's biography "pointed the way for subsequent studies . . . eventually *of every human being*"? This is the recurrent strain in Kaufmann's late work: his indifferent fielding of such pronouns as "every" (man) and "most" (people) and "the best" (judges)—and of ("most") works, "almost all" of which . . . , and so on. Where is the data to color in such ghosts? Let us see what continues to be on offer here. I fear it will be the good *and* the less good.

Principle four turns on Goethe's quarrel with Newton, "his refusal [again, unlike Kant] to equate science with Newtonian science." Goethe appeals to Kaufmann as one whose approach, like his own, is "visual and concrete" and where, in a wonderful phrase from Goethe's *Doctrine of Colors*, "every attentive look into the world involves *theorizing*" (D1 38, 42). Recalling, too, Kaufmann's claim to have rewritten some passages in the essays in *From Shakespeare to Existentialism* twenty times, we will understand where this effort comes from and the source to which it returns, for here is Goethe being invoked: "He had the courage to reread what he had written and to go over it again and again until it met the highest standards. As long as it did not, he was in no hurry to publish it. This was a crucial aspect of his autonomy: he did not write to please others or to enhance his status but to satisfy himself" (D1 42–43). Kaufmann will also say that a book of his like *Without Guilt and Justice* was in the works for decades before its publication. On the other hand, unlike Goethe's, there are few gap years in the series of Kaufmann's publications, and the late work espe-cially could have profited from a good going-over in the hunt for dispensable repetition.

Goethe's creativity was "organic"; Kant was an apostle of ossification. Goethe was "a 'whole' human being, not divided against himself like Kant." This is a rhetorically forceful but surely untenable assertion; readers will not find it hard to get the point, which may nonetheless fall short of inspiring conviction. We read that Goethe "was not all that interested in history," but in *Man's Lot* we heard that Goethe's worldview was the absolute impetus to works on "the history of art and literature, philosophy, religion, science, and innumerable works that dealt with individuals"; all thrived on Goethe's exam-ple. Goethe "was vitally interested in *development*" (D1 44), so what we miss in Kaufmann is a precise distinction between the leading ideas of "history" and "development," but we will not find it here, where appreciation trumps analysis. This is a trait more and more marked—and intentionally so—in Kaufmann's later work.

It would appear to be enough to know that "Goethe was basically right about science"—it can thrive even with false hypotheses. As a result, on the topic of Goethe's anti-Newtonian *Doctrine of Colors*, "for our purposes it does not matter who was right" (D1 35). Nonetheless, despite one's feeling that this criterion does matter, "Goethe . . . contributed a great deal to the dis-covery of the mind" (D1 46). In doing so, it was in despite of mathematics, which he disparaged. Here it is interesting to confront Kaufmann on Goethe with a historical judgment made by Hermann Broch, whom Kaufmann very likely knew in Princeton. Broch wrote: "The two great rational ways of under-standing [*Verständigungsmittel*] in modernity are the language of science in mathematics and the language of money in bookkeeping."[15] What are the spe-cial sources, one might ask, from which Broch draws his judgment? Allow us a moment of discovery. One such source must be this very Goethe—his novel *Wilhelm Meister's Apprenticeship*. In book 1, chapter 10, Wilhelm's friend Werner praises double entry bookkeeping as "one of the most beautiful inven-tions of the human mind."[16]

Now, this sentence is certainly not an aesthetic judgment that Kaufmann means to ascribe to Goethe. In evoking Werner's passion for balancing the books, can Goethe have been writing only ironically? Mirrors upon mirrors: the archromantics Schlegel and Novalis saw *Wilhelm Meister* as dominated by its worldly prose, its *unpoetic* character, lacking all "nature and mysticism" (*Mystik*)—an unserious celebration of the bourgeois commercial mind. This novel, wrote Novalis, is "a poetized bourgeois and domestic story.... The true principle is the economic (Die Oeconomische Natur ist die Wahre)." At the same time he calls it a "farce."[17]

Kaufmann has little patience for Goethe's archromantic rivals: "What Goethe ranked above everything," Kaufmann explains, "in science as in poetry, was *Anschauung*," a word that combines the senses of seeing and contemplating—a contemplation that arises, legitimately, only from concrete visual apprehension (D1 47). The discoveries made by such "Anschauung," which is anchored in lived experience, have contributed greatly to the discovery of the mind, as "the hankering for certainty and the model of mathematics" have not; in fact the latter "have been extremely harmful" (D1 48). Before getting on one's rationalist high horse, Kaufmann would have one know that Goethe was not "an apostle of feeling" in the sense of justifying "a plea of incomprehensibility . . . [but he] felt that understanding cannot dispense with feeling." Kaufmann's appreciation for the marriage of science and feeling arises from a deep place in his work: it is the long-standing plaidoyer that builds on Nietzsche's wish for a new, full human type, the "musiktreibender Sokrates" (a musical Socrates). One demurral arises: Goethe and Kant might be antipodes, but is it not a certain privileged *feeling*—respect for the categorical imperative, the law—that occupies the center of Kant's ethical theory? We have an answer in Kant's celebrated *Grundlegung*. Kant writes, "Although respect is a feeling, it is nevertheless not a feeling *received* through some influence but one *self-caused* by a concept of reason" (D1 142). This is not, finally, a theory that could accommodate the high place of feeling in Goethe's science.

And so Kaufmann stands by "a poetic science"—although one still might wonder what sort of *science* a nonmathematical *science of feeling* might be. A disgruntled reviewer writes that, for Kaufmann, "the way Goethe lived his life was a contribution in itself—a contribution that exceeded the actual, factual contributions of Newton" and then asks, "Well, okay—but how are we going to cure polio or eradicate malaria with Goethe's poetry-science?"[18] As the objects of physical and biological science grow ever more microscopic, Goethe's science of in vivo visual contemplation would indeed seem to be of little use. If, however, Kaufmann is thinking chiefly of a *description* of the scientific mind, a generalized—though acute—*experience* had by the scientific mind, then Goethe's—and Kaufmann's—argument obviously has merit. The approach is phenomenological, in the strict sense of the term as defined "crisply" by Moritz Lazarus, "Phenomenology is a descriptive portrayal of the appearances of psychic life" (D1 213).[19] Kaufmann's argument also profits from the alternative term to a "poetic science" ready to hand—the *esprit de finesse*, the psychological tact of the novelists—Goethe's contemporaries—Balzac (1799–1850), Stendhal (1783–1842), Flaubert (1821–80), Dostoevsky (1821–81), among others. Kaufmann will actually instance Hegel, Nietzsche, and Freud as artist-psychologists.

The difficulty in drawing a firm conclusion about the mind of Goethe is that Goethe's mind is everywhere and everything. Kaufmann's entire discussion of Goethe's views on poetry, science, and commerce requires a precise footing in individual works and at individual moments of his development, which Kaufmann's rather hurried polemic does not supply. He is an impatient writer in these late books, "very demanding in everything having to do with scholarship . . . [but] less demanding in philosophical argument; where one might expect him to slow down and proceed by small, careful steps, he often hurries on, as if so aware of his goal or so sure of it that he cannot slow down even when the footing is slippery."[20]

By contrast, Kaufmann's final pages in the Goethe chapter are very engaging, despite several word-for-word internal repetitions and unacknowledged citations from the discussion of Goethe in *Man's Lot*, including, unfortunately, the futile bromide that Goethe's *The Sufferings of Young Werther* produced a wave of suicides—now, Kaufmann adds, for effect, "not only in Germany but also, for example, in France." This claim has never been proved.[21] Kaufmann recounts a pungent discussion with a Princeton University chairman of philosophy with evident accuracy, remarking, first, that

> books on philosophers and psychologists are generally written by philosophers and psychologists who know that it is not their business to write about poets, like Goethe. A philosopher who forgets this or simply does not care is apt to be told by his chairman, without having asked, that while it is wonderful how well his work has been received by highly competent reviewers he ought to know—as I was told at one point—that "your work on Goethe does not *count*" (emphasis added). (D1 52)

I don't think the pun is being noted. The chairman, though an eminent historian of philosophy, did not realize that you could not acquire "the necessary feeling for Hegel's, Nietzsche's, and Freud's mentality and universe of discourse" without having steeped yourself in the unmathematical Goethe, *as they had done*. Hegel, for one, sent Goethe an eloquent letter declaring his dependency:

"When I survey the course of my spiritual development, I see you [Goethe] woven into it everywhere and would like to call myself one of your sons; my inner nature, has . . . set its course by your creations as by signal fires". . . . Professors trained in analytical philosophy find it almost impossible to believe that Goethe's impact on German philosophy could be comparable to Kant's. (D1 51–52)

In Goethe's freely given account of himself, in lucid prose and poetry, he is fully aware that his mind is in continual development. This awareness has proven to be exemplary: Kaufmann attributes to Goethe the thought that other minds were more or less like his. Hence, the principle of development is universal. Kant, it should be noted, also assigns universal validity to his view of the mind, while claiming "to describe the human mind is it as it always is, has been, and will be," which is to say, as a static entity. What follows is Kaufmann's most daring, polemical hypothesis: Kant's "extreme obscurity"—along with Hegel's and Heidegger's—"is due," he writes, "in part to an attempt—not conscious, to be sure—to hide something from themselves. They were afraid of something that kept them . . . from contributing as much as they might have done to the discovery of the mind. *What they were afraid of was the discovery of their own minds*" (emphasis added) (D1 56).

The problem with this notion, I'll suggest, is that "obscurity" is not an objective quality of writing. Writers write in the jargon of their guild—in the restricted sense of an assumed readership, to be understood and appreciated by the cognoscenti. This enterprise may not be due to timidity or a flight response. Goethe—at least in the view of George Santayana, a philosopher— is, along with Lucretius and Dante, a philosophical poet, and much of *Faust II* is obscure. A philosophical poet like Wallace Stevens is obscure, as well as a good deal of Wittgenstein. In another essay, Kaufmann cites Norman Malcolm to make this point: "one had to attend . . . [Wittgenstein's] lectures for at least three terms 'before one could begin to get *any* grasp of what he was doing'" (emphasis added).[22] Are they all provably *afraid* of the knowledge of their own minds? We shall be eager to see what evidence Kaufmann can adduce for his aggressive surmise.

He will study first the question of Goethe's influences—alleged and true: Herder, Schiller, Fichte, Schopenhauer—all of whom turn out to be either inept or—once again—obscure, their inferiority mainly a foil for Goethe's greatness. On the claim that Herder made a lasting impact on Germany's leading philosophers—as on Hegel, as Charles Taylor has argued—there is, according to Kaufmann, not a grain of evidence for this surmise (D1 60). It is a commonplace that Herder "influenced" the young Goethe, but what he did, as Kaufmann says perceptively, is to acquaint Goethe with what was already in him and would soon burst out. Kaufmann mentions Schiller briefly, chiefly as a foil to Goethe's greatness and Kant's shortcomings. When, early on, Schiller wrote to Goethe, "So much, however, is certain: the best poet is the only true human being, and the best philosopher is only a caricature compared to him," Kaufmann is confident that he was thinking of Goethe in the first place and Kant in the second (D1 71).

It comes as a surprise to learn that Schiller was taken to task by his contemporaries for the "obscurity" of his philosophical writings, but he is nonetheless spared from Kaufmann's charge of a thinker afraid to know himself. It may be because, when compared with Schelling and Fichte, for instance, Schiller writes like an angel. Fichte, an acolyte of Kant, is doubtlessly obscure, and so it is odd and ironical that *he* should complain about Schiller's style, writing, "I first have to translate everything you write before I understand it; and others have the same experience" (D1 74). Schopenhauer, "a virtuoso of vituperation," despised Fichte but, as is well known, kept his powder dry for Hegel. His charges against Hegel reached a climax of resentment without parallel in the history of published abuse. He is mentioned here as the author of a formula bent on what Kaufmann considers the chimera of reconciliation: "Kant's weak side is that in which Goethe is great; and vice versa" (D1 80).

In beginning to study Kant—that misfortune—Kaufmann opens antiphonically: "Kant was one of the greatest and most influential philosophers of all time. . . . He was the first great philosopher since the Middle Ages who was a university professor, and in ever so many ways he is the most representative philosopher of modern times. Few philosophers since Kant have approximated his genius" (D1 83). "Kant's first *Critique* was the first unquestionably major philosophical book in German" (D1 85). "While the discussion of Kant will stress the ways in which he impeded the discovery of the mind, he was plainly one of the greatest philosophers of all time" (D1 92). "In fact, he was one of the greatest philosophers of all time" (D1 95–96). And yet, as we will soon learn in detail, he has been a disaster. His method is defective, and his rigor is spurious.

What can have so blinded his adherents—and they have been many, and they have been thinkers of mettle—to his faults? What Kant accomplished gratified a general desire: "He made room for belief in both [God and immortality] while at the same time accepting the scientific world picture"; he made autonomy and free will possible in "a deterministic Newtonian universe." In a word, he appeared to have reconciled science and religion, producing, by centering the knowledge of nature on the structure of the mind, a prima facie "anti-Copernican revolution" (D1 86–87). Kaufmann' argument is trenchant.

> Kant claimed to have accomplished a Copernican revolution. Actually, his appeal is inseparable from the fact that in his *Critique of Pure Reason* he brought off an *anti-Copernican revolution*. He reversed Copernicus' stunning blow to human self-esteem. . . . what Freud liked to call a "cosmological mortification" of man's self-love. A generation earlier, Nietzsche had remarked: "Since Copernicus man seems to have got himself on an inclined plane; now he is slipping faster and faster away from the center into—what? into nothingness? into a '*penetrating* sense of his nothingness'?" . . . Kant's impact is inseparable from his success in . . . countering . . . nihilism. . . . He tried to prove that it is the human mind that gives nature its laws. . . . [He] tried to show *what the mind had to be like* to make the certainty of Euclidean geometry and Newtonian science possible. (D1 87–88, 94)

For Kaufmann, Kant's starting-off point is misguided and the show of rigor an empty promise. Kant's legacy—including luminaries no less intense than Fichte and Schelling, Hegel and Schopenhauer—inherits these mistakes, squandering the profit of following in the footsteps of Plato, Spinoza, Goethe, and Nietzsche, none of whom were professors besotted with new coinages and endless distinctions. At the same time, Kaufmann is not blind to the glories of the first *Critique*.

> The "critique of pure reason" consists in showing how reason comes to grief when it tries to give us knowledge that transcends the phenomenal world. In particular, Kant seeks to demolish what he calls rational psychology, rational cosmology, and rational theology. No claims to offer us rational knowledge of the soul, the world as a whole, or God are tenable. (D1 101)

After describing Kant's detailed account of the "antinomies," the "theses" and their "proofs," and the "antitheses" and their "proofs," Kaufmann concludes, somewhat at odds with himself, "Perhaps there is nothing in the whole history of philosophy between Plato and Nietzsche that matches the drama of these pages." The change of mood might be explained by Kaufmann's delighted anticipation of what Kant next offers—"a devastating critique of the traditional proofs for God's existence." Such disproofs had occupied Kaufmann at the time of writing his *Critique of Religion and Philosophy* (see chapter 4). Equally,

Kant's "short book on ethics," best translated as *Laying the Foundations of the Metaphysics of Morals*, excites Kaufmann's admiration, for a time: "Its impact rivals that of the *Critique of Pure Reason*, and the volume is second to none of Kant's major works in brevity, elegance, and readability" (D1 103). On the other hand, Kaufmann is no friend of "its highly intricate scholastic terminology":

> Among his key terms are maxims and principles, motives and inducements, and pathological and practical interests. There is no good reason for not making clear at the outset what precisely is meant by each of these six terms. The resulting gain in the clarity of the whole argument would have been immense, and one seems entitled to expect no less from a professor who said repeatedly that he spurned literary elegance for the sake of rigor. . . . What I am saying is that what makes Kant so difficult to read and often so hopelessly obscure is not at all exemplary rigor but rather his appalling *lack* of rigor. (D1 105–6)

It is moot whether it is really profitable for us to prolong *our* subjective reading experience of Kaufmann on Kant, since what *he* offers is mainly a subjective reading experience; his discussion is less about Kant's work than it is about his moods in reading Kant, and they can be summed up: a half-repressed admiration for Kant's ambition and architectonic complexity and a good deal of impatient scorn for the scholastic difficulty of these texts—a difficulty that Kaufmann is not about to consider a serious marker of profundity but rather as the reverse—a cover-up for ineptitude in both perspective and presentation. Still, "however maddening his style may be, one does not have the feeling that Kant is an obscurantist" (D1 107). He can still excite dialectic, and Kaufmann does produce a substantial critique of Kant's *ethical* positions, a matter much closer to Kaufmann's core interests than Kant's epistemological niceties. Kaufmann's attitude to the latter springs out of his paraphrase of "the point of Kant's 'Critique'. . . . The things we *know* are *really* spatiotemporal; and arithmetic, Euclidean geometry, and Newtonian science gives us absolutely certain knowledge of them. . . . The human mind cannot change in any fundamental way" (D1 101). On the other hand, Kaufmann has a lively and telling response to Kant's ethical philosophy—a major insight, and it is very compelling: Kant does not leave room for *moral quandaries*: "The whole thrust of his argument is that there is nothing mysterious about what human beings ought to do. On the contrary, reason tells us clearly. . . . We escape from determinism when our actions are not prompted by any inclination but solely by respect for reason" (D1 107, 109).

As we might recall from *Without Guilt and Justice*, Kaufmann excoriates those decidophobes dependent on "moral rationalism," and so he will have none of this view, whose source is Kant—the view that "purely rational procedures" can supply the motive needed to make the right decision as to "what one ought to do or what would constitute a just society" (W 22). Genuine deciders struggle with competing alternatives; real choices are made with a leap of faith, the faith of a secular humanist, the faith of a heretic. (It would not be difficult to see a regrettable parallel here with Carl Schmitt's authoritarian "decisionism"; in Kaufmann's case, however, the "authority" that gives all the meaning to the decision is the ideally un-self-deceived, autonomous individual mind.) Kaufmann holds Kant's rationalism to be simply wrong: he may not "assume that universality is the mark of rationality, while the particular and subjective are irrational." What would be the result? "As long as I have a will of my own, I am not free!" (D1 111).

Of course, this objection is too brief a summary to be asserted apodictically, and Kaufmann also observes that "autonomy means to Kant that I obey a law I have given myself." I have evidently willed this *giving* of the law, and, following Rousseau—Kant's explicitly acknowledged educator in ethical theory—"obedience to a law one has prescribed to oneself is freedom" (*Social Contract*, book 1, chap. 8) (D1 112). At the end of the day, however, Kaufmann's objection to the denial of moral quandaries in Kant's ethics is surely justified by the "incredible" deduction, "the extraordinary claim," in Kant's *Philosophy of Right*, that "a collision of duties is unthinkable" (D1 155).

Kaufmann is productive in writing about the *several* formulations of the "categorical imperative" provided by Kant. Especially one version Kaufmann judges to be "very impressive. . . . Kant's beautiful . . . and concise formulation of an ethic derived from Moses and the prophets," namely, "Act so that you treat humanity both in your own person and in every other person always as an end *also* and never as a means *only*" (D1 113). At the same time it is subtly jarring to hear Kaufmann evoke a Hebrew biblical reference for Kant's thought when, as is well documented, Kant was an outright anti-Semite. Kaufmann extenuates Kant's late characterization of "the Palestinians living among us, [who] have acquired since their exile . . . the not unfounded reputation of deceit" (from Kant's *Anthropology* of 1798):

Like most of his contemporaries and many eminent writers after him, Kant was simply unable to see any continuity between the Jewish people of his time, of whom he lacked firsthand knowledge and whom he therefore saw through the glasses of prejudice, and either the lofty passages in the Bible that had formed his own moral sense or the Jews whom he knew personally and cherished as friends [viz. Moses Mendelssohn and Marcus Herz, among others]. (D1 125)

A similar extenuation must also have been contrived by the many German Jews—famously, the Marburg philosopher Hermann Cohen and his school—who were passionate neo-Kantians.

But we are getting a bit ahead of ourselves; before looking further at Kaufmann's (lengthy) evocation of the Jewish background of Kant's moral thought, we need to take note of a newly conjured feature of Kaufmann's argument, soon to be a signature of this entire trilogy: Kaufmann's psychobiographical approach to philosophers and philosophy. Kant's admiration for the starry heavens above us and the moral law within us, following Kaufmann, is a legacy of his education—a matrilineal one. Kant's *mother* played a key role in all this by inculcating in him an ethic that demanded, quite literally, *holiness*. Kant's biographers understand this injunction, in its very impossibility, as a sign of a higher order of existence, for how could such a demand originate or be fulfilled? "Kant had indeed based his postulate of immortality, in his *Critique of Practical Reason* (1788)," writes Kaufmann,

> on the claim that practical reason demands that the achievement of holiness should be possible. Since it is not possible in this life, "it therefore can be encountered only in a *progressus ad infinitum*," and this "is possible only if we presuppose an infinitely enduring *existence* and personality of the same rational being (which one calls the immortality of the soul)". . . . This postulate [one could say] represents an attempt to bring the Christian faith in the immortality of the soul as close as possible to Moses' categorical "You shall be holy." (D1 119–20)

Kaufmann presents Kant's intellectual parentage as the Moses of Genesis and Anna Regina Kant née Reuter (I do not mean to be facetious), but references to this pair go on and on. For example, we learn that "at crucial points Moses holds the key to . . . Kant's notorious four examples in the *Grundlegung*." In another example mentioned just above—Kant's postulate of the immortality of the soul—the word "'perfect' would actually have been a little more suitable than 'holy,' which makes it doubly remarkable that Kant used the Mosaic word instead of alluding to the Sermon on the Mount. It clearly harks back to his mother's demand" (D1 123). Would it be cruel to quote one of *Kafka's* unpublished notes at this juncture? (He has certainly *not* read Kaufmann—a counterfactual jest—but one might imagine him doing so, and then writing: "Ludicrousness in the matter of Kant[.] Nausea after too much psychology[.] If somebody has good legs and is given access to psychology, he can quickly cover whole stretches of the field in any sort of zigzag he likes, as in no other. He won't believe his eyes.") [23]

Kaufmann also brings Rilke implicitly into this philosophical family by paraphrasing the Mosaic demand—"You shall be to me a kingdom of priests and a holy people"—as a call for "transformation." (Recall Rilke's poetic admonition: "You must change your life!" cited by Kaufmann in *several* preceding chapters. In our own chapter 7 we noted that it could seem as if the one goal of the serious experience of culture were to have *every* book, painting, and piece of music say to you: "You must change your life!" (S 223). So here, once again, is the very gist of Kaufmann's ethos, Kaufmann's secular faith: "We must cease being as we are. We are summoned to rise to a higher stage. Instead of being content with, or resigned to, our lot, we are told to make something of ourselves" (D1 122–23). This smoldering Mosaic ethos also helps to explain the warm reception that Kant's writings received among contemporary Jewish intellectuals—add Solomon Maimon to Moses Mendelssohn and Marcus Herz—as well as the Jewish philosophers termed neo-Kantian, like the previously mentiond Hermann Cohen and Ernst Cassirer a century (and more) later.

Kant lambasts the moral maxim *quod tibi non vis fueri* ("what you do not want to happen to you, do not do unto others"), an argument that Kaufmann treats as Kant's repudiation of the Golden Rule: Kant "clearly meant to disparage Jesus' 'Golden Rule'. . . . Kant's strictures apply to the Golden Rule" (D1 127). But this is not at all the literal case. The Golden Rule (following Matthew 7:12) is positive and reads, "Do to others what you want them to do to you." The tag that Kant quotes, in order to dispute it, is a Latin rendering of a *Talmudic* precept. Recall the anecdote we cited in chapter 12 concerning the Gentile who wanted to know the whole of the Torah. "The man went to Hillel, who accepted him, saying: 'What is hateful to you, do not do to others; that is the whole Law'" (RE 83). One senses why Kaufmann would be reluctant to have Kant disparage *Rabbi* Hillel's superb response, but it is this maxim, and not the Golden Rule, that Kant literally rejects.

We mentioned the various examples of the categorical imperative in action in the *Grundlegung*, Kaufmann's dissatisfaction with Kant's argument, and his own excavation of Kant's implicit, wholly unacknowledged reliance on Mosaic precepts. The argument against suicide, for example, depends on Kant's claim that in legislating suicide universally, one would destroy nature, "self-love having been implanted in us for a purpose (to advance the promotion of life)" (qtd. in D1 130). Only in effectively legislating suicide universally could the act be approved. But Kaufmann, arguing quite muscularly on these pages, points out any number of decent reasons that could justify suicide short of its universal legislation, offering, for one, the example of the heroic prisoner who commits suicide fearing that under torture he will betray his comrades. All the casuistry embedding Kant's argument is, for Kaufmann, nothing but a smoke screen for a covert appropriation, *tout simple*, of "Moses' categorical demand: 'Choose life'" (Deuteronomy 30:19).

A second example leading to the same conclusion turns on Kant's repudiation of a life lived purely for enjoyment ("like the native of the South Seas"), bent solely on leisure, pleasure, and procreation; but this, argues Kant, is an impossible ethic, since, "as a rational being . . . [this native] wills necessarily that all his capacities should be developed because after all they serve him [and are given to him] for all sorts of purposes" (D1 134). Kaufmann comments with vigor:

> Some people speak of the Protestant ethic in this connection, but it certainly comes from Sinai and distinguished the Jews long before there was any Protestantism. It was only when the Reformers acquainted their followers with the Old Testament that the ancient challenge to become holy and to make something of oneself came to be heeded by large numbers of people in Europe. . . . It was from "Sinai" that Kant derived his concept of law. Morality had to his mind the form of a majestic law, and he kept stressing this term, in spite of Paul's and Luther's polemics against "the law". . . . We are called upon to will the good, and to will it not because we happen to like it or it gives us pleasure but because it is what we are commanded to do, our duty. It is our duty to choose life and to become holy. (D1 135, 137)

This is Kaufmann at his most opinionated and serious best. In light of Kant's claimed source, Kaufmann can only be pleased with him. He is also immensely displeased with Kant and, then again, intermittently pleased. Kant had no historical sense, in the sense that he had no feeling "of his own place in . . . history and his own conditioning. . . . If history put him off because it was so irrational, he had even less time for psychology," and so on. On the other hand, Kant wrote an article titled "Idea for a Universal History with Cosmopolitan Intent," "in which he made the brilliant suggestion that helped to inspire

Hegel's and Marx's interpretations of history—the idea that Hegel later called 'the cunning of reason' (*die List der Vernunft*)." This is the notion that even the irrational actions of men arising from their antagonistic behavior can produce long-term, beneficent results in society—for example, a longing for universal peace. This idea is immediately absorbed by Kaufmann into a salute once more to the genius of the Old Testament, proving, he claims, Kant's responsiveness to it. "This essay shows once again how deeply Kant was influenced by Old Testament notions—history has a purpose, and in the end, 'nation shall not lift up sword against nation, neither shall they learn war any more' (Isaiah 2.4 and Micah 4.3)" (D1 139). It is Kaufmann's special contribution to a study of Kant's ethics to maintain that it is biblical and messianic in inspiration. Kaufmann tells us that the outstanding Kant scholar Lewis Beck read his manuscript approvingly, though this is no guarantee of the reasonableness of Kaufmann's insistence; Professor Beck may have had many motives for not crossing swords with Kaufmann. Many who tried did not fare well. At such moments you can have the feeling that you are reading two trilogies in one: on the one hand, a lucid, enlightening exposition of philosophical ideas; on the other, a litany of expressions of dismay at other philosophers'—and academics'— derelictions, for "there is something so dead in Kant and in Kantian ethics and in so much academic philosophy"—a philippic punctuated by sudden bursts of affection for great writers—Goethe! —and scholars—like Lewis Beck!—who have approved his work, including himself. Caveat lector.

We have often spoken of the pattern in the carpet of Kaufmann's argumentative style: here it is vivid once again, consisting, first, of the antiphonic Yes—No: namely, "Kant was one of the greatest and most influential philosophers of all time" / "One does not have to accept any particular theory about the compulsive or obsessional type, let alone the anal character, to feel that this kind of [Kantian] rigidity is not a sign of freedom or autonomy" (D1 83, 162–64). But then, as we have seen, we have a relenting of the dichotomy—Kaufmann is an explicit enemy of the oppositional character—which comes to light as a temperate Yes:

> A critic who feels that . . . he was unfree and a creature of routine may feel nevertheless that Kant *was* a relatively free spirit and demonstrated a measure of autonomy in *what* he wrote within this compulsive framework. He was not as free a spirit or as autonomous as Goethe, but obviously did display considerable independence. And some of those who have greatly admired him have responded to this quality. (D1 165–66)

On this topic of approbation, Kaufmann objects strenuously to Kant's theory of aesthetic "Wohlgefallen," the affective uptake one takes from the contemplation of beautiful forms. The crux of Kaufmann's objection is his incredulity at a theory—Kant's—that speaks of the *disinterested* contemplation of works of art: "What is one to make of . . . [Kant's] outrageous claim that the experience of beautiful works of art is devoid of any interest?" (D1 146). One oddity of Kaufmann's brief is his way of translating Kant's word for aesthetic pleasure—"Wohlgefallen." Kaufmann offers "approbation," which gives a deadening scholastic turn to the feeling, which may be less than bliss but a lot more satisfying than approval. Of course, Kant scholars know that one good reason for Kant's withdrawing all interest "in the existence of the object" is the symmetry of "the system": experiences of "the good" and "the agreeable" (better: sensuously pleasurable) are connected with interest, and so, in his concern to distinguish the feeling of the beautiful from these other feelings, Kant employs the lever of "disinterestedness."

It would also stand to reason that Kant is not as psychologically deaf as Kaufmann makes him out to be. He supplies the criterion of "Wohlgefallen," of *disinterested* pleasure, in order to justify the judgment of the beauty of a nude that crystallizes on the far side of lust. Kaufmann is also being unusually one-sided in overlooking the centrality of the concept of "play" in the constitution of the aesthetic judgment of the beautiful. Here, faculties of concept formation and imagination play with one another—the imagination producing an endless flow of images from the forms it contemplates while understanding strives to produce concepts adequate to this sensory material . . . but cannot, as the material exceeds its capacity. This tension of nonfulfillment is felt as pleasurable and is in principle endless. At some moment, however, the faculty of judgment imputes to all other rational beings a like pleasure in the form-object, at which moment the true, disinterested aesthetic judgment arises. Kant's theory of aesthetic judgment of the beautiful and the sublime is a wide—and attractive—field and plainly worth a monograph of its own, but not the one that you are reading, which is limited to *Kaufmann's* passionate mind at work in the playing fields of German thought.

As he approaches a conclusion, Kaufmann ventures a comparison between a "Goethean imperative" and the Kantian (categorical) imperative, about which we have heard a great deal. The Goethean imperative turns out to be Rabelaisian, the motto of the idyllic community of the Abbey of Thélème, "Fais ce que voudras" (Do what you want), for "on the whole, Goethe spent his life doing what he felt like doing." I am not sure that even Kaufmann's generous admission, "It is not easy to put the decisive point very precisely," satisfies one's longing for precision in ethics (D1 164). What we do know is that the chain of maxims that Kant wound around his neck is of little help and indicates the type of "religious mentality" that puts him in the company of "countless Jesuits, orthodox rabbis, and other casuists" (D1 165). As Kaufmann warms to his diatribe—"it would be hard to find a more descriptive name [for Kant's style] than pernicious anemia"—he produces a subtext, not for the first time, which engages his own personality:

> Needing nothing less than absolute certainty, the writer forgoes the excitement of living dangerously with probabilities or bold hypotheses; but his sense of certainty is spurious and depends on the obscurity of his style, which does not allow him to see clearly. (D1 166)

Kaufmann observes that Kant's language is "the language of self-deception," but in light of the fury of Kaufmann's diatribes—Kant's work is "scandalous," "grotesque," "the language of a constipated casuist" (hadn't we already agreed to put aside the charge of "an anal character"?), in a word, "an atrocity"—doubts arise whether Kaufmann is entitled to wield so confidently against others the bludgeon of "self-deception" (D1 171, 175). And then, as if he had secretly overheard our worry, he responds with a shrewd, audacious brief suggesting that he is ahead of the game. He is fully aware of the over-the-top character of his objections—his diatribes, his microjeremiads, his philippics—he says, and he asks us to see the good in it. It is bound to excite a powerful reaction—the energy of his sentences goes over to the reader to approve or to comminate; *it is a way for the reader to discover himself.* "While I see no need to burden my discussion of these men—[Goethe, Kant, Hegel, and Nietzsche, Heidegger and Buber, Freud, Adler, and Jung]—with the discoveries I have made about myself in the course of writing about them, I believe that not hiding my emotions may make it easier *for you* to discover your feelings and your mind" (emphasis added) (D1 194).

Our third thinker, Hegel, is another disaster, but his pernicious influence on all future philosophizing might have been averted if only the Kantian element of his bizarre project of wanting to reconcile Goethe and Kant had been suppressed. Kaufmann reminds his readers of the credit due to him for having helped—or rather "exerted himself"—to rehabilitate Hegel after World War II, which should prepare the ground for readier acceptance when Kaufmann begins to find "something bizarre and incredible about his books" on his way to a repudiation (D1 200). The adjective he applied to Kant's theory of autonomy—"grotesque"—resurfaces as a description of Hegel's work as well. "Any study of the *Phenomenology* ought to begin with the admission that the book is grotesque" (D1 239).

> Specifically, Hegel's *Phenomenology of the Mind*—or *of the Spirit*—might have become one of the greatest contributions ever made to the discovery of the mind, if it had not been for Kant's disastrous influence. In many ways it is a bold, almost foolhardy book, and the conception underlying it was a work of genius [*Faust* is meant] inspired by Goethe. But Hegel was determined to produce a major philosophical treatise and felt that the only way of doing that was to follow in Kant's footsteps. (D1 201)

Rudolf Haym, the Hegel scholar whom we encountered in chapter 8 and whom Kaufmann, in his 1965 *Hegel*, cited approvingly, saw at the heart of *Phenomenology* the conflict between the rhetoric of history and the rhetoric of psychology. This idea is clearly unobjectionable, but Kaufmann finds it simply off the mark. No, the conflict—and the attempt at resolution—must be conceived as one between the Kantian and the Goethean dimensions of Hegel's "mentality," however admittedly "farfetched" this thesis might seem (D1 202). Kaufmann intends to develop it, relying chiefly on the Faustian quality of Hegel's *Phenomenology* he intuited and discussed in his *Hegel*. Hegel's disputable discussion of the intensity of brother-sister love in his *Phenomenology* also appears to have been shaped by Goethe's play *Iphigenia in Tauris*, as well as Hegel's own family experience, which Kaufmann finds illuminating. The reader wonders: Is Hegel's claim about sibling love *as such* more or less true because Hegel's sister loved him?

Kaufmann's first major thrust deals with Hegel's beginnings, which are driven by Hegel's fundamental concern not for a science of consciousness *tel quel* but for religion and morality, as Kaufmann again argued in his 1965 *Hegel* monograph. One of Hegel's first essays conceives of a "grotesque" Kantian Jesus, who declares: "What you can will to be a universal law among men, valid also against yourselves, according to that maxim act; this is a basic law of ethics, the content of all legislation and of the sacred books of all peoples" (D1 206). But this tendency is short-lived, and, in proof of his main argument, Kaufmann remarks that "in his next major effort . . . Hegel turned against Kant. . . . Instead of voicing Kant's moral doctrines," Jesus is now identified with the inspiring image of humanity from Goethe's *Iphigenia* (D1 207).

The effort to discredit Hegel for his infatuation with Kant addresses the same flaw that Kaufmann saw in Kant: Kant's *Critique of Pure Reason* was composed "in flight, as it were" (Kant), and this is also true of Hegel's first major work, the celebrated *Phenomenology*. These masterpieces were written as fast as Kant's and Hegel's quill pens could fly over the page and were never thoroughly examined before publication.[24]

> Something written carefully and reconsidered again and again needs to be read very differently from something written at breakneck speed without any time out for self-criticism. And it is noteworthy that Kant and Hegel, who claimed to emulate science and promised the readers nothing less than certainty, wrote in the latter fashion. (D1 217)

Phenomenology is again "grotesque" in its pretentions: its subject is nothing less than the journey of Geist (spirit) toward self-recognition, "a *Bildungsroman* of the human spirit," whose claim to completeness actually involves "relentless selectivity and a bold construction" (D1 227). No one today would think of "reducing history to some such single story," let alone a "necessary" story—"necessity" being another dysfunctional category from the Kantian legacy. It is disturbing that "Hegel systematically ignored the difference between demonstrating that an event was necessary and merely giving a reason for it that suggests that it was not completely fortuitous" (D1 228). But Kaufmann also finds the story wonderful in its way, especially when formulated "rather poetically" by Hegel as

> the path of the natural consciousness to true knowledge . . . the way of the soul that migrates through the series of its forms as so many stages prescribed to it by its nature so that it may purify itself and becomes spirit by attaining through its complete experience of itself the knowledge of what it is in itself. (D1 229–30)

What is evidently attractive to Kaufmann in this formula is its Goethean flair. This and similar passages constitute what he calls "*Hegel's second conception of the phenomenology of the spirit,* which I shall call the *poetic* one. As the scientific conception is derived from Kant, the poetic one was inspired by Goethe" (D1 231). There is a third: it contributes, admittedly, nothing to the discovery of the mind. Kaufmann calls it, for want of a better term, "*the restricted or the* Encyclopedia *conception*" of phenomenology, which follows from the fact that as a subject heading it was inserted into later editions of Hegel's *Encyclopedia* at an unexpected place, *below psychology* (D1 251). The point of this third conception of phenomenology is that, for Kaufmann, Hegel had no clear idea of what he meant by or meant to do with the concept.

Except for a few conclusive thrusts, many of the materials of this section bearing on the parallel between the *Phenomenology* and Goethe's *Faust* can be found in the 1965 Hegel monograph. They amount to a fierce, repetitive insistence that Hegel, for all his ingenuity, for all his "being so full of surprises, so utterly unpredictable, so richly imaginative and irrepressibly *geistreich*," was never scientific; that parts of the system—there is no single, complete system—do not cohere in a necessary way; and it is futile for commentators to attempt to produce that logic (D1 233). Hegel's rigor is spurious and his self-certainty on the Kantian model a pose. It deserves notice that for all the destructive Kant idolatry that Kaufmann imputes to Hegel, the great chapter 6 of *Phenomenology* concludes with a *criticism* of Kant's teaching on morality. And not every reader, I think, is prepared to believe that Hegel's rephrasing the title of a late section of *Phenomenology* from "Science of the Experience of Consciousness" to "Phenomenology of the *Spirit*" (stress on the German word *Geist*) "*meant* a move from Kant to Goethe and Schiller" (emphasis added). Schiller has now begun to figure as a Goethe double in the quarrel with Kant (D1 235). As we would expect, Kaufmann can also admit Hegel's power—the temperate Yes following the antinomous Yes and No; and he cites a memorable and altogether essential statement by Hegel plainly revealing his (brilliant) "mentality." In a letter from 1807, Hegel writes:

> Science alone is theodicy; it keeps one both from looking at events with animal amazement or ascribing them more cleverly to accidents of the moment or of the talents of one individual—as if the destinies of empires depended on an occupied or not occupied hill—and from lamenting the triumph of injustice and the defeat of right. (D1 236)

Kaufmann reads this text as implying on Hegel's part a preternatural terror of contingencies, a deep anxiety that he aims to conceal from himself and others by a show of absolute knowledge. This, surely, is a leap based on an a priori conviction that contingencies are all right in moderation and that it signals a serious character flaw to resist them so strenuously.

I'll add that in a remarkable text by Hölderlin, Hegel's intimate friend, in which Hölderlin reflects on the task of writing a tragedy based on Empedokles's self-immolation, Hölderlin identified the obstacle to his writing a stage-worthy tragedy as the flux of contingencies (*alles Accidentellen*) in which an action would need to be entangled if put on display. Is this fact about Hölderlin's philosophy of drama also reason enough to impute to him terror that needed to wear a mask? The masks differ—some scholars speculate that Hölderlin put on the mask of insanity; Hegel, according to Kaufmann, the mask of absolute certainty. The distaste for contingencies forced to explain fateful events—the urge of great thinkers to get to only the "load-bearing elements" —would lead, if at all, to quite different character assessments. We return to a prevailing concern in reading Kaufmann about the relation of "mentalities" to works: the relation is contingent and, supposing it can be established, will vary from case to case.

Does Hegel's writing in a style—a discourse—shared by contemporary philosophers prove that "he lacked the courage to develop his natural talents" and required "a defense mechanism, a mask, a device born of fear of himself?" (D1 239–40). Would not a Hegelian view of "natural talents" see them as the *history* of their becoming—in their passage to discursive forms altogether different from their beginnings, to which the optional term "development" can be applied? Next, how decisively do empirical details concerning the facts of the manner of *publication* of Hegel's works go to the essence of "the Hegelian mind"?

When we come right down to it, the final section of this first volume of *Discovering the Mind* can replace—muscularly, rationally—the entire mix of vexation and faint praise of Hegel that we have had till now. Here, finally, Hegel stands stripped free of his poisonous Kantian robes. It is the consummation devoutly to be wished of the hope that Kaufmann had stated at the beginning: that a de-Kantianized Hegel would be a boon to the discovery of the mind.

Many passages of this conclusion seem to have been written in response to some telling concerns by scholarly readers of the manuscript—and the result is a clear, nuclear clarification of the entire narrative. Hegel comes out into the open as a great furtherer of "spiritual" discovery, of an order of mental things remote from a reductive psychologizing.

First, the question of "influence" is refined, and we get some solid intellectual history: "It is only fair to add that Kant was not Hegel's only model, that he helped H.E.G. Paulus prepare a scholarly edition of Spinoza before he wrote the *Phenomenology*, and that he was steeped in Plato, including such late dialogues as the *Parmenides* and *Sophist*, and above all in Aristotle" (D1 260). And we have the equally temperate and constructive reflection, "Although I believe that Goethe's influence on Hegel was overwhelming, it would not matter greatly if at one point it would be more appropriate to speak of an elective affinity rather than influence" (D1 261). (Speak of the style of prevarication!) Yet no reader could fail to appreciate the effort; it is overdue.

And what, concretely, of Hegel's contribution to the discovery of the mind? It is matter, Kaufmann avers, of his *accepting*

> Goethe's model of autonomy; his idea that man is his deeds and that a history of the deeds gives us the essence; the all-important point that the mind can be understood only in terms of development; the opposition to Newtonian science and the bold notion that "the history of science is science itself"; and finally also the disparagement of mathematical certainty, which turns up in the Preface to the *Phenomenology*. (D1 260–61)

Kaufmann rethinks his conclusion again—it is a little like the many conclusions to Beethoven's Fifth Symphony—and defines Hegel's accomplishments apart from their Goethean flair: in the end, he considers Hegel's *systematic* thinking—perhaps to our surprise—to be "a stroke of genius. . . . Views and positions have to be seen as a whole" (D1 262). More, his *Phenomenology* shows "how each view must be seen in relation to the person holding it," and this leads to the proto-Freudian point that, as Hegel puts it, "the stages that the mind seems to have left behind, it also possesses in its present depth. As it has run through its stages in history, it has to run through them in the present" (D1 267). Next, "Hegel suggested that every position should be seen as a stage in a development—the development of mind or spirit" (D1 263). Furthermore, "a position needs to be seen in relation to opposing views": this is a nuclear definition of Hegel's otherwise never quite defined "dialectical movement" (D1 264). Finally, it is impossible to withhold praise of Hegel's vastly influential lectures on the philosophy of history, aesthetics, and religion, and the history of philosophy (D1 267). In Kaufmann's vanishing glimpse of Hegel, the latter's insights in such studies seem "stupendous," even if defective in being so little suited to the discovery of the *individual* human mind—and hence, presumably in this sense, "disastrous" (D1 266). Hegel significantly accelerated Goethe's drive to discover the mind: their joint achievement is immense, years before a rigorous psychology emerged. But to experience the full development of Goethe's priceless legacy, unhindered by Kantian dogmatics, we must await Nietzsche's achievement, which Kaufmann will celebrate in the following volume.

16

Opium of the Intellectuals

DISCOVERING THE MIND, VOLUME 2, NIETZSCHE, HEIDEGGER, AND BUBER

Heidegger is the opium of the intellectuals.

—ANSON RABINBACH

IN THE PRECEDING VOLUME of Kaufmann's trilogy—which treated Goethe, Kant, and Hegel—Goethe emerged as much the superior psychologist, with Hegel rich in insight too, as long as he stayed true to the Goethean line and all but cast out Kant. In this second volume, which treats Nietzsche, Heidegger, and Buber, Nietzsche has no true rival in his contributions to this adventure, earning the words originally designed for Goethe's antipode, Isaac Newton, "a mind for ever / Voyaging through strange seas of Thought, alone."[1] All throughout our book, we have noted Kaufmann's often uncritical love of his best educators, Goethe and Nietzsche. (Very well, "I love Nietzsche although my disagreements with him are legion," though one sees no disagreements with Goethe at all [D2 6].)[2] The previous volume celebrated Goethe; this volume celebrates Nietzsche, who enjoyed the distinction of "never [having been] trained as a philosopher" and hence was unbeholden to Kant:

He was a classical philologist and came to philosophy by way of ancient Greek philosophy and poetry and a profound interest in moral psychology. Like Hegel and many other German philosophers, he was steeped in Goethe, but he was free of the fateful compulsion to reconcile Goethe with Kant. (D2 4)

I do not know anyone other than Kaufmann who has chosen the idea of "reconciling [or not reconciling] Goethe with Kant" as the royal road to an understanding of great thinkers. It might be important to note that in his entire lifetime Kant never recorded a word acknowledging Goethe, and so he was primus inter pares of those to whom it never occurred that "reconciling [or not reconciling] Goethe and Kant" was a key philosophical paradigm. Goethe acknowledged Kant and had no difficulty finding in him a kindred spirit in the matter of likening "the beautiful of art" to "the beautiful of nature" and seeing in nature a latent purposiveness. Robert J. Richards, a distinguished Goethe scholar, has demarked the several epochs of Goethe's "Kantianism."[3]

This point requires further explanation: The lineages of Kant with and against Goethe was a topic of lively debate in philosophical faculties in German universities at the turn of the twentieth century, especially in the writings of Karl Vorländer, on whom Kaufmann is plainly dependent in the previous volume for elaborating this antinomy. Yet Vorländer's conclusion, once again, is a respectful acknowledgment of the view of Goethe *with* Kant and hardly a felt imperative. On the other hand, one is ready to consider Kaufmann's thesis, allowing him as it does to write with rhetorical panache—as, for example, about Schopenhauer and Kierkegaard, who, he maintains, also sought "to reconcile Kant and Goethe." "We are made to feel at every turn that these two men have a bad conscience for writing well and have a compulsion to atone for their merits by reverting to Kant's mode" (D2 17).

Of course, Kaufmann will not adopt Vorländer's conciliatory stance supporting Kant, even though, in this volume 2 of *Discovering the Mind*, Kaufmann introduces Kant as "the greatest German philosopher of all time" (D2 3). This approbation is really a Yes *but* . . . , for there remains the inextinguishable stain on the history of philosophy of Kant's "grotesque" style, specious logic, and reprehensible refusal to admit hypothesis, experiment, and error into his system. The movement we have so often seen informing Kaufmann's arguments recurs *en gros* in this trilogy. The movement proceeds as a defiant "Yes!" or "No!" to some thinker or position and is followed by a stark reversal; but then, as Kaufmann scorns such oppositions, which he calls Manichaean, his conclusion will in every case be a temperate Yes *but* or No *but* . . . . He has seen some merit in a position he has scorned.

The rhythm of Yes—No followed by a temperate Yes applies to eight of the nine thinkers, with the glaring exception of Heidegger, of whom next-to-nothing good can be said. After a glorious accommodation of Goethe followed by a repudiation of Kant, Kaufmann concluded volume 1 with a mixed opinion of Hegel, in whom both Goethe and Kant contend. In this volume 2, Buber, at the end, will come off much less poorly than Heidegger, who remains a non placet. Kaufmann intends his "attitude toward Buber . . . [to be] as un-Manichaean as possible. The inclusion of the chapter on Buber should do its share to mitigate the stark juxtaposition of Nietzsche and Heidegger" (D2 6). Still, a courteous disavowal predominates.

This volume 2 begins with a lovely prelude, full of intense personal signif-icance for Kaufmann. He cites a passage from Nietzsche's seminal *Schopen-hauer as Educator*:

> Young souls should look back on their lives with the question: what have you truly loved so far, what has attracted your soul higher, what has dom-inated it and at the same time made it rejoice? . . . Your true educators and molders disclose to you what is the true primordial sense and basic substance of your nature. . . . Your educators can be no more than your lib-erators. . . . Real education is liberation. . . . To be sure, there must be other means of finding oneself, of leaving the stupor in which one usually moves as in a dismal cloud, and regaining consciousness, but I know none better than to recall one's educators and molders. (D2 7–8)

On the crucial question of self-discovery, Kaufmann, reminds us of the key perception of Goethe and Hegel, not original with "the existentialists": we have no essence other than the history of our deeds. "Nietzsche adds a psychological dimension when he says: in addition to that you might reflect on what you have especially admired. And I might add: also on what you dislike strongly" (D2 10). What follows is the strongest reference to Kaufmann's "true primordial sense and basic substance" we have had, worth being quoted at length: it will help us to see him all but face to face. It is a veiled true confession that appears to have been composed last. The piece is couched in a critique of certain "scholars" and of a "one" among them:

> The self-denial of those scholars who do not permit themselves any strong emotions, such as powerful admiration and detestation, deprives them of an important aid to self-knowledge. Typically, they think that they *know* how "one" does things and how things simply aren't done, who is to be taken seriously and who not, what counts and what doesn't count; and since they teach and write with a firm sense of consensus and hence need not use the pronoun "I" very often, their readers and students often fail

to see the blatant and uncritical dogmatism of this procedure. A lack of self-awareness is frequently mistaken for objectivity.

When one deceives oneself and is unconscious of one's own biases, one is quite likely to be left in peace by others who expect the same courtesy in return. The person who has strong likes and dislikes, on the other hand, and is aware of them and argues for them, instead of finding safety in a dogmatic consensus, is often perceived as a threat. After all, he represents a challenge to others to own up to their likes and dislikes and see what, if anything, can be said in their support. Instead of meeting this challenge many people prefer to resort to some defense mechanism and call those by whom they feel threatened dogmatic or egotistical.

One pays lip service to self-knowledge but is terrified by it and resists it. The voyage of discovery on which we are embarking does not merely concern a few dead writers. What is at stake is self-discovery, and that calls for courage. (D2 10–11)

I will jump ahead to call attention to the very last sentences in this trilogy of eleven hundred pages, to see how the beneficent snake of self-knowledge bites its tail:

Scholarship is often a form of escape. These pages, too, can be read as a diversion, perhaps even as a detective story. They could also enhance your self-understanding no less than writing them has increased mine.[4]

Here the "I" is both temperate and explicit.

Early on, a second brief prelude to writings by Schopenhauer and Kierke-gaard as incipient *depth* psychologists serves as a run-up to Nietzsche's rhetorical question, "Who among philosophers was a *psychologist* before me?" Here Kaufmann employs an encyclopedic work by Henri F. Ellenberger, *The Discovery of the Unconscious*, to cite the pregnant sentences: "It is . . . impossible to overestimate Nietzsche's influence on dynamic psychology. . . . Nietzsche may be considered the common source of Freud, Adler, and Jung" (D2 18).[5] Ellenberger appears to have unwittingly produced an advertisement for volumes 2 and 3 of Kaufmann's *Discovering the Mind*: volume 3, of course, is devoted to precisely this triad of Freud, Adler, and Jung. It would otherwise be a bit difficult to account for Kaufmann's choice of the thinkers Adler and Jung to absorb his own mature conceptual powers; he will, after all, solidly repudiate them both; and Adler and his "inferiority complex"—even in 1980—was hardly a burning topic of the day, although the fact that Adler ranked a Nietzschean will to dominate higher than Freud's pleasure principle would have contributed to his appeal. For historical background, Kaufmann's chapter includes additional, rather scattershot references to Ellenberger's *The Discovery of the Unconscious* and the *Encyclopedia of Philosophy*.

Nietzsche's depth psychological (henceforth, simply "psychological") aperçus do more than enlist him to the side of "poets" like Shakespeare and Dostoevsky, who offer only "scattered insights." He belongs with the scientist Freud for the scope and coherence of his knowledge. Kaufmann sees few genuine precursors to Nietzsche as a scientist in depth psychology, though he does take notice, as a kind of afterthought seemingly prompted by a reader, of the so-called romantic philosopher Carl Gustav Carus (1789–1869): Jung acknowledged Carus vigorously for his alleged discovery of the unconscious as the basis of the psyche. A contemporary of Carus, Franz von Baader (1765–1841), whom Gaston Bachelard called "a genius of reverie," also contributed to a romantic philosophy of the unconscious.[6]

In a lecture at Princeton some decades ago, the intellectual historian Wolf Lepenies postulated a century-long hysteresis in the history of depth psychology—hysteresis being "the principle by which history lags behind, is pitted against itself, intricately regresses within its progression."[7] His thesis, more sharply pointed than Kaufmann's, is strikingly relevant: Freud, Adler, and Jung all feed, more or less consciously, on the store of psychological reflection amassed a century before.[8]

The brunt of Kaufmann's discussion of Kierkegaard is to dismiss his contributions to psychology, Kierkegaard being too "self-centered" and "his primary source [of insight] . . . self-reflection"; yet Nietzsche's superiority as a psychologist, according to Freud, whose view Kaufmann celebrates, was owed to "the degree of introspection [he] achieved," unrivaled by anyone before (D2 20, 49). A less contentious shortcoming is Kierkegaard's failure to consider "alternatives" to the alluring absurdity of Christianity. Classical Greek religion is just as absurd, Kaufmann declares, with its indistinction between gods and men. On the other hand, Kierkegaard's reflections on anxiety are brilliant and of capital importance; and, of course, they will be taken up and elaborated notably by Heidegger and Freud.

These insights can be enumerated: (1) in Kierkegaard's words, "Dread is a *sympathetic antipathy and an antipathetic sympathy*." Kaufmann's comment is cogent: "Today we would say that it involves a deep ambivalence. We are divided against ourselves and want something that another part of us does not want" (D2 25). (2) Dread is linked to guilt. Kaufmann's comment is

again full of good sense: "When we strongly desire something that our conscience disapproves of so strongly that it does not even allow us to become
conscious of our desire, the resultant emotion is not an articulate feeling
of guilt but rather a free-floating dread or anxiety that seems to have no
object" (D2 26). (3) Finally, Kierkegaard's beautiful, memorable epigram
reads: "Dread is the dizziness of freedom." Kaufmann observes appreciatively: "Nobody before Kierkegaard had seen so clearly that the freedom
to make a fateful decision that may change our character and future breeds
anxiety" (D2 26). He has dealt with this matter in the first chapter of *Without
Guilt and Justice* (see chapter 11).

Kaufmann's contribution to the discussion above will inform a good deal of
his presentation of Heidegger and Freud. Kierkegaard, he notes, is the author
of the influential distinction between fear and anxiety, the proposition that
the object of fear is something and the "object" of dread, nothing. Kaufmann
resists this distinction:

> The experience of a deep dread or anxiety that is not accompanied by any
> awareness of an object of which one is afraid is real enough. It does not
> follow that one really is afraid of nothing, much less that this experience
> amounts to a revelation of "the nothing," as Heidegger insisted. It might
> well be the case, as Freud argued, that we dare not admit to ourselves what
> it is that fills us with anxiety and that skillful probing might reveal the
> repressed object. . . . Kierkegaard's most profound insights about dread do
> not depend on all the ado [in Heidegger as well as in Sartre, author *L'être et
> le néant*] about nothing. (D2 25)

On the irresistible subject of Heidegger, whose many derelictions we
will soon encounter, we have advance warning that Kierkegaard is the "onlie
begetter" of many of the key concepts running through Heidegger's *Being and
Time*—foremost ambiguity, chatter, and curiosity (D2 30). The latter belong
to Kierkegaard's (and Heidegger's) analysis of inauthenticity—the latter word
is Heidegger's rough coinage "Uneigentlichkeit," whose saner name is self-
deception, founded on the craving to escape the self.[9] Kierkegaard's antidote
is Christian belief; Heidegger's, anxiety and atheistic resoluteness.

Schopenhauer might deserve some attention as a major philosophical psychologist. He speaks of a basic sex drive but also links it to a *metaphysical*
reality—the Will—which doubly overturns the commonplace that his ruminations on the "Geschlechtstrieb"—sex drive, better, "species drive"—predate
Freud's "insistence on *Sexualität*." True, the claim of Schopenhauer to be a

founding figure of depth psychology can be grounded in Freud's own words: he speaks of "the great thinker *Schopenhauer* whose unconscious 'will' is to be equated with the psychic drives of psychoanalysis." But this conclusion is owed, following Kaufmann, at once to Freud's generosity and to the rhetorical advantage of enlisting to one's idea the agreement of a "great philosopher" (D2 34–35). Kaufmann ends with a smart piece of psychology in his own right:

> Freud's final observation is penetrating. People generally take no offense when a poet or novelist makes a point, or even when a philosopher makes an assertion more or less dogmatically but in passing, while they become indignant when someone offers a demonstration and marshals evidence that no longer allows one to adopt a merely aesthetic attitude, admiring the writer's wit or profundity. As soon as they are challenged to change cherished views, many people explode with resentment and strike back with purely *ad hominem* arguments, disparaging the person by whom they feel threatened. (D2 35–36)

What Kaufmann demonstrates—in agreement with Freud!—is that Schopenhauer is indeed the author of the theory of psychic repression. Schopenhauer is ruminating on the "structure" of insanity and on the information one needs to authorize a general thesis. When we realize, writes Schopenhauer,

> how much we dislike thinking of things that strongly hurt our interests, our pride, or our wishes; how reluctant we are to present such matters to our intellect for accurate and serious examination; how readily we skip, or rather creep, away from them again unconsciously. . . . In line with the above account we may thus find the origin of insanity in a forcible "banishing from one's mind" of something, but this is possible only by "putting into one's head" some other notion. (D2 36–37)

At this point, however, Kaufmann again appears to entertain a contradiction. Except for the lustrous examples above, he finds Schopenhauer, like Kierkegaard, a poor psychologist, an important reason being that "he relied very largely on literature or *Dichtung*." On the subject of insanity, he wrote, "the creatures of a genuine genius . . . have as much truth as real persons" (D2 39). Yet Kaufmann also concludes that "Nietzsche's psychology, like Freud's, has its roots primarily in imaginative literature." Alive, Kaufmann would no doubt be able to dissolve the contradiction with a creative Yes *but*. . . .

The core of *Discovering the Mind*, volume 2, consists of some 120 pages devoted to Nietzsche as a psychologist of genius—a reasonable enterprise, since, in Nietzsche's words, "A psychologist without equal speaks from my writings" (D2 47). Kaufmann's chapters consist of fresh, sometimes surprisingly personal formulations together with arguments and citations familiar from his monumental 1950 *Nietzsche: Philosopher, Psychologist, Antichrist.* Nietzsche is a perpetual model for Kaufmann of his own original thinking, good writing, and flair for the telling citation, witness Nietzsche's aperçu, "Morality has falsified all *psychologica* through and through—*moralizing* them—down to that gruesome nonsense that love is supposed to be something 'unegoistic'" (D2 50). Love, we read, is an affair of wanting to take possession, an expression of the will to power. Nietzsche continues, famously:

> Here and there on earth we may encounter a kind of continuation of love in which this possessive craving of two people for each other gives way to a new desire and lust for possession—a *shared* higher thirst for an ideal above them. But who knows such love? Who has experienced it? Its right name is *friendship.* (D2 52)

Kaufmann concluded his previous book on Goethe, Kant, and Hegel with Hegel's *five* significant achievements—all of them elaborations of Goethe's discoveries of the mind. With his penchant for microsystems, Kaufmann sees Nietzsche's "major contributions" to the discovery of the mind as also five in number. Laying out these five points with some elaboration will help to establish the basic structure of this chapter.

First and foremost is Nietzsche's skepticism about the reliability of "consciousness." It is a contribution

> so complex and ... [with] such far-flung implications that one might despair of putting the point briefly if he himself had not stated it once parenthetically in a mere four words "consciousness is a surface." In many different contexts he showed how the role of consciousness in our psychic life had been widely and vastly overestimated. (D2 54)

In this connection, Nietzsche emerges as a great theorist of repression, as Freud himself noted in *The Psychopathology of Everyday Life*, citing Nietzsche's aphorism from *Beyond Good and Evil* (2: 68): "'I have done that,' says my memory. 'I could not have done that,' says my pride and remains inexorable. Finally, my memory yields" (D2 55).

Among the most memorable and productive of Nietzsche's formulations we read:

our moral judgments and evaluations, too, are only images and fantasies about a physiological process that is unknown to us.... All of our so-called consciousness is a more or less fantastic commentary on an unknown (*ungewussten*), perhaps unknowable, but felt text. (D2 56)

Nietzsche radicalized the thesis that the substance of our dreaming consciousness is "comments," with "images and fantasies," on an unknown physiological process. He shatters the common assumption that, on the one hand, clear thoughts and, on the other, dreams come from radically different sources—different in kind and in value. This claim is supported by Nietzsche's early writings. Readers of *The Birth of Tragedy* will recall the Apollinian standard for clarity of the image: it is, surprisingly, the *dream*. Nietzsche's rich reflection on the element of fiction that all men and women insert into ordinary experience inspires a good summation from Kaufmann, *en bon pédagogue*: "Finally, there is Nietzsche's suggestion that our experiences consist largely, if not entirely, of what we lay into them." These supplements are provoked by our bodily life. Nietzsche "suggests that 'our moral judgments and evaluations' are rationalizations of unconscious physiological processes. I take it that this means that we are not indignant because an action outrages our moral sense but that the indignation is primary and the moral judgment a rationalization" (D2 57).

Nietzsche's meditations on this topic also inspire an example of what I earlier called the *romance* element of this trilogy. Here it consists of a three-page report of Kaufmann's experiences as a photographer in Calcutta, Benares, and Khajuraho, already described in *Man's Lot*; a sudden introduction of Shakespeare's *Troilus and Cressida*, to establish that Shakespeare included something of his own sensibility in classical, Homeric accounts of the Trojan War; and several of Kaufmann's own poems. "Two poems about fall should clinch this point" (D2 63–64) that no two people have the same experience of a literary or any other object (D2 59–62). Kaufmann's choice of an object is a third poem of his own. It is surely moot whether this fugue helps or distracts the reader from his willing absorption in an exposition of Nietzsche *qua* psychologist. This volume will contain many such ultrapersonal fugues, including a fleeting account of Kaufmann's visit to *est*—[Werner] Erhard Seminars Training—a highly controversial organization in the business of "self-actualization."[10] Kaufmann argues for its relevance on the grounds that it popularized Nietzsche's reflections on the self-made character of experience. Erhard's extreme claim reads: "Everything a living creature experiences is created uniquely by that living creature who is the sole source of that experience."

Erhard then adds, "You are the source of all your experience, and you don't have the least control" (D2 63–64).[11] Kaufmann thankfully finds both these claims exaggerated, but they do constitute a distraction, along with an equally elliptical, self-satisfied remark that such reflections prove Kaufmann to be the good reader whom Nietzsche asks for—"a reader as I deserve him, who reads me the way good old philologists read their Horace." The conjunction of Werner Erhard, Kaufmann, and Horace is jolting.

Kaufmann certainly rewards us in elaborating Nietzsche's originality as a theorist of *repression*. "Resistance," he writes, "this key concept of psychoanalysis—is actually encountered in Nietzsche's *Beyond Good and Evil* (Section 23): 'A proper physio-psychology has to contend with unconscious resistance in the heart of the investigator. . . .'" (D2 64–65). In the next chapter Kaufmann will discuss Freud's development of the concept of resistance to a forbidden impulse, a point that prompts, I'll add, a late, bemusing variation on the concept by Roland Barthes. In Barthes's autobiographical memoir, a chapter titled "The Book of the Self," Barthes writes: "He [Roland Barthes] *resists* his ideas: his 'self' or ego, a rational concretion, ceaselessly resists them. Though consisting apparently of a series of 'ideas,' this book is not the book of his ideas; it a book of the Self [now with a capital 'S': 'le vrai Moi'], the book of my resistances to my own *ideas*."[12] As for the distinction between the factitious ego and the deep Self, which consists of the ego's *resistance* to ideas, we have only to quote, with Kaufmann, Zarathustra's great, plangent cry: "Behind your thoughts and feelings, my brother, there stands a mighty ruler, an unknown sage-whose name is self. . . . Always the self listens and seeks: it compares, overpowers, conquers, destroys. It controls, and it is in control of the ego too."[13]

Some of Kaufmann's *personalia* are put more modestly than I've so far noted, and they can be lovely and suddenly immerse us vividly in Kaufmann's past, as this recollection, which alleges, as does Nietzsche, that the "deep Self" is *the body*: "When I was a child, German students were asked what might happen if we never felt pain. Most of them answered that in that case we might live forever. They did not realize that pain is a warning signal sent by the body to our consciousness and that it is perilous not to listen to our body" (D2 68–69). Nietzsche's first great idea now climaxes with passages from Nietzsche's celebrated fable, which he never published: "On Truth and Lie in an Extra-Moral Sense." The crux: "What, indeed, does man know of himself! Can he even once perceive himself completely?" (D2 69).[14]

"Nietzsche's *second* major contribution to the discovery of the mind was his theory of the will to power," a concept to which "he himself gave a central place in his books, beginning with *Thus Spoke Zarathustra*" (D2 70). Kaufmann is dismayed that Nietzsche scholars have failed to address so important a topic (a viral resistance?), a claim that may have been true in 1980 but is no longer cogent, as a reading of our postscript will show. Even so, Brian Leiter, who is a systematically fierce critic of Kaufmann's work, makes the contrary claim that can't be ignored: when Nietzsche reviews the life of his works in *Ecce Homo*, he nowhere considers the concept of the will to power as central to his philosophy. Nonetheless, on the strength of even its occasional mentions, it has since proved tremendously interesting. Heidegger, for one, singles out the doctrine of will to power as Nietzsche's leading idea, supporting his view of Nietzsche as the last great metaphysician of the West. Kaufmann vigorously denies that the concept of will to power has a metaphysical status for Nietzsche—for Kaufmann this idea is out of the question, as implying a two-worlds view of appearance and ulterior reality, of phenomenon and *Ding-an-sich*, which Nietzsche abhors.

How does Nietzsche profile the will to power? It stands behind his audacious argument in the preface to the second edition of *The Birth of Tragedy* on behalf of "deceptions," such "as semblance, delusion, error, interpretation, contrivance, art" as furtherers of life (D2 72–73).[15] Nietzsche will continue to write from what he describes as "the depth of this *antimoral* propensity," which now, in Kaufmann's words, "opposes Dionysus, torn to pieces but reborn, as a joyous affirmation of life to Christ crucified, whom he associated with the negation of life and of *this* world" (D2 73). Kaufmann celebrates Nietzsche's understanding of the will to life, again in opposition to Spinoza and Darwin; in Nietzsche's words:

> The wish to preserve oneself is the symptom of a condition of distress, of a limitation of the really fundamental instinct of life which aims at the *expansion of power* and, wishing for that, frequently risks and even sacrifices self-preservation [!]. . . . In nature it is not conditions of distress that are *dominant* but overflow and squandering. . . . The struggle for existence is only an *exception*, a temporary restriction of the will to live. The great and small struggle always revolves around superiority, around growth and expansion, around power—in accordance with the will to power, which is the will of life (from *The Gay Science*). (D2 80–81)

Kaufmann illustrates the point I think aptly. Not all "who risk their lives in war do so to protect the lives of others; risking one's life and living dangerously have a fatal attraction that can be understood in terms of the will to power" (D2 82). Many of his additional elaborations of the concept have been discussed in our chapter 1, on *Nietzsche: Philosopher, Psychologist, Antichrist*, as, for example, the wrong idea of thinking that Nietzsche "associated 'power' exclusively or even primarily with military or political power.... To his mind, one-upmanship, aggressiveness, jingoism, militarism, racism, conformity, resignation to a drab life, and the desire for Nirvana were all expressions of weakness" (D2 91–92). We can cite Nietzsche in *The Dawn*: "Only *the degree of reason* in strength is decisive" (D2 104). The crux of Kaufmann's argument is found in one of Nietzsche's late jottings, which Kaufmann terms the "classical formulation" of the will to power: "I assess the *power* of a *will* by how much resistance, pain, torture it endures and knows to turn to its advantage" (D2 105). The conceptual force of the drive is its demoralizing "the shamefully *moralized* way of speaking which has gradually made all modern judgments of men and things slimy" (D2 101–2). Readers of Nietzsche might object to the probity of this claim on recalling that Nietzsche also has no hesitation in flinging about charges of "strong" and "weak," but Kaufmann has an answer:

> When a way of life fascinates us but at the same time elicits strongly negative emotions, this shows that we have a strong desire to live like this ourselves but feel even more strongly that we must not do this. Whether we are fully aware of this or not, we give ourselves moral credit for not indulging in such behavior, and we resent those who do not deny themselves as we do. Nietzsche's highly emotional attacks on "the weak" are a case in point. (D2 102)

Even here a will to power is evidently in play—as it is in the highly colored, worldly examples that Kaufmann provides for the basic enjoyment and persuasion of—can one say?—the common reader. For example, on the question of whether a will to submission does not undermine a will to power, consider that the German people did not *submit* to Hitler's accession to power; they thrilled to the power they felt they acquired in identifying with his regime. This can be shown to be the case, Kaufmann claims, in every totalitarian state. In the domestic state, it is wrong to suppose that women—wives, mothers, consorts—submit to men. Their choices, too, are driven by a will to power even when these displays have a different appearance: "weakness, ill health, and dependence" can be subtle ways of dominating others (D2 109). In the course of this demonstration, Kaufmann cites two of his own poems (one is titled "Kaufmann's Laws"); quotes with admiration a very long passage from Solzhenitsyn's *The First Circle* describing the spiritual authority that comes from fearlessness; and expresses his delight in two witty, middlebrow, "psychological" best sellers of the time—Stephen Potter with *The Theory and Practice of Gamesmanship* and Eric Berne with *The Games People Play*, the Malcolm Gladwells of the time. They round out the romance element in Kaufmann's account of Nietzsche's will to power.

Nietzsche's third important contribution to the discovery of the mind is his analysis of *ressentiment*: note Nietzsche's preference for the French term, which bears more directly on his discussion of repression.[16] This concept is a lever with which he—and now others—can operate analytically on entire worldviews as they are shown to inform religions, philosophies, and other belief systems. We are dealing early on with what Karl Jaspers would later call, in the title of a famous book, "The Psychology of World Views."[17] Nietzsche was a thinker of continual concern for Jaspers.

Nietzsche locates the origin of "slave morality" in repressed rage at the power of a ruling class or human type, a revaluation producing, for one thing, the table of Christian values. Resentment of vitality inspires the value-creating "priest" to conceive "meekness" as a virtue; resentment of ostentation as "poverty of the heart"; resentment of sexual power as ascetic self-denial; and so forth. There can be no greater tribute to the animating presence of repressed resentment in Christian values than the voluptuous delight that believers will experience from their vantage point in heaven while witnessing the eternal tortures of the damned—nonbelievers by choice or by the unlucky fate of having been born too early or elsewhere. Kaufmann cites another "classical" formulation from Nietzsche's *On the Genealogy of Morals*: "The slave revolt in morality begins when *ressentiment* itself becomes creative and gives birth to values: the *ressentiment* of natures who are denied the true reaction, that of deeds, and compensate themselves with an imaginary revenge" (D2 121). But there are ways to get around revenge when you think you have been harmed: you can master that harm, grow from it, and "prove" this way, as Nietzsche's *Zarathustra* says, "that . . . [your enemy] . . . did you some good." Kaufmann is surely aware that this sublimation is easier said than done. Yet the value of this wisdom is unassailable, for "there is no nobler way to overcome resentment and transmute self-pity into a pervasive sense of gratitude" (D2 122).

The willingness to absorb criticism implies respect for alternatives. "*The essence of critical thinking is the consideration of objections and alternatives, while dogmatism ignores both.*" In their endless discussions of issues of morality and law, "Jews have cultivated the consideration of objections and alternatives for over two thousand years"—an ethos that helps to explain the prominence of twentieth-century *Jewish* philosophers and scientists. Christianity, in which authority is "much more institutionalized and centralized," is, by contrast, the "dogmatic religion *par excellence*" (though what of the Protestant schism?). "Christian church councils defined what precisely one must believe to be saved. . . . In the Roman Catholic Church, almost all intellectuals were priests who were expected to be celibate and have no offspring. A more dysgenic and anti-intellectual policy would be difficult to invent." On the curious premise that the children in large (Jewish) families—as apart from "entire generations"—are *resistant* to the convictions (Nietzsche: "lies") of their elders, Kaufmann is glad to report that Jews, by contrast, "expected rabbis to marry young and have large families" (D2 129). The result should be an abundance of freethinkers in the Nietzschean mold.

For all his willingness to embrace *hypotheses* like the primacy of a will to power and the idea of the eternal recurrence of the same, Nietzsche, too, earns the distinction of having "sided with Goethe against Kant. . . . Kant was afraid of change, while 'metamorphosis' was one of Goethe's leitmotifs, also in his life; and Nietzsche said in the poem that concludes *Beyond Good and Evil*, 'One has to change to stay akin to me.'" Kaufmann stresses that this heritage of deriding dogmatic belief systems survives in *est* ([Werner] Erhard's Seminars Training) (D2 130). Perhaps this out-on-a-limb advocacy responds to Nietzsche's notorious demand "to live dangerously."

We have arrived at the fourth (of five) of Nietzsche's major contributions to discovering the mind. This is his pioneering of *psychohistory*. We have seen Kaufmann's abundant use of this method in his descriptions of Goethe and, above all, Kant; it will define his approach throughout the entire trilogy: "I am trying to show how a psychological understanding of the principal figures . . . helps us to understand their philosophies better." It is a matter of having "some grasp of the mind or mentality of one's subject." The interpreter "must develop a feeling for what this human being could have meant or thought and what he clearly could not have meant or thought"; add to this, "an understanding of a person's individual style that can come only from prolonged immersion in the works and documents"; add to this, finally, a readiness to practice a "critical rethinking of the writer's ideas." Nietzsche practiced psychohistory in his brilliant analyses of Paul and Jesus and, in its beginnings, Luther. These portraits are less models to imitate than cogent suggestions for emulation (D2 133–34).

The last of Nietzsche's contributions to the discovery of the mind is his philosophy of masks (D2 137). In opposing the ordinary idea that masks are markers of insincerity, Nietzsche (and Kaufmann) bring high praise to this device: it makes for irony, subtlety, and appropriate reserve. Still, "the question remains how intellectual integrity and honesty . . . can be reconciled with his philosophy of masks" (D2 149). The answer is not crystal clear, and Nietzsche's remarks on this topic are rather cryptic, as form fits function. We read, from the speaker's position of strength, "Whatever is profound loves masks"; here there is no suggestion of a compromise of depth. And we also read in the same passage, rather from the position of one who has been harried, how a mask grows around "every profound spirit . . . owing to the constantly false, namely *shallow*, interpretation of every word, every step, every sign of life he gives" (D2 156). He can no longer bare his thought if it is only to invite mean thrusts. In any case, we *mask the world*: "Without accepting the fictions of logic, without measuring reality against the purely invented world of the unconditional and self-identical, without a constant falsification of the world by means of numbers, man could not live—that renouncing false judgments would mean renouncing life" (D2 152). How, then, could the temptation not arise to think that a personal fiction might be necessary for survival?

This essay ends with Kaufmann's diatribe against Karl Jaspers, unchanged from the polemic of the first existentialism anthology, which then tilts toward a wholesale dismissal of "the current French Nietzsche literature": the writings of both of Kaufmann's targets build, reprehensibly, on mere "snippets of quotations." It is worth pointing out that the many essays written by American scholars on the basis of "French theory" rely on Kaufmann's mostly unsurpassable translations; Kaufmann will recognize himself in many of these snippets (D2 166). One comes away from this lengthy essay on Nietzsche realizing how many of Kaufmann's cherished beliefs have been inspired by his "educator" Nietzsche, who demanded best and better philology. At the same time this is an impression that can have been won equally from Kaufmann's first great Nietzsche opus.

The following attack on "Heidegger's dogmatic anthropology" is one of the most powerful critical essays one is likely to read (D2 167–238). Part of this effect, in contrast with the preceding Nietzsche chapter, is owed to Kaufmann's concentration on a single item—Heidegger's masterwork *Being and Time* (1927). Kaufmann's essay is a confident, incisive, polemical assault in, once again, six theses. Here, a formidable thinker, who "proximally and for the most part," in Heidegger's own jargon, has seemed proof against analysis (in the safe position of an object of pious exegesis), finds in Kaufmann his equal at least in energy and conviction.[18]

Kaufmann ends his dismemberment with the generous request that he be refuted, if opponents dare. I cannot see how he can be. His destruction of the much-admired enterprise of *fundamental ontology* is based on a deep knowledge of Heidegger's works and of the man at work himself. Kaufmann records having spoken with Heidegger at length on Nietzsche and worked with him on translation issues in *Being and Time* (he suggested that "Dasein" be translated as "human Being") and was well aware of the copious commentaries on *Being and Time* published at the time of Kaufmann's writing his chapter.[19] Here, he asks basic questions of the text as to its intelligibility, coherence, and originality and shows no discomfort at all in being perfectly clear and direct, his strongest suit. For him, *Being and Time*, as we shall see, is a bloated, jargon-laden fragment of a larger work that never appeared, a terminological horror obscuring a patent plagiarism of Kierkegaard and Tolstoy, both of whom said it better—"it" being a large-minded meditation on a humanity condemned to die.

The opening to Kaufmann's polemic centers on a find supporting his surmise that from the start Heidegger is less a philosopher than a theologian: it is an astonishing, unpublished letter Heidegger wrote to Karl Löwith in 1921.

> Löwith had had an argument with another Heidegger student "about the 'correct' interpretation of 'my philosophy.'" Their discussion, said Heidegger, rested on "the fundamental mistake" that both measured him against "Nietzsche, Kierkegaard, Scheler and other creative and profound philosophers. You are free to do that—but it must be added that I am no philosopher, and I do not fancy that I am doing anything remotely comparable; that is not my intention."

Heidegger's climactic statement is as decisive as can be: "It is part of my factuality what I say briefly, that I am a 'Christian theologian'" (D2 170–71).

In his memoirs, Heidegger's eminent student Hans-Georg Gadamer confirms this tendency: he recalls Heidegger's devotion in early days (Marburg, 1923) to the task of "summoning to faith and to preserve in faith." *Being and Time*, continues Gadamer, arises as an answer to Heidegger's *theological* concerns. Kaufmann sees Heidegger's early thought as coming to a head in 1933 in Heidegger's barely concealed amazement at Nietzsche's dictum: "God is dead!" But in light of the evidence of Löwith and Gadamer, this awareness must surely have preceded the writing of *Being and Time*. If this despair of a loss of Being is not explicit in the 1920s, the reason is plain: "He still felt so much at home in his Christian background" (D2 170–71).

Being and Time begins with an analysis of Dasein, the human existent, which/who matters chiefly as the vehicle of the question of the meaning of "Being." But precisely at this point there is cognitive trouble for the reader. On the question of the meaning of Dasein, Heidegger is straightforward (if unhelpful): it can be (Manichaeanly) authentic or inauthentic. In a puffed-up neologism, these are Dasein's two and only two "Seinsmodi." On the question of the meaning of "Being," however, Hegel and Nietzsche have argued its futility: "Being" has no meaning. And Heidegger? Here, Kaufmann's reply is devastating:

> Heidegger himself undermines his own "fundamental question" about "the meaning of Being" as well as his repeated insistence that "the purpose of the interpretation is purely ontological" and that his ultimate concern is not with *human* existence but with the meaning of Being, when he admits— and the emphasis is his own: *"Only human Being can therefore be meaningful or meaningless."* (D2 188–89)[20]

Meanwhile, the anthropological distinction between authentic and inauthentic being is dichotomous and exclusionary and therefore worthless as a critical perspective. Kaufmann might have noted an item additionally useful to his demolition: Heidegger will go on to "distinguish" between "genuine" and "ungenuine" authenticity, a complication that further compounds the mischief.[21] The first dichotomous pair does not allow Heidegger to grasp, for one thing, the human reality of states of mind, dispositions, and drives that are at once authentic and inauthentic, such as the form taken by Heidegger's master value "resoluteness" when it commits itself to an odious cause; consider, for example, Heidegger's authentic ("own-most") commitment to Nazi Führer devotion. The entire discussion about Dasein's modes of being and Dasein's relation to Being is more obscurantist than merely dichotomous. It is shadowed by essentialism—a hunt for essences—and it is shadowed by God: "Surely, Heidegger's Being is one of the shadows of God, and there are many passages of which one can scarcely make sense until one realizes this and notes how he has substituted 'Being' for 'God.'" Kaufmann is pleased to cite the Heidegger scholar J. Glenn Gray, who wrote (brusquely): "God is dead, saith Heidegger, henceforth let us worship Being." Ergo, Kaufmann's first thesis reads literally: "Heidegger's existential ontology is dubious anthropology." One might add the codicil "dubious theology" (D2 185).

"Second thesis: Heidegger is deeply authoritarian" (D2 189). Kaufmann explains, in strident italic: "What I mean by calling Heidegger's anthropology 'dogmatic' is that *he put forward apodictically, without considering negative evidence or alternatives, commonplaces dressed up in an imposing but confusing jargon*" (D2 189). Kaufmann's objection turns on Heidegger's previously noted hostility to science—and indeed to human reason; in one of his first essays on Nietzsche, he called reason "the most stubborn adversary of thinking" (D2 193). Heidegger's indifference to *rational* inquiry runs throughout his work: he shows no feeling for the experimental character of claims and the readiness to conjure and weigh evidence to the contrary. (Defined this way, Nietzsche is an exemplary rationalist.) "The best we can do," writes Kaufmann, and not for the first time, "is to formulate hypotheses or tentative interpretations and constructions and then see what speaks for and what against them." But you will look in vain for any such awareness in Heidegger's writings. His dogmatic sentences, when they are not questions, have an essentialist character: "In his long discussion of 'Being-toward-death,' it never seems to have occurred to him to ask whether human attitudes toward death might differ." He lacks a feeling for the development of features of human being at different times and in different cultures. Heidegger's phenomenological ontology is conceived as a departure from Husserl's strictly epistemological concerns but is like Husserl's in its "quest for timeless certainty" (D2 190).

Heidegger's intellectual procedure is a subjective variant on the existential flight into authority that Kaufmann saw in the German romantics' turn to Roman Catholicism (S 78–79). Kaufmann addresses once more the ruse that he has called "exegetical thinking"; it continues to be one of his most compelling ideas. "The exegetical thinker endows his text with authority, reads his ideas into it, and then gets them back endowed with authority" (D2 191–92). What might have seemed Heidegger's unwitting though reprehensible violence done to the texts he reads—including Aristotle and Kant—becomes the brunt of Heidegger's later vigorous assertion of the inescapability of hermeneutical violence. Not doing violence to texts is not a rational option. Recall the overture to his reading of Hölderlin's ode "As When on a Holiday," where Heidegger defends the dubious textual version of the poem he supplies as deliberately suited to his interpretation (chapter 3).

It was a commonplace at the time of Kaufmann's writing this chapter, especially under the spell of French literary theory, to view the world "as a text." Kaufmann exposes a potential weakness in this ostensibly liberating trope. It now makes *everything* subject to exegetical violence. For Heidegger, writes Kaufmann, "the task consists of 'the uncovering of the [!] meaning of

Being and the fundamental structure of human Being.' Heidegger proposed to treat both as a text—into which we can read one's own ideas while purporting to describe it 'like it is'" (D2 192–93). This proposal is an invitation to authoritarianism.

Kaufmann's third thesis returns to the "shallowness" of Heidegger's discussion of authenticity and inauthenticity, categories (in Heidegger's jargon "Existentialien") that are—again—taken from Kierkegaard with scant acknowledgment. Certain scholastic readers of *Being and Time* will emulate Heidegger and immediately point out that these are not *ethical* categories, but Kaufmann, I think rightly, finds this claim preposterous. Of course, there is nothing ethically neutral about Heidegger's discussion of inauthenticity, to take the more strident case: it is mocked and castigated "while authenticity is romanticized":

> One of the three main features of inauthenticity to which Heidegger devoted a whole section each is *Gerede*, a strongly pejorative term that suggests a debasement of speech (*Rede*) and is fairly rendered by chatter. In the section on chatter, we encounter the subcategory of *Geschreibe*, which suggests worthless writing or scribbling. (D2 198)

In due course we will add the terms "curiosity" and "ambiguity."

On this topic of the names of such ostensibly value-free "Existentialien," Kaufmann points out how tone-deaf they are to ordinary German usage, where Heidegger's word for authenticity, "Eigentlichkeit," in its adjectival variant "eigentlich," has all the overtones of *inauthenticity*. In ordinary usage, it is "typically ... followed by a "but"—for example, "*really* [*eigentlich*] I shouldn't tell you, but ..." (D2 198). It should be noted that when Kaufmann, in every one of his books, uses the term "authenticity," he writes the word in English and not in German. Further on, in dealing with Heidegger's terminological olla podrida, Kaufmann is at his polemical best:

> Heidegger's distinction between *existenzial* and *existenziell*, which seems like a heavy-handed attempt to rival Kant's emphatic distinction between *transzendent* and *transzendental*, ... also has no basis in the [German] language and is so arbitrary that Kant himself frequently used one when he meant the other. (D2 199)

Kant and Heidegger hoist on the same petard!

We mentioned that, following Kaufmann, Heidegger's "Existentialien" of authenticity and inauthenticity are taken from Kierkegaard. There is more:

"His characterizations of curiosity, ambiguity, and chatter are all derived from Kierkegaard's *The Present Age* (1846), which is never even mentioned in *Being and Time*. . . . What Kierkegaard said with immense wit and brilliance . . . is repeated very ponderously in *Being and Time*—as 'fundamental ontology'" (D2 200–201). The notion of inauthenticity, in its composition, exists as a foil to the existential stance that matters most to Heidegger—resoluteness, the soul of authenticity, witness Heidegger: "This taciturn self-projection, ready for dread, into one's most authentic being guilty—is what we call resoluteness." Neither Kierkegaard nor Heidegger, however, was ever able to "establish sufficient safeguards against inhumane and brutal commitments" (D2 201), and here we are returned to Heidegger's enthusiastic participation in Nazi rituals of oppression and control.

"*Fourth thesis: Heidegger neither solved important problems nor opened them up for fruitful discussions; he covered them up*" (D2 202). Kaufmann is referring to the barren formulaic terminology with which Heidegger has "covered up" the important issues of "authenticity, ambiguity, resoluteness, guilt, conscience, and dread in the face of death," a covering up that is all the more ironic since "Heidegger never tired of telling his readers that the Greek word for truth (ἀλήθεια) means unconcealedness, and he seems to have been obsessed with the imagery of uncovering and disclosing. When will a Freudian analyze that?" (D2 203)

A good deal of the opening to *Being and Time* is concerned not with ontology but with etymology, with the primordial meaning of the words "phenomenon" and "logos"—the constituents of phenomenology. But what has this enterprise to do with its stated aim of establishing a method? "Surely," observes Kaufmann,

> one cannot establish the proper method for philosophy or for an inquiry into the nature of human Being or the human condition by discussing at length and very repetitiously the meanings of the two Greek words from which the term "phenomenology" is derived. (D2 205)

This is simply another cover-up—here, of the legitimate problem of a methodical approach to a fundamental ontology. It might be a quibble, but according to Gadamer, in *Truth and Method*, contrary to Kaufmann's account, Heidegger's core beginning concept of "understanding" is "no longer a methodological concept"; it is "the original character of the being of human life itself. Heidegger revealed the projective character of all understanding and conceived the act of understanding itself as the movement of transcendence, of moving beyond being."²² *Being and Time* delineates a "hermeneutical phenomenology" but does not *begin* by applying a time-honored hermeneutical *method*.

"*Fifth thesis: Being and Time belongs to the romantic revival in Germany*." Kaufmann is referring to the "revolutionary pathos" that Heidegger employed to great success in the seminar room and, of course, one must add, in his intellectually bruising encounter at Davos in 1929 with the cultivated, worldly humanist Ernst Cassirer.²³ "Heidegger spoke of going back to Aristotle and, a few years later, to the pre-Socratics; and he always gave the impression that his concern with Being was Greek. In fact, the pathos and passion of his enterprise were romantic and pseudo-Hellenic" (D2 205).

To find a kinship between Heidegger and the "romantics," it is true, Kaufmann selects certain features of *German* romanticism that may be less than central to the concept. It does Heidegger little good to be seen as kin to writers like Friedrich Schlegel (1772–1829) and Georg Philipp Friedrich Freiherr von Hardenberg, aka Novalis (1772–1801), as we know from Kaufmann's previous rejection of them, chiefly for Schlegel's turn to Catholicism and Novalis's love of medieval Catholicism. For Kaufmann this kinship is also based on the apodictic fragmentariness of much of their writing and their celebration of the fragment; and Heidegger never did finish the last third of part 1 of *Being and Time*, leaving it—along with the promised but missing second part—as the fragment of a postulated whole. Heidegger's promise again forms a link with the generalized romantic promise identified by Hegel as the mood of anticipation, of a future spiritual reunification with the earth that has never taken place. One is reminded of the quip variously assigned to Jean-Paul Richter, Thomas Carlyle, and Heinrich Heine: "Providence has given to the English the Empire of the sea; to the French, that of the land; to the Germans, that of—the air."²⁴

"*Sixth thesis: Heidegger secularized Christian preaching about guilt, dread, and death but claimed to break with two thousand years of Western thought.* His teaching that '*human Being as such is guilty*' . . . is a secularized version of the Christian doctrine of original sin" (D2 209). It takes little reflection to decide what credence Kaufmann would give to this "teaching." We have noted the stress he lays on Heidegger's indebtedness to Kierkegaard for his reflections on anxiety. Admittedly, Heidegger does footnote *The Concept of Dread* (1884) as a source, along with writings from Augustine and Luther, but then claims, "rather oddly, that the phenomena of dread [*Angst*] and fear [*Furcht*] . . . have never been distinguished. . . . As a matter of fact, Kierkegaard had no sooner introduced 'the concept of dread' than he added that he must 'call attention to the fact that it is different from fear and similar concepts which refer to something definite'" (D2 211). Kaufmann notes proleptically that, a decade before *Being and Time*, in *Freud's* "lecture on *Angst* in his *General Introduction to Psychoanalysis*, '*Angst*' refers to the state and disregards the object, while fear directs attention precisely toward the object.'" We can invoke Freud to discredit Heidegger's reflections on dread. But we need nothing more than ordinary daylight to see, despite Heidegger's cloud of authority, that the statements that "'Being toward death is essentially dread' and that authenticity requires dread of death" are flatly wrong (D2 213). In many places throughout his oeuvre Kaufmann has declared his independence—and a general independence—of this *enfin* Christian dogma.[25]

Kaufmann interestingly situates Heidegger in a time and place in Germany *entre deux guerres*—a way of reading *Being and Time* rarely practiced. Heidegger's idea of a necessary dread of death constitutive of human Being is, in fact, *timely*, derived from a commonplace: "Before the First World War it had been considered unmanly in Germany to be afraid in the face of death; now it was considered courageous and honest to admit one's dread." In this dictum Heidegger was merely "falling in with the chatter of the time." As for the rest of *Being and Time*, beyond its "hyperacademic language," it amounts chiefly to a repetition of "Christian commonplaces in secularized form" (D2 214). Kaufmann develops his criticism powerfully and originally:

> Heidegger never admitted that he was rejecting Nietzsche and Freud to go back to Christian ideas; he made a great show of breaking with more than two thousand years of European thought to go back to the Greeks; or he claimed to go far beyond Nietzsche, who allegedly still belonged to the Western metaphysical tradition. Rarely has a famous philosopher misunderstood so thoroughly what he was doing—and been believed so widely. (D2 214)

Bold, incisive, *knowledgeable* criticism of this caliber is proof enough that in Kaufmann we have to do with a critical thinker of distinction. Anyone preoccupying himself or herself with his oeuvre can find in such an aperçu all the justification he or she might need. It is enriched from a source that Kaufmann knows very well and extends to a criticism of Heidegger's work after *Being and Time* (1927).

Heidegger's *later* conception of the history of philosophy—the role he assigned to the *pre-Socratics*, the break with them that he found in *Plato*, and the claim that the time has come to break with the Western philosophical tradition that begins with Plato—came straight out of *Nietzsche*.... But Heidegger's later conception makes far less sense than Nietzsche's because the critique of *Christianity* has been dropped. (D2 215–16)

Even if it should be evident that Kaufmann's six objections amount to a complete rejection of Heidegger, the assault cannot resist Kaufmann's signature dialectical mode of judgment, especially remarkable after a passage that attempts to get hold of Heidegger's "geistige Persönlichkeit"—the patterned thinking of his personality. It is Kaufmann's modal logic—his No ... but Yes, en route, in this case, to a decisive No. It reads as follows:

The point is not that Heidegger is wholly inauthentic. In him—as in Hesse and Buber, Nietzsche and Sartre and everyone else—authenticity and inauthenticity are curiously mixed.... But the difference between man and man remains considerable. (D2 217–18)

Kaufmann's own power as an educator is on display in his conclusion about the mind in the making of *Being and Time*: this judgment gives his student something to hold on to for a long time, an intellectual-historical insight as full of meat as an egg has yolk or what his Princeton undergraduates would call a *'cept*:

The work [*Being and Time*] was begun when the author still saw himself as a "Christian theologian," and the "First Half"—or rather the first two-thirds of the first half—appeared when he still saw himself as a phenomenologist. After he discovered Nietzsche, he never mustered the courage to tell either his readers or at least himself to what extent he had changed his mind. (D2 218)

The hallmark of authenticity—if, despite Kaufmann's somewhat irregular support of the term, one will go on using it, since, although imprecise, it is evocative—is *Freud's* continual self-criticism, which Kaufmann develops at length in the final volume of this trilogy.

Kaufmann's penchant for a "third way" of understanding the texts and the mind of thinkers—involving neither a Yes nor a No, for that is a "Manichaean" way of thinking—shapes his analysis of Heidegger's intellectual sensibility in light of his joining the Nazi Party. Does it nullify his work—which Alfred Ayer called "nonsense," anyway, and Paul Edwards, "humbug and mystification"—or is it quite beside the point, an affair of Heidegger's merely empirical self, as many a deconstructionist thinker would have it—leaving Heidegger to be called by "his more enthusiastic supporters . . . the greatest thinker of the century, if not of the last two millennia?"[26] Kaufmann invokes Heidegger's notorious rector's address to the students of Freiburg University, in which Heidegger banishes "so-called" academic freedom as merely negative and demands that students and professors think of themselves as workers for the regime, providing "knowledge service" on the model of "labor service" and "military service" (D2 224). Is a text like this "philosophically irrelevant"? "*In method*," declares Kaufmann, a text like this is no different from the "supposedly [more] serious contribution" (D2 228). The notorious speech drips with talk of "essences" and at no point weighs conceivable objections, rival hypotheses, or alternatives. They are authoritarian dictates.

We should not leave Kaufmann's furious criticism of Heidegger without pointing up its place in the history of such encounters. This relationship has a direction that includes a turnabout. In the 1950s Kaufmann taught a Heidegger seminar to Princeton graduate students in philosophy, inviting their credulity.[27] The first 1956 edition of his influential anthology *Existentialism from Dostoevsky to Sartre* (see chapter 2) carved out a central place for Heidegger in the American reception of existentialism. By the time of the second edition of 1975, however, Kaufmann's view of Heidegger had become altogether critical.[28] From that point on, he had little besides scorn for Heidegger's mystifications. One can only speculate about this apparent turning, as does Pickus:

> Though Kaufmann knew Heidegger personally, this interaction does not seem decisive in the charges raised, as Kaufmann suggested he had already formed an opinion and then "tried to test my image of him by going to talk with him repeatedly, by attending his lectures (1955–1956) and by translating an essay of his choice with an understanding that he would answer questions about it."[29]

But there is no trace in Kaufmann's presentation of Heidegger's "The Way Back into the Ground of Metaphysics" in his 1956 anthology that anticipates the indignation of the later writings. Of course, if Kaufmann went on and on, often literally repeating his attack on Heidegger's work, character, and reputation, it might have been, as Pickus suggests, because he had not been listened to; and, to his chagrin, Heidegger's star kept rising. But this development does not explain the generosity of Kaufmann's presentation of Heidegger's work in 1956. It may be that Heidegger's charm and courtesy in 1955, as Kaufmann reports them, edulcorated for a time Kaufmann's allegedly long-standing hostile view of Heidegger's "image."

Kaufmann's remarks on Heidegger are followed by an essay in criticism on the since-forgotten Martin Buber, eyeing the confusion and affectation of his best-known treatise, *I and Thou*. That Kaufmann's review should be scathing in places is remarkable, since in an earlier essay, he lauded Buber's many achievements on behalf of a modern awareness of Judaism: his translation, with Franz Rosenzweig, of the Hebrew Bible; his exemplary manner of reading sacred texts; and the insights of this very *I and Thou*. ("In Heidegger's readings," by contrast, "there is no Thou" [ER 51].) Kaufmann's early devotion to Buber extended to his translating *I and Thou*, for which he wrote an intense introduction reprinted in the volume of essays titled *Existentialism, Religion, and Death* (1970). In "Buber's Religious Significance," the earlier essay dating from the 1950s, we hear of the finest aperçu in *I and Thou*—the definition of God as "the eternal Thou"—as "probably the most illuminating suggestion about the meaning of 'God' ever ventured" (ER 58). Furthermore, Buber's popular presentation of *The Tales of the Hasidim* is "one of the great religious books of all time, work that invites comparison with the great Scriptures of mankind" (ER 54). Kaufmann's later introduction to his translation of *I and Thou* in 1970 inaugurates a turn. Buber's *Tales of the Hasidim* retains its high value, though that praise is extenuated: once "one of great religious books of all time," it now belongs among the "few books of our century" that can display such "economy" of expression. "Among his own writings, *The Way of Man According to the Teachings of Hasidism* is a work of comparable beauty that distils Buber's own teaching in less than twenty pages"; on the other hand, *I and Thou*, "is overwritten. We are far from the clear, crisp air of a sunny autumn morning in the mountains and the bracing wit of Nietzsche's later prose. We seem even further from the simplicity of Kafka's style, schooled on the book of Genesis" (ER 71). And subsequent parts of this very introduction to a translation—normally an invitation to enter a scene of delight and instruction—warn the reader of the book's singular "blurring of all contours," its "extremely unclear language." Worse, even as Buber acknowledged its obscurity, he "endowed his own text with authority and implied that he himself could not tell its full meaning" (ER 72). Still, for all its darkness, it is clear that "*Ich und Du* is one of the great documents of Jewish faith" (ER 80).

It is interesting that Kaufmann insists on the German title to make his claim more plausible to himself—and then explains: "the choice of 'Thou' [in the English translation] did its share to make God remote and to lessen, if not destroy, the sense of intimacy that pervades Buber's book." The radically Jewish character of the book is compressed in Buber's concept of *Umkehr* (Return), meaning chiefly the return to God. The notion is simple: the sins of the man who returns to God are forgiven. The Jewish character of the concept is pronounced when contrasted with the Christian requirement for divine forgiveness: "Paul's elaborate arguments concerning the impossibility of salvation under the Torah ('the Law') and for the necessity of Christ's redemptive death presuppose that God cannot simply forgive anyone who returns. . . . Buber's whole book deals with such immediate relationships" (ER 81). But this is not to deny that "the book has many faults" (ER 86).

By 1980 Kaufmann's impatience with this book had increased. He is now altogether of another mind about its significance. He does not entirely reject *The Tales of the Hasidim*, since "it is arguable that the final one-volume collection was . . . Buber's masterpiece, although it is controversial. . . . In an important sense, [however,] the effort [of translating the Hebrew Bible into German] was a failure" (D2 243–46). As for *I and Thou*, although still very dark, *it* is clear enough—for the critic to perceive the faults of its logic.

For Kaufmann, uniquely in this case, pointing out these flaws is an admitted labor of love, but that felt love lies mainly in the past—more precisely, for a text written in 1936 and read not so many years later. Still it survives, and Kaufmann insists in one passage, quite abruptly, that his criticism is still veiled in love and admiration (D2 267). But his criticism is severe. Here is the truth—Buber's own truth—that Buber will betray: the truth of style, "as if a genuine message . . . contained a What that could be detached without any damage from its How; as if the spirit of a speech could be discovered anywhere else than in its linguistic body" (D2 253). The style *is* the logic of the book, and Buber's is defective.

Kaufmann makes a somewhat eccentric claim for including this anomalous author in a book devoted to "the discovery of the mind." Buber's strength goes not to *I and Thou* but to his theory of translation, a collaborative affair with the better intellect—Franz Rosenzweig. Their theory calls for a complete, sympathetic immersion of the "I" of the translator in the implicit "Thou" of the book to the point of selflessness and hence, objectivity, inspired by a "profound concern for the distinctive voice of the original" (D2 248–49). But this is not what actually happens when Buber goes to work as an interpreter of other people's writing. Buber's failure is *very* oddly contrasted with Kaufmann's own asserted success—or at least his good intentions:

In fact, I have extended Buber's and Rosenzweig's approach beyond the art of translation and have tried to discover the very different minds of these individuals [namely, Goethe, Kant and Hegel; Nietzsche, Heidegger, and Buber; Freud, Adler, and Jung], even as, in *Tragedy and Philosophy* I sought to discover the different mentalities of Aeschylus, Sophocles, and Euripides. One might think that this must be what Buber did, too, in his interpretations of Moses, the prophets, and the Hasidic masters, but in fact his interpretations are as a rule excessively subjective, and he tended to read his own preferences into the men he admired. This was not an incidental failing or simply a case where a man failed to live up to his own principles. This fault was a direct consequence, or a corollary, of a fatal flaw in *I and Thou*. (D2 249)

We will soon hear of this fatal flaw. Meanwhile, *I and Thou* is a striking example of what the *language* of philosophical writing must not be: highly stylized, personal, indeed private, eccentric—and finally intolerable. It is the contrived mask, the affectation of a personality. The concept of inauthenticity—if it is one—comes to mind: here "we are confronted by a pose and oracular airs without any redeeming wit or irony. But we can easily dispense with the category of inauthenticity; affectation will do" (D2 252).

Buber said that he had written *I and Thou* "under the spell of an irresistible enthusiasm. And the inspiration of such enthusiasm one may not change any more, not even for the sake of exactness. For one can only estimate what one would gain, but not what would be lost" (qtd. in D2 253). Kaufmann's comment on this extraordinary confession is a grace note: he clearly cannot be expected to like it (recall that "many a chapter in this book [*From Shakespeare to Existentialism*] was rewritten again and again, some passages easily twenty times" [SE xii]). He writes of Buber: "Those who keep having intuitions, hunches, and inspirations can afford to be ruthless with themselves, while a writer who has been under the spell of an irresistible enthusiasm only once will naturally guard its fruit more anxiously" (D2 255).

On dispensing with a critique of Buber's style, Kaufmann worries the validity of the famous Ich/Du dichotomy. Put plainly, the theory is meant to propose "a dialogical relationship. The crux of it is that neither partner in such a relationship is an object of experience or use for the other; the partners address and feel addressed by each other" (D2 252–53). Ich-Du (I-You—Kaufmann will no longer have "I-Thou") is to be contrasted with Ich-Es (I-It). But this distinction is not well argued for.

The crux of my criticism is simple: It is not true that a genuine relationship to another human being can be achieved only in brief encounters from which we must always relapse into states in which the other human being becomes for us merely an object of experience and use. (D2 257–58)

Kaufmann then unblushingly ascribes this "flaw" to Buber's having been "permanently damaged by his mother's abandonment of him when he was a small child" (D2 258). Might this be an example of Kaufmann's contextual psychologism run amok? Buber wrote: "Every You in the world is doomed by its nature to become a thing or at least to enter into thinghood again and again" (D2 262). But, for Kaufmann, Buber's "basic dichotomy cannot be accepted as it stands"—it is the efflux of a childhood trauma.

Buber is yet another example of the fateful attempt to reconcile Kant with Nietzsche, since the style of *I and Thou* is a Nietzschean pastiche, but the argument is riddled with brittle Kantian dichotomies, five of which define "basic attitudes in which there is no You: I-I, I-It, It-It, We-We, and Us-Them" (D2 258). Kaufmann's discussion of these formulae rapidly becomes unreadable: there is too much of this sort of verbiage, viz., "Of course, the You that has fallen from grace, as it were, and becomes an It may become a You again later on" (D2 262). An eloquent, final criticism reads:

> In line with his Manichaean denigration of the I-It and his unduly romantic, if not ecstatic, notion of the I-You, he refused to treat his brainchild as a good painter treats his paintings . . . subjecting them to rigorous criticism until they became better for that. Buber pretended to mistake intense emotion for revelation and did not realize sufficiently how much rational reflection is needed if we really want to encounter the You rather than an illusion. (D2 264–65)

Bringing reflection to an encounter, studying its details, attempting to realize the other person in thought need not import "a fall from grace, a relapse into inauthenticity, or a betrayal to be atoned for in another more ecstatic encounter" (D2 263).

In a letter to his fiancée, Felice Bauer, Kafka wrote, "Buber is lecturing on the Jewish myth. It would take more than Buber to get me out of my room. I have heard him before. I find him dreary, no matter what he says, something is missing." Later Kafka refers to his "tepid (*lauwarm*) writings."[30] Even more grievously, Kafka found "Buber's last books revolting, repulsive," and Freud disliked Buber's writings as well.

Since this final chapter consists of a thoroughgoing repudiation of Buber's main thought, I do not find it edifying. There are some carelessly broad brush-strokes, too, by which, for example, Adorno and Benjamin suddenly make an appearance *together with Heidegger* as writers and thinkers who were (by Kaufmann's fiat) peculiarly self-deceived (D2 256). This judgment comes as a corollary to the fact that they write in a style that Kaufmann (and many read-ers) consider more difficult, more unheard-of, than need be. But the judgment is unsubtle at least to the extent that Kaufmann does not take into account Adorno's and Benjamin's fierce resistance to Heidegger on the strength of (Heidegger's) claims that are not so impenetrable as to escape criticism. Just as one finds Kaufmann's criticism of Heidegger to be just and clear, so does one find Adorno's criticism of Heidegger's "jargon of authenticity" to be equally just and clear. Kaufmann invokes these writers to accompany Buber in a group whose prose is full of "falseness, pretense, and murkiness." Their exemplary antiself is . . . Vincent van Gogh! But is Kaufmann aware—the irony!—that Benjamin and Adorno, whom Kaufmann has lumped together with Buber on grounds of the cloudiness of style that signals self-deception, are, like him, eminent critics of Buber? In the end, the reader is asked not to seize on but to sympathize critically with Buber's "lifelong effort to create a viable humanistic religion that would be non-theological and antinomian (not conforming to the *halacha*, the traditional Jewish law). This was Buber's most ambitious and fascinating undertaking, and it was, of course, a failure" (D2 273).

An epilogue strikes a happier, a eudemonic note. It is possible to know another mind, to hear its distinctive voice, and in doing so to suffer—or, better, enjoy—change for the good. "There is no dichotomy between discovering my own mind and someone else's. I need not choose which of these two things I want to do. As I write about others, I simultaneously discover myself; and as I discover myself, I understand others better" (D2 287). Kaufmann's final pages thrill to his exhilaration at the transformative power of interpretation. His trilogy—this discovery of what other thinkers have added to the collec-tive project of discovering "the human mind"—has been a journey of *Selbst-Bildung*, of personal intellectual and spiritual formation. It then becomes all the more interesting for readers to move on to the last volume of *Discovering the Mind*, which begins with a passionate appreciation of Freud as Kaufmann's educator and an exemplary human being.

17

Unsubdued Quarrels

DISCOVERING THE MIND, VOLUME 3, FREUD, ADLER, AND JUNG

Interminable quarrels among the analysts.

Regarding the question of anti-Semitism, I have little desire to seek explanations but feel a strong inclination to surrender to my emotions and feel confirmed in my entirely unscientific attitude that human beings are after all on the average and on the whole a miserable rabble.

—SIGMUND FREUD

FREUD IS THE UNCONTESTED hero of volume 3.[1] His rivals, Alfred Adler and Carl Gustav Jung, fare badly. The gist of Kaufmann's argument is brief: Freud is a human being of impeccable character, and his work ethic is exemplary. His path to the discovery of the mind is rigorously empirical, evidence-based, and in the matter of interpretation forever hospitable to doubt, to rival hypotheses and alternatives. In these respects, Adler and Jung fall grievously short.

In arguing as he does, however, Kaufmann does not attend to the *other* Freud, who wrote, as Kaufmann (admirably) informs us: "I am actually not at all a man of science, not an observer, not an experimenter, not a thinker: I am by temperament nothing but a *conquistador*, an adventurer, if you want to translate this term—with all the inquisitiveness, daring, and tenacity characteristic of such a man."[2] Kaufmann reads this passage to mean that Freud, to his credit, never did work under the knout of nineteenth-century scientific materialism (D3 271). But the passage paints Freud very differently from the

scrupulous empiricist whom Kaufmann admires. His Freud provably enter-
tains rival hypotheses and alternatives, but Kaufmann himself does not entertain the hypothesis of Freud's—at best—irrational science.[3]

Panegyric trumps analysis: the essay is divided evenly into occasions to
praise Freud's honesty—indeed, he is the most honest human being whom
Kaufmann has *ever* encountered, namely, "I know of no man or woman who
was more honest than Freud. . . . I have never found him to be dishonest about
anything" (D3 102, 268)—and brief summaries of his major concepts, reduced
to ten in number. But from the beginning we have this question: for whom,
even in 1980, might this essay be intended? It appears to be written on the
peculiar premise that Kaufmann's reader will scarcely have heard of Freud.
But that is an exceptional idea. Kaufmann is surely convinced that the force
of his devastating criticism of Heidegger's masterwork *Being and Time* in the
previous volume of *Discovering the Mind* will not have been lost on the reader,
who—it needs to be assumed—was well-enough acquainted with *Being and
Time* for its demolition to matter. And yet, will the reader of the new volume
find the contents of Freud's *Introductory Lectures on Psychoanalysis* a revelation?

More likely, one sort of reader will be closed in advance to Freud's seemingly mystagogic talk about the mainly dysfunctional familial relations
between unconscious agencies.[4] Kaufmann's steady threnody of praise and
cursory stipulation of data points will not be nearly enough to produce his
or her conversion. And for readers already reasonably well-versed in Freud
and his conceptual armory, the absence of detailed close readings producing
aporias and objections—with one rare exception—will defeat the promise
of fresh insight. (Kaufmann is inclined to let Freud do his objecting for him.)
Kaufmann's exception, stated briefly, is his dim view of Freud's theory of art,
religion, and philosophy as arising from the frustrated gratification of appetites
for honor, wealth, and the sexual favors of beautiful women. Granting our
concerns, it will still be surprising if Kaufmann's essay on Freud changes our
judgment on Kaufmann: namely, that scarcely a line he wrote will fail to excite
either affirmation or displeasure.[5]

His essay opens with a trumpet blast: "Nobody has contributed more to
the discovery of mind than Freud" (D3 3). But whether Freud's leading concepts—such as, say, the Oedipus complex or the survival in the adult unconscious of traces of his or her seduction by a parent—should be understood
as *discoveries* and not *inventions* remains a moot affair.[6] Kaufmann proceeds
to attack covertly his colleague Carl Schorske, who had published a widely
admired essay, "Politics and Patricide in *The Interpretation of Dreams.*" Without

an argument at this juncture—though he will provide an impressive statement some three hundred pages later—Kaufmann dismisses the idea of rooting the book's leading concepts and figurative language in the artistic and political culture of fin de siècle Vienna.[7] Schorske is an implied member of a company of breeders of "legends" about Freud, of whom several "believe that the clue to his thought must be sought in the city in which he lived at the turn of the century: Vienna" (D3 3). For Kaufmann, this claim is bootless. For one thing, Freud loathed the intellectual climate of Vienna; and not a single one of the artists or writers whom Schorske cites as shaping the intellectual substance on which Freud allegedly drew—Klimt and Hofmannsthal, Kokoschka and Schoenberg among them—mattered in the least to Freud.

To get to the *real* Freud, you must see him in the light of his philosophical lineage; this is, unsurprisingly, the writings of Goethe and Nietzsche. Freud was determined from the start to study natural science—and not philosophy, which tempted him—on hearing a recitation of "Nature," a prose poem attributed to Goethe: The soul of nature is life; it embraces both the human spirit and the world of plants and animals and minerals; it suffers particular deaths in the course of developments that prepare for future avatars of its spirit.[8] And we have already heard of Freud's admiration for Nietzsche's clairvoyance in the matter of human emotion, evident in the dialogue of pride and memory: "'I have done that,' says my memory. 'I cannot have done that,' says my pride, and remains inexorable. Eventually—memory yields."[9]

Kaufmann cannot say enough about Freud's skill as a writer of prose. His talent was shaped by his intellectual legacy: in having "loved" Goethe and praised Nietzsche, he became the "spiritual child" of the two master stylists (D3 5). Kaufmann's indefatigable research has discovered an oblique confirmation of this claim in an interview published in 1929 in the *New York Herald Tribune Magazine* where a certain William Leon Smyser wrote, "Like Goethe, Freud would have liked to become a sort of scientist-poet." Kaufmann comments: "It seems unlikely that an American journalist would have made that up out of whole cloth, and the quotation goes well with the picture of Freud and his poetic science presented in the present volume" (D3 301).

The elegance and vitality of Freud's German does not translate easily. Kaufmann's own talent as a German translator is on hand to produce attractive new coinages. Freud speaks of *Fehlleistungen* or what are commonly called "slips of the tongue" but which in the technical literature have come over as "parapraxes." These are such errors as "misspeaking, misreading, mislaying, forgetting, or misremembering. Freud aims to show that such mistakes are not mere accidents but rather due to some unconscious motive that makes mischief" (D3 24). Kaufmann brightly suggests "misachievements."

It comes as no surprise that Kaufmann has strong opinions—pro and contra—about rival biographers of Freud. He is especially dismissive of Frank Sulloway's *Freud, Biologist of the Mind*; it made a great splash on publication in 1979 for its show of scientific expertise in six hundred pages.[10] Sulloway's leading idea is Freud's dependency on the work of nineteenth-century biologists like Ernst Haeckel and, of course, Charles Darwin, for an approach to the human mind as a *development*; but the concept of a development attributed to biologists *without mention of Goethe* can only have acted as a red flag. Fritz Wittels, on the other hand, the author of the much earlier *Freud and His Time* (1931), gets high marks for profiling Freud's devotion to Goethe's essay on nature, as well as advancing the notion of an "artistic science," which Kaufmann would vary slightly in his text as "poetic science."[11] Kaufmann's coinage preceded his encountering Wittels's (though he confesses disappointment at not having been the first). Yet today there are few who would think of all or many of Freud's writings as poetry—witness the last several "theoretical" pages of the *Interpretation of Dreams*—let alone as "science." It is helpful, I think, to consider another description of psychoanalysis made at about the time of Kaufmann's writing by Stuart Hampshire, Kaufmann's colleague in the philosophy department at Princeton, which seems to be on target:

> a body of doctrine [that] is no part of medical science and is no part of philosophy either, but rather is a speculative and irresistibly vivid picture of some activities of the mind, and of some mental dispositions—dispositions which are exciting, and sometimes also amusing, and which are not normally noticed.[12]

Note the qualifier "medical" and the claim that psychoanalysis is not philosophy—also, that psychoanalysis is irresistibly vivid, exciting, and sometimes amusing—and we can conclude that Kaufmann would find nothing objectionable in this description, as it still leaves room for the qualities of "poetic" and "scientific." In celebrating Freud's literary style, Kaufmann indeed literally confirms (part of) Hampshire's account: "Before long Freud created a new literary genre: the case history that can be as fascinating as any short story or novel" (D3 42). Here Kaufmann is writing—for this reader—in a positive spirit; but there is always his contentious manner, lowering under wraps and bound to provoke a well-tempered attack attitude in this or any reader, though now one is jousting on what to Kaufmann is sacred ground. He has the bold-ness to write:

> The popular conceit that there are two major twentieth-century philoso-phies, Anglo-American analytical philosophy and "Continental philoso-phy," which is thought to consist of phenomenology and existentialism, is blind. These two kinds of philosophy are variations on a single academic philosophy that goes back to Kant, and the radical alternative to both of them is the tradition whose high points are Goethe, Hegel (who tried to reconcile Goethe with Kant), Nietzsche, and Freud.

What is common to both is their preclusion of "hypotheses and empirical psychology" (D3 44).

The outcome of this claim would be the death of the facultative discipline commonly called philosophy, although Kaufmann still wishes to keep the term for an "alternative tradition" of his devising. There is only one truly sig-nificant history of philosophy to be written, building on Goethe, Hegel (to the extent that he belongs to a Goethean lineage), Nietzsche, and Freud. But as Kaufmann—and Hampshire—would agree, neither Goethe nor Freud is a philosopher by anyone's reckoning. Kaufmann even cites Freud's explicit mention of "the philosopher" as the Other, for he—the philosopher—is likely to insist that psychic phenomena are those of *consciousness* only, yet "he does not know the material whose study compelled the analyst to believe in uncon-scious acts of the soul. He has not paid attention to hypnosis nor exerted him-self to interpret dreams" (qtd. in D3 56).

In criticizing Sulloway's scientistic biography of Freud's "mind," Kaufmann enthusiastically cited the words of the critic Peter Brooks, who reviewed the same book: "Of Mr. Sulloway's 'principal ambitions' . . . the ambition to 'produce a comprehensive intellectual biography of Freud' must be judged mostly a failure" (D3 29). With some readerly hesitation, the same words might well apply to Kaufmann's attempt to found an exclusive intel-lectual tradition on four German load bearers. Here, as generally, I consider bold criticism and not laudation to be Kaufmann's better nature. We recall that this project is based on the allegedly reprehensible sameness of both Continental philosophy and Anglo-American analytical philosophy in deriv-ing from a Kant-based academic tradition. On the topic of this sameness, namely, difference, we might also recall "Bernard Williams's old canard. . . . 'Contrasting "analytical" and "Continental" philosophy,' he remarked, 'is rather like classifying cars into "front-wheel drive and Japanese,"' while declaring that he [Williams] couldn't care less whether what he wrote was called 'analytical' philosophy'; all he aimed for was 'clarity'." The contrast mocked by Williams might be fatuous, but the difference between these two philosophical styles is not done away with so easily: a start would base the analytical tradition on its valorizing logical language over sublimated reports of Continental "experience." Kaufmann began writing on existentialism as a philosophy attentive to lived experience, but his later repudiation of the academic—indeed, Kantian—sides of Heidegger and Sartre undid this beginning. The upshot is that Kaufmann has staked the power and value of his entire last trilogy—*Discovering the Mind*, volumes 1, 2, and 3—on a "great tradition" of his own devising.[13]

Some of the numbing effect of such extravagance and polemic is immediately offset by one of Kaufmann's fascinating aperçus into the wider German intellectual tradition that we encountered in *Nietzsche* as a special source of the pleasure and instruction he provides. Kaufmann notes: "We do not think of Nietzsche as having read Freud, and he collapsed before psychoanalysis was born, but his knowledge of [John Stuart] Mill was actually based in large measure *on Freud's translation*, which he owned" (emphasis added) (D3 47).

In the matter, finally, of how Continental philosophy is to be understood in relation to analytical philosophy, Kaufmann is on better ground in distinguishing, in a later chapter, between the two jarring strains of thought held to constitute the one thing called Continental philosophy: namely, phenomenology and existentialism, while deploring the fact that both are often taught together as this one sort of philosophy. These differences appear on a chart, which enriches the earlier discussion of existentialism in chapter 2 and of phenomenology in chapter 10.[14]

We need to return to Freud. The main thrust of Kaufmann's analysis arises from Freud's devotion to Goethe—this we know—and to a worldview derivative from it. Since Goethe's essay "Nature" is monist, Freud, his devoté, is neither dualist nor materialist:

> Spirit or mind or soul is also nature. But it ["Nature"] did not say this in a reductionist or materialist sense; it did not deprive the world of soul, beauty, or mystery. Neither did the essay oppose determinism or espouse some form of metaphysical idealism, denying the reality of matter. (D3 40)

Ergo, if the medical establishment was indeed so resistant to psychoanalysis—and especially to its positing of an unconscious—it was "due to . . . [its] materialistic-mechanistic training" (D3 55). Freud is very informative on this point: after noting that the work of Charcot and Breuer has "taught us that the physical symptoms of hysteria . . . are *psychogenic*," he writes:

> This new insight was taken up by psychoanalysis, which thus began to ask what might be the nature of these psychical processes which produce such unusual consequences. But this direction of research was not congenial to the contemporary generation of physicians. The medical profession had been educated to esteem highly only anatomical, physical, chemical factors. . . . They clearly doubted that psychic things admit of any exact scientific treatment. . . . In this materialistic—or better: mechanistic—period medicine made magnificent advances, but also failed myopically to recognize the noblest and most difficult problems of life. (qtd. in D3 55)

This admirably balanced way of writing prompts Kaufmann to write, in turn, of Freud's "clarity and consistency":

> When he changes his mind about something, he calls attention to it. He constantly admits hypotheses into his work and points out that this is all they are; he distinguishes between bold speculations for which there is as yet no evidence and hypotheses that have been confirmed again and again. (D3 60)

Kaufmann is incisive in questioning the propriety of linking Marx, Nietzsche, and Freud as the kingpins of university courses on makers of the modern mind. Undoubtedly, Nietzsche and Freud can be treated together: indeed, more than once, "We see Nietzsche's 'gay science' [celebrating doubt, a life lived without faith] as the major link between Goethe's non-Newtonian, nonmathematical science and Freud's psychoanalysis" (D3 101). But Freud's absolute resistance to Marxism invalidates the bigger link. There is, for Freud, no possibility of eradicating the unpredictable variety of noxious behaviors arising from man's aggression and possessiveness and the fundamental inequality of human types. In section 5 of his *Civilization and Its Discontents*, on the topic of aggression, Freud wrote apropos of Soviet Marxism: "One sees how it is comprehensible that the attempt to construct a new Communist culture in Russia should find psychological support in the persecution of the bourgeois." And indeed, once they had finished off the bourgeoisie, who would be their next target? (D3 61). History tells. The gulags never lacked for subjects; Jews were harassed to death; out-of-favor artists and intellectuals were treated no better; and then came the Nazi oppressors, well suited as objects for aggressive retaliation. At the same time, Freud's rejection of Marx,

I will add, need not invalidate the profit of a comparison of the two on such topics as repression, ideology, and false consciousness.

On the next of man's humors—possessiveness—Freud wrote, "If one removed the personal right to the possession of things, there would still be the privileges in sexual relations which are bound to become the source of the strongest ill will and the most violent hostility among human beings placed on a footing of equality in other ways." We are dealing here with an "indestructible trait of human nature." And so the task of psychoanalysis is not to lay out a blueprint for the elimination of conflict in civil society. Friction follows from individuality, and, as Kaufmann writes admiringly, in reproducing Freud, "He was . . . an unrepentant individualist who felt that the kind of character he admired depended on alienation" (D3 63). Readers may recall Kaufmann's defense of "alienation" as a spur to creativity in his *Without Guilt and Justice*. Now his argument includes an attack on the idealizing American socialists of the 1960s, foremost Herbert Marcuse, who believed that a socialist society could replace alienated labor with authentic, liberated, libidinally saturated work. Surely, though, irreversible distinctions in the energy of libido would continue to cause trouble. Freud continues:

> To be sure, when this fight ["against the inequality of possessions among human beings and what follows from that"] relies on the abstract demand of justice in the name of the equality of all human beings, the objection is too obvious that nature, by means of the highly unequal physical equipment and intellectual-spiritual (*geistige*) gifts of individuals, has established injustices against which there is no redress. (D3 68)

What, then, *does* analysis aim to achieve? It certainly does not aim, as Freud writes, to "unburden patients by admission to a . . . socialist community." Something else. It wants "to enrich them from their own inner resources by making accessible to the ego the energies that through repression are tied up in their unconscious as well as those others that the ego must squander in an unfruitful way to maintain the repression" (qtd. in D3 64). Kaufmann adds, not unexpectedly, but still amazingly, that this "ideal is—as in Nietzsche— Goethean autonomy, and much of what has been quoted in this section is very close to Nietzsche indeed" (D3 64). Ergo, on this Nietzschean standard, Freud's competence, Freud's truthfulness, meets the norm.

Or Kaufmann himself can vouch for Freud's character, and not for the first time:

One might say that he . . . considered it a point of principle to be free of illusions, but never felt that this entailed discouragement or resignation. . . . Above all, Freud's standards of honesty were very high; in fact, psychoanalysis give honesty a new dimension. Few people before Freud had realized how difficult it was to be really honest with oneself. Freud not only realized it but refused to derive from this insight any license for self-deception. (D3 74)

This picture of Freud was to be forcefully disputed by an implacable antagonist—Frederick Crews—whose arguments we will consider later in these pages.

Once again, however, on a happier note, I'll mention the refreshment one takes, on a sometimes wearisome journey over polemics and generalizations, from an intellectual-historical aperçu enabled by Kaufmann's unique erudition:

Holzwege is the title of one of Heidegger's books . . . and Heidegger went to some lengths to assure us that the peasants in the area from which he came knew the meaning of this term, suggesting how close he was to what the Nazis called "blood and soil." Roughly forty years earlier (February 25, 1913), Freud had used the term casually in a letter to [Ludwig] Binswanger; he considered it probable at that time that Jung with his innovations might be on a Holzweg. (D3 n109)

At this juncture, Kaufmann returns to defend his possibly captious view of the discipline he calls "poetic science," of which Freud is the greatest practitioner. One of his best synthesizing arguments deserves to be cited at length:

Freud repeatedly modified his theories in the light of negative evidence and, what is more, told his readers what considerations had led him to do this. Hegel, Heidegger, Buber, and Sartre published major books that were conceived as the first volumes of larger works, then found themselves unable to build on the foundations they had laid, but never gave the public or themselves any account of what had gone wrong. Heidegger's style in Being and Time is very different from that of Buber's I and Thou, but these books share a systematic failure to consider objections and alternatives. In a crucial sense these books are uncritical and unscientific while Freud's are critical and scientific. (D3 90)

Shrewd as this point is, it is overstated in the case of Heidegger, Kaufmann's bête noir. In a later expansion of the charge that Heidegger lacked any sense of self-awareness in his thought, Kaufmann writes:

Instead of giving himself and his readers some account of the ways in which he had changed and developed, he considered it a point of honor to insist on the elements of continuity. As long as the fundamental conflict in his thought and intentions was repressed, it could never be worked out and solved. He was stuck. (D3 461)

But this charge is literally false to Heidegger, who made much, explicitly, of the *Kehre* (turning) in his thinking, shortly after the publication in 1927 of *Being and Time*. On the one hand, Heidegger conceives of the turning as an event in the history of Being, with the result that "Being appears primordially in the light of concealing withdrawal." On the other hand, it is a turning within Heidegger's philosophical enterprise. It marks his full response to the turning in the previous sense—a response that begets "another mode of thinking that abandons subjectivity." In this manner of thinking "every kind of anthropology and all subjectivity of man as subject is. . . . left behind." This movement of thought is on offer in the 1929 book *What Is Metaphysics?*, the introduction to which *Kaufmann himself translated*. In this work, and in others that follow, thought turns "from the oblivion of Being into the truth of Being" as "the simultaneity of disclosure and concealment."[15]

We return to Freud's poetic science, which Freud himself appears to justify, for he claims exemption from the usual standard of the scientific verification that involves quantification. The claim is additionally interesting, I'd like to suggest, for employing a rhetorical figure developed by Kafka, who was an avid though skeptical reader of Freud. Freud wrote: "I always envy the physicists and mathematicians who can stand on firm ground. I hover, so to speak, in the air. Mental events seem to me immeasurable and probably always will be" (D3 100). Kafka wrote, of his not unrelated enterprise:

What will be my fate as a writer is very simple. My talent for portraying my dreamlike inner life has thrust all other matters into the background; my life has dwindled dreadfully, nor will it cease to dwindle. Nothing else will ever satisfy me. But the strength I can muster for that portrayal is not to be counted upon: perhaps it has already vanished forever, perhaps it will come back to me again, although the circumstances of my life don't favor its return. Thus I waver, continually fly to the summit of the mountain, but then fall back in a moment. Others waver too, but in lower regions, with greater strength; if they are in danger of falling, they are caught up by the kinsman who walks beside them for that very purpose. But I waver on the heights; it is not death, alas, but the eternal torments of dying.[16]

This figure can also be found in Nietzsche—and he is not alone—before either Freud or Kafka.

In asking about the value of the term "poetic science," we are led to consider, via Kaufmann's ten data points, Freud's contributions to discovering the mind. The first (in italic) is this very "creation of a *poetic science* of the mind." Kaufmann develops his thesis in ways that we can anticipate. Freud created a new field of inquiry on the strength of his literary sensibility along with "the rigor and self-discipline of the scientist," a fusion of abilities that allowed him to "spurn the safety of laboratory psychology, quantification, and statistics." Once again, "no unpoetic psychologist has contributed half as much to human self-understanding as did Goethe, Nietzsche, and Freud" (D3 109).

Freud's second major achievement is his *"discovery of the importance of childhood experiences for character development."* In fact, if this were his only contribution," adds Kaufmann, "it would still amount to a revolution in human self-understanding" (D3 110). This claim prima facie ignores the more than trivial contributions to such awareness by Jean-Jacques Rousseau, Johann Heinrich Jung-Stilling, William Wordsworth, and other pre-, post-, and regular romantics. But what sort of importance is this? How does this knowledge differ from case to case, and what means are at hand to determine the specific effects of childhood experience? Kaufmann is bold in specifying the conditions (or lack of conditions) for establishing such causes and effects in a nonmathematical, nonempirical experimental discipline:

> If it should be found that such a triangle [meaning: the Oedipal triangle] is not at the core of *every* neurosis, or that children raised without any visible father, or in nonpatriarchal societies, or without any family structure, should be importantly different, it would not follow at all that Freud's discovery of the Oedipus complex was not a major contribution. (D3 115)

"Freud's discovery of the importance of sex is the third major contribution." Here, Kaufmann makes the captious claim that "the sex drive and its significance in human life and culture . . . were almost nonexistent before Freud published *The Interpretation of Dreams.*" This point is unconvincing. It was richly forecast at least by Nietzsche, who wrote, as Kaufmann notes, that "the degree and kind of the sexuality of a human being reach up into the ultimate pinnacle of his spirit." In a recently published study of nineteenth-century German writing on sex, especially homosexuality, the cultural historian Robert Deam Tobin explores the work, well before Freud, of such luminaries as Heinrich Zschokke, in his novella *Eros* of 1821 and Heinrich Hössli, author

of a monumental two-volume apology for male-male love, published in the 1830s, called *Eros: Die Männerliebe der Griechen, ihre Beziehung zur Geschichte, Erziehung, Literatur und Gesetzgebung aller Zeiten* (Eros: The male love of the Greeks, its relationship to history, education, literature, and legislation of all times).[17] Kaufmann is not unaware of several of these earlier contributions but trivializes them—from personal recollection?—writing, "And if only by comparison with [the way Freud opened up the subject of sex] . . . the writings of those pioneers of sexology seem to cater to some extent to a prurient interest" (D3 117). (*Par contre*, in his philippics, Frederick Crews has no hesitation in referring to *Freud's* "prurient mind," so the adjective in this exchange of abuse has very little semantic value.[18]) But Kaufmann is surely right to claim that "like no one before him"—which is indisputable—"Freud explored *child sexuality*" (emphasis added) (D3 118). After rehearsing the normal passage of libido from its attachment to the notorious three, eye-catching erogenous zones, Freud wrote, decisively: "The direction of this development and all the dispositions that attach to it are determined by the prior infantile early blossoming of sexuality" (D3 119). This proposition in context is surely new to world history.

The fourth of Freud's major contributions is his interpretation of dreams. Kaufmann advances to a rare criticism: he considers it a wrong idea that *all* dreams represent wish fulfillments (D3 120). Few would fail to agree with this provision. But Freud is surely right and greatly creative if we take a step back from this specific claim. Kaufmann writes:

> Freud sought to show that dreams are meaningful. . . . There must be some reason for everything. And I mean *reason*, not just some *cause*. Nowhere is it plainer that Freud was not rooted in nineteenth-century mechanism and materialism. He insisted on finding a reason, a purpose, an intention, a desire to communicate something—in the end, even a wish. (D3 122)

Here Kaufmann produces a wonderful aperçu: "What Freud suggested was that even during the dream we do not want to hear what our dream is telling us"; hence, we need the fiction of the censor (D3 123). But he draws back from Freud's conception that "the dream work is motivated entirely by the need to get past the censor" (D3 125). I judge that a well-trained, Anglo-American language philosopher would have no difficulty in showing this debate to be nonsensical. But it is significant that Kaufmann is prompted here—a rare occasion—to query Freud's contributions.

"*Freud's psychopathology of everyday life constitutes his fifth major contribution*" (D3 126). Freud writes:

Egotistical, jealous, hostile feelings and impulses that are under pressure from our moral education, employ in healthy people not infrequently the path of misachievements to express somehow their undeniably existing power that is not recognized by the higher courts of the psyche. (D3 131)

Kaufmann points out smartly that, following Freud, we retain the detritus of our mistakes. "The whole thrust of *The Psychopathology of Everyday Life* is to enlarge the area of our responsibility by including in it not only our deliberate actions but even our misachievements" (D3 133). As Nietzsche would argue, there is no escaping any single item in our history. We *are* these effects.

In his dispute with Sartre, Kaufmann employs an attractive figure of speech to affirm Freud's idea of the unconscious.

Sartre's conception of "the total translucency of consciousness" is utterly dogmatic. Consciousness is not like a room that is well and evenly lit. It is more like a cellar in which one area near a stairwell has enough light for us to see easily, while the regions that are farther away are quite dim, and beyond them almost everything seems to be dark. (D3 139)

Readers of German literature contemporary with Freud's writing may be reminded of a figure in a celebrated essay by Hugo von Hofmannsthal that adds luster to Kaufmann's image. In "Der Dichter und diese Zeit" (The poet and this time), Hofmannsthal compares the poet to a "seismograph vibrating to the faintest and most remote tremor," conjuring the unconscious of a poet and a scientist. The poet's moods and affects are these "twitchings of the seismograph"; "his pains are inner constellations, configurations of objects inside him, which he lacks the power to decipher." Where is he to be found?

The poet is found there where he does not seem to be, and is always at a place other than where he is supposed to be. He dwells in an odd way in the house of time, under the staircase, where everyone has to climb past him and no one notices him . . . this unknown dwelling in one's own house.[19]

With his unimaginably rich unconscious, which holds sway over him, the poet is the delectable object of a psychoanalysis waiting to begin.

"*Freud's interpretation of mental illness constitutes his sixth major contribution.* . . . More than anyone else, Freud tore down the wall that had long divided the mentally ill from the supposedly normal human being" (D3 142).

I have written elsewhere—taking my cue, with the reader's permission, from Kaufmann to self-cite—that, for Freud,

> *all* notions and feelings and moods—whether judged normal or abnormal on pragmatic or conventional grounds—represent a play of forces aiming . . . at discharge and also at inhibition, since the gratification, as well as the unpleasurable build-up of the thrust toward gratification, of repressed unconscious wishes imperils the well-being of the psyche. Indeed, "the degree of our psychical normality" is "indicated by the measure of such suppression."[20]

The mentally ill can be said to have failed to achieve the normal play of forces aiming at gratification and, likewise, inhibition, but the difference between such failure and normal success is a difference of degree and not of kind.

Here we have Freud's seventh contribution—his new mode of therapy—the *talking cure*, which involves "free associations, the interpretation of dreams, and transference . . . the crux of . . . [which] is that the patient falls in love [or hate] with the analyst." Sandor Ferenczi, whom Kaufmann judges to be Freud's closest friend, chose to kiss his patients! Freud found out and wrote to Ferenczi with considerable wit and equanimity, using a quite wonderful word: "Soon we shall have accepted in the technique of analysis the whole repertoire of demiviergeries and petting parties, resulting in an enormous increase of interest in psychoanalysis among both analysts and patients" (D3 147–48). We should not lose sight of the fact that our chief concern throughout these pages is Walter Kaufmann, not Sigmund Freud. And so it is apt and bemusing to learn that, at the time of writing, Kaufmann had not been psychoanalyzed and did not intend to be. On the other hand, his admiration of Freud knows no bounds, and so it comes as no surprise that he would be prepared to make an exception "if Sigmund Freud were still alive and willing to take me on." His admiration is owed in no little degree to a genius who "loved language and was exceptionally sensitive to words, nuances, overtones"—a love that Kaufmann shares (D3 149). For both thinkers, the route of therapy is verbal, an affair of creativity in language.

Adopting Kaufmann's simile, the therapeutic form of Freudian psychoanalysis has changed within its original frame just as the kind of ocean liner that brought Kaufmann to America in 1939 has since been outfitted as a cruise ship for the wealthy. Kaufmann explains: "Most forms of psychotherapy since Freud have built on his foundations and are profoundly indebted to him, even various form of group therapy and even *est*, which is not really a form of therapy and more eclectic than most." The last item finds a place owing to Kaufmann's idiosyncratic enthusiasm for this questionable cult. "Many people, including myself, have gained insight into themselves and others as a result of the *est* 'training'" (D3 472). Kaufmann does not tell us what this est-enabled insight was. *The Book of est* describes an especially capable trainer shouting at his captives: "You're assholes! No more, no less," meaning to produce in clients a love-death of the ego.[21]

Kaufmann is uncertain whether Freud's interpretation of jokes amounts to an important—eighth—contribution to the discovery of the mind, owing to its conceptual affinity with Freud's interpretation of dreams, which, we recall, already counted as his fourth contribution. After all, "Freud goes to considerable lengths to show how jokes depend on condensation as well as the other mechanisms that transform the latent dream thoughts into the manifest dream content" (D3 151). The main source of tendentious jokes, as Freud's biographer Ernest Jones pointed out—Kaufmann relies on Jones's testimony in "one of the finest biographies of all time" (D3 188)—is either aggressive or erotic instincts; and this fact, as Kaufmann notes, helps to support Freud's later postulation of these two drives as basic.

Freud's ninth contribution is his interpretation of literature, art, and religion, but here Kaufmann asserts some vigorous caveats: indeed,

> his [Freud's] results are often unacceptable and in one especially important case crucially wrong. . . . His essays "A Childhood Memory of Leonardo" (1910), "The Moses of Michelangelo" (1914), "Dostoyevsky and Parricide" (1928), and "The Future of an Illusion" (1927) do not stand up well, and his last book, *Moses and Monotheism* (1939), is, though beautifully written, probably his worst book.

Kaufmann could hardly conclude otherwise about the latter essay, since it denies the very originality of the Jewish religion, the vital substance of Kaufmann's thought. For Freud, Michelangelo's Moses is "superior to the historical or traditional Moses"; this is a superiority Kaufmann is ready to grant to sculpted passion but not to the Egyptian Moses of "Moses and Monotheism" (D3 152–53), which Freud himself called a "historical novel." In his essay on Michelangelo, Freud wrote eloquently of the sculptor's stroke of genius, which

> brought into the figure of Moses something new and superhuman, and the powerful mass of his body and the musculature that is swelled with strength merely become a physical means of expression for the supreme psychic

achievement that is possible for a human being, for the subduing of one's own passion for the sake of and in obedience to a vocation to which one has dedicated oneself. (qtd. in D3 153)

It is not hard to consider this great sentence as shaping the central tenet of Kaufmann's *Nietzsche*: Nietzsche is the philosopher who glorified passion for the sake of the control it would exact from the superior man intent on self-overcoming.

But what, then, is this great blunder in Freud's writing on literature, art, and religion? As we have already indicated: it is to reduce the religious aspiration to the desolate human being's need for consolation in the face of his cosmic puniness. We've also encountered earlier, especially in chapter 4, a far nobler account of man's "aspiration." And even less tenable is Freud's idea that the creative impulse behind art and religion, philosophy and science may be a blocked sexual drive seeking "substitutive gratification":

> Freud misses the obvious point that while the sex drive, no less than hunger, *can* attain complete satisfaction, this satisfaction is not enduring in either case. Soon the appetite awakens again, and satisfying it again and again does not satisfy all our other appetites and aspirations and certainly cannot give sufficient content and meaning to our lives. It may be an illusion to suppose that anything can provide enduring satisfaction, but the attraction of art and religion, science and philosophy, is inseparable from this hope, and that is true not only of creative artists, scientists, and philosophers but also of the far more numerous people who love art, science, or philosophy more passively. (D3 163–64)

We have arrived at Freud's tenth contribution—which may be his greatest—his exemplary character: "He was one of the most remarkable human beings of all time. . . . It may well be felt that even if Freud was a great man in some sense, it does not follow that this constitutes a contribution to the discovery of the mind. But I believe that we learn about man and humanity very largely from examples—from exemplary human beings." We recall from the previous chapter Kaufmann's description of "paradigmatic individuals." Freud was one such; to reflect on him is to heighten one's sense of an available human greatness (D3 166–67). Kaufmann notes powerfully an overlooked feature of Freud's entire enterprise. He removed the stain of guilt that attaches to many human wishes, "the sense of guilt that poisoned not only sexuality but also many other wishes. . . . He was a new Adam, and through his transformation we were transformed" (D3 168).

Not only at this juncture, but also throughout his essay, Kaufmann holds Freud to be the alpha and omega of an overmastering honesty. The conversation about Freud's honesty has since advanced considerably beyond this point. The dialectically minded reader is referred especially to the oppositional writings of Frederick Crews.

Although writing in a style that less cool heads might term obsessive and sadistic, Crews has recently indicated disturbing points in Freud's intellectual itinerary calling for harsher judgment. Peter Gay, the distinguished biographer of Freud, and cooler head, observes, "*The New York Review of Books*, with its impressive circulation and educated readership a powerful cultural force, has given generous room to the repeated, and repetitive, harangues of Frederick Crews, who has made the destruction of Freud and all his works a personal crusade."[22] All the same, no reader of this misology can fail to revisit Kaufmann's chapter without some concern, owing to the pungent claims of this articulate critic. Greeted by many Freudians, in his own generously inspired phrase—"like a rabid skunk"—Crews continues to boast of being "completely lacking in respect for Freud" while determined "to denounce . . . Freud's scientific and ethical standards." He does cite, apparently noncommittedly, the view of Freud's many admirers, including Kaufmann, that

> Freud proved once and for all that unconscious beliefs and emotions play a large role in our behavior; that the human mind is at once capable of the clearest distinctions and the most devious twists and that mental illness stems in large part from an imbalance within the human being between real and ideal, between our rational and irrational selves, and between what we want to do and what we have to do.

But that is scarcely enough—or really to the point. According to Crews, Freud's standard of scientific proof with respect to Freud's more specific constructions was "abysmally low." One of Crews's philippics begins by scorning, as "a dead letter," the main item of Freud's etiology of neurosis: Oedipal repression. Furthermore, in the matter of attributing meaning to symptoms, dreams, and errors,

> for example, [in] Freud's attribution of "Dora's" asthmatic attacks to her once having witnessed an act of parental intercourse—we find that the symptomatic interpretations rest on vulgar thematic affinities (heavy breathing in coitus = asthma) residing in Freud's own prurient mind. So, too, the heart of his dream theory, the contention that every dream expresses a repressed infantile wish [a view that Kaufmann also rejects], was merely an

extrapolation from his etiology of neurosis. . . . As for the theory of errors . . . it suffers from Freud's usual overingeniousness and wanton insistence on universal psychic determinism. . . . [Finally], Freud's speculations about conscious, preconscious, and unconscious mental systems, or about the ego, the superego, and the id, or about instincts of self-preservation and sex, or of life and death, went far beyond any data that he could legitimately claim to have unearthed. Where, then, are Freud's authenticated contributions not to ethics or mores or hermeneutics but to actual knowledge of the mind? So far as I am aware, no uniquely psychoanalytic notion has received independent experimental . . . support—not repression, not the Oedipus or castration complex, not the theory of compromise formation, nor any other concept or hypothesis. . . . Nor is this negative result anomalous in view of the reckless, conquistadorial manner in which psychoanalytic theory was launched and maintained in the teeth of rational criticism.[23]

This is merely the hem of the Nessus's robe that Crews wraps around Freudian psychoanalysis.

It would be wonderful to read Kaufmann's response to this assault. We can imagine some of it. First of all, he would simply dispute the truth of several of Crews's claims. I have not noted all of them: Crews wrote that psychoanalysis has no demonstrable therapeutic value: the patients of the master would abandon him. Kaufmann denies that this is the case, writing, along with many other similar sentences, "In Freud's experience, a successful reconstruction [of an occluded piece of the patient's history] was accompanied by drastic improvement" (D3 88). Crews speaks of Freud's adherence to a "universal psychic determinism." As we have frequently noted, Kaufmann admits not a whit of it. On the usefulness of putative confirmation of Freud's major concepts by experimental psychology, Kaufmann is scathing.

Since Freud's death, growing numbers of psychologists have tried to devise tests with control groups to see whether predictions entailed by Freud's theory of repression, to give a single example, were borne out by the facts. Quite a number of research scientists reported "findings supporting the concept of repression," but critics have claimed again and again that other explanations of the test results could not be ruled out or that the tests were deficient in some other way. . . . A lot of the tests are busy-work that may be more "scientific" than Freud's books but adds nothing much to human knowledge or self-understanding. (D3 93–94)[24]

Crews dismisses the Oedipus complex as a "dead letter," but another sort of proof of its vitality appears, thus Kaufmann, in "what may well be the most exciting footnote in world literature"—Freud's application of the Oedipus complex to *Hamlet* and *Oedipus Rex* (D3 96). It is a wonderful conceptual tool. Crews calls up Wittgenstein to repudiate the usefulness of free association as the royal road to the unconscious; Kaufmann calls up Wittgenstein for his own cause:

> You see, I know that it's difficult to think *well* about "certainty," "probability," "perception," etc. But it is, if possible, still more difficult to think, or *try* to think, really honestly about your life & other people's lives. And the trouble is that thinking about these things is *not thrilling*, but often downright nasty. And when it's nasty, then it's most important. (qtd. in D3 83)

But owing to the pains of chronology, we cannot imagine Kaufmann's reply in detail. Crews, like Karl Popper before him, terms psychoanalysis a pseudoscience; Kaufmann devotes many pages to querying the common conception of science that Crews buys into: that it permits of the *certain* verification of its hypotheses; that it possesses in every case a *means* of verification for such hypotheses; that hypotheses can be sorted into two kinds: thoroughly verified and thoroughly false, and one can build on the former but must dismiss the latter. How little pertinence these distinctions have to the real living psychology—a "poetic science," rich in imagination, rich in the consciousness of error—one finds in Goethe, Nietzsche, Freud . . . Thus Kaufmann, generally. But, again, owing to the calamity of his early death, we cannot imagine Kaufmann's response to Crews's *specific* complaints.

There is at least one instructive feature to all of this: When Crews defends his own good nature, and the reasonableness of his enterprise, as one who brings the norms of good science—"noncontradiction, clarity, testability, cogency, and parsimonious explanatory power"—to his critique of Freud—he may be unwittingly copying Kaufmann.[25] Thinking of Freud—and, surely, in a minor key, of himself—Kaufmann writes:

> The writer who takes account of objections to his story and indicates how he proposes to meet them, and who discusses rival views and shows why he cannot accept them and why, in effect, his own story is the best he has been able to come up with, is often experienced as egoistic, threatening—and dogmatic. (D3 81)

Crews is articulate in warning off his critics, applying this logic of unde-served abuse to his own worthy case, but he leaves out several elements of Kaufmann's protocol: Crews is very brief in his proofs before 2018 of *why* he cannot accept the views of rivals and offers not even a hint of "the better story" of a "knowledge of the mind" he is proposing instead.[26] Meanwhile, it is interesting—and for Kaufmann "extraordinary how Freud managed not to be nasty . . . about individuals who were widely regarded as authorities. In his books, he refrained almost completely from polemics and almost never gave vent to anger or resentment" (D3 83). For the rest, I believe that Kaufmann's rebuttal would follow along the lines of the response to Crews by the Univer-sity of Chicago philosopher Jonathan Lear.[27] Perhaps the final significance of this exchange lies in its testifying to the incessant, ever-expanding controversy, in the decades following *The Discovery of the Mind*, about the value of Freud's contribution.

The remaining three hundred pages of Kaufmann's volume 3 are devoted to Adler and Jung, chiefly in their contentious relations to Freud, followed by Kaufmann's self-revealing essay called "Mind and Mask." This essay is both metaphorically and literally his final published statement and deserves our attention, I confess, more than these chapters on one disremembered—if qui-etly appropriated—"individual psychologist" (Adler) and one dishonored Aryanizing, self-deceived mystagogue and "analytical psychologist" (Jung). One rarely speaks today of Adler's signature contributions—the "inferiority complex" and "masculine protest"—and Jung's espousing Nazi ideology from his safe eyrie in Switzerland makes him a hard pill to swallow.

There is also the unusual manner in which Kaufmann proceeds to deal with Adler: the essay is hostile from the start (with very rare "No—but—Yes" con-cessions) and concerns itself at great length with secondary sources: an alto-gether undistinguished biography of Adler by Phyllis Bottome and, once again, Henri Ellenberger's *The Discovery of the Unconscious*.[28] Ernest Jones continues to be an indispensable reference. What does leap out from these first pages is a rather out-of-place but by now expectable diatribe against the "wretched state of the humanities in general and the philosophy of mind in particular" (D3 184). This sentence was written circa 1979 at a particularly exciting time in the fields of literature and languages and Continental philosophy with the influx of invigorating (if contentious) works especially from "Parisian" thinkers like Louis Althusser, Roland Barthes, Gilles Deleuze, Jacques Derrida, Michel Fou-cault, Jacques Lacan, Georges Poulet . . . and countless others; the Germans Jürgen Habermas, Manfred Frank, Friedrich Kittler . . . and countless others;

the Americans Harold Bloom, Paul de Man, Geoffrey Hartman, J. Hillis Miller, Richard Rorty . . . and countless others. As his writings suggest, together with tirades reported from his seminars, Kaufmann had little patience for this "new" thought, suspecting that it was through and through untenable scholarship in the service of an anithumanistic agenda. This resistance would explain, as well, his omitting, from his ongoing reflections on Nietzsche, critical impulses stemming from the linguistic turn in twentieth-century philosophy, which, as Erich Heller, for one, had shown, Nietzsche and Wittgenstein helped induce.[29] (The phrase "linguistic turn" was coined by Gustav Bergmann and given fresh currency by Richard Rorty, Kaufmann's colleague at Princeton.[30]) Nietzsche's phrase, "in the prison-house of language" [actually, "im sprachlichen Zwange"—"under the constraint of language"—which is not quite so cruelly imposing as a prison house], is not one that Kaufmann ever cites.

Kaufmann remains far more comfortable with an older German intellectual tradition, not hesitating to invoke Hölderlin to confirm Freud's superiority to Adler; this is the Hölderlin who declared in his Orcus ode that he could die happily if he were able to write one last great poem. Freud, following Kaufmann, achieved more than one masterpiece of his "poetic science"; these essential works stress the shaping force of a sexually charged unconscious. Adler, by contrast, had nothing comparable to offer. His gesturing in incoherent prose toward the centrality of the ego (bare of an unconscious) in its will to power over its social environment does not amount to his justification (D3 203).

Kaufmann alleges that the questions of whether (1) Adler was Freud's disciple and whether (2) Freud can have "excommunicated" him for his "heresies" have generated considerable heat, even though Kaufmann also gives reasons for Adler's being virtually unknown even at the time of his writing (ca. 1980): "The more one learns about Adler as a man, the better one understands why he is not known better" (D3 210). The answer to the first question is a resounding Yes: Adler was a pupil of Freud; and to the second question, a resounding No: their break was due to an unmysterious clash of personalities and ideas. Both were in favor of a strict parting of the ways. The point concerns Kaufmann so deeply because the implication of an excommunication for heresies paints Freud as a dogmatic pretender to papal authority. This rumor should be scotched. The real cause of their falling out was "the fact that Freud and many others felt that he [Adler] had departed from psychoanalysis, with its emphasis on the unconscious, and stressed 'ego psychology' exclusively" (D3 206). In the signature "No—but Yes" pattern of his thought, Kaufmann notes, importantly:

Perhaps I should say expressly that, of course, I do not hold it against Adler that he left the [Vienna Psychoanalytic] Society, or that he developed views very different from Freud's. For all my obvious admiration for Freud, I realize how difficult it must have been for men who were not born followers to develop fully and freely in his shadow or, if you prefer, in the immediate vicinity of so much brilliance joined with such consuming honesty. (D3 210)

The work of the historian of psychoanalysis Paul Roazen, which is marked by "extreme bias" against Freud, comes in for sustained attack throughout four chapters. Before Crews, there was Roazen (D3 211, 219).[31] For Kaufmann, it is maddening to think that Roazen's work, which is less scholarship than "repeating gossip," commanded an admiring readership for so many years. (Is Kaufmann aware that he is quoting from Heidegger's infamous *Sein und Zeit*?) In a "No—but Yes" move, Kaufmann exculpates Roazen—his colportage on Freud's relations with his followers is not the product of "deliberate deception" but not for that reason any more reliable. For example, "that 'Freud [ever] outrightly denounced Adler' is . . . untrue and reflects the author's exceedingly unscientific . . . approach" (D3 219–20).

Kaufmann's account of the relation of the Freud circle to the eminent Karl Kraus is very interesting and worth noting:

At the meeting of January 12, 1910, Fritz Wittels had analyzed Karl Kraus, the editor of *Die Fackel*, and called his talk "The *Fackel* Neurosis." He knew Kraus, having once worked for him, and they had had their difficulties. Freud said in the discussion: "Analysis is, indeed, supposed to make one tolerant, and such a vivisection could justly be reproached as being inhumane." As was his manner, he coupled such reproaches with great appreciation of the speaker as a person. But the essential point here is that he added: "He will surely guard against making his affects accessible to a wider circle, who would not have scientific esteem for them." Nevertheless, word of this meeting reached Kraus and led him to change his attitude toward psychoanalysis, which had been friendly until then. . . . From now on, however, Kraus could not resist punning on "psycho-anal," and his resentment of Freud knew no bounds. (D3 221)

It is again interesting that Kaufmann undertook to excoriate Kraus in the *New York Review of Books* in response to Erich Heller's laudation of this controversial, vexatious figure.

Kaufmann offers us a portrait of the philosopher as young reader:

I confess that I first encountered Adler and Jung in the pages of Freud's *History of the Psychoanalytical Movement*. I was probably seventeen at the time and certainly not more than eighteen, and I realize that first impressions, especially those received in one's youth, often have great staying power. Nevertheless, I have generally found in the fields in which I did research that what I read as an undergraduate turned out to be untenable. It was only to be expected, therefore, that upon rereading Freud's account after I had done so much further reading, it would strike me as embarrassing. Far from it, I now find it more masterly than I could realize before. (D3 224)

Discovering the Mind, volume 3, revives an ancient memory: it returns to Kaufmann's readerly beginnings and proceeds with gathering gusto, as if a sluice had opened. His energy is associative: Freud and Adler come together with Nietzsche, since Adler founded his psychoanalysis on the ego's will to power (though on the basis of a very weak grasp of Nietzsche). If "Adler championed Nietzsche's will to power against Freud's libido theory," Freud's thought was still closer to Nietzsche's—despite Freud's puzzling admiration for the unrivalled depth of Nietzsche's self-awareness while claiming scarcely to have read him. The three are joined by Shakespeare, whose sonnet 29—"When, in disgrace with Fortune and men's eyes / I all alone beweep my outcast state"—Kaufmann uses to illustrate, and denigrate, Adler's theses on inferiority, masculine compensation, and the drive to be "on top." Here, even Kaufmann's participation in *est* makes an appearance, since *est* and Adlerism are cut from the same burlap: "Instead of telling people that they are not really inferior, *est* tells them in so many words: Of course, you are; so what? You are 'perfect,' nevertheless" (D3 254).

Kaufmann is relentless in refuting published opinion that Freud's breaks with either of his quondam disciples—Adler and Jung—diminish him. On the contrary, his honesty, intelligence, decency, and measured irony throughout these troubles do him great credit. On the testimony of Lou Andreas-Salomé, "Ebullient and aggressive rivals in his immediate vicinity disturbed Freud in his own work and kept forcing him to come to terms with ideas prematurely, before he was fully prepared to deal with them" (D3 231). His well-temperedness under these circumstances is all the more admirable.

Kaufmann's argument continues confidently and enthusiastically, uncovering *en bon psychiatre* Adler's (and thereafter Jung's) self-deceptions. In one remarkable instance, he generously indicts a confusion by Freud himself. Freud, as we have heard, admired the degree of penetration in Nietzsche's self-knowledge but at the same time denied having read him, so how could he have come to any conclusion about Nietzsche? If, now, at the same time, Freud "ran himself down" as being in no way of comparable "nobility," that judgment must be seen, according to Kaufmann, as an unconscious expression of guilt for having denied what had really happened: Freud had read a good deal of Nietzsche, especially in the 1880s and then circa 1909 (D3 266, 272).

In a procedure somewhat unusual for him, as all but abandoning his "anti-Manichaean" pattern, Kaufmann shows scant intellectual charity to Adler: "The inadequacy of Adler as a writer was due to his inadequacy as a thinker" (D3 243). Neither Adler's early ruling ideas of *organ* inferiority nor *feeling* of inferiority—Adler is confusing on this point—does any work as a principle of psychic development. One may be of short stature (as was Adler—and Kaufmann) but not all such organ-inferior persons develop—to say the least—in similar ways. Finally,

> Adlerians familiar with the messianic tinge of the later Adler and his constant emphasis on "community feeling" may well be baffled ... [by Freud's point that] "the image of life that emerges from Adler's system is founded entirely on the aggressive drive; it leaves no room for love. . . ." But what Adler projected before the First World War was above all aggression, masculine protest, the desire to be on top, and—in person—resentment. (D3 227)

Thinking of Adler's ego-centered psychoanalysis, Freud wrote, with energizing consequences for the great surge of Freudian revisionism in Paris in the 1960s, especially in the work of Jacques Lacan, "That a psychoanalyst could be so fooled by the ego, I should not have expected. *After all, the ego plays the role of the clown in the circus*" (emphasis added) (D3 228). To be fair, Kaufmann, at the end, can find a good word for Adler, though it is (humorously?) elliptical: "Adler's many explanations of behavior in terms of the will to power provide a good deal of material ... *that lends support to Nietzsche's theory*" (emphasis added) (D3 263).

It is hard to overlook the fact that as part of his long-standing, deep, overdetermined dislike for Karl Jaspers, Kaufmann stops to chastise him for vacuous, false remarks about Freud, the object of Jaspers's "perennial resentment." "In 1950, five years after the collapse of National Socialism, Jaspers published in Germany, *Reason and Anti-Reason in Our Time*, and pointed to Marxism and psychoanalysis as the two great examples of anti-reason in our time." The charge is absurd, especially in context, since Jaspers goes on to praise "the far greater psychologists Kierkegaard and Nietzsche." To this non sequitur, add Jaspers's judgment of Freud as a notably opaque personality, when it might reasonably be said that after Nietzsche—whom Freud judged to have the profoundest self-awareness of any modern thinker—it is Freud himself, on Kaufmann's authority, who deserves that distinction (D3 236–37). Following Kaufmann, "most attacks on Freud—as distinguished from reasoned criticism of his theories—have been irrational and contradictory" (D3 240). Would that he were alive to review the latest Frederick Crews!

Kaufmann is aware that comparing Adler and Freud is a mug's game: "We do Adler no favor if we keep on juxtaposing him with Freud. . . . He needs to be seen as a link to those who walked the path he was the first to choose." Adler, as we have heard, is neither a distinguished thinker nor writer: if you merely *read* Adler, you will not get "it." His path entails the self-invention of the *guru*, which, following an elegant distinction made by David Bromwich, is a type opposite to the *sage*, who can be read, understood, and reasoned with (D3 245, 258).[32] The success of the guru relies on affective, rhetorical persuasion, on generating an intense, irrational intersubjectivity that impresses words on the supine client. In the absence of the guru, these words are not easily understood: it is a travesty of the "talking cure." After Adler,

> Fritz Perls, who saw Freud in 1936 and felt rebuffed, became the bridge to another generation of gurus who had no direct ties to Freud or his pupils. . . . If one sees Perls, who liked to be known as "Fritz," at the beginning of this secondary development, one might see Werner Erhard [the founder of *est*], who likes to be known as "Werner," as its culmination. (D3 258)

Jung, too, would qualify as a guru, at best, and least of all a sage, in the sense that his theoretical writings are confused and drowned in recondite and irrelevant erudition. "Much of the literature on archetypes and the collective unconscious ['this descent into the distant past'] is distinguished by utterly tedious, pointless erudition coupled with a stunning lack of any even elementary concern with objections and alternatives." Erudition is not scholarship, an affair of "intellectual self-discipline," which involves "the scrupulous consideration of objectives and alternatives" (D3 353, 359). Book knowledge of a fiendish range is no stay against dogmatism. It is finally telling that "Jung never wrote the kind of introduction or survey that Freud wrote. There is no one work by him that integrates his many publications into a single whole. Although he wrote copiously [and Kaufmann will add, 'badly'] his bent was really strikingly unsystematic" (D3 292). "Analytical psychology" cannot be properly judged, and in this sense it is "regressive, or, if you prefer, counterrevolutionary. It provided new forms of escape" (D3 357).

If Freud got over their break in a psychologically economical manner, Kaufmann is concerned to show that Jung never did—and the cruelty and, incidentally, falseness of his writings about Freud never came to a natural end. Especially in these passages, he reveals a schizoid personality, aflame with resentment. In Freud, Kaufmann concludes, "a combination of a residue of homosexual leanings and excessive fatherliness had led him to be, if anything, too generous" (D3 341). This led Jung, all the more insistently, to project onto Freud a ukase, excommunicating him (in this way Jung would escape the feeling of guilt for having betrayed his father figure), but this was never really the case. "It is simply false, however often it has been claimed, that Freud excommunicated Jung for heresy [for his having diluted the principal psychic motive of libido]. Jung decided to strike out on his own" (D3 324). Nevertheless, Jung "never got over his guilt feelings vis-à-vis Freud, but instead of understanding this and taking appropriate steps to make it up to Freud and get rid of his guilt feelings, he used his erudition as blinders—and kept slandering Freud" (D3 363).

It should be noted that the claim that Freud *banned* Jung still persists and has recently been endorsed by a scholar of considerable authority. In a witty essay, "How Kafka Anticipated Psychoanalysis," Peter-André Alt writes, "Freud did not condemn his son [C. G.] Jung to death by drowning but he did ban him": Alt is referring to the conclusion of Kafka's breakthrough story "The Judgment." Focusing on the reversal of roles between father and son—the father is infantilized as his son carries him to bed—Alt holds this scene to be an astonishing preview of the moment at a psychoanalytic congress in Munich, in 1912, when Freud fainted and Jung, until then considered by Freud to be his spiritual son, picked up the supine figure and carried it to a sofa, whereupon Freud, on awakening, looked up at Jung, according to Jung's report, as a son to his father.[33]

One of Kaufmann's sharpest complaints about Jung actually troubles the reader, since Jung's brief—that Freud is a pansexualist and therefore to be rejected—is found in comparable form in Kaufmann's writing about this same troublesome point—Freud's one great theoretical error. Kaufmann excoriates Jung for claiming, in an article that appeared in 1932, that

Freud constructed "a rigid system that might rightly be charged with abso-lutism"; he casually mentioned "his greater contemporary Nietzsche," as the Nazis did, just to put down Freud, without taking the trouble to dis-cover or spell out Nietzsche's psychological insights; he said of Freud that "one of his favorite maxims is Voltaire's 'Écrasez l'infâme,'" although this motto, which is actually found in the penultimate line of Nietzsche's *Ecce Homo*, is nowhere to be found in Freud's work, and then he proceeded: "With a certain satisfaction he [Freud] invariably points out the flaw in the crystal; all complex psychic phenomena like art, philosophy, and religion fall under his suspicion and appear as 'nothing but' repressions of the sexual instinct." (D3 377)

Kaufmann proceeds to denounce this screed as a web of lies and projec-tions, attacking the first item and, as we have seen, exposing, with his charac-teristically superior scholarship, Jung's blunder about Freud and Voltaire. First of all, Voltaire was attacking the *Catholic* clergy, and this was hardly Freud's leading animadversion. Secondly, Jung's attribution of the curse to Freud is not entirely innocent considering that Jung, in 1932, would soon be distinguishing between a truly creative Germanic, Aryan unconscious and a parasitic and resentful—an "infamous"—Jewish one. But it is noteworthy that Kaufmann does not attack Jung's penetrating claim about Freud's derivation of all higher creativity from the stress of ungratified libido aside from Kaufmann's adding a sarcastic "Nothing but . . ." Earlier, however, Kaufmann quoted Freud on this very matter and, like Jung, forcefully disagreed with him; the citation from Freud is not at odds with Jung's claim, if posed in a more refined manner. Supplying Freud's words, Kaufmann writes that "the inability of the sex drive to give full satisfaction" has been "the source of the most magnificent cultural achievements that are brought about by the ever advancing sublimation of its instinctual component" (D3 163).

It would not be difficult to find in Freud the even more drastic charac-terization of art, literature, and music as "substitutive gratification." And so, here, Jung is not wide of the mark, but, following Kaufmann, there is no shortage of his other errors. There is, for example, his totally impracti-cal, never secure opposition between the "introverted" and "extraverted" character. In one of Jung's classifications of psychological types, "Kant and Nietzsche turn out to be the same type and in fact the two most striking examples of the 'introverted thinking type.' A typology that has no place for the immense differences between these two types surely leaves much to be desired" (D3 309). Once widely used, this distinction of character has become obsolete.

Given Jung's shabby treatment of Freud in Jung's *Memories* (1962), it would take little more to heighten Kaufmann's animus against him. But there is an abundance of helping evidence, as, for example, Jung's egregious misunderstanding of Nietzsche, in which Wagner figures as "an advocate of love" to be played off against Nietzsche as "an advocate of power" (the quoted words are Jung's) (D3 293–94). And "Nietzsche, of course, was far from identifying the will to power [as Jung has it] with the instinct of self-preservation; he contrasted them" (D3 295). Jung's mistreatment of Freud is more significant and prompts Kaufmann to employ a Freudian tool of thought: "I conjecture that he projected upon Freud some things he found in himself and did not like." One of those "things" is the temptation to reduce nobility to one or another sort of "banal reality" (Jung). Another is his attribution to Freud of the "conformist features" of the "extraverted character," such as the need for public approval.

> The Jung we meet in [the book] *C. G. Jung Speaking* is pretentious, self-important, and unhumorous, quite lacking in the ironical self-disparagement that was so characteristic of Freud, who took great pride in his work but felt nevertheless that he himself was not important and that . . . *"the public has no claim to my person"* (Freud) (emphasis added). (D3 304)

Jung finally emerges as a tool of his *ressentiment*; this would seem to be a relatively innocuous fact—which is to say, not world-historical in its implications, except that in Jung's case it fails this test. Kaufmann is eloquent: "When *ressentiment* exploded in Germany and prepared for mass murder, Jung felt a profound kinship with what happened across the border and coined a phrase that included him too: the Germanic soul" (D3 395).

The final chapter of *Discovering the Mind* is titled "Mind and Mask," an attempted summing up of all three volumes. The reappearance of the term "mask" is a marker of Kaufmann's intellectual integrity, for it was clear from his earlier discussion of this troublesome image/concept in Nietzsche that it was hard for him—or any reader—to make sense of it. How, after all, could one read a writer "honestly" if he proclaimed that each of his propositions was only the mask of another proposition or of nothing at all? In his earlier discussion of the term in volume 2, Kaufmann quoted the most extreme formulation of the principle of the mask. In *Beyond Good and Evil*, Nietzsche conjures a hermit, a "vice-exister" of the author, who declares: "Every philosophy also *conceals* a philosophy; every opinion is also a hideout, every word also a mask." It is fair to say that by "every" he meant *every* and not what Kaufmann concludes: "We have seen that many of Nietzsche's words are indeed masks; but is *every* word also a mask? Hardly" (D2 161). Let us add to hermit Nietzsche's mask these sentences from the revised introduction to *Dawn*: "Finally, however: why should we have to say what we are and what we want and do not want so loudly and with such fervor? Let us view it more coldly, more distantly, more prudently, from a greater height; let us say it, as it is fitting it should be said between ourselves, so secretly that no one hears it, that no one hears us!"[34] This is scarcely an argument for intersubjective validation. We are clearly at a loss, and Kaufmann's valiant effort to dissolve the paradox that also lauds Nietzsche quite particularly for his intellectual conscience does not—cannot—succeed.

For the rest, "Mind and Mask" is full of cogent—but also contestable—short summaries of arguments that Kaufmann previously developed, as for example: "None of ... ['the so-called existentialists'] made Goethe's legacy his own as Freud did, and none of them paid heed to Nietzsche's *psychology*. *All of them* were corrupted by Kant" (emphasis added) (D3 459). "The excitement generated by Heidegger and Sartre was *always* due to the Nietzschean element in their work" (emphasis added) (D3 463). "Goethe and Beethoven, Leonardo and Michelangelo, Nietzsche and Freud did not have to satisfy needs of this kind ['the desires for security, reassurance, and conquests'] through sexual intercourse. But even Freud and Nietzsche never fully understood this" (D3 467).

Kaufmann paints his conclusion with extraordinarily broad brushstrokes. Consider his humiliation of Sartre, who

> failed to understand clearly how phenomenology and existentialism stand opposed to each other. .... His concern for academic respectability [his writing "in the manner of 'Hegel, Husserl, Heidegger'"] was a symptom of a more profound lack of courage. .... Recoiling from the radical insecurity of his highly individualistic "existentialism," he then sought refuge in Marxism. (D3 461–62)

This section also contains some striking disclaimers. Despite his steady laudation of Freud, Kaufmann confesses at the close that he believes neither in Freud's practice nor in Freud's theories! (The latter exclusion might once again be owed in part to his hostility to the literary theory flowing in from Paris and Yale, Cornell, Johns Hopkins Universities, and the University of California at

Irvine at the time of his writing this chapter.) Discoveries of the mind don't require theories or general principles that might faultlessly predict outcomes. A late paragraph meant to solidify this point is, however, very odd for the company it keeps:

> That the discovery of the mind does not stand or fall with theories and that theories are often overvalued is no new idea. This insight has been central to Zen Buddhism from the start, many centuries ago, and something of the sort is also implicit in Buber's *I and Thou* and, again in very different form, in Werner Erhard's *est*. (D3 470)

Now, however, for the bigger jump: this chapter is regrettably banal in many places—a plain letdown following Kaufmann's detailed, scintillating, and altogether coherent analysis of Jung. And so we learn, in the conclusion to a trilogy of one thousand pages, that "students and professors, but also many people outside the academy, pretend they see what in fact they do not see, because otherwise they might be considered incompetent or stupid" (D3 441). On the other hand, "to discover something one has to look or listen, and most people are afraid of doing that" (D3 447). Finally, "Just ask yourself whether you might be better off if you did [let go of negative emotions], and if you would like yourself better" (D3 455), and so on. These sentences would fit better in a self-help book at the top of a list of best-selling nonfictions.

At this juncture, an observation by Kaufmann's sympathetic, perceptive friend Ben-Ami Scharfstein hits the mark: Kaufmann was distressed at the little attention his later writings received from professional philosophers, but that, Scharfstein observes, is due to the great generality of his questions, for which there can be no dispositive answers.[35] But if Kaufmann were truly distressed by his unpopularity in the guild, it did not help him to write, again and again:

> Some philosophers have a genius, many more a talent—most philosophy professors a meager talent—for concealing urgent problems from themselves—and hiding—behind a web of words that they call concepts. They divert themselves and their students and readers by playing chess with words. Every move is a proposition or a series of propositions that is called an argument. (D3 445)

This is an impatient description of rationality.

Kaufmann was drawn, admirably, to address urgent problems, but his positive philosophy—his answers to these problems, namely, *What Is Man?* or (with Buber) "What about God?"—is less powerful than his critical-analytic work, which, when done carefully, is memorable.[36] His destruction of Heidegger's masterwork *Being and Time,* for one, is a triumph of critical reason. To argue the shortage of dispositive answers is not to say, however, that he is not our educator: the essence of philosophy—he would have it—is the untrammeled drive not to "invoke universal laws or elaborate theories" but "to ask illuminating questions," and here he is exemplary (D3 465).

Epilogue

He died before his own self-discovery (which he says was furthered by this series of books) reached the limit of which, granted a longer life, he was capable. . . . He remained unfinished and (like all of us?) even enigmatic.

—BEN-AMI SCHARFSTEIN

A man's life of any worth is a continual allegory—and very few eyes can see the mystery of his life—a life like the scriptures, figurative.

—JOHN KEATS

WALTER KAUFMANN'S SENSE of life is of a tragic predicament requiring a lucid consciousness sustained until the end.[1] This attitude was given to him as a Jew in Nazi Germany. It harbors the dark gaiety of self-making, "gaiety transfiguring all that dread."[2]

Kaufmann's response to this demand, which is ever present—"The Last Judgment is a summary court martial" (Kafka)—is a commitment to thinking in depth—to philosophy, understood as a full activity of mind and body, an energetic practice, altogether different from problem-solving in theory.[3] As a philosopher, one lives as a perpetual test of one's autonomy—one's heretical faith in critical thinking—no matter how inconvenient the result.

Philosophy involves the free use of the mind in its full commitment to human life—a tragic humanism. It implies a life-or-death stake, where "death," before physical extinction, means a loss of intellectual freedom, a submission to another's rule or fact. In Schiller's play *Don Carlos*, which nurtured Kaufmann, the Marquis von Posa declaims to the absolutist King Philipp

II of Spain, "Sire, Geben Sie Gedankenfreiheit!" (Sir, Give [us] freedom of thought!).[4] Kaufmann himself displays the spirit of Blake's Los: "I MUST Create a System, or be enslav'd by another Man's."[5]

Kaufmann did not create a system but what Germans call "ein Werk"—a substantial, coherent, interrelated body of work, an ensemble of books that can stand together. He experienced and gave form to an astonishing flow— he preferred the word "flight"—of ideas, critiques, "hortations," translations, interpretations—poems. For one reader, *The Faith of a Heretic* contains "improvisations, soliloquies, reasoned arguments and passionate outbursts, dispassionate discourse and personal reference—in short it has a Nietzschean feel."[6] Kaufmann explored and commented on countless books, countries, religions, architectural ruins, and works of visual art in his books and articles, photographs, lectures, and university seminars.

He was indefatigable in his pursuit of accurate information and scholarly stimulation: he had no qualms as a very young man about writing to Hermann Hesse and Karl Jaspers and thereafter to Heidegger and the playwrights Carl Zuckmayer and Rolf Hochhuth and to Ernest Jones, Freud's biographer, among others. His work ethic was unrivaled; it was also fueled by a root egotism—we shall come to that—and a desire to know enough to be able to punish those who, like Plato's cave dwellers, live in darkness, including, especially, other scholars, whom he judged to be self-deceived.

It is enlightening to review the itinerary of his publications—until the end, which is not notably happy. His monograph on Nietzsche in 1950 and his anthology of existentialist writers in 1956 were seized on by a large reading public who brought him fame and fortune. *Nietzsche*, which has since gone into five editions, was read and admired by readers of all classes—famous intellectuals like Thomas Mann and Jacques Maritain, professors, college students, and thousands of bright readers in America, Italy, and Germany. (Resistance—the charge that he had defanged Nietzsche—came decades later.) Kaufmann's introduction to America of existentialist writers like Sartre, Jaspers, and the thoroughly misunderstood Heidegger was a sensation.

These existentialists, Kaufmann argued, considered themselves loners, *like him* belonging to no school,[7] even if they display family resemblances. These affinities, in Kaufmann's case, are evident between himself and other humanist cultural historians and critics of his time, like Erich Heller, Peter Gay, and George Steiner, or the somewhat older Lionel Trilling and Isaiah Berlin. From a higher perch, they comminated against mass culture and its slack obeisance to institutions in power. The younger generation, too, fed on the theory and practice of alienation: their passionately preferred stance was "outside" and "against."

Soon after the publication of *Existentialism*, Kaufmann's irrepressible self-confidence and creativity led to his publishing, in the space of four years, 1958–61—anni mirabiles—four large books, totaling some eighteen hundred pages: *Critique of Religion and Philosophy* (1958); a collection of his essays, *From Shakespeare to Existentialism* (1960); an anthology of writings on religion, *Religion from Tolstoy to Camus* (1961); and *The Faith of a Heretic* (1961). This account ignores his publication, in 1961, as well, of his influential translation of Goethe's *Faust* and in 1962 an edition and translation of *Twenty German Poets* and a volume of his own poems, *Cain and Other Poems*. The range of Kaufmann's intellectual concerns in these works is exceptional; his erudition—as even Karl Jaspers, no friend of Kaufmann, noted—remarkable; and the pace of production almost uncanny.

These four books were by and large successes with his reading public.[8] They profile the German Bildungsideal of higher culture and self-perfection and the scathing critique of empty pursuits. In *The Faith of a Heretic*, Kaufmann excoriated "people who do not know what to do with themselves in this life, but fritter away their time reading magazines" (F 386). He declared in an interview: "One has only to write an article on matters of religion in a popular magazine to be swamped with letters, little pamphlets, and big books that claim to offer nothing less than God's own truth; but, alas, they are far from agreeing with each other. . . . How are we to choose if evidence and reason are thrown out of court?"[9] These remarks did not go without occasional—and indignant—disclaimers from professors of philosophy and Christian historians and theologians, which Kaufmann answered with his native vivacity. Susan Sontag especially minded the specious attribution of religiosity to several of the writers in *From Tolstoy to Camus*—Camus, above all. Kaufmann's next big book, a monograph on Hegel (1965), may have been stimulated by one professor's complaint that, without compelling expertise, Kaufmann had no business writing on Shakespeare and other writers outside the German field of poetry and philosophy: it was time to for him to get back to elucidating the German (mandarin) mind. The book on Hegel, though well received, did not command the audience of his earlier icebreakers.

Kaufmann's impassioned study *Tragedy and Philosophy* (1968) called for a good deal of fresh intellectual labor, but, once again, technical parts of the work, like his criticism of Aristotle's *Poetics*, were rejected by classicists; and Kaufmann may have goaded his colleague Francis Fergusson into delivering a singularly loveless review in of all places the *New York Review of Books*, where Kaufmann had hitherto been courteously mentioned. He would have been chagrined to be repudiated there. But aside from his concrete analysis of characters and plots, his book is in places discursive and incoherent in its theorizing (see chapter 9), and one does not come away feeling it has supplied a clear and usable definition of tragedy.[10]

Some of the criticisms provoked by these books surely whetted Kaufmann's appetite for conflict, and in his later works he begins to excoriate too readily too many important ideas. In *Without Guilt and Justice: From Decidophobia to Autonomy* (1973), for one, he called ideas of justice and equality "decrepit." Our chapter 11 supplied the context for the startling adjective in quotes, but I will reproduce it:

> To those whose minds are not liberated, wars, revolutions, and radical movements will never bring freedom but only an exchange of one kind of slavery for another. That is one of the most tragic lessons of the twentieth century.
>
> Liberation of the mind is no panacea, but without it angry rhetoric and cruel bloodbaths are of no avail, and tyranny endures. Most of those who see themselves as radicals and revolutionaries still cling to decrepit ideas like justice and equality and depend on guilt and fear, as our fathers and mothers did. What we need is a new autonomous morality. (W vii)

In that chapter I asked, What sort of "mind" needs to be liberated from a passion for justice? One scholar concluded his sympathetic review, "I find Professor Kaufmann's concept of moral autonomy important, original, and challenging. But his arguments on guilt, justice, and equality are unpersuasive. They do not do justice—if the word is permissible—to his other work, which I greatly admire."[11] A less charitable reviewer wrote,

> In the main what Kaufmann proposes are nostrums of autosuggestion for mandarins yearning to be cavalier; while for "those who see themselves as radicals and revolutionaries," and join in comradely struggle to eliminate oppression and exploitation, he proffers a bad conscience: guilt feelings.[12]

It still needs to be noted that Kaufmann was a vigorous and outspoken opponent of the Vietnam War, and he made his feelings public in books and newspapers. In 1977, he published a striking piece, "Selective Compassion," deploring a general aversion to addressing the ethnic cleansing of millions of Sikhs from the Punjab and the murder of some three million Bengalis, victims of Bangladesh's war of independence from Pakistan.[13] Nonetheless, despite Kaufmann's growing reputation as a public intellectual, interest in his scholarly work, following *Without Guilt and Justice*, began to fall off—precipitously. The diminishing number of reviews of his later work makes this point: the evidence of a falling off has been quantified.[14]

Many of Kaufmann's ideas, above all the plea to dispense with the idea of justice, since it is too difficult to compute precisely, and other extreme positions (he began to valorize *extremity*), like his call for a *"poetic* science," have not stood the test of time. Neither will many of Kaufmann's literary judgments.[15] On the other hand, he rarely wrote a line, true or false, that does not excite energetic agreement or indignation. He argued that only writing that made plain the author's "likes and dislikes" would set the reader on a journey of self-discovery, just as writing passionately furthered his own.

Looked at closely, much of his later work, already notably in *Hegel*, is a mix of painstaking scholarship in regard to dates, quotes, and editions; the reception history of the philosophers; and general—often overgeneral ideas— about their work . . . interrupted by striking polemical thrusts. A review of Kaufmann's last work, *Discovering the Mind*, is instructive:

> His scrupulousness in matters of translation and bibliography, his symmetrical organization, and his meticulously informative table of contents, all serve his truculent independence of contemporary philosophy. Obviously, he is not tempted by any current philosophical fashion, Anglo-American or Continental. The problems that concern him most are so general that Anglo-American philosophers now for the most part neglect them, either because they feel them beyond the reach of philosophy as they think it should be practiced or because they are too difficult to deal with in the attentive fragmentation and precise technicality that mark so much philosophical writing today.[16]

On the question of his truculence, Kaufmann's review of Charles Taylor's *Hegel* illustrates his stance. He praises Taylor by concluding, "The reader is always in the presence of a highly intelligent author, and will never feel like exclaiming: 'How stupid!'"[17] Faint praise indeed that many others had to do without. On this subject of his polemical stance, the attack attitude, one would have to note, however late in the day—and adopting his very own psychobiographical approach, which he owed to Nietzsche—that he was short of stature and, as an adolescent immigrant beginning his new life in anti-Semitic America in the late 1930s and speaking English with an accent, was fiercely determined to "push" the ethic of that unheard-of thing, the energetic Bildungsbürgertum, his social class.

In later years, Kaufmann began to be described with faint derision by analytic philosophers with whom he did not engage as an "existentialist," a "poet," and, in later years "a photographer." So-called Continental philosophers saw him as a curiosity—a passionate, unrelenting critic of Heidegger and French existentialism and the contamination of literary study by American and Parisian theory. He was not used to faint or illegible praise. It made him more determined to go his own way. From the start, his *Nietzsche* monograph displays his drive to publish work that would mean more to him than work that might have gotten him kinder reviews—such as small-scale problem-solving or the pious exegesis of canonical philosophical texts. In his later work, he insisted, again and again, that the interpretation of other people's books matters only when engaged readers pronounce them "Right!" or, more frequently, "Wrong!" Only then does such work make a difference to you as a stage in your personal Bildung.

His final trilogy, *Discovering the Mind*, concludes with a blunt turn to the question of self-knowledge: "Scholarship is often a form of escape. These pages, too, can be read as a diversion, perhaps even as a detective story. They could also enhance your self-understanding no less than writing them has increased mine" (D3 473). Still, despite his indisputable creativity, intensity, and erudition, Kaufmann's late writing can seem egotistical and abrasive, and he made academic enemies, unnecessarily. He might have tempered these proclivities. He preferred not to. If his criticism seemed nasty, *tant pis*: he could point to its good Socratic lineage in putting down persons and ideas claiming undeserved authority.[18] And yet again, as Ben-Ami Scharfstein, his good friend and interlocutor observes, "In spite of his defiance of current philosophical attitudes, he was hurt by the failure of philosophical journals to review or ascribe importance to his later books. Professionally speaking, he was a loner and a lonely man."[19]

Kaufmann's late work aimed for a wider audience, but he might have confused writing casually with a fluency that would prove attractive. He would never again have the success of his grand first book on Nietzsche or the books he wrote during the anni mirabiles of 1958–61. He seemed no longer able to find big new ideas in himself or the writings of others. It cannot have helped that by the late 1960s the three dominant avatars of existentialism—Heidegger, Jaspers, and Sartre—had renounced that program entirely. By relegating the surge of deconstructive and rhetorical French writing on Nietzsche during

the late 1970s to a symptom of resistance to Nietzsche's main doctrines—
books and essays that "discount what mattered most to Nietzsche himself"—
Kaufmann regrettably swept away an opportunity to sharpen his own positions
by reference to writers like Gilles Deleuze, Jacques Derrida, Michel Foucault,
Paul de Man, and others.[20] Contrast the productive literary agon of Sophocles
and Euripides, whom Sophocles is said to have called the "whetstone" of his
art! (D2 71). One can only speculate about Kaufmann's motives in shunning
this opportunity for debate, but there is reliable gossip about his departmental
tirades: "*They*—the rhetorical, the deconstructive types—are destroying the
humanities!" And in his later years, he would not think he needed to defend
positions that he had set in stone for three decades, especially the psychobiographical attitude, sheerly antithetical to the "Parisian" ethos. This stance
would cost him much of his university audience. Advanced undergraduates
and graduate students in several departments—of the temper of those who
once, in the 1950s, were attracted to Kaufmann's existentialism—were now
attracted to the fusées of a new generation of French thinkers, also felt to be
revolutionary.

What followed from his burning mind in later years tends to be miscellaneous work. He turned to photography and his own poetry. He began to cite
earlier writings excessively, repeating Rilke's demand: "*Du mußt dein Leben
ändern*" (You must change your life!). Martin Jay has offered this salty rejoinder
to Kaufmann's refrain: "The imperative 'to change one's life,' in italics or not, is
pace Rilke, pretty empty rhetoric. It can, after all, mean becoming a born-again
Christian convert, having a sex change operation, deciding to become a jihad-
ist, turning into a dropout hippie, etc. Or is it just radical self-alteration that is
somehow a virtue in itself, no matter what you change into? If so, why?"[21] In
addressing the presumably like-minded, Kaufmann's humanist optimism—
and thinking of Nietzsche's habitual summoning to harder heights—cannot
imagine that Rilke's poem meant anything other than a change toward the
more virtuous stance. You are to make yourself more valuable to mankind's
project of producing superior human beings—the artist, the philosopher, the
saint. But is this reading consistent with Kaufmann's more bizarre experiments
in self-renewal? Witness his attendance at meetings of the questionable cult
est and, in 1979, at the Reverend Moon's Eighth International Conference on
the Unity of the Sciences.

His last book on Freud, Adler, and Jung contains flashes of idiosyncratic
enthusiasm: "Many people, including myself, have gained insight into themselves and others as a result of the *est* 'training'" (D3 472). Kaufmann does not

tell us what this est-enabled insight was. *The Book of est* describes a highly competent trainer shouting at his clients, "I am here because my life works, and you are here because your lives don't work. . . . You have great theories about life, impressive ideas, intelligent belief systems. You are . . . very *reasonable*. . . . But just look at your own [obscenity] . . . lives, and you *know* they don't work."[22] I have to imagine that Kaufmann here was thinking more of the pertinence of this claim to "others," and that the insight he received lay elsewhere.

In 1978, Kaufmann chose to participate in a conference organized by the cult of the Reverend Sun Myung Moon, a wealthy entrepreneur and likewise the messianic founder of the Church of Unification. Moon had been roundly accused of making anti-Semitic remarks, married couples en masse, served a term in a US federal penitentiary for tax evasion, and was an ardent supporter of Richard Nixon. When Nixon was being harried by the Watergate scandal, members of the United Church, called "Moonies," fasted for three days in front of the US Capitol Building, praying for his vindication. In the *New Scientist* of June 25, 1981, one reads that Kaufmann asked himself—and then answered—the relevant question, "Is it sinful to be here?"

> During the last few weeks I have received many letters from people who urged me not to attend. . . . I am here although I am not much of a conference goer because there are so many excellent participants, because the level of discussion is exceptionally high, and because these conferences are superbly international and interdisciplinary. I have no worry that my participation could be taken to signify agreement with the religious views on other activities of the founder of his church.

There were many sympathetic to him at the time who begged him to worry, but he was not easily driven off course.[23]

In the course of his more than thirty years at Princeton, Kaufmann's students and especially his younger colleagues never failed to admire or at least to concede his energy, his independence of mind, and his astonishing erudition. He was tireless, as I have said, making his own way through the thickets of historical philosophy, religion, and psychology, bent on constituting by example the human being of humility, ambition, love, honesty, and courage. To many of those outside his circle, he failed. In one mordant view,

> many of . . . [Kaufmann's] later works were jeremiads written in an apocalyptic or vatic tone. He repeated himself frequently and pontificated in ways that too often expressed his prejudices more than demonstrating a

charitable reading of the figures, texts, or traditions at issue. . . . He reveled in his self-image as a lonely heretic crying in the proverbial wilderness about the sterility of the culture around him, and the decline of appreciation for the geniuses in his canon of greatness.[24]

But that sort of sweeping judgment does not form itself effortlessly, like a shapely cloud lifting off his texts under scrutiny. Through the close reading this book has attempted to supply, one finds in Kaufmann's work from beginning to end all sorts of precise, incontrovertible insights, flashes of wit, and love. Fair judgment lies in the detail. True, at the outset of this epilogue, I spoke of Kaufmann's root egoism and his desire to know enough to confute fools. David Pickus, a historian who has published many articles on Kaufmann's mind and work, comments privately, with little enthusiasm, on this sentence, a psychobiographical account of motive: "Yes, Kaufmann was probably driven by root egotism, but it is a good guess that so too are the people who write little to nothing, particularly authors of vicious reviews. It is of course true that few combine Kaufmann's ambition, drive, and diligence. All of these engines were running full pedal in Kaufmann's life."

We can only imagine Kaufmann's intimate experience. He has deliberately left few or no traces—the Walter Kaufmann archive at the Princeton University Library consists entirely of manuscripts of published books. There are no letters, no diaries, no unpublished manuscripts.[25] His books, which are rarely personal, imply all that he wished others to know of him. What he calls his journey to self-discovery leading, perhaps, to more explicit self-revelation, was indeed abruptly ended by his early death. He noted in the year before he died, "We are not finished until we are dead. While we live we are like a speaker in midsentence who cannot be understood fully until he has had a chance to finish" (D3 446). As Kaufmann's interlocutor Ben-Ami Scharfstein concludes, death cut off his friend in midsentence. His pen was lifted above the page to write, but that deadly strike did nothing to destroy the substantial edifice of his thought and knowledge, still standing.

Postscript

Contra *Nietzsche*

NIETZSCHE AND ITS CRITICS

Pulling *Nietzsche*'s claws.

—JOSEPH FRANK

A REMARK TYPICAL of the tone of critical readers of Kaufmann's *Nietzsche* in the decades following its first publication in 1950 is the jibe I overheard delivered by one misbegotten wag: "Kaufmann's arguments are perfectly clear . . . and perfectly wrong." One half of that aperçu is right; the other, occasionally right. We will try to see where Kaufmann, in the view of his critics, has erred but also why he had to commit himself to his interpretations and none other.

In 1965, in *Nietzsche as Philosopher*, Arthur Danto, a young professor at Columbia University, attacked Nietzsche with an arsenal of "analytic philosophical" tools, an approach that Kaufmann did not reject except to declare that it was one-sided, just as he considered one-sided the opposite but also productive perspective that saw Nietzsche as a protoexistentialist.[1] Danto's book, which amounts to a counterrevolution in the wake of Kaufmann's *Nietzsche* (Kaufmann's book having been termed "a revolution"), calls for discussion.[2]

Danto means to bring Nietzsche into a system not natural to him, one founded on the attention Nietzsche demonstrably paid to a few famous and traditional questions: for example, What can we know? What is the self? What can we will? This attention on Nietzsche's part is the hallmark of qualification as a "philosopher." There is nothing in this argument opposite to the thrust of Kaufmann's book. But Danto has in mind another notion of the qualities of genuine philosophical thought: it must be consistent with ordinary language philosophy and mathematically informed logical analysis, which is to say, "analyses in terms of logical features which ... [Nietzsche] was unable to make explicit but toward which he was unmistakably groping."[3] Danto then proceeds to treat, for example, the doctrine of the eternal recurrence with a detailed analytic precision exceeding Kaufmann's.

As Danto, not alone, has observed, many of Nietzsche's claims are elusive and contradictory, but Danto means to get to the bottom of (at least some of) them—and does so in an ingenious way. He notes that Nietzsche produces confusion by offering as a principle what is in fact its illustration, a procedure especially troubling when principle and illustration go by the same name. For example, Nietzsche's (and Kaufmann's) discussion of the religious character under the head of asceticism does not allow for the distinction between the man who is *religious* in the wide sense of worshiping God yet "*antireligious* in the narrow sense when he calls religion into question in the name of something else, such as reason, or science, or historical criticism, or truth ... [for both are] *personae* of the religious impulses which only incidentally are expressed in actual religious forms" (172). Again, "If the *Übermensch* has been taken to be a bully, whose joy is in the brute exercise of strength, Nietzsche has only himself to blame. His illustrations have obscured his principles" (182). Here Danto stretches the point, since Nietzsche never offers explicit illustrations of the Übermensch, although Kaufmann inclines to say he does (Danto finds Kaufmann's translation of "Übermensch" as "overman" "prissy"); it is still true that Nietzsche does admire excessively such superior men as Napoleon, Michelangelo, Julius Caesar—and above all Goethe:

> *Goethe* is exemplary: the impetuous naturalism which gradually becomes severe dignity. As a stylized human being, he reached a higher level than any other German ever did.[4]

This sort of mistake, the confusing of the illustration with the principle, is one that only an analytic philosopher, Danto appears to be saying, is able to sort out. As such, this claim, too, acts like a date stamp, for since this mistake involves not only confusion between the particular instance of a thesis and its general form but rests on a punning verbal confusion, the same mistake might be grasped as a feature of Nietzsche's rhetoric and hence a subject better suited to a rhetorical (read: deconstructionist) critique exceeding Danto's competence. Interestingly, Danto's preface to the 1980 edition of his book does indeed reimagine his thesis as dealing essentially with Nietzsche's claims for language (viz., "we have learnt to see conformably with our language"), but in fact it rarely does so. In the last resort, *Nietzsche as Philosopher* reveals its pre-deconstructive "naiveté" precisely by subordinating Nietzsche's rhetoric to an imputed authorial intention and moral purpose, witness Danto's scathing phrase: "the irresponsibility of Nietzsche's style," which makes of style the vehicle of the "lurid, expressionist illustration" marring the "more philosophical and abstract text" (211).[5]

Danto's first explicit mention of Kaufmann is to admire him, as is typical of most scholars in the following decades even when on the prowl for his shortcomings. Danto praises Kaufmann's reading of "idols" in Nietzsche's *The Twilight of the Idols* "in the sense in which Bacon used it, where idols are merely pernicious habits of beliefs which hold men in thrall to error" (108).[6] His admiration soon gives way to temperate respect, but then to irritation, as he turns on Kaufmann's reading of a key aphorism concerning Nietzsche's idea of "spirit" (*Geist*) (*Twilight*, X, 14). Since all of Danto's criticisms have a salutary bite, and will take us ever more deeply into Kaufmann's Nietzsche interpretation, I will consider them at some length. Danto notes that

> Nietzsche writes that "the weak have more spirit." But this once more is hardly a compliment when we look to the context from which it comes. It is always a problem, when citing Nietzsche, to make sure one includes enough of the context so that the meaning of what he says is sufficiently plain and consonant with his intentions. Even so able an expositor as Professor Kaufmann, who has been a devastating critic of those who have quoted Nietzsche to their *own* purposes by lifting passages out of context, cannot always avoid this himself. Thus, in his *Nietzsche: Philosopher, Psychologist, Antichrist, . . .* p. 294,[7] he cites Nietzsche as saying that "Darwin forgot the spirit (*Geist*)." Nietzsche does say this, in exactly the passage from which I [Danto] have been quoting in *The Twilight of the Idols* ["The species does not grow in perfection: the weak are forever prevailing over the strong" (X, 14)]. But now Kaufmann goes on to make the claim that Nietzsche is implying that you cannot explain human behavior in purely material terms without reference to man's "spiritual life," and that this was what Darwin overlooked. Nietzsche of course was not a materialist, regarding "matter" as a fiction. But his point against Darwin is *not at all* what Kaufmann says it is. The passage continues: "One must need spirit in order to acquire spirit—one loses it when one no longer needs it. The strong dispense with spirit." He [Nietzsche] defines "spirit"—which by itself sounds very exalted—as follows: "By spirit I understand caution, patience, cunning, dissembling,

great self-control, and whatever is mimicry. To the latter belongs a good bit of so-called virtue." This has almost nothing to do [according to Nietzsche] with Darwin not thinking about mental factors. Rather, it is used to make the point that "spirit" is something the herd has, but which the strong do not need, although through spirit the herd is able to triumph over the strong. The spirit leads to the debasement of the species. . . . This, I think it plain, is Nietzsche's point. (169–70)

It is easy to see how vexatious this reading would be for Kaufmann, who indeed considers "Geist" (spirit) the equivalent of reason and the root of the *difference* between perfected man and the other "species"—the masses and the beasts.

Danto then addresses a section of the *Gay Science* that poses the question "To what extent are we still pious?," writing, "[Nietzsche] . . . answers this [question] by saying that we are so insofar as we continue to believe in *truth*." He quotes Nietzsche:

> One sees that even science rests upon a belief. There is no science without preconceptions. The question whether truth is needed must not merely be affirmatively answered, but be affirmed to such a degree that the proposition, the belief, the persuasion that "nothing is needed more than truth and in relation to this everything else has a secondary value" demands expression. . . .

But [writes Danto] this is to say that science feels it necessary that there be an order and a reality which it must try to discover and with which it must seek to bring its judgments into conformity. Nietzsche continues:

> And insofar as one affirms this other world—well? Must one not therewith deny its opposite, namely *this* world? *Our* world? Thus it may be grasped what I mean when I claim that our belief in science rests upon *a metaphysical belief*. And that even we knowing ones of today, we godless and antimetaphysical ones, even *we* take *our* fire from the torch which a belief a thousand years old has kindled, that belief of Christ's which was also Plato's belief, that God is truth, that truth is divine. . . .

[Danto continues:] Let us pause to draw an inference. Zarathustra says that God is dead. If he is right, and God is identified with truth, then *truth* must be dead. Is this not another way of stating that there is perhaps no truth, no objective order, *nothing* which we must acknowledge as higher than ourselves, as fixed, eternal, and unchanging? Which is *nihilism*? Nietzsche indeed means this inference to be drawn, and the passage I [Danto] have been citing at such length ends with this crucial question to which his entire philosophy is in an answer:

> But what if this were increasingly unworthy of belief, what if nothing any long[er] proves itself divine? What if God turns out to be our most enduring lie?

Here I [Danto] must take strong exception to Professor Kaufmann's thesis. He makes a great deal of the passage I have just quoted from *The Gay Science* [above]. He cites it in his own book to support his thesis that belief in the truth is Nietzsche's faith, and that in this sense he remained a "pious" man. See Kaufmann, p. 359. He does *not* however cite the last sentence, which I have just quoted, in which Nietzsche precisely rejects this interpretation, making it plain that he is not *fromm* [pious].

The complete sentence of Nietzsche that Danto references, in Kaufmann's translation, is "But what if this belief is becoming more and more unbelievable, if nothing turns out to be divine any longer unless it be error, blindness, lies—if God himself turns out to be our *longest lie*?"[8] Danto continues:

> Nor does Kaufmann reprint this sentence in his anthology, though he does reprint the rest of the lengthy aphorism. Here is a plain example of how much mischief suspended dots can do, and how even the best-intentioned of writers about Nietzsche will often ascribe to him their *own* views, and by ample citation, give the appearance of documenting them. This, I am afraid, is Professor Kaufmann's admirable enough faith, but hardly Nietzsche's.... Kaufmann's claim is inconsistent with the attack against truth in *The Genealogy of Morals* (III, 24), where a fragment of this passage from *The Gay Science* is actually quoted.... This fragment includes the last sentence which Kaufmann omits in two places. Perhaps he did so because he could not see the point of including it, which is quite possible when one is convinced that one has a correct interpretation. (172–74)

"The strong exception" that Danto takes to Kaufmann's attempt to erase Nietzsche's suggestion that God might be our longest, most enduring lie has merit, and on it stands the pillar of his reading of Nietzsche. Danto concludes:

> I fear we must take seriously Nietzsche's claim that everything is false.... The motto of Book Five of *The Gay Science* is: "*Carcasse, tu trembles: tu tremblerais bien davantage, si tu savais ou je te mène.*" It is hard to suppose that he then had in mind something so comforting as truth exists and God is truth. The *destruction* of this idea was what was frightening and intoxicating. (174)

This passage from Danto has the collateral merit of identifying *Kaufmann's* ("admirable enough") *faith* in truth, but Kaufmann would hardly appreciate the tone of this mention.

The thrust of Danto's arguments is to underscore Nietzsche's destruction of "spirit," faith, truth, piety, even essay form.[9] In a work stemming from the so-called school of "analytical philosophy," one nonetheless discovers here and there a poststructuralist flair literally *avant la lettre.*

Kaufmann's reply is at once vigorous and technical, so technical that I shall include the whole of it in a supplement to this chapter and merely summarize now what I take to be its most effective points. Kaufmann returns Danto's charge that his citations silently omit important elements and adds that Danto's German is deplorable, but he does not specify just how these faults invalidate Danto's criticism, which alleges that Kaufmann has improperly ascribed to Nietzsche a humanist faith in truth. Kaufmann refers Danto to his (Kaufmann's) commentary on this passage from *Genealogy* on Kaufmann's page 359, which, in an unspecified way, should render untenable Danto's "interpretation" of Nietzsche's attack on truth. A careful reading of this intricate section 3: 24 of *Genealogy*, however, does lend support to Kaufmann's reading.

This section describes a human type with positive attributes—"men of knowledge, . . . hard, severe, abstinent, heroic spirits who constitute the honor of our age." They participate in the ascetic ideal even as they suppose they are liberated from it. Hence, "they are far from being free spirits: for they still have faith in truth. . . . It is precisely in their faith in truth that they are more rigid and conditional than anyone. . . . That which constrains these men, however, this unconditional will to truth, is faith in the ascetic ideal itself." Ergo, to upset this high valuation of "these last idealists of knowledge" would be to upset Nietzsche's frequent, if intermittent, high valuation of the ascetic ideal. It is on this point, by looking toward the wider context of Nietzsche's celebration of the ascetic ideal, that Kaufmann supports his claim to Nietzsche's "pious" faith in truth.

If, at the close of 3: 24 of *Genealogy*, Nietzsche puts this very will to truth in question, that doubt might be considered, I'll add, as the energetic thrust of a will to truth bold enough even to question itself. That act of questioning does not dissolve the commitment to the drive. We might view both scholars—Kaufmann and Danto, both practitioners of the ascetic ideal—as exercising, according to their lights, an "unconditional will to truth" in their reading of *Genealogy* 3: 24. Each claims to renounce all mere interpretation—as Nietzsche puts it in this very section 3: 24 of *Genealogy*—all "forcing,

adjusting, abbreviating, omitting, padding, inventing, falsifying and whatever else is of the essence of interpretation" in the name of the basic text of
Nietzsche's thought. With what result? Only a community of readers in the
fullness of time—generating what Kafka calls a "chorus of lies" in which truth
might be found—could get to the heart of the matter.[10]

Kaufmann's sharpest rebuttal concerns Nietzsche's description of Geist
(spirit) about which he and Danto disagree. It is quite true that Danto fails
to quote a crucial parenthesis in the passage from *The Twilight of the Idols*.
The passage in Nietzsche, we recall, reads: "Darwin forgot the spirit (that is
English!); the weak have more spirit. One must need spirit to acquire spirit;
one loses it when one no longer needs it. The strong dispense with spirit."
Here, now, is the omitted parenthesis in question: ("Let it go!" they think in
Germany today; "the Reich must still remain to us.") This provision, declares
Kaufmann, "shows that the reading urged against me is wrong" (N 359). In my
view Kaufmann is right.

The crux of this logomachy would seem to be that Kaufmann cannot take
Danto's criticisms seriously, since their implication, when widened out, would
leave nothing of the "educator" in Nietzsche. Nietzsche would have destroyed
Geist, truth, and piety, leaving nothing in its place, nothing suggesting the
possibility of courage, of seizing hold of one's vitality in the service of a higher
organization of self and world. Danto's contempt for his subject, if followed
through, would undo the entirety of Kaufmann's Nietzsche. Worse still, perhaps—as we follow Danto burying Pelion under Ossa—Nietzsche would
have achieved his vacuous result by merely worthless leaps of untrained
thought.

After Danto, a variant of his criticism, an excoriation of Kaufmann's alleged
ignorance of what might be called Nietzsche's politics of cruelty, began to surface.[11] In 1970, Conor Cruse O'Brien, the Irish diplomat and scholar, published
an essay titled "The Gentle Nietzscheans," which contains very likely the single
most trenchant criticism of Kaufmann's position on Nietzsche.[12] O'Brien's
Nietzsche is a far cry from—and a good deal less good-natured than—
Kaufmann's acolyte of Socrates, French enlightenment wits, and Goethe.
O'Brien bears down hard on Nietzsche's alleged infatuation with Machiavelli
(a strain with which Kaufmann disagrees, citing Nietzsche's only infrequent
mentions). But, for O'Brien, once is enough, and the link between the two
has been firmly established—a link that will subsequently accommodate that
"predator" and "beast of prey"—the syphilitic Cesare Borgia—as well. This
connection is damning.[13] In a language full of gaiety and verve, Machiavelli

recommends lies and cruelty as constructive *ragion di stato*, as *Staatsräson*. O'Brien writes:

> The category of thinkers about whom Nietzsche was enthusiastic is very small indeed, and the Machiavelli of *The Prince* is high among them. Consider this from *Beyond Good and Evil*:
>
>> Machiavelli in his *Principe* lets us breathe the dry thin air of Florence and cannot resist presenting the most serious matters in an ungovernable allegrissimo—perhaps not without a malicious artist's inkling of the antithesis he is venturing on: thoughts that are long, difficult, hard and dangerous—in a tempo of galloping along in the best and most playful high spirits.[14]
>
> Really [writes O'Brien], praise of this order hardly has to be frequent to justify a linking of names . . . of this type. For no one who reads Nietzsche at all could fail, one would think, to miss the point here: the adjectives he lavishes on Machiavelli—difficult, hard, dangerous, playful—are not only his terms of highest praise but, by no coincidence, *those he likes to apply to his own work* (emphasis added).

In his unpublished writings, continues O'Brien, Nietzsche celebrated actions that might be accomplished *by a state* when they are too violent for any individual, such as creating a rigid social hierarchy of master and slave and eliminating the unfit. The largest number of the unfit would be Christians and Jews, with the brunt of Nietzsche's contempt falling on the Jews, who were the first to perform the inversion of master values that would then infect the Christians. The weight of Nietzsche's praise of the Jews as tough and enlivening-for-the Germans is slight—following O'Brien—next to his hatred of their ethical poison. The same inversion upends the customary argument of Kaufmann and other (unidentified) gentle Nietzscheans that sees Nietzsche as a dedicated anti-anti-Semite. According to O'Brien, Nietzsche's transvaluation of all values made him the most radical anti-Semite who ever lived.

O'Brien's essay was published in 1970, giving Kaufmann the opportunity to respond; Kaufmann would write a strong, combative letter to the *New York Review of Books* in 1973, but the subject is not O'Brien's fierce Nietzsche but Erich Heller's beneficent Karl Kraus, and he did not reply to O'Brien.[15] If I were to reply to O'Brien for Kaufmann, I would stress the fact that O'Brien's harshest claims are drawn from Nietzsche's *Will to Power*, which consists of jottings Nietzsche never published. If one opts for an absolute distinction of authority between the published and the unpublished writings, as Kaufmann does, then the relative *absence* in the published writings of the likes of such murderous, proto-Nazistic diction takes on greater importance, and one is entitled to bracket out or mollify in Nietzsche's notes the uglier features of his master morality. Several passages in *On the Genealogy of Morals* praise the coexistence in well-constituted individuals of both moral types. For example,

> There are still places where the struggle is as yet undecided. One might even say that it has risen ever higher and thus become more and more profound and spiritual; so that today there is perhaps no more decisive mark of a *"higher nature,"* a more spiritual nature, than that of being divided in this sense and a genuine battleground of these opposed values.[16]

Similarly, in *Beyond Good and Evil*, we read,

> In all the higher and more mixed cultures there also appear attempts at mediation between these two moralities—and yet more often the interpenetration [confusion, *Durcheinander*] and mutual misunderstanding of both—and at times they occur directly [*hart*] alongside each other—even in the same human being, within a *single* soul.[17]

It is after all "slave morality" that first made man an "interesting animal":

> It is only fair to add that it was on the soil of this *essentially dangerous* form of human existence, the priestly form, that man first became *an interesting animal*, that only here did the human soul in a higher sense acquire *depth* and become *evil*—and these are the two basic respects in which man has hitherto been superior to other beasts![18]

There are vicious moments in Nietzsche that cannot be overlooked and which Kaufmann, with the best will in the world, could not mitigate or excuse. But the danger is that despite heaps of evidence to the contrary, these moments will be made to define Nietzsche absolutely. Addressing the political complaint directly, the Nietzsche scholar Keith Angell-Pearson declared:

> The real problem with the labeling of Nietzsche as a Fascist, or worse, a Nazi, is that it ignores the fact that Nietzsche's aristocratism seeks to revive an older conception of politics, one which he locates in the Greek *agon*.

This view, Angell-Pearson adds, is not unlike Hannah Arendt's, which should give us pause. Once you elaborate this affinity, he writes, "the absurdity of describing Nietzsche's political thought as 'Fascist,' or Nazi, becomes readily apparent."[19]

The thrust of O'Brien's concern was renewed in a note by the urbane Czech English Germanist J. P. Stern:

Walter Kaufmann's *Nietzsche: Philosopher, Psychologist, Antichrist* (1950, 1974) presents the richly illustrated but oddly idealized portrait of a classical German philosopher in the Kant-Hegel-Schopenhauer tradition, a little neater, a little more systematic and good a deal less contentious then the real Nietzsche?[20]

The question mark points to a modesty, a cautiousness in the criticism that would soon give way to a far harsher tone in others. Stern goes on address a side of Nietzsche that, he alleges, escaped Kaufmann's notice:

The knowledge and science [Nietzsche] ... talks about are states of mind of individual persons, wholly private phenomena whose *social implications* are left largely unexplored; while his notion of "life," too, alternates between the private and the cosmic spheres, *leaving out the social and political world* which, Nietzsche believes, is either governed by the individual will or made ungovernable by the democratic mob (emphasis added).[21]

For Stern, Nietzsche is fundamentally a political thinker, and the politics that follows from this separation—"a heroism of strenuousness"—is a will to power over *others* and is in principle murderous. This, of course, is not entirely wrong, as consider the long note Nietzsche composed (but did not publish) in 1885:

Inexorable, hesitating, terrible as fate, the great task and question is approaching: how shall the earth as a whole be governed? And *for what* shall "man" as a whole—no longer just one people, one race—be raised and bred?

What morality is required for this project? "A morality whose intention is to breed a ruling caste—the future masters of the earth."[22]

But Kaufmann does not in the least ignore what he takes to be Nietzsche's principal idea, namely, "The *goal of humanity* cannot lie in the end but only in *its highest specimens*." Kaufmann writes:

For Nietzsche, the mass of men has no worth whatever and is essentially continuous with the animal kingdom. ... Most men are ... distinguished only by a potentiality that few of them realize: they can, but rarely do, rise above the beasts. Man can transcend his animal nature and become a "no-longer-animal" and a "truly human being"; but only some of "the philosophers, artists, and saints" rise to that point (*Unzeitgemässe Betrachtungen* [Untimely Meditations] III 5). (N 152)

These pronunciamentos—several of Kaufmann's critics declare—have a *political* import that Kaufmann does not develop. Again, there is merit to this claim, but it is not as if Kaufmann were ignorant of it. Readers may recall Kaufmann's caveat discussed in chapter 1, beginning:

> It is one of Nietzsche's most serious shortcomings—and has contributed seriously to his "influence"—that he failed to give any emphasis to this common human potentiality and did not consider the possibility that this potentiality might be quite sufficient to re-establish that "cardinal distinction between man and animal" which Darwin seemed to Nietzsche to have denied. (N 286)

In 1983, three years after Kaufmann's death, the Germanist Walter Sokel again launched an attack like O'Brien's and Stern's (also discussed in chapter 1). It has since acquired a good deal of notoriety, though it is less trenchant than the others. Sokel's indignation is present early, in its title: "Political Uses and Abuses of Nietzsche in Walter Kaufmann's Image of Nietzsche." "In contrast to Kaufmann," writes Sokel, "[J. P.] Stern brings back to us the embarrassingly political Nietzsche, whom Kaufmann's influence had almost made us forget." Sokel then quotes a flagrant passage from Nietzsche's *Beyond Good and Evil*:

> The age of small-scale politics is over, already the next century [Nietzsche speaks of ours] will bring the struggle for world domination—and with it, the *necessity* to engage in politics on a grand scale.

"By denying this vitally important aspect of Nietzsche," Sokel continues, "Walter Kaufmann has given us an antiseptic image of him which cannot remain credible for long."[23] The attentive reader of Kaufmann will puzzle at the truth of this specific charge.

On page 194 of *Nietzsche*, while writing on *The Dawn*, Kaufmann deals expressly with the question "whether Nietzsche's conception of power has not been whitewashed. We should face the question whether Nietzsche did not, after all, have in mind political might. It so happens that *The Dawn* is quite unequivocal on this point." The fact that it is unequivocal is owed to Nietzsche's ranking expressions of the will to power on a quantitative scale. Yes, "The 'history of culture' is to be explained in terms of man's will to overwhelm, outdo, excel, and overpower his neighbor. The barbarian does it by torturing his neighbor." But this is a low degree of the striving for excellence, inferior even to the striving to inspire admiration in others, and very much inferior to that exercise in *self*-torture that produces the *saint*.

If this rank-order seems all too pat, Kaufmann has the intellectual will to advance Nietzsche's scandalous conjecture that "an ascetic's torture of his beloved neighbor" might function "as a new form of self-torture," with the Christian God as the overlord of such behavior. This surmise discredits, to say the least, the alleged top position of the saint. But it also discredits the association of a genuine exercise of will to power with political power, another form of the will to torture one's neighbor, to Nietzsche's mind "essentially a form of barbarism." And in this discussion we have Nietzsche's thought that will serve Kaufmann throughout: "Only *the degree of reason* in strength [*der Grad der Vernunft in der Kraft*] is decisive" (emphasis added) (N 197).

Sokel's claim that Kaufmann ignores Nietzsche's political passion also neglects section 7 of Kaufmann's book: this is the chapter titled "Nietzsche's Repudiation of Christ," which deals with "Nietzsche's alleged glorification of war." Here, Kaufmann means to erect a barrier against the criticism he anticipated—a criticism summed up, too, in a phrase of Henning Ottmann we have heard: "To counteract the demonization of Nietzsche, Kaufmann harmonized and depoliticized his philosophy to the point where the Übermensch was nothing more than the moral ideal of individual self-overcoming."[24] The implication is that the Übermensch would be . . . what?

In chapter 1, I alluded to the Nazi abuse of the figure, whom Nietzsche indeed somewhat ironically aligns with Cesare Borgia, notorious for freewheeling violence, cunning, and deceit and whose disturbing presence Conor Cruse O'Brien has noted. I say "ironic," even now when I will invoke a tone more sinister. Did a fact about Borgia especially attract Nietzsche—who allegedly suffered from syphilis—namely, that upon Borgia's death, when his killers abused his corpse, he was allegedly stripped of a leather mask covering parts of his face *disfigured by syphilis*? The violence beyond good and evil that marks Borgia's reputation might have stimulated Nazi propagandists to evolve him, as a model of the Übermensch, into the type of the uniformed, amoral, truncheon-swinging thug. On the other hand, what then would be the less repellent view of the Übermensch, whom Kaufmann's critics imagine in indignant repudiation of Kaufmann's concept of the perfectly "stylized," self-transfigured man? If, citing Zarathustra, they were to say *no one* yet—he cannot be imagined, he is merely a *figure* for a virtual, a necessary metamorphosis—they would not be wrong. But in order to indict Kaufmann, the thrust of his critics has been to *politicize* this figure, to lend him an empirical identity—again, as something from the Nazi playbook. Now, to take up this gage, in agreeing to *politicize* him—which is wrong—to give him authority over others, as a supreme legislator, how might he be imagined within the annals of our historical experience? As a sort of supreme commander, on the model of . . . whom? Dwight D. Eisenhower with a warrior-artist's panache? The Übermensch is *not* a political figure. Following Kaufmann,

> [One] may generalize that in most of his notorious remarks about "war," notably including the chapter "On War and Warriors" in *Zarathustra*, the word is used metaphorically. It should be noted that this chapter is immediately followed by Nietzsche's attack on the State as "The New Idol" and that Nietzsche is plainly not speaking of soldiers:
>
>> And if you cannot be saints of knowledge, at least be its warriors. They are the companions and forerunners of such sainthood. I see many soldiers: would that I saw many [such] warriors! "Uniform" one calls what they wear: would that what it conceals were not uniform! You should have eyes that always seek an enemy—*your* enemy. . . . You should seek your enemy and you should wage your war—for your thoughts. And if your thought be vanquished, your honesty should still find cause for triumph in that. You should love peace as a means to new wars—and the short peace more than the long. . . . Let your work be a struggle, let your peace be a victory.
>
> [Kaufmann writes:] "You should love peace as a means to new wars—and the short peace more than the long," has often been cited out of context to show that Nietzsche was a fascist. Nietzsche, however, is surely not speaking of "war" in the literal sense any more than he is speaking of soldiers. . . .
>
> To be sure, there are passages in which Nietzsche speaks of wars to come, meaning literally wars, and—with *amor fati*—seems glad of it; but even then he points out that men "throw themselves with delight into the new danger of *death* because they think that in the sacrifice for the fatherland they have at long last that long sought permission—the permission *to dodge their goal*: war is for them a detour to suicide, but a detour with a good conscience" [*Die Fröhliche Wissenschaft* (The Gay Science) 338].
>
> In that respect, war is classed with the altruism of the weak who find in it an escape from their hard task of self-perfection. In the end, Nietzsche—believing that "the time for small politics is gone," that "the next century will bring the fight for the dominion of the earth—the *coercion* to great

politics"—hopes that the vast wars to come will bring to an end nationalism and "the comedy" of the existence of many states: he envisages "such
an increase of the menace of Russia" that Europe will be forced, in self-
defense, to become "One Europe" [*Die Fröhliche Wissenschaft* (The Gay
Science) 362; *Jenseits von Gut und Böse* (Beyond Good and Evil) 208]. "The
era of national wars" itself is but an *"entr' acte"*—a necessary evil, a period
that "may indeed help such an art as Wagner's to a sudden glory, without
thereby guaranteeing it a *future*"; in fact, "the Germans themselves have no
future" (*Nietzsche contra Wagner* IV). (N 386–88)

At the end of his book, in the epilogue, Kaufmann sums up his view on
Nietzsche's politics.

> Nietzsche is perhaps best known as the prophet of great wars and power
> politics and as an opponent of political liberalism and democracy. That is
> the idol of the "tough Nietzscheans" and the whipping boy of many a critic.
> The "tender Nietzscheans," on the other hand, insist—quite rightly—that
> Nietzsche scorned totalitarianism, denounced the State as "The New Idol"
> (*Also Sprach Zarathustra* I 11), and was himself a kindly and charitable
> person; but some of them infer falsely that he must therefore have been a
> liberal and a democrat, or a socialist. We have tried to show that Nietzsche
> opposed both the idolatry of the State and political liberalism because he
> was basically *"antipolitical"* (*Ecce Homo* 1: 3) and, moreover, loathed the
> very idea of belonging to any "party" whatever. (N 412)[25]

Admittedly, these disclaimers do not take care of the question once and for
all. Certainly, going back to O'Brien's diatribe, there are elements in Nietzsche
elided by Kaufmann that made him fair game for a Nazi appropriation. Derrida reminds us that "the only politics that really elevated him as one of its
highest official banners was Nazi." At the same time, Derrida adds, it does
not follow that "this 'Nietzschean' politics is the only one possible, nor that it
corresponds to the best reading of this heritage.... But since, in the still open
contours of an epoch, the only politics called 'Nietzschean' were Nazi, this is
necessarily significant and must be questioned as to its entire significance."[26]

There is some trouble with this approach, as Derrida points out, since the
Nazi perspective on Nietzsche is itself unclear. I will summarize his view via
Ernst Behler's sharp formulation of it: "We can't dismiss the question whether
Nietzsche's 'large-scale politics' already lie behind us or are 'just now coming
toward us,' that is, '*on the other side* of an upheaval of which National Socialism

and Fascism were only episodes.'"[27] Derrida's contribution, which stresses the uncertainty of whatever significance Nietzsche's "great politics" might have, is not superior to Kaufmann's discussion, nor does it amount to an effective criticism of it. Kaufmann describes Nietzsche's "great politics" as a war for the truth of his ideas—which include a marked repudiation of *nationalist* petty politics, in the service of a European *unity*, and, in the long view, a thorough-going revaluation of values, not obviously to be obtained by blood and iron, though certainly in line with Bismarck's animosity toward Russia.

In the decades following the criticisms of Stern and Sokel, the reaction to Kaufmann's intellectual hegemony was to become less temperate, more impatient, and increasingly less considerate of Kaufmann's text. The Nietzsche scholar Paul Bishop, it is true, acknowledges Kaufmann's work as a "revolution" but remarks, in 2013, in an excessively anodyne way, that "although Kaufmann has fallen out of favor in recent years, this study, along with the study titled *Nietzsche, Heidegger, and Buber* (1980), ... are by no means without their value as introductory guides."[28] The meekness of his recommendation appears to be dictated by editorial prudence—he is publishing a "Companion" to Nietzsche studies—in an academic climate otherwise marked by the drastic criticism of philosophers like Michael Tanner and Robert Pippin. The tone reaches a *nec plus ultra* of disdain in a casual thrust by Brian Leiter, a very visible scholar. Asked on his web blog by a young student about how to begin to read Nietzsche, Leiter declares: "Kaufmann's old *Nietzsche: Philosopher, Psychologist, Antichrist* is extremely unreliable, and should be avoided."[29] Instead, the student is instructed to get a good grasp of Nietzsche by reading selected passages from *Beyond Good and Evil* with Leiter's own chapters at his side for depth and serious edification, Kaufmann being merely "superficially philosophical." Leiter proffers this judgment without a grain of evidence, assuming it to be prima facie inducible from his own abundant writings on Nietzsche.[30] Are contemporary Anglophone philosophers superior readers (as indeed Leiter would have it) by virtue of their philosophical *training*—one that bypassed Kaufmann—by the accumulation of "techniques and categories" from disciplinary philosophy?[31] The jury is out.

In his introduction to a 2012 Cambridge volume *Introductions to Nietzsche*, which he edited, Robert Pippin begins by writing eloquently of Kaufmann's work:

After the Second World War, all things German were under suspicion of some sort of intellectual complicity with Nazism. Many thinkers like Hegel, Nietzsche, and Heidegger . . . were listed as enemies of "the open society," and Germany itself was thought to be haunted by a dark, romantic, irrationalist, counter-Enlightenment specter. In the case of Nietzsche, this rehabilitation or decontamination in Anglophone philosophy in essence began in 1950 with the publication of Walter Kaufmann's *Nietzsche: Philosopher, Psychologist, Antichrist*. Kaufmann occupied a position of great academic importance in America (he was a philosophy professor at Princeton) and was a noted translator and critic as well. His book argued in detail against characterizations of Nietzsche as anti-Semitic, as a totalitarian thinker, or as a German nationalist, and he tried to show that Nietzsche was not just an avant-gardist of importance to the literary and artistic worlds, but that he was a challenging, even a great, original philosopher in his own right.

Kaufmann's work, continues Pippin, laid the foundation for the subsequent view in Anglophone scholarship "that Nietzsche, whatever else he was doing in his books, was making philosophical claims and devising ways to defend them."[32] It is therefore all the more disconcerting to read Pippin's subsequent lapse into the most extreme bipolar view of Kaufmann. In an essay on Alexander Nehamas's *Nietzsche: Life as Literature*—the thesis that, following Nietzsche, an exemplary life be lived *as* literature—Pippin once again reviewed the modern history of Nietzsche scholarship in America. "When Alexander Nehamas's path-breaking, elegantly conceived and executed book . . . first appeared in 1985, the reception of Nietzsche in the Anglo-American philosophical community was still in its initial, hesitant stages, even after the relative success of Walter Kaufmann's much earlier, 1950 book *Nietzsche: Philosopher, Psychologist, Antichrist*, and its postwar 'decontamination' of Nietzsche after his appropriation by the Nazis."[33] This is consistent with Pippin's account in 2012, but here he feels it necessary to add the comment: "The book was *such* a sanitizing that it now [in 2014] seems bowdlerizing; Nietzsche de-fanged."[34] "Bowdlerizing," for anyone who might value a refresher course in intellectual cheating, means "removing or altering those parts of a text considered offensive, vulgar, or otherwise unseemly." Using this word to define Kaufmann's procedure is egregious, for it would have to follow that Kaufmann's project, as Pippin defined it—"to argue in detail against characterizations of Nietzsche as anti-Semitic, as a totalitarian thinker, or as a German nationalist, and . . . to show that . . . he was a challenging, even a great, original philosopher in his own right"—was fraudulent.

With her acclaimed study *American Nietzsche*, the historian Jennifer Ratner-Rosenhagen entered the fray.[35] Her voluminous, industrious intellectual history of an "icon" (Nietzsche) treats his "ideas" as they were received in America from Emerson to Hugh Hefner. A lengthy chapter deals with Kaufmann and the reception of his *Nietzsche* in the American intellectual context of around 1950; it is full of arresting information and elegant commentary. The piece concludes with an account of what, in Ratner-Rosenhagen's view, are the gravest internal shortcomings of Kaufmann's book. Unfortunately, these criticisms are the simplest common denominator of those we have so far encountered.

The first is one of the endlessly repeated pieces of the Kaufmann myth. Ratner-Rosenhagen writes, "[Kaufmann's] image of Nietzsche as a Goethean figure struggling for authentic selfhood fails to capture the philosopher's repeated emphasis on the warring instincts in, not the unified mastery of, the self" (261). On page 244 of Kaufmann's *Nietzsche*, however (p. 213 in the first edition), we read: "Another consequence of Nietzsche's emphasis on the negative and on the fate of the individual may be seen in the tremendous importance he attached to suffering and cruelty—the negative aspect of self-overcoming." Readers may recall from the previous chapter the tip of the iceberg of Kaufmann's extensive commentary on the topic of aggression and violence in the epigram: "The will to power is, as it were, *always at war with itself. . . .* All that exists strives to transcend itself and is thus engaged in the fight against itself (emphasis added)" (N 242, p. 211 in the first edition). References to the eristic character of this effort at "authentic selfhood" are found everywhere throughout his study. Perhaps Ratner-Rosenhagen means by "warring instincts" instincts aimed *exclusively* at killing other people. Does she really believe that Kaufmann is deaf to this charge? Earlier in this chapter we quoted him at length.

> One may generalize that in most of his notorious remarks about "war," notably including the chapter "On War and Warriors" in *Zarathustra*, the word is used metaphorically. It should be noted that this chapter is immediately followed by Nietzsche's attack on the State as "The New Idol" and that Nietzsche is plainly not speaking of soldiers.

>> And if you cannot be saints of knowledge, at least be its warriors. They are the companions and forerunners of such sainthood. I see many soldiers: would that I saw many [such] warriors! "Uniform" one calls what they wear: would that what it conceals were not uniform! You should have eyes that always seek an enemy—*your* enemy. . . . You should seek your enemy and you should wage your war—for your thoughts. (N 386)

Kaufmann sums up the matter: "The will to power is the backbone of Nietzsche's philosophy—but one should not accept Santayana's picture of Nietzsche: 'the meaning he chiefly intended [was one of] ... wealth and military power.'" We can recall Nietzsche's great aphorism from *The Gay Science*. It reads in part:

> For one thing is needful: that a human being attain his satisfaction with himself. ... Whoever is dissatisfied with himself is always ready to revenge himself therefor; we others will be his victims ... [*Die Fröhliche Wissenschaft* (The Gay Science) 290].

It is not that Kaufmann has failed to note Nietzsche's sensitivity to cruelty and violence. He holds this aphorism to be a "faithful reflection of *much* of Nietzsche's thought" (emphasis added) (N 421, p. 367 in the first edition). And the rest? In Ratner-Rosenhagen's view, Kaufmann has "failed" by dint of not "capturing" the rest (261). But Kaufmann has said he will not represent the rest in all its fullness because it is *not* a faithful reflection of Nietzsche's core thought. The power, not the failure, of Kaufmann's interpretation lies in this decision.

Ratner-Rosenhagen lists several other charges. The second reads, "By severing his work from the question of influence, Kaufmann's study presents a picture of Nietzsche as timeless, hence impervious to historicization" (261). It is hard to know what these words mean. Kaufmann's "failure" to consider the question of influence appears to mean that he presents Nietzsche as a thinker who was not influenced and influenced no one else. This charge does not signify. Nietzsche, in Kaufmann's book, is forever presented in light of his sources, his works shown to be the product of spirited engagement with the Bible, Plato, Spinoza (1632–77); the French epigrammatists, namely, La Rochefoucauld (1613–80) and Vauvenargues (1715–47); Leibniz (1646–1716); Rousseau (1712–78); Goethe (1749–1832); Hegel (1770–1831); Schelling (1775–1854); Stendhal (1783–1842); Schopenhauer (1788–1860); August Comte (1798–1857); Kierkegaard (1813–55), to name a few; and such contemporaries as Charles Darwin (1809–82); David Strauss (1808–74); Richard Wagner (1813–83); Ernest Renan (1823–92), and so on. It is true that the first edition of his book Kaufmann does not do the obvious thing and list Nietzsche's well-known influence on writers who read him. At the close of the fourth edition, however, he signals this issue concisely, in full awareness that he cannot add hundreds more pages to his already big book, noting:

In the present book Nietzsche's philosophy has been stressed far more than his literary genius or that dimension of his work which inspired many of the greatest writers of the twentieth century: Thomas Mann no less than Hesse; Rilke as well as Gottfried Benn; André Malraux and André Gide; Jean-Paul Sartre and Albert Camus; George Bernard Shaw, W. B. Yeats, and Eugene O'Neill. With Nietzsche's immense influence on Rilke and Sartre I have dealt elsewhere; Thomas Mann, Benn, Gide, Camus, and Shaw have written essays on Nietzsche (for these seven men see the Bibliography); Gide also speaks of Nietzsche again and again in his *Journals*; Malraux drew on Nietzsche's life in *La Lutte avec l'ange* and Mann in *Doktor Faustus*; and O'Neill paid tribute to Nietzsche when accepting the Nobel Prize and often stressed his great debt to him. (N 419)

Is Kaufmann therefore "impervious to historicization"? This presumably means that on reading *Nietzsche* we are rendered incapable, as in the commonplace, of "situating" Nietzsche in "a historical context." In addition to the context defined by this backward and thereafter forward of influence, Kaufmann's opening fifty-page chapter (thirty-odd closer-printed pages in the first edition) is titled "Nietzsche's Life as Background of His Thought." I daresay that the parentheses about Nietzsche's life do allow us to situate him in a historical context. We must grant Ratner-Rosenhagen credit for pointing out that Kaufmann does not discuss in detail the political, cultural, and economic life of Germany, Switzerland, and Italy during all the years of Nietzsche's life (1844–1900) nor readers' reception of Nietzsche during this period, but the answer to the second part of this charge is that up until about 1888 he went essentially unnoticed.

There are, I hasten to add, exceptions to this point: *The Birth of Tragedy* was well received and richly discussed in Vienna, for one, shortly after its appearance and then attacked viciously by Wilamowitz—a polemic that Nietzsche took in stride. (We read about that exchange in Kaufmann's translation of *The Birth of Tragedy*).[36] Jewish Viennese writers were especially avid readers of Nietzsche, seeing in him a spur toward the constitution of an identity independent of social prejudice and hence amounting to a precedent for Kaufmann's distinctive way of understanding him.[37] The important cultural historian and philosopher Wilhelm Dilthey took notice of Nietzsche[38]—but this story of Nietzsche's reception is the subject of another book. Still, nothing in Kaufmann's presentation of his subject stands in the way of a monograph on this aspect of his "historicization"; in fact, the "influence and reception of

Friedrich Nietzsche" has been sketched out creatively by the author of the Wikipedia piece of this name (261). As for Nietzsche's receptiveness to the thought of his time, Brian Leiter recently asserted in the *Times Literary Supplement* that "Anglophone Nietzsche studies have improved dramatically in the past two decades in terms of historical scholarship," especially in respect of historical scholarship, to which Leiter has been himself a major contributor, "devoted to showing how ignorance of the intellectual history of nineteenth-century Germany, in particular the rise of German materialism, has distorted readings of Nietzsche."[39] Leiter might well have cited an earlier, pioneering study of Nietzsche's "real" politics by Peter Bergmann.

Bergmann's book is titled *Nietzsche, "the Last Antipolitical German"*; the quote is meant as a scandal to be refuted. Accordingly, it criticizes Kaufmann's *selective* account of "Nietzsche's involvement in the issues of his time"—we hear only of his quarrel with Wagner and his opposition to German imperialism and much anti-Semitism.[40] As a result we see "only those aspects of Nietzsche's political life which appeal to the apologist's own values and politics."[41] How would Bergmann dodge the boomerang of this charge of self-interested scholarship? His answer is that like him one must insist on grasping "Nietzsche's politics *as a whole*," which, in his study, concludes with Nietzsche's "furious polemic against 'the four great democrats'—Socrates, Christ, Luther, and Rousseau."[42] I'll add that Christian Emden's recent *Friedrich Nietzsche and the Politics of History* scrutinizes in even greater detail the link between history and politics in Nietzsche's writings, with differentiated ethical results.[43] As a result, to return to Ratner-Rosenhagen, I fail to see how Kaufmann's account of Nietzsche's thought is "impervious"—read: "proof against" such scholarship, which modifies or complements (but does not annihilate) Kaufmann's own conclusions (261).

Ratner-Rosenhagen's study of Nietzsche's reception in America is, on the whole, learned and incisive, but on this point—Kaufmann's Nietzsche's imperviousness to historicization—her criticism seems so nugatory that we must try to understand it better. Perhaps it is not Nietzsche but rather Kaufmann's "picture" of Nietzsche—in a word, Kaufmann's *book*—that actively resists being "historicized" (261). But do books about philosophers generally say why its "picture," in the act of being drawn, will connect, on publication, with the depths of its readership, projected in seismographic detail? One is again baffled and turns to Ratner-Rosenhagen's final objection in the hope of understanding the preceding ones better. Here one learns that Kaufmann fails by "casting Nietzsche as an apolitical thinker indifferent to the manifestations of will to power outside the self . . . [with the result that] *Kaufmann's*

interpretation makes the untenable claim that an individual's power has no conse-
quences for others" (emphasis added) (261). Readers of *Nietzsche* are invited to
brood over this absurdity at their leisure.

The whip-smart Duncan Large—in his *Nietzsche and Proust,* a first-
rate comparative study published in 2001—amazes us with the upsurge of
Nietzsche studies he has noted:

> the growth of interest in Nietzsche and the proliferation of perspectives on
> his work (comparative and otherwise) have been phenomenal. The second
> edition of Reichert and Schlechta's *International Nietzsche Bibliography* ...
> published in 1968, lists a total of 4,539 items; for the period 1968–92, Hilliard
> and Nitschke's bibliographies just of Nietzsche scholarship in English list
> a further 1,912 items.[44]

One can only begin to imagine the scope of a current bibliography, seventeen years later. I cite these statistics to dramatize the fact that in a great (the
greatest?) number of the items published in the time between Kaufmann and
Large, Kaufmann's *Nietzsche*—as even in Large's own study—continues to be
cited. Kaufmann's name appears in one index after another just under "Kant"
and often with a greater number of page references. The legacy of *Nietzsche*
will continue to occupy us, although the range of relevant contributions is no
longer surveyable: here I must be very selective, aiming at what I take to be
the most interesting claims against Kaufmann.

Kaufmann's main understanding of the *will to power* and the *eternal recur-*
rence of the same has provoked a great deal of productive criticism. On behalf
of Kaufmann's achievement, Hays Steilberg notes that "Kaufmann ... concentrated strongly on the question of what forms of human existence are to
be admired, to be 'valued'" then proceeds critically: "Admittedly, this is one
of the principal ideas in Nietzsche's thought, but Kaufmann's examination of
Nietzschean perspectivism, in contrast, pales next to his treatment of power
philosophy and *Entlarvungspsychologie* (the psychology of unmasking)."[45]
Steilberg then rounds out his critique by addressing the crucial concept of
"nihilism, the necessity of which for Nietzsche Kaufmann neglects to include
in his system."[46] This objection, however, is hardly true, witness Kaufmann:

> To escape nihilism—which seems involved both in asserting the existence
> of God and thus robbing *this* world of ultimate significance, and also in
> denying God and thus robbing *everything* of meaning and value—that is
> Nietzsche's greatest and most persistent problem. (N 101)

Again:

Nietzsche attacked the value problem that stares our generation in the face—the dilemma that haunts modern man and threatens our civilization:
> The end of the *moral* interpretation of the world, which no longer has any *sanction* after it has tried to escape into some beyond, leads to nihilism. "Everything lacks meaning." . . . Since Copernicus man has been rolling from the center toward "x." . . . What does nihilism mean? *That the highest values devaluate themselves.* The goal is lacking; the answer is lacking to our "Why?" [*Der Wille zur Macht* (The Will to Power) 1–2].

Nietzsche's basic problem is whether a new sanction can be found in this world for our values. (N 122)

It is clear that Nietzsche's concern with nihilism is being addressed here—but in Kaufmann's preferred perspective: namely, as a crisis in values. The charge that a less elaborated treatment of nihilism faults Kaufmann's work appears to stem from Danto's *Nietzsche*, a work with which, as we have seen, Kaufmann took strenuous and justified issue.

On reflection, can one seriously claim, in this instance, that Kaufmann's study, with its persistent focus on the devaluation of moral values, makes no contribution to the topic of nihilism? The link between nihilism and moral exhaustion is patent, as above, and so the question informing this entire chapter continues to linger: where did Kaufmann *go grievously wrong, fail to read* the Nietzsche that he *so confidently* cited? Going wrong by not citing other pieces in Nietzsche that would have tilted his perspective by degrees is another matter. I cannot once again see his principle of selection as "bowdlerizing" (Pippin) or "whitewashing" Nietzsche (Steilberg) in light of what Kaufmann set out to do: legitimize Nietzsche as an object worthy of philosophical study in an established tradition of philosophical reflection.[47]

Ofelia Schutte is one of the many scholars who have criticized Kaufmann's account of self-overcoming in Nietzsche and one of the few who have done so in a truly productive way. In *Beyond Nihilism: Nietzsche without Masks*, Schutte asks what it would mean to overcome the shape or form of the self *perpetually*?[48] The self, as self, has its boundaries. It is "a *household* of the soul."[49] Schutte cites Zarathustra, for whom all of existence is a process of will to power engaged in self-overcoming, and comments:

> In the process of intensification of life, the boundaries of the self are not only dissolved but lose their authoritative and controlling function over

the organism. . . . [This process brings about an] intensification of life by which all divisive (even if conserving) boundaries on life are destroyed or transcended. Self-overcoming involves the overcoming of the Apollonian principle of individuation and drive to permanence in favor of the greater reality of the Dionysian flow of existence in which the boundaries between subject and object, time and eternity disappear.[50]

When *generally* applied to Nietzsche's treatment of the self—and Kaufmann's understanding of this topic—Schutte's account calls for further discrimination. In another book, I have set down a sort of synopsis of the problem, meaning to echo and sustain Nietzsche's views—views consonant with Kaufmann's while complicating the matter in the direction of Schutte's.[51] For Nietzsche, the strong self is one thing—not at once itself and something else. But like the biological cell, it is not strictly speaking "a separate entity." Here I cite the biologist Lewis Thomas: "The marks of identity, distinguishing self from non-self, have long since been blurred." Nonetheless, the cell is informed by "mechanisms for preserving individuality," for "the discrimination between self and non-self," which are able to generate "precise unequivocal directions about . . . how to establish that one is, beyond argument, one's self."[52] In Nietzsche's formulation, the self "desires to 'preserve' itself only indirectly" because it is not a separate entity but a relation of self-surpassing.[53] Yet it keeps "a fundamental certainty about itself," without which, indeed, no outrage to itself could be resisted.[54]

Schutte's account of the dissolution of the self under the pressure of perpetually surpassing itself dovetails with Pippin's concern. In his introduction to a new translation of *Thus Spoke Zarathustra*, he asks:

> How could this aspiration towards something believed to be higher or more worthy than what one is or has now *be directed*, if all the old language of external or objective forms of normative authority is now impossible? On what grounds can one say that a desire to cultivate a different sort of self, to overcome oneself, is really in the service of a "higher" self? Higher in what sense?[55]

Does Nietzsche, then, after all, dispossess the self of all distinctive shape—or rather, does the matter remains undecided? There is a substantialist drift to Nietzsche's thinking on the self: the self, deep down, is its granite-like fate, as Nietzsche once has it: "At the bottom of us, really 'deep down,' there is . . . some granite of spiritual *fatum*."[56] Or is the self, rather, an ineffable striving, as in his most telling description: "No subject 'atoms.' . . . No 'substance,' rather something that in itself strives after greater strength, and that wants to preserve itself only indirectly (it wants to *surpass* itself—)"?[57] Kaufmann holds both views without sufficiently marking their tension—that is true. It will be the task of his postmodern commentators to repair the fault—writers who, under the sway of neostructuralist theory, are especially alert to *difference.*

An important critic, Bernard Reginster, whose objections we encountered earlier, also criticizes Kaufmann's formulation of self-overcoming, referring to his "blandly moralistic interpretation of self-overcoming in terms of the restraint of unbridled passion."[58] I think this criticism is worth taking up in detail, not only for the importance of its subject matter but as an indication that, to my mind, there is, like this one, scarcely a critique of Kaufmann's book that entirely hits the mark.

Reginster's objection invites a variety of responses. It is true that Kaufmann stresses the factor of self-restraint in the action of self-overcoming and stresses the *rational* control of inclination (*Neigung,* also: drive, affection). But in doing so he intends to define a "generic" essence of morality—one that would include Kant's categorical imperative "as well as, say, the Ten Commandments, . . . and the element of self-overcoming is no less essential to the utilitarian position. Self-overcoming may thus be considered the common essence of all moral codes from 'totem and taboo' to the ethics of the Buddha" (N 213). In this, Kaufmann is following Nietzsche, who, in *The Will to Power,* speaks of the "moralist's madness that demands, instead of the restraining of the passions, their extirpation (*Der Wille zur Macht* 383; cf. *Der Antichrist* 45)" (N 223). So, if Kaufmann has put the matter blandly, it is only for the moment, and on Nietzsche's authority, maintaining the generality of a discussion that intends to include Nietzsche, as well, in a family of moral philosophers.

Secondly, Kaufmann's talk of "reason" (*Vernunft*) and "inclination, drive, affection" (*Neigung*) is dictated by the philosophical canon of German aesthetic idealism that runs in his veins and is hardly a source of shame—Schiller's essay *Anmut und Würde* (Grace and dignity), in particular, speaks of a sought-after harmony of "Vernunft und Sinnlichkeit, Pflicht und Neigung" (reason and sensuousness, duty and inclination). As early as the "Preface to the First Edition (1950)," Kaufmann outlined a perspective on Nietzsche as a thinker concerned "to develop a new picture of human dignity" (N xiv).

Finally, and this is my most telling point: in the pages that Reginster criticizes, Kaufmann is bent on developing *Nietzsche's* own argument—again, by distinguishing a rationale of the control of passion from a rationale of its "extirpation." Hence, he stresses the aspect of control—not really a "bland" insistence when you consider the contrast. "We should ask," notes Kaufmann, "how Nietzsche himself would picture the 'overcoming' of the impulses: whether he meant that they should be extirpated, abnegated, controlled—or whether he had in mind yet another way of mastering them" (N 216). That "other way" will be via their *sublimation*. Note that grouping a discipline of control with extirpation and abnegation could appear to diminish its value and cogency: Kaufmann's narrative is soon captivated by the *sublime* newness of this other category. And so the discipline of control is promptly reinvigorated—indeed, performatively sublimated—for in his summary argument, Kaufmann writes: "This contrast of the abnegation, repudiation, and extirpation of the passions on the one side, and *their control and sublimation* on the other, is one of the most important points in Nietzsche's entire philosophy" (emphasis added) (N 233).[59]

Brian Leiter has argued productively against Nietzsche's asserted capacity for self-creation by underscoring Nietzsche's view of the *fated* character of the self. In this way the self is impervious to its alleged radical sublimation into any being it was not fated to be. In contrast with Kaufmann, Leiter denies that Nietzsche sponsored an unproblematic possibility of self-stylization in even the higher type. Here is a piece of Leiter's evidence:

> One might worry . . . that Nietzsche's comment about "Accepting oneself as if fated" (*Ecce Homo*, "Why I am so Wise," VI) suggests that he does not really believe in fatalism; hence, the "as if." Here Kaufmann's rendering is problematic (and probably reflects his own discomfort with finding Nietzsche to be a fatalist): for Nietzsche says simply "wie," not "as if." Thus, the phrase might have been rendered, more aptly, as "accepting oneself as fated"—which, on Nietzsche's view, one really is.[60]

Leiter's objection could be sustained by a crucial passage from *Beyond Good and Evil*, part of which we have heard:

> at the bottom of us, really "deep down," there is, of course, something unteachable, some granite of spiritual *fatum*, of predetermined decision and answer to predetermined selected questions. Whenever a cardinal problem is at stake, there speaks an unchangeable "this is I"; about man and woman, for example, a thinker cannot relearn but only finish learning—only discover ultimately how this is "settled in him." At times we find certain solutions of problems that inspire strong faith in us; some call them henceforth

their "convictions." Later—we see them only as steps to self-knowledge, signposts to the problem we *are*—rather, to the great stupidity we are, to our spiritual *fatum*, to what is unteachable very "deep down."[61]

Again, Nietzsche's *The Antichrist* begins with these very lines:

Let us face ourselves. We are Hyperboreans; we know very well how far off we live. "Neither by land nor by sea will you find the way to the Hyperboreans"—Pindar already knew this about us. Beyond the north, ice, and death—our life, our happiness. We have discovered happiness, we know the way, we have found the exit out of the labyrinth of thousands of years. Who *else* has found it? Modern man perhaps? "I have got lost; I am everything that has got lost," sighs modern man. *This* modernity was our sickness: lazy peace, cowardly compromise, the whole virtuous uncleanliness of the modern Yes and No. . . . Rather live in the ice than among modern virtues and other south winds! We were intrepid enough, we spared neither ourselves nor others; but for a long time we did not know where to turn with our intrepidity. We became gloomy, we were called fatalists. Our *fatum*—the abundance, tension, the damming of strength. We thirsted for lightning and deeds and were most remote from the happiness of the weakling, "resignation." In our atmosphere was a thunderstorm; the nature we are became dark—*for we saw no way*. Formula for our happiness: a Yes, a No, a straight line, a goal [*Der Antichrist* 1].[62]

The task for scholars fundamentally convinced by Kaufmann is how to refine his insistence on an uncontainable will to power that operates within a striving, desiderative self. The question is answered most creatively, I think, by Henry Staten, in an essay titled "Toward a Will to Power Sociology." Here, to pay tribute to good ecology, is a good summary by Staten's editor, Gudrun von Tevenar:

Staying within the theme of will to power, Henry Staten takes issue with the view, most forcefully expressed by [Brian] Leiter, that consciousness is merely a passive observer of the internal conflicts and competitions amongst drives where will to power exemplifies itself in that the strongest drive always wins. Yet if that is indeed the case, if consciousness is really merely epiphenomenal, then what precisely is the point of any conscious striving to effect change such as Nietzsche is engaged in when he urges us to grow, to overcome, to change? Staten proposes a scheme whereby the relation between thought and drives, i.e. between consciousness and unconsciousness, is credited as open to the determinations and historical sedimentations of cultural and sociological forms. And because thought is internally structured by cultural and sociological forms, it has a certain independence from drives, which Staten describes as "semi-autonomy." Thought can thus be taken as constitutive of a distinctive kind of causality.[63]

We have often cited Goethe as Nietzsche's prime educator in Kaufmann's view, a stress that will appear again and again in Kaufmann's late writings. It is true that Kaufmann's extraordinary attachment to this figure can lead to hyperbole. Kaufmann typically writes: "Goethe . . . served Nietzsche as the model of that paganism which he opposed to Christianity; here was the 'new barbarian'—the overman [Übermensch] with the 'Dionysian faith'" (N 378). In *Beyond Nihilism*, Schutte sharply opposes the implication that Nietzsche, unlike Kaufmann, saw Goethe as a Übermensch. She is quite fierce in her criticism:

> Kaufmann concludes his brief exposition of the overman idea in the same confused manner, stating that the person who has become an overman "has overcome his animal nature, organized the chaos of his passions, sublimated his impulses, and given style to his character." As an example, Kaufmann refers to Nietzsche's praise of Goethe. But the quotation from Nietzsche describes Goethe as a free spirit. Kaufmann goes on to blend "free spirit" with "overman."[64]

It is again true, following Schutte, that the attempt to square the Übermensch, which is a symbolic idea, with persons who live or have lived, might be confuted in advance by *Zarathustra*: "Never yet has there been an overman. Naked I saw both the greatest and the smallest man. They are still all-too-similar to each other. Verily even the greatest I found all-too-human" (*Also Sprach Zarathustra* II 4).[65] In light of this passage, Zarathustra becomes, in Benno Wagner's precise formulation, only "the impersonation of a line of flight beyond the limits of the herd man," a limit idea, something to be *worked toward*—an ideal only.[66] Kaufmann's admittedly puzzling response to Zarathustra's statement is to say: "It matters little," since "the Übermensch cannot be dissociated from the conception of *Überwindung* (overcoming)." He quotes Nietzsche in support: "Man is something that should be overcome"; and continues: the man who has overcome himself has become a Übermensch (N 309–10).

In fact, this aporia runs through the best critical literature on the subject. You see something of this unavoidable paradox in Pippin's comment on Kaufmann's translation of a passage in *Thus Spoke Zarathustra*. Zarathustra is saying to his "guests, you strange ones":

> I wait for others . . .
>
> —for higher, stronger, more victorious, more cheerful ones, those who are built right-angled in body and soul: *laughing lions* must come!
>
> Oh my guests, you strange ones—have you not yet heard anything of my children? And that they are on their way to me?
>
> Speak to me of my gardens, of my blessed isles, *of my beautiful new species*—why don't you speak to me of that? (final emphasis added)[67]

Pippin writes: "Kaufmann in his translation deleted the word 'species' (*Art*), writing instead: 'Speak to me of my gardens, of my blessed isles, of my new beauty.' Nietzsche referred to the overman [Übermensch] as a new species, even while he insisted that the current human being cannot be 'leaped over' in the pursuit of the overman."[68]

Is the Übermensch then immanent in "the current human being" or only in a lost historical exemplar or in neither of the two? Schutte continues to argue forcefully for the radical separation of the noble type and the postulated Übermensch.

> There is a very strong line of demarcation in Nietzsche between the *Übermensch*, who has not yet existed, and the superior type of human being, which includes literary geniuses, military heroes, great philosophers, and other exceptional persons. The *radical* transformation of the self that is implied by the symbol can in no way be reduced to the personality structure of a superior or free-spirited type. . . . In Nietzsche's psychological sketches these human beings are called higher men and free spirits. They are not *Übermenschen*. . . . The problem is that Kaufmann's interpretation is based on a misleading fusion of three Nietzschean ideas: the higher man, the *Übermensch*, and the artist-free spirit. The latter is characterized by Nietzsche as a type of higher man, but it is certainly not his sole conception of what constitutes an exceptional human being. Kaufmann's confusion is most noticeable when he states that "Caesar came closer to Nietzsche's ideal" of the overman than Goethe. Here Kaufmann mixes together three different types. Goethe is an example of a free spirit, Caesar, of a military higher man, and neither of them, of the *Übermensch*.[69]

Kaufmann's presentation of the Übermensch envisions him/it as possessing concrete *qualities* of spirit. When he sees Nietzsche detecting these qualities in such great men as Socrates and Goethe—like "the omnipresence of sarcasm [*Bosheit*] and frolics," which for Kaufmann is proof of "self-overcoming"—he associates these figures with the Übermensch, quite as Nietzsche does. For, in the matter of progress toward a "better or stronger" mankind, Nietzsche writes:

> The European today is vastly inferior in value to the European of the Renaissance: further development is altogether *not* according to any necessity in the direction of elevation. . . . In another sense, success in individual cases is constantly encountered in the most widely different places and cultures: here we really do find *a higher type* that is, in relation to mankind as a whole, *a kind of Übermensch*. Such fortunate accidents of great success have always been possible and *will* perhaps always be possible [*Der Antichrist* 3, 4]. (emphases added) (N 312)

If Schutte, and other readers, find Kaufmann confusing on this point, it is because Nietzsche does not maintain the same conception of the Übermensch throughout, relying, as we see from the above, on degrees of approximation with real living types, "the higher type."

Despite his measured praise for Kaufmann's Nietzsche study, as described in chapter 1, Nehamas also has several concerns. In his Nietzsche book, he writes:

> Walter Kaufmann, in *Nietzsche: Philosopher, Psychologist, Antichrist . . .* (chapter 6) argues that the will to power represents an empirical generalization. According to Kaufmann, Nietzsche observed human behavior and saw that much of it can be explained if we assume that it is motivated by the quest for power. He then generalized the view to all human action and then to animal behavior. Eventually, he applied it to the universe as a whole. Kaufmann finds the psychological version of the view, at least in connection with human behavior, deeply illuminating, but he rejects outright the broader, cosmological, version (204–207).[70] However, Maudemarie Clark has shown that there are very serious problems even with the psychological version, if we consider it as an empirical hypothesis ("Nietzsche's Doctrines of the Will to Power," *Nietzsche-Studien*, 12 1983, 458–468). Her own view is that the will to power is a self-conscious "myth" (page 461).[71]

Readers interested in the linked question of whether Nietzsche's "thought" of eternal recurrence also is chiefly ethical or ontological in its consequences are encouraged to follow up the work especially of Maudmarie Clark—and of others who have addressed this matter with an adjacent interest in finding Kaufmann wrong.[72]

Nehamas also objects to Kaufmann's writing that Nietzsche "would like us to conform to neither [master nor slave morality] and become autonomous" (N 297). But Kaufmann gives no reason why Nietzsche would equate accepting a code of conduct with "conforming" to it in a sense that would preclude being autonomous. "On the contrary," continues Nehamas, "we have seen that Nietzsche is concerned to show that without codes and customs there can be no action whatsoever, let alone action that is noble and admirable. The serious question, therefore, concerns the particular code involved in each case."[73]

An answer to this objection is implied by the ideal case, which we have already encountered: "There is a sense," writes Kaufmann, "in which every great individual is an embodiment of new norms, an incarnate value-legislation, and a promise and challenge to posterity" (N 415). That is the sort of freedom that Kaufmann postulates.

I earlier mentioned Duncan Large's comparative study of Nietzsche and Proust (2001), and in this work too, Kaufmann makes his typical appearance: he is excoriated, *and* he is relied on for his exemplary formulation of difficult matters. The scolding begins early, with Large speaking of "Walter Kaufmann's rather disparaging comment in . . . his *Nietzsche: Philosopher, Psychologist, Antichrist* concerning precisely such comparative studies as this [Nietzsche and Proust]."[74] The comminatory tone recurs even in a brief account of Kaufmann's indisputably proper criticism—of which Large appears to approve—of Karl Schlechta's version of *The Will to Power*, in the course of which, as we recall, Kaufmann "managed to attack (as was his wont) every previous edition and translation."[75] We hear too of the "historical importance of [Arthur] Danto's book, [which] *like Kaufmann's before it*, was to establish conclusively that Nietzsche can and must be treated 'as philosopher,' although the success of both their enterprises depended on *the severely reductive domestication of the term 'philosopher' itself*" (emphasis added).[76] Shame on Duncan Large for tarring Kaufmann with the same brush—that unreflected cliché—he employed on Danto; the philosophical depth of their studies are incomparable, to Kaufmann's credit; and in attacking Danto, Large is only echoing Danto's complaint about Nietzsche, now in Large's own formulation:

Danto is quite unashamed in regretting the "total conceptual permissiveness" of Nietzsche's "piecemeal elaborations,"[77] and in wishing that

Nietzsche had lived beyond his own ill-conceived *Daybreak* to witness the new dawn of contemporary analytical philosophy in all its systematic splendor—when, had he known what was good for him, he might well have signed up for some of Prof. Danto's classes. Danto reaches his patronizing peak in arguing: "Because we know a good deal more philosophy today, I believe it is exceedingly useful to see his [Nietzsche's] analyses in terms of logical features which he was unable to make explicit, but toward which he was unmistakably groping. His language would have been less colorful had he known what he was trying to say." (26)[78]

We will find this impertinent trope of argument directed at Kaufmann in even more current literature, as in Brian Leiter's "Philosophy Blog," someone for whom Kaufmann's work is, predictably, altogether shallow, as we have heard.[79]

But the comminations above are only half of Large's story, and indeed less than half, and this story will stand in for much of the entire enterprise of Anglophone meta-ethicists this past half century who find it equally impossible, while complaining about Kaufmann, not to rely on his authority. Large, for one, will soon elaborate his argument *altogether "mindful" of Kaufmann's caveats* about such comparative studies of "Nietzsche and *X*" as Large's own, making certain that he, Large, will include "a reading of Nietzsche which attends to the eminently Proustian problematics of involuted temporality and involuntary memory, the experience of transcendence ("moments bienheureux"), and the status of 'essences'" (emphasis added).[80] Respect for Kaufmann's obiter dicta demands such seriousness.

The scolding mood disappears altogether when Large cites Kaufmann's formulations as exemplary:

> In the wake of the interpretations of Nietzsche given by writers such as Bertram and Ludovici, Oehler, Bäumler, and Rosenberg . . . it was indeed necessary to carry out some urgent repair-work on Nietzsche's reputation, to reclaim Nietzsche's merits, and the task with variously undertaken . . . in America by Kaufmann above all.[81]

Thereafter, Large quotes Kaufmann in discussing Nietzsche's break with Wagner:

> The battle with Wagner . . . should not be viewed merely as an instance of Nietzsche's "transcending"—and certainly not as proof of his incapacity for

any lasting human attachments. . . . Few philosophers have written more eloquently in praise of friendship than Nietzsche. (N 36)[82]

In launching his study, Kaufmann, as a Jewish émigré from Nazi Germany, and as a member of the US Army of Occupation in Germany, did not—like "Doctor Faustus," in Thomas Mann's novel of that name—make things easy for himself: "Mayhap to God it seemeth I sought the hard and laboured might and main."[83] He came to his study with ideological baggage, some of which a web reviewer calling himself "Goosta" (coding, perhaps, "Giusta": "real," "true," "authentic") has cleverly—provocatively—analyzed in a bizarre over-the-top rhetoric.[84] I shall be looking closely at his tirade, which at first struck me as engaging for its "geopolitical," better "georeligious" dimension.

For Goosta, Kaufmann's "sanitized, literalized, 'honest' Nietzsche" is the product of a geopolitical circumstance. ("Literalized" is presumably a misprint for "liberalized," which is Goosta's gist.) The geopolitical factor is interesting and relevant; the point about "liberalization," however, is not literally faithful to Kaufmann, who wrote: "We have tried to show that Nietzsche opposed both the idolatry of the State and political liberalism because he was basically '*antipolitical*' . . . [*Ecce Homo* 1: 3]) and, moreover, loathed the very idea of belonging to any 'party' whatever" (N 412).[85] Goosta continues: Kaufmann, as a liberal Jew writing at the end of the War, is proof against the more searching, darker question of what prompts and enables his salvaging of Nietzsche for the liberal sensibility. This is Goosta's central, provocative—and unfounded—claim. None of us has direct insight into Kaufmann's ideologically driven motives—conscious or unconscious— while composing his book, but it strikes me and others, like Ivan Soll, as more plausible to think of him as salvaging Nietzsche for a German tradition, that of the Bildungsbürger, whose politics, including that of its Jewish members, tended to be right of center.[86] Kaufmann's eye was not primarily on America but on the traditions of a lost Germany and, if on America, then only secondarily, as a place or time in which to shelter the memory of that loss. Goosta spells out the geopolitical implications of its composition as a

most profitable historical circumstance, [for Kaufmann] as a Jew in post-war American triumphalism. . . . America had just destroyed Germany, the backbone of Europe. End of story, no questions asked, for "who controls the past controls the future, and who controls the present controls the past" [George Orwell in *1984*].

Not so fast! Kaufmann knew that America (with the help of the Soviet Union, Britain, and France) had destroyed a certain pathological excrescence of German life but not an idea of the German mind. Yet, here is Goosta: With the end of the Second World War, Old Europe died: "There was only America left on the planet, the consummation of Liberalism. The war stood for the victory of tolerance, humanitarianism, peace and 'goodwill' over the forces of darkness, discrimination, violence, judgment, extremism." This may well have been true, but this is not the "right-of-center" politics of self-stylization that Kaufmann profiled in Nietzsche.

For Goosta, "Kaufmann rode that tidal wave of American, Liberal post-war exuberance. . . . All of Nietzsche's politically incorrect comments about Jews and race . . . greatly outnumber the ones accepted by liberals." Yet here I would refer to Peter Gay, the better historian: "[Nietzsche's] infrequent anti-Jewish remarks, normally surrounded by declarations of admiration for the Jews, could be stripped of this praise, so that they ['servile commentators'] could misdescribe Nietzsche's philo-Semitism as anti-Semitism."[87]

Goosta continues: These anti-Semitic comments "were explained away in the glibbest manner by Kaufmann. . . . Where Kaufmann could not explain away, he said nothing, as in the case of women, liberalism, America, letting the smothering post-war moralism that everyone scurried back under work its magic." To the first point, Peter Gay is again apposite: "What of Nietzsche's heartless, condescending observation, 'Everything about woman has a solution: it is called pregnancy'? Though such Nietzschean views leave an unpleasant aftertaste, most can be satisfactorily clarified by the context and the dominant style of thinking that pervades his thought."[88] This account fairly describes Kaufmann's interpretive aim. It is no secret—though it goes unmentioned by Kaufmann—that Nietzsche has other and more interesting things to say about women, who, in at least one instance, we read, might be Truth, and as such more than a riddle.[89] Aphorisms from *The Gay Science* also suggest an intimate link between authorship and male parturition, namely, "Constantly," Nietzsche writes, "we [philosophers] have to give birth to our thoughts out of our pain and, like mothers, endow them with all that we have in us of blood, heart, fire, pleasure, passion, agony, conscience, fate, catastrophe."[90]

To Goosta's complaint about the liberal appropriation of Nietzsche, we know that Nietzsche was no liberal in any sense of the word. He plainly despised the ideology of the French revolution—if this is to be the main sense of liberalism—for proclaiming the equality of all men. Certainly, however, at no point ever does Kaufmann call Nietzsche "liberal." It is true that Kaufmann rides past Nietzsche's misogyny, but, as for America, it is well known that Nietzsche was hopeful of being properly read in the New World. Goosta concludes:

> So Kaufmann achieved his objective; to use the blindness of American liberalism in its hour of victory to hide one of the most powerful origins of its opposition. Kaufmann then is just an extension of the war, part of an intellectual Nuremberg. He really did all this to destroy Nietzsche by diffusing him, placing him outside of context as a mere wisdom writer and intellectual curiosity. That is this Jew's personal revenge against Germany and Europe, half disguised as part of the war effort, and to the stupid and oblivious, or equally insidious, as "scholarship."

End Goosta, who epitomizes, however crassly, the criticism of Kaufmann's Nietzsche coming from the Ludovician right. He deserves a hearing, even if in his rhetorical haste he appears to be asking us to cherish, protect, and set free a *Nazi* Nietzsche hauled protesting into a courtroom in Nuremberg. But, to proceed in slower motion, note that in light of our discussion of the ethical philosophy of Bildung, Goosta could not be more wrong in writing that Kaufmann had "placed him outside of context." And to call *Nietzsche* the Jew's "personal revenge against Germany" is, finally, crude and wrong: it is crude not to accept Kaufmann's repeated insistence, based on Zarathustra, that seeking "revenge" is vile; and it is wrong, because the Germany that Kaufmann was defying was only the odious transmogrification of an authentic Germany— one of whose epiphenomena was the instrumentalization of Nietzsche's work for rotten purposes.

We must draw to an end, and so I will now merely exhibit the fine snapshot of Nietzsche's North American legacy taken by Steven Taubeneck: "Recent North American readings of Nietzsche have sought to modify Kaufmann's picture in many different directions. . . . In the process, the contributions of Gilles Deleuze, Michel Foucault, Jacques Derrida, Sarah Kofman, and Pierre Klossowski," who do not write directly about Kaufmann, "were adapted or criticized according to the demands of the argument"—such arguments as we have been looking at. "Arthur Danto, Bernd Magnus, and Richard Schacht, each with his own suggestions, offer principles different from Kaufmann's as alternative bases for understanding Nietzsche. Alexander Nehamas and David Krell highlight . . . the roles of Nietzsche's many styles. Allan Bloom . . . retains [Kaufmann's] . . . humanistic-anthropological emphasis and adds a critique of the politics; Richard Rorty downplays the politics and drops the belief in a foundational human nature."[91] I have not been able to deal with all these approaches. But it can be said with assurance that they would not have been possible, with the rigor and finesse that marks the best of them, without Kaufmann's *Nietzsche* as their basis.[92]

Supplement

I cite at length Kaufmann's rebuttal to Danto's critique of his interpretation of certain key passages in Nietzsche:

> In a chapter on "Religious Psychology," which deals mainly with the *Genealogy*, Danto argues for a different interpretation of Nietzsche's attitude toward truth, and in two footnotes he takes issue with me (pp. 169, 173).[93] But the level of his argument borders on the incredible. . . . The translations abound in serious mistakes and omissions that are not indicated: on pages 171–176, I checked the nine quotations set off in slightly smaller type, and every single one of them is disfigured by important mistranslations or unacknowledged omissions, or both. These omissions range from a few crucial words to nine lines. An extended reply to this kind of misreading of Nietzsche would be useless. But three points can be made briefly.[94]
>
> First, he [Danto] leans largely on the *Genealogy of Morals*, III 24ff., and on *The Gay Science*, 344, which is quoted in *Genealogy* III 24. In my commentary on the *Genealogy* [N 252–53], I have offered a detailed interpretation of these sections and, without mentioning Danto, demonstrated that his interpretation is untenable.

It is not obvious how Kaufmann's pages 252–53 respond to Danto's specific objection to Kaufmann's reading of Nietzsche's "piety." They do, however, address it through the linked issue of Nietzsche's faith in the ascetic ideal. Kaufmann continues his response:

> Because Nietzsche thought that the highest degree of power consists in self-mastery, he considered the ascetic one of the most powerful of men. From his early praise of the "saint" as, together with artist and philosopher, the only truly human being, we can trace Nietzsche's esteem of the ascetic through the *Dawn*, where it is claimed that no other type of man has achieved a greater feeling of power, to the third inquiry of the *Genealogy*, where man is considered to have been a mere animal—"except for the

ascetic ideal." The asceticism of the most powerful men, however, consists in the sublimation of their impulses, in the organization of the chaos of their passions, and in man's giving "style" to his own character. . . .

This exposition furnishes an excellent illustration of Nietzsche's dialectic, of his keen emphasis on the negative, and of his ultimate recognition and affirmation of the value of the apparently negative.

Kaufmann's rebuttal continues:

Second: The other passage about which Danto takes issue with me is *The Twilight of the Idols*, IX, 14. Here (on Danto's page 169), he . . . [fails to quote] Nietzsche's parenthesis, which shows that the reading urged against me is wrong.

The passage in Nietzsche, we recall, reads: "Darwin forgot the spirit (that is English!); the weak have more spirit. One must need spirit to acquire spirit; one loses it when one no longer needs it. The strong dispense with spirit." And here, now, is the omitted parenthesis in question: "('Let it go!' they think in Germany today; 'the Reich must still remain to us')." This ironical provision does turn around Danto's sense of the thrust of the aphorism.

[Danto] . . . also ignore[s] *The Gay Science*, 2, cited on the same page[s] [230–31] of my Chapter 8, section I, and indeed all the evidence I present.

This crucial passage from *The Gay Science*, 2, reads:

What is good-heartedness, refinement, and genius to me, when the human being who has these virtues tolerates slack feelings in his faith and judgments, and when the demand for certainty is not to him the inmost craving and the deepest need—that which distinguishes the higher from the lower men. Among certain pious ones, I found a hatred of reason and appreciated it: at least they thus betrayed their bad intellectual conscience [*Die Fröhliche Wissenschaft* (The Gay Science) 2; cf. 359].

Kaufmann concludes:

Third: It is pointless to base interpretations of Nietzsche on a few snippets from his writings, paying no attention to the context—this is deliberate in Danto's case (p. 6)—or to what Nietzsche says elsewhere on the same subject.

In writing of Danto's deliberate use of "snippets," Kaufmann is presumably referring to Danto's sentence: "[Nietzsche's] structural incapacities made it difficult for him to think protractedly or to hold a problem in his mind until it yielded a solution" (p. 6). Kaufmann concludes:

> If Danto's avowed attempt to link Nietzsche with analytic philosophy were not so timely, and if he were not a respectable philosopher, one might simply ignore his book. But when a reputable writer strays out of his field, most readers have no way of telling that the book exceeds the author's competence. (N 359)

ACKNOWLEDGMENTS

I AM HAPPY to salute friends who have helped me in the writing of this book with their wisdom and generosity. I am very grateful to Rob Tempio and Mark Bellis, my editors, for their skill in bringing this vessel into port. Rob composed the book's title and encouraged me to write an *intellectual* biography, including intimate details of Walter Kaufmann's life only as they might add color and force to his ideas. With fine equanimity, Mark bore with me through several travails, including the forcible fall of a very large maple tree on my study at the approach of a serious deadline. David Pickus's readiness to share his unsurpassed knowledge of Kaufmann's work was a continual inspiration. Robert Norton's splendid encouragement was a great gift at a time I was glad to receive it. Alexander Nehamas was brilliant at lunch after lunch and a cherished source of insight into my subject. The choice wit of Christopher Prendergast, *mon Mon at Kings*, stood me in good stead the whole way. Marcel Lepper of the Deutsches Literaturarchiv Marbach spontaneously sent me photocopies of Kaufmann's letters to such notables as Hermann Hesse, Karl Jaspers, and Carl Zuckmayer—how thoughtful! In its creativity and erudition, Martin Jay's contribution exceeded every expectable norm of constructive criticism: his name, like Abou ben Adhem's, "led all the rest." Finally (and not finally), I wish to thank Kathleen Kageff, my copy editor, for her admirably relentless demand for exact documentation. My gratitude to these helpers in no way means to underestimate the kindness, acuteness, and grace of David and Georganne Bromwich, Noel and Emily Corngold, Lisa Ellis, Emery and the late Mary George, Irene Giersing, Eugene Goodheart, John Hamilton, Walter Hinderer, Christian Jany, Michael Jennings, John Squire Kirkham, David Farrell Krell, Vivian Liska, Barbara Nagel, Rafaël Newman, Serguei Oushakine, Gerhard Richter, Kim Scheppele, Karin Schutjer, Henry Staten, Benno Wagner, Anne Walker, Natascha Weisert, Caroline Wiedmer, and Michael Wood (with apologies to those deserving friends not named by name). This book is dedicated to my wife, the indescribably wonderful Regine Üllner.

NOTES

Preface

1. Walter Kaufmann, *The Faith of a Heretic* (Garden City, NY: Doubleday, 1961). This work was reprinted by Princeton University Press in 2015.

2. Amazon reviews of *The Faith of a Heretic,* http://www.amazon.com/The-Faith-Heretic -Walter-Kaufmann/product-reviews/B000HMB4JW/ref=dpx_acr_txt?showViewpoints=1.

3. "A new generation, mostly unacquainted with the risks of uncompromising and hard-edged compassion, deserves Malamud even more than the one that made up his contemporary readership." Cynthia Ozick, "Judging the World," *New York Times,* March 16, 2014, 12.

4. Molly Worthen, "Wanted: A Theology of Atheism," *New York Times,* May 31, 2015, https://www.nytimes.com/2015/05/31/opinion/sunday/molly-worthen-wanted-a-theology -of-atheism.html.

5. Walter Kaufmann, "A Plea for Socrates' Heritage (a Response)," in *Ethics and Social Justice,* ed. Howard E. Kiefer and Milton K. Munitz (Albany: State University of New York Press, 1968), 20, 17.

6. Kaufmann's heretical faith is argued with wide historical and textual knowledge and verbal precision—altogether proof against the charge, say, of "undergraduate atheism" or "contemptuous flippancy" that has been leveled against the arguments for atheism by Richard Dawkins and Christopher Hitchens. The first phrase is by Mark Johnston, *Saving God: Religion after Idolatry* (Princeton, NJ: Princeton University Press, 2009), 38; the second, by Thomas Nagel, quoted in Eugene Goodheart, "Darwinian Hubris," *Michigan Quarterly Review* L, no. 1 (Winter 2011), http://hdl.handle.net/2027/spo.act2080.0050.103.

7. George Eliot, *Middlemarch* (London: Penguin, 1995), 208.

8. Trude Weiss-Rosmarin, "An Interview with Walter Kaufmann," *Judaism* 30 (Winter 1981): 121.

9. "Oh my brothers, your nobility must not gaze backward but *outward*! You must be exiles from all fatherlands (*Vaterländer*) and forefatherlands (*Urväterländer*)! You must love your children's-land (*Kinder Land*): let this love be your new nobility." "Of Old and New Tables," 12, in *Thus Spoke Zarathustra,* tr. Walter Kaufmann, *Portable Nietzsche* (New York: Viking, 1954), 354.

10. Walter Kaufmann, *Nietzsche: Philosopher, Psychologist, Antichrist,* 4th ed. (Princeton, NJ: Princeton University Press, 1974), 330. It would be an engaging exercise to imagine Nietzsche's reaction to the news that in 1923 Jewish socialist activists founded a Camp Kinderland in the Berkshires. "Yiddish spoken here!" Did the founders have in mind the imprecation of Zarathustra? See the compelling memoir of Eugene Goodheart, *Confessions of a Secular Jew* (Woodstock, NY: Overlook, 2001), 3.

11. Friedrich Nietzsche, *Beyond Good and Evil: Prelude to a Philosophy of the Future*, tr. with commentary by Walter Kaufmann (New York: Random House, 1966), 27.

12. "Insofar as possible we must take the author's positions more seriously than he himself took them." Walter Kaufmann, *Hegel: A Reinterpretation*. Anchor Books (Garden City, NY: Doubleday 1966), x.

13. In his correspondence with Hannah Arendt, Karl Jaspers, with whom Kaufmann repeatedly jousted over the years on the topic of Nietzsche's allegedly unsalvageable "whirl" of contradictions, conceded Kaufmann's "phenomenal memory," adding, "[he has] read everything." *Hannah Arendt/Karl Jaspers Briefwechsel 1926–1969*, ed. Lotte Köhler and Hans Saner (Munich: Piper, 1985), 269.

14. Walter Kaufmann, *Tragedy and Philosophy* (Princeton, NJ: Princeton University Press, 1992 [originally 1968]), xi.

15. Walter Kaufmann, *Time Is an Artist*, the second book of *Man's Lot: A Trilogy* (New York: Reader's Digest Press/McGraw-Hill, 1978), 58.

16. "Reading should not be an auratic experience." Benjamin Bennett, *The Dark Side of Literacy: Literature and Learning Not to Read* (New York: Fordham University Press, 2008), 41.

17. Walter Kaufmann, "Existentialism Tamed," review of *The Existentialist Revolt* by Kurt F. Reinhardt, *The Existentialists* by James Collins, and *The Mind of Kierkegaard* by James Collins in *Kenyon Review* 16, no. 3 (Summer 1954): 487, http://www.walterkaufmann.com /articles/1954_Review_Revolt_Reinhardt.pdf.

18. Walter Kaufmann, *Discovering the Mind*, vol. 2, *Nietzsche, Heidegger, and Buber* (New York: McGraw-Hill, 1980), 134.

19. For a historical defense of the legitimacy of paraphrase, see Andrew Piper, "Paraphrasis: Goethe, the Novella, and Forms of Translational Knowledge," *Goethe Yearbook* 17 (2010): 179–201.

20. Kaufmann, *Hegel*, 216.

21. Ben-Ami Scharfstein, review of Walter Kaufmann, *Discovering the Mind*, 3 vols. (New York: McGraw-Hill, 1980), *Journal of the History of Philosophy* 21, no. 2 (April 1, 1983): 256.

22. *Discovering the Mind*, vol. 3, *Freud, Adler, and Jung* (New York: McGraw Hill, 1980), 325.

23. H. Meyer, review of Walter Kaufmann, *Tragedy and Philosophy*, *Books Abroad* 43, no. 4 (Autumn 1969): 609; Charles Segal, review of *Tragedy and Philosophy*, *Classical World* 62, no. 5 (January 1969): 191.

Introduction

1. Some passages in this introduction are taken from Stanley Corngold, "Foreword," in Walter Kaufmann, *The Faith of a Heretic* (Princeton, NJ: Princeton University Press, 2015), xi–xxv.

2. Carl Schorske died on September 13, 2015.

3. Joseph Frank, *Responses to Modernity: Essays in the Politics of Culture* (New York: Fordham University Press, 2012).

4. Kaufmann, *Faith of a Heretic*, 404.

5. Ibid.

6. Alexander Nehamas, *On Friendship* (New York: Basic Books, 2016), 12.

7. Kaufmann, *Faith of a Heretic*, 68.

8. Stephen Spender, "The Truly Great," in *New Collected Poems 1928–1953* (London: Faber and Faber, 2004), 16.

9. Weiss-Rosmarin, " Interview,"123. A similar account of Kaufmann's life appears in Jennifer Ratner-Rosenhagen, *American Nietzsche—A History of an Icon and His Ideas* (Chicago: University of Chicago Press, 2012), 224–26. Her book employs many of the sources I do: they are limited, since Kaufmann left next to no written testimony to his personal life. Persons interested in "his life as a man" are chiefly dependent on the interview cited above and the contribution by Ivan Soll, a devoted student of Kaufmann, to the *American National Biography Online*, https://doi .org/10.1093/anb/9780198606697.article.2001574. With this one exception, all other biographical dictionaries are derivative, and most are inaccurate in many of their details. Hence, the available narrative is linear, with few options. For my essential disagreement with Ratner-Rosenhagen's approach to Kaufmann's *Nietzsche: Philosopher, Psychologist, Antichrist*, see postscript.

10. Weiss-Rosmarin, "Interview," 125.

11. At the time, Leo Baeck was president of the Reichsvertretung der deutschen Juden, "a federation of Jewish organizations and regional and local Jewish communities, founded in 1933, that aimed to provide a unified voice for German Jewry in dealing with the Nazi authorities" (http://findingaids.cjh.org/?pID=431121).

12. Leo Baeck, *Judaism and Christianity: Essays by Leo Baeck*, tr. Walter Kaufmann (Philadelphia: Jewish Publication Society of America, 1958). Martin Buber, *I and Thou*, tr. with an introduction by Walter Kaufmann (New York: Scribners, 1970).

13. In 1962–63, Kaufmann was a Fulbright research professor at the Hebrew University in Jerusalem and again in 1975, visiting fellow of the Institute of Philosophy at the Hebrew University. Edward P. Antonio, "Kaufmann, Walter Arnold (1921–80)," *Dictionary of Modern American Philosophers*, vol. 1, ed. John R. Shook (Bristol, UK: Thoemmes Continuum, 2005), 1284.

14. Weiss-Rosmarin, "Interview," 125.

15. Eric v. d. Luft, "Kaufmann, Walter Arnold." *Dictionary of American Biography* (New York: Charles Scribner's Sons, 1995), supp. 10, 401–2.

16. Ibid., 401.

17. In his 1976 opus *Religions in Four Dimensions: Existential and Aesthetic, Historical and Comparative*, Kaufmann declared his debt to Pratt: "At Williams College I was exceedingly fortunate in being able to study comparative religion, as well as the psychology of religion, with James Bissett Pratt. His courses were the most valuable I ever took in college or in graduate school; he opened up for me *The Sacred Books of the East* and other texts; and he made me write thirteen long papers" (New York: Reader's Digest Press, 1976), 473.

18. V. d. Luft, "Kaufmann, Walter Arnold," 401.

19. Under the guise of relaying a "consensus among his contemporaries at Princeton," v. d. Luft declares that Kaufmann's "world consisted of nineteenth- and twentieth-century German thought and literature—*and very little else*" (emphasis added). "Kaufmann, Walter Arnold," 402. At the moment I hold in my hands Kaufmann's five-hundred-page volume *Religions in Four Dimensions*, a work dealing with *ten* religions. Kaufmann's earlier works deal significantly—though, of course, not exclusively—with the Bible, Eastern religious writings, Greek tragedy (in an entire volume titled *Tragedy and Philosophy*), Plato, Aristotle, Shakespeare, Thomas Aquinas, Hume, Kierkegaard, Dostoevsky, Sartre, Camus, Toynbee, Styron, organized religion in America, and many more.

20. Walter Kaufmann, *Without Guilt and Justice: From Decidophobia to Autonomy* (New York: Peter Wyden, 1973), 261.

21. Walter Kaufmann, *Cain and Other Poems* (New York: Doubleday, 1962), 157.

22. A. J. Wecker, "Kaufmann Discusses Nazis," *Daily Princetonian*, 103, no. 53 (April 24, 1979): 8. Kaufmann's later work, the grand study *Tragedy and Philosophy*, contains an extraordinary footnote relevant to this matter. Kaufmann discusses the figure of Kurt Gerstein, a provisional Nazi party member, who appears in Rolf Hochhuth's play *The Deputy*. This "SS officer risked his life again and again to help the condemned. . . . Gerstein really lived--and died. . . . To illustrate the contribution the play made on this score, one might cite Norman Podhoretz's pre-*Deputy* claim that 'no person could have joined the Nazi party, let alone the S.S., who is not at the very least a *vicious* anti-Semite' [Norman Podhoretz, *Doings and Undoings*, Noonday Press (New York: Farrar, Straus and Giroux, 1964), 348]. . . . Similar notions were extremely common in the United States. Now one no longer needs to draw *on abundant personal experience* to refute them" (emphasis added) (*Tragedy and Philosophy*, 335)." Kaufmann approached the murders he witnessed, without forgetting Nazism and with the same revulsion as did Alexander Solzhenitsyn, who describes his loathing of such crimes in his *Prussian Nights*. I owe this reference to David Pickus, who adds: "It could be that out of this simple willingness to see murder wherever it was found that Kaufmann came to deplore thinking in black and white. In this context, it is significant that he was to dedicate his decidophobia book in 1973 to Solzhenitsyn, 'autonomy in action.'" (*See Without Guilt and Justice*, 34). From a personal communication.

23. Ivan Soll, "Kaufmann, Walter Arnold," *American National Biography Online*.

24. "Walter Kaufmann, Reinhold Niebuhr to Speak Sunday," *Daily Princetonian* 82, no. 134 (December 5, 1958): 1.

25. The memorial to Walter Kaufmann composed by the Princeton Philosophy Department recounts the story of Kaufmann's first meeting with Albert Einstein. Einstein asked Kaufmann about his recently completed thesis, and on hearing that it dealt with Nietzsche, "Einstein's wonderful face expressed great shock, and he said, 'But that is simply dreadful.' This gives some idea of Nietzsche's reputation in 1947: one associated him with brutality, madness, and the Nazis" (https://philosophy.princeton.edu/about/past-faculty/walter-Kaufmann).

26. Mark F. Bernstein, "O Ethan Where Art Thou? The Student Life of a Famous Filmmaker," *Princeton Alumni Weekly*, April 20, 2016, 29.

27. Joyce Carol Oates, "Princeton Idyll," in *Dear Husband* (New York: Ecco, 2009), 92, 101.

28. Walter Kaufmann, *Critique of Religion and Philosophy* (Princeton, NJ: Princeton University Press, 1958), 410.

29. Walter Kaufmann, *From Shakespeare to Existentialism* (Princeton, NJ: Princeton University Press, 1980), ix.

30. Walter Kaufmann, *Critique of Religion and Philosophy*, "Preface to the Princeton Paperback Edition," (Princeton, NJ: Princeton University Press, 1978), xi.

31. "Walter A. Kaufmann," https://philosophy.princeton.edu/about/past-faculty/walter-kaufmann.

32. Antonio: "Kaufmann was by no means . . . an original philosopher. Indeed, there were some in the guild of philosophers who simply refused to think of him as a philosopher." One can safely be indifferent to this grand refusal. "Kaufmann, Walter Arnold (1921–80)," 1284.

33. Soll, "Kaufmann, Walter Arnold." This essay supplies important details about Kaufmann's life and work mentioned in this introduction. The passage from *Faith of a Heretic* cited by Soll is found on page 17. Soll also contributed substantial introductions to Kaufmann's final work, the three-volume study titled *Discovering the Mind* (New Brunswick, NJ: Transaction, 1991–92).

34. Rebecca Goldstein, *Plato at the Googleplex: Why Philosophy Won't Go Away* (New York: Pantheon, 2014), 9–10.

35. Colin Campbell, "The Tyranny of the Yale Critics," *New York Times*, February 9, 1986, http://www.nytimes.com/1986/02/09/magazine/the-tyranny-of-the-yale-critics.html ?pagewanted=6. One reads in the Wikipedia piece on Paul de Man (https://en.wikipedia.org /wiki/Paul_de_Man) that as early as college days, like Kaufmann, de Man was especially interested in religious mysticism; and, like Kaufmann, he was to deal with "religious" rhetoric in essays on Pascal and Kierkegaard. An intriguing essay topic emerges: the hypothetical intellectual affinity—and cogent disparity—between Kaufmann and de Man. This suggestion must proceed, however, with a certain caveat. It is entirely possible that de Man's remark to J. Hillis Miller was ironic—after all, only a citation. Was he aware of an essay by Hans-Georg Gadamer, "Martin Heidegger and Marburg Theology," in which Gadamer remarks: "Whatever he [Heidegger] taught, whether it was Descartes or Aristotle, Plato or Kant who furnished the point of departure . . . it was theological questions that were surging up in him from the beginning" (*Discovering the Mind*, vol. 2, 171). Gadamer's essay is reprinted in Otto Pöggeler, ed. *Heidegger: Perspektiven zur Deutung seines Werkes* (Cologne: Kiepenheuer und Witsch, 1969). I will add, finally, that the gentle reader of this endnote will find mentions—often critical—of the work of Paul de Man in several of the following chapters. He work was, for me, far and away the most important intellectual influence: I studied it—and find it, again and again, of such considerable range that I cannot avoid invoking it at crucial moments in this narrative. Kaufmann and de Man, who were well acquainted, were opposed in (almost) every detail to one another's work. This opposition might have been a source of irritation for each of them, but the result is finally productive, for it highlights their individual positions.

36. Weiss-Rosmarin, "Interview," 120.

37. "Much of what the major religions have done to people I find quite outrageous, nor can I accept most of the views of the so-called existentialists. It is my concern with problems we share that leads me to deal with existentialism and religion again and again." Walter Kaufmann, *Existentialism, Religion, and Death: Thirteen Essays* (New York: New American Library, 1976), ix–x.

Chapter 1: Nietzsche Redivivus

1. Epigraph: Kaufmann, *Discovering the Mind*, vol. 2, 6.

2. In indexes in studies of Nietzsche, he sits just under "Kant." Another matter: I noted earlier that Jennifer Ratner-Rosenhagen's *American Nietzsche* foregrounds passages in Kaufmann's study that I will also emphasize. Ratner-Rosenhagen's main focus, however, is very different from my own, which purports to do a close encounter—a personal, literary, *literal* analysis of Kaufmann's book in 2014–18—meaning to catch its style of thought. Professor Ratner-Rosenhagen, an intellectual historian, is interested chiefly in answering the question of why *Nietzsche* can have had such an impact on an American readership in 1950 and the decades following. She reads him as if she were reading him *then* and then resourcefully reconstructs his

American audience. In the postscript to this book titled "Contra *Nietzsche*," where Kaufmann's book is meant, I take issue with her criticisms of that work.

3. Cf. David Pickus: "It is not overly subtle to suggest that the depreciation and condescension he has received is a backhanded way of testifying to the force of his arguments." "The Walter Kaufmann Myth: A Study in Academic Judgment," *Nietzsche-Studien* 32 (2003): 236.

4. Erwin Panofsky, *Studies in Iconology: Humanist Themes in the Art of the Renaissance* (New York: Oxford University Press, 1939).

5. Erich Auerbach, *Mimesis: The Representation of Reality in Western Literature*, tr. Willard R. Trask (Princeton, NJ: Princeton University Press, 1953); originally, *Mimesis: Dargestellte Wirklichkeit in der abendländischen Literatur* (Bern: A. Francke, 1946).

6. Ernst Curtius, *European Literature and the Latin Middle Ages*, tr. Willard R. Trask (Princeton, NJ: Princeton University Press, 1953); originally, *Europäische Literatur und lateinisches Mittelalter* (Bern: A. Francke, 1948).

7. Walter Kaufmann, *Nietzsche: Philosopher, Psychologist, Antichrist*, 4th ed., Princeton Paperbacks (Princeton, NJ: Princeton University Press, 1974), 234. Pages from this text will henceforth be shown in parentheses as (N + page number).

8. Franz Kafka, *Briefe an Milena*, "Prag, 26. August 1920." One comment of many in the later work establishes a basis for Kaufmann's frequent citations of Kafka: "All three men—van Gogh, Kafka, and Freud—were distinguished by an amazing capacity for detachment from themselves and could see themselves from above" (*Discovering the Mind*, vol. 2, 256). Look at the company Kafka keeps! In a word (of Kaufmann's), all three were (virtually) free of self-deception.

9. Theodor Adorno, "Notes on Kafka," in *Prisms*, tr. Samuel Weber and Shierry Weber (London: Spearman, 1967), 246.

10. I am referring to the cover of the fourth edition.

11. *The Gay Science*, ed. and tr. Walter Kaufmann (New York: Vintage, 1974), 35–36.

12. The comments by Mann and Maritain are found on the back cover of the Princeton Paperback of the fourth edition of Kaufmann's *Nietzsche*. It is significant that Kaufmann's combative will to truth does not spare the missteps of his admirers. In the later *Critique of Religion and Philosophy*, we read: "Throughout the work of Gilson and Maritain, one can hardly fail to be struck by the vast difference between their treatment of Thomas [St. Thomas Aquinas] and their often very cavalier criticism of other philosophers" (144).

13. Catherine Belsey's definition of "liberal humanism" is immediately relevant: "Man, the center and hero of liberal humanism, was produced in contradistinction to the objects of his knowledge." *The Subject of Tragedy* (Oxford: Routledge, 2014), 9.

14. *Primus inter pares* is Steven E. Aschheim, *The Nietzsche Legacy in Germany, 1890–1990* (Berkeley: University of California Press, 1992). Kaufmann was particularly concerned to correct the emphasis on Nietzsche as a protofascist in the work of the Harvard historian Crane Brinton. Kaufmann's full entry reads: "Brinton, Crane, *Nietzsche*. Cambridge, Mass., Harvard University Press, 1941; New York, Harper Torchbook [paperback] with new preface, epilogue, and bibliography, 1965. In the new edition, the numerous errors of the original edition remain uncorrected, but in a short Preface Brinton disowns the chapter, 'Nietzsche in Western Thought.' The rev. bibliography adds serious new errors" (N 497). The Wikipedia entry (2013) titled "Influence and Reception of Friedrich Nietzsche" is well done: https://en.wikipedia .org/wiki/Influence_and_reception_of_Friedrich_Nietzsche.

15. Stanley Corngold and Geoffrey Waite, "A Question of Responsibility: Nietzsche with Hölderlin at War, 1914–1946," in *Nietzsche: Godfather of Fascism? On the Uses and Abuses of a Philosophy*, ed. Jacob Golomb and Robert S. Wistrich (Princeton, NJ: Princeton University Press, 2002), 196–214. Kaufmann points out, "When the *Historisch-Kritische Gesamtausgabe* of Nietzsche's *Werke* and *Briefe*, begun in 1933, was abandoned during the war, after publication of four volumes of letters and five of 'works,' all chronologically arranged, it had not even reached Nietzsche's first book, much less his last works" (N 427).

16. Duncan Large is an accomplished Nietzsche scholar and translator and author of *Proust and Nietzsche—a Comparative Study* (Oxford: Clarendon, 2001), 22n66. His views on Kaufmann's work are discussed in my postscript. In the citation above, Large is referring chiefly to Kaufmann's attack on earlier editions of *The Will to Power*.

17. The third of Nietzsche's four *Untimely Meditations* is titled "Schopenhauer as Educator." In a later work, *Discovering the Mind*, vol. 2, Kaufmann concludes: "In describing the qualities ... [Nietzsche] most admired in Schopenhauer, he was actually depicting his own ideal self, what he aspired to become, or in brief 'Nietzsche as Educator'" (D2 9).

18. Pickus, "Walter Kaufmann Myth."

19. Each new edition contained a fiercely annotated bibliography of secondary works that had appeared during the interval between editions. On the point that critics imputed arguments to Kaufmann that he had never made, Pickus offers a trenchant example, in Walter Sokel's charge, that Kaufmann wrote his book "to spiritualize Nietzsche and to narrow at all costs the gulf between him and Christianity." Pickus, "Walter Kaufmann Myth," 256. Pickus's criticism is directed at Walter H. Sokel, "Political Uses and Abuses of Nietzsche in Walter Kaufmann's Image of Nietzsche," *Nietzsche-Studien* 12 (1983): 438.

20. De Waehlens speaks of Kaufmann's "care, method, erudition, and *probity*" (emphasis added). But none of these qualities, de Waehlens adds, rules out the reader's task of "choosing among several Nietzsches." It is Kaufmann's faithfulness to the text that makes such a thing possible, he continues, and that is admirable. "Walter A. Kaufmann, *Nietzsche: Philosopher, Psychologist, Antichrist*," *Revue Philosophique de Louvain* 50, no. 26 (1952): 341–42.

21. In *Nietzsche's Jewish Problem: Between Anti-Semitism and Anti-Judaism* (Princeton, NJ: Princeton University Press, 2016), Robert C. Holub vigorously contests Kaufmann's widely circulated view that Elisabeth-Förster Nietzsche's distortion of Nietzsche's unpublished papers in her book *The Will to Power* turned him into the protofascist and Judaeophobe he never was. If *The Will to Power* is such noxious propaganda, Holub asks, why did Kaufmann choose to edit, translate, and publish it, as he did in 1967 (224n284)?

22. The value of "ambiguity" will suffer a sea change (it is valorized) in Kaufmann's later work.

23. Bertram's highly contestable tour de force of Nietzsche criticism, first published in 1918, was much admired by Wölfflin, Gide, Hesse, Benn, and Thomas Mann: it is composed in an extraordinarily exalted, neologistic, pseudovitalist manner—possibly beautiful—an exemplar of the high exegetical style of German prose between Weimar and the Nazis. Bertram's book has recently been translated, with a lucid introduction, in a rare act of philological piety, by Robert Norton: *Ernst Bertram, Nietzsche: Attempt at a Mythology* (Urbana: University of Illinois Press, 2009).

24. Aschheim, *Nietzsche Legacy*, 4.

25. German titles of Nietzsche's works in citations from Kaufmann's text refer to the Musarion edition of the *Gesammelte Werke* (Collected Works) (23 vols., 1920–29).

26. Alexander Nehamas is a former junior colleague of Kaufmann, a friend and intellectual interlocutor. Nehamas subsequently became a professor in the Princeton Philosophy Department, teaching advanced seminars on Nietzsche. His study, *Nietzsche: Life as Literature* (Princeton, NJ: Princeton University Press, 1985), is one of the most highly regarded books on Nietzsche written in the decade following the appearance of Kaufmann's fourth edition.

27. Nehamas, *Nietzsche*, 188.

28. Henry Staten, *Nietzsche's Voice* (Ithaca, NY: Cornell University Press, 1990), 6.

29. Nehamas, *Nietzsche*, 15.

30. Schacht is mainly concerned with Kaufmann's treatment of Nietzsche's relatively early works—*Human, All Too Human* (1878) and *The Dawn* (1881)—as little more than a run-up to this development. Richard Schacht, "Human, All Too Human," in *Introductions to Nietzsche*, ed. Robert B. Pippin (Cambridge: Cambridge University Press, 2012), 99.

31. It should be pointed out, as the writer and radio host Patrick McCarty has reminded me, that the word *sublimiren* figures rather infrequently in Nietzsche's corpus. But these uses are remarkable: for one thing, the word stands out in the very first aphorism in the first part of Nietzsche's *Human, All Too Human*, viz.,

> Historical philosophy, on the other hand, which can no longer be separated from natural science . . . has discovered in individual cases . . . that there are no opposites . . . and that a mistake in reasoning lies at the bottom of this antithesis: . . . there exists, strictly speaking, neither an unegoistic action nor completely disinterested contemplation; both are only sublimations [*Sublimirungen*], in which the basic element seems almost to have dispersed and reveals itself only under the most painstaking observation (*Human, All Too Human*, tr. R. J. Hollingdale [Cambridge: Cambridge University Press, 1996], 12).

At the same time it is only in subsequent appearances that the word acquires its modern psychological connotation. In this case, according to Kaufmann, Nietzsche is the first to have used the word so. In *Beyond Good and Evil*, "Part 3: The Religious Nature, [aphorism 58]," we read, "The practical indifference to religious matters into which he ['the scholar'] has been born and brought up is generally sublimated (*sublimirt*) in him into caution and cleanliness that shun contact with religious men and matters. . . ." [tr. Walter Kaufmann, 70]. Again: "My task: to sublimate [*sublimiren*] all drives in such a way that my perception of what is strange [foreign, other] is extensive and is yet bound up with enjoyment; the drive of honesty with myself, of justice toward things so strong that the enjoyment of it outweighs the value of the other sorts of pleasure and they, when necessary, are sacrificed to this drive in part or whole." *Nietzsches Werke: Kritische Gesamtausgabe*, vol. 6, *Nachgelassene Fragmente: Anfang 1880 bis Frühjahr 1881*, aphorism 67. There are several others uses of a similar tendency. Kaufmann's claim has encountered resistance. In *Nietzsche, "the last Antipolitical German,"* Peter Bergmann writes, "Kaufmann . . . argues that both Nietzsche and Hegel 'found a single word that epitomized their entire dialectic; and the two words, though not identical, have literally the same meaning. . . . Nietzsche's sublimation actually involves, no less than does Hegel's *aufheben*, a simultaneous preserving, canceling, and lifting up' (*Nietzsche*, 236). But Nietzsche's use of the term sublimation hardly warrants the place which Kaufmann assigns to it. It neither approached Freud's usage nor rivaled the place which *aufheben* assumed in Hegel's work" (Bloomington: Indiana University Press, 1987), 189n18. For more current, detailed studies of the concept of sublimation in Nietzsche, written in pragmatic response to P. Bergmann, see Ken Gemes, "Freud and Nietzsche on Sublimation," *Journal of Nietzsche Studies*, no. 38 (Fall 2009): 38–59 and Joseph Swenson, "Sublimation and Affirmation in Nietzsche's Psychology," *Journal of Nietzsche Studies* 45, no. 2 (Summer 2014): 196–209.

32. The *nec plus ultra* of this drive is dramatized by Dostoevsky in the figure of the madman Kirillov in *The Possessed*, a book that Nietzsche read and which made a great impression on him. For a lead, see Joseph Frank, *Dostoevsky: The Years of Ordeal, 1850–1859* (Princeton, NJ: Princeton University Press, 1983), 149n. Under the head of "The Logic of Atheism," Nietzsche writes:

> If God exists, everything depends on his will, and I am nothing outside of his will. If he does not exist, then everything depends on me, and I must prove my independence. Suicide is the most complete way of proving its independence. [This is] the classical formula of Kirillov in Dostoevsky: I am the first to reject the fiction of God. To kill another man—that would be the lowest form of independence: I want to achieve the highest point of independence. Previous suicides had reasons. I, however, have no reason, except to prove my independence.
>
> *Nietzsches Werke: Kritische Gesamtausgabe*, vol. 8/2, *Nachgelassene Fragmente: Herbst 1887 bis März 1888*, aphorism 11[334].
>
> Recast: Kirillov has pronounced God dead and divinized his own will to power. Now he must test his will against its most obdurate resistance: the naked will to live, the fear of death. He shoots himself.

33. Bernard Reginster, "The Will to Power and the Ethics of Creativity," in *Nietzsche and Morality*, ed. Brian Leiter and Neil Sinhababu (Oxford: Clarendon, 2007), 33. See also: Bernard Reginster, *The Affirmation of Life: Nietzsche on Overcoming Nihilism* (Cambridge, MA: Harvard University Press, 2006), 286n3.

34. *The Birth of Tragedy*, tr. Walter Kaufmann (New York: Random House, 1967), 3–4.

35. Pickus, "Walter Kaufmann Myth," 238. In a valuable, unpublished essay titled "Art and Two Kinds of Lies: Nietzsche and Schiller on the Value of Aesthetic Semblance," Timothy Stoll of Princeton University discusses Nietzsche's normative value of "strength" in the context of Schiller's aesthetics of "der schöne Schein" (the beautiful semblance). Schiller's influence on Nietzsche is treated in Paul Bishop and R. H. Stephenson, *Friedrich Nietzsche and Weimar Classicism* (Rochester, NY: Camden House, 2005), 31 and 151–84. "In certain places," writes Stoll,

> Nietzsche takes a seemingly uncharacteristically negative attitude towards falsehood. In one well-known passage, for example, he says that "the strength of a spirit would be measured according to how much of the 'truth' it could still bear, more clearly, to what degree it *required* it to be thinned out, disguised, sweetened, blunted, falsified" (*Beyond Good and Evil*, tr. Kaufmann, 39). To the extent that "strength" functions as the normative standard in Nietzsche's philosophy, this [claim] makes it sound as though it is precisely facing the truth head on that is his ideal, even if an ideal that no one of us could ever fully achieve.

Stoll supplies this footnote: "This is the standard line in Nietzsche interpretation going back to Vaihinger in the early 20th century." See Hans Vaihinger, *Nietzsche als Philosoph* (Berlin: Reuther und Reichard, 1902). For recent arguments to the effect that strength or power is such a normative standard for Nietzsche, see Reginster, *The Affirmation of Life*, 148–200, and Nadeem Hussain, "The Role of Life in the *Genealogy*," in Simon May, ed., *Nietzsche's* On the Genealogy of Morality (Cambridge: Cambridge University Press, 2011), 142–69.

36. Henning Ottmann, "Englischsprachige Welt," in *Nietzsche Handbuch: Leben-Werk-Wirkung* (Stuttgart-Weimar: J. B. Metzler, 2000). Ottmann adds, graciously, "But without Kaufmann's path-breaking book and his brilliant translations, the rediscovery of Nietzsche in the Anglophone world would not have been possible" (433).

37. This is a surmise from which Professor Ottmann is certainly exempt and which can safely be left to the likes of Heinrich Himmler and Martin Bormann. One should read Nietzsche's Zarathustra, who chants: "You highest men whom my eyes have seen, this is my doubt about you and my secret laughter: I guess that you would call my Übermensch—devil. / What is great is so alien to your souls that the Übermensch would be terrifying to you in his *goodness*" (Friedrich Nietzsche, *Ecce Homo*, in *Basic Writings of Nietzsche*, ed. and tr. Walter Kaufmann (New York: Modern Library, 2000), 787.

38. Friedrich Nietzsche, in *Portable Nietzsche*, 519–20.

39. Nietzsche, *Birth of Tragedy*, 22.

40. Cf. Slavoj Žižek on the same question, here in regard to readings of Hegel: "The best interpretations of Hegel are always partial: they extrapolate the totality from a particular figure of thought or of dialectical movement." *Less Than Nothing: Hegel and the Shadow of Dialectical Materialism* (New York: Verso, 2013), 280.

41. From "The Despisers of the Body," *Thus Spoke Zarathustra*, in *Portable Nietzsche*, 140–41. That Nietzsche here equates the self with the *body* calls for a discussion that Kaufmann does not undertake. These passages appear again in *Discovering the Mind*, vol. 2, 67–68.

42. The theme of "large-scale" politics or Grand Politics is introduced in Nietzsche, *Beyond Good and Evil*, tr. Kaufmann, 131.

43. *Faust II*, "Klassische Walpurgisnacht," "Pharsalische Felder," Akt II. [Erichtho]: "Denn jeder, der sein inneres Selbst /Nicht zu regieren weiß, regierte gar zu gern/ Des Nachbars Willen, eignem stolzem Sinn gemäß."

44. See, in this respect, Pickus's debunking of this wave of Kaufmann criticism in "Walter Kaufmann Myth."

45. Peter Thompson, "Kafka, Bloch, Religion and the Metaphysics of Contingency," *Kafka und die Religion in der Moderne: Kafka, Religion, and Modernity*, Oxford Kafka Studies 3, ed. Manfred Engel and Ritchie Robertson (Würzburg: Königshausen und Neumann, 2014), 178.

46. "At the end of section 15 [of *The Birth of Tragedy*], we find another self-portrait: 'the Socrates who practices music'" (395). Kaufmann again evokes this image in his translation of *The Birth of Tragedy*, calling it "surely an idealized self-portrait: Nietzsche played the piano and composed songs." *Birth of Tragedy*, 98n10.

47. The consensus at the Princeton University Press evidently holds Kaufmann's work to be far-reaching, eloquent, and apt to our moment; and so Princeton is considering republishing an entire *series* of his books, beginning with this *Nietzsche* (2013) and *The Faith of a Heretic* (2015).

48. Alexander Nehamas, "Foreword," Walter Kaufmann, *Nietzsche: Philosopher, Psychologist, Antichrist*, 5th ed. (Princeton, NJ: Princeton University Press, 2013), ix. To prove Ne-

hamas's case, here is the sort of inspiration that *Nietzsche* is still able to produce. In 2010, a young philosophy professor, Chris Terry, wrote in the *Times Higher Education*:

> Kaufmann's *Nietzsche* challenged the prevailing assumption in British philosophy that only structured argument in analytical thought systems can permit reliable insight. Studying Nietzsche, he argued, showed that experimental thinking and an atypical aphoristic presentation could acquire clarity, coherence and incisiveness by accumulation, irony and wit. Moreover, he highlighted a tradition of dissent in philosophy, showing that Nietzsche, who was no logical positivist, sidestepped rigid systematic argument to demolish inner walls, explore the springs of conviction, investigate truths in contradictions, discover vitality in a continuous process of self-pillorying thought-evolution.

"The Canon: *Nietzsche: Philosopher, Psychologist, Antichrist*, by Walter Kaufmann," *Times Higher Education*, January 14, 2010, https://www.timeshighereducation.com/books/the-canon -nietzsche-philosopher-psychologist-antichrist-by-walter-kaufmann/409972.article.

And David Rathbone's essay "Kaufmann's Nietzsche," is a scintillating appreciation, especially in its smart expansion of Kaufmann's linkage of the Übermensch with the joy of affirming the Eternal Recurrence: "for if the Übermensch is an allegory for that perspective on existence we call freedom, and eternal return is a symbol for thinking time as a finite whole, then the two allegories in conjunction figure an autonomy possible only on the basis of finitude." In *Interpreting Nietzsche: Reception and Influence*, ed. Ashley Woodward (London: Continuum 2011), 55.

49. *Morgenröte* (Dawn), "Gedanken über die moralischen Vorurteile (1881)," http://www .textlog.de/20274.html.

50. On "fated," see esp. Brian Leiter, "The Paradox of Fatalism and Self-Creation," in *Nietzsche*, Oxford Readings in Philosophy, ed. John Richardson and Brian Leiter (Oxford: Oxford University Press, 2001), 281–321. Kaufmann's proleptic reply is found in the "Preface to the Third Edition" of *Nietzsche: Philosopher, Psychologist, Antichrist* (1968): "If anything 'compelled' me to occupy myself so intensively with Nietzsche it was my love of his books" (v).

51. This description of Staten's argument is adapted from my "The Subject of Nietzsche: Danto, Nehamas, and Staten," in *Nietzsche in American Literature and Thought*, ed. Manfred Pütz (Columbia, SC: Camden House, 1995), 263–77.

52. The original sense of dialectical process as found in Hegel differs from the conception of dialectic I discuss in Kaufmann, a sense consistent with Kaufmann's own account of that process. Žižek offers a suggestive revision, although Kaufmann's intuitive fidelity to Hegel is not at stake in this chapter. "The beginning of Hegel's logic as well as the beginning of his 'logic of essence,'" writes Žižek, "which deal with the notion of reflection are just two . . . examples that demonstrate how misleading, even outright wrong, is the standard notion of the dialectical process which begins with a positive entity, then negates it, and finally negates this negation itself, returning at a higher level to the positive starting point. Here we see a quite different logic: we begin with nothing, and it is only through the self-negation of nothing that something appears." *Absolute Recoil: Towards a New Foundation of Dialectical Materialism* (London: Verso, 2014), 154.

53. It would not be difficult to return this caveat to Kaufmann's own later writings!

54. John Milton, *Samson Agonistes*, closing chorus, lines 1755–56, https://www.dartmouth .edu/~milton/reading_room/samson/drama/text.shtml.

55. In "A Representative Destiny," an essay centering on Nehamas's Nietzsche study, *Life and Literature*, George Scialabba speaks of "Nietzsche's almost unrivalled capacity to teach us 'how to live' as well as 'how to read.'" *The Modern Predicament* (Boston: Pressed Wafer, 2011), 47.

56. Gotthold Ephraim Lessing, *Anti-Goeze* (1778), tr. in Christopher Hitchens, *God Is Not Great* (New York: Twelve [Hachette], 2007), 277.

57. Pickus, "Walter Kaufmann Myth," 236–37.

58. David Sorkin, *The Transformation of German Jewry, 1780–1840* (Oxford: Oxford University Press, 1987), 15.

59. The *Bildungsbürgertum* crystallizes around the idea of *Bildung* as self-making. The concept is additionally developed in Hegel's *Phenomenology of Spirit*, viz., Hegel's claim about the individual in §489:

> His true original nature and substance is the alienation of himself as Spirit from his natural being. This externalization is, therefore, both the purpose and the existence of the individual; it is at once the means, or the transition, both of the [mere] thought-form of substance into actuality, and, conversely, of the specific individuality into essentiality. *This individuality molds itself by culture into what it intrinsically is, and only by so doing is it an intrinsic being that has an actual existence; the measure of its culture is the measure of its actuality and power.* Although here the self knows itself as this self, yet its actuality consists solely in the setting-aside of its natural self (emphasis added).

Georg Wilhelm Friedrich Hegel, *Phenomenology of Spirit*, tr. A. V. Miller and ed. J. N. Findlay (Oxford: Oxford University Press, 1977), 298.

In his lustrous treatment of German Idealist thought, Márton Dornbach situates Hegel's idea of *Bildung* in a general theory of transmissible culture, "the propogation of insight." *Receptive Spirit: German Idealism and the Dynamics of Cultural Transmission* (New York: Fordham University Press, 2016), 179, and, further, 180–82 and 206–7.

60. Ian Buruma, "A Very Superior German Liberal," review of *Not I: Memoirs of a German Childhood by Joachim Fest*, tr. Martin Chalmers, ed. Herbert A. Arnold (New York: Other, 2014), *New York Review of Books* 61, no. 13 (August 14, 2014): 67.

61. Kaufmann adds: "Even after World War II, many German professors seemed to feel that way about themselves, and in the 1950s many of their students still accepted this view. In the late 1960s they went to the opposite extreme." *Without Guilt and Justice*, 199–200.

62. Ivan Soll writes,

> Although he received his higher education entirely in the United States, Kaufmann's intellectual interests were to a large extent already formed before he emigrated as a teenager. While at the *Gymnasium* in Berlin, he had been invited by one of his teachers to join a small group of particularly gifted students who read and discussed important works in German literature. Kaufmann continued to view his participation in this group as an important source of his intellectual interests and enthusiasms. Whatever the closer contours of his intellectual development may have been, Kaufmann arrived in the United States not only with great native intelligence, energy, and the impressive general *Bildung* (culture) that one acquires in a good German *Gymnasium* (secondary school), but also with a precocious intellectual maturity and well-developed intellectual interests. One has the impression that he was not so much educated by the

two American institutions [Williams College and Harvard University] he attended as a student, as that he, much more than most, used them as the required institutional backdrop for an intellectual and personal development whose mainsprings and general configuration already lay within him.

"Walter Kaufmann and the Advocacy of German Thought in America," *Paedagogica Historica: International Journal of the History of Education* 33, no. 1 (1997): 121–22.

63. Sorkin, *Transformation of German Jewry*, 136.

64. Buruma, "Very Superior," 67.

65. Fritz Ringer, *The Decline of the German Mandarins* (Cambridge, MA: Harvard University Press, 1969), 87.

66. Ibid., 245–46.

67. David Pickus, "Walter Kaufmann and the Future of the Humanities," *Journal of Thought* 42, nos. 3–4 (Fall–Winter 2007): 90.

68. We can be reasonably specific about the shape of this "configuration" as remarked in Soll, "Walter Kaufmann and the Advocacy," 121–22. Consider another description of the "fixed and undisputed canon of literary works" constituting the German national tradition; it is one that, according to Kafka's biographer Reiner Stach, "was the task of the Gymnasium to pass on . . . to the next generation largely intact. The textbooks used in Kafka's German class and the excerpts of texts compiled in them give a clear picture of the makeup of this canon: Lessing, Goethe, Schiller, and German romanticism formed the core, and secondary texts such as Eckermann's *Conversations with Goethe* and writings about literary criticism (Herder, Lessing) provided the supplements." *Franz Kafka: The Early Years*, tr. Shelley Frisch (Princeton, NJ: Princeton University Press, 2016), 145.

69. Walter Kaufmann, *From Shakespeare to Existentialism*, Princeton Paperback edition (Princeton, NJ: Princeton University Press, 1980), 241.

70. *Letters of Thomas Mann, 1889–1995*, tr. Richard Winston and Clara Winston (New York: Knopf, 1971), 97.

71. Ibid., 184.

72. Thomas Mann, *Betrachtungen eines Unpolitischen, Reden und Aufsätze*, vol. 4, *Gesammelte Werke*, vol. 12 (Frankfurt a.M.: Fischer, 1960), 84.

73. Mann, *Letters*, 370. This paragraph derives from my "Mann as a Reader of Nietzsche," in *The Fate of the Self: German Writers and French Theory* (Durham, NC: Duke University Press, 1994), 129–30, 259.

74. Kaufmann, *From Shakespeare*, 241.

75. *Hannah Arendt/Karl Jaspers, Correspondence, 1926–1969* (New York: Harcourt Brace, 1992), 231–33. Kaufmann's displeasure with *any* philosopher having but one foot in the Enlightenment was additionally vexed when that philosopher also wrote books on Nietzsche and, hence, was quite unable to see that, according to Kaufmann, Nietzsche had both feet in the Enlightenment, always. "The notion . . . that Nietzsche sympathized with the Enlightenment . . . only in his middle period, while he later broke with this tradition . . . is entirely unwarranted" (*Nietzsche*, 295). Graeme Garrard, however, argues persuasively that this "continuist" thesis is untenable, and Nietzsche first had two feet in the Enlightenment and thereafter, in the 1880s, none. "Nietzsche for and against the Enlightenment," *Review of Politics* 70, no. 4 (Fall 2008): 595–608.

76. Marc Redfield, *Phantom Formations: Aesthetic Ideology and the Bildungsroman* (Ithaca, NY: Cornell University Press, 1996). Fritz Breithaupt, "The Ego-Effect of Money," in *Rereading Romanticism*, ed. Martha B. Helfer (Amsterdam: Rodopi, 2000), 229.

77. See Nietzsche on the essential vitality of the "schöne Seele," viz., "der Künstler, dem es an der schönen Seele gebricht," must make do with artifice, "the glass eye." *Nietzsche, Werke, Kritische Gesamtausgabe*, ed. Giorgio Colli and Mazzino Montinari, *Menschliches Allzumensch-liches*, Zweiter Band, *Nachgelassene Fragmente, Frühling 1878 bis November 1879* (Berlin: Walter de Gruyter, 1967), 77. Afterward, Nietzsche will excoriate the indolence of the "beautiful soul," its instinct for decadence: "die Trägheit: er will nicht mehr sich verändern, nicht mehr lernen, er sitzt als 'schöne Seele' in sich selber." Ibid. Achte Abteilung, Dritter Band (Berlin: Walter de Gruyter, 1972), 416.

78. *Gay Science*, 349, cited in *Discovering the Mind*, vol. 2, 81.

79. *Will to Power* (no. 382), cited in ibid., 93. Pickus points out that "*Bildung* as both ideal and practice has an indwelling aggressive side to it. One preserves some things, but roots out, and frankly, demolishes the pretenses of partial views of oneself and others as the only way to travel on to something higher." "Walter Kaufmann Myth," 242. John Andrew Bernstein's lucid study *Nietzsche's Moral Philosophy* (Teaneck, NJ: Fairleigh Dickinson University Press, 1987) undertakes to show, however, that Nietzsche's "basic moral attitudes were less coherent and frequently far less humane than one would gather from Kaufmann's distinguished book" (15). To Nietzsche's claim that the feeling of power is proportional to the hardness of the obstacle to be overcome, Bernstein observes: "This dominance [of pain] is most conspicuous when any notion of a particular goal for which pain is endured is absent, and one is instead treated to a purely abstract praise of heroic endurance for no definite goal beyond the ability to endure itself" (33). This criticism runs in line with that of Nietzsche's (and Heidegger's) *decisionism*. See below, p. 626n5.

80. Reginster, *Affirmation of Life*, 286n31.

81. Michael Tanner of Cambridge University is the worst offender, writing that Kaufmann "*peddled* a view of Nietzsche which certainly eliminated any possibility of offence being given to anyone of liberal humanist outlook" (emphasis added). "Organizing the Self and the World," *Times Literary Supplement*, May 16, 1986, 519.

82. The point is developed in William McGrath, *Dionysian Art and Populist Politics in Austria* (New Haven, CT: Yale University Press, 1974). McGrath notes that "the close ties between Jews and Austrian liberalism seems [*sic*] to have had the effect of making Jews of the younger generation during the 1870s particularly sensitive to the failures of [an anti-aristocratic, bureaucratic-leaning] liberalism" (6–7). They were inclined, rather, to buy into an "aristocratic" Nietzschean ideal of personal self-transcendence and artistic creation—a sort of *Bildungsideal* in despite of the state.

83. Friedrich Nietzsche, *The Will to Power*, ed. Walter Kaufmann and tr. R. J. Hollingdale and Walter Kaufmann (New York: Vintage, 1968), 9–40.

84. Nietzsche, *Werke, Kritische Gesamtausgabe*, 2: 213.

85. The key word "organize" can have come to Nietzsche's attention from an essay by Friedrich Hölderlin, a fragment of his novel titled *Hyperion* (I assert this connection despite Nietzsche's mean-spirited ambivalence toward the beloved author of his Schulpforta days [see the remarkable work by Geoffrey Waite: "Nietzsche/Hölderlin: A Critical Reevaluation," PhD

diss., Department of German, Princeton University, 179–420]). Hölderlin writes of "two ideals of existence":

> a state of the highest simplicity, where our needs are reciprocally attuned to themselves, and to our powers, and to everything with which we are connected, through the mere organization of nature, without our cooperation, without experience; and a state of the highest cultivation (*Bildung*), where the same would take place amid infinitely multiplied and intensified needs and powers, *through the organization that we are able to give ourselves* (emphasis added).

Friedrich Hölderlin, "Fragment von Hyperion," *Sämtliche Werke und Briefe,* ed. Günter Mieth (Munich: Hanser, 1970), 11: 483–84.

86. Nietzsche, *Basic Writings*, 124.

87. This argument derives from my "Nietzsche: Neo-Gnosticism and Nihilism," in *Nietzsche, Nihilism and the Philosophy of the Future,* ed. Jeffrey Metzger (London: Continuum, 2009), 37–53.

88. Kaufmann points out that "the Preface of Nietzsche's *Meditation* on history opens with a quotation from Goethe, and Goethe is cited over half a dozen times in the essay itself" (N 144n23).

89. Goethe's contemporaries spoke of "a discontinuousness in him of mood and behavior . . . his fickleness and his sudden turns of mind. . . . Everywhere we find this disconcertingly rapid and irregular tempo, as if his mind were set at too fast and too uncertain a pace for others to keep up with it. Nothing ever seems to retard him; on he goes at high velocity, flitting incessantly from mood to mood." Fairley Barker, *A Study of Goethe* (Oxford: Clarendon, 1947), 4, 11.

90. From "The Despisers of the Body," *Thus Spoke Zarathustra,* in *Portable Nietzsche*, 140–41.

91. Sokel, "Political Uses and Abuses," 438–39.

92. Pickus, "Walter Kaufmann Myth," 257.

93. Cited in Gerhard Neumann, "Autobiographie und Karriere: Ein Selbstporträt des literarischen Fachs am Einzelfall [Chronik der Lektüren: Portrait eines Fachs]," in *Wissenschaft und Universität: Das Selbstporträt einer Generation; Wolfgang Frühwald zum 70. Geburtstag,* compiled by Martin Huber and Gerhard Lauer (Köln: Dumont, 2005), 242.

94. It can be argued that Nietzsche's interest in *Weltanschauungen* would conflict with any claim, such as Kaufmann's, that Nietzsche's sensibility was rooted in the Enlightenment, since *Weltanschauungen* are at odds with the universalist claims normally associated with Enlightenment rationality.

Chapter 2: Raw Life

1. Department of Philosophy, Princeton University. Epigraph: Jean-Paul Sartre, *Being and Nothingness,* tr. Hazel Barnes (New York: Philosophical Library, 1956), 565.

2. *From Shakespeare to Existentialism,* 1st ed. (Boston: Beacon, 1959); new ed., with additions (Garden City, NY: Doubleday, 1960). Epigraph: Walter Kaufmann, *From Shakespeare to Existentialism* (Princeton, NJ: Princeton University Press, 1980), 22. The core of two of the twenty chapters was published even before the appearance of *Nietzsche* in 1950. "Goethe and the History of Ideas" is based on an October 1949 article in the *Journal of the History of Ideas* 10 (October 1949): 503–16, and "Goethe's Faith and Faust's Redemption"

on a November 1949 essay in *Monatshefte* (University of Wisconsin) 41, no. 7 (November 1949): 365–75.

3. *Existentialism from Dostoevsky to Sartre* (New York: Meridian, 1956).

4. *Existentialism from Dostoevsky to Sartre*, edited, with an introduction, prefaces, and new translations by Walter Kaufmann, rev. and expanded (New York: Plume [Penguin], 1975 [originally, 1956]). Pages from this text will henceforth be shown in parentheses as (E + page number).

5. A leading question hovers over much of Kaufmann's ethical thinking: Does not this very "demand for decision" open him up to the charge of *irrational* decisionism—a charge that has often been leveled against Ernst Jünger, Carl Schmitt, and Martin Heidegger? This objection is powerfully formulated in a remarkable early work by Christian Graf von Krockow, *Die Entscheidung* [*The Decision*] (Stuttgart: Ferdinand Enke, 1958). Von Krockow stresses the disastrous presupposition of a decision at all costs—costs literally accruing from the reduction of the "world" to a Nothingness of merely "instrumental" relations, requiring, it is claimed, a primary vivification through a subjective projection of possibilities. "However, the more radically and exclusively (*einseitiger*) subjectivity strives to put the 'world' under the spell of its 'project,' the more helplessly it is subjected to the brute power of the 'facts'" (144). In chapter 8, Kaufmann discusses the way reason must participate in but cannot exclusively found decisions.

6. Calvin Schrag, review of *Existentialism from Dostoevsky to Sartre*, by Walter Kaufmann, *Journal of Religion* 37, no. 3 (July 1957): 221.

7. Antonio, "Kaufmann, Walter Arnold (1921–80)," 1284.

8. Erich Heller (1911–1990) wrote *The Disinherited Mind* (1952, expanded in 1957) and *The Artist's Journey into the Interior* (1966); Peter Gay [Fröhlich] (1923–2015) wrote *The Dilemma of Democratic Socialism: Eduard Bernstein's Challenge to Marx* (1952) and *The Enlightenment, An Interpretation: The Rise of Modern Paganism* (1966); George Steiner (1929–) wrote *The Death of Tragedy* (1961) and *Language and Silence: Essays on Language, Literature, and the Inhuman* (1967); Isaiah Berlin (1909–1997) wrote *The Hedgehog and the Fox: An Essay on Tolstoy's View of History* (1953) and *Four Essays on Liberty* (1969). One might add the cultural elitist Lionel Trilling (1905–15), who wrote *The Liberal Imagination: Essays on Literature and Society* (1950) and *Beyond Culture: Essays on Literature and Learning* (1965). Both older scholars—Trilling and Berlin—lectured at the Gauss Seminars at Princeton, Trilling in 1970–71 ("Sincerity and Authenticity") and Isaiah Berlin in 1973 ("The Origins of Cultural History"). Kaufmann was an energetic member of the Gauss Seminar Committee, serving as its acting director in 1967–68, 1971–72, and 1975–76. He would have participated in the invitation to both scholars. One could readily conclude a consanguinity of temperament among these three humanists.

9. A variation of an aperçu by Mark Greif, who, studying American intellectual life in the 1950s, wrote: "The mantle of philosophy was passing to the émigrés." *The Age of the Crisis of Man: Thought and Fiction in America, 1933–1973* (Princeton, NJ: Princeton University Press, 2015), 46.

10. George Cotkin, *Existential America* (Baltimore: Johns Hopkins University Press, 2003), 1.

11. See David Pickus's judicious defense of Kaufmann's objections to Jaspers's work—especially on Nietzsche—in "Wishes of the Heart: Walter Kaufmann, Karl Jaspers, and Disposition in Nietzsche Scholarship," *Journal of Nietzsche Studies*, no. 33 (Spring 2007): 5–24.

12. Kaufmann was a Fulbright research professor at the University of Heidelberg in 1955–56.

13. Walter Kaufmann, "Existentialism Tamed," *Kenyon Review* 16, no. 3 (Summer 1954): 488.

14. Walter Muschg, "Zerschwatzte Dichtung," in *Die Zerstörung der deutschen Literatur* (Bern: Francke, 1956), 214–30.

15. *The Antichrist*, in *Portable Nietzsche*, 635.

16. Ibid. Nietzsche's affirmation of the dignity of philology is being vigorously resuscitated—for one, by the eminent Sanskritist Sheldon Pollock. In "Philology and Freedom," an as yet unpublished paper delivered at Princeton University on April 10, 2014. Pollock wrote: "Philology may well represent *the* exemplary disciplinary form for the twenty-first century global university: in its best aspects it encourages the cultivation of values central to our intellectual, political, and ethical lives: commitments to truth, to human solidarity, and to critical self-awareness." (To be sure, the plea for a generalized "human solidarity" would not be part of Nietzsche's program.) The revolutionary centrality of the concept of philology for early nineteenth-century German idealist philosophers—a claim that touches Nietzsche—is set forth with panache in an excellent work by Sarah M. Pourciau, *The Writing of Spirit: Soul, System, and the Roots of Language Science* (New York: Fordham University Press, 2017), esp. 98–99.

17. Jessica Berry, *Nietzsche and the Ancient Skeptical Tradition* (Oxford: Oxford University Press, 2011), 130–31.

18. Nietzsche, *Notebooks* (Summer 1886–Fall 1887). This is Kaufmann's translation in *Portable Nietzsche*, 458.

19. Franz Kafka, *The Castle*, tr. Mark Harman (New York: Schocken, 1998), 231.

20. This citation is found everywhere on the web, where it is reproduced as the motto of article after article, book chapter after chapter. But one wise scholar points out that Nietzsche *never* wrote these sentences. Still, you might think Nietzsche did, because another writer, and he alone—the author of "Vanishing Meaning, the Ideology of Value-Addition, and the Diffusion of Broadband Information Technology," in *Globalism with a Human Face*, ed. Jung Min Choi and John Murphy (Westport, CT: Praeger, 2004), 98—provides the hotly desired reference. Here it is: "Friedrich Nietzsche, *The Will to Power* (New York: Random House, 1967), p. 60 ff." But what would "ff." mean in this case? Is the quotation to be found on page 60 or not? Answer: it is not. The reference is invented—in the nicest case, an affair of interpretation normatively "overcoming" mere fact in the service of the scholar's will to power.

21. Nietzsche, *Will to Power*, 47.

22. Ibid., 165.

23. Ibid., 302.

24. Ibid., 330.

25. Ibid., 340.

26. Ibid., 342.

27. Ibid., 358.

28. Luther, "Operationes in Duos Psalmorum," in *D. Martin Luthers Werke: Kritische Gesamtausgabe* (Weimar: Böhlau, 1883–2009), 6: 562, 24–26.

29. *The Antichrist*, in *Portable Nietzsche*, 635.

30. *A Letter From Luther to Melanchthon*, letter no. 99, August 1, 1521, from the Wartburg (Segment), tr. Erika Bullmann Flores from *Dr. Martin Luther's Saemmtliche Schriften*, Dr. Johannes Georg Walch, ed. (St. Louis: Concordia, n.d.), vol. 15, cols. 2585–90.

31. Kaufmann wrote a foreword to John Wilcox's *Truth and Value in Nietzsche*, in which Wilcox shows Nietzsche to be predominantly a "cognitivist"—meaning, in Kaufmann's words, that Nietzsche "believed his own theories, and especially his own ethic, to be objectively true in some sense." Thereafter Kaufmann praises the fact that "Wilcox goes out of his way to consider the passages [in Nietzsche] that apparently contradict his interpretation. This is . . . sound method" (emphasis added). (Ann Arbor: University of Michigan Press, 1974), vii, ix.

32. Reinhard Mehring, *Heideggers Überlieferungsgeschick: Eine dionysische Selbstinzenierung* (Würzburg: Königshausen und Neumann, 1992), 140n7.

33. John Milton, *Samson Agonistes*, closing chorus, lines 1755–56.

34. Martin Heidegger, *Holzwege* (Frankfurt a.M.: Klostermann, 1957), 247.

35. Muschg, 214–30. Peter Szondi, *Der andere Pfeil: Zur Entstehungsgeschichte von Hölderlins hymnischem Spätstil* (Frankfurt a.M.: Insel, 1963), 14–17.

36. Martin Heidegger, *Elucidations of Heidegger's Poetry*, tr. Keith Hoeller (Amherst, MA: Humanity Books, 2000), 74.

37. Friedrich Hölderlin, *Poems and Fragments*, tr. Michael Hamburger (Cambridge: Cambridge University Press, 1980), 377.

38. Paul de Man writes, "*It is the fact that Hölderlin says exactly the opposite of what Heidegger makes him say.* Such an assertion is paradoxical only in appearance. At this level of thought it is difficult to distinguish between a proposition and that which constitutes its opposite. In fact, to state the opposite is still to talk of the same thing though in an opposite sense, and it is already a major achievement to have, in a dialogue of this sort, the two interlocutors manage to speak of the same thing." Paul de Man, "Heidegger's Exegeses of Hölderlin's Poetry," *Blindness and Insight*, rev. 2nd ed. (Minneapolis: University of Minnesota Press, 1983), 255.

39. "Among the most striking features of *Notes from Underground* is its artistic singularity and unprecedentedness; it seems to come, formally speaking, from nowhere; but, in fact, it probably comes from the feuilleton." Joseph Frank, *Dostoevsky: The Seeds of Revolt, 1821–1849* (Princeton, NJ: Princeton University Press, 1976), 237.

40. Marcus Bullock, *The Violent Eye: Ernst Jünger's Visions and Revisions on the European Right*, Kritik: German Literary Theory and Cultural Studies Series (Detroit: Wayne State University Press, 1992), 234.

41. Joseph Frank, *Dostoevsky: A Writer in His Time*, ed. Mary Petrusewicz (Princeton, NJ: Princeton University Press, 2010), 413–14.

42. Ibid., 414–15.

43. Franz Kafka, *Complete Stories*, tr. Edwin Muir and Willa Muir (New York: Schocken, 1971), 239.

44. Frank, *Dostoevsky*, 416.

45. Antonio, "Kaufmann, Walter Arnold," 1285.

46. Walter Cerf, review of *Existentialism from Dostoevsky to Sartre*, by Walter Kaufmann, *Philosophy and Phenomenological Research* 18, no. 2: 280. For Cerf's mordant views on the German university, see "Existentialist Mannerism and Education," *Journal of Philosophy* 52, no. 6: 141–52. It is best read in good company with Kaufmann's own report on the teaching of philosophy in German universities in "German Thought after World War II," in *From Shakespeare to Existentialism* (Princeton, NJ: Princeton University Press, 1980; originally, Boston: Beacon, 1959), 371–85. Cerf's account was subsequently criticized by Ludwig Land-

grebe in "The Study of Philosophy in Germany: A Reply to Walter Cerf," *Journal of Philosophy* 54, no. 5: 127–31.

47. This point is elaborated by Ann Fulton in her *Apostles of Sartre: Existentialism in America, 1945–1963* (Evanston, IL: Northwestern University Press, 1999):

> Sartre's readiness to include sexuality as an appropriate topic for philosophy was another facet of the charge that Sartre was unacademic. Kaufmann believed that Sartre's frank discussions of the philosophical implications of sex in *Being and Nothingness* sent more than one American philosopher into mild shock and were an important undercurrent in their cool reception. This aspect surfaced more clearly now, brought on in 1953 by the publication of *Existential Psychoanalysis*, which included chapters from *Being and Nothingness* that discussed the philosophical significance of sexual behavior. Kaufmann felt it necessary to remind readers in 1956 that Sartre's treatment of sex "is designed to increase our understanding of important problems, never to arouse desire" (92).

48. Jean-Paul Sartre, *Being and Nothingness: An Essay on Phenomenological Ontology*, tr. Hazel Barnes (New York: Philosophical Library, 1956), 508.

49. Henry Hatfield, review of *Existentialism from Dostoevsky to Sartre*, by Walter Kaufmann, *German Quarterly* 30, no. 4 (November 1957): 299.

50. Walter Cerf, review of *Nietzsche: Philosopher, Psychologist, Antichrist*, by Walter Kaufmann, *Philosophy and Phenomenological Research* 12, no. 2 (December 1951): 287.

51. Cerf, review of *Existentialism*, 280.

52. Weiss-Rosmarin, "Interview," 121.

53. Schrag, review of *Existentialism*, 221–22.

54. Kaufmann, *Nietzsche*, 161.

55. David Pickus, "Paperback Authenticity: Walter Kaufmann and Existentialism," *Philosophy and Literature* 34, no. 1 (April 2010): 17–31.

56. Stephen Crowell, "Existentialism," *Stanford Encyclopedia of Philosophy*, http://plato.stanford.edu/entries/existentialism/. Crowell's rather unreflected use of the term "authenticity" elides Adorno's scathing criticism of the term in *The Jargon of Authenticity*, tr. Knut Tarnowski and Frederic Will (Evanston, IL: Northwestern University Press, 1973); originally *Jargon der Eigentlichkeit: Zur deutschen Ideologie* (Frankfurt a.M.: Suhrkamp (1965). Adorno has in view the scandalous aura of the word, its suggestion (in Heidegger) of a splendid simplicity, rootedness in some old familiar place, its surreptitious participation in Being, its ignorance of the derelict social world in which it travels about by word of mouth, etc.

57. Gerhard Neumann, "Umkehrung und Ablenkung: Franz Kafkas 'Gleitendes Paradox,'" in *Franz Kafka, Wege der Forschung*, ed. Heinz Politzer (Darmstadt: Wissenschaftliche Buchgesellschaft 1973), 475. I discuss both this and the Mann quote below in the preface to my *Complex Pleasure: Forms of Feeling in German Literature* (Stanford, CA: Stanford University Press, 1998), xi–xviii.

58. Thomas Mann, *Doctor Faustus*, tr. H. T. Lowe-Porter (New York: Vintage, 1948), 485.

59. Philip Rieff, *The Feeling Intellect: Selected Writings*, ed. Jonathan B. Imber (Chicago: University of Chicago Press, 1990).

60. Tom Stern, "On Analysis," *Times Literary Supplement*, September 5, 2014, 10.

61. Kaufmann exults in what he represents as Nietzsche's unconditional valuation of "life," but is he aware that Nietzsche and now Heidegger may not be made to share the same pew,

630 NOTES TO CHAPTER 2

since Heidegger is a determined critic of *Lebensphilosophie*, which he links with the other cardinal ills of modernity: scientism, technology, historicism, etc.? See Martin Heidegger, *Interpretation of Nietzsche's Second Untimely Meditation* (Bloomington: Indiana University Press, 2016).

62. Nietzsche, *Birth of Tragedy*, 158.

63. Nietzsche, *Ecce Homo*, in *Basic Writings*, 677.

64. Ibid., 756–57; *Portable Nietzsche*, 295–96.

65. Nietzsche, *Ecce Homo*, in *Basic Writings*, 756–57.

66. Nietzsche, *Will to Power*, 270.

67. Frank Ankersmit, "Narrative, an Introduction," in *Re-figuring Hayden White*, ed. Frank Ankersmit, Ewa Domanska, and Hans Kellner (Stanford, CA: Stanford University Press, 2005), 79.

68. Paul de Man, "Autobiography as De-facement," *Rhetoric of Romanticism* (New York: Columbia University Press, 1984), 81.

69. Karl Jaspers, *Philosophie* (Berlin: J. Springer, 1932). The volumes are titled (1) *Philosophische Weltorientierung*; (2) *Existenzerhellung*; (3) *Metaphysik*.

70. Gerald Bruns, *Heidegger's Estrangements: Language, Truth, and Poetry in the Later Writings* (New Haven, CT: Yale University Press, 1989).

> Obviously, we are not speaking here of the utopian comedy of wish-fulfillment . . . rather it is comic in the darker, more satirical sense of the outsider—the philosophical outcast—who resists 'abiding integration' in behalf of scandal and freedom: a nomadic rather than vegetal comedy—a comedy of *eris* rather than *eros*, of rift rather than reconciliation. . . . The comedy of thinking is its uncontainability, its refusal of control, its lapse from reason . . . its nearness to poetry, its ability (which it perhaps shares with poetry) to live with skepticism. This is the prodigal, nomadic, cold, anarchic comedy from which even Nietzsche pulls up short (186–87).

Bruns's aperçu is interesting and engaging and shrewd for its time: it is now a lot harder to reconcile Heidegger's "darker comedy" with the dissociated propaganda of the *Black Notebooks*.

71. Cited in Hugo Ott, *Martin Heidegger: A Political Life*, tr. Allan Blunden (London: HarperCollins, 1993), 339.

72. It is unclear who has made this translation: a rival but also very adequate translation is found in Martin Heidegger, *Being and Time: A Revised Edition of the Stambaugh Translation*, tr. Joan Stambaugh and revised by Dennis Schmidt (Albany: State University of New York Press, 2010), 123.

73. J. P. Stern, "Heil Heidegger," review of Hugo Ott, *Martin Heidegger: Unterwegs zu seiner Biographie* (Frankfurt a.M.: Campus Verlag, 1988), *London Review of Books* 11, no. 8 (April 20, 1989): 8.

74. On Johann Peter Hebel, idolized by intellectual workers for the Nazis, see Charles Bambach, *Heidegger's Roots: Nietzsche, National Socialism, and the Greeks* (Ithaca, NY: Cornell University Press, 2003), 331.

75. Bruns, *Heidegger's Estrangements*, xix.

76. *Being and Time*, tr. Stambaugh and rev. Schmidt, xxiii.

77. For contrasting statements, see *Nietzsche as Political Philosopher*, ed. Manuel Knoll and Barry Stocker (Berlin: de Gruyter, 2014). Consider, too, R. Lanier Anderson's remarks, in recommending Tamsin Shaw's *Nietzsche's Political Skepticism* (Princeton, NJ: Princeton Univer-

sity Press, 2007): "It has become standard to think that Nietzsche lacked a serious (or at least an interesting) political philosophy. That conventional wisdom encourages the treatment of his many comments about politics and culture as digressions from his central philosophical concerns. This book is the most compelling challenge to date against that conventional wisdom" (https://www.amazon.com/Nietzsches-Political-Skepticism-Tamsin-Shaw-ebook/dp /Boo2WJM6BI). Equally, consult Storm Heter's detailed essay titled "Sartre's Political Philosophy" in the *Internet Encyclopedia of Philosophy*, http://www.iep.utm.edu/sartre-p/.

78. Kaufmann, *Without Guilt and Justice*, 15–18.

79. A brief account of Steven W. Laycock's *Nothingness and Emptiness: A Buddhist Engagement with the Ontology of Jean-Paul Sartre* (Albany: State University of New York Press, 2001) reads:

> Rooted in the insights of Madhyamika dialectic and an articulated meditative (zen) phenomenology, *Nothingness and Emptiness* uncovers and examines the assumptions that sustain Sartre's early phenomenological ontology and questions his theoretical elaboration of consciousness as "nothingness." Laycock demonstrates that, in addition to a "relative" nothingness (the for-itself) defined against the positivity and plenitude of the in-itself, Sartre's ontology requires, but also repudiates, a conception of "absolute" nothingness (the Buddhist "emptiness"), and is thus, as it stands, logically unstable, perhaps incoherent. The author is not simply critical; he reveals the junctures at which Sartrean ontology appeals for a Buddhist conception of emptiness and offers the needed supplement (http://muse.jhu.edu/books/9780791490969).

These lines should suggest the ongoing interest, especially among Asian (Thai, Chinese, Japanese) scholars of Buddhism, in associating Buddhist thought with phenomenological and existential philosophy.

80. Nehamas, *Nietzsche*, 179.

81. Schrag, review of *Existentialism*, 221.

Chapter 3: Cleaning the Stables

1. *Critique of Religion and Philosophy* (Princeton, NJ: Princeton University, 1958). Pages from this text will henceforth be shown in parentheses as (C + page number).

2. One needs to go outside this book for answers to these questions. That Kaufmann was married is a fact known personally to me, for I visited his home in Princeton and met his wife, Hazel. His liking of cold water and apples is a surmise following a passage in a later volume offering examples of "short spans of happiness": "an early morning walk, seeing a flower or a fine tree, a drink of cold water, or biting into a crisp apple." *Without Guilt and Justice*, 207.

3. This insistence is supported, at the least, by Kaufmann's reading of Johann Huizinga's *Homo Ludens*. Kaufmann's mouthpiece, Satan, in his coming dialogue with "The Theologian," notes Huizinga's identification of "the play element in the performance of the Sophists; he emphasizes the origin of Greek philosophy in leisure and the similarity of philosophic puzzles to non-philosophic puzzles; and he cites Plato in his own behalf" (C 230).

4. "He enjoys *ad hominem* asides, digs, parodies, and japes; but these are inspired, if not always controlled, by a desire to humanize philosophy and religion." Julian Hartt, review of *Critique of Religion and Philosophy*, by *Walter Kaufmann*, *Philosophical Review* 70, no. 2 (April 1961): 289.

5. Arthur Danto, *Nietzsche as Philosopher*, expanded ed. (New York: Columbia University Press, 2005), 108. Danto is referring to the "Introductory Remarks" to Walter Kaufmann's translation of *The Twilight of the Idols*, in *Portable Nietzsche*, tr. and ed. Walter Kaufmann (New York: Viking, 1954), 463–64.

6. James Joyce, *Ulysses* (Ware, Herefordshire: Wordsworth Editions, 2010), 444.

7. The Levinas scholar Benjamin Wurgaft puts the difference succinctly. For Levinas, "Philosophy might aim for a universal mode of 'Greek' thought, but it would always be *as Jews* that Jews encountered the universal" (http://www.myjewishlearning.com/article /emmanuel-levinas/).

8. "As Bernard Williams once remarked, the contrast of 'analytical' and 'Continental' philosophy is rather like classifying cars into 'front-wheel drive and Japanese.'" Christopher Prendergast, review of *Dictionary of Untranslatables: A Philosophical Lexicon*, ed. Emily Apter, Jacques Lezra, and Michael Wood (Princeton, NJ: Princeton University Press, 2014), *London Review of Books* 37, no. 17 (September 10, 2015): 36. This is a vivid but all too succinct way of criticizing the distinction between "analytical" and "existential" or "Continental" philosophy. In the view of three very capable philosophers, Stephen Mulhall (New College, Oxford), Béatrice Han-Pile (Essex), and Hans Johann-Glock (Zurich), the distinction is by no means nugatory (https://www.youtube.com/watch?v=xiISBhwxaYo).

9. Friedrich Nietzsche, *Beyond Good and Evil*, in *Basic Writings*, 217.

10. Paul Berman, reflecting on what "we" can do to stop the deranged murderers of the political movement ISIS, concludes, "We lift a finger. Just now, we have lifted two fingers. Maybe three! But we moderns have had trouble motivating ourselves to do even this much, and that is because, not believing in evil, we do not believe in free will, either, not even for ourselves." "Evil Is a Dirty Word, *Tablet*, October 8, 2014, http://tabletmag.com/jewish-news-and-politics /186118/evil-is-a-dirty-word. The narrator of the eponymous novel *Elizabeth Costello* by John Coetzee remarks: "She [Elizabeth] no longer believes very strongly in belief." Elizabeth reflects: "I have beliefs but I do not believe in them" (London: Penguin, 2003), 39, 200.

11. "Ich habe kein literarisches Interesse, sondern bestehe aus Literatur, ich bin nichts anderes und kann nichts anderes sein" (letter to Felice Bauer, August 14, 1913).

12. See Daniel Heller-Roazen, *The Inner Touch: Archaeology of a Sensation* (Brooklyn, NY: Zone, 2007).

13. Cited, ⸱ ith commentary, in Corngold, *Fate of the Self*, 25.

14. Stefa..os Geroulanos, *An Atheism That Is Not Humanist Emerges in French Thought* (Stanford, CA: Stanford University Press, 2010), 308–9.

15. This is the main topic of Corngold's *Fate of the Self*.

16. The third stanza of Kaufmann's own poem begins:

> To build! Not like a child that moulds the sand
> and lays his little will before the waves—
> no, not for pleasure, heedless of the morrow!
> Nor like a man who makes himself a mansion,
> the mirror of his mind that some admire:
> some spend their youth in it, and some old age,
> one adds a wing and one tears down some part,
> and in the end it is a striking ruin

in the museum of the human mind.
To build the spirit's fortress for mankind,
using the columns left us by the Greeks
and, as the Normans do in Sicily,
link them with walls and Arab vaults, providing
new columns where required to support
the Biblical mosaics of the ceiling.

To build—not a small chapel for myself,
using what stones my native land provides,
but, drawing on the best the world can give,
the wisdom of the Greeks, the subtle learning
of Jews and Arabs, and the Holy Scriptures,
construct the universal church of man. (C 143)

17. In an extensive and, I believe, fair-minded review of Kaufmann's *Critique of Religion and Philosophy* and *The Faith of a Heretic*, James Woelfel, a professor of philosophy at the University of Kansas, argues that, in faulting "empiricism," Kaufmann fails to distinguish between an atomistic "classical" empiricism deserving of his criticism and a radical empiricism, vividly present in William James, Alfred North Whitehead, and John Dewey that anticipates and fulfills Kaufmann's plea for relevance. "Religious Empiricism as '-ism': The Critical Legacy of Walter Kaufmann," *American Journal of Theology and Philosophy* 15, no. 2 (May 1994): 186–87.

18. In his review of Kaufmann's *The Portable Nietzsche*, James Gutmann, a professor of philosophy at Columbia University, wrote:

My only serious criticism of Dr. Kaufmann's work concerns *Der Antichrist* and, specifically, his translation of the title. I raised the point in a review of his earlier book in this journal [*Journal of Philosophy* 48, no. 21 (October 11, 1951): 645], perhaps unfairly since he had called the reader's attention to the ambiguity which the German term involves and which cannot be duplicated in English. Certainly no statement of the issue could improve on the one which Kaufmann now presents in his Editor's Preface on page 565: "The title is ambiguous. It first calls to mind the apocalyptic Antichrist, and this more sensational meaning is in keeping with the author's intention to be as provocative as possible. But the title could also mean 'The Anti-Christian,' and this interpretation is much more in keeping with the contents of the book, and in sections 38 and 47 the word is used in a context in which this is the only possible meaning." The concluding sentence of this statement seems to me to be conclusive evidence in favor of the translation.

The Anti-Christian (*Journal of Philosophy* 52, no. 17 [August 18, 1955]: 474). Kaufmann subsequently returned to his original, more "provocative" reading of the term.

19. I owe the stimulus to these reflections to an unpublished paper by Benjamin Steege of Columbia University titled "Debussy and the Aesthetics of 'Dehumanization.'"

20. This driving out of psychology from "pure" philosophy—especially, epistemology—precedes Heidegger. This thrust is central to the work of Frege and Husserl. In *Psychologism: A Case Study in the Sociology of Philosophical Knowledge*, Martin Kusch explores the struggle for academic priority in German universities in the nineteenth and twentieth centuries between "pure" philosophy and the new experimental psychology (London: Routledge, 1995).

21. In this context Kaufmann would have been glad to see Peter Unger's *Empty Ideas: A Critique of Analytic Philosophy* (Oxford: Oxford University Press, 2014). "Except when offering parochial ideas, . . . mainstream philosophy still offers hardly anything beyond concretely empty ideas" (http://www.amazon.com/Empty-Ideas-Critique-Analytic-Philosophy /dp/0199330816).

22. Sigmund Freud, *Die Traumdeutung*, Studienausgabe (Frankfurt a.M.: S. Fischer, 1972), 2: 227.

23. In *Patriotism and Other Mistakes*, the political philosopher George Kateb argues that "human conduct often exhibits a stronger preference for many aspirations and attainments than for morality," a view that he defines as a certain reprehensible "unrationalized aestheticism." "People and thinkers constantly demonstrate that they prefer, that they love, quite a number of ideal aims more than they love morality. They tacitly demonstrate an, as it were, innocent preference for, or love of, certain things despite the high, sometimes infinitely high, moral cost, or they expressly assert the subordination or irrelevance of morality" (New Haven, CT: Yale University Press, 2006), 118. A critical review of *Critique* by Denis J. B. Hawkins, a Catholic theologian, employs this very idea. Commenting on Kaufmann's emphasis on "man's aspirations," he remarks: "Moral aspiration without moral principle is apt to lead to odd results" (*Times Literary Supplement*, July 31, 1959, 450). Hawkins appears to have his finger on Kaufmann's unacknowledged Faustianism, "man's aspiration to transcend himself" (C 355).

24. Nietzsche, *On the Genealogy of Morals*, in *Basic Writings*, 516.

25. J. L. Austin, "Pretending," *The Symposia Read at the Joint Session of the Aristotelian Society and the Mind Association at Southampton, 11th to 13th July, 1958* (London: Harrison and Sons, 1958), 261–78.

26. *The Dawn*, in *Portable Nietzsche*, 83–84.

27. Kaufmann's work on Hegel proceeds as a lengthy expansion of an earlier and much-cited essay, "The Hegel Myth and Its Method" (1951), thereafter reprinted in *From Shakespeare to Existentialism* (1959), along with "The Young Hegel and Religion" and "Hegel: Contribution and Calamity." Hegel appears in important places in *The Faith of a Heretic* (originally published 1961) and then as the subject of the volume mentioned above: *Hegel: Reinterpretation, Texts, and Commentary*. Part 2 of this work, *Hegel: Texts and Commentary*—chiefly a translation of and commentary on the preface to Hegel's *Phenomenology of Spirit*—was reprinted in a popular Anchor paperback edition in 1966. Thereafter, Kaufmann edited *Hegel's Political Philosophy* (1970) and discussed him at length in volume 1 of *Discovering the Mind, Goethe, Kant, and Hegel*, published in 1980, the year of his death.

28. V. d. Luft, "Kaufmann, Walter Arnold," 402.

29. Immanuel Kant, "Remarks in the *Observations on the Feeling of the Beautiful and Sublime*," in *Observations on the Feeling of the Beautiful and Sublime, and Other Writings*, tr. Thomas Hilgers, Uygar Abaci, Michael Nance, and Paul Guyer (Cambridge: Cambridge University Press, 2011), 95, 105.

30. Georg Gurwitsch, "Kant und Fichte als Rousseau-Interpreten," *Kantstudien* 27 (1922): 140.

31. John Coetzee, *Elizabeth Costello*, paperback (New York: Viking Penguin, 2004), 213.

32. Kafka, *The Great Wall of China*, tr. Willa Muir and Edwin Muir (New York: Schocken, 1960), 298.

33. N.b., "Empirical risk" is a tautology, since being "empirical," in the Greek origin of the word, means "performing an experiment, putting something on trial, risking something." "'*Empirical*' derives from the Latin *empiricus*, which is a transliteration of the Greek *empiricos* (empirical, experienced; ἐμπειρικός) from *empiria* (experience; ἐμπειρία) from *en-* (in, with) + *pira* (experience, trial; πείρα), from the verb *pirao* (make an attempt, try, test, get experience, endeavour, attack; πειράω)" (http://ewonago.blogspot.com/2009/02/etymology-of-empirical-empiric.html).

34. Bernard Williams, *Truth and Truthfulness* (Princeton, NJ: Princeton University Press, 2002), 205.

35. Paul de Man, "Genesis and Genealogy in Nietzsche's *The Birth of Tragedy*," in *Allegories of Reading* (New Haven, CT: Yale University Press, 1979), 100.

36. "A Letter from Paul de Man," *Critical Inquiry* 8, no. 3 (Spring 1982): 512.

37. Nietzsche, *Will to Power*, 265.

38. Ibid., 249.

39. Geoff Waite, *Nietzsche's Corps/e: Aesthetics, Politics, Prophecy, or, The Spectacular Technoculture of Everyday Life* (Durham, NC: Duke University Press, 1996), 435n.

40. V. d. Luft, "Kaufmann, Walter Arnold," 401.

41. Nietzsche, *Will to Power*, 262.

42. Trust is also an affair of belief: even if our trust has been factually established on one occasion, it will take belief to assume that it will be established once again. This relation complicates the difference between knowledge and belief, which Kaufmann posed earlier in this chapter, where belief is taken to be the defective substitute for knowledge. In fact, knowledge of the truth cannot do without it: there must be trust in the validity of evidence. Here the work of Glenn W. Most is relevant: in his study of the vicissitudes of the figure of Doubting Thomas, Most writes: "Whether what is involved is a lyric poem or a declaration of love, instructions for escaping from a hotel room in case of fire or a message of religious salvation, nothing else can be achieved by a text if it does not in the first instance inspire the reader's trust in it— the 'willing suspension of disbelief' of which Coleridge spoke is a premise required not only by literary works of art but by all means of communication." *Doubting Thomas* (Cambridge, MA: Harvard University Press, 2005), 7–8. Even where a text is not literally involved, one must believe in the evidence of one's senses. The chapter titled "Truth, Assertion, and Belief" in Bernard Williams's lustrous work *Truth and Truthfulness* (Princeton, NJ: Princeton University Press, 2004) can be read profitably together with Kaufmann's ruminations on truth and trust. Williams inverts their relationship: "Statements which are plainly true . . . remind us that we share the same world and find the same thing salient and help us to discover where we do and do not agree" (72). The point at which we agree is a nacreous point for the formation of trust.

43. *Die Bedeutung von Kants Begründung der Ästhetik für die Philosophie der Kunst* (Cologne: Kölner-Universitäts-Verlag, 1959), 145. This lucid and informative work is still worth consulting today.

44. Max Scheler (1874–1928) constructed at length a phenomenology of the affective life. One of his many influential philosophical works is *Wesen und Formen der Sympathie* (Essence and forms of sympathy) (1923). In an early (unpublished) essay on two poems of Hölderlin (1914), Walter Benjamin described "courage" as a sort of mood—as "the feeling for life of the man who surrenders himself to danger, so that in his death it expands into a danger to the world

and at the same time overcomes it." "Two Poems by Friedrich Hölderlin: 'The Poet's Courage' and 'Timidity,'" tr. Stanley Corngold, in Walter Benjamin, *Selected Writings, 1, 1913–1926*, ed. Marcus Bullock and Michael Jennings (Cambridge, MA: Harvard University Press, 1996), 33. In *Wahrheit und Ästhetik: Untersuchungen zum Frühwerk Walter Benjamins* (Würzburg: Königshausen und Neumann, 1991), Rudolf Speth discusses the "existential dimension of Benjamin's concept of courage"—more particularly, its revelation of "the disclosive character of the affects" (50).

45. Davis S. Miall, "The Alps Deferred: Wordsworth at the Simplon Pass," *European Romantic Review* 9 (1998): 87.

46. William Wordsworth, *The Prelude*, 1805, book 6, "Cambridge and the Alps," lines 525–29 (New York: Norton, 1979), 216.

47. Ibid., lines 538–42.

48. Ian Mackean on William Wordsworth, *The Prelude*, book 6, "Cambridge and the Alps," http://www.literature-study-online.com/essays/wordsworth-prelude.html.

Chapter 4: Transcending the Human

1. Epigraph: Harold Bloom, *The Daemon Knows: Literary Greatness and the American Sublime* (New York: Spiegel and Grau, 2015), 3.

2. "Aspirations" also preface Kaufmann's essay collection *From Shakespeare to Existentialism*, published a year later: "People use moral terms without thinking about them. They confound devotion with devoutness, and humility with meekness. Yet nothing makes one more conscious of one's limitations than bold aspirations, which are not self-effacing" (S xiii).

3. Coral Davenport, "Why Republicans Keep Telling Everyone They're Not Scientists," *New York Times*, October 30, 2014, http://www.nytimes.com/2014/10/31/us/why-republicans-keep-telling-everyone-theyre-not-scientists.html.

4. Gérard Deledalle, review of Kaufmann's *Critique, Les Études philosophiques*, n.s., 14e, no. 3 (July–September 1959): 376.

5. The King James translation of John 14:6 reads, "Jesus saith unto him, I am the way, the truth, and the life: no man cometh unto the Father, but by me." He is addressing the apostle Thomas, later to emerge as "Doubting Thomas." The fate of this figure is traced vividly in the study by Most, *Doubting Thomas*.

6. Christopher Hitchens, http://www.openculture.com/2011/11/christopher_hitchens_no_deathbed_conversion_for_me_thanks_but_it_was_good_of_you_to_ask_.html.

7. "Father Divine"—its full form: "Reverend Major Jealous Divine"—was the assumed name of George Baker (alias "God"), whose effective preaching for peace and equality contributed to the inspiration behind the civil rights movement.

8. James Bisset Pratt, *The Religious Consciousness* (New York: Macmillan, 1940), 446.

9. The topic of miracles—cogent, not easily dismissed tout court—is a long abiding research interest of the philosopher of religion Hent de Vries. A major book on this topic, in which Wittgenstein is an important reference, is in the works. The 2001 article "Of Miracles and Special Effects," *International Journal for Philosophy of Religion* 50 (1/3): 41–56, is a run-up to this magnum opus.

10. Kaufmann, *Portable Nietzsche*, 452.

11. Étienne Gilson, *The Christian Philosophy of St. Thomas Aquinas* (New York: Random House, 1956), 160.

12. C. D. Broad, *Religion, Philosophy and Psychical Research* (London: Routledge and Kegan Paul, 1953). Broad was an eminent (Cambridge) University Professor of Moral Philosophy; new works by him—on Leibniz (1975), Berkeley (1976), Kant (1978), and general ethics (1985)—kept appearing even after his death in 1971.

13. In a lively review of *Critique*, Margaret Wiley Marshall identifies the thread in the carpet of the entire work as "'ambiguity' (it might have been 'paradox' or 'contradiction' or 'inconsistency') to shadow forth the clash, or the amalgam of opposites, which he [Kaufmann] considers the hallmark of truth." Marshall observes the *many* applications of the word to various systems of thought throughout the book, viz., "Thus Kaufmann characterizes as ambiguous all statements about God, the stories of the Old Testament, the poetry of Taoism, the Zen concept of *satori*, the writings of Sophocles and Kafka, the Haggadah exegesis of Hebrew scripture, and indeed all the ultimate statements of human conviction." *Journal of Higher Education* 30, no. 8 (November 1959): 463–64.

14. Kaufmann quotes "Hegel, *Encyclopaedia*, 3rd edition, 1830, par. 482."

15. Martin Luther, *Sämtliche Schriften*, ed. Johann Georg Walch, 24 vols. (St. Louis: Concordia, 1880–1910), 5: 425.

16. The psychoanalyst Adam Phillips disputes the profit of the emotion of self-contempt. See chapter 7.

17. "Nicht Selbstabschüttelung sondern Selbstaufzehrung." Franz Kafka, *Nachgelassene Schriften und Fragmente II*, ed. Jost Schillemeit (Frankfurt a.M.: Fischer, 1992), 77.

18. Rudolf Bultmann, *Das Urchristentum im Rahmen der antiken Religionen* (Zurich: Artemis, 1949), 102.

19. Albert Schweitzer, "The Idea of the Kingdom of God," *The Theology of Albert Schweitzer*, tr. E. N. Mozley (New York: Macmillan, 1951), 19, 18.

20. Rudolf Bultmann, *Theology of the New Testament*, tr. K. Grobel (New York: Scribner's, 1951–55), 10.

21. In at least one engaging instance, Kaufmann's inclination to avoid the *tu quoque* of gerrymandering will not succeed. In an amiable review of *Critique* and *The Faith of a Heretic*, Professor Jakob Petuchowski indicts Kaufmann for the very fault that Kaufmann excoriates in others—a criticism that, of course, does not invalidate Kaufmann's own accurate exposé of gerrymandering in others. Petuchowski's example is Kaufmann's selective use of the Book of Malachi (the last of the twelve minor prophets) to make a ruthlessly particularistic text redound to an alleged Jewish universalism. "In a passage of the *Critique* (pp. 364ff) in which the first chapters of Genesis are discussed," writes Petuchowski,

> Kaufmann quotes with approval the Talmudic statement that Adam was created as a solitary human being, so that it might not be said that some races are better than others. So far, so good. Kaufmann then proceeds to show that "this is how the beginning of Genesis was understood even in Biblical times." We have no quarrel with that, either. But when Kaufmann cites as his "proof-text" Malachi 2:10 ("Have we not all one father? Has not one God created us?"), we have as clear an instance of gerrymandering as we could wish to find in order to illustrate Kaufmann's own thesis. If Kaufmann had only taken the trouble to consult the context of this Malachi verse, he would have discovered

that the Prophet was fulminating against mixed marriages, that he accused his contemporaries of being faithless against their *fellow-Jews* by marrying non-Jewish wives! This,
within its actual context, has very little to do with the Universal Fatherhood of God and
the Brotherhood of Man.

"*Critique of Religion and Philosophy* and *The Faith of a Heretic*, by Walter Kaufmann" (book
review), *Judaism* 11, no. 2 (Spring 1962): 183.

22. William Shakespeare, *The Merchant of Venice*, act 1, scene 3.

23. Friedrich A. Kittler, *Discourse Networks 1800–1900*, tr. Michael Meteer (Stanford, CA:
Stanford University Press, 1990), 21.

24. Kaufmann's association of philosophy with play will have been stimulated by his reading of Johann Huizinga's *Homo Ludens* (C 230), as discussed in the preceding chapter.

25. Walter Benjamin, *Ursprung des deutschen Trauerspiels*, in *Gesammelte Schriften*, ed. Rolf
Tiedemann and Hermann Schweppenhäuser (Frankfurt a.M.: Suhrkamp, 1974), 1: 404.

26. For further appreciation of this figure, consider this citation from David Bromwich: "To
keep for a moment with [Alexander] Pope: in the line 'Or stain her honor, or her new brocade,'
the rhetorical scheme is zeugma, with abstract and concrete nouns sharing a verb." "Literature
and Theory," in *Beyond Structuralism: The Speculations of Theory and the Experience of Literature*,
ed. Wendell Harris (University Park: Pennsylvania State University Press, 1996), 204.

27. Thomas Mann, *Doctor Faustus*, tr. H. T. Lowe-Porter (Harmondsworth: Penguin, 1968),
263. It is well known that Adorno supplied Mann with a number of leading ideas and abundant
musicological detail for his novel.

28. Rainer Maria Rilke,

> Wolle die Wandlung. O sei für die Flamme begeistert,
> drin sich ein Ding dir entzieht, das mit Verwandlungen prunkt;
> jener entwerfende Geist, welcher das Irdische meistert,
> liebt in dem Schwung der Figur nichts wie den wendenden Punkt.

"Die Sonette an Orpheus" (2/12, in *Werke in drei Bänden* [Frankfurt a.M.: Insel, 1966], 1:
514). Translation by Stephen Mitchell, *Duino Elegies* and *Sonnets to Orpheus* (New York: Vintage, 2009), 157.

29. From a website for Christian apologetics: "*Logos* originally meant 'an opinion, word,
speech, or reason,' but the Stoics came to affiliate it with the spiritual creative force in the universe—reason within the physical. This is related to Plato's 'form,' which he defined as the
ultimate, perfect model held in the mind or realm of the Creator on which earthly things are
based" (http://www.gotquestions.org/Hellenism.html#ixzz3KZO7T5lI).

30. Kaufmann will be preoccupied with the idea of justice. His thoughts come to a head in
his 1973 volume *Without Guilt and Justice*, studied in chapter 11.

31. W. D. Davies, *Paul and Rabbinic Judaism: Some Rabbinic Elements in Pauline Theology*
(London: S.P.C.K., 1948, 1955). David Daube, *The New Testament and Rabbinic Judaism* (London: Athlone, University of London, 1956).

32. Eric Santner, *On Creaturely Life: Rilke, Benjamin, Sebald* (Chicago: University of Chicago Press, 2006) and *The Royal Remains: The People's Two Bodies and the Endgames of Sovereignty* (Chicago: University of Chicago Press, 2011). In "Art and Religion," Richard Shusterman comments in this vein on "the very Catholic religious rhetoric" of Arthur Danto's study
of modern art, *The Transfiguration of the Commonplace*. It does not matter that this "Catholic

rhetoric of transfiguration does not reflect his personal religious beliefs but is merely a façon-de-parler. . . . But does the religious dimension really disappear by calling it a mere manner of speaking? . . . If the religious tenor of transfiguration did not still somehow resonate with our religious sensibility, with our religious experience, faith, or imagination (however displaced and disguised it may be), then this manner of speaking would not be as captivating and in-fluential as it has proven to be" (http://www.deweycenter.uj.edu.pl/tekst_shusterman.html).

33. Omar Moad, "Dukkha, Inaction, and Nirvana: Suffering, Weariness, and Death? A Look at Nietzsche's Criticisms of Buddhist Philosophy," *Philosopher* 92, no. 1, http://www.thephiloso pher.co.uk/buddhism.htm.

34. Kafka, *Great Wall of China*, 299; Kafka, *Nachgelassene Schriften II*, 132.

35. This point has been disputed by R.B.Y. Scott, who makes it clear that Paul was not original in referring to the Torah as "the Law." "It had been a commonplace for centuries (cf. Deuteronomy 1:5; Nehemiah 8:1–2; Sirach, Prologue and 24:23, where תורה is translated nomos, 'law,' in the Old Greek version of Jewish origin)." "Princetonian 'Guerre de Plume': An Encounter in Two Stages," *Christian Century* 79, no. 5 (January 31, 1962): 129. On encoun-tering this revision, Kaufmann published in the same article his displeasure at the imputation of his "ignorance of the fact that Paul did not originate this usage" (132). To the claim that Judaism is without a theology or theologies, Louis Jacobs declares this assertion (of Judaism's "dogmalessness") an unfounded dogma in its own right. "Jewish Theology Today," *Problems in Contemporary Jewish Theology*, ed. Dan Cohn-Sherbok (Lewiston, NY: Edwin Mellen, 1991), 1–20. More recently, Cass Fisher has written an excellent book whose title says it all: *Contemplative Nation: A Philosophical Account of Jewish Theological Language* (Stanford, CA: Stanford University Press, 2012). Kaufmann's assumption that Judaism is without a theology is highly contested.

36. In *Saving God: Religion after Idolatry*, Mark Johnston sees the singular distinction of Christianity in its abridgement of Jewish law. "In undermining the Law, or righteousness, as the key to salvation, Christ's death killed off the idea of just desert under the Law. . . ." The "special significance of Christ's death and suffering . . . is a new dispensation . . . founded on outpouring love." If Kaufmann is right in his repeated insistence that Christianity does *not* originate a break from the ethical consequences of Jewish law, then Johnston's claims are incorrect (Princeton, NJ: Princeton University Press, 2009), 182–83.

37. Luke 10:27.

38. Johnston, *Saving God*, 15, xi. Johnston also wonders how the "ethical and spiritual as-pirations" at the core of man might find expression in a world without religion (40). Unlike Kaufmann, Johnston's ethical view is based entirely on the "self-revelation" of the numinous, the wholly Other, which man is powerless to elicit; and Johnston is particularly fierce about the genocidal depredations of Yahweh. Interestingly, however, Socrates also plays a role in John-ston's theological ruminations, where he likens "Socrates' attempt to vanquish and transcend myth" to the purification of the God-name "Yahweh" into the Tetragrammaton, "I am that I am" (71). A key difference between Kaufmann and Johnston is Johnston's reluctance to think of Socrates's death as exemplary.

39. Matthew 7:28.

40. See, among many other writers, Benjamin Lazier, "Overcoming Gnosticism: Hans Jonas, Hans Blumenberg, and the Legitimacy of the Natural World," *Journal of the History of*

Ideas 64, no. 4 (October 2003): 619–37, as well as the same author's *God Interrupted: Heresy and the European Imagination between the World Wars* (Princeton, NJ: Princeton University Press, 2008), especially for its bearings on twentieth-century German writers (e.g., Max Weber, Gershom Scholem, and Leo Strauss). See, too, Michael Allen Gillespie, *The Theological Origins of Modernity* (Chicago: University of Chicago Press, 2008).

41. Luther, *Sämtliche Schriften*, 3: 1321.

42. The intellectual historian Paul North takes pains to complicate Plato's "idea of truth, [which] implies that there are two worlds, a world of truth and a world of semblance. This idea of truth is a caricature of Plato . . . because the two-world 'theory' is taken as a truth of his system *rather* than as a teaching tool, a useful analogy, or a problem to be discussed. And we know for Plato that teaching by means of analogies or 'myths' . . . brought the question of semblance right back into the center to plague the assertion of a true world." For the rest, North lends support to Kaufmann's persistent refrain: "It is never wrong to see Plato as a literary artist." *The Yield: Kafka's Atheological Reformation* (Stanford, CA: Stanford University Press, 2015), 199.

43. Luther, *Sämtliche Schriften*, 3: 215.

44. Pratt, *Religious Consciousness*, 410.

45. De Certeau cites three examples of such elements:

> They concern the precondition of discourse (a division that establishes contractual relations); the status of a discourse (a locus where the Spirit speaks); and the figuration of discourse as a content (an image of the 'I'). In these three modes—conventions to be established, a place of locution to circumscribe, and a representation on which to base a narrative—the relation of a traditional language to the possibility of its being spoken is renewed. Most fundamentally still, what is renewed is the relation between the signifier and the constitution of the subject: do we exist to the other, or be spoken by him?

Mystic Speech," tr. Brian Massumi, in *The Certeau Reader*, ed. Graham Ward (Oxford: Blackwell, 2000), 197.

46. Franz Kafka, "Researches of a Dog," *Kafka's Selected Stories*, tr. Stanley Corngold (New York: W. W. Norton, 2007), 153.

47. Ibid., 157.

48. In a magazine piece titled "The Faith of a Heretic," the run-up to the book of this name, Kaufmann wrote: "Even if one has experiences that some men would call mystical—and I have no doubt that I have had many—it is a matter of integrity to question such experiences and any thoughts that were associated with them as closely and as honestly as we should question the 'revelations' of others." *Harper's Magazine*, February 1959, 3.

49. Kafka, "Researches," 159.

50. Isaiah 10:20–22.

51. Rainer Maria Rilke, *Duino Elegies*, "The First Duino Elegy," tr. Edgar Snow, http://clockworkfoundry.com/the-jumpers-library/the-first-duino-elegy-rainer-maria-rilke/.

52. Can this fugue on human "aspiration" be justified as "Nietzschean"? It is Nietzschean in the optative mode; the association is fair. In *Gay Science*, Nietzsche writes: "One could conceive of such a pleasure and power of determination, such a freedom of the will that the spirit would take leave of every faith and every wish for certainty, being practiced in maintaining himself on insubstantial ropes and possibilities and dancing even near abysses. Such a spirit

would be the free spirit par excellence." See Robert Pippin, "How to Overcome Oneself: Nietzsche on Freedom," in *Nietzsche on Freedom and Autonomy*, ed. Ken Gemes and Simon May (Oxford: Oxford University Press, 2009), 85.

53. Ivan Soll, "Introduction to the Transaction Edition," *Discovering the Mind*, vol. 2, *Nietzsche, Heidegger, and Buber* (New Brunswick, NJ: Transaction, 1992; originally published by McGraw-Hill in 1980), xlix.

54. Martin Buber, *I and Thou*, tr. with a prologue and notes by Walter Kaufmann (New York: Scribner's, 1970). In the "Prologue" Kaufmann explains that he had "first seen and heard . . . [Buber] in Lehnitz (between Berlin and Oranienburg) where he had come with Ernst Simon at his side to teach young people *Bibel lesen*—to read the Bible" (2).

55. Soll, "Introduction," xlix.

56. Martin Buber, *Königtum Gottes*, 2nd rev. ed. (Berlin: Schocken, 1936), 82.

57. I am alluding to the eloquence of such a work (as of many others by André Malraux) as *The Voices of Silence*, tr. Stuart Gilbert (Princeton, NJ: Princeton University Press, 1978).

58. The Scots essayist Iain Bamforth, who is at home in German literary and intellectual culture, thinking of the poem as too "inward, [too] compacted," comments: "K. knew what he was doing when the left it [the poem] untranslated!" for it lacks the touch of "the sprightly, lucid . . . Nietzsche poems" that Kaufmann quoted in his edition of *The Gay Science* (https://wmjas.wordpress.com/2010/06/06/walter-Kaufmanns-epitaph/).

In conversation, David Pickus pointed out the consonance between Kaufmann's poem and at least one other poem in *The Gay Science*, "Ecce Homo":

> Yes, I know from where I came!
> Ever hungry like a flame,
> I consume myself and glow.
> Light grows all that I conceive,
> Ashes everything I leave:
> Flame I am assuredly.
> —*GS*, "Joke, Cunning and Revenge:
> Prelude in German Rhymes," 62.

59. R.B.Y. Scott is not wrong in noting that Kaufmann's attitude to the Old Testament in *Critique* and in *The Faith of a Heretic* (to come) is "curiously ambivalent, showing to traditional Jewish orthodoxy a marked deference which sits uneasily with his rationalism." "Princetonian," 130.

60. As Arnulf Zweig pointed out in his review of *Critique*, "Curiously, the term 'love' is used without any clarification, though Kaufmann devotes an earlier chapter (chap. 29) to exposing the extreme ambiguity and vagueness of this term." *Ethics* 69, no. 4 (July 1959): 296.

61. Compare, Johnston, *Saving God*: "Perhaps the most distinctive part of Christian revelation is that the Highest One is by its nature Love, a revelation concretely presented in such details as the intimate way in which Jesus addresses the Creator as *Abba* or 'Dada.' . . . There is indeed an analogy between self-giving love and the outpouring of Existence Itself by way of its exemplification in ordinary existents" (113).

62. The phrase "self-incurred minority" is from Kant, *What Is Enlightenment?*

63. Oscar Wilde, "The Decay of Lying," in *Complete Works of Oscar Wilde* (New York: Barnes and Noble, 1994), 973. Cited in Shusterman, "Art and Religion."

64. Stephan Mallarmé, *Message Poétique du Symbolisme* (Paris: Nizet, 1947), 2: 321. Cited in Shusterman, "Art and Religion."

65. Matthew Arnold, "The Study of Poetry," in *The Portable Matthew Arnold*, ed. Lionel Trilling (New York: Viking, 1949), 300. Cited in Shusterman, "Art and Religion."

66. Arthur Danto, *After the End of Art* (Princeton, NJ: Princeton University Press, 1997), 188, and *The Madonna of the Future* (New York: Farrar, Strauss, and Giroux, 2000), 338. Cited in Shusterman, "Art and Religion."

67. Georg Wilhelm Friedrich Hegel, "Vorrede" to the *Phänomenologie des Geistes* (Bamberg: Goebhardt, 1807), tr. as "Preface," *The Phenomenology of Mind* (New York: Macmillan, 1931), 4–5. Text translation by J. B. Baillie modified.

68. Kaufmann, *Discovering the Mind*, vol. 2, 265.

Chapter 5: The Riches of the World

1. *From Shakespeare to Existentialism*, 1st ed. (Boston: Beacon, 1959); new ed., with additions (Garden City, NY: Doubleday, 1960). Epigraph: Walter Kaufmann, *From Shakespeare to Existentialism* (Princeton, NJ: Princeton University Press, 1980), 22. Pages from this text will henceforth be shown in parentheses as (S + page number).

2. In his study of Hegel's intellectual development, Kaufmann wonders counterfactually what philosophy might look like today (ca. 1959) if Hegel had stayed within a "first tradition" "represented by Lessing's antitheological polemics, by some of Kant's essays, and by Schiller. . . . There would have been no need for the excesses of the existentialist revolt, or for the extremes to which the positivists went" (S 173).

3. Consider a relatively recent compendium of tragic theory—*Rethinking Tragedy*, ed. Rita Felski (Baltimore: Johns Hopkins University Press, 2008)—which contains only one single mention of the word "absurdity," and there it is applied to the post-Socratic repudiation of the body and the senses in Western philosophy (113). In Terry Eagleton's *Sweet Violence: The Idea of the Tragic* (Oxford: Blackwell, 2003), the word refers chiefly to the various absurdities in the writings of other theorists of tragedy (16).

4. "On one important point, Shakespeare seems to be closer to the Christian view than to that of some existentialists. He appears to believe in absolute moral laws" (S 19). The translated sentence from Günther Bornkamm is found in *Der Lohngedanke im Neuen Testament* (Lüneburg: Heliand Verlag, 1947), namely, "das N.T. [kennt nicht] die Idee der guten Tat, die ihren Wert in sich selbst trägt" (7–8).

5. Mark Johnston may be such a man. In *Saving God*, he writes: "Only if we see that there can be no reward, does Christ's suffering and death bring our self-love and false righteousness to an end" (182).

6. Cf. Nietzsche's Zarathustra's revulsion at the spirit of revenge (*Thus Spoke Zarathustra*, 2: 42, "On Redemption."). Kaufmann's attribution to Shakespeare of a tragic vision *without resentment* comes very likely from his long immersion in Nietzsche's particular animus against the *ressentiment* of the ill-favored—the "small-souled" men. "To have claws and not to use them, and above all to be above any *ressentiment* or desire for vengeance, that is, according to Nietzsche, the sign of true power" (N 372).

7. The phrase does not originate with Stendhal: it is found in Coleridge's lectures, viz., "Milton attempted to make the English language obey the logic of passion as perfectly as the Greek and Latin [elsewhere in the lecture, 'the logic of passion or universal logic']" and in early writings on Kant and Hegel, where it appears as "die Logik des Gefühls." Samuel Taylor Coleridge, *The Complete Works*, ed. by W.G.T. Shedd (New York: Harper and Brothers, 1884), 4: 303. Otto Siebert, *Geschichte der neueren deutschen Philosophie seit Hegel* (Göttingen: Vandenhoeck und Ruprecht, 1898), 353.

8. "Goethe was the first German who discovered . . . Stendhal and the only one who, before Nietzsche, penetrated and understood him." Charles Simon, "Le Sillage de Stendhal en Allemagne," *Revue de littérature comparée* 6 (1926): 609. Cited in Henry H. H. Remak, "Goethe on Stendhal: Development and Significance of his Attitude," *Goethe Bicentennial Studies*, Humanities Series (Bloomington: Indiana University Publications, 1950), 22: 232.

9. *Gesammelte Werke* (Munich: Musarion, 1924), 15: 217.

10. Stendhal, *The Charterhouse of Passion*, tr. C. K. Scott Moncrieff, http://gutenberg.net .au/ebooks03/0300301.txt.

11. Blaise Pascal, *Thoughts*, tr. W. F. Trotter, *The Harvard Classics*, ed. Charles W. Eliot, section 4, "Of the Means of Belief," no. 277 (New York: P. F. Collier and Son, 1909–14), http://www.bartleby.com/48/1/4.html.

12. Ramon Salvidar, *Figural Language in the Novel* (Princeton, NJ: Princeton University Press, 1984), 75. Salvidar is building on Etienne Rey, "Préface," *De l'Amour* (Paris: Bernard Grasset, 1912), i–xcix.

13. The statement that Hegel furthered the belief in "inalienable human rights" ("*unalienable*" in the final printing of the American Declaration of Independence) is too blanket a statement to have cognitive value. Hegel was a determined critic of the theories (*dit* "liberal") of *natural* rights in such Enlightenment thinkers as Hobbes, Locke, and Kant. What might be inalienable, for Hegel, is the *possibility* of a free personality but solely in the setting of "the institutions of ethical life—family, civil society, and the state . . . as the necessary categorial framework within which our individual powers and capacities can flourish." Steven B. Smith, *Hegel's Critique of Liberalism: Rights in Context* (Chicago: University of Chicago Press, 1989), 130.

14. Balduin Schwarz, *Der Irrtum in der Philosophie: Untersuchungen über das Wesen, die Formen und die psychologische Genese des Irrtums im Bereiche der Philosophie, mit einem Ueberblick über die Geschichte der Irrtumsproblematik in der abendländischen Philosophie* (Münster: Aschendorff, 1934), 275.

15. T. S. Eliot, "Shakespeare and the Stoicism of Seneca," *Shakespeare Criticism*, ed. Anne Brady (Delhi, Uttar Pradesh: Atlantic, 2001), 177.

16. Oscar Wilde, *The Picture of Dorian Gray* (Leipzig: Bernhard Tauchnitz, 1908), 77–78.

17. "Besondere Methode des Denkens. Gefühlsmäßig durchdrungen: Alles fühlt sich als Gedanke, selbst im Unbestimmtesten (Dostojewski)." *Tagebücher in der Fassung der Handschrift*, ed. Michael Müller (Frankfurt a.M.: S. Fischer, 1990), 568.

18. This rich and productive line of thought is explored, as noted above, by Márton Dornbach in his study of a hitherto underemphasized aspect of German idealism—hermeneutics. *Receptive Spirit: German Idealism and the Dynamics of Cultural Transmission* (New York: Fordham University Press, 2016).

19. Frederick C. Beiser, *The Romantic Imperative: The Concept of Early German Romanticism* (Cambridge, MA: Harvard University Press, 2002), 55.

20. Nietzsche, *Will to Power*, note 981, 513.

21. Kaufmann is referring to Rudolf Otto, *The Idea of the Holy*, tr. J. W. Harvey (Oxford: Oxford University Press, 1923).

22. Rainer Maria Rilke, *Duino Elegies, The First Elegy*, tr. Stephen Mitchell, http://homestar .org/bryannan/duino.html.

23. Kafka, *Nachgelassene Schriften II*, 89.

24. J. W. von Goethe, *Goethe's Faust*, tr. and with an introduction by Walter Kaufmann, Anchor Books (New York: Random House, 1963), 189.

25. This essay precedes Hamlin's collection of critical essays in Goethe, *Faust*, tr. Walter Arndt, ed. Cyrus Hamlin (New York: Norton, 1976).

26. Ibid., 373–74.

27. This discussion of the putative unity of *Faust* is adapted from my "Reading Experience in Goethe's *Faust*," *Literary Studies and the Pursuits of Reading*," ed. Richard Benson, Eric Downing, and Jonathan Hess (Rochester, NY: Camden House, 2012), 251–65.

28. Irving Singer, *The Nature of Love*, vol. 2, *Courtly and Romantic* (Chicago: University of Chicago Press, 2009), 439.

29. In the second chapter of Kaufmann's *Tragedy and Philosophy*, we hear of one remarkable exception: Hochhuth's *The Deputy*. "So far from being anti-Christian *The Deputy* is a modern Christian tragedy . . . perhaps even the only Christian tragedy" (329).

30. *The Diaries of Franz Kafka, 1910–1913*, tr. Joseph Kresh (New York: Schocken: 1948), 157.

31. Siegmar Hellerich, *Religionizing, Romanizing Romantics: The Catholico-Christian Camouflage of the Early German Romantics; Wackenroder, Tieck, Novalis, Friedrich and August Wilhelm Schlegel* (Bern: Peter Lang, 1995).

32. The first quote is by Poulet in *Les Métamorphoses du cercle* (Paris: Plon, 1961), 136; the second, by Szondi, in *Satz und Gegensatz* (Frankfurt: Insel, 1964), 9–10.

33. De Man, "The Sublimation of the Self," in *Blindness and Insight*, 49–50.

34. Paul de Man, "Wordsworth and Hölderlin," *The Rhetoric of Romanticism* (New York: Columbia University Press, 1984), 40.

35. Arch Llewellyn, "In Frye We Trust," commenting on Northrop Frye's treatment of the Bible as a unity held together by typological anticipations (http://www.amazon.com /dp/0156027801/ref=rdr_ext_sb_ti_sims_1). Nietzsche called this exegetical appropriation "that unheard-of philological farce. . . . I mean the attempt to pull the Old Testament [from] under the feet of the Jews with the assertion that it contained nothing but Christian teaching and *belonged* to the Christians as the *true* people of Israel, the Jews being only usurpers." Nietzsche, *Daybreak: Thoughts on the Prejudices of Morality*, tr. R. J. Hollingdale (Cambridge: Cambridge University Press, 1982), 84. Cited in Karin Schutjer's excellent *Goethe and Judaism: The Wandering Ways of Modernity* (Evanston, IL: Northwestern University Press, 2015), 12.

36. Frye's major works in this regard are *The Great Code: The Bible and Literature* (New York: Harcourt Brace Jovanovich, 1982) and *Words with Power: Being a Second Study of "The Bible and Literature"* (New York: Harcourt Brace Jovanovich, 1990). Frye's reflections on the unity of the Biblical narrative are found in his note from the early 1960s, and the quoted

words are from *The Educated Imagination*, published in 1963 by the Canadian Broadcasting Corporation, 66.

37. Frye, *Educated*, 66.

38. Robert Alter, *Canon and Creativity: Modern Writing and the Authority of Scripture* (New Haven, CT: Yale University Press, 2013).

39. Frye, *Educated*, 66.

40. Schutjer, *Goethe and Judaism*, 9, 12. The quote from Goethe is *Sämtliche Werke, Briefe, Tagebücher und Gespräche*, ed. Dieter Borchmeyer et al., 40 vols. (Frankfurt a.M.: Deutscher Klassiker Verlag, 1985–99), 1.13: 273.

41. Erich Heller, "Goethe and the Avoidance of Tragedy," in Erich Heller, *The Disinherited Mind* (Cambridge: Bowes and Bowes, 1952), 37.

42. Heller had already treated both writers together with an original intensity in *The Disinherited Mind*, ibid., hence, several years before Kaufmann began his essay. How vexatious it must have been for Kaufmann to see his antiself T. S. Eliot's lavish praise printed on its cover, but how generous of Kaufmann to salute Heller's book in a following essay in *From Shakespeare to Existentialism*, declaring how much he had learned from it.

43. George Gordon Byron, Don Juan, "Canto the Third," lines 790–93, https://kalliope.org/en/text/byron1999040903.

44. The German reads: "Der weiche Gang . . . / ist wie ein Tanz von Kraft um eine Mitte, / in der betäubt ein großer Wille steht." Kaufmann's skill as a translator of poetry is evident in his *Goethe's Faust* and *Twenty-Five German Poets: A Bilingual Collection* (New York: Norton, 1975).

45. Franz Kafka, "A Starvation Artist," *Kafka's Selected Stories*, 94. Original at http://www.gutenberg.org/files/30655/30655-h/30655-h.htm.

46. Friedrich Nietzsche, "Aus höhen Bergen," http://www.theNietzschechannel.com/poetry/poetry-dual.htm.

47. *The Gay Science*, ed. and tr. Walter Kaufmann (New York: Vintage, 1974), 35–36.

48. From a letter of Rilke to Countess Margot Sizzo-Noris-Crouy, dated April 12, 1923, in *Selected Letters of Rainer Maria Rilke*, ed. Harry T. Moore (Garden City, NY: Doubleday, 1960), 353.

49. This point is contestable in Nietzsche to the extent that he confesses longings for a transformation *in kind*. See the previously noted formula: "Life—that means for us constantly transforming all that we are into light and flame," which suggests a modern Gnosticism.

50. Max Baeumer, "Nietzsche and the Tradition of the Dionysian," *Studies in Nietzsche and the Classical Tradition*, ed. James C. O'Flaherty (Chapel Hill: University of North Carolina Press, 1976), 177, 189. Discussed in Tim Murphy, *Nietzsche, Metaphor, Religion* (Albany: State University of New York Press, 2001), 55.

51. Nietzsche, *Portable Nietzsche*, 519–20.

52. Ibid., 436.

53. Nietzsche, *Gay Science*, 228.

54. Erich Heller, "Rilke and Nietzsche," in *The Importance of Nietzsche* (Chicago: University of Chicago Press, 1988), 122.

55. Here is more to the countercurrent that also finds its place, from to time, in Kaufmann's view of literary art. Quite apart from what he generally holds it to be—"the authentic and incomparable record of experiences" (S 263)—he writes: "Human art has fashioned works

of such perfection that men have thought the world must be a copy of what are in fact human *creations*" (S 261) (emphasis added). Experience is *of* the world; "world-less" *experience* is nonsensical. If the world in this view is in fact a human creation, then we deal with the possibility of a purely "created"—read: "imagined"—experience, coexistent with the production of the poem. There are many prototypes of this view. For Oscar Wilde, "the basis of action [viz., experience] is lack of imagination"; "personal experience [is] . . . a most vicious and limited circle"; and "language [is] the parent, and not the child, of thought" (http://www.gutenberg .org/files/887/old/ntntn1oh.htm#startoftext). The thought of the primacy of poetic language also keeps occurring to Kaufmann, as in the following chapter "Philosophy versus Poetry." For the great artist, he writes, "Language is no longer dominated by the stern demands of ritual tradition and asserts her sovereignty, changing and inventing and alluding at her pleasure. But when language, freed from bondage, defies the restraints of custom, she sometimes gains mastery over the man who had hoped to use her—Nietzsche, for example, as he wrote his *Zarathustra*. . . . It is as if, intoxicated with a sense of her own possibilities, she seduced the master to make merry with her" (S 263). Here we see Kaufmann writing in a very vivid (Karl) Kraus-ian vein. Kraus also sexualizes rhetorical entanglement as the embrace of a wayward woman sovereign called Language, writing, "I am not the master of language; but language masters me completely. She is not the servant of my thoughts. I have a liaison with her; I receive thoughts, and she can do with me what she wishes. I parry her word for word, for from the word the young thought springs toward me and retroactively forms the language that created it. . . . Thought is servant and language is mistress; if someone knows how to invert the relationship she makes herself useful in his house but forbids him her privates" (Karl Kraus, *Dicta and Contradicta*, tr. Jonathan McVity [Urbana: University of Illinois Press, 2001], 96). But this perspective will not suit Kaufmann for long: notice his flight from the hapless seduction: the master has been seduced into reasserting his control. And Kaufmann will not go so far as to propose art as experience's surrogate—or, indeed, as with Wilde, the lucid indictment of its nullity. This *inversion* of the commonsense view as to the primacy of lived experience reaches a crescendo in Kafka, for whom artistic freedom is the "freedom of true description that releases one's foot from lived experience (*Erlebnis*)" (*Diaries 1910–1913*, 100; *Gesammelte Werke in zwölf Bänden, nach der kritischen Ausgabe*, ed. Hans-Gerd Koch [Frankfurt a.M.: Fischer Taschenbuch Verlag, 1952], 9: 71).

56. Philippe Lacoue-Labarthe, *Poetry as Experience*, tr. Andrea Tarnowksi (Stanford, CA: Stanford University Press, 1999).

57. T. S. Eliot, "Tradition and the Individual Talent," *Selected Essays* (London: Faber and Faber, 1932), 21.

58. Cf. "Sophocles' plot [of *Antigone*] was not dictated by tradition but shaped by him as a vehicle for his experience of life" (T 215). But how does this claim, which Kaufmann repeats for many great writers, jibe with his view that (some) experience is accessible only through the work of art, where it is constituted and not "vehiculated"?

59. Heidegger would be eminently criticizable for his vatic invocation of the "Four-fold" (*Das Geviert*), for example, in his "Building Dwelling Thinking," in *Poetry, Language, Thought*, tr. Albert Hofstadter (New York: HarperCollins, 1971); or his "concept" of "ungenuine authenticity" (*unechte Eigentlichkeit*) in *Being and Time* (*Sein und Zeit*), tr. John Macquarrie and Edward Robinson (New York: Harper and Row, 1962), 186. (I am captivated by this conjunction

and will allude to it more than once.) Similar objections arise years before the 2014 publication of *The Black Notebooks*.

60. See "Dialogue between Satan and a Theologian," "Dialogue between Satan and a Christian," and "Dialogue between Satan and an Atheist," *Critique of Religion and Philosophy*, 228–59.

61. *Goethe's Faust*, 203.

Chapter 6: A Contempt for Popularity

1. Epigraph for the present chapter: Kaufmann's description of Captain Ahab in *The Faith of a Heretic* (Princeton, NJ: Princeton University Press, 2015), 334. Pages from this text will henceforth be shown in parentheses as (F + page number).

2. R.B.Y. Scott, "Princetonian 'Guerre de Plume,'" 129.

3. Walter Kaufmann, *Without Guilt and Justice*, 93–94.

4. The critic Leon Wieseltier finds words for this point, writing in 2015: "A complacent humanist is a humanist who has not read his books closely, since they teach disquiet and difficulty. In a society rife with theories and practices that flatten and shrink and chill the human subject, the humanist is the dissenter." "Among the Disrupted," *New York Times*, "Sunday Book Review," January 7, 2015, http://www.nytimes.com/2015/01/18/books/review/among-the -disrupted.html?_r=0.

5. Citing Kaufmann's own plainer language in *Without Guilt and Justice*: faith might "supply the psychic energy for good works" (W 113). The immediate binding together of notions of faith and practice is a long established figure of thought in Kaufmann's work, viz., "If the philosophers do not keep Socrates' heritage alive, who will? If none of us apply our hard-won skills to questions of *faith and practice*, we abdicate one of our crucial responsibilities" (emphasis added). Kaufmann, "A Plea for Socrates' Heritage (a Response)," in *Ethics and Social Justice*, 17.

6. Nietzsche, *The Antichrist*, section 54, cited in *Discovering the Mind*, vol. 2, 126.

7. Weiss-Rosmarin, "Interview," 123.

8. Steven Aschheim, *Culture and Catastrophe: German and Jewish Confrontations with National Socialism and Other Crises* (New York: New York University Press, 1997), 47. Cited in Vivian Liska, "Exil und Exemplarität: Jüdische Würzellosigkeit als Denkfigur," in *Literatur und Exil: Neue Perspektiven*, ed. Doerte Bischoff and Susanne Komfort-Hein (Berlin: de Gruyter, 2013), 241.

9. Weiss-Rosmarin, "Interview," 121.

10. T. S. Eliot, *After Strange Gods: A Primer of Modern Heresy* (London: Faber and Faber, 1934), 20.

11. In a work published some twenty years later, *Discovering the Mind*, vol. 1, discussed in our chapter 15, Kaufmann elaborated the point:

> For Kant, holiness represented a commandment [it is Mosaic in its inspiration]. For many other human beings, perfection is the object of a profound interest. In Plato's *Symposium*, we read that "love is a longing for immortality," but it would be better to say—and Plato meant this also—that *love is a longing for perfection*. . . . The longing for perfection is also central in the *moral* experience of many people, and Kant's dichotomy of interests as well as his whole analysis of the foundations of ethics misses the mark as far as human beings of this type are concerned.

Discovering the Mind, vol. 1, *Goethe, Kant, and Hegel* (New Brunswick, NJ: Transaction, 1991), 154. One does not need to ask twice whether Kaufmann regarded himself as a "human being of this type."

12. Denis J. B. Hawkins, review of *Critique of Religion and Philosophy*, *Times Literary Supplement*, July 31, 1959, 450.

13. Freeman Dyson, "Heretical Thoughts about Science and Society," *Edge*, August 7, 2007, https://edge.org/conversation/heretical-thoughts-about-science-and-society.

14. Stanley Corngold and Irene Giersing, *Borrowed Lives* (Albany: State University of New York Press, 1991), 37.

15. Kaufmann's version of the discourse of the prophets is open to the charge of one-sidedness. In his introduction to Kaufmann's anthology of religious writings—*Religion from Tolstoy to Camus*—the conservative political philosopher Paul Gottfried writes:

> One wonders . . . whether the Hebrew prophets were as concerned about modern so-cial justice as Kaufmann presumes. Note that eschatological and ritual matters such as the end of history and the rebuilding of the Temple come up repeatedly in Isaiah and Ezekiel. In his many tributes to the prophets, Kaufmann may be overgeneralizing from selected passages about justice drawn primarily from Amos, Micah, and Malachi. Even less clear is how this privileged strain of prophetic tradition is seen to develop into Rabbinic Judaism. Kaufmann interprets Jewish religion, from the prophets on down, as being predominantly about ethics. He thereby gives short shrift to the bulk of Talmudic literature and to the accompanying glosses produced by medieval and later rabbis— and to anything in the Jewish tradition that treats of ceremonial and dietary laws. . . . Kaufmann remained a religious rationalist, who respected whatever in religion could be made to serve human intellectual and social advancement. Perhaps also like [Moses] Mendelssohn and [Leo] Baeck, he believed that Judaism was riper than Christianity for his desired reformation because of what he imagined to be its rationalist-ethical core.

Walter Kaufmann, ed., *Religion from Tolstoy to Camus* (New Brunswick, NJ: Transaction, 2000), xii.

16. Compare Hegel's remarks in the essay that Hermann Nohl, the editor of the *Theologische Jugendschriften*, titled "The Spirit of Christianity and Its Fate": "Faith is the spirit's recognition of spirit; and only equal spirits can recognize and understand each other." Kaufmann comments, "This is faith without transcendence, faith without another world, faith that precludes any notion that I am impotent filth while God alone is good and omnipotent" (*Discovering the Mind*, vol. 1, 208).

17. This passage is taken from Sartre's speech titled "The Responsibility of the Writer," delivered at the Sorbonne in 1946 at the first general meeting of UNESCO.

18. William Butler Yeats, "The Fascination of What's Difficult," https://www.poetry foundation.org/poems/43286/the-fascination-of-whats-difficult.

19. I wrote similar words about Kafka, whose "atheology," for one thing, Kaufmann shares ("Introduction," *The Metamorphosis by Franz Kafka* [New York: Modern Library 2013], xxxvi). Likenesses—and differences—can be totted up: it is perhaps interesting to see whether the list of credits outweighs the debits. Leaving out degrees of genius, both are close, fascinated readers of the Old Testament; both are Jewish heretics in Kaufmann's sense, exploders of higher commonplaces; both are captivated (with critical arrière-pensées) by Kierkegaard;

both were read, in the 1950s, as "existentialists"; both suffered, mainly, through their institutional affiliation; both were bent on justification through writing—and *reading*. In *The Future of the Humanities*, Kaufmann's plaidoyer for close-reading runs: "We must allow ourselves to be addressed by a text; we must hearken for its distinctive voice; we must try to discern how it differs from all other voices. We must permit it to challenge shock and offend us" (FH 63). Compare Kafka's 1904 letter to Oskar Pollak: "A book must be the axe for the frozen sea inside us." *Letters to Friends, Family, and Editors*, tr. Richard Winston and Clara Winston (New York: Schocken, 1977), 16.

20. The expression "humbition"—this virtuous quality, fusing humility and ambition—seems unfortunate, probably owing to its phonic propinquity to "humbug." Sidney Hook also considers it "a curious virtue whose unlovely name suggests a cross between Uriah Heep and Horatio Alger" ("In Defense of 'Justice': A Response," *Ethics and Social Justice*, 81). It is intriguing to imagine the conversation between Kaufmann and his editor Anne Freedgood, whom he much admired, about the aptness of this word. Obviously, Kaufmann won—the word survives—but what a struggle it must have been. A year later, in writing of Freud's nobility, he preferred to withhold "humbition" from the character of his great educator, settling for a "rare combination of humility, ambition, love, courage and honesty." "Freud and the Tragic Virtues," *American Scholar* 29, no. 4 (Autumn 1960): 481.

21. Ernest Jones, *The Life and Work of Sigmund Freud* (New York: Basic Books, 1953–57), 3: 459–60.

22. The eminent geneticist Jerry Coyne cites Kaufmann's definition of faith verbatim in his assault on the alleged compatibility of science and religion, an elliptical proof that Kaufmann is still being read in the higher court of the academy. *Faith vs. Fact: Why Science and Religion Are Incompatible* (New York: Viking, 2015), 67.

23. A brief meditation by the Norwegian novelist Karl Ove Knausgård nicely complements Kaufmann's views on the indispensability of faith, a faith in the rectitude accessible to the man who strives for it.

> The disillusioned perspective distinguishes continually between faith and reality, between life as we want it to be and life as it actually is—for it is faith that joins us together with our undertakings and with the world, faith that accords them value. Without faith, no value. That's why so many people find the disillusioned perspective so provoking: It lacks faith, sees only the phenomenon itself, while faith, which in a sense is always also illusion, for most people is the very point, the profoundest meaning. To the disillusioned, morals, for instance, are not so much a question of right or wrong as of fear.

From a review of *Submission* by Michel Houellebecq, "Sunday Book Review," *New York Times*, November 2, 2015, http://www.nytimes.com/2015/11/08/books/review/michel-houellebecqs-submission.html.

Knausgård's conclusion is apt to Kaufmann's own reflections, especially when we consider the very first sentence of Kaufmann's *Without Guilt and Justice*, "Humanity has always lived in the shadow of fears" (1).

24. R.B.Y. Scott, Kaufmann's fiercest critic, objects to this statement, as follows:

> To say, as Mr. Kaufmann does (page 141, [actually p. 129]), that in the prophets 'love, justice and humility appear to be all that is asked of man, and questions of belief [are]

entirely peripheral' is absurd, in the light of Amos 9, Hosea 11, Isaiah 7, 31, 40, Jeremiah 2 and a host of similar passages. The prophets were not merely 'solitary individuals who criticized the inconsistencies, hypocrisies and . . . the organized religion of the time' (page 263 [actually p. 252]). To assert this is to ignore the prophets' own overwhelming sense of a divine will which compelled them to speak as they had no wish to speak, as was the case notably with Isaiah and Jeremiah. This is of the essence of Hebrew prophecy as the Bible describes it, but it does not fit Mr. Kaufmann's line of interpretation—so he leaves it out. R.B.Y. Scott, "Princetonian 'Guerre de Plume,'" 130.

Kaufmann is not rendered speechless by this charge and replies: "I should be happy if readers would reread the chapters in the prophets that Mr. Scott cites, though I doubt that many will find those chapters relevant to any point at issue. Mr. Scott takes a phrase out of context and manufactures a fault by adding a crucial word: 'The prophets were not merely "solitary individuals who criticized. . . ."' It is easy to convert true statements into false ones by adding 'merely'" (R.B.Y. Scott, ibid., 133).

25. E. R. Dodds, *The Greeks and the Irrational* (Berkeley: University of California Press, 1951; Boston Beacon, 1957), 136.

26. Harry Elmer Barnes and Negley King Teeters, *New Horizons in Criminology*, 2nd ed. (New York: Prentice-Hall, 1951), 184–87.

27. In a thoughtful reading of Kaufmann's philosophy of religion, James Woelfel, professor of philosophy at the University of Kansas, also singles out this passage as essential. "Religious Empiricism," 194.

28. William Horosz, professor of philosophy at the University of Oklahoma, reviewing *The Faith of a Heretic* in *Philosophy and Phenomenological Research*, no. 1 (September 1964): 145–46.

29. Jakob Petuchowski, reviewing *Critique* and *Faith of a Heretic*, 183.

30. Jan Assmann, *Moses the Egyptian: The Memory of Egypt in Western Monotheism* (Cambridge, MA: Harvard University Press, 1997), 24.

31. "Freud was not deterred by the established fact that Ikhnaton's innovations barely survived his early death and were ruthlessly suppressed long before the end of the fourteenth century: indeed, the very name of Aton was scratched out on all accessible works of the period" (F 175).

32. It might be asked, with respect to the charge of Christian particularism, which damns the unbeliever, how Jewish universalism can cohabit with the prophets' excoriation of those infidels who worship lesser gods? Some biblical scholars claim that it is not for their beliefs but for their (evil) actions that idolatrous peoples reap the rage of the prophets. This distinction remains at the center of fierce controversy.

33. "Theology is a comprehensive, rigorous, and systematic attempt to conceal the beam in the scriptures of one's own denomination . . . antithetic to the Sermon on the Mount" (F 105).

34. A radio broadcast, "Thomas Mann's War," BBC Radio 4 FM, December 5, 2005, 0.15.

35. Professor Mark David Hall writes of "our Christian roots . . . : Christian ideas underlie some key tenets of America's constitutional order," etc., and makes the link between this claim and the main dependence of morality on religion, writing of "the Founders' insight that democracy requires a moral people and that faith is an important, if not indispensable, support for morality" (http://www.heritage.org/research/lecture/2011/06/did-america-have-a-christian-founding).

36. Jeffrey Tayler writes:

> Christianity as the "foundation of our country" . . . ? That Christian zealots initiated
> the mass European migration to North America no one disputes. They did not, howev-
> er, found the country; the secularist Founding Fathers, who mostly regarded religion
> with deep suspicion, did. Check no further than Jefferson's "wall of separation between
> church and state" and, obviously, the Constitution's First Amendment (which protects
> free speech from faith by forbidding Congress from establishing a state religion), as
> well as the more obscure Article VI, which declares that "no religious test shall ever
> be required as a qualification to any office or public trust under the United States."
> If Christianity really were the "foundation of our country," . . . the Founding Fathers
> would have included an amendment making Bible study mandatory for all aspirants
> to public office.
> Jeffrey Tayler, "Bill Maher [an Atheist] Terrifies Bill O'Reilly [a Christian]: An Athe-
> ist Has the Fox News Host Running Scared," *Salon*, April 12, 2015 (http://www.salon
> .com/2015/04/12/bill_maher_terrifies_bill_oreilly_an_atheist_has_the_fox_news
> _host_running_scared/).

The atheist Tayler continues his diatribe in 2015, entirely in the spirit of Kaufmann (who,
according to Trude Weiss-Rosmarin, nonetheless called himself an agnostic):

Early on in *The Faith of a Heretic*, however, Kaufmann quoted a report from late 1960, stating that "the U. S. Supreme Court agreed to rule on the constitutionality of a requirement in
Maryland that officeholders profess belief in God. The Maryland Court of Appeals had ruled
against a professed atheist who wanted to be commissioned as a notary public, for, the court
had said, a person who does not believe in God is 'incompetent to hold office, to give testimony, or serve as a juror.' *U.S. News and World Report*, November 21, 1960, p. 16." Furthermore,
continues Kaufmann, "Bishop James A. Pike says in 'The Right to be an Atheist' (*Coronet*,
April 1961): 'In Maryland, Pennsylvania, Tennessee and Arkansas, in order to hold public office
a man must believe in the being of God. In many places, testimony of a witness in court may
be impeached if it can be shown that he is an atheist'" (F 28). Has anything changed? The very
thoughtful philosopher Mark Johnston, whose work we have discussed above, noted in 2010:
"Like it or not, in this country, the present conventions are such that to openly avow atheism
and materialism is thereby to create the presumption that you are a reprobate, a morally un-
principled person. You will then have, for example, little chance of being elected sheriff, let
alone congressman, senator, or president" (*Surviving Death* [Princeton, NJ: Princeton University Press, 2010], 4.

The atheist Tayler continues his diatribe in 2015, entirely in the spirit of Kaufmann (who,
according to Trude Weiss-Rosmarin, nonetheless called himself an agnostic):

> Both Bill O'Reilly and Ann Coulter—Christian apologists—argue from a premise so
> widely accepted that they leave it unstated: that those who believe, without proof, fan-
> tastical, far-reaching propositions about the nature of our cosmos and how we should
> live our lives have nothing to explain, nothing to account for, while those of us who
> value convictions based on evidence, reasoned solutions, and rules for living deriving
> from consensus must ceaselessly justify ourselves and genuflect apologetically for voic-
> ing disagreement.
> Beneath this unstated premise lies another more insidious notion: that there are two
> kinds of truth—religious and otherwise. That, say, the assertion that God created the
> earth in six days and rested on the seventh might not be literally true, but it merits

respect as "religious truth" (or, as Reza Aslan puts it, "sacred history"), as a metaphor for some ethereal verity, one so transcendental that boneheaded rationalists obsessed with superfluities like evidence cannot grasp it.

This is sophistry of the most contemptible variety. By such unscrupulous subterfuge the faithful (and their apologists) commit treason against reason, betray honest discourse, and hope to render their (preposterous) dogmas immune to disproof and open to limitless interpretation, depending on their needs of the moment. Either an objective proposition (say, that Jesus was the son of God, or that the Prophet Muhammad flew to heaven on a winged horse) is true or it is untrue. It cannot be whatever the one advancing it says it is; much less, true for some, but not for others.

37. *Salon*, October 15, 2007, http://www.salon.com/2007/10/15/pinker_goldstein/07:45 AM EDT. Cf. Nietzsche: "The man of faith is not free to have any conscience at all for questions of 'true' and 'untrue': to have integrity on this point would at once destroy him" (N 355).

38. Kaufmann, "Beyond Black and White: A Plea for Thinking in Color," in *Existentialism, Religion, and Death*, 120. The essay was first published in 1969.

39. This idea crops up in Kaufmann's *Without Guilt and Justice* in connection with his theory of the origin of justice: it arises from the sense that a figure of authority has betrayed one's expectations. "A casual rebuke from a person one respects greatly is felt to be crushing and never forgotten, even if the critic himself fails to remember the incident" (101). This "trauma" is the engine for a burning sense of (in)justice.

40. This letter, dated August 30, 1920, was sent to the great German historian Friedrich Meinecke, who had offered Rosenzweig a university lectureship on the strength of the latter's important 1920 study of Hegel's political thought in *Hegel und der Staat*, ed. Frank Lachmann, suhrkamp taschenbuch wissenschaft no. 1941 (Berlin: Suhrkamp, 2010).

41. If I seem unsympathetic to Kaufmann at this juncture, this criticism is nothing compared to the review of his *Critique* and *The Faith of a Heretic* published by the aforementioned Christian theologian and Old Testament scholar R.B.Y. Scott, Danforth Professor of Religion at Princeton while Kaufmann was his colleague in the Department of Philosophy. But Kaufmann was never helpless to respond. Scott's main brief takes the "unlovely" form (it is his word) of a *tu quoque*: you attack Christianity as a malicious religion by an argument that is itself defective; worse (according to Scott), "Such anti-Semitism-in-reverse [meaning: such anti-Christianity] is just as reprehensible and unlovely as the original article." R.B.Y. Scott, "Princetonian 'Guerre de Plume,'" 129.

42. Kaufmann writes:

> One can avoid... [the complications of religious belief without theology] by the simple expedient of refusing to think about religion. But if one does that, is one a Christian? ... But if one insists on thinking about it without gerrymandering and double-speak, one has to say: this I accept, this not; this I believe, this not; this I admire, this not. And if one employs no double-standard, one will have to add: in other scriptures and religions, too, I find things I accept, believe, and admire, including much that compares very favorably with much in my own tradition. Still, one may conceivably conclude, it is my own tradition that I love best, though I really agree with no more than a fraction of it. And if that is what one does, one may wish to be a Christian, but one is, literally, a heretic. (F 131)

43. Kaufmann adds: "Emphatically, theology does not closely resemble either a science or philosophy. The model of the law is far more illuminating. So is another model that may well be more than merely a model: literary criticism" (F 114).

44. Paul North, *The Yield, Kafka's Atheological Reformation* (Stanford, CA: Stanford University Press, 2016).

45. Martin Heidegger, *Die Grundbegriffe der Metaphysik: Welt, Endlichkeit, Einsamkeit*, lectures delivered in 1929/1930 (Frankfurt a.M.: Vittorio Klostermann, 1983), 9; translated as *Fundamental Concepts of Metaphysics: World, Finitude, Solitude*, tr. William McNeill and Nicholas Walker (Bloomington: Indiana University Press, 1995), 6.

46. Neal Ascherson, "Raging towards Utopia," review of *Koestler the Indispensable Intellectual* by Michael Scammel (London: Faber, 2010), *London Review of Books*, April 22, 2010, 2.

47. Cited from Jacques Derrida, *Circumfession*, in Benoit Peeters, *Derrida: A Biography* (Cambridge, UK: Polity, 2013), ix.

48. *Hegel: Reinterpretation, Texts, and Commentary* (Garden City, NY: Doubleday, 1965). *Hegel's Political Philosophy* (Atherton, CA: Atherton, 1970), reprinted as *Debating the Political Philosophy of Hegel* (2010).

49. The reference is to the heroes of the *Iliad*. Walter Kaufmann, *What Is Man?*, the third book of *Man's Lot: A Trilogy* (New York: Reader's Digest Press/McGraw-Hill, 1978), 64.

50. *Existentialism, Religion, and Death: Thirteen Essays* (New York: New American Library, 1976). Pages from this text will henceforth be shown in parentheses as (ER + page number).

51. The translation is given in Wikipedia without attribution, https://en.wikipedia.org/wiki/Nänie. The German original of the lines reads:

> Daß das Schöne vergeht, daß das Vollkommene stirbt.
> Auch ein Klaglied zu sein im Mund der Geliebten ist herrlich;
> Denn das Gemeine geht klanglos zum Orkus hinab.

52. The German original reads:

> Vor dem Tod erschrickst du? Du wünschest unsterblich zu leben?
> Leb' im Ganzen! Wenn du lange dahin bist, es bleibt.

53. Will and Ariel Durant, *Rousseau and Revolution: The Story of Civilization*, vol. 10 (New York: MJF Books, 1967), 599. This is the point elaborated in the moral theory of the excellent Victorian philosopher Henry Sidgwick: "As a rational being, each of us is required to aim at good generally . . . not at a particular part of it. The rational ideal . . . would be to subordinate one's own point of view completely . . . to the point of view of the Universe." Thomas Nagel, "Ways to Help," *Times Literary Supplement*, November 20, 2015, 3.

54. The German original reads:

> Immer strebe zum Ganzen, und kannst du selber kein Ganzes
> Werden, als dienendes Glied schliess an ein Ganzes dich an!

55. For English translation: https://www.goodreads.com/quotes/1055633-to-the-parcae-a-single-summer-grant-me-great-powers

> An die Parzen
> Nur Einen Sommer gönnt, ihr Gewaltigen!
> Und einen Herbst zu reifem Gesange mir,
> Daß williger mein Herz, vom süßen
> Spiele gesättiget, dann mir sterbe.

Die Seele, der im Leben ihr göttlich Recht

Nicht ward, sie ruht auch drunten im Orkus nicht;

Doch ist mir einst das Heilige, das am

Herzen mir liegt, das Gedicht, gelungen,

Willkommen dann, o Stille der Schattenwelt!

Zufrieden bin ich, wenn auch mein Saitenspiel

Mich nicht hinab geleitet; Einmal

Lebt ich, wie Götter, und mehr bedarfs nicht.

56. David Pickus, "Once I Lived Like the Gods: Walter Kaufmann and the Death Work Ethic," *Mortality* 22, no. 3: 240–54.

57. Personal communication. All further comments from David Pickus in this chapter are from e-mails received in August 2015.

58. Personal communication from David Pickus.

59. Ibid.

60. Corliss Lamont, "Mistaken Attitudes toward Death," *Journal of Philosophy* 62, no. 2 (January 21, 1965): esp. 29–31.

61. William Watson, "Short-Lived Genius," *Queries* 4, no. 5 (May 1888): 135.

62. *Tragedy and Philosophy*, 166.

63. Weiss-Rosmarin, "Interview," 127.

64. English needs a word to translate the German adjective "genial," an adjective describing the productions of a genius. Burton Pike, the very skilled translator of Robert Musil's *The Man without Qualities*, proposes "geniative," and I am glad to borrow it: "Goethe later was relying on Kant when he defined the geniative [*genial*] with the words: 'to have many objects present and easily relate the most remote ones to each other: this free of egotism and self-complacency.'" Robert Musil, "From the Posthumous Papers," ed. and tr. Burton Pike, *The Man without Qualities* (New York: Knopf, 1995), 2: 1340–41.

65. Rainer Maria Rilke, "Orpheus.Euridice.Hermes," tr. A. S. Kline, http://www.poetryin translation.com/PITBR/German/MoreRilke.php.

66. John Moran, review of *Without Guilt and Justice: From Decidophobia to Autonomy*, in *Science and Society* 40, no. 1 (Spring 1976): 82.

67. William Butler Yeats, "The Choice," https://allpoetry.com/The-Choice.

68. *Letters to Felice*, tr. James Stern and Elizabeth Duckworth (New York: Schocken, 1973), 21.

69. Personal communication from David Pickus.

70. Personal communication from Henry Staten.

Chapter 7: Stories of Religion

1. Epigraph: Walter Kaufmann, *Religion from Tolstoy to Camus* (New Brunswick, NJ: Transaction, 2000), 42. Pages from this text will henceforth be shown in parentheses as (R + page number). The second Torchbook edition (New York: Harper and Row, 1964) bears the subtitle on the cover: "Basic Writings on Religious Truth and Morals—a Companion Volume to *Existentialism from Dostoevsky to Sartre*"—a publisher's claim that might be hard to justify, resting on an untested idea, in this case, of "companionship." Finally, a third edition, with a new

introduction by Paul Gottfried, appeared with Transaction Publishers in 1994, with a third printing in 2000, to which I refer.

2. My impression is confirmed by the fact of the book's republication in 1994 and its many printings before and after: today it is sold by Amazon in "12 formats and editions" (https://www.amazon.com/Religion-Tolstoy-Camus-Walter-Kaufmann/dp/1560007060).

3. Kaufmann noted its secularization, so to speak, in his second preface to the book (1964), where he describes the different ways in which the writings might lend themselves to a syllabus.

4. Susan Sontag, *Essays of the 1960s and 1970s*, ed. David Rieff (New York: Library of America, 2013), 236–38. The harsh criticism of Kaufmann appears in an essay titled "Piety without Content," originally published in *Against Interpretation* (New York: Farrar, Straus, and Giroux, 1961), 249–55.

5. Sontag makes an apparently trenchant criticism:

> Camus was not, nor ever claimed to be, religious. In fact, one of the points he makes in his essay ["Reflections on the Guillotine"] is that capital punishment derives its only plausible rationale as a religious punishment and is therefore entirely inappropriate and ethically obscene in our present post-religious, secularized society. . . . If Camus is a serious writer and worthy of respect, it is because he seeks to reason according to the post-religious premises. He does not belong in the "story" of modern religion (Sontag, *Essays*, 237–39).

But see the main text above for a rebuttal.

6. How very interesting to find the same thought expressed in T. S. Eliot's review of two books by A. N. Whitehead, originally meant to appear in 1927. Eliot writes:

> There was once a time when the terms 'Christian,' 'atheist' and 'agnostic' meant something definite. If they are to continue to mean anything definite, then a fourth term must be invented for that large class of persons which includes Professor Whitehead. They are 'religious,' without holding to any religion; they are also 'scientific,' in that they believe devoutly in the latest theory of any and every particular science; and they must be cast out by any congregation of Christians, Buddhists, Brahmins, Jews, Mohammedans or Atheists.

T. S. Eliot, "The Return of Foxy Grandpa," http://www.nybooks.com/articles/2015/10/08/ts-eliot-return-foxy-grandpa/.

7. Sontag, *Essays*, 238.

8. In his introduction to the third edition of *Religion*, Paul Gottfried writes, "Kaufmann devoted his life to expounding the religious implications of literary and philosophical texts" (R xi).

9. Under the heading of "the justification of faith," one can introduce the following subheads: "faith and evidence," "the problem of evil," "faith and its meaning," "the appeal to scripture." Under the heading of the relevance of religion to morals and society, one can group the stories and essays of, among others, Tolstoy, Dostoevsky, Nietzsche, Cohen, Schweitzer, Buber, and Camus. See Kaufmann, *Religion from Tolstoy*, 2nd ed., vii–viii.

10. Arnold Beichman, *Herman Wouk: The Novelist as Social Historian* (New Brunswick, NJ: Transaction Books, 1984), 81–82.

11. Herman Wouk, *This Is My God*, rpt. ed. (New York: Back Bay Books, 1992), 313.

12. Rabbi Nathan Lopes Cardozo, "On Bible Criticism and Its Counterarguments: A Short History," http://www.aishdas.org/toratemet/en_cardozo.html.

13. William Foxwell Albright, *From the Stone Age to Christianity: Monotheism and the Historical Process* (Baltimore: Johns Hopkins Press, 1940, 1946); rev. ed., with a new introduction (New York: Anchor Books, 1957), 88.

14. Wouk, *This Is My God*, 313.

15. *Nietzsche—Godfather of Fascism? On the Uses and Abuses of a Philosophy*, ed. Jacob Golomb and Robert S. Wistrich (Princeton, NJ: Princeton University Press, 2002), x.

16. Wouk, *This Is My God*, 333.

17. Ibid., 330.

18. "According to an American Embassy report [1982], the Chinese are strongly interested in the Holocaust and other aspects of the Jewish experience." Beichman, *Herman Wouk*, 77–78.

19. Lionel Trilling, *The Opposing Self, Nine Essays in Criticism* (New York: Viking, 1955), 68.

20. Sontag, "In place of a hermeneutics we need an erotics of art." *Essays*, 20.

21. Compare Eric Santner's comment on reading Max Weber's *The Protestant Ethic*: "It's quite Nietzschean in its claim that asceticism can be an extreme manifestation of *jouissance*." Private communication.

22. Adam Phillips, "Against Self-Criticism," *London Review of Books* 37, no. 5 (March 5, 2015): 13.

23. Leo Tolstoy, *Anna Karenina* (Modern Library; New York: Random House, 1950), 887.

24. Ibid., 892.

25. Ibid., 888.

26. Ibid., 894.

27. Johann Wolfgang von Goethe, *Faust*: "Ich, Ebenbild der Gottheit, das sich schon/Ganz nah gedünkt dem Spiegel ew'ger Wahrheit" (lines 617–18). Franz Kafka, diary entry for September 25, 1917: "Zeitweilige Befriedigung kann ich von Arbeiten wie 'Landarzt' noch haben, . . . Glück aber nur, falls ich die Welt ins Reine, Wahre, Unveränderliche heben kann." Kafka, *Tagebücher*, 838.

28. Morris Rafael Cohen, "The Dark Side of Religion," in Kaufmann, *Religion from Tolstoy*, 281.

29. Department of Philosophy, Princeton University (https://philosophy.princeton.edu /about/past-faculty/walter-kaufmann).

30. Gotthold Ephraim Lessing, *Anti-Goeze* (1778), tr. in Christopher Hitchens, *God Is Not Great* (New York: Twelve [Hachette], 2007), 277.

31. Frank, *Dostoevsky: A Writer*, 794.

32. Ibid., 771.

33. Anatoly Lunacharsky, "Dostoyevsky's Plurality of Voices (re. the Book Problems of the Works of Dostoyevsky by M. M. Bakhtin)" (1929), *On Literature and Art* (Moscow: Progress, 1973), https://www.marxists.org/archive/lunachar/1929/bakhtin-dostoyevsky.htm.

34. Étienne Gilson, "How to Read the Encyclicals," *The Church Speaks to the Modern World: The Social Teachings of Leo XIII* (Garden City, NY: Image Books, 1954), 21.

35. Nietzsche, *Portable Nietzsche*, 603.

36. Ibid., 606.

37. For a more judicious account of the shortcomings of Clifford's essay—the dogmatic claim that "it is wrong always, everywhere, and for anyone, to believe anything upon insufficient evidence" (Clifford); and *equally* of James's fierce attack on it—it is not true, as James

claims, that Clifford's scruple would paralyze moral choice—see David A. Hollinger, "James, Clifford, and the Scientific Conscience," in *The Cambridge Companion to William James*, ed. Ruth Anna Putnam (Cambridge: Cambridge University Press, 1997), 69–83. In "A Reevaluation of Clifford and His Critics," *Southern Journal of Philosophy* 60 (2002): 437–57, Brian Zamulinski objects to Hollinger's "evenhanded verdict," produced to contradict the prevalent view that James's "The Will to Believe" annihilated Clifford, since, Zamulinksi maintains, it does not go far enough in rehabilitating Clifford. Zamulinski's argument that "James does not provide us with any good reason to reject Clifford entirely" is the weak form of Kaufmann's full-throated endorsement of Clifford (447).

38. Kafka, *Tagebücher*, 313.

39. Malcolm Hay, *Europe and the Jews: The Pressure of Christendom over 1900 Years* (Chicago: Academy Chicago, 1992); originally published under the title *The Foot of Pride* (Boston: Beacon, 1950).

40. Preface to ibid., xxviii–xxix.

41. Ibid., xxix.

42. Coyne, *Faith vs. Fact*, 30, 67, 207–8.

43. Martin Jay, "Politics of Translation: Siegfried Kracauer and Walter Benjamin on the Buber-Rosenzweig Bible," *Leo Baeck Institute Yearbook* 21, no. 1 (1976): 24. Brian Britt, on the other hand, argues that "Benjamin and Kracauer were engaged in projects that aspired to the same kind of romantic ideals as the Buber-Rosenzweig Bible." See his "Romantic Roots of the Debate on the Buber-Rosenzweig Bible," *Prooftexts* 20, no. 3 (Fall 2000): 262.

44. Sontag, *Essays*, 237–39.

45. Kaufmann's account of "the Church" during the Nazi persecution of the Jews omits many exceptional expressions, at all levels, of deepest concern and plaidoyers for charity. Kaufmann's judgment requires the differentiation provided by the sort of exact scholarship found (admittedly, some fifty years later) in John Connelly, *From Enemy to Brother: The Revolution in Catholic Teaching on the Jews, 1933–1965*. Connelly quotes Jacques Maritain, for one, who distinguishes between "the theological mystical body of Israel and the historical Jewish people. The former was unfaithful and 'repudiated,' the latter was not." Maritain calls for an "unprecedented" "Christian solidarity with the Jews" (Cambridge, MA: Harvard University Press, 2012), 139.

46. The full remark of Alphonse Karr, the French critic and journalist who argued in favor of capital punishment, reads, "Si l'on veut abolir la peine de mort, en ce cas, que MM. les Assassins commencent" (*Les Guêpes* [a monthly journal], January 31, 1840). This riposte can be spelled out as "If we are to abolish the death penalty, I should like to see the first step taken by those gentlemen the murderers" (http://www.devoir-de-philosophie .com/dissertation-veut-abolir-peine-mort-cas-assassins-commencent-alphonse-karr-gue-34147.html).

Chapter 8: Living with Hegel

1. First epigraph: Walter Kaufmann, *Hegel: A Reinterpretation*, Anchor Books (Garden City, NY: Doubleday, 1966), viii. Pages from this text will henceforth be shown in parentheses as (H + page number). Second epigraph: H 130.

2. "It is a loose collection of 'studies' which he [Kaufmann] has tried unsuccessfully to weave into a coherent whole. . . . It is regrettable, therefore, that he has wasted his talents and energies in this book upon subjects on which he is neither very interesting nor very enlightening." W. E. Kennick, review of *From Shakespeare to Existentialism*, by Walter Kaufmann, *Philosophical Review* 70, no. 1 (January 1961): 140.

3. This essay was subsequently published, along with "The Young Hegel and Religion" (1954) and "Hegel: Contribution and Calamity" (1956), in Kaufmann, *From Shakespeare to Existentialism*, 95–128, 129–62, 163–74, respectively.

4. J. N. Findlay, *Hegel: A Re-examination* (London: Allen and Unwin, 1958), reviewed by Kaufmann in *Mind* 70, no. 278 (April 1961): 264–69. The citation is on p. 269. Findlay would certainly be a fit rival to Kaufmann for love of Hegel, if love were a matter of time put in. In his autobiography, Findlay writes of Hegel's *Logic*: "It has been my constant companion throughout my life, and Hegel, like the moon, has taken up his stance at the end of every vista, shedding light as readily on naturalism and realism as on idealism and mysticism, and being reflected in Wittgenstein or *Principia Mathematica* as much as in Neo-Platonism or Scholastic Theology." "My Life," in R. S. Cohen, R. M. Martin, and M. Westphal, *Studies in the Philosophy of J. N. Findlay* (Albany: State University of New York Press, 1985), 4.

5. Thomas Mann, *Betrachtungen eines Unpolitischen*, in *Reden und Aufsätze, Gesammelte Werke* (Frankfurt: Fischer, 1960), 4: 84. The great artist found by Schopenhauer was . . . Thomas Mann himself, author of *Buddenbrooks*. His German readers would know that!

6. J. N. Findlay, review of *Hegel: A Reinterpretation, Texts, and Commentary*, by Walter Kaufmann, *Philosophical Quarterly* 16, no. 65 (October 1966): 366–68.

7. Soon after Kaufmann returned from war service, he went on to Harvard and in 1947 finished his dissertation. In *The Faith of a Heretic*, he recalls,

> I was appointed an instructor at Princeton. Soon I rewrote my thesis entirely and added a great deal more to make a book of it. Before long, friendly scholars urged me to follow it up with a similar book on Hegel.
>
> Had I survived to write monographs on Nietzsche first, then on Hegel, and perhaps eventually on Kant? . . . There is a haunting passage in William James, in quite a different context, that comes closer to the point, provided only it is read as a challenge not to others but to oneself: "If the generations of mankind suffered and laid down their lives; if prophets confessed and martyrs sang in the fire . . . for no other end than that a race of creatures of such unexampled insipidity should succeed, and protract . . . their contented and inoffensive lives, why, at such a rate . . . better ring down the curtain before the last act of the play, so that a business that began so importantly may be saved from so singularly flat a winding up." I do not mean to disparage scholarship or painstaking work of a highly technical nature. I should like to think that I myself have made some contributions of that sort, and I hope to make more. Certainly I respect some men who write monographs on other philosophers; but for me right now this would not do. This is a personal matter, and that is the reason for giving a personal account of it. I was confronted not with a drab life but with the question whether I had become a traitor. Writing on Hegel and translating Nietzsche and Goethe did not help unless it helped to make me a better writer and added to my armory. In 1958 I

finally published a book of a different kind, *Critique of Religion and Philosophy*, and a year later another volume, on which I had been working during the same years, *From Shakespeare to Existentialism*. Critical discussion of the work of others became a point of departure for attempts to develop my own views. Criticism predominated, but scholarship had become engaged (F 7–8).

8. Anthony Quinton, "Spreading Hegel's Wings," *New York Review of Books*, May 29, 1975, http://www.nybooks.com/articles/archives/1975/may/29/spreading-hegels-wings.

9. "Hegel's book on objective spirit, *The Philosophy of Right*, is available in a good English translation by T. M. Knox, which is philologically sound and supported by a wealth of informed notes. In a companion volume, Knox has also made available Hegel's minor *Political Writings*, to which Z. A. Pelczynski has contributed a long and scholarly introductory essay. Moreover, Marcuse has dealt with this phase of Hegel's thought in *Reason and Revolution: Hegel and the Rise of Social Theory*" (H 247).

10. Quinton, "Spreading Hegel's Wings."

11. *Genesis and Structure of Hegel's* "Phenomenology of Spirit," tr. Samuel Cherniak and John Heckman (Evanston, IL: Northwestern University Press, 1974, originally *Genèse et structure de la "Phénoménologie de l'Esprit" de Hegel* [Paris: Aubier, 1946]). Kaufmann actually cites Hyppolite in order to point out that he has utterly misunderstood Hegel's view of *Faust*: Hegel certainly does not take *Faust* as an incitement to "despise understanding and science," except as the shortest way to go to the devil (H 124).

12. Theodor W. Adorno, "Aufzeichnungen zu Kafka," in *Gesammelte Schriften*, ed. Rolf Tiedemann (Frankfurt a.M.: Suhrkamp, 1977), 10/1: 257.

13. When, in his *Tragedy and Philosophy*, Kaufmann praises Xenophanes and Heraclitus for their bold criticism of the mythical thinking of Homer and Hesiod, he writes, "They broke with exegetical thinking; they were anti-authoritarian" (5).

14. A scholar of this period, like the Germanist Walter Hinderer, will see this epoch as a *continuum*, as no longer defined, in the words of Werner Frick, by the "notorious antithesis, the normative dichotomy" of Classic versus Romantic. It is, rather, "a dense, richly differentiated aesthetic and conceptual constellation, a field for the thought-experiments of historians of ideas, . . . full of [various] currents of intellectual energy, transitions, resonances, and responses." Werner Frick, Laudatio auf Professor Walter Hinderer zur Verleihung der Goldenen Goethe-Medaille der internationalen Goethe-Gesellschaft in Weimar am 28. Mai 2015 im Deutschen Nationaltheater Weimar, 4–5.

15. Friedrich Hölderlin, *Hyperion*, "Vorletzte Fassung" in Friedrich Hölderlin, *Kritische Textausgabe* (Frankfurter Ausgabe), ed. D. E Sattler (Darmstadt: Neuwied, 1984), 10: 163. See my "Anmerkungen zu Hölderlin und Hegel in Frankfurt," in *Hölderlin-Jahrbuch 31 (1998/99)* (Eggingen: Isele, 2000): 73–74.

16. Bernhard Böschenstein, "Hölderlins späteste Gedichte," in *Über Hölderlin*, ed. Jochen Schmidt (Frankfurt: Insel, 1970), 174.

17. "The Tables Turned," https://www.poetryfoundation.org/poems/45557/the-tables-turned.

18. *Der Trompeter von Säckingen* (The Trumpeter of [Bad] Säckingen) (1853) is a popular epic poem by Joseph Viktor von Scheffel. It reappeared in 1884 as an opera of this name by Viktor Nessler, performed in Leipzig in 1888, the year in which Nietzsche first called Schiller the "trumpeter of morals."

19. Donald Phillip Verene, *Hegel's Recollection: A Study of Images in the Phenomenology of Spirit* (Albany: State University of New York Press, 1985), 7.

20. Friedrich Kittler, *Aufschreibesysteme 1800/1900* (Munich: Fink, 1985). English edition: *Discourse Networks*.

21. *Goethe's Faust*, 153.

22. Kittler, *Discourse Networks*, 17.

23. Paul Asveld, *La pensée religieuse du jeune Hegel: Liberté et aliénation* (Louvain: Publications universitaires de Louvain, 1953).

24. Herman Nohl, ed., *Hegels theologische Jugendschriften, nach den Handschriften der Kgl. Bibliothek in Berlin* (Tübingen: Mohr [Paul Siebeck], 1907), 266.

25. *The Works of Jeremy Bentham: Rationale of Judicial Evidence* (New York: Russell and Russell, 1962), 523.

26. Kaufmann's close reading of the preface, which he translates and comments, appears in the second part of his book. These chapters also contain his translation of Hegel's witty and accessible essay "Who Thinks Abstractly?"

27. Meyer Abrams, *Natural Supernaturalism: Tradition and Revolution in Romantic Literature* (New York: Norton, 1971), 92.

28. *Goethe's Faust*, 189.

29. Terry Eagleton, *Sweet Violence*, 30. The interior quote is from Kaufmann, *Tragedy and Philosophy*, 81.

30. Danto, *Nietzsche as Philosopher*, 182.

31. Robert Pippin, "You Can't Get There from Here: Transition Problems in Hegel's *Phenomenology of Spirit*," *The Cambridge Companion to Hegel*, ed. Frederick Beiser (Cambridge: Cambridge University Press, 1993), 52–89.

32. *Genesis and Structure*, 156–57.

33. *Macbeth*, act 2, scene 2.

34. The affinity between the idea of Hölderlin's maxim, which speaks of "the truest truth" and Hegel's infinitely wider expansion of this idea in the *Phenomenology*, is evident. The maxim reads:

> Only that is the truest truth wherein error too becomes truth, because truth places it in the whole of its system, into its time and place. . . . But here swift conceptual grasp [schneller Begriff] is most necessary. How can you make use of something at the right place when you still shyly tarry over it, and do not know how much meaning it has, how much or little to make of it? That is eternal serenity, divine joy—one's putting everything particular in its place, in the whole where it belongs. Therefore, without understanding or a thoroughly organized feeling, no excellence—no life. (*Sämtliche Werke*, "Frankfurter Ausgabe" [Frankfurt: Roter Stern, 1979], 14: 59.

In Hölderlin's phrase, "schneller Begriff" means "facility in understanding." "Emphasis goes on the process of conceptualizing; its active character is stressed by the qualifier 'swift.' . . . Stress falls on the mode of action, not on the concept moved about or the concept obtained." See Corngold, *Complex Pleasure*, 61. One detects a physicalizing of the concept, the suggestion of an embodied mind in action.

35. Marcuse, *Reason and Revolution*, 146.

36. This claim has been much debated—and resisted, for one, by the Hegel scholar Michael Forster. His objection reads:

Hegel certainly criticizes the manner in which this model has been utilized by previous philosophers, especially Schelling's reduction of it to a 'lifeless schema' externally applied to a subject matter (instead of being allowed to emerge therefrom). But he does not criticize the model itself; on the contrary, he quite clearly assumes its correctness, saying, for example, that since Kant it has 'been raised to its absolute significance and with it the true form in its true content has been presented, so that the Concept of Science has emerged.' (Similarly, in *Science of Logic*, pp. 836–37/WdL II pp. 564–65, Hegel resists undue emphasis on the numerical aspect of the model, its triplicity, suggesting that the method may, if desired, be divided up into more than three steps. But this does not imply any rejection of the 'thesis, anti-thesis, synthesis' model itself; on the contrary, Hegel's comments occur in the context of an explanation of the method that accords it this structure).

Hegel's Dialectical Method," *Cambridge Companion to Hegel*, 162.

37. In the words of Iris Murdoch, "What Hegel teaches us is that we should attempt to describe phenomena. . . . What we are all working upon, it might be said, is le monde vécu, the lived world, what is actually experienced, thought of as itself being the real, and carrying its own truth criteria with it—and not as being the reflection or mental shadow of some other separate mode of being which lies behind it in static parallel. . . . To sum things up in a rather shocking way: as far as method goes, we are all Hegelians nowadays." "The Existential Political Myth," in *Existentialists and Mystics: Writings on Philosophy and Literature*, ed. Peter Conradi (London: Chatto and Windus, 1997), 131–32.

38. See, however, Michael Forster's essay "Hegel's Dialectical Method" above. Andrew Cole, *The Birth of Theory* (Chicago: University of Chicago Press, 2014), 19. Cole's book is one among several very thoughtful recent attempts to make Hegel new—in Cole's case, cogent to an understanding of contemporary literary theory. Žižek's massive *Less Than Nothing* means to show that Hegel's epistemological and ontological thought has an immense explanatory value for our current political and economic crises. For a lucid discussion of Žižek's achievement, see Robert Pippin, "Back to Hegel?": Žižek "has written a serious attempt to re-animate or re-actualize Hegel (in the light of Lacanian meta-psychology and so in a form he wants to call 'materialist')." *Mediations* 26, nos. 1–2, http://www.mediationsjournal.org/articles/back-to-hegel.

39. That book might be the previously noted *Cambridge Companion to Hegel*, since it is conceived in the light of Beiser's imperative, stated in his "Introduction: Hegel and the Problem of Metaphysics": "If the modern philosopher wants to know the roots of his own position, sooner or later he will have to turn to Hegel," 1.

40. "Asked by his interviewer whether he still believed that the Germans had specific qualifications for confronting the problems of the modern age, Heidegger replied: 'Yes. . . . I am thinking of the special inner affinity of the German language with the language of the Greeks and with their thinking. This has been confirmed to me again and again by the French. When they begin to think they speak German. They insist that they could not get through with their own language.'" Martin Heidegger, "Spiegel Interview," cited in Charles R. Bambach, *Heidegger's Roots: Nietzsche, National Socialism, and the Greeks* (Ithaca, NY: Cornell University Press, 2003), 202.

41. W. H. Walsh, "Hegel: *Reinterpretation, Texts, and Commentary*, by Walter Kaufmann," *Philosophical Review* 76, no. 2. (April 1967): 240. Kaufmann is committed to the importance of a fact that other Hegel scholars have ignored: though the 1812 edition is rarely consulted, it

is the primary text and offers, in parallel with the later, definitive edition, a view onto Hegel's ongoing development of his logic. This project is on offer to scholarly readers rather than one significantly developed in Kaufmann's text.

42. Review of *Hegel* by Charles Taylor (Cambridge: Cambridge University Press, 1975), titled "Coming to Terms with Hegel," *Times Literary Supplement*, January 2, 1976, 13–14. Here Kaufmann remarks that "well over a thousand books and articles on Hegel have been published in the 1970s [alone]," 13. No one, with the possible exception of Kaufmann, can have mastered this literature.

43. Terry Pinkard, *Hegel: A Biography* (Cambridge: Cambridge University Press, 2000); Robert Pippin, *Hegel's Idealism: The Satisfactions of Self-Consciousness* (Cambridge: Cambridge University Press, 1989); *Hegel's Practical Philosophy: Rational Agency as Ethical Life* (Cambridge: Cambridge University Press, 2008); and *Hegel on Self-Consciousness: Desire and Death in "The Phenomenology of Spirit"* (Princeton, NJ: Princeton University Press, 2011).

44. Stephen D. Crites, "A Critique of Kaufmann's Hegel," *Journal of the History of Ideas* 27, no. 2, (Apr.–Jun., 1966): 303–4.

45. Findlay, review of *Hegel*, 367.

46. Findlay is exercised by the boldness of Kaufmann's claims:

> The following statement of Professor Kaufmann is so extreme that it takes my breath away: "The central point of our philological excursus is, of course, to show how Hegel himself handled his system: not as so much necessary truth, deduced once and for all in its inexorable sequence, but rather as a very neat and sensible way of arranging the parts of philosophy—not even the neatest and most sensible possible, but only the best he could do in time to meet the printer's deadline" (p. 249). Whatever the arrangement of the Encyclopedia may be, it cannot be called neat and sensible: only the plea that it is supremely profound and illuminating—though not inexorably consequential—could make it worth anyone's while to master its intricacies. (Ibid., 368)

47. Kaufmann took Marcuse seriously. In a 1969 essay titled "Black and White," he charged Marcuse's book *Repressive Tolerance* with maintaining a simplistic discrimination between parties of the Left and parties of the Right—Manichean in its absoluteness. However, he added, "Marcuse has the contagious vitality of a vigorous fighter who issues a call to war. It is an ancient battle: the war of the children of light against the children of darkness." *Survey*, no. 73 (Autumn 1969): 35–36. Kaufmann continued to cite Marcuse positively, observing that Marcuse's discussion of Hegel's concept of alienation in *Reason and Revolution* was original (in works in English) in employing that concept productively. "The Inevitability of Alienation," an introduction to Richard Schacht, *Alienation* (Garden City, NY: Doubleday 1971), xx.

48. Both citations from Sartre are found in Sartre's "Existentialism Is a Humanism," which Kaufmann reprinted in his anthology *Existentialism from Dostoevsky to Sartre*, pp. 291, 300. See chapter 3.

49. Kafka, *Letters*, 10. Or consider this fusée:

> I feel too tightly constricted in everything that signifies Myself: even the eternity that I am is too tight for me. But if, for instance, I read a good book . . . it rouses me, satisfies me, suffices me. Proofs that previously I did not include this book in my eternity, or had not pushed on far enough ahead to have an intuitive glimpse of the eternity that necessarily includes this book as well.—From a certain stage of knowledge on, weariness,

insufficiency, constriction, self-contempt must all vanish: namely, at the point where I have the strength to recognize as my own nature what previously was something alien to myself that refreshed me, satisfied, liberated, and exalted me.

Dearest Father, tr. Ernst Kaiser and Eithne Wilkins (New York: Schocken, 1954), 91.

50. A reference to the counterculture becomes altogether explicit when Kaufmann turns to the "young people who . . . feel attracted to existentialism" (H 269).

51. "In the late sixties, Trilling was no longer the same kind of critic that he had been in the forties. If the younger Trilling had imitated the manner of Victorian men of letters like Arnold, the older man was moving toward a Central European mode of cultural criticism, a philosophical history of consciousness in the Hegelian mode." Mark Krupnick, "The Neoconservatives," in *Lionel Trilling and the Critics: Opposing Selves*, ed. John Rodden (Lincoln: University of Nebraska Press, 1999), 393.

52. The critic Jonathan Arac observes that Stephen Donadio, author of *Nietzsche, Henry James, and the Artistic Will*, conceives of his work of literary criticism "along the lines of Lionel Trilling and Walter Kaufmann" (New York: Oxford University Press, 1978). I am glad to see the "lines" I have proposed drawn by two scholars of distinction. Arac observes that Donadio's literary criticism, "normal" in 1980, turns on concepts of art and the self. Paul de Man's jolting countercriticism substitutes concepts of rhetoric (for art) and reading (for the self). "The reality of literature for Donadio [and, by implication, for Trilling and Kaufmann] was aesthetic, for de Man linguistic." See "Paul de Man and Deconstruction: Aesthetics, Rhetoric, History," in *Critical Genealogies: Historical Situations for Postmodern Literary Studies* (New York: Columbia University Press, 1987), 239–40.

53. Kaufmann's *Existentialism: From Dostoevsky to Sartre* (1956) had an enormous impact on college students; the book was very widely bought and circulated. Pickus, "Paperback Authenticity," 17–31.

54. Steven B. Smith, *Hegel's Critique of Liberalism: Rights in Context* (Chicago: University of Chicago Press, 1989), 130.

55. George Armstrong Kelly, *Hegel's Retreat from Eleusis* (Princeton, NJ: Princeton University Press, 1978), 3, 116.

56. This volume, edited by Kaufmann, consists of essays by various hands (Avineri, Sidney Hook, et al.) and reprints Kaufmann's own essay "The Hegel Myth," which we have treated in chapter 5. *Hegel's Political Philosophy*, Walter Kaufmann, ed. (New York: Atherton, 1970).

57. Shlomo Avineri, *Hegel's Theory of the Modern State* (Cambridge: Cambridge University Press, 1972), 178–79.

58. Es haben aber an eigner
Unsterblichkeit die Götter genug, und bedürfen
Die Himmlischen eines Dings,
So sinds Heroen und Menschen
Und Sterbliche sonst. Denn weil
Die Seligsten nichts fühlen von selbst,
Muß wohl, wenn solches zu sagen
Erlaubt ist, in der Götter Namen
Teilnehmend fühlen ein Andrer,
Den brauchen sie.
—8TH STROPHE

http://www.zeno.org/Literatur/M/Hölderlin,+Friedrich/Gedichte/Gedichte+1800
–1804/%5BHymnen%5D/Der+Rhein.

Translation by David Constantine,

https://www.academia.edu/4064313/Selected_Poems_by_Friedrich_Hölderlin.

59. "Das was man ist kann man nicht ausdrücken, denn dieses ist man eben; mitteilen kann man nur das was man nicht ist, also die Lüge. Erst im Chor mag eine gewisse Wahrheit liegen." Kafka, *Nachgelassene Schriften II*, 348.

60. Martin Heidegger, *Being and Time*, tr. Joan Stambaugh, rev. and with a foreword by Dennis J. Schmidt (Albany: State University of New York Press, 2010), 17.

61. Theodor W. Adorno, *An Introduction to Dialectics*, ed. Christoph Ziermann, tr. Nicholas Walker (Cambridge: Polity, 2017), 32.

62. Alexandre Kojève, "Phenomenological Method in Hegel," https://www.marxists.org /reference/subject/philosophy/works/fr/kojeve.htm.

63. *Hegel: Texts and Commentary*, tr. and ed. Walter Kaufmann (Notre Dame, IN: Notre Dame University Press, 1977); originally published in 1965 by Doubleday. Pages from this text will henceforth be shown in parentheses as (Hp + page number).

64. George Lichtheim, "Restoring Hegel," *New York Review of Books*, July 15, 1965, http://www.nybooks.com/articles/1965/07/15/restoring-hegel/.

65. G.W.F. Hegel, *Theorie-Werkausgabe*, ed. Eva Moldenhauer and Karl Markus Michel (Suhrkamp: Frankfurt: 1986), 11: 574.

66. Alexander Koyré, "Note sur la langue et la terminologie hégéliennes," *Revue philosophique* (1931), reprinted in *Études d'histoire de la pensée philosophique* (Paris: A. Colin, 1961), 175–204. Cited in John Heckman, "Translator's Preface," *Genesis and Structure*, xi.

67. Heckman, "Translator's Preface," xi.

68. Pippin, "You Can't Get There from Here," 58–59.

Chapter 9: The Philosophy of Tragedy

1. Epigraph: Walter Kaufmann, *Tragedy and Philosophy* (Princeton, NJ: Princeton University Press, 1992), 101 (1st ed., Doubleday, 1968). Pages from this text will henceforth be shown in parentheses as (T + page number).

2. Terry Eagleton, *Sweet Violence*, 5. These grounds for acclamation are somewhat shaky, since Kaufmann does at times distinguish the tragic from the pitiful, and at other times does not, but Eagleton has other reasons to praise him, as we shall see.

3. Ibid., 30. The inner quotes are from Kaufmann, *Tragedy and Philosophy*, 182, 81, respectively.

4. Thirty-five years later the philosopher Fred Rush asks the question of the *value* of language in its relation to human suffering.

> In particular, one might think that issues of the therapeutic potential of language, in particular in relation to *suffering*, are especially pressing in the twentieth century. Nietzsche famously held that it is not suffering that is intolerable for humans, but rather suffering without meaning. Language is a primary manner in which the world is taken to be meaningful, so questions of the value of language to alleviate, increase, or otherwise give form to suffering naturally arise. Is language in twentieth-century Europe still a resource in this regard, or has a combination of intensified, large-scale suffering and

a concurrent depletion of linguistic imagination foreclosed this possibility? Anglo-American philosophy of language registers absolutely no interest in this topic.

Fred Rush, "Bernhard, Suffering, and the Value of Language," *German Quarterly* 87, no. 3 (Summer 2014): 351.

5. A. C. Grayling, https://en.wikipedia.org/wiki/A._C._Grayling. I hasten to add that as a public intellectual Grayling is the author of theses that do very plainly implicate human suffering. I cite these "debates," however, as informing the general program of contemporary humanist philosophy, which, for Kaufmann, had been insufficiently sensitive to "extreme situations." Compare chapter 3 of *Man's Lot*, "Western Philosophy," which begins, "Philosophy is a branch of literature in which suffering and extreme situations have traditionally been largely ignored" (*Life at the Limits*, the first book of *Man's Lot: A Trilogy* [New York: Reader's Digest Press/McGraw-Hill, 1978], 90).

6. Walter Benjamin, http://www.sfu.ca/~andrewf/CONCEPT2.html.

7. Contrast the opposing view of the prophets Amos 3:6 and Isaiah 45:5.

8. Plato is closer, in his complaint, to Ezekiel 18:2: "What do you mean by using this proverb about the land of Israel, 'The fathers have eaten sour grapes, and the children's teeth are set on edge'? As I live, says the Lord God, this proverb shall no more used by you in Israel." In *The Faith of a Heretic*, Kaufmann discusses this theodicean evolution in the Hebrew Bible (F 140–45).

9. Compare Alexander Nehamas's views on the parallel between Plato's repudiation of tragic poetry and our early contemporary repudiation of television as a popular mass medium: "Simply put, the greatest part of contemporary criticisms of television depends on a moral disapproval which is identical to Plato's attack on epic and tragic poetry in the fourth century B.C." "Plato and the Mass Media," in "Aesthetics and the Histories of the Arts," spec. issue of *Monist* 71, no. 2 (April 1988): 222.

10. I referred in chapter 1 to this classic study as a work whose interest has guaranteed its survival, certainly until now—a status I then attributed to Kaufmann's *Nietzsche*. This association of two important works on the grounds of their longevity should not preclude, however, Kaufmann's explicit dissatisfaction with Auerbach's study.

> Erich Auerbach's celebrated contrast of an exceedingly terse story in *Genesis* with a lovingly elaborated passage in the *Odyssey*, in the first chapter of his *Mimesis*, is unsound methodologically because it takes the features of two diametrically opposed genres for basic traits of the two cultures in which they are found; comparing a passage from the David stories with a suitably selected one from Sophocles he would have got a very different contrast. (T 162)

This judgment is bold—and I think acute.

11. Gunter Gebauer and Chrisoph Wulf, *Mimesis: Culture—Art—Society*, tr. Don Reneau (Berkeley: University of California Press, 1995), 318, 189.

12. I am referring to Meyer Abrams's epochal study *The Mirror and the Lamp: Romantic Theory and the Critical Tradition* (New York: Oxford University Press, 1953).

13. Francis Fergusson, an eminent scholar, reviewed *Tragedy and Philosophy* for the *New York Review of Books* (see also below). The title of his essay is "It's a Tragedy," which says it all. He is particularly exercised by Kaufmann's alleged misunderstanding of Aristotle's concept of "action," viz.,

> He completely fails to notice what Aristotle means by the "action" the dramatist imitates; he never discusses that crucial concept. In the *Poetics* "action" means something

like "motive": "mainly a psychic energy working outwards," as [S. H.] Butcher put it. If one understands action that way it is easy to see that music or lyric poetry may imitate it; if one does not, most of the *Poetics* loses its force, its consistency, and its suggestiveness. *New York Review of Books*, November 20, 1969, http://www.nybooks.com/articles/1969/11/20/its-a-tragedy/.

Kaufmann has read Butcher's *Aristotle's Theory of Poetry and Fine Art* and relies on him; Fergusson thinks he has read him carelessly.

14. The phrase from Freud is found in his *Vorlesungen zur Einführung in die Psychoanalyse—Kapitel 2* (Introductory Lectures on Psychoanalysis—chapter 2), http://gutenberg.spiegel.de/buch/-926/2.

15. Cited in Jean-Paul Sartre, *Baudelaire*, tr. Martin Turnell (New York: New Directions, 1950), 66.

16. Adorno, "Notes on Kafka," in *Prisms*, 246.

17. The philosopher Giorgio Agamben likens the heroes of Greek tragedy to the chief figures—scarcely "heroes"—of Kafka in their arrestation in the unbridgeable time of the interval between "what has happened" (Aristotle) and what is to be.

> At the time of Greek tragedy, when the traditional mythic system had begun to decline under the impulse of the new moral world that was being born, art had already assumed the task of settling the conflict between old and new, and had responded to this task with the figure of the guilty innocent, of the tragic hero who expresses in all his greatness and misery the precarious significance of human action in the interval between what is no longer and what is not yet. Kafka is the author of our time who has most coherently assumed this task.

Giorgio Agamben, *The Man without Content*, tr. Georgia Albert (Stanford, CA: Stanford University Press, 1999), 112.

For relevant commentary, see Anke Snoek, *Agamben's Joyful Kafka: Finding Freedom beyond Subordination* (New York: Bloomsbury, 2012), 131. Kaufmann is no less interesting in employing "Kafka" as a model for the peculiar temporality in which the Homeric hero lives and dies. He has in mind a scene from *The Trial*, in which the whippers are engaged in their dirty work *forever*. Kaufmann notes that Homer's people undergo no inner development, no change of character. His "heroes are eternally the same age. . . . Odysseus [is not] changed by his wanderings, nor Penelope transformed in the course of waiting for him; in this respect, Homer's world resembles Kafka's: whenever we open the door, we behold Penelope still sitting there; and if we look in another direction, we see the same old Odysseus" (T 185). The hero of Kafka's *The Trial* ruins his life through passivity—still, for Kaufmann, it is his *decision* to let his life slide in such a fashion. The hero of *The Castle*, on the other hand, takes his destiny into his own hands; but his "activism," as Kaufmann generously suggests, is no more effective than passivity in evading his own ruin. According to Max Brod, he would die, exhausted, never having obtained from the castle the recognition he craves (T 208–9). Finally, Reiner Stach, in his biography of Kafka, finds the root of Kafka's special way of dealing with Greek mythological figures in his *Gymnasium* classes:

> Kafka did not engage systematically with the culture and language of antiquity once he had the *Matura* examination out of the way, yet he did not simply make do with the set of quotations he had learned by rote. He continued to read ancient authors who

interested him, Plato in particular. Figures from the world of antiquity also appear in his literary texts, though not as they were presented to him in school, but as protagonists wrenched out of their historical context. "The Silence of the Sirens," "Poseidon," "Prometheus," "The New Attorney": none of these parable-like pieces displays a historical interest in its characters but instead uses the prominence of their names to expose them to the harsh light of modernity. That the ancient myth is disrespectfully dismantled and reassembled—as in the case of Poseidon, whom Kafka portrays as an ill-tempered executive—was part of the literary game. *Kafka: The Early Years*, 145.

On the other hand, there is Kafka's feeling for tragedy. Stach notes that there are no extant tragedies written by Kafka, "although he would soon grow far more familiar with this genre as a reader and spectator." The tragic impulse is disconnected from his readings of Greek tragedy and secreted into his novels, witness Kafka's own judgment on *The Missing Person* (*Amerika*). In a journal entry dated September 30, 1915, he compared the hero of the latter work—Karl Rossmann—with Joseph K., the hero of *The Trial*, noting: "Rossmann and K., the innocent and the guilty, in the end both killed punitively without distinction, the innocent one with a gentler hand, more shoved aside than struck down." Franz Kafka, diary entry of September 30, 1915, https://www.odaha.com/sites/default/files/Tagebucher.pdf.

18. "Ruth" is a bold choice for a key term in this discussion that will and must recur as absolutely constitutive of tragedy: it designates the ability of tragic drama to "arouse," in the words of the OED, "the feeling of sorrow for another; compassion, pity."

19. The quotes are conveniently brought together in a fine essay by Irving Wohfarth, "Et Etcetera? The Historian as Chiffonier," in *Walter Benjamin: Critical Evaluations in Cultural Theory*, ed. Peter Osborne (New York: Routledge, 2004), 190.

20. Henry Staten, *Wittgenstein and Derrida* (Lincoln: University of Nebraska Press, 1986), 19.

21. Martin Hägglund, *Radical Atheism: Derrida and the Time of Life* (Stanford, CA: Stanford University Press, 2008), 212–13.

22. Richard Sheppard, "The Problematics of European Modernism: Theorizing Modernism," in *Essays in Critical Theory*, ed. Steve Giles (London: Routledge, 1993), 14, 18. At another level, in another medium, Kaufmann shows he is well aware of the intense aesthetic effect of "breaks and fissures" when time has worked on the texture of stone (T 103). But this is not what he is looking for in literary works of art.

23. I discuss this topic throughout my *Complex Pleasure*.

24. Corngold, *Fate of the Self*, xvii.

25. *Italo Calvino: Letters, 1941–1985*, selected and with an introduction by Michael Wood and translated from the Italian by Martin McLaughlin (Princeton, NJ: Princeton University Press, 2014), 394.

26. Walter Benjamin, "The Task of the Translator: An Introduction to the Translation of Baudelaire's *Tableaux Parisiens*," tr. Harry Zohn, in *The Translation Studies Reader*, ed. Lawrence Venuti (London: Routledge, 2000), 15.

27. See Stanley Corngold, "Sebald's Tragedy":

> For my part, I understand tragedy as an ensemble of characteristics none of them stable in the reflection on tragedy since Aeschylus. The ensemble includes these features: 1. the drastic, disproportionate suffering of an individual or individuals; 2. capable of reasoning as to design; 3. who judge their suffering as the effect of a cause "high" enough to

be intelligible in principle; 4. yet find this cause inscrutable (the lament at undeserved suffering); 5. who then struggle additionally to grasp the intelligibility of that cause; 6. in a community, where the suffering is visible to many and the task of attributing a cause may be undertaken by many.

Rethinking Tragedy, ed. Rita Felski (Baltimore: Johns Hopkins University Press, 2008), 218.

28. This is a view defended with considerable rigor by Peter Juhl in *Interpretation: An Essay in the Philosophy of Literary Criticism* (Princeton, NJ: Princeton University Press, 1980). Juhl's essay also aroused considerable resistance on the grounds that it was inadequate to the complexities of literary interpretation, viz., the vigorous review by Gary Lee Stonum, *SubStance* vol. 10, no. 4, and vol. 11, no. 1 (1981/1982), 136–37, http://www.jstor.org/stable/3684539.

29. De Man, *Blindness and Insight*, 25.

30. Nietzsche, *On the Genealogy of Morals*, in *Basic Writings*, 203.

31. Anthony Julius, *T. S. Eliot, Anti-Semitism and Literary Form* (Cambridge: Cambridge University Press, 1995), 1.

32. Kaufmann, *Discovering the Mind*, vol. 2, *Nietzsche, Heidegger, and Buber*, 157.

33. De Man, *Blindness and Insight*, 107.

34. Cleanth Brooks, *The Well Wrought Urn: Studies in the Structure of Poetry* (New York: Reynal and Hitchcock, 1947); René Wellek and Austin Warren, *Theory of Literature* (New York: Harcourt Brace, 1949); W. K. Wimsatt Jr. and Monroe C. Beardsley, *The Verbal Icon: Studies in the Meaning of Poetry* (Lexington: University of Kentucky Press, 1954).

35. It should have come as no surprise to Kaufmann when his book received a scathingly negative review in the *New York Review of Books* with the title "It's a Tragedy" (November 20, 1969). The author? We have already identified him as Francis Fergusson. Kaufmann could have avoided the trouble by omitting this cavil with Fergusson, a celebrated scholar, who had taught at Princeton before Kaufmann's arrival; was the founder of the very Gauss lecture series that Kaufmann would direct one day; and was certainly personally known to him. On the other hand, Kaufmann might have dismissed Fergusson's criticism both on the grounds of a clash of personalities and on the fact that the *New York Review of Books* rather specializes in the welcome it gives to reviewers keen on overthrowing the reputation of established scholars. Kaufmann might also have written off Fergusson's assault in the manner with which Kaufmann deals with H.D.F. Kitto's abuse of "John Jones's suggestive book *Aristotle and Greek Tragedy* (1962), which he misquotes (5) and misrepresents (6) *with the cheerful abandon of a journalist*" (emphasis added) (T 148). It's the italicized phrase that's important. But this is old hat—the nasty review—the price one pays for sinning boldly, i.e., publishing.

36. Rainer Maria Rilke, *The First Duino Elegy*, tr. Stephen Mitchell (Boston: Shambhala, 1992), http://homestar.org/bryannan/duino.html.

37. In *Oedipus at Colonus*, Oedipus tells Creon that he has acted in self-defense in killing his father:

> As you love your life, I'm sure, you would strike back
> The culprit and not look around first for a warrant.
> Into this plight the gods thrust me. (T 130)

I leave it to classicists to decide how these lines jibe (or do not) with Kaufmann's insistence that the tragic situation into which Oedipus falls is of his own making and not one arranged by the gods—i.e., by an inhuman fate.

38. We find virtually the same lines at the conclusion of *The Faith of a Heretic* (F 354).

39. Walter Kaufmann, *Without Guilt and Justice.*

40. Personal communication. On pp. 168–69, Kaufmann deals scathingly with critics who, over the years, have uttered "singular superlatives in literary criticism." Here is an example. Ezra Pound writes, "The *Trachiniae* presents the highest peak of Greek sensibility registered in any of the plays that have come down to us, and is, at the same time, nearest the original form of the God-Dance." Kaufmann responds: "Let us resist the temptation to indulge in a singular superlative. It is more constructive to request that one of Pound's many admirers provide a graph showing, however approximately, the height of Greek sensibility and the proximity to the original form of the God-Dance attained by each of the extant Greek plays; if possible, accompanied by a brief explanation of the nature of the 'God-Dance' and the meaning of 'peak of Greek sensibility.'" Without such (impossible) evidence, superlatives like this, adds Kaufmann, along with "almost all singular superlatives in literary criticism are grotesque." Well and good, but is Kaufmann as immune to such a habit as he implies? Of several examples, he writes that his reason for choosing to test his principles against *Oedipus Tyrannus* is that "the best interpreters of literature for over twenty centuries, from Aristotle to Freud and the present . . . [have] agreed that it is as great a tragedy as any ever written" (T 102). And on the same page on which he mocks Pound's judgment, he writes of Aeschylus's *The Persians* as having been "written well before he [Aeschylus] had reached *the height of his powers*" (emphasis added). An unkind critic, perhaps a devoté of Pound, would deplore, quid pro quo, Kaufmann's not having supplied graphs of any kind to support these assertions.

41. Eagleton, *Sweet Violence*, 5.

42. Gilbert Murray, *Aeschylus: The Creator of Tragedy* (Oxford: Clarendon, 1940, 1962), 205.

43. William Blake, *Jerusalem*, "The Words of Los," f. 10, lines 20–21, http://www.bartleby.com/235/307.htm.

44. Contrast George Steiner, "Where the causes of the disaster are temporal, where the conflict can be resolved by technical or social means, we may have serious drama [think Ibsen!], but not tragedy." *The Death of Tragedy* (New York: Knopf, 1961), 8. Kaufmann's invocation of the *Eumenides* gives a place in tragedy to instrumental, social reason.

45. "Wer sucht findet nicht, wer nicht sucht, wird gefunden." Kafka, *Nachgelassene Schriften II*, 63.

Chapter 10: Tragedy as Philosophy

1. First epigraph: G.W.F. Hegel, cited on H 195. Second epigraph: Joseph Brodsky, http://www.nobelprize.org/nobel_prizes/literature/laureates/1987/brodsky-lecture.html.

2. "Reflections, or Sentences and Moral Maxims," by François de La Rochefoucauld, http://www.thomaswhichello.com/?page_id=831.

3. Giorgio Agamben, *The Man without Content*, tr. Georgia Albert (Stanford, CA: Stanford University Press, 1999), 112.

4. Adolf Muschg, "Zum Tode von Emil Staiger: 'Begreifen, was uns ergreift,'" http://www.zeit.de/1987/20/begreifen-was-uns-ergreift.

5. Karl Eibl, *Das monumentale Ich—Wege zu Goethes "Faust,"* Insel Taschenbuch 2663 (Frankfurt a.M.: Insel, 2000), 331.

6. "The translations, while creating a German so alien that Goethe, Schiller, and Voß thought it fit for parody, oscillate between radical literality that strains and sometimes breaks through the syntactic and semantic limits of German and a deliberate indifference to the Greek

original." Silke Weineck, *The Abyss Above: Philosophy and Poetic Madness in Plato, Hölderlin, and Nietzsche* (Albany: State University of New York Press, 2002), 62. Her discussion of Hölderlin's translations on this and successive pages brings out their uncanny power.

7. Sophocles, *The Three Theban Plays: Antigone; Oedipus the King; Oedipus at Colonus,* tr. Robert Fagles, with notes by Bernard Knox (New York: Penguin, 1984), 102. Subsequent references to this edition will be given in the text as (Ant + page number).

8. Sophocles, *The Three Theban Plays: Antigone; Oedipus the King; Oedipus at Colonus,* tr. Robert Fagles, with notes by Bernard Knox (New York: Penguin, 1984). Knox's note to this line reads: "The Greek word *oukoun* can be negative or positive, depending on the accent, which determines the pronunciation; since these written accents were not yet in use in Sophocles' time, no one will ever know for sure which meaning he intended"—"crowned" or "not crowned." Translator and commentator opt for good reasons for "not crowned." The chorus is mocking and tormenting Antigone.

9. "They . . . say that when he heard that Euripides had died, Sophocles himself appeared in a grey cloak, and in the proagon brought his chorus and actors forward without garlands, and the [Athenian] people wept." C. W. Marshall, *The Structure and Performance of Euripides' Helen* (Cambridge: Cambridge University Press, 2014), 248.

10. Thus Mephisto, in *Goethe's Faust,* 207.

11. Hermann Broch wrote, admittedly not of Aeschylus and Sophocles but of his contemporaries Kafka and Musil: "Nonetheless there is something I share with . . . [them]: all three of us have no real biography; we lived and wrote, and that's all." Christian Eschweiler, "Hermann Broch, *Die Schlafwandler: Der Zerfall der Werte und seine bedrohlichen Folgen,*" http://www.christian-eschweiler.com/downloads/schlafwandler.pdf. Also see, more recently, Žižek, in *Less Than Nothing*: "Slavoj Žižek was born, writes books, and will die" (ii).

12. E. R. Dodds, "Euripides the Irrationalist," in *Classical Review* 43 (1929): 97–104.

13. Ibid., 97.

14. Wilhelm Dilthey, *Gesammelte Schriften,* 5: 13. This work appeared in eighteen vols. from 1914 to 1977, vols. 1–13 (Leipzig: B. B. Teubner; Göttingen: Vandenhoeck und Ruprecht), vols. 14–18 (Göttingen: Vandenhoeck und Ruprecht). Wilhelm Windelband is cited in Ernst Cassirer, *The Philosophy of the Enlightenment* (Boston: Beacon, 1964), 278. The entire passage in Cassirer reads, "Windelband said of Kant's *Critique of Judgment* that it constructs, as it were, *a priori* the concept of Goethe's poetry, and that what the latter represents as achievement and act is founded and demanded in the former by the pure necessity of philosophic thought." Both texts are briefly discussed in Corngold, *Fate of the Self,* 22, 234.

15. To be more precise, its existentialism is not that of Sartre's signature lecture "Existentialism Is a Humanism" written in 1946, three years after *The Flies.* In the later work Sartre argued in a Kantian—and least of all Nietzschean—vein: "Nothing can be better for us unless it is better for all" (T 262).

16. If decent men do not exercise this principle, Trilling wrote, "We will learn that imagination and mind are politics, and of a kind we will not like." *The Liberal Imagination* (New York: New York Review of Books, 2008), 100.

17. "Among Shakespeare's tragic heroes, only Richard III belongs in this company [of villains, viz., Claudius and Edmund]; and Shakespeare gives him such incredible vitality, re-

sourcefulness, and ingenuity, coupled with courage and a sense of humor, that we almost think of him, despite our better judgment, as an engaging rogue" (T 276). We recognize courage and a sense of humor as central players in Kaufmann's account of the genuinely ethical life.

18. This topic is explored in lively detail—again in the perspective of the many theoreticians who have addressed the Hamlet problem—by the philosopher Simon Critchley and the Lacanian psychoanalyst Jamieson Webster in *Stay, Illusion! The Hamlet Doctrine* (New York: Vintage, 2015).

19. Ibid., 142–43.

20. Cited in Eugene Goodheart, "Darwinian Hubris," *Michigan University Quarterly* L, no. 1 (Winter 2011), http://hdl.handle.net/2027/spo.act2080.0050.103.

21. "Walter Kaufmann has an incredible memory and has read everything." *Hannah Arendt/ Karl Jaspers, Correspondence, 1926–1969* (New York: Harcourt Brace, 1992), 233.

22. Martin Heidegger, *Being and Time, A Revised Edition of the [Joan] Stambaugh Translation*, tr. Dennis Schmidt (Albany: State University of New York Press, 2010), 32.

23. In a later book, *Without Guilt and Justice*, Kaufmann argues as follows: "What has happened to justice and desert in our time is similar to what has happened to God. . . . As Satan once said to a Christian: 'I think you don't know yourself what you mean. You are repeating words that once designated very understandable superstitions. Now you denounce these superstitions but cling to the same words and believe that you are still saying something'" (W 105). Only by consulting a discreet note at the end of the book will the un-clued-in reader become aware that Kaufmann is citing from the imaginary dialogue between "Satan" and "A Christian" he composed for his earlier work of 1958, *Critique of Religion and Philosophy* (C 254).

24. Marc Weitzmann, "The Failure of Intelligent Explanations," *Tablet* (a web magazine), November 25, 2015, http://www.tabletmag.com/jewish-news-and-politics/195371/france -intelligent-explanations.

25. Liel Leibovitz, "The Left's Ideas Deficit Strengthens Islamists," *Tablet* (a web magazine), November 25, 2015, http://www.tabletmag.com/jewish-news-and-politics/195349 /lefts-ideas-deficit.

26. Following especially Walter Benjamin's reflections in *Ursprung des deutschen Trauerspiels*, careful readers would make a distinction between (ancient Greek) tragedy (*Tragödie*) and the German *Trauerspiel* (literally, mourning play), a form of serious drama different from tragedy chiefly in its provocative relation of action to time, inviting allegory. But this distinction was not generally observed before Benjamin's reception, and Hochhuth may not have been conversant with it—or, being conversant with it, intended the word ironically. "Colloquially," Kaufmann notes, "Germans sometimes use *Trauerspiel* to refer to a man's wretched treatment of his fellow men" (T 330). In any case, the main point is that Kaufmann thinks of *Der Deputy* as a tragedy in the sense that he has been employing throughout.

27. Daniel Jonah Goldhagen, *A Moral Reckoning: The Role of the Church in the Holocaust* (New York: Vintage, 2013).

28. For an excellent study of this case, see D. D. Guttenplan, *The Holocaust on Trial* (New York: Norton, 2001).

29. Barbara Tuchman, "The Case of Woodrow Wilson," *Atlantic*, August 2014, http://www .theatlantic.com/magazine/archive/2014/08/the-case-of-woodrow-wilson/373464/.

30. Sigmund Freud and William C. Bullitt, *Thomas Woodrow Wilson: Twenty-Eighth President of the United States—a Psychological Study* (New Brunswick, NJ: Transaction, 1999).

31. Kaufmann shows that he is aware of this point in explaining the small pleasure and instruction he takes from Brecht: "Brecht's anti-sentimentality was refreshing in its day; and though it was not at all unusual in Germany in the twenties, Brecht was a master of this tone. . . . When anti-sentimentality had developed into anti-humanism and celebrated its outrageous triumphs in the crimes of Stalin and Hitler, Brecht still expected audiences to feel delightfully shocked by his plays" (T 347).

32. "Tragedy invites people to . . . see the same situation in different perspectives and think about the relative merits of each. In this process . . . we are led to question what in ordinary life we took for granted; we are made more critical, more skeptical, and more humane" (T 351).

33. Several details in the text of the drama would have convinced Kaufmann of Hochhuth's sensibility and culture, not least the comments on Nietzsche Hochhuth ascribes to the priest Riccardo Fontana in an exchange with the unspeakably vicious Nazi doctor at Auschwitz. Fontana: "Is Nietzsche to blame / if weak-headed visionaries, brutes and murderers / have stolen his legacy? / Only madmen take him literally." Even the doctor agrees: "Right, only madmen, men of action. / It suits *them* perfectly that Nietzsche / looked to beasts of prey for his criterion / of manly virtues—. . . . No wonder, when the inventor of that monstrosity / wrote in language so intoxicated, / and with such sovereign arrogance it seemed / he had champagne instead of ink in his pen." Rolf Hochhuth, *The Deputy*, tr. Richard and Clara Winston (New York: Grove, 1964), 251–52. *Der Stellvertreter—ein christliches Trauerspiel* (Reinbeck bei Hamburg: Rowohlt, 1998), 334–35.

34. Cited without reference in Žižek, *Less Than Nothing*, 121.

35. Leo Tolstoy, *War and Peace*, tr. Nathan Haskell Dole (New York: T. Y. Crowell, 1898), 244.

36. Žižek, *Less Than Nothing*, 121.

37. It has been seriously maintained that much of Hochhuth's script was supplied him by a KGB agent. John Follain, "KGB and the Plot to Taint 'Nazi Pope,'" *Sunday Times* (London), February 18, 2007.

38. Žižek, *Less Than Nothing*, 121–22.

39. W. G. Sebald, *On the Natural History of Destruction*, tr. Anthea Bell (London: Hamish Hamilton, 2003). In his eloquent review, John Banville wrote:

> The bombing campaign, directed by Sir Arthur "Bomber" Harris and approved, though somewhat uneasily, by Churchill, involved the dropping of a million tons of bombs on 131 cities and towns in Germany, with the resulting deaths of 600,000 civilians. The statistics with which Sebald presents us—31.1 cubic meters of rubble for every inhabitant of Cologne, 6,865 corpses burned on pyres by the SS in Dresden in February 1945, flames leaping 2,000 meters into the sky over Hamburg after a combined British and US air raid with the grisly codename "Operation Gomorrah"—inevitably numb the reader's mind, as it seems to have numbed the minds of the survivors. And this is precisely Sebald's theme, the eerie fact that 'the sense of unparalleled national humiliation felt by millions [of Germans] in the last years of the war had never really found verbal expression, and those directly affected by the experience neither shared it with each other nor passed it on to the next generation.'

Guardian, February 22, 2003, http://www.theguardian.com/books/2003/feb/22/higher education.history.

In an exchange of letters with Hochhuth, Kaufmann suggested changes to the text of *The Soldiers* bearing on atmosphere and milieu; Hochhuth was glad to accept them (T 337).

Chapter 11: Against Decrepit Ideas

1. *The Future of the Humanities* (New York: Reader's Digest Press, 1977). Pages from this text will henceforth be shown in parentheses as (FH + page number). First epigraph: *Without Guilt and Justice: From Decidophobia to Autonomy* (New York: Peter Wyden, 1973), vii. Pages from this text will be shown in parentheses as (W + page number). Second epigraph: Friedrich Nietzsche, "On the Adder's Bite," *Thus Spoke Zarathustra*, Modern Library, ed. and tr. Walter Kaufmann (New York: Random House, 1995), 68. Cited in (D2 124).

2. Nietzsche, *Basic Writings*, 677.

3. One finds an interesting confirmation of this surmise in a talk Kaufmann gave in 1967 at an International Philosophy Year program, subsequently published as "Doubts about Justice": "Not only has war eroded moral standards, but service in armies of occupation has accelerated the growth of moral skepticism. So has the fact that more and more people live in big cities where—though not quite as much as in an army abroad—one can get away with behavior unthinkable in the small home town." In *Ethics and Social Justice*, 54.

4. Thus Meyer Abrams, writing on the Romantic nature lyric: "The speaker begins with a description of the landscape. . . . In the course of this meditation the lyric speaker achieves an insight, faces up to a tragic loss, comes to a moral decision, or resolves an emotional problem." "Structure and Style in the Greater Romantic Lyric," *The Correspondent Breeze: Essays on English Romanticism* (New York: Norton, 1984), 75.

5. In a review of Niall Ferguson's biography of Henry Kissinger (also a German Jewish immigrant, barely two years younger than Kaufmann), Richard Vinen writes: "The army was, in fact, the most important institution in Kissinger's early life. It made him an American." "K for Kant," review of *Henry Kissinger 1923–1968: The Idealist*, *Times Literary Supplement*, December 11, 2015, 9. It is reasonable to suppose that the same judgment applies to Kaufmann.

6. Walter Kaufmann, "Doubts about Justice," *Ethics and Social Justice*, 52.

7. Arthur Koestler, "The Yogi and the Commissar," *Horizon*, June 1942, 381–82.

8. From a letter to Nietzsche's sister, who married an anti-Semitic headman, Bernhard Förster, dated December 1887: "One of the greatest stupidities you have committed—for yourself and for me! Your association with an anti-Semitic chief expresses a foreignness to my whole way of life which fills me ever again with ire or melancholy. . . . It is a matter of honor to me to be absolutely clean and unequivocal regarding anti-Semitism, namely opposed, as I am in my writings." *Portable Nietzsche*, 456.

9. Žižek, *Less Than Nothing*, 622–23.

10. Andrew Piper and Richard Jean So, "Quantifying the Weepy Best Seller," *New Republic* (a web magazine), December 18, 2015, https://newrepublic.com/article/126123 /quantifying-weepy-bestseller.

11. There will be exceptions, of course. In the case just considered, Andrew Piper (see ibid.) found his way to computerized analysis quite independently of his formal college training.

12. Compare the following set of propositions by Kaufmann and Paul de Man: Having asserted that "there are no opposites in nature," Kaufmann writes, "Playing with fire and rolling in the snow are not opposites—far from it—but hot and cold are. No specific degree of heat or coldness has any opposite, only the concepts do" (W 25) Here, now, is Paul de Man:

> Whenever a binary pair is being analyzed or "deconstructed," the implication is never that the opposition is without validity in a given empirical situation (no one in his right mind could maintain that it is forever impossible to tell night from day or hot from cold) but only that the *figure* of opposition involved in all analytical judgments is not reliable, precisely because it allows, in the realm of language to which, as figure, it belongs, for substitutions that cannot occur in the same manner in the world of experience. When one moves from empirical oppositions such as night and day to categorical oppositions such as truth and falsehood, the epistemological stakes increase considerably because, in the realm of concepts, the principle of exclusion applies decisively.

"A Letter," *Critical Inquiry* 8, no. 3 (Spring 1982): 509.

One might ask: How good is it for the rigor or usefulness of deconstruction that, evidently, in *some* cases it is impossible to distinguish between allegedly simple perceptions of hot and cold? If I put my frostbitten hand under cold water, it burns. Has "nature," then, deconstructed itself in advance of my refusal of the binary opposition? In what spheres of experience is deconstruction valid and useful and in what spheres, not? In a certain sense both writers agree that *conceptual* distinctions are not reliable, but their understanding of the meaning of "not reliable" in this context differs in an interesting way. Discounting their futility in organizing sensuous experience, Kaufmann nonetheless insists that for "analytical philosophers," opposing "concepts and abstractions are . . . indispensable" (W 21).

13. This proposition is a simplification. Kaufmann repeats it later in the chapter, writing, "It is actually the existentialists who operate with a Manichaean scheme of two modes of existence: authentic and inauthentic. Here Buber's *I and Thou* (1923) and Heidegger's *Being and Time* (1927) are similar" (W 124). As I've noted, Heidegger speaks of "echte" (genuine) and "unechte" (ungenuine) "Eigentlichkeit" (authenticity, sometimes "proper-being"), introducing a second "Manichean" subdivision into the first "Manichean" formulation. See, also, the entry "Ereignis," in *Dictionary of Untranslatables: A Philosophical Lexicon*, ed. Barbara Cassin, tr. and ed. Emily Apter, Jacques Lezra, and Michael Wood (Princeton, NJ: Princeton University press, 2014), 278.

14. The discussion of this idea, important to intellectual historians, is alive even today. Martin Jay writes:

> I was always very unhappy with Marcuse's repressive tolerance thesis, and not only because it seemed to me self-evident that that it would backfire on the Left. Once you begin to say there shouldn't be an argument that, say, supports the Vietnam War or is pro-Zionist or whatever, then people on the other side have every right to respond, "Well, I don't want somebody supporting, say, Hugo Chavez's version of socialism in Venezuela" or "I have no interest in having a Hamas representative come to my campus." Repressive intolerance is, after all, a two-way street. I've always thought that one can challenge an idea without having to shout it down. One can refuse to go to hear somebody but not stop other people from hearing them. I can't shake a simple ACLU libertarian faith in the value of free speech.

Jamie Keesling and Spencer A. Leonard, "Critical Theory, Marxism, Social Evolution: An Interview with Martin Jay," *Platypus Review* 83 (February 2016), http://platypus1917 .org/2016/01/30/critical-theory-marxism-social-evolution-an-interview-with-martin-jay/.

15. Paul Reiwald, *Society and Its Criminals*, tr. and ed. T. E. James (London: Heinemann. 1949), 14.

16. Robert Gerwarth, *Hitler's Hangman: The Life of Heydrich* (New Haven, CT: Yale University Press, 2011).

17. Einestages, "Heydrich-Biografie: 'Abstoßend ist vor allem seine antrainierte Kälte,'" *Spiegel Online*, September 21, 2011, http://www.spiegel.de/einestages/heydrich-biografie -a-949446.html.

18. *Hamlet*, act 2, scene 2, lines 555–57, http://www.folgerdigitaltexts.org/html/Ham.html.

19. Ibid., lines 558–59.

20. Father Byron continues: "See William C. Taylor and Polly Labara, *Mavericks at Work*." William J. Byron S.J., "Humbition: Excellence in Jesuit Business Education," *Conversations on Jesuit Higher Education* 39, article 6 (February 1, 2011), http://epublications.marquette.edu /cgi/viewcontent.cgi?article=1625&context=conversations.

21. Clive James, *Cultural Amnesia: Necessary Memories from History and the Arts* (New York: Norton, 2007), 55.

22. Hannah Arendt/Karl Jaspers, *Correspondence*, 233.

23. Private communication.

24. Nietzsche, *Beyond Good and Evil*, tr. Kaufmann, 50.

25. Consult Richard Schacht, *Alienation*, with an Introductory Essay by Walter Kaufmann (Garden City, NY: Doubleday, 1970).

26. Cited in Scott McLemee, "A Worried Mind," in George Scialabba, *What Are Intellectuals Good For? Essays and Reviews* (Boston: Pressed Wafer, 2009), xiii–xiv.

27. Nietzsche's poem of homelessness titled "Vereinsamt" (Grown lonely) was written in 1884; he variously titled the poem "Der Freigeist" and "Abschied." An abridged version appeared in 1894 in *Das Magazin für Literatur*, but it was not published in full until 1900, shortly after his death: http://literaturkritik.de/public/rezension.php?rez_id=21324.

28. J. W. Goethe, *Goethe's Faust*, 319.

29. On the sense of homelessness in fin de siècle artists in Vienna and Berlin, see Stanley Corngold, "Schoenberg, Rilke, and Musil: Exemplary Figures in Fin-de-Siècle Viennese Modernism," in *Cambridge History of Modernism*, ed. Vincent Sherry (Cambridge: Cambridge University Press, 2017), 750–71.

30. Thomas G. Masaryk, *Suicide and the Meaning of Civilization*, tr. William B. Weist and Robert G. Batson, intro. Anthony Giddens (Chicago: University of Chicago Press).

31. Benno Wagner, in Stanley Corngold and Benno Wagner, *Franz Kafka: The Ghosts in the Machine* (Evanston, IL: Northwestern University Press, 2011), 46.

32. Masaryk, *Suicide*, 68.

33. Ibid., 67.

34. Ibid., 68.

35. Douglas Sturm, "Autonomous Morality and the Question of the Decrepitude of Justice," *Journal of Religion* 55, no. 1 (January 1975): 123.

36. More literally, "Truly high respect one can have only for those who do not *seek* themselves." Nietzsche, *Basic Writings*, 405.

37. Yeats, "The Choice," https://allpoetry.com/The-Choice.

38. Moran, review of *Without Guilt and Justice*, 84.

39. Bertolt Brecht, "Ballade über die Frage: 'Wovon lebt der Mensch?'" (Ballad on the question, What does man need to live?), *Die Dreigroschen Oper* (Three penny opera).

40. Hook, *Ethics and Social Justice*, 79.

41. Douglas Sturm, review of *Without Guilt and Justice*, *Journal of Religion* 55, no. 1 (January 1975): 124.

42. Judith Agassi and Joseph Agassi, "The Ethics and Politics of Autonomy: Walter Kaufmann's Contribution," *Methodology and Science* 18 (1985): 170.

43. Moran, review of *Without Guilt and Justice*, 85.

Chapter 12: The Places of Religion

1. In the same year Kaufmann also published *Existentialism, Religion, and Death: Thirteen Essays*. Epigraph: *Religions in Four Dimensions: Existential and Aesthetic, Historical and Comparative* (New York: Reader's Digest Press, 1976), 14. Pages from this text will henceforth be shown in parentheses as (RE + page number).

2. Friedrich Hölderlin, *Selected Poems and Fragments*, Penguin Classics, ed. Jeremy Adler, tr. Michael Hamburger (London: Penguin, 1998), 79.

3. Susan Sontag, *Essays*, 237–39.

4. Wayne Proudfoot, *Religious Experience* (Berkeley, CA: University of California Press, 1985), 217.

5. This procedure, which I impute to Kaufmann, is not unlike that of Joseph Raz, who, in his treatment of human of dignity, endorses "the humanistic principle . . . right away to simplify the discussion" (see chapter 13).

6. Jacob B. Agus, review of Walter Kaufmann, *Religions in Four Dimensions*, *Jewish Quarterly Review* 69, no. 1 (July 1978): 57.

7. Ibid.

8. Elijah White continues:

> He [Kaufmann] finds that most religions begin with one such visionary, though he seems at times to value the visionary capacity per se regardless of the vision's content. The new religion then comes to a dreadful crossroads, choosing either to flourish by degrading its original teachings in order to gain sufficient acceptance for survival or to remain true to its founding precepts, fail to make enough converts, and therefore wither. What then? Not much.

"Paucity of Humanism," *Living Church* 175 (July 3, 1977): 4.

9. Catherine Belsey, "The Subject of Tragedy: Identity and Difference," in *Renaissance Drama* (London: Routledge, 1985), 9.

10. In fact, this entire section of *Religions in Four Dimensions*, as Kaufmann notes, is mostly a reprise of the earlier pages. But it does no harm to have its strong points once again, valuable for the way they go to the heart of a vast and complex ensemble of concepts, stories, and motifs. It is, however, a marker that Kaufmann is not immune in his later work to the "good ecology" of repeating occasional passages from his earlier books. When one has once said what one wanted—and can say—about a crucial topic, it is not always reasonable to expect a wholly original contribution to the same topic. Writers repeat themselves; good writers don't fail to indicate this fact.

11. *Hamlet*, act 5, scene 2, line 422–28, http://www.folgerdigitaltexts.org/html/Ham .html.

12. "The State of Israel," in *The Jewish Political Tradition*, vol. 1, *Authority*, ed. Michael Walzer, Menachem Lorberbaum, Noam J. Zohar (New Haven, CT: Yale University Press, 2000), 465.

13. Kaufmann, *Cain*, 157.

14. Michaela Hoenicke Moore, *Know Your Enemy: The American Debate on Nazism, 1933–1945* (Cambridge: Cambridge University Press, 2010), 229. Robert Gilbert Vansittart (1881–1957) was an English diplomat, fiercely critical of Germany. He called for "a prolonged occupation by the allied forces; the complete destruction of the German army; drastic control of German heavy industry; the total disarmament of Germany; and the reeducation of the German people. This was the essence of Vansittartism." Norman Rose, *Vansittart: Study of a Diplomat* (London: Heinemann, 1978), 260.

15. Cf. Nietzsche, *Ecce Homo*, in *Basic Writings*, 784. The notion of "taking back" comes from Thomas Mann's *Doctor Faustus*, where the Nietzsche-persona Adrian Leverkühn announces that he will "take back" Beethoven's Ninth Symphony. Thomas Mann, *Doctor Faustus: The Life of the German Composer Adrian Leverkuhn as Told by a Friend*, tr. John E. Woods (New York: Vintage, 1999), 514.

16. Robert Charles Zaehner, "Zoroastrianism," *The Concise Encyclopedia of Living Faiths* (New York: Hawthorn, 1959), 222.

17. John Gordon Davies, *The Early Christian Church* (New York: Holt, Rinehart, and Winston, 1965), 33–34.

18. Michael Allen Williams, *Rethinking "Gnosticism": An Argument for Dismantling a Dubious Category* (Princeton, NJ: Princeton University Press, 1966).

19. Readers interested in the penetration of Gnostic elements into modern literature and philosophy may wish to consult "Kafka (with Nietzsche) as Neo-Gnostic Thinkers," in Corngold and Wagner, *Franz Kafka: Ghosts in the Machine*, 151–76.

20. This phrase first surfaces powerfully in Voegelin's *New Science of Politics* in his discussion of "the person and the work of Joachim of Flora" as representative of "the desire for a re-divinization of society." This desire, in Voegelin's view, is an error, since

> there is no eidos of history; . . . the eschatological supernature is not a nature in the philosophical, immanent sense. The problem of an eidos in history, hence, arises only when Christian transcendentalist fulfillment becomes immanentized. Such an immanentist hypostasis of the eschaton, however, is a theoretical fallacy. . . . The course of history as a whole is no object of experience; history has no eidos, because the course of history extends into the unknown future. The meaning of history, thus, is an illusion; and this illusionary eidos is created by treating a symbol of faith as if it were a proposition concerning an object of immanent experience.

The New Science of Politics (Chicago: University of Chicago Press, 1952), 110, 123.

21. Charles Harold Dodd, *The Parables of the Kingdom* (New York: Scribner, 1936), 193.

22. Voegelin, *Science, Politics, and Gnosticism* (Wilmington, DE: ISI Books, 2004), 64–65.

23. Nietzsche, *Ecce Homo*, in *Basic Writings*, 756.

24. Benjamin Lazier, *God Interrupted: Heresy and the European Imagination between the World Wars* (Princeton, NJ: Princeton University Press), 2008), 56–57. The citation is from

Jonas, *The Gnostic Religion: The Message of the Alien God and the Beginnings of Christianity* (Boston: Beacon, 1958), 324–25.

25. "Politics, in a literary work, is like a pistol shot in the middle of the concert; something loud and out of place to which we are nonetheless compelled to pay attention." *The Charterhouse of Parma*, tr. Margaret Mauldon (New York: Oxford University Press, 1997), 414.

26. The second quote is from Richard Rovere, "Letter from Washington," *New Yorker*, April 22, 1950, https://www.newyorker.com/magazine/1950/04/22/letter-from-washington-11; the quote within this quote are Taft's words, as supplied by Rovere.

27. "Die Schrift ist unveränderlich und die Meinungen sind oft nur ein Ausdruck der Verzweiflung darüber." Franz Kafka, *Der Proceß*, ed. Malcolm Pasley (Frankfurt a.M.: Fischer, 1990), 298.

28. "For example, he devotes four pages to the fall of Massada and only eight pages to Jewish history from 73 to 1873, twelve pages to the events from Jeremiah to Massada and ten pages for the establishment of the State of Israel." Agus, review of Walter Kaufmann, *Religions in Four Dimensions*, 55–56.

29. Isaiah Berlin, in Walter Kaufmann, *Hegel: A Reinterpretation*, Anchor Books, back cover.

30. Kaufmann's complete formulation is engaging: "It became the custom for priests in the West, but not in the East, to remain celibate. Since precisely many of the most intelligent elected to become monks or priests, these institutions became a genetic disaster. Christian scholars and intellectuals died without progeny—a kind of natural selection in reverse" (R 141).

31. Cited from G. G. Coulton, *Five Centuries of Religion* (Cambridge: Cambridge University Press, 1923), 1: 444.

32. Fernando Bermejo-Rubio, "(Why) Was Jesus the Galilean Crucified Alone? Solving a False Conundrum," *Journal for the Study of the New Testament* 36, no. 2: 127–54.

33. Tovia Singer, "A Closer Look at the 'Crucifixion Psalm': A Lutheran Doesn't Understand Why Rabbi Singer Doesn't Believe in Jesus," *Outreach Judaism*, outreachjudaism.org/crucifixion-psalm/. Singer's polemic prompted an ideological rebuttal, http://www.heartofisrael.net /chazak/articles/ps22.htm. It may be of interest that Sir Lancelot C. L. Brenton's translation of the Greek Septuagint Bible reads: "They have now cast me out and compassed me round about: they have set their eyes so as to bow them down to the ground. They laid wait for me as a lion ready for prey, and like a lion's whelp dwelling in secret places." There is no talk of hands and feet pierced (http://www.ecmarsh.com/lxx/).

34. A ready journalistic sampling of these issues can be found in the balanced essay of Glen Bowersock, "Who Was Saint Paul?," *New York Review of Books*, November 5, 2015, http://www.nybooks.com/articles/2015/11/05/who-was-saint-paul/; and an earlier essay by Mark Lilla, scathing in his view of the "New Paul" of political theology: "A New, Political Saint Paul?" *New York Review of Books*, October 23, 2008, http://www.nybooks.com /articles/2008/10/23/a-new-political-saint-paul/. See, too, Vivian Liska's treatment of the errancies of this tendency in her excellent *German-Jewish Thought and Its Aftermath: A Tenuous Legacy* (Bloomington: Indiana University Press, 2017), esp. pp. 41–64. It is the view, as some have sardonically suggested, that if the conceptual legacy of the Zionist state were eliminated, universal peace would follow. Liska's major contribution is to show how the mutual embrace in Jewish writers (Walter Benjamin foremost) of Halacha and Aggadah, of law and literature, counters the Pauline accusation of an inhuman harshness exerted by Jewish law.

35. Adolf Hitler, Salzburg, August 7, 1920, http://www.phdn.org/archives/www.ess.uwe
.ac.uk/genocide/statements.htm.

36. Ian Kershaw, *Hitler, 1936–45*, vol. 2, *Nemesis* (New York: Norton, 2000), 470.

37. *The Cambridge Medieval History*, ed. J. R. Tanner, C. W. Previté-Orton, and Z. N. Brooke
(New York: Macmillan, 1929), 6: 752.

38. Christianity has been described as "Judaism's great daughter religion" by Lavinia and
Dan Cohn-Sherbok in *Judaism* (Oxford: One World, 1997), 1. Kaufmann maintains that the
intellectual content of Islam is also an offspring of Judaism—notably in its belief in one God
and not a trinity of gods. But its relation to its "spiritual father" is unlike Christianity's relation
to Judaism in an important respect: "The Koran did not have to compete with an indigenous
literature; it more nearly filled a vacuum" (R 167). Islam is also unlike Christianity in the extent
of its intimacy with figures from the Hebrew Bible: in the entirety of the Meccan Koran, Jesus
is mentioned four times, Moses, however, more than a hundred" (R 165).

Chapter 13: This Priceless Heritage

1. First epigraph: *The Future of the Humanities*, xvii. Second epigraph: Tony Judt, *The Memory Chalet* (New York: Penguin, 2010), 207.

2. For relevance, compare Christopher Hitchens: "I myself am a strong believer in the study
of religion, first because culture and education involve a respect for tradition and for origins,
and also because some of the early religious texts were among our first attempts at literature."
"Introduction," *The Portable Atheist: Essential Readings for the Nonbeliever* (Philadelphia: da
Capo, 2007), xvii.

3. Kaufmann defines the classics that will make up most of the syllabus of humanities
courses as "books or poems that are presumed to be worth reading more than once because
they are considered inherently important and not merely sources of information about something else" (FH 47).

4. "The memory of the persecution he [Kaufmann] saw and experienced [in Germany, in
the 1930s] colored his approach to writing and lent it an air of existential urgency. In a world
where so many did not survive, or were forced to live without their freedom, Kaufmann would
make his engagement with the humanities matter." David Pickus, "Walter Kaufmann and the
Future of the Humanities," 89.

5. "Even if one has experiences that some men would call mystical—and I have no doubt
that I have had many—it is a matter of integrity to question such experiences and any thoughts
that were associated with them as closely and as honestly as we should question the 'revelations' of others." "The Faith of a Heretic," *Harper's Magazine*, February 1959, 34.

6. It is difficult to make this criticism square with Kaufmann's explicit statement in *Religions
in Four Dimensions* that "one cannot begin to understand the origins of totalitarianism until
one realizes that the Inquisition provided the great model" (R 152).

7. Edward Said, *The World, the Text, and the Critic* (Cambridge, MA: Harvard University
Press, 1983).

8. Said instances Ferdinand de Saussure, Georges Bataille, Claude Lévi-Strauss, along with
a resuscitated Marx, Nietzsche, and Freud. Ibid., 3.

9. Ibid., 1.

10. Ibid., 2.

11. Stanley Fish, "Will the Humanities Save Us?," *New York Times*, January 6, 2008, https://opinionator.blogs.nytimes.com//2008/01/06/will-the-humanities-save-us/.

12. Philip Rieff, *Fellow Teachers* (New York: Harper and Row, 1973), 52–53.

13. Paul de Man, *Romanticism and Contemporary Criticism: The Gauss Seminar and Other Papers*, ed. E. S. Burt, Kevin Newmark, and Andrzej Warminski (Baltimore: Johns Hopkins University Press, 1993).

14. Paul de Man, *The Resistance to Theory* (Minneapolis: University of Minnesota Press, 2002), 19.

15. Brian Vickers, "De Man's Schismatizing of Rhetoric," in *Renaissances of Rhetoric*, ed. S. Ijsseling and G. Vervaecke (Leuven, Belgium: Leuven University Press, 1991), 193–247.

16. *Kritische Friedrich Schlegel Ausgabe*, ed. Ernst Behler et al. (Munich: F. Schöningh, 1958–?), 18: 63.

17. Paul de Man, "The Return to Philology," in *Resistance to Theory*, 23.

18. Geoffrey Hartman, "Looking Back on Paul de Man," *Reading de Man Reading*, ed. Lindsay Waters and Wlad Godzich (Minneapolis: University of Minnesota Press, 1989), 6.

19. Michael Wood, "Empson's Intentions," *London Review of Books*, February 4, 2016, 7.

20. Hartman, "Looking Back," 5.

21. Corngold, *Fate of the Self*, 1.

22. Stanley Corngold, "Error in Paul de Man," *The Yale Critics: Deconstruction in America*, ed. Jonathan Arac, Wlad Godzich, and Wallace Martin (Minneapolis: University of Minnesota Press, 1983), 90–108.

23. Paul de Man, "Semiology and Rhetoric," *Diacritics* 3, no. 3 (Autumn 1973): 27–33.

24. Jamie Keesling and Spencer A. Leonard, "Critical Theory, Marxism, Social Evolution: An Interview with Martin Jay," *Platypus Review* 83 (February 2016), http://platypus1917.org/2016/01/30/critical-theory-marxism-social-evolution-an-interview-with-martin-jay/.

25. Gerhard Neumann, "Chronik der Lektüren," in *Wissenschaft und Universität: Selbstporträt einer Generation; Wolfgang Frühwald zum 70. Geburtstag*, ed. Martin Huber and Gerhard Lauer (Köln: Dumont, 2005), 250.

26. Walter Benjamin, "The Task of the Translator," tr. Harry Zohn, *Selected Writings, 1913–1926*, 1: 253. For an incisive although unrelentingly negative review of Benjamin's essay, see David Bellos, "Halting Walter," *Cambridge Literary Review* 1, no. 3: 207–20.

27. "Von Intelligenz kann nur in einem Reiche die Rede sein, wo etwas verfehlt werden kann, wo der Irrthum stattfindet—im Reiche des Bewußtseins," in *Nietzsches Werke: Kritische Gesamtausgabe III/3, Nachgelassene Fragmente Herbst 1869 bis Herbst 1872*, aphorism 5 (83). I discuss the matter in detail in "Error in Paul de Man," 90–108.

28. Nietzsche, *Will to Power*, 265–66.

29. Walter Kaufmann, *Discovering the Mind*, vol. 1, *Goethe, Kant, and Hegel*; vol. 2, *Nietzsche, Heidegger, and Buber*; vol. 3, *Freud, Adler, and Jung*.

30. In an essay by Vlad Chituc and Paul Henne, "The Data against Kant," we read: "In the last decade or so, the 'experimental philosophy' movement has argued for greater use of empirical science to inform and shape the discussion of philosophical problems. We [the authors] agree: Philosophers ought to pay more attention to their colleagues in the psychology department (even if they can't)." *New York Times*, February 19, 2016, https://www.nytimes.com/2016/02/21

/opinion/sunday/the-data-against-kant.html. Kaufmann's idea of what psychology ought and can't do is no doubt different in its procedure from that of the authors—Kaufmann's methods are empathy, intuition, rational introspection, and empathy (or licensed projection)—but even "experimental philosophy" would surely deserve consideration as an "alternative."

31. From "Dead Letters: Kafka and Disjunction," in "Things Passed Over: Narrating the Modernist Ensemble," a highly original doctoral thesis by Sanders Creasy of the University of California at Berkeley. Creasy writes of Kafka's breakthrough story "The Judgment": "The figures of Georg [Bendemann] and his father are not characters with coherent minds, intentions or histories; nor are they integral bodies with metaphorically or symbolically significant gestures. They are mere sites of disjunctive ensemble operations."

32. Moran, review of *Without Guilt and Justice*, 84.

33. Donald B. Kuspit, review of *Without Guilt and Justice*," *Philosophy and Phenomenological Research* 34, no. 2 (December 1973): 294–95.

34. Kenneth Burke, *Language as Symbolic Action: Essays on Life, Literature, and Method* (Berkeley: University of California Press, 1966), 167.

35. Thomas Mann, *The Magic Mountain*, tr. John E. Woods (New York: Knopf, 1995). Compare pages 699 and 702 as divergent translations of Mann's word "Donnerschlag."

36. David Bromwich, "A White Father at the 'Indian Camp,'" *New York Review of Books* 63, no. 4 (March 10, 2016): 50.

37. Nietzsche, *Werke: Kritische Gesamtausgabe*, ed. Giorgio Colli and Mazzino Montinari (Berlin: De Gruyter, 1967–present). Colli died in 1979, Montinari in 1986. The edition is being completed by other hands.

38. Franz Kafka, *Nachgelassene Schriften II*, 348.

39. "A few years ago [ca. 1975], criticism was still a very analytical activity, very rational, subject to a superego of impartiality and objectivity, and I wanted to react against this approach." "Roland Barthes on Roland Barthes (1979)," *The Grain of the Voice: Interviews 1962–1980*, tr. Linda Coverdale (New York: Hill and Wang, 1985), 331.

40. Adam Kirsch, "Heirs to the Throne," *New Republic*, May 11, 2010, https://newrepublic .com/article/74801/heirs-the-throne.

41. James Wood, "Books: 'Desert Storm,'" review of Robert Alter's translation of *The Book of Psalms* (New York: Norton, 2007), *New Yorker*, October 1, 2007, http://www.newyorker.com /magazine/2007/10/01/desert-storm.

42. Mark Greif, *The Age of the Crisis of Man: Thought and Fiction in America, 1933–1973* (Princeton, NJ: Princeton University Press, 2015), 103. Greif is of the opinion that the truly "meaningful intellectual trajectory" of the crisis of man and humanism in America had, by 1951, found its place in "the novel." I would certainly look for its further development, not (only) in the novel, but in *critique*, as in Kaufmann's *Critique of Religion and Philosophy* (above, chapters 3 and 4).

43. Peter Sloterdijk, *Regeln für den Menschenpark: Ein Antwortsschreiben zu Heideggers Brief über den Humanismus* (Frankfurt a.M.: Suhrkamp, 1999), cited in Grief, *Age of the Crisis of Man*, 103.

44. George Kateb, *Human Dignity* (Cambridge, MA: Belknap, 2011); Michael Rosen, *Dignity: Its History and Meaning* (Cambridge, MA: Harvard University Press, 2012).

45. Rosen, *Dignity*, 130–31, citing Joseph Raz, *The Morality of Freedom* (Oxford: Oxford University Press, 1982), 194.

Chapter 14: What Is Man's Lot?

1. First epigraph: *Life at the Limits*, 82. Pages from this text will henceforth be shown in parentheses as (LL + page number). Second epigraph: Henry James, "The Art of Fiction," *Longman's Magazine* 4 (September 1884), http://public.wsu.edu/~campbelld/amlit/artfiction .html. Third epigraph: Walter Kaufmann, *Tragedy and Philosophy*, 363. Fourth epigraph: David Pickus, personal communication.

2. *Essays of Michel de Montaigne*, Gutenberg edition, chapter 19, "That to Study Philosophy Is to Learn to Die," http://www.gutenberg.org/files/3600/3600-h/3600-h.htm.

3. Kafka, *Kafka's Selected Stories*, 153.

4. Julian Barnes's brilliant book-length essay *Nothing to Be Frightened Of* (New York: Knopf, 2008) considers death precisely this Nothing of which one cannot but be afraid!

5. *What Is Man*, the third book of *Man's Lot*, 118. Pages from this text will henceforth be shown in parentheses as (WM + page number).

6. Walter Benjamin, "The Task of the Translator," in *Selected Writings, 1913–1926*, 253.

7. Goethe, Kaufmann's educator and very likely ego ideal, finished *Faust II* at eighty-two, then "tied it up in a parcel and refused to discuss the ending even with friends who inquired about it. It was to be published after his death. It was not that he was afraid of anyone, nor was there anything to be afraid of. He simply did not write to please others, least of all the public. He did not care to know how others might react to his work. He was not heteronomous but autonomous" (D1 20).

8. Greif, *The Age of the Crisis*, 96.

9. Ibid., 97.

10. *Tractatus Logico-Philosophicus* (6.522). These comments on Wittgenstein are cited and adapted from Anat Biletzki and Anat Matar, "Ludwig Wittgenstein," *The Stanford Encyclopedia of Philosophy* (Fall 2016 ed.), ed. Edward N. Zalta, http://plato.stanford.edu/archives/fall2016 /entries/wittgenstein/.

11. Clive James, *Cultural Cohesion: The Essential Essays* (New York: Norton, 2013), 215.

12. Walter Kaufmann, "Solzhenitsyn and Autonomy," in *Solzhenitsyn: A Collection of Critical Essays*, ed. Kathryn Feuer (Englewood Cliffs, NJ: Prentice-Hall, 1976). Reprinted in Andreea Deciu Ritivoi, *Intimate Strangers: Arendt, Marcuse, Solzhenitsyn, Said in American Political Discourse* (New York: Columbia University Press, 2013), 171.

13. Byron, *Don Juan*, "Canto the Third," lines 790–93.

14. W. E. Kennick, review of *From Shakespeare to Existentialism*, 140.

15. Theodor Adorno, "Cultural Criticism and Society," in *Prisms*, tr. Samuel and Shierry Weber (Cambridge, MA: MIT Press, 1967), 34.

16. T. S. Eliot, "Tradition and the Individual Talent, *The Sacred Wood: Essays on Poetry and Criticism*, http://www.bartleby.com/200/sw4.htLL.

17. Adam Zagajewski, "Rereading Rilke: Introduction," in *The Poetry of Rilke*, tr. and ed. Edward Snow (New York: North Point, 2009), xx.

18. Kaufmann also gives another source for these repeated reflections on Rilke: Walter Kaufmann, "Nirvana or Creation," *Times Literary Supplement*, December 5, 1975, 1442.

19. August C. Krey, *The First Crusade: The Accounts of Eye-Witnesses and Participants* (Princeton, NJ: Princeton University Press, 1921), 261.

20. "Interpretation/Meaning of Romanesque Sculptural Iconography," http://www.visual-arts-cork.com/sculpture/romanesque.htm.

21. "Decoration Reflects Secular Uncertainty and Religious Certainty," http://www.visual-arts-cork.com/architecture/romanesque.htm.

22. Meyer Schapiro, *Romanesque Architectural Sculpture* (Chicago: University of Chicago Press, 2006), 203–4. On p. 117, Schapiro illustrates the separation of the saved from the damned on the lintel of the Abbey Church of Sainte Foy in Conques.

23. Franz Kafka, *Diaries*, August 6, 1914.

24. Robert Hughes, *Goya* (New York: Knopf, 2004), 382.

25. Hannah Arendt, "What Is This New Philosophy They Call 'Existentialism'?," *Nation*, February 23, 1946, https://www.thenation.com/article/french-existentialism/.

26. Odin Lysaker, "Humanity in Times of Crisis: Hannah Arendt's Political Existentialism," in *Philosophy of Justice*, ed. Guttorm Fløistad (Dordrecht: Springer, 2015), 293.

27. See Richard Wolin, "Carl Schmitt, Political Existentialism, and the Total State," *Theory and Society* 19, no. 4 (August 1990): 389–416.

28. Immanuel Kant, *The Critique of Judgment*, http://plato.stanford.edu/entries/kant-aesthetics/#2.7.

29. Nietzsche has a casual awareness of Hindu thought and imagery, which would not rule out Kaufmann's surmise. On the other hand, "ideas from India penetrated Nietzsche as little as drops of water penetrate a goose's feathers." Mervyn Sprung, "Nietzsche's Hinduism, Nietzsche's India," in *The Great Year of Zarathustra (1881–1981)*, ed. David Goicoechea (Lanham, MD: University Press of America, 1984), 177.

30. "The reason for calling this [book] *The Faith of a Heretic* was that I thought, and still think, that I do not belong to any school, that I am a loner. From any number of points of view, religious as well as philosophical, I am a heretic—a dissenter." Weiss-Rosmarin, "Interview," 121.

31. *Time Is an Artist*, the second book of *Man's Lot* (New York: Reader's Digest Press/McGraw-Hill, 1978). Pages from this text will henceforth be shown in parentheses as (TA + page number).

32. From the inside back cover of *Man's Lot*.

33. *History Detox*, "Pythagoras, Plato, and India," http://historydetox.com/pythagoras-plato-and-india/.

34. Arnaldo Momigliano, *Alien Wisdom: The Limits of Hellenization* (Cambridge: Cambridge University Press, 1971), 76–77.

35. *Jewish Virtual Library*, "Ancient Jewish History: The Greeks and the Jews (332–63 BCE)," http://www.jewishvirtuallibrary.org/jsource/History/Greeks.html.

36. "The essential nature—or eidos—of this subjective experience of photography is defined by an irreducible singularity of the photographic image, as an index indicating, 'that-has-been.'" Roland Barthes's *Camera Lucida—Reflections on Photography* (New York: Hill and Wang, 1981), annotation by Kasia Houlihan, http://csmt.uchicago.edu/annotations/barthescamera.htm.

37. My criticism bears only on the absence of reflection on the temporality of the photograph in a place in the book where one could expect it. Three paragraphs from the very end of the very last page of *Man's Lot*, the thought of the transience of the studied image occurs

to the author, but it is rendered harmless: "This particular picture [of a torso] is an invitation to see this sculpture as well as other torsos and sculptures better. In other cases, the sunset I photographed is gone, the street scene will never be the same, the faces have changed or belong to persons now dead. But there are other sunsets, street scenes, and faces, and having seen the photographs one may see them differently" (WM 139).

38. A few pages of "Photographs" in *Life at the Limits* (LL 120–25) say little beyond the fact that photographs profile aspects of the thing they study; they do not capture the whole.

39. Kafka, *Nachgelassene Schriften I*, 9–10.

40. Friedrich Nietzsche, "Miscellaneous Maxims and Opinions" (*Vermischte Meinungen und Sprüche*), http://www.lexido.com/EBOOK_TEXTS/MISCELLANEOUS_MAXIMS _AND_OPINIONS_.aspx?S=408.

41. True, "the examination of Goethe and in particular the *Werther* literature indicates that at least a few imitation suicides actually occurred." Jan Thorson and Oper-Arne Öberg, "Was There a Suicide Epidemic after Goethe's *Werther*?" *Archives of Suicide Research* 7 (2003): 69–72. But "a few" over several centuries does not constitute an epidemic.

42. Recall the look in Rembrandt's eye, in the self-portraits painted when he was in his forties—signally in the self-portrait of 1650—"a probing look by which the beholder may well feel challenged to reexamine himself and his life" (WM 122). In *The Faith of a Heretic*, Kaufmann recorded this experience as his own.

Chapter 15: Philosophy as Psychology

1. For a coherent interpretation of Kaufmann's trilogy as a whole, readers are referred to Ivan Soll's excellent introduction to each of these volumes and an incisive essay by David Pickus, "To Discover a Mind: Walter Kaufmann's Celebration of Goethe, Critique of Kant, and Evisceration of Heidegger," *South Central Review* 16, no. 2/3 (Summer–Autumn 1999): 68–90. First epigraph: Walter Kaufmann, *Discovering the Mind*, vol. 2, 15. Second epigraph: Walter Kaufmann on Immanuel Kant, *Discovering the Mind*, vol. 1, 93.

2. Walter Kaufmann, *Goethe, Kant, and Hegel*, vol. 1 of *Discovering the Mind* (New Brunswick, NJ: Transaction, 1991). Pages from this text will henceforth be shown in parentheses as (D1 + page number).

3. The suggestion comes from David Pickus in the course of our many conversations about Kaufmann's work.

4. "About the Romance Genre," https://www.rwa.org/Romance.

5. An allusion to the novel of Jack Kerouac typed in three weeks on a continuous roll of paper.

6. Kaufmann was able to announce in *Man's Lot* the coming of *Discovering the Mind* because, as he explains, "A first draft of the entire trilogy was completed in 1976 but laid aside to permit me to complete *Man's Lot*" (D1 287). He plainly intended to revise and publish that draft, but owing to his sudden death in 1980, he did not live to see the published book.

7. Friedrich Nietzsche, *Die Götzen-Dämmerung—Twilight of the Idols*, "text prepared from the original German and the translations by Walter Kaufmann and R. J. Hollingdale," http://www.handprint.com/SC/NIE/GotDamer.html.

8. Karl Vorländer, *Kant—Schiller—Goethe* (Leipzig: Felix Meiner, 1923), 260.

9. The often-overlooked but important distinction between "rationality" (unreliable) and "intelligence" (a move in the right direction) was discussed by David Z. Hambrick and Alexander P. Burgoyne in "Gray Matter," "The Difference between Rationality and Intelligence," *New York Times*, September 16, 2016, http://www.nytimes.com/2016/09/18/opinion/sunday /the-difference-between-rationality-and-intelligence.html.

10. Nicholas Boyle, *Goethe: The Poet and the Age*, vol. 1, *The Poetry of Desire (1749–1790)* (Oxford: Oxford University Press, 1991), 393.

11. Scharfstein, review of Walter Kaufmann, *Discovering the Mind*, 247.

12. *Being and Time*, tr. by Macquarrie and Robinson, 153. It is not as if Kaufmann were not aware of the philosophical venture of founding the humanities on a hermeneutic circle of understanding. In a discussion of the shortcomings of *Being and Time* in volume 2 of *Discovering the Mind*, Kaufmann remarks that this project is already fully developed in the works of Heinrich Rickert (Heidegger's teacher) and Wilhelm Dilthey, who plays a major role in *Being and Time*. It is admittedly debatable to what extent Heidegger's contribution represents an advance on the work of his educators (189–90).

13. On the Bildungsroman as a "phantom genre," see Marc Redfield's excellent *Phantom Formations: Aesthetic Ideology and the Bildungsroman* (Ithaca, NY: Cornell University Press, 1996).

14. Goethe remarked to Eckermann: "National literature is now a rather unmeaning term; the epoch of world literature is at hand, and everyone must strive to hasten its approach." I shall quote from the excellent discussion of this topic by the critic Adam Thirwell to suggest something of the change in the character of literary scholarship since 1980, the date of Kaufmann's mention of "world literature":

> There it is—*Weltliteratur*, languidly entering the literary lexicon in a conversation. That exchange is dated January 1827; Johann Peter Eckermann's *Conversations with Goethe* came out in 1836; and just a decade later, in 1848, the idea had become so normal that Marx and Engels could nonchalantly use it in their *Communist Manifesto*: "The intellectual creations of individual nations become common property. National one-sidedness and narrow-mindedness become more and more impossible, and from the numerous national and local literatures, there arises a world literature."
>
> And yet already the excited *Weltlittérateur* must pause. It might look like an ideal, but in the *Manifesto* it represents just one more example of bourgeois tentacular expansion: "The need of a constantly expanding market for its products chases the bourgeoisie over the entire surface of the globe. It must nestle everywhere, settle everywhere, establish connections everywhere. The bourgeoisie has through its exploitation of the world market given a cosmopolitan character to production and consumption in every country." World literature, so august, so aesthetic, might in fact be a phantasmal symptom of world capital.

Adam Thirwell, "All the World's a Page: Nationalism, Creolization, Emptiness and the Persistent rise of World Literature," *Times Literary Supplement*, May 20, 2016, 3.

15. Hermann Broch, *Die Schlafwandler: Eine Romantrilogie* (Frankfurt a.M.: Suhrkamp Taschenbuch Verlag, 1994), 537–38.

16. In this, Goethe's second novel, the bureaucrat Albert, the antipode to the poetic visionary Werther in *The Sufferings of Young Werther*, reappears, figuratively, as the type of the businessman that Wilhelm is unable to transcend. In the work of Terry Eagleton cited in chapter 9,

we read: "Wilhelm Meister begins by elevating the Muse of Tragedy over the figure of Commerce, but by the end of the novel, having met with no particular success on stage, he will acknowledge commerce as the true form of nobility." Eagleton, *Sweet Violence*, 191.

17. Novalis (Friedrich von Hardenberg), "Wilhelm Meisters Lehrjahre," in Stephen Prickett, ed., *European Romanticism: A Reader* (London: Bloomsbury, 2010), 148.

18. "Review of 'Discovering the Mind,'" *Celebrity Types*, http://www.celebritytypes.com /blog/2013/05/review-of-discovering-the-mind/. A rival scholarly voice gives Kaufmann's claim a chance:

> Goethe's scientific studies may have been speculative and of scant practical use because a skeptical attitude to utilitarianism predisposed him against treating the cosmos as a well-oiled machine. A visceral opposition to scientific materialism led him to reject Newton's theories, but 200 years on, the same theories are being questioned by quantum physicists straining to unpick the Cartesian model in favor of a participatory strategy that Goethe would have applauded. He became the first post-Newtonian thinker by virtue of realizing that all observations contain something that exceeds the testimony of our senses. His treatise "The Experiment as Mediator between Object and Subject" . . . contends that the process of observation is what brings the observed object into being.

Osman Durrani, "Many Aspects of Goethe," a review of works by Ritchie Robertson, *Goethe: A Very Short Introduction* (Oxford: Oxford University Press, 2016), and Matthew Bell, ed., *The Essential Goethe* (Princeton, NJ: Princeton University Press, 2016), *Times Literary Supplement*, July 13, 2016, http://www.the-tls.co.uk/articles/public/fragments-of-confession/.

19. Moritz Lazarus, *Das Leben der Seele*, vol. 2 (Berlin: Heinrich Schindler, 1857), 219. Lazarus, an academic philosopher and psychologist, was one of the founders of the Berlin Lehranstalt für die Wissenschaft des Judentums (Institute for Judaic Studies), which Kaufmann attended.

20. Scharfstein, review of Walter Kaufmann, *Discovering the Mind*, 247.

21. Consult Klaus R. Scherpe, *Werther und Wertherwirkung: Zum Syndrom bürgerlicher Gesellschaftsordnung im 18. Jahrhundert* (Bad Homburg v.d.H.: Gehlen, 1970).

22. Walter Kaufmann, "Coming to Terms with Hegel," review of Charles Taylor, *Hegel* (Cambridge: Cambridge University Press, 1975), *Times Literary Supplement*, January 2, 1976, 13. This article-length review contains many of the arguments of the first volume of *The Discovery of Mind*. In fact, in this review Kaufmann refers to a book he is writing on the subject of Goethe's anti-Newtonian science, which, as yet, in late 1975, is incomplete. It was to become this book, published after his death in 1980.

23. Franz Kafka, "Lächerlichkeit betr. Kant [.] Übelkeit nach zuviel Psychologie [.] Wenn einer gute Beine hat und an die Psychologie herangelassen wird, kann er in kurzer Zeit und in beliebigem Zickzack Strecken zurücklegen, wie auf keinem andern Feld. Da gehen einem die Augen über." *Nachgelassene Schriften I*, 423.

24. For the alleged haste with which Kant composed *Critique of Pure Reason*, leading to gaps and obscurities that needed a second edition to correct, Kaufmann relies on Kant's letters, available in Norman Kemp Smith's famous commentary on the first Critique. Kemp Smith writes:

> Seldom, in the history of literature, has a work been more conscientiously and deliberately thought out, *or more hastily thrown together*, than the *Critique of Pure Reason* (em-

phasis added). The following is the account that Kant in a letter to Moses Mendelssohn (August 16, 1783) has given of its composition: "[Though the *Critique* is] the outcome of reflection which had occupied me for a period of at least twelve years, I brought it to completion in the greatest haste within some four to five months, giving the closest attention to the content, but with little thought of the exposition or of rendering it easy of comprehension by the reader—a decision which I have never regretted, since otherwise, had I any longer delayed, and sought to give it a more popular form, the work would probably never have been completed at all. This defect can, however, be gradually removed, now that the work exists in a rough form." . . . But the *Critique* is not merely defective in clearness or popularity of exposition. That is a common failing of metaphysical treatises, especially when they are in the German language, and might pass without special remark. What is much more serious, is that Kant flatly contradicts himself in almost every chapter; and that there is hardly a technical term which is not employed by him in a variety of different and conflicting senses. As a writer, he is the least exact of all the great thinkers.

"Kant's Method of Composing the *Critique of Pure Reason*," *Philosophical Review* 24, no. 5 (September 1915): 526–27.

Chapter 16: Opium of the Intellectuals

1. Walter Kaufmann, *Discovering the Mind*, vol. 2, *Nietzsche, Heidegger, and Buber* (New Brunswick, NJ: Transaction, 1992). Pages from this text will henceforth be shown in parentheses as (D2 + page number). The lines of poetry are by William Wordsworth, *The Prelude*, book 3, lines 62–63.

2. Several of Kaufmann's disagreements with Nietzsche are described in chapter 1.

3. Robert J. Richards, "Nature Is the Poetry of Mind, or How Schelling Solved Goethe's Kantian Problems," http://home.uchicago.edu/~rjr6/articles/Schelling-Goethe.pdf.

4. Walter Kaufmann, *Discovering the Mind*, vol. 3, *Freud, Adler, and Jung* (New Brunswick, NJ: Transaction, 1992), 473. Pages from this text will henceforth be shown in parentheses as (D3 + page number).

5. Henri F. Ellenberger, *The Discovery of the Unconscious: The History and Evolution of Dynamic Psychiatry* (New York: Basic Books, 1970), 276.

6. Gaston Bachelard, *The Poetics of Reverie*, tr. Daniel Russell (Boston: Beacon, 1971), 89.

7. Andrew Gibson, *Intermittency: The Concept of Historical Reason in Recent French Philosophy* (Edinburgh: Edinburgh University Press, 2012), 9–10.

8. Interestingly, Fredric Jameson, the literary critic and Marxist political philosopher, describes postmodernism as replacing "various depth models" of the psyche [read: Freud, Jung, et al.] in favor of a set of multiple surfaces consisting of 'practices, discourses, and textual play.'" Michael Hardt and Kathi Weeks, eds., *The Jameson Reader* (Oxford: Blackwell, 2000), 198.

9. Michael Theunissen cites several passages from Kierkegaard "enabling us to estimate the influence [it is considerable!] that Kierkegaard exercised especially on Heidegger's critique of inauthenticity (*Uneigentlichkeit*)." "Das Erbauliche im Gedanken an den Tod: Traditionale Elemente, innovative Ideen und unausgeschöpfte Potentiale in Kierkegaards Rede; An einem Grabe," *Kierkegaard Studies Yearbook*, 2000 (no. 1), 49.

10. *Est* was a consciousness-raising, "self-actualization" program, established in the wake of Scientology (but without "religion") and still alive, with small differences, under the name "Landmark." It proceeded by attempting to annihilate the ordinary daily consciousness of the trainee as a way of having him or her come into contact with his or her "true self." This program turns, superficially, on the point made by Nietzsche in *Also Sprach Zarathustra*, "Behind your thoughts and feelings, my brother, there stands a mighty ruler, an unknown sage—whose name is self. In your body he dwells; he is your body." *Portable Nietzsche*, 146.

11. These quotes give a rather edulcorated version of the diction of the *est* trainer. In the volume from which Kaufmann cites these phrases, we read a different text—a trainer shouting at his audience of captive trainees that their "fucking lives . . . don't work." Luke Rhinehart, *The Book of est* (New York: Holt, 1976), 8.

12. Roland Barthes, *Barthes on Barthes*, tr. Richard Howard (New York: Hill and Wang, 1977), 173–74.

13. *Portable Nietzsche*, 146.

14. "Ja, vermöchte er auch nur sich einmal vollständig . . . zu perzipieren?" (https://www .uni-erfurt.de/fileadmin/publicdocs/Literaturwissenschaft/ndl/Material_Schmidt /Nietzsche_Über_Wahrheit.pdf).

15. Nietzsche does not establish clear distinctions between various *forms* of lies. Cf. "Art and Two Kinds of Lies: Nietzsche and Schiller on the Value of Aesthetic Semblance," an unpublished paper by Timothy A. Stoll, Department of Philosophy, Princeton University.

16. On the distinction between "resentment" and "*ressentiment*" in Nietzsche's hands, see the subtle analysis by Didier Fassin:

> For [Adam] Smith, resentment represents a passion, which can be a legitimate response to a wrong committed against the person and lead to a fair punishment of the perpetrator. . . . There is a moderate tone in his criticism of resentment, which he assimilates to a form of indignation related to an injury. For Nietzsche, *ressentiment* defines a condition that characterizes the repressed feelings of the dominated and legitimizes their reaction against the dominant. There is a radical stance in his critique of *ressentiment*, which he views as a vengefulness based on envy and impotence. . . . With Smith, we are in the realm of the psychological and within the limits of morality: the objective is to explain and justify social interactions involving injuries. With Nietzsche, we are in the domain of the genealogical and at the foundations of morality: the goal is to interpret and shake the obviousness of our moral certainties.

"On Resentment and *Ressentiment*: The Politics and Ethics of Moral Emotions," *Current Anthropology* 54, no. 3 (June 2013): 251.

17. Karl Jaspers, *Psychologie der Weltanschauungen* (Berlin, Heidelberg: Springer, 1925).

18. John Macquarrie and Edward Robinson, the eminent translators of Heidegger's *Sein und Zeit* (*Being and Time*), translate Heidegger's recurrent logical trope "zunächst und zumeist" as "proximally and for the most part." See, e.g., page 37. This English phrase has now acquired a life of its own.

19. Kaufmann also translated the introduction to Heidegger's later *Was ist Metaphysik?* as "The Way into the Ground of Metaphysics" (E 265–79).

20. Heidegger, *Being and Time*, tr. Macquarrie and Robinson, 193.

21. "Authentic understanding, no less than that which is inauthentic, can be either genuine or not genuine." Ibid., 186.

22. Hans-Georg Gadamer, *Truth and Method*, tr. William Glen-Doepel (London: Shed and Ward, 1975), 230, 229.

23. See Peter E. Gordon, *The Continental Divide: Heidegger, Cassirer, Davos* (Cambridge, MA: Harvard University Press, 2012).

24. *Wit, Wisdom, and Philosophy of Jean Paul Fred.* [*sic*] *Richter*, ed. Giles P. Hawley (New York: Funk and Wagnalls, 1884). The editor adds: "To appreciate the force of this brilliant epigram one needs to recall to mind the time when it was written. It was while the victories of the English navies under Nelson, and of the French armies under Napoleon, and the not less significant conquests of [Gottfried Wilhelm] Leibniz [1646–1716], [Immanuel] Kant [1724–1804], and [Johann Gottlieb] Fichte [1752–1814] in the world of thought, were still fresh in the world's attention" (43). Kant and Fichte were contemporaries of the cited Romantic authors; the philosopher Fichte can be included among the latter.

25. A passage from John Williams's novel *Stoner* restates Kaufmann's point too well to omit:
> He [William Stoner] wondered again at the easy, graceful manner in which the Roman lyricists accepted the fact of death, as if the nothingness they faced were a tribute to the richness of the years they had enjoyed; and he marveled at the bitterness, the terror, the barely concealed hatred he found in some of the later Christian poets of the Latin tradition when they looked to that death which promised, however vaguely, a rich and ecstatic eternity of life, as if that death and promise were a mockery that soured the days of their living.

John Williams, *Stoner* (New York: New York Review of Books, 1965), 41.

26. Cited in Thomas Sheehan, "Caveat Lector: The New Heidegger," *New York Review of Books*, December 4, 1980, http://www.nybooks.com/articles/1980/12/04/caveat-lector-the-new-heidegger/.

27. David Pickus, "What Does Walter Kaufmann's Heidegger Critique Have To Offer the 21st Century?," in "Re-reading Heidegger," spec. issue of *Studia Philosophiae Christianae*: 50 (2014): 1, 209.

28. A draft of the essay on Heidegger in *From Shakespeare to Existentialism*, titled "Heidegger's Castle" —a scathing criticism—appeared as early as 1958 in Hebrew "in a book *Divrey Iyyun*, dedicated to Martin Buber on the occasion of his eightieth birthday (Jerusalem: The Magnes Press of the Hebrew University, 1958)" (S 430). Kaufmann's initial enthusiasm for Martin Buber will also suffer a sea change (D2 241–92).

29. Pickus, "Kaufmann's Heidegger Critique," 214. The inner quote is from (D2 229).

30. Franz Kafka, *Letters to Felice*, ed. Jürgen Born and Erich Heller, tr. James Stern and Elizabeth Duckworth (New York: Schocken, 1973), 157.

Chapter 17: Unsubdued Quarrels

1. Epigraph: Sigmund Freud, letter to Arnold Zweig, December 2, 1927, Walter Kaufmann, *Freud, Adler, and Jung*, vol. 3 of *Discovering the Mind* (New Brunswick, NJ: Transaction, 1992), 68. Pages from this text will henceforth be shown in parentheses as (D3+ page number).

2. Sigmund Freud, from a letter to Wilhelm Fliess, cited in Ronald Clark, *Freud, the Man and the Cause* (New York: Random House, 1980), 212.

3. On December 17, 1911, Freud wrote to Jung: "I am not at all cut out to be an inductive researcher; my bent is wholly intuitive, and I have imposed an extraordinary discipline on myself when I set out to establish psychoanalysis, which can be discovered purely empirically" (D3 327). It remains moot, for many, whether the discoveries of psychoanalysis did actually eventuate this way.

4. Or, in the brightly colored, vitriolic style of Freud's recent, most insistent opponent—whom we will encounter again in the main text of this chapter—"the Freudian 'dynamic unconscious' turns out to be . . . an ontological maze peopled by absurd homunculi possessing their own inexplicable sets of warring motives." Frederick Crews, "Confessions of a Freud Basher," *Times Higher Education Supplement*, March 3, 1995, http://human-nature.com/freud/crews.html.

5. In this respect Kaufmann shares a good deal of the Freud effect. In an incisive review of Ronald Clark's Freud biography, Stuart Hampshire writes, "Even from the grave Freud seems still to provoke and to irritate, and to call either for total submission or for some answering aggression or resistance." "Accepting Freud," *London Review of Books* 2, no. 23 (December 4, 1980): 3.

6. Ibid.

7. This and several others of Schorske's essays on Austrian writers were subsequently published together in his much-admired *Fin de Siècle Vienna: Politics and Culture* (New York: Random House, 1979).

8. The text was actually compiled by one Georg Christoph Tobler, a younger man devoted to Goethe, who wrote down the things he heard Goethe say.

9. Nietzsche, "Epigrams and Interludes," *Beyond Good and Evil*, no. 68, in *Basic Writings*, 270.

10. Frank J. Sulloway, *Freud, Biologist of the Mind: Beyond the Psychoanalytic Legend* (New York: Basic Books, 1979).

11. Fritz Wittels, "Goethe und Freud," *Die psychoanalytische Bewegung* 2, no. 5 (September–October 1930): 431–66, included in *Freud and His Time*, tr. Louise Brink (New York: Liveright, 1931).

12. Hampshire, "Accepting Freud," 3.

13. Kaufmann's enterprise bears a suggestive resemblance to that of F. R. Leavis, who, in his *The Great Tradition*, established *the* English novel on works by, once again, four load bearers: Jane Austen, George Eliot, Henry James, and Joseph Conrad.

14.

Phenomenology	*Existentialism*
"Strict science"	Closer to literature than to science
Kant's unholy trinity of certainty, completeness, and necessity	Emphasis on uncertainty, caprice, absurdity, and opposition to systems
Intuition of essences ("*Wesensschau*")	Opposition to "essentialism"
Hyperacademic and scholastic	Antiacademic
Great appeal to Roman Catholic philosophy professors, including Pope John Paul II	Specifically condemned by Pope XII in his encyclical *Humani Generis*, in 1950
Stresses cooperative research	Stresses the solitary individual
Stresses in personal and objective knowledge	Stresses anxiety, despair, and decision

15. This passage is paraphrased from Stanley Corngold, "Heidegger's *Being and Time*: Implications for Poetics," in *Fate of the Self*, 197–98.

16. Franz Kafka, *Diaries*, August 6, 1914.

17. *Peripheral Desires: The German Discovery of Sex* (Philadelphia: University of Pennsylvania Press, 2015).

18. Crews, "Confessions."

19. Hugo von Hofmannsthal, "Der Dichter und diese Zeit," 1907, in *Der Brief des Lord Chandos: Schriften zur Literatur, Kunst und Geschichte*, ed. Mathias Mayer (Stuttgart: Reclam, 2001), 116.

20. Stanley Corngold, "1900: Sigmund Freud, *Die Traumdeutung*," *The New History of German Literature*, ed. David Wellbery (Cambridge, MA: Harvard University Press, 2004), 647.

21. Rhinehart, *Book of est*, 8.

22. Peter Gay, *Freud: A Life for Our Time* (New York: Norton, 1998), vii.

23. Crews, "Confessions."

24. Crews would claim to find confirmation in a work more recent than the one Kaufmann has in mind: Edward Erwin, *A Final Accounting: Philosophical and Empirical Issues in Freudian Psychology* (Boston: MIT Press, 1996).

25. Crews, "Confessions."

26. In the meantime, Crews has elaborated his charges against Freud in a book recently published to a mixed reception, approximately divided between anger and satisfaction. It has come too late for me to work it in. Frederick Crews, *The Making of an Illusion* (New York: Metropolian Books/Henry Holt, 2017).

27. Jonathan Lear, "A Counterblast in the War on Freud: The Shrink Is In," *New Republic*, December 25, 1995, http://human-nature.com/articles/lear.html. Crews has not been silent; here he attempts to dismiss Lear's rebuttal: http://human-nature.com/articles/crews.html.

28. Phyllis Bottome, *Alfred Adler, a Biography* (New York: G. P. Putman's Sons, 1939).

29. Erich Heller, *The Importance of Nietzsche* (Chicago: University of Chicago Press, 1988), 152–53.

30. The analytic philosopher Gustav Bergmann introduced this phrase in his review of P. F. Strawson's *Individuals: An Essay in Descriptive Metaphysics* (London: Methuen, 1959). Gustav Bergmann, "Strawson's Ontology," *Journal of Philosophy* 62, no. 19 (September 5, 1960): 603. Richard Rorty, Kaufmann's colleague in the Department of Philosophy at Princeton, included a number of Gustav Bergmann's essays in his influential anthology *The Linguistic Turn: Essays In Philosophical Method* (Chicago: University of Chicago Press, 1967). We must conclude that Kaufmann looked at the book with faint enthusiasm.

31. Paul Roazen, *Brother Animal: The Story of Freud and [Viktor] Tausk* (New York: Knopf, 1969); Roazen, *Freud and His Followers* (New York: Knopf, 1979).

32. David Bromwich, "Slow Deconstruction," *London Review of Books* 15, no. 19 (7 October 1993), 22–23.

33. "Er [Freud] verurteilte den Sohn [C. G.] Jung nicht zum Tod durch Ertrinken, aber er verbannte ihn." Peter-André Alt, "Wie Kafka der Psychoanalyse zuvorkam," *Zeitschrift für Ideengeschichte* 10, no. 4 (Winter 2016): 62.

34. Nietzsche, *Daybreak (Dawn): Thoughts on the Prejudices of Morality*, tr. R. J. Hollingdale, ed. Maudemarie Clark, and Brian Leiter (Cambridge, UK: Cambridge University Press, 1997), 5.

35. Scharfstein, review of Walter Kaufmann, *Discovering the Mind*, 247.

36. Kaufmann, "Buber's *I and Thou*," in *Existentialism, Religion, and Death*, 77.

Epilogue

1. First epigraph: Scharfstein, review of Walter Kaufmann, *Discovering the Mind*, 247. Second epigraph: John Keats, letter to George and Georgiana Keats, February 18, 1819, in *John Keats, Selected Letters*, ed. Robert Gittings (Oxford: Oxford University Press, 2002), 203.

2. William Butler Yeats, "Lapis Lazuli": "All perform their tragic play, / . . . They know that Hamlet and Lear are gay, / Gaiety transfiguring all that dread" (https://www.poetryfoundation.org/poems/43297/lapis-lazuli).

3. The aphorism reads in full: "Nur unser Zeitbegriff läßt uns das Jüngste Gericht so nennen, eigentlich ist es ein Standrecht" (It is only our conception of time that has us call the Last Judgment by this name. In fact, it is a summary court martial). Kafka, *Nachgelassene Schriften II*, 25.

4. Friedrich Schiller, *Don Karlos, Infant von Spanien*, act 1, scene 10, https://www.martinschlu.de/kulturgeschichte/klassik/schiller/doncarlos/1/110.htm.

5. Blake, *Jerusalem*, "The Words of Los," f. 10, lines 20–21.

6. Martin E. Marty, "Doubts of a Freethinker," review of Walter Kaufmann, *The Faith of a Heretic*, *New York Times*, August 6, 1961, https://timesmachine.nytimes.com/timesmachine/1961/08/06/issue.html?action=click&contentCollection=Archives&module=LedeAsset&region=ArchiveBody&pgtype=article.

7. Antonio, "Kaufmann, Walter Arnold," 1284.

8. In 2003, forty-two years after the initial publication of *From Tolstoy to Camus*, Donald Weiss, for one, a professor of philosophy at SUNY Binghamton, wrote, "This is one of the best anthologies of modern religious thought and philosophy. It is ably edited, with a long and useful introduction by Professor Kaufmann. I will use it as the centerpiece of the course in the philosophy of religion I will be teaching this fall," https://www.amazon.com/gp/customer-reviews/RQYCXQRWQ57P6/ref=cm_cr_dp_d_rvw_ttl?ie=UTF8&ASIN=1560007060.

9. This was 1961: the article is an early version of *The Faith of a Heretic* and the magazine, *Harper's*. "The Faith of a Heretic," *Harper's Magazine*, February 1959, pp. 33–39.

10. Out of charity I will not quote too conspicuously from the furious review that appeared at Christmas 1968 in the very conspicuous *Saturday Review*:

> *Tragedy and Philosophy* contains very little wrestling with such philosophical concerns as logic, beauty, finitude, death, process, ethical dilemma, the validity of analogical statement, or reason vs. passion—any of which might be thought pertinent in a philosopher's treatment of tragedy. Kaufmann realizes this and says "it depends on what your conception of philosophy is." My conception includes the notion that it is rigorous, fascinated by major problems difficult of solution, and willing to follow up the ontological implications of the statement Kaufmann makes—only to leave it unexamined— that tragedies function "on different levels of reality." Philosophy to me has intellectual courage.

Tom Driver, "Is Melpomene Dead? A Maverick Princeton Philosopher Attacks the Pronouncements on Tragedy Made by His Predecessors, Beginning with Plato," *Saturday Review*, December 28, 1968, 27–28.

This is one of the more anodyne of the diatribes featured in this review. Driver was the Paul J. Tillich Professor of Theology and Culture at the Union Theological Seminary. It should be noted, in turn, that in his *Critique of Religion and Philosophy*, Kaufmann was a scathing critic of Paul Tillich!

11. Philip H. Rhinelander, review of Walter Kaufmann, *Without Guilt and Justice: From Decidophobia to Autonomy*, *University of Pennsylvania Law Review* 122, no. 3 (January 1974): 745–61.

12. Moran, review of *Without Guilt and Justice*, 85.

13. Kaufmann, "Selective Compassion," *New York Times*, September 22, 1977, 17.

14. See www.walterKaufmann.com/reviewers/.

15. Kaufmann described Rolf Hochhuth's *The Deputy* as the world's only Christian tragedy. He wrote of Solzhenitsyn's "sympathetic portrayal of General Samsonov, the commander of the encircled Russian army," in his novel *August 1914* as "one of the glories of world literature." Indeed, "if anyone after Tolstoy or Dostoevsky has written novels that can be compared to theirs," he wrote, "it is . . . Solzhenitsyn" (LL 73). Solzhenitsyn's work has been all but forgotten.

16. Scharfstein, review of Walter Kaufmann, *Discovering the Mind*, 247.

17. Walter Kaufmann, review of Charles Taylor, *Hegel* (Cambridge: Cambridge University Press, 1975), *Times Literary Supplement*, January 2, 1976, 13.

18. Kaufmann defends the *justified* criticism of others—criticism that is improperly dismissed as stemming from the "*need* to put down the work of others"—i.e., dismissed as irrational nastiness (emphasis added). He is also rather insistent on the absence of all traces of nastiness of whatever kind in all of Freud's writing (D3 82).

19. Scharfstein, review of Walter Kaufmann, *Discovering the Mind*, 247.

20. Gilles Deleuze, *Nietzsche et la philosophie* (Paris: Presses Universitaires de France, 1962); Jacques Derrida, *Éperons: Les styles de Nietzsche* (Paris: Flammarion, 1978); Michel Foucault, *Nietzsche, la généalogie, l'histoire* (Paris: Presses Universitaires de France, 1971); Paul de Man, *Allegories of Reading: Figural Language in Rousseau, Nietzsche, Rilke, and Proust* (New Haven, CT: Yale University Press, 1979).

21. A communication from Martin Jay.

22. Rhinehart, *Book of est*, 8.

23. The author of this article, Ziauddin Sardar, comments reasonably: "Whatever the standard and outcome of the conferences, they serve their basic purpose admirably—they provide intellectual respectability for Reverend Moon and his Church of Unification. He may be genuinely concerned with 'better serving the general welfare of mankind,' as he says. But his jamborees, costing, at a conservative estimate, one million pounds a go, do little for mankind and everything for the Church of Unification." "Intellectual Respectability," *New Scientist*, June 25, 1981, 862.

24. A letter from Martin Jay, June 30, 2017.

25. A few, rather impersonal letters of Kaufmann have been retrieved from the archives of several distinguished correspondents, viz., Joseph Frank, Hermann Hesse, Karl Jaspers, and Immanuel Velikovsky. Michael D. Gordin paraphrases a letter written by Kaufmann, a "huge fan" of Velikovsky, the proponent of catastrophism, on February 23, 1976, "urging his friend into more scholarship, not public propagandizing or sniping with critics." *The Pseudoscience Wars: Immanuel Velikovsky and the Birth of the Modern Fringe* (Chicago: University of Chicago Press, 2012), 170.

Postscript

1. Arthur Danto, *Nietzsche as Philosopher*, expanded ed. (New York: Columbia University Press, 2005), xxv. In his *Nietzsche*, Kaufmann wrote: "There is a strong positivistic streak in Nietzsche's thought, and it has not gone entirely unnoticed that he bears some similarities to Wittgenstein. But a good study of this aspect of Nietzsche's philosophy is still needed" (N 422). But Danto's entry into this field has often been discredited. Brian Leiter—who, as we've sadly reported, termed "Kaufmann's old *Nietzsche: Philosopher, Psychologist, Antichrist . . .* extremely unreliable" and to "be avoided"—also wrote, "Danto also gave the genre a bad name, both because of the author's condescending attitude towards his subject and because of the sloppy scholarship *that Walter Kaufmann and others have long since exposed*" (emphasis added). *Nietzsche on Morality* (London: Routledge, 2002), xiii.

2. Paul Bishop, "Introduction," *A Companion to Friedrich Nietzsche: Life and Works* (Rochester, NY: Camden House, 2012), 4.

3. Danto, *Nietzsche as Philosopher*, xxv. Pages from this text will henceforth be shown in parentheses in the body of this chapter.

4. This notebook comment was written in preparation of the second *Untimely Meditation* (N 155).

5. This discussion draws on some of the language in my "The Subject of Nietzsche: Danto, Nehamas, and Staten," in *Nietzsche in American Literature and Thought*, ed. Manfred Pütz (Columbia, SC: Camden House, 1995), 263–77.

6. Danto, *Nietzsche as Philosopher*. He is referring to the "Introductory Remarks" to Walter Kaufmann's translation of *The Twilight of the Idols*, in *Portable Nietzsche*, 463–64.

7. I have silently corrected Danto's pagination to apply to the fourth edition of Kaufmann's *Nietzsche*, the one we are using throughout.

8. Nietzsche, *On the Genealogy of Morals* and *Ecce Homo*, tr. Walter Kaufmann and R. J. Hollingdale (New York: Vintage [Random House], 1967), 152.

9. Danto criticizes Kaufmann's view of Nietzsche's wholeness and the wholeness of his texts:
> "Even those who suppose, erroneously, that *Beyond Good and Evil* is a collection of aphorisms that may be read in any order whatever," Walter Kaufmann wrote, having in mind by "those" specifically me, "generally recognize that the *Genealogy* comprises three essays." This in his view brings the book closest to what we Anglo-American philosophers expect philosophical writing to be, all the more so in that "Nietzsche's manner is much more sober and single-minded than usual." But the manner of the essayist is a marvelous camouflage for the sort of moral terrorist Nietzsche really was, as the essay itself is a kind of literary camouflage for the sharpened stakes of aphorism he has concealed from the unwary, making this in a deep sense the most treacherous book he ever compiled, one almost impossible to read without being cut to ribbons.

Danto, *Nietzsche as Philosopher*, 256.

10. Kafka, *Nachgelassene Schriften II*, 348.

11. David Pickus, in his essay on "the Kaufmann myth," sums up the matter well: "*Bildung* as both ideal and practice has an indwelling aggressive side to it. One preserves some things, but roots out, and frankly, demolishes the pretenses of partial views of oneself and others as the only way to travel on to something higher." "Walter Kaufmann Myth": 242.

12. Conor Cruse O'Brien, "The Gentle Nietzscheans," *New York Review of Books* 15, no. 8 (November 5, 1970), http://www.nybooks.com/articles/archives/1970/nov/05/the-gentle-Nietzscheans/.

13. O'Brien speaks of that rare nineteenth-century German who, of course led on by Machiavelli, "picks out Cesare Borgia as a heroic archetype." This is Nietzsche, but it is certainly not Kaufmann's Nietzsche, whose account of Borgia in *Nietzsche* is far more nuanced than O'Brien makes out. Nietzsche neither admires nor glorifies Borgia; the argument is different:

> Nietzsche found it ridiculous to consider a Cesare Borgia unhealthy in contrast to an emasculated man who is alleged to be healthy. . . . To be moral is to overcome one's impulse; if one does not have any impulses, one is not therefore moral. In other words, Cesare Borgia is not a hero, but—Nietzsche insists—we are no heroes either if our own impulses are merely too weak to tempt us. . . . In his last work, Nietzsche insisted once more that his point was merely that there was more hope for the man of strong impulses than for the man with no impulses: one should look "even for a Cesare Borgia rather than for a Parsifal." (N 224)

14. O'Brien cites Kaufmann as the translator of this passage in Nietzsche, *Beyond Good and Evil*, tr. Walter Kaufmann, 41. But in fact O'Brien uses another man's or woman's.

15. Walter Kaufmann, "On Karl Kraus": "In the end he [Kraus] remained a pedant whose flashes of wit did not compensate sufficiently for his consuming resentment, his appalling lack of judgment, his bigotry, and his unscrupulous methods." Among Kaufmann's reasons for disdaining Kraus is surely Kraus's judgment on Nietzsche: "In 1921 Kraus wrote of Nietzsche: "He was untimely and thirty years ahead of his time. Now he is timely; in twenty years not one sentence of his will survive." *New York Review of Books*, August 9, 1973, http://www.nybooks.com/articles/1973/08/09/on-karl-kraus/. Erich Heller had defended Kraus in the review that prompted Kaufmann's letter—a review dealing with Kraus's complete works. "Dark Laughter," *New York Review of Books*, May 3, 1973, http://www.nybooks.com/articles/1973/05/03/dark-laughter/. Heller now replied to Kaufmann, with relevance to our present concern:

> And the—by no means consistently—negative relationship Karl Kraus had to Nietzsche is almost as complex and often contradictory as that of Nietzsche to Socrates. Altogether Nietzsche! I share with Kaufmann an absorbing interest in Nietzsche's work, a fascination publicly affirmed. Yet would we not both be able to compose a long list of opinions uttered by Nietzsche that, stated in isolation, would sound at least as abhorrent as Karl Kraus's "anti-Semitism"? This, regrettably, is not the place to discuss the grand and too-much-avoided task of distinguishing between opinions, occasionally held, and the enduring quality of the minds that hold them.

This reply follows Kaufmann's letter in *New York Review of Books*, August 9, 1973, http://www.nybooks.com/articles/1973/08/09/on-karl-kraus/.

16. Nietzsche, *On the Genealogy of Morals*, in *Basic Writings*, 488. This passage and the next are conveniently brought together, although in different translations, in Lawrence Hatab, *On the Genealogy of Morality: An Introduction* (Cambridge: Cambridge University Press, 2008), 67.

17. Nietzsche, *Beyond Good and Evil*, tr. Kaufmann, 204.

18. Nietzsche, *On the Genealogy*, tr. Kaufmann, 453.

19. Keith Ansell-Pearson, *An Introduction to Nietzsche as Political Thinker: The Perfect Nihilist* (Cambridge: Cambridge University Press, 1994), 33–34. On the other hand, Timothy Snyder's essay "Hitler's World" will make one wonder:

> For Hitler the bringer of the knowledge of good and evil on the earth, the destroyer of Eden, was the Jew. It was the Jew who told humans that they were above other animals, and had the capacity to decide their future for themselves. It was the Jew who introduced the false distinction between politics and nature, between humanity and struggle. Hitler's destiny, as he saw it, was to redeem the original sin of Jewish spirituality and restore the paradise of blood.

Black Earth: The Holocaust as History and War (New York: Random House, 2015), 8.

From whom does Hitler claim the knowledge of the Jew's "ethical poison"? Can this man be *Nietzsche's* late competitor for the title of the most radical anti-Semite who ever lived?

20. J. P. Stern, *A Study of Nietzsche* (Cambridge: Cambridge University Press, 1979), 37.

21. Ibid., 106.

22. Nietzsche, *Werke, Kritische Gesamtausgabe* (Berlin: de Gruyter, 1994), 11: 580.

23. Pickus shows that an important piece of the "evidence" of Kaufmann's underestimation of the cruelty of power in Nietzsche is faulty and based on a blatant misreading: Sokel literally misreads Kaufmann's word "more" as "mere" with artificially sinister results ("Walter Kaufmann Myth," 245). Walter Sokel, "Political Uses and Abuses of Nietzsche in Walter Kaufmann's Image of Nietzsche," *Nietzsche-Studien* 12 (1983), 441–42.

24. Henning Ottmann, "Englischsprachige Welt," in *Nietzsche Handbuch: Leben-Werk-Wirkung* (Stuttgart-Weimar: J. B. Metzler, 2000), 433.

25. Some reflection on the courage of German writers preceding Nietzsche, living under provincial autocrats, might not lead to the view of "antipolitical" as a badge of honor. After studying writers of the eminence of Georg Forster ("A German Jacobin"), Friedrich Schiller ("and the Police"), Johannes von Müller ("The Historian in Search of a Hero"), Heinrich von Kleist ("and the Duel with Napoleon"), Wilhelm von Humboldt ("as Diplomat"), Friedrich Hölderlin ("and the Barbarians"), Nikolaus Lenau ("as Political Writer"), and Heinrich Heine ("and the Germans"), the historian Gordon A. Craig concludes: "The fact that so many of them lost heart and withdrew from the conflict in the subsequent period gives us no reason to forget these pioneers of commitment, who refused to believe that indifference to politics was a mark of moral or intellectual superiority." Gordon A. Craig, *The Politics of the Unpolitical: German Writers and the Problem of Power, 1770–1871* (Oxford: Oxford University Press, 1995), xiv.

26. Jacques Derrida, "Nietzsches Otobiographie oder Politik des Eigennamens: Die Lehre Nietzsches," *Fugen: Deutsch-Französisches Jahrbuch für Text-Analytik*, ed. Manfred Frank, Friedrich A. Kittler, Samuel Weber (Olten/Freiburg, 1980), 91. Cited in Ernst Behler, *Confrontations: Derrida, Heidegger, Nietzsche* (Stanford, CA: Stanford University Press, 1991), 123.

27. Behler, *Confrontations*, 123.

28. Bishop, "Introduction," *Companion*, 4, 11–12.

29. "Brian Leiter's Nietzsche Blog: Thinking Out Loud about Nietzsche's Philosophy," http://brianleiterNietzsche.blogspot.com/2004/12/where-should-beginner-start-with.html.

30. On a podcast called "Philosophy Bites," Leiter discussed several issues that would count as grounds to discredit Kaufmann's presentation of Nietzsche. Recall from chapter 1

that "it is at the midpoint of Kaufmann's book, which aims to establish the unity of Nietz-sche's key thinking, that we touch 'the crown of Nietzsche's philosophy: the dual vision of the Übermensch and the eternal recurrence; its key conception is the will to power'" (N 121). Leiter points out that anything like a sustained vision of the Übermensch as an ideal and greatly-to-be-desired human being—one never before realized—is found in only one work of Nietzsche's, the relatively early *Thus Spoke Zarathustra* (1883–85). As for the will to power, it is notable that when Nietzsche reviews the life of his works in *Ecce Homo*, he no-where assigns major importance to this concept or suggests that it is the organizing theme of his philosophy. At the same time, I'll add, it is a dominant and impressive theme of *Beyond Good and Evil* and must be taken seriously (philosophybites.com/2009/09/brian-leiter-on -Nietzsche-myths.html).

31. In an earlier work Leiter put his concerns quite persuasively: "If we are to *understand* Nietzsche, then we must be able to articulate his views in terms that amount to more than *paraphrase* (the bane of the Nietzsche literature). Analytic philosophy, as it developed during the 20th century, gave us an enormous repertoire of finely tuned philosophical categories and arguments for thinking about ethics, epistemology, metaphysics—in short, all the issues that engaged Nietzsche." *Nietzsche on Morality* (London: Routledge, 2002), xiii.

32. Robert Pippin, *Introductions to Nietzsche* (Cambridge: Cambridge University Press, 2012), 4.

33. Robert Pippin, "Self-Interpreting Selves: Comments on Alexander Nehamas's *Nietzsche: Life as Literature*," *Journal of Nietzsche Studies* 45, no. 2 (Summer 2014): 118.

34. Ibid., 131.

35. Ratner-Rosenhagen, *American Nietzsche*, 224–62. Pages from this book will be shown in parentheses in the body of this chapter.

36. *Birth of Tragedy*, 4–5.

37. See "Jacob Golomb, "Nietzsche and the Marginal Jews," in *Nietzsche and Jewish Culture*, ed. Jacob Golomb (London: Routledge, 1997), 158–92.

38. Dilthey, for one, made reference to *The Genealogy of Morals*. See Jan de Mul, *The Tragedy of Finitude: Dilthey's Hermeneutics of Life*, tr. Tony Burrett (New Haven, CT: Yale University Press, 2004), 210. Nietzsche was also well aware of Dilthey: see Corngold, "Self and Subject in Nietzsche," in *Fate of the Self*, 96.

39. Brian Leiter, "The Analytic Nietzsche," *Times Literary Supplement*, September 12, 2014, 6.

40. P. Bergmann, *Nietzsche*.

41. Ibid., 1.

42. Ibid., 1, 81.

43. Christian Emden, *Friedrich Nietzsche and the Politics of History* (Cambridge: Cambridge University Press, 2008).

44. Duncan Large, *Nietzsche and Proust* (Oxford: Clarendon, 2001), 1.

45. Hays Steilberg has treated Kaufmann's work on Nietzsche in an instructive, fair-minded way in a chapter titled "From Dolson to Kaufmann," in *Nietzsche in American Literature and Thought*, ed. Manfred Pütz, 239–62, 258.

46. Ibid., 256.

47. Pippin, "Self-Interpreting Selves," 118; Steilberg, "From Dolson," 258.

48. Ofelia Schutte, *Beyond Nihilism: Nietzsche without Masks* (Chicago: University of Chi-cago Press, 1984), 86.

49. Nietzsche, *Beyond Good and Evil*, in *Basic Writings*, 217.

50. Schutte, *Beyond Nihilism*, 86.

51. Corngold, *Fate of the Self*, 127.

52. Lewis Thomas, *The Lives of a Cell: Notes of a Biology Watcher* (New York: Bantam Books, 1974) 3, 8, 9, 21, 18. One is encouraged to write about the self in Nietzsche—as related to questions of the identity of the biological cell—by Nietzsche's reflections "Biology of the Drive to Knowledge" in *Will to Power*, 272.

53. Ibid., 270.

54. Nietzsche, *Basic Writings*, 418.

55. Robert B. Pippin, "Introduction," *Thus Spoke Zarathustra*, tr. Adrian del Capo, ed. Adrian del Capo and Robert B. Pippin (Cambridge: Cambridge University Press, 2006), xxviii.

56. Nietzsche, *Beyond Good and Evil*, tr. Walter Kaufmann, 162.

57. Nietzsche, *Will to Power*, 270.

58. Bernard Reginster, *The Affirmation of Life: Nietzsche on Overcoming Nihilism* (Cambridge, MA: Harvard University Press, 2009), 286. He is referring to his discussion on pages 213–16.

59. At this point in our narrative, the Nietzsche scholar John Richardson refines Kaufmann's conception of sublimation:

> Kaufmann (*Nietzsche*, 218ff.) helpfully surveys Nietzsche's uses of "sublimation" but misses the important point at hand. He takes sublimation to occur when the undifferentiated will to power, displaced from its (for example) sexual expression, directs itself toward quite different, nonsexual ends; all that remains constant is will to power itself. But would it then be apt to call this "sublimation of the sex drive"? In the examples Nietzsche gives, we find a greater continuity: ends are modified, not replaced, viz. *Will to Power*, 312: "[One] has refined cruelty to tragic pity, so that it may be disavowed as [cruelty]. In the same way sexual love [has been refined] to *amour-passion*; the slavish disposition as Christian obedience." I take "spiritualization" to be an especially effective form or means of sublimation, for Nietzsche.

John Richardson, "Nietzsche's Power Ontology," in *Nietzsche*, Oxford Readings in Philosophy, ed. John Richardson and Brian Leiter (Oxford: Oxford University Press, 2001), 158.

60. Brian Leiter, "The Paradox of Fatalism and Self-Creation in Nietzsche," *Nietzsche*, Oxford Readings in Philosophy, ed. John Richardson and Brian Leiter (Oxford: Oxford University Press, 2001), 286.

61. Nietzsche, *Beyond Good and Evil*, tr. Kaufmann, 231.

62. Nietzsche, *The Antichrist*, in *Portable Nietzsche*, 569.

63. Gudrun von Tevenar, ed., *Nietzsche and Ethics* (Oxford: Peter Lang, 2007), 139–69. Von Tevenar's summary is found on page 11.

64. Schutte, *Beyond Nihilism*, 122.

65. *Thus Spoke Zarathustra*, in *Portable Nietzsche*, 205.

66. In Benno Wagner's complete formulation, "Nietzsche's protagonist, the Übermensch ('no one' as yet, and hence the object of Zarathustra's search), is less another cultural type than an impersonation of a line of flight beyond the limits of the herd man." Corngold and Wagner, *Franz Kafka: Ghosts in the Machine*, 20.

67. "Auf *Andere* warte ich hier in diesen Bergen . . . / —auf Höhere, Stärkere, Sieghaftere, Wohlgemuthere, Solche, die rechtwinklig gebaut sind an Leib und Seele: *lachende Löwen*

müssen kommen! // Oh, meine Gastfreunde, ihr Wunderlichen,—hörtet ihr noch Nichts von meinen Kindern? Und dass sie zu mir unterwegs sind? // Sprecht mir doch von meinen Gärten, von meinen glückseligen Inseln, *von meiner neuen schönen Art,*—warum sprecht ihr mir nicht davon?"

68. *Thus Spoke Zarathustra*, tr. del Caro, ed. Pippin, 220.

69. Schutte, *Beyond Nihilism*, 122.

70. Kaufmann's view of the "cosmological" hypothesis is somewhat elliptical, but I see no grounds for affirming that he "*rejects outright* the broader, cosmological, version." In fact Kaufmann writes that one will find "*much further evidence*" in Nietzsche's later writings for affirming the will to power as the fundamental drive of all living beings, "*as well as the still more extreme hypothesis that the will to power is the basic force of the entire universe*" (emphasis added) (N 207).

71. Nehamas adds: "A general discussion of the will to power can be found in Wolfgang Müller-Lauter, 'Nietzsches Lehre vom Willen zur Macht,' *Nietzsche-Studien* 3 (1974): 1–60. The most extensive treatment is in Heidegger's two-volume *Nietzsche* (Pfullingen: Neske, 1961), parts of which have now appeared in English." Nehamas, *Nietzsche*, 243.

72. Thus we have Gregory Bruce Smith, in his *Nietzsche, Heidegger, and the Transition to Post-modernity* (Chicago: University of Chicago Press, 1996), curiously describing Kaufmann's project as the attempt "to translate Nietzsche's philosophy into the categories of Anglo-American thought, that is, into the mold of prior systematic philosophy, paving the way for two decades of such attempts." The crux is Smith's commentary citing "Kaufmann, *Nietzsche,* 307–33." These pages sketch out Kaufmann's view on the cosmological bearing of the eternal recurrence, which Smith finds untenable. Kaufmann writes: "Nietzsche thought that the eternal recurrence might be implied by modern science; it appeared to him in the same light in which a later generation received the theory that the *universe* is 'running down'" (emphasis added). Kaufmann quotes Nietzsche: "Let us think this thought in its most terrible form: *existence* as it is, without sense and aim, but recurring inevitably without a finale of nothingness: '*the eternal recurrence*' (WM 55)" (first emphasis added). Kaufmann comments: "The doctrine means that *all events* are repeated endlessly, that there is no plan nor goal to give meaning to history or life, and that we are mere puppets in an absolutely senseless play" (emphasis added). Kaufmann's discussion is interpreted by Smith as follows: "As part of this undertaking, Kaufmann went so far as to dismiss as an ill-considered cosmological position the doctrine of eternal recurrence, which Nietzsche considered his central thought" (68n4). There is a considerable literature maintaining in no uncertain terms that Nietzsche lost interest entirely in attempting further "scientific" proofs of the applicability of this "terrible" thought to the physical cosmos. Smith's objection is inconclusive in several ways.

73. Nehamas, *Nietzsche: Life as Literature*, 254n7.

74. Large, *Nietzsche and Proust*, 1.

75. Ibid., 22n66.

76. Ibid., 27.

77. Danto, *Nietzsche*, 12, 13.

78. For a comparable criticism, see my "Subject of Nietzsche," 263–77.

79. Brian Leiter, writing in "Brian Leiter's Philosophy Blog," terms Kaufmann's work, as we have heard, "unreliable" and "to be avoided." In his blog, well known to a legion

of readers, Leiter also took fierce objection to the *New York Times*'s appointment of Professor Simon Critchley as moderator of *The Stone*. *The Stone* is a print blog featuring "the writing of contemporary philosophers and other thinkers on issues both timely and timeless." In the course of his (savage) criticism of Critchley, Leiter recommends a critical work on continental philosophy much superior to that of Critchley's—namely, his own edited work, with Michael Rosen as coeditor, *The Oxford Handbook of Continental Philosophy* (New York: Oxford University Press, 2007)—described on the press page as "The *only* accessible and authoritative guide to the continental traditions in philosophy" (emphasis added). At this point it is bemusing to take up a rival work, by David West, titled *Continental Philosophy: An Introduction* (Cambridge, UK: Polity, 2010), a book mentioning Nietzsche that has the distinction of never having been denounced by Leiter and which is, moreover, enthusiastically recommended by the redoubtable scholar Philip Pettit. David West takes the opportunity to recommend, against Leiter, Critchley's *Continental Philosophy: A Very Short Introduction* (New York: Oxford University Press, 2001) for further reading and moreover cites copiously from Kaufmann, ceding him considerable authority in defining "the Dionysian." One might now be inclined to recall Steven Aschheim's stress on "Nietzsche's congeniality to so many contrary tendencies and interests," his "capacity to elicit open-ended responses," as if transmitting even and especially to his critics "his determination to attack problems from a plurality of perspectives" (*Culture and Catastrophe*, 8).

80. Large, *Nietzsche and Proust*, 23.

81. Ibid., 41.

82. Ibid., 96. Large finds Kaufmann important to quote once again, after Kaufmann has commented on Nietzsche's effort, greater than any other modern philosopher, "to re-experience the spirit of Socrates and his disciples" (N 366). "What is interesting about Kaufmann's account," Large writes, "is that he addresses the obvious corollary, that Nietzsche was homosexual, and balks at the notion (suggested in a 1917 article by Wilhelm Stekel), dismissing it flatly: 'Stekel suggests that Nietzsche was a homosexual without himself knowing it'" (N 34n10). Large then finds Kaufmann's invocation of the overheated and strained heterosexual imagery of Zarathustra altogether cogent.

83.   https://100vampirenovels.com/pdf-novels/doctor-faustus-by-thomas-mann-free/80 -page. This website conveniently reprints the complete text of Thomas Mann's *Doctor Faustus* as translated from the German by H. T. Lowe-Porter (New York: Knopf, 1948).

84. No longer Web-accessible.

85. Ratner-Rosenhagen in *American Nietzsche* offers a fuller description of what she takes to be the ideological foundation of the American reception of Kaufmann's *Nietzsche*. Though Kaufmann took pains *to say* that Nietzsche *was no liberal*, his large picture of Nietzsche did not flesh out Nietzsche's antiliberalism vividly enough to offend a nascent "liberal imagination." And so, concludes Ratner-Rosenhagen, Kaufmann's *Nietzsche* was well-liked.

86. The politics of one burgher does not make up the politics of an entire social class, but it is significant that "right of center" characterizes the politics of another important family of Berlin Jewish burghers—that of the young Walter Benjamin. "Hilda Benjamin, the wife of Benjamin's brother Georg . . . describes the family as typical liberal bourgeoisie with an orientation just right of center." Howard Eiland and Michael W. Jennings, *Walter Benjamin: A Critical Life*

(Cambridge, MA: Harvard University Press, 2014), 20. The conjunction of the terms "liberal" with "right of center" politics in late nineteenth-century Germany gives "liberalism" a meaning that Goosta does not intend.

87. Peter Gay, "Introduction," Nietzsche, *Basic Writings*, x.

88. Ibid. Gay's citation of this phrase from *Thus Spoke Zarathustra* is not quite right. The aphorism reads: "Everything about women is a riddle, and everything about women has one solution: that is pregnancy." *Portable Nietzsche*, 178.

89. Nietzsche, "Preface," *Beyond Good and Evil*, tr. Kaufmann, 1.

90. *The Gay Science*, ed. and tr. Walter Kaufmann (New York: Vintage, 1974), 35–36.

91. Steven Taubeneck, "Afterword: Nietzsche in North America—Walter Kaufmann and Afterward," in Ernst Behler, *Confrontations: Derrida, Heidegger, Nietzsche*, tr. Steven Taubeneck (Stanford, CA: Stanford University Press, 1991), 176–77. Taubeneck's list of scholars constitutes a brief, selective bibliography of some of the best critical works on Nietzsche, to which the more recent critics we have cited above should be added. In his afterword, Taubeneck briefly discusses the contribution of each.

Gilles Deleuze, *Nietzsche and Philosophy*, tr. Hugh Tomlinson (New York: Columbia University Press, 1983).

Michel Foucault, "Nietzsche, Genealogy, History," in *The Foucault Reader*, ed. Paul Rabinow (New York: Pantheon Books, 1984), 76–100.

Jacques Derrida, *Spurs: Nietzsche's Styles (Éperons: Les Styles de Nietzsche)*, tr. Barbara Harlow (Chicago: University of Chicago Press, 1978).

Sarah Kofman, *Nietzsche et la métaphore* (Paris: Payot, 1972).

Pierre Klossowski, *The Vicious Circle*, tr. Daniel W. Smith (Chicago: University of Chicago Press, 1997).

Arthur Danto, *Nietzsche as Philosopher*.

Bernd Magnus, *Nietzsche's Existential Imperative* (Bloomington: Indiana University Press, 1978).

Richard Schacht, *Nietzsche* (London: Routledge and Kegan Paul, 1983).

Alexander Nehamas, *Nietzsche: Life as Literature*.

David Farrell Krell, *Exceedingly Nietzsche: Aspects of Contemporary Nietzsche Interpretation*, ed. with David Wood (London: Routledge and Kegan Paul, 1988).

Allan Bloom, *The Closing of the American Mind* (New York: Simon and Schuster, 1987).

Richard Rorty, *Contingency, Irony, Solidarity* (Cambridge: Cambridge University Press, 1989).

92. "Even writers who disagree with the conclusions of Jaspers and Kaufmann do not have to begin from square one. The groundwork here has been laid for them. Scholars today can take up comprehensive accounts of Nietzsche's work as elaborated by Jaspers and Kaufmann and alter or expand them without ever mentioning these original studies." David Pickus, "Wishes of the Heart: Walter Kaufmann, Karl Jaspers, and Disposition in Nietzsche Scholarship," *Journal of Nietzsche Studies*, no. 33 (Spring 2007): 7.

93. I have covertly corrected Kaufmann's pagination to apply to the expanded 2005 edition of Danto's *Nietzsche as Philosopher*.

94. Kaufmann's scathing and extended criticism of Danto is found on (N 359n13).

INDEX

Abbey Church of Sainte Foy (Conques), 453

Abel, Lionel, 284

Abrams, Meyer, 248, 285–86, 673n4

Achilles, 473

Adhem, Abou ben, 417

Adler, Alfred: and discovery of mind, 532, 551–56; ego in, 552, 555; and Freud, 552–53, 554; and inferiority complex, 551; and masculine protest, 551; and Nietzsche, 506–7, 554, 555; psychology of, 476; and will to power, 552, 554, 555

Adorno, Theodor W., 12, 32, 90, 112, 234, 272, 287, 288, 293, 368, 448, 531, 629n56, 638n27

Aeschylus, 88, 193, 281, 290, 304, 308–9, 311, 328, 339, 349, 358, 473, 667–68n27; and Aristotle, 314; catastrophic vs. irenic endings of, 311; and Euripides, 323, 324; *hamartia* in, 313; and Hegel, 316; and Homer, 310, 313, 317, 322; justice in, 311, 312, 314, 318; moral collision in, 318–19; and Nietzsche, 307, 308, 314; optimism in, 308, 309; Platonic element in, 314; reason in, 309, 311, 312; and Sartre, 326, 327; and Shakespeare, 317; and Sophocles, 322; and suffering, 312, 313; and tragedy, 340; tragic heroes of, 313; and victories of Marathon and Salamis, 315; wisdom in, 313; WORKS: *Agamemnon*, 287–88, 313, 341; *Eumenides*, 309, 311, 312, 313, 341, 669n44; *Oresteia*, 308–9, 311, 313, 314, 318, 326; *The Persians*, 669n40; *Prometheus Bound*, 358; *The Suppliants*, 309

aesthetics, 87, 156, 207, 423, 441; and Kant, 496; and Nietzsche, 461; and philosophy, 225, 443; and religion, 380; and Schiller, 238; as theology, 226. *See also* art

Agamben, Giorgio, 312, 404, 666n17

Agassi, Joseph, 377

Agassi, Judith Buber, 377

agnosticism, 110, 169–70, 396, 655n6

Agus, Jacob, 381, 395

Ajanta, caves at, 437

Akhenaten (Ikhnaton), 175–76, 381, 650n31

Akiba, Rabbi, 110, 116, 393, 395, 420

Albright, W. F., *From the Stone Age to Christianity*, 204

Alexander the Great, 458

alienation, 41, 45, 60, 352, 368, 369–73, 376, 539, 565, 622n59, 662n47

Alt, Peter-André, "How Kafka Anticipated Psychoanalysis," 557

Alter, Robert: *Canon and Creativity*, 145; *Pen of Iron*, 433

Althusser, Louis, 551

Analects, 161, 200, 434

analytic philosophy, 86, 87, 166, 232, 536–37, 568, 572–73, 602, 697n31; and existentialism, 73–74, 79; and Nietzsche, 608

Anaxagoras, 179

Anaximander, 46

Anderson, Quentin, 6

Andreas-Salomé, Lou, 148, 554

Angell-Pearson, Keith, 580

Angkor Thom (Cambodia), 437

Ankersmit, Frank, 65–66

Anselm, St., 100, 105

Antigone, 121, 473

anti-Semitism, 166, 297, 354, 567, 614n22;
and anti-Judaism, 347; and Arendt,
414; French, 224; and Freud, 373; and
Goldhagen thesis, 367; and Kolbe, 347;
and Luther, 409; and Moon, 570; and
Nietzsche, 579, 604, 617n21, 673n8,
695n15

Antonio, Edward P., *Dictionary of Modern
American Philosophers*, 55, 56

Aquinas, St. Thomas, 80, 101, 171, 177, 409,
616n12; and Aristotle, 104; censure of,
179; and Dante, 325; and justice, 364; and
Kierkegaard, 59; and Leo XIII, 214; and
Shakespeare, 129; *Summa Theologica*, 104,
408. *See also* Thomism

Arabs, 81

Arac, Jonathan, 663n52

Arendt, Hannah, 32, 34, 45, 345, 368, 369,
373, 408, 419, 580, 612n13; *Eichmann in
Jerusalem*, 414; *The Human Condition*,
457; "Marx and the Western Political
Tradition," 414; *The Origins of Totalitarianism*, 414, 457

Aristotelianism, 356

Aristotle, 64, 70, 128, 158, 273, 322, 665–
66n13; and Aeschylus, 314; and Aquinas,
104; art in, 286; and Brecht, 349;
catastrophe in, 292, 302, 328; catharsis
in, 284, 287, 289; and Christianity, 113;
dramatic unities in, 290; on *eleos* and
phobos, 287–90, 292, 310, 328; emotion
in, 283–84, 287–90, 310; and Euripides,
308; as fleeing Athens, 179; formalism of,
292–93; and great-souled man, 130, 131;
hamartia in, 284, 290–91, 292, 329; and
Hegel, 249, 315, 501; and Heidegger, 520,
523; history in, 286, 287; and hybris, 291;
and justice, 360; and knowledge, 427;
knowledge of, 450; *mimēsis* in, 284, 285,
286; music in, 285; nature in, 286; and
peripeteiai and *anagnōriseis*, 289–90, 292,
299; and philosophy, 286; and Plato, 281;

plot *(mythos)* in, 289–90, 291–92; and
reason, 117; and self-sufficiency, 137; and
Shakespeare, 129, 328–29; and Sophocles,
303; *spoudaios* in, 286, 340; and suffering,
292, 317; and tragedy, x, 278, 283–93, 310,
311, 312, 339, 340; WORKS: *Nicomachean
Ethics*, 136, 291; *Physics*, 286; *Poetics*, 284,
285–93, 328–29, 565; *Rhetoric*, 289

Arius, 110

Arnold, Matthew, 125, 126

art, 78, 450–59; as Apollinian, 451; in Aristotle, 286; and author's psychology, 296–
97; and Benjamin, 295; and Calvino, 294;
Christian, 452; and demand to change,
207, 493; depersonalization in, 82; and
existentialism, 56; and experience, 298,
449, 455, 462, 478, 645–46n55; felt objects vs. feelings in, 82; form in, 298; and
Freud, 533, 546–47, 558; and Goethe, 478;
in Hegel, 246, 263, 264, 270; Hindu, 459;
historical context of, 298, 455; and history, 296; and humanism, 452; in India,
458, 459, 460; intellectualized, 462; and
intentions, 295–97, 299, 455; and Kant,
496; and mood, 97; and Nature, 463;
and nature of man, 295; and Nietzsche,
390; and Old Testament, 459; as opiate,
438; and Ortega y Gasset, 82; and
personality, 478; and philosophy, 298,
442–43, 445, 449; priceless heritage of,
412–13; process of, 448; receiver of, 295;
recognition from, 294; and religion, 125,
126, 412, 444; repose and control in, 293;
Romanesque, 452, 453–54; and Schiller,
238; and science, 225; and suffering,
478; symbolic, 443; and transcendence,
294; transcendental authority of, 293; as
triumph of form over finitude, 293; true
understanding of, 156–58; as upsetting
certainties, 154. *See also* aesthetics

Ascherson, Neal, 184

Aschheim, Steven E., 15, 161; *The Nietzsche
Legacy in Germany, 1890–1990*, 616n14

Ashbery, John, 70

Ashoka, 437, 458, 470

Aslan, Reza, 651–52n36

aspiration, 100, 117, 124, 168; and Faust, 208, 209; and Goethe, 132, 139; for ontological richness, 124; and religion, 120, 121, 126, 209; as soul of religion, 162; and Tolstoy, 209; to truth, 100–101, 167

Assmann, Jan, 175–76

Asveld, Paul, 242

Athanasius, St., 110

atheism, viii, 112–13, 169

Athene, 404

Athens, 314–15

atom bomb, 171, 315

Auerbach, Erich, 285; *Mimesis*, 12, 665n10

Augustine, St., 89, 110, 113, 129, 177, 389, 409, 459, 523

Auschwitz, 310, 315, 332, 345–46. *See also* Holocaust

Austin, John, 87, 106

Australia, 440

authenticity, 60, 200, 207, 357; in Buber, 525; and existentialism, 44; and Freud, 525; and guilt, 365; in Heidegger, 68–69, 508, 519, 521–22, 525, 687n9; and Kierkegaard, 508; and Sartre, 525; and state, 268, 269

authoritarianism, 86; of Heidegger, 129, 519–21, 526; and religion, 116, 120, 127, 659n13116; and Schmitt, 491; and Xenophanes and Heraclitus, 659n13

autonomy, 368; and alienation, 370, 373; and civic responsibility, 377; in decisions, 358; and distributive injustice, 377; freedom of, 353; and Freud, 479, 539; of Goethe, 478–79, 483, 502; and happiness, 374–75; and Hegel, 502; and individuality, 479; and justice, 373–74; and Kant, 479, 491, 495, 497–98; life as test of, 563; of mind, 368; moral, 566; new conception of, 352; and Nietzsche, 43, 479, 601; and self-criticism, 376; and will to power, 375

Avineri, Shlomo, 268–69

Ayer, Alfred, 525

Baader, Franz von, 507

Babylonians, 391, 396

Bach, J. S., 387; *St. Matthew Passion*, 201, 444

Bachelard, Gaston, 507

Bacon, Francis, 76, 78–79, 574

Bad Day at Black Rock (1955), 450

Badiou, Alain, 355, 404

Baeck, Leo, 3, 159, 613n11, 648n15; *Judaism and Christianity*, 3, 7

Baeumer, Max, 151

Balinese Barong dance, 439

Balzac, Honoré de, 445, 486

Banville, John, 672n39

Barker, Ernest, 407

Barnes, Julian, 439

Barth, Karl, 58, 226

Barthes, Roland, 84, 421, 433, 512, 551; *Camera Lucida*, 468

Baudelaire, Charles, 287

Bauer, Felice, 530

Baumann, Gerhart, 425

Bäumler, Alfred, 13

Beardsley, Monroe, 299

beauty, 126, 412, 413, 421, 425, 433; and death, 191, 197; in Euripides, 316; of Genesis, 434; in Goethe, 504; and Hegel, 248; in Hölderlin, 236; in Homer, 305; and horror, 460–61; of Jesus's sayings, 400; in Kafka, 470; in Kant, 463, 496, 504; and Lago di Como, 351, 352, 367; and love, 175; and morality/ethics, 441; of Nefertiti, 451; in Nietzsche, 22, 25, 41, 153, 472; in Plato, 282, 283; in Rilke, 138; in Schiller, 188; of Shakespeare's tragedies, 445; and sublime, 463; and suffering, 449; and time, 469–70; and tragedy, 335; in Wordsworth, 238

Beauvoir, Simone de, 457

Beck, Lewis, 495

Beckett, Samuel, 70, 293, 350, 447; *Endgame*, 455

Beethoven, Ludwig van, 375, 412, 560; Fifth Symphony, 467, 502; late quartets of, 444; Ninth Symphony, 444

Behler, Ernst, 585–86

Beichman, Arnold, 202

Beiser, Frederick, 136, 661n39

belief. *See* faith/belief

Belsey, Catherine, 382, 616n13

Benigni, Roberto, 332

Benjamin, Georg, 700–701n86

Benjamin, Hilda, 700–701n86

Benjamin, Walter, 77, 97, 280, 635–36n44, 657n43, 678n34, 700–701n86; and art, 293, 294–95, 297, 425, 440; and Buber and Rosenzweig, 227; and Heidegger, 531; James on, 368–69; and Satan, 111; as self-deceived, 531; *Ursprung des deutschen Trauerspiels*, 327, 671n26

Benn, Gottfried, 590, 617n23

Bergmann, Gustav, 552, 691n30

Bergmann, Peter, *Nietzsche, "the Last Antipolitical German,"* 591, 618n31

Berkeley, George, 86, 180

Berlin, Isaiah, 44–45, 396, 564; "The Origins of Cultural History," 626n8

Berman, Paul, 632n10

Bermejo-Rubio, Fernando, 401

Bernal, Martin, *Black Athena*, 465

Berne, Eric, *The Games People Play*, 515

Bernstein, John Andrew, *Nietzsche's Moral Philosophy*, 624n79

Berry, Jessica, *Nietzsche and the Ancient Skeptical Tradition*, 48

Bertram, Ernst, 15, 617n23

Bhagavad-Gita, 112, 434, 459

Bible, 81, 85, 107, 161; Alter's translations of, 434; Buber-Rosenzweig translation of, 227, 657n43; and exegetical thinking, 356; exposure to, 200; and Frye, 145; gerrymandering of, 110–11, 165; and God as being-in-itself, 107; and Goethe, 111; higher criticism of, 203, 204, 221–22; and humanism, 434–35; and humanities, 412; Jewish vs. Christian, 77; King James translation of, 434, 464; and Luther, 409; and Mann, 384; and Nietzsche, 589; and Shakespeare, 137; and Spinoza, 180, 450;

and suffering, 391; and Tolstoy, 221; and truth, 96; and Wellhausen, 203

Bible, Hebrew (Old Testament), 77, 107, 117, 147, 159, 185, 381–82, 641n59; Abraham in, 473; antimonarchical strain in, 384–85; and art, 459; challenge of, 186; and Christianity, 281; David and Absalom in, 436; David in, 473; Elijah in, 137, 171; and evil as independent principle, 392–93; and Frye, 145; genocide in, 383; and German and English literature, 144–45; and Goethe, 144, 145–46, 147; and higher criticism, 221–22; humility in, 168; ideal society in, 385; inhumanity in, 382–83; and Jewish statehood, 385; and Judaism, 115; justice in, 168, 360, 385, 459; and Kafka, 106, 648n19; and Kant, 491, 492–94, 495; love in, 168, 459; Masoretic recension of, 394, 395; and modern literature, 145; morality/ethics in, 164, 165, 169, 172, 385, 392–93; and myth, 382; and Nietzsche, 147; paradigmatic individuals in, 473; and Paul, 403; prophets in (*see* prophets, Hebrew); and prosperity vs. persecution, 223; required knowledge of, 433; righteousness in, 121; Satan in, 392–93; Saul in, 473; Septuagint translation of, 394–95; slaves in, 382; and social justice, 383; sublimity of, 175; suffering in, 393; Ten Commandments, 595; time in, 467; and Zionism, 397; and Zoroastrianism, 392–93

Bible, Hebrew (Old Testament), books of: Amos, 137, 185, 392, 459, 665n7; Daniel, 115; Deuteronomy, 494; Exodus, 122–23; Ezekiel, 115, 392, 665n8; Genesis, 298, 392, 434–35, 436, 464, 467, 665n10; Habakkuk, 173; Hosea, 131, 392; Isaiah, 105, 109–10, 115, 120, 177–78, 185, 385, 391, 392, 401, 403, 405, 423, 452, 459, 665n7; Isaiah (second), 137, 392; Jeremiah, 115, 137, 159, 170, 171, 172, 391, 392; Joshua, 382–83; Judges, 384; Lamentations, 115, 391; Job, 77–78,

172, 220, 316, 317, 329–30, 334, 392–93; Leviticus, 382, 399; Micah, 385, 392, 459; Psalms, 397, 401–2, 434; Samuel, 383, 384; Song of Songs, 131

Bible, New Testament, 112, 113, 131, 171, 186; admirable elements of, 400; Beatitudes in, 216; and Buddhism, 379; contemporary knowledge of, 173; flesh and spirit in, 390; and Frye, 145; and higher criticism, 221–22; humility in, 168; and inequality, 471; Jesus in, 216; and Judaism, 383; justice in, 168, 359, 360; love in, 168, 360; Manichean elements in, 390; mercy in, 360; moral core of, 172; and morality, 169; and "Q," 222; required knowledge of, 433; and retributive justice, 359; Sermon on the Mount, 116, 131, 177, 216, 226, 242, 360, 398, 492; syncretism of, 404–5; and truth, 388

Bible, New Testament, books of: Gospels, 397; Matthew, 102, 222, 493; Mark, 102, 222, 400; Luke, 102, 177, 222; John, 102, 223, 388, 404, 436; Romans, 109; 1 Corinthians, 217–18, 404; 1 John, 82, 125; 2 John, 82

Bildung, 38, 250, 565, 568, 605, 622n59, 624n79, 624–25n85, 694–95n11; and alienation, 372, 373; and aristocracy, 32, 35; and civic responsibility, 377; and Discovering the Mind, 531; and humanism, 435; ideal of, 30; and Judaism, 31; and Man's Lot, 444; and self-aggrandizement, 367; translation of, 35; and will to power for self-creation, 34–35

Bildungsbürger, 30, 31, 603

Bildungsbürgertum, 30, 31, 35, 95, 386, 568, 622n59

Bildungsroman, 481, 499

Binswanger, Ludwig, 540

Bishop, Paul, 586

Bismarck, Otto von, 33, 586

Bizet, Georges, 62

Blake, William, 105, 309, 564

Blanchot, Maurice, 70

Bloch, Ernst, 23, 368

Bloom, Allan, 605, 701n91; The Closing of the American Mind, 45

Bloom, Harold, 100, 552; Stories and Poems for Extremely Intelligent Children of All Ages, 448

Böll, Heinrich, The Lost Honor of Katharina Blum, 415

Borgia, Cesare, 578, 583, 695n13

Bormann, Martin, 620n37

Bornkamm, Günther, 131

Borobodur (Java), 437

Boswell, James, 102

Bottome, Phyllis, 551

Bourke-White, Margaret, You Have Seen Their Faces, 468

Bradley, A. C., 316–17

Bradley, F. H., 179

Brahms, Johannes, 188

Brazil (1985), 332

Brecht, Bertolt, vii, 308, 324, 327, 376, 672n31; Life of Galileo, 348–49

Breithaupt, Fritz, 35

Brentano, Clemens, 262

Breuer, Joseph, 538

Brinton, Crane, 616n14

British philosophy, 86–87, 166

Britt, Brian, 657n43

Broad, C. D., 86, 637n12; Religion, Philosophy, and Psychical Research, 104

Broch, Hermann, 484, 670n11

Brod, Max, 666n17

Brodsky, Joseph, 311

Bromwich, David, 556

Brooks, Cleanth, 299

Brooks, Peter, 536

Brower, Reuben, 421–22

Brueghel, Pieter, the Elder, Landscape with the Flight into Egypt, 436

Brunelleschi, Filippo, 437

Brunner, Emil, 226

Bruns, Gerald, 66, 70; Heidegger's Estrangements, 630n70

Buber, Martin, 2, 58, 129, 175, 201, 562, 689n28; authenticity and inauthenticity in, 525;

Buber, Martin (*continued*)
change in thought of, 540; and Christianity, 528; and discovery of mind, 503, 505; and Freud, 530, 540; and God, 527–28; and Hasidic masters, 175, 529; and Hebrew prophets, 529; and Ich/Du dichotomy, 529–30; and Judaism, 527; and Kafka, 527, 530; and Kant, 530; Kaufmann's meeting with, 3, 122; and Moses, 529; mother's abandonment of, 530; and Nietzsche, 527, 530; and Paul, 528; on photography, 441; psychology of, 476; and sin and guilt, 365; theory of translation of, 528–29; translation of Hebrew Bible, 227, 429, 527, 528, 657n43; WORKS: *Die Frage an den Einzelnen*, 59; *I and Thou*, 3, 122, 227, 441, 527–31, 540, 561, 674n13; *Königtum Gottes*, 123; *The Tales of the Hasidim*, 227, 527, 528; *The Way of Man According to the Teachings of Hasidism*, 527
Buddha, 76, 108, 161, 172, 173, 200, 301, 379, 385; and compassion, 459; psychology in, 82; and Sartre, 71–72, 73
Buddhism, 108, 113–14, 124, 174, 409, 410, 437, 456, 458, 561; and Hinduism, 466; and Judaism, 379; and knowledge, 114; and medicine, 460; and Nietzsche, 335; and Sartre, 631n79. *See also* Zen
Bullitt, William C., *Thomas Woodrow Wilson*, 344
Bullock, Marcus, 53
Bultmann, Rudolf, 58, 79, 109–10, 113, 226; *Das Urchristentum*, 109
Bunam, Rabbi, 470
Burckhardt, Jakob, 37
Burke, Kenneth, *Language as Symbolic Action*, 429–30
Burma, 440
Buruma, Ian, 30, 31
Butcher, S. H., 291; *Aristotle's Theory of Poetry and Fine Art*, 665–66n13
Byron, Lord, 38, 148, 448; *Don Juan*, 447
Byron, William, 365–66

Calcutta, 460–61
Calderón de la Barca, Pedro, 327, 447
Caldwell, Erskine, 468
Calvin, John, 110, 129, 161, 200, 409
Calvinism, 89
Calvino, Italo, 294
Camus, Albert, 44, 54, 55–56, 158, 200, 227–29; and Arendt, 457; and Catholic Church, 228; and death, 184, 194; and Homer, 305; and Nietzsche, 62, 590; and religion, 228, 565; and Tolstoy, 199, 228; and Wouk, 205; WORKS: *The Myth of Sisyphus*, 56, 62; *The Plague*, 199, 228; "Reflections on the Guillotine," 226, 228, 655n5
Caravaggio, Michelangelo Merisi da, 436
Cardozo, Nathan Lopes, 203
Carlyle, Thomas, 523
Carus, Carl Gustav, 507
Cassirer, Ernst, 493, 523
Catholic Church, 212, 224, 228, 406, 516
Catholicism, 89, 143, 213–14, 365, 520, 523
Catholic Mass, 388
Cavell, Stanley, *The World Viewed*, 471
Celan, Paul, 448
Céline, Louis-Ferdinand, 432
Cerf, Walter, 56, 57–58, 628n46
Certeau, Michel de, 119, 640n45
Cervantes, Miguel de, *Don Quixote*, 445
Cézanne, Paul, 142
Charcot, Jean-Martin, 538
Cherniak, Samuel and John Heckman (translators), Jean Hyppolite, *Genesis and Structure of Hegel's "The Phenomenology of Spirit,"* 233, 276
Chernyshevsky, Nikolay Gavrilovich, 53, 54
Chicago School, 286
China/Chinese thought, 379, 410, 436, 466
Chituc, Vlad, 680n30
Christian Churches, 228, 657n45
Christianity, 16, 76–77, 82, 101, 107–13, 115–16, 124, 159, 397–411; and America, 180, 650n35, 651n36; and apocalyptic literature, 392, 397; and art, 452–54; belief in, 166;

and Buber, 528; celibacy in, 399; children of light and children of darkness in, 160; conception of pride in, 291; contemporary criticisms of, 165–66; conversion by, 384; cruelty of, 228, 406–7, 449; and death, 194; different churches in, 405–6; and dogmatism, 516; and Dostoevsky, 212–13; and ethics, 381; and evidence, 101–2; and existentialism, 326; faith in, 217; and finitude, 365; forgiveness in, 178; founding of, 397; and Goethe, 598; Golden Rule of, 173; and Greeks, 112–13, 178; guilt in, 365; heaven in, 280; and Hebrew Bible, 144, 281; and Hegel, x, 134, 242–43, 245, 255, 265, 270; and Heidegger, 518, 523–26; and Hellenistic philosophy, 112–13; and heresy, 164, 389, 405, 406, 408, 409, 453; and Hinduism, 461; and Islam, 379, 406, 679n38; and Israel, 397; and Judaism, 118, 160, 217, 223–24, 228, 281, 381, 383, 384, 392, 395, 397–98, 399–400, 403, 404, 409, 639n36, 657n45, 679n38; and Kant, 492; Kaufmann's rejection of, 2, 159, 160, 161; and Kierkegaard, 60, 147, 507, 508; love in, 107–8, 125, 131, 164, 360, 641n61; and Manichaeism, 398; and martyrdom, 405; and medicine, 460; mercy in, 360; and monasticism, 399; monks in, 405; and morality/ethics, 116–17, 164, 381; and Nazis, 223, 657n45; and Nietzsche, 27, 38–40, 165, 215–16, 598; and ordinary language philosophy, 83; particularism of, 650n32; and Paul, 111, 402–4; pride in, 291; reward in, 216–17; right action in, 121; ritual in, 164; and romanticism, 136; and Rome, 395, 397, 398, 400–401, 405; salvation and damnation in, 107–8, 164, 174, 177, 186, 194, 212, 387–88, 397, 398–99, 403, 408, 460, 471, 515; schisms in, 406; and Schopenhauer, 333; and self-realization, 109; sex and body in, 399; and Shakespeare, 317; sin in, 117, 217, 365; and slave morality, 515; and social ethic of compassion, 459; and social justice, 164, 165, 397; and Spinoza, 180; as

state religion, 395, 405; and Stendhal, 134; and suffering, 177, 280–81, 452–54, 460; and suffering in tragedy, 346; and theology, 652n42; and Tolstoy, 200, 212, 213; and torture, 453; and tragedy, 131, 132, 143, 278, 346; and tragic humanist worldview, 302; Trinity in, 160; and Zoroastrianism, 386, 387–88, 397, 401

Christian mosaics, 436

Christians, 80; and intolerance of Jews, 395; and Jews, 657n45; and Nietzsche, 579; and Septuagint, 395

Church, 209, 213

Churchill, Winston, 348

Church of Unification, 570, 693n23

Cicero, 316, 438–39, 471–72

Clark, Maudemarie, "Nietzsche's Doctrines of the Will to Power," 600–601

Clement IV, 409

Clifford, William Kingdon, 656–57n37; "The Ethics of Belief," 218–19

Clytemnestra, 323, 324, 341, 358, 473

Coen, Ethan, 5–6

Coetzee, John, Elizabeth Costello, 90

Cohen, Hermann, 493

Cohen, Morris Raphael, "The Dark Side of Religion," 209–10

Coke, van Deren, The Painter and the Photograph, 468

Cold War, 91

Cole, Andrew, 255; The Birth of Theory, 661n38

Coleridge, Samuel Taylor, 219, 635n42, 643n7

Colli, Giorgio, 430–31

Collins, James, 46

Columbus, Christopher, 225

comedy, 315, 336, 349–50, 446

Communism, 223

computational analysis, 356

Comte, August, 589

conformity, 183, 186; criticism of, 166; and existentialism, 267; and heresy, 165, 170, 186; to law, 360; and philosophy, 42, 166,

conformity (*continued*)
179, 183, 296; and Tolstoy, 222. *See also* conventions

Confucius, 161, 200, 379, 385, 434

Connelly, John, *From Enemy to Brother,* 657n45

Conrad, Joseph, *The Secret Agent,* 341

Constantine, 406, 409

Continental philosophy, 536–37

conventions, 171; and heresy, 179; independence of, 71, 90, 315; and truth, 100–101, 150. *See also* conformity

Copernicus, Nicolaus, 59, 489, 593

Corneille, Pierre, 327, 341, 447

Cornell University, 560

Coulter, Ann, 651n36

Council of Florence, 407

courage, 124, 280; of Camus, 199; and death, 187; and decisions, 353, 358; and great-souled man, 130; and philosophy, 179; and scholarship, 171, 174; in Shakespeare, 123, 131; and tragedy, 295; and violence, 377; virtue of, 167, 168, 211, 366, 374

Coyne, Jerry, 649n22; *Faith vs. Fact,* 225

Craig, Gordon A., 696n25

Crane, Ronald, 286

creativity/creation, 124, 184, 190, 193, 211, 375, 449; and Goethe, 484; and Kant, 484; mimesis as, 285; and reason, 376; and suffering, 12

Crébillon, Claude-Prosper Jolyot de, 87

Crews, Frederick, 540, 543, 548–51, 553, 556, 690n4, 691n26, 691n27

Critchley, Simon, 699–700n79

Critchley, Simon and Jamieson Webster: *Stay, Illusion! The Hamlet Doctrine,* 331

Crites, Stephen, 260–61

critical thinking, 86, 165–66, 171, 210, 515

Cromwell, Oliver, 384

Crowell, Stephen, 60

Crusades, 406–8, 409, 452–53, 454

culture, 2, 14, 23, 35, 103, 264, 319, 369; and death, 189, 196–97, 198; and history, 15; studies of, 356. *See also* German culture

Curtius, Ernst, *European Literature and the Latin Middle Ages,* 12

Cynics, 301

Cyrenaics, 301

Daesh (Islamic State), 341–42

Dante, 131, 487; and Aquinas, 325; *The Divine Comedy,* 248, 445; and Goethe, 141; and justice, 362; and knowledge, 427; *Paradiso,* 387; and retributive justice, 359

Danto, Arthur, 76, 126, 250, 420–21, 601–2, 605–8, 694n9, 701n91; *Nietzsche as Philosopher,* 572–78, 593, 694n1

Darius I, 385

Darwin, Charles, 26, 472, 513, 535, 574–75, 578, 582, 589, 607

Daube, David, 113

Daumier, Honoré, 468

Davies, John Gordon, 389

Davies, W. D., 113

Dawkins, Richard, 334

death, 1, 184–85, 193, 307; and beauty, 191, 197; and Camus, 194; and Christianity, 194; and cultural immortality, 189, 196–97, 198; with dignity, 197; and existentialism, 194, 195; fear of, 439; and Freud, 194; and Goethe, 192–93, 194, 306; and Goya, 456, 462; and Heidegger, 56, 194, 199, 439, 518, 520, 524; in Hölderlin, 189, 306; in Homer, 304, 305, 306, 307; and incest, 195; and Jews, 466; and justification, 189–90, 195, 197; and Kierkegaard, 518; as loss of intellectual freedom, 563; and love, 190–91; meaning of, 172; and meaning of life and human condition, 471; and Nietzsche, 193–94; and philosophy, 438–39; and poetry, 192, 193; and Sartre, 194; in Schiller, 306; and Tolstoy, 518; and work, 189

death work ethic, 187–98

decidophobia, 374, 491, 614n22; and allegiance to movements, 355, 356; defined, 353; and drifting, 355; and exegetical thinking, 356; and future riders, 358; and justice, 362; and Manichaeism, 356–57; and moral rationalism, 357; and pedantry, 358; and religion, 354–55; strategies for, 354–58

decisionism, 353, 491, 624n79, 626n5

Declaration of Independence, 382

deconstruction, 143, 155, 164, 244, 474, 674n12; and decidophobia, 356; and de Man, 92, 297, 419, 421, 422; and dialectical reading, 423; and Heidegger, 106, 525–26; and humanities, 569; and Jaspers, 66; and Manichaeism, 357; and Nietzsche, 568–69, 573; and philosophy, 293; and tragedy, 292. See also neostructuralism

Deledalle, Gérard, 101

Deleuze, Gilles, 551, 569, 605, 701n91

de Man, Paul, 233, 552, 663n52, 674n12; Blindness and Insight, 298; and death, 66; on error and mistake, 338; and Heidegger, 52, 628n38; on Hölderlin, 197; and irony, 65; and Nietzsche, 92–94, 419, 426, 569; and objective structure of literary work, 297; and reading, 419–20, 421–22; and religion, 8, 180, 615n35; and romanticism, 143–44

Dembowski, Métilde, 133

Derrida, Jacques, 106, 186, 233, 293, 421, 551, 569, 585–86, 605, 701n91

Descartes, René, 56, 59, 78–79, 427, 450

Dewey, John, 29, 421

Dhammapada, 161, 200, 412, 433, 456, 462

Dickens, Charles, 445

Dickinson, Emily, 448

Diderot, Denis, Rameau's Nephew, 250

Dilthey, Wilhelm, 156, 326, 590, 685n12

Diogenes Laertius, 245

Dionysus, 15–16, 151, 439

Dodds, E. R., 325; The Greeks and the Irrational, 170

Dominicans, 409

Donadio, Stephen, 663n52

Donatello, 436

Dornbach, Márton, Receptive Spirit, 622n59

Dostoevsky, Fyodor, 29, 44, 45, 445, 486; and existentialism, 54–56; freedom of choice in, 53; and Goethe, 138–39; Grand Inquisitor in, 210–11, 212, 213, 214, 414, 457; and Heidegger, 57; and Jaspers, 57; and Kafka, 54; and Kierkegaard, 57, 60; and Nietzsche, 33, 52–53, 54, 507; Underground Man in, 44, 53, 54–55, 60; as upsetting certainties, 154; and Wisdom, 225; WORKS: The Brothers Karamazov, 210, 211, 212–14, 220, 315, 414, 457; Notes from Underground, 1, 52–55, 57, 60, 61; The Possessed, 619n32

Dr. Strangelove (1964), 332

Dresden, 315

Driver, Tom, 692–93n10

Dubos, L'Abbé, 332

Durant, Will and Ariel, 188

Dyson, Freeman, 164

Eagleton, Terry, 249, 279, 306, 310, 342, 664n2, 685–86n16

Eckermann, Johann Peter, 685n14

Edwards, Paul, 525

Egypt, ancient, 122, 171, 172, 175–77, 381, 404, 450–51, 466, 546

Eichmann, Adolf, 359, 414

Einstein, Albert, 396, 412, 614n25

Eisenhower, Dwight D., 171, 584

Elea, school of, 465

Eliot, George, 445; Middlemarch, viii

Eliot, T. S., 132, 146, 297, 432, 448, 645n42, 655n6; After Strange Gods, 162; and Dante, 131; and experienced emotion in poetry, 155; and Goethe, 146, 156; and Joyce, 138; and Shakespeare, 123, 129, 131, 135

Ellenberger, Henri F., The Discovery of the Unconscious, 506, 507, 551

Else, Gerald, 284–85, 286

Emden, Christian, Friedrich Nietzsche and the Politics of History, 591

Emerson, Ralph Waldo, 588

emotion(s): in Aristotle, 283–84, 287–90, 310; as complexes of thoughts, 97; and

emotion (*continued*)
　great-souled man, 136; life full of intense, 192; and poetry, 154–55, 448; and reason, 135; and romanticism, 136; and thought, 61; truth in, 97

Empson, William, 422

Encyclopedia Britannica, 472

Encyclopedia of Philosophy, 507

Encyclopedia of Religion and Ethics, 472

Enlightenment, 134, 136, 173, 245, 268, 625n94

Enslin, Morton Scott, 221, 222, 223

Epicureans, 301

Epicurus, 472

equality/egalitarianism, 45, 352, 372, 471, 566

Erhard, Werner, 511–12, 556, 561. See also *est* (Werner Erhard's Seminars Training)

Eros and Thanatos, 449

est (Werner Erhard's Seminars Training), 511–12, 516, 546, 554, 556, 561, 569–70, 688n10

Euripides, 235, 300, 349, 473; and Aeschylus, 323, 324; and Aristotle, 308; beauty in, 316; and Brecht, 349; Dodds on, 325; and humanism, 322; moral collision in, 318–19; and Nietzsche, 307, 308, 314, 322, 324; and nobility, 341; and optimism, 322, 324; and Plato, 322; and Platonic dialogue, 314; responsibility in, 324; ruth and terror in, 341; and Sartre, 323, 324; skepticism of, 315; and Socrates, 322, 325; and Sophists, 322; and Sophocles, 322–23, 324–25, 569; and suffering, 294, 297; and tragedy, 342; WORKS: *Alcestis,* 315; *The Bacchae,* 316, 317, 334; *Electra,* 322–25; *Hippolytus,* 282, 317, 473; *Ion,* 315; *Iphigenia in Aulis,* 294; *Iphigenia in Taurus,* 334; *Medea,* 282, 328, 473; *The Trojan Women,* 294, 345, 447

Europe, 36, 44, 45, 265, 585, 604

evil, 378; and Arendt, 414; and Aristotle on tragedy, 283; and Christianity, 109, 165; and Dostoevsky, 53; and Gnosticism, 389–90; and Goethe, 146; and Hegel, 249; and Hegel on tragedy, 316, 317; and Hitler, 696n19; and Job, 220; and Judaism, 391, 392, 650n32; and Kafka, 91, 114; and McTaggart, 225–26; and Nietzsche, 378, 387, 580, 583, 585; and Plato on tragedy, 281, 282; and Romanesque architecture, 454; and Royce, 220; and Shakespeare, 317, 362; and Tolstoy, 209; and Zarathustra, 386, 387–88, 391; and Zoroastrianism, 392. *See also* morality/ethics

exegesis, 174, 234, 284, 419, 420

exegetical thinking, 356, 520

existentialism, 6, 43–74, 128, 200, 269, 278, 536, 564, 615n37, 674n13; and analysis, 85, 86; and analytic philosophy, 73–74, 79, 86; and anti-system sensibility, 60; and Arendt, 457; and art, 56; and authenticity, 44; and Buddhism, 72; and Bultmann, 110; and Camus, 227; characteristics of, 44, 73; and Christianity, 326; and conformity, 267; and death, 194, 195; and Dostoevsky, 54–55, 56; and essence and deeds, 505; and Euripides, 323–24; and exegetical thinking, 356; and experience, 439, 537; family resemblances in, 57; and godlessness, 44; and Goethe, 560; and Hegel, 265; and Heidegger, 69, 323, 526, 568; and individualism, 44; and Jaspers, 323, 568; and Kant, 560; and Kaufmann's photography, 462; and Kierkegaard, 57–60; Lacan on, 331; and literature, 55–56; and negation, 44, 58, 60; and Nietzsche, 39, 59, 62–64, 572; and nothingness, 44; and Ortega y Gasset, 82; and phenomenology, 560; and philosophy, 44, 55–56, 60; political, 457–58; and Protestantism, 110; as radical subjectivity, 60; and reason, 60; and religion, 57–58, 79–80, 380; and responsibility, 326; and Rilke, 82; and Sartre, 69, 149–50, 317, 318, 323, 326, 560, 568; and science, 57, 60; and Shakespeare, 129; and sin and guilt, 365; and systematic thinking, 44; and

Thomism, 110; and Tillich, 110; and times of transition, 237; and tragedy, 130, 314

experience: and art, 298, 449, 455, 462, 478, 645–46n55; and existentialism, 439, 537; extreme, 439; and language, 98; of limits, 438–39, 440, 441, 442, 444; literary works as records of, 156; lived, 196; and memory, 98; and music, 439, 444; and mysticism (*see* mysticism); naming of nonobjective, 97; in Nietzsche, 71, 93–94, 511; and poet, 298; and poetry, 154–56; and reading, 427; and religion, 4, 379–80, 381; in Sartre, 71; of thought, 71, 81; and tragedy, 323; and words, 98; and writing, 196

Fagles, Robert, 320

faith/belief, 655n9; and agnostics, 169; and assent of every reasonable person, 80; and Clifford, 219; common, 98; and critical thinking, 165–66; criticism of, 94; and defective knowledge, 75; defense of, 180–81; and established religion, 163, 167; and evidence, 101–3, 168; examination of, viii; and good works, 647n5; and Hegel, 242, 648n16; of heretic, 163, 166–67, 179, 185; of heretic vs. true believer, 168; justification and, 225; Kierkegaard on, 57; Knausgård on, 649n23; and knowledge, 80; and Luther, 409; of modern American Christianity, 165; motivations for, 103–4; need for as weakness, 161; and Nietzsche, 161, 179, 652n37; and philosophy, 165; psychophysiological criticism of, 94; and reason, 168; and religion, 8, 80; secular, 166; and suffering, 172, 178; suspicion of, 90–91; and Wittgenstein, 89–90. *See also* God; religion

Fassin, Didier, 688n16

Faulkner, William, 328

Ferenczi, Sandor, 545

Fergusson, Francis, 299, 565–66, 665–66n13, 668n35

Fest, Joachim, 31

Fest, Johannes, 31

Feuerbach, Anselm, 188

Fichte, J. G., 34, 135, 232, 248, 254, 420, 487, 488, 489

Findlay, J. N., 261–62, 263–64, 271, 658n4, 662n46; *Hegel*, 230–31

Fish, Stanley, 416–17

Flaubert, Gustave, 70, 445, 486

Flew, Antony, 225

Forster, Bernhard, 673n8

Forster, Georg, 696n25

Forster, Michael, 660–61n36

Förster-Nietzsche, Elisabeth, 15

Foucault, Michel, 233, 421, 551, 569, 605, 701n91; *Surveiller et punir,* 359

France, 238, 341

Francis, St., 161, 200, 409

Franciscans, 409

Frank, Joseph, 1, 53–55, 61, 84, 212, 213; *Dostoevsky: The Years of Ordeal, 1850–1859,* 619n32

Frank, Manfred, 551

Frankfurt school, 368–69

Frederick II, 38

Freedgood, Anne, 649n20

freedom, 4, 63; academic, 67, 416, 526; and alienation, 370; and Arendt, 457; and Benjamin, 111; and decidophobia, 353; and Declaration of Independence, 282; and Dostoevsky, 54, 210, 211, 212; and existentialism, 60; of great individuals, 601; and happiness, 374–75; Hegel on, 249, 251, 264–65, 266–69; and Heidegger, 67, 526; and Kafka, 149, 645–46n55; and Kant, 237, 491, 495; and Kierkegaard, 58, 60, 508; in Lacan, 331; at Masada, 394; of mind, 418, 563, 564, 566; and Nietzsche, 22, 36, 41, 71, 620–21n48, 640–41n52; of pure music, 443; and Schiller, 239

French Muslims, 341

French Revolution, 236, 238, 605

French theory, 421, 422, 517, 520, 560–61, 568–69. *See also* literary theory; Parisian theory

Freud, Sigmund, xi, 82, 94, 99, 123, 172, 183, 287, 293, 355; and Adler, 552–53, 554; and aggression, 538; and Akhenaten, 650n31; and alienation, 373; and ambivalence, 207, 208; and anti-Semitism, 373; on anxiety, 508; and art, 533, 546–47, 558; as artist-psychologist, 486; and authenticity, 525; autobiography of, 373; and autonomy, 479, 539; and biographers of, 535; and Buber, 530, 540; and castration complex, 549; and character development, 542; character of, 2, 533, 547–48, 554; and childhood, 542; and child sexuality, 543; and Copernicus, 489; and creativity and libido, 558; and Darwin, 535; and death, 194; and dialectical reader, 426; and discovery of mind, 532–51; and dogmatism, 552; and dreams, 104, 545, 546, 548–49; and ego, 555; and empiricism, 532, 533; on fear vs. dread, 524; and free association, 545, 550; and Goethe, 479, 534, 535, 537, 538, 539, 542, 560; and great-souled man, 130; and guilt, 547; and Hegel, 258, 275, 502, 540; and Heidegger, 524, 540; and Hölderlin, 552; honesty of, 533, 540, 548, 554; and human nature, 539; and hysteria, 538; and interpretation of dreams, 543; as intuitive researcher, 690n3; and irrational science, 533; and Jaspers, 555–56; and jokes, 546; and Jung, 540, 554, 556–59; and Kafka, 541; Kaufmann's lack of belief in, 560–61; and Kierkegaard, 507; and Kraus, 553; and libido, 554; and literature, 509, 546–47, 558; and Marx, 538–39; and materialism, 532, 537; and medical profession, 537, 538; and mental illness, 544–45; and Michelangelo, 546–47; and Moses, 546–47; and music, 558; and negative evidence, 540; and neurosis, 548, 549; and Nietzsche, 18, 167, 506, 507, 510, 534, 537, 538, 539, 542, 544, 547, 554–55, 558; and nuances, 426; and Oedipus complex, 533, 542, 548, 549, 550; and pansexualism, 557; as paradigmatic individual, 476, 547; and parapraxes, 534–35; and philosophy, 533, 534, 536, 547; and pleasure principle, 507; and poetic science, 534, 535, 540, 541, 542, 550, 552; prose of, 534, 535; and psychic determinism, 549; and psychoanalysis, 535, 537–38, 539, 540, 545–46, 549, 552; psychology of, 476; and religion, 103, 104, 533, 546–47; and repression, 549; on resistance to forbidden impulse, 512; and Sartre, 540, 544; and Schopenhauer, 508–9; and science, 83, 534, 547, 548–49; and seduction by parents, 533; and self-deception, 540, 616n8; and sexuality, 533, 542–43, 547, 552; and socialism, 539; and Sophocles, 303; and Soviet Marxism, 538; and sublimation, 558; and substitutive gratification, 547; and talking cure, 545–46; and transference, 545; and unconscious, 537–38, 544, 548, 550, 552; in Vienna, 534; and Wilson, 344; and Wisdom, 225; and wish fulfillment, 543; and women, 533; WORKS: "A Childhood Memory of Leonardo," 546; *Civilization and Its Discontents*, 103, 538; "Dostoyevsky and Parricide," 546; *The Future of an Illusion*, 104, 220–21, 302, 546; *General Introduction to Psychoanalysis*, 524; *History of the Psychoanalytical Movement*, 554; *The Interpretation of Dreams*, 83, 299–300, 535, 542; *Introductory Lectures on Psychoanalysis*, 533; *Moses and Monotheism*, 176, 546; "The Moses of Michelangelo," 546; *The Psychopathology of Everyday Life*, 510, 543–44

Frick, Werner, 659n14

Fromm, Erich, 121, 368, 373

Frye, Northrop, 145, 644n35, 644–45n36

Fulton, Ann, *Apostles of Sartre*, 629n47

Fussell, Paul, 202

Gadamer, Hans-Georg, 518; "Martin Heidegger and Marburg Theology," 615n35; *Truth and Method*, 522

Gandhi, Mahatma, 269

Garrard, Graeme, "Nietzsche for and against the Enlightenment," 623n75

Gassier, Pierre and Juliet Wilson, *Life and Complete Work of Francisco Goya,* 455, 456

Gay, Peter, 44–45, 548, 564, 604

Gebauer, Gunter, 285

Geertz, Clifford, 439

Gentile, Giovanni, 211

George, Stefan, 15, 371; circle of, 38

German culture, 33, 34, 387, 524; and Bildung, 32; and intellectual tradition, 14; and Nietzsche, 603; and pietism, 435; and self-cultivation, 30. *See also* Bildung; culture

German romanticism, 33, 144, 151, 193, 235–36, 520, 523

Germans, 361, 386–87; and Goldhagen thesis, 367; and Hitler, 514

Germany, 265, 406, 605; and France, 238; and Mann, 34

Geroulanos, Stefanos, *An Atheism That Is Not Humanist Emerges in French Thought,* 81

Gerstein, Kurt, 614n22

Gewarth, Robert, 361

Ghiberti, Lorenzo, 436–37

Gibbon, Edward, 375

Gide, André, 590, 617n23; *The Counterfeiters,* 78

Gilbert, Martin, 202

Gilgamesh, 423

Gilliam, Terry, 332

Gilson, Étienne, 104, 146, 214, 616n12

Gladwell, Malcolm, 515

Gnosticism, 117, 178, 389–91, 399, 677n19

God, 2, 111, 124, 168–69, 185; ambiguous statements about, 106, 107; as being-in-itself, 107; and Buber, 527–28; in Christianity, 107–13; death of, 364, 518; and evidence and reason, 162, 169; existence of, 100, 105, 106, 169; and Hebrew prophets, 649–50n24; Hegel on, 240–41, 255, 266, 270–71; and Heidegger, 519; in Judaism, 115; Judaism without, 178; and Kant, 488, 489; kingdom of, 226–27; as love, 124–25; man and woman as created in image of, 108, 176; and Moses, 122–23; name of, 97–98; and Nietzsche, 151, 518, 575–76, 592, 619n32; and Old Testament, 381, 382; ontological proof of existence of, 100, 105; perfection of, 105; and religion, 101; and Rilke, 151; and Shakespeare, 129; as sole ruler, 384; and Spinoza, 180; as Thou or You, 382; Tillich on, 106–7; and Tolstoy, 222; and truth, 96. *See also* faith/belief

Goebbels, Joseph, 205

Goethe, Johann Wolfgang von, 20, 31, 43, 157, 183, 189, 209, 232, 288, 375, 412, 445, 447; and academic philosophy, 536; and Anschauung, 485; anti-Catholicism of, 141; and art, 478; and aspiration, 132, 139; autonomy of, 478–79, 483, 502; beauty in, 504; and Bible, 111; and Bildung, 35; and Burckhardt, 37; as cabinet minister, 477; on character, 481; character of, 2, 479–80; and Christianity, 598; and classic vs. romantic visions, 235–36; and commerce, 484–85, 486; contemporary knowledge of, 174; contributions of, 479–80; and creativity, 484; and Dante, 141; and death, 192–93, 194, 306; and decisions, 358; and discovery of mind, 484, 485, 503, 505; and Dostoevsky, 138–39; and Eliot, 146, 156; on essence vs. deeds, 481, 505; and existentialism, 560; experimentation by, 481; and Fichte, 487; and Freud, 479, 534, 535, 537, 538, 539, 542, 560; and great-souled man, 130; and Greeks and Romans, 144; and Hebrew Bible, 144, 145–46, 147; and Hegel, 234, 235, 248–49, 279, 325, 326, 331, 486–87, 498, 499, 500, 501–2, 503, 505, 536; and Herder, 487, 488; and history, 484; and Hölderlin, 142–43; and human development, 473–74, 481–82, 484, 487; influences on, 487–88; and Judaism, 145–46; and Kafka, 208; and Kant, 90, 326, 477–78, 479, 482,

Goethe, Johann Wolfgang von (*continued*)
483, 484, 485, 487, 488, 489, 495, 496,
497, 503–4, 516; and Kierkegaard, 504;
and knowledge, 427; and Lessing, 487;
logic of passion in, 134–35; and Mann,
34; and materialism, 686n18; measure in,
132; and metamorphosis, 516; on mind,
481–82; mind of, 477–88; misinterpreta-
tion of, 156; and nature of man, 470; and
Newton, 483, 484, 485, 503, 686n18; and
Nietzsche, 21, 24, 36, 37, 38, 40, 132, 141,
142, 152, 371, 376, 472, 477, 479, 503–4, 516,
573, 578, 588, 589, 598, 599–600, 625n88;
and Orcus-motif, 319; paganism of, 144;
as paradigmatic individual, 473–74, 476;
and passion, 38, 139, 141; and philosophy, 486–87; and poetic science, 485,
486, 550; poetics of, 305; and poetry,
485; poetry of, 482; powers of renewal
of, 482; presence of in work, 129; and
present moment, 142, 152; psychology
of, 297, 476; and reflective wit, 141; as
role model, 40–41; and romanticism,
136, 143, 146; and Schelling, 143, 325;
and Schiller, 487, 488; and Schlegel,
484; and Schopenhauer, 325, 334, 487,
504; and science, 474, 483, 484–85, 538,
686n18; and Shakespeare, 129, 137–38,
139, 143; and Socrates, 479; and Stendhal,
132; suffering in, 313; and suicide, 473,
486; and tragedy, 146; tutelary role of,
37; unity of art of, 140–41; as upsetting
certainties, 154; and world literature,
685n14; and writing about self, 482;
and writing standards, 483; WORKS:
Doctrine of Colors, 481, 483, 484; *Faust*, 7,
111, 112, 137–38, 139–41, 145–46, 159, 241,
248–49, 277, 313, 346, 371–72, 481, 482,
498, 500, 565, 659n11; *Faust, a Tragedy*,
482; *Faust—a Fragment*, 235; *Faust I*,
140–41, 208; *Faust II*, 23, 140–41, 381, 487,
682n7; "Immortality," 188; *Iphigenia in
Tauris*, 131, 235, 237, 242, 278–79, 334, 498;
From My Life: Poetry and Truth (*Dichtung
und Wahrheit*), 141, 481–82, 483; "Nature,"
534, 537; "Prometheus," 381; *The Sufferings of Young Werther*, 38, 192, 381, 473,
486, 685–86n16; *West-Eastern Divan*, 482;
Wilhelm Meisters Lehrjahre, 133, 139–40,
326, 481, 484–85; *Xenien*, 188

Goldhagen, Daniel, 343

Goldhagen thesis, 367

Goldstein, Rebecca, 8, 180

Golomb, Jacob and Robert S. Wistrich,
Nietzsche—Godfather of Fascism?, 205

Gorz, André, 333

Gottfried, Paul, 655n8

Goya, Francisco, 463, 468; album "C"
drawings of, 457; *The Disasters of War*,
454; "The Dog," 455–56, 462; "Duel with
Cudgels, 454–56

Graf-Wellhausen hypothesis (Documentary
Theory), 203–4

Gray, J. Glenn, 519

Grayling, A. C., 279–80, 665n5

great-souled man, 130, 131, 136–37

Greek philosophy, 77, 118

Greeks, ancient, 59, 81, 237; and Africa and
Asia, 465; and Bible, 473; Christianity,
178; and Goethe, 144; and good vs. bad,
286; and Hegel, 243, 330; and history,
466; and Jews, 467; and morality, 286;
and Nietzsche, 503; paintings of, 451;
and religion, 507; and Schiller, 238–39;
sculpture of, 451. *See also* tragedy

Gregory IX, 408, 409

Greif, Mark, 435, 441, 626n9, 681n42; *The
Age of the Crisis of Man*, 470

Grünewald, Matthias, Isenheim altarpiece,
201, 333

Gryphius, Andreas, 327

Guardi, Francesco Lazzaro, 436

guilt, 207, 352, 377, 566; and atonement, 365;
and change, 366; in Christianity, 365; and
Freud, 547; and humbition, 365–66, 367;
and Judaism, 365; and justice, 363–65; in
Kierkegaard, 507–8; and morality/ethics,
365; and moral vs. technical failure,

366–67; as mutilating personality, 365, 366; in Sartre, 73; in Shakespeare, 73; and tragedy, 187, 312, 317–18

Gutmann, James, 633n18

Habermas, Jürgen, 551
Hadas, Moses, 6
Haeckel, Ernst, 535
Haering, Theodor, 232
Hägglund, Martin, 293
Hall, Mark David, 650n35
Hallmann, Johann Christian, 327
Hall of a Thousand Pillars (Srirangam), 459
Hamann, Johann Georg, 151
Hamlin, Cyrus, "Reading Faust," 140
Hammurabi, 450
Hammurabi, Code of, 176, 364, 381–82, 391
Hampshire, Stuart, 535, 536, 690n5
Handel, Georg Friedrich: "Hallelujah Chorus," 444; *Messiah,* 392
Hare, Richard, 225
Harper's Magazine, 162, 415, 692n9
Härtle, Heinrich, 13
Hartman, Geoffrey, 552
Hatfield, Henry, 57
Haugwitz, August Adolf von, 327
Hawkins, Denis J. B., 162
Hay, Malcolm, 228; *Europe and the Jews,* 223–24
Haym, Rudolf, 246, 247, 248, 250, 498
Hebel, J. P., 70
Hefner, Hugh, 588
Hegel, G. W. F., ix, 43, 65, 70, 84, 103, 126, 132, 143, 147, 204, 230–77, 292, 341, 426, 468, 620n40; absolute spirit in, 246, 248, 264; on actual, 266; and Aeschylus, 316; as afraid of own mind, 487; and alienation, 373; as another Odysseus, 259; on Antigone, 473; antinomies in, 259; and Aristotle, 249, 315, 501; art in, 246, 263, 264, 270; as artist-psychologist, 486; and *aufheben,* 258, 618–19n31; and *Aufhebung,* 243, 244, 276; and autonomy, 502; and beauty, 248; *Begriff* and *begreifen* in, 252;

being and non-being in, 259; being and nothing in, 256; being in, 261, 519; and brother-sister love, 498; categories in, 256–57, 259, 260, 271; change in thought of, 540; and Christianity, x, 108, 134, 165, 242–43, 245, 255, 265, 270; and civil disobedience, 269; consciousness in, 250, 260–61, 263, 277, 499; and contingencies, 500–501; criticism of, 175; culture in, 264; and Dante, 248; and development of mind, 502; dialectic in, 253–54, 255, 256, 621n52, 660–61n36; and discovery of mind, 497–502, 503, 505; and dreams, 244; editing of, 431–32; elaborate punning of in German, 274; and empiricism, 244, 257; on English playwrights, 330; and Enlightenment rights, 268; and essence and deeds, 502, 505; and existentialism, 265; and faith, 242, 648n16; family experience of, 498; and *Faust,* 659n11; Faustian quality of, 498; and Fichte, 248; finite and infinite in, 256; on freedom, 251, 264–65, 266–69; and Freud, 258, 275, 502, 540; and *Geist,* 239; and German romanticism, 235–36; on God, 240–41, 255, 266, 270–71; and Goethe, 234, 235, 248–49, 279, 325, 326, 331, 486–87, 498, 499, 500, 501–2, 503, 505, 536; and great literature, 248–51; and great-souled man, 130; on Greeks, 243; on happiness, 266; and Heidegger, 261; and Herder, 275, 487–88; and hermeneutic theory, 256; on historical development of oppositions, 243; history in, 237–38, 254, 261, 264, 266, 271, 273, 495, 499; and history of philosophy, 264, 271, 277; and Hölderlin, 236, 270, 325, 379, 500, 660n34; and humanism, 242, 270, 271; and Idea, 271; on immanence of spirit, 245; and individual, 622n59; on individual, 268; on individual identity, 265; infinite and eternal in, 245; infinite in, 239, 240, 241; intellectual development of, 642n2; Jesus in, 242, 498; jokiness of, 87, 88; joy of, 258;

Hegel, G. W. F. (*continued*)
on Judaism, 270; and Kafka, 267, 271; and
Kant, 89, 236–37, 242, 245, 248, 255, 275,
489, 497, 498–99, 500, 501, 503, 505, 536;
and Kierkegaard, 59, 273; and knowledge,
499; knowledge of, 450; language in,
256, 257–58; late modernity of, 258; and
literary art, 247; logic of passion of,
134–35, 236; and Marx, 254; and Marxism,
272–73; and master-slave relation, 234,
251; and mathematical certainty, 502; and
Mendelssohn, 275; metaphysics in, 256,
261; mind of, 478; and morality/ethics,
237, 245–46, 263, 269, 498; on nature, 264;
and nature of man, 470; and Newton,
502; and Nietzsche, 29, 33, 88, 233, 255, 265,
273, 589; objective spirit in, 246; and passionate error, 134; personal life of, 246–47,
255, 262; *Phänomenologie* as term in, 253;
on philosophical history, 264–65; philosophical science in, 263; on philosophy,
243, 246, 264, 270, 271–72, 276–77; on
philosophy and common sense, 244; and
philosophy of history, 243, 264; and Plato,
501; and poetry, 325; and pre-Socratics,
272; psychology of, 94, 476; and rationality of tradition, 134; reason in, 134,
242, 243, 245, 261, 495; religion in, 242,
246, 263, 264, 270, 379, 498; reputation
of, 232–33; rhetorical powers of, 258–59;
and rhetoric of history vs. rhetoric of
psychology, 498; on Right, 264; on rights,
643n13; and Sartre, 253, 265, 273; *Schein* in,
253; and Schelling, 248, 275, 660–61n36;
and Schiller, 234, 235, 239, 240, 245, 249,
251, 331, 500; and Friedrich Schlegel, 248;
and Schopenhauer, 275; and science,
244, 247–48, 252, 253, 254, 257, 259, 263,
276, 478, 499, 500, 502; and science of
consciousness, 498; self-concealment by,
500–501; self-consciousness in, 251–52;
self-knowledge of, 471; sentences in,
252; on Sermon on the Mount, 242; and
Shakespeare, 249, 252, 328, 330–32; and

Sittlichkeit, 242, 263, 267, 269, 279; and
Sittlichkeit and *Moralität,* 237, 245, 246;
and skepticism, 234, 244, 251, 252, 257;
Socrates in, 242; and Sophocles, 249, 316;
on stages of mind, 502; on stages of soul,
499; state in, 229, 237, 246, 264, 266–67,
268–69; and stoicism, 234, 251, 252; style
of, 247–48, 255; on subjective spirit, 264;
on suffering, 265, 317–18, 478; systematic thinking of, 502; system in, 260–61;
system of, 263; terminology of, 252–53,
275–76; and tragedy, 187, 269, 311, 315,
316–17, 319, 330–32, 337, 338; transitions
in, 250–51, 262, 264; and truth, 660n34;
and unhappy consciousness, 234; and
virtue, 242; Wilson on, 414–15; on world-
historical individual, 265; and world
spirit, 237, 243, 271, 275; WORKS: *Aesthetics,* 317, 325; "Difference of the Fichtean
and Schellingian System of Philosophy,"
243, 244, 478; *1820,* 266; *Encyclopedia,*
262–64; "Faith and Knowledge," 235, 245;
Logic, 254, 255–64, 256, 271, 272; *Logic*
(1812 edition), 661–62n41; *The Phenomenology of Spirit,* 88, 94, 134, 233, 234, 236,
238, 239, 240, 244, 246–55, 252, 256, 257,
258, 259, 260, 263, 274–77, 325, 422, 478,
498, 499–500, 501, 502, 622n59, 660n34;
Philosophy of History, 236; *Philosophy of
Right,* 264, 317–18; *Science of Logic,* 240;
"The Spirit of Christianity and Its Fate,"
242, 648n16
Heidegger, Martin, 44, 46, 50–52, 56, 84,
122, 130, 155, 158, 233, 234, 568, 626n5; and
Adorno, 531; as afraid of own mind, 487;
on anxiety and atheistic resoluteness,
508; and Arendt, 457; and Aristotle, 520,
523; and Augustine, 523; on authenticity and inauthenticity, 521–22, 525; on
authentic or inauthentic Dasein, 519;
authoritarianism of, 129, 519–21, 526; *Befindlichkeit* in, 97; on Being, 261, 519, 521;
and Benjamin, 531; change in thought of,
540–41; and Christianity, 518, 523–26; as

comic figure, 449; cover-up by, 522–23; criticism of, 175; on Dasein, 519; *das Man* in, 68–69; and death, 56, 184, 194, 199, 439, 518, 520, 524; and discovery of mind, 503, 504, 505, 517–27; dogmatism of, 519–21; and Dostoevsky, 57; on dread and fear, 523–24; essentialism of, 519, 520; and etymology, 522; and exegesis, 174, 356, 419, 420; and existentialism, 69, 323, 526; existentialism renounced by, 568; and *existenzial* and *existenziell*, 521; and "Four-fold" *(Das Geviert)*, 646n59; and Freud, 524, 540; *Gelassenheit* in, 67; and *Gerede,* 521; and German culture, 524; and German language, 258, 661n40; and German romantic revival, 523; and *Geschreibe,* 521; and God, 519; god term in, 106; Graecophilia of, 77; and guilt, 365; and Hegel, 261; on hermeneutical violence, 520–21; and history of Being, 68; and Hitler, 68; and Hölderlin, 50, 51–52, 520; on human Being, 521; and humanities, 480–81; and Husserl, 520; inauthenticity in, 68–69, 508, 687n9; and Jaspers, 64, 66–68; and Kant, 46, 520, 521, 537; Kaufmann's abhorrence of, 129; Kaufmann's letters to, 564; Kaufmann's relationship with, 518, 526–27; and Kierkegaard, 507, 508, 518, 521–22, 523–24, 687n9; lack of self-awareness of, 540–41; language in, 69–70; and Luther, 523; and Manichaeism, 357; and morality/ethics, 357, 521; and Nazis, 77, 357, 519, 522, 525–26, 540; and Nietzsche, 46, 62, 67–68, 505, 513, 518, 520, 524–25, 560, 629–30n61; ontology of, 106, 107, 272, 520; and original sin, 523; and phenomenology, 520, 525; and Plato, 524–25; and pre-Socratics, 523, 524–25; and psychology, 82, 476; and reason, 520; and religion, 379; and representation, 69–70; and Sartre, 69; and science, 520; and self-deception, 508, 531; as theologian, 518; and Tillich, 107; and Tolstoy, 518;

and *venia legendi,* 67; "Vorgriff" in, 256; and will to power, 513; WORKS: *Being and Time,* 44, 64, 66, 68–69, 73, 81, 82, 110, 272, 337, 508, 517–27, 533, 540, 541, 553, 562, 674n13; *Black Notebooks,* 106, 129; *Fundamental Concepts of Metaphysics,* 183; *Holzwege,* 540; "Letter 'On Humanism,'" 69; letter to Karl Löwith, 518; "My Way to Phenomenology," 70; rector's address to students of Freiburg University, 526; *What Is Metaphysics?,* 541

Heine, Heinrich, 31, 523, 696n25

Heinse, Wilhelm, *Ardinghello,* 151

hell, 107–8, 110, 115, 125, 174

Heller, Erich, 44–45, 150, 154, 552, 553, 564, 579, 695n15; *The Disinherited Mind,* 645n42

Hellerich, Siegmar, *Religionizing, Romanizing Romantics,* 143

Henne, Paul, 680n30

Heraclitus, 29, 174, 179, 234, 358, 472, 659n13

Herder, Johann Gottfried von, 151, 275, 487–88

heresy, 160, 163, 166–67, 168, 223; and Christianity, 164; and critical thinking, 165; definition of, 163–64; in Dostoevsky, 211; and Hebrew prophets, 185; and Milton, 219; and non-conformity, 186; and philosophy, 179–80; Scott on, 163; and theologians, 171; and Tolstoy, 222. *See also* faith/belief

hermeneutic circle, 481, 685n12

Herz, Marcus, 492, 493

Herzl, Theodor, 396

Hesiod, 281, 284, 659n13

Hesse, Hermann, 2, 355, 525, 564, 590, 617n23

Heydrich, Reinhold, 361

Hillel, Rabbi, 110, 393–94, 400, 493

Himmler, Heinrich, 620n37

Hinderer, Walter, 659n14

Hinduism, 108, 174, 410, 458, 459, 465–66; and Buddhism, 466; and Christianity, 461; and Hebrew prophets, 460;

Hinduism (*continued*)
and Judaism, 459, 460; and Nietzsche, 683n29; profundity of, 461; spirituality in, 460; temples and idols in, 466; time and history in, 466

Hiroshima, 315

history: and ancient Greeks, 466; in Aristotle, 286, 287; and art, 296; caprice as factor in, 358; cultural, 15; and distributive justice, 359–60; and Goethe, 484; and Hegel, 237–38, 254, 261, 264–65, 266, 271, 273, 277, 495, 499; and Heidegger, 68; and Kant, 494–95; and Kaufmann's *Nietzsche*, 15; and Marx, 495; and Nietzsche, 25; philosophy of, 264; and reading, 425–26; and religion, 380

Hitchens, Christopher, 102, 679n2

Hitler, Adolf, 21–22, 68, 109, 175, 211–12, 223, 359, 408, 514, 696n19

Hobbes, Thomas, 427, 450, 643n13

Hochhuth, Rolf, 308, 672–73n39; *The Deputy, A Christian Tragedy*, 327–28, 343–48, 614n22, 644n29, 671n26, 672n33, 693n15; Kaufmann's letters to, 564; *Soldiers: Necrologue for Geneva; A Tragedy*, 348

Hofmannsthal, Hugo von, 371, 534; "Der Dichter und diese Zeit," 544

Hölderlin, Friedrich, 13, 45, 144, 192, 696n25; beauty in, 236; death in, 189, 306; de Man on, 197; and Empedokles, 500–501; and Freud, 552; and Goethe, 142–43; and Hegel, 236, 270, 325, 379, 500, 660n34; and Heidegger, 46, 50, 51–52, 70, 174, 234, 356; and Orcus-motif, 319; and truth, 660n34; tutelary role of, 37; WORKS: "Andenken," 50; "Bread and Wine," 151; *Dichterberuf* ("The Poet's Vocation"), 379; "How When on a Holiday," 520; *Hyperion*, 81, 236, 624–25n85; "The Ister," 379; "The Rhine," 270–71; "To the Parcae," 189, 190, 198, 306, 460, 552; translation of Sophocles's *Oedipus Tyrannus*, 318; "Wie Wenn am Feiertage" (As when on a holiday), 51–52

Hollinger, David A., 656–57n37

Holmes, Oliver Wendell, Jr., 182

Holocaust, 185, 193, 201, 202, 224, 310, 315, 332, 343–44, 345–46, 361

Holub, Robert C., *Nietzsche's Jewish Problem*, 617n21

Homer, 281, 282, 283, 301, 450, 471, 473, 659n13; and Aeschylus, 308–9, 310, 313, 317, 322; beauty in, 305; and Camus, 305; continuum of personality in, 306; death in, 304, 305, 306, 307; humanity of, 304; *Iliad*, 284, 301, 304–7, 308–9, 317, 319, 356–57, 359–60, 446, 447; and irrationality, 305–6, 314; life portrayed by, 305; *Odyssey*, 284, 309, 323, 665n10; and Sartre, 305, 314; and Sophocles, 319; suffering in, 304; and tragedy, 304–7, 310, 317

honesty, 167, 168, 174, 211, 280, 404; decision authorized by, 353; and Hay, 224; in inquiry, 374; quest for, 172, 182; in Sophocles, 300, 301, 317; and violence, 377; virtue of, 123, 366, 374

Hook, Sidney, 339, 649n20; "In Defense of Justice (A Response)," 376

Hopkins, Gerard Manley, 70

Horace, 149, 512

Horkheimer, Max, 90, 368

Hössli, Heinrich, *Eros*, 542–43

Hughes, Robert, 456

Huizinga, Johann, *Homo Ludens*, 631n3

humanism, viii, 30, 81–82, 100, 160, 279–80, 287, 306; and art, 452; and Bible, 434–35; and classics, 435; and dignity, 435–36; and Euripides, 322; and guilt, 365; and Hegel, 270, 271; heroic, 187; and humbition, 303; and importance of human being, 427; Jewish-inflected, 381; justification of, 167; liberal, 33, 35, 382, 616n13, 624n81; and morality/ethics, 366; and psychology, 427; and religion, 242; root of, 435; and Shakespeare, 322; and Sophocles, 319, 321–22; and tragedy, 349; tragic, 322, 563; and virtue, 569; and Wieseltier, 647n4 humanities, 411–37, 551–52; in America, 32, 33; and Bible, 412; book reviewing in, 428–29; and comparative religion, 412; and deconstruction, 569; and goals of human existence, 412; and Heidegger, 480–81; and hermeneutic circle, 685n12; journalists in, 419; and Kant, 477–78; reading in, 419–28, 432–33; reasons for teaching, 412; and religion, 433–37; scholastics in, 412, 413, 415, 417, 419, 427; and science, 480; Socratics in, 413–14, 415, 416, 417, 419; visionaries in, 412–13, 415, 419

humbition, 167, 168, 172–73, 211, 280, 303, 649n20; and guilt, 365–66, 367; and violence, 377; virtue of, 123, 366, 374

Humboldt, Wilhelm von, 696n25

Hume, David, 86, 102, 180, 244, 328, 450; *History of England*, 427, 450; "On Tragedy," 332–33

Husserl, Edmund, 71, 82, 253, 336, 337, 520

Hyppolite, Jean, 251; commentary on Hegel's *Phenomenology of Spirit*, 233, 276

ibn Gabirol, Shlomoh ben Judah (Avicebron), 396

Ibsen, Henrik, 447

Ikhnaton. *See* Akhenaten (Ikhnaton)

India, 379, 410, 440, 458, 459, 461, 464, 465

Indian literature, 473

individual, 183–84; and autonomy, 479; and Dostoevsky, 53; and Enlightenment, 136; and existentialism, 44; Hegel on, 265, 268, 622n59; and Kierkegaard, 59; in Luhmann, 40; and Nietzsche, 39, 59, 268; paradigmatic, 472–73, 476; Sartre on, 265; and state, 268–69

Innocent III, 409

Inquisition, 212, 408, 409, 453, 457, 679n6

Iran, 466

Irenaeus of Lyon, 389

irony, 66

Irving, David, 344

Islam, 379, 386, 387–88, 396, 406, 407, 410, 459, 679n38. *See also* Muslims

Israel, 359, 379; Bet Alpha synagogue, 436; Kaufmann's visits to, 3

Israel, ancient, 175–76, 379, 397

Israel, state of, 310, 384, 385, 395, 397

Jabès, Edmond, 70

Jacobi, F. H., 478

Jainism, 379, 385, 410, 458

James, Clive, 368–69, 446

James, Henry, 438

James, William, 120, 221; "The Will to Believe," 218, 219–20, 225, 656–57n37

Jameson, Fredric, 687n8

Japan, 379, 391, 437

Jaspers, Karl, 34, 42, 44, 45–46, 47, 50, 56, 129, 130, 146, 295, 335, 369, 439, 449, 517, 612n13; and Dostoevsky, 57; and existentialism, 323; *Existenz-philosophie* of, 68; and Freud, 555–56; and guilt, 365; and Heidegger, 64, 66–68; Kaufmann's letters to, 564; and Kierkegaard, 556; and Nietzsche, 62, 64–65, 67–68, 515, 556; and religion, 58; renunciation of existentialism by, 568; suspense in, 65–67; and *venia legendi*, 67; WORKS: *Nietzsche,* 64–65; *Philosophie,* 66; "The Psychology of World Views," 515; *Reason and Anti-Reason in Our Time,* 555–56

Java, 440

Jay, Martin, 227, 424, 569, 674n14

Jefferson, Thomas, 353, 359, 382

Jerome, St., 399, 408

Jesus Christ, 2, 101, 102, 107, 171, 215; apocalyptic expectations of, 109; authority of, 116; beauty of sayings of, 400; conception of own person of, 216; crucifixion of, 397, 398, 400–401, 403; and Dostoevsky, 212; in early and Romanesque art, 452; in Hegel, 242, 498; and Hillel, 394; and Jewish legalism, 110; Johnston on, 116; and Judaism, 397; and Kant, 493; and love, 399–400; and Luther, 117; and Manichaeism, 390; as Messiah, 403; and morality, 399–400; and Moses, 172;

Jesus Christ (*continued*)
  Nietzsche on, 215–16, 513, 516; and Paul, 528; and perfection, 117; and pre-exilic prophets, 178; as prophet, 400; and Schweitzer, 226–27; and social justice, 164; teachings of, 397; and Tolstoy, 210, 222; and truth, 388
Jewish Enlightenment (*haskalah*), 31
Jewish Hellenism, 178
Jews, 30, 31, 81, 494; and Austrian liberalism, 624n82; canonical writing of, 395–96; as chosen people, 383; and Christian art, 453; Christian desolation of, 228; Christian hatred of, 223–24, 395, 409; and Christians, 657n45; conversion by, 384; and Crusades, 407–8, 452; and death, 466; and destruction of Jerusalem and second temple, 394; Eliot on, 162; of Germany, 109; and Greeks, 467; Haredi sect, 384; and history, 466; and Hitler, 696n19; and Hochhuth, 345–46; homeland in Palestine for, 224; and Kolbe, 347; and law, 115, 494, 515–16, 528, 639n35, 678n34; learning of, 395–96; and Luther, 409; and marriage, 516; at Masada, 394; and medicine, 460; and morality, 185, 515–16; and Nazis, 223, 457; and Nietzsche, 579; and ritual, 4; and Romans, 395; and Shoah, 185; and time, 466; and universalism, 177
John Paul II, 347
Johns Hopkins University, 292, 560
Johnston, Mark: *Saving God: Religion after Idolatry*, 115–16, 639n36, 639n38, 642n5; *Surviving Death*, 651n36
Jonas, Hans, 391
Jones, Ernest, 546, 551, 564
Josephus, Flavius, *History of the Jews*, 394
journalism, 368–69, 378, 418, 428, 449
journalists, 414–15, 428
Joyce, James, 70, 82, 138, 445; *Finnegans Wake*, 84; *Ulysses*, 145
Judaism, 108, 109, 159, 381–86; and Babylonian exile, 398; and Buber, 527; and Buddhism, 379; and Christianity, 118, 160,

217, 223–24, 228, 281, 381, 383, 384, 392, 395, 397–98, 399–400, 403, 404, 409, 639n36, 657n45, 679n38; codification of ritual in, 393; conversion to, 395; and divinization, 383, 384; everlasting perdition in, 109–10; God in, 115, 381; and Goethe, 145–46, 147; and Halacha, 404; Hegel on, 270; and Hinduism, 459, 460; intellect in, 118; and Islam, 459, 679n38; and Jesus, 397; justification on earth in, 178; Kaufmann's conversion to, 2–3; Kaufmann's rejection of, 161; and law, 115, 494, 515–16, 528, 639n35, 678n34; and liberal humanism, 382; and Lutheranism, 118; and monotheism, 175–77; moral teachings of, 124; and Moses and prophets, 392; and Near Eastern religions, 392, 393; and New Testament, 383; and Paul's theology, 111; and Pharisees, 394; Rabbinic, 648n15; rabbinical exegesis in, 398; and rabbis, 393; as religion without theology, 115; right action in, 121; ritual in, 164; and Sadducees, 394; and Schopenhauer, 333, 334; and sin and guilt, 365; and social justice, 648n15; social justice in, 398; and Spinoza, 180; suffering in, 177–78; and Ten Commandments, 282; and theology, 639n35; and tragedy, 278; universalism of, 178, 650n32; as way of life, 114–15, 217; without God, 178; without theology, 178; and Wouk, 202–3; and Zoroastrianism, 385–86, 391, 392
Judeo-Christian tradition, 107, 178, 379
Judt, Tony, 411
Juhl, Peter, 668n28
Julian the Apostate, 405
Julius, Anthony, 297
Julius Caesar, 38, 375, 573, 599
Jung, Carl Gustav, 554, 561; and Carus, 507; and discovery of mind, 532, 551, 556–59; and Freud, 540, 554, 556–59; *Memories*, 559; and Nazis, 551; and Nietzsche, 506, 559; on psychological types, 558–59; psychology of, 476; and *ressentiment*, 559
Jünger, Ernst, 626n5

Jung-Stilling, Johann Heinrich, 542

justice, 211, 352, 567, 652n39, 671n23; in
Aeschylus, 318; and autonomy, 373–74;
and Christianity, 164, 165, 168, 397; and
death of God, 364; and desert, 364–65;
distributive, 357, 359–60, 362, 374,
376–77; and equality, 362–63, 364; and
guilt, 363–65; in Hebrew Bible, 385; and
Hebrew prophets, 160, 164, 165, 168, 226,
334, 360, 397, 459, 648n15; higher law
assuring, 364; as ideal, 314; and laws, 363–
64; and liberation of mind, 418, 566; and
love, 175; in New Testament, 360; in Old
Testament, 360, 383; and punishment,
360–61; retributive, 314, 318, 357, 358–61,
362; and Royce, 220; social, 164, 165, 226,
357, 397, 417, 648n15; in Sophocles, 302,
317, 318. See also morality/ethics

justification, 166

Juvenal, 395

Kabbalah, 396

Kafka, Franz, 12, 44, 138, 309, 578, 662–
63n49; and aesthetic distance, 288;
ambiguity in, 106; and art vs. philosophy, 55–56; atheology of, 182, 648n19;
on beauty, 470; and Buber, 527, 530; on
consuming of self, 109; and decisions,
358; and Dostoevsky, 54; education of,
623n68; and Freud, 541; and Goethe, 208;
and Greek literature, 666n17; and guilt,
363; and Hebrew Bible, 106; and Hegel,
267, 271; and Heidegger, 70; on Judaism,
381; and justification, 197; on Kant,
492–93; and Kierkegaard, 648n19; and
knowledge of good and evil, 114; and literature, 81; and marriage, 358; and modernism, 293; and Nietzsche, 542; novels of
as fragments, 83–84; and Old Testament,
648n19; and psychology, 493; and Rilke,
148–49; and self-deception, 616n8; and
self-destruction, 91–92; on subjectivity
and truth, 432; on thought and feeling,
135; and tuberculosis, 358; Vergeistichung in, 221; WORKS: The Castle, 48,
84, 666n17; Diaries, 143; "In the Penal
Colony," 149, 259; "The Judgment," 557;
letter to Felice Bauer, 530; letter to Oskar
Pollak, 648–49n19; "The Metamorphosis," 83–84, 149, 198; The Missing Person
(Amerika), 145, 666–67n17; "Researches
of a Dog," 119, 439; "A Starvation Artist,"
149; "The Stoker," 149; The Trial, 394,
455–56, 666–67n17

Kanki, Keizō, 454–55

Kant, Anna Regina (née Reuter), 492

Kant, Immanuel, 28, 31, 33, 79, 82, 86, 105,
149, 232, 273, 339, 470; and academic
philosophy, 536; and aesthetic "Wohlgefallen," 496; anti-Semitism of, 491–92;
and art, 496; astronomical theory
of, 450; and autonomy, 479, 491, 495,
497–98; beauty in, 37, 463, 496, 504; and
Buber, 530; and categorical imperative,
485, 491, 493, 595; and change, 516; and
Christianity, 165, 492; and concept
formation and imagination, 496; and
Copernicus, 489; and creativity, 484; dialectic in, 253–54; and discovery of mind,
488–97, 503, 505; and error, 135; and existentialism, 560; as Faust, 482; and Fichte,
489; and God, 488, 489; and Goethe,
90, 326, 477–78, 479, 482, 483, 484, 485,
487, 488, 489, 495, 496, 497, 503–4, 516;
and Golden Rule, 493; and Grundlegung,
485, 492, 493; and Hebrew prophets, 491;
and Hegel, 89, 234, 235, 236–37, 242, 245,
248, 255, 275, 489, 497, 498–99, 500, 501,
503, 505, 536; and Heidegger, 46, 520, 521,
537; and heresy, 180; and history, 494–95;
and holiness, 492, 647n11; and humanities, 477–78; and immortality, 488,
492; and Jaspers, 34; and Jesus, 493; and
Kierkegaard, 504; and Kleist, 325; and
knowledge, 427; language of, 497; and
life lived for enjoyment, 494; and limits
on understanding, 420; on mind, 482,
487; mind of, 477–78; mood in, 97;

Kant, Immanuel (*continued*)
and moral duty, 436; and *Moralität,* 242;
and *Moralität* and *Sittlichkeit,* 237, 245;
and morality/ethics, 73, 90, 182, 245, 436,
479, 485, 490–94, 495, 500; and Moses,
491, 492, 493–94; and Newton, 489; and
Nietzsche, 29, 90, 477, 489, 503–4, 516;
and Old Testament, 491, 492–94, 495;
and passion, 236–37; and Plato, 489; and
poetry, 325; psychobiographical approach
to, 492; and psychology, 476; psychology
of, 297; and reason, 237, 248, 479, 485,
489, 490–91, 494; and religion, 488–89;
and retributive justice, 359; and rights,
643n13; and Rousseau, 90, 491; and Sartre,
537; and Schelling, 489; and Schiller, 238;
scholastic difficulty of, 490; and Schopenhauer, 489, 504; and science, 477–78, 483,
488–89, 499; and Sermon on the Mount,
492; and Spinoza, 489; and sublime, 37,
460, 463; and suicide, 494; and university
scholars, 171; WORKS: *Anthropology,* 236–
37, 491; *Critique of Judgment,* 97; *Critique
of Practical Reason,* 90, 235, 492; *Critique
of Pure Reason,* 34, 84, 90, 248, 478, 488,
489, 490, 498–99, 686–87n24; "Idea for
a Universal History with Cosmopolitan
Intent," 494–95; *Laying the Foundations of
the Metaphysics of Morals,* 490; *Philosophy
of Right,* 491; *Third Critique,* 325, 326; *What
Is Enlightenment?,* 123
Karr, Alphonse, 229, 657n46
Kästner, Erich, 448
Kateb, George: *Human Dignity,* 435; *Patriotism and Other Mistakes,* 634n23
Kaufmann, Bruno, 2, 201
Kaufmann, Edith née Seligsohn, 2
Kaufmann, Felix, 1
Kaufmann, Hazel, 631n2
Kaufmann, Walter: academic career of,
6–7, 42, 44, 183–84, 563–71; in American
Army, 4–5, 30, 95, 352, 386, 658n7; argu-
mentative style of, 12, 50, 65, 72, 76, 142,
143, 160–61, 172–74, 289, 314, 477, 483–84,

486, 495, 500, 504, 525, 551, 552–53; bar
mitzvah of, 2–3; and Bildungsbürgertum,
30–31, 95, 386; biography of in *Dictionary of American Biography,* 4; birth
of, 1; break of with organized religion,
380; character of, 3, 5–6; conversion to
Judaism, 95, 159, 161, 190, 354; creation
of "ein Werk" by, 564; death of, 1; death
of mother of, 474; decision to leave
Lutheran Church, 190, 354; dedications
of, 201; education of, ix, 3, 4, 5, 31, 32–33,
77, 95, 159, 161, 613n17, 622–23n62, 658n7;
as émigré from Nazi Germany, 95, 352,
354, 567; and *est* (Werner Erhard's
Seminars Training), 511–12, 516, 546, 554,
556, 561, 569–70, 688n10; family of, 3–4,
193; and Gauss Seminar Committee,
626n8; and German patriotism, 32; at
Gymnasium, 3, 622–23n62; at Harvard,
31, 32, 622–23n62, 658n7; Hebrew studies
of, 159; at Hochschule für die Wissenschaft des Judentums (Institute for
Judaic Studies), 3, 31, 77, 159; intellectual
formation of, 77; Jewish heritage of,
159; parents of, 232; photography of,
683–84n37; at Princeton, 5, 31, 33, 44,
231–32, 413, 658n7; Princeton Philosophy Department's encomium of, 184,
210; role models of, 40, 183; stay at Villa
Serbelloni in Bellagio, 351; stay in Jerusalem (1962), 279; and Stuart Professorship
of Philosophy, 5; as teacher, 6; thought
pattern of, 374; travels to Israel, 3; travel
to Palestine, 3; ultimate concern of, 187;
uncles of, 3–4; at University of Heidelberg, 66; at Williams College, 4, 32, 161,
613n17, 622–23n62; work ethic of, 95, 564;
WORKS: *Basic Writings of Nietzsche,*
278; *Beyond Guilt and Justice,* 397; "Black
and White," 662n47; "Buber's Religious
Significance," 527; *Cain and Other Poems,*
4, 7, 172, 352, 386–87, 444–45, 447, 565;
Critique of Religion and Philosophy, 4, 6,
7, 44, 47, 58, 72, 75–99, 100–127, 129, 162,

201, 203, 204, 214, 219, 221, 278, 281, 289, 302, 346, 380, 411, 447, 489, 565, 616n12, 652n41, 658–59n7, 671n23; *Discovering the Mind*, 303, 426, 475, 476–77, 567, 568; *Discovering the Mind, vol. 1, Goethe, Kant, and Hegel*, 476, 477–502, 537; *Discovering the Mind, vol. 2, Nietzsche, Heidegger, and Buber*, 52, 122, 129, 297, 503–31, 537; *Discovering the Mind, vol. 3, Freud, Adler, and Jung*, 302, 506, 532–62; "Doubts about Justice," 673n3; "The Eichmann Trial," 447; *Existentialism, Religion, and Death: Thirteen Essays*, 8, 43, 72, 128, 158, 187, 527; "Existentialism and Death," 195; *Existentialism from Dostoevsky to Sartre*, 43–44, 45–74, 79, 82, 97, 128, 200, 206, 526, 564; "The Faith of an Agnostic" (proposed title), 163 ; "The Faith of a Heretic," 163, 415, 640n48, 692n9; *The Faith of a Heretic*, viii, 1, 2, 3–4, 6, 7, 42, 44, 58, 79, 114, 123, 158, 159–98, 199, 201, 209, 210–11, 215, 216, 217, 218–19, 220, 226, 231, 300, 301–2, 303, 321, 355, 366, 383, 415, 444, 447, 450, 564, 565, 651n36, 652n41, 658n7; forward to John Wilcox's *Truth and Value in Nietzsche*, 628n31; *The Future of the Humanities*, 351, 352, 369, 411–37, 450, 457, 648–49n19; *Hegel*, x, 279, 420, 498, 565, 567; *Hegel: A Reinterpretation*, ix, 231–77; *Hegel: Reinterpretation, Texts, and Commentary*, 88, 187; "The Hegel Myth and Its Method," 230, 233, 264; *Hegel's Political Philosophy*, 187, 268; "History and Honesty," 224; introduction to Martin Buber's *I and Thou*, 527–28; introduction to translation of Nietzsche's *The Birth of Tragedy*, 19; "Jaspers in Relation to Nietzsche," 46; "A Journal in Verse," 447; "Kaufmann's Laws," 514; *Man's Lot*, 196, 197, 410, 438–75, 479, 482, 483, 484, 486, 511; *Man's Lot: Life at the Limits*, 440, 441–62, 463, 468, 474; *Man's Lot: Time Is an Artist*, 440, 462–70, 474; *Man's Lot: What Is Man?*, 440–41, 470–75; "Mind and Mask," 551; *Nietzsche, Heidegger, and Buber*, 129, 297, 586; *Nietzsche: Philosopher, Psychologist, Antichrist*, xi, 5, 7, 11–42, 43, 50, 59, 61, 62, 70–71, 76, 85, 100, 162, 178–79, 201, 214–15, 258, 510, 514, 537, 564, 568, 572, 574, 581, 582, 586, 587, 588, 592, 601; "Nietzsche's Theory of Values," 5; "Occupation," 4–5; "On Karl Kraus," 695n15; *Philosophic Classics*, 7; photography of, 86, 378–79, 440–41, 443, 450, 460–61, 462–63, 468–69, 474, 511, 568, 569; poetry of, 158, 172, 196, 378–79, 443, 474, 511, 514, 569; *Religion from Tolstoy to Camus*, 7, 167, 199–229, 565; *Religions in Four Dimensions: Existential and Aesthetic, Historical and Comparative*, 72, 378–410, 437, 444, 452, 458, 459, 464, 613n19; review of Findlay's *Hegel*, 230–31; "Selective Compassion," 566–67; *From Shakespeare to Existentialism*, 6, 7, 43, 46, 47, 73, 128–58, 193, 201, 230, 234, 236, 278, 340, 447, 449, 482, 483, 529, 565, 658–59n7; "Solzhenitsyn and Autonomy," 446; "To build—not a small chapel for myself," 81, 632–33n16; *Tragedy and Philosophy*, x, xi, 73, 121, 187, 193, 198, 249, 278–310, 311–50, 425, 443, 445, 529, 565–66, 614n22; translation and commentary on preface to Hegel's *Phenomenology*, 274–77; translation of Baeck's *Judaism and Christianity*, 7; translation of Buber's *I and Thou*, 122, 527; translation of Goethe's *Faust*, 7, 241, 482, 565; translation of Nietzsche's *Beyond Good and Evil*, 278; translation of Nietzsche's *Ecce Homo*, 278; translation of Nietzsche's *On the Genealogy of Morals*, 278; translation of Nietzsche's *The Birth of Tragedy*, 278, 590; translation of Nietzsche's *The Case of Wagner*, 278; translation of Nietzsche's *Thus Spoke Zarathustra*, viii; translation of Nietzsche's *Will to Power*, 278; translations of, 43, 148, 172; *Twenty German Poets*, 7, 565; *Without Guilt and Justice: From Decidophobia*

Kaufmann, Walter (*continued*)
  to Autonomy, 150, 302, 314, 351, 352,
    353–77, 378, 391, 403–4, 418, 428, 432, 446,
    479, 483, 508, 539, 566, 567, 647n5, 652n39,
    671n23; "The Young Hegel and Religion,"
    133–34
Keats, John, 144, 146, 353, 448, 563; "Ode to
    a Nightingale," 447
Kelly, George Armstrong, *Hegel's Retreat
    from Eleusis,* 268
Kennedy, John F., 367
Kennick, William, 230, 447–48
Kerouac, Jack, "On the Road," 477, 684n5
Kertész, André, 463
Kestner, J. C., 478
Kierkegaard, Søren, 43, 54, 56, 57–60, 61–62,
    89, 101, 160, 415; and anxiety, 507–8; and
    Christianity, 507, 508; criticism of, 175; and
    death, 518; on decision making, 508; and
    de Man, 615n35; as depth psychologist,
    506; and Dostoevsky, 57, 60; on dread,
    507–8; and exegetical thinking, 356; on
    fear vs. anxiety, 508; and Freud, 507;
    and Goethe, 504; and great-souled man,
    130; on guilt, 507–8; and Hegel, 273; and
    Heidegger, 507, 508, 518, 521–22, 523–24,
    687n9; and inauthenticity, 508; and
    Jaspers, 556; and Kafka, 648n19; and Kant,
    504; and moral irrationalism, 357; and
    Nietzsche, 39, 59–60, 589; prose style of,
    147; as psychologist, 509; and psychology,
    507; romanticism of, 147; and Sartre, 57;
    and Schelling, 60; and Shakespeare, 129;
    and suffering, 449; WORKS: *The Concept
    of Dread,* 523; *Concluding Unscientific
    Postscript,* 59; *Either/Or,* 358; *Fear and
    Trembling,* 324; *The Present Age,* 522
King, Martin Luther, Jr., 352–53
Kirsch, Adam, 433
Kissinger, Henry, 343, 673n5
Kittler, Friedrich, 551; *Discourse Networks,
    1800/1900,* 111, 241
Klee, Paul, *Angelus Novus,* 280

Kleist, Heinrich von, 37, 143, 144, 192, 325,
    696n25
Klimt, Gustav, 534
Klossowski, Pierre, 605–6, 701n91
Knausgård, Karl Ove, 649n23
knowledge, 83, 100; attainment of, 88, 427,
    450; and Buddhism, 114; and faith, 75,
    80; and Hegel, 499; and Kafka, 114; and
    logic of passion, 133; and Nietzsche, 427,
    584, 588; and philosophy, 88; and Plato,
    117, 427; and reason, 79; and Schiller, 245;
    and tragedy, 281, 292
Knox, Bernard, 320
Koch, Robert, 408
Koestler, Arthur, 184; "The Yogi and the
    Commissar," 353
Kofman, Sarah, 605, 701n91
Kojève, Alexandre: *Introduction to the Rea-
    ding of Hegel,* 233; "Phenomenological
    Method in Hegel," 273
Kokoschka, Oskar, 534
Kolbe, Maximilian, 346–48
Koran, 388, 433
Koyré, Alexander, 275–76
Kracauer, Siegfried, 227, 368, 657n43
Kraus, Karl, 553, 579, 645–46n55, 695n15
Krell, David Farrell, 605, 701n91
Krockow, Christian Graf von, *Die Entschei-
    dung,* 626n5
Krupnick, Mark, 663n51
Kubrick, Stanley, 332
Kusch, Martin, *Psychologism,* 633n20
Kuspit, Donald, 428

Lacan, Jacques, 207, 233, 234, 347, 355, 551,
    555; "The Mirror Stage as Formative of
    the I-Function," 331
Lacoue-Labarthe, Philippe, *Poetry as Expe-
    rience,* 155
Lambert, Johann Heinrich, 253
Lamont, Corliss, 189, 196; "Mistaken Atti-
    tudes toward Death," 190–92, 193
language, 645–46n55; and de Man, 419–20;
    and experience, 98; and Heidegger, 258,

661n40; logical, 537; and New Critics, 421, 424; and Nietzsche, 552, 573–74; and philosophy, 79; of scribe and tribe, 98; and sexuality, 645–46n55; and suffering, 664–65n4. *See also* ordinary language philosophy

Laokoon, 451

Lao-Tze, 160, 161, 200

Large, Duncan, 13, 700n82; *Nietzsche and Proust,* 592, 601–3

La Rochefoucauld, François, duc de, 312, 589

Laws of Manu, 161, 200, 364, 471

Laycock, Steven W.: *A Buddhist Engagement with the Ontology of Jean-Paul Sartre,* 72; *Nothingness and Emptiness,* 631n79

Lazarus, Moritz, 485–86

Lazier, Benjamin, *God Interrupted,* 391

Lear, Jonathan, 551, 691n27

Leavis, F. R., *The Great Tradition,* 690n13

Leibniz, Gottfried Wilhelm, 84, 427, 450, 589

Leibovitz, Liel, 341

Leiter, Brian, 421, 513, 586, 591, 596, 597, 602, 694n1, 696–97n30, 697n31, 699–700n79

Lenau, Nikolaus, 696n25

Leon, Moses de, 396

Leonardo da Vinci, 560

Leo XIII, *Aeterni Patris,* 213, 214

Lepenies, Wolf, 507

Lessing, Gotthold Ephraim, 28, 29, 31, 210–11, 232, 234, 235, 285, 326, 487; *The Education of Mankind,* 235

Levinas, Emmanuel, 77, 632n7

liberalism, 223, 585, 603, 604, 605, 700n85. *See also* humanism, liberal

Lichtheim, George, 274

Lincoln, Abraham, 353

Liska, Vivian, 678n34

literary theory, 259, 273, 278, 560–61. *See also* French theory

Locke, John, 643n13

Lohenstein, Daniel Caspar von, 327

love, 167, 184, 193, 211, 280, 378; and beauty, 175; and Christianity, 107–8, 125, 131, 164, 641n61; and death, 190–91; God as, 124–25; and Hebrew prophets, 168, 459; in Hegel, 498; and Hölderlin, 236; and Jesus, 399–400; and justice, 175; and logic of passion, 132–33; in New Testament, 168, 360; in Nietzsche, 510; and Paul, 403–4; in Plato, 647n11; and Rule of St. Francis, 409; of self, 207; in Shakespeare, 131–32; and social justice, 164; of truth, 90–91; and violence, 377; as virtue, 123, 175, 366, 374, 403–4

Löwith, Karl, 518

Lucretius, 487

Luft, Eric von der, 4, 88, 94–95, 613n19

Luhmann, Niklas, 40, 183, 184

Lukács, Georg, 373

Lunarchasky, Anatoly, 213

Luria, Isaac, 396

Luther, Martin, 215, 216; brutality of, 409; dualism in, 117–18; and Heidegger, 523; and Hellenism of Fourth Gospel and Paul, 113; and justification, 334; Kaufmann's encounter with, 161, 165, 200; and law, 494; and Mann, 33, 34; and Nietzsche, 29, 49, 516; and reason, 101, 108, 409; and salvation, 116, 302; and schism, 406; and St. Francis, 409; word and reason in, 117–18

Lutheranism, 405, 406

Lysaker, Odin, 457

Machiavelli, Niccolò, 578–79, 695n13; *The Prince,* 579

Magnus, Bernd, 605, 701n91

Maimon, Solomon, 493

Maimonides, Moses (Moses ben Maimon; Rambam), 110, 118; *Moreh Nevukhim (A Guide to the Perplexed),* 396

Malamud, Bernard, viii

Malcolm, Norman, 487

Mallarmé, Stephan, 70, 82, 125, 126, 157

Malraux, André, 29, 123, 590; *La Lutte avec l'ange,* 590

Mani, 357, 388–89, 399

Manichaeism, 356–57, 358, 389–90, 398

Mann, Thomas, 179, 445, 564, 617n23, 658n5; on Kaufmann's *Nietzsche*, 13; as liberal humanist, 33; and Nietzsche, 33–34, 231, 590; at Princeton, 33; and Schopenhauer, 34, 231; WORKS: *Doctor Faustus*, 33, 34, 61, 85, 111, 112, 193, 384, 435, 590, 638n27, 677n15; *The Magic Mountain*, 430; *Reflections of an Unpolitical Man*, 231

Marcel, Gabriel, 58

Marcion, 389

Marcuse, Herbert, 368, 373, 539, 674n14; *Reason and Revolution*, 233, 254, 264, 662n47; *Repressive Tolerance*, 357–58, 662n47

Maritain, Jacques, 13, 110, 146, 564, 616n12, 657n45

Markham, Edwin, "The Man with the Hoe," 448

Marlowe, Christopher, 447

Marshall, Margaret Wiley, 637n13

Marx, Karl, 65, 79, 368; and alienation, 373, 376; and distributive injustice, 376; and Freud, 538–39; and Hegel, 254; and history, 495; and scientific materialism, 272; WORKS: *Das Kapital*, 71, 356, 376; *Economic and Philosophic Manuscripts of 1844*, 233, 369, 376, 432; *The German Ideology*, 233

Marx, Karl and Friedrich Engels: *Communist Manifesto*, 685n14

Marxism, 44, 356, 368; and alienation, 369–70; and Hegel, 272–73; and Jaspers, 555–56; and Sartre, 71, 560

Mary, 118, 405; Immaculate Conception of, 214

Masaryk, Thomas, *Suicide and the Meaning of Civilization*, 372–73

McCarthy, Joseph, 171, 391

McCarty, Patrick, 618n31

McGrath, William, *Dionysian Art and Populist Politics in Austria*, 624n82

McTaggart, John, "God, Evil, and Immortality," 225–26

Meinecke, Friedrich, 652n40

Mendelssohn, Moses, 275, 396, 492, 493, 648n15, 686–87n24

Mephistopheles, 111, 141, 157, 482

Mesopotamia, 404, 466

metaphysical anxiety, 178

metaphysics, 8, 79, 213; and Bradley, 179; and Buddhism, 114; and Danto, 126; in Hegel, 256, 261; and Nietzsche, 68, 697n31; and Old Testament, 382; and Plato, 79; and religious experience, 380; and Sartre, 69; and scientific empiricism, 244

Michelangelo, 147, 412, 436, 463, 560, 573; "Last Judgment," 469

Mill, John Stuart, 363, 537

Miller, Arthur, *Death of a Salesman*, 328, 345

Miller, J. Hillis, 8, 552, 615n35

Miller, Jacques-Alain, 355

Miller, John William, 4

Milton, John, 28, 154, 384; *Areopagitica*, 218–19; "On His Blindness," 296; *Paradise Lost*, 445; *Samson Agonistes*, 431

mimēsis, 284, 285, 286, 443

Mitchell, Basil, 225

modernism, 69, 70, 82, 83–84, 142, 236, 293

Mohenjo Daro, 458

Momigliano, Arnaldo, 466–67

Monophysites, 406

Montaigne, Michel de, 71, 396, 438–39, 472

Montinari, Mazzino, 430–31

Moon, Sun Myung, 569, 570, 693n23

Moore, G. E., 87, 232; "Refutation of Idealism," 273

morality/ethics, 79, 121, 150, 280, 352, 353, 462; absolute, 182; and agnosticism, 169–70; and allegiance to movements, 355; and autonomy, 566; and beauty, 441; bourgeois, 83; and Camus, 227–28; and Christianity, 116–17, 164, 381; dualism in, 386–89, 391; and failure, 366–67; and Greeks, 286; and guilt, 365; Hawkins on, 162; in Hebrew Bible, 172, 385, 392–93; and Hebrew Bible vs. New Testament, 169; and Hebrew prophets, 164, 165; and

Hegel, 237, 245–46, 263, 269, 498; and Heidegger, 357, 521; and humanism, 366; impulse and action in, 169; and Jews, 185, 515–16; and Job, 220; and Judaism, 124; of judiciary introspection, 207; and Kant, 73, 90, 182, 245, 436, 479, 485, 490–94, 495, 500; Kateb on, 634n23; and Kierkegaard, 57, 59; and Kolbe, 347; and Lacan, 347; and Nietzsche, 29, 218, 240, 393, 510, 515, 579, 580, 581, 583, 585, 593, 595, 601, 605, 697n31; of openness, 168; and Plato, 281–82; and punishment, 361; and rationalism, 357, 358; and religion, 8, 168, 169, 170, 182, 354; and Rilke, 149; and Royce, 220; and Schiller, 240; and self-scrutiny, 181; slave, 515; and Steichen, 441; and survival, 367–68; and Tolstoy, 206, 209; and tragedy, 302, 340–41; and universality, 479; and Žižek, 347. *See also* evil; justice

Moran, John, 377, 428

Mormonism, 174

Moses: and Akhenaten, 175–76; and Buber, 529; and deification, 473; and Freud, 546–47; and God, 122–23; and Hinduism, 460; and humbition, 172–73; as innovator, 412; and justice, 364; and Kant, 491, 492, 493–94; and kingdom of priests, 109, 493; and normative Judaism, 392; originality of religion of, 176–77; as paradigmatic individual, 479; and Paul, 404; and Rilke, 449, 493; and Tetragrammaton, 122–23; and Wellhausen, 203

Most, Glenn W., *Doubting Thomas*, 635n42

Mozart, Wolfgang Amadeus, 142, 387, 446–47, 450; *Don Giovanni*, 444; "Eine kleine Nachtmusik," 444

Müller, Johannes von, 696n25

Murdoch, Iris, 255, 661n37

Murray, Gilbert, 284, 309

Muschg, Walter, *The Destruction of German Literature*, 46, 51

music, 52, 53, 294, 318, 349, 387, 443; in Aristotle, 285, 289, 290, 665–66n13; and Bildungsbürgertum, 30; and British philosophers, 87; and demand to change, 207, 493; and German culture, 387; and Kafka, 119; liberation through, 62; and limit experience, 439, 442, 444; and Mann, 34, 61, 638n27; and Nietzsche, 62, 132, 485, 620n46; as opiate, 438; and philosophy, 62; religious context of, 412; as substitutive gratification, 558

Musil, Robert: *The Man without Qualities*, 83, 97; *The Perplexities of Young Törless*, 97, 293

Muslims, 118, 452, 453, 460. *See also* Islam

Mussolini, Benito, 211

mysticism, 484; and British philosophy, 87; and de Man, 615n35; and faith, 103; Jewish, 107, 396; Kaufmann's experience of, 54, 161, 380, 413, 640n48, 679n5; and Koestler, 353; and Pratt, 4; and previous knowledge, 118–19; and Wittgenstein, 443. *See also* religion

Nagasaki, 315

Nag Hammadi, 389

Napoleon I, 38, 88, 134, 238, 246, 573

Nazis, 3, 5, 13, 28, 30, 68, 95, 160, 193, 201, 344, 614n22; and Bildungsbürgertum, 31; and Christianity, 223, 657n45; and Goldhagen thesis, 367; and Heidegger, 77, 357, 519, 522, 525–26, 540; and Hochhuth, 345–46; and Jews, 223, 457; and Jung, 551; and Kolbe, 347; and Luther, 34; and Mann, 34, 384; and Niemöller and Schneider, 223; and Nietzsche, 13, 30, 31, 204–5, 580, 583, 584, 585–86, 587, 605, 614n25, 617n15; and Pius XII, 343–44; and racialism, 52; and Übermensch, 52; and Wouk, 202

Nefertiti, 451

Nehamas, Alexander, 2, 23–24, 72–73, 605, 665n9, 701n91; "Foreword," Walter Kaufmann, *Nietzsche*, 620–21n48; *Nietzsche: Life as Literature*, 16, 587, 600–601, 618n26

neostructuralism, 142, 143, 292, 423–24. *See also* deconstruction

Nessler, Viktor, 659n18

Nestorianism, 406

Neumann, Gerhard, 61, 425

New Comedy, 315

New Criticism, 106, 273, 421–22, 423–24

New Guinea, 440

Newton, Isaac, 483, 484, 485, 489, 502, 503, 686n18

New Yorker, 414

Nicene Creed, 405

Niebuhr, Karl Paul Reinhold, 79

Niemöller, Martin, "The Salt of the Earth," 223

Niethammer, Friedrich Immanuel, 246

Nietzsche, Elisabeth-Förster, *The Will to Power,* 617n21

Nietzsche, Friedrich Wilhelm, 11–42, 44, 45, 74, 80, 84, 86, 108, 122, 183, 296, 302, 410; and academia, 413; and academic philosophy, 536; and Adler, 506–7, 554, 555; admiration and detestation in, 505; and Aeschylus, 314; and aesthetics, 17, 441, 461; affirmation of life on earth in, 43; and analytic philosophy, 572–73, 608; and Antichrist, 82; and anti-Semitism, 579, 587, 591, 604, 617n21, 673n8, 695n15; aphoristic style of, 16–17; and apocalyptic literature, 392; Apollinian in, 19, 25, 37; and appearance and ulterior reality, 513; aristocratism of, 35, 580; and art, 390; as artist, 22, 23; as artist-psychologist, 486; and asceticism, 22, 23, 35, 40, 515, 577, 606–7; and autonomy, 43, 479, 601; beauty in, 22, 25, 41, 153, 472; on Being, 519; and Benn, 590; and Bible, 589; and Biblical prophets, 24; and Bildung, 30–31, 38; and Bildungsbürgertum, 30; and Bizet, 62; and Borgia, 578, 583, 695n13; and Buber, 527, 530; and Buddhism, 114, 335; and Burckhardt, 37; and Camus, 62, 590; centers in, 37; and change, 516; character of, 2; and Christianity, 27, 38–40, 165, 215–16, 579, 598; coherence of corpus of thought of, 18; and communication,

298; and Comte, 589; contradictory propositions in, 64–65; and Copernicus, 489, 593; and Darwin, 513, 574–75, 578, 582, 589, 607; and death, 193–94; and decadence, 16, 17; and decisions, 358; on deep Self as body, 512; and de Man, 92–94, 419, 426; as dialectical monist, 25; and dialectical reader, 426; Dionysus and Dionysian in, 17, 20–21, 25, 26, 27, 33, 36, 37, 57, 151, 461, 513; and discovery of mind, 503, 505–17; and divine providence or purpose of nature, 17; and Dostoevsky, 33, 52–53, 54, 507; on dreaming consciousness, 511; and dualism, 387–88; early (proto-Nazi) interpreters of, 18; as educator, 29, 30, 31; and Einstein, 614n25; and Enlightenment, 623n75, 625n94; *ephexis* in, 48, 49, 50, 65; and Epicurus, 472; on error, 93–94, 95, 426; and eternal recurrence, 21, 26–27, 36, 142, 152, 393, 573, 592, 601, 620–21n48, 696–97n30, 699n72; and ethics, 35; on Euripides, 314, 322, 324; European nihilism in, 36; exhortation to live dangerously, 193; and existentialism, 39, 62–64, 572; experience in, 93–94, 511; experience of thought in, 71; on explanation vs. text, 94; and facts vs. interpretations, 48, 49; and faith, 161, 179, 652n37; and fascism, 23; and fated character of self, 596–97; and fragmentation, 17; and freedom, 22, 36, 41, 71; and French enlightenment, 578; and French revolution, 605; and French theater of absurd, 336; and Freud, 18, 167, 506, 507, 510, 534, 537, 538, 539, 542, 544, 547, 554–55, 558; friendship in, 36–37; and Geist, 429, 574–75, 578; and German imperialism, 591; as German nationalist, 587; and German tradition, 603; and Gide, 590; and Gnosticism, 390–91; and God, 151, 518, 575–76, 592, 619n32; and Goethe, 21, 24, 36, 37, 38, 40, 132, 141, 142, 152, 371, 376, 472, 477, 479, 503–4, 516, 573, 578, 588, 589, 598, 599–600, 625n88; and great-souled man, 130, 136; and Greek philosophy and poetry, 503; and Hebrew Bible, 147, 473; and Hegel, 29, 33, 88, 233, 255, 265, 273, 589; and Heidegger, 46, 62, 67–68, 505, 513, 518, 520, 524–25, 560, 629–30n61; and Heraclitus, 472; and Hesse, 590; and Hinduism, 683n29; historicization of, 589–90, 591–92; and history, 25; and Hitler, 21–22; and Hochhuth, 672n33; idols in, 76; and imaginative literature, 509; and individual, 39, 268; influence of, 589–90; influences on, 589; and injunction to suffer change, 149; on inner experience and outer world, 93–94; inspiration in, 63–64, 71; on intelligence, 92–93; interpretation in, 65; and Jaspers, 34, 62, 64–65, 67–68, 515, 556; and Jesus Christ, 513, 516; and Jews, 579; joy in, 62–64, 71; and Julius Caesar, 599; and Jung, 506, 559; on justice and guilt, 363; and Kafka, 149, 542; and Kant, 29, 90, 477, 489, 503–4, 516; and Kierkegaard, 39, 59–60, 589; and knowledge, 427, 584, 588; and Kraus, 695n15; and language, 573–74, 645–46n55; and La Rochefoucauld, 589; and Leibniz, 589; and liberalism, 585, 603, 604, 605, 700n85; on lies, 688n15; and life as work of art, 188; and linguistic turn in philosophy, 552; and living dangerously, 449; on love, 510; and Luther, 49, 516; and Machiavelli, 578–79; and Malraux, 590; and Mann, 33–34, 231, 590; man vs. animal in, 26; and masks, 516–17, 559–60; master and slave in, 515, 579, 580, 601; meaning and purpose in, 36; and metaphysics, 68, 697n31; and microscopic reading, 423; and Montaigne, 472; on mood, 97; and morality/ethics, 17, 29, 218, 240, 387–88, 393, 510, 515, 579, 580, 581, 583, 585, 593, 595, 601, 605, 697n31; and music, 62, 620n46; and nature of man, 470, 472; and Nazis, 13, 30, 31, 204–5, 580, 583, 584, 585–86, 587, 605, 614n25, 617n15; and nihilism, 36,

37, 592, 593; and not being at home, 371; and nuances, 426; and O'Neill, 590; and organic unity, 16–17, 18; organization in, 35–37; as paradigmatic individual, 476; parekbasis in, 65–66; on party man as liar, 354; and Pascal, 472; and passion, 547; and Paul, 215, 217–18, 402–3, 516; personality in, 28; and personhood, 16; and phenomenon and Ding-an-sich, 513; philology in, 47–48, 49, 94; as philosopher, 18, 23; philosophy of method of, 17; and piety, 577, 578, 606; and pity, 288; and Plato, 17, 472, 589; and poetic science, 550; and politics, 23, 39, 581–86, 591, 603, 604, 605, 630–31n77, 696n25; and power, 624n79, 696n23; and present moment, 142; principle and illustration in, 573; and prison-house of language (sprachlicher Zwang), 552; and privileged moment, 152; as problem-thinker, 17; and prostitute in Dresden brothel, 33; psyche of, 94; and psychohistory, 516; as psychologist, 18, 82, 506–7, 509–12; and psychology, 297, 476, 560; questions vs. answers in, 17; rationality in, 22; and reason, 28, 117–18, 429, 520; reason and impulse in, 25; on reliability of consciousness, 510–12; and religion, 38–40, 573; and Renan, 589; renewal in, 150; and repression, 510, 512, 515; and resentment, 215, 688n16; resistance to, 568–69; and ressentiment, 218, 515–16, 642n6, 688n16; and retributive justice, 359; and revenge, 215, 605; and reward, 216–17; rhetoric of, 121; and Rilke, 147–48, 150–54, 325, 590; as role model, 40; on romantic and Dionysian art, 239; and romanticism, 136, 143; and Rousseau, 472, 589; and Salomé, 148; and Sartre, 62, 70–71, 72, 73, 326, 336, 560, 590; and Schelling, 589; and Schiller, 239–40, 659n18; and schöne Seele, 624n77; and Schopenhauer, 25, 29, 36, 39, 335, 472, 589, 617n17; and science, 573, 575, 581;

Nietzsche, Friedrich Wilhelm (*continued*)
self-actualization in, 25–26; on self and
body, 620n41; and self-contestation,
19; and self-creation, 16, 18, 34–35,
596–97; self-cultivation in, 35; and
self-fashioning, 19; self in, 65; and self-
making, 35, 43, 76, 511; and self-mastery,
607; and self-overcoming, 20, 39, 547,
588, 593–96; self-perfection in, 20, 21,
23, 35; and self-stylization, 18, 20, 30;
and self-sufficiency, 137; self-vivification
in, 22; and sexuality, 515, 542, 698n59,
700n82; and Shakespeare, 129, 328, 335,
507; and Shaw, 590; and Shiva, 458,
461–62; on slave morality, 515, 580, 601;
and Socrates, 179, 308, 578, 600; and Sophocles, 307, 308, 314, 315–16; and special
pleading, 83; and Spinoza, 472, 513, 589;
and state, 585, 588, 603; statement and
counterstatement in, 68; and Stendhal,
132, 365, 369, 589; and Strauss, 589; strength and value in, 19–20; struggle in, 43;
and sublimation, 21, 35, 596, 618–19n31,
698n59; and *sublimiren*, 618–19n31; and
suffering, 664–65n4; and sun worship,
13; and system building, 17; terms used
by, 92–94; tone of, 27; and totalitarianism, 587; and tragedy, 281, 304, 307–8,
309, 314, 315–16, 339; and transformation,
645n49; and truth, 575–78, 606, 619n35;
and Übermensch, 20–21, 23, 36, 153, 250,
377, 573, 583–84, 598–600, 620–21n48,
696–97n30, 698n66; on unconscious
physiological processes, 511; and unified
self, 19; and unity, 18; unity of thought
of, 21; and universal moral law, 29; on
university scholars, 170–71; and van
Gogh, 474; and Vauvenargues, 589;
and virtue, 30, 569; and Wagner, 33, 559,
589, 591, 603; and war, 583, 584–85, 588;
and weakness, 514; will and power in,
391; will to life in, 35, 513; and will to
power, 18, 19, 20–21, 22, 23, 25, 26, 28,
34–35, 36, 39, 49, 95, 510, 512–15, 554, 581,
582–83, 588–89, 592, 597–98, 600–601,
696–97n30, 698n59, 699n70; and Wittgenstein, 694n1; and women, 604–5,
701n88; writing in, 63–64, 71; Yea-saying
of, 36, 62; and Yeats, 590; Zarathustra
in, 152, 153, 357, 385–89, 392, 474, 512;
and Zoroastrianism, 387–88; WORKS:
*On the Advantage and Disadvantage
of History for Life*, 150; *Also Sprach
Zarathustra*, viii–ix, 43, 65, 142, 148,
178–79, 387, 513, 515, 584, 585, 588, 598,
599, 688n10, 696–97n30; *The Antichrist*,
43, 47, 214, 215, 216–18, 388, 595, 597, 600,
633n18; *Beyond Good and Evil*, 369, 510,
512, 516, 559–60, 579, 580, 582, 585, 586,
596, 618n31, 694n9, 696–97n30; *The
Birth of Tragedy from the Spirit of Music*,
15, 16, 17, 18, 21, 37, 92, 132, 240, 284, 304,
307–8, 309, 322, 323, 335, 461, 511, 513;
Colli and Montinari edition of, 430–31;
The Dawn, 402–3, 514, 560, 582, 602, 606,
618n30; *Ecce Homo*, 16, 23, 24, 179, 193,
351–52, 390, 513, 558, 585, 696–97n30;
"Ecce Homo," 641n58; *Der Fall Wagner
(The Case of Wagner)*, 16; *The Gay
Science*, 18, 20, 239, 378, 513, 575–76, 584,
585, 589, 604–5, 606, 607, 640–41n52,
641n58; *On the Genealogy of Morals*,
22, 41, 103–4, 218, 286, 359, 515, 576,
577–78, 580, 606, 607, 694n9; *Human,
All Too Human*, 472, 618n30, 618n31;
Musarion edition of, 5, 30; *Nietzsche
contra Wagner*, 43, 585; "On Truth and
Lie in an Extra-Moral Sense," 512; *The
Portable Nietzsche*, 43; *Revaluation of All
Values*, 63; *Schopenhauer as Educator*,
505, 617n17; *Songs of Zarathustra*, 63; *The
Twilight of the Idols*, 16, 21, 36, 40, 41, 43,
63, 76, 194, 574, 578, 607; "Vereinsamt,"
675n27; *The Will to Power*, 36, 49, 65, 93,
151, 426, 579, 595, 698n59; Zarathustra's
Drunken Song, 152; Zarathustra's "On
Self-Overcoming," 153; Zarathustra's
"On Those Who Are Sublime," 153

Nirvana, 449

Nixon, Richard, 570

North, Paul, 182; *The Yield,* 640n42

Novalis (Georg Philipp Friedrich Freiherr
    von Hardenberg), 61, 144, 192, 235,
    484–85, 523

Oates, Joyce Carol, "Princeton Idyll," 6

O'Brien, Conor Cruse, 582, 583, 585, 695n13;
    "The Gentle Nietzscheans," 578–81

Oehler, Richard, 13

Olson, Elder, 286

O'Neill, Eugene, 590

Opitz, Martin, 327

Orcus theme, 187–88, 196, 319, 460

ordinary language philosophy, 79, 82, 83, 89,
    572–73

O'Reilly, Bill, 651n36

Orff, Carl, 318

Origen, 110

Orpheus, 151

Ortega y Gasset, José, 44, 56; *The Dehu-
    manization of Art,* 82; *The Revolt of the
    Masses,* 370

Orwell, George, *1984,* 603

Osiris, 404

Ottmann, Henning, 20, 583; "Englischspra-
    chige Welt," 620n36, 620n37

Otto, Rudolf, 137

Ozick, Cynthia, viii

Paine, Thomas, 102

Palestine, 3, 224, 382, 396, 407. *See also* Israel

Panofsky, Erwin, *Studies in Iconology,* 12

Papal Infallibility, 214

Parisian theory, 81, 244, 292, 551, 568, 569.
    See also French theory

Parmenides, 174, 234

Pascal, Blaise, 61, 71, 133, 472, 615n35

Pascal's wager, 105, 220

Pasteur, Louis, 225

Paul, 107, 165; and Buber, 528; and Christia-
    nity, 111, 402–4; forgiveness in, 178; and
    Gnosticism, 178; and Greeks, 101; and

Hebrew prophets, 178; and Jesus Christ,
    528; and Jewish law, 115, 494, 528, 639n35,
    678n34; and Luther, 113; and Nietzsche,
    215, 216, 217–18, 402–3, 516; and Plato, 178;
    predestination in, 178; and salvation, 116,
    528; and Taubes, 77; and virgin birth, 102

Paulus, H. E. G., 501

Pelagius, 110

Perls, Fritz, 556

Perry, R. B., *The Present Conflict of Ideals,*
    38–39

Persia, ancient, 385, 391

Petrashevsky circle, 213

Petuchowski, Jakob, 637–38n21

Pharisees, 394, 397, 400, 403

phenomenology, 356, 485–86, 536, 537; and
    existentialism, 560; and Heidegger, 520,
    525; and sin and guilt, 365; and tragedy,
    336–38

Phillips, Adam, 207, 208, 637n16

Philo, 395

Philoctetes, 345

philology, 49, 65, 94, 627n16

philosopher(s), 94–95; biography of, 255; as
    critic and diagnostician, 296; opposition
    by, 183, 296; psychobiographical ap-
    proach to, 492; and radical questions, 42

philosophy, 166, 303; abstractness and artifi-
    ciality of, 79; and aesthetics, 225, 443; and
    alienation, 369–70; Anglo-American, 567;
    apologetic and conservative tendencies of,
    179; in Aristotle, 286; and art, 298, 442–43,
    445, 449; and aspiration, 85; and begin-
    nings and endings, 83–84; and challenge
    to change one's life, 89, 92; commitment
    to, 223; and conformity, 42, 166, 179, 183,
    296; Continental, 536–37, 567; as critical
    and diagnostic, 179, 183; and critical
    thinking, 8, 165, 166, 210, 515–16, 563; and
    criticism of beliefs, 90–91, 94; and death,
    438–39; and decidophobia, 356; and
    existentialism, 44, 55–56, 60; and extreme
    experiences, 439; and faith, 165; and forms
    of consciousness, 255; and Freud,

philosophy (*continued*)

533, 534, 547; as full activity of mind and body, 563; and German culture, 387; and Goethe, 486–87; and greatness, 85; and heresy, 179–80; history of, 264, 271, 277; and humanism, 81–82, 563; and idols, 92; and knowledge, 88; and language, 79; laughter in, 87; linguistic turn in, 552; literary style in, 83–84; and longing, 85; and moral work, 92; and music, 62; origins of Greek, 464–65; and poetry, 99, 129, 158, 325; psychobiographical approach to, 492; and psychology, 82, 680–81n30; and rationalization of valuations of society, 29; and reading, 427; and reason, 165; and religion, 210; as revolutionary, 166; and self-destruction, 92; and self-making, 92; and Shakespeare, 129, 328; and skepticism, 244; and stages in life of spirit, 88; standards of, 75–76; as subversive, 154; and suffering, 279; tradition of, 7–8; and truth, 85; writing in, 75

Pickus, David, 438, 614n22; on Kaufmann and Bildungsideal, 32, 624n79, 694–95n11; on Kaufmann and death, 195; on Kaufmann and Heidegger, 526; on Kaufmann and Holocaust, 193; on Kaufmann and humanism, 30; on Kaufmann and humanities, 679n4; on Kaufmann and Jaspers, 45; on Kaufmann and Kierkegaard, 59–60; on Kaufmann and Nietzsche, 14, 19, 39, 59–60, 617n19, 641n58, 696n23; on Kaufmann's critical stance, 304; on Kaufmann's death work-ethic, 95, 189, 190, 197; on Kaufmann's egoism, 571

Pico della Mirandola, Giovanni Francesco, *De hominis dignitate*, 435

Pike, Burton, 654n64

Pilate, 388, 397, 400, 401

Pinkard, Terry, *Hegel*, 260

Pinker, Steven, 180–81

Piper, Andrew, 673n11

Pippin, Robert, 277, 586–87, 599; *Hegel on Self-Consciousness*, 260; *Hegel's Idealism*, 260; *Hegel's Practical Philosophy*, 260; introduction to Nietzsche's *Thus Spoke Zarathustra*, 594–95; "You Can't Get There from Here," 251

Pius IX, "A Syllabus of Errors," 214

Pius XII, 343–44, 346

Plato, 29, 158, 273, 395, 412, 665n8; absolutist dualisms in, 117; and Aeschylus, 314; and Arendt, 457; and Aristotle, 281; and ban on theater, 471; beauty in, 282, 283; and Christianity, 113; criticism of, 175; and democracy, 391; dialogues of, 84; as educator, 174; and Euripides, 314, 322; founded knowledge and untenable belief in, 117; and Hegel, 501; and Heidegger, 524–25; and human nature, 471; and Indian thought, 379, 464, 465; and Jaspers, 64; and justice, 360, 364; and Kant, 489; and Kierkegaard, 59; and knowledge, 427; and love and perfection, 647n11; and metaphysics, 79; and morality, 281–82; mythmaking of, 281; and myth of Er, 282; and Nietzsche, 17, 472, 589; and Paul, 178; and poetry, 281; and Pythagoras, 464; and reason, 117; and Sartre, 69; and science, 117; and Socrates, 283, 301, 473; and Sophocles, 281, 303, 304; and suffering, 283; and theory of Forms, 282; and tragedy, 281–83, 284, 289, 293, 314, 665n9; and truth, 640n42; WORKS: *Apology of Socrates*, 79; *Greater Hippias*, 472; *Laws*, 281, 282–83, 284, 414; *Parmenides*, 465, 501; *Phaedo*, 283; *Republic*, 212, 281–82, 283, 298, 334; *Sophist*, 501; *Symposium*, 647n11

Plautus, *The Comedy of Asses*, 471

Podach, Erich, 14

Podhoretz, Norman, 614n22

poetry, 447; and death, 192, 193; and Eliot, 155; and emotion, 154–55, 448; and experience, 154–56, 298; and Goethe, 482, 485; and Hegel, 325; and Heidegger, 51; and Kant, 325; and Nietzsche, 503; and philosophy, 99, 129, 158, 325; and Plato,

281; and psychology, 478; and science, 126, 485, 486, 567; as subversive, 154; and suffering, 445

Polgar, Alfred, 369

politics, 355; and Bildung, 32; and Nietzsche, 23, 39, 581–86, 591, 603, 604, 605, 630–31n77, 696n25; and university, 418

Pollock, Sheldon, "Philology and Freedom," 627n16

Popper, Karl, 233, 550; *The Open Society and Its Enemies,* 232

postmodernism, 47, 142, 293

post-postmodernism, 293

poststructuralism, 577

Potter, Stephen, *The Theory and Practice of Gamesmanship,* 515

Poulet, Georges, 143, 147, 551

Pound, Ezra, 669n40

Pratt, James Bissett, 4, 103, 118, 613n17

pre-Socratics, 70, 356, 523, 524–25

Princeton, New Jersey, 440

Prometheus, 473

prophets, Hebrew, 464, 648n15; and Buber, 529; and Christian Bible, 77; and education, 200; excoriation of infidels by, 650n32; and God, 649–50n24; and Hay, 224; as heretics, 185; and Hinduism, 460; and humility, 168; and Jesus, 178; and justice, 168, 334, 360, 397, 459, 648n15; and Kant, 491; and law, 110; and love, 108, 168, 459; and morality, 164, 165; and Near Eastern religions, 392; and normative Judaism, 392; oppositional stance of, 76, 137; and Paul, 178, 404; and self-sacrifice, 116; and social justice, 160, 164, 165, 226; and Socrates, 77

Protestantism, 2, 79, 89, 106, 110, 190, 226, 494, 516

Proudfoot, Wayne, 380

Proust, Marcel, *In Search of Lost Time,* 83

Prussia, 266

pseudo-Tertullian, 389

psychoanalysis, 252, 356

psychobiography, 569

psychology, 82–83, 94–95; of author, 296–97; of Buber, 476; empirically based, 82; of Goethe, 476; of Hegel, 476; of Heidegger, 476; and humanism, 427; of Kant, 476; modern, 83; and Nietzsche, 297, 476, 506; and phenomenology, 337; and philosophy, 82, 680–81n30; and poetry, 478; and reading, 426; and religion, 103; and special pleading, 83

Pynchon, Thomas, 70

Pythagoras, 464, 465

Quinton, Anthony, 232–33, 273

Rabelais, François, 496

Racine, Jean, 327, 447

Rathbone, David, "Kaufmann's Nietzsche," 620–21n48

Ratner-Rosenhagen, Jennifer, 588–90, 591–92; *American Nietzsche,* 613n9, 615–16n2, 700n85

Rawls, John, *A Theory of Justice,* 359

Raz, Joseph, 676n5; *The Morality of Freedom,* 435–36

reason, 12, 75, 163, 167, 595; and Aeschylus, 309, 311, 312; and Aristotle, 117; and Chernyshevsky, 53, 54; commitment to, 223; and conditions of choice, 357; and creativity, 376; and Dostoevsky, 53, 54; and Enlightenment, 136; and existentialism, 60; and faith, 79, 168; and feeling, 135; and great-souled man, 136; and Hegel, 134, 242, 243, 245, 261, 495; and Heidegger, 51, 520; and Kant, 237, 248, 479, 485, 489, 490–91, 494; and Kierkegaard, 59, 61; and knowledge, 79; and Luther, 101, 108, 117–18, 409; and Nietzsche, 25, 28, 117–18, 429, 520; and philosophy, 165; and Plato, 117; and religion, 162; and Rilke, 148; and Schiller, 238, 245; and self-transcendence, 108–9; and Tolstoy, 222; and tragedy, 307, 308, 312–13; and truth, 325

Redfield, Marc, 35

Reginster, Bernard, 19, 35, 595; *The Affirmation of Life,* 19

Reinhardt, Kurt F., 46

Reiwald, Paul, 360

religion, 99, 100, 137, 159–98, 378–410; and aesthetics, 380; ambiguity in, 106; and ancient Greeks, 507; and art, 125, 126, 381, 444; and aspiration, 101, 120, 121, 162, 209; and authoritarianism, 116, 120, 127; and belief, 80; and Camus, 228, 565, 655n5; common sense of, 165, 169; comparative, 380, 412, 433; contemporary, 89; critical attitude toward, 4; and culture, 103; and deception, 104; and decidophobia, 354–55; and de Man, 615n35; and devotion, 8; and Dostoevsky, 212; effect of on human existence, 8; and empiricist movement, 87; epistemology of, 224; and evidence, 105, 162; and existentialism, 57–58, 79–80, 380; and experience, 4, 379–80, 381; and finitude, 303; and Freud, 103, 104, 220–21, 533, 546–47; and God, 101; and Hegel, 242, 246, 263, 264, 270, 379, 498; and history, 380; and Hitler, 223; humanistic, 121, 242; and humanities, 433–37; importance of beliefs in, 380; and inhumanity, 228; intellectual interest in, 8; and James, 120, 219–20, 221; and Kant, 90, 488–89; and literature, 381; and morality/ethics, 8, 168, 169, 170, 182, 354; and Nietzsche, 38–40, 573; and perfection, 121; and persecution, 223; and philosophy, 161, 210; propositions in, 101–3; and psychology, 103; and reason, 162; and revelation, 103; and salvation, 174; and science, 225; and society, 229; and stories, 201, 227; study of, 380; and suffering, 172; and term "religious," 200–201; and theology, 437; and tradition, 103; and tragedy, 121–22; as wishful thinking, 104. *See also* faith/belief; mysticism

Rembrandt Harmenszoon van Rijn, 142, 437, 463, 469, 473, 479, 684n42; "Large Self-Portrait," 6–7, 443

Renan, Ernest, 589

Richards, I. A., 284

Richards, Robert J., 504

Richardson, John, 698n59

Richter, Jean-Paul, 523

Rickert, Heinrich, 685n12

Rieff, Philip: *The Feeling Intellect,* 61; *Fellow Teachers,* 45, 417, 418

Rig-Veda, 471

Rilke, Rainer Maria, 44, 54, 55–56, 68, 112; angels in, 152–53; beauty in, 138; and Dionysian affirmation of life, 151; emotions in, 154; and Eternal Recurrence of the Same, 152; and ethics, 149; and God, 151; and great-souled man, 130; and Hebrew Bible, 147; and Heidegger, 46, 70, 356; and injunction to change, 149, 493, 569; inspiration in, 155–56; and Kafka, 148–49; and logic of passion, 154; and Moses, 449, 493; and Nietzsche, 147–48, 150–54, 325, 590; renewal in, 150; and Salomé, 148; stature of, 448–49; striving in, 153; and virtue, 569; war poetry of, 448; WORKS: "Archaic Torso of Apollo," 149, 150, 443; *Duino Elegies,* 138, 151, 152–53, 155–56, 300, 371; *Neue Gedichte,* 148; *The Notebooks of Malte Laurids Brigge,* 293; "Orpheus. Eurydice. Hermes," 195; "The Panther," 148–49, 150; "The Song of the Idiot," 148; *Sonnets to Orpheus,* 151, 153–54, 155, 449; "thing"-poems of, 82

Ringer, Fritz, *The Decline of the German Mandarins,* 32

Roazen, Paul, 553

Robertson, D. W., 146

Romanesque churches, 452

romanticism, 35, 135–36, 143, 151, 192, 447; and childhood, 542; and de Man, 143–44; and Goethe, 143; and Hölderlin, 236; medievalizing, 146; and *mimēsis,* 285–86; and Nietzsche, 136, 143, 239; as resurgent Gothic medievalism, 144

Rome, ancient, 144, 395, 397, 398, 400–401, 405, 406

Ronell, Avital, 180

Roos, Carl, *Kierkegaard og Goethe*, 273

Roosevelt, Eleanor, 358, 470

Rorty, Richard, 421, 552, 606, 701n91

Rosen, Michael, *Dignity*, 435–36

Rosenkranz, Karl, 248, 263

Rosenzweig, Franz, 227, 527, 528–29, 652n40, 657n43; *The Star of Redemption*, 181–82

Rosmarin-Weiss, Trude, 8

Ross, W. D., 289

Roth, Joseph, 369

Roth, Philip, 157

Rouault, Georges, *Crucifixion*, 201

Rousseau, Jean-Jacques, 29, 71, 90, 174, 236, 339, 472, 491, 542, 589; *Profession de foi du vicaire savoyard*, 90

Royce, Josiah, 220, 225

Rozanov, V. V., 53

Rule of St. Francis, 409

Rush, Fred, 664–65n4

Russell, Bertrand, *History of Western Philosophy*, 232

Russia, 585

Ryle, Gilbert, 86

Sadducees, 394, 397

Sade, Marquis de, 290

Said, Edward, *The World, the Text, and the Critic*, 416

Saladin, 396

Santayana, George, 423, 487, 589

Santner, Eric, 113, 656n21

Sardar, Ziauddin, 693n23

Sarto, Andrea del, 436

Sartre, Jean-Paul, 43, 50, 55–56, 87, 149–50, 224, 233, 446, 564; and Aeschylus, 326, 327; and Arendt, 457; atheism of, 71–72; authenticity and inauthenticity in, 525; and Buddha, 71–72, 73; change in thought of, 540; and Communist Party, 355; and consciousness, 544; and death, 194; and empty self, 72; and Euripides, 323, 324; and exegetical thinking, 356; and existentialism, 69, 149–50, 317, 318, 323, 326, 560, 568; experience in, 71; and Freud, 540, 544; and Gorz, 333; guilt in, 73; and Hegel, 253, 265, 273; and Heidegger, 69; and Homer, 305, 314; and Husserl, 253; on individual, 265; and Kant, 537; and Kierkegaard, 57; and Marxism, 560; and metaphysics, 69; and nature of man, 470; and Nietzsche, 62, 70–71, 72, 73, 326, 336, 560, 590; nothingness in, 72, 631n79; and phenomenology, 560; and philosophy, 450; and Plato, 69; and political Marxism, 71; and religion, 58; and sexuality, 629n47; and Shakespeare, 73; and Sophocles, 326, 327; and suffering, 326–27; and tragedy, 326–27; WORKS: *Being and Nothingness*, 56–57, 629n47; *Dirty Hands (Les mains sales)*, 327; *L'être et le néant*, 62, 508; "Existentialism Is a Humanism," 69, 670n15; *The Flies (Les Mouches)*, 323, 324, 326–27, 451, 670n15; *Les mots*, 327; *Nausea (La Nausée)*, 336; "Portrait of the Anti-Semite," 57; "The Responsibility of the Writer," 166

Satan, 111–13

Schacht, Richard, 18, 605, 701n91; "Human, All Too Human," 618n30

Schapiro, Meyer, 452, 454

Scharfstein, Ben-Ami, xi, 480, 561, 563, 568, 571

Scheffel, Joseph Viktor von, *Der Trompeter von Säckingen*, 659n18

Scheler, Max, 97, 339, 635n44; "On the Phenomenon of the Tragic," 336–38

Schelling, Friedrich Wilhelm Joseph, 39, 244, 326; and Goethe, 143, 325; and Hegel, 248, 275, 660–61n36; and Jaspers, 64; and Kant, 489; and Kierkegaard, 60; and Nietzsche, 589

Schiller, Friedrich, 31, 189, 192, 232, 326, 447, 696n25; beauty in, 188; death in, 306; and freedom, 239; and *Geist*, 239; and Goethe, 487, 488; and Hegel, 234, 235, 239, 240, 245, 249, 251, 331, 500; and infinity, 239;

Schiller, Friedrich (*continued*)
and Kant, 238; on knowledge and philosophical reason, 245; and morality, 240; and Nietzsche, 239–40, 659n18; and Orcusmotif, 319; and reason,245, 238; WORKS: *On the Aesthetic Education of Man*, 235, 237, 238–39, 242, 275; *Anmut und Würde*, 595; *Don Karlos*, 563–64; "Friendship," 240; "Immortality," 188, 306; "Nänie," 187–88; *Trompeter von Säckingen*, 240; *Xenien*, 188

Schlechta, Karl, 601

Schlegel, August Wilhelm, 144, 235

Schlegel, Friedrich, 65, 135, 144, 235, 248, 420, 484, 523

Schleiermacher, Friedrich, 235, 326

Schmitt, Carl, 353, 457, 491, 626n5

Schneider, Paul, 223

Schoenberg, Arnold, 534

Scholem, Gershom, 391

Schopenhauer, Arthur, 14, 33, 488; and Euripides, 334; and Freud, 508–9; and Goethe, 325, 334, 487, 504; and Hegel, 275; and Kant, 489, 504; and Mann, 34, 231; and Nietzsche, 25, 29, 36, 39, 335, 472, 589, 617n17; on poetic justice, 333–34; as psychologist, 506, 508–9; and repression, 509; and resignation, 334; and sex drive, 508; and Shakespeare, 328, 334; and Sophocles, 334; on tragedy, 332, 333–35; and unconscious will, 509

Schorske, Carl, 1, 612n2, 690n7; "Politics and Patricide in *The Interpretation of Dreams*," 533–34

Schrag, Calvin, 44, 58, 61, 73

Schutjer, Karin, 146

Schutte, Ofelia, *Beyond Nihilism*, 593–94, 598, 599–600

Schwarz, Balduin, 135

Schweitzer, Albert, 109, 226–27; *The Quest of the Historical Jesus*, 226

Scialabba, George, "A Representative Destiny," 622n55

science, 88, 101, 173; and absolute dualisms, 117; and art, 225; and Brecht, 348; and Chernyshevsky, 53; and contemporary prejudices, 183; and Dyson, 164; and existentialism, 57, 60; and feeling, 485; and Freud, 83, 533, 534, 535, 540, 541, 542, 547, 548–49, 552; and Goethe, 40, 474, 483, 484–85, 538, 550, 686n18; and Hegel, 244, 247–48, 252, 253, 254, 259, 263, 276, 478, 499, 500, 502; and Heidegger, 520; and humanities, 480; and Kant, 477–78, 483, 488–89, 499; and Nietzsche, 550, 573, 575, 581; and Plato, 117; poetic, 485, 486, 534, 535, 540, 541, 542, 550, 552, 567; priceless heritage of, 412–13; and religion, 220, 225; and scholarship, 480

Scott, R. B. Y., 163, 639n35, 641n59, 649–50n24, 652n41

Sebald, W. G., *On the Natural History of Destruction*, 348, 672n39

Seneca, 471

Servetus, 110, 161, 200

Sesostris III, bust of, 450–51

Sextus Empiricus, 244

Shakespeare, William, 31, 38, 158, 183, 201, 227, 277, 327, 450, 472; and Aeschylus, 317; and Aquinas, 129; and Aristotle, 129; and Armada, 315; and Augustine, 129; and Calvin, 129; and catastrophe, 302, 328, 329; character of, 2; and Christianity, 317; and communication, 298; courage in, 131; and Eliot, 129; and Goethe, 129, 137–38, 139, 143; and great-souled man, 130, 136, 137–38; guilt in, 73; and *hamartia*, 328–29; and Hegel, 249, 252, 330–32; and humanism, 322; and Kierkegaard, 129; love in, 131–32; and Nietzsche, 129, 328, 335, 507; nonpsychological motivation in, 137; and Old Testament, 147; and philosophy, 129, 328; and recognition, 329; and Sartre, 73; and Scheler, 338; and Schopenhauer, 328, 334; and self-sufficiency, 137; and Socrates, 129; and Sophocles, 129, 319; style in, 252; and tragedy, 129, 131, 137, 278, 328–35, 338, 340, 642n6; as upsetting certainties, 154; and world literature,

447; WORKS: *Antony and Cleopatra*, 131; *Coriolanus*, 123, 131, 146; *Hamlet*, 121, 123, 128, 131, 137–38, 139, 286, 298, 328–29, 330, 331, 333, 335, 362, 383–84, 445, 550; *Julius Caesar*, 131; *King Lear*, 123, 128, 130, 131, 329, 330, 341, 345, 445; *Macbeth*, 137–38, 139, 252, 329, 330, 341, 343; *The Merchant of Venice*, 110; *Othello*, 131, 329, 330, 340; *Richard III*, 328, 330; sonnet 29, 554; sonnet 94, 136; *Timon of Athens*, 132, 329; *Troilus and Cressida*, 511

Shammai, Rabbi, 393–94

Shaw, George Bernard, 324, 414, 590

Shelley, Percy Bysshe, 353, 448

Sheppard, Richard, 293–94

Shintoism, 410

Shiva, 458, 461–62, 466

Shlomoh Yitzhaki (Rashi), 396

Shoah. *See* Holocaust

Shusterman, Richard, "Art and Religion," 125–26

Shwe Dagon pagoda (Rangoon), 437

Sidgwick, Henry, 653n53

Sikhism, 379, 410, 458

Sikorski, Władysław, 348

Singer, Irving, 141

Singer, Tovia, 401

Sloterdijk, Peter, 435

Smith, Adam, 688n16

Smith, Gregory Bruce, 699n72

Smith, Ronald Gregor, 122

Smith, Steven B., 268

Smyser, William Leon, 534

Snyder, Timothy, "Hitler's World," 696n19

socialism, 212, 213, 539

Socrates, 29, 75, 89, 115, 128, 237, 369, 375, 639n38; and analytic philosophy, 79; and Bacon and Descartes, 78–79; as critical and diagnostic, 42, 183, 296; death of, 315; and decisions, 358; Dodds on, 325; and Euripides, 322, 324, 325; and existentialism, 74, 79; and Goethe, 479; and great-souled man, 130; and Hebrew prophets, 77; in Hegel, 242; as heretic, 183; and iconoclasm, 76; on man and truth, 85; as model for humanities, 413–14; and Nietzsche, 179, 307, 308, 578, 600; as perishing for heresy, 179; and Plato, 283, 301, 473; as Plato's ideal man, 79; and Satan, 112; scorn for intellectual inferiors of, 90; serenity and happiness of, 301; and Shakespeare, 129; and tragedy, 281; and Wittgenstein, 89–90; and writing, 84

Sodoma (Giovanni Antonio Bazzi), 436

Sokel, Walter H., 39, 40, 586; "Political Uses and Abuses of Nietzsche in Walter Kaufmann's Image of Nietzsche," 582, 583, 617n19, 696n23

Solger, Karl Wilhelm Ferdinand, 144

Soll, Ivan, 7, 32, 603, 613n9; "Walter Kaufmann and the Advocacy of German Thought in America," 622–23n62, 623n68

Solzhenitsyn, Alexander, 445–46; *August 1914*, 446, 693n15; *The First Circle*, 514–15; *Prussian Nights*, 614n22

Sontag, Susan, 201, 205, 207, 210, 228, 380, 565, 655n5; *Essays of the 1960s and 1970s*, 200; *Against Interpretation*, 200; *On Photography*, 468

Sophists, 322, 324

Sophocles, 128, 183, 201, 227, 292, 309, 349, 448, 464, 473; and Aeschylus, 322; and Aristotle, 303; and Asian architecture, 443; Athenian audience of, 301; blindness in, 300, 302; catastrophe in, 302; catastrophic vs. irenic endings of, 311–12; character in, 324–25; and consciousness of finitude, 302–3; and Euripides, 322–23, 324–25, 569; and fate, 300, 301; and Freud, 303; and *hamartia*, 299; and Hegel, 249, 316; and Heidegger, 174, 234; and heroic ethos, 318, 319, 341; and heroic humanism, 319, 321–22; and Homer, 319; honesty in, 300, 301, 317; humility in, 303; and inevitability of tragedy, 301; justice in, 302, 317, 318; and moral collision, 319; and Nietzsche, 307, 308, 314, 315–16; and Oedipus story, 121, 299, 473; and Plato,

Sophocles (*continued*)
281, 303, 304; radical insecurity in, 300,
302; and Sartre, 326, 327; and Scheler, 338;
and Schopenhauer, 334; and Shakespeare, 129, 319; suffering in, 300, 319, 321;
and tragedy, 329; and truth, 300, 301;
worldview of, 316; WORKS: *Ajax,* 319;
Antigone, 131, 237, 250, 269, 274, 282, 290,
291, 300, 301, 303–4, 307, 315, 317, 319–21,
339, 646n58; *Electra,* 282, 300, 307, 322–23,
324, 326; *Oedipus at Colonus,* 198, 307, 316,
341, 668n37; *Oedipus Tyrannus,* 139, 288,
298, 299–304, 301, 304, 307, 311–12, 315,
316, 317, 318, 319, 328, 339–40, 345, 447, 550,
669n40; *Philoctetes,* 289, 307, 414; *The Women of Trachis,* 288, 289, 300, 307, 669n40
Sorkin, David, 30, 31
Spain, 396
Sparta, 314–15
Spender, Stephen, 2
Speth, Rudolf, 636n33
Spinoza, Baruch, 40, 84, 413, 501; and Bible,
180, 450; as heretic, 179–80; and Jaspers,
64; and Kant, 489; and knowledge, 427;
knowledge of, 450; and Nietzsche, 472,
513, 589
Stace, W. T., *The Philosophy of Hegel,* 232
Stach, Reiner, 666–67n17
Staiger, Emil, 313
Stalin, Joseph, 211–12
Stambaugh, Joan, 70
state: and authenticity, 268, 269; and Hegel,
229, 237, 246, 264, 266–67, 268–69;
and individual, 268–69; murder by,
229; and Nietzsche, 585, 588, 603; and
self-perfection, 268; separation of church
and, 136
Staten, Henry, 189–90, 198, 293; *Nietzsche's
Voice,* 17, 25–26; "Toward a Will to Power
Sociology," 597–98
Steichen, Edward, *The Family of Man,*
440–41
Steilberg, Hays, 592, 697n45
Steiner, George, 44–45, 564, 669n44

Stendhal (Marie-Henri Beyle), 7, 135, 391,
445, 486, 643n7; *The Charterhouse of
Parma,* 132–33, 134, 365; and Goethe,
132; logic of passion in, 132–33; and
Nietzsche, 132, 365, 369, 589
Stern, J. P., 68–69, 581, 582, 586
Stern, Tom, 61
Stevens, Wallace, 448, 487
stoicism, 234
Stoics, 301, 395
Stoll, Timothy, "Art and Two Kinds of Lies,"
619n35
The Stone, 699–700n79
Strauss, David, 589
Strauss, Leo, 32, 391
Stravinsky, Igor, *Akedah Yizhak,* 437
Strindberg, August, 447
structuralism, 81, 292, 294
Sturm, Douglas, 373–74, 376–77
Styron, William, 328
sublime, 460–61, 463
suffering, 177–78, 184, 185, 193, 449; in
Aeschylus, 312, 313; and aesthetics, 441;
and alienation, 373; in Aristotle, 292; and
art, 478; and beauty, 449; and Bible, 391;
in Christian art, 452–54; and Christianity, 177, 280–81, 460; and Christian
tragedy, 346; and creation, 12; and
Dostoevsky, 55, 210, 220; and Euripides,
294, 297; and faith, 172, 178; in Goethe,
313; in Hebrew Bible, 393; Hegel on, 265,
317–18, 478; in Homer, 304; and Hume,
332, 333; inevitability of, 318, 319; and Job,
220, 330; in Judaism, 177–78; and Kierkegaard, 449; and language, 664–65n4;
and Nietzsche, 664–65n4; and philosophy, 279; and Plato, 283; and poetry,
445; problem of, 172; and religion, 172;
and Royce, 220; and Sartre, 326–27; in
Sophocles, 300, 319, 321; and theism, 172;
and tragedy, 280, 295, 311, 312, 317–18, 335,
336, 339, 340, 342, 344, 349
suicide, 194, 195, 197, 331, 354–55, 442; and
Goethe, 192, 473, 486; and Kant, 494;

and Kleist, 37; and Masada, 394; and
Samson, 473; and Sophocles, 448
Sulloway, Frank, *Freud, Biologist of the Mind*,
535, 536
Szathmary, Arthur, 1
Szondi, Peter, 51, 143, 147

Taft, Robert A., 391
Talmud, 3, 159, 167, 395–96
Tamir, Yael, 385
Tammuz, 404
Tanner, Michael, 35, 586
Tao Teh Ching, 412, 434
Taubeneck, Steven, 605–6, 701n91
Taubes, Jacob, 77, 404
Tayler, Jeffrey, 651n36
Taylor, Charles, 487–88; *Hegel*, 260, 567
Terry, Chris, 620–21n48
Tertullian, 409
Tevenar, Gudrun von, 597
theology, 58, 171, 380, 652n42, 653n44;
aesthetics as, 226; critique of, 78–79, 80;
and Heidegger, 129; Judaism without,
178; literary criticism as form of, 182, 226;
masquerade of, 172
Theunissen, Michael, 687n9
Thirty Years' War, 405
Thirwell, Adam, 685n14
Thomas, Lewis, 594
Thomism, 64, 110, 214, 356. *See also* Aquinas,
St. Thomas
Thompson, Hunter S., *Hell's Angels*, 449
Thompson, Peter, 23
Thucydides, 287, 315, 324, 375, 450
Tieck, Johann Ludwig, 144
Tiepolo, Giovanni Battista, 436
Tillich, Paul, 58, 79, 110, 226; *The Courage
to Be*, 106–7; *Systematic Theology, Part I*,
106–7
time, 463, 464–65, 466, 467, 468, 469–70
Titian, 436
Tiye, ebony head of, 451
Tobin, Robert Deam, 542

Tolstoy, Leo, 160, 161, 201, 206–10, 445–46;
and Camus, 199, 228; and Christianity,
200; and death, 518; and Faust, 208,
209; and God, 222; and Heidegger, 518;
and Higher Criticism, 221, 222; and
knowledge, 427; and reading, 206–7; and
Wisdom, 225; WORKS: *Anna Karenina*,
206–10, 211; *The Death of Ivan Ilyitch*, 199,
207, 208; "My Religion," 208, 209, 222; "A
Reply to the Synod's Edict of Excommunication," 199, 208, 219; *Resurrection*, 228;
War and Peace, 347
Torah, 115, 144, 203, 393, 395, 398, 420, 493,
528, 639n35
totalitarianism, 211, 212, 408, 457, 514, 587,
679n6
Toynbee, Arnold J., 129, 130
tragedy, 123, 172, 356–57, 445, 447; and
Aristotle, x, 278, 283–93, 310, 311, 312, 339,
340; and authors' intentions, 295–97; and
beauty, 335; and catastrophe, 307, 308,
328, 339, 340; and catharsis, 303–4; Christian, 346, 644n29, 693n15; and Christianity, 131, 132, 143, 278; colliding forces in,
330; and comedy, 315, 336, 349–50; and
courage, 295; courage in, 336; death of,
307–8, 312, 314; definition of, 295, 566,
667–68n27; *eleos* and *phobos* in, 287–90,
292, 310, 311, 328, 338; *eleos* (ruth) in, 308,
315, 319, 327, 345, 667n18; Elizabethan,
341; as enjoyable, 332–33, 335; and error,
338; and Euripides, 342; and events, 338;
and existentialism, 130, 314; failure in, 187;
as form of knowledge, 292; and Goethe,
146; greatness in, 339; Greek, 56, 137,
311–27, 328, 334, 338, 339–41, 342, 344–45,
349, 427, 451; and guilt, 187, 312, 317–18;
and *hamartia*, 284, 290–91, 292, 299, 313,
328–29; Hegel on, 187, 269, 311, 315, 316–17,
319, 330–32, 337, 338; heroic failure in,
345; hero of, 187, 339; and Homer, 304–7,
310, 317; and humanism, 349; Hume on,
332–33; and inevitability, 339, 340; and
involvement, 308, 315; and Judaism, 278;

tragedy (*continued*)
and Kafka, 666–67n17; and knowledge, 281; in life, 340, 341–43; and life experience, 323; modern, 338, 344–45; moral conflict in, 316–17, 318–19, 339, 340, 341; and morality, 302, 340–41; and myth vs. history, 345; Nietzsche on, 281, 284, 304, 307–8, 309, 314, 315–16, 339; nobility in, 286, 295, 336, 339, 340, 341; and numinous, 137; and optimism, 315, 322; and phenomenology, 336–38; and Plato, 281–83, 284, 289, 293, 314, 665n9; and reason, 307, 308, 312–13; and religion, 121–22; and responsibility, 317–18; and Sartre, 326–27; Schopenhauer on, 332, 333–35; and self-sacrifice, 131; and Shakespeare, 129, 131, 137, 278, 328–35, 338, 340, 642n6; social and cultural conditions enabling, 315; and Sophocles, 301, 329; and sorrow, 295; and suffering, 280, 295, 311, 312, 317–18, 335, 336, 339, 340, 342, 344, 349; symbolic action in, 295; and sympathy, 284, 288, 308, 311, 315, 336; terror in, 327; and *tragōidia*, 284–85; and *tragōidoi*, 284–85; view of life in, 131, 310, 311, 312. *See also* Aeschylus; Aristotle; Euripides; Sophocles

Trakl, Georg, 46, 51, 70, 236, 356

translation, 428, 429–30, 434

Trauerspiel, 327, 343, 346, 671n26

Trilling, Lionel, 6, 206, 211, 267, 273, 327, 564, 663n51, 663n52, 670n16; "Sincerity and Authenticity," 626n8

truth: aspiration to, 100–101, 167; and Bible, 96; and Clifford, 218; and coherence, 95, 96; and conventions, 100–101, 150; and correspondence, 95; as correspondence of appearance and reality, 96; as correspondence of expectation and fulfillment, 96; in emotion, 97; and God, 96; and guilt, 365; and Hegel, 660n34; and Hölderlin, 660n34; and Jesus, 388; and Kafka, 432; and Lessing, 211; and logic of passion, 133; love of, 90–91; and Milton, 218; and New

Testament, 388; and Nietzsche, 575–78, 577, 606, 619n35; of one's condition, 101; and perception of error, 135; and philosophy, 85, 100; and Plato, 640n42; and promise, 96; propositional, 114; and reason, 325; and relationship between God and man, 96; Socrates on, 85; and Sophocles, 300, 301; as what is trustworthy, 95–96

Tuchman, Barbara, 344

Turner, Joseph Mallord William, 463

Twain, Mark, 470

United States, ix, 603–4, 605; after World War II, 45; and Bildung, 32; and Christianity, 650n35, 651n36; Constitution of, 267; culture of, 369; humanities in, 32, 33; politicians in, 101; slavery in, 266

University of California, Irvine, 560–61

Untermeyer, Louis, 448

Upanishads, 161, 200, 423, 458, 464, 465, 466

Vaihinger, Hans, 19

Valentinus, 389

van Gogh, Vincent, 142, 170, 470, 473, 474, 479, 531, 616n8

Vansittart, Robert Gilbert, 386–87, 677n14

Vauvenargues, 589

Vedas, 388, 459, 466

Vega, Lope de, 447

Vellacott, Philip, 309

Verdi, Giuseppe, 444

Verene, Donald Phillip, 240–41, 251

Verrocchio, Andrea Del, *Equestrian Monument of Bartolommeo Colleoni*, 459

Vickers, Brian, 420

Vietnam War, viii, 279, 306, 342–43, 566

Villon, François, 142

Vinen, Richard, 673n5

La vita è bella (1997), 332

Voegelin, Eric, 391; *The New Science of Politics*, 390, 677n20; *Science, Politics, and Gnosticism*, 390

Voltaire (François-Marie Arouet), 71, 174, 558

Vorländer, Karl, 504; *Schiller-Goethe-Kant*, 477

Vries, Hent de, 636n9

Wackenroder, Wilhelm Heinrich, 144

Waehlens, Adolphe de, 15, 617n20

Wagner, Benno, 598, 698n66

Wagner, Richard, 33, 34, 559, 589, 591, 603

Waite, Geoffrey, 369

Walsh, W. H., 259–60

war, 583, 584–85, 588, 673n3

Warren, Austin, 299

Weimar Republic, 32

Weiss, Donald, 692n8

Weitzmann, Marc, 341

Wellek, René, 299

Wellhausen, Julius, 203–4

Werfel, Franz, 448

White, Elijah, 381, 676n8

Whitman, Cedric, 291, 319, 321

Whitman, Walt, 448; *Leaves of Grass*, 266; "Roaming in Thought *(After Reading Hegel)*," 266

Wieseltier, Leon, 647n4

Wilcox, John, 61; *Truth and Value in Nietzsche*, 628n31

Wilde, Oscar, 125, 126, 174, 645–46n55; "The Doer of Good," 201; "The Master," 201; "The Nightingale and the Rose," 201; *The Picture of Dorian Gray*, 135

Williams, Bernard, 92, 536–37; *Truth and Truthfulness*, 635n42

Williams, John, *Stoner*, 689n25

Williams, Michael, *Argument for Dismantling a Dubious Category*, 390

Wilson, Colin, *The Outsider*, 45

Wilson, Edmund, 369; *To the Finland Station*, 414

Wilson, Woodrow, 344

Wimsatt, W. K., 299

Winckelmann, Johann Joachim, 151

Windelband, Wilhelm, 326

Winnicott, D. W., 181, 268

Wisdom, John, "Gods," 224–25

Wittels, Fritz, 553; *Freud and His Time*, 535

Wittgenstein, Ludwig, 89, 166, 284, 413, 443, 487, 550; and linguistic turn in philosophy, 552; and Nietzsche, 694n1; and Socrates, 89–90; *Tractatus*, 84

Woelfel, James, 650n27; "Religious Empiricism as '-ism,'" 633n17

Wölfflin, Heinrich, 617n23

Wolin, Richard, 457–58

women, 284, 369, 382, 412, 415, 451, 461, 473; and conquest of Palestine, 382; and Euripides, 324; and Freud, 533; and Nietzsche, 604–5, 701n88; and Shakespeare, 131; and Sophocles, 300, 321; and time and art, 469; and tragedy, 332, 340, 349; and will to power, 514

Wood, James, 434

Wood, Michael, 422

Woods, John E., 430

Wordsworth, William, 75, 144, 146, 238, 448, 542; *The Prelude*, 98–99, 248; "The Tables Turned," 238

world as text, 520–21

World War II, 315, 331, 342, 344, 348, 367, 603, 604, 672n39

Worthen, Molly, viii

Wouk, Herman, 201–2, 221, 222; *The Caine Mutiny*, 202; *This Is My God*, 202–5; *War and Remembrance*, 202; *The Winds of War*, 202

Wouk, Sarah, 201

Wulf, Christoph Otto, 285

Wurfgaft, Benjamin, 632n7

Xenophanes, 179, 659n13

Yale University, 560

Yeats, William Butler, 167, 423, 448, 590; "The Choice," 195, 376

Yudah ben Halevi, "To Zion," 396

Zaehner, Robert Charles, 388

Zagajewski, Adam, 448

Zamulinski, Brian, 656–57n37

Zen, 116, 410, 437, 561. *See also* Buddhism

Zionism, 396–97, 678n34

Žižek, Slavoj, 347, 348, 355, 404, 620n40, 621n52; *Less Than Nothing*, 661n38

Zohar, 396

Zola, Émile, *Germinal*, 170

Zoroastrianism, 379, 385–89; and apocalyptic literature, 392; and Bible, 392–93; and Christianity, 387, 392, 397, 401; and Judaism, 391, 392; and Nietzsche, 387–88

Zschokke, Heinrich, *Eros*, 542

Zuckmayer, Carl, 564

Zweig, Arnold, 167

Zweig, Arnulf, 641n60